Bromberg and Ribstein on Limited Liability Partnerships, The Revised Uniform Partnership Act, and The Uniform Limited Partnership Act (2001)

by Christine Hurt and D. Gordon Smith

Highlights of the 2014 Edition

In this new edition, authors and leading authorities on partnership law Christine Hurt and Gordon Smith provide comprehensive and practical guidance on three important areas of partnership law:

- **Limited Liability Partnerships.** The interpretation and application of limited liability provisions, which have been adopted in all 51 jurisdictions, continue to be important in light of ongoing corporate investigations and litigation which carry the potential for significant liability of professional firms, many of which are organized as limited liability partnerships (LLPs). The authors have updated their discussion of LLPs, including the latest statutory provisions and cases. Of special interest is the applicability of liability shield provisions in light of recent bankruptcies of high-profile law firm LLPs.

- **Revised Uniform Partnership Act.** Currently, 40 jurisdictions have adopted to some extent the Revised Uniform Partnership Act (RUPA). It has become the new statutory law of partnership and the basis for future case law in the field. The authors have updated their analysis of RUPA, including discussion of the latest state variations.

- **Uniform Limited Partnership Act (2001).** The revised version of the Uniform Limited Partnership Act (ULPA) was promulgated by the National Conference of Commissioners on Uniform State Laws in 2001 (ULPA 2001), has already been adopted by 20 states, and is expected to be adopted by many other states as the successor to the 1985 version of the Uniform Limited Partnership Act. The authors have updated their coverage of ULPA, including which states to date have adopted this Act.

Wolters Kluwer
Law & Business

The book discusses these developments in light of not only the case law and statutory law of partnership, but also tax and regulatory considerations, broader theoretical implications, and impact on planning, drafting, and choice of form.

In addition, this edition contains updated charts of the state laws pertaining to numerous aspects of LLPs, and an updated appendix of state statutes reflecting legislative changes through September 2013.

12/13

For questions concerning this shipment, billing, or other customer service matters, call our Customer Service department at 1-800-234-1660.

For toll-free ordering, please call 1-800-638-8437.

BROMBERG AND RIBSTEIN ON
**LIMITED LIABILITY PARTNERSHIPS, THE
REVISED UNIFORM PARTNERSHIP ACT,
AND THE UNIFORM LIMITED PARTNERSHIP
ACT (2001)**

BROMBERG AND RIBSTEIN ON
LIMITED LIABILITY PARTNERSHIPS, THE REVISED UNIFORM PARTNERSHIP ACT, AND THE UNIFORM LIMITED PARTNERSHIP ACT (2001)

2014 Edition

CHRISTINE HURT
Professor of Law
Director, Program in Business Law and Policy
University of Illinois College of Law

D. GORDON SMITH
Glen L. Farr Professor of Law
J. Reuben Clark Law School
Brigham Young University

ALAN R. BROMBERG
University Distinguished Professor of Law
Southern Methodist University
Of Counsel, Jenkens & Gilchrist, P.C., Dallas

LARRY E. RIBSTEIN
Late Richard and Marie Corman Professor of Law
University of Illinois College of Law

This Edition supersedes the 2013 and all other previous Editions.

Wolters Kluwer
Law & Business

Copyright © 2014 Alan R. Bromberg, the Estate of Larry E. Ribstein, and CCH Incorporated. All Rights Reserved.

Published by Wolters Kluwer Law & Business in New York.

No part of this publication may be reproduced or transmitted in any form or by any means, including electronic, mechanical, photocopying, recording, or utilized by any information storage or retrieval system, without written permission from the publisher. For information about permissions or to request permissions online, visit us at *www.aspenpublishers.com/licensing/default.aspx*, or a written request may be faxed to our permissions department at 212-771-0803.

Wolters Kluwer Law & Business serves customers worldwide with CCH, Aspen Publishers and Kluwer Law International products.

Printed in the United States of America

1 2 3 4 5 6 7 8 9 0

ISBN 978-1-4548-2691-0

Library of Congress Catalog No. 96-79065

SUSTAINABLE FORESTRY INITIATIVE

Certified Chain of Custody
Promoting Sustainable Forestry

www.sfiprogram.org
SFI-01347

About Wolters Kluwer Law & Business

Wolters Kluwer Law & Business is a leading global provider of intelligent information and digital solutions for legal and business professionals in key specialty areas, and respected educational resources for professors and law students. Wolters Kluwer Law & Business connects legal and business professionals as well as those in the education market with timely, specialized authoritative content and information-enabled solutions to support success through productivity, accuracy and mobility.

Serving customers worldwide, Wolters Kluwer Law & Business products include those under the Aspen Publishers, CCH, Kluwer Law International, Loislaw, ftwilliam.com and MediRegs family of products.

CCH products have been a trusted resource since 1913, and are highly regarded resources for legal, securities, antitrust and trade regulation, government contracting, banking, pension, payroll, employment and labor, and healthcare reimbursement and compliance professionals.

Aspen Publishers products provide essential information to attorneys, business professionals and law students. Written by preeminent authorities, the product line offers analytical and practical information in a range of specialty practice areas from securities law and intellectual property to mergers and acquisitions and pension/benefits. Aspen's trusted legal education resources provide professors and students with high-quality, up-to-date and effective resources for successful instruction and study in all areas of the law.

Kluwer Law International products provide the global business community with reliable international legal information in English. Legal practitioners, corporate counsel and business executives around the world rely on Kluwer Law journals, looseleafs, books, and electronic products for comprehensive information in many areas of international legal practice.

Loislaw is a comprehensive online legal research product providing legal content to law firm practitioners of various specializations. Loislaw provides attorneys with the ability to quickly and efficiently find the necessary legal information they need, when and where they need it, by facilitating access to primary law as well as state-specific law, records, forms and treatises.

ftwilliam.com offers employee benefits professionals the highest quality plan documents (retirement, welfare and non-qualified) and government forms (5500/PBGC, 1099 and IRS) software at highly competitive prices.

MediRegs products provide integrated health care compliance content and software solutions for professionals in healthcare, higher education and life sciences, including professionals in accounting, law and consulting.

Wolters Kluwer Law & Business, a division of Wolters Kluwer, is headquartered in New York. Wolters Kluwer is a market-leading global information services company focused on professionals.

WOLTERS KLUWER LAW & BUSINESS
SUPPLEMENT NOTICE

This product is updated on a periodic basis with supplements to reflect important changes in the subject matter. If you have purchased this product directly from Wolters Kluwer Law & Business, we have already recorded your subscription for the update service.

If, however, you purchased this product from a bookstore and wish to receive future updates and revised or related volumes billed separately with a 30-day examination review, please contact our Customer Service Department at 1-800-234-1660 or send your name, company name (if applicable), address, and the title of the product to:

Wolters Kluwer Law & Business
Distribution Center
7201 McKinney Circle
Frederick, MD 21704

Important Contact Information

- To order any title, go to *www.aspenpublishers.com* or call 1-800-638-8437.
- To reinstate your manual update service, call 1-800-638-8437.
- To contact Customer Service, e-mail *customer.service@wolterskluwer.com*, call 1-800-234-1660, fax 1-800-901-9075, or mail correspondence to Order Department—Aspen Publishers, Wolters Kluwer Law & Business, PO Box 990, Frederick, MD 21705.
- To review your account history or pay an invoice online, visit *www.aspenpublishers.com/payinvoices*.

SUMMARY OF CONTENTS

CONTENTS

≡*2*≡

FORMATION OF THE LLP   43

Contents

≡*3*≡

PARTNER LIABILITY FOR PARTNERSHIP DEBTS   109

Contents

≡*4*≡

EFFECT OF LLP STATUS ON OTHER PARTNERSHIP RULES 175

Contents

≡5≡

LIMITED PARTNERSHIP AS LLP: THE LLLP   197

≡6≡

FOREIGN LLPs: CHOICE-OF-LAW
AND OTHER LITIGATION ISSUES   209

≡*7*≡

APPLICATION OF NON-PARTNERSHIP LAW   231

≡*8*≡

THE REVISED UNIFORM PARTNERSHIP ACT   271

Contents

≡9≡

UNIFORM LIMITED
PARTNERSHIP ACT (2001) 401

Contents

Contents

≡*Appendix A*≡

UNIFORM PARTNERSHIP ACT (1997)

≡*Appendix B*≡

≡*Appendix C*≡

≡*Appendix D*≡

PREFACE

This book covers three important developments in partnership law. The first is the registered limited liability partnership (LLP) provisions, which have been adopted in all jurisdictions since their inception in Texas in 1991. These provisions are discussed in detail in Chapters 1–6, with a discussion of related law in Chapter 7. Though the number of general partnerships has been slowly decreasing in the past decade, the number of LLPs have been increasing just as steadily as LLPs remain a popular choice for professional firms.

The other two important developments are the adoption of new uniform partnership laws. The Revised Uniform Partnership Act (R.U.P.A.) was promulgated by the National Conference of Commissioners on Uniform State Laws in 1994 and has been adopted to some extent in 40 jurisdictions. It has become the new statutory law of partnership and the basis of future case law in the field. The revised version of the Uniform Limited Partnership Act (U.L.P.A. 2001) was promulgated by the National Conference of Commissioners on Uniform State Laws in 2001 and has already been adopted by 20 U.S. jurisdictions as the successor to the 1985 version of the Uniform Limited Partnership Act.

This book discusses the LLP statutes adopted through approximately August 15, 2013. It includes R.U.P.A. with the 1996 LLP amendments and the 1997 amendment to Section 801, together with official comments to the 1994 and 1996 amended versions, reprinted in Appendix A; the Prototype Limited Liability Partnership Act, reprinted in Appendix B; significant state variations on R.U.P.A. enacted in California and Delaware, along with New York LLP provisions, reprinted in Appendix C; and the Uniform Limited Partnership Act (2001), reprinted in Appendix D. The book discusses these developments in light of the existing case and statutory law of partnership and its tax and regulatory context. It also discusses the broader theoretical implications of these developments and their impact on planning, drafting, and choice of form.

The assistance of Richard Walker and Sali Guirguis is gratefully acknowledged.

Christine Hurt
D. Gordon Smith

September 2013

BROMBERG AND RIBSTEIN ON

LIMITED LIABILITY PARTNERSHIPS, THE REVISED UNIFORM PARTNERSHIP ACT, AND THE UNIFORM LIMITED PARTNERSHIP ACT (2001)

≡ *1* ≡

BACKGROUND and INTRODUCTION

This chapter introduces the limited liability partnership (LLP). Section 1.01 discusses the history of the LLP form. Section 1.02 provides an overview of the features of LLPs. Section 1.03 briefly reviews some general theoretical considerations concerning LLPs that are relevant throughout this book. Sections 1.04 to 1.06 discuss matters that relate to the choice of the LLP form by new and existing firms. Section 1.07 briefly reviews the two statutory contexts of LLP provisions—that is, the Uniform Partnership Act (U.P.A.) and the Revised Uniform Partnership Act (R.U.P.A.)—which are discussed throughout this book.

§ 1.01   HISTORY OF THE LLP FORM

This section sketches the origin and development of the LLP form. Section (a) discusses the background and structure of the first LLP statute in Texas, which initially shielded LLP partners from personal liability only for tort-type claims. Section (b) discusses Delaware's adoption and expansion of the form and other early adoptions. Section (c) considers the extension of the LLP liability shield to all liabilities. Section (d) discusses LLP provisions based on the Revised Uniform Partnership Act. Section (e) completes the history of the LLP through late 2000.

(a) The Texas Statute

The limited liability partnership (LLP) originated in Texas in 1991 to protect against a limited list of torts. It was inspired by the government suits against law and accounting firms that had done work for the freewheeling savings and loan and thrift associations that failed in large and costly numbers in the 1980s along with the collapse of real estate values they had helped to inflate. The suits alleged joint and several liability claims under U.P.A. § 15 for various kinds of malpractice or other tortious misconduct. The claims were against all partners including many who had nothing to do with the failed associations. The suits highlighted the vicarious liability of partners for each other's conduct, a liability that did not exist in other forms of professional organization.

To protect the innocent partners from vicarious liability claims of this sort, Lubbock, Texas lawyers James H. Milam, Philip W. Johnson, and Robert L. Duncan, proposed and State Senator John Montford introduced S.B. 302 in the 72d Texas Legislature.[1] It would have amended the joint and several liability portion of the Texas version of U.P.A. § 15 to create permanent protection from vicarious liability by adding:

> A partner in a professional partnership is not individually liable, except to the extent of the partner's interest in partnership property, for the errors, omissions, negligence, incompetence, or malfeasance committed in the course of rendering professional service on behalf of the partnership by another partner, employee, or representative of the partnership.[2]

By definitions of professional partnerships and professional service, the protection from liability was limited to a short list of professionals that included doctors, lawyers, architects, engineers, and accountants.[3]

The protected liabilities — for errors, omissions, negligence, incompetence, or malfeasance — were tort types. The words were copied from the Texas

---

[1] For a history of the Texas law, see Fortney, Seeking Shelter in the Minefield of Unintended Consequences — The Traps of Limited Liability Law Firms, 54 Wash. & Lee L. Rev. 717 (1997). *See also* In re Rambo Imaging, L.L.P., 2008 WL 2778846, at 6 (Bankr. W.D. Tex. July 15, 2008) (noting that the Texas statute "came from a cry for protection from personal liability claims from unincorporated and accounting firms").

[2] S.B. 302, 72d Tex. Legis. § 2 (1991).

[3] S.B. 302, 72d Tex. Legis. § 1.

Professional Corporation Act[4] and Professional Association Act[5] in order to give professionals in partnerships the same limited immunity as professionals organized under those statutes.

In the quoted form, S.B. 302 passed the Texas Senate with little attention or comment. In the House of Representatives S.B. 302 was supported by firms (mostly law firms) that wanted limited liability but disliked incorporation for tax, professional tradition, or other reasons. But it was criticized for:

(1) Including only professionals, particularly lawyers,
(2) Relieving partners from responsibility for misconduct of those they directed or supervised (such as a doctor's nurse or technician, a lawyer's junior associate),
(3) Failing to signal to patients and clients that their professionals' liability was limited in complete reversal of historic and familiar partnership law, and
(4) Failing to provide any substitute source of recovery for injured patients and clients.

In response to these criticisms, S.B. 302 was amended to provide for:

(1) Extending the liability limitation to all partnerships,
(2) Denying protection to partners for misconduct of those working under their supervision or direction,
(3) Requiring annual registration with the state and inclusion of "L.L.P." or "registered limited liability partnership in the firm name," and
(4) Requiring liability insurance in an arbitrary and admittedly often inadequate amount of $100,000.

Representative Steve Wolens added these provisions to the Texas version of the U.P.A. by floor amendment to a different bill he sponsored creating limited liability companies and amending other business organization statutes. In this form they became law as follows:

Definition of Terms
> Sec. 2. In this Act . . .
> "Registered limited liability partnership" means a partnership registered under Section 45-A and complying with Sections 45-B and 45-C.

----

[4] Tex. Rev. Civ. Stat. Ann. art. 1528e-16.
[5] Tex. Rev. Civ. Stat. Ann. art. 1528f-24.

Nature of Partner's Liability in Ordinary Partnership and in Registered Limited Liability Partnership

Sec. 15. (1) Except as provided by Paragraph (2) of this Section, all partners are liable jointly and severally for all debts and obligations of the partnership including those under Sections 13 and 14.

(2) A partner in a registered limited liability partnership is not individually liable for debts and obligations of the partnership arising from errors, omissions, negligence, incompetence, or malfeasance committed in the course of the partnership business by another partner or a representative of the partnership not working under the supervision or direction of the first partner at the time the errors, omissions, negligence, incompetence, or malfeasance occurred, unless the first partner:

(a) was directly involved in the specific activity in which the errors, omissions, negligence, incompetence, or malfeasance were committed by the other partner or representative; or

(b) had notice or knowledge of the errors, omissions, negligence, incompetence, or malfeasance by the other partner or representative at the time of occurrence.

(3) Paragraph (2) does not affect the joint and several liability of a partner for debts and obligations of the partnership arising from any cause other than those specified in Paragraph (2).

(4) Paragraph (2) does not affect the liability of partnership assets for partnership debts and obligations.

Registered Limited Liability Partnerships

Sec. 45-A. (1) To become a registered limited liability partnership, a partnership must file with the secretary of state an application stating the name of the partnership, the address of its principal office, the number of partners, and a brief statement of the business in which the partnership engages.

(2) The application must be executed by a majority in interest of the partners or by one or more partners authorized by a majority in interest of the partners.

(3) The application must be accompanied by a fee of $100 for each partner.

(4) The secretary of state shall register or renew any partnership that submits a completed application with the required fee.

(5) Registration is effective for one year after the date the registration is filed, unless voluntarily withdrawn by filing with the secretary of state a written withdrawal notice executed by a majority in interest of the partners or by one or more partners authorized by a majority in interest of the partners.

(6) The secretary of state may provide forms for application for or renewal of registration.

Name of Registered Limited Liability Partnerships

Sec. 45-B. A registered limited liability partnership's name must contain the words "registered limited liability partnership" or the abbreviation "L.L.P." as the last words or letters of its name.

Insurance of Registered Limited Liability Partnerships

Sec. 45-C. (1) A registered limited liability partnership must carry, if reasonably available, at least $100,000 of liability insurance of a kind that is designed to cover the kinds of errors, omissions, negligence, incompetence, or malfeasance for which liability is limited by Section 15(2).

(2) If the registered limited liability partnership is in compliance with the requirements of Subsection (1), the requirements of this section shall not be admissible nor in any way made known to the jury in determining the issue(s) of liability for or extent of the debt or obligation or damages in question.[6]

This first LLP statute was popular and elicited many filings, mostly by law firms, including some plaintiffs' firms that had objected to any legislative limitation of partner liability.[7]

The original LLP sections were discussed and drafted hurriedly and under pressure late in a short session (the Texas Legislature meets regularly for only four months in alternate years). The need for refinement and clarification was already apparent and became clearer in publicizing the statute.[8] Redrafting began quickly in hopes that a special session of the Legislature would be called and amendments could be passed. But there was no special session and the amendments had to wait until 1993 for enactment.

A principal difficulty with the original LLP sections was that insurance was not always available to satisfy the insurance requirement. Policies often used language different from the narrowly worded list of actions in the statute. And many policies contained exclusions of conduct that might otherwise be within the statutory language. The original solution was to allow some flexibility by describing the insurance as "of a kind that is designed to cover the kinds" of specified misconduct and by conditioning the liability shield on insurance "if reasonably available." That meant there was no substitute protection if the insurance was not of the right "kind" or was not "reasonably available." Moreover, it raised questions of the meaning of the quoted terms. The rethought solution was

---

[6]Tex. Rev. Civ. Stat. Ann. art. 6132b-2, 15, 45-A, 45-B, 45-C.

[7]Within two years of enactment of the Texas law, there were 569 law firm LLPs. *See* Why 569 Texas Law Firms Just Switched to LLP, Law Off. Mgmt. & Admin. Rep., Apr. 1994, at 941; Fortney, supra, note 1.

[8]So far as possible without further legislation, efforts were made to resolve various issues in comments accompanying or following publication of the statute. Bromberg, Source and Comments, 17 Tex. Rev. Civ. Stat. Ann. 86, 109–11, 142–44 (Vernon Supp. 1992). *See also* Anderson, Bromberg, Egan, Griffin, Schoenbrun & Szalkowski, Registered Limited Liability Partnerships, 28 Bull. Bus. L. Sec. 1 (State Bar of Texas, No. 3, Sept. 1991), *reprinted* 55 Tex. Bar. J. 728 (1992).

to permit a $100,000 trust fund, letter of credit, or equivalent as an alternative to $100,000 of liability insurance. With "if reasonably available" deleted, the liability shield required either the right "kind" of insurance or trust fund or equivalent.

Other revisions also were required. On reflection, it was agreed that a partner's knowledge or notice of another's misconduct should not subject the partner to liability if he or she took reasonable steps to prevent or cure it. There was a need to clarify what the original provisions probably intended: that the partnership must be an LLP both at the time of the misconduct and at the time a liability is alleged and tried, that "representative" included employees, servants and agents, that a change in the partners in a registration year did not affect the validity of the registration, and that a limited partnership could become an LLP. Additionally, the registration procedure called for a number of housekeeping or administrative details.

These changes became law as part of a wholly new Texas Revised Partnership Act in 1993, which evolved parallel to and in some respects following the national R.U.P.A.:

Art. 6132b-1.01   General Definitions

In this Act: . . .

(15) "Registered limited liability partnership" means a partnership registered under Section 3.08(b) and complying with Sections 3.08(c) and (d)(1).

Art. 6132b-3.08   Liability in and Registration of Registered Limited Liability Partnership

(a) Liability of Partner. (1) A partner in a registered limited liability partnership is not individually liable for debts and obligations of the partnership arising from errors, omissions, negligence, incompetence, or malfeasance committed while the partnership is a registered limited liability partnership and in the course of the partnership business by another partner or a representative of the partnership not working under the supervision or direction of the first partner unless the first partner:

(A) was directly involved in the specific activity in which the errors, omissions, negligence, incompetence, or malfeasance were committed by the other partner or representative; or

(B) had notice or knowledge of the errors, omissions, negligence, incompetence, or malfeasance by the other partner or representative at the time of occurrence and then failed to take reasonable steps to prevent or cure the errors, omissions, negligence, incompetence, or malfeasance.

(2) Subsection (a)(1) does not affect:

(A) the joint and several liability of a partner for debts and obligations of the partnership arising from a cause other than the causes specified by Subsection (a)(1);

(B) the liability of a partnership to pay its debts and obligations out of partnership property; or

(C) the manner in which service of citation or other civil process may be served in an action against a partnership.

(3) In this subsection, "representative" includes an agent, servant, or employee of a registered limited liability partnership.

(b) Registration. (1) In addition to complying with subsections (c) and (d)(1), to become a registered limited liability partnership, a partnership must file with the secretary of state an application stating:

(A) the name of the partnership;

(B) the federal tax identification number of the partnership;

(C) the street address of the partnership's principal office in this state and outside this state, as applicable;

(D) the number of partners at the date of application; and

(E) in brief, the partnership's business.

(2) The application must be executed by a majority-in-interest of the partners or by one or more partners authorized by a majority-in-interest of the partners.

(3) Two copies of the application must be filed, accompanied by a fee of $200 for each partner.

(4) A partnership is registered as a registered limited liability partnership on filing a completed initial or renewal application, in duplicate with the required fee, or on a later date specified in the application. A registration is not affected by later changes in the partners of the partnership.

(5) An initial application filed under this subsection and registered by the secretary of state expires one year after the date of registration or later effective date unless earlier withdrawn or revoked or unless renewed in accordance with Subdivision (7). . . .

(c) Name. A registered limited liability partnership's name must contain the words "registered limited liability partnership" or the abbreviation "L.L.P." as the last words or letters of its name.

(d) Insurance or Financial Responsibility. (1) A registered limited liability partnership must:

(A) carry at least $100,000 of liability insurance of a kind that is designed to cover the kinds of errors, omissions, negligence, incompetence, or malfeasance for which liability is limited by Subsection (a)(1); or

(B) provide $100,000 of funds specifically designated and segregated for the satisfaction of judgments against the partnership based on the kinds of errors, omissions, negligence, incompetence, or malfeasance for which liability is limited by Subsection (a)(1) by:

(i) deposit in trust or in bank escrow of cash, bank certificates of deposit, or United States Treasury obligations; or

(ii) a bank letter of credit or insurance company bond.

(2) If the registered limited liability partnership is in compliance with Subdivision (1), the requirements of this subsection shall not be admissible

or in any way be made known to the jury in determining an issue of liability for or extent of the debt or obligation or damages in question.

(3) If compliance with Subdivision (1) is disputed:

(A) compliance must be determined separately from the trial or proceeding to determine the partnership debt or obligation in question, its amount, or partner liability for the debt or obligation; and

(B) the burden of proof of compliance is on the person claiming limitation of liability under Subsection (a)(1).

(e) Limited Partnership. A limited partnership may become a registered limited liability partnership by complying with applicable provisions of the Texas Revised Limited Partnership Act (Article 6132a-1, Vernon's Texas Civil Statutes) and its subsequent amendments.[9]

---

[9]Tex. Rev. Civ. Stat. Ann. art. 6132b-3.08. Additional housekeeping provisions on withdrawal, renewal, amendment, and related matters were the following, many of which were adopted by other states:

(6) A registration may be withdrawn by filing in duplicate with the secretary of state a written withdrawal notice executed by a majority-in-interest of the partners or by one or more partners authorized by a majority-in-interest of the partners. A withdrawal notice must include the name of the partnership, the federal tax identification number of the partnership, the date of registration of the partnership's last application under this section, and a current street address of the partnership's principal office in this state and outside this state, if applicable. A withdrawal notice terminates the status of the partnership as a registered limited liability partnership as of the date of filing the notice or a later date specified in the notice, but not later than the expiration date under Subdivision (5).

(7) An effective registration may be renewed before its expiration by filing in duplicate with the secretary of state an application containing current information of the kind required in an initial application and the most recent date of registration of the partnership. The renewal application must be accompanied by a fee of $200 for each partner on the date of renewal. A renewal application filed under this section continues an effective registration for one year after the date the effective registration would otherwise expire.

(8) The secretary of state may remove from its active records the registration of a partnership whose registration has been withdrawn or revoked or has expired and not been renewed.

(9) The secretary of state may revoke the filing of a document filed under this subsection if the secretary of state determines that the filing fee for the document was paid by an instrument that was dishonored when presented by the state for payment. The secretary of state shall return the document and give notice of revocation to the filing party by regular mail. Failure to give or receive notice does not invalidate the revocation. A revocation of a filing does not affect an earlier filing.

(10) The secretary of state may provide forms for application for or renewal of registration.

(11) A document filed under this subsection may be amended or corrected by filing in duplicate with the secretary of state articles of amendment executed by a majority-in-interest of the partners or by one or more partners authorized by a majority-in-interest of the partners. The articles of amendment must contain the name of the partnership, the tax identification number of the partnership, the identity of the document being amended, the date on which the document being amended was filed, the part of the document being amended, and the amendment or correction. Two copies of the articles of amendment must be filed, accompanied by a fee of $10 plus, if the amendment increases the number of partners, $200 for each partner added by amendment of the number of partners.

(12) A document filed under this subsection may be a photographic, facsimile, or similar reproduction of a signed document. A signature on a document filed under this section may be a facsimile.

It was politically impractical to increase the modest amount of required insurance or substitute trust or letter of credit, although logic suggested that the amount should be proportional to the number of partners in the firm or some other measure of the firm's potential liability for misconduct.

The Texas statute has been amended since 1993. Among other changes, Texas now offers liability protection for both tort and contract claims[10] and has deleted the insurance requirement.[11] The most recent version of the Texas statute is discussed and compared with other statutes throughout this book.

(b)   The Delaware Expansion and Other Early Adoptions

The 1992 Louisiana statute followed the original Texas model but omitted the insurance requirement and added that a protected partner is not a proper party in a suit to enforce the partnership's liability. By 1993 it had broadened the types of protected liability to include willful or intentional misconduct.[12]

While Texas was making its 1993 amendments, Delaware, the District of Columbia, and North Carolina adopted the Texas LLP provisions with variations and elaborations. The most extensive changes were in Delaware, consistent with its policy of becoming the most favorable state for business organizations. Its principal intentions were to enlarge the liability shield and articulate its conflict-of-laws position that its law should apply to its outbound LLPs wherever they might operate. Delaware's specific changes were:

(1)   Broadening the list of protected activity by adding "wrongful acts or misconduct" to negligence and dropping the narrower terms of the Texas act.[13]

(2)   Narrowing a partner's liability for misconduct of someone under the partner's supervision or direction by confining that to "direct supervision

---

(13) A person commits an offense if the person signs a document the person knows is false in any material respect with the intent that the document be delivered on behalf of a partnership to the secretary of state for filing. An offense under this subdivision is a Class A misdemeanor.

(14) The secretary of state is not responsible for determining if a partnership is in compliance with the requirements of Subsection (d)(1).

(15) The secretary of state may adopt procedural rules on filing documents under this subsection.

Tex. Rev. Civ. Stat. Ann. art. 6132b-3.08.

Subsection (14) was included to relieve the concern of the Secretary of State's office that any filing with it imposed some responsibility on it to assure that the filing organization was what it purported to be. This concern and the need for fuller administrative provisions are among the reasons why the Governor never signed the bill but allowed it to become law without her signature.

[10] Tex. Bus. Org. § 152.805.
[11] 2011 Texas Laws ch. 139, effective Sept. 1, 2011.
[12] La. Rev. Stat. Ann. § 9:3431.
[13] Del. Code Ann., tit. 6, § 1515(b).

and control," although it did not make this an explicit exception from the LLP shield.[14]

(3)   Enlarging the insurance requirement to $1,000,000, while eliminating the original Texas phrase, "if reasonably available."[15]

(4)   Specifically authorizing its LLPs to operate outside the state as well as inside, and expressing its policy that its law govern them.[16]

(5)   Leaving lawyer eligibility for LLP status to rules of its Supreme Court.[17]

(6)   Capping the registration fee at the maximum corporate franchise tax level.[18]

In 1994 Delaware added further to the liability shield:

(7)   Broadening protected activity to include misconduct "whether characterized as tort or contract or otherwise."[19]

(8)   Clarifying (and perhaps amplifying) innocent partners' protection from indirect liability by specifying that they are not liable "either directly or indirectly, by way of indemnification, contribution, assessment or otherwise" for the otherwise protected misconduct.[20]

These last two important changes are considered further in Chapter 3. The latter of the two represents a first effort to deal with aspects of general partnership law that are affected by the LLP possibility that some but not all partners will be relieved from individual liability for partnership obligations. Chapter 4 deals with other effects.

Delaware, like Texas, became a full-shield statute.[21] Delaware has adopted a version of the Revised Uniform Partnership Act.[22] The Delaware statute is discussed and compared with other statutes throughout this book.

The District of Columbia in 1993 adopted the 1991 Texas provisions without substantive change except to require insurance "of not less than the amount

---

[14] Del. Code Ann., tit. 6, § 1515(c).

[15] Del. Code Ann., tit. 6, § 1546.

[16] Del. Code Ann., tit. 6, § 1547.

[17] Del. Code Ann., tit. 6, § 1515(d).

[18] Del. Code Ann., tit. 6, § 1544(c).

[19] Del. Code Ann., tit. 6, § 1515(b). This did not go as far as giving protection from all contract liability as New York and Minnesota later did. Rather, it was intended to cover the kind of misconduct that could also breach a contract such as malpractice, which might be simultaneously a tort and a breach of the attorney-client engagement agreement.

[20] Del. Code Ann., tit. 6, § 1515(b).

[21] 1997 Delaware Laws Ch. 114 (S.B. 115), approved June 30, 1997, and effective on enactment (amending Del. Code Ann., tit. 6, § 1515(b)).

[22] Del. Code Ann., tit. 6, §§ 15101 to 151210.

carried by the individual partner carrying the greatest amount of individual liability insurance" if greater than $100,000,[23] while eliminating the original Texas phrase, "if reasonably available." As the location of branch offices of many law firms, some of them Texas-based, the District permitted foreign limited liability partnerships to file locally and be governed by the liability limitations and other laws of the state in which they were formed.[24] It thus became the first jurisdiction to accept in legislation the conflict of laws provision that the internal affairs and liability limitations of inbound LLPs are governed by the laws of their place of organization or registration. A number of states later enacted similar hospitality to foreign LLPs. North Carolina in 1993 adopted the 1991 Texas provisions without substantive change except to omit the insurance requirement.[25]

In 1994, 13 states adopted LLP provisions, most copying the Texas or Delaware model with minor differences. As discussed below, LLP provisions made their way into R.U.P.A. in 1996, and today all states have adopted LLP provisions.

(c)   The Extension to All Liabilities

Of the 1994 LLP adoptions, only New York and Minnesota made major alterations, further enlarging the liability shield to approximate that for corporations and limited liability companies. New York was the more expansive of these two and at the same time the more restrictive. It was expansive—much like corporate or limited liability company law—in shielding the partners from vicarious liability for virtually all partnership obligations, whether from contracts, torts, or otherwise:

> [N]o partner of a partnership which is a registered limited liability partnership is liable or accountable, directly or indirectly (including by way of indemnification, contribution or otherwise), for any debts, obligations or liabilities of, or chargeable to, the registered limited liability partnership or each other, whether arising in tort, contract or otherwise, which are incurred, created or assumed by such partnership while such partnership is a registered limited liability partnership, solely by reason of being such a partner or acting (or omitting to act) in such capacity or rendering professional services or otherwise participating (as an employee, consultant, contractor or otherwise) in the conduct of the other business or activities of the registered limited liability partnership.[26]

---

[23] D.C. Code Ann. § 41-145 (repealed).
[24] D.C. Code Ann. § 41-147 (repealed).
[25] N.C. Gen. Stat. §§ 59-45, 59-84.2, 59-84.3.
[26] N.Y. P'ship Law § 26(b).

New York was restrictive in allowing only professional partnerships to be LLPs. It defined these as general partnerships that hold New York professional licenses, or that have at least one member who holds a New York professional license, or that are related to New York LLPs.[27] The favored professions were lawyers, medical doctors, dentists, professional engineers, accountants, land surveyors, and architects.[28]

There were exceptions to New York's broad protection from liability. A partner remained personally liable for his or her own negligent or wrongful acts or misconduct and for those of persons under his or her direct supervision and control.[29] Unlike any earlier statute, the New York statute provided that an LLP partner became prospectively liable "to the extent at least a majority of the partners shall have agreed unless otherwise provided in any agreement between the partners."[30] Thus it permitted the majority to contract away the LLP shield for some or all of its partners for some or all liabilities. In addition to the signal of altered status in the name requirement, New York mandated — consistently with its limited partnership provisions — that an LLP publish notice of its status for six weeks.[31] The state prescribed continuation of the liability shield through dissolution, winding up, and termination of the partnership.[32]

Minnesota expanded liability protection beyond misconduct. The original version included "anything chargeable to the partnership under Section 323.12 and Section 323.13, or for any other debts or obligations of the limited liability partnership."[33] The referenced sections are U.P.A. §§ 13 and 14 (wrongful acts and breaches of trust). By adding "any other debts or obligations," the expansion shielded contract liability at the same time it deleted liability for supervised and directed misconduct.

Recognizing that it had made the limited liability of an LLP substantially equivalent to that of a corporation, Minnesota included an implied invitation to override the liability protection by "piercing the veil" on grounds used in corporate law:

> (a) Except as provided in paragraph (b), the case law that states the conditions and circumstances under which the corporate veil of a corporation may be pierced under Minnesota law also applies to limited liability partnerships.

---

[27] N.Y. P'ship Law § 121-1500(a).
[28] N.Y. P'ship Law § 2, defining "profession" by reference to N.Y. Education Law Title 8.
[29] N.Y. P'ship Law § 26(c).
[30] N.Y. P'ship Law § 26(d).
[31] N.Y. P'ship Law § 121-1500(a).
[32] N.Y. P'ship Law § 26(f).
[33] Minn. Stat. Ann. § 323.14(2). The original Minnesota LLP Act has been replaced by provisions modeled on RUPA. *See* Minn. Stat. Ann. §§ 323a.1-01 to 12-03.

    (b) The use of informal procedures or arrangements for managing the limited liability partnership or conducting its business is not a ground for piercing the veil of the limited liability partnership.[34]

The original Minnesota statute also imposed liability on a partner for receiving distributions greater than would have been allowed if the LLP had been a corporation subject to prohibition of distributions when insolvent in the equity sense.[35] In addition, Minnesota preserved the right of the partnership and partners to sue a particular partner for breach of duty to the partnership or partners and for failure to contribute to losses and liabilities other than those for which the particular partner's liability is shielded.[36] And it prescribed continuation of the liability shield through dissolution, winding up, and termination of the partnership.[37]

    In 1995 there were moves toward eliminating even the moderate restrictions on limited liability included in the Minnesota and New York statutes. The American Bar Association, Business Law Section, Committee on Partnerships and Unincorporated Business Organizations, Working Group on Registered Limited Liability Partnerships, prepared Prototype Limited Liability Partnership provisions for inclusion in the Revised Uniform Partnership Act. These provisions, like New York's, eliminated vicarious liability for all kinds of debts without the corporate-type restrictions on distributions that are included in the Minnesota statute or a limitation to professionals as in New York. This act provided:

    A person is not, solely by reason of being a partner, liable, directly or indirectly, including by way of indemnification, contribution, assessment or otherwise, for debts, obligations or liabilities of, or chargeable to, the partnership, whether sounding in tort, contract or otherwise, which are incurred, created or assumed by the partnership while the partnership is a registered limited liability partnership.[38]

    Along similar lines, Georgia adopted an LLP act that provides for a complete and unrestricted liability limitation:

    [A] partner in a limited liability partnership is not individually liable or accountable, either directly or indirectly (by way of indemnification, reimbursement,

---

[34] Minn. Stat. Ann. § 323.14(3).

[35] Minn. Stat. Ann. § 323.14(5), referring to Minn. Stat. Ann. § 302A.551, whose general rule permits distributions "only if the board determines . . . that the corporation will be able to pay its debts in the ordinary course of business after making the distribution." The revised Minnesota statute cited in note 33, above, is closely based on R.U.P.A., which does not include the distribution restriction. For discussion of statutes that restrict distributions, see Section 4.04(d), below.

[36] Minn. Stat. Ann. § 323.14(2).

[37] Minn. Stat. Ann. § 323.14(4). The revised Minnesota statute cited in note 33 above, does not include either of these provisions.

[38] American Bar Association, Prototype LLP Act § 306(c).

contribution, assessment or otherwise) for any debts, obligations or liabilities of, or chargeable to, the partnership or another partner, whether arising in tort, contract or otherwise, that are incurred, created or assumed by such partnership while such partnership is a limited liability partnership, solely by reason of being such a partner or acting (or omitting to act) in such capacity or otherwise participating in the conduct of the activities of the limited liability partnership.[39]

By mid-1995, several more states had LLP statutes that eliminated partners' vicarious liability — new statutes in Colorado, Idaho, Indiana, Missouri, Montana, North Dakota, and South Dakota, and an amended version of the Maryland statute. These were joined in 1996 by Alabama, California, Connecticut, Massachusetts, Oregon, and Virginia. In 1997, the District of Columbia and the following additional states passed "full-shield" statutes: Arkansas, Delaware, Nebraska, New Mexico, Oklahoma, and Texas. In 1998 and 1999 the list of full-shield statutes expanded to include Florida, Iowa, Mississippi, and Vermont. The march toward full-shield protection continues, and in 2013 only nine states retain partial-shield statutes. The full list is in Chapter 3, Table 3-1. Under full-shield statutes, which are discussed in more detail in Section 3.03, the limited liability of partners in LLPs is substantially indistinguishable from that of corporate shareholders or members of LLCs. However, an LLP differs from a corporation in those states, just as it differs from a partnership there and elsewhere.

(d)   R.U.P.A.-based LLP Provisions

Until mid-1995, all the LLP provisions to date except Texas' 1993 revision were embodied in state versions of U.P.A. As noted above, the Prototype LLP Act proposed LLP provisions for inclusion in R.U.P.A. In August 1996, the National Conference of Commissioners on Uniform State Laws approved Limited Liability Partnership Amendments to the Uniform Partnership Act (1994). These amendments, coupled with the Prototype Act, assisted states in thoroughly integrating LLP provisions into R.U.P.A. A NCCUSL fact sheet lists states and territories adopting the various versions of R.U.P.A.[40] Specific citations to the 38 statutes based on R.U.P.A. at current writing are also listed in the Table in Chapter 8. State variations on R.U.P.A. are reflected in tables throughout this book.

---

[39] Ga. Code Ann. § 14-8-15(a).
[40] *See* http://uniformlaws.org/LegislativeFactSheet.aspx?title=Partnership Act.

(e)   The Current Status of the LLP

All U.S. jurisdictions have adopted LLP provisions. California[41] joined New York in permitting only professional firms to be LLPs (*see* Section 2.03(a)(3), below).

The LLP form was increasingly accepted through the 1990s but seems to have stabilized since the turn of the century. According to data reported by the Internal Revenue Service,[42] the number of limited liability partnerships filing information returns grew only slightly from 2001 to 2010. During that same time period, the filing of information returns by general partnerships declined while the filing of information returns by limited liability companies more than doubled. Nevertheless, the LLP form remains important in the professions. For example, Goldman, Sachs & Co. announced in May 1996 that it would convert to LLP form at the end of its fiscal year after 127 years as a general partnership. [43] The firm's senior partner noted considerations like those that apply to many firms—that "ownership, governance and partnership arrangements won't change in this new world," and that the firm simply wanted to improve "strength and stability" by protecting "against any kind of danger that a cyclical industry might face." The article noted a possible concern that capital withdrawal by partners, as happened in 1994, could deplete the firm's capital base. Previously reluctant large New York law firms have also adopted the LLP form in the wake of corporate scandals creating a risk of potentially huge liability. [44]

The LLP form also has been recognized outside the United States. The United Kingdom has enacted the Limited Liability Partnerships Act 2000.[45] The act provides that limited liability partnerships shall be treated as a "legal persona-

---

[41] *See* Cal. Corp. Code § 16101(6).

[42] *See* http://www.irs.gov/pub/irs-soi/10pasnapshot.pdf.

[43] O'Brian, Goldman Chooses Limited Liability For New Structure, Wall St. J., May 21, 1996, at C13.

[44] For an empirical study of the adoption of the LLP form by New York law firms, see Scott Baker & Kimberly D. Krawiec, The Economics of Limited Liability: An Empirical Study of New York Law Firms, 2005 U. Ill. L. Rev. 107. Since the publication of that study, most other major law firms in New York have adopted the LLP form.

[45] *See* United Kingdom Statute, Ch. 12, *available at* http://www.hmso.gov.uk/acts/acts2000/00012-a.htm-c.htm. For commentary on the Act, see Explanatory Notes to Limited Liability Partnerships Act 2000 (July 20, 2000), *available at* http://www.hmso.gov.uk/acts/en/2000en12.htm; Milman, Limited Liability Partnerships: The Waiting Goes On, International Company and Commercial Law Review 11(10) 329 (2000).

lity separate from that of its members."[46] However, details such as the extent to which the entity's default provisions are based on partnership law or the law of other business entities were left to be determined in separate regulations.[47] Limited liability partnership provisions also have been adopted in the Canadian provinces of Ontario and Alberta, after having been considered at the federal level in Canada.[48]

§ 1.02 INTRODUCTION TO THE LLP FORM

(a) LLP as a General Partnership

An LLP is, in fact, a general partnership.[49] Most LLP statutes provide that an LLP must be a "partnership" to register as such (*see* Section 2.02, below) and also explicitly define "partnership" to include LLPs (*see* Table 2-1).

(b) Limited Liability

LLPs' most significant feature is that their members have some form of limited liability. As discussed above in Section 1.01, the vast majority of LLP statutes provide that LLP partners are not, solely by virtue of their status as such, individually liable for partnership debts, whether based on contract or on the negligence or other misconduct of other partners or employees.

---

[46] *See* Limited Liability Partnerships Act 2000, note 45, supra, Section 2.

[47] *See id.*, *passim*, and Explanatory Notes, supra, note 45.

[48] *See* Alberta Partnership Act, R.S.A., 1980, c. P2. Ontario P'ships Act, R.S.O., 1990, c. P5; Manzer, A Practical Guide to Canadian Partnership Law (1996), LLP Supplement (October 2000).

[49] *See* Institute of Physical Med. & Rehabilitation, LLP. v. Country Wide Ins., 193 Misc. 2d 803, 752 N.Y.S.2d 232 (N.Y. City Civ. Ct. 2002) (LLP is a "partnership" for purposes of bringing claim in commercial division of small claims part). Some cases have distinguished LLPs from general partnerships for some purposes. *See* In re Promedicus Health Group, LLP, 416 B.R. 389, 391 (Bankr. W.D.N.Y. 2009) (held that LLP partners' potential personal liability for wrongful acts under the N.Y. statute did not make them general partners for purposes of determining the partnership's insolvency under bankruptcy law; the court noted that "[i]t is simply incorrect to think of the 'universe' of partnerships in the State of New York as consisting only of general partnerships and limited partnerships. Consequently, it is incorrect to think of the universe of *partners* as being only general partners and limited partners" [emphasis in original]); Largo Realty, Inc. v. Purcell, 77 Mass. App. Ct. 162, 928 N.E.2d 999, 1001–02 (2010) (noting that LLP is one of three types of partnerships, along with general and limited partnerships, differing according to the partners' liability).

In analyzing LLPs and comparing them with other types of business associations, it is important to keep in mind that LLP statutes vary regarding the nature of LLP partners' liability. Under some statutes LLP partners *are* liable for several categories of conduct, including conduct that is no more than a breach of contract (*see* Section 3.02, below). Under other statutes LLP partners have limited liability for all categories of claims (*see* Section 3.03, below). However, under both types of statutes partners may be liable for participating in or supervising wrongful conduct (*see* Section 3.04, below).

As discussed throughout this book, the limited liability of LLP members raises many questions. These concern not only the extent of partners' liability but also the internal rules governing LLPs (*see* Chapter 4), the treatment of LLPs under nonpartnership statutes (*see* Chapter 7), and choice of the LLP form (*see* Section 1.04, below).

(c) Registration and Related Duties

In return for their limited liability, LLP members sacrifice some of the informality of general partnership. LLP provisions prescribe registration formalities, restrict the name of the LLP and, in some cases, require the firm to carry insurance or ensure the availability of specified minimum assets (*see* Chapter 2).

(d) Recognition of Foreign LLPs

LLP provisions introduce important choice of law issues into partnership law. Formerly, choice-of-law issues were minimal in partnership law because of the uniformity of partnership law and the fact that most issues were settled by agreement rather than by the statute. However, LLP provisions include statutory formalities and rules regarding limited liability that cannot be settled entirely by contract among the partners. Also, there is much more diversity across the states regarding LLP provisions than there used to be in partnership law. These factors raise questions concerning the enforceability of LLP provisions in non-LLP states (*see* Chapter 6).

(e) Entity Nature of an LLP

Whether a partnership is an entity or an aggregate has long been a disputed issue,[50] though R.U.P.A. § 2.01(a) states definitively that a partnership is an entity distinct from its partners.[51] Where the characterization of a partnership remains in doubt, limited liability makes entity characterization of LLPs more certain.[52]

§ 1.03 THEORETICAL ISSUES REGARDING LLPs

This section presents a brief overview of some theoretical issues raised by the overall concept of the LLP—that is, by permitting general partners to limit their liability. These issues, which have been important in the evolution of LLP statutes, the use of LLPs by firms, the tax and regulatory treatment of LLPs, and the application and enforcement of LLP provisions by courts. The issues will be discussed in more detail throughout this book.[53]

(a) Limited Liability

As discussed in more detail below in Section 3.01, the main issue raised by LLP provisions is whether statutes ought to limit the liability of general partners. If

---

[50] *See* Bromberg & Ribstein on Partnership, § 1.03 (hereinafter "Bromberg & Ribstein").

[51] The U.P.A. does not explicitly characterize the partnership and contains both aggregate features, such as technical dissolution on dissociation of a member, and entity features, such as the partnership's power to take title to property. Bromberg & Ribstein, § 1.03(c)(1).

[52] For cases recognizing the entity nature of an LLP, see United States v. Stein, 463 F. Supp. 2d 459, 464 (S.D.N.Y. 2006) (Del. law; partner of large accounting LLP treated as employee for purposes of applying attorney-client privilege to communications between partner and firm's counsel given that partnership has "over one thousand partners who probably are not exposed to unlimited liability for partnership obligations," citing Delaware law both on LLP liability limitation and general characterization of partnership as entity); In re Zecher, 2006 WL 3519316 (Bankr. D. Mass. Dec. 6, 2006) (Mass. law; transfer of LLP's property to partner was transfer from a separate entity which resulted in limitation of partner's homestead exemption); Resource Bankshares Corp. v. St. Paul Mercury Ins. Co., 323 F. Supp. 2d 709 (E.D. Va. 2004) (LLP was a "person" under liability policy providing coverage for "making known to any person or organization written or spoken material that violates a person's right of privacy"); Hecht, Solberg, Robinson, Goldberg & Bagley v. Superior Court, 137 Cal. App. 4th 579, 595, 40 Cal. Rptr. 3d 446, 457 (2006) (LLP is a separate entity from its individual partners who have privacy rights, though court assumes without deciding that the LLP also has privacy rights). *See also* Marin v. Gilberg, 2008 WL 2770382 (S.D. Tex. July 11, 2008) (holding that LLP cannot appear pro se and must be represented by counsel).

[53] For an overview of theoretical issues regarding modern unincorporated firms generally and comparing specific forms, see Ribstein, The Rise of The Uncorporation, ch. 7 (2010).

members who directly participate in management can limit their individual liability for the firm's debts, they have a greater incentive to engage in activities that have high potential payoffs for the owners but that impose risks on the creditors.

It is important to refine the policy issue concerning limited liability in three respects. First, there never has been any question concerning partners' ability to enter into specific "nonrecourse" contracts with their creditors (*see* Section 3.01, below). Designating a firm as one having limited liability can be considered a kind of nonrecourse contract with those who extend credit knowing of the designation. Thus, the main issue in LLPs concerns whether the statute ought to grant partners' immunity for claims as to other creditors, including tort claimants who have no opportunity to contract for liability.

A second refinement of the limited liability issue concerns professional firms. Professional malpractice liability is similar to contract liability in the sense that, unlike many torts, it arises out of a consensual relationship in which the client has an opportunity to bargain with the firm. However, professional firms are subject to special regulation based on the idea that clients ought to be assured of a high level of service irrespective of their contract. This is important because of the heavy use of the partnership form by professional firms. This aspect of the limited liability issue is explored in Chapter 7. Also, large law and accounting firms may have special responsibilities in representing to the public the truthfulness of their clients' disclosures. They may, therefore, be held liable to those who were not directly their clients, such as shareholders in the client, for aiding and abetting securities fraud or under other theories.

Finally, it is important to keep in mind that the limited liability issue as it arises regarding LLPs is not whether firms' owners ought to be able to limit their liability in general, but whether they ought to be able to do so through this particular form of business. This actually involves two subissues, discussed in the following subsections: (1) To what extent does the particular form of business provide protection for third-party creditors? (2) Is it appropriate to offer limited liability as part of a form that is otherwise designed on the assumption that its members will be personally liable? The first question primarily implicates third parties, while the second relates primarily to the members themselves.

(b)   Prerequisites of Limited Liability: Formalities and Other Mandatory Rules

Limited liability is available to members of other types of firms, most notably LLCs, corporations, and limited partnerships. Accordingly, the policy issue concerning limited liability is not whether the liability should be limited at all, but whether it should be limited specifically in the LLP form. This, in turn, depends on differences among the types of firms that use the various business forms, and concerning how LLP provisions protect involuntary creditors as compared with other limited liability forms. Unlike limited partnerships and corporations, LLP members can directly participate in management and therefore can cause the firm to engage in activities that injure creditors. However, LLPs do not differ in this respect from close corporations or from LLCs, both of which permit direct member participation in management. Also, unlike all other forms of limited liability firms, most LLP statutes generally do not restrict distributions or compromise of contribution obligations that could increase the third parties' risks of relying on the firm's assets (exceptions are discussed in Section 4.04(d), below). In this respect, the LLP form does present genuine issues regarding the expansion of limited liability. Potential problems are mitigated, however, by two important factors. First, some LLP statutes require LLP firms to carry substantial insurance or equivalent liability protection (*see* Section 2.06, below). Second, most LLP statutes provide for only a restricted form of limited liability. In particular, under most statutes LLP members may be held liable to the extent that they participate in or supervise wrongdoing even if their activity is not tortious in itself (*see* Section 3.02, below).

(c) Limited Liability and the Partnership Standard Form

A critical issue concerning limited liability as it applies specifically to LLPs is that it may create problems in terms of determining and applying other aspects of partnership law (*see* Chapter 4). Partnership statutes are designed in light of members' personal liability for the firm's debts. In particular, general partnership statutes provide, subject to contrary agreement, for equal and direct participation in management, equal financial rights, restricted transferability of management rights, the power to voluntarily withdraw from the firm, and for dissolution on dissociation of a member. All of these provisions are designed to accommodate the interests of personally liable members who need to control their potential personal liability, and whose shares in the firm should reflect their contributions of personal assets or credit. If, instead, members have limited liability, equal financial rights may not properly reflect the members' contributions to the firm. Also, the costs in terms of continuity of the firm of giving each member the right to veto major transactions or amendments and the right to exit at any time may exceed the benefits in terms of protecting individual members from exposure to personal liability. And combining limited liability with provisions designed for personally liable members may make the courts' job of interpreting and filling gaps in the statute and the parties' agreement more difficult. This can increase the uncertainty and costs of resolving partnership disputes.

These differences raise issues concerning whether courts should develop a separate jurisprudence to LLPs and to non-LLP partnerships. They also make it important for partners to consider carefully whether they want the statutory default rules to apply to their firm.

The potential problems involved in including limited liability provisions in a statute that is designed for firms whose members have personal liability are, however, offset to some extent by the advantages of the combination. These advantages include the availability of partnership precedents to resolve LLP disputes, the ease of converting from general partnership to LLP form (*see* Section 2.04, below), and the greater certainty that LLPs will be treated as partnerships for tax and regulatory purposes (*see* Chapter 7).

§ 1.04   CHOICE OF FORM: GENERAL COMPARISONS WITH OTHER BUSINESS FORMS

In deciding whether to become an LLP, a firm must make three types of evaluations. First, how does the LLP differ from other types of business association "standard forms" the firm could adopt? This section provides a brief overview of some general differences between LLPs and other types of business associations that relate to this determination. It focuses on the differences that appear from the business association statutes themselves. Section 1.07 below discusses these and other differences in more detail.

Second, an existing firm must decide whether the costs of the transition to a new form outweigh the benefits of this transition rather than maintaining the firm's current organizational form. Considerations that are relevant to the second question are discussed below in Section 1.05.

Third, the firm must choose a particular statute under which to organize — that of a state in which it will operate, or a more favorable statute in another state. An important consideration is the relative benefits of a nonoperation-state statute. Section 1.06 summarizes some of the main variations among LLP statutes.

Section 1.07 combines all of these considerations and presents an overview of the factors relating to the choice of form and choice of statute determinations.

(a)   Comparison with General Partnerships

As discussed above in Section 1.02(a), an LLP is defined explicitly or implicitly as a partnership under partnership law. Nevertheless, LLPs differ from other general partnerships in at least two important respects: the limited liability of LLP members (*see* Section 1.02(a), above) and the formalities and other prerequisites of obtaining this limited liability (*see* Section 1.02(b), above). These express statutory differences might support other, subtler, differences between the two types of firms. First, courts could interpret provisions of the general partnership statute or apply general partnership case law differently in cases involving LLPs than in cases involving other types of partnerships. For example, compliance or failure to comply with LLP formalities might affect an LLP's existence as a partnership in addition to its LLP status (*see* Section 2.07(d), below), or LLP partners' fiduciary duties might be interpreted differently from those of other types of partners (*see* Section 4.05, below).

A second subtle difference between LLPs and other partnerships concerns partnership agreements. Even if partnerships share default statutory provisions with LLPs, the partners might decide to allocate financial rights in their agreement differently depending on the extent to which the partners bear personal liability for the firm's debts (*see* Sections 2.09(g) and 4.04, below).

(b) Limited Partnerships

LLPs differ in the following respects from limited partnerships:[54]

(1) Unlike general partners in many limited partnerships, LLP partners are not individually liable for all debts of the business.[55]

(2) Unlike limited partners, LLP partners under some statutes are liable for some debts of the LLP (*see* Section 1.02(b), above).

(3) Unlike limited partners,[56] LLP partners' limited liability does not depend on whether they participate in the general management and control of the firm. Rather, under most LLP statutes, nonmanaging LLP partners may be liable only for participating in or supervising particular conduct or partners (*see* Section 3.04, below).

[54] These differences are based on the Revised Uniform Limited Partnership Act (1985), some version of which is in effect in most states. The difference concerning partner liabilities may not apply if the limited partnership has registered as an LLP as discussed below in Chapter 5. Many of the other differences listed here, including the "control" rule noted in (3) and the extent of "linkage" with the general partnership statute noted in (8), are affected by the revision of the Revised Uniform Limited Partnership Act by the National Conference of Commissioners on Uniform State Laws, referred to as U.L.P.A. (2001), which is set forth in Appendix D and discussed in detail below in Chapter 9. U.L.P.A. (2001) has been adopted by 18 states and the District of Columbia.

[55] *See* Verizon Yellow Pages Co. v. Sims & Sims, P.C., 15 Mass. L. Rptr. 734, 2003 WL 836087 (Mass. Super. Feb. 24, 2003) (holding that, because LLP partner had no exposure to liability, he could not represent the LLP pro se, distinguishing case involving limited partnership's representation by general partner).

[56] U.L.P.A. § 303 (2001), which eliminates the "control rule," is discussed infra in Chapter 9, § 9.303.

(4)   The formalities and other organizational prerequisites of LLPs differ from those in limited partnerships (*see* Sections 2.03–2.06, below). LLPs are subject to some requirements that do not apply to limited partnerships, such as yearly renewals of registration and minimum insurance.

(5)   An LLP that does not comply with formalities is probably a general partnership both internally and among the members (*see* Section 2.07(d), below), while a limited partnership that does not comply with formalities probably remains a limited partnership among the members, and may or may not be a general partnership vis-à-vis third parties.[57]

(6)   Limited partnership statutes generally restrict distributions and the effect of compromising member contribution obligations,[58] while most LLP statutes do not.

(7)   LLP statutes apply general partnership rules regarding equal financial and management rights among partners, while limited partnership statutes differentiate in many important respects between limited and general partners.

(8)   More generally, limited partnership statutes include many provisions that apply only to limited partnerships, including provisions on management and control, member dissociation, distributions, contributions, and dissolution,[59] while LLP statutes include only a few provisions that apply specifically to LLPs and otherwise apply general partnership rules to LLPs.

(c)   Limited Liability Companies

LLPs differ in several respects from limited liability companies (LLCs). The differences tend to make the LLP form better suited to very closely held informal firms or professional firms, while the LLC may be better suited to more formal firms.[60]

---

[57] *See* Bromberg & Ribstein, § 12.04.

[58] *See id.* § 12.08; R.U.L.P.A. §§ 502(c), 607–08.

[59] Again, this difference may become more pronounced with the promulgation of U.L.P.A. (2001), which "delinks" limited and general partnership law. *See* § 9.101(b), infra.

[60] *See* Stover and Hamill, The LLC versus LLP Conundrum: Advice for Businesses Contemplating the Choice, 50 Alabama L. Rev. 813 (1999) (discussing advantages of LLP form for informal firms). LLC statutory provisions are tabulated in appendices in Ribstein & Keatinge on Limited Liability Companies (2d ed. 2004) (hereinafter "Ribstein & Keatinge"), Chapters 4–13.

(1) LLP members are individually liable for some partnership debts under some statutes (*see* Section 1.02(b), above), while LLC members are not liable solely by virtue of being members in an LLC.[61]

(2) LLPs, like other general partnerships, are governed by statutory default rules that give members equal financial rights. By contrast, default provisions of LLC statutes often allocate financial rights according to capital contributions.

(3) Statutory default rules may be varied only by written agreement under many LLC statutes. Agreements in general partnerships, including LLPs, generally need not be in writing to be enforceable.

(4) LLC statutes provide that the firm can elect to be governed by default rules that provide for centralized management and nonparticipation of non-managing members. By contrast, LLP partners, like those in other general partnerships, have equal rights to participate in management. Partners may vary the rule among themselves by contrary agreement. However, since every partner is an agent of the partnership, it may be difficult to prevent non-managing partners from binding the firm vis-à-vis third parties.

(5) LLC statutes may provide by default for amendment of the agreement by majority vote. LLPs are subject to the usual general partnership unanimity default rule for amendment and other important acts.

(6) LLC statutes may limit dissociation and dissolution, while general partnership default provisions that apply to LLPs permit dissociation and dissolution at will.

(d) Corporations

LLPs differ from corporations in the following respects:

(1) Under some LLP statutes LLP members have only a restricted form of limited liability, as distinguished from corporate shareholders who have no liability solely by virtue of being shareholders.[62]

(2) Unlike shareholders in the "standard form" corporation, LLP partners participate directly in management and control unless they otherwise

---

[61] LLC members, like LLP members, also may be held liable under common law principles for participation in wrongdoing. At the same time, as discussed in Section 1.01, supra, the clear trend in LLP statutes is toward a complete limited liability shield. Accordingly, there may be little difference in member liability between the two types of firms in most cases.

[62] As with LLCs, however, shareholders may be liable under common law principles for participating in wrongdoing. At the same time, most LLP statutes provide for a complete limited liability shield. *See* Section 1.01, supra. Accordingly, there may not be a significant difference in this respect between LLP partners and shareholders.

agree. Even if they otherwise agree, each LLP partner, unlike a corporate shareholder, has the power to bind the firm vis-à-vis third parties who are unaware of limitations on the partners' authority.

(3)   Default rules relating to internal corporate governance differ significantly from the partnership rules that apply to LLPs in many other respects. In a "standard form" corporation, ownership interests are freely transferable, dissociation of a member does not dissolve the firm, and distributions to members are subject to restrictions that are intended to protect creditors. Although close corporations may be operated somewhat like partnerships, general corporate rules apply except to the extent that the firm specifically opts out of those rules·or that special statutory close corporation rules apply.

(4)   General partnerships must change their form through a conversion, merger, or related procedure to become a corporation, but not to become an LLP.

(5)   Organizational formalities and requirements regarding insurance and annual renewal differ significantly between corporations and LLPs (*see* Sections 2.03–2.06, below).

§ 1.05   DECISION TO CHANGE BUSINESS FORM

This section discusses considerations that relate primarily to an existing partnership's decision whether to change its business form, and in particular to register as an LLP — the situation for which the LLP provisions were primarily designed.[63]

(a)   Revising and Writing the Parties' Agreement

One problem in converting to a limited liability firm is that the parties may need to revise their agreement. By requiring only a simple registration by an existing firm, LLP statutes ostensibly make this process less burdensome than for other forms of business associations. Since other partnership default rules continue to

---

[63] For an empirical and theoretical analysis of law firms' decision to adopt the LLP form, see Baker & Karwiec, The Economics of Limited Liability: An Empirical Study of New York Law Firms, 2005 Ill. L. Rev. 107. It has been suggested that lawyers may face potential malpractice liability for advice in connection with selection of the LLP form, a risk exacerbated by Kentucky's decision to tax LLPs as corporations. *See* Rutledge & Vestal, Making the Obvious Choice Malpractice: LLPs and the Lawyer Liability Time Bomb in Kentucky's 2005 Tax Modernization, 94 Ky. L.J. 17 (2005–2006).

apply, the partners need not review their agreement in light of new default rules. Moreover, partners may amend their agreements orally, while LLC statutes provide that only written operating agreements may override statutory provisions.[64] Drafting agreements may require renegotiation and, in turn, may force underlying disagreements to the surface, which could even lead to a breakup of the firm.

The contrast with other forms in this respect is not, however, as stark as it may first appear. Although LLP registration does not specifically require redrafting agreements, it may make revisions advisable. Most importantly, the parties may need to revise their shares in the firm to reflect the reduction in risk to which partners in some aspects of the firm's business are exposed (*see* Sections 2.09(g) and 4.04, below), and revise provisions on contribution and indemnification (*see* Sections 2.09(c)–(e), below). The need to renegotiate is virtually ensured by the fact that a majority, if not all, of the partners must approve the filing (*see* Section 2.04, below). If the agreement is changed, it is safer to do so in writing.

(b) Legal Aspects of Conversion or Registration

Registering as an LLP does not technically involve the creation of a new business or legal entity and, therefore, generally should not trigger strong consequences under either agreements or statutes (*see* Section 4.08, below). In particular, most LLP statutes permit approval of registration by only a majority or majority-in-interest of the partners (*see* Section 2.04, below).

By contrast, a change from the general partnership form to an LLC or corporation may involve dissolution and termination of the partnership and a transfer of assets to the new firm. This may require approval of all partners, cause the termination of existing contracts, and create the possibility of continuing personal liability for post-dissolution debts.[65] However, as discussed in Section 8.902 and Section 8.905, below, some partnership statutes provide for conversion or mergers of partnerships into other business entities, including LLCs.[66] Although this procedure eliminates the need for termination and transfer of assets, it may provide for somewhat less continuity than LLP registration.[67]

---

[64] *See* Ribstein & Keatinge, § 4.16 and App. 4-1 (tabulating state statutory provisions).

[65] *See* Bromberg & Ribstein, § 7.21 (discussing the analogous situation of incorporation of a general partnership).

[66] Conversions also may be provided for in LLC or multiple-entity statutes. *See* Ribstein & Keatinge, App. 11-1.

[67] For example, Town of Vernon v. Rumford Assocs. IV, 53 Conn. App. 785, 732 A.2d 779 (1999) held that an entity that converted into an LLC was not subject to any bankruptcy stay that might have applied to the LLC when it filed for bankruptcy because the LLC was not automatically a party to the foreclosure. Had the case involved a partnership that registered as an LLP, the court might not have separated the two entities. For a discussion of the effect of LLC conversion provisions, see Ribstein & Keatinge, § 11.13.

One of the main potential categories of legal consequences of the change in form is tax law. When firms change business form, this could be regarded as a termination of the prior entity. There are no tax consequences merely from the conversion to a different form, as where a partnership converts to an LLC.[68] There may, however, be tax consequences from the change in the partners' responsibility for losses. Partners share liabilities according to their risk of loss. In a conversion to a limited liability type of firm, such as an LLC, the members would, by default, share the debt by profit ratios. Moreover, decreases in the members' share in the liabilities as a result of the conversion would be effective taxable distributions to those members, while members who bear personal liability for the debts, as through guarantees, would be making effective contributions to the firm. This analysis probably would hold for LLPs *if* members would no longer bear personal liability. However, under some statutes LLP members retain liability to voluntary creditors for ordinary contracts (*see* Section 1.02(b), above). Since the misconduct-based liabilities for which partners retain personal responsibility are only contingent in most firms, the change to LLP status may not cause a reshuffling of financial contributions and distributions, as does the complete limited liability in LLCs (*see* Section 3.02, below).

§ 1.06   VARIATION AMONG STATUTES

It is important to keep in mind that firms not only have a choice of *forms*, but also a choice of *statutes* (*see* Section 2.08, below). A firm technically may be able to choose to register under an LLP statute located in a state different from the firm's chief executive office or operational base. This statute may offer a better cost-benefit tradeoff than the local LLP or other limited liability statute. However, this alternative may not be available for some firms, such as professional firms that must, in any event, comply with local rules restricting forms of business in general and liability limitation in particular (*see* Section 7.04, below). Moreover, the cost in terms of registration and other fees of operating as a foreign firm in the operation state may outweigh any advantages of choosing a particular statute.

There are two significant types of variations in LLP statutes. The first involves the nature of the liability limitation. Most importantly, while a few LLP statutes retain individual partner liability for contract-type debts, most provide for limited liability for both contract-type and tort-type debts (*see* Section 3.03 and Table 3-1, below). The second type of variation concerns the general nature

---

[68] *See* Ribstein & Keatinge, § 17.16. As to business entity conversions generally, see Frost, The Federal Income Tax Consequences of Business Entity Conversions, J. Real Est. Tax. 83, Winter 1999.

of the partnership statute on which the LLP provisions are based. As of this writing some LLP statutes are still based on the original version of the U.P.A. However, as discussed in Section 1.01(d), most LLP provisions are now included in partnership acts that are based at least to some extent on R.U.P.A., as most states have now adopted that Act.

There are also many variations in LLC and corporate statutes, particularly regarding closely held firms. The discussion in the next section focuses on standard variations of each.[69]

§ 1.07 SUMMARY OF CHOICE-OF-FORM CONSIDERATIONS

This section elaborates on the general considerations discussed in Sections 1.04–1.06 relating to a firm's decisions as to the organizational form and statute under which it should organize. It presents a three-stage model of the decision-making process. Subsection (a) assumes that the decision is being made by a brand new firm that can choose any business organization statute in the country without being penalized for operating outside the formation state. Subsection (b) changes these facts by assuming that the firm is an existing business that is deciding whether and how to change its organizational form. This brings in the considerations discussed in Section 1.06. Subsection (c) further complicates the decision by introducing costs of operating outside the formation state. Subsection (d) then presents an overall summary of a firm's decisionmaking process. Table 1-1 summarizes the choice-of-form considerations discussed below for LLPs, LLCs, and corporations.

(a) New Firm — Any Statute

Several factors drive the organizational decisionmaking process of a new firm that can choose any statute. A firm should begin by considering the factors discussed in this first subcategory. The factors are listed in approximate order of importance. Any one of the first few factors may be important enough for most firms to outweigh combination of factors further down the list.

(1) Federal Tax Classification

This factor once loomed large but has now been diminished by the "check-the-box" rule (*see* Section 7.05). The following discussion does not deal in depth

---

[69] LLC statutes are discussed and summarized in detail in Ribstein & Keatinge.

with the complicated tax issues presented by the choice between the partnership, corporate, and Subchapter S forms.[70]

(2) Eligibility of Form for Type of Business

The decisionmaking process discussed in this section takes for granted the basic business characteristics of the firm, including the nature of the business and number of owners. Once these characteristics are determined, the firm obviously cannot select a business form that does not permit these characteristics.

(i) Professional

These firms must determine whether they are eligible to choose a particular business form under the business association statute or licensing or ethical rule. The LLP form is perhaps the most readily available for most professional firms, but there are exceptions under statutes and local rules as to both the firm's ability to practice in the LLP form and the application of the LLP tort shield (*see* Section 7.04).

(ii) Nonprofit

Partnership statutes generally exclude these firms from using the partnership, and therefore the LLP, form (*see* Section 2.02(c)).[71] However, they may be able to organize under some LLC statutes[72] or under nonprofit corporation statutes.

(iii) One-member

One-member firms cannot be LLPs (*see* Section 2.02(c)), but may incorporate, and may also be LLCs under many statutes.[73]

(3) Liability Shield

In the absence of tax classification concerns, the scope and other characteristics of the liability shield are probably the most important factors now

---

[70] For a discussion of the latter choice, see Lee, A Populist Political Perspective of the Business Tax Entities Universe: "Hey the Stars Might Lie but the Numbers Never Do," 78 Tex. L. Rev. 885 (2000).

[71] However, the Delaware statute provides that a partnership may be formed not for profit if there is intent to form a partnership. Del. Code Ann., tit. 6, § 15-202.

[72] *See* Ribstein & Keatinge, § 4.10.

[73] *Id.* § 4.03.

driving choice of statute and form. The considerations relating specifically to choice of a particular LLP statute are discussed below in Section 2.08.

Most firms will want a full liability shield — that is, one that provides that members are not personally liable for the firm's debts of any type. This would limit the firm to the LLC or corporate form or to a "full-shield"-type LLP statute that limits members' liability for all kinds of debts (*see* Section 3.03). A firm has several options if it expects to deal exclusively or primarily with creditors who want the members to have vicarious liability. It could choose to organize under a partial-shield LLP statute that excepts contract-type debts from the shield, or could organize under a full-shield LLP or LLC statute that provides a clear procedure for waiving some or all liabilities. The latter choice may be preferable for many firms, since organizing under a partial-shield statute leaves the members vulnerable to potentially narrow judicial interpretations of the shield (*see* Section 3.02). On the other hand, creditors may prefer the security of default liability to relying on a waiver of a default liability shield.

The firm also should consider whether the statute provides for direct liability for supervising or monitoring partners (*see* Section 3.04). This type of liability may be a significant cost of choosing the statute, depending on how broadly it is interpreted and on whether the firm is exposed to such liability in any event under professional ethics rules (*see* Section 7.04(b)).

(4) Taxes and Registration Fees

The taxes and fees the formation state imposes on the firm may be a significant consideration in choice of form, particularly if other factors are equally balanced. A few states require registration and renewal fees for LLPs, sometimes based on the number of partners (*see* Section 2.03 and Table 2-5). These fees may be rather high, particularly for large partnerships.

State taxes usually are not a consideration in choice of form or statute because most states follow the federal classification scheme.[74] However, in Pennsylvania and Texas, which impose corporate income taxes on LLCs but not on LLPs,[75] it may be cheaper to organize as an LLP.

(5) Insurance or Financial Security Requirements

These requirements in LLP statutes are discussed in Section 2.06, and their relevance to the choice of a particular LLP statute is discussed in Section 2.08.

---

[74] For specific state-by-state tax differences between LLCs and LLPs, see Ely & Grissom, LLC and LLP Scorecard: An Update, 93 Tax Notes 695 (Oct. 29, 2001).

[75] 15 Pa. C.S.A. § 8925 (although being phased out by 2009); Vernon's Tex. Tax Code Ann. § 171.002. However, several states impose per-partner fees on LLPs. *See* Section 2.03(b)(11) and Table 2-5, infra.

The requirements may be less than the insurance or security many firms would have to obtain for their own protection and in any event may be imposed by local professional licensing rules. Nevertheless, statutory requirements may cause a problem even for such firms since failure to comply may cost the firm its liability shield. This is especially important in light of the difficult interpretation problems under some of these statutes.

(6) Other Financial Regulations

Whether the statute regulates distributions to partners may be particularly important (*see* Section 4.04(d)). In professional firms, rigid prohibitions on distributions by "insolvent" firms may be a severe problem for firms that normally compensate partners by paying out all or most net earnings. Although fraudulent transfer rules may restrict distributions by all types of firms, additional statutory restrictions add another potentially costly layer of regulation. Note that the choice of form may matter under fraudulent conveyance or fraudulent transfer rules since it is not clear how these rules apply to LLPs (*see* Section 4.04(d)).

(7) Formalities and Loss of Liability Shield

The more formalities a statute requires, the greater the potential organizational cost and the greater the chance of inadvertent loss of the liability shield.

Initial registration disclosures for LLPs are set forth in Table 2-2 and discussed in Section 2.03(b). Perhaps the most burdensome requirement is the partners' names and addresses, which some owners would prefer not to disclose. A few LLP statutes require disclosure of partners' identities. LLC statutes go no further than requiring disclosure of *initial* organizers or owners.

Many LLP statutes require annual renewal or reports, although the statutes commonly require notice before cancellation of the registration and some permit retroactive reinstatement (*see* Section 2.03(c)). While corporate and LLC statutes normally do not include such requirements, they are not particularly burdensome (apart from the fees discussed immediately above). Moreover, all firms have an incentive to ensure that they do not maintain stale information on their public records.

LLC and LLP statutes generally require few operational formalities, such as meetings, although LLC statutes may provide for some formalities.[76] Corporation statutes, on the other hand, often provide by default for numerous operational formalities that potentially may apply even to closely held firms.

Apart from explicit statutory provisions regarding the loss of the liability shield, noncompliance with formalities may support a veil-piercing claim, at least

---

[76] *See* Ribstein & Keatinge, §§ 8.03–8.04.

where other factors, such as undercapitalization, are also present. The relative absence of operational formalities in LLPs therefore gives this form an edge regarding the security of the shield. This and other differences between LLPs and corporations with regard to veil-piercing are discussed in Section 3.08.[77]

(8)   Suitability of Default Rules: In General

LLC and partnership statutes are well designed for closely held firms. In general, their default rules assume that owners will be involved in management, will make significant capital and labor investments, and want an exit mechanism in the form of the ability to sell their interests back to the firm. At the same time, the rules give the members ample flexibility to vary these default rules.

By contrast, corporate default rules assume that members will delegate management to directors and officers, provide for standardized financial interests, and assume that members will rely on public securities markets to exit the firm. Although close corporation provisions vary these default rules, there are often gaps in the rules, particularly regarding exit from the firm. Courts may fill the gaps in unpredictable ways, such as by assuming the parties wanted to be treated like partners even if they incorporated.

There are some important variations within these generalizations. General partnership default rules, which apply to LLPs that are not limited partnerships (*see* Chapter 4), are adapted for very closely held firms. They assume that owners are not only co-equal, but are each so important to the firm that the firm should dissolve when a member leaves and each member should be able to veto additional members. As discussed in more detail in Paragraphs 9 through 11 below, LLC statutes and R.U.P.A. are better suited to closely held firms that want to have passive members and to continue following member dissociation.

(9)   Restricting Management Authority

A particular respect in which LLCs are better adapted than partnerships to closely held firms concerns restrictions on nonmanaging members' ability to bind the firm. While any partner can bind the firm in ordinary matters (*see* Section 4.03(a)), corporations, limited partnerships, and LLCs can readily confine agency power to directors or officers, general partners, or managing members, respectively. However, the LLC's advantage in this respect over general partners is mitigated by uncertainties regarding the agency power of nonmanaging members and who will be characterized as a manager.[78] Also, the Revised Uniform Limited Liability Company Act has no default provision regarding the apparent

---

[77] Veil-piercing in LLCs is discussed in *id.* § 12.03.
[78] *See* Ribstein & Keatinge, § 8.09.

authority of LLC members and managers, implicitly leaving this to agency law.[79] Since the common law of agency is unclear as to the authority of LLC members and managers, RULLCA would significantly reduce the clarity of LLC law on this issue and thus reduce or eliminate this advantage of LLCs over LLPs. There may be better partnership-based alternatives. In particular, the firm could choose to be an LLLP and restrict management to the general partners (*see* Section 5.05, below). Also, the statement of partner authority R.U.P.A. provides for (*see* Section 4.03(b), below) closes this gap between LLCs and partnerships.

(10) Continuity of Firm

As noted in Paragraph 8, general partnerships have less continuity than other business forms because under the traditional U.P.A. rule they dissolve when a single member leaves. Although the members can provide in the partnership agreement for a measure of continuity of the business, they cannot avoid dissolution of the *entity*. This may threaten the continuity of title[80] and of ongoing contracts. This problem is mitigated to some extent but not fully solved by R.U.P.A. § 801 (*see* Section 8.201, below).

Another potential source of discontinuity in a partnership is that creditors of general partners may be able to compel the dissolution of the partnership by obtaining the debtor's interest through foreclosure.[81] It is less clear that creditors of LLC members have this right.[82]

(11) Buyout Rights

LLC[83] and partnership (*see* Section 4.07) statutes traditionally provide by default for buyout of partners who wish to leave. This is an important right in closely held firms in which members commonly have no public market into which to exit. Lock-in of members can give rise to oppression that could trigger complex and uncertain judicial remedies. On the other hand, exit at will can place a cash-flow burden on the firm and increase the tax valuation of membership

---

[79] *See* RULLCA § 301 (2006).

[80] *See* Fairway Dev. Co. v. Title Ins. Co., 621 F. Supp. 120 (N.D. Ohio 1985) (holding that the "new" partnership resulting from a partner's death did not have standing to enforce a title insurance policy issued to the "old" partnership), discussed in § 8.201, infra.

[81] *See* Bromberg & Ribstein, § 3.05(d)(3)(v). For discussions of foreclosure under limited partnership statutes, see Kleinberger & Bishop, Charging Orders and the New Uniform Limited Partnership Act Dispelling Rumors of Disaster, Prob. & Prop. 30 (July/Aug. 2004); Schurig & Jetel, A Charging Order Is the Exclusive Remedy Against a Partnership Interest: Fact or Fiction?, Prob. & Prop. 57 (Nov./Dec. 2003).

[82] *See* Ribstein & Keatinge, § 7.08. The Revised Uniform Limited Liability Company Act, § 503(c) (2006) clearly provides for a disclosure right.

[83] *See id.* § 11.03.

interests.[84] Accordingly, the members may want to draft around the exit right or, for tax valuation purposes, choose a statute that does not provide for a default exit right. All general partnership statutes include a default exit right. Moreover, agreements that eliminate this right are unenforceable under R.U.P.A. § 103(b)(6) (*see* Section 8.602, below) and are not clearly valid under the U.P.A.[85] It is not clear to what extent the partnership agreement can impose financial penalties on withdrawing partners under the U.P.A.[86] or R.U.P.A. (*see* Section 8.602, below). On the other hand, LLC statutes clearly permit the members to eliminate members' power to dissociate, and most now provide that members have no default right to withdraw and be paid for their interests.[87]

Although there are potential disadvantages in terms of exit under both partnership and LLC statutes, on balance LLC statutes are a better choice from this perspective for most firms. Firms that want to provide for exit may be partnerships or may be LLCs and contract for exit under statutes that do not provide for a default exit right. On the other hand, firms that want to prevent exit at will are probably better off under most LLC statutes since even those with a default exit right are generally subject to contrary agreement. In short, from the standpoint of buyout rights, the general partnership form is likely to be better only for firms that do not engage in substantial advance planning and drafting (and which probably would not engage in a lengthy choice-of-form analysis).

(12) Later Transition to Incorporation

A start-up venture that organizes as a partnership or LLC may be contemplating a later phase of activity in which it sells interests to the public. As discussed in Paragraph 9, corporate default rules suit publicly held firms. Although other business forms, particularly including the LLC and limited partnership, can be adapted to public ownership, they may meet some market resistance because of uncertainty about how these rules will be interpreted and applied and because of lingering questions from the collapse of the market for publicly traded limited partnership interests.

---

[84] Under I.R.C. § 2704, 26 U.S.C.A. § 2704, a restriction on liquidation rights can be disregarded in valuing the estate for tax purposes even in the absence of a transfer of value. In particular, in valuing an interest in a family-controlled partnership, restrictions on liquidation that are "more restrictive than the limitations that would apply under the State law generally applicable to the entity in absence of the restriction" are ignored. Treas. Reg. § 25.2704-2(b), 26 C.F.R. § 25.2704-2(b) (defining "applicable restriction"). *See also* I.R.C. § 2704(b)(3)(B) (providing that an "applicable restriction" does not include "any restriction imposed, or required to be imposed, by any Federal or State law"). *See* Ribstein & Keatinge, §§ 11.02 and 17.18.

[85] *See* Bromberg & Ribstein, § 7.03(b).

[86] *See* Bromberg & Ribstein, § 7.13(i).

[87] *See* Ribstein & Keatinge, § 11.02 and App. 11-1.

These considerations raise the question whether a firm that is contemplating later public ownership would be better off initially organizing as a corporation than initially organizing as a partnership or LLC and later converting to the corporate form.[88] The answer depends on two types of questions. First, does the initial statutory form readily permit conversion or merger into the corporate form? Most LLC statutes do.[89] But the same is true of many general partnership statutes based on R.U.P.A.[90]

Second, what are the tax consequences of changing the form of the business? Conversion from any flow-through form (including Subchapter S) to a Subchapter C corporation will almost certainly entail some tax consequences. The basic question in this respect is whether the tax cost of conversion is likely to exceed the cost of operating as a separately taxable entity plus the costs of choosing a form that is poorly suited for the firm's closely held phase.

(13) Employment Regulation

The form selected by the business may matter with respect to the application of employee-protection legislation, particularly state worker compensation laws and state and federal employment discrimination laws (*see* Section 7.03). General partners are traditionally regarded as co-owners even if they work in the business, while shareholders, LLC members, and, perhaps, limited partners may be viewed as less active in management and therefore as employees. The role of choice of form has, however, been placed in doubt by the Supreme Court's decision in *Clackamas Gastroenterology Associates, P.C. v. Wells* (*see* Section 7.03(b)(3)).

(14) Bankruptcy

As discussed in Section 7.02, it may matter for several reasons whether a firm is characterized as a partnership for bankruptcy law purposes, including the vote necessary for a voluntary bankruptcy, the availability of stays and injunctions against nondebtor partners, and the application of fraudulent conveyance rules.

---

[88] For a general discussion of the choice of the corporate form by Silicon Valley firms, see Bankman, The Structure of Silicon Valley Start-ups, 41 UCLA L. Rev. 1737 (1994).

[89] *See* Ribstein & Keatinge, § 11.16.

[90] *See* R.U.P.A. art. 9, discussed in §§ 8.901–8.908, infra.

(15) Securities Law

Just as partners' participation in the firm may make them ineligible for employee protection regulation, it may also make them ineligible for investor protection under federal and state securities laws, particularly under state securities laws that explicitly deal with LLC interests. However, the application of the securities laws to LLPs, as to interests in other types of firms, depends on a highly factual inquiry. *See* Section 7.01. Application of the securities laws may, in turn, matter to the firm's ability to use cash-based rather than accrual-based accounting.[91]

(16) Tax

Although tax classification now matters only for the choice between the corporate and related forms on the one hand and unincorporated business forms on the other, there remain some tax considerations that relate to the choice among unincorporated business forms. In particular, the special treatment of distributions to exiting members under I.R.C. § 736, which is mainly now available only to professional firms, may depend, at least for the time being, on whether the member is technically a "partner" (*see* Section 7.05). Also, the application of self-employment tax may depend, again at least for now, on whether the member is a "limited partner."[92] As discussed below in Section 5.05, the latter consideration may be one of the main reasons for choosing the LLLP form. However, these factors may no longer be important once the relevant tax rules are appropriately designed to accommodate the LLC form.

(17) The Novelty Problem

An overriding consideration that runs through many of the above topics concerns the relative novelty of the LLP as compared with the corporate and partnership forms. Novelty raises at least three important problems: the absence of accepted customs and forms, the paucity of case law,[93] and uncertainty as to how the business form will be classified under tax and regulatory statutes. With respect to the latter point, in addition to the discussions above of tax, bankruptcy, securities, and employment law, it is important to consider the tax accounting

---

[91] *See* I.R.C. § 461(i)(3)(A) (organization that is required to register offering is a tax shelter and therefore may not be able to use accrual accounting).

[92] This conclusion has been weakened somewhat by the Tax Court opinion in Renkemeyer, Campbell & Weaver, LLP v. C.I.R., 136 T.C. No. 7 (U.S. Tax Ct. Feb. 9, 2011), discussed below in Section 7.05, nn.202–205.

[93] Liberty Mut. Ins. Co. v. Gardere & Wynne, LLP, 1994 WL 707133 (D. Mass. Dec. 6, 1994) suggests the problems that may result from the novelty of the LLP form. The court transferred a malpractice claim against a Texas law LLP to Texas largely because of the many issues that needed to be decided under Texas law, including questions concerning the application of the Texas LLP act.

questions that arise for LLCs and LLPs, which have been largely settled for Subchapter S corporations. Indeed, these problems may explain why closely held firms continue to incorporate despite the unsuitability of the corporate form in other respects (*see* Section 1.07(a)(8)).

In general, it is important to keep in mind that the novelty problem is to some extent, *illusory*, *transitory*, and *relative*. The problem is often *illusory* because the concept of closely held limited liability firms is inherently new irrespective of choice of form. Thus, it may be a false hope to avoid the LLP form because it is slightly newer than the LLC, or to choose it on the theory that this makes applicable the existing body of partnership law when there are so many questions about the extent to which this law should apply (*see* Chapter 4). The problem is *transitory* since customs, forms, and regulatory recognition are certain to accelerate with the widespread adoption and acceptance of these new business forms. Indeed, the LLP now has been around long enough that courts and legislatures have had an opportunity to address several of the initial questions. Finally, the problem is *relative* because the costs of novelty should be compared with the benefits of these new forms. Thus, for example, it may be a false economy to suffer the restrictions of Subchapter S on financial allocations and number and type of member in order to avoid the uncertainties of LLP or LLC tax accounting.

(b)   Existing Firms

A firm that already exists when it chooses a statutory form faces considerations in addition to those discussed above. As discussed in Section 1.05(b), it may be easier for an existing partnership to register as an LLP than to turn itself into an LLC by merger, conversion or other mechanism. The vote required for registration may be only a majority or majority in interest, and LLP registration appears to preserve the existing entity. However, statutory provisions that permit easy conversion into the LLC form are reducing this difference. Moreover, the ease of registration may be illusory. As discussed in Section 1.05(a), above, the most important aspect of registration is redrafting of the partnership agreement, a chore that may have to be done regardless of the mechanism for a partnership's transition to limited liability. On the other hand, forming an LLP lets the members avoid this task where renegotiation is likely to be costly, as by engendering disagreement.

(c)   Foreign Operation

Subsections (a) and (b) assumed that a firm could choose from any U.S. LLC, corporate or LLP statute. The reality, discussed in the following subsections, is that there may be significant advantages to choosing to organize under a statute of the state in which the firm will operate and avoiding characterization as a "foreign" firm even if there are theoretically better statutes elsewhere. (This, of course, does not apply to a firm that intends to operate in several states and therefore necessarily will operate as a foreign firm in some states.)

(1) Recognition of Formation State Law

As discussed in Chapter 6, while the LLC and LLP forms are recognized virtually everywhere, operation states may apply their own regulatory statutes, and may not enforce a foreign firm's formation state law on member liability. In this regard, as discussed in Section 7.04(c), it is important for professional firms to consider not only the LLP or LLC statute but also local licensing and ethical rules. In light of these rules, a firm may gain no advantage by, for example, "shopping" for a better liability shield.

These considerations may affect choice of form as well as choice of statute. A firm may be better off organizing as a local LLC under a full-shield LLC statute than organizing under another state's full-shield LLP law, even if the LLP form is preferable in other respects, because of questions about local recognition of the LLP shield.

(2) Cost of Foreign Organization

Though a firm may be tempted to form in a low-fee state, it may find that it has to pay equally high fees in the operation state as a foreign firm (*see* Table 2-5) in addition to the registration fees in the formation state.

(d) Summary: A Decision Tree

The long but still incomplete list of factors to consider for choice of form may be simplified somewhat by asking a series of questions. In each case, the question assumes the optimal statute or form available in any state, unless the advantages of home state formation outweigh the costs (*see* subsection (c), above):

(1) Which types of statutes are available in light of the nature of the firm's business — e.g., nonprofit, single-member, or professional (Subsection (a)(1))?

(2)   How important are restrictions on the LLP liability shield (Subsection (a)(3))?

(3)   What are the costs and fees associated with a particular statute or form (Subsection (a)(4))?

(4)   What are the costs of insurance, other financial regulation or formalities imposed by the particular form (Subsection (a)(5)–(6))?

(5)   Is the firm currently a general partnership? If so, it may be easier for it to continue to be a partnership and to register as an LLP than to convert to, or merge into, a separate form of business (Subsection (b)).

(6)   To what extent does the form accommodate particular contracting alternatives that are appropriate for the firm, including separation of management and ownership (Subsection (a)(8)), continuity of the firm when a member dissociates (Subsection (a)(10)), and restrictions on member dissociation (Subsection (a)(11))?

(7)   If the firm is planning on later going public, how difficult will the later conversion to corporate form be (Subsection (a)(12))?

(8)   Will the firm be making sensitive promotion and termination decisions concerning owner–employees, or will its owner–employees work in injury-prone positions in the firm, to which employee-protection legislation may apply (Subsection (a)(13))?

(9)   Is the firm likely to want bankruptcy law provisions relating to partners and partnerships, or those relating to corporations, to apply (Subsection (a)(14))?

(10) Is the firm planning to sell interests to outside investors in transactions to which the securities law may apply (Subsection (a)(15))?

(11) Does the firm have passive members who will want to be able to avoid the self-employment tax (Subsection (a)(16))?

(12) Is the firm likely to want to make deductible distributions to exiting members under I.R.C. § 736 (Subsection (a)(16))?

This list of questions reveals that *professional* firms often have strong reasons for choosing the LLP form. For reasons discussed in more detail in Subsection (a) and in later sections of the book cross-referenced there, the answers to questions 1, 2, 4, 6, 8, 9, and 12 point toward use of the LLP form by professional firms in many cases. Question 5 also will often point in this direction, since many professional firms are already partnerships. Nonprofessional firms are also likely to want to use the LLP form if they are already partnerships (question 5) and other factors do not weigh against the LLP form. A firm that is selling interests to outside investors may have a particular incentive to be an LLP. Also, at least for the time being, a firm with passive members may want to be an LLLP in order to avoid the self-employment tax. Nonprofessional closely held firms to which these special circumstances do not apply probably will want to be LLCs.

TABLE 1-1.   COMPARISON OF BUSINESS FORMS

Characteristics*	Book Section	LLP	LLC	Corp.	LP**
Must be subject to federal corporate tax	7.05	No	No	Yes	No
May be used by professionals	7.04	Yes	Yes	Yes[1]	No
May be used by nonprofit firms	2.02(c)	No	Some	Yes[2]	No
May be used by one-member firms	2.02(c)	No	Yes[3]	Yes	No
Owners have limited liability for all debts of firm	3.03	Some	Yes	Yes	No[4]
Insurance requirement	2.06	Some	No	Some[5]	No
Distribution restrictions	4.04(d)	Some	Yes	Yes	Yes
Decision-making formalities	4.02	No	No	Yes	No
Centralization of decision-making power	4.02	No	Yes	Yes	Yes
Firm necessarily dissolves on member dissociation	4.07	Some[6]	No	No	No
Default buyout right	4.07	Yes	Some	No	Some
Federal securities laws apply	7.01	?	?	Yes	Yes
State securities laws apply	7.01	?	Some	Yes	Yes
Convert or register from other business form	Ch. 2	Yes[7]	Some	Some	Some[8]
Formation state law governs	6.02(d)	Yes	Yes	Yes	Yes

*Refers to characteristics determined wholly or mostly by governing business association statute.

**Some of these features, notably including partners' liability, default buyout rights, and conversion, may be changed by Re-R.U.L.P.A.

Table 1-1   **1. Background and Introduction**

Table 1-1 (cont'd)

Yes = Applies to firms governed by most or all statutes
No = Does not apply to firms governed by most or all statutes
Some = Applies to firms governed by some statutes
? = Application of feature is unsettled or varies from state to state

Notes
1. Applies under professional corporation statutes.
2. Applies under nonprofit corporation statutes.
3. All but Massachusetts.
4. Does not apply to limited partners or to LLLPs.
5. Applies to professional corporations.
6. Applies under U.P.A.-based but not R.U.P.A.-based statutes.
7. Registration by existing general or limited partnerships.
8. R.U.P.A. permits conversion from general partnership.

≡2≡

FORMATION of the LLP

§ 2.01 INTRODUCTION

This chapter discusses formation of limited liability partnerships (LLPs). In general, LLP statutes add to general partnership statutes provisions requiring registration and other formalities. These provisions help alert creditors to the limited liability nature of the firm and help ensure that they have ready access to current information about the firm. The formation of the underlying partnership is discussed in Section 2.02. Filing formalities are discussed in Section 2.03. Section 2.04 discusses rules concerning partners' approval of the registration of LLPs. Sections 2.05–2.06 discuss, respectively, name and insurance requirements in LLP statutes. Section 2.07 considers the status of firms that have not complied with the formalities discussed in this chapter. Section 2.08 and Section 2.09 discuss two important matters that arise on formation — the firm's choice of the state of registration and changes that the firm might need to make in the partnership agreement as a result of registration.

§ 2.02 FORMATION OF THE UNDERLYING PARTNERSHIP

As shown in Table 2-1, LLP statutes generally provide that an LLP is a "partnership."[1] This means that the firm must fit the definition of partnership under the partnership statute — that is, it must be "an association of two or more persons to carry on as co-owners a business for profit."[2] This section discusses factors particularly relating to LLPs that bear on formation of the underlying partnership.

---

[1] The North Dakota statute provides a twist. "Limited liability partnerships" are treated in a separate statute, which distinguishes them from "partnerships." *See* N.D. Cent. Code § 45-22-01(13)–(18).

[2] U.P.A. § 6(1) (1914); R.U.P.A. § 202 (1994). *See generally* Bromberg and Ribstein on Partnership ch. 2 (1998) (hereinafter "Bromberg & Ribstein"). It follows that a law firm operating as a sole proprietorship would not be an LLP even if it registered as such. *See* Ribstein, *Ideoblog*, "Dreier: Economic and legal ramifications" (Dec. 10, 2008), *available at* http://busmovie.typepad.com/ideoblog/2008/12/dreier-economic-and-legal-ramifications.html.

Thomas H. Lee Equity Fund V, L.P. v. Mayer Brown, Rowe & Maw LLP, 612 F. Supp. 2d 267, 271, n.1 (S.D.N.Y. 2009) (Ill. law) noted the question of whether an alleged "combination" of an Illinois LLP and an LLP formed under English law had "legal status," but treated the two as one entity where the combined entity did not move to dismiss.

(a)   Relevant Factors

Formation of the underlying partnership does not depend on formalities, but rather on whether the parties intended to be partners.[3] Partnership intent, in turn, is either "subjective" or "objective." "Subjective" intent means that the parties have expressed their desire to be treated as partners either orally or in writing through documents such as tax and assumed name filings.[4] "Objective" intent means that the parties have engaged in the act of carrying on a business as co-owners, which places their relationship within the definition of partnership, even if the parties did not subjectively desire to be treated as partners.[5] The objective elements of partnership include profit and loss sharing, and co-ownership and contribution of property.[6]

(b)   Effect of Filing LLP Registration

The filing of an LLP registration strongly indicates that the relationship that is subject to the filing is a partnership since, as noted above, an LLP is defined in most statutes as a "partnership." If the filing happens to include partners' names (*see* Section 2.03(b) and Table 2-1, below), the filing may be evidence of the named persons' subjective intent to be partners,[7] or constitute a representation of partnership that establishes partnership by estoppel.[8] Similarly, an LLP filing that purports to name the partners but fails to include a person's name might be evidence against subjective intent of the persons named in the filing to form a partnership with the unnamed person.

Although a firm must be a partnership to be a limited liability partnership, it does not necessarily follow that a firm that has made a filing is a partnership. In general, whether a firm that calls itself a "partnership" actually is one depends on the partners' intending to form a relationship that includes the statutory elements of partnership.[9] One might argue that the owners' limited liability increases the possibility that they will not be characterized as partners if other standard partnership elements — that is, profit sharing, management sharing and contribution, and sharing of property — are minimal or absent. The problem with this argu-

---

[3] Bromberg & Ribstein, § 2.05.

[4] Bromberg & Ribstein, § 2.05(b).

[5] Bromberg & Ribstein, § 2.05(c).

[6] Bromberg & Ribstein, § 2.07.

[7] Although the filing indicates the existence of a partnership relationship among some of the partners, it may not be conclusive as to precisely who the partners are because membership may change over time. It is not clear whether the inclusion of persons in the registration may support partnership by estoppel. *See* Section 3.10, below.

[8] *See* Dow v. Jones, 311 F. Supp. 2d 461 (D. Md. 2004) (D.C. law).

[9] *See* Bromberg & Ribstein, § 2.05.

ment is that it suggests that an LLP could never be a "partnership," which would be inconsistent with the definition of an LLP discussed immediately above.

Even apart from the effect of loss-sharing, characterizing an LLP as a non-partnership is, generally, only a remote possibility, with some possible exceptions discussed in the next subsection. The parties' "partnership" characterization usually has been controlling.[10] The cases involving a clear conflict between the parties' characterization and the underlying elements of the relationship so far have focused on the issue of whether a relationship characterized as a *nonpartnership* nevertheless should be treated as a *partnership*.[11] Only a couple of cases have held that the parties' characterization of their relationship as a "partnership" was not conclusive.[12] Although the courts may want to avoid injury to third parties, declaring the relationship to be a nonpartnership is usually not the way to do this since it not only invalidates the registration but also cuts off any underlying vicarious liability. This reasoning would not, however, prevent a court from characterizing an LLP as a nonpartnership, or some apparent members of the firm as nonpartners, for employment discrimination or other nonpartnership law purposes (*see* Section 7.03, below).

A partnership that files an LLP registration continues to be the same entity that preceded the filing (*see* Section 4.08, below).

(c) The "Two-owner," "Profit," "Business," and Property Co-ownership Requirements

In some situations there may be no underlying partnership even if the partners have characterized it as such by an LLP filing or otherwise. One is where only one person exercises meaningful control or receives a share of the profits. This may not be a partnership because it is not "an association of two or more persons [who] carry on as co-owners. . . ." Firms in which there is any significant question whether the two-owner requirement is satisfied would be well advised to consider forming as limited liability companies (LLCs), since no LLC statute requires LLCs to have two or more members.[13]

This raises the policy issue of whether partnership statutes ought to clarify that a one-owner firm can be a partnership, and therefore an LLP. Under statutes that hold members individually liable for partnership contracts, the two-member requirement does not matter regarding liability for the firm's debts because a sole owner could not limit his liability for wrongdoing in any event. But the

---

[10] Bromberg & Ribstein, § 2.07(d).

[11] *See, e.g.,* Taylor v. Getty Oil Co., 637 F. Supp. 886 (E.D. La. 1986).

[12] *See* In re Washington Commc'ns Group, Inc., 18 B.R.W. 437 (D.D.C. 1982); Chaiken v. Employment Sec. Comm'n, 274 A.2d 707 (Del. Super. 1971).

[13] *See* Ribstein & Keatinge on Limited Liability Companies (2d ed. 2004), App. 4-1 (hereinafter "Ribstein & Keatinge").

two-owner requirement does bar sole proprietors from availing themselves of the LLP-type liability limitation in states in which members have limited liability for contracts as well as torts. Thus, some have suggested that requiring two owners for limited liability discriminates against sole proprietors.[14] A possible argument for the two-owner restriction as applied to partnerships is that co-ownership is an important distinguishing characteristic of the partnership not only under the definition of partnership, but in the sense that an assumption of co-ownership underlies the structure of partnership default rules. For example, partnership statutes provide for joint management and sharing of profits. Also, the charging order remedy restricting the rights of a partner's creditor from reaching partnership assets is designed for multiple-owner firms. One-owner partnerships therefore raise problems that would have to be resolved through extra litigation, concerning the application of these rules to this new form of business.[15] Moreover, one-owner partnerships would be inconsistent with the basic contractual nature of a partnership since a contract ordinarily requires two parties. On the other hand, one-owner corporations have been recognized for some time. Sole proprietorships arguably ought to be able to decide for themselves whether the benefits of the LLP liability limitation outweigh the problems resulting from unsuitable default rules. Perhaps the best long-run solution would be to make limited liability available to sole proprietorships as a form of business distinct from partnership.[16]

The definition of partnership also excludes other relationships — where individuals share space and expenses or jointly own property but do not "carry on . . . a business";[17] or where the individuals carry on a business but not "for profit."[18] As with the two-member requirement, while these restrictions reflect the nature of the relationship for which the partnership structure is designed, they raise the issue whether this should be reason enough to prevent the parties to other types of relationships from choosing the partnership (and therefore LLP) form of business.

---

[14] See Madden v. Aldrich, 346 Ark. 405, 58 S.W.3d 342 (2001) (holding that a sole proprietor could be held liable for her employee's misconduct, with strong dissent recognizing the anomaly of extending limited liability to firms but not to sole proprietors); Hamilton, Registered Limited Liability Partnerships: Present at the Birth (Nearly), 66 U. Colo. L. Rev. 1065 (1995); Klein & Zolt, Business Form, Limited Liability and Tax Regimes: Lurching Toward a Coherent Outcome?, 66 U. Colo. L. Rev. 1001 (1995).

[15] See Ribstein, Reverse Limited Liability and the Design of Business Associations, 30 Del. J. Corp. L. 199 (2005).

[16] See Crusto, Extending The Veil to Solo Entrepreneurs: A Limited Liability Sole Proprietorship Act (LLSP); 2001 Colum. Bus. L. Rev. 381. Ribstein, The Loneliest Number: The Unincorporated Limited Liability Sole Proprietorship, 1 J. Asset Protection 46 (May/June 1996).

[17] See U.P.A. § 7(2); R.U.P.A. § 202(c)(2); Bromberg & Ribstein, § 2.06(a)–(b).

[18] See Bromberg & Ribstein, § 2.06(c). However, the Delaware statute provides that a partnership may be formed not for profit if there is intent to form a partnership. Del. Code Ann., tit. 6, § 15-202.

§ 2.03   THE LLP REGISTRATION

In addition to being a "partnership," an LLP must satisfy statutory formalities. The legal requirements for becoming an LLP are considerably simpler— and in most cases cheaper to satisfy— than forming a limited partnership, limited liability company, corporation, or other organization with limited liability.

Subsection (a) considers which partnerships can be LLPs. The transition from partnership to LLP is typically a two-part process. Subsection (b) discusses the first part, an initial filing with a state official. Section 2.05 discusses the second part, a name requirement identifying the firm as an LLP. Section 2.06 discusses a third part that is required in a few states: liability insurance or a segregated asset alternative. The annual or other periodic filings needed in some states to maintain LLP status are discussed in Subsection (c). The partner approval required for the initial filing is discussed in Section 2.04.

Subsections (a)–(c) generally treat LLP in the context of the prevailing Uniform Partnership Act (U.P.A.). Subsection (d) considers what LLPs will be like under the Revised Uniform Partnership Act (R.U.P.A.).

(a)   What Partnerships Can Be LLPs

(1)   Need for Written Contract

There is no requirement that a partnership have a written partnership agreement in order to be an LLP. However, the advantages of a written agreement in any partnership[19] are perhaps even greater in an LLP because LLP status may make it desirable to have somewhat different and more clearly stated terms than in an ordinary partnership. These aspects are discussed in Section 2.09, below, and in Chapters 3 and 4.

(2)   Number of Members

A partnership is an "association of two or more persons." Section 2.02(c), above, considers the policy argument surrounding the two-owner requirement.

(3)   Type of Business

LLP provisions are typically found in states' general partnership statutes, as amendments to the sections describing partner liability and as additional sections prescribing LLP requirements. The implication is that any partnership described in

---

[19] *See* Bromberg & Ribstein, § 2.05(d).

those statutes can become an LLP. California and New York confine LLP status to partnerships performing professional services. New York permits LLP registration only by (i) partnerships each of whose partners is a professional authorized by law to render professional service in the state[20] and (ii) partnerships authorized or licensed to render professional service in the state and (iii) partnerships that are "related" in a specified way to a professional LLP.[21] California permits registration only by certain professional partnerships, foreign professional firms, or firms that have an ownership relationship to such firms to be LLPs.[22] Whether professional partnerships in other states can be LLPs is discussed in Section 7.04(a). Section 2.02(c), above, discusses nonprofit firms and individuals who are not carrying on a business.

(4) Foreign Partnerships

Can a partnership formed under the law of State X (a foreign partnership) operate as an LLP under the law of State Y? Since all states now have LLP statutes, the issue is mainly important if X's and Y's LLP provisions differ. The definition of "partnership" is substantially the same across the states. The answer to this question therefore depends on whether the statute permits a partnership to operate as an LLP under the law of another state. Most states' definitions of "limited liability partnership" or "registered limited liability partnership" include only partnerships that are registered under their statute. As shown in Table 2-1, some statutes define an LLP as a partnership complying with their LLP provisions and thus seem indifferent to what law governs other aspects of the partnership. As discussed in Section 6.02(b), this would permit firms to partially "domesticate" under one state's law while being governed in other respects by another's. However, R.U.P.A. makes clear what is at least implicit in most states—that a firm cannot register under its law but agree to be governed by the law of another state.[23] Finally, most states permit inbound foreign LLPs—those formed under another state's laws but doing business locally—to have their internal affairs and partner liability be governed by the foreign state's laws. The various treatments of foreign LLPs are discussed further in Section 2.03(b)(16) below, and Chapter 6.

---

[20] A law firm, Jacoby & Meyers, challenged this restriction, arguing that New York's Partnership Law would not prohibit a registered limited liability partnership from practicing law, even if the partnership admitted non-lawyer equity investors, but a federal court rejected this argument. Jacoby & Meyers, LLP v. Presiding Justices of the First, Second, Third, & Fourth Dep'ts, Appellate. Div. of the Supreme Ct. of N.Y., 847 F. Supp. 2d 590, 598 (S.D.N.Y. 2012) ("if J & M allowed a non-lawyer to own an equity interest in the firm, it could not operate as a limited liability partnership").

[21] N.Y. P'ship Law ch. 34, § 121-1500(a). "Related" and "foreign related" LLPs are defined in detail in *id.* § 2.

[22] *See* Cal. Corp. Code § 16101(8).

[23] *See* R.U.P.A. § 101(4) (defining "limited liability partnership" as a partnership that has filed a statement of qualification under this law but not elsewhere); R.U.P.A. § 106(B) (providing that this statute governs limited liability partnerships); R.U.P.A. § 103(B)(10) (providing that this choice-of-law rule cannot be altered by contrary agreement).

(5)   Limited Partnerships

Limited partnerships that choose to be LLPs—commonly known as "LLLPs"—are discussed in Chapter 5. Some states expressly permit a limited partnership to become an LLP (*see* Chapter 5, Table 5-1). Others expressly authorize only general partnerships to be LLPs[24] or define LLPs as general partnerships that comply with LLP requirements.[25] New York achieves that result by allowing only "a partnership without limited partners" to be an LLP.[26] Whether a limited partnership can become an LLP absent an explicit authorizing or denying statute is considered in Section 5.04. U.L.P.A. §§ 102(9) and 201(a)(4) (2001), discussed in Chapter 9, Section 9.201, below, require limited partnerships to elect either LLLP or non-LLLP status.

(6)   Newly Created Partnerships

Can a partnership be newly created as an LLP? As discussed in Section 2.02, above, LLP statutes generally permit a "partnership" to become an LLP, implying that a partnership already exists. That implication is strengthened by the common requirements, discussed below in Section 2.03(b), that a majority of the partners sign the LLP filing or authorize someone to do so. The California act provides separately for registration by a partnership to be an LLP[27] and for conversion by a general partnership to an LLP[28] but does not make clear whether the latter procedure is only for existing partnerships. Thus caution suggests formation of the partnership before — if only momentarily before — filing for LLP status.

(b)   Initial Filing

To become an LLP, a partnership must file with a designated official a document — variously called an application, certificate, or registration — requesting or stating LLP status and containing the additional information summarized in this subsection. The contents of such registrations required by the states are tabulated in Table 2-1. Highlights are summarized below.

(1)   Firm Name

All filings to become an LLP must include the firm name. The requirements for the firm name are discussed in Section 2.05, below.

[24] Cal. Corp. Code § 16953.
[25] Utah Code Ann. § 48-1d-102(10).
[26] N.Y. P'ship Law § 121-1500(a).
[27] Cal. Corp. Code § 16953.
[28] Cal. Corp. Code § 16955.

(2)   Office and Agent

All LLP filings must include an address (e.g., to facilitate service of process) and some must include more than one office and an agent for process. The usual pattern is address of the principal office and, if that office is not in the state, the registered local office and registered agent.

(3)   Partner Information

Some states require the filing to include the number of partners. Some of these base the filing fee, discussed in Section 2.03(b)(11) below, on the number of partners. In other states the number of partners has no operative significance, although it is information that may be relevant to someone dealing with or planning to sue the partnership. As indicated in Table 2-2, some states require disclosure of the names of at least some partners. None require information concerning partner contributions to the firm or their shares of profit or loss.

(4)   Business Description

Most LLP statutes require the registration to describe the LLP's business or purpose. Most states have no limit on the kind of business that can be an LLP. However, as noted in Section 2.03(a)(3), above, a few states allow only professional partnerships to be LLPs. A state's limitations or regulations on the kinds of business a partnership may conduct also apply to LLPs.

(5)   Other Required Matters

As shown in Table 2-2, the states require a variety of other matters to be disclosed in LLP registrations. These include the latest date upon which the partnership is to dissolve if the partnership has a specific date of dissolution, specification of any partners who are to be liable as partners for all or specified partnership debts or obligations (i.e., have contracted away the LLP liability shield),[29] and the federal

---

[29] N.Y. P'ship Law § 121-1500(a)(8). A New York LLP partner is liable prospectively for partnership debts or obligations "to the extent at least a majority of the partners shall have agreed unless otherwise provided in any agreement between the partners." N.Y. P'ship Law § 121-1500, § 26(d). *See* Section 3.05, infra.

tax identification number of the partnership (to help distinguish partnerships with similar names).

(6) Other Permitted Matters

Most states expressly allow the LLP filing to contain any other matter the partnership decides to include and a partnership probably can include other matters without such a provision. Some states provide that the inclusion of other information in the filing is notice of that information.[30] Without a section like that, the effect of inclusion of other matters is uncertain.

(7) Place of Filing

A single state filing is the prevailing pattern. The usual requirement is to file with the local Secretary of State.[31] Elsewhere it is the Department of Assessments and Taxation,[32] the Department of State,[33] or the Commission.[34] Georgia requires filing in the superior court of any county in which the partnership has an office.[35]

(8) Effect of Errors

As shown in Table 2-6, some statutes provide that a filing is effective if there has been substantial compliance with the statute, similar to the rule most states have for limited partnerships.[36] Some statutes provide that LLP status is not

---

[30] *E.g.*, Ind. Code § 23-4-1-45.

[31] *E.g.*, Del. Code Ann., tit. 6, § 15-105; Idaho Code § 53-3-105; Iowa Code Ann. § 486A.105; Kan. Stat. Ann. § 56a-1201(a); La. Rev. Stat. Ann. § 9-3432A; Minn. Stat. Ann. §§ 323A.1003; N.C. Gen. Stat. Ann. § 59-84.2(a); Ohio Rev. Code Ann. § 1776.81(C).

[32] Md. Code Ann., Corps. & Ass'ns § 9A-1001).

[33] N.Y. P'ship Law § 121-1500(a).

[34] Va. Code Ann. § 50-73.132.

[35] Ga. Code Ann. § 14-8-62(a).

[36] U.L.P.A. § 2(2); R.U.L.P.A. § 201(b). *See* Bromberg & Ribstein, § 12.03. On substantial compliance with LLC formation requirements, see Ribstein & Keatinge, § 4.15.

affected by errors in the filing.[37] Even without a statute of that sort, errors should not affect LLP status unless they mislead persons dealing with the partnership.[38]

(9) Effect of Changes

Changes will inevitably occur over time in partnerships. Most states permit amendment of an LLP registration to reflect changes,[39] or generally permit amendment or correction of the registration.[40] As shown in Table 2-3, some statutes require amendment when changes in certain of the filed information occur, though generally without specifying a penalty for failure to amend. Table 2-3 also lists statutes that provide for continuity of the LLP liability shield despite changes in the information in a filing, such as the number of partners or the members of the partnership, admission or dissociation of partners, or dissolution, winding up, and liquidation of the partnership as to a liability incurred while an LLP. Cautious firms will keep their registrations in effect and current to avoid possible loss of LLP protection.

(10) Signature; Power of Attorney

In an effort to ensure that the important transition to LLP status is the act of the partnership, most jurisdictions have requirements concerning who signs the filing. Requirements, which are set forth in Table 2-4, include one or more authorized partners, an authorized person, one or more partners, two or more partners, or all partners. Signature by power of attorney may be explicitly authorized[41] and is probably available elsewhere as a matter of agency law without special statutory authorization. A limited partnership's filing must be signed by at least one general partner in one of the few states that has legislated on that point.[42]

Section 2.04, below, discusses procedures within the partnership to authorize LLP filing. Caution suggests having a written record of authorization. This may be in a written partnership agreement, minutes of a partnership meeting, or otherwise.

---

[37] E.g., Prototype LLP Act § 914(a) (LLP status not affected if filing was in good faith); R.U.P.A. § 1001(e); Cal. Corp. Code § 16953(e); Del. Code Ann., tit. 6, § 15-1001(e); Idaho Code § 53-3-1001(e); Ind. Code § 23-4-1-45 (errors in filing do not affect LLP status); Mass. Gen. L. ch. 108A, § 45(4); Nev. Rev. Stat. § 87.440; N.H. Rev. Stat. Ann. § 304-A:44(III); W. Va. Code § 47B-10-1(h).

[38] Section 2.07(b), infra, considers further the effect of noncompliance with the filing or other LLP requirements.

[39] E.g., Prototype LLP Act § 914(d).

[40] E.g., N.Y. P'ship Law § 121-1500(j).

[41] See Conn. Gen. Stat. Ann. § 34-410.

[42] Del. Code Ann., tit. 6, § 17-214(b)(1).

(11) Fees

Fees are set forth in Table 2-5. Most states charge a modest fee in the $50–$200 range for an LLP filing. A few states charge more substantial fees based on the number of partners. There will commonly be additional fees for renewals or periodic reports. There may be state or local taxes; federal income taxes are considered in Chapter 7.

(12) When Effective

The preconditions to effectiveness of the registration are summarized in Table 2-6. Since the LLP filing requirements are simple, there is little reason for them to be reviewed other than to see that they contain the information required by statute and that the fees are paid. Accordingly, several statutes declare LLP status effective on filing or on filing plus payment of fees. Some statutes, however, suggest the need for review or approval by the filing authority. Delaware and other states provide that the filing is effective if there is substantial compliance. This can be double-edged because it suggests both that strict compliance is unnecessary and that mere filing or other facial compliance is insufficient. Several states permit registration to become effective on a post-filing date specified in the filing.

The statutory language on effectiveness does not refer to other prerequisites of existence, including the name requirement and any insurance or alternate financial responsibility requirement. Failure to meet these additional requirements leaves in question whether a firm that has satisfied the filing requirement is an LLP or enjoys the liability shield. Section 2.07, below, discusses this issue.

(13) Publication

In deference to the local press, a state may require publication in local newspapers within prescribed periods after filing for LLP status.[43]

(14) Operation in Other States: Outbound

A state may authorize its LLPs to do business in other states.[44] However, it is highly probable that partnerships can do business outside a state without statutory authority from that state. Statutes authorizing outbound business do not

---

[43] New York requires publication once a week for six weeks in two newspapers in county of principal office. N.Y. P'ship Law § 121-1500(a).

[44] E.g., S.C. Code Ann. § 33-41-1140.

ensure LLP status when inbound in the other states. As shown in Table 6-2, many LLP states address this issue by providing that the internal affairs of their LLPs (including the liabilities of the partners) should be governed by their own laws rather than, by implication, the laws of the inbound states in which the partnerships may be doing business. These provisions are designed to receive full faith and credit in the inbound states. R.U.P.A. provides that LLPs formed under the statute are governed by it.[45] The effect of this provision is unclear in a state that has not adopted R.U.P.A. (*see* Section 6.03, below).

(15) Operation in Other States: Inbound

As discussed in Section 6.02 and Section 6.03, all but a handful of states now explicitly permit LLPs formed in another state to operate in their state and to be governed by the law of the state of formation. Most of these states require qualification or registration in the inbound state, although formation-state law may apply even without registration.

In general, an LLP registered in one state and contemplating business in other states should review its own statutes and those in other relevant states and decide whether it may operate as a foreign LLP in those states. Chapter 6 considers the statutory, constitutional, and conflict of laws principles that may influence that decision.

(16) Application of Other Law

An LLP, like any other partnership, is subject to the general partnership law and to a variety of other laws that may include licensing, assumed or fictitious name filing, and assorted regulatory and tax laws.

(c) *Periodic Filing or Renewal*

Requirements for periodic renewal or reports are summarized in Table 2-7. Most states provide for one-year duration for LLP status and annual renewal. Others require periodic reports, usually annually. Renewal and reporting serve to keep current the filed information and to produce some revenue for the state. They also serve as a reminder to remain in compliance with other LLP requirements such as name and (if applicable) insurance and registered agent and office. Exceptions to these rules include Georgia, which provides that LLP status continues until

---

[45] R.U.P.A. § 106(b) (providing that "limited liability partnership" is governed by the statute); R.U.P.A. § 101(5) (defining "limited liability partnership" as partnership which has filed a statement of qualification under the statute).

canceled by a filing executed by a majority of the partners or one or more authorized partners.[46]

Both renewal and report-type statutes commonly provide for administrative revocation of registration, typically after the LLP receives notice of noncompliance, sometimes with an opportunity to reinstate for a specified time, with the reinstatement relating back to the time of revocation (*see* Table 2-7). Even with notice and reinstatement provisions, firms need to have procedures to ensure that they comply with the periodic requirements, particularly because partners may be exposed to personal liability for debts incurred when the firm's LLP status has lapsed.[47]

The LLP registration may terminate on a variety of events other than administrative revocation, including voluntary withdrawal or cancellation, or dissolution or termination of the underlying entity (*see* Section 2.03(b)(9), above, and Section 3.12, below).

(d)   *Registration under R.U.P.A.-based Statute*

The LLP registration requirements need not be any different under an R.U.P.A.-based statute than under a U.P.A.-based statute. However, the complication presented by R.U.P.A. is coordinating the LLP registration with R.U.P.A. statements of partnership authority,[48] dissociation,[49] dissolution,[50] and merger.[51] These statements probably should be integrated in some way with LLP statements—that is, the statute should permit LLP registrations to also operate as R.U.P.A. statements of partnership authority, dissolution, and merger. This would reduce third parties' information costs and potential conflicts between multiple filings. For example, if the registration constitutes notice of the facts stated therein, the registration might limit or expand partners' authority in ways that the statement of partnership authority could not.

The Prototype LLP and Virginia acts deal with this problem by providing that an LLP registration has the effect of a R.U.P.A. statement of partner authority, dissolution or merger or an amendment, cancellation, or limitation of such a statement, if its title states the purpose for which it was filed and it complies with the provision that applies to the particular statement.[52] Under this provision, if an

---

[46] Ga. Code Ann. § 14-8-62(c).

[47] *See* Apcar Inv. Partners VI, Ltd. v. Gaus, 161 S.W.3d 137 (Tex. App. 2005) (partners individually liable for lease executed three years after LLP status expired).

[48] R.U.P.A. § 303.

[49] R.U.P.A. § 704.

[50] R.U.P.A. § 805.

[51] R.U.P.A. § 907.

[52] Prototype LLP Act § 914(b); Va. Code. § 50-73.136(B). The provision that the registration must comply with the formalities that apply to the other statement means, among other things, that the

LLP registration that purports also to serve as another R.U.P.A. statement is filed after a specific R.U.P.A. statement, the LLP registration would control by virtue of the R.U.P.A. rules that later statements nullify prior ones.[53] In any event, there would be no conflict between a registration statement and any other statement, since either the registration or the specific other statement, but not both, would control as to the subject matter of the specific statement.

§ 2.04   PARTNER APPROVAL OF REGISTRATION

This section discusses voting requirements for partners' approval of LLP registrations. Voting requirements for LLLP registration are discussed in Section 5.01(c), below.

(a)   No Specific LLP Voting Provisions

Some LLP statutes have no explicit voting requirement — that is, they are either silent or provide only for registration by a person authorized to file the registration. Under these statutes it is unclear what voting rule applies. With respect to statutory voting rules, the U.P.A. and R.U.P.A. both provide that "ordinary" matters are decided by majority vote.[54] U.P.A. requires unanimity for acts "in contravention of any agreement between the partners,"[55] while R.U.P.A. requires unanimity for acts "outside the ordinary course of business of a partnership" or that amend the agreement.[56] Changing the nature of the firm from unlimited liability to full or partial limited liability is almost certainly an extraordinary act or an amendment that requires unanimity under the default voting rule. As discussed throughout this book, LLP registration has potential effects on such matters as partners' responsibilities for liabilities (*see* Chapter 3), and application of nonpartnership statutes (*see* Chapter 7). For example, registration may result in a reallocation of the risk of liability from all of the partners to those who are engaged in the highest-risk businesses, while the partners continue to share the profits on the same basis as before registration (*see* Section 2.09(g), n.120, below). Accordingly, this is the sort of matter on which partners in a "default" partnership would expect to have a veto.[57]

---

partners cannot avoid the duty to disclose partners imposed by R.U.P.A. § 303 (*see* analysis of § 303 in § 8.303, infra) by attempting to use an LLP registration as a statement of partnership authority.

[53] *See, e.g.,* R.U.P.A. § 303(d)(1).

[54] U.P.A. § 18(h) (1914); R.U.P.A. § 401(j) (1994).

[55] U.P.A. § 18(h).

[56] R.U.P.A. § 401(j).

[57] Partners do have a de facto veto power through their right to dissociate and, perhaps, demand liquidation of the firm. However, this veto does not exist under the current version of R.U.P.A. § 801. Moreover, it may not be effective in many situations, as where the dissociation would be wrongful because it is prior to expiration of a definite term or undertaking, or where the dissociation would

(b) Specific LLP Voting Provisions

Some LLP statutes include specific provisions on voting for the registration, at least in the absence of contrary agreement. These are summarized in Table 2-8. Variations include unanimous approval, execution, or authorization of the registration by a "majority-in-interest" or "majority" of the partners. As indicated in Table 2-8, statutes may implicitly provide for the requisite authorization in their requirements as to who may execute the registration. Some statutes provide for a voting rule by cross-reference — that is, by characterizing the registration as an ordinary matter (thereby in effect providing that a majority vote is sufficient), or by requiring approval by the vote necessary to amend the agreement.

Statutes that permit registration by majority or other subunanimous vote raise difficult policy and constitutional issues.[58] LLP registration may, in effect, redistribute exposure to liability from the partners generally to those partners who are closely enough involved in the liability-generating aspects of the practice to be exposed to direct liability for monitoring or supervision lapses (*see* Section 3.04, below). Directly affected partners arguably ought to be able to block the registration. On the other hand, a default unanimity rule might so greatly increase the bargaining costs associated with registration that some firms may be unable to become LLPs. The appropriate balance between these competing considerations may vary from firm to firm. Thus, as discussed in subsections (c) and (d) below, it is important to determine whether a particular partnership has agreed to vary the default voting rule.

Because a majority voting rule for registration might significantly alter the partners' contract, it may even be unconstitutional under the Contract Clause to apply such a rule to existing partnerships.[59] On the other hand, permitting LLP registration is a new development that partnerships in existence on adoption of the LLP statute did not anticipate in drafting their agreement. It is reasonable to suppose that many partnerships would have contracted for limited liability from the outset if they had been allowed to do so.[60]

---

trigger damages, a low valuation of the interest, or a noncompetition clause under the partnership agreement.

[58] *See* Ribstein, Possible Futures for Unincorporated Firms, 64 U. Cin. L. Rev. 319 (1996). Similar issues may be presented by statutes that permit transition by conversion or merger from partnership to a limited liability type of business association.

[59] U.S. Constitution, Article I, Section 10 provides: "No state shall . . . pass any . . . Law impairing the obligations of contracts." *See generally* Butler & Ribstein, The Contract Clause and the Corporation, 55 Brook. L. Rev. 767 (1989).

[60] *See generally* Ribstein, The Deregulation of Limited Liability and the Death of Partnership, 70 Wash. U. L.Q. 365 (1992).

(c)   Effect of Agreement: No Statutory Voting Rule on Registration

A statute that does not provide a specific voting rule on registration raises the issue of whether the partnership agreement provides the relevant voting rule. LLP registration should probably be considered an extraordinary decision comparable to amending the agreement, and therefore one that must be approved unanimously. It is not clear whether a partnership agreement that provides for partner approval of important matters by a less-than-unanimous vote should be applied to LLP registration even if the agreement does not explicitly deal with registration.

A court may decide that the parties must explicitly contract out of the partners' right to veto important decisions, so that the veto may apply to an unanticipated type of decision in the absence of a specifically applicable contract provision.[61] On the other hand, a court could decide that the parties intended through a general subunanimous voting provision to waive the statutory default voting rule for all important matters, and therefore apply the agreement to the decision to register.[62]

If the agreement permits subunanimous voting only for specific decisions, such as for mergers but not for amendments of the agreement, a court could decide that the agreement only waives the statutory default for those provisions. If the agreement permits majority voting for some types of decisions but subunanimous supermajority voting for others, it would be clear that the parties intended to generally contract around unanimity, but not what vote they wanted to require for registration. In this case, a court should apply the most closely analogous provision, such as the provision that applies to amendments rather than to merger or dissolution.

(d)   Effect of Agreement: Specific Voting Provisions on Registration

Under statutes that provide specific majority or majority-in-interest voting rules for LLP registration it is necessary to determine the effect of agreements that

---

[61] See McCallum v. Asbury, 238 Or. 257, 393 P.2d 774 (1964) (dictum that "fundamental" change in governance structure would not be authorized by general provision for amending the agreement by majority vote). But see Day v. Sidley & Austin, 394 F. Supp. 986 (D.D.C. 1975), aff'd sub nom. Day v. Avery, 548 F.2d 1018 (D.C. Cir. 1976), cert. denied, 431 U.S. 908 (1977) (permitting merger over plaintiff partner's objection under provision that specifically allowed admission of partners by majority vote).

[62] See Bailey v. Fish & Neave, 8 N.Y.3d 523, 868 N.E.2d 956, 837 N.Y.S.2d 600 (2007) (interpreting general majority vote to authorize change from accrual to cash system, permitting significantly lower payment to plaintiff when he withdrew than he would have received under the prior system).

provide for general unanimity or supermajority voting rules on specified or all important matters or on LLP registration in particular.

An agreement that explicitly requires a high or unanimous vote for LLP registration ought to be enforced like other partnership voting rules.[63] It is not clear whether an agreement that includes only a general unanimity voting rule should be interpreted to override majority-vote provisions in LLP statutes. Some statutes explicitly make their voting rules subject to contrary provision in the partnership agreement.[64] Others do not explicitly prohibit such agreements. However, the voting rules in LLP provisions are intended to substitute a specific voting rule on LLP registrations for the *statutory* unanimity vote on major decisions. It arguably follows that an *agreement* to make all or specified decisions unanimously should not be deemed to vary the LLP voting rule. Conversely, an *agreement* to generally make decisions by *majority* vote arguably should not be deemed to vary a specific *statutory* requirement for a *unanimous* vote on registration. Nevertheless, statutes that make their default rule broadly subject to contrary agreement imply that a general majority voting rule in the agreement may vary the LLP voting rule. Finally, assuming that a contractual voting rule that does not explicitly refer to LLP registration may override the statutory voting rule, this raises the same issue as statutes that do not provide for a voting rule as to whether the contractual voting rule is intended to apply to LLP registration.

Statutes such as those in New York, which provides that the registration shall be considered ordinary business, present a further complication. The statute presumably applies either the statutory or, if inconsistent, the contractual voting rule on ordinary business. It is not clear whether an agreement to vote unanimously only on specified ordinary matters would be applied to the LLP registration decision, or even whether an explicit agreement to vote unanimously on LLP registration would be enforced. However, these statutes could be interpreted as providing for a majority voting rule on LLP registration unless the agreement provides for some other vote for this decision.

By specifically cross-referencing the vote to amend contribution obligations, R.U.P.A. clarifies the rule that applies when there are different votes on different types of amendments. Since LLP registration potentially affects the allocation of liabilities among the partners, it seems logical to cross-reference the vote on contributions that may have a similar effect.

---

[63] *See* U.P.A. § 18 (providing that voting and other rules are subject to contrary agreements); R.U.P.A. § 103(b) (not listing voting rules among nonwaivable provisions).

[64] *E.g.,* Prototype LLP Act § 910(c); Va. Code. § 50-73.132(c). This may be the case under R.U.P.A. § 103(b) and statutes based on this provision, which does not list the LLP voting provision as one of the Act's nonwaivable provisions.

(e)   Effect of Unauthorized Filing

There may be an issue concerning the effect of unauthorized filings, particularly if registration must be approved unanimously. Such filings probably should be binding as to third parties under the estoppel reasoning discussed in Section 2.07(c), below. However, this raises difficult issues concerning the apportionment of the liability among the partners. Forcing partners who did not agree to the filing to face direct liability alone for participating in the wrongdoing could result in the sort of shift of responsibilities without partner consent that unanimity requirements are intended to guard against. Accordingly, courts may permit such partners to seek indemnification from their co-partners under some circumstances. The rules on indemnification where there is an effective registration are discussed below in Section 4.04(b).

(f)   Drafting Voting Rules Dealing with LLP Registration

A partnership whose members do not wish to register as an LLP should consider adding a provision to their agreement that provides for voting on a potential future LLP registration. If the members want to ensure that they can veto future registrations, they should amend their agreement specifically to provide for a unanimity vote on LLP registrations. Note that the partners should do this even if the partnership law currently applicable to their firm includes LLP provisions that do not provide for majority approval of a registration, since the firm may be able to register under the LLP statute of a different jurisdiction (*see* Chapter 6).

§ 2.05   NAME REQUIREMENTS

All LLP statutes require that LLPs so identify themselves in their names. Statutory provisions concerning the name of the LLP are summarized in Table 2-9. States also may require the LLP designation in their rules governing professional firms.[65] The usual requirement is that "LLP" (with or without periods), "Limited Liability Partnership," or the equivalent for "Registered Limited Liability Partnership," be the last letters or words in the name. Some states are similar but do not insist that the designation come at the end of the name. Where a limited partnership becomes an LLP, the requirement is a doubling of designations such as "Registered Limited Liability Limited Partnership" or "LLLP,"[66]

---

[65] *See* Section 7.04, below.
[66] *See* Del. Code Ann., tit. 6, § 17-214(a)(2).

or other combinations of the limited partnership and LLP statutory name requirements.[67]

As summarized in Table 2-9, many states require that the name of an LLP not be the same as or deceptively similar to the name of another business entity filed with the state, for example, a corporation, limited partnership, limited liability company, or LLP. There is no practical way for the state to know whether an LLP has a name the same as or deceptively similar to that of an entity whose name is not filed with the state. But common law may similarly require that the LLP name not be the same as or deceptively similar to the name of an unfiled entity.

A name the same as or similar to another organization's name may be permitted with the consent of the other organization.[68] If several partnerships with similar names want to be LLPs, the first to file or reserve a name can bar the others unless it gives consent or the others change their names. Some states permit a foreign LLP to have and use a name like a domestic LLP if the foreign LLP agrees to identify its foreign state.[69] Even without explicit statutory authorization, such identification of the foreign jurisdiction may result in a name that is sufficiently different from that of the domestic firm to comply with the statute.

The consequences of not using the required name are uncertain. *See* Section 2.07, below.[70] Statutes should give guidance on this point, especially where they protect from liability for contract. An asserted LLP's failure to identify itself as such may misrepresent the partners' liability to one who is contracting with the firm. If so, estoppel will operate to bar liability protection. On the other hand, partners of a law firm that did not include the LLP designation in its letterhead did not lose limited liability in the absence of a statutory requirement conditioning protection on whether a third party knows that he or she is dealing with an LLP.[71]

---

[67] The Prototype LLP Act would amend R.U.L.P.A. to this effect or permit various combinations of words that the initials represent. The R.U.P.A. comments suggest an amendment to the Uniform Limited Partnership Act (1985), which requires a limited partnership registering as a limited liability partnership to comply with the LLP statute. R.U.P.A. § 101, cmt. This, in effect, would require adding the LLP or equivalent designation to the limited partnership's name, which, in turn, must include the words "limited partnership." *See* R.U.L.P.A. § 102(1). U.L.P.A. § 108 (2001) provides that an LLLP name "must contain the phrase 'limited liability limited partnership' or the abbreviation 'LLLP' or 'L.L.L.P.' and must not contain the abbreviation 'L.P.' or 'LP.' " *See* Section 9.108, infra.

[68] *E.g.*, Del. Code Ann., tit. 6, § 15-108(c).

[69] *E.g.*, Or. Stat. § 67.625 (must state name under which created, followed by "a limited liability partnership of (identify registration jurisdiction)").

[70] Illinois provides that a foreign limited liability partnership may not use an assumed or fictitious name to intentionally misrepresent its geographic origin or location, and for fines of up to $1,000 for each day of violation. *See* Ill. Comp. Stat. Ann. ch. 805, § 805 ILCS 206/1002.

[71] Chamberlain v. Irving, 2006 WL 3290446 (Conn. Super. Oct. 26, 2006).

Because tort creditors (other than those whose claims also can be characterized as contractual) cannot very well rely on whether partners have ordinary partner liability as opposed to LLP liability, the use of the required LLP name is unlikely to be significant for them. It arguably follows that courts should recognize the LLP shield in tort cases even though the partnership has not used the required name. While this result could tend to undermine compliance with the name requirement, it arguably balances the parties' interests where the failure to use the required name was inadvertent. To minimize risk of loss of LLP protection, LLP firms should use their LLP designation wherever they use their names, not only in contracts, but also in advertisements, correspondence, directory listings, and business cards.

As shown in Table 2-9, name reservation before filing is permitted in some states.

§ 2.06   INSURANCE AND FINANCIAL RESPONSIBILITY REQUIREMENTS

(a)   Insurance

Texas initiated the requirement of insurance as a substitute for partners' joint and several liability.[72] An arbitrary $100,000 was chosen. Recognizing that insurance is not always available, it qualified the requirement as carrying "if reasonably available, at least $100,000 of liability insurance of a kind that is designed to cover the kinds of errors, omissions, negligence, incompetence, or malfeasance for which liability is limited."[73] Its 1993 revision retained the insurance requirement but deleted "if reasonably available" and provided an alternative described below in subsection (c).[74] The 2010 revision deleted the insurance requirement.[75]

A few jurisdictions have followed the original Texas requirement of placing liability insurance requirements in the LLP statute as a substitute for partner's individual liability:

California: Accounting firms — $100,000 per licensed person up to $5 million with minimum of $1,000,000 for firms with five or fewer members, partner guarantees for the difference between liability and insured amount or an affirmation of net worth of more than $10 million; law firms — same, but maximum of $7.5 million and net worth of $15 million.[76]

---

[72] See Section 1.01(a), above.

[73] Tex. Rev. Civ. Stat. Ann. art. 6132b-45C(1).

[74] Tex. Bus. Org. Code § 152.804. A creditor can pursue judgment against partner of LLP where the partner was insured but the firm was not as required by the statute. See Edward B. Elmer, M.D., P.A. v. Santa Fe Props., Inc., 2006 WL 3612359 (Tex. App. Dec. 13, 2006).

[75] 2011 Texas Laws ch. 139, effective Sept. 1, 2011.

[76] Cal. Corp. Code § 16956.

Connecticut: $250,000.[77]

Massachusetts: Professional LLPs must carry the insurance "designated" by the applicable regulating board.[78] Most boards have not yet designated minimum amounts.

Rhode Island: $50,000 times the number of professional employees but not less than $100,000 or more than $500,000 with deductible of no more than $25,000 for each claim multiplied by the number of professional employees.[79]

South Carolina: $100,000 "beyond the amount of any applicable deductible" and any higher insurance coverage required by their licensing authorities.[80]

Washington: Professionals must maintain professional liability insurance of $1 million to $3 million, taking into account the nature and size of business within the profession or specialty.[81]

Note that even in states whose LLP statutes do not require insurance or financial responsibility the firm may be subject to such requirements under licensing or other statutes. Some states have financial responsibility requirements for professional firms that apply to LLPs.[82]

There is some intended flexibility in the type of insurance the firm must carry. But there is resulting uncertainty when a policy employs insuring language different from the statute or excludes conduct that is protected by the statute. It has been held that where the statute does not permit only "substantial compliance" with statutory requirements "the partnership must be in strict compliance with the insurance or financial responsibility requirements."[83] In some cases the court may decide as a matter of law (including interpretation of the insurance

---

[77] Conn. Gen. Stat. § 34-327(e).

[78] Mass. Gen. L. ch. 108A, § 45(8).

[79] R.I. Gen. L. § 7-12-58.

[80] S.C. Code Ann. § 33-41-1130(A)(1)–(2). This stipulation concerning the deductible is probably implicit in all the dollar requirements.

[81] Wash. Rev. Code § 25.05.125(4).

[82] Colo. S. Ct. Rule 265.I.A.4 ($100,000 per lawyer up to $500,000 per claim and $300,000 per lawyer up to $2,000,000 for all claims in a year); Ill. Comp. St. S. Ct. Rule 722(b) ($100,000 per claim and $250,000 annual aggregate per lawyer up to $5,000,000 per claim and $10,000,000 annual aggregate); Mass. Sup. Ct. Rule 3:06 ($50,000 plus $15,000 per lawyer up to $500,000); Del. Sup. Ct. R. 67(h) (greater of $1,000,000 or $100,000 per lawyer per claim and greater of $2,000,000 or $200,000 per lawyer for all claims during the policy year); Burns Ind. Att'y Disc. Rule 27(g) ($50,000 per lawyer up to $5,000,000 per claim and $100,000 per lawyer up to $10,000,000 for all claims during the policy year); Neb. S. Ct. Rule for Lim. Liab. Prof. Org. I(C)(7)(b)(iv) ($250,000 per lawyer up to $1,000,000 per claim and $500,000 per lawyer up to $5,000,000 for all claims in a policy year); N.J. Rules of Ct. Rule 1:21-1C(3) ($100,000 per lawyer up to $5 million per claim); Ohio St. Govt. Bar Rules, Rule 3, § 4 ($50,000 per lawyer up to $5,000,000 per claim or $100,000 per lawyer up to $10,000,000 for all claims in a policy year). Like the LLP statutory provisions discussed below in subsections (b) and (c), most of these rules provide for individual liability for failing to insure and permit compliance by financial segregation.

[83] Edward B. Elmer, M.D., P.A. v. Santa Fe Props., Inc., 2006 WL 3612359, *2 (Tex. App. Dec. 13, 2006) (though partner had insurance the partner did not have statutory liability protection because the firm was not insured as required by the statute).

policy contract) whether the policy satisfies the statute. In others, it may be a fact question for the jury if there is one. The burden may be on the partners who claim liability protection to prove that the partnership has complied with the statute.[84] For the fact question, the relevant aspects include availability of insurance in the market, good faith effort to satisfy the statute, and how closely the policy approximates the range of conduct whose liability is protected (as distinct from the particular conduct in suit). Firms that want greater assurance than their policy gives should consider the asset segregation alternative discussed below in Section 2.06(b). The availability of the alternative may influence a court to construe strictly the insurance requirement.

Most LLP states have omitted an insurance requirement, presumably relying on partners' rational self-interest to insure.

(b)   Penalty for Noncompliance

An LLP that fails to comply with the insurance requirement loses the liability shield at least up to the amount that should have been covered by insurance.[85]

(c)   Financial Responsibility through Segregation

As an alternative to insurance that might not be available, or that might be too costly, Texas created an alternative:

> $100,000 of funds specifically designated and segregated for the satisfaction of judgments against the partnership based on the kinds of errors, omissions, negligence, incompetence, or malfeasance for which liability is limited . . . by:
>
>> (A) deposit of cash, bank certificates of deposit, or United States Treasury obligations in trust or bank escrow; (B) a bank letter of credit; or (C) insurance company bond.

---

[84] This is explicit in W. Va. Code § 47B-10-5.

[85] For an example of a rule embodying this result, *see* Ill. Comp. St. S. Ct. Rule 722(b)(2) (providing for joint and several liability for lawyers in a firm that has obtained minimum insurance up to the amount of the deductible or retention unless the firm has provided proof of financial responsibility of at least the amount of the deductible or retention). Failure to have the requisite insurance may result in complete loss of the liability shield in states that do not specify a lesser penalty. For a case imposing this penalty, see Edward B. Elmer, M.D., P.A. v. Santa Fe Props., Inc., 2006 WL 3612359 (Tex. App. Dec. 13, 2006), discussed at note 83, supra.

All of the other states that require insurance have comparable provisions in the same amount as the insurance they require. California provides for aggregation of insurance and other financial security, and the ability to aggregate may be implicit in the other statutes.[86]

(d) Impact on Veil-piercing

A statutory insurance or segregation requirement can be argued as a determination of adequate protection that militates against piercing the limited liability veil, as noted below in Section 3.07.[87] However, hinting at the possibility of piercing the limited liability veil, South Carolina legislates that nothing in the insurance or segregation alternative shall "constitute a determination of the adequacy of capitalization of a registered limited liability partnership for any purpose."[88]

(e) Admissibility of Insurance Requirements

To avoid influencing jury verdicts on liability and measure of damages, most states with insurance requirements prohibit telling the jury about the insurance.[89]

(f) Time of Compliance

Insurance or asset segregation is a substitute for partner individual liability.[90] The substitute concept clearly contemplates that the insurance or segregation be in effect at the time of suit for such purposes as obtaining dismissal of a protected partner. The concept equally contemplates that the insurance or segregation be in effect at the time of judgment.

Most of the statutes that require insurance or segregation also require that the protected conduct occur "while the partnership is a registered limited liability

---

[86] The Illinois Supreme Court rule also provides for segregation. *See* Ill. Comp. St. S. Ct. Rule 722(b)(3).

[87] Dow v. Jones, 311 F. Supp. 2d 461 (D. Md. 2004) (D.C. law) indirectly supports this by holding that the insurance requirement, not veil-piercing, provided a reason for suing an LLP despite its lack of assets.

[88] S.C. Code Ann. § 33-41-1130(D)(2).

[89] Cal. Corp. Code § 16956(d); Mass. Gen. L. ch. 108A, § 45(8)(b); R.I. Gen. L. § 7-12-58(c); S.C. Code Ann. § 33-41-1130(B); W. Va. Code § 47B-10-5(c). Hecht, Solberg, Robinson, Goldberg & Bagley v. Superior Court, 137 Cal. App. 4th 579, 40 Cal. Rptr. 3d 446 (2006) (held that the California provision did not prevent *discovery* of insurance because it may be relevant to causation and damages).

[90] It follows from this that the insurance company should not be able to assert the partners' immunity from liability as a defense. *See* W. Va. Code § 47B-10-5, which makes this explicit.

partnership."[91] Particularly where the statute defines an LLP in terms of compliance with the statute (*see* Section 2.07(a), below), this demands that the insurance or segregation that the statute requires for LLPs be in effect at the time of the misconduct. A statute that omitted the quoted phrase (since repealed)[92] was copied from the original Texas LLP statute that was probably intended, and was soon amended, to specify that the protected conduct occur while the partnership is an LLP (*see* Section 1.01(b), above).

§ 2.07   EFFECT OF NONCOMPLIANCE WITH STATUTORY REQUIREMENTS

The statutory requirements for LLPs discussed above in this chapter raise questions concerning the consequences of noncompliance with these requirements. Because the statutes generally define an LLP as a partnership that has complied with these requirements, this suggests that the liability limitation generally does *not* apply to liabilities incurred while the firm is not in compliance with the requirements. Moreover, as noted immediately above in Section 2.06(f), some statutes explicitly grant the limitation only for liabilities incurred while the firm is an LLP. This section discusses the potential effect of noncompliance with these requirements on LLP partners' limited liability.

(a)   *Statutory and Judicial Qualifications on Strict Compliance*

As shown in Table 2-1, the statutes generally define an LLP as one that is registered as provided in the statute or that is registered and otherwise complies with the statute. The rules limiting liability, in turn, apply only to a partnership that is a limited liability partnership.[93] Under these provisions, if an LLP registration is defective, or (under the statutes that include other compliance in the LLP definition) the LLP fails to comply in some other respect with the LLP statutory requirements, the liability limitation does not apply. However, as discussed in the following subsections, even if partners do not comply strictly with statutory requirements, they may be entitled to the protection of the LLP provisions on one of several grounds: substantial compliance (Section 2.07(b)); noncompliance with an annual reporting requirement (Section 2.07(b)); and estoppel (Section

---

[91] *E.g.*, S.C. Code Ann. § 33-41-370(B).

[92] D.C. Code Ann. § 33-445 (repealed).

[93] *See, e.g.*, R.U.P.A. § 306(c). As discussed in § 3.09, infra, the qualifications in LLP statutes of partners' duties to contribute toward losses are subject to the main liability provision, and therefore also apply only to LLPs.

2.07(c)). Section 2.07(d) considers the effect of noncompliance with formalities on the existence of the underlying partnership.

(b) Substantial Compliance

Noncompliance with statutory requirements may have been de minimis, so that the firm is in "substantial compliance" with statutory requirements. For example, the noncompliance may not materially impact required public disclosures and financial responsibility. On the other hand, failure to have insurance or asset segregation when this is required will almost certainly forfeit the liability limitation.[94] As discussed in Section 2.03(b)(8) and shown in Table 2-6, many LLP statutes require only "substantial compliance" with the statute or excuse good faith errors, or both. For example, the Delaware statute explicitly requires only "substantial compliance."[95] As discussed in Section 2.03(b)(9) and shown in Table 2-3, some statutes provide that changes after the filing do not affect the firm's status as an LLP. In the absence of a specific "substantial compliance" provision it is possible that courts may nevertheless excuse minor defects. Failure to have the right "kind" of required insurance may be excused because of the flexibility in the phrasing of the requirement, as noted above in Section 2.06(a). However, it is important to keep in mind that such excuses, if taken too far, could nullify statutory prerequisites for LLP status. Thus, it has been held that a member of a partnership that made effort to register as an LLP was not a de facto LLP so that the partners were subject to liability under general partnership law.[96]

The most important question regarding the effect of noncompliance with LLP provisions is whether firms' failure to file annual renewals can cause loss of LLP status. Most firms can be expected to comply with formalities that apply on formation, just as they comply with analogous provisions in statutes concerning other types of business associations. However, the duty to renew annually the registration or to file periodic reports as a prerequisite of continued existence is unique to LLPs, and easily could trap unwary firms. Also, annual renewals are relatively unimportant in informing third parties about the LLP's limited liability status.

---

[94] *See* Edward B. Elmer, M.D., P.A. v. Santa Fe Props., Inc., 2006 WL 3612359 (Tex. App. Dec. 13, 2006) (partner had no liability protection though he had insurance because the firm did not have insurance as required by the statute, citing absence of "statutory compliance" language in the statute).

[95] Del. Code Ann., tit. 6, § 15-1001(e).

[96] American Import-Export of Goods, LLC v. World of Colors, LLP, Slip Copy, 2010 WL 3974846 (E.D. Mich. Oct. 8, 2010) (Mich. law).

Thus, courts may hold that a firm that has complied in all other respects with the necessary formalities is in "substantial compliance" with statutory requirements. LLP statutes often do, and probably should, provide that LLP status does not end automatically on failure to make an annual report, but rather must be revoked by an administrative proceeding after notice and failure to comply. Some provide that the partnership may be reinstated and deemed not to have lost its LLP status. *See* Section 2.03(c), above, and Table 2-7. However, it has been held under a statute that did not include a "substantial compliance" provision or a grace period for a renewal application that the partners in a firm formed as an LLP were personally liable for a lease entered into three years after the registration expired.[97] The court distinguished limited partnership cases arising under statutes that included "substantial compliance" language.

(c)   LLPs by Estoppel

The creditor may be estopped from denying the firm's LLP status because the parties transacted business on the assumption that the firm was an LLP.[98] If the firm has clearly represented itself to a third party as a limited liability partnership, this arguably creates a contract for nonrecourse liability with that party. If such a contract would be enforced in the absence of LLP provisions, arguably it should be enforced after such statutes are passed.

There is, however, authority against enforcing LLP status based on mere representation of the firm as an LLP without registration.[99] One argument against enforcing LLPs by estoppel is that the statutes literally condition LLP status on compliance with formalities. This interpretation is reinforced to some extent by provisions discussed above in subsection (b) for limited relief from technicalities — in particular, those that provide that post-filing changes do not affect the LLP's status. By a "negative pregnant" construction, this language suggests that other inaccuracies do affect the LLP's status, and, therefore, the members' liability. On the other hand, it may be significant that LLP statutes generally do

---

[97] Apcar Inv. Partners VI, Ltd. v. Gaus, 161 S.W.3d 137 (Tex. App. 2005).

[98] For cases recognizing corporations by estoppel, see Cranson v. IBM Corp., 234 Md. 477, 200 A.2d 33 (1964); Harry Rich Corp. v. Feinberg, 518 So. 2d 377 (Fla. Dist. Ct. App. 1987); HF Phillipsborn & Co. v. Suson, 59 Ill. 2d 465, 322 N.E.2d 45 (1975); Sherwood & Roberts-Oregon, Inc. v. Alexander, 269 Or. 389, 525 P.2d 135 (1974). For cases recognizing LLCs by estoppel see Leber Assocs., LLC v. Entertainment Group Fund, Inc., 2003 WL 21750211 (S.D.N.Y. July 29, 2003); Ruggio v. Vining, 755 So. 2d 792 (Fla. App. 2000). For a discussion of LLCs by estoppel, see Ribstein & Keatinge, note 13, supra, § 4.15, n.5. For a discussion of the application of partnership-by-estoppel or purported-partner liability to LLPs, see § 3.10, infra.

[99] *See* Campbell v. Lichtenfels, 2007 WL 447919 (Conn. Super. Jan. 26, 2007) (merely putting "LLP" initials on checks and letterheads does not protect the partners from liability for a co-partner's malpractice where the firm has failed to register as an LLP).

not provide, analogously to some corporate and LLC statutes,[100] for liability of those who assume or purport to act as LLPs without having fully complied with filing requirements.[101]

From a policy standpoint, permitting firms to be "estoppel" LLPs might confuse third parties who would otherwise assume that the LLP has complied fully with statutory requirements. Thus, a court in determining whether to enforce the limited liability of partners in a defective LLP should consider whether noncompliance with requirements significantly reduced the protection the legislature sought to provide. Material failure to comply with insurance or bonding requirements probably should bar limited liability despite estoppel. Perhaps partners should be personally liable even if compliance with insurance requirements would not have enabled the firm to pay its claims. This result would increase the deterrence effect of the statute. On the other hand, rigid enforcement even in the absence of harm to third parties might unnecessarily reduce the utility of the LLP form, particularly in light of the uncertainty and complexity of insurance and bonding requirements. This consideration provides a rationale for statutes that limit liability to harm caused by noncompliance with insurance requirements (*see* Section 2.06(b), note 85, above).

It is not clear whether an estoppel should arise if a third party believes the firm is an LLP but the LLP has failed adequately to represent itself as such to the world, as by failing to comply with the statutory requirements for disclosing LLP status. Once again, the issue is whether it is appropriate to base liability on the prophylactic purposes of the statutory requirements.

(d) Effect of Noncompliance with Formalities on Existence of Underlying Partnership

Noncompliance with LLP formalities usually affects only the status of the firm as an LLP, and not its existence as a partnership.[102] The Indiana statute provides that

---

[100] *See* Model Business Corporation Act (MBCA) § 2.04; Ribstein & Keatinge, note 13, above, § 4.15 (discussing LLC provisions).

[101] North Dakota does provide for such liability. *See* N.D. Cent. Code § 45-22-07.

[102] *See* In re Lim, 2007 WL 58711 (Mo. Jan. 9, 2007) (non-registration did not prevent law firm from being a valid partnership and therefore did not violate ethical rule by misrepresenting partnership status). In re Hawthorne Townhomes, L.P., 282 S.W.3d 131 (Tex. App. 2009) held that an LLP that "converted" to a limited partnership did not cease to exist when it withdrew its registration as an LLP and then registered the same day as a limited partnership, with the result that an arbitration agreement entered into by the LLP could be enforced against the limited partnership. The court applied the conversion provision of the Texas Revised Partnership Act, which provides that the converted entity continues to exist. However, this provision does not relate to the effect of withdrawal of LLP registration. Moreover, it is not clear from the case that the LLP had, in fact, converted pursuant to the partnership statute. Therefore, while the withdrawal of the registration alone would not affect the existence of the underlying partnership, it is not clear that the limited

the existence of a partnership is not affected by the filing or failure or omission to file a registration, the expiration of the partnership's status as an LLP, or the filing of a withdrawal.[103]

In the absence of such a statutory provision, noncompliance with LLP formalities may bear on the existence of the underlying partnership. In particular, the absence of LLP registration may be critical in marginal cases in which the other evidence of partnership is weak. Noncompliance with corporate, limited partnership, or limited liability company formalities has been held to affect the formation of the firm itself. As discussed above at note 100, many corporate and LLC statutes make this clear by imposing liability on those who assume or purport to act prior to formation. Limited partnership statutes commonly provide that the limited partnership is formed on "substantial compliance" with the filing requirement[104] and provide for relief in the event of a mistaken failure to file.[105] The critical question is whether the failure to comply with formalities means these firms not only do not provide limited liability vis-à-vis third parties, but that the business association is unenforceable among purported shareholders, limited partners, or LLC members.

There is authority enforcing limited partnership agreements among the partners even if formalities have not been complied with.[106] There is also authority enforcing LLP agreements among the partners despite noncompliance with formalities.[107] On the other hand, one could argue that members did not intend to form any business association in the event the firm failed to meet the critical condition of limited liability of the members. Similarly, in an LLP the parties may have realigned their profit and management shares in order to reflect the partners' limited liability. Thus, their failure to comply with the LLP provisions enforcing the apparent underlying agreement may not reflect the parties' intent. The counterargument is that the LLP provisions assume that the firm that is registering is a "partnership" (*see* Section 2.02) and the partnership statutes that include LLP provisions have independent rules defining the existence of a "partnership." This arguably supports construing the statute to provide that abortive LLPs are still partnerships.

---

partnership should have been deemed to be the same entity for purposes of application of the arbitration agreement. *See* Bromberg & Ribstein, § 7.21(f).

[103] Ind. Code § 23-4-1-7(5).

[104] *See* R.U.L.P.A. § 201(b) (1985); U.L.P.A. § 201(c) (2001).

[105] R.U.L.P.A. § 304; U.L.P.A. § 306 (2001).

[106] *See* Bromberg & Ribstein, § 12.04(b).

[107] Joachim v. Flanzig, 2004 WL 383225 (N.Y. Sup. Feb. 25, 2004) (enforcing agreement despite failure to comply with statutory requirements of filing and publication); Hart v. Theus, Grisham, Davis & Leigh, L.L.P., 877 So. 2d 1157 (La. App. 2004) (noting that although failure to renew registration causes loss of limited liability protection, the partnership continues).

§ 2.08 CHOICE OF REGISTRATION STATE

This section considers the criteria that will usually be most important in choosing where to become an LLP. Section (a) discusses the degree and kind of protection in the state of formation. Section (b) discusses protection in states where operations are conducted. Section (c) notes other factors.

(a) Protection in Formation State

In choosing where to register as an LLP the first place to consider is the home base where the partnership's principal or executive office is. If that jurisdiction affords the desired degree of LLP protection from liability, it is a logical choice because the firm and its lawyer probably will have greater familiarity with the local law and procedure and less expense than finding and filing in another jurisdiction. But other jurisdictions may be better. In evaluating the degree of protection of an LLP statute these aspects should be considered: Are contract liabilities as well as tort liabilities protected? What tort liabilities are protected? Do indemnification or contribution provisions dilute protection? What is the duration of the protection?

(1) Contract Protection

The broadest protection is afforded by the states that limit liability for contract as well as for tort liability (*see* Sections 1.01(d)–(e), above, and Section 3.03 and Table 3-1, below).

(2) Tort Protection

There is also significant variation in statutory protection against tort liabilities. Several partial-shield statutes protect partners from liability for "negligence, wrongful acts or misconduct, whether characterized as tort, contract or otherwise."[108] Many statutes, whether or not they protect only against tort-type liabilities, provide that the shield "shall not affect the liability of a partner in a registered limited liability partnership for his own negligence, wrongful acts or misconduct or that of any person under his direct supervision and control."[109] However, several

---

[108] This is based on language in the original Delaware statute, Del. Code Ann., tit. 6, § 1515(b) before Delaware adopted a full-shield approach and, later, R.U.P.A. Similar statutes are listed in Table 3-1.

[109] This, too, is based on the original Delaware provision, Del. Code Ann., tit. 6, § 1515(c), now superseded by R.U.P.A. Similar statutes are listed in Table 3-1 and discussed in Section 3.04, infra.

statutes as well as the Prototype LLP Act and R.U.P.A. include language that is less suggestive of vicarious liability for persons acting under partners' supervision or control, or at least narrow the potential scope of any such liability (*see* Section 3.04(a) and Table 3-1).

(3) Dilution of Protection

As discussed more fully below in Section 3.09 and Section 4.04, the LLP protection against liability can be diluted or diminished by the operation of the usual U.P.A. right to be indemnified and obligation to contribute. If a partner is liable for her own misconduct and receives indemnification from the firm, the innocent partners have in effect shared that liability, particularly if they also must contribute to losses resulting from their co-partner's misconduct. The partnership agreement can make appropriate adjustments in indemnification and contribution, but statutory adjustments would save contracting costs. State laws vary in this respect and merit comparison.[110] The R.U.P.A. is as succinct and effective as any: "A partner is not personally liable, directly or indirectly, including by way of contribution or otherwise, for such a partnership obligation solely by reason of being or so acting as a partner."[111]

(4) Duration of Protection

As discussed more fully in Section 2.03(c), above, states vary concerning length of time an LLP registration remains in effect. All states with fixed lengths permit renewal, and states with long or indefinite duration require periodic reporting on pain of possible revocation. There is an advantage in registering in a state with longer duration of protection. But this is less important than the scope of protection.

---

[110] Indemnification and contribution are affected by U.P.A. §§ 18(a), 18(b), 34, 36(4), and 40(d). Most LLP statutes adjust each of these sections by an exception for or a reference to the limitation of liability in their versions of U.P.A. § 15. Statutory provisions are listed in Table 3-2. Some jurisdictions do not adjust any other obligations, while others do not adjust their equivalents of § 18(b). The latter omission is not particularly surprising, since that subsection refers only to the *partnership's* duty to indemnify and not to the *partners'* duty to contribute toward any resulting loss. Most statutes provide that partners shall not be personally liable as a result of the partnership's indemnification for shielded liabilities. Indemnification and contribution are affected (directly or indirectly) by R.U.P.A. §§ 307(b), (d), 401(c), 703(b), 806(b), 807(b)–(d), 903(e), 906(c). All these sections are adjusted for LLP limitations in the Prototype and the R.U.P.A. LLP amendments. R.U.P.A. § 306(c) not only adjusts the default rule concerning partners' indemnification and contribution, but also overrides the preregistration partnership agreement on the assumption that the partners would want to change that agreement to reflect the liability limitation. This provision is discussed in § 4.04(b), infra.

[111] R.U.P.A. § 306(c).

Perhaps more important is that protection remain in effect with changes in partners or structure of the firm. For example, R.U.P.A. provides that LLP "status remains effective, regardless of changes in the partnership."[112] As shown in Table 2-3 and discussed in Section 2.03(b)(9), some states provide for continued LLP status after dissolution. However, equivalent results can be achieved by renewals if the dissolved partnership remembers to make them.

Liability protection may come to an end because the firm ceases to be the type that may be an LLP under the applicable law. As discussed above in Section 2.03(a)(3), California and New York restrict registration to general partnerships in specified professions. New York includes most of the major ones,[113] and requires that the firm or some or all of the members hold New York professional licenses.[114] A New York LLP partner loses protection and becomes prospectively liable "to the extent at least a majority of the partners shall have agreed unless otherwise provided in any agreement between the partners."[115] Thus a partner's protection is at the sufferance of some majority of the partners.

(b) Protection in Operation State

Another set of protection concerns affects the choice of place to become an LLP. This concern relates to where the partnership will be operating. If an operating state has LLP protection only for firms registered there, registering there initially may be more beneficial than registering in a state with broader liability protection. If the operation state has formation state protection for foreign LLPs it may be a good idea to register initially in the state that offers the broadest liability protection or is otherwise the most desirable. Sections 2.03(a)(3) and 2.03(b)(16), above, and 6.02, below, discuss LLP status in operation states.

(c) Other Factors

Numerous other factors, many of which are discussed in Section 1.07, may influence the choice of state in which to become an LLP. A fundamental one is the basic partnership law there: U.P.A. (or variations from it) or R.U.P.A. (or variations from it). Another factor relates to costs of LLP protection, including filing fees (see Section 2.03(b)(11)), state taxes (see Section 1.07(a)(4)) and

---

[112] R.U.P.A. § 1001(d).

[113] The eligible professions include lawyers, medical doctors, dentists, professional engineers, land surveyors, architects, and accountants. N.Y. P'ship Law ch. 34 § 2, defining "profession" by reference to N.Y. Educ. Law tit. 8.

[114] N.Y. P'ship Law ch. 34 § 2, § 121-1500(a).

[115] N.Y. P'ship Law ch. 34 § 2, § 26(d). Section 3.05, below, discusses this and related issues of waiving limited liability.

insurance or financial responsibility requirements (*see* Section 2.06). Since firms concerned about liability will normally carry insurance anyway, an LLP insurance requirement may not be significant. But firms that want to avoid this kind of cost may prefer a state that has no insurance or financial responsibility requirement.

Some states expressly permit limited partnerships to register as LLPs (*see* Section 2.03(a)(4), above, and Chapter 5, below). Whether it can validly register in other states that do not prohibit it is an open question (*see* Section 5.04, below).

With the continuing proliferation and amendment of LLP statutes it is important to keep in mind that the choice of place of formation is not irrevocable. An LLP may withdraw from one state and reform in a more favorable state.

§ 2.09　IMPACT OF LLP STATUS ON THE PARTNERSHIP AGREEMENT; CHECKLIST AND DISCUSSION

A partnership that is becoming or is deciding whether to become an LLP faces a host of considerations that are discussed throughout this book. As already discussed above in Section 2.08, the partnership must decide where to become an LLP and where to register as a foreign LLP. It must also ensure that the registration is approved by the appropriate vote (*see* Sections 2.03(b)(1) and 2.04, above). This section discusses what changes the partners should consider making in their partnership agreement as a result of LLP registration. The section cross-references the relevant sections of this book.[116]

(a)　Maintenance of LLP Status

Perhaps most importantly, a partnership that registers as an LLP must consider provisions in the agreement to ensure that the firm continues to comply with statutory prerequisites for LLP status. These include:

(1)　Maintenance of insurance or alternate financial responsibility (Section 2.06).

(2)　Maintenance of LLP registration, including annual filings where applicable (Sections 2.03(b)(14), 2.03(c), 2.08(a)(4)).

---

[116] *See* Marquis, Creating a Michigan Limited Liability Partnership, 74 Mich. B.J. 698 (1995) (listing a series of partnership provisions that must be reviewed and amended when changing a firm to an LLP).

(3) Appropriate use of partnership name, including LLP designation, in correspondence and otherwise (Section 2.05).

(4) Ensuring that the requisite number of partners have authorized the LLP registrations, preferably in writing in states where the partners are not required to execute the registration itself (Sections 2.03(b)(10), 2.04).

These compliance matters — particularly the first two — may be made the responsibility of an administrator or manager. The agreement also should make clear the partners' agreement to maintain the requisite statutory insurance. In addition, the partners may want to provide that a failure to perform these duties constitutes a breach of the manager's or administrator's duty of care (*see* Section 2.09(i), below).

(b) Partners' Direct Liability

The partners should consider provisions in the partnership agreement that can minimize potential direct liability of individual partners to third parties (Section 3.04). Direct liability may be a major new source of concern for partners as courts, under prodding from plaintiffs' lawyers, may expand this liability to compensate somewhat for the elimination of vicarious liability. The agreement might provide that a partner who is an administrator or manager is not thereby liable for the errors of others unless they are performed under the administrator's or manager's direct supervision.

The partners also should consider other liability-limitation provisions to help deal with the situations like those outlined below in Section 3.04(b), such as the following:

(1) A partner in a law or accounting partnership who has overall responsibility for a particular client is not thereby responsible for all work done on behalf of that client.

(2) A specialist who gives advice on a particular matter does not thereby have any supervisory or monitoring responsibility in connection with that matter.

These sorts of provisions should be tailored to the direct liability language of the applicable statute. The partnership agreement cannot prevent a holding that the administrator, the client-responsible person, or the specialist is liable to third parties, for the facts may establish the kind of supervision, control, or participation that leads to direct liability. But in close cases the partnership agreement may help determine the extent of their activities. *See* the related discussion of duties in Section 2.09(i), below.

(c)   Loss Sharing and Contribution Obligations

Losses are the excess of expenses over revenues in a given operating period and the excess of liabilities over assets on liquidation. *Liabilities* are particular debts owed by the firm. Partnership agreements generally include provisions that allocate operating losses to the partners' capital accounts. These losses may create negative balances in the partners' capital accounts. Whether or not the partners' liability is limited, these negative balances may create obligations to compensate for co-partners' capital contributions or advances to the firm.[117] Thus, even in an LLP the agreement may provide for payment to the partnership on account of the negative balances.

In contracting for contribution obligations in an LLP the agreement should limit the partners' contribution obligation to give effect to the statutory liability shield (*see* Section 3.09(b)). Otherwise, the partnership's trustee in bankruptcy or other creditor representative may enforce the partner's contribution obligation, even if it is intended only for the benefit of the other partners (*see* Section 4.04(b)). The agreement might also be interpreted as a waiver of the liability shield (*see* Section 3.05).

Apart from deliberate contribution obligations, the partners should be careful about language in the agreement that suggests that they are individually liable for partnership debts. Such language may be interpreted as a waiver of the liability shield (*see* Section 3.05). Even if the partners are not careful, R.U.P.A. § 306(c) may override partnership agreement provisions that are inconsistent with the shield (*see* Section 4.04(b), below).

Partners may have direct liability for a loss produced by their misconduct or attributable to a debt that antedated the LLP registration. The statutes provide with varying precision for partner contribution in such situations (*see* Section 3.09). The partnership agreement may more precisely allocate the liability by treating it as an expense of the partnership, to be specially allocated to the partner who is liable. Thus it will affect both that partner's profit share and capital account but not the profit share or capital account of other partners. The result will protect the other partners from indirect sharing in the liability.

(d)   Indemnification of Partners

Indemnification of partners is discussed in Section 4.04(b), below, while its effect on the partners' contribution obligations is discussed below in Section 3.09(c). As those sections show, LLP statutes leave many questions about the

---

[117] *See* Section 3.09(b), infra.

allocation of responsibility for liabilities among the partners that the partners should consider addressing in their partnership agreements.[118]

Partners who pay partnership liabilities to third parties have a right under the statute,[119] and often under express provisions of the partnership agreement, to obtain indemnification from the partnership. Indemnification rights technically lie only against the partnership assets with the liability then adjusted among the partners through contribution. Partners should be called upon to pay the debt in proportion to their obligations to contribute toward partnership losses.

Indemnification is less important given the decline in partners' direct liability to creditors. Even where partners are vicariously liable for partnership debts, creditors normally must first exhaust partnership assets (*see* Section 3.08). This is especially likely to be true in contract-type claims, the main category of claims for which LLP partners might be liable under some LLP statutes (*see* Section 3.02 and Section 3.03).

Indemnification may, however, be significant where partners must pay claims that resulted from their own errors or misconduct or errors or misconduct of those acting under their direct control (*see* Section 3.04). As discussed in Section 4.04(b), an important issue may arise when a partner's indemnification right triggers partner contribution obligations in apparent contravention of the liability shield. The agreement might give the paying partner a direct right against the other partners, even where the paying partner may have been to some extent responsible for the loss. Because LLP statutes may permit direct liability even where the partner has not engaged in any misconduct (*see* Section 3.04(a)), refusing to indemnify in this type of situation will create extra exposure for partners who are in risky areas of the partnership's business or who undertake supervisory responsibilities. If these partners are denied indemnification they may be reluctant to engage in these activities, may seek alternative types of compensation so that they can, in effect, insure against the risk, or may refuse to be partners in LLPs. On the other hand, the non-liable partners would not want to provide for a right of indemnification that is so broad that it would encourage carelessness. Thus, partners should have some right to be indemnified against direct liability that is not based on their negligence or more serious misconduct. A possible middle ground would be to provide for indemnification for particular activities that engender a high risk of liability but that are important to the partnership, such as serving as a manager or administrator or serving on an oversight committee.

---

[118] *See* Fortney, Seeking Shelter in the Minefield of Unintended Consequences—The Traps of Limited Liability Law Firms, 54 Wash. & Lee L. Rev. 717 (1997); Ribstein, Possible Futures for Closely Held Firms, 64 U. Cin. L. Rev. 319 (1996).

[119] *See* U.P.A. § 18(b); R.U.P.A. § 401(c).

To the extent that the partner seeking indemnification has a right against the individual partners, this could have the unwanted effect of requiring the partners to contribute toward payment of tort-type claims for which they have no vicarious liability under the statute (*see* Section 3.09(c), below). On the other hand, limiting partners' indemnification right to the partnership assets could effectively deny them relief in most cases, thereby significantly reducing the value of the indemnification right.

Even if the partners provide only for an indemnification claim against the partnership assets, this may indirectly obligate partners to outside creditors. The indemnification may leave insufficient partnership assets to pay other contract or other claims for which the partners remain liable under some statutes, thereby forcing partners to pay these claims out of personal assets (*see* Section 3.09(c), below). The partners could minimize, although perhaps not completely eliminate, this problem by contracting in the partnership agreement that, notwithstanding any provision to the contrary in their agreement, their liability is limited to the maximum extent provided for in the applicable statute.

Note that an existing general partnership that registers as an LLP must be sure to adjust its agreement concerning indemnification and contribution to reflect the registration. A provision imposing a direct obligation for indemnification on the partners may be innocuous when the partners are in any event liable to contribute toward all partnership losses, but quite significant when the partners are generally shielded from such liabilities. This raises the question whether the statute should reflect the parties' probable expectations by overriding such provisions in LLPs unless the partners expressly provide otherwise (*see* Section 4.04(b), below).

The above discussion gives rise to another planning consideration in addition to drafting the agreement. The partners could reduce the possibility that an indemnification obligation will give rise to "back door" individual liability by organizing under a statute that provides for the most complete possible limited liability shield — that is, provides that the partners have no liability merely because they are partners (*see* statutes summarized in Table 3-1). While partners still may be liable to creditors for their own misconduct under this provision, this type of provision makes it less likely that partners would be liable to tort claimants for the sort of non-negligent supervisory conduct for which they may expect indemnification.

(e) Indemnification by Partners

The partnership agreement may provide that partners who incur partnership liabilities as a result of their negligence, or outside the scope of the agreement or the usual course of business, must indemnify the partnership.

(f) Management and Voting Rights

Although LLP registration does not necessarily require a restructuring of contractual management and voting rights, it may justify more complete judicial enforcement of centralization of management (*see* Section 4.02, below). On the other hand, it is important to keep in mind that a reason for organizing as an LLP rather than as an LLC or close corporation is to minimize regulation of the firm. It follows that the parties may want to ensure that their agreement is written so as to ensure that this objective is realized. This may entail, among other things, providing that members have strong management and voting rights so that they are not treated as passive investors under the securities laws (*see* Section 7.01, below) or employees under the employment discrimination laws (*see* Section 7.03, below).

In addition to general management rights, LLP registration triggers a potential concern about the partners' authority to waive the limited liability shield (*see* Section 3.05, below). The agreement should provide clearly for the vote (probably unanimous, but at least supermajority) required to authorize any such waiver.

(g) Profit Sharing

LLP registration may trigger a reevaluation of profit sharing ratios in the partnership agreement (*see* Section 4.04(c), below). Partners who are in the more liability-prone aspects of the partnership business may be exposed to new risks as a result of protecting the partners generally from vicarious liability. If indemnification does not fully protect the newly exposed partners (*see* subsection (d), above), these partners may demand higher compensation to offset their increased risk. This could entail a reallocation of ownership interests.[120]

(h) Distributions

Partnership agreements often require cash distributions according to a formula or procedure. However, LLP registration may trigger a reevaluation of this approach because it introduces potential conflicts of interest that do not exist in non-LLP

---

[120] In Hart v. Theus, Grisham, Davis & Leigh, L.L.P., 877 So. 2d 1157 (La. App. 2004), a partner who had not been compensated for the extra risk cited this basis for arguing for non-enforcement against him of the partnership agreement's arbitration provision. The partner claimed that the LLP registration had created a new entity, terminating the pre-LLP agreement. The court rejected the argument and enforced the provision. The appropriate remedy for this problem is permitting the partner to veto the LLP registration unless the agreement is revised to accommodate the reallocation of responsibility. *See* § 2.04(a), note 57, supra.

partnerships (*see* Section 4.04(d), below). First, particularly under statutes that provide for a complete liability shield, partners may have an incentive to distribute partnership assets to themselves to avoid having to pay partnership claims. LLP statutes generally do not include corporate-type restrictions on distributions by insolvent or thinly capitalized firms. Exceptions are discussed in Section 4.04(d), below. However, the courts may recognize veil-piercing, fraudulent transfer, or other remedies in this situation. As a result, it may be prudent to insert provisions in the agreement that ensure against distributions that would leave the firm undercapitalized.

A second kind of conflict as to distributions that may arise under LLP provisions is one between partners. Partners who can be sure of limited liability may have an incentive to distribute assets while partners who are exposed to direct liability for faulty monitoring or other conduct may want to ensure that the partnership retains the assets to pay claims that they may otherwise have to face alone. Depending on their bargaining power the partners may agree to maximize distributions, to restrain them so much that they are reasonably likely to cover liabilities, or to distribute available cash, retaining only enough to protect against veil-piercing or other creditor-protection remedies.

(i)   Fiduciary and Other Partner Duties

LLP registration introduces new opportunities for partner harm to co-partners that may require contracting for additional fiduciary duties. First, it may be necessary to provide that a manager's failure to perform a duty to maintain LLP registration and other prerequisites of LLP status (*see* Section 2.09(a), above) gives rise to a breach of the duty of care.

Second, because LLP registration removes some or all of the partners' vicarious liability, it puts new emphasis on partners' direct liability. The partners, accordingly, may want to try to avoid direct liability by avoiding supervisory tasks that are most likely to trigger this liability. The partners can reduce this problem to some extent by ensuring the affected partners that they will be indemnified against potential liability. They may also need to specify partner duties more carefully in the agreement, such as by providing explicitly for the assignment of monitoring or supervisory tasks. *See* the related discussion of responsibilities in Section 2.09(b), above.

(j)   Dissociation and Dissolution

LLP registration probably will not trigger a significant restructuring of the dissociation and dissolution provisions in the agreement (*see* Section 4.08, below). Under the "check-the-box" tax classification rule (*see* Section 7.05, below), the partners need no longer ensure that they have the requisite management, transferability, and dissolution provisions for partnership tax status.

In drafting dissolution and dissociation provisions the partners should consider the potential effect of these events on the partnership's LLP registration (*see* Section 3.12(a)–3.12(b), below). In circumstances in which the partnership business is intended to continue following a partner's dissociation, the agreement should provide that, for purposes of the effect of the registration, the continuing partnership is the successor of, or the same entity as, the partnership that antedated the partner's event. While this will not necessarily be enough to ensure the continued validity of the registration, it may help persuade a court if the issue is deemed otherwise close.

(k) Applicable Law

The partnership agreement should clearly provide for the applicable law. To eliminate, as much as possible, any doubt on the applicable law, the contractually selected law should be the same as the state of registration (*see* Section 6.02, below).

The agreement also should make clear the states in which the partnership will operate (*see* Sections 2.03(a)(3), 2.03(b)(16), above). This will help clarify the states in which the partnership should register and help ensure that the LLP does not operate in states that may not respect the liability shield provision of the formation state.

TABLE 2-1. DEFINITION OF LLP

State	Section[†]	Categories
Alabama	10A-8-1.02(7)	1, 2, 3
Alaska	32.06.995(7)	7
Arizona	29-1001	1, 2, 5
Arkansas	4-46-101(5)	7
California	16101(8)	1, 2, 3*
Colorado	7-64-101(13)	8
Connecticut	34-301(20)	1, 2, 4
Delaware	15-101(8)	7
District of Columbia	29-601.02(7)	7
Florida	620.8101(6)	7
Georgia	14-8-2(6.1)	1, 2, 3
Hawaii	425-101	7*
Idaho	53-3-101(7)	7

Table 2-1   **2.   Formation of the LLP**

State	*Section*[†]	*Categories*
Illinois	206/101	7
Indiana	23-4-1-2	1, 2, 3, 4
Iowa	486A.101(5)	1, 2, 3*
Kansas	56a-101(e)	7
Kentucky	362.1-101(8)	7
Louisiana	9:3435	1
Maine	1001(5)	7
Maryland	9A-101	8
Massachusetts	108A, § 2	1, 2, 4
Michigan		*
Minnesota	323A.0101	7
Mississippi	79-13-101(5)	7
Missouri	358.020(8), .510	1, 2, 3, 4, 5
Montana	35-10-102(4)	1, 2*
Nebraska	67-402(5)	7
Nevada	87.020(5)	1, 2, 3, 4
New Hampshire	304-A:2(VII)	1, 2, 3, 4
New Jersey	42:1A-2	7
New Mexico	54-1A-101	7
New York	2	1, 2, 3, 4, 5*
North Carolina	59-32(7)	1, 2, 4
North Dakota	45-22-01(3), (13)	1, 2, 3*
Ohio	1776.01(J)	7
Oklahoma	1-101	8
Oregon	67.005	7
Pennsylvania	8201(c), 8202	1, 2*
Prototype	101(11)	1, 2, 3
Revised Uniform Partnership Act	101(5)	7
Rhode Island	7-12-13(7)	1, 2, 3, 4
South Carolina	33-41-20(6)	1*, 2, 3, 4
South Dakota	48-7A-101(5)	7
Tennessee	61-1-101	7
Texas	1.002(48)	1*
Utah	48-1d-102(10)	7*
Vermont	3201(5)	7
Virginia	50-73.79	2
Washington	25.05.005	7*
West Virginia	47B-1-1(13)	1, 2, 3
Wisconsin	178.01(2)	1, 2, 3
Wyoming	17-21-101(a)(vi)	1, 2, 3, 4

[†]*See* Table 2-10 for full statutory citations.

Table 2-1 (cont'd)

Categories

LLP definition contains following elements:

*   *See* Notes, below.

1.   "Partnership."

2.   Formed or registered under the statute.

3.   Governed by law of this state.

4.   Complying with statute.

5.   Limited partnerships, at least if they register under the statute.

6.   General partnerships.

7.   R.U.P.A. (*see* below).

8.   Same as 7, excluding language that firm must not have filed a similar statement in any other jurisdiction.

Notes

California: Cannot be limited partnership and must be licensed to practice law, architecture or accountancy or provide related services.

Colorado: Limited partnerships may register as LLLPs.

Hawaii: Follows R.U.P.A. but no provision that the LLP is necessarily governed by the law of the state in which it registers irrespective of the parties' agreement to be governed by other law.

Michigan: No definition.

Montana: Includes domestic and foreign LLPs.

New York: Must be partnership without limited partners of professionals authorized to practice in New York.

North Dakota: Applies to "domestic LLP." "LLP" refers to either a domestic or a foreign LLP.

Pennsylvania: Although definition does not include "governed by" language, 15 Pa. C.S.A. § 8201(c) says LLP registered under this chapter shall be governed by Pennsylvania general or limited partnership law.

Revised Uniform Partnership Act: Categories 1 and 2, plus firm must not have filed a similar statement in any other jurisdiction. Although the definition does not include "governed by" language, §§ 106(b) and 103(b)(10) provide that the law of the state in which it registers necessarily governs an LLP irrespective of the parties' agreement to be governed by other law.

South Carolina: LLP "includes" partnership that meets these definitional elements.

Texas: "A partnership governed as a limited liability partnership."

Utah: § 48-1b-101(2)(p) creates "tribal limited liability partnerships."

Washington: Law governing language is in § 25.05.030.

Table 2-2   2.   Formation of the LLP

TABLE 2-2.   REGISTRATION CONTENTS

State	Section[†]	Categories
Alabama	10A-8-10.01(a)	1
Alaska	32.06.91(e), (h)	4
Arizona	29-1101	3
Arkansas	4-46-1001(c)	4
California	16953	1
Colorado	7-64-1002	2
Connecticut	34-419	1
Delaware	15-1001(c)	4*
District of Columbia	29-610.01	4
Florida	620.9001(3)	4
Georgia	14-8-62	*
Hawaii	425-153	4*
Idaho	53-3-1001(c)	4
Illinois	206/1001	4
Indiana	23-4-1-45	1
Iowa	486A.1001(3)	4
Kansas	56a-1001	4
Kentucky	362.1-931(3)	4
Louisiana	9:3432	3
Maine	822; tit. 5 § 105(1)	1*
Maryland	9A-1001	2
Massachusetts	108A, 45(1), (7)	1*
Michigan	449.44	1*
Minnesota	323A.1001	2
Mississippi	79-13-1001(c)	4
Missouri	358.440	3
Montana	35-10-701	*
Nebraska	67-454	2
Nevada	87.440	4*
New Hampshire	304-A:44	1
New Jersey	42:1A-47	4
New Mexico	54-1A-1001	2
New York	121-1500(a)	1*
North Carolina	59-84.2	1*
North Dakota	45-22-03(3)	4*
Ohio	1776.81	4
Oklahoma	1-1001	4

Table 2-2 (cont'd)

State	Section[†]	Categories
Oregon	67.590	1*
Pennsylvania	8201	*
Prototype	910	2
Revised Uniform		
Partnership Act	1001	4
Rhode Island	7-12-56	*
South Carolina	33-41-1110	3
South Dakota	48-7A-1001	4
Tennessee	61-1-1001	1
Texas	152.802(a)	*
Utah	48-1d-1101	4
Vermont	3291	4
Virginia	50-73.132	2
Washington	25.05.500	3
West Virginia	47B-10-1(a)	1*
Wisconsin	178.40	*
Wyoming	17-21-1101	2

[†]*See* Table 2-10 for full statutory citations.

Categories

* Other required contents (*see* Notes, below).
1. Must include name, address (e.g., of principal office or place of business or of registered office and agent), and nature of business or purpose.
2. Name and address only.
3. Same as 1 only add number of partners.
4. RUPA: Name, address, statement that firm is applying to be LLP and any deferred effective date.

Notes

Delaware: Add number of partners at time of registration.
Georgia: Add name, business, that partnership elects to be LLP, and that election is duly authorized.
Hawaii: Same as R.U.P.A. except no deferred effective date.
Illinois: Same as R.U.P.A. except also include number of partners.

Table 2-2   2. Formation of the LLP

Table 2-2 (cont'd)

Maine: Name of clerk or registered agent.

Massachusetts: Add federal employer identification number, names of partners authorized to execute real property conveyances, and, for each partner in a professional LLP, name, business address, and certificate from licensing board.

Michigan: Add federal employer identification number or, if none, social security number of person or persons signing registration.

Montana: Name and business mailing address, date of first use in commerce of LLP, description of business transacted, and name and business mailing address of each partner.

Nevada: Names and addresses of managing partners in the state.

New York: Any delayed effective date and, if applicable, statement that all or specified partners assume liability for all or specified debts.

North Carolina: Add delayed effective date and fiscal year end.

North Dakota: Add name and address of each managing partner, or of all partners if the LLP is engaged in farming or ranching in the state or leasing land for that use; statement indicating whether LLP engaged in farming or ranching in the state or owning or leasing land in the state which is used for farming or ranching; nature of business.

Oregon: Add federal employer identification number and names and addresses of at least two partners.

Pennsylvania: Add name, address, and statement that the registration has been authorized by at least a majority in interest of the partners.

Rhode Island: Add name and address, names and addresses of resident partners, place where partnership business records are maintained, number of partners, and statement of partnership's business.

Texas: Name, federal tax identification number, address, number of partners at the date of application, and brief statement of the partnership's business.

West Virginia: Add e-mail address to send notices and reminders of annual filings, names and addresses of partners authorized to execute instruments for partnership, and that partnership is registering as LLP.

Wisconsin: Add name and address and formation jurisdiction of foreign LLP.

TABLE 2-3.   EFFECT OF CHANGES

State	*Section*[†]	*Categories*
Alabama	10A-8-10.01(l), (m)	4, 5
Alaska	32.06.911(e), (f)	7

Table 2-3 (cont'd)

State	Section[†]	Categories
Arizona	29-1101	7
Arkansas	4-46-1001	7
California	16953(e)	2
Colorado	7-64-1002	6
Connecticut	34-419(b)	2
Delaware	15-1001	7
District of Columbia	29-610.01	7
Florida	620.9001	7
Georgia	14-8-62(d), (f)	2, 5
Hawaii	425-154, -155	1, 2
Idaho	53-3-1001	7
Illinois	206/1001(e), (f)	7
Indiana	23-4-1-45, -46	5
Iowa	486A.1001	7
Kansas	56a-1001(d), (e)	7
Kentucky	362.1-931(4)	7
Louisiana		6
Maine	822(3), 823	1, 2
Maryland	9A-1001	3, 5
Massachusetts	108A, 45(4)	2
Michigan	449.44(5)	2
Minnesota	323A.1001	7
Mississippi	79-13-1001(e)–(f)	7
Missouri	358.440(12), (13), (20)	1, 5
Montana	35-10-702(3), (4), 30-13-209	1*, 4, 5
Nebraska	67-454	7
Nevada	87.540	2
New Hampshire	304-A:48; :44(III)	1*, 2
New Jersey	42:1A-47(f)	7
New Mexico	54-1A-1001	7
New York	121-1500	1, 2, 4, 5
North Carolina	59-84.2(g)	2
North Dakota	45-22-03(9)	7
Ohio	1776.81(E), (F)	7
Oklahoma	1-1001	2
Oregon	67.610	2, 4, 5
Pennsylvania	8204(c), 8201(d), 8205	4, 5, 6
Prototype	914(a), (d)	1, 2

Table 2-3   **2. Formation of the LLP**

Table 2-3 (cont'd)

State	Section[†]	Categories
Revised Uniform Partnership Act	1001(d), (e)	7
Rhode Island	7-12-56(f), (h)	2, 5
South Carolina	33-41-1110(F)	2
South Dakota	48-7A-1001	7
Tennessee	61-1-1001	1*, 2, 4, 5
Texas	152.802(d)	3
Utah	48-1d-1101	2
Vermont	3291	7
Virginia	50-73.136(D)	1
Washington	25.05.500	2
West Virginia	47B-10-1	1*, 2
Wisconsin	178.41	3, 4, 5
Wyoming	17-21-1102(c)–(d)	2, 4, 5

[†]*See* Table 2-10 for full statutory citations.

Categories
* *   *See* Notes, below.
1. Amendment required to reflect changes or inaccuracy.
2. Changes in filed information do not affect LLP status.
3. Membership changes do not affect LLP status.
4. Liability shield persists through dissolution as to liability incurred while the partnership was an LLP (*see* Section 3.12(a)(2)).
5. Registration survives dissolution or carries over to successor partnership.
6. No general provision about changes.
7. R.U.P.A. provision described below.

Notes
Idaho: Amendment required to notify of change in registered office or agent.
Montana: Section 30-13-209 (assumed business name registration) requires amendment within one year if certain changes occur.
New Hampshire: Must file change of name notice if name changes. May file notice of change for other information, but annual notice must include all material changes.
New Jersey: Annual report must indicate material changes.
New Mexico: Annual report must indicate material changes.

Table 2-3 (cont'd)

Revised Uniform Partnership Act: Categories 2 and 4. Section 1001(d) provides that LLP status "remains effective, regardless of changes in the partnership, until it is canceled pursuant to Section 105(d) or revoked pursuant to Section 1003." Although the Comment to this section asserts that this means that "the former partners of a terminated partnership would not be personally liable for partnership obligations incurred while the partnership was a limited liability partnership," this effect is questionable for the post-termination period (when the LLP is no longer a "partnership") in the absence of more explicit statutory language.

Tennessee: Annual report must indicate material changes.

West Virginia: Annual report must indicate material changes.

TABLE 2-4.   SIGNATURE

State	*Section*[†]	*Categories*
Alabama	10A-8-10.01(b)	1
Alaska	32.06.970	4
Arizona	291005(c)	4
Arkansas	4-46-105	4
California	16953(a)	1
Colorado	7-90-301(2)	*
Connecticut	34-410	1*
Delaware	15-105(c)	6
District of Columbia	29-102.01(a)(4)	6
Florida	620.8105	4
Georgia	14-8-62(b)	2
Hawaii	425-1.8	3
Idaho	53-3-105(b)	4
Illinois	206/105(c)	4
Indiana	23-4-1-45	1
Iowa	486A.105(3)	4
Kansas	56a-105(c)	4
Kentucky	362.1-105(3)	4
Louisiana	9:3432(B)	2
Maine	826	1
Maryland	9A-105	6
Massachusetts	108A, § 45(1)	1

Table 2-4   **2.   Formation of the LLP**

Table 2-4 (cont'd)

State	*Section*[†]	*Categories*
Michigan	449.44(2)	2
Minnesota	323A.0105(c)	4
Mississippi	79-13-105(c)	4
Missouri	358.440(2)	2
Montana	35-10-701(2)	4
Nebraska	67-406	4
Nevada	87.440(2)	2
New Hampshire	304-A:51	1
New Jersey	42:1A-6(c)	4
New Mexico	54-1A-105	4
New York	121-1500(b)	3
North Carolina	59-84.2(a1)(ii)	6*
North Dakota	45-22-01(24); 45-22-03(3)	*
Ohio	1776.05(C)	1
Oklahoma	1-105	4
Oregon	67.520	6
Pennsylvania	8201(a)	3*
Prototype	No provision	
Revised Uniform Partnership Act	105(c)	4
Rhode Island	7-12-56(b)	2
South Carolina	33-41-1110(B)	2
South Dakota	48-7A-105	4
Tennessee	61-1-1001	1
Texas	152.802(b)	2
Utah	48-1d-110	1
Vermont	3205(c)	4
Virginia	50-73.83(C)	4
Washington	25.05.025	4
West Virginia	47B-10-1(b)	1
Wisconsin	178.46(3)(a)	1*
Wyoming	17-21-1101(b)	1

[†]*See* Table 2-10 for full statutory citations.

Categories

* *See* Notes, below.

1.   One or more authorized partners.

Table 2-4 (cont'd)

2. Majority in interest (or similar vote) or one or more authorized partners. *Georgia* (majority or one or more authorized partners, subject to contrary agreement); *Michigan* and *Texas* (majority in interest or individuals authorized by majority in interest); *Missouri* (majority or one or more partners authorized by majority in interest).
3. One or more partners.
4. R.U.P.A.: Two or more partners.
5. All partners.
6. Authorized persons.

N.B. *See also* Table 2-8 (Partner Approval of Registration), below, Categories 4 and 5.

Notes

Connecticut: Or certain promoters or receivers; person executing may do so as attorney in fact.

Colorado: No provision.

North Carolina: As provided in the agreement.

North Dakota: Must be signed by a "managing partner." "Signed" defined to mean that document signed by person authorized by this chapter or by vote of requisite number of partners.

Pennsylvania: A general partner.

Wisconsin: Or as otherwise provided in the partnership agreement.

TABLE 2-5. REGISTRATION FEES

State	Section[†]	Domestic: Initial/ Subsequent	Foreign: Initial/ Subsequent
Alabama	10-8A-1001(c), (e), 10A-1-4.31	$150/$100	$150/$__
Alaska		Not specified	Not specified
Arizona	29-1005(F)	Not specified	Not specified
Arkansas	4-46-1207	$50/n.a.*	$300/n.a.*
California	West's Ann. Cal. Gov. Code § 12189	$70/$70	$120/$70
Colorado	7-90-303	Not specified	Not specified
Connecticut	34-413	$60/$20	$60/$10

Table 2-5   **2.   Formation of the LLP**

Table 2-5 (cont'd)

State	Section[†]	Domestic: Initial/ Subsequent	Foreign: Initial/ Subsequent
Delaware	15-1207	$200 fee for filing statement and $200 per partner per year*	Same
District of Columbia	29-102.12	Not specified	Not specified
Florida	620.81055	$50/$25 filing fees	$25 filing fee
Georgia	14-8-62	Not specified	Not specified
Hawaii	425-168	$25	$25
Idaho	53-3-105A	$100*	$100
Illinois	206/108	$100 per partner*	$500
Indiana	23-4-1-45, -49	$90*	$90*
Iowa	486A-1202(1)	$50*	$100
Kansas	56a-105(f), (g); 56a-1201, -1202, -1203	Not specified/$40	Not specified/$40
Kentucky	362.1-109(1)(a)	$40	$90
Louisiana	9:3432, 49:222	$150/$25	$150/$25
Maine	871(8), (10), (18), (18-A)	$175/$85	$250/$150
Maryland	1-203(b)(3)	$100/$300	$100/$300
Massachusetts	108A, § 45(1), (3); 47(4)	$500/$500	$500/$500
Michigan	449.44(2), (4), 47	$100/$100	$100/$100
Minnesota	323A.0101(5)	$135/$135	Not specified
Mississippi	79-13-105(f)	$250	$250
Missouri	358.440(3), (9), (19)	$25 per partner/$100*	$100/$20
Montana	30-13-217; 2-15-405	Not specified	Not specified
Nebraska	67-462	$200/$10	$200/$10
Nevada	87.440(3), .510	$75/$125	Not specified
New Hampshire	304-A:51	$50/$100	$50/$100
New Jersey		Not specified	Not specified
New Mexico	54-1A-1206	$50/$50	$50/$50
New York	121-1500(c), (g), 1502(a), (f)	$200/$20	$250/$50
North Carolina	59-35.2(a)	$125/$200	$125/$200
North Dakota	45-22-22	$35*/$25	$60*/$25
Ohio	111.16(F)	$125/Not specified	Not specified

Table 2-5 (cont'd)

State	Section[†]	Domestic: Initial/ Subsequent	Foreign: Initial/ Subsequent
Oklahoma	1-105	$100/$100	$100
Oregon	56.140, 67.525	$100/$100	$275/$275
Pennsylvania	8221(b)	$200 per partner per year*	$200 per partner per year*
Rhode Island	7-12-56(c), 7-12-59(d)(9)	$100 per partner*/$100 per partner*	$1,000 for two years
South Carolina	33-41-1110(C), 1160(d)	$100/$100	$100/$100
South Dakota	48-7A-1208	$125/$50	$125/$50
Tennessee	61-1-1004	$50 per partner per year*	$50 per partner for two years
Texas	4.158	$200 per partner/ $200 per partner	$200 per partner/$200 per partner, $750 maximum
Utah	63J-1-504	Not specified	Not specified
Vermont	3310	$75/$15	$100/$100
Virginia	50-73.83(F)(1), (2)	$100/$50	$100/$50
Washington	25.05.500	Not specified	Not specified
West Virginia	47B-10-1(c), (e), (r)	$250/$500	Not specified
Wisconsin	178.48(1)(a)	$100	$100
Wyoming	17-21-1101(n)	$100/*	

[†]*See* Table 2-10 for full statutory citations.

Categories
*   *See* Notes, below.

Notes
Arkansas: Section 4-43-1104 provides for same fees for LLLPs.
Delaware: Up to $120,000.
Florida: For partners residing or incorporated in Florida; $10,000 maximum.
Hawaii: Domestic: $10,000 maximum. Foreign: $1000 for 1 to 9 partners, $5000 for 10 to 49 partners, and $10,000 for 50 or more partners.
Idaho: $120 if application not typed or if attachments included.
Illinois: $200 minimum, $5000 maximum.
Indiana: $75 if filed electronically.
Iowa: Section 488.1206 provides for $100 fee for LLLP statement of qualification.

Table 2-5   **2. Formation of the LLP**

Table 2-5 (cont'd)

Missouri: $25 per partner for initial registration, but no more than $100. $100 for renewal plus $50 per partner for each added partner, but no more than $200.

North Dakota: $3 per each managing partner over two up to $250.

Ohio: Section cross-references Ohio Stat. § 111.16(F).

Pennsylvania: For partners residing or incorporated in Pennsylvania. Fee increased for inflation every year beginning December 31, 1997.

Rhode Island: $2500 maximum.

Tennessee: Minimum $250, maximum $2500.

Wyoming: Fee same as for corporations.

TABLE 2-6. EFFECTIVENESS OF REGISTRATION

State	*Section*[†]	*Categories*
Alabama	10A-8-10.01(g)	4, 5
Alaska	32.06.91(e), (h)	1, 5
Arizona	29-1101(d)	1, 5
Arkansas	4-46-1001(e)	1, 5
California	16953(c), (e)	2, 5*
Colorado	7-64-1002; 7-90-304(1)	1
Connecticut	34-411	3
Delaware	15-1001(d), (e)	4, 5
District of Columbia	29-610.01	1, 5
Florida	620.9001(4)	1, 5
Georgia	14-8-62(c), (e)	1, 5
Hawaii	425-155	1
Idaho	53-3-1001(e)	1, 5
Illinois	206/1001	2, 5*
Indiana	23-4-1-45	1, 5
Iowa	486A.1001(5)	1, 5
Kansas	56a-1001(d)	1, 5
Kentucky	362.1-110(1)	1, 5*
Louisiana	9-3432(E)	2
Maine	828	3
Maryland	9A-1001	1, 5
Massachusetts	108A, § 45(4)	2
Michigan	449.44(3)	2
Minnesota	323A.1001	1, 5

Table 2-6 (cont'd)

State	Section[†]	Categories
Mississippi	79-13-1001(e)	1, 5
Missouri	358.440(5)	2
Montana	35-10-701(3), (4)	4
Nebraska	67-454	1, 5
Nevada	87.440(5)	1
New Hampshire	304-A:44(III)	4, 5*
New Jersey	42:1A-47(f)	1, 5
New Mexico	54-1A-1001	1, 5
New York	121-1500(d)	2, 5*
North Carolina	59-84.2(a1), (f1)	*
North Dakota	45-22-03(2), (4)	2, 3, 5
Ohio	1776.81(E)	1, 5
Oklahoma	1-1001	1, 5
Oregon	67.530	1, 5
Pennsylvania	8201(b)	1
Prototype	910(a), 914(a)	1*, 5
Revised Uniform Partnership Act	1001(d)	1, 5
Rhode Island	7-12-56(d)	3
South Carolina	33-41-1110(D), -1110(E)	
South Dakota	48-7A-1001	1; 5
Tennessee	61-1-1001	4
Texas	152.802(c)	1, 5
Utah	48-1d-1101, 48-1d-113	1, 5
Vermont	3291(e)	1, 5
Virginia	50-73.132; –73.83(J)	1, 2
Washington	25.05.500(6)	1
West Virginia	47B-10-1(f)	1, 5
Wisconsin	178.49	1, 5*
Wyoming	17-21-1101	1

[†]*See* Table 2-10 for full statutory citations.

Categories

* *See* Notes, below.
1. On filing.
2. On filing and payment of fees.
3. On filing if meets statutory requirements.

Table 2-6   **2.   Formation of the LLP**

Table 2-6 (cont'd)

4.   On filing if substantial compliance with statutory requirements. District of Columbia ("satisfactorily completed"); Maine and North Dakota ("conforms to law"); New Mexico ("properly completed"); Rhode Island ("completed").
5.   Permits post-filing effective date.
6.   No provision.

Notes

California: Section 16953(c) refers to registration by the Secretary, while subsection (e) provides for formation on filing.

Illinois: Provision that secretary of state shall register LLP that submits completed statement with the required fee.

Kentucky: Requirements included in Kentucky Entity Filings Act, § 14, 2010 Ky. Laws Ch. 151.

New Hampshire: Within 90 days.

North Carolina: Effectiveness provided for in partnership agreement.

New York: Within 60 days.

Prototype: Section 914(c) adds that filing is conclusive as to third parties.

West Virginia: Within 60 days.

Wisconsin: Within 90 days.

TABLE 2-7.   PERIODIC RENEWAL OR REPORT

State	*Section*[†]	*Categories*
Alabama	10A-8-10.01(e)	1, 5
Alaska	32.06.913	3*, 5, 6
Arizona	29-1103	2, 5, 6
Arkansas	4-46-1003	2, 5, 6
California		4
Colorado	7-64-1007, 7-90-501	3*
Connecticut	34-420, 34-422	2*, 5
Delaware	15-1002	2, 5, 6*
District of Columbia	29-102.11	3*
Florida	620.9003	2, 5, 6
Georgia	14-8-62	4
Hawaii	425-163	2
Idaho	53-3-1003	2, 5, 6
Illinois	206/1003	1
Indiana		4
Iowa		4

Table 2-7 (cont'd)

State	Section[†]	Categories
Kansas	56a-1201, -1202, -1203	1
Kentucky	362.1-121	1, 5, 6
Louisiana	9-3432(E)	1
Maine	808-A-808-C, 873	2, 5
Maryland	9A-1011-14	2, 5, 6
Massachusetts	108A, § 45(2), (6), (7)	2*, 5
Michigan	449.44, .47	4
Minnesota	323A.1003	2, 6*
Mississippi		4
Missouri	358.440(6), (8), (9)	1
Montana	30-13-206	3*
Nebraska	67-456	1, 5, 6
Nevada	87.510, .520, .530	1, 5, 6
New Hampshire	304-A:47	1, 5
New Jersey	42:1A-(49)	1, 4, 5, 6
New Mexico	54-1A-1003	2
New York	121-1500(g)	3, 5*, 6
North Carolina	59-84.4	2, 5, 6
North Dakota	45-22-21.1	2, 6
Ohio	1776.83	3*, 5, 6
Oklahoma		4
Oregon	67.645, .655, .660, .665, .670	2, 6
Pennsylvania	8221	1
Prototype	912	2, 6
Revised Uniform Partnership Act	1003	2, 5, 6
Rhode Island	7-12-56(e)	1
South Carolina	33-41-1110(E)	1
South Dakota	48-7A-1003	2, 5, 6
Tennessee	61-1-1001	2
Texas	152.802(e), (g)	1
Utah	48-1d-1109	1
Vermont	3293	2, 5, 6
Virginia	50-73.134	2, 5, 6
Washington	25.05.500	1, 2, 5
West Virginia	47B-10-1(e)	2
Wisconsin		4
Wyoming	17-21-1101	2

[†]See Table 2-10 for full statutory citations.

Table 2-7   2.   Formation of the LLP

Table 2-7 (cont'd)

Categories
*   *See* Notes, below.
1.   Annual renewal.
2.   Annual report (including requirement to update registration information).
3.   Reports required at longer than annual interval.
4.   No renewal or reporting requirement.
5.   State must give notice of failure to renew or report prior to cancellation of registration.
6.   Noncomplying firm may reinstate for specified time retroactive to time of cancellation.

N.B. Renewal or annual fees are listed in Table 2-5.

Notes
Alaska: Biennial report.
Colorado: Secretary may permit biennial report.
Connecticut: Electronic filing required, with exceptions.
District of Columbia: Biennial report.
Kentucky: Kentucky Entity Filings Act, §34(5), 2010 Ky. Laws Ch. 151 provides for notice by the Secretary if an annual report does not contain the required information.
Massachusetts: LLPs rendering professional services must include certification that each partner is still licensed, as well as other information.
Minnesota: Secretary may send annual registration form which includes notice that failure to file form by December 31 will result in revocation of the statement of qualification without further notice.
Montana: This requirement incorporated by reference in § 35-10-701.
New York: Report every five years.
Ohio: Biennial report.

TABLE 2-8.   PARTNER APPROVAL OF REGISTRATION

State	*Section*[†]	*Categories*
Alabama	10A-8-10.01(k)	2
Alaska	32.06.911	9
Arizona	29-1101	6

Table 2-8 (cont'd)

State	Section[†]	Categories
Arkansas	4-46-1001(b)	9
California	16955(a)	2*
Colorado	7-64-1002	1*
Connecticut	34-410	7*
Delaware	15-1001(b)	9
District of Columbia	29-610.01(b)	9
Florida	620.9001(2)	9
Georgia	14-8-62(b)	2*
Hawaii	425-152	9
Idaho	53-3-1001(b)	9
Illinois	206/1001(b)	9
Indiana	23-4-1-45(1)(A)	7
Iowa	486A.1001(2)	9
Kansas	56a-1001	4
Kentucky	362.1-1001(2)	9
Louisiana	9:3432(B)	5
Maine	821	9
Maryland	9A-1001	7
Massachusetts	108A, § 45(1)	2
Michigan	449.44(2)	5
Minnesota	323A.1001	9
Mississippi	79-13-1001(a)–(b)	9
Missouri	358.440(2)	5
Montana	35-10-701	7
Nebraska	67-454	9
Nevada	87.440(2)	3
New Hampshire	304-A:44(II)	7
New Jersey	42:1A-47(b)	9
New Mexico	54-1A-1001(b)	9
New York	121-1500(1)	8
North Carolina	59-84.2(a1)	7
North Dakota	45-22-03(6)	2, 8
Ohio	1776.81(C)	9
Oklahoma	1-1001	9
Oregon	67.500(3)	9*
Pennsylvania	8201(a)(4)	3*
Prototype	910(c)	2
Revised Uniform Partnership Act	1001	9

Table 2-8   **2.   Formation of the LLP**

Table 2-8 (cont'd)

State	Section[†]	Categories
Rhode Island	7-12-56(b)	4
South Carolina	33-41-1110(B)	4
South Dakota	48-7A-1001	9
Tennessee	61-1-1001	2*
Texas	152.802(b)	5
Utah	48-1d-1101(2)	9
Vermont	3291(b)	9
Virginia	50-73.132(C)	6
Washington	25.05.500	9
West Virginia	47B-10-1(b)	7
Wisconsin	178.46(3)(a)	7
Wyoming	17-21-1101	7

[†]*See* Table 2-10 for full statutory citations.

Categories
*   *See* Notes, below.
1.   Unanimous.
2.   Majority.
3.   Majority-in-interest.
4.   Execution by majority in interest or one or more partners authorized to execute an application.
5.   Execution by majority in interest or one or more partners authorized by a majority in interest.
6.   Vote necessary to amend agreement.
7.   No default voting requirement or general reference to persons authorized.
8.   Registration defined as ordinary matter.
9.   R.U.P.A. provision (vote necessary to amend agreement, or vote necessary to amend contribution obligations if the agreement specifically so provides).

Notes
California: Conversion by partnership to LLP. Section 16953 provides that the registration must be executed by one or more partners authorized to execute a registration.
Colorado: Or in manner provided in partnership agreement.
Connecticut: Filed document shall be executed by one or more partners authorized to execute such a document or, if LLP has not been formed, by person(s) forming it, or if in hands of receiver, by the receiver.

Table 2-8 (cont'd)

Georgia: Subject to contrary partner agreement, majority or one or more authorized partners.

Oklahoma: Also requires execution by one or more partners.

Oregon: The same vote is necessary to cancel under § 67.595.

Pennsylvania: Registration must include statement that registration has been authorized by a majority in interest of the partners.

Tennessee: If general partnership, approval by majority of partners or as otherwise provided in partnership agreement; if limited partnership, all partners irrespective of contrary agreement unless formed after July 1, 1995, and agreement provided for conversion to LLP without consent of all partners.

TABLE 2-9.   NAME

State	*Section*[†]	*Categories*
Alabama	10A-1-5.07	1, 5
Alaska	32.06.912	1
Arizona	29-1102	2, 4
Arkansas	4-46-1002	1
California	16952	1
Colorado	7-90-601(3)(d), 602	2, 4, 6
Connecticut	34-406, 407	1, 4, 6
Delaware	15-108	1, 4, 6
District of Columbia	29-103.01–.02	2, 4
Florida	620.9002	1
Georgia	14-8-63	1
Hawaii	425-151	2
Idaho	53-3-1002	1
Illinois	206/1002	1
Indiana	23-4-1-45	1
Iowa	486A.1002	1
Kansas	56a-1002	1
Kentucky	14A.3-010(4)	1*
Louisiana	9-3433	1a
Maine	803-A, 804-A	2, 4, 6
Massachusetts	108A, § 46	1
Maryland	9A-1003, 1004	1, 3*, 6
Michigan	449.45	1
Minnesota	323A.1002	2, 4

Table 2-9   2.   Formation of the LLP

Table 2-9 (cont'd)

State	Section[†]	Categories
Mississippi	79-13-1002	1
Missouri	358.450, .460	1, 4, 6
Montana	35-10-703, 30-13-211	2*, 6
Nebraska	67-455	1, 4
Nevada	87.450	1
New Hampshire	304-A:45(I), :46	1, 3*, 6
New Jersey	42:1A-48	1
New Mexico	54-1A-1002	1
New York	121-1501	2*
North Carolina	59-84.3; 55D-20–55D-21	2
North Dakota	45-22-04, -05, -06	2*, 3, 5, 6, 7
Ohio	1776.82	2*
Oklahoma	1-1002	1
Oregon	67.625	1*, 4
Pennsylvania	8203	6*
Prototype	911	1
Revised Uniform Partnership Act	1002	1
Rhode Island	7-12-57	1, 3
South Carolina	33-41-1120	1a
South Dakota	48-7A-1002	1
Tennessee	61-1-1003	2*, 4, 6, 7
Texas	152.803; 5.063	1a
Utah	48-1b-1002	1, 4
Vermont	3292	1
Virginia	50-73.133; 73.78	1
Washington	25.05.505	2
West Virginia	47B-10-3	1
Wisconsin	178.42	1, 4
Wyoming	17-21-1103	1, 3,* 4

[†] *See* Table 2-10 for full statutory citations.

Categories

*   *See* Notes, below.

1.   Name must end with "LLP" with or without periods, "Limited Liability Partnership," or equivalents for Registered Limited Liability Partnership, and for limited liability limited partnerships if applicable.

1a.   Same as 1, but no option for "LLP."

Table 2-9 (cont'd)

2. Same as 1, but no requirement that designation be at end of name.
3. Name may not be the same as or deceptively similar to that of other business associations.
4. Name must be distinguishable on state records from that of other business associations.
5. Partners contracting or consenting to contract on behalf of the LLP without required portion of name lose liability shield as to relying third parties.
6. Permits name reservation.
7. Name must be in English or Roman characters.

Notes

Delaware: Also provides that name may contain the name of a partner and certain designated words.

Kansas: Must end with abbreviation "LLP" (does not list option with periods).

Kentucky: Cross-references Kentucky Business Entity Filing Act, 2010 Ky. Laws ch. 151, § 23(4), which provides that LLP name shall contain "Registered Limited Liability Partnership" or the abbreviation "LLP" as the last words or letters of its name.

Maine: May refuse filing if name is obscene, contemptuous, inappropriately promotes abusive or unlawful activity, or falsely suggests association with public institution.

Maryland: May not contain word or phrase that indicates organization for any purpose not stated in certificate or filing.

Montana: Or other words or abbreviations required or authorized by formation state, including "Professional Limited Liability Partnership" or its abbreviation. Section 30-13-211 permits name reservation.

Minnesota: Section 319A.07 requires professional L.L.P. name to end with "Professional Limited Liability Partnership" or "P.L.L.P."

New Hampshire: Also cannot be deceptively similar to state or federal agency or instrumentality.

New York: May use "R.L.L.P." or "RLLP."

North Dakota: May not contain word or phrase that indicates organization for any purpose not stated in certificate or filing, or for which LLP may not be formed by state law or LLP chapter.

Ohio: Name may also contain in "P.L.L." or "PLL" or "Registered Partnership Having Limited Liability."

Oklahoma: If name "conflicts" with another filed name, cannot register under it unless other party consents and agrees to change name, withdraw from the state, or dissolve.

Oregon: Name cannot contain specified words indicating it is another type of business association. May use names of individual present or former partners of the partnership or a predecessor partnership, as permitted by ethics rules and professional regulation.

Table 2-9   **2.   Formation of the LLP**

Table 2-9 (cont'd)

Pennsylvania: Name shall not be unavailable for use by corporation under corporate statute and "shall contain the term 'company,' 'limited,' or 'limited liability partnership' or an abbreviation of one of those terms, or words or abbreviations of like import in English or any other language."

Tennessee: Foreign LLP may use designations allowed in the jurisdiction where it is registered.

Texas: Must contain "limited liability partnership" or abbreviation.

Wyoming: Refers to registered trademark or service mark.

TABLE 2-10.   FULL STATUTORY CITATIONS

State	*Citation Information*
Alabama	Ala. St. § —
Alaska	Alaska Stat. § —
Arizona	Ariz. Rev. Stat. Ann. § —
Arkansas	Ark. Code § —
California	Cal. Corp. Code § —
Colorado	Colo. Rev. Stat. § —
Connecticut	Conn. Gen. Stat. § —
Delaware	Del. Code Ann. tit. 6, § —
District of Columbia	D.C. Code Ann. § —
Florida	Fla. Stat. Ann. § —
Georgia	Ga. Code Ann. § —
Hawaii	Haw. Rev. Stat. § —
Idaho	Idaho Code § —
Illinois	Ill. Comp. Stat. Ann. Ch. 805
Indiana	Ind. Code § —
Iowa	Iowa Code § —
Kansas	Kan. Stat. Ann. § —
Kentucky	Ky. Rev. Stat. Ann. § —
Louisiana	La. Rev. Stat. Ann. § —
Maine	Me. Rev. Stat. Ann. tit. 31, § —
Maryland	Md. Code Ann., Corps. & Ass'ns § —
Massachusetts	Mass. Gen. L. ch. 108A, § —
Michigan	Mich. Comp. Laws § —
Minnesota	Minn. Stat. § —
Mississippi	Miss. Code Ann. § —
Missouri	Mo. Rev. Stat. § —

Table 2-10 (cont'd)

State	*Citation Information*
Montana	Mont. Code Ann. § —
Nebraska	Neb. Rev. Stat. § —
Nevada	Nev. Rev. Stat. § —
New Hampshire	N.H. Rev. Stat. Ann. § —
New Jersey	N.J. Rev. Stat. § —
New Mexico	N.M. Stat. Ann. § —
New York	N.Y. P'ship Law ch. 39, § — (Consol.)
North Carolina	N.C. Gen. Stat. § —
North Dakota	N.D. Cent. Code § —
Ohio	Ohio Rev. Code Ann. § —
Oklahoma	Okla. Stat. tit. 54, § —
Oregon	Or. Rev. Stat. § —
Pennsylvania	15 Pa. Cons. Stat. § —
Prototype	Prototype Registered Limited Liability Partnership Act, § —
Revised Uniform Partnership Act	Uniform Partnership Act (1994) with 1996 Amendments, § —
Rhode Island	R.I. Gen. Laws § —
South Carolina	S.C. Code Ann. § —
South Dakota	S.D. Codified Laws Ann. § —
Tennessee	Tenn. Code Ann. § —
Texas	Tex. Bus. Org. Code § —
Utah	Utah Code Ann. § —[121]
Vermont	Vt. Stat. Ann., title 11, § —
Virginia	Va. Code Ann. § —
Washington	Wash. Rev. Code § —
West Virginia	W. Va. Code § —
Wisconsin	Wis. Stat. § —
Wyoming	Wyo. Stat. § —

---

[121] Utah provisions cited in the text are effective July 1, 2013 for new entities and Jan. 1, 2015 for existing entities. *See* Utah Code Ann. § 48-1b-1205.

≡*3*≡

PARTNER LIABILITY for PARTNERSHIP DEBTS

Partners are, in general, vicariously liable for the debts of their partnership.[1] This chapter discusses the characteristic of limited liability partnerships (LLPs) that distinguishes them from other general partnerships — the members' limited liability.[2] Section 3.01 discusses the general policy issues concerning limiting the liability of partners. This discussion helps inform the discussion throughout this chapter of the liabilities of partners in LLPs. Section 3.02 discusses the scope of limited liability under statutes that limit vicarious liability only for co-partners' misconduct. Section 3.03 discusses statutes that provide for complete limitation of vicarious liability. Section 3.04 discusses members' liability for their own misconduct under both LLP statutes and the common law. Section 3.05 and Section 3.06 discuss contracts by LLP members for more or less personal liability than the statutes provide for. Section 3.07 discusses loss of statutory liability by the application of common law "veil-piercing" rules. Section 3.08 and Section 3.09 discuss the effect of LLP provisions on enforcing partner liability among the partners and to third-party creditors. Section 3.10 discusses liability of purported members of LLPs. Sections 3.11–3.12 discuss the timing of the liability shield—when the registration must be in effect and the effect of dissolution, winding up, and termination. Section 3.13 compares LLP partners' limited liability with that of members of other limited liability business associations.

The special regulation and policy issues relating to limiting the liability of members of professional firms are discussed in Chapter 7.

§ 3.01 POLICY ISSUES CONCERNING LIMITING THE LIABILITY OF PARTNERS

This section discusses the policy issues relating to the liability of partners for debts of partnerships and to limitations of that liability in LLP statutes. The purpose of this discussion is to establish a framework for evaluating and interpreting the statutory provisions limiting liability, to provide a means of predicting how courts may apply these provisions, and to give some guidance as to how

---

[1] *See* Uniform Partnership Act § 15; Revised Uniform Partnership Act § 306; Bromberg and Ribstein on Partnership, § 5.08 (1988 & Supp.) (hereinafter "Bromberg & Ribstein").

[2] For other reviews of statutory provisions and policy considerations, see Fortney, Seeking Shelter in the Minefield of Unintended Consequences—The Traps of Limited Liability Law Firms, 54 Wash. & Lee L. Rev. 717 (1997); Goforth, Limiting the Liability of General Partners In LLPs: An Analysis of Statutory Alternatives, 75 Or. L. Rev. 1139 (1996); Hamilton, Registered Limited Liability Partnerships: Present at the Birth (Nearly), 66 U. Colo. L. Rev. 1065 (1995); Ribstein, Limited Liability of Professional Firms after Enron, 29 J. Corp. L. 427 (2004). One federal court failed to understand this basic distinction. *See* United States v. 175 Inwood Assocs. LLP., 330 F. Supp. 2d 213 (E.D.N.Y. 2004) (CERCLA case treating general partners in an LLP like general partners in non-LLP partnerships under N.Y. law).

statutory provisions may be improved or refined. Subsection (a) briefly discusses the default rule under which partners are vicariously liable for partnership debts. Subsections (b) and (c) discuss considerations relevant to limiting liability for the separate categories of contract-type and tort-type liabilities. This discussion is important to understanding the distinction in many LLP statutes between these categories of liabilities. Subsections (d)–(g) then discuss considerations relevant to limiting liability in LLPs as distinguished from other types of firms.

(a)   The Default Rule: Partners' Vicarious Liability

Partners' vicarious liability for the debts of the partnership has long been an identifying characteristic of the partnership form of business. Because partners are, by definition, co-owners of the partnership,[3] they are co-principals from an agency law standpoint. As co-owners and profit-sharers, partners' have the power to participate directly in the management of the firm and the incentive to maximize the productivity of the firm. This puts them in a better position than outside creditors to ensure that the firm's assets will be sufficient to pay its debts.[4] It arguably follows that, if partnerships and creditors bargained over the partners' liability, partners ordinarily would rather take responsibility for their firm's ability to pay its debts than pay the higher credit costs creditors would demand if the partners did not have this responsibility. If that is the deal partnerships ordinarily would reach with their creditors, it follows that the statutory standard form can reduce transaction costs by providing that deal as a default rule. On the other hand, as discussed below in Section 3.03, there are substantial arguments for making limited liability the default rule.

Even assuming that the default partnership would prefer vicarious liability, there are surely many partnerships that do not fit the characteristics of the default partnership and would want to opt out of vicarious liability. Firms can limit their liability by contracting with their creditors or by forming one of several types of limited liability firms, including corporations, limited liability companies (LLCs), and limited partnerships. The following subsections consider some policy considerations that come into play in permitting *general partnerships* to opt out of vicarious liability.

(b)   Limited Liability and Voluntary Creditors

Partners can, of course, enter into enforceable "nonrecourse" contracts with creditors providing that the creditors may not have recourse to the partners' indi-

---

[3] *See* U.P.A. § 6(1); R.U.P.A. § 202.
[4] *See* Bromberg & Ribstein, § 2.07(a). *See also* Sykes, The Economics of Vicarious Liability, 93 Yale L.J. 1231 (1984).

vidual assets.[5] It arguably follows that they should have limited liability to voluntary creditors through a statutory "standard form" contract such as the LLP, which provides notice to creditors of the liability by means of name and registration requirements. One might argue that such a statute simply reduces the costs of contracting separately with individual creditors.[6] There are, however, some arguments, discussed below in Section 3.03, against LLP statutes that limit liability for contracts.

(c)   Limited Liability and Involuntary Creditors

The most important policy question regarding limited liability is whether owners should be able to limit their liability to tort victims, those to whom the firm may be indirectly liable, such as for aiding and abetting a securities fraud, or others who do not deal intentionally with the firm before the claim arises. Some commentators question the advisability of permitting corporate shareholders to limit liability in this situation.[7] These criticisms are based on the premise that limited tort liability involves the potential of increased costs for creditors who are not in a position to adjust their credit charges to reflect the costs. Members may have less incentive to be careful in their own activities, including monitoring their co-members, if they know that creditors cannot touch their own assets. Also, limited liability owners who receive all the benefits from the firm but can shift some costs to creditors may manage the firm in a risky or careless manner with the result that the firm cannot pay its debts.[8]

The important question is whether *society* is better off because the benefits to owners of limited liability discussed above outweigh the potential benefits to tort plaintiffs of personal liability. This depends on the potential costs and benefits of not legally compelling firms' owners to be individually responsible to tort victims. The following are some considerations that bear on this cost-benefit decision:

---

[5] *See* Dominion Nat'l Bank v. Sundowner Joint Venture, 50 Md. App. 145, 436 A.2d 501 (1981) (recognizing enforceability of nonrecourse contracts); Union Trust Co. v. Poor & Alexander, Inc., 168 Md. 400, 177 A. 923 (1935) (enforcing nonrecourse contract in "investment trust"); Ribstein, Limited Liability and Theories of the Corporation, 50 Md. L. Rev. 80, 112–13 (1991).

[6] *Id.* at 113–14.

[7] *See* Halpern, Trebilcock & Turnbull, An Economic Analysis of Limited Liability in Corporation Law, 30 U. Toronto L.J. 117 (1980); Hansmann & Kraakman, Toward Unlimited Shareholder Liability for Corporate Torts, 100 Yale L.J. 1879 (1991) (advocating pro rata liability in corporations); Leebron, Limited Liability, Tort Victims, and Creditors, 91 Colum. L. Rev. 1565 (1991) (suggesting unlimited tort liability in some situations); Schwartz, Product Liability, Corporate Structure, and Bankruptcy: Toxic Substances and the Remote Risk Relationship, 14 j. Leg. Stud. 689 (1985) (suggesting unlimited liability if assets and insurance insufficient to satisfy knowable tort claims).

[8] *See* Woodward, Limited Liability in the Theory of the Firm, 141 J. Inst. & Theo. Econ. 601, 606 (1985); Ribstein, note 5, supra, at 97–98.

(1) Owners will not necessarily ignore risks to third parties even if they are not personally liable for these risks. Firms would be careful even in the absence of liability in order to protect their reputations. Even limited liability firms insure against tort liability because owners have reason to be concerned about loss of corporate assets.[9] Employee-members and nonmember managers could lose their jobs if the firm becomes insolvent because of tort claims. Also, the firm may have to insure to appease unsecured voluntary creditors who would have to share with tort creditors in the event the firm becomes insolvent. If the company does have to insure, its insurance rates, and the availability of insurance, depend on how carefully the business is operated. Thus, limited tort liability is likely to impose high costs on creditors only with respect to the relatively small class of firms that have little reputation to be concerned about, few assets to protect from tort claims, and large potential tort liabilities.

(2) In evaluating the costs and benefits of limited liability, it is important to keep in mind that unlimited liability is not a panacea for creditors. Partners can evade personal liability by, for example, shifting assets to family members, as partners in professional firms commonly do.

(3) Even if owners and managers face a significantly higher risk of loss of wealth from torts under unlimited liability, this may not give them much additional incentive to be careful. Owners, like firms, can insure. Also, owners and agents have incentives to act carefully, even if they will not face personal liability for failing to do so, in order to preserve their personal reputations for probity and care.

(4) Assuming personal liability would increase owners' incentives to be careful, this increase may not be a good thing. Some tort or malpractice cases impose liability for unknowable risks, or for injuries that were easily preventable by plaintiffs.[10] Unlimited liability may even *reduce* overall incentives for care by deflecting lawsuits from immediately negligent parties to remote non-negligent owners. The result may be to make firms *too* careful—for example, wholly avoiding socially beneficial products, or causing individual partners to engage in duplicative monitoring activities.

(5) Unlimited liability causes a shift from first-party insurance, such as accident and worker-compensation policies, to third-party insurance. This shift may increase overall insurance costs by, among other problems, causing over-insurance in relation to the expected loss, higher administrative costs, higher costs of diversifying risks for insurance companies, and less ability to separate insureds into risk pools.[11]

---

[9] *See* Easterbrook & Fischel, Limited Liability and the Corporation, 52 U. Chi. L. Rev. 89 (1985); Ribstein, The Deregulation of Limited Liability and the Death of Partnership, 70 Wash. U. L.Q. 417 (1992).

[10] *See* Kornhauser, An Economic Analysis of the Choice Between Enterprise and Personal Liability for Accidents, 70 Cal. L. Rev. 1345 (1982).

[11] *See* Priest, The Current Insurance Crisis and Modern Tort Law, 96 Yale L.J. 1521 (1987).

(6) Unlimited tort liability imposes potential costs on firms that must be balanced against its benefits in order to determine whether unlimited tort liability is good for society. Among other things, owners have to incur costs in monitoring their co-owners. Indeed, they may not be able to fully delegate decision making to other managers or owners. These costs are not imposed on owners who invest after the unlimited liability rule goes into effect. Rather, the costs may hurt society by decreasing the size and number of large firms in which the imposition of monitoring and other costs may be particularly troublesome.

In summary, since it is unclear how unlimited liability affects owners' incentives and whether any effect on incentives benefits society, unlimited liability may or may not be socially beneficial.

(d) Limiting Liability in Closely Held Firms

Limited liability is, of course, now widely available through corporations, limited partnerships, and LLCs. Thus, even if criticisms of limited liability are generally well founded, there is a further question of why it should not be extended to general partnerships. One reason, discussed in this subsection, is that there is a concern about the efficiency of limited liability in closely held firms. Other potential objections to limited liability in LLPs are discussed in later subsections. It is not obvious why closely held firms would want to limit the owners' liability. The owners presumably have to pay higher credit costs to third parties in return for limiting their liability to reflect creditors' increased risks of nonpayment. Despite these increased costs, limited liability may be worth the increased credit costs to owners in *publicly traded* firms because, as some commentators have pointed out, limited liability facilitates transferability of shares, and therefore makes efficient securities markets possible.[12]

The cost-benefit tradeoff is harder to see in closely held firms such as general partnerships in which shares normally are not freely transferable. Even in closely held firms, limited liability reduces the owners' need to monitor their co-owners' activities.[13] But while the advantages of limited liability to owners are less in closely held firms, the increased risks to creditors may be even higher than in publicly held firms. So why would general partners ever be willing to pay the higher credit costs of limited liability?

One reason may be that the costs to creditors are not as great as one might suppose. Creditors' benefits from members' personal liability depend on their comparison under limited and personal liability of the likelihood that (1) the firm's assets will be unavailable and (2) the owners' assets will be unavailable. Moreover, the creditors have to consider their costs of determining what the

---

[12] *See* Easterbrook & Fischel, note 9, supra.
[13] *See* Ribstein, note 5, above, at 101–06.

owners own, making sure that personally liable owners do not transfer their own assets out of reach prior to collection, and the creditors' costs of collecting from owners' personal assets.[14]

The costs of collecting debts from individual partners may be high in view of exhaustion requirements under state law and co-debtor stays and injunctions under federal bankruptcy law (*see* Section 3.08, below). In a colorful example of creditors' travails in this respect, a creditor unsuccessfully sought judgment against the partners in South Carolina, then got a judgment of pro rata liability in Ohio, but failed to have this judgment enforced against partner assets in Indiana.[15]

Even for larger debts, personal liability may not offer much additional protection where firms have either significant assets or minimally capitalized corporate owners or individuals with highly liquid financial assets that are costly for creditors to monitor. At any rate, under a limited liability default rule, owners could opt out by guaranteeing particular debts. The costs, benefits, and practical problems associated with such contracts are discussed below in Section 3.05.

Assuming limited liability is a problem for closely held firms, this alone would not explain why limited liability should be available for many types of closely held firms, including corporations, limited partnerships, and LLCs, but not for general partnerships. The following subsections explore considerations that may apply only to certain business forms.

(e)   Limited Liability and Management Structure

One reason why limited liability may particularly be a problem for general partnerships concerns management structure. One of the costs of limited liability is that it may encourage managers to run the firm in a way that imposes risks on creditors. In a "standard form" corporation, this risk is mitigated by the fact that the firm is run by directors. To be sure, managers may own substantial stock or options that may increase in value through risky investments. But nonowner managers may be more likely than owners to avoid risk because their jobs are at stake in the event of a possible bankruptcy. Although managers are supposed to serve the interests of the owners, there may be enough "slack" in the owners' power to control the managers to leave room for the managers to act in some respects more in creditors' than owners' interests. Partnerships, by contrast, generally combine ownership and control in the same people. Coupling this management structure with limited liability may present special risks to creditors.

The fact that the partnership management structure is unsuited to limited liability may explain the law's initial reluctance to permit shareholders to take

---

[14] *See* Ribstein, note 9, above, at 428–33.
[15] Thompson v. Wayne Smith Constr. Co., Inc., 640 N.E.2d 408 (Ind. App. 1994).

over direct management of the corporation.[16] It may also explain the limited partnership control rule, which inhibits limited partners from taking over management functions without, at the same time, losing their limited liability.[17]

Concerns about partnership management structure do not, however, distinguish LLPs from other modern closely held firms now that restrictions on management form have been relaxed. The control rule in R.U.L.P.A. includes a long list of safe harbors and a reliance requirement that prevents creditors from holding limited partners liable unless they were misled into thinking that they were general partners.[18] Moreover, the control rule has been eliminated in U.L.P.A. § 303 (2001) (*see* Section 1.04(b), note 54, above, and Section 9.303, below). Owners of close corporations may directly participate in management[19] and owners of LLCs have complete flexibility on the form of management.[20] This liberalization raises serious questions about the appropriateness of restricting limited liability in general partnerships.

(f) Limited Liability and Partnership Taxation

Limited liability is arguably inappropriate for firms that are taxed as partnerships. Because members of such firms generally are taxed on income as the firm earns it, they have a strong incentive to cause the firm to distribute all of its earnings leaving little, if any, cushion for creditors.[21] Moreover, this argument fails to distinguish the LLP from other types of closely held firms that are taxed as partnerships and therefore have comparable tax incentives to distribute earnings, including LLCs, Subchapter S corporations, and limited partnerships.

(g) Statutory Creditor Protection Provisions

The partnership statutes in which LLP provisions are included generally do not include provisions like those in most other limited liability business association statutes that help protect against inadequate capitalization by regulating

---

[16] *See, e.g.*, Manson v. Curtis, 223 N.Y. 313, 119 N.E. 559 (1918).

[17] *See* U.L.P.A. § 7 (1916); R.U.L.P.A. § 303 (1985).

[18] *See* R.U.L.P.A. § 303 (1985).

[19] *See, e.g.*, Del. Code Ann., tit. 8, §§ 350, 351, 354 (permitting statutory "close corporations" to enter into agreements that remove functions from, or dispense with, the board).

[20] *See generally* Ribstein & Keatinge on Limited Liability Companies ch. 8 (3d ed. 2008).

[21] Some commentators have argued for links between the corporate tax and limited liability based on potential misincentives by managers vis-à-vis owners. *See* Kanda & Levmore, Taxes, Agency Costs and The Price of Incorporation, 77 Va. L. Rev. 211 (1991); Snoe, The Entity Tax and Corporate Integration: An Agency Cost Analysis and a Call for a Deferred Distributions Tax, 48 U. Miami L. Rev. 1 (1993). However, these arguments relate more to the owners' choice of form than to the need for creditor protection.

members' capital contributions and distributions. The arguments for and against including such provisions in LLP statutes are discussed below in Section 4.04.

§ 3.02   LIMITED "TORT" LIABILITY IN LLPs

In general, the liability shields that apply under each statute are summarized in Table 3-1. This section discusses the LLP statutes that limit liability for particular categories of conduct — that is, for negligence or other misconduct by a co-partner or other agent or employee of the firm. The model for these provisions is a prior version of the Delaware statute, which provides that a partner "is not liable for debts and obligations of or chargeable to the partnership arising from negligence, wrongful acts, or misconduct, whether characterized as tort, contract or otherwise, committed while the partnership is a registered limited liability partnership and in the course of the partnership business by another partner or an employee, agent, or representative of the partnership."[22]

As discussed above in Section 3.01(b), there are arguments favoring limiting vicarious liability generally, and specifically in LLPs. The policy question concerning limited tort liability in LLPs is whether this can be reconciled with retaining vicarious liability for contracts. In other words, if vicarious liability for contracts is an appropriate default rule, how is it possible to justify limited liability for those who are not in a good position to protect themselves by contract? The difficulty of justifying this rule may be one factor in the move toward full-shield provisions discussed below in Section 3.03.

The policy arguments concerning the bifurcated rule for contracts and torts are discussed more fully in Section 3.03, below. This section will discuss the main argument in favor of the rule: limiting partners' vicarious liability for co-partners' misconduct eliminates the category of vicarious liability that is most costly and provides the least benefits to creditors. Limited liability for misconduct provides "peace of mind" insurance against potentially disastrous liability for such uncontrollable events as bank failures[23] and punitive damage awards. Partners can, to a significant extent, control or opt out of contract liability. By contrast, partners may find it hard to control co-partners' negligence or other misconduct. As long as they did not fail to monitor or participate in wrongdoing,

---

[22] Del. Code Ann., tit. 6, § 1515(b). This section was first amended to provide protection for all kinds of claims (*see* 1997 Delaware Laws Ch. 114 (S.B. 115), approved June 30, 1997) and was later replaced by a provision based on R.U.P.A.

[23] *See* Hamilton, supra note 2. The role of the savings and loan crisis in spurring the original LLP provision in Texas is discussed in Section 1.01, supra.

for which partners may be directly liable under LLP statutes or the common law (*see* Section 3.04, below), there is little the partners could have done to prevent other categories of liabilities. Imposing personal liability for other misconduct, therefore, does little to increase partners' incentives to act on creditors' or clients' behalf.[24] Accordingly, vicarious tort liability beyond monitoring failures may impose costs on partnerships that exceed the social benefits of vicarious liability.

Statutes that limit partners' liability only for misconduct-based claims raise some questions about the types of vicarious liability that are limited.[25] The language clearly applies to any form of negligence or misconduct. It is important to keep in mind that the statutes do not explicitly distinguish between "torts" and "contracts." Professional malpractice liability arising out of partners' negligence is certainly included in the exception to vicarious liability despite the fact that this liability probably could be characterized as arising out of the contractual relationship between the professional and the client. Nevertheless, plaintiffs' lawyers may try to exploit any ambiguity in the statute by arguing that at least some kinds of malpractice are not shielded because they are breaches of contract.[26] Thus, it is significant that the original partial-shield Delaware statute was amended in 1994 to provide that it limits vicarious liability for conduct "whether characterized as tort, contract or otherwise."[27] The R.U.P.A. shield similarly applies to conduct "whether *arising in* contract, tort or otherwise."[28] In any event, a distinction that required conduct to be characterized as a "tort" or a "breach of contract" would be extremely difficult to make.[29]

---

[24] *See* Section 3.01(c), supra.

[25] *See* U.S. Claims, Inc. v. Saffren & Weinberg, LLP, 2009 WL 2179738 (E.D. Pa. July 22, 2009) (Pa. law; partner may be liable for breach of contract claims to the extent that they are attributable to the partnership as a whole, as well as for tort claims to the extent that partner committed or participated in fraudulent representations).

[26] *See* Dzienkowski, Legal Malpractice and The Multi-state Law Firm: Supervision of Multi-state Offices; Firms as Limited Liability Partnerships; and Predispute Agreements To Arbitrate Client Malpractice Claims, 36 S. Tex. L. Rev. 967, 985–86 (1995).

[27] *See* 1994 Del. Laws Ch. 259 (S.B. 311), § 3, amending Del. Code Ann., tit. 6, § 1515(b); Section 1.01(c), supra. The Delaware provision has been replaced by R.U.P.A.-based language given immediately below. Statutory variations are shown in Table 3-1.

[28] R.U.P.A. § 306(c) (emphasis supplied).

[29] *See* FDIC v. Clark, 978 F.2d 1541, 1552 (10th Cir. 1992) (stating that even if the relationship between a professional and the client originates in contract, malpractice still sounds in tort); Ribstein, Tort and Contract in Georgia, 30 Mercer L. Rev. 303 (1978).

§ 3.03 LIMITED LIABILITY FOR ALL
TYPES OF CLAIMS

As shown in Table 3-1, most statutes provide that liability is limited for all partnership debts and obligations. For example, the Revised Uniform Partnership Act provides:

> An obligation of a partnership incurred while the partnership is a limited liability partnership, whether arising in contract, tort, or otherwise, is solely the obligation of the partnership. A partner is not personally liable, directly or indirectly, including by way of contribution or otherwise, for such a partnership obligation solely by reason of being or so acting as a partner.[30]

Subsection (a) discusses the scope of the type of liability limitation. Subsection (b) discusses policy issues raised by these statutes. Subsection (c) discusses a potential ramification of extending limited liability to general partnerships—the possibility that limited liability could replace vicarious liability as the default rule for all kinds of firms.

(a) Scope of Liability Limitation

LLP statutes that eliminate partners' *vicarious* liability for all types of claims mean that a partnership creditor is not entitled to a judgment against the partner personally solely on account of the partner's status as such.[31] However, these

---

[30] R.U.P.A. § 306(c).

[31] Ciecka v. Rosen, 908 F. Supp. 2d 545 (2012) (partners in an LLP not liable for other partner's alleged tortious interference with contract); Vohra v. Cadigan Arbor Park, 2010 WL 1102428 (Cal. App. Mar. 25, 2010) (thus partner is not a proper party to an action against an LLP); Colliers, Dow & Condon, Inc. v. Schwartz, 2004 WL 1246004 (Conn. Super. May 24, 2004); Santos v. 305 West 56th St. Realty LLC, 21 Misc. 3d 174, 862 N.Y.S.2d 435 (2008); Falcone v. Karagiannis, 2009 WL 3817477 (N.Y. Sup. Nov. 4, 2009); Regency Found. v. Robson, 14 Misc. 3d 1209(A), 836 N.Y.S.2d 489 (N.Y. Sup. Ct. 2006); Mantell v. Samuelson, 4 Misc. 3d 134(A) (N.Y. Sup. App. Term 2004); Bennett v. Cochran, 2004 WL 852298 (Tex. App. Apr. 22, 2004). Cordier v. Tkach, 2006 WL 2407051, Nonpublished/ Noncitable (Cal. App. Aug. 22, 2006) reversed a jury verdict against a partner in an LLP where the court erroneously instructed the jury that the plaintiff could recover against a partner in an LLP for breach of a retainer agreement based on the fact that the contract was intended for the partner's benefit. The court reasoned that this transformed third-party beneficiary doctrine into vicarious liability contrary to both the common law and the statutory liability shield.

iCore Networks, Inc. v. McQuade Brennan LLP, 2008 WL 4550988 (E.D. Va. Oct. 7, 2008) (D.C. law) dismissed a complaint alleging that a partner "assumed responsibility" for his accounting partnership's work. The court reasoned that the complaint merely stated a legal conclusion rather than factually supporting the theory that the partner had a duty separate from the duties of the firm. A later opinion upheld an amended complaint alleging additional facts in support of the duty. *See* statutes nevertheless preserve partners' liability for their own misconduct, including faulty supervision of other partners, discussed below in Section 3.04, and contracts for liability, discussed below in Section 3.05. Also, it is important to keep in mind that the *partnership* retains vicarious liability for its partners' acts.[32] Partners therefore remain liable at least up to their investment in the firm, and perhaps beyond this if they have agreed with their co-partners to contribute toward partnership losses.[33]

(b) Policy Issues

The more general issue of whether partners should be able to limit their liability is discussed above in Section 3.01. If they should, then complete limited liability statutes obviously are sound. If they should not, then policy issues remain concerning whether the statutes should retain personal liability for contracts even though they limit partners' vicarious tort liability.

Even if one believes that general partnerships should not be able fully to limit their liability, limiting liability for tort-type debts might be difficult to reconcile with personal liability for contract-type debts. The best argument for the distinction is the need to preserve the basic vicarious liability nature of partnership, particularly in order to help ensure that LLPs will continue to be treated as

iCore Networks, Inc. v. McQuade Brennan LLP, 2009 WL 36596 (E.D. Va. Jan. 5, 2009) (D.C. law) discussed in Section 3.04, n.45, infra. Roe v. Ladymon, 2010 WL 2978293 (Tex. App.-Dallas July 30, 2010) held that an LLP partner's signature on contract indicating he was signing solely on behalf of the LLP does not render him personally a party to the contract. The court noted LLP partners' limited liability in reasoning that the partner had not taken personal responsibility for the debt merely by his signature. For discussion of similar issues concerning the border between individual and firm responsibility in the limited liability company context, see Ribstein & Keatinge on Limited Liability Companies, § 12:4, n.1; Gunnings v. Internet Cash Enter. of Asheville, LLC, 2007 WL 1931291 (W.D.N.C. 2007); Estate of Countryman v. Farmers Co-op. Ass'n, 679 N.W.2d 598 (Iowa 2004) (imposing liability on a managing member for a firm's tort); (holding individual defendants liable for directing their LLC to make usurious loans).

Largo Realty, Inc. v. Purcell, 77 Mass. App. Ct. 162, 928 N.E.2d 999 (2010) held that, because recovery is limited to an LLP's assets, plaintiff could not sue a partnership simply by naming a partner. Although the court distinguished general and limited partnerships, it is not clear why the partner's liability for partnership debts should matter as to whether the partnership should be named. As to suits against the partnership, *see* Bromberg & Ribstein, § 5.12. The court may have meant that, unlike a non-LLP general partnership, plaintiff cannot reach any assets at all simply by suing a partner in an LLP.

[32] *See* Canada Life Assur. Co. v. Estate of Lebowitz, 185 F.3d 231, 236 n.4 (4th Cir. 1999) (Md. law).

[33] United States v. 175 Inwood Assocs. LLP., 330 F. Supp. 2d 213 (E.D.N.Y. 2004) held partners in a N.Y. LLP individually liable for damages under the Comprehensive Environmental Response, Compensation, and Liability Act of 1980 (CERCLA). The court acknowledged that the partners could not be held individually liable "solely by reason of being such a partner," but nevertheless held that they "are not protected as individuals from liability incurred by the partnership if the assets of the partnership are insufficient to satisfy the liability," citing cases involving non-LLP general partnerships.

"partnerships" under regulatory statutes (*see* Chapter 7). As discussed above in Section 3.02, the LLP form accomplishes this while relieving the owners from the most burdensome type of liability.

On the other hand, there are several arguments against bifurcated liability. First, the distinction is inconsistent with concerns discussed above in Section 3.01(b) that involuntary creditors cannot bargain for protection from the extra risks imposed by limited liability. Indeed, this extra concern for victims of misconduct is reflected in the U.P.A. distinction between "joint" liability for contract-type debts and "joint and several" liability for tort-type debts.[34] With joint liability, creditors must exhaust remedies against the firm before pursuing the assets of individual partners. With joint and several liability, creditors can proceed directly against the partners without exhaustion.[35] Thus, *if* personal liability to contract creditors is appropriate, there is a strong argument that it also should be extended to tort-type creditors.

Second, preserving vicarious contract liability may impair tort creditors' rights against the partnership. As discussed below in Section 3.09(b), limiting liability only for misconduct-type claims gives partners an incentive to protect their own wealth by paying contract claims first out of partnership assets, leaving nothing for the tort-type creditors.

Third, personal liability for contract-type debts arguably is an inappropriate default rule. A problem with partners' vicarious liability is that it is costly for creditors to monitor partners' wealth and guard against possible wealth transfers by owners. It also may be costly to pursue claims against partners' assets, perhaps through several jurisdictions and in the face of federal bankruptcy rules and state law exhaustion requirements (*see* Sections 3.01(d), above, and 3.09, below). Thus, creditors holding smaller claims may not be much interested in personal liability. If so, the partnership would want to contract around the personal liability default with respect to these creditors. Yet because these claims are too small to justify personal liability, they may also be too small to justify the costs of contracting around the personal liability default rule. Conversely, under a default rule of limited liability, it would be cost-justified for the creditors with larger claims to bargain for individual partner liability as discussed below in Section 3.05. In short, under these assumptions about collection costs and contracting, limited liability is the appropriate default rule.

(c)   The Next Step: Limited Liability as a Default Rule?

If limited liability becomes the rule for all types of claims in LLPs, this raises the question whether limited liability should be the *default* rule. In other words,

---

[34] *See* U.P.A. § 15 (1914).
[35] *See* Bromberg & Ribstein, § 5.08.

perhaps the rule should be that *no one* — either partners or sole proprietors — promises to back business debts with personal wealth in the absence of a specific contract.[36]

If virtually all firms can be expected to opt for limited liability, vicarious liability may become a trap for the unlucky or unwary, such as those who did not even know they were partners. Requiring formalities in order to take advantage of limited liability makes no sense unless the formalities required by the LLP provisions give creditors substantial protection and notice. Yet registration itself adds little but notice that the firm is an "LLP." This notice would be irrelevant once every firm is treated as an LLP.

Even if LLP statutes generally go no further than limiting liability for tort-type claims, there is a strong argument that at least this type of limited liability should be available for all partnerships. The theory underlying allowing this liability limitation is that the costs of such liability to partnerships exceed the social benefit as discussed above in Section 3.02. Moreover, the formalities and name restrictions necessary for this liability limitation obviously are irrelevant to most tort-type creditors. Any minimum insurance requirements that are deemed appropriate could be applied to both LLP and non-LLP partnerships.

§ 3.04 PARTNERS' DIRECT LIABILITY

Nothing in the LLP statutes or in statutes relating to other types of limited liability business associations relieves owners from liability for their own misconduct. "Limited liability" means only that the owners are not, solely as owners,[37] vicariously liable for the firm's debts. Thus, while a release of a partnership also released partners who were vicariously liable for partnership debts, and whose liability was therefore derivative of the partnership's liability, it did not release partners of an LLP who were directly liable for their own wrongful acts but not named in the release.[38]

Subsection (a) reviews the statutory language on the scope of partners' direct liability. Subsection (b) discusses how some specific cases might be resolved under the statutes. Subsection (c) discusses potential conflicts of interest

---

[36] *See* Klein & Zolt, Business Form Limited Liability and Tax Regimes, 66 U. Colo. L. Rev. 1001 (1995).

[37] The Indiana statute also provides that one is not liable for "acting or failing to act as a partner, or participating as an employee, a consultant, a contractor, or otherwise in the conduct of the business or activities of the limited liability partnership. . . ." Ind. Code § 23-4-1-15(2)(b).

[38] *See* Schuman v. Gallet, Dreyer & Berkey, 180 Misc. 2d 485, 689 N.Y.S.2d 628 (Sup. Ct. 1999), *aff'd*, 280 A.D.2d 310, 719 N.Y.S.2d 864 (Mem.), 2001 N.Y. Slip Op. 00976 (Feb. 8, 2001). While this case applies both to LLPs and non-LLP partnerships, it is particularly applicable to LLPs, none of whose partners are vicariously liable.

that may arise from partners' individual liability in LLPs. Subsection (d) discusses the nature of partners' direct liability.

(a)   Review of Statutory Provisions

The statutes both preserve whatever liability partners may have had under the common law[39] and, perhaps, provide for an additional statutory category of liability for misconduct. Variations are summarized in Table 3-1. An important model is the original version of the Delaware statute, which provides that the liability limitation "shall not affect the liability of a partner in a registered limited liability partnership for his own negligence, wrongful acts, or misconduct, or that of any person under his direct supervision and control."[40] As shown in Table 3-1, statutes provide for such liability under a variety of formulations.

It is uncertain under the supervision-type of provision whether the partner must be negligent or at fault in order to be held liable. Stating that the LLP provisions "shall not affect" the partner's liability suggests that the statute only continues any liability partners may have had for their own misconduct or for negligently failing to monitor or supervise others. But it is not clear to what preexisting supervisory liability the statute might be referring other than partners'

---

[39] See Blackmon v. Hale, 1 Cal. 3d 548, 83 Cal. Rptr. 194, 463 P.2d 418 (1970) (liability for breach of attorney's duties as co-trustees of funds for surrendering trust funds to defalcating attorney).

[40] Del. Code Ann., tit. 6, § 1515(c). For applications of similar language in the Connecticut statute, see Colliers, Dow and Condon, Inc. v. Schwartz, 88 Conn. App. 445, 871 A.2d 373 (2005) (holding that partner is not liable for negligently failing to inform plaintiff that the firm had converted to an LLP in the absence of evidence that plaintiff, who was aware of the partnership's LLP status, was harmed by any negligence by the individual partner); City of Bridgeport v. C.J. Fucci, Inc., 2007 WL 1120537 (Conn. Super. March 28, 2007) (complaint stated negligence claim in connection with renovation project against individual professionals who owned design firm LLP). The Delaware provision was replaced by a provision based on R.U.P.A., but adding that the liability limitation "shall not affect the liability of a partner in a limited liability partnership for such partner's own negligence or willful misconduct." Del. Code Ann., tit. 6, § 15-306(d). That subsection was deleted in a subsequent revision, as explained in the Synopsis, "to eliminate unnecessary language and confirm the liability standard of a partner in a limited liability partnership under existing law." Del. Laws 2001, ch. 85 (effective August 1, 2001). For an application of the Texas LLP statute providing for liability of a partner who was directly involved in the wrongful conduct or who had notice of the partner's negligence and failed to take reasonable steps to prevent or cure it, see Software Publishers Ass'n v. Scott & Scott, LLP, 2007 WL 92391 (N.D. Tex. Jan. 11, 2007) (refusing to dismiss allegations that the managing partner controls the partnership's activities complained of in the complaint). U.S. Claims, Inc. v. Saffren & Weinberg, LLP, 2009 WL 2179738 (E.D. Pa. July 22, 2009) (Pa. law) held that a partner may be held liable for committing or participating in fraudulent representations under a statute that limited partners' liability for "negligent or wrongful acts or misconduct committed by another partner," but provided for liability for debts arising from other causes. In re Promedicus Health Group, LLP, 416 B.R. 389 (Bankr. W.D.N.Y. 2009), applying the Delaware-type language in the New York statute, held that LLP partners' potential personal liability for wrongful acts did not make them general partners for purposes of determining the partnership's insolvency under bankruptcy law.

vicarious liability under traditional partnership law, which is supposedly eliminated by LLP registration.

As shown in Table 3-1, not all LLP statutes include potentially confusing language on supervisory or other indirect liability. Some provide for liability only for the partner's own wrongs or omit any extra language on liability of individual members and provide in varying terms that a partner in an LLP is not individually liable merely because of her partnership status. This preserves partners' common law liability for their own misconduct without the risk of creating new categories of statutory liability.[41]

Partners in law and other professional firms have *ethical* duties to monitor others in the firm, which may or may not give rise to liability even in the absence of specific language in the LLP statute (*see* Section 7.04(b), below). However, it has been held that Connecticut's direct supervision provision supersedes ethical obligations under Connecticut's Model Rule of Professional Conduct 5.1 requiring lawyers to exercise supervision.[42]

(b) Scope of Direct Liability: Some Specific Cases

It seems clear under the "direct supervision and control" type of provision that non-negligent partners would not be liable for the acts of a co-partner who acted independently, as indicated perhaps by the acting partner's retention of fees on her own matters.[43] However, in many other types of cases the result may not be so clear. To fully understand the scope of partners' individual liability under statutory language or the common law it is necessary to analyze some specific

---

[41] *See* Katz v. Image Innovations Holdings, Inc., 2008 WL 4840880 (S.D.N.Y. Nov. 4, 2008) (N.Y. law); Dow v. Donovan, 150 F. Supp. 2d 249, 268 (D. Mass. 2001) (discussed further in note 46, infra; holding under Massachusetts LLP statute that follows this approach that "[t]he liability of each [partner] depends on proof of some wrongful act or omission by that individual partner. This statute does not mean that partners in a Limited Liability Partnership can *never* be liable in a discrimination suit. It means that the plaintiff must demonstrate that the individual partner was negligent or committed some other kind of wrongful act, error, or omission that produced discrimination against the plaintiff."). *See also* Scarborough v. Napoli, Kaiser & Bern, LLP, 63 A.D.3d 1531, 880 N.Y.S.2d 800 (2009) (reinstating complaint against individual defendants who had not established as a matter of law that they committed no negligent or wrongful act for which they could be held individually liable). This type of provision has the indirect effect of minimizing the possibility that LLP partners will have "back door" personal liability for tort-type claims because of the need to indemnify partners against direct liability for non-negligent conduct. *See* §§ 2.09(d), supra, and 3.09(c), infra.

[42] *See* Kus v. Irving, 736 A.2d 946 (Conn. Super. 1999). Model Rule 5.1 is discussed in § 7.04(b), notes 141–145.

[43] *See Kus*, 736 A.2d 946, note 42, supra (holding that lawyers were not liable for co-partner's alleged taking of excessive fees under Connecticut's direct supervision provision where they filed unrebutted affidavits "that they had no personal knowledge of the dealings between the plaintiff and Irving [the alleged wrongdoer], nor did they have any supervision or control of Irving and that under the partnership agreement, Irving retains all fees for his activities and does not share any of them with the other partners").

examples under the various interpretations of the statutory language discussed above:[44]

(1) Partner has overall responsibility for a client, but other lawyers or accountants do all the work, including the negligence or other misconduct that triggers liability, and partner has no knowledge of any misconduct. Partner might be liable under the common law for negligently delegating work or under a statute that imposes liability on partner for the misconduct of another acting under her "supervision." One question in this regard is whether partner must engage in actual supervision of *specific work* to be held liable, or whether merely having overall responsibility for the *client* is enough to constitute "supervision." The language like that in the original Delaware statute imposes liability only for acts under a partner's "direct" supervision. This at least clarifies that a law firm's managing partners are not personally liable for all misconduct committed by any partner. Partner may be able to show that under customs and practices in large law or accounting firms, client responsibility carries with it only responsibility for billing and client contact rather than for all work done for the client. Even if partner is regarded as a supervisor, partner also must have "control" under an original-Delaware-type statute. Partner's general management power, coupled with the partner's relationship with the client, may be enough to constitute "control."[45]

(2) Partners on a law firm's "opinion committee" review a tax opinion prepared primarily by other lawyers. The client misstates the facts underlying the tax opinion but no one on the opinion committee is aware of this. Partners may be deemed to have enough notice to be negligent — as where the facts as presented were illogical or unclear. If they are not negligent, they might still have statutory liability for supervising the opinion. In this case, service on the opinion committee necessarily involves a supervisory role. The opinion committee has "control" in the form of the ability to decide whether to issue the opinion. However, it has been held that partners were not individually liable for an opinion letter that was issued by a law firm rather than by individual lawyers where the alleged misrepresentations were those collectively of the firm rather of any individual.

(3) Partner is an antitrust law specialist who is consulted concerning the antitrust aspects of a transaction being primarily handled by lawyers in a law firm's corporate department. The negligence or misconduct does not concern the

---

[44] For a discussion of some of these situations, see Hamilton, note 2, above.

[45] Dean Foods Co. v. Pappathanasi, 2004 WL 3019442 (Mass. Super. Dec. 3, 2004). In a variation on this fact situation, the court upheld a complaint against an individual accounting partner for liability for embezzlement by the accounting firm's employee. iCore Networks, Inc. v. McQuade Brennan LLP, 2009 WL 36596 (E.D. Va. Jan. 5, 2009) (D.C. law). The partner allegedly gave the client assurances as to the performance of the firm's employee when negotiating to be retained by the client, and these assurances allegedly induced the client to place "special confidence" in the partner. This opinion followed the dismissal of an initial complaint which alleged only that the partner had "assumed responsibility" for the LLP's performance. *See* iCore Networks, Inc. v. McQuade Brennan LLP, 2008 WL 4550988 (E.D. Va. Oct. 7, 2008), discussed in § 3.03, n.31, supra.

antitrust advice. Partner may have enough notice of the misconduct to be negligent for not preventing harm to the client. Partner probably would not be regarded as supervising the conduct, and has no more "control" than has any other partner. Partner may be "cooperating" in misconduct under some statutes, but those statutes impose liability only on negligent partners.

(4) Partners on a law firm's management committee set associates' compensation in a way that discriminates on the basis of race or sex. Such partners probably are committing direct wrongful acts for which they would be liable under all of the statutes.[46]

(5) Partners on a law or accounting firm's management or policy committee set rules such as methods of determining partner compensation or performing audits that are found to have been a factor in inducing or encouraging conduct that caused harm. It is not clear whether or under what circumstances such partners would be committing direct wrongful acts for which they would be liable under all of the statutes. However, one case refused to dismiss a complaint by a law firm associate for wrongful retaliatory dismissal against the LLP's managing partner, alleging that the partner "guided every aspect of those firms' operation and existence during the [relevant] period of time."[47]

(6) Several lawyers participate in a case in which an associate negligently misses a deadline for filing of a notice of appeal or negligently mishandles service of process on the defendant. No one other than the associate knows or should know either of the specific negligent act or of any information that would make it negligent to delegate the task to the associate. Although only the

---

[46] In Dow v. Donovan, 150 F. Supp. 2d 249 (D. Mass. 2001), plaintiff sued for gender discrimination in being denied partnership. The court denied plaintiff's motion for summary judgment against the partnership and the individual partners and ordered a separate trial against the partnership on its liability. The court held that the partnership's unanimity voting rule on admitting partners would not necessarily preclude the partnership's liability, but accepted neither the plaintiff's contention that this rule would justify individual partner liability nor the defendant's argument that it would preclude such liability. Rather, the court reserved the issue of partners' vicarious liability for later determination, holding that a single lawyer could represent the partnership in the first trial on partnership liability, but that conflicts might preclude such single representation in any later trial on the partners' liability. In Parsells v. Manhattan Radiology Group, L.L.P., 255 F. Supp. 2d 1217, n.7 (D. Kan. 2003) (Kan. law), the court rejected plaintiff's argument for holding LLP partners vicariously liable for discrimination, stating that plaintiff had cited:

> no authority suggesting that [the] default rule of partnership law would supersede those cases that hold, in the specific context of employment discrimination, that individual liability is not appropriate. The court, in its own research, has found no cases discussing this issue. Thus, in the absence of such authority, the court declines to adopt plaintiff's argument.

> Similar results might occur under other legislation, including the Federal Debt Collections Practices Act. *See* Garcia v. Jenkins/Babb LLP, 2013 WL 3789830 (N.D. Tex. July 22, 2013) (holding that though no specific acts were alleged that violated the FDCPA on other grounds, whether a partner/employee could be held liable for his own acts that violated the act was an open question).

[47] Connolly v. Napoli, Kaiser & Bern, LLP, 2006 WL 901675 (N.Y. Sup. April 4, 2006).

associate is negligent, partners with direct supervisory responsibility might be liable under the statutory language.[48]

(7) A lawyer in a Washington, D.C. branch office of a law firm engaging in specialized regulatory law that differs from other work generally done by the firm commits malpractice. Depending on the statutory language and the nature of the misconduct, partners in the branch office may be liable for failing to supervise the lawyer. Managing or other partners in the home office may be liable under some statutes for negligent hiring, and may have ethical responsibilities to ensure that appropriate procedures are in place in the branch.[49]

In general, the main effect of LLP statutes may be to clarify a partner's expectation that he will not be individually liable except in situations where the partner was clearly in a position to prevent the loss.[50] Under the analysis in Section 3.01, above, this is the situation in which vicarious liability has the least benefits and the most potential for imposing excessive risk-avoidance costs, such as duplicative monitoring by multiple "supervisors." Courts should interpret the statutes consistently with this analysis by refusing to expand the direct liability category to include what is, in effect, vicarious liability. However, under pressure from plaintiffs' lawyers, courts might expand partners' individual liability for their own misconduct to partially compensate for the elimination of vicarious liability, perhaps by imposing liability on partners who are not involved in the misconduct but who merely learn of it and fail to act on this knowledge.

(c)   Incentive Effects of Partners' Direct Liability

Partners' liability for participating in or supervising misconduct, coupled with their limited liability for other partnership debts, may have perverse incentive effects. Even without vicarious liability, partners have incentives to monitor their

---

[48] For discussions of breach of ethical duties to monitor in this situation, see In re Yacavino, 494 A.2d 801, 801-03 (N.J. 1985); Dzienkowski, supra note 26, at 977 (1995). Note that the liable supervising attorney may be able to recover in tort from the negligent associate. *See* Kramer v. Nowak, 908 F. Supp. 1281 (E.D. Pa. 1995); Pollack v. Lytle, 120 Cal. App. 3d 931, 175 Cal. Rptr. 81 (1981). *But see* Beck v. Wecht, 48 P.3d 417 (Cal. 2002) (declining to follow *Pollack*).

[49] For a general discussion of potential supervisory responsibility in the branch office situation, see Dzienkowski, supra note 26, at 978-79.

[50] With respect to an LLP partner's expectation of limited liability, see First American Title Ins. Co. v. Lawson, 177 N.J. 125, 827 A.2d 230 (2003). The court refused to void an innocent LLP partner's insurance coverage on account of his co-partner's fraud, reasoning in part (177 N.J. at 142, 827 A.2d at 240):

> [B]y organizing the firm as a limited liability partnership, Snyder had every reason to expect that his exposure to liability would be circumscribed in accordance with the Uniform Partnership Law. Stated differently, voiding Snyder's coverage solely because of his partners' wrongful conduct potentially would expose Snyder to uninsured liability in a manner inconsistent with his expectations under the UPL.

co-partners in order to protect the firm's reputation.[51] But it is important to keep in mind that the partners' personal liability for participating in misconduct would exceed their partners' share of the firm's liability. Thus, partners may find that they can best reduce their liability risk if they avoid monitoring that might trigger liability for participating in misconduct under a negligence theory or under statutory language that focuses liability on direct supervisors or partners who have notice or knowledge of misconduct.[52] For example, specialists may refuse to learn about cases in which they are not directly involved, and firms may abolish opinion committees. This may hurt both firms and their clients. Firms could attempt to deal with this problem by imposing specific duties on partners or adjusting financial responsibility through indemnification (*see* Section 4.04(b), below). Courts might deal with the problem through fiduciary duty rules (*see* Section 4.05, below).

Partners' personal liability may also introduce conflicts of interest regarding payout policies and insurance. Partners who are either defendants to lawsuits or who are involved in areas of the firm's activities that pose a high risk of personal liability may insist on maintaining high levels of insurance and on retaining high levels of cash. The firm may have to negotiate protection for these partners in order to retain their services or to persuade the requisite number of partners to approve an LLP registration (*see* Section 2.04(b)).

(d)   *Nature of Partners' Direct Liability*

Whatever the *scope* of partners' liability for negligent monitoring or participation, there is a further issue concerning the *nature* of this liability. Specifically, it is not clear whether this liability should be characterized as wholly personal, or whether it is a continuation of the partners' vicarious responsibility for liabilities of the firm. This issue matters for the question of whether creditors must exhaust remedies against the firm before pursuing individual partners (*see* Section 3.08(b)).

§ 3.05   CONTRACTING FOR LIABILITY

LLPs or individual partners can contract for liability that is broader than that under the applicable statute. For example, one or more partners might personally

---

[51] *See* Fortney, Am I My Partner's Keeper? Peer Review In Law Firms, 66 U. Colo. L. Rev. 329 (1995); Oedel, Deming, TQM and the Emerging Managerial Critique of Law Practice, 37 Ariz. L. Rev. 1209 (1995).

[52] *See* DeMott, Our Partners' Keepers? Agency Dimensions of Partnership Relationships, 58 J.L. & Contemp. Prob. 109, 128–29 (Spring 1995) (noting that a statute like the one in D.C. or Texas that imposes liability based on knowledge of misconduct might deter partners from obtaining information); Fortney, Seeking Shelter in the Minefield of Unintended Consequences—The Traps of Limited Liability Law Firms, 54 Wash. & Lee L. Rev. 717 (1997); Ribstein, Possible Futures for Closely Held Firms, 64 U. Cin. L. Rev. 319 (1996).

guarantee particular debts of the firm.[53] Some statutes provide explicitly for liability for debts for which the partners agreed to be liable.[54] As discussed above in Section 3.01, such contracts would provide individual liability for those creditors who place the highest value on this protection. Partners also might contract for individual liability in connection with the firm's audit, legal opinion, or other work, even in situations in which they would not be held liable under the standards discussed above in Section 3.04. A partner's merely saying that she will take responsibility for an associate's work should not be construed as a contract for personal liability, although such a statement may be evidence that the partner acted as a supervisor for purposes of imposing statutory liability.

Partners may not only guarantee individual debts, but may agree in the partnership agreement to waive the statutory liability shield as to all debts. Where only some managing partners opt out of limited liability, the firm may resemble a limited partnership. As shown in Table 3-1, several statutes provide for waiver of the liability limitation as to all or specified partners and all or specified debts, and for modification or revocation of the waiver, by a specified vote, usually less than unanimous, unless otherwise provided in the partnership agreement. The statutes provide that the modification or revocation does not affect partners' liability for debts created or assumed prior to the modification or revocation. Although R.U.P.A. does not include an analogous provision, it states in commentary that intentional waiver in the partnership agreement and as well as private contractual guarantees may modify the liability shield.[55]

Statutory subunanimous voting rules on waiver of the shield raise issues similar to those regarding subunanimous approval of the LLP registration (see Section 2.04, above), except that the greater negative impact on dissenting partners argues even more forcefully for a unanimity rule in this situation.

It is not clear under the statutory waiver provisions whether a general voting provision that does not deal explicitly with waiver of the liability shield would alter the statutory voting requirement. As with statutory provisions on voting to register (see Section 2.04), a strong argument could be made that, since the statutory provision on waiver is a special voting rule, it probably can be varied only by an agreement that explicitly waives this rule.

The statutes that provide for the partnership's waiver of the shield (see Table 3-1) generally provide that they do not affect partners' individual ability to

---

[53] See Apcar Inv. Partners VI, Ltd. v. Gaus, 161 S.W.3d 137 (Tex. App. 2005). The guaranty is separate from any liability the partners may have as such. Thus, Apcar held that the two-year limitation on the guaranty did not affect the partners' individual liability arising from the fact that the lease was executed after the firm's LLP registration had expired.

[54] See Table 3-1. See Rappaport v. Gelfand, 197 Cal. App. 4th 1213 (Cal. App. July 28, 2011) (partner not individually liable for the buyout price to a dissociating partner in the absence of the requisite agreement under the California statute).

[55] See Comment to § 306. This appears consistent with R.U.P.A. § 103(b)(10), which provides that a partnership agreement may not "restrict" third parties' rights under the act, and therefore does not apply to expansion of third parties' rights.

act as guarantors or sureties for, provide collateral for, or otherwise be liable for the debts, obligations, or liabilities of an LLP. This seems logical, since a general waiver of the shield by partner vote differs from assumption of a particular liability in a particular contract. However, the statutory waiver provisions raise questions concerning their application to other liability agreements. For example, an agreement that a single partner shall be liable for a given debt closely resembles a guaranty. Moreover, an agreement to require partner contributions to the payment of specified debts is functionally similar to holding the partners individually liable for those debts.[56] Given these similarities, issues may arise as to whether the statutory voting requirement for waiver will be applied to these other transactions.

For statutes that, like R.U.P.A., do not deal explicitly with waiver of the liability shield, considerations similar to those applicable to the LLP registration (*see* Section 2.04) should apply in determining the applicable voting rule. Waiver should be regarded as an extraordinary act or amendment to the agreement under general partnership statutory voting rules.[57] If the agreement provides for majority or other subunanimous voting on extraordinary events or amendments, these provisions arguably should apply to waivers unless they are limited to certain events, not including waiver of the liability shield. On the other hand, given the potentially serious consequences of waiver of the liability shield, a strong argument may be made that unanimity should be required in the absence of a contrary explicit agreement on the vote necessary for waiver.

§ 3.06   NONRECOURSE DEBTS

LLP provisions do not prevent LLP partners from contracting for nonrecourse debts just as they could prior to the adoption of LLP provisions (*see* text at note 4, above). Partners may thereby reduce or eliminate their personal liability for "contract-like" debts that is imposed under most LLP provisions. For example, LLPs could agree with lessors that the partnership's office lease is enforceable against the partnership assets only and not against the partners individually.

§ 3.07   VEIL-PIERCING RULES

Even if the LLP has complied with all statutory formalities, courts may impose liability on LLP partners for the firm's debts, just as they have on corporate

---

[56] Despite this potential similarity, the Comment to R.U.P.A. § 306 asserts that such contribution liability can be reconciled with the liability shield.

[57] *See* U.P.A. § 18(h); R.U.P.A. § 401(j); Bromberg & Ribstein, § 6.03.

shareholders, under a "piercing the veil" theory.[58] The many corporate cases involve a variety of factors. It is often difficult to determine from courts' opinions which factors are the most important.[59] These cases tend to hold shareholders liable mainly to voluntary creditors where misleading as to the nature of the firm or the amount of its capitalization may be relevant.[60] One prominent commentator also argues that veil-piercing is used largely to police siphoning of funds that might constitute or border on fraudulent conveyances.[61] In general, to the extent that veil-piercing is based on such activities as misrepresentation or other fraud on creditors it may be difficult to distinguish from direct liability for fraud.

The important question for present purposes is whether corporate-type veil-piercing rules apply to LLPs.[62] As shown in Table 3-1, a few statutes explicitly provide for application of corporate law standards regarding veil-piercing. But there are at least three inherent differences between LLPs and corporations that justify the application of different rules in the two contexts. First, inadequate capitalization raises different questions in LLPs than in corporations. A professional firm that has not engaged in misleading or siphoning of funds may be considered inadequately capitalized if it has not maintained adequate means of

---

[58] Skidmore Energy, Inc. v. KPMG LLP, 2004 WL 3019097 (N.D. Tex. Dec. 28, 2004) held under Texas law that the alter ego theory was inapplicable to liability of a U.S. accounting firm organized as an LLP for the debts of a Moroccan member of the international organization. The court cited a limited partnership case holding that alter ego theories are inapplicable to partnerships because they are unnecessary. This reasoning is appropriate for a limited partnership because the statutory "control rule" that applies to that entity reduces the need for common law liability. However, there is no equivalent rule for LLPs. In any event, the issue of liability of an LLP for debts incurred by a related but arguably separate legal entity differs from that of whether members of an LLP are liable for the firm's debts because the LLP shield itself is not intended to apply in this situation.

For other cases involving liability among branches of international accounting firms, see In re Parmalat Securities Litigation, 2005 WL 1670246 (S.D.N.Y. July 18, 2005) and In re Parmalat Securities Litigation, 2005 WL 1527674 (S.D.N.Y. June 28, 2005). These cases involved the spectacular multibillion dollar collapse of the Italian company, Parmalat. The court allowed claims to proceed on agency and joint venture grounds against the international parents of auditing firms for securities fraud and alleged misconduct by the Italian arms of the auditing firms, but denied liability against the U.S. arms of the firms.

[59] For analyses of the cases, see Hackney & Benson, Shareholder Liability for Inadequate Capitalization, 43 U. Pitt. L. Rev 837 (1982); Krendl & Krendl, Piercing the Corporate Veil: Focusing the Inquiry, 55 Den. L.J. 1 (1978); Hamilton, The Corporate Entity, 49 Tex. L. Rev. 979 (1971).

[60] See Thompson, Piercing the Corporate Veil: An Empirical Study, 76 Cornell L. Rev. 1036 (1991) (surveying 1,500 veil-piercing cases, and finding, among other things, that the veil was pierced in only 70 tort cases altogether, of which more than two-thirds involved corporate shareholders).

[61] See Clark, The Duties of the Corporate Debtor to its Creditors, 90 Harv. L. Rev. 505 (1977).

[62] Some courts have applied corporate-type veil-piercing rules to LLPs. See, e.g., Svenningsen v. Corbin, 52 Conn. L. Rptr. 300 (Conn. Super. Ct. July 11, 2011). Nevertheless, a commentator recently observed, "There are . . . virtually no cases in which limited liability partners are held liable on a veil-piercing theory." Mark J. Loewenstein, Veil-Piercing to Non-Owners: A Practical and Theoretical Inquiry, 41 Seton Hall L. Rev. 839, 839 n.5 (2011).

meeting predictable malpractice claims. As discussed above in Section 2.06, some LLP statutes provide for specific insurance or bonding requirements. Even if the statutory minimum insurance proves inadequate for a particular LLP, legislatures arguably intend that compliance with the minimum is enough.[63] Conversely, if the firm does not maintain insurance that is either required by statute or that is customary in the industry, this may support liability under an inadequate capitalization theory. Veil-piercing liability for withdrawal of funds from the firm also may pose special problems in LLPs. Restrictions on distributions in professional LLPs may be burdensome in light of partners' needs to distribute income pursuant to compensation agreements and to meet partners' tax liabilities. On the other hand, while these problems may justify not imposing specific statutory restrictions on distributions (*see* Section 4.04(d), below), courts may use more flexible common law veil-piercing doctrine to substitute for the absence of statutory restrictions on distributions.[64]

Second, LLPs arguably are distinguishable from corporations with regard to the failure to observe formalities. LLP statutes do not provide for formalities such as directors' and owners' meetings as do corporate and some LLC statutes. It follows that a creditor will rarely be able to argue that a firm that called itself an "LLP" was run so informally that it gave the appearance of being something else. Indeed, the Colorado statute, which provides for application of corporate-type standards, also provides that the use of informal procedures is not alone a ground for piercing the veil.[65]

A third difference between LLPs and corporations with regard to veil-piercing is that under many statutes LLPs have limited liability only in tort cases. In these cases, some reasons why courts pierce the veil may not be present — that is, creditors cannot be misled about the nature of the firm or its capital. Indeed, corporate veil-piercing in tort cases has been very rare.[66]

---

[63] *See* Walkovszky v. Carlton, 18 N.Y.2d 414, 223 N.E.2d 6, 276 N.Y.S.2d 585 (1966) (corporate veil-piercing case in which court, in refusing to pierce veil for inadequate capitalization, cited defendant's compliance with statutory insurance requirement).

[64] *See* Dzienkowski, supra note 26, at 985:

> [P]artners must be careful not to undercapitalize their law firms. A limited liability law firm with a policy of distributing firm assets to the partners each month may be vulnerable to an argument by plaintiffs' lawyers that the partners should contribute assets back to the entity for the purposes of the litigation. Some firms may argue that the minimum insurance requirements or the minimum capital fund requirements should preclude arguments for piercing the LLP veil. However, courts are likely to look at conduct of individual firms, taking into account circumstances surrounding the withdrawal of funds from the LLP. Courts are more likely to uphold a regular distribution of assets occurring under a set policy than a last minute withdrawal of funds immediately before a malpractice verdict.

[65] *See* Colo. Rev. Stat. § 7-64-306. This statute was applied in Middlemist v. BDO Seidman, LLP, 958 P.2d 486 (Colo. App. 1997).

[66] *See* Thompson, note 60, supra.

§ 3.08 ENFORCEMENT OF PARTNER
LIABILITY BY CREDITORS

General partners' personal liability may be enforced directly in suits by creditors, and indirectly through their contribution obligation. Both sets of rules are, of course, modified for LLPs. Direct actions are discussed in this section, while the next section discusses the contribution obligation.

(a) Suits Against Partners

Many LLP statutes provide that LLP partners may not be sued individually with respect to debts for which they have limited liability.[67] While the U.P.A. does not provide for suits against partners, R.U.P.A. does.[68] R.U.P.A. and the Prototype LLP Act provide that suits may not be brought against LLP partners for liabilities on account of which the partners' liability is limited by the LLP provisions.[69] Note, however, that such provisions should not prevent partners from being sued where there are fact questions about such matters as the partners' responsibility for supervision or about whether the liability arose while the shield was in place, which can only be determined through litigation. The statutes provide in varying terms that the partners cannot be sued to recover damages with respect to which their liability is limited. Thus, suit *can* be brought against the partner as long as it alleges a proper ground of recovery against the partner.

(b) Exhaustion of Remedies: Partners' Vicarious Liability

Under state law, creditors in many cases must exhaust partnership assets before proceeding against individual partners.[70] Plaintiffs traditionally must exhaust only in cases of joint — that is, contract-type — liabilities[71] and not where

---

[67] *See* Table 3-1.

[68] R.U.P.A. § 307.

[69] *See* R.U.P.A. § 307(f); Prototype LLP Act § 306(d).

[70] *See* Bromberg & Ribstein, § 5.08(d). Exhaustion does not necessarily require plaintiff actually to collect partnership assets, but only to attempt to collect or to show that the partnership cannot satisfy the judgment. *See* U.S. Trust Co. of New York v. Bamco 18, 183 A.D.2d 549, 585 N.Y.S.2d 186 (1992) (plaintiff must only show partnership cannot or will not satisfy the judgment); British Land (B of C), Inc. v. 43 West 61st St. Assocs., 177 A.D.2d 458, 576 N.Y.S.2d 554 (1991), *leave to appeal dismissed*, 79 N.Y.2d 1040, 584 N.Y.S.2d 449, 594 N.E.2d 943 (1992) (plaintiff's obligation satisfied by the six executions it delivered to the sheriff).

[71] *See* Tilcon Capaldi, Inc. v. Feldman, 249 F.3d 54, 63 (1st Cir. 2001) (R.I. law); Moseley, Hallgarten, Estabrook & Weeden, Inc. v. Ellis, 849 F.2d 264, 271 (7th Cir. 1988) (Ill. law); Wisnouse v. Telsey, 367 F. Supp. 855, 858-60 (S.D.N.Y. 1973) (N.Y. law); In re Stanfield, 6 B.R. 265, 267 (Bankr. D. Nev. 1980) (Nev. law); In re Peck, 206 N.Y. 55, 99 N.E. 258 (1912); Ira Rubin, P.C. v. A. C. Kluger & Co., 86 Misc. 2d 1014, 383 N.Y.S.2d 828, 831 (Civ. Ct. 1976); Diamond Nat'l. Corp. v. Thunderbird Hotel, Inc., 85 Nev. 271, 454 P.2d 13, 15 (1969); Arbor Village Condo.

liability for partnership obligations is joint and several.[72] Several states have modified the U.P.A. to prescribe joint and several liability of partners for all partnership obligations, including those based on contract as well as those based on tort.[73] Some courts apparently have recognized a general exhaustion requirement,[74] particularly where the applicable statute lets plaintiffs sue partnerships in the firm name along with some or all the partners.[75] The spread of

---

Ass'n v. Arbor Vill. Ltd., L.P., 95 Ohio App. 3d 499, 642 N.E.2d 1124 (Ohio App. 1994). U.P.A. § 15(b) makes partners jointly liable for "debts and obligations of the partnership" other than those specified in U.P.A. §§ 13 (wrongful acts, e.g., torts) and 14 (breaches of trust), for which the liability is joint and several by U.P.A. § 15(a). The obligations for which U.P.A. § 15 creates joint liability include contracts and the obligations to perform them. See Hartford Fin. Sys., Inc. v. Florida Software Servs., Inc., 550 F. Supp. 1079, 1088 (D. Me. 1982) (Maine law), *appeal dismissed*, 712 F.2d 724 (1st Cir. 1983) (obligation to arbitrate pursuant to agreement); Bank of Commerce v. DeSantis, 114 Misc. 2d 491, 451 N.Y.S.2d 974, 978 (Civ. Ct. 1982).

[72] See Foster v. Daon Corp., 713 F.2d 149, 151 (5th Cir. 1983) (Tex. law) (with joint and several liability, "plaintiff has a direct right of action against [a partner] for enforcement of this obligation, without the necessity of first proceeding against the partnership"); In re Kelsey, 6 B.R. 114, 118-19 (Bankr. S.D. Tex. 1980) (Tex. law); Catalina Mortg. Co. v. Monier, 800 P.2d 574 (Ariz. en banc 1990) (on certified question: limited partnership's creditor may obtain judgment against general partner and reach his assets prior to exhaustion of partnership assets; limited partnership was in bankruptcy reorganization); Phillips v. Cook, 239 Md. 215, 210 A.2d 743, 746–747 (1965); Fowler Commc'n. Co. v. Charles Land & Co., 248 S.W. 314 (Tex. Comm. App., adopted 1923). See Martinez v. Koelling, 228 Neb. 1, 421 N.W.2d 1, 2–3 (1988) (distinguishing joint from joint and several liability). For general discussions of exhaustion, see § 8.306, infra; Bromberg & Ribstein, § 5.08(d)–(h).

[73] See, e.g., Ga. Code Ann. § 14-8-15; N.C. Gen. Stat. § 59-45.

[74] See National Hygienics, Inc. v. Southern Farm Bureau Life Ins. Co., 707 F.2d 183, 187 (5th Cir. 1983) (Miss. law; saying that a partner "is generally only personally liable after all the assets of the partnership have been exhausted" so that the fact that a partner protected himself by settling a partnership claim and obtaining a release of general partners was not notice to the claimant that the partner lacked authority); In re Norman, 32 B.R. 562, 565 (W.D. Mo. 1983) (saying that Missouri law "appears" to require exhaustion, so that a partner's liability for the debts of a solvent partnership were not noncontingent and therefore did not have to be counted toward the maximum allowed for a small businessperson bankruptcy filing under Bankruptcy Code (11 U.S.C.) ch. 13, §§ 1301 *et seq.*); Ohio Cas. Ins. Co. v. Harbor Ins. Co., 66 Cal. Rptr. 340, 346 (Ct. App. 1968) (holding that insurer of a joint venturer was entitled to recover from the insurer of the coventurer and of the joint venture the first insurer's contribution toward the settlement of a tort claim against the venture and the venturers; second insurance was an asset of the venture and was to be exhausted before resort to the first insurance, an individual asset of the first venturer). Courts also may stretch the definition of "joint" liability in order to impose an exhaustion requirement. In Arbor. Vill. Condo. Ass'n v. Arbor Vill. Ltd., L.P., 95 Ohio App. 3d 499, 642 N.E.2d 1124 (Ohio App. 1994), the court held that, where the partnership, through an agent, failed to disclose repairs in a condominium sale, it was a partnership breach of duty, not partner breach, under U.P.A. § 13, so that the creditor had to exhaust remedies.

[75] See Ill. Code Civ. Proc. § 2-411(b) (by implication from authorization of unsatisfied judgment creditor of partnership to enforce liability of a partner); Koppers Co. v. Mackie Roofing & Sheet Metal Works, 544 So. 2d 25, 26 (La. Ct. App. 1989) (by implication from La. Civ. Code arts. 2817 (partnership as principal obligor is primarily liable for its debts) and 737 (partners may not be sued unless partnership is joined)); Leger v. Townsend, 257 So. 2d 761, 763 (La. Ct. App. 1972); Security State Bank v. McCoy, 219 Neb. 132, 361 N.W.2d 514 (1985) (Neb. Rev. Stat. § 25-316 requires judgment against partnership and insufficiency of its assets before execution against

R.U.P.A. has accelerated this trend by imposing a conditional exhaustion requirement in all types of cases.[76]

The exhaustion requirement in state partnership law, where applicable, works together with both LLP provisions and with recent cases under federal bankruptcy law to block creditors' access to partners' assets. Several cases have enjoined creditor actions against nonbankrupt partners.[77] There is also some authority for automatically staying actions against non-bankrupt partners.[78] This authority may be reinforced by a R.U.P.A. provision that partners' contribution obligations are enforceable by "a person appointed by a court to represent creditors of a partnership."[79] This language suggests that the contribution obligation is property of the estate, and therefore that actions by the partnership's creditors against individual partners may be stayed under bankruptcy law.[80] Conversely, it has been held that where LLP partners had no obligation to contribute to their partnership's bankruptcy estate under the full-shield Massachusetts LLP statute, permitting the partnership's creditors to collect from non-debtor partners will not deplete the partnership's bankruptcy estate, thereby removing a basis for enjoining and releasing claims against such partners.[81]

---

individual assets); Horn's Crane Serv. v. Prior, 182 Neb. 94, 152 N.W.2d 421 (1967); Hall v. Oldfield, 117 Ohio St. 247, 158 N.E. 191, 192-93 (1927). For other cases reaching the same conclusion under firm-name statutes but without discussing whether the statute negates the exhaustion requirement, see Sargeant v. Grimes, 70 F.2d 121, 122 (10th Cir. 1934), *cert. denied*, 293 U.S. 568 (1934) (Colo. law); Heiden v. Beuttler, 11 F. Supp. 290, 291 (N.D. Iowa 1935) (Iowa law); Leach v. Milburn Wagon Co., 14 Neb. 106, 15 N.W. 232 (1883) (Iowa judgment creditor failed to show no partnership assets in Nebraska); Young v. Mayfield, 316 P.2d 162, 165 (Okla. 1957) (dictum); Fowler v. Brooks, 146 P.2d 304, 307, 308 (Okla. 1944).

[76] See R.U.P.A. § 307(d). Specifically, the Act would require an unsatisfied judgment against the partnership unless the partnership is bankrupt, the claimant and the partner have agreed that exhaustion is not necessary, or the court finds that partnership assets in the state are insufficient, that exhaustion is excessively burdensome, or that the court's inherent equitable powers are appropriately exercised to permit direct recovery against individual assets.

[77] See generally Buschman & Madden, The Power and Propriety of Bankruptcy Court Intervention in Actions Between Nondebtors, 47 Bus. Law. 913, 942 (1992) (noting entry of temporary injunctions against creditors' suits where the partners contribute to a reorganization plan); Glassman, Third-Party Injunctions in Partnership Bankruptcy Cases, 49 Bus. Law. 1081 (1994); Ribstein, The Illogic and Limits of Partners' Liability in Bankruptcy, 32 Wake Forest Law Review 31 (1997); Zaretsky, Co-Debtor Stays In Chapter 11 Bankruptcy, 73 Corn. L. Rev. 213, 254-59 (1988).

[78] See In re Litchfield, 135 Bankr. 797 (W.D.N.C. 1992). *But see* In re Hudgins, 153 B.R. 441 (E.D. Va. 1993) (reasoning that, despite the partner's apparent "rights" in specific partnership property under the U.P.A., these rights are insufficient to justify invoking the stay); Chase Bank of Ariz. v. Acosta, 880 P.2d 1109 (Ariz. App. 1994) (holding that a stay entered in a partnership bankruptcy does not bar a direct action against a partner); Macey & Kennedy, Partnership Bankruptcy and Reorganization: Proposals for Reform, 50 Bus. Law. 879, 912 (1995); Bromberg & Ribstein, § 5.08(i).

[79] R.U.P.A. § 807(f).

[80] See 11 U.S.C. § 362(a)(3).

[81] See In re Mahoney Hawkes, LLP, 289 B.R. 285 (Bankr. D. Mass. 2002).

Even in states that preserve the traditional distinction between joint and joint and several liability, the LLP provisions would preclude liability, and therefore direct suit, in the category of "tort-like" joint and several liability cases in which direct suit had been permitted without exhaustion. The state law rules requiring exhaustion in joint liability cases, coupled with bankruptcy rules that can bar direct suit against partners of bankrupt partnerships, could operate to bar direct suits to enforce the "contract-type" liability that is preserved by LLP provisions.[82]

Even if creditors are barred from suing partners directly on their vicarious liability, they have two other options. First, they could attempt to have the partners' liability characterized as direct rather than vicarious (*see* Section 3.08(c), below). Second, they might obtain recovery from the partnership, with contributions by individual partners (*see* Section 3.09, below).

(c) Exhaustion of Remedies: Partners' Direct Liability

The exhaustion requirement applies only to partners' vicarious liability for partnership debts, and not to partners' liability for their own debts, which might include liability for negligent participation in or failure to monitor wrongs of co-partners.[83]

§ 3.09 PARTNERS' DUTIES TO CONTRIBUTE TOWARD LOSSES

In general, partners must contribute on dissolution toward the satisfaction of partnership liabilities. This is an obligation among the partners, in contrast to the partners' liability directly to third parties. This inter-partner obligation may be modified for LLP partners to avoid the contribution obligation becoming a kind of end-run around the LLP liability shield. Issues concerning this modification are discussed in the following subsection.

---

[82] *See* Brackley & Voelkel Const., Inc. v. 3421 Causeway, Ltd., 712 So. 2d 716 (La. App. 1998) (applying Louisiana "discussion" (i.e., exhaustion) provisions to LLP in contract case under Louisiana partial-shield statute, although holding that discussion was waived because not specifically raised prior to answer or judgment by default).

[83] *See* §§ 3.02(b), 3.03, supra. This is made clear by R.U.P.A. § 307(d)(5) (§ 307(d)(2) of the Prototype LLP Act), which excuses exhaustion if "liability is imposed on the partner by law or contract independent of the existence of the partnership." *See* § 8.307, below.

(a)   Review of Relevant U.P.A. Provisions

LLP statutes commonly provide that partners do not have to contribute toward liabilities that are limited by the LLP provisions. For example, the original Delaware version of U.P.A. § 15 on which several LLP statutes were based provides that LLP partners are not liable "either directly or indirectly, by way of indemnification, contribution, assessment or otherwise. . . ."[84]

Some states (*see* Table 3-2), also make the following changes in the standard U.P.A. language (indicated by italics):

U.P.A. § 18(a): "Each partner shall be repaid his contributions, whether by way of capital or advances to the partnership property and share equally in the profits and surplus remaining after all liabilities, including those to partners, are satisfied; *except as provided in [U.P.A. § 15], each partner* must contribute towards the losses, whether of capital or otherwise, sustained by the partnership according to his share in the profits."[85]

U.P.A. § 34: "Where the dissolution is caused by the act, death or bankruptcy of a partner, each partner is liable to his co-partners for his share of any liability created by any partner acting for the partnership as if the partnership had not been dissolved unless . . . (3) *The liability is for a debt or obligation for which the partner is not liable as provided in [U.P.A. § 15].*"[86]

U.P.A. § 40: "In settling accounts between the partners after dissolution, the following rules shall be observed, subject to any agreement to the contrary: (1) The assets of the partnership are . . . (b) The contributions of the partners specified in clause (4) of this paragraph . . . (4) *Except as provided in [U.P.A. § 15]: (a) The partners shall contribute, as provided by section 18 (1) the amount necessary to satisfy the liabilities; and (b)* if any, but not all, of the partners are insolvent, or, not being subject to process, refuse to contribute, the other partners shall contribute their share of the liabilities, and, in the relative proportions in which they share the profits, the additional amount necessary to pay the liabilities."[87]

Inter-partner loss sharing under LLP provisions raises several questions that are covered in the following subsections. Subsections (b)–(g) discuss how the limitation on partners' vicarious liability to third parties applies in determining the partners' obligations among themselves to contribute toward partnership debts. Subsection (h) discusses the effect of the LLP liability limitation on partners' liability to their co-partners for their shares in the partnership.

---

[84] Del. Code Ann., tit. 6, § 1518(1), § 1515(b). This language has been incorporated into Delaware's version of R.U.P.A., Del. Code Ann., tit. 6, § 15-306(c).

[85] This language is from the original version of the Delaware statute, Del. Code Ann., tit. 6, § 1518(1).

[86] Del. Code Ann., tit. 6, § 1534.

[87] Del. Code Ann., tit. 6, § 1540.

(b) Effect of Liability Limitation on Contribution Obligations

As noted in subsection (a), LLP statutes commonly provide that partners' obligations to contribute toward the satisfaction of liabilities are subject to the LLP provisions limiting partners' individual liability to third parties. LLP members may be personally liable for "contract-type" claims, and under all statutes are personally liable for claims that arose before registration or while the firm was not an LLP for some other reason. It is not clear how to translate partners' nonliability for *particular* claims into nonliability for the deficit remaining after subtracting *all* liabilities from assets. This question is particularly important in light of the fact that, under exhaustion rules (*see* Section 3.08, above), creditors' claims are channeled first into the partnership rather than directed at particular partners. Suppose, for example, that an LLP has assets (not including partners' contribution obligations) of $50,000, $50,000 in "contract-type" debts to third parties for which partners are personally liable, and $50,000 for "tort-type" liabilities for which some partners are not individually liable under the LLP provisions. There are three main alternatives, assuming only the LLP is liable:[88] (1) Pay the "contract-type" claims in full out of partnership property, leaving neither partnership property nor partner contribution obligations for tort-type claims; (2) pay the tort claims in full out of partnership property and the contract-type claims out of partner contributions; or (3) prorate the $50,000 short-fall between contract-type and tort-type claims, so that partners would be personally liable for $25,000. The example could be complicated further by substituting pre-registration claims for "contract-type" claims, or by including both types of claims for which all partners are personally liable.

Partners' liability for these claims would be determined under the U.P.A.'s loss-sharing scheme. U.P.A. § 18(a) requires each partner to "contribute towards the losses, whether of capital or otherwise, sustained by the partnership according to his share in the profits." U.P.A. § 40(d) requires partners to contribute as provided by § 18(a) toward the payment of liabilities. Under U.P.A. § 40, loss-sharing is administered by making up a "pot" that includes both partnership property and partners' contributions necessary to pay partnership liabilities (subsection (a)). Liabilities are ranked beginning with liabilities owed to nonpartner creditors (subsection (b)). Assets are applied to payment of these liabilities in the order of, first, partnership property and, second, partners' contributions (subsection (c)).

LLP provisions based on the original Delaware statute change the U.P.A. by adding that partners are not liable "either *directly or indirectly*, by way of indemnification, contribution, assessment or otherwise . . ." with respect to claims for which their liability is limited. The problem is that U.P.A. § 15 relates to

---

[88] The question of what happens when individual partners are directly liable is discussed below in Section 3.09(d).

partners' liability for particular debts, while the partners' contribution obligations relate to the overall shortfall left after paying all of the liabilities. Thus, the original Delaware scheme does not make clear which creditors bear the shortfall. The question can be answered in one of two unsatisfactory ways—either by denying liability to creditors who have tort-type claims, or by forcing the partners to contribute on account of a deficit created by debts for which their personal liability was supposed to be limited. The problem is mitigated under statutes that provide that partners have limited liability for all types of debts (*see* Section 3.03, above). However, even under these statutes it would be necessary to allocate liabilities that were, and were not, incurred while the partnership was an LLP.

In general, the statutes should be clarified along lines that compromise the objectives of paying claims and of insulating partners from liabilities by providing for alternative (3), above — proration of partners' contribution obligations. However, partners would still have an incentive to exhaust partnership assets by paying contract claims prior to dissolution in order to avoid having to pay these claims out of their own pockets. Perhaps the best solution is to rely on creditors' ability to protect themselves by contract, and the bankruptcy court's ability to characterize these payments as voidable preferences if they were paid within 90 days of insolvency.[89]

(c) Effect of Liability Limitation on Indemnification

The statutory provisions discussed above deal explicitly only with the partners' *contribution* liability—that is, the liability of individual partners to their co-partners on account of partnership losses. However, the Delaware-type of statute indicates that it affects more than just contribution obligations by providing that a partner is not liable "either directly or indirectly, by way of indemnification, contribution, assessment or otherwise. . . ."[90]

LLP provisions probably do not affect "indemnification" or "assessment." Indemnification refers to the partners' rights against the *partnership* on account of liabilities paid by the partners[91] or the partnership's rights against a wrong-doing partner (*see* Section 4.04(c), below). Thus, indemnification does not relate directly to partnership creditors' rights against partners. Not surprisingly, therefore, most statutes do not adjust indemnification rights to take account of the liability shield. Some statutes provide that an indemnification obligation shall not

---

[89] *See* Bankruptcy Code § 547 (11 U.S.C.). Note that the partners may be able to avoid this rule by paying the contract claims while tort claims were merely potential or pending and long before bankruptcy.

[90] Del. Code Ann., tit. 6, § 1515(b); tit. 6, § 15-306(c).

[91] *See* Ohlendorf v. Feinstein, 697 S.W.2d 553 (Mo. App. 1985) (partner cannot be held individually liable for attorneys' fees); Bromberg & Ribstein, § 6.02(f).

require a partner to make a payment inconsistent with the liability shield.[92] This probably refers to the indirect effect of indemnification in triggering a partner's contribution obligation discussed below.

Partners' rights to indemnification against the partnership probably will arise only in connection with partners' direct personal liability for their own wrongdoing.[93] Partners normally must contribute toward the firm's liabilities only after creditors have exhausted their remedies against the partnership (*see* Section 3.08, above), by which time any action by the partners against the firm is likely to be pointless. Thus, it is unlikely in this situation that partners will have made a payment for which they seek indemnification.

Assuming the firm must indemnify a partner, this triggers a contribution obligation when the partnership's liabilities, including its indemnification liability, exceed its assets apart from partners' contributions. The question in this situation is whether the partners are liable for a deficit that arises in part when the partnership indemnifies a partner on account of a claim for which the partners' liability is supposed to be limited under the statute. The partners might be liable to a partner seeking indemnification under the express terms of the partnership agreement (*see* Section 2.09(d), above, and Section 4.04(d), below). They may also be liable under the statute because, although the claim that gave rise to the indemnification is a tort-type claim for which liability is limited, the indemnification liability itself is in the nature of a contract claim for which liability is not limited under some statutes. The better approach would be for the indemnification to trigger a contribution obligation in such a situation only under the proration approach discussed above in Section 3.09(b).[94] Of course this issue does not arise when the shield applies to both contract and tort-type claims.

An "assessment" is a contractual obligation owed by an individual partner. Since LLP statutes are intended to undo only *statutory* liability and not liability created under contracts among the partners, the partners should be able to agree to assess LLP partners for partnership liabilities even if the partners are not individually liable for these obligations under the LLP statute. Nor should LLP registration affect a provision for assessment in the existing partnership agreement

---

[92] *See* the Delaware and New York provisions noted in Table 3-2 and the discussion of the New York statute in § 3.09(h), nn. 112–114, infra. The original California LLP provision in effect takes account of the liability shield by providing that the partnership must indemnify only to the extent of its assets. Cal. Corp. Code § 15018(b). This provision is not included in the analogous section of the California version of R.U.P.A., Cal. Corp. Code § 16401.

[93] Partners may have a right of indemnification against the firm despite their wrongdoing where they are merely negligent or the statute imposes liability even on non-negligent partners. *See* § 4.04(b), infra.

[94] The same analysis also should apply if an innocent partner voluntarily pays a tort-type claim for which his liability is limited under the statute. This situation is likely to be rare, since partners could easily defend against such actions based on the statute. Indeed, such a "voluntary" payment is most likely to be made in settlement of a claim in which the partner's direct liability is at issue.

(*see* Section 4.04(b), below). Even if the statute purports to prohibit such contracts, the partners could accomplish similar results by, for example, reducing partners' compensation. There is no policy reason why the partners should be forced to resort to such indirect means of allocating responsibility within the firm. However, like indemnification, an assessment liability among the partners should not create a liability to creditors on account of a claim for which liability is otherwise limited under the statute.

(d)   *Contributions by Wrongdoing Partners*

As discussed above in Section 3.04, partners may be held liable on the ground that they monitored, supervised, or were otherwise involved in the wrong. The question in this situation is whether these partners' liability is only to third parties or whether it affects their contribution obligations. The partners' direct liability for their own wrong arguably should be distinguished from their obligation to contribute toward partnership losses. Thus, although creditors could recover the full amount of the liability from wrongdoing partners, they cannot in this way recover indirectly from wrongdoing partners by contribution.

On the other hand, since original-Delaware-type statutes limit partners' contribution obligations only to the extent their liability is limited (*see* Section 3.08(b), above), it arguably follows that wrongdoing partners do have contribution obligations. If so, it would be necessary to determine the deficit for which these partners are liable.[95] It is not clear how this amount would be calculated. The calculation might be made in a manner similar to the allocation among all the partners of limited liability and personal liability claims—by determining the proportion of each category of claims in the total and dividing this amount among the wrongdoing partners.

Even if wrongdoing partners do not have contribution obligations under the partnership statute, they may have a duty to indemnify their co-partners (*see* Section 4.04(b), below) or to contribute as joint tortfeasors under general tort law.

---

[95] An analogous problem is involved when a partnership deficit must be allocated among partners who were such when the liability was incurred and those who entered later and therefore are not personally liable under U.P.A. §§ 17 and 41(7), discussed in Bromberg & Ribstein, § 7.18. *See* In re CS Assocs., 160 B.R. 899 (E.D. Pa. 1993) (Pa. law; general partner of limited partnership is not "personally liable" under 11 U.S.C. § 723 for deficiency to bankrupt estate for debt arising before admission); In re Miramar Mall Ltd. P'ship, 152 B.R. 631 (S.D. Cal. 1993) (based on U.P.A. § 17, general partner of limited partnership not liable for deficiency under Bankruptcy Code § 723(a) (11 U.S.C.) for claims arising before the partner became a general partner).

(e) *Effect of Liability Limitation on Duty to Contribute Toward Post-dissolution Debts*

The original-Delaware-type provisions limit partners' obligations to contribute not only toward pre-dissolution claims, but also toward claims incurred after dissolution. This is the effect of revising U.P.A. § 34 to provide that a partner is not liable for his share of post-dissolution debt if the debt is one for which the partner is not liable under the LLP limitation, whether or not the acting partner acted with knowledge or notice of the dissolution (*see* Section 3.09(a), above). Unlike the limitation in § 40, the effect of this provision in terms of its relation to the liability limitation is clear, since it is applied to specific liabilities rather than to the liabilities as a whole.

(f) *R.U.P.A. Provisions*

R.U.P.A., unlike the U.P.A., does not provide explicitly for contribution by partners to the payment of *liabilities*. On dissolution, the partner is required to contribute "an amount equal to any excess of the charges over the credits in the partner's account"[96]— that is, toward the payment of partnership losses. Where partners fail to contribute, the other partners must contribute in proportion to their loss share toward satisfaction of partnership obligations.[97]

The Prototype and some other statutes listed in Table 3-2 provide that the contribution obligation is limited to an amount "that is attributable to an obligation for which the partner is liable under § 306." These statutes also provide that, when partners fail or are not obligated to contribute, each partner must contribute in the proportion in which such partner shares losses any additional amounts necessary to satisfy partnership contributions for which such partner is liable.

These provisions do not fully solve the problem of adapting R.U.P.A.'s contribution obligations for LLPs. It is not clear how a general loss is "attributable" to a specific obligation for which the partner's liability is limited. In particular, as under the U.P.A., questions will arise as to whether liabilities for which partners are vicariously liable may be paid first, leaving no partnership assets to pay claims for which the partners have no vicarious liability (*see* Section 3.11, below). Nor is the ambiguity resolved by R.U.P.A.-based statutes that require partner contributions "except as provided" in the liability shield.[98]

---

[96] R.U.P.A. § 807(b).

[97] R.U.P.A. § 807(c).

[98] *See* Table 3-2. Cal. Corp. Code § 16807(b) is even more ambiguous, since it simply provides that the contribution obligation is "except for registered limited liability partnerships and foreign limited liability partnerships."

This simply places the burden on a bankruptcy or other court to determine how to adjust the partners' contribution obligation.

The LLP amendments to R.U.P.A. exclude from the calculation of a partner's obligation to contribute to the excess of charges over credits "charges attributable to an obligation for which the partner is not personally liable under Section 306."[99] This eliminates some of the ambiguity under the Prototype because, rather than attempting to determine whether a loss is attributed to shielded debts, the deficit is calculated for each partner by excluding particular shielded debts. It is not clear how much of a *partnership* debt should be attributed respectively to shielded and unshielded *partners*. This could be resolved by allocating debts to partners based on their loss-sharing percentages. Of course, as under the Prototype and the U.P.A., this provision would still let the partnership pay unshielded debts in order to minimize partners' individual exposure.

R.U.P.A. also provides for charging a partner's account for "the partner's share of the partnership losses"[100] and that a partner is "chargeable with a share of the partnership losses...."[101] R.U.P.A. and the Prototype Act make no alteration in the basic loss-sharing provision. This is appropriate, since R.U.P.A. § 401(a)(2) and (b) and equivalent provisions in R.U.P.A.-based statutes, unlike the loss sharing provision in the U.P.A., refer to the ongoing crediting and charging of partners' accounts. There is no reason why, despite the liability shield, a partner's capital account may not be diminished by partnership losses in a particular year. Exempt liabilities need to be distinguished only to the extent that they would produce a contribution obligation.[102] Thus, the R.U.P.A. commentary to § 401 confuses the issue by asserting that "a partner's obligation to contribute to a partnership's losses beyond previously agreed contributions is limited to the partner's share of partnership obligations for which that partner is personally liable under Section 306"[103] without making clear this difference between the contribution liability under § 807 and charging partner accounts under § 401. A few statutes based on R.U.P.A. go even further by altering their black letter to provide that the charging of partnership losses under section 401 is subject to the liability shield.[104] These provisions should be interpreted to refer only to partners' contribution obligations on dissolution and winding up. This point could be clarified by providing in R.U.P.A. § 401 that a partner is liable on

---

[99] R.U.P.A. § 807(b).

[100] R.U.P.A. § 401(a)(2).

[101] R.U.P.A. § 401(B).

[102] There is a further question whether there is any need for such a provision on the charging of partner accounts beyond simply a general provision, like R.U.L.P.A. § 503, which generally allocates profits and losses.

[103] R.U.P.A. § 401, cmt.

[104] *See* Table 3-2.

account of an excess of charges over credits in the account only to the extent provided for in R.U.P.A. § 807.[105]

The Prototype makes a change in the default indemnification provision in R.U.P.A. § 401 by making the indemnification right subject to the following proviso:

> . . . provided, however, no partner in a registered limited liability partnership shall be required as a consequence of such indemnification to make any payment for the partnership to any other partners to the extent that such payment would be inconsistent with [the liability limitation in § 306].[106]

As under the U.P.A.-based statutes discussed above in Section 3.09(c), this proviso is probably unnecessary because indemnification technically relates only to the partnership's liability rather than to that of the individual partners. But the proviso does help to clarify that, where the indemnification is on account of a claim for which the partners have limited liability, the liability limitation should carry over to any contribution liability that is triggered by the indemnification. Despite this clarification, however, the uncertainty discussed above in Section 3.09(c) remains as to how the resulting contribution liability would be calculated when it results from a combination of shielded and unshielded claims.

(g)   Enforcement of Contribution Obligations in Bankruptcy

The most important context for application of the principles discussed in this section is in bankruptcy court, since contribution obligations matter most for insolvent firms. In bankruptcy, the trustee exercises creditors' rights under state law, including the right to enforce the contribution obligations of a bankrupt partnership.[107] Thus, it is significant that the Bankruptcy Code has been amended to provide explicitly for LLPs. The Code now provides that partners are liable for deficiencies only "to the extent that under applicable nonbankruptcy law such general partner is personally liable for such deficiency."[108] The legislative com-

---

[105] This is so provided in W. Va. Code § 47B-4-1(b). The same statute adds that partners may be personally liable on account of liabilities charged to their accounts only to the extent that the liabilities are unshielded. W. Va. Code § 47B-4-1(1)(b). This added provision is probably unnecessary given the cross-reference to the dissolution distribution section, which cross-references the shield provision. However, the additional language may be useful since it does tend to eliminate any possible doubt about the relationship between the shield and the charging of liabilities to the partners' accounts.

[106] Prototype LLP Act § 401(c).

[107] See U.P.A. § 40(e); R.U.P.A. § 807(f).

[108] Bankruptcy Code § 723(a) (11 U.S.C.). See In re Hoover WSCR Assocs. Ltd., 268 B.R. 227 (Bankr. C.D. Cal. 2001) (trustee has no claim under § 723 against general partner who is not

ment to this section says that "a partner of a registered limited liability partnership would only be liable in bankruptcy to the extent a partner would be personally liable for a deficiency according to the registered limited liability statute under which the partnership was formed."[109] However, the "black letter" refers only to "*applicable* nonbankruptcy law (emphasis added)," which presumably refers to whatever law would be applied under state choice-of-law principles (*see* Chapter 6).

As discussed above in Section 3.09(f), state partnership law leaves unclear how particular partnership debts are allocated among shielded and unshielded partners. This is complicated by the additional problem of dividing whatever amounts are recovered from partners among various creditors. The National Bankruptcy Review Commission would continue the basic principle of the Code provision discussed immediately above and clarify that recoveries from partners pay deficiencies only on claims for which the partners are personally liable under applicable nonbankruptcy law.[110] The Commission recommends dividing liabilities among partnership creditors in proportion to partners' liability to each creditor under state law.[111]

(h)   Partners' Liability for Co-partners' Shares

The discussion above in this Section shows that LLP statutes in effect protect partners from being held liable "indirectly" to third parties (to use the language in many statutes) via their obligations among themselves to contribute toward partnership debts. There is a separate issue as to whether LLP statutes limit debts arising solely among the partners relating to their liability for repayment of capital and other losses. Of course these partnership losses may be attributable to some extent to debts to third parties that are shielded from the LLP liability limitation. However, broadly shielding the partners from all inter-partner obligations would seem to be inconsistent with the purpose of the LLP liability limitation, which is to limit partners' liabilities to creditors rather than to generally reallocate the burden of partnership losses among the partners.

Consistent with this analysis, it has been held that the LLP liability limitation under the New York statute, which included the "directly or indirectly" language discussed above, does not limit partners' individual liability to account

---

personally liable under state law because creditor had not obtained judgment against partner before state statute of limitations had run).

[109] *See* 140 Cong. Rec. 10752-01, 10768, Oct. 4, 1994.

[110] *See* Bankruptcy: The Next Twenty Years, National Bankruptcy Review Commission Final Report (October 20, 1997), Recommendation 2.3.9.

[111] *Id.*

to withdrawing partners for repayment of their partnership share.[112] New York trial and appellate courts held that defendants were not entitled to dismissal under New York's LLP liability shield, reasoning that this provision applies to debts to third parties and not to partners' duty to account to co-partners for partnership assets. (Although the plaintiff, as a former partner, was technically a creditor of the firm, the debt was owed him as a partner and therefore not subject to the liability shield.) The Court of Appeals observed that the LLP statute was a response to the savings and loan crisis of the 1980s, which threatened lawyers and accountants with massive personal liability to third parties. The shield was not intended to adjust partners' liabilities to each other. Although the LLP shield refers broadly to "any debts," the court noted that this language occurs in a provision that deals only with debts to third parties.[113] The court concluded that the parties have recourse to their agreement:

> Partners might agree, as among themselves, to limit the right to contribution or indemnification or to exclude it altogether. In this case, however, there was no written partnership agreement; therefore, the provisions of the Partnership Law govern.[114]

In short, the LLP liability shield does not extend to the allocation of ordinary business risks and responsibilities, which the partners can readily deal with in their partnership agreement.

It might seem odd that LLPs are treated differently from other limited liability firms such as LLCs and corporations where innocent members are not personally liable to former partners to make up shortfalls in partnership assets. But partnerships, including LLPs, fundamentally differ from these other firms because partnerships were designed to be personal-liability entities. Adding the LLP liability limitation thus takes care only of the particular problem of liability to third parties while leaving the rest of the statute intact.

---

[112] Ederer v. Gursky, 9 N.Y.3d 514, 881 N.E.2d 204, 851 N.Y.S.2d 108 (2007). *See also* Kuslansky v. Kuslansky, Robbins, Stechel & Cunningham, LLP, 50 A.D.3d 1100, 858 N.Y.S.2d 213 (2008) (same result, following *Ederer*). For an analysis of *Ederer*, see Ribstein, Ideoblog, LLP partners are liable to each other (Feb. 17, 2008), *available at* http://busmovie.typepad.com/ideoblog/2008/02/llp-partners-ar.html.

[113] 9 N.Y.3d at 524, 881 N.E.2d at 211, 851 N.Y.S.2d at 115.

[114] 9 N.Y.3d at 526, 881 N.E.2d at 212, 851 N.Y.S.2d at 116.

§ 3.10   LIABILITY OF PURPORTED PARTNERS

A firm that is not a partnership but that represents itself to third parties as such is treated as a partnership by estoppel under the U.P.A.[115] Such a firm is not an LLP because LLPs normally are defined as "partnerships," which includes only actual partnerships (*see* Section 2.07(c), above). However, one could be a partner by estoppel of a firm that is actually an LLP. Also, a firm that represents itself as an LLP could be a partnership by estoppel. This section considers the liability of the estoppel members in these two situations.

(a)   Liability of Estoppel Partner in LLP

A person may be represented to be a member of an actual LLP. If such a person is an estoppel partner, she might be held to have either the full liability of a general partner in a non-LLP general partnership or the liability of a general partner in an LLP, which may include personal liability for contract-type debts. One who is a partner by estoppel in an LLP arguably should have the same liability that an actual LLP partner would have, just as an estoppel partner of a non-LLP also would have liability comparable to that of a non-LLP member.[116]

Registrations normally need not name partners (*see* Section 2.03(b)(3), above, and Table 2-2). Statutes that require disclosure of the number of partners do so only as a way to compute the tax due from the partnership to the formation state. Accordingly, third parties should not be able to rely on the registrations as statements of current membership. This result is consistent with a Delaware provision that the inclusion of persons in filings cannot be used as evidence in determining whether such persons are partners.[117] It is also consistent with the provision in R.U.P.A. that "[a] person is not liable as a partner merely because the person is named by another in a statement of partnership authority."[118]

(b)   Liability of Estoppel Partner in LLP by Estoppel

As discussed above in Section 2.07(c), an LLP that has not complied with formalities could be an LLP by estoppel, though there are policy reasons contra,

---

[115] U.P.A. § 16. R.U.P.A. § 308 provides comparable rules for "purported partnerships."

[116] U.P.A. § 16 provides that, when a partnership liability results from a representation, the partner "is liable as though he were an actual member of the partnership." R.U.P.A. § 308(a) similarly provides that the purported partner is liable "as if the purported partner were a partner."

[117] Del. Code Ann., tit. 6, § 15-1001(h).

[118] R.U.P.A. § 308(c). R.U.P.A. § 303(b) does not require disclosure of partner names in the statement, but only of an agent who keeps a list of partners.

including protecting third parties from being misled and encouraging compliance with LLP provisions. If the firm's LLP status is not recognized, it would follow a fortiori that one who is only an estoppel partner in the firm should not be treated better than an actual partner. If, on the other hand, purported firms are held to be entitled to limited liability, one who is only an estoppel partner in the firm arguably should be treated the same as a purported partner in an actual LLP — the situation discussed above in Section 3.10(a).

The Montana statute, which is generally based on R.U.P.A., provides that the purported partner is liable only if he would have been personally liable "if the purported partner had been a partner."[119] This suggests that a purported partner is entitled to the LLP liability limitation even if the firm is not a partnership and therefore not an LLP.

§ 3.11   WHEN REGISTRATION MUST BE IN EFFECT

LLPs are usually continuations of vicarious-liability firms, and the underlying partnership business may continue despite a loss of registration. This raises issues about whether a registration applies to a debt that was arguably attributable to the period before or after the registration was in effect.[120]

(a)   Misconduct-based Claims

The LLP liability limitation in statutes that limit liability only for misconduct-type claims typically applies to "misconduct" committed while the partnership is an LLP. Thus, the liability limitation does not apply to misconduct committed before the registration.[121] This should be the case even if the injury occurs thereafter. This is consistent with the statutes' functions of informing third parties that

---

[119] Mont. Code Ann. § 35-10-308(1)(b).

[120] In Bastys v. Rothschild, 2000 WL 1810107 (S.D.N.Y. Nov. 21, 2000), plaintiff claimed that the wrong was incurred when the firm was not registered, so that partners were not insulated from liability under the New York statute providing protection "while such partnership is registered as a limited liability partnership." The court noted that plaintiff had not shown the firm's status at any relevant time, but that it did not need to reach the question because it was dismissing the claims on other grounds.

[121] See Griffin v. Fowler, 260 Ga. App. 443, 579 S.E.2d 848, n.1 (2003) (law partners had potential liability for plaintiff's claim based on co-partner's malpractice, fraud and breach of fiduciary duty based on evidence that defendant law firm performed legal services for plaintiff prior to registering as LLP). But see Parsells v. Manhattan Radiology Group, L.L.P., 255 F. Supp. 2d 1217 (D. Kan. 2003) (Kan. law, discussed in Section 3.04(b), note 46; rejecting plaintiff's argument that partners should be jointly and severally liable for employment discrimination that occurred prior to LLP registration).

the firm's liability is limited and, where relevant, providing insurance or asset segregation.[122] However, where the claim is by an involuntary tort victim and the firm's insurance or asset segregation is in effect for the claim, perhaps it should be enough that the registration is in effect when the partners are sued or a judgment is recovered (*see* Section 2.06, above).

The shield arguably should continue for misconduct that occurred while the firm was registered even if the firm's LLP status later ended because of failure to renew, report, or satisfy name or applicable insurance or asset segregation requirements. Statutory language applying the shield to acts committed while the firm is an LLP supports the argument that the liability limitation is fixed at the time of the misconduct. However, the typical statutory language also states that "a partner in a registered limited liability partnership is not liable. . . ."[123] This supports the argument that the liability limitation does not apply if the partnership is not an LLP (and therefore the defendant is not a partner in an LLP) at the time of suit, when the limitation is asserted.[124] The argument is particularly strong when the firm has lost its registration because the insurance or asset segregation required for LLP status is no longer in place (*see* Section 2.06(f), above). Partnerships that want sure protection should keep their LLP status intact.[125]

---

[122] R.U.P.A. § 306, cmt., provides an additional reason for using the time of misconduct—it prevents a partnership from registering to limit liability for misconduct it has already committed. It is not clear, however, why this is any worse than committing the misconduct knowing that the liability shield is already in place.

[123] This is based on the original Delaware LLP provision, Del. Code Ann. tit. 6, § 1515(b). The effect of other language, including that in R.U.P.A. § 306, is discussed below in Section 3.12(b). Delaware has now adopted language similar to that in R.U.P.A. *See* Del. Code Ann. tit. 6, § 306(c).

[124] Evanston Ins. Co. v. Chargois & Ernster, LLP, 2009 WL 490013 (S.D. Tex. Feb. 25, 2009) (Tex. law) held that the liability limitation did not apply where both the partnership's wrong and the suit occurred while the partnership was an LLP. After the partnership dissolved and the registration expired the partners carried on the business in a general partnership without a new registration. The trademark owner thereafter won a judgment for attorney and expert fees and sued the new general partnership. The court noted the defendants' argument that the wrong occurred while the firm was an LLP but, without citing the statutory language, held that the partners were liable because they continued the prior firm as general partners without discharging its debts.

[125] The Colorado statute clarifies this issue by providing that:

> A partner in a limited liability partnership does not become liable, directly or indirectly, for partnership obligations incurred, created, or assumed while the partnership was a limited liability partnership merely because the partnership ceases to be a limited liability partnership.

Colo. Rev. Stat. § 7-64-306. However, this provision still leaves the ambiguity inherent in the "merely because" proviso: It is not clear what will cause the partner to be liable after the partnership ceases to be an LLP.

(b)   Contract Liability: Post-registration Accrual

The scope of liability shields that apply to contracts as well as misconduct-based claims presents all of the questions discussed immediately above as well as some additional questions. The registration clearly does not apply to contract liabilities where the contract was entered into *and* the debt became due prior to the registration, or while the firm's registration had expired.[126]

It is not clear, however, whether the registration must be in effect both at the time of the initial contract and after later obligations relating to this contract accrue, such as when rent or interest is due or the partnership draws on a line of credit. Cases discussed below dealing with partners' post-dissolution liability on contracts entered into prior to dissolution and new partners' liability for pre-admission debts (*see* Section 3.12(a), below) are relevant here by analogy. As discussed below, some of these cases hold that new partners are not personally liable on pre-admission contracts even for debts that accrue after they are partners.[127] Under this approach, the parties' responsibility is fixed under the applicable rules as of the time of the contract. This is the relevant time for determining the parties' expectations.[128] More specifically, creditors usually set their credit terms based on information, including the existing partners' assets, as of the time the underlying obligations were created. Thus, if the firm is an LLP at the time of the contract, the liability limitation arguably should be binding for all payments that accrue after the contract regardless of the later status of the firm's registration. By the same token, where an obligation relating to a contract that was entered into prior to registration accrues after a firm becomes an LLP, creditors arguably could expect partners to continue to be personally liable for amounts accruing under the contract. Note, however, that the debt may have been so contingent at the time of the initial contract that the parties could be said to be entering into separate contracts with respect to later installments. This situation may not be clearly distinguishable from the one discussed in the next subsection

---

[126] *See* Apcar Inv. Partners VI, Ltd. v. Gaus, 161 S.W.3d 137 (Tex. App. 2005) (holding partners individually liable for lease executed three years after expiration of LLP registration where the firm failed to file renewals). Evanston Ins. Co. v. Dillard Dep't Stores, Inc., 602 F.3d 610 (5th Cir., 2010), held under Texas law that the shield was unavailable where the trademark infringing conduct occurred when the partnership was registered but the judgment was rendered after the firm was no longer an LLP. The court reasoned that the debt was not incurred under the statute until the judgment was rendered. The court noted that the subsection applying to partner misconduct showed that the Texas legislature knew how to focus on commission of the relevant conduct, and that this subsection was inapplicable to this case because it involved a partner's liability for another partner's misconduct. It is not clear that the misconduct subsection is as limited as the court assumed, although it is clearly aimed at individual partner misconduct rather than acts arguably committed by the firm as a whole — in this case, trademark infringement by the law firm's website.

[127] *See* note 148, infra.

[128] *See* R.U.P.A. § 306, cmt., noting that "the reasonable expectations of creditors and the partners are paramount."

involving a "new" post-registration debt owed to a creditor who dealt continuously with the firm before and after registration.

The statutory language does not clearly support either of these interpretations. Language that applies to "obligations or liabilities . . . which are incurred, created or assumed"[129] while the partnership was an LLP could be interpreted to refer *both* to the time of the creation of the underlying obligation (that is, the signing of the lease) *and* to the time period for which the rental liability was due. Thus, such liability shields arguably would apply to the entire amount of the rent due under a lease that was entered into while the partnership was an LLP *and* for any rental payments due while the partnership was an LLP, though *not* for rental payments due after the firm is no longer an LLP.

LLP statutes generally provide that the liability limitation applies to "a partner in a registered limited liability partnership."[130] As discussed immediately above, this language implies that after the registration is no longer valid the partner has vicarious liability even for debts that arose while the registration was effective. It arguably should follow that the partner has vicarious liability for later-accruing obligations. On the other hand, this result makes somewhat less sense than in the misconduct situation, since insurance or asset segregation is irrelevant to contract claims.

Some statutes provide further clarification on the relation-back issue. The Maryland statute provides that the liability shield does not affect

> (3) The liability of a partner for debts and obligations of the partnership, whether in contract or in tort, that arise from or relate to a contract made by the partnership prior to its registration as a limited liability partnership, unless the registration was consented to in writing by the party to the contract that is seeking to enforce the debt or obligation.[131]

The Minnesota statute attempts to clarify relation-back of debts for purposes of the LLP shield by providing:

> (1) All partnership debts and obligations of the partnership, whether in contract or in tort, that arise from or relate to a contract made by the partnership prior to its registration as a limited liability partnership, unless the registration was consented to in writing by the party to the contract that is seeking to enforce the debt or obligation and obligations under or relating to a note, contract, or other agreement are incurred when the note, contract, or other agreement is entered into.

---

[129] Statutes that use this language include the Prototype, Alaska, California, Georgia, New York, and Virginia. The Alabama statute uses "assumed." Full statutory citations to liability shield provisions are listed in Table 3-1.

[130] The effect of other language, including that in R.U.P.A., is discussed in § 3.12(b), infra.

[131] Md. Code Ann., Corps. & Ass'ns § 9A-307(d)(3).

(2) An amendment, modification, extension, or renewal of a note, contract, or other agreement does not affect the time at which a partnership debt or obligation under or relating to that note, contract, or other agreement is incurred, even as to a claim that relates to the subject matter of the amendment, modification, extension, or renewal.

This subsection does not affect any law, rule, or period pertaining to any statute of limitations or statute of repose.[132]

These provisions obviously leave some room for courts to determine which liabilities "arise from or relate to a contract made by the partnership prior to its registration" under the Maryland statute, or "arise from or relate to a note, contract, or other agreement" under the Minnesota statute. Also, despite the statutory language, a court may hold that an amendment or modification that creates, rather than merely relates to, an obligation may be the relevant time for determining the existence of the shield.

(c) *Contracts Entered into Following Registration*

Contracts entered into and other liabilities incurred after the registration normally should be covered by the registration.[133] However, just as a creditor expects the default liability rule that governs the initial contract to control, so a creditor with a linked series of contracts arguably would expect the liability to apply until she contracts otherwise. This raises the question whether these creditor expectations should control despite the fact that the post-transition dealings technically comprise a separate contract.

When a partnership dissolves and reforms as an LLC or corporation, creditors continue to have the benefit of personal liability unless they have actual or constructive notice of the change.[134] Although LLP statutes do not explicitly require such notice, similar rules arguably should apply in some situations where a partnership continues to deal with a creditor after registration in technically separate contracts. For trade creditors and others who deal with many buyers in relatively small transactions, it is probably more costly for creditors to monitor their

---

[132] Minn. Stat. § 323A.0306(d). This section does not contain all the language in the quote— subsection (d)(1) now says: "All partnership debts and obligations under or relating to a note, contract, or other agreement are incurred when the note, contract, or other agreement is entered into." Language similar to that in the Minnesota statute concerning "amendment, modification, extension or renewal" is included in the Comment to R.U.P.A. § 306.

[133] *See* Cordier v. Tkach, 2006 WL 2407051, Nonpublished/Noncitable (Cal. App. Aug. 22, 2006) (no vicarious liability for breach of retainer agreement where agreement was entered into and services performed after the firm's registration as an LLP).

[134] U.P.A. § 35 and R.U.P.A. § 804 both provide that a partner may bind the dissolved partnership for winding-up transactions and where the other party lacks notice of the change in entity.

customers' changes than for the customers to inform the creditors when changes occur. It may be enough to protect such creditors for the LLP simply to use the "LLP" designation in its post-registration dealings as the statutes require (*see* Section 2.05, above). Although LLP statutes do not necessarily condition the liability limitation on use of the designation in all of the firm's dealings, the courts might hold LLP partners liable under a veil-piercing theory (*see* Section 3.07, above) to relying post-registration creditors if the LLP does not use the required designation, or by stretching the pre-resignation accrual theory discussed above in Section 3.11(b) to extend to a course of dealings that began prior to registration.

Clients of professional firms have a particularly strong argument for notice based on the theory that all of their dealings arise out of a single engagement agreement that began prior to the registration. Thus, for example, law firm partners may be personally liable if their firm commits malpractice after registration in representing a client who engaged the firm prior to registration.[135] If the engagement is viewed as a pre-registration contract, the firm may have to fully inform the client of the nature and consequences of the registration and give it an opportunity to withdraw.[136] The duty to fully inform the client is based either on the professional's ethical obligation[137] or on a fiduciary duty to make affirmative disclosures. In any event, the attorney at least has an ethical duty to inform clients of the fact of the registration, breach of which may trigger possible professional sanctions.[138]

The extent of the duty to inform the client raises many questions. It is not clear, for example, whether the standard of informed consent for a law client is comparable to that for consenting to conflicts of interest, and whether the client's consent can be informed if the client is not advised by another lawyer. The information would probably have to include at least a description of the partners' former personal liability and a description of the matters (perhaps excluding current cases) that are subject to the liability limitation.[139]

---

[135] *See* Redman v. Walters, 88 Cal. App. 3d 448, 152 Cal. Rptr. 42 (1979) (holding law partner liable for malpractice that occurred prior to his dissociation where client did not receive notice of dissociation).

[136] The Maryland statute discussed in § 3.11(b), supra, provides that the registration does not affect liability under a prior contract unless "the registration was consented to in writing by the party to the contract that is seeking to enforce the debt or obligation." *Cf.* Beane v. Paulsen, 21 Cal. App. 4th 89, 26 Cal. Rptr. 2d 486 (1993) (requiring explicit client consent to release partner from liability for pre-dissolution malpractice).

[137] *See* Model Rule 1.8(h), discussed in § 7.04(b), infra (providing that "a lawyer shall not make an agreement prospectively limiting the lawyer's liability to a client for malpractice unless permitted by law and the client is independently represented in making the agreement").

[138] Use of the "LLP" or similar designation may be sufficient. *See* § 7.04, notes 120–122, infra.

[139] *See* Dzienkowski, supra note 26, at 985 n.82:

If the limited liability of partners and shareholders for torts of others in the firm were a contractual matter with individual clients, the client would need to have independent representation in

(d) Effect of Specific Contractual Provisions Dealing with
   Change of Organizational Form

A creditor or other third party who is dealing with a non-LLP partner may attempt to protect against the consequences of registration by means of a specific contract provision that deals with this eventuality. For example, the contract may provide for a continuation of partner liability notwithstanding the registration or for termination of the contract if the partnership registers as an LLP.[140] There is no reason why such a contract should not be enforced. However, it is important to keep in mind that a third party may not be protected by a general provision to the effect that contract rights cannot be enforced by a different "entity," since LLP statutes commonly provide that the post-registration firm is the same partnership or entity as it was prior to registration (*see* Section 4.08, below).

§ 3.12 EFFECT OF FUNDAMENTAL
CHANGES ON LLP STATUS

This section discusses the effect of dissociation, admission, dissolution, conversion, and merger on the partners' liability limitation.

(a) Dissociation, Dissolution, and Successor Firms
   Under the U.P.A.

This subsection discusses several issues related to the effect of the liability shield in connection with dissolution of a partnership under LLP provisions based on the U.P.A.

(1) Effect of Dissolution and Termination on
     LLP Status

Partner dissociation dissolves the partnership under U.P.A. § 31. A dissolved partnership continues for purposes of winding up under U.P.A. § 30. It arguably follows that the LLP registration continues to apply to the dissolved

---

entering into the arrangement. It is also foolish to believe that the majority of clients will understand what the designation at the end of the law firm name means in practice. Perhaps all states should have a requirement that law firms relying on the limited liability entity should have to disclose in plain language the effect of the state law on the client's ability to bring an action against the firm in the future.

[140] This option obviously does not help third parties with contracts that were entered into prior to the advent of the LLP.

partnership as long as the partnership maintains its registration. Partnerships should make sure by keeping their status intact until termination. Some statutes make clear that an LLP registration continues to apply through winding up and that the dissolved partnership may continue its LLP status after dissolution by continuing its filings through termination.[141] Other statutes make clear that an LLP registration continues to apply after dissolution.[142] On the completion of winding up the partnership terminates and, therefore, its LLP status probably ceases.

(2) Application of Liability Shield After Termination or Dissociation to Pre-existing Liabilities

Dissociation, dissolution, and termination do not terminate partners' liability for liabilities that arose prior to these events.[143] Even if the termination of a partnership or the dissociation of a partner from an LLP ends the application of the liability shield as to new debts, the old shield may continue to apply to pre-termination or pre-dissociation debts. This is similar to the issue regarding the effect of a lapsed registration discussed above in Section 3.11. The liability limitation probably applies to a post-termination claim that arises out of a contract or misconduct made or occurred while the LLP registration was in effect. As shown in Table 2-3, some statutes clarify that dissolution or termination does not affect a partner's liability for a debt incurred while the partnership was an LLP. The Pennsylvania statute goes a step further and completely insulates partners who withdraw from continuing partnerships even from liabilities for which they had no liability limitation prior to withdrawal.[144]

On the other hand, consistent with the discussion in Section 3.11, statutes applying the liability shield to "a partner in a registered limited liability partnership" imply that after termination or dissociation ends membership in an LLP, the shield no longer applies even to debts that arose while the registration was effective. An argument against this interpretation is that the U.P.A. provides that dissolution does not "discharge" any pre-existing obligation. It follows that the dissolution should not, in effect, create a liability that would not otherwise exist. Nevertheless, it may be wise for the firm to retain tail coverage on liability policies until limitations have run against possible claims.

As also discussed above in Section 3.11, even if the shield continues as to liabilities that are fully attributable to the pre-dissociation or pre-termination

---

[141] N.D. Cent. Code § 45-22-14 and -15 (dissolved partnership may continue its LLP status after dissolution by continuing its filings through termination).

[142] See Table 2-3.

[143] See U.P.A. § 36(1).

[144] Pa. Stat. Ann. tit. 15 Pa. C.S.A. § 8205. The withdrawing partner remains liable for his own misconduct. Also, the liability limitation is conditioned on the filing of a statement of withdrawal, and is lost if the partnership dissolves within a year after the dissociation unless the dissolution is by partner death or by retirement pursuant to a pre-existing retirement policy.

period, it might not apply to obligations such as rent, interest, or draws on lines of credit that arguably relate to the post-dissociation or post-termination period. Courts have held that partners are personally liable for continuing obligations on contracts entered into while they are partners even if they leave or the firm dissolves after the contract but before part of the obligation accrues.[145] These cases are supported by the principle that a creditor contracts only for the credit of the partners as of the time of the debt.[146] By a parity of reasoning, the liability shield also should be deemed to continue into effect for these claims.

Finally, it is not clear whether the liability shield continues to apply to dissociated partners as to debts for which such partners are liable as a result of partners' continuing apparent and actual authority to bind a dissolved firm under U.P.A. § 35. Since the liability is based on a continuation of the partner's status as such for certain purposes, by a parity of reasoning the shield also should continue to apply.

(3) Application of Liability Shield to New Partners of Continuing Partnerships

Partners who are admitted into LLPs certainly have the protection of the LLP liability shield as to debts that arise after their admission. They, like the

---

[145] *See* In re Judiciary Tower Assocs., 175 B.R. 796, 809 (D.D.C. 1994) (holding partner liable to contractor on contract entered into while defendant was a partner even if some work was performed after he left); Travers v. Rainey, 888 P.2d 372 (Colo. App. 1994) (dissolution does not necessarily end partner's liability on lease entered into prior to dissolution); Nolan Road West Ltd. v. PNC Realty Holding Corp., 248 Ga. App. 248, 544 S.E.2d 750 (2001) (former general partner in limited partnership liable for lease commission obligations that arose after withdrawal under a commission agreement signed while he was partner); Shea v. State Farm Fire & Cas. Co., 198 Ga. App. 790, 403 S.E.2d 81 (1991) (partners continued to be personally liable for worker compensation insurance premiums due after they incorporated and before they advised insurer of change in status); 8182 Maryland Assocs., Ltd. P'ship v. Sheehan, 14 S.W.3d 576 (Mo. 2000) (partner who signed lease was jointly and severally liable for all obligations under the lease and the liability was not terminated by partner's withdrawal); Bromberg & Ribstein, § 7.14 (discussing partners' continuing liability for obligations existing at time of dissolution). *See also* In re Securities Group 1980, 74 F.3d 1103 (11th Cir. 1996) (N.Y. law; holding limited partners to contribution obligations for lease claims although default did not occur under leases until after partners' withdrawal date). *But see* Oxford Mall Co. v. K & B Miss. Corp., 737 F. Supp. 962 (S.D. Miss. 1990) (Miss. law) (partners who left before breach of a lease contract not liable even if they were partners at the time of the making of the contract); Two Wall St. v. Anderson (N.Y. Sup. Ct. 1991), N.Y.L.J., at p.23, col. 1 (Aug. 15, 1991), *aff'd on other grounds*, 183 A.D.2d 490, 583 N.Y.S.2d 436 (1992) (partner who was such at time of lease but not at time of default not liable under lease that provided for joint and several liability of named partners, including the former partner, and their successors, but that did not provide for liability of partners who left prior to default).

[146] *See* In re Judiciary Tower Assocs., note 145, supra (reasoning that "[a] creditor contracting with a general partnership does so in the rightful expectation that all of the general partners stand behind that contract, and that a partner's withdrawal will not release that partner's responsibility on the contract").

other partners, may or may not be protected with respect to liabilities that are related to contracts that were entered into when no shield was in effect. Newly admitted partners may not need the LLP shield for these debts, since for "obligations of the partnership arising before his admission" their liability is in any event limited to the firm's assets.[147] Some cases have held that partners who entered a partnership after the date of a note were not liable for payments due later.[148] The creditors arguably did not take into account the credit of later-admitted partners. This is the same reasoning discussed above in Section 3.11, and supports carrying over a liability shield to liabilities that accrue on earlier obligations.

(4) Successor Partnerships

It is not clear if the liability shield continues to protect a successor *partnership* just as it does new and continuing *partners* as to liabilities that accrue on obligations entered into under a prior registration. This result is supported by the fact that, under the U.P.A., the liabilities of the old firm carry over to the new firm after a dissolution and sale of assets where the assets are sold to one or more people who were partners in the old partnership.[149] It arguably should follow that limitations on liability, including the effect on these liabilities of an LLP registration, also should continue as to the assets of the new firm.

On the other hand, since the successor is technically a new "entity," one might argue that a wholly new LLP registration — rather than an amendment that reflects the changes — is required to preserve LLP status. In other words, because of the creation of a new entity, the partner may no longer be in a "registered limited liability partnership," as most statutes require for application of the liability limitation. Some statutes eliminate this ambiguity by providing that the registration carries over to a successor partnership (*see* Table 2-3).[150]

---

[147] *See* U.P.A. § 17 and § 41(7).

[148] *See* Citizens Bank of Mass. v. Parham-Woodman Med. Assocs., 874 F. Supp. 705 (E.D. Va. 1995) (Va. law) (holding that new partners were not liable for disbursements made to the partnership pursuant to pre-existing construction loan agreement after the partners joined the partnership); 8182 Maryland Assocs., Ltd. P'ship v. Sheehan, 14 S.W.3d 576 (Mo. 2000) (former partners who were not partners at time of lease agreement and who withdrew before default were not personally liable for lease); Weisenberg v. Mount Royal Assocs., 666 A.2d 1103, 1108 (Pa. Super. 1995) (holding that partner who was not such at time note was executed not personally liable under the clear terms of U.P.A. § 17). *See also* Resolution Trust Corp. v. Teem P'ship, 835 F. Supp. 563 (D. Colo. 1993) (Colo. law; new partner not personally liable on pre-existing note, but liable only for increase in loan amount after he became partner, even if new note reaffirmed old one and partner accepted benefits; partner agreed to be liable only to extent of assessments by partnership).

[149] U.P.A. § 41; Bromberg & Ribstein, § 7.18.

[150] For an application of the New York provision, see Conolly v. Thuillez, 800 N.Y.S.2d 344 (2005) (holding that partners of successor partnership were not required to make additional filing). The U.P.A. provision applies only where the business is continued by one or more former partners, and not where it is continued by a new entity such as a corporation.

Even if the registration and shield apply to successors, there remains the question of what constitutes a successor. U.P.A. § 41 provides for transfer of liabilities to a "partnership. . . continuing the business" of the dissolved partnership only where there is continuation by one or more former partners, and not by a new entity such as a corporation.[151] Also, this provision implicitly contemplates a single firm that is continuing the firm intact. Thus, if the partners scatter to several firms the LLP registration probably does not follow all of these partners into their respective firms.[152] This result is particularly likely to follow under statutes such as the Alabama and Wisconsin statutes listed in Table 2-3, which provide that the registration carries over to successor firms only if the registered firm does not liquidate. Courts may hold, or legislators may provide, that the firm to which a majority of the partners or of the assets move is the successor firm. In any event, partners should file new registrations if they want to ensure continuation of their liability shield.

(b) Dissociation and Dissolution Under R.U.P.A.

This subsection discusses the special issues that arise in connection with dissociation and dissolution when LLP provisions are added to R.U.P.A.

(1) Effect of Dissociation, Dissolution, and Termination on LLP Status

R.U.P.A. differs from the U.P.A. in that a partner may dissociate from a R.U.P.A. partnership without causing dissolution.[153] It follows that an LLP registration continues in effect despite any partner dissociation.

R.U.P.A. further provides that LLP status remains effective regardless of changes in the partnership until it is canceled or revoked.[154] The Comment to this section states that this means that dissolution does not alter LLP status. However, this does not clearly follow from the black letter, which arguably applies only to changes in the facts stated in the statement of qualification rather than in the entity itself.

---

[151] Bromberg & Ribstein, § 7.19.

[152] *See* Hamilton, note 2, supra. *Cf.* Woo, The Business of Law, Wall St. J., Sept. 2, 1994, at B3, col. 4, noting that, on the dissolution of Lord, Day, & Lord, Barrett Smith, "because Morgan Lewis expects to hire Lord Day lawyers individually, subject to a vote of that firm's partners, it wouldn't have to pay the debts of the dissolving firm."

[153] R.U.P.A. §§ 601, 603.

[154] R.U.P.A. § 1001(d). Prototype LLP Act § 910(e) is similar.

When a partner is dissociated from a partnership, the partnership causes the dissociated partner's interest to be purchased for a buyout price.[155] The purchase of the dissociating partner's interest is an obligation of the LLP, not of the individual partners.[156]

(2) Application of Liability Shield After Termination or Dissociation to Pre-existing Liabilities

As under the U.P.A., a R.U.P.A. partner continues to be liable on debts that accrued prior to dissociation or termination of the firm. Indeed, R.U.P.A. § 703(a) arguably broadens this liability by providing that a partner is liable after dissociation for any "obligation" incurred prior to dissociation, and not merely a "liability" as under U.P.A. The liability shield under R.U.P.A. § 306(c) applies to "an obligation of a partnership incurred while the partnership is a limited liability partnership." Prototype LLP Act § 306(c) similarly provides that a partner is not liable as such for debts, obligations or liabilities "incurred, created or assumed by the partnership while the partnership is a registered limited partnership."[157] Both R.U.P.A. and the Prototype further clarify the scope of the shield by extending it to a "partner," and eliminating the extra language that requires the partner to be one in an LLP. The Virginia and Colorado statutes take this a step further by specifying that a "person" is not liable solely by reason of being a partner, so that the shield clearly applies to one who is no longer a partner.[158] Unlike the U.P.A.-based provisions, R.U.P.A. and the Prototype also make clear that the dissociated partner retains the protection of the LLP provisions for post-dissociation debts that are created by the continuing partners' post-dissociation apparent or actual authority.[159]

---

[155] R.U.P.A. § 701(a).

[156] Rappaport v. Gelfand, 197 Cal. App. 4th 1213, 129 Cal. Rptr. 3d 670, 683 (Cal. App. 2011).

[157] California's statute provides that this limitation on liability "shall not apply to claims based upon acts, errors, or omissions arising out of the rendering of professional limited liability partnership services of a registered limited liability partnership providing legal services unless that partnership has a currently effective certificate of registration issued by the State Bar." Cal. Corp. Code § 16306(f). The failure to register with the State Bar does not affect the rights or obligations of the partners among themselves or to the partnership. Davis v. Heubeck, 2012 WL 2165916 (Cal. App. June 14, 2012).

[158] Colo. St. § 7-64-306; Va. Code. § 50-73.96. It is not clear, however, if the shield applies to one who is no longer a partner, since the statute refers only to "being," and not "having been," a partner. *But see* Evanston Ins. Co. v. Chargois & Ernster, LLP, 2009 WL 490013 (S.D. Tex. Feb. 25, 2009) (Tex. law; discussed in § 3.11, n.124, supra; holding that partners who continued an LLP after dissolution and expiration of its registration were liable for a wrong and judgment that occurred while the partnership was an LLP because the partners continued the prior firm as general partners without discharging its debts).

[159] R.U.P.A. § 703(b); Prototype LLP Act § 703(b).

(3) Application of Liability Shield to New Partners of Continuing Partnerships

R.U.P.A., similar to the U.P.A., provides that a new partner is not personally liable for obligations "incurred before" his admission.[160] The application of the liability shield to new partners accordingly should be similar to that under the U.P.A.

(4) Successor Partnerships

R.U.P.A. does not provide explicitly for successor partnerships (*see* Section 8.703, below). As noted above, the firm does not necessarily dissolve when a partner dissociates. Even if the firm does dissolve, it continues until termination, as under the U.P.A. The problem arises when the entity winds up and terminates by selling its assets as a going concern. As discussed in Section 3.12(a)(4), under the U.P.A., the firm, and by implication its registration, would continue under certain circumstances — specifically, when continued by some of the initial partners. But under R.U.P.A. the firm may not continue in this situation, so that the new firm must file its own registration.

(c) *Conversion or Merger Under R.U.P.A. and the U.P.A.*

R.U.P.A. Article 9 provides for conversion and merger between limited and general partnerships (*see* Section 8.902 and Section 8.905, below). R.U.P.A. Sections 903 and 906 make the necessary adjustments for the LLP shield with respect to the effect of conversion and merger on partners' liabilities.

However, it may not be clear under R.U.P.A. what the effect would be of an LLP registration of a firm that is a party to a conversion or merger. Under R.U.P.A. § 904, a partnership that is a party to a conversion "is for all purposes the same entity that existed before the conversion." It seems to follow that the LLP registration would carry over to the converted firm, as where an LLP converts to a limited partnership. On the other hand, R.U.P.A. § 906 provides for the cessation of the "separate existence" of partnerships that are parties to mergers. This suggests that an LLP registration of a predecessor firm does not apply to the new firm. Although R.U.P.A. § 1001(d) provides that a partnership's registration continues until canceled or revoked, the registration arguably ends if the registered firm ceases to exist. It is not clear why conversions and mergers should have different effects in this regard. R.U.P.A. should clarify whether the LLP registration carries over in mergers and conversions.

---

[160] R.U.P.A. § 306(b). The formulation is slightly different from U.P.A. § 17, which refers to obligations "arising before" admission, but the Comment to § 306(b) says no change is intended.

Under the U.P.A., conversion and merger would essentially involve the dissolution and sale of the old firm to a new firm. Thus, the analysis in subsection (b), above, including the discussion of successor partnerships, would apply to mergers and conversions under the U.P.A.

§ 3.13   COMPARISONS WITH MEMBER LIABILITY IN OTHER BUSINESS ASSOCIATIONS

This section compares the liability of partners in an LLP with that of members of other types of business association. In general, the differences in this respect between firms are more a matter of degree than kind, and indeed may be minimal in some respects because of fact-specific variations and customized contracts. This comparison helps to determine how to differentiate other rules within the LLP from analogues in other types of firms, and how to categorize LLPs for regulatory purposes.

(a)   LLP Versus Non-LLP Partners

The limited liability of general partners in LLPs is not as different from the liability of general partners in non-LLPs as it might appear at first blush. That is because LLP partners have general partners' liability in several situations. At the same time, general partners have some protection from liability. These two aspects of the comparison between LLPs and non-LLP partnerships are discussed separately below.

(1)   Risk of Liability for Partners in an LLP

Nonregistration. LLP partners are personally liable for liabilities arising from conduct prior to registration.

Noncompliance with other requirements. LLP statutes generally define an LLP as one that complies with the statutory requirements. Because the liability limitation is linked with LLP status, partners may be personally liable if the partnership fails to maintain the required insurance, include the appropriate LLP designation in its name or to renew its registration as of the time the liability arises (*see* Section 2.03(f), above).

Partners' own misconduct. None of the statutes excuses the partner from liability arising out of his or her own misconduct or malpractice (*see* Section 3.04, above).

Other partners' misconduct. Most statutes explicitly impose personal liability on partners who were involved in or had notice of other partners' or employees' errors or omissions (*see* Section 3.04, above). As also discussed in Section 3.04, courts might also characterize as partner malpractice the failure adequately to supervise co-partners or employees or to take corrective steps after learning of a co-partner's or employee's malpractice.

Liability for other misconduct. Under some LLP statutes partners are personally liable for conduct undertaken in the course of the partnership business other than the errors-and-omissions liability explicitly excepted by the statute (*see* Section 3.02). This would include failure to pay a loan or rental or to fulfill some other contractual obligation.

(2) Nonliability of Non-LLP Partners

Limited scope of firm's liability. A partner is not liable for co-partner conduct for which the firm is not responsible. Thus, the misconduct must itself be a tort, and it must be sufficiently connected with the firm's business that it should be attributed to the firm.[161]

Contractual limitations. A non-LLP partner can limit partners' personal liability by contract with third parties (*see* Section 3.06, above).

Exhaustion of remedies. Even as to debt for which liability is not limited, creditors may not be able to execute against individual partners unless they have exhausted their remedies against the firm's assets (*see* Section 3.08(b), above).

(3) Comparison of LLPs and Non-LLPs

Based on the above discussion, LLP status reduces the exposure of partners' personal assets to creditor claims only if all of the following conditions are satisfied:

(1) The plaintiff is able successfully to prove a claim against the partnership.
(2) The partner is subject to process and has personal assets.
(3) The claim arose while the partnership was registered, designated as an LLP, and in some jurisdictions was insured or otherwise financially responsible.
(4) In some jurisdictions, only if the claim is based on negligence or other partner misconduct.

---

[161] *See* Bromberg & Ribstein, §§ 4.07, 5.11.

(5)   The partner did not commit malpractice or other misconduct, did not negligently fail to monitor co-partners, and was not otherwise involved in or aware of the misconduct.

In general, partners in both LLPs and non-LLPs share attributes of both personal and limited liability. Partners of both kinds often can rely on the firm's assets and insurance to protect them from personal exposure, while both kinds of LLP partners face personal exposure to substantial debts such as long-term loans and lease payments if the firm's assets are wiped out by malpractice liability and must pay some attention to the activities of their co-partners to avoid personal liability. So partners in both LLPs and non-LLPs have comparable incentives to exercise care in hiring, supervising, and evaluating co-partners.

Thus, the main difference between the two types of firms is that non-LLP partners face a risk of vicarious liability for the conduct of partners that they cannot easily control by instituting better monitoring and supervision. This may cause non-LLPs to be overly cautious. For example, law firms may avoid representing high-risk start-up ventures that may give rise to lawsuits in connection with securities violations. Finally, it is important to keep in mind that, even if a particular claimant cannot recover against a partner, this may leave more individual partner assets available to others whose claims arose while the firm was unregistered or uninsured or who are able to show the requisite partner misconduct or involvement in the malpractice or other misconduct.

(b)   Limited Partnerships

General partners in limited partnerships are, of course, treated like general partners in general partnerships with regard to liability. Where limited partnerships can register as LLPs, general partners' liability would, of course, be the same as in a general partnership LLP.[162]

In comparing limited partnerships and LLPs it is important to consider potential differences between the liability of limited partners and of general partners in LLPs. Limited partners do not, as such, have any personal liability for the debts of their limited partnership unless, under R.U.L.P.A., they participate in control of the business. Even then, limited partners will rarely be deemed to be participating in control given the extensive safe harbor under the Revised Uniform Limited Partnership Act (R.U.L.P.A.).[163] By contrast, as discussed above in

---

[162] The effect of LLP registration of limited partnerships on the liability of both general and limited partners is discussed in Chapter 5. Both general and limited partners in limited partnerships would have full limited liability by default under the revision of R.U.L.P.A. *See* § 1.04(b), note 54, supra. Under U.L.P.A. §§ 102(9) and 201(a)(4) (2001), the firm must elect between LLLP and non-LLLP status in its certificate. *See* § 9.201, infra.

[163] *See* R.U.L.P.A. § 303(b) (1985). Even this liability has been eliminated in U.L.P.A. § 303 (2001). *See* § 1.04(b), note 54, supra, and § 9.303, infra.

subsection (a), under most statutes LLP members have vicarious liability for several types of partnership debts whether or not they take part in control of the partnership. Note, however, that there is a similarity between limited partnerships and LLPs in that LLP partners may be liable if they participate in particular actionable conduct (*see* Section 3.04, above).

(c)   *Limited Liability Companies and Corporations*

The limited liability of limited liability company (LLC) members and corporate shareholders is more certain than that of limited partners in that LLC members and shareholders do not lose their liability shield for participating in control. LLC members and shareholders, like partners in LLPs, are liable for their own tortious conduct, including negligent failure to monitor. However, LLC members' and shareholder' liability is more limited than that of LLP members under the LLP statutes that provide for personal liability for contract-type debts.

TABLE 3-1.   LIABILITY SHIELD

State	*Section†*	*Categories*
Alabama	10A-8-3.06(c), (d)	3, 5*, 7, 9*
Alaska	32.06.306(c)	3a, 7a, 9a
Arizona	29-1026	3a*; 7a, 9a, 11, 12
Arkansas	Ark. Code § 4-46-306(c)	3a, 7a, 9a
California	16306, 16956, 16957	3*, 6, 9, 10, 11, 13
Colorado	7-64-306, -1004, -1009	3, 8*, 11, 12*
Connecticut	34-327	3, 4, 10
Delaware	15-306(c)	3*, 11
District of Columbia	29-603.06(c)	3a, 7a. 9a
Florida	620.8306	3a*, 7a, 9a
Georgia	14-8-15	3, 6, 9*, 13
Hawaii	425-117	3a, 7a, 9a
Idaho	53-3-306	3a, 7a, 9a
Illinois	206/306	3a, 7a, 9a
Indiana	23-4-1-15	3*, 6, 13
Iowa	486A.306	3a, 7a, 9a
Kansas	56a-306	3a, 7a, 9a
Kentucky	362.1-306(3)-(4)	3a, 7a, 9a
Louisiana	9:3431	2a, 2b, 6, 13

Table 3-1   **3. Partner Liability for Partnership Debts**

Table 3-1 (cont'd)

State	*Section*[†]	*Categories*
Maine	1034(3)	3a, 7a, 9a
Maryland	9A-306-307	3*, 5*, 9a, 13
Massachusetts	108A, §§ 15, 45(8)	3*, 6, 10
Michigan	449.46	1, 4, 13, 14*
Minnesota	323A.0306, -.0307	3a, 7a, 9a, 11, 13
Mississippi	79-13-306	3a, 7a, 9a
Missouri	358.150	3*, 4, 13
Montana	35-10-307	3, 4, 5*, 8*, 13
Nebraska	67-418	3a, 7a, 9a
Nevada	87.150	1, 4, 13
New Hampshire	304-A:15	1, 4, 13
New Jersey	42:1A-18	3a, 7a, 9a
New Mexico	54-1A-306; 54-1-47	3, 4, 7, 9a, 10
New York	26	3, 4, 9*
North Carolina	59-45	2b*, 13, 14
North Dakota	45-22-08.1, -10	3a,* 7a, 9a, 11
Ohio	1776.36	3a, 7a, 9a
Oklahoma	1-306; -309	3a, 7a, 9a, 10
Oregon	67.105; .615	3*, 4, 7, 9a, 11
Pennsylvania	8204, 8207(c)	2b, 4, 8*, 9
Prototype	306	3, 7
Revised Uniform Partnership Act	306	3a, 7a, 9a
Rhode Island	7-12-26; 7-12-58	3, 4, 10, 13
South Carolina	33-41-370, -1130	2b, 4, 5*, 6*, 10
South Dakota	48-7A-306	3a, 7a, 9a
Tennessee	61-1-306	1, 4, 13, 14
Texas	152.801	3
Utah	48-1d-306	3a, 7a, 9a
Vermont	3226	3a, 7a, 9a
Virginia	50-73.96	3, 7
Washington	25.05.125	3a, 7a, 9a, 10
West Virginia	47B-3-6; 47B-10-5	1, 4, 10
Wisconsin	178.12	1, 4, 13
Wyoming	17-21-306	3*, 4, 9, 13

[†]*See* Table 3-3 for full statutory citations.

Table 3-1 (cont'd)

Categories and Related Notes
*   *See* Related Notes, below.
1. Errors and omissions only. Original Delaware (language clarifying (1) that the partner is not liable directly or indirectly, by way of indemnification, contribution, assessment or otherwise; and (2) that the errors and omissions shield applies regardless of whether the liability is characterized as tort, contract or otherwise).
2a. Errors and omissions only, but no references to indirect liability for indemnification or contribution.
2b. Errors and omissions only, but no language clarifying tort-contract characterization. North Carolina (includes language on indirect liability).
2c. Errors and omissions.
3. Full shield. California (pursuant to § 16306(f), no liability limitation for claims based on legal services unless LLP "has a currently effective certificate of registration issued by the State Bar"); Delaware (liability limitation extends to obligations "arising out of or related to circumstances or events occurring while the partnership is a limited liability partnership"); Indiana (limiting liability for "acting or failing to act as a partner, or participating as an employee, a consultant, a contractor or otherwise"); Maryland (limiting liability for "acting or omitting to act" as partner or "rendering professional services or otherwise participating, as an employee, consultant, contractor, or otherwise, in the conduct of the business or activities of the partnership"); Massachusetts and Oregon (professional partners have liability comparable to shareholders in professional corporations); Missouri (LLP partners shielded from liability to each other); North Carolina (no modification of law applicable to professionals); Wyoming (limiting liability for "acting or omitting to act" as a partner "or otherwise participating (as an employee, consultant, contractor or otherwise) in the conduct of the other business or activities" of the LLP).
3a. Revised Uniform Partnership Act: "An obligation of a partnership incurred while the partnership is a limited liability partnership, whether arising in contract, tort, or otherwise, is solely the obligation of the partnership. A partner is not personally liable, directly or indirectly, including by way of contribution or otherwise, for such a partnership obligation solely by reason of being or so acting as a partner. This subsection applies notwithstanding anything inconsistent in the partnership agreement that existed immediately before the vote required to become a limited liability partnership . . .". Arizona (Notwithstanding contrary provisions in a partnership agreement existing prior to the effective date of a statement of qualification, the filing of a statement pursuant to § 291101 creates a presumption that the partners have agreed to the applicability of this subsection). Kentucky (inserts in first sentence "An obligation of a partnership *arising out of or related to circumstances or events occurring or* incurred while . . .). North Dakota (last sentence omits "that existed immediately before . . .").
4. Does not affect liability for partner's own acts or those under partner's direct supervision and control (*see* Section 3.04).

Table 3-1 (cont'd)

5. Liability for participation, knowledge or notice (see Section 3.04). Alabama (§ 1010 provides that professional LLP partner or employee rendering professional services is liable for wrong in which he participates as if he were sole practitioner); District of Columbia (if directly involved in specific activity in which misdeeds were committed, or had written notice or knowledge of the misdeeds at time of occurrence); Maryland and South Carolina (if negligent in appointing, directly supervising, or cooperating with other partner, employee, or agent); Montana (liable for "partner's own negligence, wrongful act, or misconduct, including without limitation an act under § 35-10-628(2) [acts inappropriate for winding up], or that of any person under the partner's direct supervision and control").

6. Liability for partner's own wrongs. South Carolina (one who renders professional services is liable for own acts as if he were sole practitioner).

7. Not liable merely because of partner status.

7a. Revised Uniform Partnership Act version of 7 (*see* 3a).

8. Liability for debts for which partners agreed to be liable. Colorado (except as otherwise provided in a written partnership agreement); Pennsylvania (except debts for which the partner has agreed in writing to be liable); Montana (limitation does not affect partner's ability to act as a guarantor or surety for, provide collateral for, or otherwise agree to be primarily or contingently liable for LLP's debts).

9. Provision for partnership's waiver of liability shield. Alabama (unanimous vote); Georgia and Kentucky (nonliability is except as otherwise provided in the partnership agreement); New York and Wyoming (majority vote).

9a. Revised Uniform Partnership Act (the shield is not in the § 103(b) exclusive list of matters that cannot be waived by the partnership agreement); Delaware (adds that waiver applies if third party consents); Florida (adds that partnership antedating adoption of R.U.P.A. LLP provisions can waive liability shield within six months of adoption of act); Oregon (adds that section does not affect partner's ability to be released from obligation).

10. Insurance requirement (*see* Section 2.06) (indicates only requirements in LLP statutes; as for requirements in state professional regulation, *see* Section 2.06, n.82).

11. Restrictions on distributions (*see* Section 4.04(d)).

12. Veil-piercing under corporate standards except informality not alone a ground for piercing the veil. Arizona (provides for informalities, but not for corporate standard).

13. LLP partner is not proper party to suit to recover damages for which liability is limited.

14. Liability for tax obligations. Michigan (§ 418.647 provides that LLP partners also are jointly and severally liable for worker compensation).

TABLE 3-2.   AMENDMENTS TO REFLECT
LIABILITY SHIELD

State	Section[†]	Categories
Alabama	10A-8-4.01, -703, -806, -807	2
Alaska	32.06.807	3
Arizona	29-1077	3
Arkansas	4-46-807	3
California	16401, 16807	2*
Colorado	7-64-807(8)	4*
Connecticut	34-335, 377, 378	2
Delaware	15-401(c); 15-807	3*
District of Columbia	29-608.07(b)	4
Florida	620.8807	3
Georgia	14-8-18, -34, -36, -40	1
Hawaii	425-144	3
Idaho	53-3-807	3
Illinois	206/807	3
Indiana	23-4-1-18, -34, -36, -40	1
Iowa	486A.807	3
Kansas	56a-807	3
Kentucky	362.1-807	3
Louisiana		5
Maine	1087(2)	3
Maryland	9A-807	3
Massachusetts	108A, § 18, 34, 36, 40	1
Michigan	449.18, .34, .36, .40	1
Minnesota	323A.0807	3
Mississippi	79-13-807	3
Missouri	358.180, .340, .360, .400	1
Montana	35-10-401, -621, -629	2
Nebraska	67-445	3
Nevada	87.180, .340, .360, .400	1
New Hampshire	304-A:18, :34, :36, :40	1
New Jersey	42:1A-45	3
New Mexico	54-1A-401(b), -703, -806, -807	3
New York	40, 65, 67, 71	1*
North Carolina		5

Table 3-2   **3.   Partner Liability for Partnership Debts**

Table 3-2 (cont'd)

State	Section[†]	Categories
North Dakota	45-22-08.1	*
Ohio	1776.37(C)	3
Oklahoma	1-807	3
Oregon	67.315	3
Pennsylvania		5
Prototype	401, 807	4
Revised Uniform Partnership Act	807	3
Rhode Island	7-12-29, -45, -47, -51	
South Carolina	33-41-510, -960, -1060	1
South Dakota	48-7A-807	3
Tennessee	61-1-807	5
Texas	152.707(d)	2,*
Utah	48-1d-906	2, 3
Vermont	3277	3
Virginia	50-73.99, -73.123(B)	4
Washington	25.05.330(2)	*
West Virginia	47B-4-1, -8-7(b)	4
Wisconsin	178.15, .29, .35	1
Wyoming	17-21-401, -703, -807, -808	4

[†]*See* Table 3-3 for full statutory citations.

Categories

Partnership act provisions are amended as follows to reflect the liability shield:

*   *See* Notes, below.

1.   Adjustments to U.P.A. loss-sharing and contribution provisions based on original Delaware statute.

2.   R.U.P.A.-based provisions making loss-sharing and contribution obligations except as provided in the liability shield.

3.   Official adjustments to R.U.P.A., excluding shielded liabilities from the calculation of the partner's contribution obligation.

4.   Prototype variation on R.U.P.A.: Contribution obligation under § 807 is limited to an amount "that is attributable to an obligation for which the partner is liable under 306."

5.   No adjustments of other partnership provisions. *But see* Table 3-1, which lists shield provisions that clarify partners' nonliability for indemnification or contribution.

Table 3-2 (cont'd)

Notes

California: Partner's contribution obligation is "except for registered limited liability partnerships and foreign limited liability partnerships."

Colorado: "[N]o partner shall be obligated to contribute under this section with respect to any amounts that are attributable to a partnership obligation incurred while the partnership is a limited liability partnership."

Delaware: Section 15-401(c) provides that indemnification obligation is except as provided in liability shield.

New York: Section 40(2) provides that indemnification obligation is except as provided in liability shield.

North Dakota: Liability shield does not limit the partnership's or its partners' rights to make claims against a partner on the ground of the partner's breach of duty to the partnership or the other partners.

Texas: Section 152.801(e) also provides that the LLP liability limitation "prevails over the other parts of this Act regarding the liability of partners, their chargeability for the obligations of the partnership, and their obligations regarding contributions and indemnity."

West Virginia: Similar to 3, above, but loss-sharing provision clarifies that partner is liable for excess of charges over credits only to the extent provided in shield provision.

Washington: LLP partner contributes to the extent of his or her share of unpaid partnership obligations for which the partner is personally liable under Wash. Rev. Code § 306.

TABLE 3-3.   FULL STATUTORY CITATIONS

State	*Citation Information*
Alabama	Ala. St. § —
Alaska	Alaska Stat. § —
Arkansas	Ark. Code § —
Arizona	Ariz. Rev. Stat. Ann. § —
California	Cal. Corp. Code § —
Colorado	Colo. Rev. Stat. § —
Connecticut	Conn. Gen. Stat. § —
Delaware	Del. Code Ann. tit. 6, § —
District of Columbia	D.C. Code Ann. § —
Florida	Fla. Stat. Ann. § —
Georgia	Ga. Code Ann. § —

Table 3-3   3. Partner Liability for Partnership Debts

Table 3-3 (cont'd)

State	*Citation Information*
Hawaii	Haw. Rev. Stat. § —
Idaho	Idaho Code § —
Illinois	Ill. Comp. Stat. Ann. Ch. 805
Indiana	Ind. Code § —
Iowa	Iowa Code § —
Kansas	Kan. Stat. Ann. § —
Kentucky	Ky. Rev. Stat. Ann. § —
Louisiana	La. Rev. Stat. Ann. § —
Maine	Me. Rev. Stat. Ann. tit. 31, § —
Maryland	Md. Code Ann., Corps. & Ass'ns § —
Massachusetts	Mass. Gen. L. ch. 108A, § —
Michigan	Mich. Comp. Laws § —
Minnesota	Minn. Stat. § —
Mississippi	Miss. Code Ann. § 79-13 —
Missouri	Mo. Rev. Stat. § —
Montana	Mont. Code Ann. § —
Nebraska	Neb. Rev. Stat. § —
Nevada	Nev. Rev. Stat. § —
New Hampshire	N.H. Rev. Stat. Ann. § —
New Jersey	N.J. Rev. Stat. § —
New Mexico	N.M. Stat. Ann. § —
New York	N.Y. Partnership Law ch. 39, § — (Consol.)
North Carolina	N.C. Gen. Stat. § —
North Dakota	N.D. Cent. Code § —
Ohio	Ohio Rev. Code Ann. § —
Oklahoma	Okla. Stat. tit. 54, § —
Oregon	Or. Rev. Stat. § —
Pennsylvania	15 Pa. Cons. Stat. § —
Prototype	Prototype Registered Limited Liability Partnership Act, § —
Revised Uniform Partnership Act	Uniform Partnership Act (1994) with 1996 Amendments, § —
Rhode Island	R.I. Gen. Laws § —
South Carolina	S.C. Code Ann. § —
South Dakota	S.D. Codified Laws Ann. § —
Tennessee	Tenn. Code Ann. § —
Texas	Tex. Bus. Org. Code § —

Table 3-3 (cont'd)

State	*Citation Information*
Utah	Utah Code Ann. § —[164]
Vermont	Vermont St., tit. 11, § —
Virginia	Va. Code Ann. § —
Washington	Wash. Rev. Code § —
West Virginia	W. Va. Code § —
Wisconsin	Wis. Stat. § —
Wyoming	Wyo. Stat. § —

---

[164] Utah provisions cited in the text are effective July 1, 2013 for new entities and Jan. 1, 2015 for existing entities. *See* Utah Code Ann. § 48-1b-1205.

≡4≡

EFFECT of LLP
STATUS on OTHER
PARTNERSHIP RULES

§ 4.01 INTRODUCTION

This chapter analyzes the implications of limited liability partnership (LLP) provisions for aspects of partnership law other than those that deal explicitly with the terms or conditions of the partners' limited liability.

Limited liability and formalities may fundamentally change the partners' relationship. Much of partnership law implicitly or explicitly assumes that the partners are personally liable for partnership debts. Personally liable partners need, among other things, strong management rights, the power to veto new members, a strong exit right, and financial rights that reflect contributions of credit as well as of capital. Different rules may be appropriate for LLPs.

In most respects, however, the default rules of the partnership laws do apply to LLPs. An important function of LLP provisions is to add limited liability to general partnerships. Changing the partnership statute to accommodate LLPs obviously would interfere with this function. However, as discussed throughout this chapter, judicial interpretation of partnership agreements and the default provisions of the statute may depend on whether the partnership is an LLP.

It is important to keep in mind that the partners can vary statutory default rules in their partnership agreement. Although this chapter emphasizes the interpretation and application of the default rules in partnership statutes, it also highlights the need of partners in LLPs to consider whether their agreements should be modified when they register as LLPs. Considerations relevant to drafting the partnership agreement are summarized above in Section 2.09.

§ 4.02 MANAGEMENT AND CONTROL

Partnership law provides that a general partner has equal voting management and voting rights[1] and a power to veto extraordinary decisions or amendments to the partnership agreement[2] and the admission of new members.[3] These rights are particularly important to personally liable partners, since they ensure that partners will not be exposed to additional personal risk as a result of business decisions with which they disagree. This raises the question whether partners should have different management and control rights in LLPs. This section discusses four aspects of partners' management and control rights: (1) participation in

---

[1] U.P.A. § 18(e); R.U.P.A. § 401(f); Bromberg and Ribstein on Partnership, § 6.03(b) (2012) (hereinafter "Bromberg & Ribstein").

[2] U.P.A. § 18(h); R.U.P.A. § 401(j); Bromberg & Ribstein, § 6.03(c).

[3] U.P.A. § 18(g); R.U.P.A. § 401(i); Bromberg & Ribstein, § 6.03(d).

management ; (2) voting rights; (3) the decision in the event of disagreement; and (4) the power to veto new members.

(a) Partner Management Rights

Partnership law provides that partners have "equal rights in the management and conduct of the partnership business."[4] Thus, unless otherwise agreed, partners have rights to participate in the initiation as well as approval of all management decisions and to be employed in the business.[5] Partners who are excluded from management may be entitled to a judicial dissolution of the partnership.[6]

Whether a default "equality" rule is appropriate depends in part on whether most firms that adopt the partnership form would prefer this rule.[7] The limited liability of LLP partners is an important consideration in determining the appropriate default management rule. Partners who have limited liability, and therefore limited exposure to the consequences of mismanagement, are less likely to suffer harm from delegating management responsibilities than are partners who have personal liability.

It does not necessarily follow, however, that partnership statutes should apply a different rule regarding partner participation in management to LLPs than to non-LLP partnerships. First, a default right to participate in management may be appropriate even for limited liability partners where these partners are employed in the firm. Management decisions have important consequences for partners who are employed in the firm even if they are not personally liable for the firm's debts. Partners cannot diversify risks to their earning power as can those who invest only financial capital.

A second reason why the statutory default regarding management participation should not change for LLP partners is that, under many LLP statutes, LLP partners remain liable for some debts. These include "contract-type" debts (*see* Section 3.02, above) or debts arising out of misconduct in which they participate or for which they have some supervisory responsibility (*see* Section 3.04, above). LLP partners' liability for "contract-type" debts means that they have as much incentive as non-LLP partners to participate in management decisions. LLP partners' liability for faulty supervision means that LLP partners would

---

[4] U.P.A. § 18(e); R.U.P.A. § 401(f).
[5] *See* Bromberg & Ribstein, § 6.03(b).
[6] *See* Bromberg & Ribstein, § 7.06(c).
[7] It also depends on whether this rule is better suited to *informal* firms that will accept rather than contract around the statutory defaults. A default equality rule may be suitable for informal general partnerships even if many firms will opt out of the rule. However, because of the formalities required by LLP provisions, this is less likely to be a consideration with respect to LLPs.

want to ensure that they have a say in determining the scope of the business and monitoring procedures and lines of authority regarding activities for which they may later be determined to have had some supervisory responsibility.

Third, LLP partners would prefer default rules that provide for direct participation in management if such rules helped ensure favorable treatment under regulatory statutes. In particular, retaining default partnership rules regarding management responsibility may be significant in determining whether the firm should be treated as a "partnership" under securities and employment discrimination statutes (*see* Chapter 7).

The partners can, of course, agree to vary the default rule of equal participation by delegating responsibility to managing partners. Partners may be more likely to do so in LLPs, and the partnership's status as an LLP may affect the interpretation and enforcement of such agreements. There is some authority for interpreting an agreement that delegates management powers as not excluding nonmanaging partners from participation in decisionmaking. In *Wilzig v. Sisselman*,[8] the court interpreted an agreement that delegated management functions to 5 of 11 partners as not providing for survivorship of management rights after the death of a managing partner, partly because this might concentrate control in one manager over a period of years. The court said:

> [T]he right of a partner to be heard on fundamental and vital aspects of the partnership enterprise, matters that could substantially affect the investment and liability of a partner, should not be deemed surrendered unless the intention to do so is clearly expressed. Management rights are extremely important since partners are generally liable jointly for all obligations arising from the conduct of partnership business.[9]

Under this approach, in a non-LLP partnership total exclusion of a nonmanaging partner will be enforced only under an explicit and unambiguous agreement.[10] However, LLP partners' limited liability removes the rationale for strict interpretation expressed by the *Wilzig* court. The question remains whether courts will rigidly follow old partnership precedents in the somewhat different context of the LLP.

---

[8] 182 N.J. Super. 519, 442 A.2d 1021 (1982).

[9] 182 N.J. Super. 519, 535, 442 A.2d 1021, 1030. Similarly, Berk v. Sherman, 682 A.2d 209 (D.C. App. 1996) (Md. law) held that the delegation of power to a managing partner in a brother-sister partnership to "develop, lease, sell and convey the property" did not prevent the non-managing partner from bringing a malpractice claim against the partnership's lawyers although the managing partner had refused to sue. The court reasoned that authority not specifically delegated by the other partners to a managing partner under an express agreement is presumed to be withheld.

[10] *See* Bromberg & Ribstein, § 6.03(c)(5).

(b)   Partner Voting Rights

The statutory default rule that partners have "equal rights in the management and control of the partnership business"[11] means that partners vote according to a rule of one-person-one-vote—that is, "per capita"—rather than "pro rata" according to financial investments as in corporations.[12] The difference between partnerships and corporations partly reflects the different types of member contributions. While corporate shareholders' contributions are mainly financial, partners also contribute their personal credit in the form of liability for partnership debts, and in many cases services. In addition, joint and several liability may treat small and large allocation partners equally for purposes of liability to third partners.[13] Accordingly, even partners who make relatively small capital contributions would have a reason to insist on a substantial say in management.

It follows from this analysis that LLP partners would have less reason to prefer a voting rule based other than on financial contributions. However, for reasons similar to those discussed above regarding participation in management (*see* Section 4.02(a), above), this consideration does not necessarily justify a different default rule in LLPs. Even without personal liability, LLP partners may make significant contributions of their time and energy, and LLP partners may have personal liability for contract-type and some tort-type claims. Moreover, without an easy way to value and keep track of contributions and returned con-tributions, a default rule of pro rata management rights might be difficult to administer, particularly in informal firms.[14]

(c)   Decision in the Event of Disagreement

Partnership law provides for a default rule of decisionmaking by a majority vote for ordinary decisions, and by unanimous vote for extraordinary decisions or amendments of the agreement.[15] This rule arguably is inappropriate for LLPs. A veto rule can impose significant costs on the partnership.[16] A unanimity rule can lead to impasses given the likelihood that the partners will disagree on important matters, and gives each partner the power to "hold up" the partnership on major decisions in order to exact concessions from the other partner. Moreover, a unanimity rule is hard to administer because of the difficulty of determining the types of decisions on which unanimity is required and those that require only a

---

[11] *See* U.P.A. § 18(e).

[12] *See* Bromberg & Ribstein, § 6.03(b).

[13] *See* R.U.P.A. § 306(a).

[14] *See* Ribstein & Keatinge, Ribstein & Keatinge on Limited Liability Companies, § 5.02 (2d ed. 2004) (hereinafter "Ribstein & Keatinge").

[15] U.P.A. § 18(h); R.U.P.A. § 401(j); Bromberg & Ribstein, § 6.03(c).

[16] *See* Bromberg & Ribstein, § 6.03(c)(2).

majority vote. These significant costs of a unanimity rule are justified only if an across-the-board majority vote rule would impose even higher costs on individual dissenting partners. That may be the case in a non-LLP partnership mainly because of the high potential costs to personally liable partners of having to go along with management decisions with which they disagree. The limitation of liability in LLPs is arguably enough to change the cost-benefit balance of a unanimity rule.

On the other hand, there are arguments favoring applying the same veto rule to LLPs and to non-LLPs. First, LLPs have chosen to obtain limited liability through the general partnership form rather than in some other way, and therefore would prefer application of general partnership default rules. If the parties would want default rules better suited to limited liability, they could choose to form a limited liability company (LLC). Most LLC statutes that specify voting rights provide for majority or, at least, subunanimous, approval of LLC decisions.[17] Second, LLP members may have personal liability for some liabilities, including contract-type debts for which partner voting rights may be significant. Accordingly, a veto power may be more justified in LLPs than in LLCs.

The limited liability of LLP partners may be relevant to judicial interpretation of agreements that vary the default rule. There is some authority for refusing to enforce agreements that override partners' veto power.[18] Most relevant cases have enforced such agreements.[19] In any event, authority for limitations on enforcement is weaker as to LLPs than as to non-LLP general partnerships because the majority's decisions have less impact on limited liability than on personally liable partners.

(d)   Admission of New Members

One of the partners' most important management rights under the partnership statutes is the right to veto the admission of new members.[20] This rule of "delectus personae" (choice of the person) is a fundamental aspect of partnership law.

---

[17] *See* Ribstein & Keatinge, § 8.03.

[18] *See* McCallum v. Asbury, 238 Or. 257, 260-61, 393 P.2d 774, 775-76 (1964) (enforcing subunanimous creation of executive committee under agreement permitting amendments by majority vote, but stating that "[f]undamental changes in a partnership agreement may not be made without the consent of all the parties").

[19] *See* Day v. Sidley & Austin, 394 F. Supp. 986 (D.D.C. 1975), *aff'd sub nom.* Day v. Avery, 548 F.2d 1018 (D.C. Cir. 1976), *cert. denied*, 431 U.S. 908 (1977) (not requiring unanimous approval of merger); Bailey v. Fish & Neave, 8 N.Y.3d 523, 868 N.E.2d 956, 837 N.Y.S.2d 600 (2007) (enforcing amendment to the partnership agreement approved by a majority in accordance with the agreement that changed from an accrual to a cash system, resulting in a significantly lower payment to plaintiff when he withdrew than he would have received under the prior system); Aztec Petroleum Corp. v. MHM Co., 703 S.W.2d 290 (Tex. Civ. App. 1985) (permitting limited partners to add removal power to agreement and then remove general partner over general partner's objection). *See generally* Bromberg & Ribstein, § 6.03(c)(5).

[20] U.P.A. § 18(g); R.U.P.A. § 401(I); Bromberg & Ribstein, § 6.03(d).

The members' right to choose their associates is justified by: (1) a new partner's power to create partnership liabilities, and therefore personal liabilities for co-partners, (2) the partners' equal shares in partnership profits, which would be diluted by admission of a new partner, (3) partners' power to be heard on and to veto partnership decisions, and (4) each partner's power to dissolve and compel the liquidation of the partnership.

As with other partner management powers, the need to veto admission of new members is diminished by LLPs' limited liability. This suggests that perhaps the power should be relaxed in LLPs. However, as discussed immediately above, there are other bases for the power besides partners' personal liability. Even in an LLP, admission of a new partner still alters the existing management and financial organization of the firm. Also, under many statutes LLP partners are liable for contracts that might be made by incoming partners. Finally, the power to choose co-members relates to treatment of partnerships under nonpartnership law (*see* Chapter 7). For example, *Breedon v. Catron*[21] held that a partnership is not an executory contract that can be assumed by a bankrupt partner's trustee, in part because the partnership delectus personae rule is an applicable state law that excuses a nondebtor party from accepting performance from an entity other than the debtor. Changing this default rule could, therefore, have the indirect result of requiring the continuation of the partnership after bankruptcy.

Even if LLP statutes preserve the power to veto admission of new members, members nevertheless can agree to alter this right. As with the management rights discussed elsewhere in this section, the courts may strictly interpret waiver of such an important right in the context of a general partnership.[22] However, these precedents arguably should not be applied with equal force to LLPs because the costs to partners of waiving their power to veto new associates are lower where new partners have less ability to create liabilities for which their co-partners are personally liable.

§ 4.03 PARTNERS' AGENCY POWER

LLP status could affect partners' agency power in two ways. First, it could affect judicial interpretations of the scope of agency power; and, second, it could affect provisions for filings of statements of partner authority.

---

[21] In re Catron, 158 B.R. 624 (Bankr. E.D. Va., 1993), *aff'd,* 158 B.R. 629 (E.D. Va. 1993), *aff'd,* 25 F.3d 1038 (4th Cir. 1994).

[22] *See* Sunshine Cellular v. Vanguard Cellular Sys., Inc., 1993 WL 212675 (S.D.N.Y. 1993) (Md. law); Rapoport v. 55 Perry Co., 50 A.D.2d 54, 376 N.Y.S.2d 147 (1975) (strictly interpreting a provision in the partnership agreement that permitted intra-family transfer of a partnership *interest* as inapplicable to transfers of management rights); Bromberg & Ribstein, § 6.03(d).

(a) Scope of Partner Authority

Each general partner is an agent of the partnership and has the power to bind the partnership as to any act that is "for apparently carrying on in the ordinary course the partnership business or business of the kind carried on by the partnership" unless the partner is not actually authorized and the third party knows this.[23] Also, the partnership is liable for wrongful acts committed by partners acting in the ordinary course of the business[24] or for funds misapplied by partners who were apparently authorized to receive them.[25] LLP status does not affect a partner's authority to bind the partnership under these provisions.[26] However, the fact that the firm is an LLP may affect the scope of authority in close cases. Thus, it has been held that an innocent partner did not lose insurance coverage on account of his co-partners' fraud in the insurance application, citing the partner's expectation of limited liability in an LLP.[27]

(b) Statements of Partner Authority

The Revised Uniform Partnership Act (R.U.P.A.) § 303 provides that a partnership may file a statement of partnership authority that states the authority or limitations on the authority of some or all of the partners. The statement binds the partnership in favor of third parties or transferees for value who lack contrary knowledge, while a restriction on authority to transfer real property is effective against transferees for value.[28] Other states added provisions to their versions of the Uniform Partnership Act (U.P.A.) for filed statements of partner authority that bind third parties in real property transactions[29] and, under one statute, also bind the partnership.[30] The statement of partner authority probably should be combined with the LLP registration in order to economize on filings and prevent possible conflicts between statements in two separate filings (*see* Section 2.03(d), above).

---

[23] U.P.A. § 9; R.U.P.A. § 301; Bromberg & Ribstein, §§ 4.01–4.03.

[24] U.P.A. § 13; R.U.P.A. § 305(a); Bromberg & Ribstein, § 4.07.

[25] U.P.A. § 14; R.U.P.A. § 305(b); Bromberg & Ribstein, § 4.07(f).

[26] *See* Jones v. Foundation Surgery Affiliates of Brazoria Co., 403 S.W. 3d 306 (Tx. App.-Houston [1st Dist.] 2012) (physician group LLP was liable for physician's tortious acts, even though it argued that the partners only had "authority" to conduct surgical procedures with "reasonable care"); Dow v. Jones, 311 F. Supp. 2d 461 (D. Md. 2004) (D.C. law) (client retainer); First American Title Ins. Co. v. Lawson, 177 N.J. 125, 827 A.2d 230 (2003) (fraud in insurance application).

[27] *See Lawson,* note 26, supra, discussed and quoted in § 3.04(b), note 50, supra.

[28] R.U.P.A. § 303(d)–(e).

[29] Cal. Corp. Code §§ 15010.5–15010.6; Fla. Stat. Ann. § 620.605; Ga. Code Ann. § 14-8-10A. The California and Florida provisions have been superseded by those states' adoptions of R.U.P.A. § 303.

[30] Ga. Code Ann. § 14-8-10A. *See* Bromberg & Ribstein, § 4.04(e).

§ 4.04   FINANCIAL RIGHTS

LLP status has several potential effects on partners' financial rights. First, it potentially affects the interpretation and application of the statutory default rule of equal sharing of profits. Second, LLP status affects allocation among the partners of partnership liability through indemnification and contribution. Third, firms' adoptions of LLP status could trigger major revisions of partnership agreements. Fourth, LLP status could lead to judicially imposed or statutory limitations on partnership distributions.

(a)   Equal Profit Share

Partnership law provides by default that partners share equally in partnership profits irrespective of partners' capital contributions.[31] Equal sharing is based on partners' contributions of services and credit in addition to cash. As with management rights (*see* Section 4.02(a), above), limiting partners' liability arguably weakens the argument for sharing that is disproportionate to financial contributions. Under the LLP statutes that continue partners' personal liability for contract-type claims, the default rule arguably should provide for sharing of liability risk by equalizing profit shares.

The argument for corporate-type sharing according to capital contributions is stronger in firms that are governed by statutes that provide for complete limited liability. Even in these firms, however, partners may make varying service contributions that would be inconsistent with capital-based sharing. Moreover, equal sharing may be the only practicable method of dividing profits in the absence of an easy way to value contributions and track return of contributions (*see* text accompanying note 14, above).

Finally, partners' choice of the LLP form over the LLC and other limited liability business forms signals that partners prefer to be bound by partnership default rules.

(b)   Allocating Liabilities Among Partners: Indemnification and Contribution

Under the general law of partnership, the partnership generally must indemnify a partner who pays a partnership debt in the absence of contrary agreement.[32] If the partnership's liabilities, including liability for indemnification, exceed its assets, the partners must contribute to the losses. Where creditors proceed against the partnership assets rather than directly against the partners, contribution and

---

[31] U.P.A. § 18(a); R.U.P.A. § 401(b); Bromberg & Ribstein, § 6.02(b).
[32] *See* U.P.A. § 18(b); R.U.P.A. § 401(c); Bromberg & Ribstein, § 6.02(f).

indemnification are, in effect, telescoped into a single proceeding involving creditors, partners and the partnership.[33] A partner whose intentionally wrongful conduct caused the liability probably cannot seek indemnification, and must indemnify the partnership.[34] A partner who was merely negligent may be entitled to indemnification under the agreement or default provisions of the statute, and in any event probably has no duty to indemnify the partnership for the whole amount of the loss.

The indemnification context is modified in LLPs. It is important to keep in mind that indemnification normally will be an issue mainly as to claims creditors can pursue directly against the partners without exhausting remedies against the partnership. If an outside creditor has come up empty-handed against the partnership, the partner seeking indemnification is likely to fare no better. Partnership statutes require exhaustion at least in contract claims, and increasingly in all types of claims (*see* Section 3.08(b), above). Thus, indemnification may not be very helpful even under the tort-only LLP shield. A creditor might sue directly a partner who is liable for her own misconduct or for supervising or failing to monitor the misconduct of others (*see* Section 3.08(c), above).

It is important to keep in mind in this connection that the liability shield in LLP statutes has been held not to preclude such partners from obtaining contribution in the absence of contrary agreement (*see* Section 3.09(c), above). Also, a partner may be held liable for agreed contributions irrespective of the statutory default rule, subject to any applicable statutory provisions regarding the effectiveness of pre-registration agreements discussed below.[35] Thus, if the partners want to ensure their limited liability even in actions among themselves, they must be careful to address this issue clearly in the partnership agreement.

The partners may make clear in their agreement an obligation to indemnify partners whose faulty supervision or monitoring led to direct liability (*see* Section 2.09(d), above). Such agreements may be necessary to induce partners who are involved in risky activities to agree to LLP registration that ends other partners' participation in the risk. The agreement may even make clear that the partners must make good any indemnification by contributing to the partnership out of their personal assets. Courts should enforce the agreement even if it

---

[33] In some cases, creditors must exhaust remedies against the partnership or are barred in bankruptcy from proceeding against the partners. *See* § 3.08, supra.

[34] *See* Rubin Quinn Moss Heaney & Patterson, P.C. v. Kennel, 832 F. Supp. 922 (E.D. Pa. 1993) (holding that law firm was entitled to indemnification from a partner for funds the firm paid to clients on account of the partner's misappropriation of client funds); Gramercy Equities Corp. v. DuMont, 72 N.Y.2d 560, 534 N.Y.S.2d 908, 531 N.E.2d 629 (1988) (denying indemnification to joint venturer who alone defrauded third parties); Flynn v. Reaves, 135 Ga. App. 651, 218 S.E.2d 661 (1975) (wrongdoing partner not entitled to indemnification); Bromberg & Ribstein, § 4.07(h), n.94.

[35] *See* Henry v. Masson, 333 S.W.3d 825 (Tex. App. 2010) (liability under agreement for contributions during winding up necessary to discharge debts; interpreting the agreement to require the payments even if funds are not available from the sale of partnership property).

requires payments by partners whose liability to creditors is limited under the statute. The statutes are intended only to cover the liability of partners to *creditors* rather than inter-partner adjustments. In any event, the partners ought to be able to waive statutory consequences that apply among themselves.

Note that a creditor's representative such as a bankruptcy trustee can enforce a partner's contribution obligation.[36] A court might permit such enforcement even of an obligation that arises under the partnership agreement. On the other hand, a court might permit enforcement only by the intended beneficiary of the agreement, the indemnified partner, particularly if a contrary interpretation would undercut the LLP liability shield.

In general, the potential for triggering contribution obligations suggests that partners should be careful in drafting indemnification provisions in LLP agreements (*see* Section 2.09(d)).

Partners' agreements to pay partnership liabilities raise troublesome issues when they are included in the pre-registration partnership agreement and it is not clear whether the partners intended the provisions to survive registration. R.U.P.A. § 306(c) attempts to deal with this problem by providing that the section that limits partner liability "shall apply notwithstanding anything inconsistent in the partnership agreement that existed immediately before the vote required to become a limited liability partnership." As shown in Table 3-1, some states have adopted this language. This provision deals with situations where partners have not engaged in the detailed planning necessary to align their agreement with LLP registration. Indeed, a major function of business association statutes is to reduce the need for such detailed contracting.[37] Thus, LLP statutes arguably should provide a default term that rewrites contracts consistent with the parties' presumed expectations. However, the parties' expectations may not be clear. In particular, they may have intended that the indemnification and contribution provisions survive registration and were unaware that they had to explicitly so provide. Moreover, it is not clear which "inconsistent" partnership agreement provisions the statute overrides. For example, does it apply to an agreement to make additional contributions or assessments when voted by the partners or managers? The official comment to this section says that it does not, but this is far from clear, particularly where the additional contributions are demanded specifically in order to pay extraordinary liabilities. The better approach therefore may be to assume that the partners themselves will make necessary changes in the partnership agreement to reflect registration.[38]

---

[36] *See* U.P.A. § 40(e); R.U.P.A. § 807(f).

[37] *See* Ribstein, Statutory Forms for Closely Held Firms: Theories and Evidence from LLCs, 73 Wash. U. L.Q. 369 (1995).

[38] The need to adjust the agreement suggests the importance of a default unanimity voting rule on LLP registration. *See* § 2.04, supra.

(c)   Agreements on Partner Compensation and Profit-shares

Although, as discussed above in Section 4.04(a), the appropriate partnership default rule probably should not change for LLPs, LLP registration may affect partnership agreements on compensation. The effect of the LLP provisions is to shift partner liability for misconduct-type claims from a regime in which each partner may have to pay all partnership debts to one in which a partner must pay out of nonpartnership assets only for misconduct in which she is implicated. In general, this shifts some risk from partners who are remote from the wrong to any partner who is closely associated with the wrongdoing.

The partners may want to reflect this reallocation of risk in the allocation of profit shares. For example, under the current regime, a professional partnership may have a "lockstep" seniority-based compensation system that gives the highest compensation to the most senior partners who have the most wealth and, therefore, the largest liability risk under a vicarious liability system.[39] If the firm registers as an LLP, the partners may want to change their compensation method to one in which the partners in the more liability-prone departments are compensated for taking the largest risk of personal liability.[40] The partners whose riskier activities earn substantial revenues for the firm could demand, in effect, to share the risk of personal liability with the partners who gain from these revenues. Indeed, unless affected partners are compensated for the increased risk, their risk-adjusted compensation will decline as a result of the registration.[41]

These potential changes in the agreement concerning partner compensation raise both legal and practical issues. The legal issue is whether reducing a partner's compensation on account of a potential claim for which the statute limits liability would amount to imposing liability contrary to the statute. It is highly unlikely that the statute would be so interpreted. As discussed above in Section 4.04(b), it is not even clear that the statute applies to inter-partner adjustments through indemnification. Even if the statute applies to indemnification, a change in compensation would reflect liabilities only in an attenuated and indirect way. And even if the statute technically applies in this situation, it is arguably only a default rule that the parties can waive by agreement.

The more important issue raised by changes in compensation is a practical one. Because LLP provisions reallocate risk among the partners, and because partners may be able effectively to block LLP conversion either by voting against it (*see* Section

---

[39] There are other possible reasons for a seniority-based compensation system in a law firm, including enabling the partners to diversify the risks associated with revenue shifts among specialties. *See* Gilson & Mnookin, Sharing Among the Human Capitalists: An Economic Inquiry into the Law Firm and How Partners Split Profits, 37 Stan. L. Rev. 313 (1985).

[40] *See* Hamilton, Registered Limited Liability Partnerships: Present at the Birth (Nearly), 66 U. Colo. L. Rev. 1065 (1995).

[41] On the other hand, changing the profit share could defeat the risk-allocation attributes of the existing compensation scheme. *See* note 39, supra.

2.04, above) or by dissociating, LLP registration is likely to trigger renegotiation and rewriting of the agreement. Even partners who do not bear an increased liability risk could use their blocking power to insist on changes in the agreement. These costs of rewriting the agreement could outweigh any benefits from the registration.

In general, problems with renegotiating the agreement depend on how much the partners as a whole gain from the registration and how they share these benefits. For example, in a relatively small, non-departmentalized firm composed of partners with relatively equal wealth whose work involves relatively equal liability risk, the registration may significantly lessen the partners' individual liability risk and may benefit all partners relatively equally. Accordingly, there may be little problem in obtaining all partners' consent to the registration. In a larger departmentalized firm, the registration may help partners in less risky parts of the firm's practice but have relatively little effect on partners in the riskier areas who retain personal liability for their own misconduct or that of partners or employees acting under their supervision. In a firm that has some senior partners near the end of their careers and some relatively young partners, the registration may benefit the younger partners far more than the older ones.

(d)   Distributions to Partners

LLP provisions introduce two types of conflicts regarding distributions to partners. First, such statutes—particularly those that completely shield partners from vicarious liability—give partners an incentive to distribute assets to themselves in order to avoid paying claims against the partnership. Second, partners who can be sure of being protected against vicarious liability may have an incentive to distribute assets while those who might have direct liability for faulty monitoring or other conduct may want to ensure that the partnership retains enough assets to pay claims that they may otherwise have to face alone.

With respect to the first potential conflict—that between partners and creditors—partnership statutes, unlike limited partnership, corporation, and LLC statutes, generally do not include restrictions on partnership distributions or on making or compromise of capital contributions. Exceptions are the original Minnesota statute[42] and the North Dakota statute, which apply their corporate dividend restrictions to LLPs;[43] the Colorado and Oregon statutes, which restrict distributions by LLPs unless their assets exceed liabilities;[44] the Arizona statute, which prohibits distributions in violation of the fraudulent transfer statute;[45] the

---

[42] Minn. Stat. Ann. § 323.14. The Minnesota statute has been revised so that it is closely based on R.U.P.A., which does not include the distribution restriction. *See* Minn. St. Ann. § 323A.0306.

[43] N.D. Cent. Code § 45-22-10.

[44] Colo. Rev. Stat. §§ 7-64-1004–1005 (also restricting return of contributions); Or. Rev. Stat. § 67.615.

[45] Ariz. Rev. Stat. § 29-1026(F).

Delaware statute, which imposes liability only on partners in LLPs who knowingly receive dividends in violation of the restriction;[46] and the California statute, which restricts distributions both when the firm cannot pay debts when they come due and when liabilities and amounts needed to satisfy preferential rights exceed assets.[47]

The usual partnership rule reflects the fact that, since creditors of partnerships need not rely on the firm's assets, they need no assurance that the firm will have assets available for the payment of debts. The situation changes, of course, in LLPs. Some LLP statutes in effect compensate for the lack of restrictions on capitalization and distributions through insurance and bonding requirements (*see* Section 2.06, above). However, most statutes do not have insurance or bonding requirements, and any mandatory insurance may be inadequate to cover large liabilities. The courts may compensate for any shortfall in insurance requirements or other statutory protection by imposing veil-piercing liability on firms that distribute a high proportion of their earnings and thereby leave little capital for the payment of claims (*see* Section 3.07, above). Moreover, distributions by insolvent firms may trigger fraudulent conveyance liability. It is not clear whether partnership fraudulent conveyance law will be applied to LLPs (*see* Section 7.02, below).[48]

Restrictions on distributions by partnerships may have a serious impact on professional firms.[49] Such firms tend to distribute all of their earnings to the partners.[50] Indeed, some partnerships compensate partners based on "profit center" approach that bills and credits to the partners their shares of revenue and expense items.[51] Such firms operate more as centers for distributing income to partners than as independent profit-generating entities. Viewed in this light, the statutes that apply corporate restrictions on dividends to LLPs could create significant problems if they are interpreted to require LLPs to retain significant earnings. Moreover, statutes that require partners to disgorge distributions by insolvent firms create a possibly anomalous distinction between partners

---

[46]Del. Code Ann., tit. 6, § 15-309. The Colorado statute has a similar limitation. *See* Colo. Rev. Stat. § 7-64-1004 (2).

[47]Cal. Corp. Code § 16957.

[48]If an LLP's solvency for fraudulent conveyance purposes is determined, as for a non-LLP partnership, by taking into account partners' net assets, then an LLP's conveyances may not be fraudulent even if the firm's liabilities exceed the firm's assets. Courts more likely will consider partner net assets in determining solvency only to the extent the partners must contribute these toward the payment of the firm's liabilities. In any event, it is not clear that the fraudulent transfer rules for determining partnership insolvency would differ from those applicable under special LLP distribution provisions.

[49]For example, former partners of Brobeck, Phleger & Harrison agreed to pay more than $22 million to settle claims arising out of payment to these partners of distributions and bonuses while the firm was insolvent. *See* Sandburg, The Recorder, Feb. 23, 2005, *available at* http://www.law.com/jsp/article.jsp?id=1109120820688.

[50]*See* Hamilton, note 40, supra.

[51]*See* Bromberg & Ribstein, § 6.02(b).

whose earnings are in the form of salaries and those who receive profit distributions.

The Colorado, California, Delaware, North Dakota, and Oregon statutes include language that may deal with these problems of distributions by professional firms. Colorado exempts from distribution restrictions "reasonable compensation to the partners for their participation as employees in the business of the partnership regularly or customarily paid to partners or their estates in the normal course of the partnership business."[52] Oregon is similar.[53] Delaware exempts "amounts constituting reasonable compensation for present or past services or reasonable payments made in the ordinary course of business pursuant to a bona fide retirement plan or other benefits program."[54] The North Dakota statute exempts employee partners from liability for distributions "regularly paid to the partner on account of engagement in the partnership business to the extent the distribution is reasonable compensation for the partner's services to or on behalf of the partnership."[55] Of course, "reasonable," "regularly," "customarily," and "normal course" may be in dispute, particularly where individual partners' compensation varies significantly from year to year and is not determined by a precise formula. The California statute provides that "a distribution for purposes of this section means the transfer of money or property by a registered limited liability partnership to its partners without consideration."[56] This language may be broad enough to permit the firm to compensate for services without violating the distribution restrictions.

The second type of conflict regarding distributions—that among the partners with differing exposure to liability—may be dealt with in the partnership agreement (*see* Section 2.09(h), above) or through judicially imposed fiduciary duties as discussed immediately below (*see* Section 4.05, below).

§ 4.05   FIDUCIARY DUTIES

A partnership's LLP status does not change the basic rule that partners owe fiduciary duties to one another, and probably does not necessitate a change in the statutory provisions that very generally describe partners' duties.[57] However, LLP status may significantly affect the duties courts apply in specific cases. The nature of fiduciary duties in any particular contractual relationship is affected by

---

[52] Colo. Rev. Stat. § 7-64-1004.
[53] Or. Rev. Stat. § 67.615.
[54] Del. Code Ann., tit. 6, § 15-309(a).
[55] N.D. Cent. Code § 45-22-10(3).
[56] Cal. Corp. Code § 16957(c).
[57] U.P.A. § 21; R.U.P.A. § 404.

the express and implied terms of the relevant contract.[58] A partnership's LLP status is an important contextual factor that the courts must take into account in determining the scope of fiduciary duties in the partnership.

LLP status may have different effects on partners' duties of loyalty and care. The duty of loyalty includes the duty to refrain from self-benefiting use of the partnership's property, from using management control to enter into self-benefiting deals with the partnership, and from competition with and usurping opportunity of the partnership.[59] The duty of care involves exercising caution in supervising the partnership activities and in entering into particular deals.[60]

LLP status is unlikely to have any direct effect on partners' incentives to engage in self-dealing or take partnership property or opportunities. However, LLP status may create conflicts of interest that are unique to this type of firm. For example, partners who have potential direct liability for participating in or failing to monitor misconduct may attempt to prevent the firm from distributing earnings that could be used to pay the claim and proportionately reduce their responsibility.[61] Courts may or may not hold that this involves a conflict of interest. It is not clear, however, whether the exposed partners' interests in retaining income are superior to those of the other partners in distributing it. Accordingly, the partners probably should make clear in the partnership agreement any limitations they wish to impose on distributions (*see* Section 2.09(h), above).

LLP status also may affect the partners' duty of care. Where all partners are personally liable for the debts of the firm, they have a substantial incentive to exercise caution in supervising the firm in order to avoid having to pay partnership debts out of personal assets. Limited liability reduces this incentive. Moreover, a stricter duty of care might be necessary to offset possible partner incentives to remain remote from conduct in order to insulate themselves from personal liability for participating in or failing to monitor misconduct (*see* Section 3.04(b), above). Accordingly, a fiduciary duty of care may be more necessary in this context to ensure that partners exercise caution. On the other hand, this analysis applies largely to smaller firms. In large partnerships the risk of personal liability for partnership debts is remote enough that LLP registration makes little change in the partners' incentives.

The above discussion concerns default fiduciary duties. LLP status also arguably should relate to whether the partners ought to be able to modify or

---

[58] *See* Ribstein, The Revised Uniform Partnership Act, Not Ready for Prime Time, 49 Bus. Law. 45, 52 (1993).

[59] *See* R.U.P.A. § 404(b); Bromberg & Ribstein, § 6.07(b)–(e).

[60] *See* R.U.P.A. § 404(c); Bromberg & Ribstein, § 6.07(f).

[61] *See* Hamilton, note 40, supra. Whether this strategy is successful depends on whether the partners' direct liability is in the nature of a duty to contribute to the partnership's liability, or whether the "guilty" partners must contribute as independent joint tortfeasors. *See* § 3.09(d), supra. In the latter case, payments by the partnership may not reduce the wrongdoing partners' proportionate share.

eliminate fiduciary duties. It may be that, where partners are personally liable for the firm's debts, they are exposed to greater risk from fiduciary breach, and have less ability to exit the firm, than where the partners have limited liability. Thus, LLPs arguably should have the same power to opt out of fiduciary duties that LLCs and limited partnerships have in some states.[62]

§ 4.06 LITIGATION AND REMEDIES

LLP status may affect litigation by and against the LLP. Partnerships historically were not legal entities for litigation purposes.[63] Although this is changing for non-LLP partnerships, it continues to be the rule in some places. Because registration as an LLP creates limited liability, it forces plaintiffs to look to the firm's assets, and therefore increases the importance of suing the firm as an entity. If suits can be brought against the LLP in its name, it arguably should follow that the LLP should be able to sue in its name. Thus, it has been held that an LLP can sue and be sued in its name despite cases to the contrary involving non-LLP general partnerships.[64]

Federal diversity jurisdiction is discussed below in Section 6.05, since it is an aspect of LLPs operating outside their home jurisdiction.

LLP status also may affect remedies among the partners. Historically, the most important remedy among partners is the action for an accounting.[65] A partnership's LLP status could not, itself, affect a partner's right to an accounting. The need for a way to resolve partners' claims will not change for LLPs, in which partners can be expected to have the same sorts of disputes as in non-LLP partnerships.

What could change as a result of LLP status is the exclusivity of the accounting remedy. Under the exclusivity rule, the partners must sue each other in accounting.[66] Exclusivity is rooted in ancient history—the aggregate theory of partnership and the separation of law courts from the equity courts in which partners' claims against each other could be heard.[67] But exclusivity also is based on the practical consideration that all claims between the partners must be resolved and a balance struck in order to resolve any individual claims.[68] One

---

[62] *See, e.g.,* 6 Del. Code § 17-1101 (permitting limited partnerships to modify or eliminate fiduciary duties); *id.* § 18-1101 (same for limited liability companies).

[63] *See* Bromberg & Ribstein, §1.03(c)(3).

[64] Brown Rudnick Berlack Israels LLP v. Brooks, 311 F. Supp. 2d 131 (D. Mass. 2004) (Mass. law).

[65] *See* U.P.A. § 22 (providing for right to account); R.U.P.A. § 405 (providing for accounting and other remedies); Bromberg & Ribstein, § 6.08.

[66] *See* Bromberg & Ribstein, § 6.08(c).

[67] Bromberg & Ribstein, § 6.08(c) at n.18.

[68] Bromberg & Ribstein, § 6.08(c) at nn.19–31.

reason for having to resolve all claims together is that the partners traditionally not only share profits but have a duty to contribute toward losses. Once the duty to contribute toward losses is eliminated or mitigated, an important source of cross claims between partners also disappears, and with it one of the arguments for requiring partner claims to be resolved in an accounting.

There are, of course, other reasons why the partners would be bringing claims against each other that should be resolved in a single proceeding, and most LLP statutes do not completely eliminate the partners' duty to contribute toward losses. But there are already strong reasons for eliminating the accounting exclusivity rule in non-LLP partnerships, including the superiority of modern joinder and permissive cross-claim rules to the rigid accounting exclusivity rule and the merger of law of equity. There is also case law support for eliminating the exclusivity rule[69] and the rule has been eliminated in the R.U.P.A.[70] Moreover, there is no accounting exclusivity rule in any other type of firm, including the closely similar LLC. Thus, even a marginal reduction in the practical underpinning of the accounting rule may be enough to push its demise in some jurisdictions.

The relief granted in an accounting action will be affected by the LLP's impact on contribution and indemnification discussed in Sections 3.09(b)–(d) and 4.03(b), above.

§ 4.07 DISSOCIATION, DISSOLUTION, AND OTHER FUNDAMENTAL CHANGES

The effect of LLP status on partner contribution obligations in connection with dissolution was discussed above in Section 3.11(c). This section discusses the impact of LLP status on the partners' rights in connection with dissolution and dissociation.

Partnership law gives each partner the power to exit the partnership at any time. U.P.A. § 31 provides that a partner may dissolve the partnership by express will at any time, irrespective of any contrary provision in the partnership agreement. Under the U.P.A., this dissolution triggers a liquidation of the partnership unless the partners have agreed otherwise[71] or the partnership is for a specific term or undertaking that has not expired at the time of the dissolution.[72] Under

---

[69] *See* Sertich v. Moorman, 162 Ariz. 407, 783 P.2d 1199 (1989).

[70] *See* R.U.P.A. § 405 (permitting actions by a partner against the partnership or another person "with or without an accounting").

[71] U.P.A. § 38(1) (unless otherwise agreed, partners may have partnership property applied to discharge liabilities).

[72] U.P.A. § 38(2).

R.U.P.A., a partner may withdraw at any time[73] irrespective of any contrary provision in the partnership agreement.[74] Subject to contrary agreement,[75] a partner may trigger dissolution of the partnership if the partnership is at will.[76] If the partnership is for a definite term or particular undertaking and a partner dissociates wrongfully or by bankruptcy or death (or an equivalent event for a partner who is not an individual), the partnership dissolves if a majority express their will to do so within 90 days thereafter.[77] If there is no dissolution, the partnership must buy out the dissociating partner.[78]

LLP status should not change the basic default rule that a partner can exit at any time. This right of exit and buyout provides necessary liquidity by compensating for the inherent difficulty of selling partnership interests that is associated with the nontransferability of management rights (*see* Section 4.02(d), above).

Nor should LLP status change the partnership default rule that the partnership is dissolved and liquidated on partner dissociation or express will unless otherwise agreed or unless the partnership is for a term, at least under LLP statutes that provide that partners have personal liability for contract-type debts. To be sure, there are strong arguments for abandoning this rule even in non-LLP partnerships.[79] But the relevant issue is whether LLP status should change this rule. The strongest basis for dissolution-at-will is the partners' need to settle partnership liabilities that otherwise would continue to bind exiting partners. This continues to apply under LLP statutes that preserve the partners' liability for contract-type claims, which are the most important category of outstanding debts that need to be settled on liquidation. Tort-type claims often will not be known or capable of being settled on dissolution. Accordingly, as long as LLP status provides only limited protection from vicarious liability the default rule should not change. The conclusion may differ, however, under LLP statutes that fully limit partners' liability (*see* Section 3.03, above). Since there are strong arguments for abandoning dissolution-at-will even in non-LLP partnerships,[80] without personal liability dissolution-at-will is harder to justify.

LLP status should change the rule that refuses to give effect to partners' agreements that prohibit dissociation at will. The need to restrict dissociation in family firms (*see* Section 5.02(b)) may spur such a change. The main argument against enforcing such agreements is that the partners' inability to stop their continuing responsibility for partnership claims would impose such an onerous

---

[73] R.U.P.A. § 601(1), 602.
[74] R.U.P.A. § 103(b)(6).
[75] R.U.P.A.'s dissolution and buyout provisions are not listed as unwaivable in R.U.P.A. § 103(b).
[76] R.U.P.A. § 801(1).
[77] R.U.P.A. § 801(2).
[78] R.U.P.A. §§ 603(a), 701.
[79] *See* Ribstein, note 58, supra, at 69–70; Ribstein, A Statutory Approach to Partner Dissociation, 65 Wash. U. L.Q. 357 (1987).
[80] *See* articles cited in note 79, supra.

obligation on partners that any agreement to bear the obligation is suspect. But even in non-LLP general partnerships non-dissociation agreements should be enforced, particularly in light of the exhaustion requirement (*see* Section 3.08(b), above), which, if applicable, reduces the "sting" of partners' liability.[81] The rationale for non-enforcement disappears in LLPs. LLP partners are not vicariously liable to involuntary creditors, and therefore should be able to limit their continuing liability by contract. Conversely, they should be able to give contractual assurances to lessors and other creditors that they will not suddenly withdraw their personal credit from the firm.

§ 4.08   EFFECT OF LLP REGISTRATION ON CONTINUATION OF THE PARTNERSHIP

The LLP registration should have no effect on the continuity of the underlying partnership. Many LLP statutes provide that a partnership that files an LLP registration continues to be the same partnership or entity as before, or does not dissolve as a result of, the registration.[82] This has been confirmed by case law.[83] These statutes and cases may be effective to prevent disruption in such contexts as property ownership and pending litigation. LLP registration therefore may provide greater continuity than conversion or merger (*see* Section 1.05(b), above). The rule is arguably justified by the fact that the registration is simply a change in some of the terms affecting the partnership, particularly including the partners' liability, and not in the underlying entity. By agreeing to the registration (*see* Section 2.04), the partners are, in effect, agreeing only to amend their

---

[81] *See* Ribstein, Prime Time, note 58, supra, at 64.

[82] *See, e.g.,* Minn. Stat. § 323A.201(b); Mont. Code Ann. § 35-10-637(1); N.M. Stat. Ann. § 54-1A-201 (continues to be same entity); Okla. Stat. tit., § 54-1-201 (continues to be same entity); Va. Code. § 50-73.132(E); W. Va. Code § 47B-10-2; Wis. Stat. § 178.41(2)(a); Prototype LLP Act § 910(e). *See also* Ind. Code § 23-4-1-7(5) (partnership's existence is not affected by registration); N.D. Cent. Code § 45-22-03(7) (LLP registration does not dissolve general partnership).

[83] *See* Hart v. Theus, Grisham, Davis & Leigh, L.L.P., 877 So. 2d 1157 (La. App. 2004) (enforcing arbitration provision of pre-LLP agreement over partner's argument that the agreement should not be enforced after LLP registration because it changed the partners' relative risk of liability; *see* § 2.09(g), note 120, supra); Sasaki v. McKinnon, 124 Ohio App. 3d 613, 707 N.E.2d 9 (1997) (holding that LLP was the successor of the pre-LLP partnership but the same entity); Howard v. Klynveld Peat Marwick Goerdeler, 977 F. Supp. 654 (S.D.N.Y. 1997) (stating that when firm became an LLP "[t]he partnership was not dissolved and continued without interruption with the same partners, principals, employees, assets, rights, obligations, liabilities and operations as maintained prior to the change. Thus, Peat Marwick LLP is in all respects the successor in interest to Peat Marwick"). For a discussion of the analogous partnership/LLC conversion situation, see § 1.05(b), note 68, supra; Ribstein & Keatinge, § 11.13.

agreement. By the same token, cancellation of the LLP registration alone should not be considered to cause dissolution of the partnership. On the other hand, a "same entity" provision in the statute should not necessarily override an agreement with a creditor or among the partners that specifically provides for termination or other consequences on registration of the firm as an LLP (*see* Section 3.11(d)).

≡5≡

LIMITED PARTNERSHIP as LLP:
THE LLLP

As shown in Table 5-1, some state limited liability partnership (LLP) acts allow limited partnerships to register as LLPs.[1] This chapter discusses rules that apply to the business association that results from such a registration — a "limited liability limited partnership," or "LLLP." These rules concern the liability limitation (Section 5.02), and effect of LLP status on other limited partnership

---

[1] Oregon, which is restricted to professional firms, explicitly prohibits a limited partnership from registering as an LLP. Or. Rev. Stat. § 67.500(1). The Pennsylvania act provides that the LLP provisions apply to limited partnerships that register as LLPs. 15 Pa. C.S.A. § 8201(a).

rules (Section 5.03). Section 5.04 discusses the application of LLP provisions that do not explicitly provide for LLLLPs. Section 5.05 discusses some important considerations in choosing the LLLP form. Foreign LLLPs are discussed below in Section 6.02(a).

Limited partnership acts also deal with LLLP registration. The Prototype LLP Act and R.U.P.A. § 101, cmt., both suggest amendments to R.U.L.P.A. U.L.P.A. §§ 102(9) and 201(a)(4) (2001) now expressly deal with LLPs by requiring the firm to elect between LLLP and non-LLLP status in the certificate (*see* Section 9.201, below). As with other aspects of limited partnership law, U.L.P.A. (2001) has "delinked" limited and general partnership law, providing for all of the requirements and consequences of LLLP status in the limited partnership law. LLLP provisions are likely to move in this direction.

As discussed in Section 5.02(b), an LLLP is closely similar to a centrally managed LLC, particularly when limited partners have no control liability under the applicable LLP or limited partnership provisions. In general, as discussed in more detail below in Section 5.05, a firm may choose to be an LLLP rather than an LLC or LLP if it wants secure centralized management or wants for some reason to be subject to the rules governing limited partnerships.

§ 5.01   FORMATION OF LLLP

(a)   *Formation of the Underlying Limited Partnership*

The LLP provisions shown in Table 5-1 permit LLP registration of "limited partnerships." Thus, a firm that is not a "limited partnership" because, for example, it has failed to comply with the filing or other requirements of the limited partnership statute, cannot be an LLLP. This raises the question whether the abortive limited partnership should be treated as a general partnership, which would be an LLP if it has complied with the LLP provisions. General and limited partners arguably should not have less liability protection by attempting to become a limited partnership than if they had organized as a general partnership and then registered as an LLP. But the "erroneous partner" provisions in limited partnership statutes[2] create express general partner liability for the abortive limited partner who does not file or correct a certificate to show actual status and whom a third party transacting business with the firm in good faith believes

---

[2]R.U.L.P.A. § 304 (1985). *See* Bromberg & Ribstein, § 12.04(e), (f) (1988 & Supp.).

to be a general partner. Given literal application of these provisions, an abortive limited partner would have general partner liability, while the intended general partners presumably would be treated like general partners in a general partnership and receive the protection of the LLP registration. The only possible justification for this strange result would be to deter noncompliance with limited partnership formalities. But since general partners normally are the ones who are responsible for compliance, punishing the limited partners would not have the desired effect. Moreover, it is questionable whether the potential injury from noncompliance with formalities is enough to justify this draconian result. The only reasonable result would be to treat the abortive limited partners as general partners protected by the LLP registration.

(b) Compliance with LLP Requirements

The LLP statutes that permit registration by LLLPs require compliance with the requirements of LLP statutes, including those relating to registration, name, and insurance. Many limited partnership acts have provisions relating to LLLPs.[3] The statutes also have special name requirements for LLLPs (*see* Section 2.05, above).

(c) Approval of Registration

As shown in Table 5-1, most LLLP provisions have specific requirements for partner approval of the LLLP registration. An important model is the Delaware statute, which provides for registration:

> . . . as permitted by the limited partnership's partnership agreement or, if the limited partnership's partnership agreement does not provide for the limited partnership's becoming a limited liability limited partnership, with the approval (i) by all general partners, and (ii) by the limited partners or, if there is more than 1 class or group of limited partners, then by each class or group of limited partners, in either case, by limited partners who own more than 50 percent of the then current percentage or other interest in the profits of the limited partnership owned by all of the limited partners or by the limited partners in each class or group, as appropriate. . . .[4]

This section of the Delaware statute provides the voting rule at least for all limited partnership agreements that antedate the LLP statutes, since such firms are

---

[3] Statutory provisions are summarized in Table 5-1.
[4] Del. Code Ann., tit. 6, § 17-214.

not likely to have agreements that provide for LLP registration. The statute also provides the rule for limited partnerships that are formed after the LLP statute but do not provide specifically for LLP registration.

Another important model that has already been adopted by some states and is likely to be adopted by others is the LLLP provision suggested in R.U.P.A., which, as for LLP registration, requires approval "by the vote necessary to amend the limited partnership agreement except, in the case of a limited partnership agreement that expressly considers contribution obligations, the vote necessary to amend those provisions."[5]

These and other default voting requirements are shown in Table 5-1. They include, subject to contrary provision in the agreement, unanimity or the vote required to amend the agreement. The Virginia statute provides for a vote permitted by a *written* partnership agreement, or the vote required to amend a *written* partnership agreement.[6] As appears from comparing the statutory provisions summarized in Table 5-1 with those summarized on Table 2-8, some statutes, provide different voting rules for limited partnerships than they prescribe for general partnerships. This includes Delaware, whose LLP rule is based on R.U.P.A.

Note that, as discussed above in Section 2.04, there are potential questions concerning what provisions of the partnership agreement determine voting on LLP registration when there is no explicit reference to such registration. The Tennessee provision, shown on Table 5-1, addresses this question by applying the vote that applies explicitly to LLP registration.

Issues analogous to those regarding approval of registration relate to relinquishment of LLLP registration. A firm may want to relinquish this status because the requirements and cost of maintaining it are no longer worth the minor difference in liability protection. U.L.P.A. § 1110 (2001) requires the consent of a partner who will have personal liability unless the partners have specifically agreed to permit this particular action without such consent. *See* Section 9.1110, below.

(d)   *Effect of Noncompliance with Requirements*

A limited partnership that purports to be an LLLP but that fails to comply with registration, name, or insurance requirements probably will be treated analogously to a general partnership in similar circumstances. In other words, it may be deemed to be an LLLP by "substantial compliance" with statutory requirements (*see* Section 2.07(b), above), or an LLLP by estoppel (*see* Section 2.07(c), above). As with a defective LLP, the noncompliance with LLLP requirements

---

[5] *See* R.U.P.A. § 101, Comment to Amendments.
[6] Va. Code Ann. § 50-73.78(A)(1).

probably has no effect on the existence of the underlying limited partnership (*see* Section 2.07(d), above). The effect of noncompliance with limited partnership formalities is discussed above in Section 5.01(a).

§ 5.02   LIABILITY OF LLLP PARTNERS

(a)   Liability of General Partners

The general partners in an LLLP are liable to the same extent as general partners in an LLP.[7] LLLP general partners may be able to waive the liability limitation (*see* Section 3.05, above). Such a firm would be, essentially, a limited partnership, except that it would not be subject to the control rule because the liability of the limited partners would not depend on whether they participated in control.

(b)   Vicarious Liability of Limited Partners and the Control Rule

As shown in Table 5-1, most states apply the LLP liability limitation not only to general partners but also to limited partners who are liable for the partnership's debts under the limited partnership act.[8] The Pennsylvania statute simply provides that the LLP provisions apply to limited partnerships that register as LLPs,[9] leaving unclear whether the LLP provisions apply to both general and limited partnerships.

The main effect of applying the LLP liability limitation to limited partners is to reduce the effect of the "control rule," pursuant to which limited partners may be liable for taking part in the control of the business.[10] Some firms may want to use the LLLP form to avoid the control rule's potential impact on limited partners. Locking limited partners out of control might increase limited partners' vulnerability to incompetent or dishonest general partners. The "control rule" normally has little impact because the R.U.L.P.A. provides for a creditor reliance requirement, as well as broad safe harbors that permit extensive limited partner control through positions in corporate general partners and otherwise.[11] However,

---

[7] *See generally* Chapter 3.

[8] These provisions may become decreasingly important if states follow U.L.P.A. § 303 (2001) in eliminating the "control" rule. *See* text accompanying note 13, below.

[9] 15 Pa. C.S.A. § 8201(c).

[10] R.U.L.P.A. § 303 (1985).

[11] R.U.L.P.A. § 303(b) (1985).

the control rule may be a significant constraint as the firm nears insolvency.[12] Although firms can protect themselves from liability by becoming LLCs, they may prefer to organize as LLLPs for the reasons discussed in Section 5.05.

Note, however, that issues regarding limited partners' limited liability in LLLPs have been mooted by the elimination of the control rule in U.L.P.A. (2001) (*see* Section 1.04(b), note 54, above). Two states already had eliminated control liability prior to U.L.P.A.[13]

Even if some firms may have a good reason for becoming limited partnerships without a control rule, it is not clear the firms should be able to accomplish this by becoming LLLPs if this might mislead creditors. Limited partnership statutes would continue to provide for the control rule, while the rule's teeth would be pulled by the possibly unexpected operation of the LLP statute. Thus, it might be better for statutes to make the control rule optional through an explicit waiver in the certificate or to eliminate it as a default rule rather than by permitting an "end run" through the LLP.

(c)   Direct Liability of Limited Partners

Limited partners in LLLPs may be subject to LLP statutory provisions that impose liability on partners who participate in or fail adequately to monitor the wrongdoing of others (*see* Section 3.04, above). Most LLLP provisions provide that the LLP provisions apply to limited partners who are liable for the partnership's debts under the limited partnership act. This suggests that limited partners may lose their protection from limited liability to the extent that they engage in the sort of conduct for which other LLP partners would be liable.

§ 5.03   EFFECT ON OTHER LIMITED PARTNERSHIP RULES

An LLLP is a very different sort of firm from a standard-form limited partnership. Not only would the general partners have limited liability, but the

---

[12] Indeed, application of the rule may be beneficial in this situation because limited partners otherwise might be tempted to take control and engage in risky strategies knowing that they can benefit from success while putting the cost of failure on the creditors.

[13] *See* Ga. Code Ann. § 14-9-303; Mo. Rev. Stat. § 359.201.

limited partners are apparently exempt from the control rule (*see* Section 5.02(b), above). This suggests the possibility that other rules in LLLPs should be changed to accommodate the changes effected by limited partners' liability. However, despite the limitation of liability, LLLPs would retain the limited partnership's basic bifurcated management structure of passive investors and active managers. Thus, the usual limited partnership rules concerning such matters as management, transfers, distributions, and dissolution continue to apply. Nevertheless, courts should be wary about applying limited partnership precedents in this new context. For example, limited partners who have been freed from the constraints of the control rule may no longer need the strong fiduciary protections of limited partners in standard limited partnerships. The effects of LLLP registration are also a consideration to be taken into account in drafting the limited partnership statute.[14]

§ 5.04   LLP STATUTES WITH NO LLLP PROVISIONS

Most LLP statutes do not explicitly provide for LLLPs. Uniform Partnership Act (U.P.A.) § 6(2) provides that the partnership act applies to limited partnerships except to the extent that limited partnership provisions are inconsistent. R.U.L.P.A. § 1105, which is in effect in most states, applies the general partnership statute "in any case not provided for in this Act." LLP provisions probably would not apply *to limited partners* under either the general partnership or the limited partnership statute since the LLP provisions would vary applicable provisions of the limited partnership statute. R.U.L.P.A. § 403(b) also provides that a general partner of a limited partnership has the liabilities of a partner in a partnership without limited partners. Under this provision, the LLP provisions arguably would apply to general partners in limited partnerships. However, a state that has adopted a limited partnership statute based on U.L.P.A. (2001) but without the statute's provisions for LLLPs would not recognize LLPs. U.L.P.A. (2001) explicitly delinks general and limited partnership law (*see* Section 9.101(a), below), thereby precluding application of the general partnership statute's LLP provisions to limited partnerships.

---

[14] *See* Ribstein, Limited Partnerships Revisited, 67 U. Cin. L. Rev. 953 (1999) (discussing this issue in the context of the project to revise R.U.L.P.A.).

§ 5.05   CHOICE-OF-FORM CONSIDERATIONS

Given the apparent similarity between the LLLP form and centralized management LLCs, it is important to analyze the choice between these two business forms. In general, the LLLP, by combining the advantages of the limited partnership form with those of limited liability for all partners, offers a unique type of centralized management in an unincorporated business association. There are several possible reasons why firms might want to be LLLPs rather than LLCs or other forms of business despite the apparent similarity of these two business forms:

(1) Firms may want to escape burdens such as state taxes that may be imposed on LLCs but not limited partnerships.

(2) "Family limited partnerships" might use the LLLP to assign equity interests without management or buyout rights or vicarious liability to family members by making them limited partners.[15] In this context, it may be enough to deny management rights to the family members and to restrict their authority to bind the firm without also giving a potential remedy to creditors if the family members do exercise management powers. The firm could not necessarily accomplish the same thing by becoming an LLP and delegating management rights to the senior managers because there is some question whether partnership law allows the necessary restriction on partner dissociation rights (*see* Section 4.07, above).

(3) LLLPs may provide a way to avoid the self-employment tax, which is not imposed on those who are classified for this purpose as limited partners.[16]

(4) The LLLP form helps ensure that only the designated managers — that is, the general partners — can manage the firm and bind it in transactions with third parties. In an LLC, even one that is centrally managed, there may be some question about who the managers are and about the scope of their authority (*see* Section 1.07(a)(9), above).

Assuming a firm wants to combine the limited partnership structure with limited liability for all partners, it has the additional option of forming a non-LLLP limited partnership and then incorporating the general partner.[17] One disadvantage of this approach is that it forces the firm to maintain a separate entity. Another potential disadvantage is that incorporating the general partner does not protect the limited partners from liability for participating in control of the business (*see* Section 5.02(b), above). This is obviously not a drawback under statutes that do not provide for control liability (*see* note 13, above) or do not

---

[15] The tax implications of restricted buyout rights in family firms are discussed in § 1.07(a)(11), note 84.

[16] *See* I.R.C. § 1402(a), discussed in § 7.05(f), infra.

[17] *See generally* Ribstein, An Applied Theory of Limited Partnership, 37 Emory L.J. 835, 868-71 (1988).

protect limited partners in LLLPs. A possible advantage of incorporating the general partner over forming an LLLP is that this involves less risk of interstate non-recognition of the liability shield (*see* Section 6.02(a), below).

TABLE 5-1. LLLP PROVISIONS

State	Section[†]	Categories
Alabama	10A-9-2.01, -2.04, -3.03, -4.04	1, 2b 3a
Alaska		4
Arizona	29-367; 29-1101, -1102, -1026(D)	1, 2c, 3
Arkansas	4-47-201(a)(4), -303, -404(c)	1, 3a
California		4
Colorado	7-64-306(3)–(4), -1001(1), -1002; 7-90-301	1, 2b, 3
Connecticut		4
Delaware	17-214	1, 2a, 3
District of Columbia	29-702.01(a)(4), -.04(a)(2); -703.03; -704.04	1, 2b, 3a
Florida	620.1404(3); 1102(10)	1, 3
Georgia	14-8-62(g), 14-9-403	1, 2b
Hawaii	425E-201(a)(4), -303; -404(c)	1, 2d, 3a
Idaho	53-2-201(a)(4), -303; -404(3)	1, 3a
Illinois	215/201(a)(4), -303, 404(c)	1, 2b, 3a
Indiana		4
Iowa	488.201(1)(d), .303, .404(3)	1, 2b, 3a
Kansas		4
Kentucky	362.2-201(2), 303 -404(3)	1, 2b, 3a
Louisiana		4
Maine	1321(1)(d), 1354(3), (4)	1, 3a*
Maryland	9A-1006	1, 2e, 3
Massachusetts		4
Michigan		4
Minnesota	321.0201, .0204(a)(2), 303, 404(a)	1, 2b, 3a
Mississippi		4
Missouri	358.510	1, 2a
Montana	35-12-601, -604(1)(b), -703, -803	1, 2b, 3a
Nebraska		4
Nevada	88.606-609	1, 2b, 3a
New Hampshire		4
New Jersey		4
New Mexico	54-2A-201(A)(4), -303, -404,	1, 2e, 3a

Table 5-1 (cont'd)

State	Section[†]	Categories
New York		4
North Carolina	59-210	1, 2e
North Dakota	45-23-01–45-23-09	1, 2b, 3a
Ohio	1782.64	1, 2c, 3
Oklahoma	500-201A, -204A, -303A, -404A	1, 2b, 3a
Oregon		4
Pennsylvania	8201	1
Prototype	920	1, 2c, 3
Revised Uniform Partnership Act	101 (cmt.)	1, 2c, 3
Rhode Island		4
South Carolina		4
South Dakota	48-7-1106	1, 2d, 3
Tennessee	61-1-1001	1, 2b
Texas	152.805 and 153.351–153.353	1, 2c, 3
Utah	48-2e-201(2)(d) -203(1)(b) -303, -404	1, 2b, 3a
Vermont		4
Virginia	50-73.142	1, 2c, 3
Washington	25.10.201, .231, .401	1, 2b, 3
West Virginia		4
Wisconsin		4
Wyoming	17-14-301(a)(xiv)	1

[†]*See* Table 5-2 for full statutory citations.

Categories

*   *See* Notes, below.

1.   Limited partnerships may register as LLPs, including by statement in the limited partnership certificate).

2.   Default approval provisions (if not otherwise agreed):
   a. Delaware model: by all general partners and half or more by class of ownership interests of limited partners (Delaware provides for more than 50 percent).
   b. All general partners (**North Dakota** permits partners to unanimously agree to approval by a lesser number, and provides for conversion of LLP to a limited partnership; **Tennessee** is notwithstanding contrary provision in limited partnership agreement for limited partnership formed before effective date of the act or for those formed after unless original limited partnership agreement provided for a lesser vote for converting the limited partnership to an LLP).

Table 5-1 (cont'd)

   c. Vote required for amendment (**Virginia** refers to *written* agreement).
   d. R.U.P.A. (and **Minnesota and North Dakota**): vote, if any, necessary to amend contribution obligations.
   e. No default voting provision or reference to persons authorized.
3. Liability limitation applies to limited as well as general partners.
   a. Statute includes U.L.P.A. (2001) provision eliminating limited partners' liability for participating in control. **Maine** provides for joint and several liability of partner of professional limited liability limited partnership for participating in or controlling or supervising conduct.
4. No LLLP provision.

TABLE 5-2. FULL STATUTORY CITATIONS

State	*Citation Information*
Alabama	Ala. St. § —
Alaska	Alaska Stat. § —
Arizona	Ariz. Rev. Stat. Ann. § —
Arkansas	Ark. Code § —
California	Cal. Corp. Code § —
Colorado	Colo. Rev. Stat. § —
Connecticut	Conn. Gen. Stat. § —
Delaware	Del. Code Ann. ch. 15, tit. 6, § —
District of Columbia	D.C. Code Ann. § —
Florida	Fla. Stat. Ann. § —
Georgia	Ga. Code Ann. § —
Hawaii	Haw. Rev. Stat. § —
Idaho	Idaho Code § —
Illinois	805 Ill. Comp. Stat. Ann.
Indiana	Ind. Code § —
Iowa	Iowa Code § —
Kansas	Kan. Stat. Ann. § —
Kentucky	Ky. Rev. Stat. Ann. § 362.2
Louisiana	La. Rev. Stat. Ann. § —

Table 5-2   **5.   Limited Partnership as LLP: The LLLP**

Table 5-2 (cont'd)

State	*Citation Information*
Maine	Me. Rev. Stat. Ann. tit. 31, § —
Maryland	Md. Code Ann., Corps. & Assns., § —
Massachusetts	Mass. Gen. L. ch. 108A, § —
Michigan	Mich. Comp. Laws § —
Minnesota	Minn. Stat. § —
Mississippi	Miss. Code Ann. § —
Missouri	Mo. Rev. Stat. § —
Montana	Mont. Code Ann. § —
Nebraska	Neb. Rev. Stat. § —
Nevada	Nev. Rev. Stat. § —
New Hampshire	N.H. Rev. Stat. Ann. § —
New Jersey	N.J. Rev. Stat. § —
New Mexico	N.M. Stat. Ann. § —
New York	N.Y. Partnership Law ch. 39, § — (Consol.)
North Carolina	N.C. Gen. Stat. § —
North Dakota	N.D. Cent. Code § —
Ohio	Ohio Rev. Code Ann. § —
Oklahoma	Okla. Stat. tit. 54, § —
Oregon	Or. Rev. Stat. § —
Pennsylvania	15 Pa. Cons. Stat. § —
Prototype	Prototype Registered Limited Liability Partnership Act, § —
Revised Uniform Partnership Act	Uniform Partnership Act (1994) with 1996 Amendments, § —
Rhode Island	R.I. Gen. Laws § —
South Carolina	S.C. Code Ann. § —
South Dakota	S.D. Codified Laws Ann. § —
Tennessee	Tenn. Code Ann. § —
Texas	Tex. Bus. Org. Code § —
Utah	Utah Code Ann. § —[18]
Vermont	Vermont St., tit. 11, § —
Virginia	Va. Code Ann. § —
Washington	Wash. Rev. Code § —
West Virginia	W. Va. Code § —
Wisconsin	Wis. Stat. § —
Wyoming	Wyo. Stat. § —

---

[18] Utah provisions cited in the text are effective July 1, 2013 for new entities and Jan. 1, 2015 for existing entities. *See* Utah Code Ann. § 48-1b-1205.

≡ 6 ≡

FOREIGN LLPs: CHOICE
of LAW and OTHER
LITIGATION ISSUES

This chapter discusses issues that arise when limited liability partnerships (LLPs) operate outside the jurisdiction in which they were formed. At one time, choice of law in partnerships was not a significant issue because the Uniform Partnership Act (U.P.A.) was in effect in virtually every state. Now, with the Revised Uniform Partnership Act (R.U.P.A.) in effect in 37 states and D.C., conflicts may occur. In addition, LLP statutes in each state both increase the problem of nonuniformity and help to solve that problem by including provisions that permit foreign LLPs to operate in other states, usually under the law of the formation state. Section 6.01 begins by discussing general policy considerations that are relevant in determining whether the law of the state of formation should apply to LLPs wherever they do business. Foreign LLP provisions are then discussed in Section 6.02. Section 6.03 discusses the application to LLPs of the choice-of-law rule in the R.U.P.A.

In general, a firm that has registered as an LLP is recognized as such (unless it opts out of this treatment under R.U.P.A. § 101(4)), including for liability purposes, in any state in which the LLP transacts business.[1] The principle of applying the registration state's law was recognized by *Liberty Mutual Insurance Co. v. Gardere & Wynne, LLP,*[2] in which the client of a Texas LLP sued for malpractice in Massachusetts, where some of the work was done. The judge ordered the case transferred to Texas for resolution of LLP and other partnership issues under Texas law. The main exceptions to interstate recognition of the liability shield concern local application of regulatory statutes, particularly including regulation of the legal profession and state securities laws. As shown in Table 6-2, this is explicit in some states. As discussed in Section 6.02(d), local law may apply to such matters even under statutes that do not make this explicit.[3]

Section 6.04 and Section 6.05 discuss long-arm and federal diversity jurisdiction applicable to foreign LLPs.

§ 6.01 GENERAL POLICY CONSIDERATIONS

Enforcing contractual choice of law serves valuable functions. These include facilitating exit from inefficient mandatory terms, promoting jurisdictional competition, furthering development of efficient standard form terms, resolving problems of multiple state regulation, and reducing uncertainty about which law applies.[4]

The problems concerning multiple state regulation are a particularly strong reason for enforcing contractual choice of law. Applying a separate set of governance and financial rules in each state in which a partnership transacts business would impose significant costs on multi-state firms.[5] If, for example, a different

---

[1] Firms that are not registered as LLPs are subject to general choice-of-law principles that are beyond the scope of this book. *See generally* O'Hara & Ribstein, The Law Market (2009); O'Hara & Ribstein, From Politics to Efficiency in Choice of Law, 67 U. Chi. L. Rev. 1151 (2000); Ribstein, From Efficiency to Politics in Contractual Choice of Law, 37 Ga. L. Rev. 363 (2003); Ribstein, Delaware, Lawyers and Choice of Law, 19 Del. J. Corp. L. 999 (1994), *reprinted in* 37 Corp. Practice Commentator 151 (1995); Ribstein, Choosing Law By Contract, 18 J. Corp. L. 245 (1993).

[2] 1994 WL 707133 (D. Mass. 1994). *See also* Dow v. Jones, 311 F. Supp. 2d 461 (D. Md. 2004) (discussed in § 6.02(d), note 28, infra; applying D.C. law to LLP registered in D.C.).

[3] *See* Dzienkowski, Legal Malpractice and the Multi-state Law Firm: Supervision of Multi-state Offices; Firms as Limited Liability Partnerships; and Predispute Agreements to Arbitrate Client Malpractice Claims, 36 S. Tex. L. Rev. 967, 988 (1995). For a discussion of an approach to choice of law for multi-jurisdictional law firms, see Ribstein, Ethical Rules, Law Firm Structure, and Choice of Law, 69 U. Cin. L. Rev. 1161 (2001).

[4] The costs and benefits of enforcing contractual choice of law are discussed in the articles cited in note 1, supra.

[5] *See* Ribstein, note 3, supra.

state's law applied to members residing in each state, the firm would have to have, in effect, separate classes of management and financial rights consisting of members in each state.

More important for LLPs, if a partnership is treated as an LLP in some states but not others, partners in some states would have limited liability while those elsewhere would not. Given the significant implications of limited liability for financial, governance, dissolution, transfer, and other member rights (*see* Chapter 4), this might, in effect, require a separate partnership agreement in each state. Moreover, the partnership would have to represent itself differently in each state through advertising, name, and letterheads (*see* Section 2.05, above). If the firm erred and mistakenly represented itself as a non-LLP in an LLP state, this could have disastrous consequences for the partners in that state. Even if the firm could maintain its separate identities in each state, this could confuse clients who deal with the firm in both LLP and non-LLP states. In general, applying different state laws relating to member liability would require the firm to operate completely separately in each state in which it did business. This could reduce or eliminate economies of scale and scope and the overall feasibility of multi-state partnerships.

The benefits of allowing parties to be governed under the partnership law of the state of their choice, including the LLP provisions of that law, must be balanced against the potential costs. These include possible confusion of third parties as to the variations in the liability shield in each state discussed in Chapter 3 and summarized in Table 3-1. Also, allowing firms to choose LLP provisions would allow partners to evade the restrictions on limited liability that are imposed in stricter states that are intended for the protection of third parties. These problems with enforcing contractual choice of law may or may not outweigh the significant benefits of allowing the parties to choose the applicable law. States obviously could eliminate problems caused by variation by adopting the same partnership law. Although the vast majority of states currently have adopted the R.U.P.A., many states have adopted idiosyncratic, modified versions of R.U.P.A., including its LLP provisions, as reflected in Table 3-1 and the discussions of state variations throughout Chapter 8. Thus, the problems of exposing firms to different laws in each state in which they operate will remain. Moreover, complete uniformity is not necessarily advantageous, since it would eliminate the possibility of experimentation and innovation and the potential advantages of permitting different types of firms to choose from among different statutes.[6]

---

[6] *See generally* Ribstein & Kobayashi, An Economic Analysis of Uniform State Laws, 25 J. Legal Stud. 131 (1996).

§ 6.02　FOREIGN LLP PROVISIONS

All LLP statutes include provisions relating to LLPs formed under the law of another jurisdiction (the "formation state") that transact business in another "operation" state. These statutes raise several issues that are addressed in this section. Section 6.02(a) discusses what types of firms are included in definitions of a foreign LLP for purposes of being recognized by and subject to the requirements of the statute. Subsection (b) discusses registration requirements. Subsection (c) discusses recognition of foreign LLPs as foreign limited liability companies (LLCs) or other types of firms under the statutes providing for those firms. Subsection (d) discusses the extent to which formation state law is applied to foreign LLPs under LLP registration provisions.

(a)　Definition of a Foreign LLP

The various state definitions of foreign limited liability partnership are summarized in Table 6-1. Most foreign LLP provisions define as a "foreign registered limited liability partnership" only a firm that is registered as an LLP under the laws of another jurisdiction (which could include foreign country) or state.[7] This could be called the "label" approach in that it defines a foreign LLP as one that is labeled as such rather than one that has certain characteristics. This provides a measure of certainty.

As shown in Table 6-1, some states include in their definitions of foreign LLPs firms that are not only denominated as such under the law of the organization state but that also meet some sort of similarity test.[8] This ensures against firms seeking protection under a state's LLP law although they are radically different from local LLPs. The tradeoff is a loss of clarity. To the extent that a state is concerned about unwanted variations, it could deal with the problem directly by limiting the extent to which foreign law applies as discussed below in Section 6.02(d). Alternatively, the statute could limit foreign LLP treatment to firms registered in a state or the District of Columbia, thereby taking advantage of the substantial consensus within the U.S. concerning the basic nature of the LLP.

The New York statute modifies the label approach. It includes any professional partnership without limited partners operating under an agreement governed by the laws of any other jurisdiction or a partnership "related" in a

---

[7] See, e.g., Ohio Rev. Code Ann. § 1776.01(I).

[8] See, e.g., D.C. Stat. § 29-601.01(5) (defining a foreign limited liability partnership as "a foreign partnership whose partners have limited liability for the debts, obligations, or other liabilities of the foreign partnership under a provision similar to § 29-603.06(c)").

specified way to a foreign professional partnership.[9] The California statute is similarly worded.[10]

In the absence of a statutory provision clarifying the treatment of foreign LLPs, common law choice-of-law rules relating to partnerships may apply.[11] This could mean the application of the law of the creditor's state, rather than that of the state of formation.[12]

A firm formed under an agreement that is governed by State X's law either by an explicit choice-of-law clause or a default choice-of-law rule may want to register as a *domestic* LLP in State Y to, for example, take advantage of lower registration fees or less onerous registration requirements. Some statutes leave the door open to this result by defining an LLP solely in terms of whether it is registered under the statute without regard to whether it is "governed by" the law of that state.[13] However, as discussed below in Section 6.03(b), the R.U.P.A. LLP amendments make clear that the registration state's law applies irrespective of any contrary agreement.

R.U.P.A. § 101(4) permits a firm to file a statement of election not to be a foreign LLP. This statement would allow firms to avoid potential uncertainty created by statutes that do not apply the label approach, or to avoid the burdens of LLP status by registering under the foreign entity provisions of an LLC or other statute where this is permitted. The law applicable to an electing firm is discussed below in Section 6.03(b). As noted on Table 6-1, no state has yet adopted this election provision.

A foreign *limited partnership* that is registered as an LLP in its formation state — that is, an LLLP (*see* Chapter 5, above) — might be treated in other states as an LLLP, an LLP, or something else. The difference is significant, since the characterization would determine which statute's rules on registration and choice of law would apply. Under "label" statutes, such a firm would seem to be a foreign LLP if it is designated as such by the formation state. But such a firm might also be a foreign limited partnership. The New York statute provides that a foreign limited partnership that is denominated as an LLP under the formation statute is recognized as a foreign limited partnership but not as a foreign limited liability partnership or a New York registered foreign limited liability partnership.[14] The Missouri LLP act permits a foreign limited partnership that may

---

[9] N.Y. P'ship Law § 2.

[10] Cal. Corp. Code § 16101(6)(A).

[11] *See* Rutledge, To Boldly Go Where You Have Not Been Told You May Go: LLCs, LLPs, and LLLPs in Interstate Transactions, 58 Baylor L. Rev. 205, 238–40 (2006) (discussing the definition of corporation for conflict-of-laws purposes under Restatement (Second) of Conflicts, § 298 (1971)).

[12] *See id.*; Restatement (Second) of Conflicts, § 295 (1971).

[13] *See* Ribstein, Delaware, Lawyers and Choice of Law, 19 Del. J. Corp. L. 999, 1022-25 (1994) (discussing issue of law applicable to such "platypus" firms).

[14] N.Y. P'ship Law § 121-1502(*l*).

register and has registered as an LLLP or its equivalent in its home jurisdiction to become an LLLP by complying with the Missouri LLLP provisions.[15] As for domestic LPs,[16] general partners may also receive liability protection by registering as an LLLP.

In the absence of a statutory provision clarifying the treatment of foreign LLLPs, common law choice-of-law rules relating to partnerships may apply.[17] This could mean application of the law of the creditor's state, rather than that of the state of formation.[18] Even if the statute clearly treats the foreign firm as an LLLP, the applicable rules may not be clear. In particular, U.L.P.A. (2001) § 901 provides that foreign law controls the limited liability of the limited partners, but does not clarify what law governs the general partners' liability.[19]

(b)   Registration or Qualification

As shown in Table 6-2, most states provide that a foreign LLP must register prior to transacting business in the state,[20] while some provide that a foreign LLP may transact business without registration. These statutes generally apply the law of the formation jurisdiction to foreign firms even if they do not register as required by the statute. Even where registration is required, the main penalties for not registering may be an inability to sue in the state's courts and exposure to substituted service on the secretary of state.[21]

---

[15] Mo. Rev. Stat. § 358.510.2.

[16] See Mo. Rev. Stat. § 359.172.2.

[17] See Rutledge, To Boldly Go Where You Have Not Been Told You May Go: LLCs, LLPs, and LLLPs in Interstate Transactions, 58 Baylor L. Rev. 205, 241–42 (2006) (discussing the definition of corporation for conflict-of-laws purposes under Restatement (Second) of Conflicts, § 298 (1971)).

[18] See id; Restatement (Second) of Conflicts, § 295 (1971).

[19] See Rutledge, supra note 17 at 241–42.

[20] As to what constitutes transacting business, see KEB Enters., L.P. v. Smedley, 140 Idaho 746, 101 P.3d 690 (2004) (applying same test as for foreign limited liability company, excluding mere acquisition of mortgage and indebtedness, and therefore not requiring mortgagee to register before suing for foreclosure).

[21] See, e.g., R.U.P.A. § 1103(b); Prototype LLP Act § 918. See Cadlerock Props. Joint Venture, L.P. v. Schilberg, 2001 WL 950233, 30 Conn. L. Rptr. 85 (Conn. Super. July 17, 2001) (genuine dispute as to whether foreign LLP transacted business in Connecticut and therefore barred from suing there for failure to register); Westmoreland v. Jordan Partners, LLLP, 306 Ga. App. 575, 703 S.E.2d 39 (2010) (LLP could not maintain action where had it failed to register not only when it filed suit but also as of the filing of the motion to dismiss). See also KEB Enters., L.P. v. Smedley, 140 Idaho 746, 101 P.3d 690 (2004) (mortgagee was not transacting business in the state and therefore did not have to register before suing to foreclose).

(c) Application of Other Statutes: Foreign LLPs as Domestic Non-LLPs

Some states may require an LLP to register as a limited partnership, LLC, or corporation. In particular, a limited liability partnership may fit the operation state's definition of a foreign "limited liability company."[22] Many of the others use a "label" approach and define as a "foreign limited liability company" only an entity designated as such by the organization statute.[23] This type of definition would exclude firms designated as "limited liability partnerships."

Some LLC statutes define a "foreign limited liability company" for purposes of the statute's registration and choice-of-law provisions in terms that do not necessarily exclude foreign limited liability partnerships. These definitions include firms that are substantially similar to LLC,[24] or unincorporated associations formed under laws other than of this state that affords members limited liability.[25] The Montana and Louisiana statutes do not include any definition of foreign LLC. In such a state, an LLP might have to register as a foreign LLC, perhaps in addition to registering as an LLP, even if it was designated as an LLP under the organization statute.[26] However, partial-shield LLPs may be excluded by all definitions of foreign LLCs because they do not provide for the requisite limited liability or because they are not substantially similar to LLCs in the critical respect of limited liability. Also, the fact that every LLP state provides for LLCs in a separate statute implies that the home state not only characterizes its LLPs differently from LLCs, but also characterizes LLPs as non-LLCs. Operation states may accept the formation state's unambiguous characterization.

An LLP that is not an LLLP probably is not a "foreign limited partnership."[27] Such firms are not characterized as such in the formation state or are provided for under a separate statute. Also, as discussed above in Section 1.04(b),

---

[22] *See* § 21 V.S.A. § 3001(10) (foreign limited liability company defined as "an entity organized under laws, other than the laws of this state, which afford limited liability to its owners comparable to the liability" of LLC members).

[23] *See* Ribstein & Keatinge on Limited Liability Companies, App. 13-1 (table summarizing state provisions) (1994 and Supp.) (hereinafter "Ribstein & Keatinge").

[24] *See* Ala. Code § 10A-5-1.02(4) (defining a "foreign limited liability company" as "[a]n organization formed under the laws of any jurisdiction other than Alabama that is substantially similar to a limited liability company").

[25] *See* Ky. Rev. Stat. § 275.015(9); Miss. Code Ann. § 79-29-105(i), (o); Or. Rev. Stat. § 63.001(11). Many statutes include a similar definition but add the stipulation that the firm need not register under any other statute. *See* Ribstein & Keatinge, App. 13-1. This stipulation would exclude LLPs in most, if not all, of the states that provide for this definition.

[26] The operation state need not apply the organization state's characterization of the firm, but rather may make an independent characterization based on the firm's attributes. *See* Restatement (Second) of Conflicts § 298 (application of corporate choice-of-law rules); Hemphill v. Orloff, 277 U.S. 537 (1928) (holding that Michigan could require a firm chartered in Georgia as a Commercial Investment Trust to register as a foreign corporation in Michigan in order to do business there).

[27] Note, however, that Delaware allows foreign-country LLPs to be "domesticated" as Delaware limited partnerships, including limited liability partnerships. *See* Del. Code Ann., tit. 6, § 15-904.

the firms may differ in important respects from limited partnerships from the standpoint of the members' liability, the management and control structure of the firm, and the "control rule" that conditions limited partners' liability limitation on their nonparticipation in control.

(d) Issues to Which Formation State Law Applies

As shown in Table 6-2, most LLP statutes provide that the law of the formation state of a foreign LLP governs organization, internal affairs, and the liability of the partners. These statutes make clear the parties' power contractually to select the choice of law by choosing their organization state.[28] The statute may add that the LLP shall not be denied registration or prohibited from doing business in the state by reason of any difference between the formation state and the operation state.[29]

Notwithstanding these general provisions, local regulatory law clearly applies to certain matters. Foreign LLP provisions do not permit a foreign LLP to engage in business from which domestic LLPs are barred. The statute may clarify that a foreign LLP has no greater rights or powers than a domestic LLP.[30] In particular, as discussed further in Section 7.04(c), a professional LLP would be subject to the same restrictions, including limitation of liability, that are applied to domestic LLPs of the same type. The New York statute makes this clear by adding that partners who perform professional services in the state have the same liability as partners in domestic LLPs and are subject to New York professional practice rules.[31] Other statutes explicitly provide that professional and other firms are subject to laws regulating specific types of business.[32] Even in the absence of such provisions, local professional licensing laws and other regulation probably apply to all firms operating in the state even if they are foreign LLPs.

As noted above, foreign LLP provisions normally apply the formation state's liability limitation whether it is broader or narrower than the limitation in the operation state, subject to the qualification discussed in the previous paragraph concerning liability limitations that apply to specific types of firms. By a parity of reasoning, the formation state's law on other matters relating to liabilities also should apply, including any requirement that the creditor exhaust

---

[28] See iCore Networks, Inc. v. McQuade Brennan LLP, 2008 WL 4550988 (E.D. Va. Oct. 7, 2008) (applying Virginia-choice-of-law rule, holding that D.C. law applied in determining the liability of a partner in a D.C. LLP); Dow v. Jones, 311 F. Supp. 2d 461 (D. Md. 2004) (applying D.C. law as to liability and agency power of partner in LLP registered under D.C. law).

[29] See R.U.P.A. § 1101.

[30] See R.U.P.A. § 1101 (application of foreign law does not authorize foreign LLP to engage in business in which a domestic LLP may not engage).

[31] N.Y. P'ship Law § 121-1502(*l*).

[32] See, e.g., Mass. Gen. L. ch. 156C, § 47; Nev. Rev. Stat. § 87.560(2).

remedies against the partnership before pursuing individual partners (*see* Section 3.08(b), above).

There is a border area of matters that relate to partner liabilities but that may nevertheless be governed by the law of the operation state. Statutes that provide that formation state law applies to partner liabilities probably refer only to the scope of partners' liability for the firm's debts. Thus, operation state law probably applies to the scope of the *partnership's* liability to third parties, including partners' power to bind the firm, at least in the absence of a choice-of-law clause or other reasons for applying the law of the formation state. By the same token, operation state law might determine the scope of partners' direct liability for their own wrongs. It is not clear whether this would include liability for monitoring or participation in misconduct (*see* Section 3.04, above).

It has been held that the registration state's law applies in determining the existence of the partnership.[33] This involves some circularity, since the firm may not be an LLP, and therefore not subject to the LLP choice-of-law rule, if it is not a partnership (*see* Section 2.02, above).

One of the most difficult choice-of-law questions concerns the law applicable to veil-piercing. Because veil-piercing generally results in holding partners vicariously liable for wrongdoing by the firm, it arguably follows that formation state law should apply on this issue as it does on other issues relating to the scope of members' liabilities for the firm's debts. From a policy standpoint, applying the law of operation states would impose significant compliance burdens on multi-state firms. On the other hand, veil-piercing liability is, to some extent, liability for direct misconduct by the partners. Moreover, applying formation state law might impose excessive research costs on third parties and violate fundamental policies of the operation state concerning limited liability firms' duties to creditors. The extra burden of applying multi-state law is mitigated to some extent by the fact that veil-piercing law is fact-intensive and involves basic principles of fraud and creditor protection that do not vary widely between the states. Cases based on other types of unincorporated firms have reached mixed results.[34]

---

[33] *See* Morson v. Kreindler & Kreindler, LLP, 616 F. Supp. 2d 171 (D. Mass. 2009) (Mass. law; holding that Massachusetts resident was not a partner under New York law, the law of the registration state, for purposes of determining existence of diversity jurisdiction).

[34] *See* Trans Union L.L.C. v. Credit Research, Inc., 2001 WL 648953 (N.D. Ill. 2001) (whether two companies are sufficiently "intertwined" to be liable for each other's actions decided under the law of the state of organization); Abu-Nassar v. Elders Futures, Inc., 1991 WL 45062 (S.D.N.Y. Mar. 28, 1991) (applying Lebanese law to determine the compliance of limited liability company with formalities of organization, but forum (New York) law to determine whether veil should be pierced); Matjasich v. State Dep't of Human Res., 21 P.3d 985 (Kan. 2001) (applying Utah wage law holding LLC members individually liable for unpaid wages under Kansas LLC provision providing that formation state law applies to member liability); Ribstein & Keatinge, § 13.03.

(e)   Effect of Formation State Rules on Operation in Other States

As shown in Table 6-2, most LLP statutes provide that it is the policy of the enacting state that an LLP formed under the act shall be recognized by other states. The Table identifies statutes with language similar or identical to the following:

(1) A registered limited liability partnership organized and existing under this chapter may conduct its business, carry on its operations, and have and exercise the powers granted by this chapter in any state, territory, district, or possession of the United States or in any foreign country.

(2) It is the intent of the Legislature that the legal existence of registered limited liability partnerships formed in this state be recognized outside the boundaries of this state and that, subject to any reasonable requirement of registration, a domestic registered limited liability partnership transacting business outside this state be granted the protection of full faith and credit under the Constitution of the United States.

These provisions (despite their "full faith and credit" language) probably have no direct constitutional impact. They do help eliminate any doubt about the parties' intent to contract for the application of the statute under which they form the LLP and help establish the "interest" of the formation state in having its law applied in other states. However, neither is very important now that virtually all states have foreign LLP provisions.

§ 6.03   R.U.P.A. CHOICE-OF-LAW PROVISION

The Revised Uniform Partnership Act (R.U.P.A.) § 106 provides that "[t]he law of the jurisdiction in which a partnership has its chief executive office governs relations among the partners and relations between the partners and the partnership." This provision is to some extent subject to the parties' contrary agreement. Issues regarding these provisions are discussed below in Section 8.106. The present section discusses the effect of foreign LLP provisions, including those added to R.U.P.A. by the LLP amendments.

A state that simply adds foreign LLP provisions to the original (non-LLP) version of R.U.P.A.[35] raises questions concerning the relationship between the foreign LLP provisions and the general choice-of-law provision. In the absence of any reconciling language, it is not clear whether the law of the chief executive

---

[35] An example is the prior version of the New Mexico statute, N.M. Stat. Ann. § 54-1-46. New Mexico has now adopted R.U.P.A.

office state or of any other jurisdiction selected in the agreement would control rather than that of the registration state. Montana's R.U.P.A.-based act provides that, "notwithstanding" the general choice-of-law provision, the laws of "the jurisdiction in which the partnership is formed" govern a foreign LLP.[36] This suggests that the registration state controls, but it does not preclude determination of the formation jurisdiction by agreement rather than registration.

R.U.P.A. with the 1996 LLP amendments and the Prototype LLP Act provide that the internal affairs and partner liability of foreign limited liability partnerships[37] are governed by the law of the formation jurisdiction.[38] The general choice-of-law sections in these acts provide that the law of this state governs relations among the partners and their liability for debts in an LLP registered in this state[39] and this cannot be waived by contrary agreement.[40] Thus, an LLP that registers in a state that includes these provisions necessarily accepts that state's law as the law governing its agreement. This election clearly controls in the registration state over contrary provisions in the agreement for the application of another state's law. In other words, an LLP that registers under a statute that includes this provision is thoroughly "domesticated" in that state. The R.U.P.A. LLP provision also probably would determine the law under which the LLP was formed in any other state in which the LLP operates unless that state provides for some other mandatory basis for choosing the applicable law, such as the location of the chief executive office. On the other hand, if the LLP registers in a state that does not include this provision but operates in a state that does, the "laws of the jurisdiction which govern the agreement under which it was formed" *probably* would be the state of registration, but *might* be some other state selected in the agreement or in which the firm's operations or offices are located.

A "partnership" that elects not to be a foreign LLP under R.U.P.A. § 101(4) may not be governed by the law of the registration state. If the firm is a partnership, R.U.P.A. § 106(a) would apply. This section provides that "the law of the jurisdiction in which a partnership has its chief executive office governs relations among the partners and between the partners and the partnership." As discussed below in Section 8.106, the parties can choose a different law in their agreement, but the law of the jurisdiction in which the chief executive office is located necessarily applies under § 1.03 insofar as the chosen law restricts the rights of

---

[36] Mont. Code Ann. § 35-10-710(5).

[37] Prototype LLP Act § 101(4) defines foreign LLPs to include LLPs registered under another jurisdiction's law. R.U.P.A. § 101(4) defines a foreign LLP to include a firm that is formed under other law, has the status of an LLP under that law, and has not elected not to be a foreign LLP. Since all LLP statutes require registration for a firm to be an LLP under the state's law, the R.U.P.A. definition would seem to be the same in effect as the Prototype's except for the R.U.P.A. election not to be a foreign LLP, discussed infra.

[38] R.U.P.A. § 1101(a); Prototype LLP Act § 919(e). Va. Code. § 50-73.141(E) is similar to the Prototype.

[39] R.U.P.A. § 106(b); Prototype LLP Act § 106(b).

[40] R.U.P.A. § 103(b)(9); Prototype § 103(b)(9).

third parties. On the other hand, if the electing firm is not a "partnership," the R.U.P.A. choice-of-law provision would not apply and the applicable law would be chosen under general choice-of-law rules. In either event, the firm would not be an LLP under the laws of the operation state and its members therefore may not have limited liability. Accordingly, it is not clear why a firm might make this election, unless limited liability is unimportant and the firm seeks to escape some tax, fee, default rule, or regulation that applies only to LLPs.[41]

§ 6.04   LONG-ARM JURISDICTION

The provisions on foreign limited liability partnerships may be relevant in determining whether the long-arm jurisdiction statute applies. In *UOP v. Andersen Consulting*,[42] a Connecticut court held that the state long-arm statute applied to an Illinois LLP because it was a foreign limited liability partnership under the Connecticut LLP statute, and therefore was a foreign partnership under the long-arm statute. The court rejected the argument that the residence of any partner determined the partnership's citizenship for long-arm purposes.

§ 6.05   DIVERSITY JURISDICTION

A firm's access to federal court may be significant, particularly for interstate firms that might face a local bias in remote state courts. Federal courts have jurisdiction in suits that do not allege federal claims only if federal diversity jurisdiction applies. There is federal diversity jurisdiction if the amount in controversy exceeds $75,000 and, most importantly, no plaintiff has the same state of citizenship of any defendant.[43] In diversity cases, forum state law determines whether the firm can sue or be sued.[44]

Citizenship of partnerships is determined by looking through the firm to individual members, irrespective of the entity nature of the firm for state law. This follows from *Carden v. Arkoma Associates*,[45] in which the Supreme Court so held for limited partnerships. The Court said:

---

[41] For a general discussion of the problem of firms' need to accept regulation or unsuitable default rules as a price of limited liability, see Ribstein, Limited Liability Unlimited, 24 Del. J. Corp. L. 407 (1999).

[42] 1995 WL 784971 (Conn. Super. Dec. 21, 1995).

[43] *See* 28 U.S.C. § 1332 (providing for diversity jurisdiction); Strawbridge v. Curtiss, 7 U.S. (3 Cranch) 267 (1806) (requiring complete diversity of citizenship).

[44] *See* Fed. R. Civ. Proc. 17(b).

[45] 494 U.S. 185 (1990).

The 50 States have created, and will continue to create, a wide assortment of artificial entities possessing different powers and characteristics, and composed of various classes of members with varying degrees of interest and control. Which of them is entitled to be considered a "citizen" for diversity purposes, and which of their members' citizenship is to be consulted, are questions more readily resolved by legislative prescription than by legal reasoning. . . . We have long since decided that, having established special treatment for corporations, we will leave the rest to Congress; we adhere to that decision.[46]

This broad reasoning seemingly would extend to all unincorporated firms,[47] and particularly LLPs, which traditionally are even less like "entities" than limited partnerships. *Carden* is indefensible in basic principle since it applies an aggregate theory that hardly fits general, much less limited, partnerships. However, it was apparently based partly on an antagonism to diversity jurisdiction and an unwillingness to extend such jurisdiction without explicit congressional authorization, particularly given the line-drawing burden this would impose on the courts in a world of proliferating business entities.

Some early cases relating indirectly to LLPs suggested some uncertainty about applying *Carden* in this context. In *Carlos v. Adamany*,[48] the court suggested without support that only decisionmaking members of an LLC would determine citizenship for diversity purposes. *Carlos* is hard to reconcile with *Carden* other than by noting that, since *Carden* involved a partnership, as *Carlos* indicates, there may be somewhat more room to argue for a different test with respect to non-partnership firms such as LLCs. This suggests that *Carlos* will not be applied to LLPs.[49] In *Lowsley-Williams v. North River Insurance Co.*,[50] the court held that a Lloyd's of London syndicate with which the plaintiff was associated most closely resembled an LLP, and ultimately concluded on other grounds that diversity had to be determined with reference to the individual investors (or "Names"). But the court noted that Congress needed to assist the judiciary in applying diversity jurisdiction to "the wide array of non-traditional legal entities which currently exist and which are continuously being created."[51]

---

[46] 494 U.S. 185, 197. Several cases have applied *Carden* in dismissing derivative suits by partners because the partnership must be joined as a defendant and this destroys diversity. *See* Bromberg & Ribstein, § 5.14(c). For cases applying *Carden* to limited liability companies, see Ribstein & Keatinge, § 10.06.

[47] It has not been applied, however, to a professional corporation, despite its similarity to a partnership. *See* Hoagland ex rel. Midwest Transit, Inc. v. Sandberg, Phoenix & von Gontard, P.C., 385 F.3d 737 (7th Cir. 2004).

[48] 1996 WL 210019 (N.D. Ill. 1996).

[49] In Keith v. Black Diamond Advisors, 48 F. Supp. 2d 326 (S.D.N.Y. 1999), the court refused to follow *Carlos* as to a limited liability company, noting that the conclusion was "dicta and unsupported by authority" and that it ignored *Carden*).

[50] 884 F. Supp. 166 (D.N.J. 1995).

[51] 884 F. Supp. 166, 170.

More recent cases dealing explicitly with LLPs have left little doubt that *Carden* applies in most cases.[52] *Reisman v. KPMG Peat Marwick LLP*[53] applied *Carden* in a case involving common law fraud claims against a public accounting firm organized (like other large public accounting firms) as an LLP. The court noted that the firm would now be virtually immune from diversity suits everywhere in the United States, but conversely would also be denied access to such litigation. *Mudge Rose Guthrie Alexander & Ferdon v. Pickett*[54] held that a New York LLP suing to recover legal fees is, for diversity purposes, a citizen of every state in which its members are citizens. After noting *Carden*'s cautionary language about judicial distinctions between business entities, the court said it was not inclined to distinguish LLPs from limited partnerships. Although characterization for diversity purposes is a federal question, the court noted that state law supports applying *Carden* because it defines "partnership" to include LLPs. The limited liability of LLP partners is not determinative for diversity, and in any event does not distinguish limited partners and partners in LLPs. Indeed, the court noted that LLP partners have some liability exposure under New York law for pre-registration liabilities, for malpractice by the partners themselves or those under their supervision, and to the extent a majority of the partners agree. This discussion of LLP partners' liability suggests that the court believed that LLPs are even less like corporations than the limited partnership involved in

---

[52] In addition to the earlier cases discussed immediately below, see Swiger v. Allegheny Energy, Inc., 540 F.3d 179 (3d Cir., 2008) (finding diversity jurisdiction where no member of LLP law firm shared citizenship with plaintiff); Moreno Energy, Inc. v. Marathon Oil Co., 884 F. Supp. 2d 577 (2012) (ordering a revised Notice of Removal alleging the citizenship of all members of an LLP); Lee v. Brown, 2009 WL 3157542 (D. Conn. Sept. 25, 2009) (allegation that LLPs had places of business in a state different from those in which plaintiffs reside insufficient to state grounds of court's jurisdiction); MCF Limited P'ners v. Seneca Specialty Ins. Co., 2012 WL 6681813 (M.D. Pa. Dec. 21, 2012); Watson v. Bretz & Coven LLP, 2013 WL 765361 (S.D.N.Y. Feb. 28, 2013); Morson v. Kreindler & Kreindler, LLP, 616 F. Supp. 2d 171 (D. Mass. 2009) (discussed in § 6.02(d), n.33, supra); Scantek Med., Inc. v. Sabella, 2008 WL 2518619 (S.D.N.Y. June 24, 2008); RD Legal Funding, LLC v. Erwin & Balingit, LLP, 2008 WL 927570 (S.D. Cal. April 4, 2008); Thompson v. Deloitte & Touche LLP, 503 F. Supp. 2d 1118 (S.D. Iowa 2007); Dixie Aire Title Servs., Inc. v. SPW, L.L.C., 2007 WL 464704 (W.D. Okla. Feb. 8, 2007) (defendant LLP law firm seeking to remove suit to federal court must show the citizenship of its members and of the members of any entities that are LLCs or LLPs); Koetters v. Ernst & Young LLP, 2005 WL 1475533 (E.D. Ky. June 21, 2005) (requiring complete diversity for removal); Burton v. Coburn, 2005 WL 607912 (D.D.C. March 16, 2005); City of Golden v. Parker, 138 P.3d 285 (Colo. 2006); Schlichtmann v. Ivey & Ragsdale, 352 F. Supp. 2d 6 (D. Me. 2005) (one designated "managing partner" was subject to complete diversity requirement); Paul Reid, LLP v. U.S. Fire Ins. Co., 2005 WL 1676805 (W.D. Wis. July 18, 2005) (requiring complete diversity for removal); Bosshard Bogs, LLP v. Cliffstar Corp., 2002 WL 32350544 (W.D. Wis. Oct. 23, 2002) (holding that requisite diversity shown); Bosshard Bogs, LLP v. Cliffstar Corp., 2002 WL 32360299 (W.D. Wis. Sept. 16, 2002) (requiring plaintiff to show evidence of diversity). *But see* Wigfall v. Wolpoff & Abramson, LLP, 2005 WL 3213955 at 1, n.1 (D.D.C., Nov. 1, 2005) (assuming without deciding that, unlike common law partnerships, LLPs do not reside where their partners reside, and noting that diversity jurisdiction had not been challenged).

[53] 965 F. Supp. 165, 176–77 (D. Mass. 1997).

[54] 11 F. Supp. 2d 449 (S.D.N.Y. 1998).

Carden. In *Cohen v. Kurtzman*,[55] the court went so far as to impose Rule 11 sanctions for alleging diversity jurisdiction in a case involving an LLP.

One potential group of cases that may be exceptions to this now well-accepted rule that diversity jurisdiction of an LLP depends on the citizenship of its partners are class action lawsuits subject to the Class Action Fairness Act (CAFA).[56] Though earlier policies may have encouraged broader definitions of citizenship to restrict access to federal courts, one purpose of CAFA was to channel class action lawsuits into federal courts. Therefore, CAFA provides that for those lawsuits "an unincorporated association shall be deemed to be a citizen of the State where it has its principal place of business and the State under whose laws it is organized."[57] Because of the relative newness of the statute, whether limited liability partnerships will be considered "unincorporated associations" is an open question. The Fourth Circuit has held that limited liability companies are "unincorporated associations" and so have the citizenship of its organizing states and its principal place of business, not each of its members.[58] Because of this case and other district court cases like it, LLPs will probably also be treated as unincorporated associations. In that event, an LLP would be a citizen of the state in which it registered and in the state of its principal place of business. The principal place of business of the LLP would most likely be determined by the "nerve center" test applied to corporations for purposes of federal diversity of citizenship.[59]

TABLE 6-1.   DEFINITION OF FOREIGN LLP

State	*Section*[†]	*Categories*
Alabama	10A-8-1.02(2)	4*
Alaska	32.06.995(6)	3a
Arkansas	4-46-101(4)	3a
Arizona	29-1001(5)	1
California	16101(6)	*
Colorado	7-90-102(24.5)	4*

---

[55] 45 F. Supp. 2d 423 (D.N.J. 1999).

[56] Class Action Fairness Act, Pub. L. No. 109-2, 119 Stat. 4 (2005).

[57] 28 U.S.C. § 1332(d)(10).

[58] *See* Ferrell v. Express Check Advance of SC LLC, 591 F.3d 698 (4th Cir. 2010); *see also* Bond v. Veolia Water Indianapolis, LLC, 571 F. Supp. 2d 905 (S.D. Ind. 2008) (citing congressional language that a "wide range of unincorporated associations" were to be treated as corporations for CAFA diversity jurisdiction); Marroquin v. Wells Fargo, LLC, 2011 WL 476540 (S.D. Cal. Feb. 3, 2011) (limited liability company as unincorporated association). In addition, at least one court has held that a limited liability limited partnership is an unincorporated association. *See* Abraham v. St. Croix Renaissance Grp., L.L.L.P., 2012 WL 6098502 (D.V.I. Dec. 7, 2012).

[59] *See* Hertz Corp. v. Friend, 130 S. Ct. 1182 (2010); Heckemeyer v. NRT Missouri, LLC, 2013 WL 2250429 (E.D. Mo. May 22, 2013) (applying the "nerve center" test to a limited liability company under CAFA).

Table 6-1   **6. Foreign LLPs: Choice of Law and Other Litigation Issues**

Table 6-1 (cont'd)

State	Section[†]	Categories
Connecticut	34-301(7)	1*
Delaware	15-101(7)	3a
District of Columbia	29-601.02(6)	3a
Florida	620.8101(5)	3a
Georgia	14-8-2(5)	1*
Hawaii	425-101	3a
Idaho	53-3-101(5)	3a
Illinois	206/101	3a
Indiana	23-4-1-2	1
Iowa	486A.101(4)	3a
Kansas	56a-101(d)	3a
Kentucky	362.1-101(7)	3a
Louisiana		2
Maine	1001(4)	1
Maryland	9A-101(e)	1*
Massachusetts	108A, § 2	*
Michigan		*
Minnesota	323A.0101(6)	3a*
Mississippi	79-13-101(4)	3a*
Missouri	358.020(5)	3a*
Montana	35-12-504(7)	*
Nebraska	67-402(4)	3a
New Hampshire	304-A:2(VIII)	1
New Jersey	42:1A-2	3a
New Mexico	54-1A-101(4)	3a
Nevada		2
New York	Ch. 39/2	*
North Carolina	59-32(4g)	3a*
North Dakota	45-22-01(10)	3a*
Ohio	1776.01(I)	3a
Oklahoma	54/1-101	3a
Oregon	67.005(5)	3a
Pennsylvania	8202	4*
Prototype	101(4)	4*
Revised Uniform Partnership Act	101(4)	3*
Rhode Island	7-12-13	1
South Carolina		2
South Dakota	48-7A-101(4)	3a
Tennessee	61-1-101(5)	3a
Texas	152.001(3)	1

Table 6-1 (cont'd)

State	Section[†]	Categories
Utah	48-1d-102(6)	4
Vermont	3201	3a
Virginia	50-73.79	1*
Washington	25.05.005	3a
West Virginia	47B-1-1(6)	1
Wisconsin	178.01(2)(dm)	1
Wyoming	17-21-101(a)(v)	1

[†]*See* Table 6-3 for full statutory citations.

Categories

* *See* Notes, below.
1. LLP formed under the laws of another jurisdiction (may be very similar to 3a, but not exact R.U.P.A. wording).
2. No definition.
3. R.U.P.A. definition, including non-waivability of formation state law and election not to be foreign LLP.
3a. R.U.P.A. definition, not including election not to be foreign LLP.
4. Only LLPs equivalent or similar to domestic LLPs included.

Notes

Alabama: Adds to 1, above: "in which no partner is personally liable for such partnership's debts, obligations, or liabilities, under the laws of such state or jurisdiction."

California: Same as 1, above, but partners must be professionals licensed in California and in other states or the firm must have a specified relationship with a professional LLP; and cannot be a limited partnership.

Colorado: LLP is an entity that is functionally equivalent to a domestic limited liability partnership and is formed or governed under the law of a jurisdiction other than this state and is recognized under the law of this state as a separate legal entity.

Connecticut: Same as 1, but specifies formation in other "state" and must be registered or denominated as LLP in that state.

Georgia: Includes LLLPs in its definition: "any limited liability partnership and any limited liability limited partnership formed under the laws of a jurisdiction other than this state."

Maryland: Excludes foreign limited partnership registered or denominated as a limited liability limited partnership under another state's laws.

Table 6-1 (cont'd)

Massachusetts: Does not specifically require that the LLP be registered under another jurisdiction's laws.

Mississippi: Adds the limitation that the LLP "affords to each of its partners, pursuant to the laws under which it is organized, limited liability with respect to all or a portion of the liabilities of the entity."

Montana: Adds to the definition of "foreign limited partnership": "Foreign limited partnership" means a partnership formed under the laws of a jurisdiction other than this state and required by those laws to have one or more general partners and one or more limited partners. The term includes a foreign limited liability partnership."

New York: Professional partnership without limited partners. Also under § 1502(*l*), a foreign limited partnership that is denominated as an LLP under the formation statute is recognized as a foreign limited partnership but not as a foreign limited liability partnership or a New York registered foreign limited liability partnership.

North Dakota: Category 3a, but specifies that firm must be "in good standing" in formation state.

Pennsylvania: A partnership that has registered under another jurisdiction's law that is similar to this subchapter, whether or not the partnership is required to register under the section relating to foreign registered limited liability partnerships.

Prototype: LLPs "or the functional equivalent thereof" that are registered as LLPs under foreign law.

Revised Uniform Partnership Act: Firms that are formed and have LLP status under other law and do not file a statement of election not to be a foreign LLP.

Virginia: LLPs "or the functional equivalent thereof" which are registered as LLPs under foreign law.

TABLE 6-2. FOREIGN LLPS AND OPERATION IN OTHER STATES

State	*Section*[†]	*Categories*
Alabama	10A-8-10.06, -10.09(b), (c), (e)	1, 3, 4
Alaska	32.06.921-922	1, 3
Arkansas	4-46-1101, -1102	1, 3
Arizona	29-1105-1106	1, 3
California	16958, 16959	1, 3*
Colorado	7-64-1010(2), 7-90-801, -805(4)	1, 3, 5
Connecticut	34-400, 34-429	1, 3, 4
Delaware	15-1101, -1102	1, 3
District of Columbia	29-601.06-07	1, 4

Table 6-2 (cont'd)

State	*Section*[†]	*Categories*
Florida	620.9101, .9102	1, 3
Georgia	14-8-44	3
Hawaii	425-156, -157, -158	1, 3
Idaho	53-3-1101, 1102	1, 3
Illinois	206/1101, 1102	1, 3
Indiana	23-4-1-44, -49	1, 3, 4
Iowa	486A.1101, .1102	1, 3*
Kansas	56a-1101, -1102	1, 3
Kentucky	362.1-951	1, 3
Louisiana		7
Maine	851, 852	1, 3*
Maryland	9A-106	1, 3, 4, 6
Massachusetts	108A, § 47	1, 3, 4
Michigan	449.47	1, 3
Minnesota	323A.1101, 1102	1, 3
Mississippi	79-13-1101, 1102	1, 3
Missouri	358.440(19), .500, .510.2	1*, 4, 6
Montana	35-10-710	1, 3, 4, 6
Nebraska	67-457, -458	1, 3
Nevada	87.560(1), (2)	1, 5*
New Hampshire	304-A:50	1, 3, 4
New Jersey	42:1A-50, -51	1, 3
New Mexico	54-1A-1101, -1102, -1103	1, 3
New York	121-1502, -1503	1*, 3, 4
North Carolina	59-90, -93; 59-45(e)–(f)	1, 3, 5
North Dakota	45-22-18, -19	1, 3
Ohio	1776.85, 86	1, 3
Oklahoma	1-1101, -1102	1, 3
Oregon	67.025 .765	1, 3*, 4
Pennsylvania	8207, 8211(b)	1*, 3, 4
Prototype	910, 919(c)	1, 4
Revised Uniform Partnership Act	1101, 1102	1, 3
Rhode Island	7-12-59	1, 3, 4*
South Carolina	33-41-1140, -1150	1, 3, 5*
South Dakota	48-7A-1101, -1102	1, 3
Tennessee	61-1-1004	1, 3, 4
Texas	152.905, 1.102, 1.104	1, 3
Utah	48-1b-101(2)(d)	1, 3

Table 6-2 6. **Foreign LLPs: Choice of Law and Other Litigation Issues**

Table 6-2 (cont'd)

State	Section[†]	Categories
Vermont	3301-3302	1, 3
Virginia	50-73.138, .141	1, 3, 4
Washington	25.05.125, .550, .555	1, 3*
West Virginia	47B-10-4	1, 3, 4
Wisconsin	178.45	1, 3
Wyoming	17-21-1104	1, 3, 4

[†]*See* Table 6-3 for full statutory citations.

Categories

*   *See* Notes, below.
1.   Foreign LLP must register prior to transacting business.
2.   Foreign LLP may transact business without registration.
3.   Formation state law applies to internal affairs and liabilities.
4.   Enacting state provides for recognition of its LLPs elsewhere; "full faith and credit" language.
5.   Enacting state provides for recognition of its LLPs or liability limitation elsewhere: other language.
6.   Formation state law applies to all partnerships, not only LLPs.
7.   No provision.

Notes

California: Application of foreign law on liability is subject to the firm's compliance with financial security provisions.

Colorado: Section 7-64-1010 provides that the section does not permit a firm to engage without authorization in a profession to which a specific statutory provision applies.

Iowa: Section 487.1303 treats a foreign LLLP as a foreign limited partnership.

Maine: Exception for liability of professional partners for their own acts or for acts of persons under their direct supervision and control.

Missouri: Requires filing of a "notice."

Nevada: To extent permitted by other jurisdiction's laws.

New York: Partners who perform professional services in the state have the same liability as partners in domestic LLPs and are subject to New York professional practice rules. Subsection (g) requires re-registration in second year and every two years thereafter; same for foreign in § 121-1502.

Oregon: Liability for foreign LLPs is the same as for domestic LLPs and professional liability is the same as for shareholders of foreign professional corporations (§ 5); foreign LLP not permitted to do what LLP may not do (§ 72).

Pennsylvania: Applies foreign limited partnership provisions.

Table 6-2 (cont'd)

Rhode Island: Section 7-12-31.1(2)(b) provides that accounting partnership is subject to Rhode Island law. Section 7-12-59(e) provides that name of foreign LLP shall end with "Registered Limited Liability Partnership," "L.L.P" or "LLP" "or such other similar words or abbreviation" as is required or authorized by formation state.

South Carolina: LLP may carry on business and exercise powers under this act in any state or foreign country; foreign LLP that renders professional services need not obtain certificate of authority unless it has an office in South Carolina.

Washington: Foreign LLP is subject to insurance requirement.

TABLE 6-3.   FULL STATUTORY CITATIONS

State	*Citation Information*
Alabama	Ala. St. § —
Alaska	Alaska Stat. § —
Arkansas	Ark. Code §§ ——
Arizona	Ariz. Rev. Stat. Ann. § —
California	Cal. Corp. Code § —
Colorado	Colo. Rev. Stat. § —
Connecticut	Conn. Gen. Stat. § —
Delaware	Del. Code Ann. ch. 15, tit. 6, § —
District of Columbia	D.C. Code Ann. § —
Florida	Fla. Stat. Ann. § —
Georgia	Ga. Code Ann. § —
Hawaii	Haw. Rev. Stat. § —
Idaho	Idaho Code § —
Illinois	Ill. Comp. Stat. Ann. Ch. 805
Indiana	Ind. Code § —
Iowa	Iowa Code § —
Kansas	Kan. Stat. Ann. § —
Kentucky	Ky. Rev. Stat. Ann. § —
Louisiana	La. Rev. Stat. Ann. § —
Maine	Me. Rev. Stat. Ann. tit. 31, § —
Maryland	Md. Code Ann., Corps. & Assns. § —
Massachusetts	Mass. Gen. L. ch. 108A, § —
Michigan	Mich. Comp. Laws § —
Minnesota	Minn. Stat. § —
Mississippi	Miss. Code Ann. §
Missouri	Mo. Rev. Stat. § —
Montana	Mont. Code Ann. § —

Table 6-3   **6.   Foreign LLPs: Choice of Law and Other Litigation Issues**

Table 6-3 (cont'd)

State	*Citation Information*
Nebraska	Neb. Rev. Stat. § —
Nevada	Nev. Rev. Stat. § —
New Hampshire	N.H. Rev. Stat. Ann. § —
New Jersey	N.J. Rev. Stat. § —
New Mexico	N.M. Stat. Ann. § —
New York	N.Y. Partnership Law ch. 39, § — (Consol.)
North Carolina	N.C. Gen. Stat. § —
North Dakota	N.D. Cent. Code § —
Ohio	Ohio Rev. Code Ann. § —
Oklahoma	Okla. Stat. tit. 54, § —
Oregon	Or. Rev. Stat. § — (section number of uncodified law)
Pennsylvania	15 Pa. Cons. Stat. § —
Prototype	Prototype Registered Limited Liability Partnership Act, § —
Revised Uniform Partnership Act	Uniform Partnership Act (1994) with 1996 Amendments, § —
Rhode Island	R.I. Gen. Laws § —
South Carolina	S.C. Code Ann. § —
South Dakota	S.D. Codified Laws Ann. § —
Tennessee	Tenn. Code Ann. § —
Texas	Tex. Bus. Org. Code § —
Utah	Utah Code Ann. § —[60]
Vermont	Vermont St. Ann., tit. 11, § —
Virginia	Va. Code Ann. § —
Washington	Wash. Rev. Code § —
West Virginia	W. Va. Code § —
Wisconsin	Wis. Stat. § —
Wyoming	Wyo. Stat. § —

---

[60] Utah provisions cited in the text are effective July 1, 2013 for new entities and Jan. 1, 2015 for existing entities. *See* Utah Code Ann. § 48-1b-1205.

≡7≡

APPLICATION of
NON-PARTNERSHIP LAW

This chapter discusses the application of regulatory statutes to limited liability partnerships (LLPs). In general, these statutes apply to firms irrespective of their form of organization. Nevertheless, adoption of the LLP form as distinguished from the limited liability company (LLC) or other form may affect whether and how these statutes apply to the activity. Federal and state securities laws are discussed in Section 7.01. The bankruptcy and employment discrimination laws are discussed in Section 7.02 and Section 7.03. Section 7.04 discusses state laws and regulations concerning professional practice as LLPs. Section 7.05 discusses some issues relating to tax classification and treatment of LLPs.

§ 7.01   LLP INTERESTS AS SECURITIES UNDER STATE AND FEDERAL SECURITIES LAWS

The federal and state securities laws may regulate sales of LLP interests.[1] If an LLP interest is considered a security, then at a minimum, the antifraud provisions of the federal securities law will apply to these sales. Because most sales of LLP interests are likely to be in relatively small offerings, they may be entitled to one or more exemptions from the registration requirements. If the firm is required to register, this may prevent it from using accrual accounting (*see* § 1.07(a)(15), note 95, above).

The federal securities laws apply to transactions involving a *security*, which includes, in addition to specific types of instruments, any investment contract.[2] The leading Supreme Court case has defined *investment contract* to mean "a contract, transaction or scheme whereby a person invests his money in a common enterprise and is led to expect profits solely from the efforts of the promoter or a third party."[3] An LLP, like other partnerships or, for that matter, other business associations, undoubtedly involves an investment of money in a common enterprise with an expectation of profits. The critical question is whether profits are expected "solely from the efforts of the promoter or a third party," so that the investors can be said to rely on disclosures concerning the management's track record and other facts bearing on the firm's prospects of success.

In most cases, general partnership interests are *not* securities. At least under federal law, even if management is centralized to some extent in a management committee, the partnership interests will not be securities as long as the partners have significant powers to oversee management. A leading case applying this rule is *Williamson v. Tucker.*[4] In *Williamson* the court articulated what has come to be known as the *Williamson* test:

---

[1] *See* Welle, When Are Limited Liability Partnership Interests Securities?, 27 J. Corp. L. 63 (2001).

[2] *See* 15 U.S.C. §§ 77b, 78c.

[3] SEC v. W. J. Howey Co., 328 U.S. 293, 298–99 (1946).

[4] 645 F.2d 404 (5th Cir. 1981). For cases applying *Williamson*, see Youmans v. Simon, 791 F.2d 341 (5th Cir. 1986) (no security where investors were sophisticated and had the power to terminate the venture and replace the manager); Casablanca Prods., Inc. v. Pace Int'l Research,

All of this indicates that an investor who claims his general partnership or joint venture interest is an investment contract has a difficult burden to overcome. On the face of a partnership agreement, the investor retains substantial control over his investment and an ability to protect himself from the managing partner or hired manager. Such an investor must demonstrate that, in spite of the partnership form which the investment took, he was so dependent on the promoter or on a third party that he was in fact unable to exercise meaningful partnership powers. A general partnership or joint venture interest can be designated a security if the investor can establish, for example, that (1) an agreement among the parties leaves so little power in the hands of the partner or venturer that the arrangement in fact distributes power as would a limited partnership; or (2) the partner or venturer is so inexperienced and unknowledgeable in business affairs that he is incapable of intelligently exercising his partnership or venture powers; or (3) the partner or venturer is so dependent on some unique entrepreneurial or managerial ability of the promoter or manager that he cannot replace the manager of the enterprise or otherwise exercise meaningful partnership or venture powers.[5]

The court's amplification of its nonsecurity examples includes this discussion:

> Thus, a general partnership in which some agreement among the partners places the controlling power in the hands of certain managing partners may be an investment contract with respect to the other partners. . . . In such a case the agreement allocates partnership power as in a limited partnership, which has long been held to be an investment contract. . . . Similarly, one would not expect partnership interests sold to large numbers of the general public to provide any real partnership control; at some point there would be so many partners that a partnership vote would be more like a corporate vote, each partner's role having been diluted to the level of a single shareholder in a corporation. Such an arrangement might well constitute an investment contract.
>
> A general partner or joint venturer who lacks the business experience and expertise necessary to intelligently exercise partnership powers may also be dependent on the investment's promoter or manager. . . . A scheme which sells investments to inexperienced and unknowledgeable members of the general public cannot escape the reach of the securities laws merely by labelling itself a general partnership or joint venture. Such investors may be led to expect profits to be derived from the efforts of others in spite of partnership powers nominally retained by them.[6]

Inc., 697 F. Supp. 1563 (D. Or. 1988) (no security because plaintiff had sufficient business expertise to enforce partnership rights).

[5] *Williamson*, 645 F.2d at 423, 424.

[6] *Williamson*, 645 F.2d at 423, 424 (citations omitted).

Williamson, therefore, mandates some factual inquiry as to the partners' actual powers and their ability to exercise them, while recognizing that one who claims that membership in a general partnership is an investment contract "has a difficult burden to overcome." A general partnership that for all intents and purposes functions as a limited partnership, however, will be treated as such for securities law purposes. This is consistent with what is commonly viewed as the "substance-over-form" approach of *Howey*.[7]

Another leading case relied exclusively on the partners' powers under the partnership statute or agreement,[8] and several courts have emphasized these powers, while allowing some room for extrinsic evidence as to whether the powers could be exercised.[9] These cases indicate that a general partnership will very rarely be a security,[10] but the possibility remains.[11]

Should LLPs be differentiated from other general partnerships because of the limited liability of the general partners? Limited liability arguably relates to the definition of a "security" because it reduces partners' incentives to be informed about the business, encourages delegation of management powers, and encourages unsophisticated investors to become partners. These effects are more likely if the limited liability extends to contracts. However, the "security" issue

---

[7] Bromberg and Ribstein on Partnership, § 2.13(e) (hereinafter, "Bromberg & Ribstein"). Note, however, that there may not be a sharp dividing line between "substance" and "form." *See* Ribstein, Form and Substance in the Definition of a "Security": The Case of Limited Liability Companies, 51 Wash. & Lee L. Rev. 807, 825 (1994).

[8] Goodwin v. Elkins & Co., 730 F.2d 99 (3d Cir. 1984) (agreement provided, inter alia, for removal of managing partner by majority vote).

[9] Holden v. Hagopian, 978 F.2d 1115 (9th Cir. 1992) (relying on *Koch*, below this note, and partners' technical powers under agreement, court reasoned that investors in horse breeding partnership who were not knowledgeable about the horsebreeding business did not show they could not have replaced the manager with someone else of similar expertise); Rivanna Trawlers Unlimited v. Thompson Trawlers, Inc., 840 F.2d 236 (4th Cir. 1988) (partners in 25-member firm removed and replaced managing partner and twice removed external managers; partnership agreement required 60% approval of partners for various matters including loans over $5000); Matek v. Murat, 862 F.2d 720 (9th Cir. 1988). For cases holding that general partnership interests may be securities—part on the basis of evidence outside the agreement—see Stone v. Kirk, 8 F.3d 1079 (6th Cir. 1993) (joint venture with a completely passive venturer, citing *Williamson* without further discussion); Koch v. Hankins, 928 F.2d 1471 (9th Cir. 1991) (question of fact whether partners in 35 related general partnerships could meaningfully exercise control over the overall enterprise); SEC v. Shreveport Wireless Cable Television P'ship, 1998 WL 892948 (D.D.C. October 20, 1998) (denying summary judgment where powers under agreement resembled those of limited partners or shareholders; there was sale of 700–1000 interests, almost half as fractional interests, which may have limited partners' input to that of corporate shareholders; and testimony that partners were precluded from participating in essential managerial decisions).

[10] *See* Ribstein, Private Ordering and the Securities Laws: The Case of General Partnerships, 42 Case W. Res. L. Rev. 1 (1992) (arguing for an even stronger rule that a general partnership is a *per se* non-security).

[11] *See* S.E.C. v. Schooler, 902 F. Supp. 2d 1341 (S.D. Cal. 2012) (granting a permanent injunction for the SEC based on a prima facie showing that general partnership interests were securities, stating "[b]ut, like any presumption, the presumption that general partnership interests aren't securities can be overcome, and therefore has limited independent force).

ultimately depends on the extent to which these effects are present in a given case and help to satisfy the *Williamson* burden, and currently the law in this area relating to LLPs is evolving at both the state and federal level.

Thus, even without a presumption, LLP interests should not be "securities" if one of the *Williamson* factors is not present. In an LLP, this will likely be possible only in extreme cases where investors lack realistic power over the management of the partnership. That may be because they are too numerous, their interests are too small, their lack of knowledge of the partnership's business is too great, the management is too specialized, or the agreement restricts their rights too tightly.

It has been held that this burden was met in a case preliminarily enjoining sales of interests in an LLP, without explicitly differentiating between LLPs and non-LLP partnerships.[12] The court held that the investors were effectively powerless in part because 85 percent of the invested proceeds were transferred to defendant-controlled entities, leaving insufficient funds to run the business (telephone companies). It is not clear whether the court would have reasoned differently if the partners had partnership-type personal liability, effectively making investors' personal assets available to the firm. Other factors supporting the sale of a security included investors' agreement to ratify all manager actions, nondisclosure of essential information, and emphasis in the offering materials of manager's experience in the telecommunications industry, despite investors' power to replace managers and their exercise of this power.

In another federal LLP case, the Eleventh Circuit reversed a trial court holding that the *Williamson* burden was not met in a case involving a scheme to raise $20 million from more than 350 investors to invest in debt pools was reversed on appeal.[13] Reserving for later the question of whether the *Williamson* presumption applied to LLP interests, the appellate court concluded that although the investors had formal powers under the agreement, including the power to remove the general partner, they lacked the effective ability to exercise these powers: despite the investors' general business experience, it was significant that they had no independent experience in the debt-purchase business; the general partner could be removed only for cause by unanimous vote; the partners were geographically dispersed and had no preexisting relationships; the general partner controlled information and did not give the investors enough data to make an informed decision as to how much the partnership's debt pool was worth; and the voting process favored the general partner because unvoted ballots were counted for management. Although other managers were available that could have managed the debt pool, the investors still lacked a realistic alternative to the incumbent general partner because the partnership had no contractual right to get

---

[12] S.E.C. v. Shiner, 268 F. Supp. 2d 1333 (S.D. Fla. 2003).
[13] *See* S.E.C. v. Merchant Capital, LLC, 483 F.3d 747 (11th Cir. 2007).

control of the assets from a third-party firm with which the general partner had contracted to manage them.

In a case a few years later, a district court in Michigan held that LLP interests were securities relying on the Court of Appeals decision in *Merchant Capital* as well as on an expert opinion that reasoned that, given LLP partners' limited liability, and therefore their reduced incentive to be active in the business, the partnership presumption against security "is not appropriate when the investment is in a limited liability partnership."[14] In 2011, the U.S. Department of Justice was also able to convince the Eleventh Circuit that LLP interests were securities in a securities fraud case. However, the court focused on the extent of management participation in the LLPs without establishing precedent on whether the *Williamson* presumption related to LLPs generally.

Some state statutes explicitly characterize interests in LLPs,[15] though some statutes apply only to LLPs in which some members are passive.[16] State administrative rulings and administrative actions against sales of LLP interests also indicate that LLPs can be securities under some circumstances.[17] Also, one case certified a class action under the Colorado Securities Act involving interests in LLPs, reasoning that the *Williamson* presumption against finding a security in a general partnership did not apply to an LLP because of the latter's limited liability.[18] These authorities show that use of the LLP form is no guarantee. The fact that both LLCs and LLPs are unincorporated limited liability firms suggests that LLC rulings may be significant for LLPs. Some rulings under state law have held that LLC interests are securities under definitions similar to the federal definition,[19] but there is some authority going

---

[14] *See* S.E.C. v. Lowery, 633 F. Supp. 2d 466, 480 (W.D. Mich. 2009).

[15] *See* Conn. Gen. St. 36b-3(19) (defining "as an 'investment contract', an interest in a limited liability company or limited liability partnership").

[16] *See* Iowa Code § 502.102(28)(e); N.H. Rev. Stat. Ann. § 421-B:2.XX(a), (b). The Iowa statute provides that LLP interests are not securities if the opponent of the security characterization can prove that all members are actively engaged in management. The New Hampshire statute includes an exception for professional LLPs.

[17] *See* Welle, When Are Limited Liability Partnership Interests Securities?, 27 J. Corp. L. 63, 65, nn.11 and 12 (2001) (citing administrative rulings in five states and administrative actions in 11 states).

[18] Toothman v. Freeborn & Peters, 80 P.3d 804 (Colo. App. 2002) (citing as rationales that LLP members have limited liability; members frequently have little management power; and as of 2002, no state or federal authorities had extended the presumption to LLPs).

[19] *See* Ak's Daks Commc'ns, Inc. v. Securities Div., 138 Md. App. 314, 333, 771 A.2d 487, 498 (2001); Nutek Info. Sys. v. Ariz. Corp. Comm'n, 977 P.2d 826 (Ariz. App. 1998); Cleland v. Express Commc'ns, Inc., Ga. Sec. Comm'r, Case No. 50-93-0075 (April 14, 1994); Order of Prohibition in In re Express Commc'ns, Ill. Sec'y of State Secs. Dep't, File No. 9200106 (Dec. 13, 1993). Cogniplex, Inc. v. Ross, 2001 WL 436210 (N.D. Ill. 2001) (refused to dismiss a claim under the Illinois securities law). In People v. Riggle, 95CA1476 (Colo. App. Jan. 15, 1998) the court held that the evidence supported the jury's guilty verdict for selling membership interests in a wireless cable Nevada LLC because, under *Williamson*, the members' dependence on manager supported by nationwide membership, the specialized nature of business, and a provision in the operating agreement stating that it was in the members' best interest to engage an experienced and

the other way.[20] Also, many state statutes now clarify to what extent LLC interests are "securities."[21] These statutes seem to either include LLC interests in the definition of security or create a rebuttable presumption of either inclusion or exclusion based on whether members are active in management.

The Securities and Exchange Commission (SEC) has alleged that LLC interests are securities and has obtained consent decrees providing for injunctions and

---

expert manager. But the court nevertheless reversed the conviction because the trial judge refused on the jury's request to supplement an instruction on the *Howey* test without elaborating on the "essential managerial efforts" part of the test. Although the defendant did not appeal the court's failure to give his tendered instruction based on *Williamson,* the court's finding that the jury lacked sufficient guidance under the *Howey* instruction, together with the court's endorsement of *Williamson,* suggests that such an instruction may be required in future cases. For discussions of state blue sky developments involving LLCs, see Sargent, Will Limited Liability Companies Punch a Hole in the Blue Sky?, 21 Sec. Rev. L.J. 438 (1994); Note, Beck, From Orange Groves to Wireless Communication Systems: Arizona Applies the *Howey* Test to Limited Liability Companies, 31 Ariz. St. L.J. 1021 (1999).

[20] *See* Tschetter v. Berven, 621 N.W.2d 372 (S.D. 2001).

[21] Alaska Stat. § 45.55.990(32) (defining LLC interest as "security"); Ariz. Rev. Stat. Ann. § 47-8103(C) (LLC or partnership interest not a security unless traded on securities exchanges or markets, its terms expressly provide that it is a security, or is an investment company security); Cal. Corp. Code § 25019 (LLC interest not a security if LLC can prove that all of its members are actively engaged as managers); Idaho Code Ann. § 30-14-102(28)(e) (including interests in LLCs as "investment contracts"); Ind. Code § 23-19-1-2(28)(e) (("security" defined to include LLC interest); Iowa Stat. § 502.102(19) (defining LLC interest as "security" unless person claiming it is not a "security" can prove that all of the members are actively engaged in management); Mich. Comp. Laws Ann. § 450.5103 (LLC interest is a security to the same extent as interest in corporation, partnership or limited partnership); Mo. Ann. Stat. § 347.185 (rebuttable presumption that an LLC interest is not a security where management is not vested in one or more managers); Neb. Rev. Stat. § 8-1101(15) ("security" expressly includes LLC interests unless the member enters into a written commitment to be engaged actively and directly in the management of the LLC, and all members of the LLC are actively engaged in the management (although unclear whether all members must enter into written commitments to actively manage); N.M. Stat. Ann. § 58-13B-2(DD)(6) (LLC interests are securities); Ohio Rev. Code Ann. § 1707.01(b) (defining LLC interests as securities); 70 Pa. Cons. St. 1-102(t) (LLC interests are "securities" unless the LLC is not managed by managers, the purchaser of the membership interest enters into a written commitment to be engaged actively and directly in the management of the company, and the purchaser of the membership interest, in fact, does participate actively and directly in the management of the company); Utah Code Ann. § 61-1-13(ee)(ii) (defining LLC interest as "security" but not in a family LLC formed as part of an estate plan or in an LLC where person claiming exemption can prove all of the members are actively engaged in the management of the LLC); Wis. Stat. Ann. § 551.102(28)(e) (presuming LLC interest to be a "security" unless each member is actively engaged in management beyond exercising voting rights or if each member in an LLC with 15 members or fewer has authority to bind the LLC). For discussions of the treatment of LLC interests by state securities laws under statutes, case law, and administrative rulings, see Ribstein & Keatinge on Limited Liability Companies, § 14.03 (1992 & Supp.) (hereinafter "Ribstein & Keatinge").

related relief in some cases in which the SEC alleged both fraud and sale of unregistered securities.[22] The few court decisions on this issue are mixed.[23]

There are several arguments against characterizing closely held LLCs, particularly member-managed LLCs, as securities.[24] First, like partnerships,

---

[22] See SEC v. Parkersburg Wireless Ltd. Liab. Co., SEC Litig. Rel. No. 14325 (D.D.C. Nov. 8, 1994), 57 SEC Docket 2725 (1994) (order to disgorge $537,637 received by one defendant, to be used by LLC's receiver for the benefit of investors in LLC interests); *id.*, 156 F.R.D. 529 (D.D.C. 1994) (contempt order against one defendant for failing to satisfy order to provide information); *id.*, SEC Litig. Rel. No. 14126 (D.D.C. June 15, 1994), 56 SEC Docket 2534 (1994) (preliminary injunction; alleged sale of over $10 million of LLC interests to 700 investors nationwide; interests in wireless cable television system LLC); *id.*, 1995 WL 79775 (D.D.C. Feb. 21, 1995) (order of liquidation of LLC and approval of receiver's plan to distribute $3 million remaining cash to investors returning 27 to 36 cents per dollar invested); SEC v. Knoxville, LLC, SEC Litig. Rel. No. 14155 (S.D. Cal. July 12, 1994), 57 SEC Docket 442 (1994) (temporary restraining order; alleged effort to raise $35 million by sale of interests in wireless cable television system LLC); SEC v. Vision Commc'ns, Inc., SEC Litig. Rel. No. 14081 (D.D.C. May 11, 1994), 56 SEC Docket 1866 (1994), SEC Litig. Rel. No. 14026 (D.D.C. Mar. 14, 1994), 56 SEC Docket 880 (Mar. 14, 1994) (permanent injunction and receivership to marshal assets for distribution to investors; order of disgorgement from two individual defendants; alleged sales $1.25 million nationwide; interests in wireless cable television system LLC).

[23] For cases holding that LLC interests were securities, see KFC Ventures, L.L.C. v. Metaire Med. Equip. Leasing Corp., 2000 WL 726877 (E.D. La. June 5, 2000) (LLC interest a security, noting that member of manager-managed LLC was not allowed to act as agent by virtue of being member, authority was limited to voting with other members, and members' power was further limited by the fact that the manager held an 85% interest in the LLC); SEC v. Shreveport Wireless Cable Television P'ship, 1998 WL 892948 (D.D.C. Oct. 20, 1998) (denying summary judgment where members' powers under partnership and LLC agreements resembled those of limited partners or shareholders, there was large-scale sale of interests and evidence that partners were precluded from participating in essential managerial decisions); SEC Parkersburg Wireless Ltd. Liab. Co., 991 F. Supp. 6, 9, n.3 (D.D.C. 1997) (holding in favor of "security" characterization and stating that, "[w]hile the investors theoretically may have possessed a right to manage the affairs of PWLLC under the terms of the Operating Agreement, the inexperience and geographic diversity of the 700-odd investors essentially precluded this from ever coming to pass"). For cases contra, see Nelson v. Stahl, 173 F. Supp. 2d 153 (S.D.N.Y. 2001) (agreements granted members authority over management of the entities although they chose to remain passive, relying on *Keith,* below); Great Lakes Chem. Corp. v. Monsanto Co., 96 F. Supp. 2d 376 (D. Del. 2000) (holding, after an extensive review of the law, including *Keith,* below, that purchase of 100% of interests of manager-managed LLC, where an operating agreement gave members the power to remove managers and dissolve the firm, was not the purchase of a security); Keith v. Black Diamond Advisors, 48 F. Supp. 3d 326 (S.D.N.Y. 1999) (dismissing a securities fraud case involving interests in a "member-managed" New York LLC, holding that these interests were not securities under *Rivanna* [840 F.2d 236] and other cases discussed in note 9, supra). For treatment of LLC interests under federal securities laws, see Ribstein & Keatinge, § 14.02.

[24] For articles that question whether LLC interests should be treated as "securities," see Goforth, Why Limited Liability Company Membership Interests Should Not Be Treated As Securities And Possible Steps To Encourage The Result, 45 Hastings L.J. 1223 (1994); McGinty, The Limited Liability Company: Opportunity for Selective Securities Law Deregulation, 64 U. Cin. L. Rev. 369 (1996); Ribstein, note 7 above; Sargent, Are Limited Liability Company Interests Securities?, 19 Pepp. L. Rev. 1069 (1992) (LLC interests normally should not be securities); Burke, Note, Limited Liability Companies and the Federal Securities Laws: Congress Should Amend the Securities Laws to Avoid Coverage, 76 Ind. L.J. 749 (2001). *But see* Branson & Okamoto, The Supreme Court's Literalism and the Definition of "Security" in the State Courts, 50 Wash. & Lee L. Rev. 1043 (1993) (LLCs should be securities under state law); Steinberg & Conway, The Limited

LLCs have the critical features of flexibility of management structure and members' opportunity to participate in control without jeopardizing their limited liability. LLC owners, like partners, therefore may have strong expectations that they will not be relying on the "efforts of others." Second, extending the *Williamson* presumption to closely held LLCs would serve the purpose of providing for a clear rule that reduces litigation and aids private ordering. Third, the Supreme Court has indicated that interests in closely held firms should not be included in the definition of a "security" in its decision in *Marine Bank v. Weaver*.[25]

Landreth Timber Co. v. Landreth[26] did apply the securities laws to the sale of "stock" of an entire closely held corporation. However, this decision does not require interests in LLCs, partnerships, or other unincorporated firms to be treated as "securities." The Court reasoned in part that "stock" is expressly included in the definition of a "security" and that investors expect the securities laws to apply in this situation. LLCs and LLPs as well as other partnerships are not expressly included in the definition of "security" and investors in them probably do not expect the securities laws to apply.[27]

Even if LLC interests are deemed to be "securities" at the federal and state level, most LLPs will not be "securities." LLPs operate under the partnership rule of equal member participation in management (*see* Section 4.02, above), which is significant under the "efforts of others" *Howey* rule. A partner's power to bind the partnership in transactions with third parties — a power not easily cut off — tends to reduce a partner's reliance on whatever centralized management there is in a managing partner or management committee. Finally, LLPs' identification as "partnerships" clearly signals the nature of the firm to third parties and typically indicates that investors do not expect the securities laws to apply. The form of the investment and the expectation of investors were both important to the Supreme Court in *Landreth*.

Assuming LLP interests are securities under federal law, offerings of the securities must be registered under the Securities Act of 1933 unless the sales are entitled to exemptions, such as those for limited offerings,[28] private offerings,[29] or

---

Liability Company as a Security, 19 Pepp. L. Rev. 1105 (1992) (LLC interests normally should be securities).

[25] 455 U.S. 551 (1982). For another prominent Supreme Court case applying the securities laws to a closely held firm, see Superintendent of Ins. v. Bankers Life & Cas. Co., 404 U.S. 6 (1971). For a discussion of policy considerations supporting exempting closely held firms from affirmative disclosure rules, see Ribstein, note 10, supra, at 22–24.

[26] 471 U.S. 681 (1985).

[27] *See* Great Lakes Chem. Corp. v. Monsanto Co., 96 F. Supp. 2d 376 (D. Del. 2000) (holding that purchase of 100% of interests of manager-managed LLC was not the purchase of a security, declining to apply *Landreth* because LLC interests are not traditional "stock").

[28] *See* Regulation D, Securities Act Rules 501–508, 17 C.F.R. §§ 230.501–230.508.

[29] Securities Act of 1933, § 4(2), 15 U.S.C. § 77d(2).

for intrastate transactions.[30] Resales of LLP interests probably are not exempt under SEC Rule 144[31] because, as closely held firms, LLPs probably do not register or report under the 1934 Act.[32] LLPs may, however, be able to use Rule 144A for resales.[33] Whether or not LLP interests are exempt from registration, if they are securities, they are subject to the anti-fraud provisions.[34] However, as long as they are not registered under the 1934 Act, LLP interests are not subject to that act's proxy[35] or short-swing trading[36] provisions or requirements for financial reporting to the SEC.[37]

Under state law, if offerings of LLP interests are registered under the 1933 Act, they could be offered by "coordination" in states that model their exemptions after the Uniform Securities Act.[38] Otherwise, they would probably have to be registered by "qualification"[39] through the filing of a registration statement and approval by the state commissioner[40] unless the offering is exempt. The Uniform Limited Offering Exemption proposed by the North American Securities Administration Association and in effect in several states permits offerings of $5 million or less under rules similar to the federal limited offering exemption.[41] Short-form registration by "notification"[42] is available only to the more large and seasoned issuers, and therefore probably not to LLPs.[43]

---

[30] *See* Securities Act Rule 147, 17 C.F.R. § 230.147.

[31] Securities Act Rule 144, 17 C.F.R. § 230.144.

[32] In general, firms must register if they are listed on an exchange or have total assets exceeding $1 million and equity securities held by more than 750 people. *See* Securities Exchange Act of 1934, § 12(a), (g), 15 U.S.C. § 78*l*(a), (g). Securities Exchange Act of 1934, § 13, 15 U.S.C. § 78m requires companies registered under the act to file reports. Under Securities Act Rule 144(c), 17 C.F.R. § 230.144(c), Rule 144 is available only for firms that are filing 1934 Act reports or that make equivalent information publicly available.

[33] *See* Securities Act Rule 144A(d)(3)(i), 17 C.F.R. § 230.144A(D)(3)(i) (making exemption available to nonlisted and non-NASDAQ-traded securities but only for sales to very large financial institutions or other "qualified institutional buyers").

[34] *See* Securities Act of 1933 Act §§ 12(2) and 17(a), 15 U.S.C. §§ 77l(2) and 77q(a); Securities Exchange Act of 1934 Act § 10(b), 15 U.S.C. § 78j(b), Securities Exchange Act Rule 10b-5, 17 C.F.R. § 240.10b-5.

[35] *See* Securities Exchange Act of 1934, § 14, 15 U.S.C. § 78n.

[36] Securities Exchange Act of 1934, § 16(b), 15 U.S.C. § 78p.

[37] Securities Exchange Act § 13, 15 U.S.C. § 78m.

[38] *See* Uniform Securities Act § 301. As of September 1, 2012, 17 states had adopted the Uniform Securities Act: Georgia, Hawaii, Idaho, Indiana, Iowa, Kansas, Maine, Michigan, Minnesota, Mississippi, Missouri, New Mexico, Oklahoma, South Carolina, South Dakota, Vermont, and Wisconsin.

[39] Uniform Securities Act § 301.

[40] Uniform Securities Act § 304(c).

[41] *See, e.g.*, Ill. Stat. § 130.420(4)(D); Ga. Code Ann. 10-5-9 (16).

[42] *See* Uniform Securities Act § 301.

[43] Uniform Securities Act § 302(a).

§ 7.02 BANKRUPTCY LAW

The treatment of a bankrupt LLP or bankrupt LLP partners depends in large extent on how the limited liability shield interacts with the bankruptcy law. This is so far unclear.[44] There are few reported bankruptcy opinions involving LLPs. Though recent years have seen a number of high-profile LLP bankruptcies involving law firms, much of the financial consequences to the partners in those firms was the result of negotiated settlements in the shadow of bankruptcy law, particularly fraudulent transfer law.[45] Other lesser-known LLP bankruptcies are further complicated because the main driver of insolvency was a malpractice or discrimination claim that may be applicable to individual partners.[46] Though still few in number, an increasing number of cases involve LLCs and have applied partnership precedents regarding nonliability aspects of entity law without explicit consideration of whether such firms generally should be treated as partnerships.[47]

Whether an LLP is a "partnership" and its members "partners" for bankruptcy law purposes rather than a corporation is significant for several reasons, including:

(1) Partners' duty to contribute to payment of partnership debts.[48]

(2) Whether partners can obtain stays or injunctions delaying actions against partners by partnership creditors.[49]

(3) In what circumstances a partnership bankruptcy is necessary given the availability of partner assets to pay creditor claims.

---

[44] *See* In re Mahoney Hawkes, LLP, 289 B.R. 285 (D. Mass. 2002) ("There is little case law in Massachusetts on the liability of individual partners in a limited liability partnership" even in non-bankruptcy cases).

[45] Creditors of Brobeck, Phleger & Harrison LLP filed an involuntary Chapter 7 Bankruptcy Petition against it on Sept. 17, 2003. Three years later, Coudert Brothers, LLP had filed a Chapter 11 Bankruptcy Petition on Sept. 22, 2006. Heller Ehrman LLP filed a Chapter 11 Bankruptcy Petition on Dec. 28, 2008. Thelen LLP filed a Chapter 7 Bankruptcy Petition on Sept. 17, 2009. After creditors of Howrey LLP filed an involuntary bankruptcy lawsuit in April 2011, Howrey filed voluntarily in June 2011. Most recently, Dewey LeBouef filed a Chapter 11 Bankruptcy Petition on May 28, 2012.

[46] *See* In re Mahoney Hawkes, LLP, 289 B.R. 285 (D. Mass. 2002); In re Labrum & Doak LLP, 237 B.R. 275 (E.D. Pa. 1999).

[47] *See* In re DeLuca (JTB Enters., L.C. v. D & B Venture, L.C.), 194 B.R. 79 (Bankr. E.D. Va. 1996) (holding that a bankrupt LLC member's interest can be terminated); In re Daugherty Constr., Inc., 188 B.R. 607 (D. Neb. 1995) (holding that LLC operating agreement is executory contract, relying on partnership precedents). For a discussion of bankruptcy treatment of LLCs see Ribstein & Keatinge, § 14.04.

[48] *See* Bankruptcy Code (11 U.S.C.) § 723.

[49] *See generally* Buschman & Madden, The Power and Propriety of Bankruptcy Court Intervention in Actions Between Nondebtors, 47 Bus. Law. 913, 942 (1992); Glassman, Third-Party Injunctions in Partnership Bankruptcy Cases, 49 Bus. Law. 1081 (1994); Ribstein, The Illogic and Limits of Partners' Liability in Bankruptcy, 32 Wake Forest L. Rev. 31 (1997); Zaretsky, Co-Debtor Stays In Chapter 11 Bankruptcy, 73 Corn. L. Rev. 213, 254–59 (1988).

(4) Whether solvent partners should be required to continue in partnership with an insolvent partner.[50]

Any person may be a debtor under Chapter 7, 11, or 12 of the Bankruptcy Code.[51] *Person* "includes individual, partnership, and corporation."[52] An LLP is undoubtedly a person;[53] however, it is not clear whether an LLP is a partnership or a corporation. The cases so far generally accept the state law definition of partnership.[54] The Code does not define partnerships, but defines corporation to specifically not include limited partnerships.[55]

Despite LLP partners' limited liability, there are strong arguments for treating LLPs as partnerships under the bankruptcy law:

(1) They are clearly defined as such under LLP provisions (*see* Section 1.02(a), above). This is significant, since bankruptcy cases generally apply the state law definition of partnership.[56]

(2) Since "limited partnerships" are excluded from the definition of "corporation," it follows *a fortiori* that *general* partnerships that have registered as LLPs also should be excluded.

(3) The Code explicitly applies state law LLP liability limitations in determining partner contribution obligations in bankruptcy (*see* Section 3.09(g), above). This strongly suggests that LLPs will be treated as partnerships under this provision.

(4) The provisions on commencement of the proceeding are as applicable to LLPs as to other partnerships. The Code provides that a petition approved by less than all the partners is treated as an involuntary proceeding.[57] LLPs are subject to

---

[50] A partner's bankruptcy is a dissolution cause under U.P.A. § 31, a cause of dissociation under R.U.P.A. § 601(6), and a potential dissolution cause under R.U.P.A. § 801. However, under Bankruptcy Code (11 U.S.C.) §§ 363(*l*), 365(e)(1), and 541(c)(1), a debtor partner's trustee in bankruptcy controls and may deal with the debtor's property, the trustee may assume executory contracts, and the debtor's interest becomes property of the estate, notwithstanding contracts or state law that otherwise would prevent these results. These provisions may or may not supercede contracts or provisions of state law permitting or compelling removal of debtor partners or dissolution of the partnership on bankruptcy of a partner. *See* Bromberg & Ribstein, § 7.05(b)(3). The law regarding continuity of LLCs after member bankruptcy is discussed in Ribstein & Keatinge, § 14.04.

[51] 11 U.S.C. § 109(b), (d), (f).

[52] 11 U.S.C. § 101(41).

[53] *See* In re ICLNDS Notes Acquisition, LLC, 259 B.R. 289, 293 (B.C. N.D. Ohio 2001) holding that "[a]s corporations and partnerships are eligible to be debtors, and because an LLC draws its character from both of those forms of doing business, an LLC is similar enough to those entities that it also comes within the definition of 'person' and is eligible for protection under the Code").

[54] *See, e.g.,* In re Labrum & Doak, LLP, 237 B.R. 275 (E.D. Pa. 1999); In re Vannoy, 176 B.R. 758 (M.D.N.C. 1994); Matter of Historic Macon Station Ltd. P'ship, 152 B.R. 358 (M.D. Ga. 1993); In re Cooper, 128 B.R. 632 (E.D. Tex. 1991); In re Indvik, 118 B.R. 993 (N.D. Iowa 1990) (use of trade name supports partnership); In re Belle Isle Farm, 76 B.R. 85 (E.D. Va. 1987).

[55] 11 U.S.C. § 101(9).

[56] *See* 11 U.S.C. § 101(41), supra note 50 and accompanying text.

[57] *See* 11 U.S.C. § 303(b)(3).

the same management rules as other types of partnerships, including each partner's default power to veto extraordinary transactions (*see* Section 4.02, above).

(5) Characterizing LLPs as corporations because of the owners' limited liability would raise serious predictability problems given the many variations in limited liability among LLPs, and between LLPs and other types of firms. Among other things, it would not be clear how to treat partial-shield LLPs (*see* Section 3.02, above) or LLPs that have elected to waive the liability shield (*see* Section 3.05, above). This policy consideration suggests that the state law partnership form of the business should matter as it arguably does for securities law purposes (*see* Section 7.01, above) and as it does for tax purposes under the "check-the-box" rule (*see* Section 7.05, below).

It follows that the same bankruptcy rules that apply to partnerships also should apply to LLPs except to the extent that the rules specifically depend on the owners' personal liability, as they do in connection with partner contributions, co-debtor stays and injunctions and, as discussed below, fraudulent transfers and conveyances. Moreover, bankruptcy should have the same effect on an LLP as on other types of partnerships. Thus, a general partner's bankruptcy should have the same effect on an LLP as on a non-LLP partnership;[58] the property of the bankrupt partnership[59] includes claims for debts owed to the LLP by members on account of members' obligations to make or return contributions (*see* Section 3.08, above); and the estate of a bankrupt partner includes the member's interest in the LLP[60] but not specific property of the LLP.[61]

A nonmanaging partner in an LLP has been treated as a shareholder in a corporation for purposes of not having standing to file an involuntary bankruptcy petition under § 303(b)(3) of the Bankruptcy Code, though a "general partner" would.[62] Citing a position in a popular bankruptcy treatise, the court reasoned that the purpose of this Code section was to protect partners who are exposed to

---

[58] The effect under partnership law is discussed in § 4.07, supra. The effect of bankruptcy law is discussed in Bromberg & Ribstein, § 7.05(b)(3).

[59] *See* 11 U.S.C. § 541(a)(1) (property of the bankrupt estate includes "all legal or equitable interests of the debtor in property").

[60] *See* In re Buckman, 600 F.2d 160 (8th Cir. 1979).

[61] *See* In re Minton Group, 46 B.R. 222 (S.D.N.Y. 1985). For a discussion of partnership property in bankruptcy, see Bromberg & Ribstein, § 3.05(d)(4).

[62] *See* In re Rambo Imaging, L.L.P., 2008 WL 2778846 (Bankr. W.D. Tex. July 15, 2008). The uncertainty regarding bankruptcy classification of LLPs is likely to remain. The National Bankruptcy Reform Commission had some relevant recommendations that would not have clarified the situation and, in any event, are unlikely to be adopted. It proposed defining "general partner" as "any entity that as a result of an existing or former status as an actual or purported general partner in an existing, former, predecessor, or affiliated partnership, is liable under applicable nonbankruptcy law for one or more debts of the partnership." See Nat'l Bankr. Review Comm'n, The Next Twenty Years: Final Report, Recommendation 2.3.1. (Oct. 20, 1997). This apparently would exclude partners in LLPs under full-shield statutes. The Commission did not have a recommendation for defining partnership.

personal liability and that there was therefore no reason to distinguish LLP partners in a "full-shield" LLP from corporate shareholders in light of the partners' liability limitation. The court also relied on the inclusion of "partnership association organized under a law that makes only the capital subscribed responsible for the debts for such association" in the Code's definition of corporation. Though it is a truism of limited liability partnerships that its partners are not liable for certain debts of the partnership, the doctrine of fraudulent conveyances may arrive at the same result as personal liability. The Bankruptcy Code provides that a transfer may be avoided if made by an "insolvent" partnership or the transfer rendered the partnership insolvent.[63] Insolvent is defined so as to take into account the non-partnership property of each "general partner,"[64] because the ability to claw back previous distributions may result in partners being pseudo-liable, even if LLP partners may not have to contribute toward the payment of debts.[65] Because of this uncertainty, partners have an incentive, even in LLPs organized in full-shield jurisdictions, to enter into settlements with the bankruptcy trustee in consideration of a release from all claims.[66]

Another legal doctrine that effectively weakens the limited liability shield in law firms' bankruptcy proceedings is the doctrine of "unfinished business."[67] As a general partnership, partners have authority, absent agreement, to wind up current partnership business and account to the partnership. In law firms, leading up to and following a dissolution or bankruptcy filing, partners disassociate from the firm and most join other firms, taking their current clients and current

---

[63] *See* 11 U.S.C. § 548(b).

[64] *See* 11 U.S.C. § 101(32)(B); Uniform Fraudulent Transfers Act, § 2(c); Uniform Fraudulent Conveyance Act, § 2(2).

[65] *See* In re Promedicus Health Group, LLP, 416 B.R. 389, 391 (Bankr. W.D.N.Y. 2009) (holding that because of their limited liability, and despite their potential personal liability for wrongful acts, LLP partners were not "general partners" under the above Bankruptcy Code definition). However, the definition of "insolvent" for an LLP might take into account contributions partners are obligated to make, including for pre-registration claims, for contracts under tort-only shields, and for claims for which partners are at fault.

[66] *See, e.g.*, First Amended Plan of Liquidation of Coudert Brothers LLP Dated May 9, 2005 (approved on Aug. 27, 2008 by Judge Robert D. Drain, U.S. Bankruptcy Court, Southern District of New York) (providing for full release of "Participating Partners."). Former Dewey & LeBoeuf partners are currently being asked to agree to a settlement with that firm's bankruptcy trustee to contribute between $5,000 and $3.5 million to avoid clawback claims under the theory that many partners took distributions knowing that the firm was in financial straits. *See* Peter Lattman, Former Dewey Partners to Return Millions in Compensation to Pay Creditors. N.Y. Times, Aug. 17, 2012, at B6 (stating that the settlement would make up one-third of the firm's deficiency to creditors, with "unfinished business" claims repaying the remainder).

[67] *See* Amanda A. Main, Applying the Unfinished Business Rule to Dissolved Law Partnerships, 33 L.A. Law. 10 (March 2010); John C. Keeney, Jr. & Lynne M. Baum, Beware of Unfinished Business, 19 Prof. Law. 24 (2009).

projects with them.[68] The new firms invite these disassociating partners to join their firms precisely because the partners bring with them current and future fee-generating business. When solvent firms voluntarily dissolve, partners amicably split up the business and go on their way. However, when firms enter into bankruptcy, the bankruptcy trustee may not be as gracious.

Bankruptcy trustees are entrusted to oversee the winding up of the insolvent partnership, even an LLP, and liquidate the assets of the LLP to discharge obligations to creditors. The assets of a service firm are its clients, which go out the door with the disassociating partners. Recently, in some very high-profile law firm bankruptcies, trustees have sued both former partners and their new law firms to retrieve fees from unfinished business of the debtor that was completed by an exiting partner. In *In re Brobeck, Phleger & Harrison LLP*, the U.S. Bankruptcy Court in the Northern District of California relied on a California case[69] involving a general partnership to hold that the unfinished business *"Jewel"* doctrine applied in the LLP context.[70] However, under the RUPA, enacted after *Jewel*, exiting partners would be entitled to "reasonable compensation for services rendered in winding up of the partnership," but not profit.[71] Furthermore, a recent case from the Southern District of New York held that the *Jewel* doctrine applied in the bankruptcy of Thelen LLP, a California LLP and that the doctrine applied both to contingency-fee legal work and fee-based legal work.[72]

Interestingly, in *Brobeck*, the partners, mindful of the *Jewel* doctrine, entered into a Final Partnership Agreement in February 2003, months before filing a bankruptcy petition. The "FPA" contained a provision waiving the LLP's interest in ongoing business in favor of the partners. The *Brobeck* court found that the *Jewel* waiver was valid; however, because the LLP was effectively transferring an asset of the LLP (the ownership of the unfinished business) within the two-year look back period, the *Jewel* waiver was a fraudulent transfer and subject to return.[73] In *In re Heller Ehrman LLP*, the same court held that a *Jewel* waiver, though otherwise effective, was also a fraudulent transfer when executed months prior to the LLP's bankruptcy, allowing the bankruptcy trustee to sue former partners and their new firms for unfinished business profits.[74] These cases

---

[68] *See* Rachel M. Zahorsky, 550 Lawyers: Where Are They Now?, 95 ABA J. 30 (April 2009) (reporting that 402 of the 550 attorneys at Heller Ehrman LLP had found new positions at other law firms shortly after that firm's demise).

[69] *See* Jewel v. Boxer, 156 Cal. App. 3d 171 (1984).

[70] *See* In re Brobeck, Phleger & Harrison LLP, 408 B.R. 318 (N.D. Cal. 2009).

[71] *See* RUPA § 401(h).

[72] *See* In re Geron v. Robinson & Cole LLP, __ B.R. __, 2012 WL 3800766 (S.D.N.Y. Sept. 4, 2012).

[73] *See* In re Brobeck, 408 B. R. 318, 39 (2009).

[74] *See* In re Heller Ehrman LLP, 2011 WL 1539796 (N.D. Cal. Apr. 22, 2011). In *Heller*, the LLP was actually organized as having professional corporations be the partners of the LLP and the individual attorneys be members of the professional corporations. The attorneys argued that the

have already resulted in bankrupt law firm trustees suing receiving law firms for unfinished business and in settlements.[75] However, these cases suggest quite strongly that a *Jewel* waiver executed and operational when insolvency is not on the horizon should be respected by the courts; however, such a waiver that only transfers the rights in the unfinished business by its terms at dissolution would seem to fall under the fraudulent transfer doctrine.

Interestingly, even though a *Jewel* waiver may be considered a fraudulent conveyance and subject the new law firm to a clawback of profits from unfinished business, the execution of the waiver and the continuation of a firm matter is not a breach of fiduciary duty of an exiting partner.[76] Here, partnership law and bankruptcy law conflict.

§ 7.03   PARTNERS AS "EMPLOYEES" UNDER EMPLOYMENT DISCRIMINATION AND RELATED LAWS

Since partners of general partnerships, including LLPs, may be both owners and workers in the firm, a question may arise as to whether they are employees who are protected by employment discrimination and worker compensation laws. These two types of laws are discussed separately below.

(a)   *Employment Discrimination*

Title VII of the Civil Rights Act of 1964, prohibits discrimination against any "employee" because of race, color, religion, sex, or national origin.[77] Under the

---

partnership-based rule of "unfinished business" did not apply to them because they were not partners in the LLP. The court looked through the structure and noted that their employment agreements specified that all attorney employees owed fiduciary duties to the partnership, which the court reasoned included the fiduciary duties underlying the unfinished business doctrine. This holding was confirmed in another proceeding in the same case. In re Heller Ehrman L.L.P., 2013 WL 951706 (Mar. 11, 2013). In that case, the court held that the waiver was not given in exchange for equivalent value, even though the presence of the waiver may have aided in a more efficient winding up of business and placing of staff.

[75] Dewey & LeBoeuf was effectively dissolved in February 2013, when former partners agreed to a bankruptcy plan requiring them to return distributions. *See* Peter Lattman, *With a Judge's Decision, Dewey is Officially Dissolved*, N.Y. Times, Feb. 28, 2013, at B5. However, in July 2013, the firm's attorneys asked to subpoena over 30 firms for information on Dewey's unfinished business. In the *Howrey* bankruptcy case, Baker Hostetler agreed to return $41.1 million in fees from unfinished business, including a $38.4 million contingency fee from an antitrust matter.

[76] *See* In re Heller Ehrman L.L.P., 2013 WL 951706 (Mar. 11, 2013) (reasoning that "the *Jewel* waiver freed the unfinished business from the Shareholders' fiduciary duty to account for profits earned in completing that business").

[77] 42 U.S.C. §§ 2000e *et seq.*

Age Discrimination in Employment Act it is "unlawful for an employer . . . to discharge any individual . . . because of such individual's age."[78] The Act defines an employee as "an individual employed by any employer."[79] These and other federal and state statutes dealing with employment discrimination raise the question whether a partner is an "employee" or is employed by an employer. There are related questions as to whether payments to retired partners are regulated by the Employee Retirement Income Security Act (ERISA).[80]

These laws clearly apply to a partnership's nonpartner employees, including the decision whether to admit an associate as a partner.[81] However, in a concurring opinion in a leading partnership employment discrimination case, Justice Powell noted that the employment discrimination laws probably do not regulate employment decisions involving those who are bona fide partners.[82] Although one important employment discrimination case ordered the admission of an associate upon a finding of discrimination, thereby holding that employment discrimination law may override partnership law,[83] the court was careful to note:

> The instant case involves only an employee's elevation to partnership; it does not involve Ms. Hopkins' retention of partnership or the regulation of the relationship among partners at Price Waterhouse. Thus, we are not confronted by the concerns expressed in Justice Powell's concurring opinion. Justice Powell emphasized that the Court in *Hishon* did not reach the question whether Title VII protects employees after they become partners; nor do we reach that question in this case.[84]

In considering how a partnership's registering as an LLP might affect whether the employment discrimination laws protect its partners, the following discussion examines cases dealing with various types of partnership-type business associations. While the cases mostly concern general partnerships, a recent Supreme Court case involving a professional corporation is applicable to all types of firms.

---

[78] *See* 29 U.S.C. § 623(a)(1).

[79] 29 U.S.C. § 630(f).

[80] Employment Retirement Income Security Act of 1974 §§ 2 *et seq.*, 29 U.S.C.A. §§ 1001 *et seq.*

[81] *See* Hishon v. King & Spalding, 467 U.S. 69 (1984); Hopkins v. Price Waterhouse, 920 F.2d 967 (D.C. Cir. 1990); Ezold v. Wolf, Block, Schorr and Solis-Cohen, 751 F. Supp. 1175 (E.D. Pa. 1990), *rev'd*, 983 F.2d 509 (3d Cir. 1993) (plaintiff failed to show that firm's preferred reasons for refusing to admit associate as partner were only a pretext); Bromberg & Ribstein, § 2.02(b)(2).

[82] *See* Hishon v. King & Spalding, 467 U.S. 69, 79 (1984) (Powell, J., concurring).

[83] Hopkins v. Price Waterhouse, 920 F.2d 967 (D.C. Cir. 1990).

[84] Hopkins v. Price Waterhouse, 920 F.2d 967, 979 (D.C. Cir. 1990).

(1) General Partnerships

Courts have held that one who is designated as a partner in a partnership may or may not be treated as an employee.[85]

Several cases have applied a test that relies on whether one is a "bona fide" partner under state law. The leading authority for this test is *Wheeler v. Hurdman*,[86] in which the court refused to apply an anti-discrimination law to a partner in a large accounting firm. The court rejected an "economic realities" test based on control or domination of the partner, holding that "bona fide general partners" are not employees for purposes of the anti-discrimination laws. The court reasoned that, despite some similarities between partners in a very large partnerships and corporate employees, there are significant differences between partners and employees, including liability for loss, profit sharing, and selectivity of admission.

Similarly, in *Simpson v. Ernst & Young*,[87] the court in an ADEA case rejected a special "economic realities" test and considered whether the plaintiff would be viewed as a partner in light of all of the factors that would be relevant under state partnership law.[88] The court held that the plaintiff was an employee, noting that his supposed capital contributions looked more like a loan, his compensation looked more like salary than a profit share, his voting rights were illusory, he had no management authority, and the firm's management committee did not treat the plaintiff like a partner in subjecting him to a layoff. Although the court noted that the plaintiff's unlimited liability was an important partnership attribute, it questioned whether the liability would be enforced against the plaintiff in view of the absence of other partnership features.[89]

---

[85] *Compare* Caruso v. Peat, Marwick, Mitchell & Co., 664 F. Supp. 144 (S.D.N.Y. 1987), 717 F. Supp. 218 (S.D.N.Y. 1989), *and* Simpson v. Ernst & Young, 850 F. Supp. 648 (S.D. Ohio 1994) (characterizing "partner" as employee), *with* Strother v. Southern Cal. Permanente Med. Group, 79 F.3d 859 (9th Cir. 1996) (reversing summary judgment against "partner" under state anti-discrimination law) *and* Wheeler v. Hurdman, 825 F.2d 257 (10th Cir.), *cert. denied*, 484 U.S. 986 (1987) (treating a partner as a non-"employee"). *See generally* Comment, Partners as Employees Under the Federal Employment Discrimination Statutes: Are the Roles of Partner and Employee Mutually Exclusive?, 42 U. Miami L. Rev. 699 (1988) (advocating an "economic realities" test under which some partners would be employees for anti-discrimination law purposes). A law partner who receives benefits under the firm's disability policy has been held to be a "beneficiary" under the Employment Retirement Income Security Act and is therefore barred from bringing state claims against the insurer. *See* Wolk v. Unum Life Ins. of Am., 186 F.3d 352 (3d Cir. 1999). The court held that a law firm partner is not an employer under the "plain language" of the act defining "beneficiary" as a "person designated by a participant, or by the terms of an employee benefit plan, who is or may become entitled to a benefit thereunder."

[86] 825 F.2d 257 (10th Cir.), *cert. denied*, 484 U.S. 986 (1987).

[87] 850 F. Supp. 648 (S.D. Ohio 1994).

[88] *See generally* Bromberg & Ribstein, ch. 2.

[89] 850 F. Supp. at 663.

On the other hand, in *Ehrlich v. Howe*,[90] the court held that the plaintiff was a nonemployee partner and therefore not entitled to an ERISA claim for termination. It noted that the plaintiff was jointly and severally liable for partnership debts, shared profits and losses, voted as a partner, had a sufficient voting interest to be able to block partnership decisions with one other partner, participated in hiring decisions, and could be terminated only by unanimous vote of the other partners.

In *Strother v. Southern California Permanente Medical Group*,[91] the court reversed judgment against a "partner" in a medical group under California anti-discrimination law. The court noted that the federal cases, which were controlling in the absence of California case law,

> reveal that determining whether an individual is an "employee" typically requires a factual inquiry which goes beyond merely the partnership agreement and the "partner" label. Courts must analyze the true relationship among partners, including the method of compensation, the "partner's" responsibility for partnership liabilities, and the management structure and the "partner's" role in that management, to determine if an individual should be treated as a partner or an employee for the purpose of employment discrimination laws.[92]

Thus, the district court wrongly determined that plaintiff was not an "employee" based solely on the complaint, the attached partnership agreement, and the fact that plaintiff was labeled a "partner." The partnership agreement provided for partnership rights, including the rights to be elected to the firm's board of directors, which managed the firm, to vote on amendments to the partnership agreement, board representatives, partner discharges, and termination of the partnership. However, plaintiff had little control over the board, was compensated based on her performance, was subject to discipline for poor performance, and was one of 2,400–2,500 "partners," suggesting rights comparable to those of an employee.[93] In light of the questions raised by these facts, judgment on the pleadings alone was improper.

Rhoads v. Jones Financial Companies[94] held that plaintiff was a partner rather than an employee of a brokerage firm. The court distinguished *Simpson* because plaintiff was liable for the loan she received to buy her interest, shared in profits and losses according to her interest in the firm, had meaningful partner powers to vote on partnership matters, remove the managing partner and examine partnership books, and was referred to and treated as a general partner in all partnership documents. As in *Wheeler,* the court held that the fact that plaintiff

---

[90] 848 F. Supp. 482 (S.D.N.Y. 1994).
[91] 79 F.3d 859 (9th Cir. 1996).
[92] 79 F.3d 859, 867 (9th Cir. 1996).
[93] 79 F.3d 859, 867–68 (9th Cir. 1996).
[94] 957 F. Supp. 1102, 1110 (E.D. Mo. 1997).

did not have full control over her working environment did not mean that she should be treated as an employee, reasoning that "possessing a few indicia of employee status did not destroy plaintiff's status as a partner."[95]

Equal Employment Opportunity Commission v. Sidley Austin Brown & Wood[96] held, in a majority opinion by Judge Posner, that there was enough question whether 32 equity partners in a 500-partner law firm demoted to "counsel" or "senior counsel" were covered by the age discrimination law that the EEOC was entitled to compliance with a subpoena to the extent that it sought documents concerning whether the demoted partners were employees under the age discrimination law. The firm was controlled by a self-perpetuating executive committee. Non-members of the committee had some authority but no firm-wide power. The demoted partners had significant capital accounts and shared profits based on points assigned by the executive committee. The court reasoned that the partners' classification as such under state law did not control their treatment under federal antidiscrimination law. Judge Easterbrook, concurring, asserted that a bona fide partner was not an "employee" under federal law, emphasizing the importance of unlimited liability and profit-sharing to the determination of whether one is an owner, and discounting concentration of decisionmaking authority. Judge Easterbrook concurred on the issuance of the subpoena on the ground that the EEOC was entitled to information bearing on the status of partners other than those who were demoted.

(2) LLPs

One recent case held that an LLP could be held liable in connection with a decision whether to admit an associate as a partner to the LLP.[97] In a case dealing with a partner in an LLP, *Siko v. Kassab, Archbold & O'Brien, L.L.P.*,[98] the court denied defendant law firm's motion for summary judgment in a claim under the Family and Medical Leave Act. The defendant asserted that it had fewer than 50 "employees" and therefore was not an "employer" under the act, since partners and of-counsel lawyers were not employees for purposes of the FMLA. Applying *Simpson,* the court reasoned:

> This matter is distinguishable from the cases Defendant relies on which hold that partners are not employees under federal anti-discrimination statutes.[5] Those cases are limited to general partnerships where the partner is either a shareholder or subject to unlimited liability. In the current matter, partners of Defendant's law firm

[95] 957 F. Supp. 1102, 1110 (E.D. Mo. 1997).
[96] 315 F.3d 696 (7th Cir. 2002).
[97] *See* Dow v. Donovan, 150 F. Supp. 2d 249 (D. Mass. 2001). For a discussion of the partners' vicarious liability in *Dow,* see Section 3.04, notes 41 and 46, supra.
[98] 1998 WL 464900, Slip at 5 (E.D. Pa. Aug. 5, 1998).

are neither shareholders nor subject to unlimited liability but, rather, part of a limited liability partnership. Thus, for the purpose of summary judgment, Defendant has failed to assert sufficient facts to support the legal conclusion that Defendant's law firm partners are not employees.

[5] Defendant cites Hull v. Rose, Schmidt, Hasley & DiSalle, 700 A.2d 996 (Pa. Super. 1997) and Wheeler v. Hardman, 825 F.2d 257 (10th Cir. 1987) for the proposition that partners are not employees under federal anti-discrimination statutes. Hull and Wheeler, however, involve general partners who are subject to unlimited liability of the corporation. As such, those partners, unlike those at Defendant's law firm, are accountable for all the benefits and pitfalls attributable of the corporation.

(3) Professional Corporations: *Clackamas Gastroenterology Associates, P.C. v. Wells*

Some courts have treated shareholders in a professional *corporation* as employees despite the firm's similarities to a partnership.[99] Most importantly, the Supreme Court to some extent clarified the resolution of the issues in the above cases by holding in *Clackamas Gastroenterology Associates, P.C. v. Wells,*[100] that whether four physician-shareholders in a medical clinic could be counted toward the 15 "employees" required for application of the Americans with Disabilities Act. The Court refused to rely either on the corporate form of the clinic, as did the Court of Appeals or on whether the shareholders were functional equivalents of partners, as did the district court. Rather, the court relied on the element of control, emphasized both by the common law in determining the existence of a master-servant relationship, and by the EEOC. The Court cited EEOC guidelines looking to whether the firm hires, fires, or supervises the worker, whether the individual reports to others or can influence the organization, the parties' intent that the individual be an employee, and whether the individual shares in the firm's profits, losses, and liabilities. The person's title, such as partner, is not determinative. The Court remanded, noting that evidence of control, profit share, and personal liability pointed to non-employee status, but that payment of salaries, and requirements that director-shareholders comply with the clinic's standards and report to a personnel manager, pointed the other way.

[99] 1998 WL 464900, Slip at 5 (E.D. Pa. Aug. 5, 1998).
[100] 538 U.S. 440, 123 S. Ct. 1673 (2003).

(4)   Summary

The pre-*Clackamas* cases indicate that both the form and substance of the relationship matter under the employment discrimination laws. Thus, it may be significant under these cases that LLP members are partners under state law (*see* Section 1.02(a), above). But the courts have also looked beneath the outward partnership characteristics. For example, the *Simpson* plaintiff believed he was a partner and had all of the outward aspects of partnership. This probably would have been enough to establish partnership intent, the critical element under state law.[101] Yet the court may also have been concerned about the possibility that employers would dress up employees in partnership clothing in order to evade the discrimination laws. In general, even if the courts purport to consider only whether the plaintiff is a "bona fide" partner under partnership law, they probably also will take into account the employment discrimination context of the decision. This is consistent with the relevance of many other contextual factors to the determination of the existence of a partnership relationship.[102]

Under an alternative formulation, the substance of the relationship not only matters, but is solely determinative to the exclusion of the parties' chosen form.[103] Under a version of this approach, "[t]he same analysis will apply regardless of the form of business organization involved," and "labels are not dispositive."[104] Under this approach, the test of whether the purported employee is actually an owner depends on whether the "employee" has a substantial role in governance (which declines with numerosity of owners) and an opportunity to share in the financial success of the firm.[105]

Form cannot, however, wholly be disregarded. The type of business association the parties have selected supplies the background rules that, in turn, determine the critical facts of the "employee's" participation in governance and other owner-like characteristics.[106] Even if the parties' agreement partly supplants the terms of the statutory standard form, the statute nevertheless helps determine how the courts will interpret this agreement. Moreover, strong practical considerations of predictability, judicial economy, and avoidance with interference of contract support emphasizing the form of the transaction.[107]

This brings us to the question of the effect of *Clackamas* on the foregoing analysis. Although *Clackamas* did not involve a partnership, it seems clear following this case that the fact that a business is a partnership under state law

---

[101] *See* Bromberg & Ribstein, § 2.05, and § 2.02, supra.

[102] Bromberg & Ribstein, § 2.02.

[103] Bromberg & Ribstein, § 2.02.

[104] *Id.* at 560–61.

[105] *Id.*

[106] *See* Ribstein, Statutory Forms for Closely Held Firms: Theories and Evidence from LLCs, 73 Wash. U. L.Q. 369 (1995).

[107] *See* Ribstein, supra note 7.

will not prevent the application of employment discrimination laws. By the same token, it should not be determinative whether the partnership has registered as an LLP. However, the firm's selection of the partnership or LLP form may bear on application of the factors relied on by the Court. Accordingly, *Wells* may signal only a change in emphasis and reasoning rather than necessarily different results than those reached in the above cases. In particular, the Court noted that the shareholders' personal liability pointed to non-employee status in *Wells*. Conversely, registration as an LLP may cause the firm's members to be treated as employees in a marginal case.

While there may be a difference between LLPs and other general partnerships for purposes of the employment discrimination laws, the difference between LLPs on the one hand and LLCs and professional corporations on the other is less clear. Under *Clackamas*, "partners" under state law are unlikely to be treated differently under the discrimination laws from those who have identical rights and obligations but are shareholders or LLC members. To the extent that courts emphasize the underlying nature of the relationship, the applicable default rules matter. Manager-managed LLCs depart significantly from the partnership-type rule of partner participation in management. Even LLPs with management committees may be distinguished from centrally managed LLCs because of the strong default rule of partner participation in management and partners' power to bind the firm in third-party transactions. Also, LLPs under statutes that provide for partner personal liability for contract-type debts may be deemed to retain enough personal liability to distinguish partners from employees. LLC statutes, on the other hand, protect members from vicarious liability. These differences may determine results in close cases, as where the size of the firm denies members realistic participation in management.

(b) Worker Compensation

In most states partners, consistent with their ownership status and the traditional "aggregate" nature of partnership, are treated as co-employers under the worker compensation statutes, although some states have made partners eligible for compensation by legislation or decision.[108] By comparison, LLC members are more likely to be treated as employees because the limited liability of LLCs lends itself more to entity treatment and the statutory centralized management may reduce the status of LLC members as compared with partners. The states have

---

[108] *See* Bromberg & Ribstein, § 1.03(c)(7).

permitted some or all members or managers to either elect[109] or to opt out of coverage.[110]

Some statutes have explicit provisions covering LLPs.[111] Where LLCs are covered and partnerships are not, and there is no explicit coverage of LLPs, LLP members may be less likely to be treated as employees than LLC members.

§ 7.04   LLPS AND PROFESSIONAL PRACTICE

Because many professional firms are partnerships, and because the partnership form is widely accepted for state professional licensing purposes, the availability of a partnership form of limited liability is particularly important for such firms. The LLP form raises two types of questions for professional firms. First, there is a question whether the firm is permitted to practice in a particular state as an LLP. Second, even if the firm can practice as an LLP, there may be a question whether the liability limitation provided for in the LLP statute will be permitted

---

[109] *See* Iowa Stat. § 85.1a (statute has been amended to add "limited liability partner" to list of those who may elect) (LLC member, like proprietor or partner, can elect to be covered); Ky. Rev. Stat. § 342.012(1); Minn. Stat. Ann. § 176.041(r) (limited liability companies with 10 or fewer members and less than 22,880 hours of payroll in the previous year may elect workers' compensation coverage for managers that are at least 25% owners); Mont. Code Ann. § 39-71-401(2)(r) (manager of a manager-managed LLC may elect coverage if he owns 20% or more either separately or if aggregated with shares owned by certain others); Neb. Rev. Stat. § 48-115(10) (an LLC member, like an individual employer, partner, or self-employed person, who is working full time in the business may elect to be covered by the act); Okla. Stat. tit. 85, § 85-3 (an LLC member who owns 10% of the capital of the LLC, like a corporate 10% stockholder-employee, is not an "employee" but may elect to be covered); Wis. Stat. Ann. § 102.075 (member who is full-time employee may elect to be covered).

[110] *See* Iowa Stat. § 85.1a (statute has been amended to add "limited liability partner" to list of those who may elect) (LLC member, like proprietor or partner, can elect to be covered); Ky. Rev. Stat. § 342.012(1); Minn. Stat. Ann. § 176.041(r) (limited liability companies with 10 or fewer members and less than 22,880 hours of payroll in the previous year may elect workers' compensation coverage for managers that are at least 25% owners); Mont. Code Ann. § 39-71-401(2)(r) (manager of a manager-managed LLC may elect coverage if he owns 20% or more either separately or if aggregated with shares owned by certain others); Neb. Rev. Stat. § 48-115(10) (an LLC member, like an individual employer, partner, or self-employed person, who is working full time in the business may elect to be covered by the act); Okla. Stat. tit. 85, § 85-3 (an LLC member who owns 10% of the capital of the LLC, like a corporate 10% stockholder-employee, is not an "employee" but may elect to be covered); Wis. Stat. Ann. § 102.075 (member who is full-time employee may elect to be covered).

[111] These include Ga. Code Ann. § 34-9-2.2 (providing that partners who are actively engaged in business may elect coverage); Mich. Comp. Laws. § 418.151(b) (including LLPs in definition of employer); *id.* § 418.647(2) (LLP owners are jointly and severally liable for worker compensation judgments); Mo. St. § 287.030(1) (LLP included in definition of employer); Mt. Code Ann. § 39-71-401 (LLP may elect to include partner working full time in the business as an employee); N.J. Stat. Ann. § 34:15-36 (LLP may elect to include partner working in the business as employee); Or. Rev. Stat. § 656.735(3)(c) (LLP members jointly and severally liable for workers' compensation penalties).

for a particular profession by the relevant licensing agency. These questions are discussed in the following two subsections.

(a) *Practice by Professional Firms as LLPs*

Every state permits professional firms to practice as partnerships or as corporations.[112] Many states also now permit professions to practice as limited liability companies.[113]

If the state restricts the form of entity in some way, there may be a question whether the state allows professional firms to practice as LLPs.[114] Even if the state allows professional corporations, it is not necessarily clear that the state would permit any kind of partnership, including an LLP.

There are usually no restrictions in the LLP statutes themselves. Indeed, some statutes provide that *only* professionals can be LLPs (*see* Section 2.03(a)(3), above). General partnership statutes generally do not restrict the types of businesses that can be conducted in the partnership form. All states have authorized public accounting firms to practice as LLPs, prompting the conversion to this form of the large accounting firms.[115] Some state statutes explicitly authorize professional LLPs.[116] Some state statutes authorize professions to practice in

---

[112] *See* Hillman on Lawyer Mobility, at 6:9 (2d ed. Supp. 2009); Kalish, Lawyer Liability and Incorporation of the Law Firm, 29 Ariz. L. Rev. 563, 563 (1987); Note, Developments in the Law — Lawyers' Responsibilities and Lawyers' Responses, 107 Harv. L. Rev. 1547, 1659 (1994); Annotation, Practice by Attorneys and Physicians as Corporate Entities or Associations under Professional Service Corporation Statutes, 4 A.L.R.3d 383.

[113] *See* Ribstein & Keatinge, § 15.13.

[114] For discussions of limitations on law firm organization form, see Christensen & Bertschi, LLC Statutes: Use by Attorneys, 29 Ga. L. Rev. 693, 695–96 (1995); Fortney, Seeking Shelter in the Minefield of Unintended Consequences — The Traps of Limited Liability Law Firms, 54 Wash. & Lee L. Rev. 717 (1997).

[115] *See* Telberg, Big 6 Race into LLPs, 8 Accounting Today, n.14 at 1, 41 (Aug. 8, 1994). For some state opinions, see Alaska Att'y Gen. Op. File No. 663-94-0210, 1994 Alaska AG Lexis 1, 1994 WL 28925 (corporations, partnerships, and out of state (at least Delaware) LLPs may register to practice public accounting); Ind. Bd. of Accountancy Definitions 862 IAL 1-0.5-1; (defining "firm" to include entities formed under Indiana law, including LLPs); La. Op. Att'y Gen. No. 94-88, 1994 WL 330115 (La. A.G. Apr. 22, 1994) (acknowledging a limited liability partnership is a partnership); Neb. Op. Att'y Gen. No. 94009, 1994 WL 62968 (Neb. A.G. Feb. 18, 1994) (allowing foreign LLP to register); Nev. Atty. Gen. Op. No. 94-04, 1994 WL 126167 (Mar. 25, 1994) (holding that out-of-state professional LLPs may register as partnership with Board of Accountancy); 1994 N.Y. Op. Att'y Gen. 14, 1994 WL 281941 (N.Y. A.G. June 6, 1994).

[116] *See* Ala. Code § 10A-8-10.10; Colo. Rev. Stat. § 12-2-117(1) (LLP may engage in practice as certified public accountants); Kan. Stat. Ann. § 1-308(a) (same); Tenn. Code Ann. § 61-1-1005 (professional firm may register as LLP subject to laws regulating professions); Utah Code § 48-1d-306, 48-1d-1301through 1310; Wash. Rev. Code § 25.05.510.

many different entity forms.[117] Several lawyer ethics rules and opinions have authorized law firms to practice in various forms, including LLPs.[118]

Where LLPs are not clearly authorized for use by lawyers or other professionals, policy considerations may be relevant in predicting the ultimate resolution. Since LLPs clearly are defined as "partnerships" under all LLP statutes (*see* Section 1.02(a), above), the only question is whether policy considerations

---

[117] *See, e.g.,* Conn. Gen. Stat. Ann. § 20-281(a) (permitting accounting "firms" to register) and § 20-279b(3) (defining "firm" to mean "any person, proprietorship, partnership, corporation, limited liability company or association and any other legal entity which practices public accounting"); Minn. Stat. §§ 319B.02, .03 (LLPs and other types of business entities to practice law); Mo. Rev. Stat. § 484.020 (same); Va. Code § 54.1-4412 (providing that a CPA may organize a firm as a "sole proprietorship, partnership, corporation, limited liability company, limited liability partnership, or any other form or organization permitted by law"); Utah Code Ann. § 48-1-48.

[118] *See* ABA Standing Comm. on Ethics and Professional Responsibility, Formal Opinion 96-401 (Aug. 2, 1996); Ala. Ethics Op. RO-96-09 (1996); Colo. Prof. Serv. Co. Rule 265.I.A; Del. Sup. Ct. Rule 67; Los Angeles County Bar Ass'n Professional Responsibility and Ethics Committee Inquiry No. 1992-2 (May 27, 1992); D.C. Bar Ethics Op. No. 235, Feb. 16, 1993) (permitting lawyers to practice as LLPs or LLCs in the District of Columbia if they include the words "registered limited liability partnership" or "limited liability company" as the last words of their names), *revised by* D.C. Bar Legal Ethics Comm. Op. 254 (1995) (hereinafter Op. 254) (deleting requirement that law firm include the words "registered limited liability partnership"); Fla. Rules of Prof'l Conduct, Rule 4-8.6; Rule 1-203(4) Rules and Regulations for the Organization and Government of the State Bar of Ga. (July 15, 1996) (providing that Georgia lawyers may practice alone or as partners, shareholders, or members of partnerships, LLPs, professional corporations, professional associations, and LLCs); Ill. Comp. St. S. Ct. Rule 721(a) (including LLPs among types of firms that may practice law); Ill. Comp. St. S. Ct. Rule 722(a) (including LLPs in definition of "limited liability entity"); Ill. Comp. St. S. Ct. Rule 722(b) (liability of members of "limited liability entity" is determined by the statute under which the entity is organized if the entity maintains minimum insurance or proof of financial responsibility); Burns Ind. Att'y Disc. Rule 27; Iowa Code of Prof'l Resp. Definition 2 (defining "law firm" for purposes of disciplinary rules to include LLP); Kan. Ethics Op. 94-03 (June 28, 1994); Ky. State S. Ct. Rule 3.022(f) (authorizing practice as employees of or partners, shareholders, members or co-owners of LLPs, professional corporations, LLCs "or any other limited liability entity organized pursuant to applicable statutes"); Mass. Sup. Ct. Rule 3:06; Neb. Sup. Ct. Rule for Ltd. Liab. Prof. Org. I(C)(1); N.J. Rules of Court., Rule 1:21-1C; N.Y. County Lawyers' Ethics Op. No. 703 (Nov. 8, 1994); N.M. State Bar Advisory Opinions Committee Op. 1996-1 (June 6, 1996) (stating that it is not unethical for a law firm to practice as a limited liability partnership as long as the lawyers forming the partnership provide for individual liability, but noting that neither the legislature nor the Supreme Court has explicitly authorized lawyers to practice as an LLP); Ohio St. Gov't Bar Rules, Rule 3, § 1; R.I. Sup. Ct. Art. II, Rule 10; Pa. Rules of Prof'l Conduct Amendment 112 (Apr. 28, 1995) amending 204 Pa. Code § 5481.3 and Rule 5.4(d), Comment (stating that "It is permissible to organize a law firm using any form of association desired, including, without limitations such non-traditional forms as a limited partnership, registered limited liability partnership, limited liability company or business trust, so long as all of the restrictions in paragraph (d) [concerning non-lawyer ownership and control] are satisfied"); Va. Code Ann. § 54.1-3902A; Va. S. Ct. Rules, Part 6, § 4, Par. 14; W. Va. L.E. I96-02; W. Va. Prof'l Cond. Rule 5.7. The Texas State Bar Professional Ethics Committee has ruled that a lawyer may not establish an LLP or other partnership with one or more non-lawyer professional if one of the activities of the LLP or other partnership would be to provide legal services, though the ruling strongly suggests an LLP could otherwise practice law. Tex. State Bar Prof'l Ethics Comm. Op. 493 (1994). Texas Disciplinary Rules of Professional Conduct, Rule 7.01(a) further supports this conclusion by providing for the name of an LLP in law practice.

militate against treating LLPs as such under professional registration statutes. The inherent flexibility of the partnership form, coupled with changes over time in the structure of both corporations and partnerships, have muddied distinctions between partnerships and corporations. Because the "partnership" restriction is not as meaningful from a policy standpoint as it once may have been, it would be inappropriate to give the restriction the sort of narrow interpretation that might be justified if it still served an important purpose. It follows that LLPs should not be characterized as non-"partnerships" merely because they deviate slightly from the traditional partnership form.

The main deviation from the partnership form is, of course, the difference between LLPs and other types of partnerships in partner liability. However, any difference in liability does not create significant differences between LLPs and other types of partnerships. First, as discussed further below in Section 7.04(b), the extent of liability of professionals is often controlled directly by local ethical rules.

Second, even if the form of business determines the nature of the members' liability, all LLP statutes provide for direct liability of partners for their own wrongdoing and some provide for liability for participating in or failing to monitor the wrongdoing of others (*see* Section 3.04, above). This liability may even go beyond that of partners in non-LLP partnerships, who are directly liable only for their own *negligence*, and who in some states cannot be held vicariously liable without exhaustion of partnership assets. Moreover, several LLP statutes require firms, as a condition of obtaining limited liability, to have insurance or show other evidence of financial responsibility (*see* Section 2.06, above). These provisions are comparable to those in state ethical rules authorizing lawyers to practice as limited liability entities (*see* Section 7.04(b), below). Also, California makes the liability limitation in law firms contingent on the LLP having registered with the California state bar.[119]

One reason for refusing to permit professional firms to practice as LLPs while permitting firms to practice as other types of limited-liability entities is the potential for confusing clients, patients, and others about the nature of the firm. Unsophisticated third parties may not understand that LLP partners, unlike those in other general partnerships, have limited liability for misconduct-type claims. The standard "LLP" designation required by the LLP statutes (*see* Section 2.05, above), as well as by some ethical rules,[120] may not go far enough to dispel this confusion.

---

[119] Cal. Corp. Code § 16306(f). An issue has been raised in the bankruptcy of the Howrey law firm as to whether its partners have personal liability because they failed to have a currently effective bar registration certificate. *See* In re Howrey LLP, Case No.11-31376, (Bankr. N.D. Cal.), Separate Opposition of The Petitioning Creditors of Howrey LLP to the Motion of Debtor for Order: (A) Authorizing Use of Cash Collateral on an Interim and Final Basis; (B) Granting Adequate Protection and Related Relief; and (C) Scheduling Final Hearing on Use of Cash Collateral (June 8, 2011).

[120] *See* N.J. Court Rules, Rule 1:21-1C(c); Wyo. Bar Ass'n Organ. & Gov't Rule 13. *See also* Minn. St. § 319B.05.

One ethics opinion, noting this problem, required the firm's name to end with "registered limited liability partnership" rather than just "LLP."[121] This highlights the firm's limited liability. Other opinions have held that the "LLP," "LLC," or similar designation was enough.[122] This is arguably a sensible approach since the liability limitation in LLPs goes no further than that in professional corporations and there is no greater likelihood of confusion with respect to "LLP" than there is with respect to "PC." Moreover, given the prevalence of the "PC" form, clients and others probably do not expect that lawyers and other professionals will have vicarious liability for the acts of their co-partners.

Even if there are policy reasons for distinguishing LLPs from other partnerships, it is important to take into account the potential costs of making such a distinction. First, if states distinguished professional LLPs from other types of professional partnerships, professionals subject to this rule would have to determine what *other* deviations from the U.P.A. might make their firms non-"partnerships." This could be a problem in light of the changes in partnership law in the Revised Uniform Partnership Act (R.U.P.A.), such as the R.U.P.A. rules that provide for exhaustion of remedies[123] and cutoff of liability for dissociating partners.[124] R.U.P.A. partnerships may be concerned that these moves toward limited liability will make them non-"partnerships" in non-R.U.P.A. states that have strictly interpreted this term to exclude LLPs. Moreover, states have adopted and will continue to adopt variations on R.U.P.A. Given the potential adverse consequences of being a non-"partnership," even a slight possibility that a regulatory board might raise a problem under a revised partnership act may be a cause for concern. Second, states should apply the partnership characterization of the LLP's home state in order to make possible interstate operation of firms that have organized as LLPs. The problem of interstate recognition is discussed further in Section 7.04(c), below.

---

[121] *See* D.C. Ethics Op. No. 235 (Feb. 16, 1993). But D.C. Ethics Op. 254 allows use of abbreviations.

[122] *See* ABA Standing Comm. on Ethics and Prof'l Responsibility, 96-401 (Aug. 2, 1996) (stating that use of the statutorily required name or abbreviation in public communications is sufficient to make such communications not misleading or deceptive under Model Rules 7.1 and 7.5(a) and that an LLP's referring to itself as a "partnership" is not an actual or implied misrepresentation, reasoning that lawyers' business form is now relatively unimportant to clients, that the abbreviation puts clients on notice that their lawyer is practicing in a particular form and encourages them to inquire if they are in doubt, and that lawyers must respond to such inquiries by clearly explaining the liability limitation); Mich. State Bar Standing Comm. on Prof'l and Jud. Ethics, Op. R-17 (1994) (holding that lawyers practicing in a professional limited liability company do not have any ethical obligations to explain the elimination of vicarious partner liability beyond adding the abbreviation "PLLC" to the firm name); Miss. Bar Op. No. 222 (Nov. 17, 1994); N.Y. County Lawyers' Ethics Op. No. 703 (Nov. 1994). Bar of the City of New York Formal Op. 1995-7 (May 31, 1995) noted that "lawyers may wish to consider whether [use of the initials LLP] is adequate in all circumstances. In addition, lawyers changing to LLC or LLP form should be prepared to answer any client questions regarding the nature of the change and its ramifications."

[123] R.U.P.A. § 307.

[124] R.U.P.A. §§ 702, 704.

States may restrict limited partnerships from engaging in professional practice.[125] LLPs clearly can be distinguished from limited partnerships. First, while LLPs are recognized under the provisions of the general partnership law, limited partnerships are formed under separate statutes. That will be even more clearly so as states adopt U.L.P.A. (2001), which "delinks" limited from general partnership law. Second, LLPs are structurally different from limited partnerships. Limited partners do not, as such, have any personal liability for the debts of their limited partnership unless they participate in control of the business.[126] By contrast, under most LLP statutes, LLP members have personal liability for contract-type debts (*see* Section 3.02, above) and for debts arising from the partners' own misconduct as well as from conduct of those working under a partner's supervision and control (*see* Section 3.04, above). Third, limited partnerships differ from LLPs in the critical respect that the limited partnership "control rule" imposes personal liability for the debts of the limited partnership on limited partners who participate in the control of the business.[127] The control rule tends to deter limited partners from ensuring that the firm establishes and observes appropriate client-protection policies. By contrast, LLPs are structured like ordinary general partnerships, in which all partners can take part in the management and control of the business.[128] It is not clear what effect U.L.P.A. § 303 (2001), which eliminates control liability,[129] might have on professionals' use of the limited partnership form, since the absence of control liability makes limited partnerships more closely resemble other limited liability business forms.

(b) Recognition of Liability Limitation

There is no reason to believe that courts will not fully enforce LLP statutory limited liability.[130] However, even if a state allows professional firms to practice as LLPs, and even if the firm organizes under an LLP statute that limits partners' vicarious liability for malpractice or for all types of liabilities, the state's rules regulating the profession nevertheless may hold the professional vicariously liable.

---

[125] Colo. Rev. Stat. § 12-2-117(1)(e) initially provided that a partnership registering with the Colorado Accountancy Board to practice accounting must be a "general partnership." Section 12-2-117(1) was amended so that "partnership" now explicitly includes LLPs and foreign LLPs. *See* 1995 Colo. Legis. Serv. H.B. 95-1061, § 25 (approved May 24, 1995). Conn. Bar Ass'n Informal Op. 94-2 (Jan. 3, 1994) permits lawyers to practice as limited partnerships.

[126] R.U.L.P.A. § 303 (1985). However, as discussed immediately below, control liability is being eliminated.

[127] R.U.L.P.A. § 303 (1985). A few states have eliminated control liability. *See* Ga. Code Ann. § 149303 and Mo. Rev. Stat. § 359.201.

[128] *See* U.P.A. § 18(e) (1914).

[129] *See* Chapter 1, notes 54 and 56, supra; § 9.303, infra.

[130] *See* § 3.03, note 31, supra; First Am. Title Ins. Co. v. Lawson, 177 N.J. 125, 827 A.2d 230 (2003) (discussed in § 3.04(b), note 50, supra).

Most states provide that shareholders in professional corporations do not have vicarious liability for the malpractice of their co-members.[131] State statutes generally apply similar rules to members of other professional entities, including LLPs.[132] Although some state courts have the inherent power to regulate the liability of members of professional firms,[133] most such courts have explicitly recognized liability limitations in professional limited liability firms,[134] subject to insurance requirements in some states (*see* Section 2.06(a), note 81, above).

Perhaps in recognition of increasing availability of limited liability through LLPs and LLCs, the American Law Institute began moving toward a uniform rule under which lawyers necessarily are vicariously liable for all wrongful acts of principals and employees in the firm.[135] The draft rule was intended to operate irrespective of the statute governing the applicable business form.[136] It was based in part on what the drafters say is the thin capitalization of law firms.[137] The draft submitted at the 1997 meeting provided:

> (2) Each of the principals of a law firm organized as a general partnership is liable jointly and severally with the firm.
> (3) A principal of a law firm organized other than as a general partnership as authorized by law is vicariously liable for the acts of another principal or employee of the firm to the extent provided by law.[138]

At the 1997 annual meeting the members added "without limited liability" after "partnership" in subsections (2) and (3).[139] This is the version that was finally

---

[131] *See* Hillman, note 112, supra, at 6:10–6:12 (summarizing and citing statutes on lawyer liability); Annotation, Liability of Professional Corporation of Lawyers or Individual Members Thereof for Malpractice or Other Torts of Another Member, 39 A.L.R. 4th 556.

[132] *See, e.g.,* Ala. Code § 10A-8-10.10, -3.06.

[133] *See* First Bank & Trust Co. v. Zagoria, 250 Ga. 844, 302 S.E.2d 674 (1983); Keatinge, The Floggings Will Continue Until Morale Improves: The Supervising Attorney and His or Her Firm, 39 S. Tex. L. Rev. 279, 294-95 (1998).

[134] *See* Colo. Prof. Serv. Co. Rule 265.I.A.4; Del. Sup. Ct. R. 67(h); Henderson v. HIS Fin. Servs., 266 Ga. 844, 471 S.E.2d 885 (1996) (reversing *Zagoria*, based on long-standing ethical rules permitting lawyers to limit their vicarious liability and the recognition in many states of law practice in professional corporations, LLCs and LLPs, although reaffirming court's inherent power); Rule 1-203(4), Rules and Regulations for the Organization and Government of the State Bar of Ga., added July 15, 1996; Fla. Bar Reg. R. 4-8.6(a) and Comment (permitting lawyers to practice as limited liability entities, although noting the need for "enabling action by this Court"); Ill. Comp. St. S. Ct. Rule 721-722 (permitting lawyers to practice as limited liability entities, including LLPs, subject to rules regarding insurance and financial responsibility); Mass. Sup. Ct. Rule 3:06(3)(a) (recognizing limited liability of members of LLPs and other limited liability entities); Neb. Sup. Ct. Rule for Ltd. Liab. Prof'l Orgs. I(C)(7)(a); N.J. Court Rules, 1969 R. 1:21-1C(a)(1); Wyo. Bar Ass'n Org. & Gov't Rule 13.

[135] ALI, Restatement of the Law Governing Lawyers, § 79 (Tent. Draft 7, 1994).

[136] The draft notes that the Council rejected a motion that would add the prefix "Except as otherwise provided by statute." *See id.* at 117, footnote*.

[137] *See id.* at 118.

[138] Restatement of the Law Governing Lawyers, § 79 (Tent. Draft 8, March 21, 1997).

[139] *See* ALI Rep., 1997 WL 1077698, Vol. 20, No. 1 (Fall 1997).

adopted.[140] Thus, the Restatement explicitly recognizes limitation of lawyers' liability in LLPs under applicable law.

Even if they do not have general vicarious liability, lawyers and other professionals may have supervisory liability under ethical rules.[141] Model Rule of Professional Conduct 5.1 provides that a law firm partner must "make reasonable efforts to ensure that the firm has in effect measures giving reasonable assurance that all lawyers in the firm conform to the Rules of Professional Conduct" and "a lawyer having direct supervisory authority over another lawyer shall make reasonable efforts to ensure that the other lawyer conforms to the Rules of Professional Conduct."[142] The law partner or supervisor is responsible for another lawyer's violation of the rules if the lawyer "knows of the conduct at the time when its consequences can be avoided or mitigated but fails to take reasonable remedial action."[143] It has been held that these rules do not give rise to vicarious liability.[144] However, the ethical rules may provide evidence of standard practice as to supervision, and the expansion of statutory limited liability in law practice through LLCs and LLPs gives plaintiffs' lawyers a new incentive to explore such chinks in the liability shield.[145] Note that ethical rules may require a minimum level of insurance as a condition of not being held vicariously liable (*see* Section 2.06(a), note 83). The ethical prohibition on attorney agreements limiting mal-

[140] *See* Restatement (Third) of the Law Governing Lawyers § 58 (2000). *Id.* Comment c notes that "[l]egislation allows lawyers to practice in professional corporations and, in many states, in limited-liability general partnerships or limited-liability companies. Such legislation generally contains language excluding liability of principals of the entity for negligence or misconduct in which they did not participate directly or as supervisors."

[141] Ill. Comp. St. S. Ct. Rule 722(c) (lawyer has liability for own acts and for those of a "person under the lawyer's direct supervision and control"); Ind: Burns Ind. A.D. Rule 27(f); N.J. Court Rules, R. 1:21-1C(a)(1); Neb. Ct. R. 3-201(C)(7)(a).

[142] The Ethics 2000 Commission Report on the Evaluation of the Model Rules of Professional Conduct (Aug. 2001) (E2K Report) proposed revising Rule 5.1(a) to also apply to "a lawyer who individually or together with other lawyers possesses comparable managerial authority in a law firm."

[143] *See* Hazard & Hodes, The Law of Lawyering, §§ 42.1–44.9 (3d ed. Supp. 2010). For a case on the ethical responsibilities of supervising attorneys, see In re Yacavino, 494 A.2d 801 (N.J. 1985). ABA Standing Comm. on Ethics and Professional Responsibility, Formal Op. 96-401 (Aug. 2, 1996) notes that lawyers are subject to the ethical rules regarding supervisory obligations even though some state statutes do not provide for supervisory liability.

[144] *See* Stewart v. Coffman, 748 P.2d 579, 581 (Utah Ct. App. 1988), *cert. granted*, 765 P.2d 1277 (Utah 1988), *cert. dismissed*, Aug. 19, 1988 (unpublished order). *See also* Kus v. Irving, 736 A.2d 946 (Conn. Super. 1999), discussed supra in § 3.04, notes 43–44, holding that the standard of liability for "direct supervision and control" under the LLP statute supersedes any liability under Rule 5.1.

[145] For articles exploring potential supervisory liability of lawyers under ethical rules, see Dzienkowski, Legal Malpractice and The Multi-state Law Firm: Supervision of Multi-state Offices; Firms as Limited Liability Partnerships; and Predispute Agreements to Arbitrate Client Malpractice Claims, 36 S. Tex. L. Rev. 967, 972-79 (1995); Fortney, Am I My Partner's Keeper?, Peer Review in Law Firms, 66 U. Colo. L. Rev. 329 (1995); Keatinge, supra note 129 at 292-94; Wolfram, Inherent Powers in the Crucible of Lawyer Self-Protection: Reflections on the LLP Campaign, 39 S. Tex. L. Rev. 359 (1998); Ribstein, Ethical Rules, Agency Costs and Law Firm Structure, 84 Va. L. Rev. 1707 (1998).

practice liability[146] probably does not apply to statutory limitations on vicarious liability.[147] Note, however, that the rule may be relevant in determining whether a firm acted properly in obtaining the consent of existing clients when it registers as an LLP (*see* Section 3.11(c), above).

Vicarious liability in professional firms does raise special issues.[148] Clients and patients not only want to make sure that specific debts are repaid, but that professionals will deliver the appropriate degree of service, including monitoring of co-partners or associates. Since professionals often have personal wealth but the firm owns little in the way of marketable assets, unlimited liability arguably helps provide this assurance.[149] Professional firms might do less monitoring if professionals could share extra income that is generated by careless procedures without risk of liability.[150]

Limited liability of lawyers and other professionals and its effect on monitoring raise additional issues in light of possible involvement by professionals in Enron and other large corporate frauds that have come to light since the fall of 2001. Some commentators have suggested that these lapses might be attributable to professionals' limited liability.[151]

The important question is whether the costs of these extra monitoring burdens outweigh the benefits. The burdens of vicarious liability may be heaviest for relatively large firms, and therefore might limit the size of professional firms.[152]

---

[146] *See* Model Rules of Prof'l Conduct, Rule 1.8(h): "A lawyer shall not make an agreement prospectively limiting the lawyer's liability to a client for malpractice unless permitted by law and the client is independently represented in making the agreement. . . ." *See also* Model Code of Prof'l Responsibility § 6-102(a).

[147] *See* ABA. Standing Comm. on Ethics and Prof'l Responsibility, Formal Opinion 96-401 (Aug. 2, 1996) (holding that Rule 1.8(h) does not prohibit practice in an LLP, and reasoning that the limitation on vicarious liability in LLPs derives from state law rather than from an agreement between an lawyer and his client); Miss. Bar Opinion No. 222 (Nov. 17, 1994) (adopting LLC form of practice is not an "agreement" to limit liability barred by Rule 1.8(h)); E2K Report, note 138, supra, Rule 1.8, Comment 14 (stating that this provision does not "limit the ability of lawyers to practice in the form of a limited-liability entity, where permitted by law, provided that each lawyer remains personally liable to the client for his or her own conduct and the firm complies with any conditions required by law, such as provisions requiring client notification or maintenance of adequate liability insurance"). *But see* Wolfram, supra note 145 at 371–72 (arguing that the anti-waiver rule applies to LLPs).

[148] *See generally*, Fortney, supra note 114; Ribstein, Limited Liability of Professional Firms after Enron, 29 J. Corp. L. 427 (2004); Ribstein, The Deregulation of Limited Liability and the Death of Partnership, 70 Wash. U. L.Q. 417, 434–35 (1992).

[149] *See* Fama & Jensen, Agency Problems and Residual Claims, 26 J.L. & Econ. 327, 336–37 (1983).

[150] *See* Carr & Mathewson, The Economics of Law Firms: A Study in the Legal Organization of the Firm, 33 J.L. & Econ. 307, 321–22 (1990).

[151] *See* Fortney, High Drama and Hindsight: The LLP Shield, Post-Andersen, 12 Bus. L. Today, Jan./Feb. 2003 at 46; Rhode & Paton, Lawyers, Ethics, and Enron, 8 Stan. J. L. Bus. & Fin. 9 (2002). For arguments against repealing limited liability of professionals, see Ribstein, Limited Liability of Professional Firms after Enron, 29 J. Corp. L. 427 (2004).

[152] *See* Ribstein, supra note 148 (discussing theories and evidence showing that vicarious liability causes law firms to be smaller than they would be without vicarious liability).

The more remote the negligence for which a professional may be held personally liable, the greater the potential monitoring costs. In smaller firms, vicarious liability may be virtually nonexistent because professionals would be liable primarily for negligent acts they committed themselves either directly, or indirectly by failing to correct problems they observed.[153] In larger firms professionals may be held liable for malpractice of which they could not have been aware even by the most stringent personal monitoring. Indeed, any increased monitoring may be useless and counterproductive to the extent that it involves second-guessing complex professional decisions. Clients themselves, such as the corporate clients of large law firms, may be able to monitor their own cases through legal departments.[154] Personal liability negates large firms' important advantage of diversification. Adding more clients, cases, specialties, and regions may even out income flows among specialties, but it simultaneously adds more risks of vicarious liability.[155] And as discussed above in Section 3.04(c), the supervisory liability imposed under some LLP statutes and ethical rules may actually discourage monitoring by penalizing lawyers who undertake supervision.

Vicarious liability not only may impose a greater burden, but also may be less necessary, for large than for smaller firms. Large firms generally have significant assets, including the marketable assets of the firm and of the primarily liable members as well as of all other members whose negligence contributed to the loss. Moreover, because the firm and primarily liable members can be expected to have substantial assets, the firm has incentives to purchase third-party malpractice insurance and to monitor co-partners to minimize their premiums and protect against liability beyond policy limits and within coinsurance and deductibles. It is also significant that large firms often have invested substantial resources over a long period of time in developing a reputation for care and probity.[156] Although injured clients cannot recover against this reputation, the reputation represents an investment of real resources for the firm, and therefore gives it an incentive to minimize malpractice. On balance, to the extent that it limits the size of large, reputable law firms, mandatory vicarious liability of professional firm partners may even reduce client protection.[157]

These considerations suggest at least that the need for vicarious liability will vary from firm to firm. Even if some mandatory vicarious liability is justified, these considerations strongly militate against a *uniform* rule like that initially proposed by the American Law Institute, which would prohibit any professional

---

[153] *See* Kelsey-Seybold Clinic v. Maclay, 466 S.W.2d 716 (Tex. 1971) (triable issue as to whether medical partnership breached duty to use reasonable means to prevent partner from improperly using his position in personal relationship with patient).

[154] *See* Carr & Mathewson, note 146, above, at 322.

[155] *See* Note, note 112 supra, at 1672–74.

[156] *See* Ribstein, note 148, above, at 435.

[157] *See id.*

law firm from adopting limited liability. The issue is debatable enough that individual states should be encouraged to make their own judgments.

(c) Interstate Professional Firms

The general choice of law rules regarding LLPs are discussed in Chapter 6. It is not clear under those rules whether, even in a state with foreign LLP provisions, a firm's power to practice must be enforced in the operation state (*see* Section 6.02(d), above). But there are strong policy reasons supporting this result. A firm that cannot operate as an LLP in one or more states must maintain separate names, letterheads, and the like for all of its clients in that state. Even if the firm does all this, it might still be misleading clients because of the LLP status of the firm in other states. Moreover, requiring the nature of LLPs to change from state to state may violate the law of, and mislead clients and other creditors, in their home states. Finally, even if the firm can maintain its dual nature vis-à-vis third parties, it may have to contract with partners in LLP states as to compensation and other matters on a different basis from partners in non-LLP states to the extent that partners' liability bears on compensation and other matters (*see* Section 4.04, above). Because of these problems, a firm that cannot practice *everywhere* as an LLP may be unable to practice *anywhere* as such. In other words, a single state's decision not to allow LLPs to register could have negative implications for LLPs nationally. In this sense, interstate enforcement of liability limitations differs from other regulation, such as licensing regulation, which does not affect the internal organization of the firm.[158]

Even if a firm can practice everywhere as an LLP, it may be subject to regulation of professional firms, including the ethical rules mandating member liability (discussed above in Section 7.04(b)), which varies from state to state.[159] Choice of law with regard to ethical rules can be complex and ambiguous.[160] This

---

[158] *See* Ribstein, Ethical Rules, Law Firm Structure, and Choice of Law, 69 U. Cin. L. Rev. 1161 (2001), discussed in note 160, infra.

[159] Some state rules explicitly permit foreign rules to apply except local insurance requirements may apply. *See, e.g.,* Del. Sup. Ct. R. 67(a); Fla. Bar Reg. R. 4-8.6(g).

[160] *See* O'Brien, Multistate Practice and Conflicting Ethical Obligations, 16 Seton Hall L. Rev. 678, 678 (1986); Committee on Counsel Responsibility, Risks of Violation of Rules of Professional Responsibility by Reason of the Increased Disparity Among the States, 45 Bus. Law. 1229, 1229-30 (1990); Rensberger, Jurisdiction, Choice of Law, and the Multistate Attorney, 36 S. Tex. L. Rev. 799 (1995); Note, Developments in the Law—Lawyers' Responsibilities and Lawyers' Responses, 107 Harv. L. Rev. 1547, 1585 (1994); Note, Professional Responsibility and Choice of Law: A Client-Based Alternative to the Model Rules of Professional Conduct, 28 U. Mich. J. L. Ref. 459 (1995). Author Bromberg notes that apart from the traditional arguments that plaintiffs will use to fit their claims within the exceptions to limited liability, it is likely that state and federal courts will be asked to override legislative judgment in favor of the fiduciary duty that lawyers owe clients and the significant state interest in regulating the attorney–client relationships. Thus, one can suspect that individual partners in the multi-state law firm will face more difficulty in using the LLP legislation to insulate themselves from liability. For author Ribstein's views

situation is not much clarified by Model Rule 8.5, which applies the rules of the jurisdiction in which the court sits for conduct in a judicial proceeding, local rules if the lawyer is licensed locally, or the rule of the jurisdiction in which the lawyer principally practices if the lawyer is licensed locally unless the lawyer's conduct has its predominant effect in another jurisdiction where the lawyer is licensed.[161] This varying regulation imposes burdens on multi-state firms comparable to those imposed by variations in restrictions on the types of firms that can practice in the states.[162]

Firms may be able to mitigate these problems by contracting for a particular ethical regime in their partnership agreement and in engagement letters with clients.[163] However, in the absence of a clear statute or ethical rule on contractual choice of law, it is not clear to what extent these clauses will be enforced. Among other problems, a specific contract with a client that applies a foreign-state liability limitation may be considered a contract waiving malpractice liability in contravention of Model Rule 1.8(h).[164]

§ 7.05   TAX TREATMENT OF LLPs

Most, if not all, LLPs are eligible to be taxed as partnerships under current federal law.[165] If a firm is a partnership for tax purposes the partners are taxed only once on income when earned in the partnership rather than incurring a second tax on distributions. They also may be able to deduct business losses against personal income under some circumstances.

Subsection (a) discusses general background considerations. Subsection (b) discusses publicly traded partnerships. Subsections (c) and (d) discuss potential tax consequences of registration — recognition of gain or loss through a termination, and sudden accrual of income through a forced change in accounting methods.

---

concerning the problems of interstate law firms and the need to let them choose to organize under a single state's rules, see Ribstein, note 158, supra.

   [161] *See* Model Rules of Prof'l Conduct, Rule 8.5. E2K Report, note 142, supra, Rule 8.5, proposes to change these rules to permit any jurisdiction in which a lawyer renders legal services to regulate a lawyer regardless of where she is licensed to practice. The proposed rule would apply the rules of the court in which the conduct occurs or, "for any other conduct, the rules of the jurisdiction in which the lawyer's conduct occurred, or, if the predominant effect of the conduct is in a different jurisdiction, the rules of that jurisdiction shall be applied to the conduct. A lawyer is not subject to discipline if the lawyer's conduct conforms to the rules of a jurisdiction in which the lawyer reasonably believes the predominant effect of the lawyer's conduct will occur."

   [162] *See* Ribstein, note 158, supra.

   [163] *See* Conflicts of Interest Task Force of the ABA Section of Business Law, Conflict of Interest Issues, 50 Bus. Law. 1381, 1426 (1995) (suggesting that firms include choice-of-law clauses in engagement letters to deal with client conflict issues).

   [164] *See* note 146, supra.

   [165] This section deals with federal taxation of LLPs. Classification of LLPs for purposes of state taxation may vary from state to state.

(a) *Federal Income Tax: In General*

Whether a business is taxed as a corporation or a partnership is answered in most cases with reference to the definitions in the Internal Revenue Code of "corporation"[166] and "partnership."[167] The term *corporation* includes "associations, joint-stock companies, and insurance companies."[168] "Partnership" is the residual category that includes "other unincorporated organizations, through or by means of which any business, financial operation or venture is carried on."

Historically, the so-called Kintner regulations[169] formerly governed the determination of what constitutes an "association." These regulations were prompted by a series of cases led by *United States v. Kintner*,[170] which involved licensed professionals seeking certain tax advantages of incorporation, particularly the ability to shelter income in corporate pension plans. Since the Internal Revenue Service (IRS) was then concerned with stopping what it believed were essentially partnerships from attaining the tax status of corporations, the *Kintner* regulations were weighted in favor of finding that a business organization was *not* a corporation. This weighting worked against the IRS in cases involving firms that are seeking to be treated as partnerships for tax purposes. The *Kintner* regulations judged corporate resemblance in terms of what the IRS believed to be the distinguishing characteristics of corporations and partnerships: continuity of life, corporate-type management, limited liability, and free transferability of interest.[171] The regulations provided that a business organization was a corporation for tax purposes only if it had at least three of these corporate characteristics.[172]

Classification of business organizations under the *Kintner* rules proved to be problematic. The classification problems during the early history of LLPs were particularly intense because LLPs fell through the gaps of then-existing regulation.

Recognizing these theoretical and practical problems, the IRS adopted a rule that drops the four-factor approach in favor of letting unincorporated firms choose to be taxed as either corporations or partnerships — that is, to "check a box."[173] Though still referred to as the "check-the-box" rule, partnership tax treatment is actually the default rule for eligible unincorporated entities. The rule provides that a domestic "eligible entity" (foreign entities are covered

---

[166] I.R.C. § 7701(a)(3).

[167] I.R.C. § 7701(a)(2) (not including corporations, trusts, and estates).

[168] *See* Treas. Reg. § 1.301-7701(2)(b), 1.301-7701-3.

[169] Treas. Reg. § 301.7701-2 (pre-1997).

[170] 216 F.2d 418 (9th Cir. 1954).

[171] Treas. Reg. § 301.7701-2(a)(2) (pre-1997).

[172] Treas. Reg. § 301.7701-2(a)(3).

[173] *See* Simplification of Entity Classification Rules, 26 C.F.R. pt. 1, 301, 602 (Dec. 10, 1996, eff. Jan. 1, 1997), Treas. Reg. §§ 301.7701-2, 301.7701-3. The test does not replace other rules, including I.R.C. § 7704, which taxes "publicly traded" partnerships as corporations.

separately), which includes business firms other than corporations, joint stock companies, insurance companies, or banks, is not treated as a corporation for income tax purposes unless it elects this treatment. An eligible entity with two or more members is a partnership for income tax purposes unless it elects to be a corporation.[174] An eligible entity with one member is taxed directly and the entity is disregarded unless the entity elects to be a corporation for tax purposes.[175]

The above discussion concerns federal tax classification. State tax classification does not necessarily follow federal law.

(b)   Publicly Traded Partnerships

The Internal Revenue Code (I.R.C.) subjects to corporate tax treatment a "publicly traded partnership" unless its gross income consists 90 percent or more of "qualifying" income.[176] "Publicly traded partnership" is defined as partnership interests that are either "traded on an established securities market" or "readily tradable on a secondary market (or the substantial equivalent thereof)."[177] Qualifying income, which is also referred to as "passive-type income,"[178] is defined to include interest, dividends, rents, and income from sale of real property or natural resource production.[179] This definition may be broad enough to reach even businesses that are closely held by conventional standards, but in recent years has been used to allow limited partnerships, particularly managers of private equity funds, to conduct initial public offerings and retain partnership tax treatment.[180] Currently, there are approximately 150 publicly traded partnerships in the U.S. receiving partnership tax treatment. An LLP that meets the qualifications of a "publicly traded partnership" will be taxed as a corporation irrespective of whether the check-the-box rule would lead to a different result.

(c)   Tax Consequences of Registration: Recognition of Gain and Loss

A partnership's registration as an LLP does not cause a termination of the partnership under I.R.C. § 708 as long as both the original partnership and the resulting LLP are classified as partnerships for tax purposes, the partners in the original partnership continue as partners in the LLP, and there is not a sale or exchange of 50 percent or more of the total interests in partnership capital and

---

[174] Treas. Reg. § 301.7701-3(b)(1)(i).
[175] I.R.C. § 7704 (1986).
[176] I.R.C. § 7704 (1986).
[177] I.R.C. § 7704(b). *See* Bromberg & Ribstein, § 12.23.
[178] I.R.C. § 7704(c).
[179] I.R.C. § 7704(d).
[180] *See* Fleischer, Taxing Blackstone, 61 Tax L. Rev. 89 (2008).

profits within a 12-month period. For federal income tax purposes the registered limited liability partnership will be considered a continuation of the partnership. A conversion of a general partnership into a limited partnership is an exchange under I.R.C. § 721[181] as long as each partner's total percentage interest in the partnership's profits, losses, and capital remains the same after the conversion and the business of the general partnership is continued after the conversion.[182] Registration of an LLP has been deemed to be a partnership-to-partnership conversion governed by this limited partnership ruling, and therefore not to cause the partnership to terminate under I.R.C. § 708.[183] Several private letter rulings have treated the conversion of a general partnership into a registered limited liability partnership as analogous to this situation.[184]

(d)   Tax Consequences of Registration: Continued Use of Cash Method of Accounting

It is important to consider whether a general partnership's registration as an LLP would force the firm to switch from cash method to accrual method of tax accounting. If it did, this could require sudden acceleration of income into the year in which the conversion occurred.

Under I.R.C. § 448, a partnership that does not have a C corporation partner can use the cash method of accounting unless, generally speaking, it is a "tax shelter."[185] That term is defined in § 461 to include an "enterprise" or a "syndicate."[186] Since "enterprise" excludes a firm whose interests are generally not

---

[181] I.R.C. § 721 of the Code provides that no gain or loss shall be recognized to a partnership or to any of its partners in the case of a contribution of property to the partnership in exchange for an interest in the partnership.

[182] See Rev. Rul. 84-52, 1984-1 C.B. 157. Conversely, if partners do dissociate, LLP registration may be a taxable event. By threatening to trigger this tax consequence, partners who object to the registration may be able to wield a kind of de facto veto even if the statute permits approval of the registration by a majority vote. The effectiveness of the veto is limited by the fact that the objecting partners might suffer tax and other adverse consequences by dissociating. See § 2.04(f), supra.

[183] Rev. Rul. 95-55, 1995-2 C.B. 313 (holding that the registration therefore does not cause the partnership to terminate under I.R.C. § 708).

[184] Priv. Ltr. Ruls. 9229016 (Apr. 16, 1992); 9412030 (Dec. 22, 1993) (LLP converting to LLC); 9420028 (Feb. 18, 1994) (formation of Delaware LLP); 9423037 (Mar. 16, 1994) (conversion of New York general partnership to Delaware LLP); 9423040 (Mar. 18, 1994) (conversion of New York general partnership to Delaware LLP); 9424036 (Mar. 21, 1994) (conversion of Illinois general partnership to Delaware LLP); 9448025 (Aug. 31, 1994) (conversion of Illinois general partnership to Illinois LLP); 9507014 (Nov. 15, 1994) (conversion of Illinois general partnership to Iowa LLP). For a general discussion of tax consequences of entity conversions, see Frost, The Federal Income Tax Consequences of Business Entity Conversions, J. Real Est. Tax. n. 83 (Winter 1999).

[185] I.R.C. § 448(b) exempts, among other things, entities with less than $5 million in gross receipts.

[186] I.R.C. § 461(i)(3). That subsection also includes tax shelter as defined in id. § 6662(d)(2)(C)(iii).

securities, it would exclude LLPs.[187] Thus, the important question is whether an LLP is a "syndicate." This term includes a partnership in which more than 35 percent of the losses are allocated to limited partners or limited entrepreneurs.[188] Assuming that limited partners are only those who are such under state limited partnership statutes, the "cash method" question in LLPs reduces to whether LLP members are "limited entrepreneurs" as defined in I.R.C. § 464(e)(2). They are not limited entrepreneurs under the Code if they will actively engage in the business.[189]

The IRS has ruled that members in a professional *LLC* who would actively engage in the business and vote on important matters are not limited entrepreneurs.[190] The IRS also has ruled that a professional LLC that represented it had been in its current business for over 100 years without reporting losses was not a "syndicate" for any year in which it does not incur losses.[191] This suggests that even passive members of the typical professional LLC, which does not normally incur losses, will be limited entrepreneurs, and so that such a firm will be able to use the cash method.[192] These concepts also should apply to LLPs, although as of this writing there is no definitive ruling.[193]

(e)   Self-employment Tax

Avoidance of the potentially substantial self-employment tax is a potential important planning and choice-of-form consideration,[194] particularly since passage of the Omnibus Budget Reconciliation Act of 1993, which removed the dollar limit on wages on the health insurance portion of the tax.[195] The tax is on net earnings from self-employment derived by an individual.[196] "Net earnings from self-employment" includes an "individual's distributive share, whether or not distributed, of income or loss from any trade or business carried on by a partner-

---

[187] *See* § 7.01, supra (concluding that LLPs may be, but generally are not, "securities"). This raises the interesting question of whether characterizing an LLP as a "security" would result in accrual of income for tax purposes.

[188] I.R.C. § 1256(e)(3)(B).

[189] *See* I.R.C. § 1256(e)(3)(C)(i).

[190] *See* Priv. Ltr. Rul. 9321047.

[191] Private Ltr. Rul. 9415005.

[192] *See* Banoff, New Ruling Adds Further Encouragement for Large Firms To Form LLCs, 81 P'ships & S Corps. No. 1 (July 1994), at 12.

[193] *See* Bishop & Donn, S Corp. as LLC Member; LLPs Use of Cash Method, 1 J. LLCs 178 (1995).

[194] The self-employment tax is 15.3% of a general partner's share of trade or business income, based on old-age, survivors, and disability insurance (OASDI) tax of 12.4% and Medicare tax of 2.9%. *See* I.R.C. §§ 3402, 3111, 1401. A 0.9% increase in the Medicare tax rate applicable to amounts earned above certain thresholds ($200,000 for single filers and $250,000 for joint filers) was enacted as part of the Patient Protection and Affordable Care Act of 2010. Pub. L. No. 103-66, Section 10906. The increase is effective for taxable years after Dec. 31, 2012.

[195] Pub. L. No. 103-66, 107 Stat. 312 (codified in scattered sections of 42 U.S.C.).

[196] I.R.C. § 1401.

ship of which the individual is a partner, unless a specific exception applies" but excluding income or loss allocated to limited partners.[197]

Under rules proposed in January, 1997 but never adopted,[198] a member of a firm that is classified as a partnership for federal tax purposes is treated as a limited partner under the proposed regulations (except in a service partnership[199]) unless the member has personal liability for the firm's debts, authority to contract on behalf of the partnership under the law under which the partnership was organized or participates in the partnership's trade or business for more than five hundred hours during the taxable year.[200] If this rule had become effective, it would provide a reason to avoid the general partnership, including LLP, form. Partnership law gives all general partners the authority to contract on behalf of the firm, thus placing the partner within one of the exceptions to limited partner status.[201]

An important 2011 Tax Court opinion, *Renkemeyer, Campbell & Weaver, LLP, v. C.I.R.,*[202] held that the legislative history of the Code's definition of "limited partner"[203] relevant Code provision "does not support a holding that Congress contemplated excluding partners who performed services for a partnership in their capacity as partners (i.e., acting in the manner of self-employed persons), from liability for self-employment taxes."[204] Accordingly, the lawyer partners of a law firm, all of whose revenues were derived from the partners' legal services, were subject to the tax. This reasoning suggests that even limited partners may be liable for self-employment tax if they perform services for the partnership, which has obvious relevance to choice of business form.[205]

---

[197] I.R.C. § 1402(a).

[198] The effectiveness of this rule was delayed by the Taxpayer Relief Act. *See* Pub. L. 105-34, § 935.

[199] *See* Prop. Treas. Reg. § 1.1402(a)-2(h)(5) (1997) (providing that if substantially all of the activities of a partnership involve the performance of services in the fields of health, law, engineering, architecture, accounting, actuarial science, or consulting, an individual who provides services as part of that trade or business will not be considered a limited partner).

[200] *See* Prop. Treas. Reg. § 1.1402(a)-2(h)(2)(ii).

[201] For a discussion of post-1997 proposals concerning the self-employment tax issue and their current status, see Ribstein & Keatinge, § 21:11 (2011).

[202] 136 T.C. No. 7 (U.S. Tax Ct. Feb. 9, 2011).

[203] I.R.C. § 1402(a)(13).

[204] 126 T.C. No. 7 at 22.

[205] For an analysis of the case focusing on its implications for limited partnerships and LLCs, see Ribstein & Keatinge, § 21:11 (2011).

≡8≡

THE REVISED UNIFORM PARTNERSHIP ACT

This chapter gives an overview of the Revised Uniform Partnership Act (R.U.P.A.), officially known as Uniform Partnership Act (1994).[1] References to Comments are to the official drafters' comments. Each Section has the number of the corresponding Section of R.U.P.A. and includes the following features:

1. A summary of the most **Important Changes** from the Uniform Partnership Act (U.P.A.).

2. An **Analysis** of each section intended to note potential areas of concern for legislators and bar committees who are considering adopting R.U.P.A. and for partners in, or those who are dealing with, partnerships that are governed by R.U.P.A.[2] States adopting significant variations on each section are highlighted in bold.

3. "**LLP Cross-references**" to each section showing the section numbers in this book where the R.U.P.A. LLP provisions are discussed. The amendments to R.U.P.A. for limited liability partnerships (LLPs) and the official drafters' comments to these amendments are set forth in Appendix A.

---

[1] *See* R.U.P.A. § 1002.

[2] References in the footnotes to "Bromberg & Ribstein" are to Bromberg and Ribstein on Partnership (1988 & Supp.). References in the footnotes to "Prime Time" are to Ribstein, The Revised Uniform Partnership Act: Not Ready for Prime Time, 49 Bus. Law. 45 (1993). There are occasional cross-references to earlier sections of this book. The footnotes give illustrative case citations. The Bromberg & Ribstein references should be consulted for a comprehensive list and the most recent cases.

8. The Revised Uniform Partnership Act

The following is a chart listing the state adoptions of R.U.P.A. as of September 1, 2011:

State	*Citation*	*Effective date*
Alabama	Ala. Code §§ 10-8A-101 to 10-8A-1109	January 1, 1997
Alaska	Alaska St. §§ 32.06.201-.997	January 1, 2001
Arizona	Ariz. Rev. Stat. §§ 29-1001 to 29-1111	July 20, 1996
Arkansas	Ark. Code §§ 4-46-101 to 4-46-1207.	January 1, 2000
California	Cal. Corp. Code, §§ 16100 to 16962	January 1, 1997
Colorado	Colo. Rev. Stat. Ann. §§ 7-64-101 to 7-64-1206	January 1, 1998
Connecticut	Conn. Gen. Stat. Ann. §§ 34-300 to 34-434	July 1, 1997
Delaware	Del. Code. Ann., tit. 6, § 15-101 to § 15-1210	January 1, 2000
District of Columbia	D.C. Code Ann. §§ 29-601.01 to 29-611.01	April 9, 1997
Florida	Fla. Stat. §§ 620.81001 to 620.9902	January 1, 1996
Hawaii	Haw. Rev. Stat. §§ 425-101 to 425-145	July 1, 2000
Illinois	805 Ill. Comp. Stat. §§ 206/100-1207	January 1, 2003
Iowa	Iowa Code §§ 486A.101 to 486A.1302	January 1, 1999
Idaho	Idaho Code §§ 53-3-101 to 53-3-1205	January 1, 2001
Kansas	Kan. St. 56a-101 to 1305	January 1, 1999
Kentucky	Ky. Rev. Stat. Ann., Chapter 362, sub Chapter 1	July 12, 2006
Maryland	Md. Code Ann., Corporations and Associations, §§ 9-101 to 9-1205	July 1, 1998
Maine	31 Me. Rev. Stat. Ann. c. 17, §§ 1001–1105	July 1, 2007
Minnesota	Minn. Stat. §§ 323A.0101 to 323A.1203.	January 1, 1999
Mississippi	Miss. Code Ann. §§ 79-13-01 to 79-10-1206	January 1, 2005
Montana	Mont. Code Ann. §§ 35-10-101 to 35-10-724	July 1, 1993

State	Citation	Effective date
Nebraska	Neb. Rev. Stat. §§ 67-401 to 67-467	January 1, 1998
Nevada	Nev. Rev. Stat. §§ 87.4301 to 87.4357	July 1, 2006
New Jersey	N.J. Rev. Stat. §§ 42:1A-1 to 42:1A-56	December 8, 2001
New Mexico	N.M. Stat. Ann. 1978 §§ 54-1-47, 54-1A-101 to 54-1A-1206	July 1, 1997
North Dakota	LLP: N.D. Cent. Code §§ 45-22-01 to 45-22-27	January 1, 1997
Ohio	Ohio. Rev. Code Ann. §§ 1776.01 to 1776.96	August 6, 2008
Oklahoma	54 Okla. Stat. Ann. §§ 1-100 to 1-1207	November 1, 1997
Oregon	Or. Rev. Stat. 67.005 to 67.810	January 1, 1998
South Dakota	S.D. Codified Laws § 48-7A-101 to 48-7A-1208	July 1, 2001
Tennessee	Tenn. Code Ann. §§ 61-1-101 to 61-1-1208	January 1, 2002
Texas	Tex. Bus. Orgs. Code §§ 152.001 to 152.914	January 1, 1994
Utah	Utah Code Ann. §§ 48-1b-101 to 48-1b-1205	July 1, 2012
Vermont	11 Vt. Stat. Ann. §§ 3201 to 3502	January 1, 1999
Virginia	Va. Code Ann. §§ 50-73.79 to 50-73.149	January 1, 1997
Washington	Wash. Rev. Stat. §§ 25.05.005 to 25.05.907	June 11, 1998
West Virginia	W.Va. Code §§ 47B-1-1 to 47B-11-5	90 days from March 19, 1995
Wyoming	Wyo. Stat.Ann., §§ 17-21-101 to 17-21-1003	January 1, 1994

§ 8.101.   DEFINITIONS

Section 101

(1) "Business" includes every trade, occupation, and profession.

(2) "Debtor in bankruptcy" means a person who is the subject of:

(i) an order for relief under Title 11 of the United States Code or a comparable order under a successor statute of general application; or

(ii) a comparable order under federal, state, or foreign law governing insolvency.

(3) "Distribution" means a transfer of money or other property from a partnership to a partner in the partner's capacity as a partner or to the partner's transferee.

(4) "Foreign limited liability partnership" means a partnership that:

(i) is formed under laws other than the laws of this State;

(ii) has the status of a limited liability partnership under those laws; and

(iii) does not file a statement of election not to be a foreign limited liability partnership.

(5) "Limited liability partnership" means a partnership that has filed a statement of qualification under Section 1001 and has not filed a similar statement in any other jurisdiction.

(6) "Partnership" means an association of two or more persons to carry on as co-owners a business for profit formed under Section 202, predecessor law, or comparable law of another jurisdiction.

(7) "Partnership agreement" means the agreement, whether written, oral, or implied, among the partners concerning the partnership, including amendments to the partnership agreement.

(8) "Partnership at will" means a partnership in which the partners have not agreed to remain partners until the expiration of a definite term or the completion of a particular undertaking.

(9) "Partnership interest" or "partner's interest in the partnership" means all of a partner's interests in the partnership, including the partner's transferable interest and all management and other rights.

(10) "Person" means an individual, corporation, business trust, estate, trust, partnership, association, joint venture, government, governmental subdivision, agency, or instrumentality, or any other legal or commercial entity.

(11) "Property" means all property, real, personal, or mixed, tangible or intangible, or any interest therein.

(12) "State" means a State of the United States, the District of Columbia, the Commonwealth of Puerto Rico, or any territory or insular possession subject to the jurisdiction of the United States.

(13) "Statement" means a statement of partnership authority under Section 303, a statement of denial under Section 304, a statement of dissociation under Section 704, a statement of dissolution under Section 805, a statement of merger under Section 907, or an amendment or cancellation of any of the foregoing.

(14) "Transfer" includes an assignment, conveyance, lease, mortgage, deed, and encumbrance.

Summary: Defines terms used in the Act.

Parallel U.P.A.:   § 2.

Important Changes: Adds definitions of distribution, partnership, partnership agreement, partnership interest, partnership at will, state, and statement. "Real property" is now "property"; "bankrupt" is now "debtor in bankruptcy"; and "conveyance" is now "transfer." These definitions are referred to below throughout this chapter. *See, e.g.,* § 103 ("partnership agreement"); § 202 ("partnership"); § 502 ("partnership interest"); § 503 ("distribution"); § 801 ("partnership at will").

LLP Cross-references: Sections 1.02(a), 6.02(a).

State variation

Ohio adds a definition of "tribunal:" as "a court, or if provided in the partnership agreement or otherwise agreed, an arbitrator, arbitration panel, or other tribunal."[3] This effectively restricts the parties from using arbitration or other alternative remedies to avoid mandatory provisions of the statute. In particular, § 1776.03(7) does not allow the agreement to "[v]ary the right of a tribunal to expel a partner in the events specified in division (E) of Section 1776.51 of the Revised Code." Also, throughout the Act, provision that apply to courts explicitly apply to the broader term "tribunal."

§ 8.102.   KNOWLEDGE AND NOTICE

Section 102

(a) A person knows a fact if the person has actual knowledge of it.

(b) A person has notice of a fact if the person:

(1) knows of it;

(2) has received a notification of it; or

(3) has reason to know it exists from all of the facts known to the person at the time in question.

(c) A person notifies or gives a notification to another by taking steps reasonably required to inform the other person in ordinary course, whether or not the other person learns of it.

(d) A person receives a notification when the notification:

---

[3] Ohio Rev. Code § 1776.02.

(1) comes to the person's attention; or

(2) is duly delivered at the person's place of business or at any other place held out by the person as a place for receiving communications.

(e) Except as otherwise provided in subsection (f), a person other than an individual knows, has notice, or receives a notification of a fact for purposes of a particular transaction when the individual conducting the transaction knows, has notice, or receives a notification of the fact, or in any event when the fact would have been brought to the individual's attention if the person had exercised reasonable diligence. The person exercises reasonable diligence if it maintains reasonable routines for communicating significant information to the individual conducting the transaction and there is reasonable compliance with the routines. Reasonable diligence does not require an individual acting for the person to communicate information unless the communication is part of the individual's regular duties or the individual has reason to know of the transaction and that the transaction would be materially affected by the information.

(f) A partner's knowledge, notice, or receipt of a notification of a fact relating to the partnership is effective immediately as knowledge by, notice to, or receipt of a notification by the partnership, except in the case of a fraud on the partnership committed by or with the consent of that partner.

Summary: Defines "knowledge" and "notice" in a manner similar to UCC § 1-201(25)–(27).

Parallel U.P.A.:   §§ 3, 12.

Important Changes: Considerably expands on U.P.A. definitions; distinguishes between "notice," which includes the concept of "reason to know," and "notification" which, like the U.P.A., is based on the acts of the party claiming notice; defines knowledge, notice, and notification to organizations; and expands the situations in which notice to or knowledge of a partner is notice to or knowledge of the partnership.

Analysis: Subsection (a) defines knowledge as actual knowledge. The Comment to this section says that this is a change from the U.P.A., which defines knowledge as including bad faith knowledge and therefore permits an inference of knowledge from other known facts. But there is actually no change. Knowledge, when it is at issue, generally usually must be proved circumstantially from other facts that came to the attention of the person charged with knowledge rather than based strictly on subjective awareness.

Subsections (b) and (d) distinguish between *receiving* notification and *having* notice. Subsection (b) provides that a person "has notice of a fact" if the person "knows" it (which is defined circularly in subsection (a)), has received notification of it, or has reason to know it exists. In short, a person may receive notification but not have notice because he neither knows nor should know it. Conversely, he may have notice even if the other party has not delivered notification. This distinction permits a party who has delivered a communication to rely on the other's receiving it even if the other plausibly maintains at trial that he did not actually have the information. Indeed, the U.P.A. § 3(2) definition of notice also is based on the act of the notice-giver.

This section is on weaker ground in defining the situations when the partnership, as distinguished with an individual, is charged with a partner's knowledge. Subsection (f) would expand on the situations in which the partnership is bound by knowledge or notice of or notification to a partner by providing that the partnership is bound by any such knowledge, notice, or notification.[4] By contrast, U.P.A. § 12 provides that the partnership is bound only by "notice" to a partner (which U.P.A. § 3 defines as equivalent to R.U.P.A.'s "notification" except that the U.P.A., unlike R.U.P.A., requires a writing) or "the knowledge of the partner acting in the particular matter, acquired while a partner or then present to his mind, and the knowledge of any other partner who reasonably could and should have communicated it to the acting partner." This recognizes that a partnership should not necessarily be bound by information that any partner happens to possess or have reason to know unless the third party justifiably relied or the partner had a good reason for acting on the information or sending it through channels.

Potential problems with the use of these terms are discussed below in connection with other sections of R.U.P.A. *See, e.g.,* the analyses of §§ 301, 302, and 702, below.

State variation

Colorado defines knowledge to include conscious awareness.[5] Receipt of notice includes giving notice under fair and reasonable circumstances.

---

[4]This provision is subject to general agency law rules on the imputation of a partner's knowledge and notice to the partnership. *See* Grassmueck v. American Shorthorn Ass'n, 402 F.3d 833, 839 (8th Cir. 2005) (applying agency law's "sole actor" doctrine to impute partner's fraud to the partnership).

[5]Colo. Rev. Stat. § 7-64-102.

§ 8.103.   EFFECT OF PARTNERSHIP
AGREEMENT; NONWAIVABLE PROVISIONS

Section 103

(a) Except as otherwise provided in subsection (b), relations among the partners and between the partners and the partnership are governed by the partnership agreement. To the extent the partnership agreement does not otherwise provide, this [Act] governs relations among the partners and between the partners and the partnership.

(b) The partnership agreement may not:

(1) vary the rights and duties under Section 105 except to eliminate the duty to provide copies of statements to all of the partners;

(2) unreasonably restrict the right of access to books and records under Section 403(b);

(3) eliminate the duty of loyalty under Section 404(b) or 603(b)(3), but:

(i) the partnership agreement may identify specific types or categories of activities that do not violate the duty of loyalty, if not manifestly unreasonable; or

(ii) all of the partners or a number or percentage specified in the partnership agreement may authorize or ratify, after full disclosure of all material facts, a specific act or transaction that otherwise would violate the duty of loyalty;

(4) unreasonably reduce the duty of care under Section 404(c) or 603(b)(3);

(5) eliminate the obligation of good faith and fair dealing under Section 404(d), but the partnership agreement may prescribe the standards by which the performance of the obligation is to be measured, if the standards are not manifestly unreasonable;

(6) vary the power to dissociate as a partner under Section 602(a), except to require the notice under Section 601(1) to be in writing;

(7) vary the right of a court to expel a partner in the events specified in Section 601(5);

(8) vary the requirement to wind up the partnership business in cases specified in Section 801(4), (5), or (6);

(9) vary the law applicable to a limited liability partnership under Section 106(b); or

(10) restrict rights of third parties under this [Act].

Summary: Provides that the "partnership agreement" (defined in § 101(5)) governs the partners' relationship except as to the matters identified in subsection (b).

Parallel U.P.A.:   None.

Important Changes: The U.P.A. did not summarize in one place the situations that cannot be varied by the agreement. Some of the situations identified in this section may be consistent with current law, while others, including the limitations on waiving fiduciary duties, probably are not.

Analysis: In general, as discussed below in connection with §§ 403, 404, 601, 603, and 801, limitations on what the partners may agree among themselves are questionable policy. Section 103(b)(10) also provides that the "partnership agreement" cannot "restrict rights of third parties under this [Act]."[6] Comment 2 points out that a restriction to which the third party has agreed is enforceable. This may be inconsistent with § 103(b)(10), which flatly provides that a partnership agreement cannot restrict third-party rights and does not include an exception for third party consent.

Section 103(b)(3)(ii) permits an interested party in a loyalty-breaching transaction to vote to authorize or ratify the transaction unless prevented by the partnership agreement. Corporate law generally bars such a person from voting.[7]

State variations

Delaware does not restrict loyalty or care waivers[8] and provides that agreements restricting third-party rights are enforceable with the consent of those third parties.[9] Also, the section provides:

> (d) It is the policy of this chapter to give maximum effect to the principle of freedom of contract and to the enforceability of partnership agreements.
>
> (e) A partner or another person shall not be liable to the partnership or the other partners or another person that is a party to or is otherwise bound by a partnership agreement for the partner's or other person's good faith reliance on the provisions of the partnership agreement.

It is not clear how this language interacts with the R.U.P.A. § 103(b) restrictions on the agreement that are included in Delaware's version of the section. Recent Delaware cases have given broad effect to the similar provision in the Delaware limited partnership statute.[10]

---

[6] *See* Keatinge, The Partnership Agreement and Third Parties: Re RULPA § 110(b)(13) v. RUPA § 103(b)(10), 37 Suffolk L. Rev. 873 (2004).

[7] *See, e.g.,* RMBCA §§ 8.62 (directors), 8.63 (shareholders).

[8] Del. Code Ann., tit. 6, § 15-103.

[9] Del. Code Ann., tit. 6, § 15-103(b)(8).

[10] *See* Bromberg & Ribstein, § 16.07(h)(5). For discussions of this provision, see Ribstein, Fiduciary Duties and Limited Partnership Agreements, 37 Suffolk U. L. Rev. 927 (2004); Ribstein, Unlimited Contracting in the Delaware Limited Partnership and its Implications for Corporate Law, 17 J. Corp. L. 299 (1991).

The section also provides:

> (c) Notwithstanding anything to the contrary contained in this section, Sections 15201, 15203 and 15501 may be modified only to the extent provided in a statement of partnership existence and in a partnership agreement.

The referenced subsections provide, respectively, that the partnership is a separate legal entity, that property acquired by a general partnership is property of the partnership and not of the partners, and that a partner is not a co-owner of partnership property. Thus, this provision clarifies the entity nature of the partnership. Language to this effect is included in the cross-referenced subsections.

The **Kentucky** version of U.L.P.A. § 110 includes a subsection (3), which provides that if a written partnership agreement requires amendments to be in writing in accordance with the agreement, then that provision shall be enforceable.[11]

New Jersey does not include the restrictions on contracting in subparagraphs (b) (1), (5) and (6) and, as to (3), provides that the agreement may not "reduce the duty of loyalty under subsection b. of section 24 or subsection b. of section 33 of this act so as to permit a partner to engage in conduct which is intentionally injurious to the partnership; no 5 or 6."[12]

Tennessee omits subparagraph (b)(10) concerning third-party rights.[13]

Texas excepts "a limitation on an individual partner's liability in a limited liability partnership as provided by this chapter [Chapter 152 of the Business Organizations Code]."[14]

Virginia, like Delaware, does not restrict loyalty or care waivers[15] and provides that agreements restricting third-party rights are enforceable with the consent of those third parties.[16]

LLP Cross-reference: Section 6.03(a).

---

[11] Ky. Rev. St. Ann. § 362.1-103(3).
[12] N.J. Stat. § 42:1A-4.
[13] Tenn. Code Ann. § 61-1-103.
[14] Tex. Bus. Orgs. Code Ann. § 152.002(b)(7).
[15] Va. Code § 73.81.
[16] Va. Code § 73.81(B)(7).

§ 8.104. SUPPLEMENTAL PRINCIPLES
OF LAW

Section 104

(a) Unless displaced by particular provisions of this [Act], the principles of law and equity supplement this [Act].

(b) If an obligation to pay interest arises under this [Act] and the rate is not specified, the rate is that specified in [applicable statute].

Summary: States that the principles of law and equity supplement the act unless displaced by the act, and gives a statutory cross-reference for the applicable rate of interest.

Parallel U.P.A.: §§ 4(2)–(3), 5. U.P.A. § (4)–(5) are covered in R.U.P.A. §§ 1001 and 1006, respectively.

Important Changes: Adds interest rate cross-reference. Although this section eliminates specific references to law of agency and estoppel in U.P.A. § 4(2)-(3) and the statement in U.P.A. § 4(1) that the rule that statutes in derogation of the common law are to be strictly construed shall have no application to this act, the Comment states that no changes are intended by these deletions.[17]

Analysis: None.

State variations

Delaware provides that restrictions on assignments of intangibles in its versions of UCC Article 9 do not apply to an interest in a domestic partnership.[18]

Tennessee provides that if an obligation to pay interest arises under this act and the rate is not specified, the rate is the applicable federal rate pursuant to 26 U.S.C. § 1274(d) or any successor law; and that the rule that statutes in derogation of the common law are to be strictly construed does not apply to this act.[19]

---

[17] *See* Grassmueck v. American Shorthorn Ass'n, 402 F.3d 833 (8th Cir. 2005) (applying agency law's "sole actor" doctrine concerning the adverse interest exception to imputing knowledge and notice, noting that R.U.P.A. did not change U.P.A. regarding the application of the law of agency).

[18] Del. Code Ann., tit. 6, § 15-104(c) (referring to *id.* §§ 9-406 and 9-408).

[19] Tenn. Code Ann. § 61-1-104.

§ 8.105.   EXECUTION, FILING, AND RECORDING
OF STATEMENTS

Section 105

(a) A statement may be filed in the office of [the Secretary of State]. A certified copy of a statement that is filed in an office in another State may be filed in the office of [the Secretary of State]. Either filing has the effect provided in this [Act] with respect to partnership property located in or transactions that occur in this State.

(b) A certified copy of a statement that has been filed in the office of the [Secretary of State] and recorded in the office for recording transfers of real property has the effect provided for recorded statements in this [Act]. A recorded statement that is not a certified copy of a statement filed in the office of the [Secretary of State] does not have the effect provided for recorded statements in this [Act].

(c) A statement filed by a partnership must be executed by at least two partners. Other statements must be executed by a partner or other person authorized by this [Act]. An individual who executes a statement as, or on behalf of, a partner or other person named as a partner in a statement shall personally declare under penalty of perjury that the contents of the statement are accurate.

(d) A person authorized by this [Act] to file a statement may amend or cancel the statement by filing an amendment or cancellation that names the partnership, identifies the statement, and states the substance of the amendment or cancellation.

(e) A person who files a statement pursuant to this section shall promptly send a copy of the statement to every nonfiling partner and to any other person named as a partner in the statement. Failure to send a copy of a statement to a partner or other person does not limit the effectiveness of the statement as to a person not a partner.

(f) The [Secretary of State] may collect a fee for filing or providing a certified copy of a statement. The [officer responsible for] recording transfers of real property may collect a fee for recording a statement.

Summary: States requirements for the statements provided for in the Act.

Parallel U.P.A.:   None.

Important Changes: The statements of authority (§ 303), denial of authority (§ 304), dissociation (§ 704), dissolution (§ 805), and merger (§ 907) are new.

Analysis: This section creates potential problems because it does not fully specify the penalties for noncompliance with formalities that have not been waived.[20] Subsection (e) says only that failure to send a copy of the statement to a partner or person named as partner does not change its effect as to non-partners. This negatively implies that other noncompliance does have an effect as to non-partners. For example, the statement may be ineffective if only one rather than two partners execute it as required in subsection (c). The courts might protect unwary partners by recognizing "de facto" compliance, but this would introduce the sort of unpredictability the statute is intended to eliminate. The statute should omit or limit the effect of requirements that are not essential to the statute's basic purpose of establishing the authority of particular partners.

§8.106. GOVERNING LAW

Section 106

(a) Except as otherwise provided in subsection (b), the law of the jurisdiction in which a partnership has its chief executive office governs relations among the partners and between the partners and the partnership.

(b) The law of this State governs relations among the partners and between the partners and the partnership and the liability of partners for an obligation of a limited liability partnership.

Summary: Provides that the law of the state in which partnership has its chief executive office governs the partnership's internal affairs.

Parallel U.P.A.: None.

Important Changes: This section supplies a choice-of-law rule for partnerships that is based on a similar rule in Article 9 of the Uniform Commercial Code.[21]

Analysis: As discussed throughout this book, R.U.P.A. effects significant changes in the law of partnership. As a result, firms whose operations are based in U.P.A. states may want to elect to be governed by R.U.P.A. Conversely, partnerships based in a R.U.P.A. jurisdiction may seek to be governed by the U.P.A. or a R.U.P.A. variant. Moreover, apart from preferring a particular law, partners may want to make the choice of law more certain in order to avoid disputes over

---

[20] Similar criticisms apply to the requirements for the individual statements. *See* the discussion of R.U.P.A. § 303(c).
[21] 5 U.C.C. § 9-103(3)(d).

this potentially difficult issue.[22] Accordingly, the choice-of-law rule provided by this section may be among the most important in the act.

"Chief executive office" is not defined either in R.U.P.A. or in the U.C.C. provision from which it is derived. A comment to the U.C.C. says that the term "means the place from which in fact the debtor manages the main part of his business operations."[23] This suggests that the court should look to the locus of administrative activity rather than to where the firm earns its money.[24] "Chief executive office" may be ambiguous for many firms, such as large decentralized interstate law and accounting firms, or informal itinerant firms that own real estate in several states but have little administrative activity.[25] Larger multi-state firms and limited liability partnerships (LLPs) (*see* below in this **Analysis**) are most likely to contract explicitly for application of a particular state's law.

R.U.P.A. 106(a) is not one of the nonwaivable provisions listed in R.U.P.A. § 103 and the Comment to § 106 describes the section as a default rule. It follows that a contract that provides for the application of the law of a state other than that in which the chief executive office is located should be treated as a "partnership agreement" under R.U.P.A. § 101(5), which effectively waives § 106.[26] But a Comment to R.U.P.A. § 106 states that the parties' ability to select the applicable law is subject to general choice-of-law rules.[27] These rules restrict the parties' freedom to contract for choice of law.[28] For example, a court in a R.U.P.A. state to which a partnership's business is closely connected may apply a

---

[22] For examples of the complications that may arise concerning choice of law, see Spitzer v. Shanley Corp., 870 F. Supp. 565 (S.D.N.Y. 1994) (Oklahoma law governs fiduciary duty concerning deals with a general partner that is a Texas corporation and whose parent is a Delaware corporation); Thompson v. Wayne Smith Const. Co., Inc., 640 N.E.2d 408 (Ind. App. 1994) (giving South Carolina judgment requiring exhaustion for joint liability full faith and credit, but not a Ohio decision as to effect of joint liability, noting "[w]hile the first state in which execution is attempted might require the creditor to whistle Dixie as a prerequisite to execution, the second state might require the creditor to stand on his head. Worse yet, a third state might require the creditor to have never whistled Dixie or stood on his head as a condition precedent to proceeding. Repetitive or perhaps contradictory procedural requirements would proliferate to no purpose"). *See generally* Bromberg & Ribstein, § 1.04(a)–(d).

[23] U.C.C. § 9-103, comment 5(c).

[24] *See* Vestal, Choice of Law and the Fiduciary Duties of Partners under the Revised Uniform Partnership Act, 79 Iowa L. Rev. 219, 233–35 (1994).

[25] *Id.* at 238–40.

[26] For a discussion of this issue, see *id.* at 243–46. The courts have enforced provisions in partnership agreements that specify the applicable law. *See, e.g.,* Diamond v. T. Rowe Price Assocs., Inc., 852 F. Supp. 372 (D. Md. 1994) (applying Netherland Antilles law pursuant to choice-of-law and forum clause in partnership agreement to settle dispute concerning distributions); Gillespie v. Seymour, 876 P.2d 193 (Kan. App. 1994) (applying Illinois law pursuant to both partnership agreement and lex loci contractus to deny successor liability for tortious acts); Bromberg & Ribstein, § 1.04(a).

[27] This is made explicit in the Texas provision quoted in note 40, infra.

[28] *See* Ribstein & Keatinge on Limited Liability Companies, § 13.04 (2d ed. 2004) (hereinafter referred to as "Ribstein & Keatinge").

R.U.P.A. limitation on contracting out of fiduciary duties[29] or restricting third-party rights[30] rather than the law of a contractually selected state that would enforce the agreement. It is not clear that the Comment can override the black letter, which makes § 106 subject to contrary agreement. As a policy matter, there are strong arguments against restricting contractual choice of law, and in any event such restrictions should be treated the same in both corporations and partnerships.[31] Legislators should consider clarifying that, like corporations, partnerships can select the law that applies to the firm.

It is not entirely clear under § 106 what are "internal affairs" that are governed by the law of the state in which a firm's chief executive office is located. The term almost certainly extends to allocation of management and financial rights among the partners. However, it may not extend to rules that affect third parties such as the determination whether a partnership is formed, effect of a statement of partnership authority[32] or creditors' need to exhaust remedies against the partnership.[33] The act should at least be changed to clarify, as in the Revised Uniform Limited Partnership Act (R.U.L.P.A.),[34] and most limited liability company (LLC)[35] and LLP[36] statutes, as well as the Texas provision quoted below, that the state of formation governs the partners' *liability*.

R.U.P.A. § 106(b), discussed in Section 6.03, provides for the law applicable to a limited liability partnership. It is not subject to contrary agreement pursuant to R.U.P.A. § 103(b)(10).

State variations

Colorado states that the formation jurisdiction law applies, but that the firm is presumed to have been formed in the jurisdiction in which it has its chief executive office.[37]

---

[29] *See* R.U.P.A. § 103(b)(3)–(5).

[30] R.U.P.A. § 103(b)(10).

[31] *See generally* O'Hara & Ribstein, Corporations and the Market for Law, 2008 Ill. L. Rev. 661; Ribstein, From Efficiency to Politics in Contractual Choice of Law, 37 Ga. L. Rev. 363 (2003); Ribstein, Choosing Law by Contract, 18 J. Corp. L. 245 (1993). *But see* Vestal, note 24, supra, at 247–50 (arguing that allowing contractual choice of law would lead to a "race to the bottom" in partnership law.

[32] R.U.P.A. § 105(a) provides that a R.U.P.A. statement such as a statement of partnership authority under § 303 has effect in the state in which it is filed. However, the statement may not be effective if it is filed by a R.U.P.A. partnership in a U.P.A. state or by a U.P.A. partnership in a R.U.P.A. state.

[33] R.U.P.A. § 307.

[34] *See* Uniform Limited Partnership Act (1985) § 901 (laws of organization state govern limited partnership's "organization and internal affairs and the liability of its limited partners").

[35] For a review and analysis of these statutes, see Ribstein & Keatinge, § 13.03(a).

[36] *See* Section 6.02(d), above.

[37] Colo. Rev. Stat. § 7-64-106.

Delaware ensures enforcement of choice-of-law clauses by providing that "[i]f (i) a partnership agreement provides for the application of the laws of the State of Delaware, and (ii) the partnership files with the Secretary of State statement of partnership existence, then the partnership agreement shall be governed by and construed under the laws of the State of Delaware."[38]

Tennessee provides that "[w]here the partners have provided that the partnership agreement is governed by the laws of a jurisdiction other than this state, the law of the jurisdiction governing the partnership agreement governs relations among the partners and between the partners and the partnership."[39]

Texas provides as follows:

Internal affairs. The internal affairs of a partnership will be governed by its jurisdiction of formation[40] "Jurisdiction of formation" means: (A) in the case of a domestic filing entity, this state; (B) in the case of a foreign entity for which a certificate of formation or similar organizational instrument is filed in connection with its formation, the jurisdiction in which the entity's certificate of formation or similar organizational instrument is filed; or (C) in the case of a domestic or nonfiling entity for which a certificate of formation or similar organizational instrument is not filed in connection with its formation:

(i) the jurisdiction the laws of which are chosen in the entity's governing documents to govern its internal affairs if that jurisdiction bears a reasonable relation to the owners or members or to the entity's business and affairs under the principles of this state that would otherwise apply to a contract among the owners or members; or

(ii) if Subparagraph (i) does not apply, the jurisdiction in which the entity has its chief executive office. For purposes of this code, the internal affairs of an entity include: (1) the rights, powers, and duties of its governing authority, governing persons, officers, owners, and members; and (2) matters relating to its membership or ownership interests.[41]

Liability to third parties. The law of the jurisdiction of formation also applies "to the liability of an owner, a member, or a managerial official of the entity in the capacity as an owner, a member, or a managerial official for an obligation, including a debt or other liability, of the entity for which the owner, member, or managerial official is not otherwise liable by contract or under provisions of law other than this code."[42]

---

[38] Del. Code Ann., tit. 6, § 15-106(c).
[39] Tenn. Code Ann. § 61-1-106.
[40] Tex. Bus. Orgs. Code § 1.103.
[41] Tex. Bus. Orgs. Code § 1.002(43).
[42] Tex. Bus. Orgs. Code § 1.104.

This provision clarifies the ambiguity under R.U.P.A. concerning the law applicable to the partners' liability. Since there is only a single choice-of-law provision, the section makes clear that the law chosen by the parties generally governs. However, the Texas provision raises the new question of whether the chosen state's law "bears a reasonable relation" to the firm. Also, as discussed above in Section 6.03, it is not clear that the "chosen" law necessarily would include the place of LLP registration.

LLP Cross-reference: Section 6.03(b).

§ 8.107. PARTNERSHIP SUBJECT TO AMENDMENT OR REPEAL OF [ACT]

Section 107

A partnership governed by this [Act] is subject to any amendment to or repeal of this [Act].

Summary: A partnership governed by the act is subject to amendment or repeal of the act.

Parallel U.P.A.: None.

Important Changes: Adds a "reserved power" clause, long a distinctive characteristic of corporations, to partnership law.

Analysis: This section broadly lets legislatures retroactively change existing partnership agreements. This may violate the contract clause of the U.S. Constitution.[43] Although legislatures arguably need some flexibility to adapt the statute to new circumstances and ideas, there is ordinarily no reason why amendments must apply to existing firms, as distinguished from allowing such firms to opt into statutory changes. Indeed, this section contrasts with R.U.P.A. § 1006, discussed below, which protects U.P.A. partnerships from being automatically altered by the enactment of R.U.P.A. The same concern for retroactivity should apply to amendments or repeal of R.U.P.A.

[43] *See* U.S. Const. art. I, § 10, cl. 6; Butler & Ribstein, The Contract Clause and the Corporation, 55 Brook. L. Rev. 767 (1989).

§ 8.201.   PARTNERSHIP AS ENTITY

Section 201

(a) A partnership is an entity distinct from its partners.

(b) A limited liability partnership continues to be the same entity that existed before the filing of a statement of qualification under Section 1001.

Summary: Provides that "a partnership is an entity distinct from its partners."

Parallel U.P.A.:   None

Important Changes: Attempts to eliminate confusion concerning the nature of a partnership that is created by the combination of entity and aggregate features in the U.P.A.

Analysis: This section has the virtue of correcting a misapprehension that a partnership is simply an aggregate of its partnerships for all purposes. Yet it may create confusion of its own. "Aggregate" and "entity" are simply shorthand ways of *describing* partnership features. For example, a partnership is an "entity" insofar as it may own property in its own name, but an "aggregate" to the extent that the partnership dissolves as a result of a change in membership. Indeed, despite § 201, R.U.P.A. includes several "aggregate" characteristics, such as personal liability of partners[44] and dissolution on dissociation of a single partner.[45] The terms can cause mischief when courts or legislatures mistakenly derive consequences from them that should, instead, be based on policy or the parties' agreement.[46]

The Comment to § 201 includes an example of the misunderstanding of the appropriate uses of the aggregate/entity distinction. The Comment states:

> Giving clear expression to the entity nature of a partnership is intended to allay previous concerns stemming from the aggregate theory, such as the necessity of a deed to convey title from the "old" partnership to the "new" partnership every time there is a change of cast among the partners. Under R.U.P.A., there is no "new" partnership just because of membership changes. That will avoid the result in cases such as *Fairway Development Co. v. Title Insurance Co.*, 621 F. Supp. 120 (N.D. Ohio 1985), which held that the "new"

---

[44] *See* the discussion below of R.U.P.A. §§ 306–307.

[45] *See* the discussion below of R.U.P.A. § 801.

[46] The problems inherent in the aggregate/entity distinction are discussed in Bromberg & Ribstein, § 1.03.

partnership resulting from a partner's death did not have standing to enforce a title insurance policy issued to the "old" partnership.

The basic question in the *Fairway* situation, however, is whether the partnership's dissolution created a "new" partnership under the title insurance contract. That depends on the terms of the contract and on what happens in dissolution, not on whether the partnership is an "entity." Moreover, even if the *Fairway* result *should* turn on whether the partnership is an "entity," it plainly *does* not. If the partnership is an "entity," dissolution only creates a new entity.

Legislators should consider amending this section to provide that "a partnership is an entity distinct from its partners *unless the context otherwise requires.*" "Context" is intended to mean the entire legal and factual context and not merely the context within the partnership statute of the specific provision that relates to the case. The latter approach, while debatable in light of the foregoing discussion, would at least provide a more accurate description of the nature of partnership and thereby reverse rules that unduly emphasize the aggregate nature of partnership. At the same, this rule would help prevent the opposite erroneous over-reliance on entity features.

State variations

Delaware provides that a "partnership is a separate legal entity which is an entity distinct from its partners unless or to the extent otherwise provided in a statement of partnership existence and in a partnership agreement."[47]

Minnesota addresses the *Fairway* problem discussed above:

Except as otherwise provided in this chapter, a partnership remains the same entity for purposes of holding title to or conveying an interest in real or personal property and for all other purposes:

(1) during the winding up of the partnership following its dissolution;

(2) whether the status of a partnership that is a limited liability partnership terminates under section 323A.105(d) or section 323A.1003; and

(3) regardless of whether the words "limited liability partnership," "professional limited liability partnership," "general partnership," "registered limited liability partnership," or the designation "L.L.P.," "LLP," "P.L.L.P.," "PLLP," "R.L.L.P.," or "RLLP" are used in an instrument conveying an interest in real or personal property to or from the partnership or in any other writing.[48]

---

[47] Del. Code Ann., tit. 6, § 15-201(a). *See also* tit. 6, § 15-103(c), quoted supra in Section 8.103.

[48] Minn. Stat. Sec. 323A.1203.

§ 8.202.   CREATION OF PARTNERSHIP

Section 202

(a) Except as otherwise provided in subsection (b), the association of two or more persons to carry on as co-owners a business for profit forms a partnership, whether or not the persons intend to form a partnership.

(b) An association formed under a statute other than this [Act], a predecessor statute, or a comparable statute of another jurisdiction is not a partnership under this [Act].

(c) In determining whether a partnership is formed, the following rules apply:

(1) Joint tenancy, tenancy in common, tenancy by the entireties, joint property, common property, or part ownership does not by itself establish a partnership, even if the co-owners share profits made by the use of the property.

(2) The sharing of gross returns does not by itself establish a partnership, even if the persons sharing them have a joint or common right or interest in property from which the returns are derived.

(3) A person who receives a share of the profits of a business is presumed to be a partner in the business, unless the profits were received in payment:

(i) of a debt by installments or otherwise;

(ii) for services as an independent contractor or of wages or other compensation to an employee;

(iii) of rent;

(iv) of an annuity or other retirement or health benefit to a beneficiary, representative, or designee of a deceased or retired partner;

(v) of interest or other charge on a loan, even if the amount of payment varies with the profits of the business, including a direct or indirect present or future ownership of the collateral, or rights to income, proceeds, or increase in value derived from the collateral; or

(vi) for the sale of the goodwill of a business or other property by installments or otherwise.

Summary: States the rules for determining when partnership relationship is created.

Parallel U.P.A.:   §§ 6, 7.

Important Changes: Revises two of the categories of protected relationships; deletes the language in U.P.A. § 6(2) that provides for application of the statute to limited partnerships.

Analysis: R.U.P.A. now includes the U.P.A. definition of partnership as both a "definition" (R.U.P.A. § 101(4)) and as what the Comment to this section describes as an "operative rule." Although Comment 1 to this section says no change is intended by this repetition, courts may derive significance from the similar but not identical "operative" and "definitional" provisions.

This section also adds the language, not found in the U.P.A. or in the R.U.P.A. definition, "whether or not the persons intend to form a partnership." The Comment says that this merely clarifies that the parties need only the intent to engage in the acts that constitute partnership rather than the intent to be partners. This is consistent with the case law.[49]

Some of the new language that redefines profit-sharing relationships that are not presumptively partnerships may present some problems. Subsection (c)(3)(iv) extends the annuity category to include payment of a "health benefit," and subsection (c)(3)(v) extends the interest-payment category to include "a direct or indirect present or future ownership interest in the collateral" of a loan. By implying that these payments are profit sharing (and therefore must be protected from the inference of partnership), the act may unintentionally expand the concept of "profits." Profits include only payments that indicate that the recipient is a residual claimant and therefore an owner of the business.[50] The receipt of fixed payments from the partnership does not support the partnership inference.[51] Accordingly, in the absence of these new provisions, such payments as health benefits would not support partnership. The effect of the changes therefore may be to bolster the argument that the new "protected" relationships *are* partnerships, even if they are not *presumptively* partnerships.

Like U.P.A. § 6(2), § 202(b) provides that "[a]n association formed under a statute other than this [act], a predecessor statute, or a comparable statute of another jurisdiction is not a partnership under this [act]." In fact, intent to form

---

[49] *See* Bromberg & Ribstein, § 2.05.

[50] *See* Bromberg & Ribstein, § 2.07(a).

[51] *See* Pinnacle Port Cmty. Ass'n, Inc. v. Orenstein, 872 F.2d 1536 (11th Cir. 1989) (finding no partnership between lender and developer based on testimony that developer received all revenues after lender's principal and interest payments despite other testimony that lender got 94% percent of total returns); In re Matis, 74 B.R. 363 (N.D.N.Y. 1987); Hull v. Comptroller of Treasury, 312 Md. 77, 537 A.2d 1188 (1988) (retired pilots receiving guaranteed payments from an association were not partners); Coon v. Schoeneman, 476 S.W.2d 439 (Tex. Civ. App. 1972) (plaintiff received all profits from sale of houses after paying fixed amount to owner). However, partnership may be supported by evidence other than the mode of payment. *See* Bernstein, Bernstein, Wile & Gordon v. Ross, 22 Mich. App. 117, 177 N.W.2d 193 (1970) (partnership although attorney received fixed salary). *See generally* Bromberg & Ribstein, § 2.07(b)(4).

another entity may be evidence of no intent to form a partnership.[52] However, R.U.P.A. deletes the U.P.A. language providing that the Act applies to limited partnerships "except in so far as the statutes relating to such partnerships are inconsistent herewith." As the Comment points out, this still leaves R.U.L.P.A. § 1105, which provides that the U.P.A. governs in cases not provided for by R.U.L.P.A.[53] This at least eliminates potential conflict between differently formulated partnership and limited partnership provisions on the application of general partnership law to limited partnerships.[54] However, this may leave some confusion in states that adopt R.U.P.A. without making clear in their older limited partnership statute that the new partnership law applies.[55] It also leaves open the larger question of whether partnership law — particularly as changed by R.U.P.A. — *should* apply to limited partnerships. In contrast with general partnerships, limited partnerships necessarily have centralized management, passive limited-liability members, and some formality. These differences in basic features should result in pervasive differences in default rules, including fiduciary duty and remedy provisions that limited partnership law has borrowed from general partnerships. Since R.U.P.A. does apply to limited partnerships, the R.U.P.A. changes must be evaluated in light of their appropriateness for limited as well as for general partnerships. Thus, states that are considering adopting R.U.P.A. should use this as an opportunity for reexamining the linkage between general and limited partnership law.[56]

The reference in § 202(b) to "a comparable statute of another jurisdiction" suggests that it excludes foreign *partnerships*.[57] However, Comment 2 to § 202 suggests that this language is intended to refer to other *forms* of business, such as corporations and limited partnerships.

---

[52] Lentz Eng'g, L.C. v. Brown, 2011 WL 4449655 (Tex. App.-Houston, Sept. 27, 2011).

[53] R.U.L.P.A. § 1105.

[54] In particular, unlike the R.U.L.P.A. language, the U.P.A. language might preclude application of the U.P.A. if R.U.L.P.A. is silent on an issue and this silence is interpreted as a negative pregnant that creates an inconsistency with the U.P.A.

[55] For example, in Montana, which has adopted R.U.P.A., the limited partnership statute states that "the provisions of the Uniform Partnership Act (Title 35, Chapter 10) govern." Mont. Code Ann. § 35-12-503 (1993). The citation is to the location of both the new and revised partnership statutes. Since the limited partnership provision was not changed following the adoption of the new general partnership law, this invites the argument that the limited partnership statute refers to the old, repealed general partnership statute.

[56] See Ribstein, Linking Statutory Forms 58 L. & Contemp. Probs. 187 (Spring 1995). R.U.P.A.'s application to limited partnerships is also discussed below in connection with R.U.P.A. Article IX, which applies the R.U.P.A. merger and conversion provisions to limited partnerships. Note that U.L.P.A. (2001) moots this issue by eliminating the linkage between general and limited partnership law. See § 1.04(b), note 54, supra, and § 9.101(b), infra.

[57] Section 6.03(a) discusses the choice-of-law implications of this interpretation.

State variations

The **Colorado** limited partnership statute clarifies linkage by providing that a limited partnership may elect whether to be governed by U.P.A. or R.U.P.A. and that U.P.A. applies in the absence of an election.[58]

Delaware provides that a partnership may be formed not for profit if there is intent to form a partnership.[59]

Oregon and Texas provide that "[a]n agreement to share losses by the owners of a business is not necessary to create a partnership" and that an "expression of an intent to be partners in the business" is merely one of five "[f]actors indicating that persons have created a partnership," together with profit, loss and control-sharing and contribution of property.[60] On the other hand, in Texas, conclusive evidence of all five factors establishes a partnership as a matter of law.[61]

LLP Cross-reference: Section 2.02.

§ 8.203.   PARTNERSHIP PROPERTY

Section 203

Property acquired by a partnership is property of the partnership and not of the partners individually.

Summary: Provides that property acquired by a partnership is property of the partnership and not of the partners individually.

Parallel U.P.A.:   §§ 8(1), 25.

---

[58] Colo. Stat. §§ 7-61-110, -129; 7-62-403(3), -1104.

[59] Del. Code Ann., tit. 6, § 15-202.

[60] Or. Rev. Stat. § 67.005; Tex. Rev. Civ. Stat. Ann. art. 6132b-§ 2.03. For applications of the Texas statute *see* Ingram v. Deere, 2009 WL 1900537 (Tex. July 3, 2009) (holding that the Texas statute does not require proof of all of the listed factors in order to show partnership, though evidence of one factor is normally insufficient, and noting (n.6) that "Oregon adopted factors almost verbatim to the factors listed in TRPA for determining whether a partnership exists. * * * Oregon and Texas are the only states to enact a statute that deviates from the UPA's rules for determining the existence of a partnership."); Reagan v. Lyberger, 156 S.W.3d 925 (Tex. App. 2005) (fact that parties signed a "profits participation agreement" supported intent to be partners under Texas Revised Partnership Act though agreement signed after facts in the case occurred, where other factors also supported partnership).

[61] *See* Ingram v. Deere, 288 S.W.3d 886, 903–04 (Tex. 2009).

Important Changes: Clarifies that partnership property is owned by the partnership and not by the partners individually.

Analysis: R.U.P.A. § 203 clarifies that partnership property is owned by the partnership itself rather than by the individual partners. This helpfully eliminates the confusion created by the U.P.A.'s "tenancy in partnership," which simultaneously made partners the nominal owners of partnership property and systematically negated their individual ownership rights.[62]

State variation

Delaware, consistent with its variation on Section 103, provides that this provision may not be modified "[u]nless otherwise provided in a statement of partnership existence and in a partnership agreement, property."[63]

§ 8.204.   WHEN PROPERTY IS PARTNERSHIP PROPERTY

Section 204

   (a) Property is partnership property if acquired in the name of:
      (1) the partnership; or
      (2) one or more partners with an indication in the instrument transferring title to the property of the person's capacity as a partner or of the existence of a partnership but without an indication of the name of the partnership.
   (b) Property is acquired in the name of the partnership by a transfer to:
      (1) the partnership in its name; or
      (2) one or more partners in their capacity as partners in the partnership, if the name of the partnership is indicated in the instrument transferring title to the property.
   (c) Property is presumed to be partnership property if purchased with partnership assets, even if not acquired in the name of the partnership or of one or more partners with an indication in the instrument transferring title to the property of the person's capacity as a partner or of the existence of a partnership.

---

[62] *See* Bromberg & Ribstein, §§ 3.04–3.05.
[63] Del. Code Ann., tit. 6, § 15-203.

(d) Property acquired in the name of one or more of the partners, without an indication in the instrument transferring title to the property of the person's capacity as a partner or of the existence of a partnership and without use of partnership assets, is presumed to be separate property, even if used for partnership purposes.

Summary: States rules for determining when property is owned by the partnership.

Parallel U.P.A.:   § 8.

Important Changes: Clarifies that property acquired in the name of the partnership or of one or more partners with an indication of the partnership's interest is partnership property; that the presumption from purchase with partnership assets applies even if the property is not acquired in partnership name or with an indication of the partnership's interest; and that property acquired in partner name without an indication of the partnership's interest and without partnership assets is presumed to be separate property.

Analysis: U.P.A. § 8 was one of the provisions in the U.P.A. that most needed to be changed. Given the informality of the "standard form" partnership that is the focus of the partnership act, questions inevitably will arise as to whether property is owned by the partnership or by the individual partners. Third parties need a low-cost method of determining what property is owned by the partnership so that they can adjust credit and other costs accordingly. The partners are in the best position to provide this information. Thus, the investigation and uncertainty costs third parties may seek to charge to the business if they cannot easily determine what it owns probably will exceed the partners' costs of clarifying property ownership.

The U.P.A. goes no further in clarifying ownership than providing in § 8(2) that property acquired with partnership funds is partnership property. R.U.P.A. adds three more precise rules for determining ownership of partnership property: (1) Property is deemed to be owned by the partnership if acquired in partnership name; (2) the partnership funds presumption takes precedence over title in individual name; and (3) property is presumed to be owned by individual partners if purchased in individual name without partnership assets.

There may be some debate as to whether the partnership statute should create a presumption in favor of individual ownership of property held in the partners' names where the property is used in the partnership business but was not purchased with partnership funds. Because of the informality of partnership, use by the partnership may be at least as reliable an indicator of ownership as individual title. Moreover, declaring a partner to be the owner of property that is important to the firm may permit that partner to appropriate value that belongs to the partnership or to extract concessions from the other partners.[64] Nevertheless, the presumption based on title in the partners' names is justified. While R.U.P.A. may disappoint some partners by causing outcomes that are inconsistent with the parties' intent, the partners would favor a rule that minimizes the costs of litigation and of conducting the business.

The 1990 draft added another useful rule, which was deleted from the final version, that property the title of which is customarily recorded and is other than in the partnership name is not partnership property even if it was purchased with partnership assets. This provision would protect a partner's creditor or other third party who relied on record title. This makes sense in light of the policy discussed in the preceding paragraph, and was consistent with law in some states.[65] It is not clear why this change was deleted from the final version of R.U.P.A. or why property purchased in partnership name should always be regarded as partnership property, but property purchased in separate name should only be presumed to be separate property.

States considering adopting the R.U.P.A. approach should consider some further refinements. First, the partnership statute arguably should provide that ownership of property is determined consistent with representations to justifiably relying third parties. In other words, there is some justification for treating third parties who rely, for example, on credit applications like those who rely on record title. The statute would thereby create a category of apparent ownership analogous to partnership by estoppel.[66] Second, the statute should clarify that the "partnership funds" presumption applies when property is purchased on partnership *credit*, with repayments to be made with partnership funds.[67]

State variation

Delaware provisions on partner contributions. It provides that "[e]ach person to be admitted as a partner to a partnership formed under either Section 15202(a)(i)

---

[64] *See, e.g.,* Pav-Saver Corp. v. Vasso Corp., 143 Ill. App. 3d 1013, 97 Ill. Dec. 760, 493 N.E.2d 423 (1986) (wrongfully dissolving partner precluded from withdrawing patent or its value from partnership where such withdrawal would have prevented the innocent partner from carrying on the business); Bromberg & Ribstein, § 3.02(b).

[65] *See* Ga. Code Ann. § 14-8-8; Morgan Guar. Trust Co. v. Alexander Equities, Inc., 246 Ga. 60, 268 S.E.2d 660 (1980); In re Estate of Allen, 239 N.W.2d 163 (Iowa 1976). Comment 1 to § 204 refers to the Georgia statute as an antecedent to § 204. For a discussion of the importance of record title under the Georgia provision, see Ribstein, An Analysis of Georgia's New Partnership Law, 36 Mercer L. Rev. 443, 481–82 (1985).

[66] *See* U.P.A. § 16.

[67] *See* Bromberg & Ribstein, § 3.02(c).

or Section 15202(a)(ii) of this Chapter may be admitted as a partner and may receive a partnership interest in the partnership without making a contribution or being obligated to make a contribution to the partnership. Each person to be admitted as a partner to a partnership formed under either Section 15202(a)(i) or Section 15202(a)(ii) of this Chapter may be admitted as a partner without acquiring an economic interest in the partnership. Nothing contained in this section shall affect a partner's liability under Section 15306."[68] It also provides that a partner's contribution "may be in cash, property or services rendered, or a promissory note or other obligation to contribute cash or property or to perform services"[69] and for enforcement of partner contribution obligations.[70]

§ 8.301. PARTNER AGENT OF PARTNERSHIP

Section 301

Subject to the effect of a statement of partnership authority under Section 303:

(1) Each partner is an agent of the partnership for the purpose of its business. An act of a partner, including the execution of an instrument in the partnership name, for apparently carrying on in the ordinary course the partnership business or business of the kind carried on by the partnership binds the partnership, unless the partner had no authority to act for the partnership in the particular matter and the person with whom the partner was dealing knew or had received a notification that the partner lacked authority.

(2) An act of a partner which is not apparently for carrying on in the ordinary course the partnership business or business of the kind carried on by the partnership binds the partnership only if the act was authorized by the other partners.

Summary: Specifies the power of a partner to bind the partnership in transactions with third parties.

Parallel U.P.A.: § 9.

---

[68] Del. Code Ann., tit. 6, § 15-205. The references to § 15-202 clarify that the provision applies to non-profit as well as to for-profit partnerships. *See* the Variations to § 202, discussed in § 8.202, supra.

[69] Del. Code Ann., tit. 6, § 15-206.

[70] Del. Code Ann., tit. 6, § 15-207.

Important Changes: Provides that a partner's apparent authority includes acts for carrying on in the ordinary course "business of the kind carried on by the partnership," and not only the business of the particular partnership; provides that a third party is bound by "notification," rather than merely knowledge, that an "apparently . . . usual" transaction is unauthorized; deletes the provision that bound a third party by knowledge that non-"apparently . . . usual" acts were unauthorized; and omits the U.P.A.'s list of events that require unanimous consent. Other changes resulting from the cross-referencing of § 303 are discussed below concerning that Section.

Analysis: R.U.P.A. changes the circumstances in which a third party is barred from holding the partnership responsible for an act within the partner's "apparently . . . usual" authority. U.P.A. § 9(1) provides that an "apparently . . . usual" act does not bind the partnership if the third party "has knowledge of the fact that [the partner] has no such authority." U.P.A. § 3(1) provides that "knowledge" includes only actual and "bad faith" knowledge. This standard does not embrace constructive notice as suggested in the Comments to this section and § 102, but rather merely clarifies that proof of knowledge does not depend on establishing subjective awareness of lack of authority.[71] The U.P.A., therefore, requires a fairly high degree of awareness of lack of authority on the part of the third party for the partnership not to be bound for apparently authorized acts. This makes sense because it gives the partnership the incentive to reduce the costs of third parties dealing with it to the extent that it can cheaply do so by clarifying partners' authority, while preventing the third party from ignoring information it already has. While the "knowledge" issue is sometimes unclear under the U.P.A., the stronger knowledge requirement and substantial U.P.A. case law[72] provide guidance and protection.

R.U.P.A. § 301(1) provides that the act is not binding as to a third party who "knew *or had received a notification* that the partner lacked authority." The italicized language arguably expands the situations in which the transaction does

---

[71] For example, a partnership avoided being bound by an issuance of title that a third party knew related to the partner's personal loan even without proving that the third party was subjectively aware that the issuance was *unauthorized. See* Investors Title Ins. Co. v. Herzig, 320 N.C. 770, 360 S.E.2d 786 (1987).

[72] *See, e.g.,* Green River Assocs. v. Mark Twain Kansas City Bank, 808 S.W.2d 894 (Mo. App. 1991) (since bank knew partnership agreement required deposit of proceeds of loan in partnership account, it could not rely on any apparent authority of general partner to deposit elsewhere, so partnership not liable for repayment of misappropriated proceeds); First Nat'l Bank and Trust Co. v. Scherr, 467 N.W.2d 427 (N.D. 1991) (under U.P.A. § 9(4) and agency law, bank that earlier relied on authority of one partner to borrow for partnership could not continue to do so after it had knowledge from partnership agreement and signature card that consent of both partners required); Evans v. Pioneer Bank of Evanston, 809 P.2d 251 (Wyo. 1991) (promissory note executed by one of two managing partners not binding on partnership where partnership agreement required consent of both to such transaction outside the regular course of business, and bank had a copy of agreement).

not bind the partnership. For example, under § 102(d), a third party may or may not have "notification" that a partner lacks authority merely because the third party has a copy of a lengthy partnership agreement that includes provisions generally limiting the partner's authority. Also, it is not clear how "notification" will be defined in the context of verbal statements. R.U.P.A. accordingly increases third parties' incentives to get written evidence of the partner's authority in *all* substantial transactions, no matter how "apparently . . . usual." R.U.P.A. § 303, discussed below, facilitates this by authorizing central filings that clarify partners' authority.

A second change R.U.P.A. makes in the partner's agency authority makes things a bit more difficult for the partnership. The U.P.A. provides that a third party is bound by restrictions on the partner's authority of which he is aware both where the restrictions apply to the partner's general power to bind in "apparently . . . usual" transactions under § 9(1), and where the restriction applies to the partner's authority created in any other way under § 9(4). R.U.P.A., however, does not include the latter provision. As a result, it is unclear whether a transaction that is within a partner's inherent agency power but is not "apparently . . . usual" binds the partnership even if a third party knows or has been notified of a limitation on authority. For example, a managing partner who has wide power to run the firm may be able to bind the partnership in an extraordinary transaction even if the third party knows that the partner lacks authority, as where the transaction is obviously for the manager's personal benefit. Comment 5 to § 301 says that § 301(1) "fully reflects the principle embodied in U.P.A. Section 9(4) that the partnership is not bound by an act of a partner in contravention of a restriction on his authority known to the other party." However, the effect of this Comment is unclear in light of the fact that the black letter of § 301(1) clearly applies only to "apparently . . . usual" transactions.

Third, R.U.P.A. omits the U.P.A.'s categories of presumptively nonbinding transactions.[73] The U.P.A.'s list needed revision in light of modern practice.[74] Some of the acts in the U.P.A. list are not helpful. For example, it is not clear what acts can be considered to "dispose of the good will of the business" within the meaning of § 9(3)(c).[75] Also, it makes little sense in light of modern practice to say that partners had no partner authority to contract to submit partnership claims to arbitration as provided by § 9(3)(e).[76] Yet such a list helpfully provides presumptive "standard form" restrictions on partners' authority for informal partnerships. Also, deleting the list leaves unclear the continuing relevance of the transaction categories. Although the R.U.P.A. Comments justify the deletion on

---

[73] *See* U.P.A. § 9(3).

[74] *See* U.P.A. Revision Subcommittee of the Committee on Partnerships and Unincorporated Business Organizations, Section of Business Law, American Bar Association, Should the Uniform Partnership Act be Revised? 43 Bus. Law. 121 (1987) (hereinafter "ABA Report").

[75] *See* Bromberg & Ribstein, § 4.03(c)(1).

[76] *See* Bromberg & Ribstein, § 4.03(c)(5).

the grounds of "flexibility," the benefits of this "flexibility" must be balanced against the costs of uncertainty and increased litigation.

§ 8.302.   TRANSFER OF PARTNERSHIP PROPERTY

Section 302

(a) Partnership property may be transferred as follows:

(1) Subject to the effect of a statement of partnership authority under Section 303, partnership property held in the name of the partnership may be transferred by an instrument of transfer executed by a partner in the partnership name.

(2) Partnership property held in the name of one or more partners with an indication in the instrument transferring the property to them of their capacity as partners or of the existence of a partnership, but without an indication of the name of the partnership, may be transferred by an instrument of transfer executed by the persons in whose name the property is held.

(3) Partnership property held in the name of one or more persons other than the partnership, without an indication in the instrument transferring the property to them of their capacity as partners or of the existence of a partnership, may be transferred by an instrument of transfer executed by the persons in whose name the property is held.

(b) A partnership may recover partnership property from a transferee only if it proves that execution of the instrument of initial transfer did not bind the partnership under Section 301 and:

(1) as to a subsequent transferee who gave value for property transferred under subsection (a)(1) and (2), proves that the subsequent transferee knew or had received a notification that the person who executed the instrument of initial transfer lacked authority to bind the partnership; or

(2) as to a transferee who gave value for property transferred under subsection (a)(3), proves that the transferee knew or had received a notification that the property was partnership property and that the person who executed the instrument of initial transfer lacked authority to bind the partnership.

(c) A partnership may not recover partnership property from a subsequent transferee if the partnership would not have been entitled to recover the property, under subsection (b), from any earlier transferee of the property.

(d) If a person holds all of the partners' interests in the partnership, all of the partnership property vests in that person. The person may execute a document in the name of the partnership to evidence vesting of the property in that person and may file or record the document.

Summary: Provides rules on the effect of purported transfers of partnership property.

Parallel U.P.A.:   § 10.

Important Changes: Deals with transfers of all property and not merely real property; enforces a conveyance that is authorized under any part of the partner-authority provision rather than only the "apparently . . . usual" portion of that provision as in U.P.A. § 10; clarifies that the partnership bears the burden of proving that transfers were not authorized; provides that subsequent transferees of property originally held in partnership name or by partners with an indication that they are such are bound by "notification," rather than merely "knowledge," that the transfer was unauthorized; provides that transferees of property held in partner name without an indication that they are partners are bound by "notification" that the property is partnership property and that the transfer was unauthorized; deletes the provisions for transfer of the partnership's equitable title; and provides for ownership of partnership property by a person who holds all of the partners' interests in the partnership.

Analysis: This provision, like U.P.A. § 10, provides that even some unauthorized transfers of partnership real property may be binding in favor of grantees that justifiably relied on record title. Several of the changes noted above fix problems with the U.P.A., including the application to transfers of property other than real property, better integration with the partner-authority provision,[77] clarification of the burden of proving authority, and deletion of provisions for equitable enforcement of transfers outside the chain of title.[78]

However, R.U.P.A. substitutes some potential problems of its own. First, the section now applies even to property transfers that do not involve record title. There is no reason why subsequent, or even immediate, grantees should receive the special protection of this section where they have not relied on a record of title. Second, the section removes some of the subsequent grantee's protection by providing that the conveyance is not binding as to a grantee who had merely

---

[77] *See* Bromberg & Ribstein, § 4.04(b)(1) (suggesting that even a transfer that was not "apparently . . . usual" should bind the partnership "if it was otherwise actually or apparently authorized").

[78] *See* Bromberg & Ribstein, § 4.04(b)(2) (suggesting that this provision should be either eliminated or changed "to clarify that the holder in this situation has no rights against those other than the partnership").

"notification," as distinguished from actual knowledge, of the lack of authority (and, as to property held in partner name, that the property was partnership property).[79] This may reduce third parties' ability to rely on record title, since it is not clear what facts regarding ownership or authority will be deemed to provide "notification" of these facts. Once again, as with ownership of property (*see* § 204), R.U.P.A. reduces third parties' ability to rely on record title.[80]

§ 8.303.   STATEMENT OF PARTNERSHIP AUTHORITY

Section 303

(a) A partnership may file a statement of partnership authority, which:
   (1) must include:
      (i) the name of the partnership;
      (ii) the street address of its chief executive office and of one office in this State, if there is one;
      (iii) the names and mailing addresses of all of the partners or of an agent appointed and maintained by the partnership for the purpose of subsection (b); and
      (iv) the names of the partners authorized to execute an instrument transferring real property held in the name of the partnership; and
   (2) may state the authority, or limitations on the authority, of some or all of the partners to enter into other transactions on behalf of the partnership and any other matter.

(b) If a statement of partnership authority names an agent, the agent shall maintain a list of the names and mailing addresses of all of the partners and make it available to any person on request for good cause shown.

(c) If a filed statement of partnership authority is executed pursuant to Section 105(c) and states the name of the partnership but does not contain all of the other information required by subsection (a), the statement nevertheless operates with respect to a person not a partner as provided in subsections (d) and (e).

(d) Except as otherwise provided in subsection (g), a filed statement of partnership authority supplements the authority of a partner to enter into transactions on behalf of the partnership as follows:

---

[79] *See* R.U.P.A. § 302(a)(3).

[80] This denigration of the record's effect is apparently inconsistent with R.U.P.A. § 303(d)(2), which provides that a grant of authority in a filed statement of partnership authority is effective in favor of transferees of real property without "knowledge to the contrary." This questionably appears to give an immediate transferee more right to rely on a statement of authority than a subsequent transferee has to rely on record title.

(1) Except for transfers of real property, a grant of authority contained in a filed statement of partnership authority is conclusive in favor of a person who gives value without knowledge to the contrary, so long as and to the extent that a limitation on that authority is not then contained in another filed statement. A filed cancellation of a limitation on authority revives the previous grant of authority.

(2) A grant of authority to transfer real property held in the name of the partnership contained in a certified copy of a filed statement of partnership authority recorded in the office for recording transfers of that real property is conclusive in favor of a person who gives value without knowledge to the contrary, so long as and to the extent that a certified copy of a filed statement containing a limitation on that authority is not then of record in the office for recording transfers of that real property. The recording in the office for recording transfers of that real property of a certified copy of a filed cancellation of a limitation on authority revives the previous grant of authority.

(e) A person not a partner is deemed to know of a limitation on the authority of a partner to transfer real property held in the name of the partnership if a certified copy of the filed statement containing the limitation on authority is of record in the office for recording transfers of that real property.

(f) Except as otherwise provided in subsections (d) and (e) and Sections 704 and 805, a person not a partner is not deemed to know of a limitation on the authority of a partner merely because the limitation is contained in a filed statement.

(g) Unless earlier canceled, a filed statement of partnership authority is canceled by operation of law five years after the date on which the statement, or the most recent amendment, was filed with the [Secretary of State].

Summary: This section permits a partnership to file "a statement of partnership authority." Subsection (d) *supplements* partners' authority by binding the partnership in favor of third parties who lack knowledge contrary to the statements in the document as to transactions generally and as to real property transactions if the statement is recorded in the office for recording transfers of that property. Subsection (e) *limits* partners' authority to transfer real property held in partnership name by providing that non-partners are deemed to know of limitations on authority provided for in a statement recorded in the office for recording transfers of that property.

Parallel U.P.A.: None.

Important Changes: The U.P.A. did not provide for such filings.

Analysis: This section provides an important way for partnerships to clarify partner authority. It is made particularly necessary by the "notification" rule in R.U.P.A. § 301, which may complicate reliance on partners' apparent authority.[81]

The main potential concerns with the statement of partnership authority relate to the required formalities. Section 105 requires that at least two partners execute any statement filed by the partnership. Section 303(a)(1) requires the statement to include the names and addresses of all partners (or of an agent who maintains a list of partners), including those whose authority is not dealt with in the statement. Section 105(e) requires a person who files a statement to send a copy to every partner and person named as a partner.

These requirements do not impose undue burdens on the partners. The duty to send copies may be waived under § 103(b)(1), and the partnership can avoid public record disclosure of partners by using an agent. Section 303(c) provides that failure to include all of the required information does not change the statement's effect as to non-partners, and § 105(e) provides that the failure to send copies to partners or others does not limit the effectiveness of the statement as to non-partners.

The formalities may, however, raise some issues. First, partnerships with confidentiality concerns may seek to avoid the requirement in § 303 that they disclose names and addresses of partners or make this information available through an agent. Section 303(c) provides that omitting required information does not make the statement ineffective as to third parties. This suggests that the partners may omit the name of the agent who holds a record of the partners' names and, by implication, the names of some or all of the partners from this record. Then is there any reason for the partnership to disclose this information if it does not want to do so?

Second, this disclosure requirement raises the further question whether including partners' names affects on their being determined actual or purported partners.[82] R.U.P.A. § 308(c) provides that a person is not liable as a partner only because she is named as such in a statement of partnership authority. This leaves the possibility, however, that being named helps establish such liability or will be deemed to be significant evidence of the intent to be partners. This is supported to some extent by the fact that R.U.P.A. § 304 offers those who are named in statements of partnership authority the opportunity to deny their status as partners, which would be unnecessary if the statement of authority had no such effect. Being named in a statement of partnership authority also could have ramifications under non-partnership law, such as bearing on whether the person is a partner or employee for purposes of the employment discrimination laws.

---

[81] *See* the analysis supra of R.U.P.A. § 301.

[82] Analogous problems are presented by disclosing partners' names in LLP registrations. *See* §§ 2.02(b), 3.10(a), supra.

Third, under §§ 105(c) and 303(c) the statement is ineffective if executed by fewer than two partners. This requirement could invalidate the statement if one of those who executed the statement is later deemed not to have been a partner at the time of execution.

There are also some questions concerning the potential effects of the statement other than those explicitly provided for in § 303. For example, subsection (f) says that, except as provided in subsections (d) and (e), "a person not a partner is not deemed to know of a limitation on the authority of a partner *merely because* the limitation is contained in a filed statement" (emphasis added). This phrase arguably would permit the statement to be used as *some evidence* that the third party knew of the limitation.

State variation

Tennessee only requires disclosure of the names of the partners authorized to execute an instrument transferring real property held in the name of the partnership.[83]

§ 8.304. STATEMENT OF DENIAL

Section 304

A partner or other person named as a partner in a filed statement of partnership authority or in a list maintained by an agent pursuant to Section 303(b) may file a statement of denial stating the name of the partnership and the fact that is being denied, which may include denial of a person's authority or status as a partner. A statement of denial is a limitation on authority as provided in Section 303(d) and (e).

Summary: Permits a person named as a partner in a statement filed under § 303 to file a statement denying his authority or status as a partner which operates as a limitation on his authority to the same extent as a limitation on authority contained in a statement of partnership.

Parallel U.P.A.: None.

Important Changes: U.P.A. did not provide for comparable filings.

---

[83] Tenn. Code Ann. § 61-1-303(a)(1)(C).

Analysis: Under §§ 303(d) and 304, a statement of denial may be effective to at least cancel the authority to bind that otherwise would arise from a statement of partnership authority under § 303. Also, the statement may be effective to limit authority to transfer real property through § 303(e). Other potential effects are unclear. In particular, one who denies his partnership status nevertheless may be a partner if he intentionally does the acts that would make him a partner under R.U.P.A. § 202.

§ 8.305.   PARTNERSHIP LIABLE FOR PARTNER'S ACTIONABLE CONDUCT

Section 305

(a) A partnership is liable for loss or injury caused to a person, or for a penalty incurred, as a result of a wrongful act or omission, or other actionable conduct, of a partner acting in the ordinary course of business of the partnership or with authority of the partnership.

(b) If, in the course of the partnership's business or while acting with authority of the partnership, a partner receives or causes the partnership to receive money or property of a person not a partner, and the money or property is misapplied by a partner, the partnership is liable for the loss.

Summary: Provides for partnership liability for torts and other wrongful acts of partners.

Parallel U.P.A.:   §§ 13–14.

Important Changes: Covers the misconduct formerly covered by the above sections of the U.P.A., as well as eliminating some gaps in U.P.A. coverage: "Actionable conduct" embraces strict liability claims, unlike the U.P.A.'s "wrongful act or omission"; the partnership may not, as it could under the U.P.A., take on the acting partner's immunity from suit;[84] and, unlike under the U.P.A., a partner can bring tort suits against the partnership.[85]

Analysis: None.

---

[84] For a discussion of this issue, see Bromberg & Ribstein, § 4.07(g).
[85] This change is reinforced by § 405(b)(3).

§ 8.306.   PARTNER'S LIABILITY

Section 306

(a) Except as otherwise provided in subsections (b) and (c), all partners are liable jointly and severally for all obligations of the partnership unless otherwise agreed by the claimant or provided by law.

(b) A person admitted as a partner into an existing partnership is not personally liable for any partnership obligation incurred before the person's admission as a partner.

(c) An obligation of a partnership incurred while the partnership is a limited liability partnership, whether arising in contract, tort, or otherwise, is solely the obligation of the partnership. A partner is not personally liable, directly or indirectly, including by way of contribution or otherwise, for such a partnership obligation solely by reason of being or so acting as a partner. This subsection applies notwithstanding anything inconsistent in the partnership agreement that existed immediately before the vote required to become a limited liability partnership under Section 1001(b).

Summary: Provides that all partners are liable jointly and severally for all partnership obligations unless otherwise agreed by the claimant or provided by law; and that a person admitted as a partner into an existing partnership is not personally liable for any partnership obligation incurred before the person's admission as a partner.

Parallel U.P.A.:   §§ 15, 17, 41(7).

Important Changes: Partners are jointly and severally liable for all partnership obligations and not only for tort-type liabilities as under U.P.A. § 15.

Analysis: Although this section broadens the application of joint and several liability, it changes the traditional meaning of that liability. *See* the Analysis below of § 307.

Section 306 continues the rule in U.P.A. § 17 that a partner's personal assets are not subject to debts incurred prior to the partner's admission. Recent cases have disagreed about whether this includes amounts that accrue after admission in connection with pre-admission contracts.[86] Perhaps this section should be

---

[86] *Compare* Citizens Bank of Mass. v. Parham-Woodman Med. Assocs., 874 F. Supp. 705 (E.D. Va. 1995) (Va. law; partners who entered partnership after date of construction loan agreement were not personally liable disbursements made after partners joined partnership), *with* Conklin Farm v. Leibowitz, 274 N.J. Super. 525, 644 A.2d 687 (N.J. Super. 1994) (new partner

clarified to provide that the obligation is incurred when the partnership enters into the underlying contract.[87] In any event, partnerships and their creditors should be careful to draft their contracts so as to clarify the liability of subsequently admitted partners.

Section 306 is not included in the § 103(b) exclusive list of R.U.P.A. provisions that the partnership agreement may not waive. Since, R.U.P.A. § 103(b)(10) provides that the agreement may not "restrict rights of third parties under this [Act]," a partnership agreement could not effectively *restrict* liability to third parties, either by limiting liability or by making it joint rather than joint and several. However, the agreement apparently could *expand* liability, for example by eliminating the exhaustion requirement under R.U.P.A. § 307. Also, R.U.P.A. § 306(a) permits enforcement of contracts varying partners' joint and several liability if agreed by the claimant. Nevertheless, R.U.P.A. § 103 does not explicitly permit the enforcement of *other* agreements that restrict third-party rights, such as agreements expanding the exhaustion requirement, even if the third party joins in the agreement. Comment 2 to R.U.P.A. § 103 says that a restriction to which the third party has agreed is enforceable, but as just noted this appears inconsistent with the "black letter."

LLP Cross-reference: The limitation on partners' vicarious liability provided for in subsection (c), and state variations on this provision, are discussed in Chapter 3.

§ 8.307. ACTIONS BY AND AGAINST PARTNERSHIP AND PARTNERS

Section 307

(a) A partnership may sue and be sued in the name of the partnership.

---

was personally liable for interest on preexisting partnership promissory note that accrued after her admission into partnership). *See generally* Bromberg & Ribstein, § 7.18(b).

[87] This issue, as well as an equivalent issue concerning the new partner's tort liability, is clarified by Tex. Rev. Civ. Stat. Ann. art. 6132b-§ 3.07, which provides that the new partner has no liability for a partnership obligation that "relates to an action taken or omissions occurring before the partner's admission to the partnership; or . . . arises before or after the partner's admission under a contract or commitment entered into before the partner's admission to the partnership." Interestingly, the Delaware legislature recently added language to § 15-306(c) to specify that partners in an LLP are not liable for obligations "incurred" while the partnership is an LLP or "arising out of or related to circumstances or events occurring while partnership is a limited liability partnership" but does not add the same clarifying language to subsection (b). Ky. Rev. Stat. § 362.1-306 makes a similar clarification in the LLP subsection only.

(b) Except as otherwise provided in subsection (f), action may be brought against the partnership and any or all of the partners in the same action or in separate actions.

(c) A judgment against a partnership is not by itself a judgment against a partner. A judgment against a partnership may not be satisfied from a partner's assets unless there is also a judgment against the partner.

(d) A judgment creditor of a partner may not levy execution against the assets of the partner to satisfy a judgment based on a claim against the partnership unless the partner is personally liable for the claim under Section 306 and:

(1) a judgment based on the same claim has been obtained against the partnership and a writ of execution on the judgment has been returned unsatisfied in whole or in part;

(2) the partnership is a debtor in bankruptcy;

(3) the partner has agreed that the creditor need not exhaust partnership assets;

(4) a court grants permission to the judgment creditor to levy execution against the assets of a partner based on a finding that partnership assets subject to execution are clearly insufficient to satisfy the judgment, that exhaustion of partnership assets is excessively burdensome, or that the grant of permission is an appropriate exercise of the court's equitable powers; or

(5) liability is imposed on the partner by law or contract independent of the existence of the partnership.

(e) This section applies to any partnership liability or obligation resulting from a representation by a partner or purported partner under Section 308.

(f) A partner is not a proper party to an action against a partnership if that partner is not personally liable for the claim under Section 306.

Summary: Provides that partnership may sue and be sued in its own name; that actions against the partnership and any or all partners may be brought together or separately; that only a judgment against a partner individually may be satisfied from a partner's assets; and that a judgment creditor may levy against a partner's assets only after an unsatisfied levy against the partnership, except in certain circumstances.

Parallel U.P.A.:   None.

Important Changes: State law on the issues in this section varies.[88] The most important change from current state law concerns the "exhaustion" requirement in subsection (d), which prevents creditors from levying against partners of non-bankrupt partnerships without first levying unsuccessfully against the partnership or convincing a court that levy would be unsuccessful. This rule is

---

[88] *See* Bromberg & Ribstein, §§ 5.08–5.13.

similar in effect to most states' rules for joint liability[89] but differs from the rule in most places that exhaustion is not required for joint and several liability claims.[90]

Analysis: An across-the-board exhaustion requirement makes some sense. It is consistent with current partnership law that requires application of partnership property to pay liabilities and partner contributions to make up any shortfall,[91] and with bankruptcy law that lets the trustee pursue general partners only if partnership assets are insufficient.[92] Requiring exhaustion obviously helps partners by saving them the expense of paying the creditor and then maintaining an indemnification action against the firm. At the same time, it may not hurt many creditors, for whom it is often not worthwhile to monitor and pursue the wealth of individual partners. Where creditors do find it worthwhile to rely on individual partners, they can and do obtain guarantees that permit direct actions against the partners. Thus, the exhaustion requirement may not significantly increase partnerships' credit costs.[93]

Yet there are also substantial arguments against switching to an exhaustion rule.[94] Requiring exhaustion for both joint and joint and several liability will increase litigation costs for tort creditors who may have no opportunity to contract around the rule. If courts require only a single return of execution, exhaustion may not be a serious problem. But exhaustion may be difficult if tort creditors must pursue partnership assets in several states. Finally, the exhaustion rule may be unnecessary protection for partners in light of the broad availability of various forms of limited liability, including limited liability companies and limited liability partnerships.[95] As long as firms easily can contract out of unlimited

---

[89] *See* Moseley, Hallgarten, Estabrook & Weeden, Inc. v. Ellis, 849 F.2d 264, 271 (7th Cir. 1988) (Ill. law); Commonwealth Capital Inv. Corp. v. McElmurry, 302 N.W.2d 222, 225 (Mich. App. 1980); Diamond Nat'l Corp. v. Thunderbird Hotel, Inc., 85 Nev. 271, 454 P.2d 13, 15 (1969).

[90] *See* Foster v. Daon Corp., 713 F.2d 149, 151 (5th Cir. 1983) (Tex. law); Head v. Vulcan Painters, Inc., 541 So. 2d 11 (Ala. 1989); Head v. Henry Tyler Constr. Corp., 539 So. 2d 196, 199 (Ala. 1988); Catalina Mortgage Co. v. Monier, 800 P.2d 574 (Ariz. 1990, en banc); Phillips v. Cook, 239 Md. 215, 210 A.2d 743, 746–47 (1965). For discussions of the exhaustion requirement, see Bromberg & Ribstein, § 5.08(d)–(g), and § 3.08, supra (as to LLPs).

[91] *See* U.P.A. § 40(a), (c), (d).

[92] *See* 11 U.S.C. § 723.

[93] *See* Ribstein, The Deregulation of Limited Liability and the Death of Partnership, 70 Wash. U. L.Q. 419, 430–31 (1992) (discussing this as a justification for limited liability in closely held firms).

[94] The arguments against the R.U.P.A. approach are well summarized in Hynes, The Revised Uniform Partnership Act: Some Comments on the Latest Draft of R.U.P.A., 19 Fla. St. U. L. Rev. 727, 730–39 (1992).

[95] The application of exhaustion rules to LLPs is discussed supra in § 3.08.

liability, there is little reason for the partnership standard form to move closer to limited liability through an exhaustion requirement.[96]

Section 307 also has potentially undesirable effects on partnership bankruptcy. Section 307(d)(2) provides that exhaustion is unnecessary if the partnership is the subject of a voluntary or involuntary bankruptcy proceeding. In other words, as soon as such a proceeding commences, the partners' individual assets are exposed to execution for partnership debts. This undoubtedly will deter partners from filing voluntary proceedings and therefore may discourage the use of Chapter 11 to reorganize partnerships. It also may encourage creditors to bring involuntary proceedings solely as a way of reaching partners' individual assets even where bankruptcy is otherwise inappropriate.

Note that R.U.P.A. provides for some potentially broad exceptions to the exhaustion requirement. Section 307(d)(3) excuses exhaustion if that "is an appropriate exercise of the court's inherent equitable powers." The statute nowhere guides the court's exercise of discretion. Subsection 307(d)(5) excuses exhaustion if "liability is imposed on the partner by law or contract independent of the existence of the partnership." This exception allows creditors to sue partners directly for their own misconduct, as where they have negligently supervised their colleagues.[97]

R.U.P.A. § 307 may introduce some confusion depending on the existing law in enacting states. What was formerly "joint" liability in some states will be "joint and several" under R.U.P.A.[98] At the same time, R.U.P.A. would defeat the main point of that recharacterization by requiring exhaustion even under joint and several liability, although many states had required it only for joint liability. Finally, R.U.P.A. would cast further doubt on that already complicated state of affairs through its exceptions to the exhaustion requirement, particularly the one for "direct" liability.

For the above reasons, legislators should proceed cautiously in deciding whether to adopt the exhaustion requirements. Also, creditors dealing with R.U.P.A. partnerships should consider the effect of the exhaustion rule and the potential advantages of obtaining direct obligations from R.U.P.A. partners.

LLP Cross-reference: None.

---

[96] Conversely, if the partnership form does move closer to limited liability through an exhaustion rule, this arguably weakens the argument against expanding limited liability through the LLC form. *See* Ribstein, note 93, supra, at 430–31.

[97] For application of this rule to LLPs, see § 3.08(c), supra.

[98] *See* PNC Bank, N.A. v. Farinacci, 964 N.E.2d 1124 (Ohio Ct. App. 2011) (applying joint liability to partnership formed prior to the effective date of the legislature's adoption of the RUPA-based Ohio Uniform Partnership Act). In addition, the court assessed liability equally among the partners, though partners had specified varying allocations of profits among themselves in the partnership agreement.

§ 8.308.   LIABILITY OF PURPORTED PARTNER

Section 308

(a) If a person, by words or conduct, purports to be a partner, or consents to being represented by another as a partner, in a partnership or with one or more persons not partners, the purported partner is liable to a person to whom the representation is made, if that person, relying on the representation, enters into a transaction with the actual or purported partnership. If the representation, either by the purported partner or by a person with the purported partner's consent, is made in a public manner, the purported partner is liable to a person who relies upon the purported partnership even if the purported partner is not aware of being held out as a partner to the claimant. If partnership liability results, the purported partner is liable with respect to that liability as if the purported partner were a partner. If no partnership liability results, the purported partner is liable with respect to that liability jointly and severally with any other person consenting to the representation.

(b) If a person is thus represented to be a partner in an existing partnership, or with one or more persons not partners, the purported partner is an agent of persons consenting to the representation to bind them to the same extent and in the same manner as if the purported partner were a partner, with respect to persons who enter into transactions in reliance upon the representation. If all of the partners of the existing partnership consent to the representation, a partnership act or obligation results. If fewer than all of the partners of the existing partnership consent to the representation, the person acting and the partners consenting to the representation are jointly and severally liable.

(c) A person is not liable as a partner merely because the person is named by another in a statement of partnership authority.

(d) A person does not continue to be liable as a partner merely because of a failure to file a statement of dissociation or to amend a statement of partnership authority to indicate the partner's dissociation from the partnership.

(e) Except as otherwise provided in subsections (a) and (b), persons who are not partners as to each other are not liable as partners to other persons.

Summary: Deals with liability of a person who is represented as a partner and effect of filed statements on partnership status, and provides that those who are not partners among themselves are not such as to third parties liability apart from this section.

Parallel U.P.A.:   §§ 7(1), 16.

Important Changes: Basically the same as U.P.A. §§ 7(1) and 16, except that subsections (c) and (d) provide that a person is not liable as a partner merely because the person is named by another in a statement of partnership authority or because of a failure to make a filing indicating the partner's dissociation from the partnership.

Analysis: The potential impact of filings on partners' estoppel liability is discussed elsewhere in this book.[99]

§ 8.401. PARTNER'S RIGHTS AND DUTIES

Section 401

(a) Each partner is deemed to have an account that is:

(1) credited with an amount equal to the money plus the value of any other property, net of the amount of any liabilities, the partner contributes to the partnership and the partner's share of the partnership profits; and

(2) charged with an amount equal to the money plus the value of any other property, net of the amount of any liabilities, distributed by the partnership to the partner and the partner's share of the partnership losses.

(b) Each partner is entitled to an equal share of the partnership profits and is chargeable with a share of the partnership losses in proportion to the partner's share of the profits.

(c) A partnership shall reimburse a partner for payments made and indemnify a partner for liabilities incurred by the partner in the ordinary course of the business of the partnership or for the preservation of its business or property.

(d) A partnership shall reimburse a partner for an advance to the partnership beyond the amount of capital the partner agreed to contribute.

(e) A payment or advance made by a partner which gives rise to a partnership obligation under subsection (c) or (d) constitutes a loan to the partnership which accrues interest from the date of the payment or advance.

(f) Each partner has equal rights in the management and conduct of the partnership business.

(g) A partner may use or possess partnership property only on behalf of the partnership.

(h) A partner is not entitled to remuneration for services performed for the partnership, except for reasonable compensation for services rendered in winding up the business of the partnership.

---

[99] *See* analyses of R.U.P.A. §§ 303 and 704, and § 3.10, supra.

(i) A person may become a partner only with the consent of all of the partners.

(j) A difference arising as to a matter in the ordinary course of business of a partnership may be decided by a majority of the partners. An act outside the ordinary course of business of a partnership and an amendment to the partnership agreement may be undertaken only with the consent of all of the partners.

(k) This section does not affect the obligations of a partnership to other persons under Section 301.

Summary: Provides for financial and management rights of partners.

Parallel U.P.A.:   § 18.

Important Changes: Subsections (a) and (b) provide that partners are "deemed" to have capital accounts; subsection (h) provides for compensation of all winding up partners; subsection (j) makes clear the voting rule implicit in the U.P.A. that unanimity is required for extraordinary matters and not merely amendments to the agreement.[100]

Analysis: R.U.P.A. § 401 generally retains the rules in U.P.A. § 18 concerning the partners' equal management and financial rights, loss sharing in relation to profits, rights to indemnification and compensation for services, and interest on advances.[101]

The major difference between U.P.A. and R.U.P.A. regarding financial rights is the requirement in subsections (a) and (b) that each partner is "deemed to have an account" that is "credited with" partner contributions and shares of profits and "charged with" distributions and partner shares of losses. This change may have uncertain consequences for the sort of informal partnerships for which the statute is most needed. Many such firms have nothing resembling partner "accounts," and indeed may not even have been intentionally organized as partnerships. A requirement that such partners are "deemed" to have accounts may mean only that, on dissolution or breakup, the court will establish capital accounts for purposes of determining the partners' shares. If so, R.U.P.A. should have provided for capital accounts only in the distribution provision, § 807. In any event, reconstructing the partners' accounts may be an unnecessarily difficult exercise in informal partnerships. In short, while a provision for capital accounts makes good sense to any lawyer who has drafted a partnership agreement, it does not necessarily make sense for a partnership statute that is designed specifically for firms that do not have agreements.

---

[100] The U.P.A. rule is discussed in Bromberg & Ribstein, § 6.03.

[101] These rules are discussed generally in Bromberg & Ribstein, §§ 6.02, 6.03.

R.U.P.A. also changes the U.P.A. by providing in subsection (h) that partners are entitled to compensation for winding-up services even where the dissolution was not caused by the death of a partner.[102] The general no-compensation rule reflects the partners' expectations, in the absence of contrary agreement, that all partners will make combined capital, labor, and credit contributions to the firm and that these contributions will be compensated through the partners' profit shares.[103] There is no reason to assume that these expectations change when the partners' participation in the firm changes from conducting the business to winding it up unless a partner's death forces a greater workload on the survivors.[104]

The same considerations apply to winding up by arduous completion of law cases or other professional work. Moreover, additional considerations justify the no-compensation rule in this context, including the fact that it is difficult to value each partner's contribution to the result.[105] There are also counter-arguments. Forcing withdrawing partners to finish cases without extra compensation can lock them into the firm, and partners who must work for no extra fee may lack adequate incentives to do the work properly. But the partners might favor a rule that promotes the firm's stability, and professionals have reputational incentives to work hard even without a fee that accurately reflects their contribution.[106]

As a result of the foregoing considerations, legislators should consider carefully whether they want to adopt the change regarding winding-up compensation, and partners should consider varying the R.U.P.A. default rule by a contrary provision in their partnership agreements.

State variations

Delaware provides that partners may delegate to others their rights and powers to manage and control the business and affairs of the partnership without jeopardizing their partner status;[107] that, subject to the partnership agreement, that a partnership may "indemnify and hold harmless any partner or other person from and against any and all claims and demands whatsoever;"[108] for contractual appraisal rights in connection with amendments to the agreement, mergers, consolidations and asset sales;[109] for agreements regarding classes and voting, in-

---

[102] *See* Mark I. Weinstein, The Revised Uniform Partnership Act: An Analysis of its Impact on the Relationship of Law Firm Dissolution, Contingent Fee Cases and the No Compensation Rule, 33 Duq. L. Rev. 857 (1995).

[103] *See* Bromberg & Ribstein, § 6.02(g)(1).

[104] *See* Bromberg & Ribstein, § 7.08(e)(2).

[105] *See* Bromberg & Ribstein.

[106] *See* Bromberg & Ribstein.

[107] Del. Code Ann., tit. 6, § 15-401(l).

[108] Del. Code Ann., tit. 6, § 15-110.

[109] Del. Code Ann., tit. 6, § 15-120.

cluding voting by written consent or proxy,[110] and for penalties for violation of the agreement.[111]

Oregon provides that a partnership agreement may establish classes and provide for future classes.[112]

Tennessee includes the above Delaware provisions for delegation of rights without jeopardizing partner status, for classes and voting and for voting by written consent.[113]

Texas reduces the confusion created by assuming the existence of accounts where there are none by providing that the partner is "entitled to be credited with an equal share of the partnership's profits and is chargeable with a share of the partnership's capital or operating losses in proportion to the partnership's share of the profits."[114]

LLP Cross-reference: Section 3.09(f).

§ 8.402.   DISTRIBUTIONS IN KIND

Section 402

A partner has no right to receive, and may not be required to accept, a distribution in kind.

Summary: A partner is neither entitled to receive nor required to accept a distribution in kind.

Parallel U.P.A.:   § 38(1).

Important Changes: Implicit in the U.P.A.

Analysis: This is a suitable default rule that follows from the partners' expectations of equal treatment in the absence of contrary agreement.

---

[110] Del. Code Ann., tit. 6, § 15-407.
[111] Del. Code Ann., tit. 6, § 15-408.
[112] Or. Rev. Stat. § 67.140(12).
[113] Tenn. Code Ann. § 61-1-401(*l*), -407.
[114] Tex. Bus. Orgs. Code § 1.152.202.

State variation

Delaware provides: "A partner, regardless of the nature of the partner's contribution, has no right to demand and receive any distribution from a partnership in kind. A partner may not be compelled to accept a distribution of any asset in kind from a partnership to the extent that the percentage of the asset distributed to the partner exceeds a percentage of that asset which is equal to the percentage in which the partner shares in distributions from the partnership. A partner may be compelled to accept a distribution of any asset in kind from a partnership to the extent that the percentage of the asset distributed to the partner is equal to a percentage of that asset which is equal to the percentage in which the partner shares in distributions from the partnership."[115] It also includes limitations on distributions that apply to all partnerships, as well as liabilities that apply only to partners in LLPs.[116]

§ 8.403. PARTNER'S RIGHT TO INFORMATION

Section 403

(a) A partnership shall keep its books and records, if any, at its chief executive office.

(b) A partnership shall provide partners and their agents and attorneys access to its books and records. It shall provide former partners and their agents and attorneys access to books and records pertaining to the period during which they were partners. The right of access provides the opportunity to inspect and copy books and records during ordinary business hours. A partnership may impose a reasonable charge, covering the costs of labor and material, for copies of documents furnished.

(c) Each partner and the partnership shall furnish to a partner, and to the legal representative of a deceased partner or partner under legal disability:

(1) without demand, any information concerning the partnership's business and affairs reasonably required for the proper exercise of the partner's rights and duties under the partnership agreement or this [Act]; and

(2) on demand, any other information concerning the partnership's business and affairs, except to the extent the demand or the information demanded is unreasonable or otherwise improper under the circumstances.

---

[115] Del. Code Ann., tit. 6, § 15-402.

[116] Del. Code Ann., tit. 6, § 15-309, discussed in § 4.04(d), supra. In addition to Delaware, several states provide for restrictions on distributions. These are listed in Chapter 3, Table 3-1, and discussed in § 4.04(d), supra.

Summary: Provides for partners' access to books and records and for partners' rights to receive information.

Parallel U.P.A.:   §§ 19–20.

Important Changes: Clarifies that the partnership has no duty to have books and records, that partners' agents and attorneys and former partners shall have access to books and records, that the time of inspection is limited to reasonable business hours, and that the partnership may charge for copies furnished.

Analysis:

Books and Records. This section, like the equivalent U.P.A. provision, awkwardly provides for a "partnership" duty to keep books and records at a particular place without stating any penalty for breach of the duty. It would be better simply to give partners the only right they care about—a right to inspect partnership records at the firm's business office.

Even more importantly, the act precludes the parties from contracting to restrict access to books and records. R.U.P.A. § 103(b)(2) provides that the partnership agreement may not "unreasonably restrict a partner's right of access to books and records under Section 403(b)."[117] There is a question whether this restriction on private ordering is appropriate. The partners may want to protect confidential information, or to ensure that obstreperous partners cannot badger the firm with burdensome information requests. The prohibition on agreements restricting access at least gives antagonistic or litigious partners a basis for challenging clear, and perhaps even "good faith," restrictions to access that fall within the nebulous "unreasonable" category. On the other hand, an absolute right of access to books and records makes it harder for partners to conceal self-dealing or other misconduct. In general, a prohibition on eliminating such a basic partner right arguably is justified on the ground that such elimination necessarily conflicts with the existence of a partnership relationship.

Other information. The most controversial aspects of the general disclosure provisions in this section concern the "demand" requirement. U.P.A. § 20 required disclosure "on demand true and full information of all things affecting the partnership." The case law has generally overlooked the U.P.A. § 20 "demand"

---

[117] This limitation apparently does not apply to restrictions on access by *former* partners. Such agreements may be particularly important in light of R.U.P.A.'s rule giving such partners access "to books and records pertaining to the period during which they were partners." On the one hand, former partners whose interests are being liquidated may want information, for example, regarding the period between the time of dissociation and the time of settlement of accounts on dissolution. On the other hand, access by former partners may raise troubling confidentiality problems. These points illustrate the difficulty of drafting specific rules that are right for all firms and, accordingly, the need to permit private contracting.

requirement and compelled disclosure in other appropriate circumstances, consistent with the expectations of those in a fiduciary relationship.[118] A change in the statute therefore would have been appropriate if only to align it with the case law. One state's variation on the U.P.A., in an attempt to align the statute with the case law, adopted a "just and reasonable" standard as a *substitute* for the demand requirement.[119] The 1990 R.U.P.A. draft adopted this variation. But the final version reflects a complicated compromise regarding demand. Subsection (c)(1) provides for disclosure *without demand* of "information concerning the partnership's business and affairs reasonably required for the proper exercise of the partner's rights and duties under the partnership agreement." Subsection (c)(2) requires disclosure *on demand* "of any other information concerning the partnership's business and affairs, except to the extent the demand or the information demanded is unreasonable or otherwise improper under the circumstances."

R.U.P.A.'s compromise is not only inconsistent with the case law under the U.P.A. but is unclear and unduly complex for the informal firms for which it is intended. Partners must now try to determine when information must be provided without demand under subsection (c)(1) because it is "reasonably required for proper exercise of the partner's rights and duties under the partnership agreement." For a partner who is involved in management, this could include anything relating to the partnership. On the other hand, under subsection (c)(2) partners may be able to resist disclosure even of demanded information if the information or demand falls within the nebulous category of "unreasonable or otherwise improper under the circumstances." These terms await clarification by generations of case law.

---

[118] *See* Witter v. Torbett, 604 F. Supp. 298 (W.D. Va. 1984) (joint venture); Reed v. Robilio, 273 F. Supp. 954 (W.D. Tenn. 1967), *aff'd*, 400 F.2d 730 (6th Cir. 1968) (purchase of estate's interest by surviving partner; duty held not breached); Sutton v. Fleming, 602 So. 2d 228 (La. App. 1992) (joint venturer breached fiduciary duty by failing to inform joint venturer that $100,000 of purchase price was actually finder's fee, portion of which was paid to co-joint venturer); Appletree Square I Ltd. P'ship v. Investmark, Inc., 494 N.W.2d 889, 893 (Minn. App. 1993) (Uniform Limited Partnership Act provision that limited partners have the right, "upon reasonable demand," to obtain information from the general partners, like the disclosure requirement in the U.P.A.s, only addresses the narrow duty of partners to respond to requests for information and does not negate a partner's broad common law duty to disclose all material facts even in the absence of limited partner demand, reasoning that "[t]o hold that partners may replace their broad duty of disclosure with a narrow duty to render information upon demand would destroy the fiduciary character of their relationship, and it would also invite fraud. Unless partners knew what questions to ask, they would have no right to know material information about the business. In this case, if respondents knew the building was contaminated with asbestos and if they reasonably should have known their partners did not know about the asbestos, they may have breached their fiduciary duty of disclosure"); Starr v. International Realty, Ltd., 271 Or. 396, 533 P.2d 165 (1975) (failure to disclose receipt of side compensation from vendor of property; active concealment not required); Johnson v. Peckham, 132 Tex. 148, 120 S.W.2d 786, 120 A.L.R. 720 (1938). *See generally* Bromberg & Ribstein, § 6.06(a).

[119] *See* Ga. Code Ann. § 14-8-20.

It is important to keep in mind that, as Comment 3 to this section points out, disclosure may be required even without demand and apart from this section under the obligation of "good faith and fair dealing" in § 404(d), discussed below, and in connection with the partner's management right under U.P.A. § 401. If so, the elimination of the "demand" requirement is superfluous and misleading.

As Comment 3 to this section makes clear, unlike the books and records duty, the general disclosure duty is subject to contrary agreement. In view of the problems discussed above with the default disclosure rules, partnerships governed by R.U.P.A. should be especially careful to define their disclosure obligations in their agreements. Legislators should consider alleviating this contracting burden by preserving the simple U.P.A. default rule and the precedential effect of the many cases that interpret this rule.

State variation

Delaware provides for a right of access on reasonable demand, an action to enforce, that the partnership agreement may provide for confidentiality, and that the partners' rights to obtain information "may be restricted in an original partnership agreement or in any subsequent amendment approved or adopted by all of the partners and in compliance with any applicable requirements of the partnership agreement."[120]

§ 8.404.   GENERAL STANDARDS OF PARTNER'S CONDUCT

Section 404

(a) The only fiduciary duties a partner owes to the partnership and the other partners are the duty of loyalty and the duty of care set forth in subsections (b) and (c).

(b) A partner's duty of loyalty to the partnership and the other partners is limited to the following:

(1) to account to the partnership and hold as trustee for it any property, profit, or benefit derived by the partner in the conduct and winding up of the partnership business or derived from a use by the partner of partnership property, including the appropriation of a partnership opportunity;

---

[120] Del. Code Ann., tit. 6, § 15-403.

(2) to refrain from dealing with the partnership in the conduct or winding up of the partnership business as or on behalf of a party having an interest adverse to the partnership; and

(3) to refrain from competing with the partnership in the conduct of the partnership business before the dissolution of the partnership.

(c) A partner's duty of care to the partnership and the other partners in the conduct and winding up of the partnership business is limited to refraining from engaging in grossly negligent or reckless conduct, intentional misconduct, or a knowing violation of law.

(d) A partner shall discharge the duties to the partnership and the other partners under this [Act] or under the partnership agreement and exercise any rights consistently with the obligation of good faith and fair dealing.

(e) A partner does not violate a duty or obligation under this [Act] or under the partnership agreement merely because the partner's conduct furthers the partner's own interest.

(f) A partner may lend money to and transact other business with the partnership, and as to each loan or transaction the rights and obligations of the partner are the same as those of a person who is not a partner, subject to other applicable law.

(g) This section applies to a person winding up the partnership business as the personal or legal representative of the last surviving partner as if the person were a partner.

Summary: Provides that the only fiduciary duties of partners are the duties of loyalty and care provided for in this section and that partners also have an obligation of good faith and fair dealing.

Parallel U.P.A.:   § 21.

Important Changes: The section adds a duty of care and the obligation of good faith and fair dealing and expands the statutory definition of the duty of loyalty. Other changes are discussed in the following **Analysis**.

Analysis: U.P.A. § 21 provides simply and comprehensively that a partner must account to the partnership for benefits appropriated without co-partner consent. An enormous body of case law has evolved under this section to deal with every variety of fiduciary breach.[121] Accordingly, U.P.A. § 21 should be changed only with great care to avoid unsettling a valuable stock of existing law.

R.U.P.A. § 404 does make some worthwhile changes to U.P.A. § 21. The duty-of-loyalty language derived from the U.P.A. omits the U.P.A.'s confusing reference to conduct in the "formation" of the firm. This language made no

---

[121] *See generally* Bromberg & Ribstein, § 6.07.

sense, since the partners can have no duties as such until their partnership relationship has been formed.[122] Also, the first sentence of the section makes clear that the duties of care and loyalty are "the only fiduciary duties a partner owes." The Reporter has said that this language would facilitate contracting around the duties.[123] Unfortunately, however, this purpose is negated by the statute's addition of the wild card good faith obligation and limitations on contracting discussed below.

Aside from the salutary changes just noted, many of R.U.P.A.'s changes regarding fiduciary duties are questionable for the reasons discussed below.

The Duty of Loyalty (§ 404(b)).   Subsection (b) revises the duty of loyalty by adding to the general U.P.A. duty not to appropriate benefits without co-partner consent specific duties to refrain from self-dealing or competition with the partnership. These provisions were added because § 404 now is intended to be an exhaustive list of duties. Since the case law under the U.P.A. had supported these duties under the U.P.A. language, or as a matter of common law, R.U.P.A. probably has only codified prior law. R.U.P.A. should be altered to clarify that the new categories are only subcategories of the original R.U.P.A. definition of the partner's fiduciary duties in order to remove any possible implication that partners' duties have been expanded from prior law.

The Duty of Care (§ 404(c)).   R.U.P.A. § 404(c) provides that a partner's duty of care is limited to refraining from engaging in "grossly negligent or reckless conduct, intentional misconduct, or a knowing violation of law." The gross negligence standard is generally consistent with current law. Courts have held that partners are not subject to a duty of ordinary care in the management of the business.[124] However, the new statutory language, such as "intentional misconduct" and "knowing violation of law," may have to be clarified by future cases.

Hopefully the new R.U.P.A. provision will not change partnership law by leading courts to apply results from cases involving other types of business associations that are based on similarly phrased standards.[125] Whether a duty of care is justified depends on a careful evaluation of the costs and benefits of the duty in

---

[122] *See* Bromberg & Ribstein § 6.02(a)(7). The effect of dissociation on partners' fiduciary duties is covered by R.U.P.A. § 603, discussed infra.

[123] *See* Weidner, The Revised Uniform Partnership Act Midstream: Major Policy Decisions, 21 U. Tol. L. Rev. 825, 856 (1990).

[124] *See* Northen v. Tatum, 164 Ala. 36a, 51 So. 17 (1909); Wirum & Cash Architects v. Cash, 837 P.2d 692 (Alaska 1992); Johnson v. Weber, 166 Ariz. 528, 803 P.2d 939 (1990); Snell v. De Land, 136 Ill. 533, 27 N.E. 183 (1891); Thomas v. Milfelt, 222 S.W.2d 359 (Mo. App. 1949); Knipe v. Livingston, 209 Pa. 49, 57 A. 1130 (1904); Ferguson v. Williams, 670 S.W.2d 327 (Tex. Civ. App. 1984); Duffy v. Piazza Constr., Inc., 62 Wn. App. 19, 815 P.2d 267 (1991) (joint venturers). *See also* Borys v. Rudd, 207 Ill. App. 3d 610, 566 N.E.2d 310 (1991) (no duty to account for business decision to settle litigation or for late payment of taxes). *See generally* Bromberg & Ribstein, § 6.07(f).

[125] Kan. Rev. Stat. Ann. § 362.1-404(5), in fact, was recently amended to clarify that the corporate law doctrine of entire fairness review does not apply to a partner's breach of the duty of loyalty.

the particular context in which it is applied. In the typical informal, very closely held business for which the partnership standard form should be designed, the duty of care may be wholly unnecessary. The partners have ample incentives to monitor their co-partners because of their liability for partnership debts and their equal contributions to the firm. The partnership statute accordingly assumes that the partners will participate equally in management rather than delegating management responsibilities. While there is authority analogizing general partners to corporate directors,[126] this is in the limited partnership context. Limited partnerships are closely analogous to corporations because of the passivity of limited partners and the common practice of incorporated general partners.[127]

"Good Faith and Fair Dealing" (§ 404(d)). Subsection (d) includes a new and undefined "obligation of good faith and fair dealing." A statutory "obligation of good faith and fair dealing" hardly seems objectionable. A partnership agreement, like other contracts, is subject to judicial interpretation of the contract language in light of the parties' expectations. That is particularly so for long-term business relationships like partnerships which the parties cannot practicably plan in detail at the outset. In effect, this interpretation process requires the parties to act in "good faith" consistent with their mutual expectations rather than merely literally complying with their agreement. Since this principle ensures that the parties' conduct conforms to their underlying deal, the parties obviously cannot contract out of it. The parties can, however, vary the application of the principle in particular cases by varying their deal.

The problem with § 404(d) is that it erroneously characterizes "good faith," like other fiduciary duties, as a "standard[ ] of partner's conduct." Including "good faith and fair dealing" as a separate obligation in the same section that defines fiduciary duties implies at least a close analogy between good faith and fiduciary duties. Yet as Comment 4 to § 404 points out, good faith "is not a fiduciary duty arising out of the partners' special relationship." Fiduciary duties are a particular type of duty owed by one who exercises a discretionary power on behalf of another.[128] By contrast, "good faith" is simply a principle that generally guides interpretation of every contract. Unlike fiduciary duties, the "good faith" obligation does not generally force contracting parties to sacrifice their own interests in making or enforcing bargains. For example, in *Market Street Associates Limited Partnership v. Frey*,[129] Judge Posner held that a lessee had no

---

[126] *See* Wyler v. Feuer, 85 Cal. App. 3d 392, 149 Cal. Rptr. 626 (1979); Trustees of Gen. Elec. Pension Trust v. Levenson, 1992 WL 41820 (Del. Ch. 1992). The Texas Revised Partnership Act applies an ordinary care standard subject to a business judgment rule taken from corporation law. Tex. Rev. Civ. Stat. Ann. art. 6132b-4.04(c), (d).

[127] *See* Ribstein, An Applied Theory of Limited Partnership, 37 Emory L.J. 835, 868-70 (1988).

[128] *See* United States v. Chestman, 947 F.2d 551 (2d Cir. en banc, 1991), *cert. denied*, 112 S. Ct. 1759.

[129] 941 F.2d 58 (7th Cir. 1991).

duty to point out to a lessor that its turning down financing would trigger an obligation under the lease to sell the property for less than market value. The confusion of these duties is apparent from Comment 3 to § 403, which says that the § 404(d) good faith obligation may require affirmative disclosure, an obligation that arises only out of a *fiduciary* relationship. In short, R.U.P.A.'s new "good faith" standard awaits clarification by case law.

Nonwaivability of Fiduciary Duties (§ 103).   R.U.P.A. § 103(b)(3)–(5) provide that the partners may not eliminate the duty of loyalty or obligation of good faith, and may not "unreasonably reduce" the duty of care. These provisions raise serious policy issues.[130] State variations on this provision broadening the effect of the agreement are discussed above in Section 8.103.

R.U.P.A. may alter decades of prior law under the U.P.A. U.P.A. § 21, the U.P.A.'s sole substantive fiduciary duty section, provides that a partner must account only for those profits derived "without the consent of the other partners." The partners also may authorize partner compensation under the lead-in to U.P.A. § 18, which is no different in effect from allowing a partner to take partnership opportunities as part of his compensation. Consistent with these provisions, the courts have enforced partnership agreements permitting partners to compete with the partnership[131] and to engage in self-dealing.[132] Delaware, a leading business jurisdiction, has enacted a comprehensive authorization of freedom of contract in limited partnerships.[133] The Comments to § 103 cite only one case in support of the anti-waiver rule, *Labovitz v. Dolan*.[134] This was a case in which a general partner abused a discretionary power over dividends for a purpose clearly not permitted by the partnership agreement—to force a distress sale by limited partners, who had to pay taxes on partnership's earnings. *Labovitz* has been limited to its facts by more recent Illinois cases.[135]

Mandatory fiduciary duties are questionable policy. Fiduciary duties can be costly to the partnership because they may unduly deter the agent from exercising

---

[130] For more extensive criticism of these provisions, see Prime Time, at 52–61. For opposing commentary critical of the extent to which R.U.P.A. permits contracting regarding fiduciary duties, see Vestal, Fundamental Contractarian Error in the Revised Uniform Partnership Act of 1992, 73 B.U. L. Rev. 523 (1993).

[131] *See* Singer v. Singer, 634 P.2d 766 (Okla. App. 1981).

[132] *See* Wilson v. Button, 404 F.2d 309 (5th Cir. 1968); Hooper v. Yoder, 737 P.2d 852 (Colo. 1987); Covalt v. High, 100 N.M. 700, 675 P.2d 999 (N.M. App. 1983). For a discussion of cases enforcing partnership provisions opting out of fiduciary duties, see Bromberg & Ribstein, § 6.07(h)(2).

[133] *See* § 8.103, supra.

[134] 189 Ill. App. 3d 403, 136 Ill. Dec. 780, 545 N.E.2d 304 (1989).

[135] *See* In re Estate of Rubloff, 645 N.E.2d 370, 206 Ill. Dec. 365 (Ill. App. 1994) (no allegations like those in *Labovitz* that would limit exercise of discretionary dissolution power); Adler v. William Blair & Co., 245 Ill. App. 3d 57, 613 N.E.2d 1264, *reconsidered on other grounds*, 153 Ill. 2d 534, 180 Ill. Dec. 300, 607 N.E.2d 194 (1993) (limited partnership agreement gave general partner discretion to invest for capital appreciation and disclosed possible conflicts of general partners, distinguishing *Labovitz* as a squeeze-out case).

his discretion, and expose the firm to wasteful litigation. Moreover, incentive compensation and other devices are available to constrain the agent to act in the principal's interests. Thus, it may be quite sensible for a firm to contract out of fiduciary duties. For example, R.U.P.A. prevents partners from (1) contracting out of a duty of care where the probability that a partner with a heavy investment in the firm and exposure to personal liability will be grossly negligent is so low as not to be worth the costs and risks of litigation; (2) protecting a managing partner who is simultaneously managing other partnerships from exposure to intractable conflicts; (3) letting a managing partner enter into contracts with the partnership on behalf of the partner's management company; or (4) clarifying that a partner can be expelled without any cause or without any special procedure.

In light of the potential costs of restricting these contracts, it is important to consider whether the restrictions are necessary to protect the partners. Non-waivable fiduciary duties provide minimum standards that most partners would contract for, and may serve useful purposes in some partnerships. Also, Comment 2 to § 103 suggests that waivers may result from "superior bargaining power" and cites cases on contract unconscionability. Indeed, mandatory duties may constrain opportunistic behavior by managing partners in general partnerships or by general partners in limited partnerships who effectively control the drafting of partnership agreements and "sell" partnership interests to passive investors who do not closely scrutinize provisions designed to restrict or eliminate the duty.

Some commentators argue that the parties to formal general and limited partnership agreements, who often negotiate in detail or are participating in sophisticated, idiosyncratic, tax-motivated deals, are unlikely to need the protection of an unconscionability rule that invalidates certain types of fiduciary waivers in all partnership agreements. Although partners are unable to foresee how a waiver might be applied, the courts can deal with unforeseen events through contract interpretation rather than broad prohibition. Common law limitations on unconscionable agreements would still be available, as is made clear in the Comment to Section 104. Moreover, efficient securities markets (for the relatively few actively publicly traded partnerships) and promoters' incentives to maintain a good reputation for future deals provide some check on fiduciary breaches. Author Bromberg believes that mandatory fiduciary duties are efficient as well as fair because of the high costs of determining the effect of their waiver.[136]

---

[136] For a general criticism of these types of constraints, see Butler & Ribstein, Opting Out of Fiduciary Duties: A Response to the Anti-Contractarians, 60 Wash. L. Rev. 1 (1990). Even the Reporter to R.U.P.A. favored opting out of fiduciary duties. See Weidner, The Revised Uniform Partnership Act Midstream: Major Policy Decisions, 21 U. Tol. L. Rev. 825, 856 (1990).

R.U.P.A.'s limited authorization of waivers raises additional questions. Section 103(b)(3)(i) permits waiver of the duty of loyalty as to "specific types or categories of activities" and § 103(b)(5) permits agreed "standards" for measuring the performance of the good faith obligation that "are not manifestly unreasonable." In other words, R.U.P.A. forbids even "reasonable" but non-"specific" waivers, and waivers that are "specific" but "unreasonable," but not waivers that are merely "unreasonable" but not "manifestly" so. As noted above in the Analysis of § 103, § 103(b)(3)(ii) permits an interest party in a loyalty-breaching transaction to vote to authorize or ratify the transaction unless prevented by the partnership agreement. As Comment 5 to Section 103 makes clear, this permits authorization or ratification of specific conduct whether or not this authorization is unreasonable. These qualifications on non-waivability await clarification by the case law.

It is important to recognize that, even without these vague statutory constraints on contracting, a court can find a fiduciary breach despite a partnership agreement that includes a broad enforceable waiver of fiduciary duties. The breach may not be within the language of the waiver, as where a partner not only competes with the firm as permitted by the waiver, but does so by making unauthorized use of confidential information.[137] Moreover, even conduct that is literally authorized by the provision may not be permitted under the "good faith" principle discussed above of enforcing the parties' basic expectations rather than the literal language of their agreement.

Statutory Limitation of Fiduciary Duties (§ 404(e)–(f)). R.U.P.A. qualifies its fiduciary duties by providing in § 404(e)–(f) that a partner does not violate a duty merely by furthering his own interest and may transact business with the partnership on the same basis as a third party "subject to applicable law." It is not clear how these provisions limit partners' duties, particularly since they seem to contradict the duty to act selflessly under § 404(b)(2), and since § 404(a) already limits partners' duties by specifying that they are "only" those specified in § 404. To the extent that the rest of § 404 explicitly limits partners' duties, it is unnecessary to add that the partner has no duties beyond those specified.

Comment 6 to § 404 says that subsection (f) is derived from a RULPA provision that partners who are creditors of the partnership are treated like outside creditors subject to applicable debtor-creditor law.[138] Although this language appears only to limit partners' obligations to creditors, putting it in a section on general standards of conduct implies that it also limits partners' duties among

---

[137] *See* Tri-Growth Centre City, Ltd. v. Silldorf, Burdman, Duignan & Eisenberg, 216 Cal. App. 3d 1139, 265 Cal Rptr. 3309 (1989).

[138] *See* R.U.L.P.A. § 107 (1985). *See* Szturm v. Huntington Blizzard Hockey Assocs. Ltd. P'ship, 516 S.E.2d 267 (W. Va. 1999) (limited partner could assert wage lien superior to claims of limited partnership's general creditors; West Virginia's adoption of R.U.L.P.A. and of R.U.P.A., which contains similar provision, reversed prior case law under U.P.A., although partner's claim remains subject to fraudulent conveyance law).

themselves. This is confirmed by Comment 6, which says that this provision would let a partner buy partnership property at a liquidation sale. Such an interpretation would leave uncertain the effect of case law under the U.P.A., which imposes duties on partners in connection with these transactions.[139]

In general, legislators considering whether to adopt the R.U.P.A. and partners deciding whether to be governed by it should carefully evaluate not only the policy arguments discussed above, but also the costs and benefits of abandoning the relative security of the developed case law under the U.P.A. for R.U.P.A.'s unknown territory.

Pre-formation Transactions. Pre-formation duties raise knotty issues.[140] Among other things, it is not clear how a partner can owe a fiduciary duty prior to the formation of a fiduciary relationship, or how such a duty can be defined or limited where the parties have not yet contracted. R.U.P.A. clarifies these issues by stating that duties arise only in connection with the "conduct and winding up" of the business.

State variations

California makes the duties of loyalty and care nonexclusive.[141]

Colorado makes the duties of loyalty and care nonexclusive and includes language on pre-formation duties.[142] The latter provision continues, if not exacerbates, the knotty state of the law under the U.P.A. It provides that "[i]f a partnership is formed, the duties a partner owes to the partnership and the other partners pertain to all transactions connected with the formation, conduct, or liquidation of the partnership."[143] This at least clarifies that there are no such duties if the relationship is never formed. The language suggests that the duties that *eventually* arise under the partnership agreement apply to pre-formation transactions. In that case, no duty actually arises prior to formation of the relationship. However, applying later duties to prior transactions means that the parties do not know what duties will eventually until after their pre-formation conduct is completed. Moreover, the parties' ability later to negate these duties in the agreement is limited by R.U.P.A. § 103, on which the analogous provision in the Colorado statutes is based.

Delaware provides: "Except as provided in the partnership agreement, a partner may lend money to, borrow money from, act as a surety, guarantor or endorser for, guarantee or assume 1 or more specific obligations of, provide collateral for and transact other business with, the partnership and, subject to other

---

[139] *See* Bromberg & Ribstein, § 7.02(c)(2).
[140] *See* Bromberg & Ribstein, §§ 6.06(b) and 6.07(a)(7).
[141] Cal. Corp. Code § 16404. The California provision deletes the word "only," which suggests but does not explicitly state that the duties are nonexclusive.
[142] Colo. Stat. § 7-64-404.
[143] Colo. Stat. § 7-64-404.

applicable law, has the same rights and obligations with respect thereto as a person who is not a partner."[144]

The **Kentucky** version of subsection (a) provides that a partner's fiduciary duties "include" the duties in the section, and the duties of loyalty and care provided for in the equivalents of subsections (b) and (c) state that the duties "include" the definitions in the respective subsections.[145] In addition, effective April 11, 2012, "that a transaction was fair to the partnership shall not constitute a defense to" the breach of the duty of loyalty.[146]

Oregon provides that partner loans must be fair, authorized by the partnership agreement, or authorized or ratified by a majority of the disinterested partners or by a number or percentage of partners specified in the partnership agreement, after full disclosure of all material facts.[147]

New Jersey omits the good faith duty in subsection (d).[148]

Texas makes the duties of loyalty and care nonexclusive and specifies that partners are not trustees and are not held to the standard of trustees.[149]

§ 8.405.   ACTIONS BY PARTNERSHIP AND PARTNERS

Section 405

(a) A partnership may maintain an action against a partner for a breach of the partnership agreement, or for the violation of a duty to the partnership, causing harm to the partnership.

(b) A partner may maintain an action against the partnership or another partner for legal or equitable relief, with or without an accounting as to partnership business, to:

(1) enforce the partner's rights under the partnership agreement;

(2) enforce the partner's rights under this [Act], including:

(i) the partner's rights under Sections 401, 403, or 404;

(ii) the partner's right on dissociation to have the partner's interest in the partnership purchased pursuant to Section 701 or enforce any other right under [Article] 6 or 7; or

(iii) the partner's right to compel a dissolution and winding up of the partnership business under Section 801 or enforce any other right under [Article] 8; or

---

[144] Del. Code Ann., tit. 6, § 15-404(f).
[145] Ky. Rev. St. Ann., § 362.1-404(1)–(3).
[146] Kan. Rev. Stat. Ann. § 1-404(5).
[147] Or. Rev. Stat. § 67.155(6).
[148] N.J. Rev. Stat. § 42:1A-24.
[149] Tex. Rev. Civ. Stat. Ann. art. 6132b-4.04.

(3) enforce the rights and otherwise protect the interests of the partner, including rights and interests arising independently of the partnership relationship.

(c) The accrual of, and any time limitation on, a right of action for a remedy under this section is governed by other law. A right to an accounting upon a dissolution and winding up does not revive a claim barred by law.

Summary: Provides for remedies between partner and partnership.

Parallel U.P.A.:   §§ 22, 43.

Important Changes: Clarifies that partners may sue both in and outside of an accounting to enforce rights under the act and the partnership agreement, and rights independent of the partnership agreement; and provides that the accrual of and time limitations on remedies under this section are governed by other law.

Analysis: The most important change from prior law is to clarify partners' right to sue outside of an accounting. U.P.A. § 22 provides only for a "right to an account," which involves a potentially lengthy proceeding resolving all pending matters among the partners.[150] Cases under the U.P.A. hold that the accounting proceeding is the partners' *exclusive* remedy for some causes of action arising out of partnership affairs.[151] Because this rule introduced unnecessary procedural complexity it was long overdue for abolition.

R.U.P.A. § 406(b) addresses exclusivity by providing that "a partner may maintain an action against the partnership or another partner for legal or equitable relief, including an accounting as to partnership business." This provision, however, does not necessarily eliminate the exclusivity rule. Partners always have been *able* to bring *some* actions other than for accounting. The statute can safely reverse the exclusivity rule only by a clear statement that an accounting is *never* a prerequisite to exercise of a partner's remedies against the firm.

At the same time, § 406(b) may make an important change by broadening individual partners' remedies. Although partners clearly should be able to bring some kinds of litigation directly, as for recovery of distributions or indemnification, it is less clear that they should be able to sue individually on actions that belong to the firm. Such a right lets any partner burden the firm with costly litigation. At the same time, the individual right of action may also preserve valuable

---

[150] *See* Bromberg & Ribstein, § 6.08(d).
[151] The exclusivity rule and its exceptions are reviewed in Bromberg & Ribstein, § 6.08(b).

rights.[152] Firms may want to avoid the potential for this kind of excessive litigation by requiring suit in the name of the firm.[153]

In light of the potential costs of litigation that may be triggered by this section, it is significant that this section is not listed in § 103 as nonwaivable. However, Comment 3 to § 405 says that partners may not "eliminate entirely the remedies for breach of those duties which are mandatory under Section 103(b)." This has no support in the "black letter." It does not necessarily follow from the fact that a *duty* is mandatory that the *remedy* is also mandatory. Moreover, it is not clear under Comment 3 when a contract would be deemed to "eliminate entirely" the remedies for breach of duty.[154]

Accordingly, legislators considering whether to adopt § 405 should consider revising the provision to clarify to what extent individual partners can or cannot sue on actions belonging to the firm. Firms should also consider whether to contractually limit partners' remedies, perhaps through arbitration clauses,[155] being wary of the uncertainty created by the Comments as to the enforceability of complete waivers.

State variation

Delaware provides that a partner may bring a derivative action, and for standing, demand and fees and expenses in such actions.[156]

§ 8.406.   CONTINUATION OF PARTNERSHIP BEYOND DEFINITE TERM OR PARTICULAR UNDERTAKING

Section 406

(a) If a partnership for a definite term or particular undertaking is continued, without an express agreement, after the expiration of the term or completion of the undertaking, the rights and duties of the partners remain the same as they were at the expiration or completion, so far as is consistent with a partnership at will.

---

[152] *See* Bromberg & Ribstein, §§ 5.03–5.05.

[153] This is similar to the default rule suggested for limited liability companies in the Prototype Limited Liability Company Act. *See* ABA Ad Hoc Ltd. Liab. Co. Comm., Prototype Limited Liability Company Act § 1102.

[154] For more extensive commentary on this section, see Prime Time at 61–62.

[155] *See* Bromberg & Ribstein, § 6.08(e).

[156] Del. Code Ann., tit. 6, § 15-405(d)–(g).

(b) If the partners, or those of them who habitually acted in the business during the term or undertaking, continue the business without any settlement or liquidation of the partnership, they are presumed to have agreed that the partnership will continue.

Summary: Provides that if partnership for a term is continued without an express agreement after the expiration of the term the partnership becomes one at will.

Parallel U.P.A.: § 23.

Important Changes: None.

Analysis: None.

§ 8.501. PARTNER NOT CO-OWNER OF PARTNERSHIP PROPERTY

Section 501

A partner is not a co-owner of partnership property and has no interest in partnership property which can be transferred, either voluntarily or involuntarily.

Summary: A partner is not a co-owner of and has no transferable interest in partnership property.

Parallel U.P.A.: §§ 24–25.

Important Changes: Eliminates the U.P.A. concept that partners own partnership property as tenants in partnership, although there may be little difference in effect because the U.P.A. defines the tenancy in partnership so as to effectively deny partners direct ownership rights in partnership property.

Analysis: This is a desirable change that eliminates potential confusion inherent in the concept of tenancy in partnership.[157] However, it is not clear what effect the change will have on existing law. For example, R.U.P.A. may not change the distinction between partners and corporate shareholders regarding

---

[157] The potential confusion is discussed in *id.* Bromberg & Ribstein, § 3.04(b).

liability for embezzlement, despite the contrary assertion in the Comment to this section. Nonliability in this context may be based on whether, as a policy matter, criminal remedies are appropriate for property disputes in closely held firms and not solely on the characterization of partnerships as aggregates rather than entities.[158]

State variation

Delaware, consistent with its variation on Section 103, provides that this provision may not be modified "[u]nless otherwise provided in a statement of partnership existence and in a partnership agreement."[159]

§ 8.502.   PARTNER'S TRANSFERABLE INTEREST
IN PARTNERSHIP

Section 502

The only transferable interest of a partner in the partnership is the partner's share of the profits and losses of the partnership and the partner's right to receive distributions. The interest is personal property.

Summary: A partner's only transferable interest is the partner's share of the profits and losses and interest in distributions.

Parallel U.P.A.:   §§ 26, 27(1).

Important Changes: More precisely defines the partner's "transferable interest" as including the partner's interest in "distributions" as well as "profits."[160]

Analysis: *See* discussion of § 503.

State variation

Delaware refers to the interest as the partner's economic interest.[161]

---

[158] *See* Bromberg & Ribstein, § 3.05(b), n.20.

[159] Del. Code Ann., tit. 6, § 15-501.

[160] R.U.P.A. § 101 defines "distribution" as a transfer "from a partnership to a partner in the partner's capacity as a partner or to the partner's transferee" and "partnership interest" as including the transferable interest "and all management and other rights."

[161] Del. Code Ann., tit. 6, §§ 15-101(6), 15-502.

§ 8.503.   TRANSFER OF PARTNER'S
TRANSFERABLE INTEREST

Section 503

(a) A transfer, in whole or in part, of a partner's transferable interest in the partnership:

(1) is permissible;

(2) does not by itself cause the partner's dissociation or a dissolution and winding up of the partnership business; and

(3) does not, as against the other partners or the partnership, entitle the transferee, during the continuance of the partnership, to participate in the management or conduct of the partnership business, to require access to information concerning partnership transactions, or to inspect or copy the partnership books or records.

(b) A transferee of a partner's transferable interest in the partnership has a right:

(1) to receive, in accordance with the transfer, distributions to which the transferor would otherwise be entitled;

(2) to receive upon the dissolution and winding up of the partnership business, in accordance with the transfer, the net amount otherwise distributable to the transferor; and

(3) to seek under Section 801(6) a judicial determination that it is equitable to wind up the partnership business.

(c) In a dissolution and winding up, a transferee is entitled to an account of partnership transactions only from the date of the latest account agreed to by all of the partners.

(d) Upon transfer, the transferor retains the rights and duties of a partner other than the interest in distributions transferred.

(e) A partnership need not give effect to a transferee's rights under this section until it has notice of the transfer.

(f) A transfer of a partner's transferable interest in the partnership in violation of a restriction on transfer contained in the partnership agreement is ineffective as to a person having notice of the restriction at the time of transfer.

Summary: Provides for the effect of a transfer of a partner's transferable interest.

Parallel U.P.A.:   §§ 27(1), 32(2).

Important Changes: Defines the transferee's right as one to receive distributions; clarifies that the transferor retains the rights and duties of partner; and provides that partnership has no duty to recognize transferee's rights until it receives notice of the transfer. Section 103 clarifies that a partner may waive the right to transfer his interest. Subsection (f) reinforces this by providing that a transfer in violation of a transfer restriction is ineffective as to a person having notice of the restriction at the time of transfer.

Analysis: R.U.P.A. § 503(b) clarifies the effect of an assignment by providing that it transfers "distributions to which the transferor would otherwise be entitled." However, the definition of "distribution" in § 101(3) as a "transfer of money or other property from a partnership to a partner in the partner's capacity as a partner or to the partner's transferee" does not clarify whether "distributions" includes such items as partner compensation and repayment of advances. The problem is that, because partners contribute labor and credit, they are more than just capital contributors, as partnership law recognizes by providing for equal profit shares despite unequal capital contributions. Thus, partners arguably receive salaries and interest *as partners.* On the other hand, a stronger argument can be made that partners are compensated through their profit shares for their labor and credit contributions purely as partners, so that payments such as wages, rent, and interest are made pursuant to other types of relationships with the firm. Indeed, if such other payments are combined with non-partner attributes such as absence of management rights, the recipients may not be partners.[162] It follows that courts should interpret "distributions" to include only the partners' share of net revenues rather than other types of compensation.

This section carries over the U.P.A. rules denying assignees both management and information rights. These rules comport with the idea that the assignee is not a partner and cannot become so without the other partners' consent. But denying the assignee all information rights is questionable. The assignee has a strong need for information for federal tax purposes and in order to protect herself from unfair dealing by the other partners. At the same time, the costs for most partnerships of providing basic financial information to assignees are relatively low. Because the lack of information rights substantially hinders assignability while conferring only a small benefit on the typical informal partnership, a fully specified partnership agreement would probably give assignees information rights. The standard form should therefore give information rights to assignees in the absence of contrary agreement, as does the Texas provision discussed below. On the other hand, firms with special concerns about confidentiality could contract to waive such rights.

---

[162] *See generally* Bromberg & Ribstein, §§ 2.07–2.09.

Section 503(d) provides that "the transferor retains the rights and obligations of a partner other than the interest in distributions transferred." While this is the likely result under the U.P.A.,[163] it is not necessarily the best rule. A partner's assignment of her entire financial interest leaves her with a power of control but without a profit share. Because of the importance of profit sharing to the determination of partnership, the assignor might be considered to have withdrawn as a partner. Firms might prefer this result because of the risk that an assignor would lack adequate incentives to exercise control for the benefit of the firm. On the other hand, automatic dissociation of assignors would be a significant limitation on the liquidity of partners' financial rights. Thus, perhaps § 601(4)(ii), which permits nonassigning partners to expel the assignor, is a reasonable compromise. Indeed, it may not differ much in effect from an automatic dissociation rule, since even under an automatic dissociation rule the nonassigning partners could agree to let the assignor remain in the firm.

State variations

Delaware provides that the partners may agree to non-transferability, that a partnership interest may be evidenced by a certificate, that until a transferee of a partnership interest becomes a partner, the transferee shall have no liability as a partner solely as a result of the transfer except as assumed by agreement, and that a partnership may acquire a partnership interest.[164]

Texas gives assignees information rights, providing: "For a proper purpose the transferee may require reasonable information or an account of partnership transactions and make reasonable inspection of the partnership books."[165]

§ 8.504. PARTNER'S TRANSFERABLE INTEREST SUBJECT TO CHARGING ORDER

Section 504

(a) On application by a judgment creditor of a partner or of a partner's transferee, a court having jurisdiction may charge the transferable interest of the judgment debtor to satisfy the judgment. The court may appoint a receiver of the share of the distributions due or to become due to the judgment debtor

---

[163] *See* Kanarek v. Gadlex Assocs., 115 A.D.2d 592, 496 N.Y.S.2d 253 (1985). *But cf.* Thomas v. Price, 718 F. Supp. 598 (S.D. Tex. 1989) (holding under the terms of a security agreement that on default the secured party owned the debtor's partnership interest and the debtor was no longer a partner). *See generally* Bromberg & Ribstein, § 3.05(c)(4).

[164] Del. Code Ann., tit. 6, § 15-503(g)–(j).

[165] Tex. Rev. Civ. Stat. Ann. art. 6132b-5.03(b).

in respect of the partnership and make all other orders, directions, accounts, and inquiries the judgment debtor might have made or which the circumstances of the case may require.

(b) A charging order constitutes a lien on the judgment debtor's transferable interest in the partnership. The court may order a foreclosure of the interest subject to the charging order at any time. The purchaser at the foreclosure sale has the rights of a transferee.

(c) At any time before foreclosure, an interest charged may be redeemed:

(1) by the judgment debtor;

(2) with property other than partnership property, by one or more of the other partners; or

(3) with partnership property, by one or more of the other partners with the consent of all of the partners whose interests are not so charged.

(d) This [Act] does not deprive a partner of a right under exemption laws with respect to the partner's interest in the partnership.

(e) This section provides the exclusive remedy by which a judgment creditor of a partner or partner's transferee may satisfy a judgment out of the judgment debtor's transferable interest in the partnership.

Summary: Provides for the rights of partners' creditors to reach partnership interests.

Parallel U.P.A.:   § 28.

Important Changes: Changes or clarifies prior law by providing that (1) an assignee's interest may be charged; (2) a charging order "constitutes a lien" on the charged interest; (3) a court may foreclose the charged interest; (4) the purchaser of a foreclosed interest has the rights of an assignee; (5) the charged interest may be redeemed by the debtor partner; (6) the charging order is the creditor's exclusive remedy; and (7) the charging order can reach distributions of all kinds, and not only "money" due the debtor.

Analysis: The provision that a charging order is a lien on the charged interest should be clarified. As it stands, it erroneously implies that the charging order alone confers priority on the charging creditor.[166]

---

[166] *See* Princeton Bank & Trust Co. v. Berley, 57 A.D.2d 348, 394 N.Y.S.2d 714 (1977) (levying creditor of an individual partner had priority over an earlier charging creditor of the partner who had not obtained ancillary order); Bromberg & Ribstein, § 3.05(d)(3)(iii). *But see* City of Arkansas City v. Anderson, 242 Kan. 875, 757 P.2d 673 (1988) (charging order created lien on partnership interest that was superior to security interest entered into prior to charging order but perfected afterward). *See also* In re Jaffe, 235 B.R. 490 (Bankr. S.D. Fla. 1999) (Fla. law; mere petition for charging order did not perfect a lien, but indicating that entry of charging order alone would have resulted in a perfected lien).

Empowering the court to foreclose on the charged interest apparently is consistent with prior law.[167] However, because a purchaser of a foreclosed interest is an assignee, and therefore has at least the power to compel judicial dissolution of a partnership at will,[168] some authorities permit foreclosure only in certain circumstances, as where the creditor is not otherwise likely to be paid within a reasonable time.[169]

Making the charging order an exclusive remedy is probably a good idea and is amply supported by authority.[170] The justification for exclusivity is that the charging order, unlike other remedies such as garnishment, is designed specifically to accommodate the interests of both partners and creditors.

State variation

Delaware clarifies the issues discussed above by adding: "(f) No creditor of a partner shall have any right to obtain possession of, or otherwise exercise legal or equitable remedies with respect to, the property of the partnership."

§ 8.601.   EVENTS CAUSING PARTNER'S DISSOCIATION

Section 601

A partner is dissociated from a partnership upon the occurrence of any of the following events:

---

[167] *See* U.P.A. § 28(2) (providing for redemption of the charged interest "before foreclosure"); Tupper v. Kroc, 88 Nev. 146, 494 P.2d 1275 (1972). *But cf.* In re Stocks, 110 B.R. 65 (N.D. Fla. 1989) (Florida law; holding that charging order on a limited partnership interest cannot be foreclosed, distinguishing general partnership interests on the basis of the different wording of the limited and general partnership statutes); Centurion Corp. v. Crocker Nat'l. Bank, 208 Cal. App. 3d 1, 255 Cal. Rptr. 794 (1989) (requiring consent by a nondebtor general partner to foreclosure sale of sole limited partnership interest, relying on cases concerning general partnership interests). *See generally* Bromberg & Ribstein, § 3.05(d)(3)(v).

[168] *See* U.P.A. § 32(2); R.U.P.A. § 801(6)(ii).

[169] *See* City of New York v. Bencivenga, 8 Misc. 2d 29, 169 N.Y.S.2d 515 (Sup. Ct. 1955) (requiring showing of need for foreclosure); Gose, The Charging Order under the Uniform Partnership Act, 28 Wash. L. Rev. 1, 16 (1953). Because of the possible disruption from foreclosure, Georgia prohibits this remedy. *See* Ga. Code Ann. sec. 14-8-28; Ribstein, An Analysis of Georgia's New Partnership Law, 36 Mercer L. Rev. 443, 490 (1985). For authority that is more favorable to foreclosure, see Hellman v. Anderson, 233 Cal. App.3d 840, 284 Cal. Rptr. 830 (1991) (holding that a creditor can foreclose on charged interest without the consent of co-partner unless co-partner bears the burden of showing that foreclosure would unduly interfere with business); Nigri v. Lotz, 216 Ga. App. 204, 453 S.E.2d 780 (1995) (holding that the Georgia prohibition on foreclosure as to general partnership interests does not apply to a limited partner's interest because assignees of limited partners cannot force judicial dissolution); Bromberg & Ribstein, § 3.05(d)(3)(v) (citing other authorities on foreclosure). Limitations on foreclosure are criticized in Hynes, The Charging Order: Conflicts Between Partners and Creditors, 25 Pac. L.J. 1 (1993) (noting the purchaser's limited right of interference in the business and the nondebtor partners' redemption power).

[170] *See* Bromberg & Ribstein, § 3.05(d)(3)(i).

(1) the partnership's having notice of the partner's express will to withdraw as a partner or on a later date specified by the partner;

(2) an event agreed to in the partnership agreement as causing the partner's dissociation;

(3) the partner's expulsion pursuant to the partnership agreement;

(4) the partner's expulsion by the unanimous vote of the other partners if:

(i) it is unlawful to carry on the partnership business with that partner;

(ii) there has been a transfer of all or substantially all of that partner's transferable interest in the partnership, other than a transfer for security purposes, or a court order charging the partner's interest, which has not been foreclosed;

(iii) within 90 days after the partnership notifies a corporate partner that it will be expelled because it has filed a certificate of dissolution or the equivalent, its charter has been revoked, or its right to conduct business has been suspended by the jurisdiction of its incorporation, there is no revocation of the certificate of dissolution or no reinstatement of its charter or its right to conduct business; or

(iv) a partnership that is a partner has been dissolved and its business is being wound up;

(5) on application by the partnership or another partner, the partner's expulsion by judicial determination because:

(i) the partner engaged in wrongful conduct that adversely and materially affected the partnership business;

(ii) the partner willfully or persistently committed a material breach of the partnership agreement or of a duty owed to the partnership or the other partners under Section 404; or

(iii) the partner engaged in conduct relating to the partnership business which makes it not reasonably practicable to carry on the business in partnership with the partner;

(6) the partner's:

(i) becoming a debtor in bankruptcy;

(ii) executing an assignment for the benefit of creditors;

(iii) seeking, consenting to, or acquiescing in the appointment of a trustee, receiver, or liquidator of that partner or of all or substantially all of that partner's property; or

(iv) failing, within 90 days after the appointment, to have vacated or stayed the appointment of a trustee, receiver, or liquidator of the partner or of all or substantially all of the partner's property obtained without the partner's consent or acquiescence, or failing within 90 days after the expiration of a stay to have the appointment vacated;

(7) in the case of a partner who is an individual:

(i) the partner's death;

(ii) the appointment of a guardian or general conservator for the partner; or

(iii) a judicial determination that the partner has otherwise become incapable of performing the partner's duties under the partnership agreement;

(8) in the case of a partner that is a trust or is acting as a partner by virtue of being a trustee of a trust, distribution of the trust's entire transferable interest in the partnership, but not merely by reason of the substitution of a successor trustee;

(9) in the case of a partner that is an estate or is acting as a partner by virtue of being a personal representative of an estate, distribution of the estate's entire transferable interest in the partnership, but not merely by reason of the substitution of a successor personal representative; or

(10) termination of a partner who is not an individual, partnership, corporation, trust, or estate.

Summary: Describes the events that cause termination of a partner's status as a partner and winding up or of the partnership under Article 8 or purchase of the partner's interest under Article 7.

Parallel U.P.A.:   §§ 29, 31, 32.

Important Changes: Separates partner dissociation from dissolution of the partnership; clarifies the nature of events that cause partner dissociation, including partner bankruptcy or analogous event (subsection 6),[171] partner death and incapacity (subsection 7), and the "death" of nonindividual partners (subsections 8–10); and provides for expulsion other than pursuant to the partnership agreement by unanimous partner vote under certain circumstances (subsection 4) and by judicial action for partner misconduct (subsection 5).

Analysis: This section improves on the U.P.A. by identifying events that cause only cessation of partner status and not necessarily dissolution and winding up. The consequences of dissociation without dissolution are described in Articles 6 and 7.

One problem with this provision is that it does not require written notice of dissociation. Without a notice requirement there is considerable uncertainty about whether the partner has withdrawn,[172] which invites costly litigation. Comment 2

---

[171] As Comment 7 notes, the bankruptcy law effect of this provision is uncertain. *See* Bromberg & Ribstein, § 7.05(c)(3).

[172] For example, in Campbell v. Miller, 274 N.C. 143, 161 S.E.2d 546 (1968), the court held that a partnership was dissolved either when defendant told plaintiff to "get out of here" or when plaintiff left as instructed. For numerous other cases illustrating the uncertainty, see Bromberg & Ribstein, § 7.02(e)(2).

to this section says that a requirement of written notice might trap unwary partners. However, the benefits of a notice requirement may outweigh the costs. In any event, R.U.P.A. already creates a potential trap by requiring "notice" while not requiring that it be in writing. Moreover, written notice of withdrawal imposes less formality than R.U.P.A.'s complex buyout rules, which are discussed below.[173]

State variation

Delaware provides for dissociation on dissolution of a partnership, LLC, trust or limited partnership that is a partner or termination of a partner who is not an individual, partnership, corporation, trust, limited partnership, limited liability company or estate.[174] It also clarifies dissociation on partner bankruptcy by revising subsection 6 as follows:

(6) the partner's: (i) making an assignment for the benefit of creditors; (ii) filing a voluntary petition in bankruptcy; (iii) being adjudged a bankrupt or insolvent, or having entered against that partner an order for relief in any bankruptcy or insolvency proceeding; (iv) filing a petition or answer seeking for that partner any reorganization, arrangement, composition, readjustment, liquidation, dissolution or similar relief under any statute, law or regulation; (v) filing an answer or other pleading admitting or failing to contest the material allegations of a petition filed against that partner in any proceeding of this nature; (vi) seeking, consenting to or acquiescing in the appointment of a trustee, receiver or liquidator of that partner or of all or any substantial part of that partner's properties; or (vii) failing, within 120 days after its commencement, to have dismissed any proceeding against that partner seeking reorganization, arrangement, composition, readjustment, liquidation, dissolution or similar relief under any statute, law or regulation, or failing, within 90 days after the appointment without that partner's consent or acquiescence, to have vacated or stayed the appointment of a trustee, receiver or liquidator of that partner or of all or any substantial part of that partner's properties, or failing, within 90 days after the expiration of any such stay, to have the appointment vacated;[175]

---

[173] *See* § 701(e), (g), and (I), discussed in the analysis of § 701.

[174] Del. Code Ann., tit. 6, § 15-601(11)–(12).

[175] Del. Code Ann., tit. 6, § 15-601(6).

§ 8.602.   PARTNER'S POWER TO DISSOCIATE; WRONGFUL DISSOCIATION

Section 602

(a) A partner has the power to dissociate at any time, rightfully or wrongfully, by express will pursuant to Section 601(1).

(b) A partner's dissociation is wrongful only if:

(1) it is in breach of an express provision of the partnership agreement; or

(2) in the case of a partnership for a definite term or particular undertaking, before the expiration of the term or the completion of the undertaking:

(i) the partner withdraws by express will, unless the withdrawal follows within 90 days after another partner's dissociation by death or otherwise under Section 601(6) through (10) or wrongful dissociation under this subsection;

(ii) the partner is expelled by judicial determination under Section 601(5);

(iii) the partner is dissociated by becoming a debtor in bankruptcy; or

(iv) in the case of a partner who is not an individual, trust other than a business trust, or estate, the partner is expelled or otherwise dissociated because it willfully dissolved or terminated.

(c) A partner who wrongfully dissociates is liable to the partnership and to the other partners for damages caused by the dissociation. The liability is in addition to any other obligation of the partner to the partnership or to the other partners.

Summary: Provides that partner has the power to dissociate at any time, and defines and states the consequences of wrongful dissociation.

Parallel U.P.A.:   §§ 31(2), 38(2).

Important Changes: Clarifies that a partner has the power to dissociate at any time, irrespective of any contrary provision in the partnership agreement; defines the circumstances in which dissociation is wrongful; and defines the remedies for wrongful dissociation. With respect to remedies, this section eliminates the U.P.A. rule that denies the wrongful partner a share in the goodwill of the partnership.

Analysis: An important aspect of this provision is that it clarifies that a partner has the power to dissociate at any time. This is reinforced by § 103(b)(6), which provides that the partners cannot waive this power other than to require notice in writing.

There are two potential, but not entirely persuasive, arguments against letting partners contract around the dissociation right. The first concerns open-ended liability. However, the potential costs of continuing liability are not as great as they might appear. R.U.P.A. reduces the sting of such liability by requiring creditors, subject to their contrary agreement with the partners, to exhaust partnership assets before proceeding against individual partners.[176] Moreover, even a partner who cannot dissociate can negotiate with his co-partners for indemnification and with creditors for a release.

A second possible argument against allowing contracts around the dissociation right is that the partners cannot predict the effects of the agreement over the course of the partnership. However, legislators are no better able to predict the long-term effects of the statutory rule for all partnerships. Moreover, courts can fill contracting gaps by considering whether partners' actions are in good faith accord with their underlying deal and by expelling partners or dissolving partnerships in cases of partner misconduct.[177] It is unnecessary to prohibit *all* agreements to protect partners from the occasional bad deal.

Thus, whatever the potential costs of open-ended liability, partners probably should be able to decide the issue for themselves.[178] Indeed, R.U.P.A. does let the partners determine the consequences of wrongful dissociation. Only subsection (a) of § 602 is listed as nonwaivable in R.U.P.A. § 103(b). This is reinforced by Comment 2 to § 602, which notes that the partnership agreement can "modify the effects of wrongful dissociation." The partners therefore can penalize withdrawal through liquidated damages, a low buyout price,[179] or a noncompetition agreement. This forces courts to decide when a penalty becomes a prohibition. In deciding this question, the courts may and should apply the same good faith interpretation principles that would condition enforcement of a straight waiver.[180] In short, the prohibition on waiving the power to dissociate may have little effect in practice.

---

[176] *See* R.U.P.A. § 307(d).

[177] *See* R.U.P.A. §§ 601(5) (judicial expulsion), 801(5) (judicial dissolution).

[178] *See* Prime Time, at 63–64; Ribstein, A Statutory Approach to Partner Dissociation, 65 Wash. U. L.Q. 357, 410–16 (1987).

The contract that should be enforced is one explicitly limiting a partner's power to dissociate. In other words, we do not suggest that a partnership for a particular term or undertaking should be interpreted as one prohibiting a partner from dissociating. For a contrary suggestion, see Hillman, Indissoluble Partnerships, 37 U. Fla. l. Rev. 691, 731 (1985).

[179] The question of whether the partners can agree not to buy the interest at all is discussed infra in the analysis of § 701.

[180] *Cf.* Rafe v. Hindin, 29 A.D.2d 481, 288 N.Y.S.2d 662 (1968), *aff'd mem.*, 23 N.Y.2d 759, 244 N.E.2d 469, 296 N.Y.2d 955 (1968) (refusing to enforce a share transfer restriction in a close corporation under circumstances indicating oppression by party seeking enforcement).

Subsection (b) defines when a partner's dissociation is wrongful: only if it is in breach of an express provision of the partnership agreement, or is a wrongful withdrawal by express will that does not follow another partners' death, incapacity, bankruptcy or wrongful dissociation,[181] or judicial expulsion for misconduct prior to the expiration of an agreed term or completion of an agreed undertaking.

A wrongful dissociation triggers liability for damages under § 602(c) irrespective of whether the dissociation causes dissolution of the partnership. Subsection (c) provides for damages for wrongful dissociation "in addition to any other liability of the partner to the partnership or to the other partners." It is not clear what "other liability" means. Comment 3 to § 602 suggests that damages should be added to "substantial expenses resulting from a partner's premature withdrawal from a term partnership, such as replacing the partner's expertise or obtaining new financing." It is not clear why such expenses are not part of the damages for wrongful dissociation.

Note that, while wrongful conduct that leads to judicial expulsion under R.U.P.A. § 601(5) triggers a right to damages, the same is not true of wrongful conduct that justifies dissolution under R.U.P.A. § 801(5).[182] This distinction reflects the fact that a partner's actionable conduct is not necessarily a cause of dissolution under § 801. However, the distinction may encourage extra litigation over identifying the precise ground for relief.

Unlike U.P.A. § 38(2)(c)(II), § 602(c) does not deny the wrongful partner a share in partnership goodwill. Changing the rule in this respect is questionable. In the informal partnership for which the statute should be designed, there is probably no goodwill associated with the firm (as distinguished from the individual continuing partners) in which the departing partner should share.[183] Thus, there is a significant risk of over-compensating dissociating partners on account of goodwill in this situation. If wrongful partners have a good chance of being overpaid, they obviously have a perverse incentive to leave prematurely.

---

[181] Subsection 602(b)(2)(i) makes clear that dissociation by express will is non-wrongful if it follows within 90 days a dissociation by another partner by death or otherwise pursuant to § 601(6)–(10).

[182] See Horizon/CMS Healthcare Corp. v. Southern Oaks Health Care, Inc., 732 So. 2d 1156 (Fla. App. 1999) (no right to damages for wrongful dissolution, whether by will of a partner or by court decree under R.U.P.A. § 801(5) based on partner misconduct that makes it impracticable to carry on the business).

[183] See generally Ribstein, A Theoretical Analysis of Professional Partnership Goodwill, 70 Neb. L. Rev. 36 (1991).

§ 8.603.   EFFECT OF PARTNER'S DISSOCIATION

Section 603

(a) If a partner's dissociation results in a dissolution and winding up of the partnership business, [Article] 8 applies; otherwise, [Article] 7 applies.

(b) Upon a partner's dissociation:

(1) the partner's right to participate in the management and conduct of the partnership business terminates, except as otherwise provided in Section 803;

(2) the partner's duty of loyalty under Section 404(b)(3) terminates; and

(3) the partner's duty of loyalty under Section 404(b)(1) and (2) and duty of care under Section 404(c) continue only with regard to matters arising and events occurring before the partner's dissociation, unless the partner participates in winding up the partnership's business pursuant to Section 803.

Summary: Provides that partner's dissociation results in either a purchase of the partner's interest under Article 7 or a winding up under Article 8; terminates the partner's right to participate in management and conduct of the business other than to participate in winding up; and terminates fiduciary duties other than the duties relating to pre-dissociation matters.

Parallel U.P.A.:   None.

Important Changes: Provides that dissociation may result in buyout without dissolution; and clarifies the effect of dissociation.

Analysis: Under the U.P.A., a partner's dissociation is virtually synonymous with dissolution. A major change in R.U.P.A. is that dissociation does not necessarily cause dissolution.

This section specifies some, but not all, of the effects of dissociation under R.U.P.A. As noted in Comment 1 to § 601 and Comment 1 to § 701, a former partner, among other rights, powers and obligations, has continuing access to books and records, power to bind the firm, and liability to creditors on pre-dissociation and some post-dissociation partnership debts.

The main problems with this section concern subsections (b)(2) and (3), which provide that the partner's duties of loyalty and care continue following partner dissociation but, except for the duty not to compete, they continue only with regard to matters arising or events occurring prior to dissociation unless the partner participates in winding up.[184] This provision raises difficult questions concerning (1) whether the partner breached his fiduciary duty; (2) whether the breach concerned "matters or events that occurred before the dissociation";

---

[184] For further criticism of this section, see Prime Time, at 64–65.

(3) whether the breach involved the duty not to compete, which does not continue after dissociation; and (4) whether the partners' agreement waived post-dissociation duties.[185]

To give an example of the confusion that may result under this provision, consider a claim that a law partner appropriated a fee from a client and a case he took with him after dissociating. If the attorney is deemed to be appropriating work in process that belongs to the firm, he may be liable if the appropriation is "with regard to" a pre-dissociation matter or event. On the other hand, if he is deemed to be competing with his former firm, or if his conduct is deemed to be with regard to a post-dissociation matter, he apparently has not breached his duty. This raises questions about the continued authority of cases under the U.P.A. that hold, for example, that former law partners may not appropriate the benefit of cases they continue to handle after leaving the firm.[186] The Comment to subsection (b) says that the post-dissociation duty of loyalty extends to "completing on-going client transactions" and "fees received from the old clients." However, this could be regarded as competition, which subsection (b)(3) permits after dissociation.

The potential confusion added by § 603 may be unnecessary. R.U.P.A. § 404 imposes fiduciary duties on any "partner." Section 603(b) assumes that "partner" does not apply to a dissociated partner. But nothing in R.U.P.A. prevents courts from holding that a dissociated partner retains some partnership attributes, including fiduciary duties.[187] R.U.P.A. recognizes fiduciary duties in connection with "winding up"[188] and that a dissociated partner may participate in winding up.[189] As a policy matter, the conditions that initially gave rise to the partners' fiduciary duties still exist as long as a former partner retains control over partnership property or management power.[190] The termination of partners' fiduciary duties, like other aspects of fiduciary duties' existence and breach, arguably should be determined by courts on a case-by-case basis, subject to the parties' power to settle their rights by contract.

Section 603 raises an additional problem by failing to make clear what determines whether a dissociation results in a dissolution and winding up. Legislators adopting the section should clarify the point by stating: "(a) A partner's disso-

---

[185] Since § 603 is not one of the non-waivable provisions under § 103, the partners apparently can waive the continuation of their fiduciary duties although, of course, under the latter section they cannot waive the duties themselves.

[186] See Little v. Caldwell, 101 Cal. 553, 36 P. 107 (1894); Rosenfeld, Meyer & Susman v. Cohen, 146 Cal. App. 3d 200, 194 Cal. Rptr. 180 (1983); Bromberg & Ribstein, § 7.08(e). See also Leff v. Gunter, 33 Cal. 3d 508, 189 Cal. Rptr. 377, 658 P.2d 740 (1983) (partner could not bid against former partner on partnership opportunity after dissolution).

[187] Comment 2 to § 404 says § 603(b)(3) "limits the application" of the duty of loyalty, suggesting that a dissociated partner would have such a duty under § 404 in the absence of § 603.

[188] See R.U.P.A. § 404(b)(1)–(2).

[189] See R.U.P.A. § 803.

[190] See Frankel, Fiduciary Law, 71 Cal. L. Rev. 795, 823, n.100 (1983). See generally Ribstein, Are Partners Fiduciaries?, 2005 Ill. L. Rev. 209 (tying existence of fiduciary duties to management responsibilities).

ciation results in a dissolution and winding up of the partnership business only if Section 801 so specifies. In that event [Article] 8 applies; otherwise [Article] 7 applies."

§ 8.701. PURCHASE OF DISSOCIATED PARTNER'S INTEREST

Section 701

(a) If a partner is dissociated from a partnership without resulting in a dissolution and winding up of the partnership business under Section 801, the partnership shall cause the dissociated partner's interest in the partnership to be purchased for a buyout price determined pursuant to subsection (b).

(b) The buyout price of a dissociated partner's interest is the amount that would have been distributable to the dissociating partner under Section 807(b) if, on the date of dissociation, the assets of the partnership were sold at a price equal to the greater of the liquidation value or the value based on a sale of the entire business as a going concern without the dissociated partner and the partnership were wound up as of that date. Interest must be paid from the date of dissociation to the date of payment.

(c) Damages for wrongful dissociation under Section 602(b), and all other amounts owing, whether or not presently due, from the dissociated partner to the partnership, must be offset against the buyout price. Interest must be paid from the date the amount owed becomes due to the date of payment.

(d) A partnership shall indemnify a dissociated partner whose interest is being purchased against all partnership liabilities, whether incurred before or after the dissociation, except liabilities incurred by an act of the dissociated partner under Section 702.

(e) If no agreement for the purchase of a dissociated partner's interest is reached within 120 days after a written demand for payment, the partnership shall pay, or cause to be paid, in cash to the dissociated partner the amount the partnership estimates to be the buyout price and accrued interest, reduced by any offsets and accrued interest under subsection (c).

(f) If a deferred payment is authorized under subsection (h), the partnership may tender a written offer to pay the amount it estimates to be the buyout price and accrued interest, reduced by any offsets under subsection (c), stating the time of payment, the amount and type of security for payment, and the other terms and conditions of the obligation.

(g) The payment or tender required by subsection (e) or (f) must be accompanied by the following:

(1) a statement of partnership assets and liabilities as of the date of dissociation;

(2) the latest available partnership balance sheet and income statement, if any;

(3) an explanation of how the estimated amount of the payment was calculated; and

(4) written notice that the payment is in full satisfaction of the obligation to purchase unless, within 120 days after the written notice, the dissociated partner commences an action to determine the buyout price, any offsets under subsection (c), or other terms of the obligation to purchase.

(h) A partner who wrongfully dissociates before the expiration of a definite term or the completion of a particular undertaking is not entitled to payment of any portion of the buyout price until the expiration of the term or completion of the undertaking, unless the partner establishes to the satisfaction of the court that earlier payment will not cause undue hardship to the business of the partnership. A deferred payment must be adequately secured and bear interest.

(i) A dissociated partner may maintain an action against the partnership, pursuant to Section 405(b)(2)(ii), to determine the buyout price of that partner's interest, any offsets under subsection (c), or other terms of the obligation to purchase. The action must be commenced within 120 days after the partnership has tendered payment or an offer to pay or within one year after written demand for payment if no payment or offer to pay is tendered. The court shall determine the buyout price of the dissociated partner's interest, any offset due under subsection (c), and accrued interest, and enter judgment for any additional payment or refund. If deferred payment is authorized under subsection (h), the court shall also determine the security for payment and other terms of the obligation to purchase. The court may assess reasonable attorney's fees and the fees and expenses of appraisers or other experts for a party to the action, in amounts the court finds equitable, against a party that the court finds acted arbitrarily, vexatiously, or not in good faith. The finding may be based on the partnership's failure to tender payment or an offer to pay or to comply with subsection (g).

Summary: States the rules governing payment to and indemnification of a dissociating partner.

Parallel U.P.A.: §§ 38(2), 42.

Important Changes: Provides a right of buyout without dissolution of the firm, unlike the U.P.A. that requires at least a technical dissolution when a partner leaves; provides a new formula for determining the buyout price and new mechanisms for setting the price when the parties disagree; changes the rules regarding deferred payment to a wrongfully dissociating partner; and provides for acceleration of amounts due by dissociating partner in determining amount of setoff against partnership's liability to partner.

Analysis: Section 701 is the counterpart to U.P.A. §§ 38(2) and 42, which also provide for buyout of a dissociated partner where the firm is continued but only following dissolution of the firm. The various rules in § 701 are discussed separately below.

Duty to Purchase.   R.U.P.A. § 701(a) provides that "the partnership shall cause the dissociated partner's interest in the partnership to be purchased. . . ." This provision raises at least two questions. First, it is not clear who will buy the dissociated partner's interest. This continues the ambiguity under U.P.A. § 42, which gives the dissociating partner a right to have the value of his interest paid but does not specify who must buy. Comment 2 to § 701 says that "cause to be purchased" accommodates a purchase by the partnership, the partners or a third party. But it is not clear how the partnership can "cause" a purchase by an entity other than the partnership. The effect of this language is probably to make the partnership liable for a failure to buy the departing interest.

Second, there is a question whether buyout is mandatory.[191] Section 701 is not listed as a nonwaivable provision in § 103(b). However, § 103(b)(6) provides that the partners cannot contract around the power to dissociate by express will under § 602, and Comment 2 to § 701 says that "[t]he buyout is mandatory." Accordingly, the parties may or may not be able to restrict the buyout by contracting for liquidated damages, a low buyout price, or a noncompetition agreement. Comment 3 to Section 701 reinforces the confusion by stating:

> The Section 701 rules are merely default rules. The partners may, in the partnership agreement, fix the method or formula for determining the buyout price and all of the other terms and conditions of the buyout right. Indeed, the very right to a buyout itself may be modified, *although a provision providing for a complete forfeiture would probably not be enforceable. See* Section 104(a). [Emphasis added.]

The cross-referenced provision, § 104, simply provides for application of rules of law and equity. It is not clear to which such rules the Comment refers. There is authority under the U.P.A. forbidding "forfeiture" provisions.[192] Yet the fact that § 701 is not among nonwaivable provisions listed in § 103 is an affirmative indication of contractual freedom that is not provided for in the U.P.A. Against this background, a court could hold that the buyout right is a fundamental aspect of the power to dissociate or, alternatively, that only termination of liability and authority is fundamental. The statute should eliminate this uncer-

---

[191] *See* Prime Time, at 64.
[192] *See* Bromberg & Ribstein, § 7.13(i)(1).

tainty and confusion about the buyout right by stating clearly that the parties have complete freedom of contract regarding the power to dissociate.

Valuation of Partner's Interest. This section provides new rules for fixing the "buyout price" of a dissociating partner's interest. Comment 3 states that this term was intended to stress the unique circumstances relevant to partnerships.

U.P.A. § 42 provides that the dissociated partner is entitled to the "value of his interest in the dissolved partnership." Section 701(b) provides in considerably more detail that the dissociated partner is entitled to the "amount that would have been distributable to the dissociating partner under Section 807(b) if, on the date of dissociation, the assets of the partnership were sold at a price equal to the greater of the liquidation value or the value based on a sale of the entire business as a going concern without the dissociated partner and the partnership were wound up as of that date."

R.U.P.A.'s distinction between "going concern" and "liquidation" value introduces new language that reduces the precedential value of the case law interpreting the U.P.A., and may confuse the courts. "Liquidation" could mean any sale, since the value of productive assets necessarily depends on how they are to be used—that is, their "going concern" value. Alternatively, liquidation might mean piecemeal sale.[193] Recently, California courts have held that "liquidation value" does not mean "a distress sale price," but "the sale price of the separate assets based upon their market value as determined by the willing and knowledgeable buyer and a willing and knowledgeable seller, neither of which is under any compulsion to buy or sell."[194]

The further qualification that the price is to be determined "without the dissociated partner" obviously makes sense. However, the reference to "going concern" indicates that goodwill can be taken into account. The "without the dissociated partner" phrase seems to require that the reputations of the *nondissociating* partners be taken into account in determining goodwill. In other words, the going concern sale of the partnership would include transfer of the partners' reputations.[195] Accordingly, this provision may change the general rule regarding goodwill in professional partnerships.[196] However, by qualifying in this way only

---

[193] This confusion is evident in the corporate appraisal rights cases that require the "net asset value" component of "fair value" to be determined on the basis of what a third party would pay for the assets on liquidation (*see* Bell v. Kirby Lumber Corp., 413 A.2d 137 (Del. 1980); Poole v. N.V. Delii Maatschappij, 243 A.2d 67 (Del. 1968)) yet exclude consideration of the investment value of the assets even if this is an important determinant of what the third party would pay (*see* Francis I. DuPont & Co. v. Universal City Studios, Inc., 312 A.2d 344 (Del. Ch. 1973), *aff'd*, 334 A.2d 216 (1975)).

[194] *See, e.g.*, Derrick v. California Cardiac Surgeons, 2012 WL 1560653 (Cal. App. May 4, 2012); Rappaport v. Gelfand, 197 Cal. App. 4th 1213, 1228 (Cal. App. 2011).

[195] A recent Washington case held that including goodwill in valuation didn't violate the Washington Rules of Professional Conduct and specifically included goodwill related to other partners' work on government defense contracts. *See* Dixon v. Crawford, McGilliard, Peterson & Yelish, 262 P.3d 108 (2011).

[196] *See* Bromberg & Ribstein, § 7.13(c).

going concern value, the stipulation deepens the confusion inherent in the contrasting "going concern" and "liquidation" descriptions of value.

The Colorado, Delaware, New Jersey, and Oregon provisions noted below eliminate much of this confusion by providing simply for payment of "value" or "fair value." While this language in itself provides little guidance, it triggers the application of the substantial case law under U.P.A. § 42.

R.U.P.A. also changes the U.P.A. by eliminating the former partner's right to be paid a share of profits attributable to use of the partner's investment in the business from dissociation until time of payment. There is no apparent reason for eliminating this important right.[197] The profits-or-interest election differs from fixing an interest prospectively to reflect the risk-adjusted time value of money. It obviously can differ significantly from a fixed statutory rate of interest. Investors generally expect to be paid for use of their invested capital. Moreover, unless the continuing partners must pay for the capital they are using, they may inefficiently prolong the business instead of winding it up. Accordingly, the parties probably would draft for this right in a fully specified agreement, and the statute should provide this rule for the many informal partners who are unlikely to think of it on formation. Indeed, courts may continue to effectuate the parties' likely expectation in this regard even without explicit statutory authority.

Deferred Debts. Subsection (c) provides that the buyout price is offset against damages due from the dissociated partner as well as "all other amounts owing, whether or not presently due." It is not clear why agreements that provide for deferred rather than accelerated payment should not be enforced.

Indemnification. The straightforward indemnification right in R.U.P.A. § 701(d) improves on muddled indemnification provisions in U.P.A. § 38. The U.P.A. provides for no indemnification for rightfully withdrawing partners, a "discharge" for expelled partners and, as to wrongfully withdrawing partners, that they were both indemnified "against all present or future liabilities" and "released" from "existing liabilities."[198] Subsection (d) clearly provides for a complete indemnification against all partnership liabilities other than those incurred by the post-dissociation act of the dissociated partner.[199]

Procedures for Payment. R.U.P.A. § 701(e), (g), and (i) provide for detailed procedures regarding tender and payment of and suit for the value of a dissociated partner's interest similar to those in the Model Business Corporation Act.[200] These procedures may surprise informal partnerships in which membership could change without anyone's realizing that they belonged to a "partnership" governed by these elaborate provisions. For example, a partner may find

---

[197] *See* Bromberg & Ribstein, § 7.13(f) (explaining reasons for profits-or-interest election).

[198] *See* Bromberg & Ribstein, § 7.13(e)(1).

[199] *See* Prime Time, at 421 (recommending this rule instead of different rule proposed in prior version of R.U.P.A.).

[200] *See* Model Bus. Corp. Act § 13.25 (1984).

himself unexpectedly barred from suit because he did not commence an action within one year after an action that could be construed as a "written demand for payment." Or the partnership may find itself unexpectedly bound to pay attorney's fees and other expenses because it unreasonably failed to tender payment. Thus, legislators should consider proposing these procedures as "opt-in" provisions that can be adopted by partnerships.

Moreover, the procedures are incomplete in that subsection (e) does not specify a time limit after the 120 days following demand for the partnership to make its payment of the estimated buyout price. Thus the partnership may indefinitely delay making any payment, subject only to a court order in a dissociated partner's suit under subsection (i). Legislatures adopting these procedures should provide a time limit for payment of the estimated price.[201]

Deferred Payments. Subsection (h) provides that a wrongfully dissociating partner is not entitled to be paid until expiration of the agreed term or undertaking "unless the partner establishes to the satisfaction of the court that earlier payment will not cause undue hardship to the business of the partnership." A deferred payment must be secured by bond. By contrast, U.P.A. § 38(2)(c) simply provides that the partner is entitled to be paid in cash or by bond approved by the court. The meaning and application of the R.U.P.A. rule will have to be determined through future litigation. At the same time, it is not clear that the rule provides much more protection to continuing partners than their ability under the U.P.A. to defer payment by providing a bond.

State variations

California provides that its equivalent to § 701 shall not apply to any dissociation that occurs within 90 days prior to a dissolution. Instead, all partners who dissociated within 90 days prior to the dissolution shall be treated as if the firm wound up subject to deduction of wrongful dissociation damages.[202]

Colorado provides that the buyout price is the "value of the partner's interest in the partnership."[203]

Delaware provides that the buyout price of a partner's interest is the "fair value of such partner's economic interest as of the date of dissociation based upon such partner's right to share in distributions from the partnership."[204]

New Jersey defines the buyout price in terms of "fair value."[205]

---

[201] *See, e.g.,* Tex. Rev. Civ. Stat. Ann. art. 6132b-7.01(g) (30 days).
[202] Cal. Corp. Code § 16701.5.
[203] Colo. Stat. § 7-64-701.
[204] Del. Code Ann., tit. 6, § 15-701(b).
[205] N.J. Rev. Stat. § 42:1A-34(b).

Oregon defines the buyout price as the "fair value" of the leaving partner's interest and adds that the price is not discounted as a result of a minority interest.[206]

Tennessee substitutes "material" for "undue" in subsection (h).[207]

§ 8.702.   DISSOCIATED PARTNER'S POWER TO BIND AND LIABILITY TO PARTNERSHIP

Section 702

(a) For two years after a partner dissociates without resulting in a dissolution and winding up of the partnership business, the partnership, including a surviving partnership under [Article] 9, is bound by an act of the dissociated partner which would have bound the partnership under Section 301 before dissociation only if at the time of entering into the transaction the other party:

(1) reasonably believed that the dissociated partner was then a partner;

(2) did not have notice of the partner's dissociation; and

(3) is not deemed to have had knowledge under Section 303(e) or notice under Section 704(c).

(b) A dissociated partner is liable to the partnership for any damage caused to the partnership arising from an obligation incurred by the dissociated partner after dissociation for which the partnership is liable under subsection (a).

Summary: Provides for limited continuation of a dissociated partner's authority to bind the partnership, and for liability of a dissociated partner for losses resulting from his post-dissociation transactions.

Parallel U.P.A.:   §§ 33, 35.

Important Changes: Provides that a dissociated partner has continuing authority where dissociation does not cause dissolution, a situation that does not exist under the U.P.A.; specifies a two-year time limit on a dissociated partner's power to bind the partnership; eliminates the partnership's ability to provide notice of dissociation by publication; and expands dissociated partners' liability to the partnership for post-dissociation transactions.

Analysis: This section provides that for two years after a partner's dissociation, the partnership may be held liable for the dissociated partner's acts if the

---

[206] Or. Rev. Stat. § 67.250.
[207] Tenn. Code Ann. § 61-1-701(h).

third party reasonably believed the dissociated partner was then a partner, did not have notice of the partner's dissociation, and is not deemed to have knowledge by reason of a statement of partnership authority under R.U.P.A. § 303 or a statement of dissociation under R.U.P.A. § 704.

The separate reasonable belief and notice rules indicate that a court could hold that a third party who reasonably believed that the partner was with the firm at the time of the transaction and was not notified of a later dissociation may hold the partner and partnership liable. Thus, if the partnership notifies the third party under § 102 it is exonerated even if the third party "reasonably believes" the dissociated partner remains in the firm. Since the notice requirements are not tied to the time of the transaction, a court could hold that a third party who reasonably believed that the partner was with the firm at the time of the transaction and was not notified of a *later* dissociation may hold the partner and partnership liable. Since a dissociated partner's power to bind the firm could continue under this provision for as long as two years as to creditors who did not receive a notification of the dissociation, the partnership has an incentive to file a statement of dissociation under § 704 in order to limit a dissociating partner's authority. *See* the discussion of that section below.

Section 702(b) in effect states a special duty to refrain from post-dissociation transactions that a partner breaches even if he has not acted carelessly or disloyally under § 404. It is not clear why the Commissioners added this special duty or why they did not apply it to other kinds of unauthorized transactions. As discussed above in the Analysis of § 603, they did not have to provide separately for the duties of a dissociated partner since a partner's duties under § 404 do not necessarily terminate after dissociation. Indeed, § 702(b) itself implies this by referring to the dissociated member as a "partner." Even if special liability is warranted, it may be difficult to isolate the "loss" from the unauthorized transaction in the sense of the excess of the transaction's cost less the revenue it generates. Comment 2 says that subsection (b) makes the partner liable for a "loss net of any gain from the transaction." It is not clear how there can be a "gain" if there is a "loss." Presumably this means that revenues must be subtracted from the expenses.

§ 8.703.   DISSOCIATED PARTNER'S LIABILITY TO OTHER PERSONS

Section 703

(a) A partner's dissociation does not of itself discharge the partner's liability for a partnership obligation incurred before dissociation. A dissociated partner is not liable for a partnership obligation incurred after dissociation, except as otherwise provided in subsection (b).

(b) A partner who dissociates without resulting in a dissolution and winding up of the partnership business is liable as a partner to the other party in a transaction entered into by the partnership, or a surviving partnership under [Article] 9, within two years after the partner's dissociation, only if the partner is liable for the obligation under Section 306 and at the time of entering into the transaction the other party:

(1) reasonably believed that the dissociated partner was then a partner;

(2) did not have notice of the partner's dissociation; and

(3) is not deemed to have had knowledge under Section 303(e) or notice under Section 704(c).

(c) By agreement with the partnership creditor and the partners continuing the business, a dissociated partner may be released from liability for a partnership obligation.

(d) A dissociated partner is released from liability for a partnership obligation if a partnership creditor, with notice of the partner's dissociation but without the partner's consent, agrees to a material alteration in the nature or time of payment of a partnership obligation.

Summary: Provides for the dissociated partner's post-dissociation liability for pre-dissociation and post-dissociation debts.

Parallel U.P.A.:   §§ 35(2), 36.

Important Changes: Changes the partner's continuing liability for post-dissociation debts along the same lines as § 702 changes the partner's authority to bind the firm; applies rules similar to those under U.P.A. § 36 regarding the release of the liability of a dissociated partner, but applies only to the situation in which the dissociation does not cause dissolution.

Analysis: As to the continuing liability of the dissociated partner, *see* the discussion above of reasonable belief/notice requirements in the **Analysis** of § 702. Note that § 703 provides for continuing liability for a pre-dissociation "obligation." The Comment says that "[t]he word 'obligation' is used instead of 'liability' and is intended to include broadly both tort and contract liability incurred before dissociation." It is not clear whether this broadens the partners' liability beyond that under the U.P.A. rule for long-term contracts entered into and for wrongdoing that occurred prior to the dissociation. Conversely, this rule may support a broad liability shield under R.U.P.A.-based LLP provisions.[208]

---

[208] *See* § 3.11(b)–(c), *supra*.

Note on Successor Liability.   U.P.A. § 41 provides for automatic assumption of the liabilities of a dissolved partnership by a successor firm that includes one or more of the partners of the dissolved firm. This continuity is valuable for creditors of the pre-dissolution firm. Without it, they would lose their direct right of action against the assets of the dissolved firm and have to pursue these assets through the partners' interests in the firm. This would frustrate creditor expectations where the business is continued under similar ownership.

There is no provision in R.U.P.A. for successor liability. The Comment to § 703 states:

> In general under R.U.P.A., as a result of the adoption of the entity theory, relationships between a partnership and its creditors are not affected by the dissociation of a partner or by the addition of a new partner, unless otherwise agreed. Therefore, there is no need under R.U.P.A., as there is under the U.P.A., for an elaborate provision deeming the new partnership to assume the liabilities of the old partnership. *See* U.P.A. Section 41.

To be sure, successor liability is less of an issue under R.U.P.A. because the firm does not necessarily dissolve on partner dissociation as it does under U.P.A. Nevertheless, there is still arguably a need for a statute to define successor firms. A winding up may entail a sale of the firm as a going concern to fewer than all of the partners of the dissolved firm in a transaction that is virtually identical to a dissociation. In that situation, creditors may be worse off than they were in the equivalent situation under the U.P.A. Under R.U.P.A., creditors not only must try to reach the dissolved firm's assets through cumbersome charging orders against individual partners, but may be unable to do so before exhausting remedies against the dissolved partnership under § 307(d). R.U.P.A. partnerships may eschew dissociation in favor of dissolution precisely in order to increase the difficulty of collection. Indeed, courts may impose successor liability whatever R.U.P.A. says and, as with corporate successors under the U.P.A., impose liability under a variety of theories, including fraudulent conveyances, disregarding the legal entity, bulk sale law, and implied assumption of liability.[209]

Note that the absence of a definition of successor firms may work against a R.U.P.A. partnership if the absence of a provision on succession of firms leads a court not to carry over a prior partner's limited liability partnership registration.[210]

---

[209] *See* Bromberg & Ribstein, § 7.19(b), (e).
[210] *See* § 3.11(b), supra.

There is also a question concerning the release of partner liabilities where the business is continued by a going concern sale without payment of debts. Section 703 provides for release only where dissociation does not result in dissolution.

LLP Cross-reference: Section 3.12(b)(2).

§ 8.704.   STATEMENT OF DISSOCIATION

Section 704

(a) A dissociated partner or the partnership may file a statement of dissociation stating the name of the partnership and that the partner is dissociated from the partnership.

(b) A statement of dissociation is a limitation on the authority of a dissociated partner for the purposes of Section 303(d) and (e).

(c) For the purposes of Sections 702(a)(3) and 703(b)(3), a person not a partner is deemed to have notice of the dissociation 90 days after the statement of dissociation is filed.

Summary: Section 704 permits the dissociated partner or the partnership to file a statement that a partner has dissociated from the partnership. Third parties are deemed to have notice 90 days after the filing of a statement of dissociation of the partner's dissociation and of the termination of the partner's authority to bind to the extent that such termination either cancels a supplement to partnership authority under R.U.P.A. § 303(d) or restricts authority to transfer real property under § 303(e).

Parallel U.P.A.:   None.

Important Changes: There was no prior mechanism for limiting a dissociated partner's power to bind the partnership or liability for post-dissociation transactions by means of a central filing, although U.P.A. § 35 did provide for giving notice of dissolution by publication.

Analysis: This device may be a reasonable way to let the partnership terminate authority and liability after partner dissociation. However, it may be unrealistic to expect that trade creditors who deal repeatedly with a partnership will constantly check the public records to determine whether partners have dissociated. Thus, the effect of this provision, like that of the exhaustion requirement in § 307, may be to cause creditors to rely more heavily on the liability of the firm than on individual partners.[211]

Note that, under Section 308(d), a person does not continue to be liable as a partner merely because of a failure to file a statement of dissociation to indicate the partner's dissociation.

§ 8.705. CONTINUED USE OF PARTNERSHIP NAME

Section 705

Continued use of a partnership name, or a dissociated partner's name as part thereof, by partners continuing the business does not of itself make the dissociated partner liable for an obligation of the partners or the partnership continuing the business.

Summary: Partnership's continued use of its name after a partner's dissociation does not alone continue the dissociated partner's liability for partnership debts.

Parallel U.P.A.:   § 41(10).

Important Changes: None.

Analysis: None.

§ 8.801. EVENTS CAUSING DISSOLUTION AND WINDING UP OF PARTNERSHIP BUSINESS

Section 801

A partnership is dissolved, and its business must be wound up, only upon the occurrence of any of the following events:

---

[211] The effect of § 704 of terminating post-dissociation authority and liability invites a reexamination of the effect of the statement of partnership authority under § 303. Section 303 allows partnerships to limit authority only in real property transactions because of the assumption that creditors will not routinely check the public record in connection with other types of transactions. Yet because § 704 forces creditors to check repeatedly for filings of statements of dissociation, letting partnerships limit authority even in non–real property transactions might not significantly increase creditors' burdens. Similar observations apply to the § 806 statement of dissolution discussed infra.

(1) in a partnership at will, the partnership's having notice from a partner, other than a partner who is dissociated under Section 601(2) through (10), of that partner's express will to withdraw as a partner, or on a later date specified by the partner;

(2) in a partnership for a definite term or particular undertaking:

(i) within 90 days after a partner's dissociation by death or otherwise under Section 601(6) through (10) or wrongful dissociation under Section 602(b), the express will of at least half of the remaining partners to wind up the partnership business, for which purpose a partner's rightful dissociation pursuant to Section 602(b)(2)(i) constitutes the expression of that partner's will to wind up the partnership business;

(ii) the express will of all of the partners to wind up the partnership business; or

(iii) the expiration of the term or the completion of the undertaking;

(3) an event agreed to in the partnership agreement resulting in the winding up of the partnership business;

(4) an event that makes it unlawful for all or substantially all of the business of the partnership to be continued, but a cure of illegality within 90 days after notice to the partnership of the event is effective retroactively to the date of the event for purposes of this section;

(5) on application by a partner, a judicial determination that:

(i) the economic purpose of the partnership is likely to be unreasonably frustrated;

(ii) another partner has engaged in conduct relating to the partnership business which makes it not reasonably practicable to carry on the business in partnership with that partner; or

(iii) it is not otherwise reasonably practicable to carry on the partnership business in conformity with the partnership agreement; or

(6) on application by a transferee of a partner's transferable interest, a judicial determination that it is equitable to wind up the partnership business:

(i) after the expiration of the term or completion of the undertaking, if the partnership was for a definite term or particular undertaking at the time of the transfer or entry of the charging order that gave rise to the transfer; or

(ii) at any time, if the partnership was a partnership at will at the time of the transfer or entry of the charging order that gave rise to the transfer.

Summary: Provides that a partnership is dissolved, and its business must be wound up if (1) the partnership is at will and receives notice from a partner who has not dissociated by some other cause of that partner's withdrawal by express will; (2) the partnership is for a definite term or particular undertaking, a partner dissociates wrongfully or by bankruptcy or death (or an equivalent event for a partner who is not an individual), and a majority decide to dissolve within

90 days thereafter; (3) an event occurs that the partners agreed should cause winding up; (4) it is unlawful to continue the business; or (5) a court so decrees.

Parallel U.P.A.:   §§ 31, 32.

Important Changes: Like the U.P.A., R.U.P.A. § 801 provides that the partnership must be wound up on occurrence of an event causing dissolution. However, unlike the U.P.A., R.U.P.A. § 801(2) provides that a partnership for a term — i.e., one that is not "at will"[212] does not dissolve, and therefore does not liquidate, upon wrongful dissociation or dissociation by death or related events unless a majority[213] of the partners agree to wind up or dissociate within 90 days after the dissociation. Thus, the partners can continue by acquiescence and the nonwrongful partners can avoid both dissolution and liquidation. Also, R.U.P.A. § 802, discussed below, provides that the partners may waive dissolution and retroactively undo the winding up at any time prior to termination.

R.U.P.A. also clarifies the effect of partnership agreements. R.U.P.A. § 801 is subject to contrary provision in the partnership agreement pursuant to R.U.P.A. § 103, except that the partners may not contract to avoid judicial dissolution or dissolution for unlawfulness under subsections 801(4)-(6). Thus, the partnership can avoid dissolution by agreement. Also, subsection (3) provides for dissolution upon "an event agreed to in the partnership agreement resulting in the winding up of the partnership business."

Other changes include the following:

1. Section 801(1) provides for dissolution of a partnership at will by "the partnership's having notice from a partner" of the partner's express will to withdraw. "Notice" is defined in R.U.P.A. § 102(b) to include knowledge and reason to know as well as receipt of "notification." Because of this broad definition of "notice," it is not clear whether or to what extent R.U.P.A. has changed prior law concerning partner acts that dissolve a partnership. Moreover, because the act explicitly provides for dissolution only if the partnership has notice of a partner's express will to withdraw, it is not clear whether the partnership dissolves if the

---

[212] R.U.P.A. § 101(6) defines a "partnership at will" as "a partnership in which the partners have not agreed to remain partners until the expiration of a definite term or the completion of a particular undertaking." As confirmed by the Official Comment, the partners must not only agree to a term, but must also agree to remain partners until the expiration of the term. Only this sort of an agreement should matter for purposes of determining whether the partners have the right to continue the firm after a co-partner's dissociation. *See* Bromberg & Ribstein, § 7.13(c)(3). Unfortunately, the Comment helps perpetuate the confusion under prior law by citing as an example of a partnership for a term Stainton v. Tarantino, 637 F. Supp. 1051 (E.D. Pa. 1986). That case involved an agreement to dissolve *no later than* Dec. 30, 2020 — i.e., an agreement for a maximum rather than minimum term.

[213] The 1994 version of R.U.P.A. provided for a "majority in interest" vote. This term was not defined in the Act but, according to Comment 5(i) to § 801, "is intended to satisfy Internal Revenue Service regulations regarding continuity of life." With the advent of the check-the-box rule, this awkward formulation was unnecessary and therefore was deleted by the 1997 amendment.

partner expresses a will to dissolve, as would have been the case under the U.P.A.

2. Section 801(4) provides for dissolution if it is unlawful to carry on the partnership, but only if it is "unlawful for all or substantially all of the business of the partnership to be continued." If the partnership cures the illegality within 90 days after it has notice of the event, the cure is effective retroactively to the date of the event. Also, under R.U.P.A. § 601(4)(i), the partners may, by unanimous vote, expel a partner if it is unlawful to carry on the partnership business with that partner. Thus, R.U.P.A. lets partnerships avoid many of the problems of dissolution for illegality discussed in this section.

3. Under § 801(5) and (6) the dissolution occurs when the relevant "judicial determination" is made. Because it is not clear whether the "determination" is an initial order, a final resolution, or some other stage of the proceeding, R.U.P.A. carries forward the uncertainty in the U.P.A. case law concerning the time of dissolution.[214]

4. Section 801(5)(i) improves somewhat on the U.P.A. by providing for judicial dissolution only when "the economic purpose of the partnership is likely to be unreasonably frustrated," rather than when the partnership can only be carried on at a "loss," as under the U.P.A. § 32(1)(e). This will prevent unintentional dissolution in tax shelter partnerships that are producing book losses. *See* Comment 7 to § 801.

5. Section § 801(5), the analog to the "equitable" ground of judicial dissolution under the U.P.A., restricts the court's discretion by specifying that the court may dissolve only when it is impracticable to carry on the business.

6. R.U.P.A. does not include an analog to U.P.A. § 39, which provides for rights of a person who was fraudulently induced to invest in a partnership.[215]

Analysis: The issue of when the partnership should dissolve and liquidate, and in particular whether it should liquidate on dissociation of a single partner, is one of the most controversial in partnership law. In analyzing this issue, consider the small, informal partnership operating without an agreement—the situation in which a partnership statute is most valuable, and therefore the situation for which the statute should be designed. Should a partner who wishes to leave have the right to compel winding up of the firm, or only the right to a buyout and indemnification against liabilities?

---

[214] *See* Bromberg & Ribstein, § 7.06(a)(3).

[215] Comment 5 to Section 405 says that "R.U.P.A. . . . leaves it to the general law of rescission to determine the rights of a person fraudulently induced to invest in a partnership. *See* Section 104(a)." However, it is not clear how that law will resolve difficult questions of defrauded partners' rights vis-à-vis innocent creditors and co-partners. *See* Bromberg & Ribstein, § 7.20.

It is important to emphasize that the question is *not* whether the partnership "should be" continued. Rather, since the partners can contract around the statute either at the time of their original agreement or at the time of a dissolution event, the appropriate question is whether the partners who wish to continue the firm should have negotiating leverage. If the leaving partner may compel liquidation, the firm nevertheless will continue if the other partners, in effect, purchase this right. If the rights are reversed, the firm will be liquidated if the leaving partner buys out the other partners and sells the firm.

In answering the critical question of whether the leaving or continuing partners should have negotiating leverage, it is important to keep in mind that the parties have made open-ended investments of their human and financial capital and personal credit in an ongoing business. It follows that the group would not want to give any member the right at any time to force the partners who want to continue to, in effect, pay for the right to do so. As a practical matter, such a liquidation right puts the whole group at the mercy of any individual partner who can time the call to facilitate a takeover of the firm at an advantageous price.[216] Although partners can draft around the statutory rule, the statute arguably should not force most firms to engage in customized drafting. Moreover, such a default rule exposes partnerships to risks from agreements that incompletely vary the statutory rule and is not a viable option for the very informal, often unintentional, partnerships for which the statute should be designed.

Notwithstanding these considerations, U.P.A. §§ 31 and 38 give the leaving partner a right to compel liquidation. This rule was probably an application of the extreme aggregate view of partnership as an association among *particular* parties that necessarily ends when one of the parties wants it to. In other words, the U.P.A. drafters probably did not consider carefully the costs of the liquidation right. Whatever the U.P.A. drafters thought, 80 years of the U.P.A. has demonstrated the inappropriateness of liquidation at will, as indicated by the standard practice of drafting around the right and the judicial decisions that have found some way to qualify it.[217]

The concern for payoff of partnership liabilities is probably the best argument for dissolution at will. However, in light of the high potential costs of the liquidation right, the problem is best addressed by the full indemnification of dissociating partners provided for in § 701(d). There is also arguably some need to protect minority partners from majority oppression. But this does not necessarily justify giving each partner the power to compel liquidation of the firm rather than merely a right to a buyout. Also, partners' rights to seek judicial

---

[216] *See generally* Ribstein, note 178, supra, at 384–89, 393–95 (discussing the risk of takeover and how a liquidation right increases this risk).

[217] Some of these cases are reviewed in *id.* at 374–75.

dissolution or expulsion mitigate potential mistreatment.[218] In any event, the potentially helpless position of the partners who wish to continue the firm discussed above is at least as serious as the plight of partners who want to leave.

Thus, R.U.P.A. is arguably misguided in preserving a partner's power to liquidate a partnership at will. But R.U.P.A. § 801(2) at least improves on the U.P.A. by permitting continuation by a majority of the partners in the event of certain types of partner dissociations from a partnership for an unexpired term or uncompleted undertaking. The U.P.A., by contrast, permits continuation in this situation only if all of the remaining partners agree. It makes no sense to give the liquidation right to a partner in a partnership for a definite term or undertaking merely because another partner has dissociated. Rather, it is logical to infer from the parties' agreement to a definite term or undertaking that premature liquidation prior to expiration of the term or undertaking would be particularly costly.

In addition to substantive problems with partnership dissolution, the term itself has been a source of confusion with the related concepts of termination and partner dissociation under the U.P.A.[219] R.U.P.A. may increase the confusion by changing the meaning of the term to an event which requires winding up when the partners do not agree to continue pursuant to § 801(2)(i) or § 802(b). The Texas provision discussed below eliminates the term.

Just as partnerships may be formed without a writing, R.U.P.A. § 801 does not require a withdrawing partner to express his will to withdraw in writing. However, a detailed agreement to dissolve may be subject to the statute of frauds if the terms create obligations that cannot be satisfied in less than one year.[220]

State variations

Arizona provides for continuation of a partnership that is left with one or no partners through addition by remaining partners and transferees of the requisite number of partners.[221]

Oregon departs from the R.U.P.A. model (rightly under the above analysis) in requiring a majority vote for dissolution of a partnership at will (and a unanimous vote for dissolution of a partnership for a term).[222]

---

[218] These remedies are provided for in R.U.P.A. §§ 601(5) and 801(4)–(6). They are also designated in R.U.P.A. § 103(5)–(6) as not subject to the parties' contrary agreement. Accordingly, the act provides for a sort of judicial "escape valve" that protects parties against oppressive effects of continuation agreements that could not have been anticipated at the time of the agreement.

[219] See Bromberg & Ribstein, § 7.01.

[220] See Knudson v. Kyllo, __ N.W.2d __, 2012 WL 3031350 (N.D. July 26, 2012).

[221] Ariz. Rev. Stat. § 29-1071(7).

[222] Or. Rev. Stat. § 67.290.

Tennessee follows original 1994 format in providing for dissolution within 90 days of dissociation unless before that time a majority in interest of the remaining partners agree to continue the partnership.[223]

Texas eliminates the term "dissolution." It defines events of withdrawal[224] similar to dissociation in R.U.P.A. § 601, and events (including certain withdrawals) which require a winding up[225] similar to R.U.P.A. § 801, and requires buyout (redemption) of a withdrawn partner unless an event requiring winding up occurs within 60 days of withdrawal.[226]

§ 8.802. PARTNERSHIP CONTINUES AFTER DISSOLUTION

Section 802

(a) Subject to subsection (b), a partnership continues after dissolution only for the purpose of winding up its business. The partnership is terminated when the winding up of its business is completed.

(b) At any time after the dissolution of a partnership and before the winding up of its business is completed, all of the partners, including any dissociating partner other than a wrongfully dissociating partner, may waive the right to have the partnership's business wound up and the partnership terminated. In that event:

(1) the partnership resumes carrying on its business as if dissolution had never occurred, and any liability incurred by the partnership or a partner after the dissolution and before the waiver is determined as if dissolution had never occurred; and

(2) the rights of a third party accruing under Section 804(1) or arising out of conduct in reliance on the dissolution before the third party knew or received a notification of the waiver may not be adversely affected.

Summary: This section provides that the partnership continues after dissolution for purposes of winding up until termination. However, at any time prior to completion of winding up, the partners may decide by unanimous vote (not

---

[223] Tenn. Code Ann. § 61-1-801(2).
[224] Tex. Rev. Civ. Stat. Ann. art. 6132b-6.01.
[225] Tex. Rev. Civ. Stat. Ann. art. 6132b-8.01.
[226] Tex. Rev. Civ. Stat. Ann. art. 6132b-7.01.

including any wrongfully dissolving partner) to waive the dissolution and continue the partnership business. If they do so the dissolution is retroactively nullified and pre-waiver liabilities are determined as if dissolution never occurred. This does not affect the rights of third parties who relied on the dissolution before receiving notice of the waiver, or entered into winding up transactions with the partnership that are binding under § 804(1).

Parallel U.P.A.:   U.P.A. § 30.

Important Changes: Under the U.P.A., the partnership necessarily is at least technically dissolved on the happening of an event that causes dissolution, and there is no way to reverse the dissolution even if the partners decide to continue the business.

Analysis: Retroactive waiver of a dissolution may be significant for both partners' internal rights and the rights of third parties. For partners, it means that winding up and paying off debts suddenly becomes a buyout and indemnification. For third parties, the dissolution and winding up may have triggered rights under contracts. Also, whether the firm is winding up or continuing affects the partners' authority to bind the firm. Section 802 substantially protects affected parties by providing that nonwrongfully dissociating partners must consent to the continuation, and that the waiver of dissolution does not affect the rights of third parties who relied on the dissolution or a member's post-dissolution authority. Indeed, the waiver may provide a windfall for some pre-waiver third parties whose contracts were unauthorized as winding-up transactions were, in effect, ratified by the firm's decision to again become a going concern (*see* Comment 3 to § 802).

Since § 802 substantially protects parties affected by a waiver of dissolution it does not raise serious policy issues.[227] However, the notice and consent requirements limit the usefulness of the section since the validity of the continuation is threatened by any member who claims oral dissent from the continuation or any creditor who relied on the dissolution. Accordingly, the members who wish to continue might be better off forming a new business association rather than by using the odd procedure provided for in this section.

---

[227] For criticism of a version of R.U.P.A. § 802, on which U.L.L.C.A. § 802 is based, which originally did not adequately protect dissociating members or third parties who might be injured by the waiver, see Prime Time, note 2, supra. Note that § 802 may have unexpected effects on LLP registration. *See* § 3.11, supra.

Note that this section does not protect wrongfully dissolving partners or third parties whose rights were automatically triggered by the dissolution but who did not act in reliance on the dissolution. These effects may give partners incentives to act opportunistically by causing and then reversing a dissolution. Although this sort of conduct may be policed by good-faith duties, third parties should be wary of the potential effects of § 802 when entering into contracts with R.U.P.A.-based partnerships.

As discussed above in connection with § 801, R.U.P.A. already provides for significant continuity by default and lets the partners contract for even more. Accordingly, partnerships and legislators should consider whether the additional continuity provided by § 802 is useful enough that it is worth the uncertainty and confusion it might create.

§ 8.803. RIGHT TO WIND UP PARTNERSHIP BUSINESS

Section 803

(a) After dissolution, a partner who has not wrongfully dissociated may participate in winding up the partnership's business, but on application of any partner, partner's legal representative, or transferee, the [designate the appropriate court], for good cause shown, may order judicial supervision of the winding up.

(b) The legal representative of the last surviving partner may wind up a partnership's business.

(c) A person winding up a partnership's business may preserve the partnership business or property as a going concern for a reasonable time, prosecute and defend actions and proceedings, whether civil, criminal, or administrative, settle and close the partnership's business, dispose of and transfer the partnership's property, discharge the partnership's liabilities, distribute the assets of the partnership pursuant to Section 807, settle disputes by mediation or arbitration, and perform other necessary acts.

Summary: Provides that a partner who has not wrongfully dissociated may participate in winding up the partnership and specifies activities that are appropriate for winding up.

Parallel U.P.A.: § 37.

Important Changes: The list of activities that a winding-up partner may engage in was not included in the U.P.A.

Analysis: This section attempts to clarify the extent of the partners' right to wind up by specifying certain acts that winding up partners can engage in. The specific list is noncontroversial, but the general statement of the power to "preserve the partnership business or property as a going concern for a reasonable time" could cause uncertainty and litigation if it is interpreted as permitting the partners to avoid winding up for an extended period.[228]

A more important problem with this section is that, like the U.P.A., it fails to clarify the extent to which fewer than all of the partners can exercise winding up powers. While some courts have held that fewer than a majority of the partners have post-dissolution authority only to conduct ordinary partnership business,[229] others have held that fewer than all of the partners can sell all of the partnership's property in connection with dissolution.[230] The latter result arguably frustrates the partners' expectation to participate in significant decisions of the firm.

§ 8.804.   PARTNER'S POWER TO BIND PARTNERSHIP AFTER DISSOLUTION

Section 804

Subject to Section 805, a partnership is bound by a partner's act after dissolution that:

(1) is appropriate for winding up the partnership business; or

(2) would have bound the partnership under Section 301 before dissolution, if the other party to the transaction did not have notice of the dissolution.

---

[228] For cases in which the courts have permitted extensive continuation, see Paciaroni v. Crane, 408 A.2d 946 (Del. Ch. 1979); Dow v. Beals, 149 Misc. 631, 268 N.Y.S. 425 (1933); Gregg v. Bernardi, 250 Or. 458, 443 P.2d 166 (1968). The Comment to § 803 approves the result in *Paciaroni.*

[229] *See* Paciaroni v. Crane, 408 A.2d 946 (Del. Ch. 1979) (two of three partners permitted to race the partnership's horse over the objection of the third); Simmons v. Quick-Stop Food Mart, 307 N.C. 33, 296 S.E.2d 275 (1982) (conveyance of partnership property in connection with dissolution not in usual scope of business but was authorized or ratified by co-partner).

[230] *See* Cunningham & Co. v. Consolidated Realty Mgmt., 803 F.2d 840 (5th Cir. 1986). *See also* Froemming v. Gate City Fed. Sav. & Loan Ass'n, 822 F.2d 723 (8th Cir. 1986) (N.D. law; jury issue whether dissolution provisions of partnership agreement required liquidation, and so excepted sale of assets on dissolution from provision requiring two-thirds vote for extraordinary transactions); Goldstick v. Kusmiersky, 593 F. Supp. 639 (N.D. Ill. 1984) (one partner allowed to sue on partnership claim despite refusal of other partner to join, relying on U.P.A. § 35(1)(a)). *See generally* Bromberg & Ribstein, § 4.04(c).

Summary: Subject to § 805 (which provides for filing of a statement of dissolution) the partnership is bound by post-dissolution acts that are either appropriate to winding up or, as to creditors who lacked "notice" of the dissolution, are within the acting partner's pre-dissolution authority.

Parallel U.P.A.:   §§ 33, 35.

Important Changes: Considered in isolation, this section expands the partnership's liability for post-dissolution acts compared to U.P.A. § 35 by omitting some limitations in partners' continuing authority regarding unknown or inactive partners, creditors who had not extended credit prior to dissolution, acts of bankrupt partners, and non–winding-up acts of partners of unlawful partnerships. However, considered together with § 805, discussed below, the effect of this section is actually to shrink partners' post-dissolution exposure.

Analysis: Under this section, the effect of dissolution in terminating a partner's authority is treated similarly to the effect of a withdrawal of authority under § 301: it affects only those creditors who have "notice" of the lack of authority.[231] Since the partnership cannot escape being bound by the transaction without notifying creditors, it has a strong incentive to file a § 805 statement of dissolution. As discussed below, if the partnership does file such a statement it can cut off partners' continuing authority more effectively than partnerships could under the U.P.A.

Note that the expanded notice requirement under § 805 treats dissolved partnerships differently from the way § 702 treats partners who dissociate from a continuing partnership: the authority of *dissociating* partners is terminated after two years even as to creditors who lack notice of the dissociation,[232] and the act is binding only as to creditors who not only do not have notice of the dissociation, but also "reasonably believe[]" at the time of the transaction that the dissociated partner is a partner. Thus, whether a partner's post-dissociation act binds the partnership may depend on whether the dissociation causes a dissolution.

---

[231] Note that under § 102, the concept of "notice" is somewhat broader than that of "notification" which controls under § 301.

[232] This distinction may be justified by the fact that winding up presumably has a limited duration while post-dissociation liability could continue indefinitely. However, the partners could effectively continue the firm by "winding up" and selling it as a going concern. This potential functional similarity between winding up and continuation casts doubt on the wisdom of sharply distinguishing the two situations for purposes of cutting off partner authority.

§ 8.805. STATEMENT OF DISSOLUTION

Section 805

(a) After dissolution, a partner who has not wrongfully dissociated may file a statement of dissolution stating the name of the partnership and that the partnership has dissolved and is winding up its business.

(b) A statement of dissolution cancels a filed statement of partnership authority for the purposes of Section 303(d) and is a limitation on authority for the purposes of Section 303(e).

(c) For the purposes of Sections 301 and 804, a person not a partner is deemed to have notice of the dissolution and the limitation on the partners' authority as a result of the statement of dissolution 90 days after it is filed.

(d) After filing and, if appropriate, recording a statement of dissolution, a dissolved partnership may file and, if appropriate, record a statement of partnership authority which will operate with respect to a person not a partner as provided in Section 303(d) and (e) in any transaction, whether or not the transaction is appropriate for winding up the partnership business.

Summary: Allows the partnership to file a statement of dissolution that is deemed to provide notice of dissolution 90 days after filing and that immediately limits a partner's authority to the extent provided for in § 303(d) and (e).[233]

Parallel U.P.A.:   None.

Important Changes: There was no provision in the U.P.A. for the filing of a statement that cuts off post-dissolution authority, although U.P.A. § 35 permits giving notice of dissolution by publication.

Analysis: The statement of dissolution potentially shrinks partnerships' exposure to post-dissolution liability as compared with the U.P.A. Given the expanded exposure to post-dissolution debts under § 804 for partnerships that do not file this statement, most partnerships undoubtedly will opt to provide constructive notice by filing a statement of dissolution. The net result is that creditors of R.U.P.A. partnerships will have to be continually on the alert for new partnership filings.

---

[233] Under R.U.P.A. § 303(d) the statement of dissolution would withdraw a supplement to partner authority contained in a statement of partnership authority. Under § 303(e) the statement of dissolution would limit partner authority to convey real property.

State variation

Delaware provides that if the partnership fails or refuses to file a statement of dissolution, a partner or dissociated partner who is or may be adversely affected by the failure or refusal may petition the Court of Chancery to direct the filing.[234]

§ 8.806.   PARTNER'S LIABILITY TO OTHER PARTNERS AFTER DISSOLUTION

Section 806

(a) Except as otherwise provided in subsection (b) and Section 306, after dissolution a partner is liable to the other partners for the partner's share of any partnership liability incurred under Section 804.

(b) A partner who, with knowledge of the dissolution, incurs a partnership liability under Section 804(2) by an act that is not appropriate for winding up the partnership business is liable to the partnership for any damage caused to the partnership arising from the liability.

Summary: Provides that after dissolution a partner is liable to the other partners for his share of winding-up liabilities, except that a partner who, with knowledge of the winding up, incurs a partnership liability by an act that is inappropriate for winding up is liable for any resulting loss.[235]

Parallel U.P.A.:   § 34.

Important Changes: This section does not vary the rules according to the cause of dissolution as does the U.P.A. Also, § 103 clarifies that the partners can contract around this provision.

Analysis: None.

LLP Cross-reference: Section 3.09(f).

---

[234] Del. Code Ann., tit. 6, § 15-805(e).

[235] Note that R.U.P.A. § 802, discussed supra, provides a special rule for the exposure of a dissociating partner to liabilities incurred during the 90-day "limbo" period.

§ 8.807. SETTLEMENT OF ACCOUNTS AND CONTRIBUTIONS AMONG PARTNERS

Section 807

(a) In winding up a partnership's business, the assets of the partnership, including the contributions of the partners required by this section, must be applied to discharge its obligations to creditors, including, to the extent permitted by law, partners who are creditors. Any surplus must be applied to pay in cash the net amount distributable to partners in accordance with their right to distributions under subsection (b).

(b) Each partner is entitled to a settlement of all partnership accounts upon winding up the partnership business. In settling accounts among the partners, the profits and losses that result from the liquidation of the partnership assets must be credited and charged to the partners' accounts. The partnership shall make a distribution to a partner in an amount equal to any excess of the credits over the charges in the partner's account. A partner shall contribute to the partnership an amount equal to any excess of the charges over the credits in the partner's account but excluding from the calculation charges attributable to an obligation for which the partner is not personally liable under Section 306.

(c) If a partner fails to contribute the full amount required under subsection (b), all of the other partners shall contribute, in the proportions in which those partners share partnership losses, the additional amount necessary to satisfy the partnership obligations for which they are personally liable under Section 306. A partner or partner's legal representative may recover from the other partners any contributions the partner makes to the extent the amount contributed exceeds that partner's share of the partnership obligations for which the partner is personally liable under Section 306.

(d) After the settlement of accounts, each partner shall contribute, in the proportion in which the partner shares partnership losses, the amount necessary to satisfy partnership obligations that were not known at the time of the settlement and for which the partner is personally liable under Section 306.

(e) The estate of a deceased partner is liable for the partner's obligation to contribute to the partnership.

(f) An assignee for the benefit of creditors of a partnership or a partner, or a person appointed by a court to represent creditors of a partnership or a partner, may enforce a partner's obligation to contribute to the partnership.

Summary: Provides for distribution of partnership property and contributions by partners on liquidation of the partnership.

Parallel U.P.A.: § 40.

Important Changes: § 807 makes several changes in the distribution scheme now provided for in U.P.A. § 40: it eliminates the priority of outside creditors over partner creditors; eliminates the priority of repayment of capital over repayment of surplus; eliminates the "dual priority" or "jingle" rule that gives partnership creditors priority as to partnership property and separate creditors priority as to separate property; provides that profits and losses are credited or charged to partners' "accounts"; provides that a partner is entitled to a distribution, or must make a contribution, in the amount of the difference between credits and charges in his account; and provides that partners must contribute toward partnership obligations not known when accounts were settled.

Analysis: This section raises many questions. First, it is not clear if R.U.P.A. requires a court to reconstruct partnership "accounts" for informal partnerships rather than determining assets and liabilities and dividing them.

Second, R.U.P.A. provides that any deficit in the partners' capital accounts constitutes a contribution obligation unless otherwise agreed. Yet these deficits may reflect only the parties' intentions regarding the tax consequences of partnership and not the duty actually to make contributions to the partnership. This has engendered some confusion under the U.P.A.[236] Partners in R.U.P.A.-based partnerships will at least know what the rule is and should be careful to draft around the default rule if it does not reflect their intention.

Third, R.U.P.A. §§ 401(b) and 807 (*see* Comment 3 to § 807) raise questions concerning the long-standing priority of capital losses under the U.P.A.[237] In other words, although capital partners receive distributions from solvent partnerships that reflect their capital contributions, when liabilities exceed assets the non-capital-contributing partners have no obligation to repay the lost capital. Priority of capital losses was clearly the rule under the U.P.A., has been applied in many cases,[238] and is arguably consistent with partners' expectations.[239] But some

---

[236] *Compare* Park Cities Corp. v. Byrd, 534 S.W.2d 668 (Tex. 1976) (requiring general partner in a limited partnership to repay on dissolution a deficit in her account resulting from depreciation charges), *with* Lamborn v. Dittmer, 873 F.2d 522 (2d Cir. 1989) (holding that an agreement requiring losses to be reflected in the partners' capital accounts did not compel the partners to make capital contributions).

[237] *See* U.P.A. § 40(b), which lists partners' capital contributions as a debt that must be paid by partner contributions.

[238] For cases recognizing the partners' obligation to repay capital losses under the U.P.A., see Cooper v. Cooper, 289 Ala. 263, 266 So. 2d 871 (Ala. 1972); Schymanski v. Conventz, 674 P.2d 281 (Alaska 1983); Hamilton Airport Adver. v. Hamilton, 462 N.E.2d 228 (Ind. App. 1984); Sinman v. Mezoff, 327 Mass. 285, 98 N.E.2d 263 (1951); Vassallo v. Sexauer, 22 Mich. App. 188, 177 N.W.2d 470 (1970); Bass v. Daetwyler, 305 S.W.2d 339 (Mo. App. 1957); Halsey v. Choate, 27 N.C. App. 49, 217 S.E.2d 740, *cert. denied*, 288 N.C. 730, 220 S.E.2d 350 (1975); Dycus v. Belco Indus., Inc., 569 P.2d 553 (Okla. App. 1977); First W. Mortgage Co. v. Hotel Gearhart, Inc., 268 Or. 213, 522 P.2d 881 (1974); Lyman v. Wood, 169 Pa. Super. 512, 83 A.2d 420 (1951); Eardley v. Sammons, 8 Utah 2d 159, 330 P.2d 122 (1985); Bromberg & Ribstein, § 6.02(c)(2).

[239] For a discussion of the rationale of the capital-loss-sharing rule, see *id.* For criticism of this change in R.U.P.A., see Prime Time, at 73–75.

courts have expressed dissatisfaction with the rule, since it seems to differentiate between contributions of labor and capital, which should be treated equivalently.[240]

R.U.P.A. § 807(b) provides that "[t]he partnership shall make a distribution to a partner in an amount equal to any excess of the credits over the charges in the partner's account. A partner shall contribute to the partnership an amount equal to any excess of the charges over the credits in the partner's account." There is no distribution priority for capital contributions. There is no R.U.P.A. distinction between capital and other losses (income tax law is contra but not controlling here) and no explicit requirement that capital losses be charged solely against the capital contributor's account.

Some commentators conclude that R.U.P.A. requires capital losses to be charged (like other losses) against all the partners' accounts — equally or according to profit shares if profit shares are not equal — absent contrary agreement. A "non-capital" partner will contribute to "capital" losses to the extent her capital account is negative as a result of sharing such losses. Comment 3 to R.U.P.A. § 402 supports this interpretation by stating that R.U.P.A. carries forward the U.P.A. equal treatment of "capital" and "ordinary" losses. The Comment says that the U.P.A. phrase "whether capital or operating" was deleted because the distinction of losses is inconsistent with contemporary accounting practice and terminology. That is quite true but has no bearing on the loss sharing and contribution structure of the statute itself. Rather, the deletion suggests that the phrase was superfluous if U.P.A. was construed in light of its structure, which is similar to that of R.U.P.A. The drafters' comment that it may seem unfair to require service partners to share capital losses merely notes a fairness issue that deserves consideration by the partners in designing their agreement.

However, there may be at least enough doubt whether R.U.P.A. adopts the U.P.A. rule regarding sharing of capital losses that courts sympathetic with service partners may be tempted to interpret R.U.P.A. as having changed the U.P.A. rule regarding sharing of capital losses. He places weight on R.U.P.A. § 401's deletion of "whether capital or operating" and the statement in Comment 3 to R.U.P.A. § 807 that "[t]he partners may, however, agree to share 'operating' losses differently from 'capital' losses, thereby continuing the U.P.A. distinction." The U.P.A. does not, of course, distinguish capital and operating losses. The R.U.P.A. drafters apparently confused the parity of capital *contributions* and operating *profits* with the separate issue of the parity of capital and operating *losses*. It is the separate treatment of capital contributions and operating results that Comment 3 to § 401 apparently refers to as inconsistent with accounting practice. The U.P.A. distinguishes between capital contributions and profits by giving the former a preferred status. This preference, in turn, creates the service partners' obligation to contribute toward capital losses. It follows that, by eliminating the preferred status of capital contributions, R.U.P.A. eliminates the default duty to contribute toward capital losses.

---

[240] *See* Kessler v. Antinora, 279 N.J. Super. 471, 653 A.2d 579 (N.J. Super. 1995) (construing agreement not to require service partner to contribute toward loss of capital).

Partners in R.U.P.A. partnerships should be careful to draft around this rule if it does not reflect their intentions. Indeed, the spread of the limited liability partnership makes it increasingly likely that the issue will arise only in the most informal partnerships that have not elected LLP status.

LLP Cross-reference: Section 3.09(f).

State variations

Delaware includes provisions for known and unknown claims against dissolved LLPs and for liability and limitations on distributions.[241]

Tennessee does not include the last clause of § 807(b) referring to LLP partners.[242]

§ 8.901. DEFINITIONS

Section 901

In this [article]:

(1) "General partner" means a partner in a partnership and a general partner in a limited partnership.

(2) "Limited partner" means a limited partner in a limited partnership.

(3) "Limited partnership" means a limited partnership created under the [State Limited Partnership Act], predecessor law, or comparable law of another jurisdiction.

(4) "Partner" includes both a general partner and a limited partner.

Summary: Includes definitions of "partner," "limited partner," "limited partnership" and "general partner" for purposes of this article, which provides for mergers of partnerships.

Important Changes: U.P.A. did not provide for mergers or conversions.

Analysis: Section 901 defines "partner" to include limited partners. This highlights the general issue of article 9's purporting to cover conversions and mergers involving limited partnerships.[243] These matters are more appropriately covered by limited

---

[241] Del. Code Ann., tit. 6, § 15-807(h)–(k). With respect to limitations on distributions in the Delaware act and other state statutes, see Chapter 3, Table 3-1, and § 4.04(d), supra.

[242] Tenn. Code Ann. § 61-1-807.

[243] For other questions and problems regarding R.U.P.A.'s application to limited partnerships, see the analysis of § 202.

partnership statutes. In particular, the general partnership statute is not the place to provide voting requirements for limited partnerships[244] or for the liability of limited partners.[245]

§ 8.902.   CONVERSION OF PARTNERSHIP TO LIMITED PARTNERSHIP

Section 902

(a) A partnership may be converted to a limited partnership pursuant to this section.

(b) The terms and conditions of a conversion of a partnership to a limited partnership must be approved by all of the partners or by a number or percentage specified for conversion in the partnership agreement.

(c) After the conversion is approved by the partners, the partnership shall file a certificate of limited partnership in the jurisdiction in which the limited partnership is to be formed. The certificate must include:

(1) a statement that the partnership was converted to a limited partnership from a partnership;

(2) its former name; and

(3) a statement of the number of votes cast by the partners for and against the conversion and, if the vote is less than unanimous, the number or percentage required to approve the conversion under the partnership agreement.

(d) The conversion takes effect when the certificate of limited partnership is filed or at any later date specified in the certificate.

(e) A general partner who becomes a limited partner as a result of the conversion remains liable as a general partner for an obligation incurred by the partnership before the conversion takes effect. If the other party to a transaction with the limited partnership reasonably believes when entering the transaction that the limited partner is a general partner, the limited partner is liable for an obligation incurred by the limited partnership within 90 days after the conversion takes effect. The limited partner's liability for all other obligations of the limited partnership incurred after the conversion takes effect is that of a limited partner as provided in the [State Limited Partnership Act].

---

[244] *See* R.U.P.A. §§ 902(b) and 905(c)(2), providing for voting by "partners" of limited partnerships.

[245] *See* R.U.P.A. §§ 902(e), 906(c).

Summary: Provides for a method of converting a general partnership into a limited partnership. The conversion must be approved by all partners unless otherwise provided in the partnership agreement. A general partner's liability for partnership debts continues in a manner similar to the continuing liability of dissociating partners under §§ 702 and 703.

Parallel U.P.A.: None.

Important Changes: The U.P.A. does not provide for conversion.

Analysis: Article 9 attempts to clarify how combinations and conversions of partnerships may be accomplished and the effects of these transactions. Under the U.P.A., these transactions were accomplished through admission and dissociation of partners and asset sales.

It may be unclear whether a conversion will be deemed to be effective under R.U.P.A., since § 902 provides for procedural requirements (the filing of a statement that includes certain information) without specifying the effect of noncompliance.

This section, like others in this Article, prescribes rules that relate to limited partnerships, including rules concerning how a person becomes a limited partner. It may not be clear whether these requirements override provisions in the limited partnership statute on, for example, the formation of a limited partnership. Legislatures should be careful to include the necessary provisions in the limited partnership statute.

State variations

Several states, including those that have not adopted R.U.P.A., provide for conversion and merger of partnerships or for comparable procedures. Conversion provisions may be scattered among statutes providing for several different business entities or statutes may provide for conversions among multiple business entities.[246] The following are examples of variations on conversion provisions in R.U.P.A.-type statutes.

California provides that a non-LLP partnership may be converted into a domestic limited partnership or limited liability company or a foreign other business entity, which is defined as "a limited partnership, limited liability company,

---

[246] For an example of a non-R.U.P.A. statute, see Ga. Code § 14-9-206.2 (corporation, LLC or general partnership may elect to become a limited partnership). For provisions in LLC statutes, see Ribstein & Keatinge, App. 11-1. For some examples of multiple entity conversion and merger provisions, see Alabama Business Entities Conversion and Merger Act, 2000 Alabama Laws Act 2000-211; Colo. Corporations and Associations Act, § 7-90-101 *et seq.*; Maine Rev. Stat. tit. 31 M.R.S.A. § 746.

or an unincorporated association (other than a nonprofit association), but excluding a partnership."[247]

Delaware provides for conversion of several different types of entities into domestic partnerships, including LLPs.[248]

Hawaii permits conversion of a domestic partnership or limited liability partnership to a foreign partnership, limited liability partnership, or any other entity.[249]

Illinois provides for merger and conversion of partnerships into LLCs.[250]

New Jersey permits mergers and consolidations among partnerships, corporations, limited partnerships, and limited liability companies.[251]

Ohio permits mergers, consolidations, and conversions between partnerships and one or more additional domestic partnerships or other domestic or foreign entities[252] and provides for appraisal rights for dissenting partners.[253]

Oregon permits conversion between a domestic partnership and several types of business entities including foreign partnership, domestic or foreign LLC, limited partnership, or professional corporation.[254]

Texas permits a partnership to convert to a foreign partnership or any other entity, and any partnership or other entity to convert to a domestic partnership.[255]

§ 8.903. CONVERSION OF LIMITED PARTNERSHIP TO PARTNERSHIP

Section 903

(a) A limited partnership may be converted to a partnership pursuant to this section.

(b) Notwithstanding a provision to the contrary in a limited partnership agreement, the terms and conditions of a conversion of a limited partnership to a partnership must be approved by all of the partners.

(c) After the conversion is approved by the partners, the limited partnership shall cancel its certificate of limited partnership.

(d) The conversion takes effect when the certificate of limited partnership is canceled.

---

[247] Cal. Corp. Code §§ 16901, 16902.
[248] Del. Code Ann., tit. 6, § 15-901.
[249] Haw. Rev. Stat. § 425-192.
[250] 805 ILCS, §§ 206/908-09.
[251] N.J. Rev. Stat. § 42:1A-46.
[252] Ohio Rev. Code § 1776.68, .69, .72, .73
[253] *Id.* § 1776.76–78.
[254] Or. Rev. Stat. § 67.340, .342.
[255] Tex. Rev. Civ. Stat. Ann. art. 6132b-9.05.

(e) A limited partner who becomes a general partner as a result of the conversion remains liable only as a limited partner for an obligation incurred by the limited partnership before the conversion takes effect. Except as otherwise provided in Section 306, the partner is liable as a general partner for an obligation of the partnership incurred after the conversion takes effect.

Summary: Provides for conversion of a limited to a general partnership. The limited partner is liable as such for pre-conversion liabilities, and as a general partner for post-conversion liabilities. The conversion must be approved by all of the partners notwithstanding a contrary provision in the limited partnership agreement.

Parallel U.P.A.: None.

Important Changes: The U.P.A. does not provide for conversion.

Analysis: The **Analysis** of § 902 applies here. As to the relationship with limited partnership statutes, the mandatory unanimity rule probably overrides a provision in the limited partnership statute that permits the parties to contract for limited partner voting rules. As noted in the Comment to Section 903, the unanimity requirement in Section 902 is intended to protect against involuntary personal liability in connection with conversions. It therefore should take precedence over a general statutory provision that does not relate specifically to conversions.[256]

This and the previous section do not say whether a partner who withdraws from the firm prior to the expiration of a term or the undertaking rather than becoming a general or limited partner pursuant to the conversion should be treated as wrongfully dissolving. However, as noted in the Comment to this section, a partner has the power to veto the transaction, and therefore the leverage to negotiate the terms of his withdrawal. *See* the discussion below of the withdrawal provision in R.U.P.A. § 906.

§ 8.904. EFFECT OF CONVERSION

Section 904

(a) A partnership or limited partnership that has been converted pursuant to this [article] is for all purposes the same entity that existed before the conversion.

(b) When a conversion takes effect:

---

[256] By analogy, R.U.P.A. Section 905(c)(2) provides for approval of mergers by all partners of a limited partnership or by "the vote required for approval of a merger" under applicable law.

(1) all property owned by the converting partnership or limited partnership remains vested in the converted entity;

(2) all obligations of the converting partnership or limited partnership continue as obligations of the converted entity; and

(3) an action or proceeding pending against the converting partnership or limited partnership may be continued as if the conversion had not occurred.

Summary: Provides that the converted firm continues to be the same entity and that all property and liabilities of the old firm become that of the new one.

Parallel U.P.A.:   None.

Important Changes: The U.P.A. does not provide for conversions.

Analysis: The statement that the entity is unchanged may cause some confusion. The "entity" is clearly changed in some sense if, for example, an agreement clearly provides for cash-out of members or acceleration of loans upon a conversion. As discussed above in the **Analysis** of § 201, there are problems associated with trying to answer specific questions with reference to the concepts of "entity" or "aggregate."[257] For example, it is not clear whether the conversion procedure avoids the obligation to pay real estate transfer fees that is, whether the conversion causes a transfer of real property to the converted firm.[258] A court may or may not interpret "same entity" language in the conversion statute to indicate a legislative intent that no transfer for value occurs. This is clarified by the Delaware provision discussed below.

It has been held that conversion of a partnership into an LLC does not involve a fraudulent conveyance because plaintiff, a former employee, continued to have the same rights against the converted firm's assets, although the employee had an equitable action against the firm based on the firm's contractual obligation to pay the plaintiff "in kind" his percentage of the net proceeds from sale of the business.[259] On the other hand, a professional LLC formed by a sole proprietor lawyer in order to escape a malpractice/fraud judgment was subjected

---

[257] For cases involving the effect of conversions into LLCs, see Ribstein & Keatinge, § 11.16, nn.82–86.

[258] *See* Wolter v. Wisconsin Dep't of Revenue, 605 N.W.2d 283 (Wis. App. 1999) (holding that a transfer of property to the LLC triggers the fee, reasoning that the transferees received value in the form of an interest in the LLC capital accounts and the limited liability of the LLC form and that an exemption in the transfer fee statute for transfers between family members did not apply).

[259] Kanefield v. SP Distrib. Co., 25 S.W.3d 492 (Mo. App. 2000).

to successor liability for the debts of the sole proprietor because the LLC was a "fraudulent attempt" by defendant to escape his obligation.[260]

It is not clear what effect conversion provisions will have on conversion-like procedures that are not done under the statute. In *C&J Builders & Remodelers v. Geisenheimer*,[261] the court applied an arbitration clause in a sole proprietor's agreement to a successor LLC, relying on Connecticut statutory provisions relating to partnership-LLC conversions as a source of legislative policy.[262]

LLP Cross-reference: Section 3.12(c).

State variation

Delaware provides that, for *purposes of Delaware law*, conversion shall not be deemed to cause a transfer of debts, liabilities or duties,[263] and the converted partnership is the same entity as the pre-conversion partnership.[264] The reference to Delaware law may limit the effect of the conversion vis-à-vis contracts and federal law. Delaware also provides that, in connection with the conversion, rights or securities of, or interests in, the converting entity may be exchanged for cash, property, rights or securities of, or interests in, the conversion partnership or another entity.[265]

§ 8.905.   MERGER OF PARTNERSHIPS

Section 905

(a) Pursuant to a plan of merger approved as provided in subsection (c), a partnership may be merged with one or more partnerships or limited partnerships.

(b) The plan of merger must set forth:

---

[260] Baker v. Dorfman, 2000 WL 1010285 (S.D.N.Y. 2000) (relying partly on *Geishenheimer*, infra).

[261] 249 Conn. 415, 733 A.2d 193 (1999).

[262] *See also* Deveraux's Carpentry Servs., LLC v. Ericson, 1999 WL 956768 (Conn. Super. 1999) (holding, relying on *Geishenheimer*, that a home contractor contracting as a sole proprietorship could enforce the contract through a lien after converting to an LLC because all of the statutory protections afforded the homeowner remained notwithstanding the conversion).

[263] Del. Code Ann., tit. 6, § 15-902(f).

[264] Del. Code Ann., tit. 6, § 15-902(g).

[265] Del. Code Ann., tit. 6, § 15-902(i). *See also* tit. 6, § 15-903 (similar provision relating to conversion of partnership into another entity; also providing that conversion does not require the partnership to wind up unless otherwise agreed).

(1) the name of each partnership or limited partnership that is a party to the merger;

(2) the name of the surviving entity into which the other partnerships or limited partnerships will merge;

(3) whether the surviving entity is a partnership or a limited partnership and the status of each partner;

(4) the terms and conditions of the merger;

(5) the manner and basis of converting the interests of each party to the merger into interests or obligations of the surviving entity, or into money or other property in whole or part; and

(6) the street address of the surviving entity's chief executive office.

(c) The plan of merger must be approved:

(1) in the case of a partnership that is a party to the merger, by all of the partners, or a number or percentage specified for merger in the partnership agreement; and

(2) in the case of a limited partnership that is a party to the merger, by the vote required for approval of a merger by the law of the State or foreign jurisdiction in which the limited partnership is organized and, in the absence of such a specifically applicable law, by all of the partners, notwithstanding a provision to the contrary in the partnership agreement.

(d) After a plan of merger is approved and before the merger takes effect, the plan may be amended or abandoned as provided in the plan.

(e) The merger takes effect on the later of:

(1) the approval of the plan of merger by all parties to the merger, as provided in subsection (c);

(2) the filing of all documents required by law to be filed as a condition to the effectiveness of the merger; or

(3) any effective date specified in the plan of merger.

Summary: Provides a method of merging partnerships with other partnerships or limited partnerships. The merger must be pursuant to a plan of merger that is approved by all of the partners of a partnership that is a party to the merger or by the number or percentage specified for merger in the partnership agreement, and by all of the general and limited partners of a limited partnership that is a party to the merger or by the vote required for approval of a merger by the law of the limited partnership's jurisdiction of organization.

Parallel U.P.A.:   None.

Important Changes: The U.P.A. does not provide for a procedure for merging partnerships.

Analysis: As with conversions, it is unclear when mergers will be deemed to comply with R.U.P.A. because § 905 provides for procedural requirements without specifying the effect of noncompliance. Specifically, § 905 requires a "plan of merger" that must contain certain information. It is not clear whether the transaction is valid if the plan omits some of the information or if the information is contained in a memorandum agreement or even an oral understanding that is not designated as a "plan of merger."

State variations

As noted with respect to Section 902, above, several states, including those that have not adopted RUPA, provide for conversion and merger of partnerships or for comparable procedures. Merger, like conversion, provisions may be scattered among statutes providing for several different business entities or statutes may provide for mergers among multiple business entities.[266] The following are examples of variations on the merger provisions in R.U.P.A.-type statutes.

California provides for merger of "(1) Two or more partnerships into one partnership; (2) One or more partnerships and one or more other business entities into one of those other business entities; (3) One or more partnerships, other than a limited liability partnership, and one or more other business entities into one partnership."[267]

Colorado Corporations and Associations Act[268] combines provisions for the merger or conversion of different types of entities.

Delaware provides for contractual appraisal rights for mergers, consolidations and asset sales.[269]

Missouri permits a domestic partnership to merge or consolidate with or into one or more general partnerships or domestic or foreign limited partnerships, limited liability companies, trusts, business trusts, corporations, real estate investment trusts and other associations or business entities.[270]

New Jersey permits mergers and consolidations among partnerships, corporations, limited partnerships and limited liability companies.[271]

Oregon permits merger between a domestic partnership and several types of business entities including foreign partnership, domestic or foreign LLC, limited partnership or professional corporation.[272]

---

[266] For merger provisions in LLC statutes, see Ribstein & Keatinge, App. 11-1. For citations to multiple entity conversion and merger provisions, see note 246, supra.

[267] Cal. Corp. Code § 16910.

[268] Colo. Rev. Stat. § 7-90-101 *et seq.*

[269] Del. Code Ann., tit. 6, § 15-120.

[270] Mo. Rev. Stat. § 358.520.

[271] N.J. Rev. Stat. § 42:1A-46.

[272] Or. Rev. Stat. § 367.340, .360.

Texas permits a domestic partnership to merge with one or more domestic or foreign partnerships or other entities.[273]

Washington permits domestic partnerships to merge with domestic partnerships, domestic limited partnerships, domestic limited liability companies, or domestic corporations, and permits foreign partnerships, foreign limited liability companies, foreign limited partnerships, and foreign corporations to merge with domestic partnerships, domestic limited liability companies, domestic limited partnerships, or domestic corporations.[274] It also provides for amendment of governing documents and for dissenters' rights.[275]

§ 8.906.   EFFECT OF MERGER

Section 906

(a) When a merger takes effect:

(1) the separate existence of every partnership or limited partnership that is a party to the merger, other than the surviving entity, ceases;

(2) all property owned by each of the merged partnerships or limited partnerships vests in the surviving entity;

(3) all obligations of every partnership or limited partnership that is a party to the merger become the obligations of the surviving entity; and

(4) an action or proceeding pending against a partnership or limited partnership that is a party to the merger may be continued as if the merger had not occurred, or the surviving entity may be substituted as a party to the action or proceeding.

(b) The [Secretary of State] of this State is the agent for service of process in an action or proceeding against a surviving foreign partnership or limited partnership to enforce an obligation of a domestic partnership or limited partnership that is a party to a merger. The surviving entity shall promptly notify the [Secretary of State] of the mailing address of its chief executive office and of any change of address. Upon receipt of process, the [Secretary of State] shall mail a copy of the process to the surviving foreign partnership or limited partnership.

(c) A partner of the surviving partnership or limited partnership is liable for:

---

[273] Tex. Rev. Civ. Stat. Ann. art. 6132b-9.02.
[274] Wash. Rev. Code § 25.05.370, 390.
[275] Wash. Rev. Code §§ 25.05.385, 420–475.

(1) all obligations of a party to the merger for which the partner was personally liable before the merger;

(2) all other obligations of the surviving entity incurred before the merger by a party to the merger, but those obligations may be satisfied only out of property of the entity; and

(3) all obligations of the surviving entity incurred after the merger takes effect, but those obligations may be satisfied only out of property of the entity if the partner is a limited partner.

(d) If the obligations incurred before the merger by a party to the merger are not satisfied out of the property of the surviving partnership or limited partnership, the general partners of that party immediately before the effective date of the merger shall contribute the amount necessary to satisfy that party's obligations to the surviving entity, in the manner provided in Section 807 or in the [Limited Partnership Act] of the jurisdiction in which the party was formed, as the case may be, as if the merged party were dissolved.

(e) A partner of a party to a merger who does not become a partner of the surviving partnership or limited partnership is dissociated from the entity, of which that partner was a partner, as of the date the merger takes effect. The surviving entity shall cause the partner's interest in the entity to be purchased under Section 701 or another statute specifically applicable to that partner's interest with respect to a merger. The surviving entity is bound under Section 702 by an act of a general partner dissociated under this subsection, and the partner is liable under Section 703 for transactions entered into by the surviving entity after the merger takes effect.

Summary: Provides for the effect of a merger between partnerships. Among other things, a merger combines the property and obligations of the constituent companies; a partner of the surviving partnership is personally liable for and must contribute toward the obligations for which he was liable before the merger; the partner is not personally liable for pre-merger liabilities of any other constituent; and a partner of a constituent entity who does not become a partner of the survivor is treated as having dissociated from the survivor and the buyout, liability and authority rules of Sections 701–703 apply to that partner.

Parallel U.P.A.: None.

Important Changes: The U.P.A. does not provide for partnership mergers.

Analysis: The difference between a "merger" and a "conversion" is unclear. The main difference between the two transactions appears to be the statement in § 904 that the converted firm continues to be the same entity. However, as discussed above in the Analysis of § 904, the meaning of that statement is unclear. Moreover, it is not clear that the non-surviving "entity" ceases to exist in a merger as provided by R.U.P.A. § 906(a)(1). Indeed, R.U.P.A. § 906(a)(4) provides that "an action or proceeding pending against a partnership or limited partnership that is a party to the merger may be continued as if the merger had not occurred."

R.U.P.A. Sections 701-703 govern the rights, powers, and liabilities of a partner who does not become a partner in the surviving entity unless there is "another statute specifically applicable to that partner's interest with respect to a merger." As with the other provisions in this Article, this may override contrary provisions in the limited partnership statute. As noted in the Comment, whether the dissociation is wrongful is essentially left to the partnership agreement or to the bargain made by the dissociated partner when he leaves the firm, having in mind the partner's default veto power over mergers under Section 905(c).

LLP Cross-reference: Section 3.12(c).

State variation

Texas provides that a partner of party is not per se liable for another party's obligation unless the former consents in connection with the specific plan.[276]

§ 8.907.   STATEMENT OF MERGER

Section 907

(a) After a merger, the surviving partnership or limited partnership may file a statement that one or more partnerships or limited partnerships have merged into the surviving entity.

(b) A statement of merger must contain:

(1) the name of each partnership or limited partnership that is a party to the merger;

(2) the name of the surviving entity into which the other partnerships or limited partnership were merged;

(3) the street address of the surviving entity's chief executive office and of an office in this State, if any; and

(4) whether the surviving entity is a partnership or a limited partnership.

(c) Except as otherwise provided in subsection (d), for the purposes of Section 302, property of the surviving partnership or limited partnership which

---

[276]Tex. Rev. Civ. Stat. Ann. art. 6132b-9.02(g)(9).

before the merger was held in the name of another party to the merger is property held in the name of the surviving entity upon filing a statement of merger.

(d) For the purposes of Section 302, real property of the surviving partnership or limited partnership which before the merger was held in the name of another party to the merger is property held in the name of the surviving entity upon recording a certified copy of the statement of merger in the office for recording transfers of that real property.

(e) A filed and, if appropriate, recorded statement of merger, executed and declared to be accurate pursuant to Section 105(c), stating the name of a partnership or limited partnership that is a party to the merger in whose name property was held before the merger and the name of the surviving entity, but not containing all of the other information required by subsection (b), operates with respect to the partnerships or limited partnerships named to the extent provided in subsections (c) and (d).

Summary: Provides for the contents and filing of an optional statement of merger that can place property of constituent partnerships in the name of the surviving partnership.

Parallel U.P.A.:   None.

Important Changes: The U.P.A. has no analogous procedures and does not provide for mergers.

Analysis: None.

§ 8.908.   NONEXCLUSIVE

Section 908

This [article] is not exclusive. Partnerships or limited partnerships may be converted or merged in any other manner provided by law.

Summary: Provides that partnerships or limited partnerships may be converted or merged in any other manner provided by law.

Parallel U.P.A.:   None.

Important Changes: The U.P.A. does not provide for mergers or conversions.

Analysis: This section leaves unclear the effect of conversion-like or merger-like transactions that are not explicitly accomplished under R.U.P.A. First, it is not clear what other law can authorize conversions or mergers. Comment 2 to § 901 says that it is likely that, despite § 908, the R.U.P.A. conversion and merger procedures "will be used in virtually all cases" since most states have no other procedures. Moreover, Comment 3 to § 103 says that, although conversion and merger rules are not listed as mandatory, noncompliance, including varying the unanimity requirement for limited partnerships, "is to deny . . . 'safe harbor' validity to the transaction." This implies that the merger and conversion provisions are, in effect, mandatory although not listed as such.

Second, even if R.U.P.A. is effectively exclusive, it is not clear whether transactions that are not explicitly characterized as R.U.P.A. conversions or mergers nevertheless can have the same effect as transactions that conform to R.U.P.A., particularly regarding partners' liability.

To be safe, partnerships that wish to merge should follow the R.U.P.A. procedures even if they might have accomplished similar effects by an asset-sale or similar transaction under the U.P.A.

Note: State provisions relating to LLPs, including some that may vary from R.U.P.A. Articles 10 and 11 even in states that have adopted RUPA, are discussed above in Chapters 2, 3, and 6.

§ 8.1001.   STATEMENT OF QUALIFICATION

Section 1001

(a) A partnership may become a limited liability partnership pursuant to this section.

(b) The terms and conditions on which a partnership becomes a limited liability partnership must be approved by the vote necessary to amend the partnership agreement except, in the case of a partnership agreement that expressly considers contribution obligations, the vote necessary to amend those provisions.

(c) After the approval required by subsection (b), a partnership may become a limited liability partnership by filing a statement of qualification. The statement must contain:

(1) the name of the partnership;

(2) the street address of the partnership's chief executive office and, if different, the street address of an office in this State, if any;

(3) if there is no office in this State, the name and street address of the partnership's agent for service of process who must be an individual resident of this State or any other person authorized to do business in this State;

(4) a statement that the partnership is applying for status as a limited liability partnership; and

(5) a deferred effective date, if any.

(d) The status of a partnership as a limited liability partnership is effective on the later of the filing of the statement or a date specified in the statement. The status remains effective, regardless of changes in the partnership, until it is canceled pursuant to Section 105(d) or revoked pursuant to Section 1003.

(e) The status of a partnership as a limited liability partnership and the liability of its partners is not affected by errors or later changes in the information required to be contained in the statement of qualification under subsection (c).

(f) The filing of a statement of qualification establishes that a partnership has satisfied all conditions precedent to the qualification of the partnership as a limited liability partnership.

(g) An amendment or cancellation of a statement of qualification is effective when it is filed or on a deferred effective date specified in the amendment or cancellation.

LLP Cross-reference: Section 2.03(b).

§ 8.1002.   NAME

Section 1002

The name of a limited liability partnership must end with "Registered Limited Liability Partnership," "Limited Liability Partnership," "R.L.L.P.," "L.L.P.," "RLLP," or "LLP."

LLP Cross-reference: Section 2.05.

State variation

Delaware provides that the name of any partnership (not only LLPs) may contain a partner's name and "the words 'Company,' 'Association,' 'Club,' 'Foundation,' 'Fund,' 'Institute,' 'Society,' 'Union,' 'Syndicate,' 'Trust' (or abbreviations of like import)."[277] It also includes provisions requiring that partnership names be distinguishable on the records from names of other entities,[278] and for reservation of names.[279]

[277] Del. Code Ann., tit. 6, § 15-108(a).
[278] Del. Code Ann., tit. 6, § 15-108(c).
[279] Del. Code Ann., tit. 6, § 15-109.

§ 8.1003.   ANNUAL REPORT

Section 1003

(a) A limited liability partnership, and a foreign limited liability partnership authorized to transact business in this State, shall file an annual report in the office of the [Secretary of State] which contains:

(1) the name of the limited liability partnership and the State or other jurisdiction under whose laws the foreign limited liability partnership is formed;

(2) the current street address of the partnership's chief executive office and, if different, the current street address of an office in this State, if any; and

(3) if there is no current office in this State, the name and street address of the partnership's current agent for service of process who must be an individual resident of this State or any other person authorized to do business in this State.

(b) An annual report must be filed between [January 1 and April 1] of each year following the calendar year in which a partnership files a statement of qualification or a foreign partnership becomes authorized to transact business in this State.

(c) The [Secretary of State] may administratively revoke the statement of qualification of a partnership that fails to file an annual report when due or to pay the required filing fee. The [Secretary of State] shall provide the partnership at least 60 days' written notice of intent to revoke the statement. The notice must be mailed to the partnership at its chief executive office set forth in the last filed statement of qualification or annual report. The notice must specify the annual report that has not been filed, the fee that has not been paid, and the effective date of the revocation. The revocation is not effective if the annual report is filed and the fee is paid before the effective date of the revocation.

(d) A revocation under subsection (c) only affects a partnership's status as a limited liability partnership and is not an event of dissolution of the partnership.

(e) A partnership whose statement of qualification has been administratively revoked may apply to the [Secretary of State] for reinstatement within two years after the effective date of the revocation. The application must state:

(1) the name of the partnership and the effective date of the revocation; and

(2) that the ground for revocation either did not exist or has been corrected.

(f) A reinstatement under subsection (e) relates back to and takes effect as of the effective date of the revocation, and the partnership's status as a limited liability partnership continues as if the revocation had never occurred.

LLP Cross-reference: Section 2.03(c).

§ 8.1101.   LAW GOVERNING FOREIGN LIMITED LIABILITY PARTNERSHIP

Section 1101

(a) The laws under which a foreign limited liability partnership is formed govern relations among the partners and between the partners and the partnership and the liability of partners for obligations of the partnership.

(b) A foreign limited liability partnership may not be denied a statement of foreign qualification by reason of any difference between the laws under which the partnership was formed and the laws of this State.

(c) A statement of foreign qualification does not authorize a foreign limited liability partnership to engage in any business or exercise any power that a partnership may not engage in or exercise in this State as a limited liability partnership.

LLP Cross-reference: Section 6.03(b).

§ 8.1102.   STATEMENT OF FOREIGN QUALIFICATION

Section 1102

(a) Before transacting business in this State, a foreign limited liability partnership must file a statement of foreign qualification. The statement must contain:

(1) the name of the foreign limited liability partnership which satisfies the requirements of the State or other jurisdiction under whose laws it is formed and ends with "Registered Limited Liability Partnership," "Limited Liability Partnership," "R.L.L.P.," "L.L.P.," "RLLP," or "LLP";

(2) the street address of the partnership's chief executive office and, if different, the street address of an office in this State, if any;

(3) if there is no office in this State, the name and street address of the partnership's agent for service of process who must be an individual resident of this State or any other person authorized to do business in this State; and

(4) a deferred effective date, if any.

(b) The status of a partnership as a foreign limited liability partnership is effective on the later of the filing of the statement of foreign qualification or a date specified in the statement. The status remains effective, regardless of changes in the partnership, until it is canceled pursuant to Section 105(d) or revoked pursuant to Section 1003.

(c) An amendment or cancellation of a statement of foreign qualification is effective when it is filed or on a deferred effective date specified in the amendment or cancellation.

LLP Cross-reference: Section 6.02(b).

§ 8.1103.   EFFECT OF FAILURE TO QUALIFY

Section 1103

(a) A foreign limited liability partnership transacting business in this State may not maintain an action or proceeding in this State unless it has in effect a statement of foreign qualification.

(b) The failure of a foreign limited liability partnership to have in effect a statement of foreign qualification does not impair the validity of a contract or act of the foreign limited liability partnership or preclude it from defending an action or proceeding in this State.

(c) Limitations on personal liability of partners are not waived solely by transacting business in this State without a statement of foreign qualification.

(d) If a foreign limited liability partnership transacts business in this State without a statement of foreign qualification, the [Secretary of State] is its agent for service of process with respect to [claims for relief] arising out of the transaction of business in this State.

LLP Cross-reference: Section 6.02(b).

§ 8.1104.   ACTIVITIES NOT CONSTITUTING
TRANSACTING BUSINESS

Section 1104

(a) Activities of a foreign limited liability partnership which do not constitute transacting business within the meaning of this [article] include:

(1) maintaining, defending, or settling an action or proceeding;

(2) holding meetings of its partners or carrying on any other activity concerning its internal affairs;

(3) maintaining bank accounts;

(4) maintaining offices or agencies for the transfer, exchange, and registration of the partnership's own securities or maintaining trustees or depositories with respect to those securities;

(5) selling through independent contractors;

(6) soliciting or obtaining orders, whether by mail or through employees or agents or otherwise, if the orders require acceptance outside this State before they become contracts;

(7) creating or acquiring indebtedness, mortgages, or security interests in real or personal property;

(8) securing or collecting debts or foreclosing mortgages or other security interests in property securing the debts, and holding, protecting, and maintaining property so acquired;

(9) conducting an isolated transaction that is completed within 30 days and is not one in the course of similar transactions of like nature; and

(10) transacting business in interstate commerce.

(b) For purposes of this [article], the ownership in this State of income-producing real property or tangible personal property, other than property excluded under subsection (a), constitutes transacting business in this State.

(c) This section does not apply in determining the contacts or activities that may subject a foreign limited liability partnership to service of process, taxation, or regulation under any other law of this State.

§ 8.1105.   ACTION BY [ATTORNEY GENERAL]

Section 1105

The [Attorney General] may maintain an action to restrain a foreign limited liability partnership from transacting business in this State in violation of this [article].

§ 8.1201.   UNIFORMITY OF APPLICATION
AND CONSTRUCTION

Section 1201

This [Act] shall be applied and construed to effectuate its general purpose to make uniform the law with respect to the subject of this [Act] among States enacting it.

Summary: Provides that the act shall be applied to effectuate its purpose make the law uniform.

Parallel U.P.A.:   None.

Important Changes: As discussed in the Analysis, may change courts' method of interpreting the partnership statute.

Analysis: This section presents interesting questions given the fact that R.U.P.A. actually works counter to uniformity by *changing* current uniform law. Thus, it is not clear under this section whether courts should construe R.U.P.A. so that it is as consistent as possible with existing law under the U.P.A., or whether they should simply maximize the uniformity of the cases under R.U.P.A.

§ 8.1202.   SHORT TITLE

Section 1202

This [Act] may be cited as the Uniform Partnership Act (1994).

Summary: Provides that the act may be cited as the Uniform Partnership Act (1994).

Parallel U.P.A.:   § 1.

§ 8.1203.   SEVERABILITY CLAUSE

Section 1203

If any provision of this [Act] or its application to any person or circumstance is held invalid, the invalidity does not affect other provisions or applications of this [Act] which can be given effect without the invalid provision or application, and to this end the provisions of this [Act] are severable.

Summary: Provides that invalidity of any provision does not affect other provisions.

Parallel U.P.A.:   None.

Important Changes: Probably consistent with current law.

Analysis: None.

§ 8.1204.   EFFECTIVE DATE

Section 1204

This [Act] takes effect _____.

Summary: Establishes an effective date of the statute. This will be determined by each legislature, and may be delayed from passage of the statute. Section 1006 provides for the consequences of R.U.P.A.'s becoming effective in a jurisdiction.

Parallel U.P.A.:   § 44.

§ 8.1205.   REPEALS

Section 1205

Effective January 1, 199___, the following acts and parts of acts are repealed: [the State Partnership Act as amended and in effect immediately before the effective date of this Act].

Summary: Provides that R.U.P.A. supersedes the partnership statute that was previously in effect.

Parallel U.P.A.:   § 45.

§ 8.1206.   APPLICABILITY

Section 1206

(a) Before January 1, 199___, this [Act] governs only a partnership formed:

(1) after the effective date of this [Act], unless that partnership is continuing the business of a dissolved partnership under [Section 41 of the prior Uniform Partnership Act]; and

(2) before the effective date of this [Act], that elects, as provided by subsection (c), to be governed by this [Act].

(b) After January 1, 199___, this [Act] governs all partnerships.

(c) Before January 1, 199___, a partnership voluntarily may elect, in the manner provided in its partnership agreement or by law for amending the partnership agreement, to be governed by this [Act]. The provisions of this [Act] relating to the liability of the partnership's partners to third parties apply to limit those partners' liability to a third party who had done business with the partnership within one year preceding the partnership's election to be governed by this [Act], only if the third party knows or has received a notification of the partnership's election to be governed by this [Act].

Summary: This section provides that this act applies to partnerships formed under the prior act or that are continuing such partnerships under U.P.A. § 41 only after a specified date unless such partnerships elect after the effective date to be covered by this act. This election operates to limit partners' liability as to third parties who had done business with the partnership within one year prior to the election only if those third parties knew or received a notification of the election.[280]

Parallel U.P.A.:   None.

Analysis: Applying the act to preexisting partnerships can change existing contracts by changing, among other things, the rules on the effect or interpretation of existing formal agreements, the default provisions that govern informal partnerships, the determinations of which relationships are partnerships, and the rules governing which third-party transactions bind the partnership.[281] Section

---

[280] The Texas Revised Partnership Act is similar but provides that the section relating to limited liability partnerships applies to all such partnerships even if they are not covered by the rest of the Act. Tex. Rev. Civ. Stat. Ann., art. 6132b-10.03.

[281] For discussions of how retroactive application might affect partnerships and of the costs and benefits of various transition rules, see Ribstein, Changing Statutory Forms, 1 J. Small & Emerging Bus. Law 11 (1997); Vestal, Should the Revised Uniform Partnership Act of 1994 Really Be Retroactive?, 50 Bus. Law. 267, 274–81 (1994). Some partnership cases have involved the retroactivity issue. With respect to the U.P.A., Howard v. Hammond, 455 S.E.2d 390 (Ga. App. 1995) held that a partner's locking a co-partner out of his office and precluding him from servicing insurance clients was a wrongful dissolution under pre-U.P.A. law. The court cited the rule that: "Laws in existence at the time a contract is executed are part of that contract." Application of the U.P.A. probably would have made no difference to the result in this case. Nor, probably, would application of R.U.P.A. The defendant might have tried to make an issue out of R.U.P.A. § 404(e), which authorizes some selfish conduct. *See* the analysis of § 404. However, it is unlikely that this

authorization extends to the type of conduct involved in *Howard*. Vestal, above, at 279-80 discusses the potential retroactive impact of this provision.

Several cases have interpreted the R.U.P.A. retroactivity provision. *See* Kindergartners Count, Inc. v. DeMoulin, 249 F. Supp. 2d 1233 (D. Kan. 2003) (Kan. law; applying U.P.A. to partnership formed prior to effective date of R.U.P.A.); In re Tsurukawa, 287 B.R. 515 (9th Cir. BAP 2002) (Cal. law; applying UPA to partnership formed prior to effective date of RUPA where no evidence of election to be covered by R.U.P.A.); Wadley v. Walton, 816 So. 2d 491 (Ala. Civ. App. 2001) (applying accounting requirement under pre-R.U.P.A. Alabama law to partnership formed prior to relevant date, relying on *Master Boat Builders*); Ex parte Master Boat Builders, Inc., 779 So. 2d 192, 197 (Ala. 2000) (holding that R.U.P.A. provision permitting action without an accounting was inapplicable to partnership formed prior to relevant date; provision applying R.U.P.A. to partnership continuing the business of dissolved partnership interpreted to apply only to partnership "doing business as a dissolved partnership" and as not referring "to a class of partnerships that are separate from those formed after" the relevant date); Hall v. TWS, Inc., 113 P.3d 1207 (Alaska 2005) (action arising out of events that occurred and rights that accrued prior to effective date of R.U.P.A. governed by U.P.A.); Dickson, Carlson & Campillo v. Pole, 83 Cal. App. 4th 436, 99 Cal. Rptr. 2d 678 (2000) (holding that U.P.A. applies in determining partners' compensation for completing unfinished partnership business); Zimmerman v. Dan Kamphausen Co., 971 P.2d 236, 239 (Colo. App. 1998); Efron v. Milton, 892 So. 2d 497 (Fla. App. 2004) (R.U.P.A. not applicable to partnerships formed prior to retroactive application date); Mock v. Bigale, 867 So. 2d 1259 (Fla. App. 2004) (holding that R.U.P.A was applicable by its terms after Jan. 1, 1998 to partnership whenever it was formed); Ascontec Consulting. Inc. v. Young, 714 So. 2d 585, 588, n.2 (Fla. App. 1998); Green v. Bellerive Condos. Ltd. P'ship, 135 Md. App. 563, 573, 763 A.2d 252, 257, n.6 (2000) (holding that U.P.A. is applicable to charging order issued before R.U.P.A. effective, but referring to R.U.P.A. because no relevant difference from U.P.A.); Della Ratta v. Larkin, 382 Md. 553, 856 A.2d 643 (2004) (applying U.P.A. to events during statutory transition period in the absence of an election to be covered by R.U.P.A.); Ross v. American Iron Works, 153 Md. App. 1, 834 A.2d 962 (2003) (applying U.P.A to partnership formed, and action commenced, prior to dates specified in Maryland version of R.U.P.A.); Parkwood Ltd. Dividend Hous. Ass'n v. State Hous. Dev. Auth., 258 Mich. App. 495, 671 N.W.2d 144 (2003) (applying U.P.A. to action commenced before relevant date specified in Minnesota R.U.P.A.); Maus v. Galic, 669 N.W.2d 38 (Minn. App. 2003) (R.U.P.A. inapplicable to action commenced before effective date and preexisting partnership that did not elect to be governed by R.U.P.A.); Brcka v. Falcon Elec. Corp., 2001 WL 641524 (Minn. App. June 12, 2001) (R.U.P.A. § 202 did not apply to the present case but that it codified the pre-R.U.P.A. common law); Gast v. Peters, 267 Neb. 18, 671 N.W.2d 758 (2003); First Am. Title Ins. Co. v. Lawson, 351 N.J. Super. 407, 798 A.2d 661 (2002) (applying U.P.A. to partner's power to bind partnership by misrepresentation with respect to contract entered into prior to effective date of R.U.P.A.), *aff'd and rev'd in part on other grounds,* 177 N.J. 125, 827 A.2d 230 (2003); Fate v. Owens, 27 P.3d 990 (N.M. App. 2001) (U.P.A. applies to limited partnership formed prior to adoption of R.U.P.A.); McDowell v. McDowell, 143 S.W.3d 124 (Tex. App. 2004) (applying definition of partnership under Texas Revised Partnership Act pursuant to provision for application to all partnerships after Dec. 31, 1998); Kahn v. Seely, 980 S.W.2d 794, 798 (Tex. App. 1998) (applying Tex. Rev. Civ. Stat. Ann. art. 6132b11.03(a), no intent to be covered by revised act, so prior law applies); Casey v. Chapman, 123 Wash. App. 670, 98 P.3d 1246 (2004) (applying U.P.A. to a 1993 transaction where R.U.P.A. adopted in the state in 1999; no reference to statutory retroactive application date). *See generally* Bromberg & Ribstein, § 1.04(e). An earlier version of RUPA, which was adopted in Wyoming, provides that the new law applies to existing partnerships. *See* Wyo. Stat. § 17-21-1003. In B & R Builders v. Beilgard, 915 P.2d 1195 (Wyo. 1996) the court applied to an existing partnership the new statutory presumption under RUPA § 204(d) that property acquired by a partner in individual name is presumed to be the partner's separate property. Since the court upheld the trial court's finding that the property belonged to the partnership, it is not clear that application of R.U.P.A. changed the result in this respect. If the property had been found to be individual property only because of the new statutory presumption, there is a potential issue whether this would "impair the obligations of a contract

1206 gives partners an ample opportunity to revise their contracts before the new law applies and third parties some notice of changes in the rules that may affect partners' and partnerships' liability. These protections are not only good policy, but help insulate the act from constitutional attack.[282] Non-retroactivity has been recognized in several cases.[283]

It has been argued that R.U.P.A. should not be applied without a deliberate election even after a transition period to give the parties an opportunity to renegotiate their deal in light of the new rule.[284] However, this argument fails adequately to accommodate the competing needs for both change and stability in the law.[285] Moving firms to the new rule without a deliberate opt-in reduces costs, including the negotiation costs necessary to make the move. Moreover, not permitting transition would complicate the law by preserving multiple statutory standards. In any event, if the parties have not changed their contract within five years, it is a fair assumption that they either favor the new rule or are unaware of the change, in which case they probably did not bargain over the rule.

Notwithstanding this section, courts may apply R.U.P.A. to interpret U.P.A.[286]

An earlier version of RUPA, which was adopted in Wyoming, provides that the new law applies to existing partnerships.[287] In *B & R Builders v. Beilgard*,[288] the court applied to an existing partnership the new statutory presumption under R.U.P.A. § 204(d) that property acquired by a partner in individual name is presumed to be the partner's separate property.[289] Since the court upheld the trial court's finding that the property belonged to the partnership it is not clear that

---

existing on January 1, 1994" in violation of Wyo. Stat. § 17-21-1003(c). For an application of the U.P.A. to a partnership-by-estoppel issue arising out of representations made prior to the act's effective date, see Ag Servs. of Am., Inc. v. Nielsen, 231 F.3d 726 (10th Cir. 2000) (New Mexico law). In Fujimoto v. Au, 95 Haw. 116, 19 P.3d 699, 743, n.22 (2001), which generally applied the U.P.A., the court noted that the plaintiffs' "ability to satisfy the judgment from the assets of individual partners may be affected" by the adoption of R.U.P.A. but did not decide this issue.

[282] *See* Total Holdings USA, Inc. v. Curran Composites, Inc., 2009 WL 3238186 (Del. Ch., Oct. 9, 2009) (applying Delaware's version of R.U.P.A. after expiration of grace period, citing and quoting Text). *See generally* Butler & Ribstein, The Constitution and the Corporation ch. 2 (1994); Butler & Ribstein, The Contract Clause and the Corporation, 55 Brook. L. Rev. 767 (1989). Note that § 1006 contrasts with R.U.P.A. § 107, discussed supra, which provides that a partnership governed by R.U.P.A. is subject to amendment or repeal of the act.

[283] *See* Zimmerman v. Dan Kamphausen Co., 971 P.2d 236, 239 (Colo. App. 1998); Ascontec Consulting. Inc. v. Young, 714 So. 2d 585, 588, n.2 (Fla. App. 1998); Kahn v. Seely, 980 S.W.2d 794, 798 (Tex. App. 1998) (applying Tex. Rev. Civ. Stat. Ann. art. 6132b-11.03(a), no intent to be covered by revised act, so prior law applies).

[284] *See* Vestal, note 281, supra, at 282–83.

[285] *See* Ribstein, supra note 281.

[286] *See* Cheesecake Factory, Inc. v. Baines, 125 N.M. 622, 964 P.2d 183 (N.M. App. 1998) (citing R.U.P.A. § 308 as to requirements regarding partnership by estoppel through public statements).

[287] *See* Wyo. Stat. § 17-21-1003.

[288] 915 P.2d 1195 (Wyo. 1996).

[289] *See* Bromberg & Ribstein, § 3.02(g).

application of R.U.P.A. changed the result in this respect. But if the property had been found to be individual property only because of the new statutory presumption, there is a potential issue whether this would "impair the obligations of a contract existing on January 1, 1994" in violation of the Wyoming provision.[290]

State variation

Delaware provides by an amendment to its version of § 1001 that a partnership that was an an LLP under prior law or would have been an LLP under prior law but for an election to be covered by the new law continues to be an LLP and that its latest statement of qualification or renewal under the old law constitutes a statement of qualification under the new law.[291]

§ 8.1207.   SAVINGS CLAUSE

Section 1207

This [Act] does not affect an action or proceeding commenced or right accrued before this [Act] takes effect.

Summary: Provides that the act does not affect an action or proceeding commenced or right accrued before the act takes effect.

Parallel U.P.A.:   None.

Analysis: Section 1207 provides protection against alteration of rights in addition to that provided by § 1206. As Comment 3 to § 1207 notes, it may not be clear when a right has accrued. As the Comment says, there is no accrued right on a contract until breach. Pre-enactment contracts are protected to some extent under § 1206. More complex issues may arise with respect to tortious conduct or injury that can be attributed to both the pre-enactment and post-enactment periods.

---

[290] *See* Wyo. Stat. § 17-21-1003(c).
[291] Del. Code Ann., tit. 6, § 15-1001(i).

§ 8.1208.   EFFECTIVE DATE

Section 1208

This [Act] takes effect _____.

§ 8.1209.   APPLICABILITY

Section 1209

(a) This [Act] does not govern a partnership that becomes a limited liability partnership before this [Act] takes effect, except (i) a partnership that is continuing the business of a dissolved limited liability partnership or (ii) a limited liability partnership that elects, before January 1, 199___, in the manner provided by the partnership agreement or by law for amending the agreement, to be governed by this [Act]. If an election is made, the provisions of this [Act] relating to the liability of a partner to a third party apply to limit the partner's liability to a third party who had done business with the partnership within 12 months next preceding the election only if the third party at the time of the election, knew or had received notification of the election.

(b) After January 1, 199___, this [Act] governs all limited liability partnerships.

(c) The existing provisions for execution and filing a statement of qualification of a limited liability partnership continue until either the limited liability partnership elects to have this [Act] apply or January 1, 199___.

§ 8.1210.   SAVINGS CLAUSE

Section 1210

This [Act] does not affect an action or proceeding commenced or right accrued before this [Act] takes effect.

398

§ 8.1211.   REPEALS

Section 1211

Effective January 1, 199___, the following acts and parts of acts are repealed: [the Limited Liability Partnership amendments to the State Partnership Act as amended and in effect immediately before the effective date of this [Act]].

≡9≡

UNIFORM LIMITED
   PARTNERSHIP ACT
   (2001)

This chapter gives an overview of the Uniform Limited Partnership Act (2001) (U.L.P.A.). Each Section except for § 9.101 has the number of the corresponding Section of U.L.P.A. and includes the following features to the extent applicable:

1. A **Summary** of the section.

2. The parallel provisions in the Uniform Limited Partnership Act 1985 (**U.L.P.A. 1985**), the Uniform Partnership Act (1994) (R.U.P.A.), and the Uniform Limited Liability Company Act (U.L.L.C.A.). With respect to the relevance of provisions in these other laws, *see* § 101(B), below. The R.U.P.A. provisions are discussed in Chapter 8 and cited throughout as § 8.___.[1]

3. The sections of **Bromberg & Ribstein** on Partnership that deal with the material covered by the particular section of the act.

4. A summary of the most **Important Changes** from the Revised Uniform Limited Partnership Act (U.L.P.A. 1985), including changes that reflect the linkage of prior law with the Uniform Partnership Act (*see* § 9.101(b)). This Chapter does not cover comparisons with the Uniform Limited Partnership Act

---

[1] The U.L.L.C.A. provisions are discussed in Ribstein, A Critique of the Uniform Limited Liability Company Act, 25 Stetson L. Rev. 313 (1995) (hereinafter U.L.L.C.A. Comments). Other frequently cross-referenced writings are Ribstein, An Applied Theory of Limited Partnership, 37 Emory L.J. 835 (1988) (*Applied*); Ribstein, Limited Partnerships Revisited, 67 U. Cin. L. Rev. 953 (1999) (Revisited); Ribstein, Linking Statutory Forms, 58 L. & Contemp. Probs. 187 (Spring 1995) (Linking); and Ribstein & Keatinge on Limited Liability Companies (Ribstein & Keatinge). *See also* Closely-Held Business Symposium: The Uniform Limited Partnership Act, 37 Suffolk U.L. Rev. 577–81 (2004); Kleinberger, A User's Guide to the New Uniform Limited Partnership Act, 37 Suffolk U. L. Rev. 583 (2004).

(1916), which is still in effect in a few states, or with the Uniform Partnership Act (1914). U.L.P.A. 1916 and U.P.A. 1914 are discussed in detail throughout Bromberg & Ribstein, and Chapter 8 includes detailed comparisons between U.P.A. 1914 and R.U.P.A.

5. An **Analysis** of each section, focusing on changes made in U.L.P.A. (1985) rather than on existing law, which is covered in cross-referenced sections of Bromberg and Ribstein on Partnership. The Analysis refers to other U.L.P.A. sections and, therefore, to the discussions of those sections in this Chapter. The Analysis discusses potential areas of concern for legislators and bar committees who are considering adopting U.L.P.A. and for partners in, or those who are dealing with, partnerships that are governed by that act (*see* § 9.101(C)–(D)). References to Comments are to the official drafters' comments.

The following is a chart listing the state adoptions of U.L.P.A. (2001) as of September 1, 2011:[2]

State	*Citation*	*Effective date*
Alabama	§§ 10-9C-101 to 10-9C-1208	January 1, 2010
Arkansas	Ark. Code §§ 4-47-101 to 4-47-1209	September 1, 2007
California	Cal. Corp. Code §§ 15900 to 15912.07	January 1, 2008
Florida	Fl. St. §§ 620.1101–620.2205	January 1, 2006
Hawaii	H.R.S. §§ 425B-101 to 425B.1205	July 1, 2004
Idaho	Idaho Code §§ 53-2-101 to 1205	July 1, 2006
Illinois	805 ILCS 215/101-1402	January 1, 2005
Iowa	Acts 2004 (80 G.A.) Ch. 1021	January 1, 2005
Kentucky	Ky. Rev. St. Ann., Chapter 362, sub Chapter 2	July 12, 2006
Maine	31 M.R.S.A. §§ 1301 to 1461	July 1, 2007
Montana	2011 Mt. Laws Ch. 216	April 18, 2011
Minnesota	M.S.A. §§ 321.0101 through 321.1208	January 1, 2005
Nevada	2007 Nev. Laws ch. 146	May 29, 2007
New Mexico	2007 N.M. Laws ch. 129	January 1, 2008
North Dakota	N.D. Code Ch. 45-10.2	June 30, 2005
Oklahoma	54 Ok. Stat. Ann., Ch. 9	January 1, 2011

---

[2]Oklahoma had initially enacted a version of the Uniform Limited Partnership Act (2001), but the act was declared unconstitutional in its entirety. *See* Weddington v. Henry, 202 P.3d 143 (Okla. 2008). Oklahoma enacted a subsequent version indicated in the table.

State	*Citation*	*Effective date*
Utah	Utah Code §§ 48-2d-101-1205 353, Ch. 2d	July 1, 2012
Washington	Wash. Rev. Code Ch. 25.10	January 1, 2010

§ 9.101.   PRELIMINARY NOTES

The Preliminary Notes discuss general considerations that apply to the discussion of U.L.P.A. (2001).

A.   Mandatory Rules

This Chapter discusses the extent to which each section can be waived by contrary agreement. This topic is dealt with generally in U.L.P.A. § 110, but application of that section raises many issues throughout the Act.

B.   Linkage

One of U.L.P.A. key objectives is "de-linking" limited partnerships from general partnership law. Until now, limited partnerships have been relegated to a variation on general partnerships. The limited partnership law is a kind of Swiss cheese, with general partnership law filling in the holes. U.P.A. § 6(2) provides that the U.P.A. "shall apply to limited partnerships except in so far as the statutes relating to such partnerships are inconsistent herewith." Under U.L.P.A. (1985), general partnership law can apply as a supplemental principle of law under § 104, as one of the rights, powers, liabilities or restrictions applied to general partners in limited partnerships under § 403, or as a case not provided for in the limited partnership statute under § 1105. The web of linkages created significant confusion.[3] With U.L.P.A., limited partnerships become a stand-alone form. In order to convey an understanding of prior law, the discussion of each section below gives references to R.U.P.A. provisions that might have been linked to the limited partnership statute under prior law.

Despite its intent, U.L.P.A. did not, and could not, accomplish complete de-linkage because courts remain free to apply cases relating to other business associations statutes to the extent they deem these analogies appropriate. These might be part of the principles of law and equity explicitly applied under

---

[3] *See* Linking; Miller, Linkage and Delinkage: A Funny Thing Happened to Limited Partnerships when the Revised Uniform Partnership Act Came Along, 37 Suffolk L. Rev. 891 (2004).

U.L.P.A. § 107. Apart from this provision, courts probably will apply cases decided under statutory provisions that have nearly identical language. This might include not only R.U.P.A., but also the Uniform Limited Liability Company Act, some provisions of which also are cross-referenced below.[4]

C.   Guidance for Adopting States

The Analysis is intended to provide guidance for states considering whether to adopt U.L.P.A. In general, each state should consider not only the intrinsic value of each provision, but also how the provision relates to existing business association and other statutes; whether uniformity is desirable and how it is affected by the adoption of the act; and the potential costs of changing the law.

D.   Guidance for Adopting Firms

The Analysis is intended to provide guidance for firms that are considering whether to form a limited partnership governed by U.L.P.A., to elect coverage of U.L.P.A., or to adjust the partnership agreement to reflect coverage by U.L.P.A.

E.   Structure of the Act

Apart from linkage issues discussed above, U.L.P.A. presents issues of statutory drafting style. The Act implicitly or explicitly cross-references, among other provisions, the extensive definitions, the provision on contrary agreements (§ 110), and the provision on notice (§ 103). The Analysis of each Section clarifies these cross-references and discusses their implications.

---

[4]These applications of cases decided under other statutes may, however, be misleading because of differences between the two statutes. Note also that U.L.L.C.A. has now been revised. *See* Revised Uniform Limited Liability Company Act (2006), *available at* http://www.law.upenn.edu/bll/archives/ulc/ullca/2006act_final.pdf. For a detailed analysis of this Act, see Ribstein, An Analysis of the Revised Uniform Limited Liability Company Act, 3 Va. L. & Bus. Rev. 35 (2008). Because U.L.P.A. drew from the earlier U.L.L.C.A., the later revised act is less relevant in interpreting U.L.P.A. and will not be reviewed here. However, the revised act and the commentary just cited should be consulted for a broader perspective on U.L.P.A.

§ 9.102. DEFINITIONS

Section 102

In this [Act]:

(1) "Certificate of limited partnership" means the certificate required by Section 201. The term includes the certificate as amended or restated.

(2) "Contribution," except in the phrase "right of contribution," means any benefit provided by a person to a limited partnership in order to become a partner or in the person's capacity as a partner.

(3) "Debtor in bankruptcy" means a person that is the subject of:

(A) an order for relief under Title 11 of the United States Code or a comparable order under a successor statute of general application; or

(B) a comparable order under federal, state, or foreign law governing insolvency.

(4) "Designated office" means:

(A) with respect to a limited partnership, the office that the limited partnership is required to designate and maintain under Section 114; and

(B) with respect to a foreign limited partnership, its principal office.

(5) "Distribution" means a transfer of money or other property from a limited partnership to a partner in the partner's capacity as a partner or to a transferee on account of a transferable interest owned by the transferee.

(6) "Foreign limited liability limited partnership" means a foreign limited partnership whose general partners have limited liability for the obligations of the foreign limited partnership under a provision similar to Section 404(c).

(7) "Foreign limited partnership" means a partnership formed under the laws of a jurisdiction other than this State and required by those laws to have one or more general partners and one or more limited partners. The term includes a foreign limited liability limited partnership.

(8) "General partner" means:

(A) with respect to a limited partnership, a person that:

(i) becomes a general partner under Section 401; or

(ii) was a general partner in a limited partnership when the limited partnership became subject to this [Act] under Section 1206(a) or (b); and

(B) with respect to a foreign limited partnership, a person that has rights, powers, and obligations similar to those of a general partner in a limited partnership.

(9) "Limited liability limited partnership," except in the phrase "foreign limited liability limited partnership," means a limited partnership whose certificate of limited partnership states that the limited partnership is a limited liability limited partnership.

(10) "Limited partner" means:
(A) with respect to a limited partnership, a person that:
(i) becomes a limited partner under Section 301; or
(ii) was a limited partner in a limited partnership when the limited partnership became subject to this [Act] under Section 1206(a) or (b); and
(B) with respect to a foreign limited partnership, a person that has rights, powers, and obligations similar to those of a limited partner in a limited partnership.

(11) "Limited partnership," except in the phrases "foreign limited partnership" and "foreign limited liability limited partnership," means an entity, having one or more general partners and one or more limited partners, which is formed under this [Act] by two or more persons or becomes subject to this [Act] under [Article] 11 or Section 1206(a) or (b). The term includes a limited liability limited partnership.

(12) "Partner" means a limited partner or general partner.

(13) "Partnership agreement" means the partners' agreement, whether oral, implied, in a record, or in any combination, concerning the limited partnership. The term includes the agreement as amended.

(14) "Person" means an individual, corporation, business trust, estate, trust, partnership, limited liability company, association, joint venture, government; governmental subdivision, agency, or instrumentality; public corporation, or any other legal or commercial entity.

(15) "Person dissociated as a general partner" means a person dissociated as a general partner of a limited partnership.

(16) "Principal office" means the office where the principal executive office of a limited partnership or foreign limited partnership is located, whether or not the office is located in this State.

(17) "Record" means information that is inscribed on a tangible medium or that is stored in an electronic or other medium and is retrievable in perceivable form.

(18) "Required information" means the information that a limited partnership is required to maintain under Section 111.

(19) "Sign" means:
(A) to execute or adopt a tangible symbol with the present intent to authenticate a record; or
(B) to attach or logically associate an electronic symbol, sound, or process to or with a record with the present intent to authenticate the record.

(20) "State" means a State of the United States, the District of Columbia, Puerto Rico, the United States Virgin Islands, or any territory or insular possession subject to the jurisdiction of the United States.

(21) "Transfer" includes an assignment, conveyance, deed, bill of sale, lease, mortgage, security interest, encumbrance, gift, and transfer by operation of law.

(22) "Transferable interest" means a partner's right to receive distributions.

(23) "Transferee" means a person to which all or part of a transferable interest has been transferred, whether or not the transferor is a partner.

Summary: Defines terms used in the Act.

Parallel U.L.P.A. 1985: § 101.

Parallel R.U.P.A.: § 101.

Parallel U.L.L.C.A.: § 101.

Important Changes: New subsections 3-6, 9, 15-19 and 21-23.

Analysis: This Chapter discusses the implications of several of these definitions, including (6) (§ 404); (8) (113, 401); (10) (113, 301); (11) (113, 801, 1101, 1206); (13) (§ 110); (18) (§ 111); (22)–(23) (§§ 701–703).

Subsection 11: The definition of limited partnership is no longer linked with the definition of partnership as under U.L.P.A. (1985), § 101(7). This may be significant in dropping the "for-profit" and "business" aspects of the definition of partnership under R.U.P.A. (*see* § 9.104, below).

The relevance of the entity's having been formed to the definition of limited partnership is discussed below in § 9.201.

Although this subsection defines a limited partnership as "having" both general and limited partners, under §§ 801(3)(B) and 801(4) there may be a period of 90 days (or more under the agreement) during which the last general or limited partner has dissociated and has not been replaced but the partnership nevertheless is not deemed to be dissolved. This could raise a question concerning whether the firm is a "limited partnership" and therefore entitled to liability shields under § 303 (for limited partners) and § 404 (for a general partner in a limited liability limited partnership, which must be a limited partnership under § 101(9)). The Comment to this subsection provides that "a limited partnership may not indefinitely delay 'having one or more general partners and one or more limited partners.'" Despite that Comment, § 101(11) and § 801 would seem to be in conflict. However, § 113 permits the same person to be both a general and a limited partner. Although § 101(11) also requires the partnership to be "formed" by two or more persons, a properly formed partnership might later "have" a general and a limited partner who are the same person. If dissociation leaves the firm with neither a general nor a limited partnership, the firm would seem to be dissolved immediately under § 801, and questions concerning a limbo period and members' limited liability would not arise.

Subsection 13: The definition clarifies that the agreement may be oral or implied or in a record. Should the Act require variation of statutory requirements in written agreements? A writing requirement arguably would reduce litigation.[5] Although such a requirement might frustrate the parties' expectations, this is less likely in usually formal limited partnerships than in general partnerships or LLCs.

Referring to the agreement in the singular, and referring ambiguously to "the partners," leaves unclear whether the agreement can constitute several agreements made at different times on different points, or one or more agreements that are made by fewer than all the members.[6] The agreement also includes records.

The operating agreement is discussed further in § 9.110. The relation between the agreement and records is discussed in § 9.201.

§ 9.103.   KNOWLEDGE AND NOTICE

Section 103

(a) A person knows a fact if the person has actual knowledge of it.

(b) A person has notice of a fact if the person:

(1) knows of it;

(2) has received a notification of it;

(3) has reason to know it exists from all of the facts known to the person at the time in question; or

(4) has notice of it under subsection (c) or (d).

(c) A certificate of limited partnership on file in the [office of the Secretary of State] is notice that the partnership is a limited partnership and the persons designated in the certificate as general partners are general partners. Except as otherwise provided in subsection (d), the certificate is not notice of any other fact.

(d) A person has notice of:

(1) another person's dissociation as a general partner, 90 days after the effective date of an amendment to the certificate of limited partnership which states that the other person has dissociated or 90 days after the effective date of a statement of dissociation pertaining to the other person, whichever occurs first;

---

[5] *See* U.L.L.C.A. Comments at 336–37.
[6] *See* U.L.L.C.A. Comments at 336.

(2) a limited partnership's dissolution, 90 days after the effective date of an amendment to the certificate of limited partnership stating that the limited partnership is dissolved;

(3) a limited partnership's termination, 90 days after the effective date of a statement of termination;

(4) a limited partnership's conversion under [Article] 11, 90 days after the effective date of the articles of conversion; or

(5) a merger under [Article] 11, 90 days after the effective date of the articles of merger.

(e) A person notifies or gives a notification to another person by taking steps reasonably required to inform the other person in ordinary course, whether or not the other person learns of it.

(f) A person receives a notification when the notification:

(1) comes to the person's attention; or

(2) is delivered at the person's place of business or at any other place held out by the person as a place for receiving communications.

(g) Except as otherwise provided in subsection (h), a person other than an individual knows, has notice, or receives a notification of a fact for purposes of a particular transaction when the individual conducting the transaction for the person knows, has notice, or receives a notification of the fact, or in any event when the fact would have been brought to the individual's attention if the person had exercised reasonable diligence. A person other than an individual exercises reasonable diligence if it maintains reasonable routines for communicating significant information to the individual conducting the transaction for the person and there is reasonable compliance with the routines. Reasonable diligence does not require an individual acting for the person to communicate information unless the communication is part of the individual's regular duties or the individual has reason to know of the transaction and that the transaction would be materially affected by the information.

(h) A general partner's knowledge, notice, or receipt of a notification of a fact relating to the limited partnership is effective immediately as knowledge of, notice to, or receipt of a notification by the limited partnership, except in the case of a fraud on the limited partnership committed by or with the consent of the general partner. A limited partner's knowledge, notice, or receipt of a notification of a fact relating to the limited partnership is not effective as knowledge of, notice to, or receipt of a notification by the limited partnership.

Summary: Defines knowledge, notice, and receipt of notification for various purposes in the Act.

Parallel U.L.P.A. 1985: § 208.

Parallel R.U.P.A.: § 102.

Parallel U.L.L.C.A.:   § 102.

Important Changes: Combines formerly linked R.U.P.A. § 102, U.L.P.A. (1985) § 208 (now § 102(c)) and new § 102(d).

Analysis:

Subsections (a), (b), (e)–(h):   *See* **Analysis** of R.U.P.A. provision in § 8.102.

Subsection (c):   This was formerly covered in U.L.P.A. § 208 (1985). Is one bound by the limited partnership's liability limitation even if she does not know she is dealing with a limited partnership despite the central filing of a certificate of limited partnership? In this situation, the third party may have no reason to check the record. Thus, *Water, Waste & Land v. Lanham,*[7] cited in the Comment to this section, held under a comparable LLC statutory provision that, because plaintiff did not know defendant was acting for an LLC (the firm's agent used only the initials "P.I.I." rather than the firm's full name "Preferred Income Investors, LLC.") the defendant could be held liable as a partially disclosed principal. In other words, the statute provided constructive notice only if the firm used a name that would put the plaintiff on notice that he was dealing with an LLC.

Note that this subsection does not provide constructive notice that one who the certificate does *not* list as a general partner is *not* a general partner. Thus, one who is not a general partner but appears to be such to a third party may be liable as a purported partner in a *general* partnership under U.P.A. § 16 or R.U.P.A. § 308 if he represents himself as such, or under U.L.P.A. (1985) § 304 or U.L.P.A. § 304 if a third party believes in good faith that the person is a general partner in a general or limited partnership. A person who represents herself as a general partner in a *limited* partnership might have been liable as such under U.L.P.A. (1985) § 303 if she participated in control, or otherwise by linkage with the above general partnership provisions.[8] U.P.A. § 6(2) might not have linked § 16 because the latter could be deemed to be "inconsistent" with the U.L.P.A. 1985's provisions for the certificate and limited partners' control liability. But since there is no such limitation under R.U.P.A., U.L.P.A. (1985) § 1105 might apply R.U.P.A. § 308 on the ground that purported partner liability is a "case not provided for" in U.L.P.A. (1985). An early draft of U.L.P.A. (2001) would have clarified the issue by importing purported partner liability.[9] Final U.L.P.A. (2001) does not include such a provision, but might apply purported partner

---

[7] 955 P.2d 997 (Colo. 1998).
[8] *See* Revisited at 972–73; Linking at 206–07.
[9] Revision of Unif. Ltd. Partnership Act (1976) with 1985 Amendments (March 1999 draft), § 403c-3. *See* Revisited, at 973.

liability as a "principle[] of law and equity" under U.L.P.A. § 107 (2001). Note that if a partnership agreement, but not the certificate, lists one as a general partner, the certificate would not control under § 201(d)(2) because of lack of third-party detrimental reliance.

As a matter of policy, a third party who knows she is dealing with a limited partnership reasonably might be expected to check the certificate to determine who the general partners are. Moreover, the nonbinding effect of the certificate in this respect under § 103(c) effectively brings a form of limited partner control liability, now formally eliminated in § 303, partially in through the back door by letting third parties claim to have been misled by a limited partner's exercise of control.[10]

For other consequences of inaccurate filings, *see* § 202(c) (as to when the certificate controls), and § 208 (liability for false statements).

Subsection (d): The effect of constructive notice in limiting the partners' power to bind and liability is also provided for in §§ 402, 606, 607, 804, 805, 1111, and 1112.

§ 9.104. NATURE, PURPOSE AND DURATION OF ENTITY

Section 104

(a) A limited partnership is an entity distinct from its partners. A limited partnership is the same entity regardless of whether its certificate states that the limited partnership is a limited liability limited partnership.

(b) A limited partnership may be organized under this [Act] for any lawful purpose.

(c) A limited partnership has a perpetual duration.

Summary: Provides for the entity nature of limited partnership, the continuation of the entity regardless of status as an LLLP, organization for any lawful purpose and perpetual duration.

Parallel U.L.P.A. 1985: §§ 106; 201(4).

Parallel R.U.P.A.: § 201(a).

---

[10]This is the reverse of the point that purported partner liability makes the control rule unnecessary. *See* Applied at 885.

Parallel U.L.L.C.A.:   § 201.

Bromberg & Ribstein: §§ 1.03; 11.03.

Important Changes: Provides for entity nature and the effect on the entity of LLLP status; expansion of permissible purpose; and provides for perpetual duration, contrary to the implication from the U.L.P.A. (1985) § 201(a)(4) requirement that the certificate state the latest date on which the limited partnership is to dissolve.

Analysis:

Subsection (a):   The confusion and practical problems resulting from an absolute entity characterization of general partnerships are discussed above in § 8.201 and in Bromberg & Ribstein, § 1.03. Similar problems apply to limited partnerships.[11] Like general partnerships, limited partnerships have some aggregate features, including general partner liability, so that characterizing the firm as an entity for all purposes may be misleading. Thus, the statute arguably should provide that the firm is an entity unless the context otherwise requires.

The parties might try to avoid negative consequences of entity characterization by contrary agreement under U.L.P.A. § 110. Since the partnership agreement may be "implied" under § 102(13), courts may reach the results consistent with non-entity characterization. However, an agreement probably would not bind third parties under § 110(b)(13).

The effect of LLLP registration on the continuation of the entity is discussed above in Section 4.08.

Subsection (b):   The Act does not require a *business* purpose. Since a non-business probably cannot be said to have conventional "profits," this suggests that the firm may be organized under the Act as a non-profit business. This is supported by the fact that, unlike U.L.P.A. (1985) § 101(7), the definition of limited partnership in § 102(11) does not link with the definition of partnership in U.P.A. § 6(1) or R.U.P.A. §§ 101(6) and 202(a), including the for-profit and business aspects of that definition (*see* §§ 8.202 and 9.102, above). However, as the Comments note, non-profit partnerships do not fit many of the default provisions of the Act. Thus, it might be preferable to leave non-profit entities to a separate statute.

The "lawful" purpose requirement is apparently subject to contrary agreement under § 110. The agreement is, of course, subject to other law, and in any event may not restrict non-partner rights under § 110(b)(13). But permitting an agreement contrary to § 104(b), coupled with the absence of any provision for

---

[11] *See* Revisited, at 996.

dissolution for unlawfulness under § 801, may mean that the partnership is fully effective as among the partners. This contrasts with the situation in general partnerships and in limited partnerships under U.L.P.A. (1985).[12]

Subsection (c): Default perpetual duration and the absence of a requirement that the partnership specify a limited duration in the certificate as under U.L.P.A. (1985) § 201(a)(4) may mean that a third party has no notice that she is dealing with a dissolved partnership. However, as with a general partnership, the limited partnership may be bound as a going concern unless the third party is given notice. *See* § 103(d).

§ 9.105.   POWERS

Section 105

A limited partnership has the powers to do all things necessary or convenient to carry on its activities, including the power to sue, be sued, and defend in its own name and to maintain an action against a partner for harm caused to the limited partnership by a breach of the partnership agreement or violation of a duty to the partnership.

Summary: Provides for the powers of a limited partnership.

Parallel U.L.P.A. 1985:   None.

Parallel R.U.P.A.:   None.

Parallel U.L.L.C.A.:   § 112.

Important Changes: Specification of powers.

Analysis: This provision's effect is unclear, since there is no limited partnership doctrine comparable to corporate "ultra vires." The Comments suggest that the power to sue and be sued is mentioned only so that § 110(b)(1) can make it non-waivable. But it is not clear why this provision should be non-waivable, since a restriction on this right usually affects only the partners themselves. Also, as discussed above in § 9.104, the partners apparently can waive the entity nature of the limited partnership, which embraces the power to engage in litigation in partnership name, at least to the extent that third parties are not adversely affected pursuant to § 110(b)(13).

---

[12] *See* Bromberg & Ribstein, §§ 2.11, 7.04, and 17.04.

The Comment also states that this provision establishes that the partnership has "standing" to enforce the agreement. However, the *power* to sue does not necessarily give the partnership itself enough of an interest in the suit to give it standing under applicable law.

§ 9.106. GOVERNING LAW

Section 106

The law of this State governs relations among the partners of a limited partnership and between the partners and the limited partnership and the liability of partners as partners for an obligation of the limited partnership.

Summary: Specifies that the law applicable to relations among and liability of partners of a limited partnership.

Parallel U.L.P.A. 1985:   None.

Parallel R.U.P.A.:   § 106.

Parallel U.L.L.C.A.:   § 1001.

Bromberg & Ribstein: § 1.04.

Important Changes: New provision.

Analysis: This section determines which state law applies and not the completely separate question of the effect of the statute and the parties' agreement, which is one of the issues determined by the applicable law.

This provision applies only to a limited partnership, which § 102(11) defines as "an entity . . . formed under this [Act]." It therefore clarifies that only this limited partnership act applies to the matters specified in the Section, and not the law of some other state, such as the state where the chief executive office is located under R.U.P.A. § 106(a). Unlike the situation covered by R.U.P.A., a limited partnership has made a deliberate choice of applicable law by choosing to form under a particular statute. Although that should be obvious in the absence of this provision, § 106, coupled with § 110(b)(2), clarifies that this choice applies in certain situations notwithstanding any other choice-of-law rules, and despite a contrary provision in the partnership agreement.[13]

This provision raises almost as many questions as it answers. First, while the provision may be binding on courts of the enacting state, courts of other states may, but need not, follow it, although they probably will apply a similar rule under foreign limited partnership provisions like § 901, below. Second, the provision's scope is unclear. For example, it is not clear whether the provision requires application of the formation state's law to a veil-piercing issue, or to an issue involving the rights of transferees of partnership interests.[14]

§ 9.107. SUPPLEMENTAL PRINCIPLES OF LAW

Section 107

(a) Unless displaced by particular provisions of this [Act], the principles of law and equity supplement this [Act].

(b) If an obligation to pay interest arises under this [Act] and the rate is not specified, the rate is that specified in [applicable statute].

Summary: Provides for application of principles of law and equity and a rule for the payment of interest.

Parallel U.L.P.A. 1985: § 1105.

Parallel R.U.P.A.: § 104.

Parallel U.L.L.C.A.: § 104.

Bromberg & Ribstein: § 1.02.

Important Changes: None.

Analysis: These general principles always have applied to limited partnership, both implicitly and by linkage through U.L.P.A. (1985) § 1105 to U.P.A.

---

[13] In other words, the parties cannot form under State A, where the filing fees may be low, and yet choose to be governed by the law of State B, whose higher filing fees may reflect the greater desirability of its law. *See* Ribstein, Delaware, Lawyers and Choice of Law, 19 Del. J. Corp. L. 999, 122–25 (1994).

[14] The Comment says that the section applies to transferees since they "derive their rights and status under this Act from partners." But whether the Act and the partners can limit the rights of transferees may be precisely the issue the court has to decide.

§ 4 and R.U.P.A. § 104. However, this Act's de-linkage of general and limited partnership by bringing provisions formerly left to general partnership law explicitly into U.L.P.A. now leaves uncertain the extent to which these provisions "displace" other general partnership statutory provisions or general principles of partnership law. For example, does the non-inclusion of partnership by estoppel or purported partnership mean that this rule no longer applies under U.L.P.A.?[15] The Comment to this Section says that the general partnership cases "may be relevant by analogy" if the differences between general and limited partnerships are "immaterial to the disputed issue." This leaves unclear when courts should apply cases interpreting similar partnership or, for that matter, corporate or LLC, provisions, to limited partnerships despite language or contextual differences.[16]

§ 9.108.   NAME

Section 108

(a) The name of a limited partnership may contain the name of any partner.

(b) The name of a limited partnership that is not a limited liability limited partnership must contain the phrase "limited partnership" or the abbreviation "L.P." or "LP" and may not contain the phrase "limited liability limited partnership" or the abbreviation "LLLP" or "L.L.L.P."

(c) The name of a limited liability limited partnership must contain the phrase "limited liability limited partnership" or the abbreviation "LLLP" or "L.L.L.P." and must not contain the abbreviation "L.P." or "LP."

(d) Unless authorized by subsection (e), the name of a limited partnership must be distinguishable in the records of the [Secretary of State] from:

(1) the name of each person other than an individual incorporated, organized, or authorized to transact business in this State; and

(2) each name reserved under Section 109 [or other state laws allowing the reservation or registration of business names, including fictitious name statutes].

(e) A limited partnership may apply to the [Secretary of State] for authorization to use a name that does not comply with subsection (d). The [Secretary of State] shall authorize use of the name applied for if, as to each conflicting name:

(1) the present user, registrant, or owner of the conflicting name consents in a signed record to the use and submits an undertaking in a form satisfactory to the [Secretary of State] to change the conflicting name to a name that

---

[15] See U.P.A. § 16 and R.U.P.A. § 308; § 9.103.

[16] For a discussion of the linkage problems that remain after formal de-linkage, see Linking.

complies with subsection (d) and is distinguishable in the records of the [Secretary of State] from the name applied for;

(2) the applicant delivers to the [Secretary of State] a certified copy of the final judgment of a court of competent jurisdiction establishing the applicant's right to use in this State the name applied for; or

(3) the applicant delivers to the [Secretary of State] proof satisfactory to the [Secretary of State] that the present user, registrant, or owner of the conflicting name:

(A) has merged into the applicant;

(B) has been converted into the applicant; or

(C) has transferred substantially all of its assets, including the conflicting name, to the applicant.

(f) Subject to Section 905, this section applies to any foreign limited partnership transacting business in this State, having a certificate of authority to transact business in this State, or applying for a certificate of authority.

Summary: Provides rules governing the limited partnership's name.

Parallel U.L.P.A. 1985:   § 102.

Parallel R.U.P.A.:   None.

Parallel U.L.L.C.A.:   § 105.

Bromberg & Ribstein: § 2.13(b); § 12.02(b)–(c).

Important Changes: The name may include a limited partner's name; "limited partnership" may be abbreviated; the name must appropriately designate whether the limited partnership is a limited liability limited partnership and must be "distinguishable in the records" from that of other firms, rather than not "deceptively similar"; authorization to use a non-distinguishable name.

Analysis: The changes align limited partnership law with most current law relating to other business entities. However, as under other statutes, the effect of a non-complying name is unclear. The requirement that the name be specified in the certificate is discussed below in § 9.201. Note that this provision does not define the "name" of the limited partnership.[17] Provisions requiring accurate identification of the nature of the firm imply that the name is more than just what is set forth in the certificate, but do not clarify the consequences of using a name

---

[17] *See* U.L.L.C.A. Comments, at 339.

that differs from the one in the certificate. This obviously affects the duty to amend under § 202, discussed in § 9.202, and the liability for false statements under § 208, discussed in § 9.208.

§ 9.109.   RESERVATION OF NAME

Section 109

(a) The exclusive right to the use of a name that complies with Section 108 may be reserved by:

(1) a person intending to organize a limited partnership under this [Act] and to adopt the name;

(2) a limited partnership or a foreign limited partnership authorized to transact business in this State intending to adopt the name;

(3) a foreign limited partnership intending to obtain a certificate of authority to transact business in this State and adopt the name;

(4) a person intending to organize a foreign limited partnership and intending to have it obtain a certificate of authority to transact business in this State and adopt the name;

(5) a foreign limited partnership formed under the name; or

(6) a foreign limited partnership formed under a name that does not comply with Section 108(b) or (c), but the name reserved under this paragraph may differ from the foreign limited partnership's name only to the extent necessary to comply with Section 108(b) and (c).

(b) A person may apply to reserve a name under subsection (a) by delivering to the [Secretary of State] for filing an application that states the name to be reserved and the paragraph of subsection (a) which applies. If the [Secretary of State] finds that the name is available for use by the applicant, the [Secretary of State] shall file a statement of name reservation and thereby reserve the name for the exclusive use of the applicant for a 120 days.

(c) An applicant that has reserved a name pursuant to subsection (b) may reserve the same name for additional 120 day periods. A person having a current reservation for a name may not apply for another 120 day period for the same name until 90 days have elapsed in the current reservation.

(d) A person that has reserved a name under this section may deliver to the [Secretary of State] for filing a notice of transfer that states the reserved name, the name and street and mailing address of some other person to which the reservation is to be transferred, and the paragraph of subsection (a) which applies to the other person. Subject to Section 206(c), the transfer is effective when the [Secretary of State] files the notice of transfer.

Summary: Provides for reservation of the exclusive right to the use of a name that complies with § 108.

Parallel U.L.P.A. 1985: § 103.

Parallel R.U.P.A.: None.

Parallel U.L.L.C.A.: § 106.

Bromberg & Ribstein: § 12.02(b).

Important Changes: Similar in effect to prior law.

§ 9.110. EFFECT OF PARTNERSHIP AGREEMENT

Section 110

(a) Except as otherwise provided in subsection (b), the partnership agreement governs relations among the partners and between the partners and the partnership. To the extent the partnership agreement does not otherwise provide, this [Act] governs relations among the partners and between the partners and the partnership.

(b) A partnership agreement may not:

(1) vary a limited partnership's power under Section 105 to sue, be sued, and defend in its own name;

(2) vary the law applicable to a limited partnership under Section 106;

(3) vary the requirements of Section 204;

(4) vary the information required under Section 111 or unreasonably restrict the right to information under Sections 304 or 407, but the partnership agreement may impose reasonable restrictions on the availability and use of information obtained under those sections and may define appropriate remedies, including liquidated damages, for a breach of any reasonable restriction on use;

(5) eliminate the duty of loyalty under Section 408, but the partnership agreement may:

(A) identify specific types or categories of activities that do not violate the duty of loyalty, if not manifestly unreasonable; and

(B) specify the number or percentage of partners which may authorize or ratify, after full disclosure to all partners of all material facts, a specific act or transaction that otherwise would violate the duty of loyalty;

(6) unreasonably reduce the duty of care under Section 408(c);

(7) eliminate the obligation of good faith and fair dealing under Sections 305(b) and 408(d), but the partnership agreement may prescribe the standards by which the performance of the obligation is to be measured, if the standards are not manifestly unreasonable;

(8) vary the power of a person to dissociate as a general partner under Section 604(a) except to require that the notice under Section 603(1) be in a record;

(9) vary the power of a court to decree dissolution in the circumstances specified in Section 802;

(10) vary the requirement to wind up the partnership's business as specified in Section 803;

(11) unreasonably restrict the right to maintain an action under [Article] 10;

(12) restrict the right of a partner under Section 1110(a) to approve a conversion or merger or the right of a general partner under Section 1110(b) to consent to an amendment to the certificate of limited partnership which deletes a statement that the limited partnership is a limited liability limited partnership; or

(13) restrict rights under this [Act] of a person other than a partner or a transferee.

Summary: Provides that this Act governs partners' relations only where the agreement does not otherwise provide, except in certain designated cases.

Parallel U.L.P.A. 1985:   None.

Parallel R.U.P.A.:   § 103.

Parallel U.L.L.C.A.:   § 103.

Bromberg & Ribstein: §§ 6.01(c), 6.07(h), 16.01(c), 16.07(h).

Important Changes: Limits the effectiveness of partnership agreement in ways similar to R.U.P.A. Changes the law for limited partnerships subject to U.P.A., which did not summarize the situations that cannot be varied by the agreement. Case law under U.P.A. may or may not be consistent with many of the limitations, including those on waiving fiduciary duties.

Analysis:

Subsection (a) provides blanket authorization for partnership agreement provisions varying the provisions of the statute, making unnecessary specific language with respect to each provision of the act. This subsection applies among the partners. Parties other than partners are covered by § 110(b)(13) and § 201(d)(2), as discussed below regarding those provisions. The Comment provides that the partnership agreement may prohibit oral modifications, and this is consistent with the failure to include the definition of partnership agreement in § 102(13) in the list of non-modifiable provisions § 110(b). The act arguably should require that any writing requirements be specified in writing.

Subsection (b): Most of these limitations are discussed in connection with the specific sections to which they refer (105, 106, 111, 204, 304, 305, 407, 408, 604, 802, 1002, and 1110), as well as in connection with the analogous R.U.P.A. provisions in Chapter 8 (*see* cross-references in discussion of above sections).

Restricting agreements among the partners raises the same issues as analogous R.U.P.A. and U.L.L.C.A. provisions. The authors' respective positions on these issues are discussed in the cross-referenced Bromberg & Ribstein sections. According to author Ribstein, the arguments against such restrictions include the following: Partners do not need special protection from their agreements beyond what applies to contracts generally, case law does not support such limitations, statutory restrictions will tend to be ineffective because they can be avoided by clever drafting, and restrictions, to the extent that they are effective, prevent valuable planning for specific situations that cannot be covered by a general statute.[18] Restrictions on contracting are particularly unwarranted in limited partnerships, which are specialized vehicles that parties tend to use only with extensive legal advice, in contrast to more general-purpose general partnerships and LLCs. Even family limited partnerships will rely on legal advice because of the tax law on estate tax discounts that motivates many such partnerships. Accordingly, the use of language from R.U.P.A. § 103 as well as U.L.L.C.A. § 103 may cause courts to apply standards and case law that are inappropriate for limited partnerships. As detailed in the cross-referenced treatise sections, author Bromberg believes that restrictions on contracting specifically applicable to limited and general partnerships may be appropriate in some circumstances.

Subsection 13 provides that the agreement may not restrict a non-partner's right under the Act. The Comment says that this subsection is intended to clarify that a contract such as a partnership agreement does not govern the rights of non-parties to the contract. The subsection raises several issues and creates many traps for the unwary.[19]

---

[18] *See* U.L.L.C.A. Comments, at 331–32; Ribstein, Fiduciary Duty Contracts in Unincorporated Firms, 54 Wash. & Lee L. Rev. 537 (1997); Revisited at 985–86.

[19] *See* Keatinge, The Partnership Agreement and Third Parties: Re RULPA §110(b)(13) v. RUPA §103(b)(10), 37 Suffolk L. Rev. 873 (2004).

First, it may not be clear when an agreement "restricts" non-partner rights. For example, a partnership agreement, which includes oral and implied provisions under § 102(13), may simultaneously provide for non-partner rights and limit these rights. Does § 110(b)(13) mean that the rights are enforceable but the restrictions are not, that neither the rights nor the restrictions on non-partners are enforceable, or that the entire agreement is unenforceable because it includes restrictions on non-partner rights (see below)? Also, the agreement may have unexpected effects on third-party rights, particularly in creating liability for excessive contributions (*see* § 9.509, below).

Second, it is not clear whether this provision precludes enforcement even of a restriction to which a non-partner has agreed.[20] The R.U.P.A. Comments state that such a restriction would be enforceable, but the statutory language does not make this clear and there is no comparable comment in U.L.P.A.[21] Section 102(13) defines a partnership agreement as "the *partners'* agreement . . . concerning the partnership" (emphasis added). It arguably follows that an agreement is *not* a "partnership agreement," and therefore is not subject to § 110(b)(13), if, or to the extent that, it applies to non-partners. Under this interpretation, the section would be a tautology: an agreement only among the partners binds only the partners. On the other hand, these provisions may mean that an agreement among the partners that purports to bind non-partners is a partnership agreement under § 102(13) and therefore cannot bind non-partners under § 110(b)(13) even if the non-partners are made parties to the agreement. Indeed, the agreement with non-partners may be invalid (and may take the whole partnership agreement down with it) even if it is separate in form if a court decides that it is part of the partnership agreement in substance.

Third, while § 110(b)(13) says that the agreement can restrict transferees' rights, neither § 110(a), which affirmatively describes the effect of the agreement, nor § 102(13), which defines the agreement, mentions transferees. In order to give § 110(b)(13) meaning, the other provisions would have to be interpreted to embrace agreements among the partners that apply to transferees. This would support the broad view of invalidity as to third parties discussed in the previous paragraph. But if an agreement among the partners can restrict transferees' rights, apparently even without their consent, it is not clear why it cannot restrict the rights of other similarly situated non-partners, such as creditors, whether or not they consent.

Fourth, it is not clear whether an agreement that restricts non-partner rights is effective even among the partners. The section says that the agreement "may not"

---

[20] *See* U.L.L.C.A. Comments, at 338.

[21] *See* R.U.P.A. § 103(b)(9), discussed in § 8.103. Although this provision is based on R.U.P.A. § 103(b)(9), it subtly differs in referring to persons "other than a partner or a transferee" rather than "third parties." It is not clear how this difference will affect application of R.U.P.A. cases to U.L.P.A. limited partnerships.

include such a restriction, implying that it is invalid to the extent that it does. The Comment unhelpfully says that it is not "automatically" unenforceable "*inter se* the partners and any transferees," leaving this issue to "other law." Even partial invalidation as to the non-partner will leave the court with a complex interpretation issue as to the effect of the non-invalid portion.

Fifth, it is not clear how the provision interrelates with § 201(d)(2), which says that the certificate or other filed document prevails over the agreement as to reasonably relying non-partner/transferees. This implicitly suggests that the agreement applies to non-partner/transferees who *do not* reasonably rely on the certificate or other filed document. As discussed above, pursuant to § 110(b)(13), the agreement might expand but not restrict such parties' rights, presumably whether or not the third party reasonably relies on the agreement.

In general, states would be well-advised not to adopt this subsection.[22] Omission of the provision would avoid the minefields discussed below, instead leaving these issues to well-established principles of contract law.

State variations

The **Illinois** version of subsection 110(b)(5) applies to "fiduciary duties" rather than only to the duty of loyalty.[23]

The **Kentucky** version of U.L.P.A. § 110 includes a subsection (3), which provides that if a written partnership agreement requires amendments to be in writing in accordance with the agreement, then that provision shall be enforceable.[24] Also, the Kentucky act contains an additional provision that, subject to Kentucky's version of U.L.P.A. § 110, "it shall be the policy of the General Assembly through this subchapter to give maximum effect to the principles of freedom of contract and the enforceability of partnership agreements."[25]

The **Maine** version of U.L.P.A. §110 does not include a restriction on waiver of care and loyalty duties, and has a separate subsection providing that, "[n]otwithstanding any other provision of this chapter, there exists, for purposes of this chapter, an implied contractual covenant of good faith and fair dealing in every partnership agreement which may not be eliminated by the terms of the partnership agreement."[26]

---

[22] Delaware, Tennessee, and Virginia modified the corresponding provision in R.U.P.A. *See* § 8.103, supra.

[23] 805 ILCS §215/110.

[24] Ky. Rev. St. Ann., § 362.2-110(3).

[25] *Id.* § 106(3).

[26] 31 Me. Rev. St. Ann. § 1310.

§ 9.111.   REQUIRED INFORMATION

Section 111

A limited partnership shall maintain at its designated office the following information:

(1) a current list showing the full name and last known street and mailing address of each partner, separately identifying the general partners, in alphabetical order, and the limited partners, in alphabetical order;

(2) a copy of the initial certificate of limited partnership and all amendments to and restatements of the certificate, together with signed copies of any powers of attorney under which any certificate, amendment, or restatement has been signed;

(3) a copy of any filed articles of conversion or merger;

(4) a copy of the limited partnership's federal, state, and local income tax returns and reports, if any, for the three most recent years;

(5) a copy of any partnership agreement made in a record and any amendment made in a record to any partnership agreement;

(6) a copy of any financial statement of the limited partnership for the three most recent years;

(7) a copy of the three most recent annual reports delivered by the limited partnership to the [Secretary of State] pursuant to Section 210;

(8) a copy of any record made by the limited partnership during the past three years of any consent given by or vote taken of any partner pursuant to this [Act] or the partnership agreement; and

(9) unless contained in a partnership agreement made in a record, a record stating:

(A) the amount of cash, and a description and statement of the agreed value of the other benefits, contributed and agreed to be contributed by each partner;

(B) the times at which, or events on the happening of which, any additional contributions agreed to be made by each partner are to be made;

(C) for any person that is both a general partner and a limited partner, a specification of what transferable interest the person owns in each capacity; and

(D) any events upon the happening of which the limited partnership is to be dissolved and its activities wound up.

Summary: Specifies information that the partnership must maintain at its designated office.

Parallel U.L.P.A. 1985:   § 105.

Parallel R.U.P.A.:   None.

Parallel U.L.L.C.A.: None.

Bromberg & Ribstein: §§ 6.05; 16.05.

Important Changes: See discussion below.

Analysis: Unlike U.L.L.C.A. and R.U.P.A., this provision requires the firm to keep certain information. The information listed in this section is subject to access by the partners under § 304 and § 407 below. The information listed here is referred to throughout the act as "required information," which is defined in § 102(18) as the information the partnership must maintain under this section. It is not clear what the consequences are of a partnership's not creating the listed records, such as superseded partnership agreements, or not maintaining the records once created. The general partners presumably are responsible for compliance and may be liable for damages resulting from failure to maintain, at least to the extent that this failure is a breach of duty under § 408. *See* Comment to § 201. Issues relating to some specific subsections are discussed below.

Paragraph 5: Unlike U.L.P.A. (1985), which requires only "then effective written partnership agreements," this section requires superseded agreements and clarifies what is meant by a "written" agreement with the language "made in a record." Section 102(17) defines "record" as "information that is inscribed on a tangible medium or that is stored in an electronic or other medium and is retrievable in perceivable form." The Comment to § 111 excludes oral agreements that are "subsequently inscribed in a record (but not consented to as such)." It is not clear how this would apply, for example, to an oral agreement that the parties orally agree should be inscribed in a record where the parties do not consent to the resulting record.

Paragraph 9: The above discussion of "record" applies here. The Comment to this subparagraph states that this is not a statute of frauds provision, although the partnership agreement can specify that only recorded contributions are enforceable.

§ 9.112. BUSINESS TRANSACTIONS OF PARTNER WITH PARTNERSHIP

Section 112

A partner may lend money to and transact other business with the limited partnership and has the same rights and obligations with respect to the loan or other transaction as a person that is not a partner.

Summary: Concerns partners' loans and other transactions with the partnership.

Parallel U.L.P.A. 1985:   § 107.

Parallel R.U.P.A.:   § 404(f).

Parallel U.L.L.C.A.:   § 409(f).

Bromberg & Ribstein: § 12.09(b).

Important Changes: None.

Analysis: The effect of this provision is unclear. Although similar language has been included in R.U.P.A. and U.L.L.C.A. provisions that deal with partners' duties, as discussed in § 8.404 as well as in the Comment to § 112, this provision has nothing to do with partners' duties among themselves, such as duties regarding purchases of partnership property at liquidation sales.[27] The Comment says that the provision means that the Act does not discriminate against creditors of limited partnerships who are partners. However, as the Comment recognizes, any such discrimination would be a matter of debtor–creditor law.[28]

§ 9.113.   DUAL CAPACITY

Section 113

A person may be both a general partner and a limited partner. A person that is both a general and limited partner has the rights, powers, duties, and obligations provided by this [Act] and the partnership agreement in each of those capacities. When the person acts as a general partner, the person is subject to the obligations, duties and restrictions under this [Act] and the partnership agreement for general partners. When the person acts as a limited partner, the person is subject to the obligations, duties and restrictions under this [Act] and the partnership agreement for limited partners.

---

[27] *See* Bromberg & Ribstein, § 7.02(c)(2).

[28] *See* Szturm v. Huntington Blizzard Hockey Assocs. Ltd. P'ship, 516 S.E.2d 267 (W. Va. 1999) (limited partner could assert wage lien superior to claims of limited partnership's general creditors; West Virginia's adoption of U.L.P.A. 1985 and of R.U.P.A., which contains similar provision, reversed prior case law under U.P.A., although partner's claim remains subject to fraudulent conveyance law).

Summary: Provides for effect of person's being both a general and limited partner.

Parallel U.L.P.A. 1985: § 404.

Parallel R.U.P.A.: None.

Parallel U.L.L.C.A.: None.

Bromberg & Ribstein: None.

Important Changes: None.

§ 9.114. OFFICE AND AGENT FOR SERVICE OF PROCESS

Section 114

(a) A limited partnership shall designate and continuously maintain in this State:
(1) an office, which need not be a place of its activity in this State; and
(2) an agent for service of process.
(b) A foreign limited partnership shall designate and continuously maintain in this State an agent for service of process.
(c) An agent for service of process of a limited partnership or foreign limited partnership must be an individual who is a resident of this State or other person authorized to do business in this State.

§ 9.115. CHANGE OF DESIGNATED OFFICE OR AGENT FOR SERVICE OF PROCESS

Section 115

(a) In order to change its designated office, agent for service of process, or the address of its agent for service of process, a limited partnership or a foreign limited partnership may deliver to the [Secretary of State] for filing a statement of change containing:

(1) the name of the limited partnership or foreign limited partnership;

(2) the street and mailing address of its current designated office;

(3) if the current designated office is to be changed, the street and mailing address of the new designated office;

(4) the name and street and mailing address of its current agent for service of process; and

(5) if the current agent for service of process or an address of the agent is to be changed, the new information.

(b) Subject to Section 206(c), a statement of change is effective when filed by the [Secretary of State].

§ 9.116.   RESIGNATION OF AGENT FOR SERVICE OF PROCESS

Section 116

(a) In order to resign as an agent for service of process of a limited partnership or foreign limited partnership, the agent must deliver to the [Secretary of State] for filing a statement of resignation containing the name of the limited partnership or foreign limited partnership.

(b) After receiving a statement of resignation, the [Secretary of State] shall file it and mail a copy to the designated office of the limited partnership or foreign limited partnership and another copy to the principal office if the address of the office appears in the records of the [Secretary of State] and is different from the address of the designated office.

(c) An agency for service of process is terminated on the 31st day after the [Secretary of State] files the statement of resignation.

§ 9.117.   SERVICE OF PROCESS

Section 117

(a) An agent for service of process appointed by a limited partnership or foreign limited partnership is an agent of the limited partnership or foreign limited partnership for service of any process, notice, or demand required or permitted by law to be served upon the limited partnership or foreign limited partnership.

(b) If a limited partnership or foreign limited partnership does not appoint or maintain an agent for service of process in this State or the agent for service of process cannot with reasonable diligence be found at the agent's address, the

[Secretary of State] is an agent of the limited partnership or foreign limited partnership upon whom process, notice, or demand may be served.

(c) Service of any process, notice, or demand on the [Secretary of State] may be made by delivering to and leaving with the [Secretary of State] duplicate copies of the process, notice, or demand. If a process, notice, or demand is served on the [Secretary of State], the [Secretary of State] shall forward one of the copies by registered or certified mail, return receipt requested, to the limited partnership or foreign limited partnership at its designated office.

(d) Service is effected under subsection (c) at the earliest of:

(1) the date the limited partnership or foreign limited partnership receives the process, notice, or demand;

(2) the date shown on the return receipt, if signed on behalf of the limited partnership or foreign limited partnership; or

(3) five days after the process, notice, or demand is deposited in the mail, if mailed postpaid and correctly addressed.

(e) The [Secretary of State] shall keep a record of each process, notice, and demand served pursuant to this section and record the time of, and the action taken regarding, the service.

(f) This section does not affect the right to serve process, notice, or demand in any other manner provided by law.

Summary: These sections provide for designation and change of office and agent for service of process, as well as for service of process in the event of the failure to designate. A foreign limited partnership initially designates its office and agent in the application for a certificate of authority under § 902(a)(4) and is subject to penalty for failure to maintain under § 906(a)(3). Limited partnerships can make changes other than under § 115 by amending the certificate or annual report under § 202 or § 210(e). Failure to change promptly can be penalized under § 208.

Parallel U.L.P.A. 1985: § 104.

Parallel R.U.P.A.: None.

Parallel U.L.L.C.A.: §§ 108–111.

Bromberg & Ribstein: § 12.02(d).

Important Changes: More detailed provisions regarding designation and change of office and agent, and addition of provision regarding substituted service.

§ 9.118.   CONSENT AND PROXIES OF PARTNERS

Section 118

Action requiring the consent of partners under this [Act] may be taken without a meeting, and a partner may appoint a proxy to consent or otherwise act for the partner by signing an appointment record, either personally or by the partner's attorney in fact.

Summary: Provides for proxies and consents to action taken without a meeting.

Parallel U.L.P.A. 1985:   None.

Parallel R.U.P.A.:   None.

Parallel U.L.L.C.A.:   § 404(e).

Bromberg & Ribstein: § 16.03(b).

Important Changes: Clarifies that consents and proxies are permissible.

Analysis: It is not clear why this provision was necessary, since the Act does not elsewhere require a meeting or specify rules regarding voting.

§ 9.201.   FORMATION OF LIMITED PARTNERSHIP; CERTIFICATE OF LIMITED PARTNERSHIP

Section 201

(a) In order for a limited partnership to be formed, a certificate of limited partnership must be delivered to the [Secretary of State] for filing. The certificate must state:

(1) the name of the limited partnership, which must comply with Section 108;

(2) the street and mailing address of the initial designated office and the name and street and mailing address of the initial agent for service of process;

(3) the name and the street and mailing address of each general partner;

(4) whether the limited partnership is a limited liability limited partnership; and

(5) any additional information required by [Article] 11.

(b) A certificate of limited partnership may also contain any other matters but may not vary or otherwise affect the provisions specified in Section 110(b) in a manner inconsistent with that section.

(c) If there has been substantial compliance with subsection (a), subject to Section 206(c) a limited partnership is formed when the [Secretary of State] files the certificate of limited partnership.

(d) Subject to subsection (b), if any provision of a partnership agreement is inconsistent with the filed certificate of limited partnership or with a filed statement of dissociation, termination, or change or filed articles of conversion or merger:

(1) the partnership agreement prevails as to partners and transferees; and

(2) the filed certificate of limited partnership, statement of dissociation, termination, or change or articles of conversion or merger prevail as to persons, other than partners and transferees, that reasonably rely on the filed record to their detriment.

Summary: States how a limited partnership is formed and the contents and effect of the certificate.

Parallel U.L.P.A. 1985:   § 201.

Parallel R.U.P.A.:   None.

Parallel U.L.L.C.A.:   §§ 202–203.

Bromberg & Ribstein: §§ 12.02–12.05.

Important Changes: Requires election of LLLP status; does not require specification of dissolution date; provides for the effect of certificate provisions that are inconsistent with provisions of the partnership agreement.

Analysis: Because the certificate is a publicly filed document, the document itself and the fact of its filing may have a different effect on third parties than the non-filed part of the agreement. But the partnership agreement clearly can have an effect among the partners independent of the certificate, as is shown by subparagraph (d)(1), analyzed below. Thus, it is not clear what the Comment means by "[a] limited partnership is a creature of statute." Issues relating to specific subparagraphs are discussed below.

Paragraph (a)(1):   The name requirements are discussed in § 9.108. As discussed there, it is not clear whether the firm's name is only that stated in the certificate or depends on usage. It is also not clear whether a non-complying

name constitutes an absence of "substantial compliance with subsection (a)" that
would affect formation of the limited partnership under § 201(c).

Paragraph (a)(3):   The effects of listing and failing to list general partners
are covered by § 103(c), discussed in § 9.103. Naming in the certificate is not a
prerequisite to becoming a general partner under § 401.

Paragraph (a)(4):   The certificate must, in effect, "check the box" as to
LLLP status. This forces the partners to face the liability issue, so that they do
not erroneously assume that the firm has a particular liability status. But this
provision raises several complications. First, the legislature must ensure that this
requirement does not conflict with other formalities or approval requirements for
LLLP status. *See* § 5.01(b)–(c). Second, it is not clear whether omitting this
"check" not only prevents the firm from being an LLLP under § 102(9), but also
prevents formation as a limited partnership under subsection (c) because the firm
is not in "substantial compliance with subsection (a)." Thus, a partnership that does
not elect to be an LLLP may be a general partnership rather than an LLP, with
personal liability for all partners. Third, it is not clear what the effect is of certificate
amendments regarding the LLLP election. *See* the Analysis of § 201, below.

Subsection (b):   By providing that the certificate is subject to § 110(b), this
subsection implies that the certificate is part of the partnership agreement. This is
also implied by the broad definition of "partnership agreement" in § 102(13). *See*
discussion of subsection (d), below.

Subsection (c):   It is not clear what this subsection means by stating that
the limited partnership is "formed" upon filing. This connects with the definition
of "limited partnership" in § 102(11) as an entity "formed under this [Act]."
These provisions involve fundamental issues concerning the relationship between
the filing requirement and the contractual aspects of the limited partnership.

The Comment says that "[a] limited partnership is a creature of statute, and
this section governs how a limited partnership comes into existence." However,
the limited partnership is clearly controlled among the partners by the agreement
pursuant to § 110 and § 201(d)(1).[29] The agreement arguably can bind third
parties to the consequences of limited partnership if these parties agree.[30] Note
that the act does not provide, as do several corporate and LLC acts, for liability
of those assuming or purporting to act as a limited partnership without complying
with formalities. On the other hand, it is not clear what the effect is of § 110(a)
and (b)(13). These provisions apparently prevent the partnership agreement from
affecting third parties' rights even if those parties consent. *See* § 9.110. Rights

---

[29] *See* Bromberg & Ribstein, § 12.04(b).
[30] *See* U.L.L.C.A. Comments, at 338.

that third parties have to recover from parties to a defective limited partnership may or may not arise under this Act. *See* § 306, discussed in § 9.306. Moreover, if a firm has not properly been "formed" as a limited partnership under § 102(11), it arguably follows that the agreement purporting to bind the third party is not a limited partnership agreement under § 102(13) because it is not one "concerning the limited partnership," and is therefore not limited in effect by § 110.

As discussed above regarding subsection (a), there are several issues concerning when there is "substantial compliance" with subsection (a). It would be better to eliminate the substantial compliance requirement and provide for formation by filing irrespective of the content of the certificate. This would be consistent with the basic notice function of the certificate and with the cases dealing with the substantial compliance requirement under current law.[31]

The precise time of formation is governed by § 206(c).

Subsection (d): Although subsection (b) and § 102(13) indicate that the certificate and other records may be part of the partnership agreement, this subsection distinguishes between the "partnership agreement" and filed record. In order to make sense of the provision, "partnership agreement" in subsection (1) should be interpreted to include the agreement that is not part of the records referred to in subsection (2).

Several issues arise with respect to the different effects of the certificate on "partners and transferees" and on others who reasonably and detrimentally rely on the certificate. First, as discussed in § 9.110, it is not clear how to reconcile this provision with § 110(b)(13), since it implies that the partnership agreement controls over the certificate as to non-relying third parties. Second, it is not clear what the effect is of a provision in the filed record that is in addition to but not inconsistent with the partnership agreement. The Comment states that the policy underlying this provision would make it equally applicable to this situation, but that seems inconsistent with the language of the provision. In any event, it is not clear how the certificate would be consistent with the agreement if it contains a material provision that the agreement does not.

A general partner may have a duty to amend a false certificate under § 202(c) and be held liable under § 208. It is not clear what effect a certificate that is inconsistent with the partnership agreement has under those provisions. In this situation, the statement arguably is true by reason of § 201(d).

---

[31] *See* Bromberg & Ribstein, § 12.03(c); Ribstein, Applied, at 879–80.

§ 9.202.　AMENDMENT OR RESTATEMENT
OF CERTIFICATE

Section 202

(a) In order to amend its certificate of limited partnership, a limited partnership must deliver to the [Secretary of State] for filing an amendment or, pursuant to [Article] 11, articles of merger stating:

(1) the name of the limited partnership;

(2) the date of filing of its initial certificate; and

(3) the changes the amendment makes to the certificate as most recently amended or restated.

(b) A limited partnership shall promptly deliver to the [Secretary of State] for filing an amendment to a certificate of limited partnership to reflect:

(1) the admission of a new general partner;

(2) the dissociation of a person as a general partner; or

(3) the appointment of a person to wind up the limited partnership's activities under Section 803(c) or (d).

(c) A general partner that knows that any information in a filed certificate of limited partnership was false when the certificate was filed or has become false due to changed circumstances shall promptly:

(1) cause the certificate to be amended; or

(2) if appropriate, deliver to the [Secretary of State] for filing a statement of change pursuant to Section 115 or a statement of correction pursuant to Section 207.

(d) A certificate of limited partnership may be amended at any time for any other proper purpose as determined by the limited partnership.

(e) A restated certificate of limited partnership may be delivered to the [Secretary of State] for filing in the same manner as an amendment.

(f) Subject to Section 206(c), an amendment or restated certificate is effective when filed by the [Secretary of State].

Summary:　Provides for method of amending and restating the certificate and for the duty to amend in certain circumstances.

Parallel U.L.P.A. 1985:　§ 202.

Parallel R.U.P.A.:　None.

Parallel U.L.L.C.A.:　§ 204.

Bromberg & Ribstein:　§ 12.02.

Important Changes: Does not require amendment to reflect continuation of the business on partner dissociation, but does require amendment to reflect appointment of a person to wind up the business.

Analysis:

Subsections (b)–(c):   The duty to amend was already antiquated in U.L.P.A. (1985)[32] and there is little justification for continuing that duty. There is no equivalent duty in corporate law. The duty might make sense in limited partnerships if there were a danger of misleading third parties. But there is no such danger to the extent that the certificate provisions are controlling[33] or other provisions ensure timely updating:

1.   Section 103(c) provides that the certificate is constructive notice that the persons it designates as general partners are such.
2.   Section 103(d) provides that that certificate amendment is notice of dissolution or dissociation, thereby giving partners a strong incentive to amend in order to limit their liability and the authority of partners acting for the firm, as was recognized in eliminating the duty to file a certificate of cancellation (see § 9.203).
3.   As discussed in § 9.108, the name stated in the certificate pursuant to § 201(a)(1) may control over any other name the partnership uses. In other words, any misleading may result from *use* of that name rather than from the certificate disclosure. This is implicit in not requiring correction of the name under § 201(b) or (c). If correction is not required because the certificate controls, it is not clear why the same would not be true of other statements as to which the certificate controls.
4.   Section 201(d) provides that the certificate controls over inconsistent terms of the partnership agreement as to a reasonably relying non-partner/transferee (*see* § 9.201).
5.   Section 208 provides for liability for false statements by persons who signed or by partners with notice sufficient to change or correct (*see* § 9.208).

The duty to amend raises several issues in addition to whether it is necessary. First, it is not clear what the consequences are to the limited partnership of not satisfying its duty to amend. Since, as the Comment notes, it is actually the general partners who have this responsibility under § 406, the limited partnership's duty essentially duplicates the general partners' duty to correct false statements

---

[32] *See* Ribstein, Applied, at 779.
[33] *See* U.L.L.C.A. Comments, at 344–45.

under subsection (c). Responsibility for correction primarily relates to possible injury to the partners resulting from liabilities to third parties created by misleading certificate statements. Liability for such injuries would be covered by the general partners' duties under § 408.

Second, it is not clear how the subparts of the section relate to each other. In other words, why do some false statements trigger a duty to amend by the "limited partnership" under subsection (b), while all false statements give rise to a duty to correct by knowing general partners under subsection (c)?

Third, although the Comment to § 201 states that an amendment deleting LLLP status must add a specification that the firm is *not* an LLLP, it is not clear what the effect of omitting this specification would be. If the certificate does not state that the firm is an LLLP, then it would not be an LLLP under § 102(9). The question is whether the partnership ceases being a limited partnership because the omission of a statement as to LLLP status prevents it from being "formed" under § 102(11). This may or may not be the result under § 201(a)(4), discussed above in § 9.201. On the one hand, once the partnership has been properly formed, it is not clear that a defective amendment would change that status. On the other hand, it is not clear why the omission of the appropriate "check" in the non-LLLP box would have a different effect on amendment than on initial formation, unless the requirement that the firm check the LLLP box on formation apparently is intended only as a reminder to the partners rather than as notice to third parties.

Fourth, it is uncertain how an amendment regarding LLLP status would relate to § 1110(b)(2), which provides that a certificate amendment deleting LLLP designation is ineffective without the consent of each general partner. It seems to follow that a third party could not hold the general partners liable even if the certificate stated that the firm was not an LLLP if a general partner did not consent to that deletion, even if the third party lacked notice of the lack of consent. This obviously presents opportunities for abuse. Moreover, it is arguably inconsistent with § 201(d), which seems to make the certificate designation that the firm is not an LLLP control regardless of whether the partners can be deemed to have agreed to the deletion of this status. Perhaps the lack of unanimous consent to deletion affects internal allocation of liabilities among the partners even if it does not affect liability to third parties.

§ 9.203. STATEMENT OF TERMINATION

Section 203

A dissolved limited partnership that has completed winding up may deliver to the [Secretary of State] for filing a statement of termination that states:

(1) the name of the limited partnership;

(2) the date of filing of its initial certificate of limited partnership; and

(3) any other information as determined by the general partners filing the statement or by a person appointed pursuant to Section 803(c) or (d).

Summary: Permits the filing of a statement of termination after the completion of winding up.

Parallel U.L.P.A. 1985:   § 203.

Parallel R.U.P.A.:   None.

Parallel U.L.L.C.A.:   § 805.

Bromberg & Ribstein: § 17.08(b)(3).

Important Changes: Prior provision required the filing of certificate of cancellation upon partnership dissolution.

Analysis: The partnership has ample incentive to file the statement because, under § 103(d)(3), the statement provides constructive notice terminating partners' authority to bind the partnership.

§ 9.204.   SIGNING OF RECORDS

Section 204

(a) Each record delivered to the [Secretary of State] for filing pursuant to this [Act] must be signed in the following manner:

(1) An initial certificate of limited partnership must be signed by all general partners listed in the certificate.

(2) An amendment adding or deleting a statement that the limited partnership is a limited liability limited partnership must be signed by all general partners listed in the certificate.

(3) An amendment designating as general partner a person admitted under Section 801(3)(B) following the dissociation of a limited partnership's last general partner must be signed by that person.

(4) An amendment required by Section 803(c) following the appointment of a person to wind up the dissolved limited partnership's activities must be signed by that person.

(5) Any other amendment must be signed by:

(A) at least one general partner listed in the certificate;

(B) each other person designated in the amendment as a new general partner; and

(C) each person that the amendment indicates has dissociated as a general partner, unless:

(i) the person is deceased or a guardian or general conservator has been appointed for the person and the amendment so states; or

(ii) the person has previously delivered to the [Secretary of State] for filing a statement of dissociation.

(6) A restated certificate of limited partnership must be signed by at least one general partner listed in the certificate, and, to the extent the restated certificate effects a change under any other paragraph of this subsection, the certificate must be signed in a manner that satisfies that paragraph.

(7) A statement of termination must be signed by all general partners listed in the certificate or, if the certificate of a dissolved limited partnership lists no general partners, by the person appointed pursuant to Section 803(c) or (d) to wind up the dissolved limited partnership's activities.

(8) Articles of conversion must be signed by each general partner listed in the certificate of limited partnership.

(9) Articles of merger must be signed as provided in Section 1108(a).

(10) Any other record delivered on behalf of a limited partnership to the [Secretary of State] for filing must be signed by at least one general partner listed in the certificate.

(11) A statement by a person pursuant to Section 605(a)(4) stating that the person has dissociated as a general partner must be signed by that person.

(12) A statement of withdrawal by a person pursuant to Section 306 must be signed by that person.

(13) A record delivered on behalf of a foreign limited partnership to the [Secretary of State] for filing must be signed by at least one general partner of the foreign limited partnership.

(14) Any other record delivered on behalf of any person to the [Secretary of State] for filing must be signed by that person.

(b) Any person may sign by an attorney in fact any record to be filed pursuant to this [Act].

Summary: Specifies who must sign certificates and other records.

Parallel U.L.P.A. 1985:   § 204.

Parallel R.U.P.A.:   None.

Parallel U.L.L.C.A.:   § 205.

Bromberg & Ribstein: § 12.02(k).

Important Changes: Provides for signing of records and other certificates; clarifies that only general partners listed in the certificate can satisfy signing requirement; specifies signing by persons appointed under § 803(c)–(d).

Analysis: Section 201(c) provides for formation upon filing of the certificate upon substantial compliance with § 201(a) without specifying that the certificate must be signed under § 204. Section 206 provides for filing of the certificate, again without requiring that the certificate have been signed. Although this section requires signing of the certificate, it is not clear what the effect is of failure to sign. This section is non-waivable under § 110(b)(3), as well as under § 110(b)(13) to the extent that waiver would restrict third parties' rights.

§ 9.205.   SIGNING AND FILING PURSUANT TO JUDICIAL ORDER

Section 205

(a) If a person required by this [Act] to sign a record or deliver a record to the [Secretary of State] for filing does not do so, any other person that is aggrieved may petition the [appropriate court] to order:
    (1) the person to sign the record;
    (2) deliver the record to the [Secretary of State] for filing; or
    (3) the [Secretary of State] to file the record unsigned.
(b) If the person aggrieved under subsection (a) is not the limited partnership or foreign limited partnership to which the record pertains, the aggrieved person shall make the limited partnership or foreign limited partnership a party to the action. A person aggrieved under subsection (a) may seek the remedies provided in subsection (a) in the same action in combination or in the alternative.
(c) A record filed unsigned pursuant to this section is effective without being signed.

Summary: Provides for an action to compel execution, delivery for filing, or filing of a record.

Parallel U.L.P.A. 1985:   § 205.

Parallel R.U.P.A.:   None.

Parallel U.L.L.C.A.:   § 210.

Bromberg & Ribstein: § 12.02(k).

Important Changes: Provides that limited partnership shall be made a party to the action if it is not the party bringing it.

Analysis: Since a limited partnership apparently can be formed without signing (*see* § 9.204), the main importance of this section may be to create responsibility for false statements in the certificate pursuant to § 208(a)(1).

§ 9.206.   DELIVERY TO AND FILING OF RECORDS; EFFECTIVE TIME AND DATE

Section 206

(a) A record authorized or required to be delivered to the [Secretary of State] for filing under this [Act] must be captioned to describe the record's purpose, be in a medium permitted by the [Secretary of State], and be delivered to the [Secretary of State]. Unless the [Secretary of State] determines that a record does not comply with the filing requirements of this [Act], and if all filing fees have been paid, the [Secretary of State] shall file the record and:

(1) for a statement of dissociation, send:

(A) a copy of the filed statement and a receipt for the fees to the person which the statement indicates has dissociated as a general partner; and

(B) a copy of the filed statement and receipt to the limited partnership;

(2) for a statement of withdrawal, send:

(A) a copy of the filed statement and a receipt for the fees to the person on whose behalf the record was filed; and

(B) if the statement refers to an existing limited partnership, a copy of the filed statement and receipt to the limited partnership; and

(3) for all other records, send a copy of the filed record and a receipt for the fees to the person on whose behalf the record was filed.

(b) Upon request and payment of a fee, the [Secretary of State] shall send to the requester a certified copy of the requested record.

(c) Except as otherwise provided in Sections 116 and 207, a record delivered to the [Secretary of State] for filing under this [Act] may specify an effective time and a delayed effective date. Except as otherwise provided in this [Act], a record filed by the [Secretary of State] is effective:

(1) if the record does not specify an effective time and does not specify a delayed effective date, on the date and at the time the record is filed as evidenced by the [Secretary of State's] endorsement of the date and time on the record;

(2) if the record specifies an effective time but not a delayed effective date, on the date the record is filed at the time specified in the record;

(3) if the record specifies a delayed effective date but not an effective time, at 12:01 a.m. on the earlier of:

   (A) the specified date; or

   (B) the 90th day after the record is filed; or

(4) if the record specifies an effective time and a delayed effective date, at the specified time on the earlier of:

   (A) the specified date; or

   (B) the 90th day after the record is filed.

Summary: Provides for delivery to and filing by the appropriate state official of the certificate and for the effective time of filing.

Parallel U.L.P.A. 1985: § 206.

Parallel R.U.P.A.: None.

Parallel U.L.L.C.A.: § 206.

Bromberg & Ribstein: § 12.02(i).

Important Changes: Requires captioning of the document and provides for delayed effective date.

§ 9.207. CORRECTING FILED RECORD

Section 207

(a) A limited partnership or foreign limited partnership may deliver to the [Secretary of State] for filing a statement of correction to correct a record previously delivered by the limited partnership or foreign limited partnership to the [Secretary of State] and filed by the [Secretary of State], if at the time of filing the record contained false or erroneous information or was defectively signed.

(b) A statement of correction may not state a delayed effective date and must:

   (1) describe the record to be corrected, including its filing date, or attach a copy of the record as filed;

   (2) specify the incorrect information and the reason it is incorrect or the manner in which the signing was defective; and

   (3) correct the incorrect information or defective signature.

(c) When filed by the [Secretary of State], a statement of correction is effective retroactively as of the effective date of the record the statement corrects, but the statement is effective when filed:

   (1) for the purposes of Section 103(c) and (d); and

(2) as to persons relying on the uncorrected record and adversely affected by the correction.

Summary: Provides for correction of records that were defective at the time of filing.

Parallel U.L.P.A. 1985:   None.

Parallel R.U.P.A.:   None.

Parallel U.L.L.C.A.:   § 207.

Analysis: Given the power to amend under § 202, the only apparent function of this section is to provide for the relation back of the correction to the record's original effective date. However, this function is limited because it does not affect constructive notice under Section 103(c) and (d) or those who have detrimentally relied on the uncorrected record.

§ 9.208.   LIABILITY FOR FALSE INFORMATION
IN FILED RECORD

Section 208

(a) If a record delivered to the [Secretary of State] for filing under this [Act] and filed by the [Secretary of State] contains false information, a person that suffers loss by reliance on the information may recover damages for the loss from:
(1) a person that signed the record, or caused another to sign it on the person's behalf, and knew the information to be false at the time the record was signed; and
(2) a general partner that has notice that the information was false when the record was filed or has become false because of changed circumstances, if the general partner has notice for a reasonably sufficient time before the information is relied upon to enable the general partner to effect an amendment under Section 202, file a petition pursuant to Section 205, or deliver to the [Secretary of State] for filing a statement of change pursuant to Section 115 or a statement of correction pursuant to Section 207.
(b) Signing a record authorized or required to be filed under this [Act] constitutes an affirmation under the penalties of perjury that the facts stated in the record are true.

Summary: Provides for liability to one who detrimentally relies on false information in a record by a person who signed or caused the signing of the record knowing the information was false or a general partner with notice the information was false in time to amend, correct or change the document prior to reliance.

Parallel U.L.P.A. 1985: § 207.

Parallel R.U.P.A.: None.

Parallel U.L.L.C.A.: § 209.

Bromberg & Ribstein: § 12.02(n).

Important Changes: Applies to any record delivered for filing and filed.

Analysis: As discussed in § 9.202, the need for liability for false statements in records is unclear. This liability to some extent duplicates liability for fraud of those who knowingly sign false statements. To the extent that liability goes beyond fraud and gives a remedy for immaterial misstatements and without requiring reasonable reliance, it may be unjustified. The Comment states that reasonable reliance is not required because the statement is perjury. It is not clear why this should justify liability in favor of one who has reason to know that a statement in the record is untrue. Moreover, a draconian damage remedy could discourage limited partnerships from giving public notice through filed documents.[34]

§ 9.209. CERTIFICATE OF EXISTENCE OR AUTHORIZATION

Section 209

(a) The [Secretary of State], upon request and payment of the requisite fee, shall furnish a certificate of existence for a limited partnership if the records filed in the [office of the Secretary of State] show that the [Secretary of State] has filed a certificate of limited partnership and has not filed a statement of termination. A certificate of existence must state:

(1) the limited partnership's name;

(2) that it was duly formed under the laws of this State and the date of formation;

(3) whether all fees, taxes, and penalties due to the [Secretary of State] under this [Act] or other law have been paid;

---

[34] *See* U.L.L.C.A. Comments, at 344–45.

(4) whether the limited partnership's most recent annual report required by Section 210 has been filed by the [Secretary of State];

(5) whether the [Secretary of State] has administratively dissolved the limited partnership;

(6) whether the limited partnership's certificate of limited partnership has been amended to state that the limited partnership is dissolved;

(7) that a statement of termination has not been filed by the [Secretary of State]; and

(8) other facts of record in the [office of the Secretary of State] which may be requested by the applicant.

(b) The [Secretary of State], upon request and payment of the requisite fee, shall furnish a certificate of authorization for a foreign limited partnership if the records filed in the [office of the Secretary of State] show that the [Secretary of State] has filed a certificate of authority, has not revoked the certificate of authority, and has not filed a notice of cancellation. A certificate of authorization must state:

(1) the foreign limited partnership's name and any alternate name adopted under Section 905(a) for use in this State;

(2) that it is authorized to transact business in this State;

(3) whether all fees, taxes, and penalties due to the [Secretary of State] under this [Act] or other law have been paid;

(4) whether the foreign limited partnership's most recent annual report required by Section 210 has been filed by the [Secretary of State];

(5) that the [Secretary of State] has not revoked its certificate of authority and has not filed a notice of cancellation; and

(6) other facts of record in the [office of the Secretary of State] which may be requested by the applicant.

(c) Subject to any qualification stated in the certificate, a certificate of existence or authorization issued by the [Secretary of State] may be relied upon as conclusive evidence that the limited partnership or foreign limited partnership is in existence or is authorized to transact business in this State.

Summary: Provides for the filing of a certificate that may be relied upon as conclusive evidence that a limited partnership or foreign limited partnership is in existence or is authorized to transact business in this State.

Parallel U.L.P.A. 1985:   None.

Parallel R.U.P.A.:   None.

Parallel U.L.L.C.A.:   § 208.

Analysis: This statement provides public notice of facts that may not be in the public record, including non-dissolution of the partnership. However, it is not clear what the effect is of reliance on the statement.

§ 9.210. ANNUAL REPORT

Section 210

(a) A limited partnership or a foreign limited partnership authorized to transact business in this State shall deliver to the [Secretary of State] for filing an annual report that states:

(1) the name of the limited partnership or foreign limited partnership;

(2) the street and mailing address of its designated office and the name and street and mailing address of its agent for service of process in this State;

(3) in the case of a limited partnership, the street and mailing address of its principal office; and

(4) in the case of a foreign limited partnership, the State or other jurisdiction under whose law the foreign limited partnership is formed and any alternate name adopted under Section 905(a).

(b) Information in an annual report must be current as of the date the annual report is delivered to the [Secretary of State] for filing.

(c) The first annual report must be delivered to the [Secretary of State] between [January 1 and April 1] of the year following the calendar year in which a limited partnership was formed or a foreign limited partnership was authorized to transact business. An annual report must be delivered to the [Secretary of State] between [January 1 and April 1] of each subsequent calendar year.

(d) If an annual report does not contain the information required in subsection (a), the [Secretary of State] shall promptly notify the reporting limited partnership or foreign limited partnership and return the report to it for correction. If the report is corrected to contain the information required in subsection (a) and delivered to the [Secretary of State] within 30 days after the effective date of the notice, it is timely delivered.

(e) If a filed annual report contains an address of a designated office or the name or address of an agent for service of process which differs from the information shown in the records of the [Secretary of State] immediately before the filing, the differing information in the annual report is considered a statement of change under Section 115.

Summary: Provides for the filing of an annual report stating certain information, such as the firm's name or address.

Parallel U.L.P.A. 1985: None.

Parallel R.U.P.A.:   None.

Parallel U.L.L.C.A.:   § 211.

Bromberg & Ribstein: § 12.02(*l*).

Analysis: It is not clear what the effect is of failure to file the report apart from an action by the state to dissolve the partnership under § 809 or revoke a foreign limited partnership's certificate of authority under § 906. Note that even if the annual report is current, there may still be liability for false statements under § 208 or a duty to amend under § 202.

§ 9.301.   BECOMING LIMITED PARTNER

Section 301

A person becomes a limited partner:
   (1) as provided in the partnership agreement;
   (2) as the result of a conversion or merger under [Article] 11; or
   (3) with the consent of all the partners.

Summary: States when a person becomes a limited partner.

Parallel U.L.P.A. 1985:   §§ 301, 704(a).

Parallel R.U.P.A.:   None.

Parallel U.L.L.C.A.:   None.

Important Changes: Provides for admission of a limited partner as the result of a conversion or merger under Article 11. Does not make admission contingent on a time specified in the records.

§ 9.302.   NO RIGHT OR POWER AS LIMITED PARTNER TO BIND LIMITED PARTNERSHIP

Section 302

A limited partner does not have the right or the power as a limited partner to act for or bind the limited partnership.

Summary: Provides that limited partner, as such, has no power to bind the partnership.

Parallel U.L.P.A. 1985: None.

Parallel R.U.P.A.: None.

Parallel U.L.L.C.A.: § 301(b).

Bromberg & Ribstein: § 14.01(c).

Important Changes: This was the effect of prior law.

Analysis: As discussed in the Comment, a limited partner may have a power to bind in some other capacity—for example, as a general partner (*see* § 113) or by virtue of a power delegated by a general partner. U.L.P.A. (1985) § 302 provides that the partnership agreement may grant voting powers to limited partners, and U.L.P.A. (1985) § 303 lists contractual control rights that would not trigger control liability. That Act provides only for the power to bind in transactions with third parties rather than internal governance rights. However, several sections require unanimous partner consent to various acts, including both general and limited partners. These sections, which are listed in the Comment to this section, are discussed below. These default voting rights protect limited partners in the situations in which they are most likely to be concerned about general partners' abuse of discretion.[35] They also provide some guidance concerning the general partners' acts that will be deemed to bind the partnership under § 402. Partnerships that want to avoid the need for limited partner approval, vary the unanimity voting rule, or provide for voting rights in situations not covered by the Act, can contract around the Act under § 110.

§ 9.303. NO LIABILITY AS LIMITED PARTNER FOR LIMITED PARTNERSHIP OBLIGATIONS

Section 303

An obligation of a limited partnership, whether arising in contract, tort, or otherwise, is not the obligation of a limited partner. A limited partner is not personally liable, directly or indirectly, by way of contribution or otherwise, for an obligation of the limited partnership solely by reason of being a limited part-

---

[35] For a discussion of theoretical considerations relating to limited partner voting rights, and comparisons between limited partnerships and other business forms in this respect, see Revisited, at 880–81.

ner, even if the limited partner participates in the management and control of the limited partnership.

Summary: Provides that a limited partner is not liable as such for the debts of the partnership.

Parallel U.L.P.A. 1985:   § 303.

Parallel R.U.P.A.:   None.

Parallel U.L.L.C.A.:   § 303.

Bromberg & Ribstein: §§ 15.13–15.15.

Important Changes: Eliminates the limited partner "control" rule, which provided that limited partners could be held liable for the firm's debts when they participated in control of the business.

Analysis: Although this section represents a significant formal departure from U.L.P.A. (1985), it actually differs little in effect from the prior provision. That section qualified control liability with a long list of powers limited partners could exercise without participating in control and by providing for liability only to those who were misled into believing that the limited partner was a general partner. Even with the elimination of the control rule, a limited partner still might be liable as a purported general partner under R.U.P.A. § 308, particularly since the certificate's failure to list the limited partner as a general partner is not deemed to provide notice that the person is not a general partner (*see* U.L.P.A. § 201 and § 9.201, above). Eliminating liability imposed on the limited partner "solely by reason of being a limited partner" does not preclude liability on some other ground, including fraud or estoppel.[36]

Although the control rule might seem to have become an anachronism given increasing prevalence of limited liability, in fact its elimination is not clearly the right result.[37] A rule that, in effect, ensured that the managers had personal liability does have some usefulness. Where parties to firms had few limited liability options, the rule might have imposed unnecessary costs on many firms. But given the many such options today, the rule provides a viable contracting alternative. This is arguably confirmed by the fact that only two states have

---

[36] *See* Bishop, The New Limited Partner Liability Shield: Has the Vanquished Control Rule Unwittingly Resurrected Lingering Partner Estoppel Liability as Well as Full General Partner Liability? 37 Suffolk L. Rev. 667 (2004).

[37] For a discussion of prior law and a policy analysis of elimination of the control rule, see Revisited, at 979–80.

eliminated the control rule.[38] States therefore should carefully consider whether they should retain the control rule.

State variations: **California**[39] and **Alabama**[40] retain the limited partner control rule.[41]

§ 9.304. RIGHT OF LIMITED PARTNER AND FORMER LIMITED PARTNER TO INFORMATION

Section 304

(a) On 10 days' demand, made in a record received by the limited partnership, a limited partner may inspect and copy required information during regular business hours in the limited partnership's designated office. The limited partner need not have any particular purpose for seeking the information.

(b) During regular business hours and at a reasonable location specified by the limited partnership, a limited partner may obtain from the limited partnership and inspect and copy true and full information regarding the state of the activities and financial condition of the limited partnership and other information regarding the activities of the limited partnership as is just and reasonable if:

(1) the limited partner seeks the information for a purpose reasonably related to the partner's interest as a limited partner;

(2) the limited partner makes a demand in a record received by the limited partnership, describing with reasonable particularity the information sought and the purpose for seeking the information; and

(3) the information sought is directly connected to the limited partner's purpose.

(c) Within 10 days after receiving a demand pursuant to subsection (b), the limited partnership in a record shall inform the limited partner that made the demand:

(1) what information the limited partnership will provide in response to the demand;

(2) when and where the limited partnership will provide the information; and

(3) if the limited partnership declines to provide any demanded information, the limited partnership's reasons for declining.

---

[38] *See* Ga. Code Ann. § 14-9-303; Mo. Rev. Stat. § 359.201.
[39] Cal. Corp. Code. § 15903.03.
[40] Ala. Code § 10-9C-303.
[41] Cal. Corp. Code. § 15903.03.

(d) Subject to subsection (f), a person dissociated as a limited partner may inspect and copy required information during regular business hours in the limited partnership's designated office if:

(1) the information pertains to the period during which the person was a limited partner;

(2) the person seeks the information in good faith; and

(3) the person meets the requirements of subsection (b).

(e) The limited partnership shall respond to a demand made pursuant to subsection (d) in the same manner as provided in subsection (c).

(f) If a limited partner dies, Section 704 applies.

(g) The limited partnership may impose reasonable restrictions on the use of information obtained under this section. In a dispute concerning the reasonableness of a restriction under this subsection, the limited partnership has the burden of proving reasonableness.

(h) A limited partnership may charge a person that makes a demand under this section reasonable costs of copying, limited to the costs of labor and material.

(i) Whenever this [Act] or a partnership agreement provides for a limited partner to give or withhold consent to a matter, before the consent is given or withheld, the limited partnership shall, without demand, provide the limited partner with all information material to the limited partner's decision that the limited partnership knows.

(j) A limited partner or person dissociated as a limited partner may exercise the rights under this section through an attorney or other agent. Any restriction imposed under subsection (g) or by the partnership agreement applies both to the attorney or other agent and to the limited partner or person dissociated as a limited partner.

(k) The rights stated in this section do not extend to a person as transferee, but may be exercised by the legal representative of an individual under legal disability who is a limited partner or person dissociated as a limited partner.

Summary: Specifies limited and dissociated limited partners' rights to inspect and copy required and other information on demand and receive information without demand that is material to the limited partner's consent.

Parallel U.L.P.A. 1985:   § 305.

Parallel R.U.P.A.:   § 403(b) (with respect to former partners).

Parallel U.L.L.C.A.:   § 408.

Bromberg & Ribstein: § 16.06.

Important Changes: Specifies rights concerning demand, provides for rights to receive information relating to consents without demand, and provides for rights of dissociated partners.

Analysis:

Subsection (a): "Required information" is defined in U.L.P.A. § 102(18) and described in U.L.P.A. § 111.

Subsection (b): In contrast to the limited partners' right to demand information under U.L.P.A. (1985) § 305, this section adds the requirements that the limited partner seek the information "for a purpose reasonably related to the partner's interest as a limited partner," that the demand be in a record "describing with reasonable particularity the information sought and the purpose for seeking the information," and that the information be "directly connected to the limited partner's purpose." The Comment suggests that these limitations reflect the concern that the limited partner has no fiduciary duty with regard to use of the information.[42] However, this concern may be outweighed by the limited partners' isolation from control and consequent need for information.[43] It is not clear how the information sought can satisfy the "reasonably related" test and yet not the "directly connected" test. It is also not clear how the request can be in good faith consistent with U.L.P.A. § 305(b) and yet not satisfy the reasonableness tests under U.L.P.A. § 304(b), with which the limited partner also must comply. Despite these ambiguities, the test is at least clearer than the one under U.L.L.C.A. § 408.[44] The procedural requirements in the section are based on MBCA § 16.02(c).

Subsection (d): This subsection makes the good faith requirement explicitly applicable, since it would not apply to a former partner under U.L.P.A. § 305(b). The same question as above concerning the relationship with the reasonableness requirement also applies here.

Subsection (f): Under U.L.P.A. § 704, the representative of a deceased limited partner may exercise the rights of a current limited partner under Section 304.

Subsection (g): The limited partnership, acting through the general partners under U.L.P.A. § 406(a), can restrict use of information apart from the agreement. It is not clear how reasonableness in this context relates to the reasonableness constraints on what the agreement can provide, discussed below, or to the reasonableness restrictions that would apply in any event under sub-

---

[42] *See also* Callison & Vestal, "They've Created a Lamb with Mandibles of Death": Secrecy, Disclosure, and Fiduciary Duties in Limited Liability Firms, 76 Ind. L.J. 271 (2001).

[43] This is consistent with defining a "security" for purposes of the application of the securities laws depending significantly on the investor's participation in management. *See generally* Ribstein, Private Ordering and the Securities Laws: The Case of General Partnerships, 42 Case W. Res. L. Rev. 1 (1991).

[44] *See* U.L.L.C.A. Comments, at 354-55.

section (b). In other words, can the limited partnership reasonably prevent the limited partner from reasonably seeking information? Also, it is not clear why the burden of justification should be on the limited partnership, as distinguished from requiring the limited partner to show that the constraints are unreasonable, as a partner must do when questioning general partners' discretion in other matters.

Subsection (i):   This is similar to a proxy disclosure rule. Requiring disclosure without requiring explicit demand is arguably justified because it is reasonable to assume that the limited partners would demand information in this situation. As under the federal proxy rules, it may be unclear what "material" information includes, and there is nothing analogous to federal proxy disclosure forms to provide guidance. Nor is it clear how, if at all, the materiality standard will be deemed to differ from the more prolix standard under U.L.L.C.A. § 408(b): "information concerning the company's business or affairs reasonably required for the proper exercise of the member's rights and performance of the member's duties under the operating agreement or this [Act]."[45]

The partnership will be deemed to know what the general partners know under U.L.P.A. § 103(h), except "in the case of a fraud on the limited partnership committed by or with the consent of the general partner." The fraud issue may arise in cases involving limited partner consent to self-dealing transactions under U.L.P.A. § 103(b)(5)(B), discussed in connection U.L.P.A. § 408, below, and R.U.P.A. § 404, above, in § 8.404. As discussed in the Comment, the duty applies to information the limited partnership knows whether or not the limited partnership (or the general partners) know it is material.

Subsection (k):   A dissociated partner, although treated as a transferee under U.L.P.A. § 602(a)(3), has information rights under U.L.P.A. § 304(d) that transferees do not generally have (*see* U.L.P.A. § 702(a)(3)).

Waiver: U.L.P.A. § 110(b)(4) provides that this section is not subject to a contrary agreement that unreasonably restricts the right to information, but that "the partnership agreement may impose reasonable restrictions on the availability and use of information obtained . . . and may define appropriate remedies, including liquidated damages, for a breach of any reasonable restriction on use." Restrictions on agreements waiving partners' fiduciary duties are discussed below in § 9.408. With respect to waiver of limited partner information rights, it is not clear what a "reasonable" restriction is, or how this reasonableness restriction relates to the restriction in subsection (g).[46]

---

[45] This standard is discussed in U.L.L.C.A. Comments, at 356.
[46] For a discussion of the similar restriction in U.L.L.C.A., see U.L.L.C.A. Comments, at 357-58.

State variation: **California** provides that a limited partnership may keep confidential from limited partners for a reasonable time "any information which the limited partnership reasonably believes to be in the nature of trade secrets or other information the disclosure of which the limited partnership in good faith believes is not in the best interest of the limited partnership or could damage the limited partnership or its business or which the limited partnership is required by law or by agreement with a third party to keep confidential."[47]

§ 9.305. LIMITED DUTIES OF LIMITED PARTNERS

Section 305

(a) A limited partner does not have any fiduciary duty to the limited partnership or to any other partner solely by reason of being a limited partner.

(b) A limited partner shall discharge the duties to the partnership and the other partners under this [Act] or under the partnership agreement and exercise any rights consistently with the obligation of good faith and fair dealing.

(c) A limited partner does not violate a duty or obligation under this [Act] or under the partnership agreement merely because the limited partner's conduct furthers the limited partner's own interest.

Summary: A limited partner has no fiduciary duty as such. The partner must act in good faith, but does not violate any duty merely by furthering her own interest.

Parallel U.L.P.A. 1985: None.

Parallel R.U.P.A.: None.

Parallel U.L.L.C.A.: § 409.

Bromberg & Ribstein: § 16.07(a)(1).

Analysis:

Subsection (a): Limited partners as such should have no fiduciary duties, since fiduciary duties constrain those who exercise management powers on

---

[47] Cal. Corp. Code § 15903.04.

behalf of others rather than solely as owners. But the elimination of the "control rule" under U.L.P.A. § 303 may lead to increased management by limited partners, and therefore arguably a need to articulate the fiduciary duties that accompany this power. An early draft of U.L.P.A. had suggested provisions based on U.L.L.C.A. and the MBCA that imposed fiduciary duties to the extent that limited partners took on management powers. These provisions, particularly the one based on U.L.L.C.A., raised significant questions, including concerning what powers triggered fiduciary duties given the wide variety of potential agreements the parties might make.[48] Also, given problems of contracting out of default duties under § 110(b), discussed below in § 9.408, the default rule matters. Accordingly, it is probably best to provide by default for no duties and let the parties agree to fiduciary duties under U.L.P.A. § 110(a) to reflect any delegation of management power.

Note that the problem of drafting statutory rules to cover a multitude of situations, and therefore the logic of allowing the parties to contract for the appropriate level of fiduciary duties, applies generally to fiduciary duties, and not just to limited partners' duties. Nevertheless, the Comment suggests that the Act distinguishes between fiduciary duties that arise by virtue of partners' "status" and those that arise by contract. A corollary of this distinction is that the Act restricts contracting with regard to duties that arise from status, as discussed below.

Subsection (b): As noted in the Comment, the good faith obligation "is *not* a fiduciary duty" that requires partners to act disinterestedly. Rather, as discussed in § 8.404, it is a principle of contract interpretation. As discussed there, it is, therefore, misleading to cover this obligation in the same section as fiduciary duties, rather than in a section on interpretation of the partnership agreement.[49] The Comment adds that "[c]ourts should not use the obligation to change *ex post facto* the parties' or this Act's allocation of risk and power." That injunction also should apply to fiduciary duties.

U.L.P.A. § 110(b)(7) provides that the agreement cannot eliminate the obligation of good faith and fair dealing under U.L.P.A. § 305(b), but "may prescribe the standards by which the performance of the obligation is to be measured, if the standards are not manifestly unreasonable." The interpretation of this provision is discussed above in § 8.404.

Subsection (c): It is not clear precisely how this provision qualifies the fiduciary duties of general partners (*see* U.L.P.A. § 408(e) and § 9.408, below, and R.U.P.A. § 404 and § 8.404, above). This provision is especially unclear in this context. Since limited partners have no default fiduciary duties, they should

---

[48] *See* U.L.L.C.A. Comments, at 983–84.
[49] New Jersey omits the analogous good faith duty from its version of RUPA. *See* N.J. Rev. Stat. § 42:1A-24.

be able to act selfishly as long as they obey the contract. Accordingly, it is not clear what "merely because" is intended to exclude.

§ 9.306.   PERSON ERRONEOUSLY BELIEVING SELF TO BE LIMITED PARTNER

Section 306

(a) Except as otherwise provided in subsection (b), a person that makes an investment in a business enterprise and erroneously but in good faith believes that the person has become a limited partner in the enterprise is not liable for the enterprise's obligations by reason of making the investment, receiving distributions from the enterprise, or exercising any rights of or appropriate to a limited partner, if, on ascertaining the mistake, the person:

(1) causes an appropriate certificate of limited partnership, amendment, or statement of correction to be signed and delivered to the [Secretary of State] for filing; or

(2) withdraws from future participation as an owner in the enterprise by signing and delivering to the [Secretary of State] for filing a statement of withdrawal under this section.

(b) A person that makes an investment described in subsection (a) is liable to the same extent as a general partner to any third party that enters into a transaction with the enterprise, believing in good faith that the person is a general partner, before the [Secretary of State] files a statement of withdrawal, certificate of limited partnership, amendment, or statement of correction to show that the person is not a general partner.

(c) If a person makes a diligent effort in good faith to comply with subsection (a)(1) and is unable to cause the appropriate certificate of limited partnership, amendment, or statement of correction to be signed and delivered to the [Secretary of State] for filing, the person has the right to withdraw from the enterprise pursuant to subsection (a)(2) even if the withdrawal would otherwise breach an agreement with others that are or have agreed to become co-owners of the enterprise.

Summary: Provides for a method by which a person who erroneously invests in a business believing that he is a limited partner can avoid thereby being liable as a general partner.

Parallel U.L.P.A. 1985:   § 304.

Parallel R.U.P.A.:   None.

Parallel U.L.L.C.A.:   None.

Bromberg & Ribstein: § 12.04(e)–(f).

Important Changes: Adds subsection (c).

Analysis: This section not only shields one who wants to avoid liability as a partner (subsection (a)), but also effectively provides, in subsection (b), the basis of the erroneous general partner's liability to a third party who enters into the transaction believing in good faith that the person is a general partner prior to the filing of the appropriate statement or certificate. This is in addition to any grounds for liability that may exist under U.P.A. § 16 or R.U.P.A. § 308 for a representation that one is a general partner in general partnership (*see* § 8.308, above), or liability for a false statement in the certificate under U.L.P.A. § 208. Erroneous partner liability is affected by the fact that the certificate is not deemed to give notice that one not listed in the certificate is not a general partner (*see* § 103(c), discussed in § 9.103, above).

§ 9.401.   BECOMING GENERAL PARTNER

Section 401

A person becomes a general partner:
(1) as provided in the partnership agreement:
(2) under Section 801(3)(B) following the dissociation of a limited partnership's last general partner;
(3) as the result of a conversion or merger under [Article] 11; or
(4) with the consent of all the partners.

Summary: Specifies how one becomes a general partner in a limited partnership.

Parallel U.L.P.A. 1985:   § 401.

Parallel R.U.P.A.:   § 401(i).

Parallel U.L.L.C.A.:   § 404(c)(7).

Bromberg & Ribstein: §§ 14.03(c)(5) and 14.03(e)(1).

Important Changes: Subsections 2 and 3 are new.

Analysis: As discussed above, the limited partnership has a duty to amend under U.L.P.A. § 202(b)(1), and there may be liability under U.L.P.A. § 208 for failing to do so. Nevertheless, as discussed in the Comment, a person's status as a general partner does not depend on certificate disclosure. Although this makes sense with respect to rights and duties among the partners, it is not clear why disclosure or nondisclosure in the certificate should not be conclusive as to third parties (*see* U.L.P.A. § 103(c) and U.L.P.A. § 304, discussed in §§ 9.103 and 9.304, above).

§ 9.402. GENERAL PARTNER AGENT OF LIMITED PARTNERSHIP

Section 402

(a) Each general partner is an agent of the limited partnership for the purposes of its activities. An act of a general partner, including the signing of a record in the partnership's name, for apparently carrying on in the ordinary course the limited partnership's activities or activities of the kind carried on by the limited partnership binds the limited partnership, unless the general partner did not have authority to act for the limited partnership in the particular matter and the person with which the general partner was dealing knew, had received a notification, or had notice under Section 103(d) that the general partner lacked authority.

(b) An act of a general partner which is not apparently for carrying on in the ordinary course the limited partnership's activities or activities of the kind carried on by the limited partnership binds the limited partnership only if the act was actually authorized by all the other partners.

Summary: Describes a general partner's power to bind the partnership.

Parallel U.L.P.A. 1985: § 403.

Parallel R.U.P.A.: § 301.

Parallel U.L.L.C.A.: § 301(a).

Bromberg & Ribstein: § 14.01(b).

Important Changes: Imports the rule for general partner authority into the limited partnership act rather than relying on linkage with the general partnership act.

Analysis: General partners have the same power in limited as in general partnerships (*see* R.U.P.A. § 301, discussed in § 8.301, above), as this provision makes explicit by bringing the partnership statutory language into the limited partnership statute. However, it is not clear how the courts will interpret this section—specifically, whether they will apply this language differently in general and limited partnership contexts. For example, the courts may have protected limited partners by putting the burden on sophisticated lenders and other third parties to determine if even "apparently . . . ordinary" general partner actions are authorized where there was a hint of general partner self-dealing.[50]

This section's application may depend on other provisions of the Act. Whether a third party is notified of lack of authority may depend on constructive notice under U.L.P.A. § 103(d). A general partner may have apparent or actual authority under this section even the partner is not listed in the certificate under U.L.P.A. § 401 and U.L.P.A. § 103(c).

§ 9.403.   LIMITED PARTNERSHIP LIABLE FOR GENERAL PARTNER'S ACTIONABLE CONDUCT

Section 403

(a) A limited partnership is liable for loss or injury caused to a person, or for a penalty incurred, as a result of a wrongful act or omission, or other actionable conduct, of a general partner acting in the ordinary course of activities of the limited partnership or with authority of the limited partnership.

(b) If, in the course of the limited partnership's activities or while acting with authority of the limited partnership, a general partner receives or causes the limited partnership to receive money or property of a person not a partner, and the money or property is misapplied by a general partner, the limited partnership is liable for the loss.

Summary: Provides for the limited partnership's liability for a general partner's misconduct or misappropriation.

Parallel U.L.P.A. 1985:   § 403.

Parallel R.U.P.A.:   § 305.

Parallel U.L.L.C.A.:   § 302.

---

[50] *See* Revisited, at 977–78.

Bromberg & Ribstein: § 14.07.

Analysis: This language was formally linked from R.U.P.A. § 305, discussed in § 8.305, above, to limited partnerships through U.L.P.A. (1985) § 403. Courts likely will continue to apply general partnership cases in the limited partnership context as they did under prior law.

§ 9.404.   GENERAL PARTNER'S LIABILITY

Section 404

(a) Except as otherwise provided in subsections (b) and (c), all general partners are liable jointly and severally for all obligations of the limited partnership unless otherwise agreed by the claimant or provided by law.

(b) A person that becomes a general partner of an existing limited partnership is not personally liable for an obligation of a limited partnership incurred before the person became a general partner.

(c) An obligation of a limited partnership incurred while the limited partnership is a limited liability limited partnership, whether arising in contract, tort, or otherwise, is solely the obligation of the limited partnership. A general partner is not personally liable, directly or indirectly, by way of contribution or otherwise, for such an obligation solely by reason of being or acting as a general partner. This subsection applies despite anything inconsistent in the partnership agreement that existed immediately before the consent required to become a limited liability limited partnership under Section 406(b)(2).

Summary: Provides for joint and several liability of general partners for all limited partnership obligations incurred after the partner became such, except while the partnership is an LLLP.

Parallel U.L.P.A. 1985:   § 403.

Parallel R.U.P.A.:   § 306.

Parallel U.L.L.C.A.:   None.

Bromberg & Ribstein: § 15.08.

Important Changes: Imports rather than linking general partnership liability rule, and provides for general partner limited liability in LLLPs.

Analysis: The U.L.P.A. drafters had to face important questions about whether to retain the traditional personal liability of general partners.[51] Providing for limited liability would recognize the strong trend toward limited liability in unincorporated firms, particularly including incorporating the general partner or permitting the firm to become an LLLP. Indeed, in the current environment, vicarious liability may be a trap for the unwary.

The Prefatory Note indicates that the drafters were persuaded to retain the existing rule by the transition problem involving the many existing non-LLLP limited partnerships. Another and perhaps more serious transition problem is that, given the long history of general partner personal liability, creditors would need to be affirmatively alerted of the change. Thus, the Act retains default vicarious liability but lets the partnership adopt LLLP status through statement in the certificate of limited partnership. *See* subsection (c), and U.L.P.A. § 102(9) and 201(a)(4), discussed in §§ 9.102 and 9.201, above. Apart from transition, retaining the current rule can be defended on the ground that the traditional limited partnership rule now offers an option of bifurcated liability that some firms might want and that other limited liability forms do not offer.

The deliberations on this provision by the NCCUSL drafting committee indicate the closeness of this issue. The drafters initially decided to "flip" the default liability rule, and then "flopped" the "flip" back to the original rule only weeks before NCCUSL finally approved the Act.[52] This suggests that there is room for disagreement and a variety of state approaches on this issue rather than a compelling reason to accept NCCUSL's ultimate conclusion.

Provisions such as partners' fiduciary duties and dissolution and dissociation rights arguably should depend on whether the firm has opted for general partner liability. However, it would be difficult to provide precise alternative rules for each type of firm. Accordingly, it is probably best to assume that the firm will adopt the traditional default rule of general partner liability and leave other internal adjustments for the partnership agreement.

---

[51] *See* Revisited, at 970–72. For a review of general partner liability under U.L.P.A. (2001), see Rall, A General Partner's Liability under the Uniform Limited Partnership Act (2001), 37 Suffolk L. Rev. 913 (2004).

[52] *See* National Conference of Commissioners of Uniform State Laws, Proposed Revisions of Uniform Limited Partnership Act (1976) with 1985 Amendments, § 404, Note 9 (April 2001), *available at* http://www.law.upenn.edu/bll/ulc/ulc_frame.htm.

§ 9.405. ACTIONS BY AND AGAINST PARTNERSHIP AND PARTNERS

Section 405

(a) To the extent not inconsistent with Section 404, a general partner may be joined in an action against the limited partnership or named in a separate action.

(b) A judgment against a limited partnership is not by itself a judgment against a general partner. A judgment against a limited partnership may not be satisfied from a general partner's assets unless there is also a judgment against the general partner.

(c) A judgment creditor of a general partner may not levy execution against the assets of the general partner to satisfy a judgment based on a claim against the limited partnership, unless the partner is personally liable for the claim under Section 404 and:

(1) a judgment based on the same claim has been obtained against the limited partnership and a writ of execution on the judgment has been returned unsatisfied in whole or in part;

(2) the limited partnership is a debtor in bankruptcy;

(3) the general partner has agreed that the creditor need not exhaust limited partnership assets;

(4) a court grants permission to the judgment creditor to levy execution against the assets of a general partner based on a finding that limited partnership assets subject to execution are clearly insufficient to satisfy the judgment, that exhaustion of limited partnership assets is excessively burdensome, or that the grant of permission is an appropriate exercise of the court's equitable powers; or

(5) liability is imposed on the general partner by law or contract independent of the existence of the limited partnership.

Summary: Provides for separate or joint actions against the partnership and the partners; general partner liability if there is a judgment against the general partner judgment against the general partner if the partner is personally liable for the claim under U.L.P.A. § 404 and other conditions are satisfied.

Parallel U.L.P.A. 1985: § 403.

Parallel R.U.P.A.: § 307.

Parallel U.L.L.C.A.: None.

Bromberg & Ribstein: §§ 15.08–15.12.

Important Changes: The R.U.P.A. rule, which is applied to limited partnerships through U.L.P.A. (1985) § 403 and § 1105, is incorporated into this section except for subsections (a) (suit in partnership name); (e) (application to purported partners); and (f) (partner is not a proper party to an action against a partnership if partner is not personally liable).

Analysis: The equivalent R.U.P.A. provision, § 307, is discussed in § 8.307, above. With respect to the differences between that provision and U.L.P.A. § 405: suit in partnership name is covered in U.L.P.A. § 105; there is no purported partner liability under U.L.P.A. (*see* U.L.P.A. § 103(c), discussed in § 9.103, above); and U.L.P.A. § 405(a) states that a partner can be joined only "[t]o the extent not inconsistent with Section 404," which provides for limited liability of general partners in LLLPs. The provision on joining a partner is unclear. Joining a partner may or may not be consistent with the partner's liability limitation under U.L.P.A. § 404, particularly since the partner may be liable under a separate obligation as provided in U.L.P.A. § 405(c)(5).

§ 9.406.   MANAGEMENT RIGHTS OF
GENERAL PARTNER

Section 406

(a) Each general partner has equal rights in the management and conduct of the limited partnership's activities. Except as expressly provided in this [Act], any matter relating to the activities of the limited partnership may be exclusively decided by the general partner or, if there is more than one general partner, by a majority of the general partners.

(b) The consent of each partner is necessary to:

(1) amend the partnership agreement;

(2) amend the certificate of limited partnership to add or, subject to Section 1110, delete a statement that the limited partnership is a limited liability limited partnership; and

(3) sell, lease, exchange, or otherwise dispose of all, or substantially all, of the limited partnership's property, with or without the good will, other than in the usual and regular course of the limited partnership's activities.

(c) A limited partnership shall reimburse a general partner for payments made and indemnify a general partner for liabilities incurred by the general partner in the ordinary course of the activities of the partnership or for the preservation of its activities or property.

(d) A limited partnership shall reimburse a general partner for an advance to the limited partnership beyond the amount of capital the general partner agreed to contribute.

(e) A payment or advance made by a general partner which gives rise to an obligation of the limited partnership under subsection (c) or (d) constitutes a loan to the limited partnership which accrues interest from the date of the payment or advance.

(f) A general partner is not entitled to remuneration for services performed for the partnership.

Summary: The partnership is managed by general partners; partners vote equally and by majority, except that unanimous general and limited partner consent required for matters listed in subsection (b); provides for indemnification and advances; partner entitled to interest on loans, but not to compensation for services performed.

Parallel U.L.P.A. 1985: § 403; § 405.

Parallel R.U.P.A.: § 401.

Parallel U.L.L.C.A.: § 404(b).

Bromberg & Ribstein: § 16.03(a).

Important Changes: Provides for rules applicable to general partners directly rather than through linkage with general partnership act; limited partner consent to certain acts; and that general partner is not entitled to compensation for winding up services.

Analysis: This section governs default rights that control among the members of the firm. They are generally subject to contrary agreement under U.L.P.A. § 110, with possible exceptions discussed below.[53]

Subsection (a): A partner can delegate management rights to limited partners or non-partners, with possible implications for the partners' fiduciary duties, as discussed below in § 9.408.

---

[53] With respect to enforceability of management arrangements in limited partnerships under prior law, see Bromberg & Ribstein, § 16.03.

Subsection (b):   Limited partner voting rights provide protection in trans-actions that are economically significant or where general and limited partners' interests are especially likely to diverge.[54] They are consistent with the voting rights of non-managing LLC members provided for in U.L.L.C.A. § 404(c).[55] The voting rights are particularly important in light of limited partners' reduced exit rights under U.L.P.A. as compared with prior law (*see* U.L.P.A. § 601, dis-cussed in § 9.601, below).

Several other provisions of the Act provide for voting rights of partners, in-cluding those listed in the Comment to U.L.P.A. § 302. These include § 301(3) and 401(4) (admission of limited and general partners); § 502(c) (compromise of partner's contribution obligation); § 601(b)(4) and 603(4) (expulsion); § 703(c)(3) (redemption of interest subject to charging order); § 801(2) and § 801(3) (dissolution); § 803(C) (appointing person to wind up the limited partnership); § 1103(a) and (b)(2) (conversion approval); § 1107(a) and (b)(2) (merger approval); and § 1110 (approval of personal liability under mergers, conversions and relinquishment of LLLP status). All but § 1110 are subject to contrary agree-ment under U.L.P.A. § 110. The partnership agreement can provide for additional voting rights, and for a vote authorizing transactions that otherwise would violate the duty of loyalty (*see* § 110(b)(5)).

Subsections (c) and (d):   The Act distinguishes limited and general part-ners with respect to default rights to receive indemnification and advances and interest on these amounts because, as the Comment says, limited partners "are assumed to be passive." Thus, limited partners are remitted to their agreements on this issue. It is not clear why the Act draws this distinction, particularly since limited partner loans are provided for in § 112. An agreement that provides for limited partner management powers also can provide for reimbursement and indemnification.

Subsection (f):   R.U.P.A. § 401(h), which applied to limited partnerships under U.L.P.A. 1985, provides for a default right to reimbursement for winding-up expenses. The Comment explains that "winding up is one of the tasks for which the limited partners depend on the general partner." But it is not clear how this differentiates limited from general partnerships.

---

[54] *See* Revisited, at 975–76.

[55] Given the elimination of the "control rule" from U.L.P.A., limited partners more closely resemble non-managing LLC members than they did under U.L.P.A. 1985.

§ 9.407.   RIGHT OF GENERAL PARTNER AND FORMER GENERAL PARTNER TO INFORMATION

Section 407

(a) A general partner, without having any particular purpose for seeking the information, may inspect and copy during regular business hours:

(1) in the limited partnership's designated office, required information; and

(2) at a reasonable location specified by the limited partnership, any other records maintained by the limited partnership regarding the limited partnership's activities and financial condition.

(b) Each general partner and the limited partnership shall furnish to a general partner:

(1) without demand, any information concerning the limited partnership's activities and activities reasonably required for the proper exercise of the general partner's rights and duties under the partnership agreement or this [Act]; and

(2) on demand, any other information concerning the limited partnership's activities, except to the extent the demand or the information demanded is unreasonable or otherwise improper under the circumstances.

(c) Subject to subsection (e), on 10 days' demand made in a record received by the limited partnership, a person dissociated as a general partner may have access to the information and records described in subsection (a) at the location specified in subsection (a) if:

(1) the information or record pertains to the period during which the person was a general partner;

(2) the person seeks the information or record in good faith; and

(3) the person satisfies the requirements imposed on a limited partner by Section 304(b).

(d) The limited partnership shall respond to a demand made pursuant to subsection (c) in the same manner as provided in Section 304(c).

(e) If a general partner dies, Section 704 applies.

(f) The limited partnership may impose reasonable restrictions on the use of information under this section. In any dispute concerning the reasonableness of a restriction under this subsection, the limited partnership has the burden of proving reasonableness.

(g) A limited partnership may charge a person dissociated as a general partner that makes a demand under this section reasonable costs of copying, limited to the costs of labor and material.

(h) A general partner or person dissociated as a general partner may exercise the rights under this section through an attorney or other agent. Any restriction imposed under subsection (f) or by the partnership agreement applies both to the attorney or other agent and to the general partner or person dissociated as a general partner.

(i) The rights under this section do not extend to a person as transferee, but the rights under subsection (c) of a person dissociated as a general may be exercised by the legal representative of an individual who dissociated as a general partner under Section 603(7)(B) or (C).

Summary: Specifies general and dissociated general partners' rights to inspect and receive information.

Parallel U.L.P.A. 1985:   § 403.

Parallel R.U.P.A.:   §§ 403(b)–(c); 503(a)(3).

Parallel U.L.L.C.A.:   § 408.

Bromberg & Ribstein: § 16.06.

Important Changes: Specifies rights concerning demand for information; clarifies that partnership can impose reasonable restrictions on use of information, but no default obligation to pay copying costs.

Analysis: This provision is similar in format to U.L.P.A. § 304 on limited partners' information rights except for changes generally to align it with the R.U.P.A. sections on disclosure and transferee rights that formerly were linked with U.L.P.A. 1985, with the differences noted above. The discussion of U.L.P.A. § 304(g) in § 9.304, above, regarding restrictions on general partners' use of information, and of restrictions on waiver under U.L.P.A. § 110(b)(4) also applies here.

§ 9.408.   GENERAL STANDARDS OF GENERAL PARTNER'S CONDUCT

Section 408

(a) The only fiduciary duties that a general partner has to the limited partnership and the other partners are the duties of loyalty and care under subsections (b) and (c).

(b) A general partner's duty of loyalty to the limited partnership and the other partners is limited to the following:

(1) to account to the limited partnership and hold as trustee for it any property, profit, or benefit derived by the general partner in the conduct and winding up of the limited partnership's activities or derived from a use by the general partner of limited partnership property, including the appropriation of a limited partnership opportunity;

(2) to refrain from dealing with the limited partnership in the conduct or winding up of the limited partnership's activities as or on behalf of a party having an interest adverse to the limited partnership; and

(3) to refrain from competing with the limited partnership in the conduct or winding up of the limited partnership's activities.

(c) A general partner's duty of care to the limited partnership and the other partners in the conduct and winding up of the limited partnership's activities is limited to refraining from engaging in grossly negligent or reckless conduct, intentional misconduct, or a knowing violation of law.

(d) A general partner shall discharge the duties to the partnership and the other partners under this [Act] or under the partnership agreement and exercise any rights consistently with the obligation of good faith and fair dealing.

(e) A general partner does not violate a duty or obligation under this [Act] or under the partnership agreement merely because the general partner's conduct furthers the general partner's own interest.

Summary: Provides that the only fiduciary duties of partners are the duties of loyalty and care provided for in this section and that partners also have an obligation of good faith and fair dealing.

Parallel U.L.P.A. 1985:   § 403.

Parallel R.U.P.A.:   § 404.

Parallel U.L.L.C.A.:   § 409.

Bromberg & Ribstein: § 16.07.

Important Changes: Virtually identical to R.U.P.A. § 404, which was linked to U.L.P.A. 1985, except that R.U.P.A. § 404(f) is in U.L.P.A. § 112, and there is no provision comparable to R.U.P.A. § 404(g), on the duties of a non-partner winding up the business.

Analysis: Because of this section's similarity with R.U.P.A. § 404, much of the Analysis of that provision in § 8.404, above, is relevant here. The following analysis will focus on the specific issues regarding limited partner fiduciary duties.[56]

---

[56] *See* Revisited, at 980–83.

Subsections (a)–(c):   The default rules arguably should focus on the relationship between the general partners as a group and the limited partners rather than among the general partners, as in the general partnership statute. This suggests that general partners should have stricter duties in limited than in general partnerships. Under U.L.P.A.'s default rules, limited partners not only lack significant voting power and participation in management (*see* U.L.P.A. § 302, discussed in § 9.302, above), but also, in contrast with U.L.P.A. 1985, are denied the ability to threaten the firm with loss of capital by withdrawing prior to dissolution (*see* U.L.P.A. § 601, discussed in § 9.601, below). These features might justify imposing a duty of ordinary care rather than the more limited duty under U.L.P.A. § 408(c), and generally applying U.L.P.A. § 408(a)–(c) differently from the same language in R.U.P.A. § 404. On the other hand, a problem with imposing stricter duties is the restrictions on the power to waive those duties under U.L.P.A. § 110(b)(5)–(7), discussed below.

Note that this section recognizes duties only to partners and not to transferees of partnership interests. This may be significant, for example, in connection with squeeze-out transactions under Article 9. *See* Comment to § 1102(b)(3).

Subsection (e):   This provision confusingly seems to contradict the general partners' duties described above in the section. It might be interpreted in the general partnership context to refer to situations in which the partners are acting for themselves as owners rather than for the firm as agents, where fiduciary duties appropriately apply. Thus, for example, the Comment to § 1102 notes that a partner who votes for a conversion or merger under a subunanimity voting rule does not thereby breach a duty to the other partners. However, this interpretation has less applicability to limited than to general partnerships, because general partnerships in the former usually can be assumed to be acting as agents for the limited partners. Thus, it is not clear how courts will apply this provision to limited partnership. On the other hand, eliminating this provision would exacerbate the problems of restricted waivability of partners' duties discussed immediately below.

Waiver: U.L.P.A. § 110(b)(5)–(7) include restrictions on waiving fiduciary and good faith duties that are similar to those in R.U.P.A. § 103, which are discussed above in § 8.404. Given the potential costs of these restrictions on contract, legislatures and attorneys should consider carefully the wisdom of adopting these provisions and advising clients to select statutes that include them.[57]

---

[57] For an analysis of the effect of partnership agreement provisions on fiduciary duties under ULPA (2001), see Ribstein, Fiduciary Duties and Limited Partnership Agreements, 37 Suffolk L. Rev. 927 (2004).

Apart from general policy considerations, these provisions reflect the difficulty of drafting statutory limitations on a particular aspect of the parties' power to contract. In particular, there are issues concerning the effect on fiduciary duties of general partners' delegation of powers to others, including limited partners. An earlier draft of U.L.P.A. would have followed U.L.L.C.A. in relieving a general partner from fiduciary duties "to the extent of the managerial authority delegated to the limited partners by the partnership agreement."[58] This presented significant interpretation problems concerning how a delegation would affect the partners' fiduciary duties and what types of delegation were permitted.[59] For example, can a general partner exercise all powers under the agreement as limited partner pursuant to U.L.P.A. § 113 and have no duties by reason of U.L.P.A. § 305?

The Comment to § 305(a) states that any limited partner duties arise by contract, thereby suggesting that the partner would have no duties in this situation if the contract did not create them. The final version of U.L.P.A. does not include the delegation provision. The Comments to U.L.P.A. §§ 406 and 408 state that delegation of power does not relieve the partner of duties but is relevant in defining them. This leaves the court with a difficult line-drawing task that would not exist if the statute straightforwardly allowed the parties to contract regarding fiduciary duties. Further difficulties are created by U.L.P.A. § 110(b)(5)(B), which provides that the agreement may "specify the number or percentage of partners which may authorize or ratify, after full disclosure to all partners of all material facts, a specific act or transaction that otherwise would violate the duty of loyalty." This literally permits the agreement to permit an interested partner to participate in the vote, contrary to corporate law.[60] Indeed, the provision literally appears to permit the agreement to provide that *only* the interested partners may participate in the vote. A court is unlikely to enforce such an extreme provision, but there are many potential ambiguities at the margins. Again, these difficulties would not exist if the statute straightforwardly permitted contracting regarding fiduciary duties.

State variations: The **Kentucky** version of subsection (1) provides that a partner's fiduciary duties "include" the duties in the section, and the duties of loyalty and care provided for in subsections (2) and (3) state that the duties "include" the definitions in the respective subsections.[61] Along similar lines, **California** omits "only" before "fiduciary duties."[62]

---

[58] *See* U.L.L.C.A. § 409(h)(4), discussed in U.L.L.C.A. Comments, at 361.

[59] *See* Revisited, at 981.

[60] *See, e.g.,* R.M.B.C.A. §§ 8.62 (directors), 8.63 (shareholders).

[61] 2006 Kentucky House Bill No. 234, Kentucky 2006 Regular Session, Chapter 362, sub-chapter 2, § 128(1)–(3).

[62] Cal. Corp. Code § 15904.08(a).

§ 9.501.   FORM OF CONTRIBUTION

Section 501

A contribution of a partner may consist of tangible or intangible property or other benefit to the limited partnership, including money, services performed, promissory notes, other agreements to contribute cash or property, and contracts for services to be performed.

Summary: Permits partners' contributions to the partnership to be in any form.

Parallel U.L.P.A. 1985:   § 501.

Parallel R.U.P.A.:   None.

Parallel U.L.L.C.A.:   § 401.

Bromberg & Ribstein: § 12.07(d).

Important Changes: Prior provision was limited to "cash, property, or services rendered, or a promissory note or other obligation to contribute cash or property or to perform services."

Analysis: This section is based on U.L.L.C.A. § 401. It eliminates outmoded restrictions on financing the firm.

§ 9.502.   LIABILITY FOR CONTRIBUTION

Section 502

(a) A partner's obligation to contribute money or other property or other benefit to, or to perform services for, a limited partnership is not excused by the partner's death, disability, or other inability to perform personally.

(b) If a partner does not make a promised non-monetary contribution, the partner is obligated at the option of the limited partnership to contribute money equal to that portion of the value, as stated in the required information, of the stated contribution which has not been made.

(c) The obligation of a partner to make a contribution or return money or other property paid or distributed in violation of this [Act] may be compromised only by consent of all partners. A creditor of a limited partnership which extends credit or otherwise acts in reliance on an obligation described in subsection (a), without notice of any compromise under this subsection, may enforce the original obligation.

Summary: Provides that partners' contribution obligations are not excused by death, disability, or other inability to perform personally; a partner may compel a partner who does not make a non-monetary contribution to contribute its monetary value stated in the required information; that compromise of an obligation to contribute or to return improperly distributed funds must be consented to by all partners; and that a creditor who relies on a contribution obligation without notice of any compromise may enforce the original obligation.

Parallel U.L.P.A. 1985: § 502.

Parallel R.U.P.A.: None.

Parallel U.L.L.C.A.: § 402.

Bromberg & Ribstein: § 12.08.

Important Changes: No statute of frauds provision; consent of all partners required for compromise of an obligation to return improper distributions.

Analysis:

Subsection (a): U.L.P.A. 1985 provides for enforcement only of written contribution obligations. This long-standing statute of frauds has the potential advantage of reducing litigation. It is not clear why the requirement was eliminated.[63] Moreover, current law is now uncertain because § 111(9)(A) requires the limited partnership to maintain a record of contribution obligations that are not set forth in a written partnership agreement. Although the Comment to § 111(9) says that failure to comply "does not render unenforceable an oral promise to make a contribution," courts may take the failure to have the required record into account as evidence that there was no such promise. The Comments to §§ 110 and 111(9) also say that the partnership agreement can impose writing requirements that make oral promises unenforceable. As noted above in the Analysis of § 110, such a provision arguably should be required to be made in a written agreement.

---

[63] *See* U.L.L.C.A. Comments, at 349–50 (commenting on U.L.L.C.A. § 402).

Subsection (b):   U.L.P.A. § 111(9) requires the agreed value of the promised contribution to be set forth in a written partnership agreement or a record. However, the Act does not say how the agreement as to value is to be made. The Comment to § 111(9) says that the person who has made or promised the contribution must concur with the valuation, although the partnership agreement can give valuation authority to the general partners. But the statute does not provide for the authority to set valuation.

Subsection (c):   This provision continues the rule from U.L.P.A. 1985 that a relying creditor can enforce a compromised obligation. The provision therefore provides some basis for an action by a limited partnership's creditor to enforce a partner's contribution obligation (*see* Bromberg & Ribstein, § 12.08(c)). This rule is questionable, given the unlikelihood of creditor reliance on contributions, particularly those other than in cash.[64] The provision also raises questions concerning the effect of the partnership agreement, which gives rise to the obligation. In particular, partners may unexpectedly find themselves being held liable to creditors for failure to pay assessments.[65] The potential for such liability hinders the use of assessment provisions, which can be a valuable tool for raising cash for firms that cannot readily access the capital markets.

This subsection also includes a new and questionable provision that the partners must unanimously consent to the compromise of an obligation to return a distribution that violates the Act. Under U.L.P.A. § 508(b), a distribution may violate the Act without violating the agreement. This suggests that the partners alone may waive a violation of the Act, even if the violated provision was intended to protect creditors. Since this provision is expressly embodied in the Act, it is apparently not subject to restriction in U.L.P.A. § 110(b)(13) on agreements restricting the rights of non-partners. But that provision apparently would prevent the partners from modifying the unanimous consent requirement.

§ 9.503.   SHARING OF DISTRIBUTIONS

Section 503

A distribution by a limited partnership must be shared among the partners on the basis of the value, as stated in the required records when the limited partnership decides to make the distribution, of the contributions the limited partnership has received from each partner.

---

[64] *See* U.L.L.C.A. Comments, at 349–50.
[65] *See* Bromberg & Ribstein, § 12.08(c); Revisited, at n.191.

Summary: Provides for sharing of distributions on the basis of the value of partners' contributions.

Parallel U.L.P.A. 1985: § 504.

Parallel R.U.P.A.: None.

Parallel U.L.L.C.A.: § 405.

Bromberg & Ribstein: § 16.02(c)(2).

Important Changes: No qualification regarding contributions that have been made and then returned to the partners.

Analysis: Note that U.L.P.A. has omitted a provision comparable to U.L.P.A. (1985) § 503 allocating profits and losses. The Comment says that "nearly all limited partnerships will choose to allocate profits and losses in order to comply with applicable tax, accounting and other regulatory requirements. Those requirements, rather than this Act, are the proper source of guidance for that profit and loss allocation." However, since the Act is supposed to provide default rules, it should not exclude a provision merely because the parties can be expected to draft for it.

With respect to the apportionment of distributions without regard to whether contributions have been returned, the Comment notes that the effect is the same as prior law as long as any distributions are allocated according to the initial contributions.

The agreement can vary the rule for sharing distributions pursuant to U.L.P.A. § 110. As the Comment notes, any such agreement must be checked for its effect on the operation of other provisions of the Act or the agreement based on the right to receive distributions.

§ 9.504. INTERIM DISTRIBUTIONS

Section 504

A partner does not have a right to any distribution before the dissolution and winding up of the limited partnership unless the limited partnership decides to make an interim distribution.

Summary: Provides that a partner has a right to pre-dissolution distributions only to the extent the limited partnership decides to make such distributions.

Parallel U.L.P.A. 1985:   § 601.

Parallel R.U.P.A.:   None.

Parallel U.L.L.C.A.:   § 405.

Bromberg & Ribstein: § 16.02(c)(2).

Important Changes: Provides for a right to interim distributions that the limited partnership "decides to make."

Analysis: The partners can provide for distribution rights in the agreement pursuant to U.L.P.A. § 110. This provision applies even in the absence of an agreement. The general partner makes the relevant decision for the limited partnership pursuant to U.L.P.A. § 406(a). This provision implies that a partner has rights as soon as the relevant decision is made. This would seem to trigger U.L.P.A. § 507. It is not clear whether the limited partnership can then negate these rights by revoking the decision.

§ 9.505.   NO DISTRIBUTION ON ACCOUNT OF DISSOCIATION

Section 505

A person does not have a right to receive a distribution on account of dissociation.

Summary: Provides that a partner is not entitled to a distribution on dissociating from the firm.

Parallel U.L.P.A. 1985:   § 604.

Parallel R.U.P.A.:   § 701.

Parallel U.L.L.C.A.:   None.

Bromberg & Ribstein: §§ 17.01(c)(2); 17.13.

Important Changes: Eliminates partner's default right to receive payment for the value of a partner's interest upon dissociation.

Analysis: This is a significant change from the default rule of payment upon dissociation under current U.L.P.A. 1985 and, for general partners, through linkage with R.U.P.A. § 701. It is consistent with several recent statutory amendments.[66] U.L.P.A. §§ 601–605 provide for causes and consequences of dissociation of general and limited partners. The effect of dissociation is now that the dissociating partner becomes a transferee of its interest (*see* U.L.P.A. §§ 602(a)(3) and 605(a)(5)). The agreement can provide for distribution rights pursuant to U.L.P.A. § 110.

This change in the uniform law has significant policy implications.[67] Limited partners' lack of default exit rights leaves them particularly vulnerable to management misconduct given their lack of a significant voice in management. Limited partners may have to resort to remedies for breach of fiduciary duty under U.L.P.A. § 408 or judicial dissolution under U.L.P.A. § 802. On the other hand, the right to withdraw and obtain payment for the interest in the firm may leave the firm vulnerable to liquidity problems and let partners abuse the threat of withdrawal. Also, blocking the exit allows the members to claim a valuation discount for estate tax purposes.[68] This may be especially important for limited partnerships, which are suitable for family-controlled businesses in which there is bifurcated power between the first and second generations.

U.L.P.A. § 505 changes the default rule of dissociation at will that applies to general partners through linkage with R.U.P.A. §§ 601 and 701, although a general partner may be able to dissolve the firm under U.L.P.A. § 801 if partners owning most of the distribution rights do not elect to continue under § 801(3). This emphasis on dissociation and continuation in limited partnerships is arguably justified by the greater likely consequences in a limited than in a general partnership of dissociation by a single general partner.

§ 9.506. DISTRIBUTION IN KIND

Section 506

A partner does not have a right to demand or receive any distribution from a limited partnership in any form other than cash. Subject to Section 812(b), a limited partnership may distribute an asset in kind to the extent each partner receives a percentage of the asset equal to the partner's share of distributions.

---

[66] *See* Bromberg & Ribstein, § 17.01, n.19.
[67] *See* Revisited, at 990–93.
[68] *See* 26 U.S.C. § 2704; Ribstein & Keatinge, ch. 18.

Summary: Provides that partner has no right to non-cash distribution, although partnership may make in-kind distributions pro rata according to distribution shares.

Parallel U.L.P.A. 1985:   § 605.

Parallel R.U.P.A.:   None.

Parallel U.L.L.C.A.:   § 405.

Bromberg & Ribstein: § 16.02(c)(2).

Important Changes: None; does not require that right to distributions in kind be stated in the certificate or in writing.

§ 9.507.   RIGHT TO DISTRIBUTION

Section 507

When a partner or transferee becomes entitled to receive a distribution, the partner or transferee has the status of, and is entitled to all remedies available to, a creditor of the limited partnership with respect to the distribution. However, the limited partnership's obligation to make a distribution is subject to offset for any amount owed to the limited partnership by the partner or dissociated partner on whose account the distribution is made.

Summary: Partner or transferee who is entitled to receive a distribution has the rights and remedies of a creditor, subject to offset for amount the partner or dissociated partner owes the partnership.

Parallel U.L.P.A. 1985:   § 606.

Parallel R.U.P.A.:   None.

Parallel U.L.L.C.A.:   § 405(c).

Bromberg & Ribstein: § 16.02(c)(2).

Important Changes: Provides for partnership's right of offset.

Analysis: This section provides for the consequences of a partner's having a right to a distribution under the partnership agreement or under U.L.P.A. § 504.

The partner entitled to a distribution is treated as an unsecured creditor under U.L.P.A. § 508(e).

§ 9.508. LIMITATIONS ON DISTRIBUTION

Section 508

(a) A limited partnership may not make a distribution in violation of the partnership agreement.

(b) A limited partnership may not make a distribution if after the distribution:

(1) the limited partnership would not be able to pay its debts as they become due in the ordinary course of the limited partnership's activities; or

(2) the limited partnership's total assets would be less than the sum of its total liabilities plus the amount that would be needed, if the limited partnership were to be dissolved, wound up, and terminated at the time of the distribution, to satisfy the preferential rights upon dissolution, winding up, and termination of partners whose preferential rights are superior to those of persons receiving the distribution.

(c) A limited partnership may base a determination that a distribution is not prohibited under subsection (b) on financial statements prepared on the basis of accounting practices and principles that are reasonable in the circumstances or on a fair valuation or other method that is reasonable in the circumstances.

(d) Except as otherwise provided in subsection (g), the effect of a distribution under subsection (b) is measured:

(1) in the case of distribution by purchase, redemption, or other acquisition of a transferable interest in the limited partnership, as of the date money or other property is transferred or debt incurred by the limited partnership; and

(2) in all other cases, as of the date:

(A) the distribution is authorized, if the payment occurs within 120 days after that date; or

(B) the payment is made, if payment occurs more than 120 days after the distribution is authorized.

(e) A limited partnership's indebtedness to a partner incurred by reason of a distribution made in accordance with this section is at parity with the limited partnership's indebtedness to its general, unsecured creditors.

(f) A limited partnership's indebtedness, including indebtedness issued in connection with or as part of a distribution, is not considered a liability for purposes of subsection (b) if the terms of the indebtedness provide that payment of principal and interest are made only to the extent that a distribution could then be made to partners under this section.

(g) If indebtedness is issued as a distribution, each payment of principal or interest on the indebtedness is treated as a distribution, the effect of which is measured on the date the payment is made.

Summary: Describes when distribution is prohibited and provides that partner owed a distribution is treated as general unsecured creditor.

Parallel U.L.P.A. 1985:   §§ 607, 608(c).

Parallel R.U.P.A.:   None.

Parallel U.L.L.C.A.:   §§ 406, 407.

Bromberg & Ribstein: § 16.02(c)(2).

Important Changes: Equity insolvency and preferential rights tests; rules for determining whether the distribution is wrongful and description of status of partner owed a distribution.

Analysis: A distribution may be excessive if it violates the partnership agreement *or* if it violates the statutory standard under subsection (b). The policy considerations relating to liability for excessive distributions and the standard of liability are discussed in § 9.509. Section 508(e) describes the status of a partner who is entitled to a distribution under § 507.

Subsection (c), like U.L.L.C.A. § 406, requires firms to make the complex determination on the basis of "reasonable" accounting practices that the distribution meets the "balance sheet" and "equity insolvency" tests.[69] These requirements unfortunately ensure that even small, informal LLCs will need legal and accounting advice in arranging day-to-day finances.

§ 9.509.   LIABILITY FOR IMPROPER DISTRIBUTIONS

Section 509

(a) A general partner that consents to a distribution made in violation of Section 508 is personally liable to the limited partnership for the amount of the distribution which exceeds the amount that could have been distributed without the violation if it is established that in consenting to the distribution the general partner failed to comply with Section 408.

(b) A partner or transferee that received a distribution knowing that the distribution to that partner or transferee was made in violation of Section 508 is

---

[69] *See* U.L.L.C.A. Comments, at 354.

personally liable to the limited partnership but only to the extent that the distribution received by the partner or transferee exceeded the amount that could have been properly paid under Section 508.

(c) A general partner against which an action is commenced under subsection (a) may:

(1) implead in the action any other person that is liable under subsection (a) and compel contribution from the person; and

(2) implead in the action any person that received a distribution in violation of subsection (b) and compel contribution from the person in the amount the person received in violation of subsection (b).

(d) An action under this section is barred if it is not commenced within two years after the distribution.

Summary: Provides for liability for distribution violating § 508 of general partner that consents to the distribution or partner or transferee that received it, and for right of impleader by general partner sued for consenting to distribution.

Parallel U.L.P.A. 1985: § 608.

Parallel R.U.P.A.: None.

Parallel U.L.L.C.A.: § 407.

Bromberg & Ribstein: §§ 15.16(d)–(g); 16.02(c)(2).

Important Changes: Imposes liability on partners consenting to distributions with a right of impleader; changes statute of limitations from one or six to two years; eliminates liability for rightfully returned contributions comparable to that in R.U.L.P.A. § 608(a).

Analysis: The liability under this section largely duplicates fraudulent conveyance liability, with the addition of liability of partners who consented to the distribution and potential liability to creditors based on violation of the partnership agreement.

This liability raises significant policy issues.[70] The liability can significantly hinder earnings distributions because the authorizing and receiving partners face liability depending on current asset valuations. This can particularly be a problem since partnerships' earnings are taxed to partners whether or not they are distributed. Also, lingering or shifting liability of transferors and transferees can hinder transfers of partnership interests (*see* U.L.P.A. § 702(d) and (g)). At the same time, creditors gain little more protection than is available from fraudulent conveyance laws and contracts. To be sure, fraudulent conveyance laws do not

___

[70] *See* Ribstein, Applied Theory, at 888–89; U.L.L.C.A. Comments, at 354; Revisited, at 986–88.

provide a cause of action against authorizing partners. Managers' liability may be justified in corporations because of creditors' difficulty of suing individual partners.[71] But, unlike corporations, partnerships are unlikely to be publicly traded because this would compromise their partnership tax status.[72] Finally, the liability does not square with the absence of such liability in most LLP statutes (*see* Section 4.04, above). It is not clear why passive *limited* partners who receive distributions should face liability to creditors, when *general* partners in LLPs do not.

Liability for distributions, like that for unperformed contribution obligations (*see* § 502(c), discussed in § 9.502, above), presents special problems to the extent that it is based on the partnership agreement. Partners may be surprised by the risks created by seemingly innocuous provisions in the agreement that can affect liability for distributions.[73] Moreover, the effect of such provisions on creditors raises questions concerning enforceability of the partnership agreement under U.L.P.A. § 110(b)(13), prohibiting agreements that restrict non-partner rights (*see* § 9.110, above). Similar issues arise regarding restrictions on compromise of partners' obligations to return distributions in U.L.P.A. § 502(c), discussed in § 9.502, above.

Subsection (a):   It may not be clear what conduct triggers liability under this section. First, it is not clear what constitutes "consent." The Comment says that "'consent' must be understood as encompassing any form of approval, assent or acquiescence, whether formal or informal, express or tacit." For example, is a partner not attending a meeting at which the distribution is approved deemed to consent immediately, or only after failing to object at some point after receiving knowledge or notice of the decision?

Second, there are issues regarding the applicable standard of care. The Comment notes that, while § 508(c) applies a "reasonableness" standard with respect to the partnership's accounting, an individual partner will not be liable unless the partner was also grossly negligent under § 408(c) or breached some other duty under § 408 for relying on the partnership's accounting standards. However, the black letter does not make clear that a partner who relies on a standard that is deemed unreasonable under § 508(c) will be exonerated under § 408.

Subsection (d):   The Comment notes that the time period applies to the commencement of an action under (a) or (b) and not to impleader under (c).

---

[71] *See* M.B.C.A. § 8.33 (providing for liability of directors).

[72] *See* I.R.C. § 7704.

[73] *See, e.g.,* Henkels & McCoy, Inc. v. Adochio, 138 F.3d 491 (3d Cir. 1998) (N.J. law) (liability for breach of provision requiring maintenance of adequate reserves).

§ 9.601. DISSOCIATION AS LIMITED PARTNER

Section 601

(a) A person does not have a right to dissociate as a limited partner before the termination of the limited partnership.

(b) A person is dissociated from a limited partnership as a limited partner upon the occurrence of any of the following events:

(1) the limited partnership's having notice of the person's express will to withdraw as a limited partner or on a later date specified by the person;

(2) an event agreed to in the partnership agreement as causing the person's dissociation as a limited partner;

(3) the person's expulsion as a limited partner pursuant to the partnership agreement;

(4) the person's expulsion as a limited partner by the unanimous consent of the other partners if:

(A) it is unlawful to carry on the limited partnership's activities with the person as a limited partner;

(B) there has been a transfer of all of the person's transferable interest in the limited partnership, other than a transfer for security purposes, or a court order charging the person's interest, which has not been foreclosed;

(C) the person is a corporation and, within 90 days after the limited partnership notifies the person that it will be expelled as a limited partner because it has filed a certificate of dissolution or the equivalent, its charter has been revoked, or its right to conduct business has been suspended by the jurisdiction of its incorporation, there is no revocation of the certificate of dissolution or no reinstatement of its charter or its right to conduct business; or

(D) the person is a limited liability company or partnership that has been dissolved and whose business is being wound up;

(5) on application by the limited partnership, the person's expulsion as a limited partner by judicial order because:

(A) the person engaged in wrongful conduct that adversely and materially affected the limited partnership's activities;

(B) the person willfully or persistently committed a material breach of the partnership agreement or of the obligation of good faith and fair dealing under Section 305(b); or

(C) the person engaged in conduct relating to the limited partnership's activities which makes it not reasonably practicable to carry on the activities with the person as limited partner;

(6) in the case of a person who is an individual, the person's death;

(7) in the case of a person that is a trust or is acting as a limited partner by virtue of being a trustee of a trust, distribution of the trust's entire transferable interest in the limited partnership, but not merely by reason of the substitution of a successor trustee;

(8) in the case of a person that is an estate or is acting as a limited partner by virtue of being a personal representative of an estate, distribution of the estate's entire transferable interest in the limited partnership, but not merely by reason of the substitution of a successor personal representative;

(9) termination of a limited partner that is not an individual, partnership, limited liability company, corporation, trust, or estate;

(10) the limited partnership's participation in a conversion or merger under [Article] 11, if the limited partnership:

(A) is not the converted or surviving entity; or

(B) is the converted or surviving entity but, as a result of the conversion or merger, the person ceases to be a limited partner.

Summary: Describes the events that cause dissociation of a person as a limited partner.

Parallel U.L.P.A. 1985:   § 603.

Parallel R.U.P.A.:   None.

Parallel U.L.L.C.A.:   § 601.

Bromberg & Ribstein: § 17.01(c)(2).

Important Changes: Eliminates limited partners' default right to dissociate upon six months' notice.

Analysis: This provision is the same as R.U.P.A. § 601, discussed in § 8.601, above, except that there is no dissociation for insolvency and related events consistent with the limited partner's limited liability, there is provision for dissociation as a result of conversion or merger, and the section provides that there is no default right to dissociate before termination. Note that a person who is both a limited and a general partner under U.L.P.A. § 113 can dissociate as one but not the other.

A limited partner may have a power to dissociate under U.L.P.A. § 601(b)(1) even if not a right to do so under § 601(a). Even if the limited partner dissociates, there is no default right to a distribution pursuant to U.L.P.A. § 505, discussed in § 9.505, above. Rather, the dissociated limited partner becomes the holder of its transferable interest. This and other effects of dissociation are covered by U.L.P.A. § 602, discussed in § 9.602, below.

The agreement can provide for a right to dissociate pursuant to U.L.P.A. § 110, discussed in § 9.110, above. It can also vary any of the dissociation causes. Compare waiver of comparable general partner rights, discussed below in § 9.604.

§ 9.602. EFFECT OF DISSOCIATION AS A LIMITED PARTNER

Section 602

(a) Upon a person's dissociation as a limited partner:

(1) subject to Section 704, the person does not have further rights as a limited partner;

(2) the person's obligation of good faith and fair dealing as a limited partner under Section 305(b) continues only as to matters arising and events occurring before the dissociation; and

(3) subject to Section 704 and [Article] 11, any transferable interest owned by the person in the person's capacity as a limited partner immediately before dissociation is owned by the person as a mere transferee.

(b) A person's dissociation as a limited partner does not of itself discharge the person from any obligation to the limited partnership or the other partners which the person incurred while a limited partner.

Summary: Describes effects of dissociation on limited partners' rights and duties.

Parallel U.L.P.A. 1985: None.

Parallel R.U.P.A.: § 603(b).

Parallel U.L.L.C.A.: § 603.

Bromberg & Ribstein: § 17.13.

Important Changes: There was no comparable provision in U.L.P.A. 1985, and it was unclear how R.U.P.A. would be applied to limited partners.

Analysis: This section applies to dissociation of a person as a limited partner, even if the person is also a general partner under U.L.P.A. § 113 and retains that status. The former partner's rights as a transferee of its transferable interest are covered by U.L.P.A. § 704, discussed in § 9.704, below. Information rights are covered in U.L.P.A. § 304(d) and (f), discussed in § 9.304, above. This section is subject to contrary agreement under U.L.P.A. § 110, and to a plan of conversion or merger under Article 11 that provides for a person's dissociation as a limited partner.

§ 9.603.   DISSOCIATION AS A GENERAL PARTNER

Section 603

A person is dissociated from a limited partnership as a general partner upon the occurrence of any of the following events:

(1) the limited partnership's having notice of the person's express will to withdraw as a general partner or on a later date specified by the person;

(2) an event agreed to in the partnership agreement as causing the person's dissociation as a general partner;

(3) the person's expulsion as a general partner pursuant to the partnership agreement;

(4) the person's expulsion as a general partner by the unanimous consent of the other partners if:

(A) it is unlawful to carry on the limited partnership's activities with the person as a general partner;

(B) there has been a transfer of all or substantially all of the person's transferable interest in the limited partnership, other than a transfer for security purposes, or a court order charging the person's interest, which has not been foreclosed;

(C) the person is a corporation and, within 90 days after the limited partnership notifies the person that it will be expelled as a general partner because it has filed a certificate of dissolution or the equivalent, its charter has been revoked, or its right to conduct business has been suspended by the jurisdiction of its incorporation, there is no revocation of the certificate of dissolution or no reinstatement of its charter or its right to conduct business; or

(D) the person is a limited liability company or partnership that has been dissolved and whose business is being wound up;

(5) on application by the limited partnership, the person's expulsion as a general partner by judicial determination because:

(A) the person engaged in wrongful conduct that adversely and materially affected the limited partnership activities;

(B) the person willfully or persistently committed a material breach of the partnership agreement or of a duty owed to the partnership or the other partners under Section 408; or

(C) the person engaged in conduct relating to the limited partnership's activities which makes it not reasonably practicable to carry on the activities of the limited partnership with the person as a general partner;

(6) the person's:

(A) becoming a debtor in bankruptcy;

(B) execution of an assignment for the benefit of creditors;

(C) seeking, consenting to, or acquiescing in the appointment of a trustee, receiver, or liquidator of the person or of all or substantially all of the person's property; or

(D) failure, within 90 days after the appointment, to have vacated or stayed the appointment of a trustee, receiver, or liquidator of the general partner or of all or substantially all of the person's property obtained without the person's consent or acquiescence, or failing within 90 days after the expiration of a stay to have the appointment vacated;

(7) in the case of a person who is an individual:

(A) the person's death;

(B) the appointment of a guardian or general conservator for the person; or

(C) a judicial determination that the person has otherwise become incapable of performing the person's duties as a general partner under the partnership agreement;

(8) in the case of a person that is a trust or is acting as a general partner by virtue of being a trustee of a trust, distribution of the trust's entire transferable interest in the limited partnership, but not merely by reason of the substitution of a successor trustee;

(9) in the case of a person that is an estate or is acting as a general partner by virtue of being a personal representative of an estate, distribution of the estate's entire transferable interest in the limited partnership, but not merely by reason of the substitution of a successor personal representative;

(10) termination of a general partner that is not an individual, partnership, limited liability company, corporation, trust, or estate; or

(11) the limited partnership's participation in a conversion or merger under [Article] 11, if the limited partnership:

(A) is not the converted or surviving entity; or

(B) is the converted or surviving entity but, as a result of the conversion or merger, the person ceases to be a general partner.

Summary: Describes the events that cause dissociation of a person as a general partner.

Parallel U.L.P.A. 1985:   § 602.

Parallel R.U.P.A.:   § 601.

Parallel U.L.L.C.A.:   § 601.

Bromberg & Ribstein: § 17.01(c)(2).

Important Changes: U.L.P.A. (1985) § 602 provided only for withdrawal on written notice.

Analysis: It was unclear whether dissociation causes other than withdrawal, such as expulsion, listed in R.U.P.A. § 601 were linked to U.L.P.A. 1985.[74] The inclusion of this provision makes this explicit. This provision is discussed above in § 8.601. It applies to the dissociation as a general partner of one who is both limited and general partner under U.L.P.A. § 113.

The partnership agreement may not override the power to dissociate by express will under subsection 1 other than to require notice in writing. As discussed above in § 8.602, this restriction on contracting is questionable. It is also not clear why the restriction is applied to general but not limited partners, since the two may now resemble each other under the partnership agreement with regard to management power and liability. The agreement may, however, override the expulsion power under § 603(5), in contrast to R.U.P.A. § 103(b)(7). This difference is also puzzling, since the expulsion power seemingly is even more important in limited than in general partnerships given the greater power of general partners and possibility for conflict with limited partners in the latter context.

§ 9.604.   PERSON'S POWER TO DISSOCIATE AS GENERAL PARTNER; WRONGFUL DISSOCIATION

Section 604

(a) A person has the power to dissociate as a general partner at any time, rightfully or wrongfully, by express will pursuant to Section 603(1).

(b) A person's dissociation as a general partner is wrongful only if:

(1) it is in breach of an express provision of the partnership agreement; or

(2) it occurs before the termination of the limited partnership, and:

[74] *See* Linking, at 194–95.

(A) the person withdraws as a general partner by express will;

(B) the person is expelled as a general partner by judicial determination under Section 603(5);

(C) the person is dissociated as a general partner by becoming a debtor in bankruptcy; or

(D) in the case of a person that is not an individual, trust other than a business trust, or estate, the person is expelled or otherwise dissociated as a general partner because it willfully dissolved or terminated.

(c) A person that wrongfully dissociates as a general partner is liable to the limited partnership and, subject to Section 1001, to the other partners for damages caused by the dissociation. The liability is in addition to any other obligation of the general partner to the limited partnership or to the other partners.

Summary: Provides that partner has the power to dissociate at any time, and defines and states the consequences of wrongful dissociation.

Parallel U.L.P.A. 1985: § 602.

Parallel R.U.P.A.: § 602.

Parallel U.L.L.C.A.: § 602.

Bromberg & Ribstein: § 17.03.

Important Changes: Definition of wrongful dissociation.

Analysis: This section makes explicit the application of the principles of R.U.P.A. § 602, discussed in § 8.602, above, which may or may not have been linked under U.L.P.A. 1985. One problem with linkage under prior law is the uncertain significance of the presence or absence of a term or undertaking (*see* § 604(b)(2), below). With respect to agreements waiving the power to dissociate, *see* U.L.P.A. § 603, discussed in § 9.603, above.

Subsection (b)(1): This subsection clarifies that wrongful dissociation refers only to the partnership agreement, contrary to the implication of some general partnership case law (*see* Bromberg & Ribstein, § 7.03(g)).

Subsection (b)(2): In contrast to R.U.P.A. § 602, this section makes dissociation prior to termination wrongful even if the partnership is *not* for a definite term or particular undertaking. This may be justified by a general partner's more important role in a limited than in a general partnership. However, because this change in the law may be a trap for the unwary, the issue is arguably better left for the partnership agreement.

As stated in the Comment, the reference to "termination" means that this subsection imposes a duty to remain a partner after dissolution. Although termination probably refers to the completion of winding up, it is not defined in the Act. U.L.P.A. § 203, discussed in § 9.203, above, permits but does not require the partnership to file a statement of termination. Thus, it may not be clear at what point a general partner's winding up duties cease.

§ 9.605.   EFFECT OF DISSOCIATION AS GENERAL PARTNER

Section 605

(a) Upon a person's dissociation as a general partner:

(1) the person's right to participate as a general partner in the management and conduct of the partnership's activities terminates;

(2) the person's duty of loyalty as a general partner under Section 408(b)(3) terminates;

(3) the person's duty of loyalty as a general partner under Section 408(b)(1) and (2) and duty of care under Section 408(c) continue only with regard to matters arising and events occurring before the person's dissociation as a general partner;

(4) the person may sign and deliver to the [Secretary of State] for filing a statement of dissociation pertaining to the person and, at the request of the limited partnership, shall sign an amendment to the certificate of limited partnership which states that the person has dissociated; and

(5) subject to Section 704 and [Article] 11, any transferable interest owned by the person immediately before dissociation in the person's capacity as a general partner is owned by the person as a mere transferee.

(b) A person's dissociation as a general partner does not of itself discharge the person from any obligation to the limited partnership or the other partners which the person incurred while a general partner.

Summary: Describes effects of dissociation on general partners' rights and duties.

Parallel U.L.P.A. 1985:   None.

Parallel R.U.P.A.:   § 603(b); § 703(a), (c) and (d).

Parallel U.L.L.C.A.:   § 603.

Bromberg & Ribstein: §§ 7.08, 17.08.

Important Changes: There was no equivalent provision in U.L.P.A. 1985. To the extent that there was linkage with R.U.P.A., the differences are described in the Analysis.

Analysis: In contrast to R.U.P.A. § 603(a), discussed in § 8.603, above, a general partner's dissociation from a limited partnership does not trigger either buyout or dissolution. Thus, the Act includes no default provisions concerning buyout comparable to R.U.P.A. § 701. Moreover, this section is not explicitly linked to U.L.P.A. as it was to U.L.P.A. 1985. However, limited partnerships that provide for a right to dissociate arguably can be expected also to provide for buyout rights in the agreement.

Subsection (a)(1):   Although U.L.P.A. § 604 provides that a general partner does not have the default right to dissociate prior to termination, this section provides a partner who does dissociate may not participate in winding up. This differs from R.U.P.A. § 603(b)(1). The reason for the distinction is not clear. It may reflect the fact that the general partner in a limited partnership often does not have a significant ownership interest to protect in winding up. However, this could be covered in the partnership agreement and does not necessarily justify a change in the default rule, particularly since the general partner is likely to have a substantial ownership interest in the relatively informal limited partnership for which the default rule is particularly important.

Subsection (a)(2)–(3):   These provisions are similar to R.U.P.A. § 603(b)(2)-(3), discussed in § 8.603, above.

Subsection (a)(4):   The statement of dissociation and certificate amendment have constructive notice effects under U.L.P.A. § 103(d) discussed in § 9.103, above. This, in turn, affects the partner's continued liability under U.L.P.A. §§ 607, 805, and 1111 and power to bind under U.L.P.A. §§ 606, 804, and 1112. With respect to the duty to amend the certificate to reflect dissociation, see U.L.P.A. § 202(b)(2), discussed above in § 9.202. With respect to signing of that amendment, see U.L.P.A. § 204(a)(5)(C) and 205.

Subsection (a)(5):   One who is both a general and a limited partner under U.L.P.A. § 113 and who dissociates as the former may remain the latter while holding the general partner's transferable interest. These dual interests must be disclosed under U.L.P.A. § 111(9)(C). U.L.P.A. § 704 provides for rights upon dissociation by death, while Article 11 provides for conversions and mergers, including for a plan of conversion or merger that may provide for the rights of one who dissociates as a result of the conversion or merger.

Subsection (b):　This subsection is equivalent to R.U.P.A. § 703(a), which probably was linked to U.L.P.A. 1985. Discharge by agreement or material alteration as under R.U.P.A. § 703(c) and (d) are covered by U.L.P.A. § 607(d)–(e).

Waiver:　This section is not listed as one of the non-waivable provisions under U.L.P.A. § 110(b). Note that while waiver of fiduciary duties is restricted under that section, waiver of the effect of duties after dissociation may not be.

§ 9.606.　POWER TO BIND AND LIABILITY TO LIMITED PARTNERSHIP BEFORE DISSOLUTION OF PARTNERSHIP OF PERSON DISSOCIATED AS GENERAL PARTNER

Section 606

(a) After a person is dissociated as a general partner and before the limited partnership is dissolved, converted under [Article] 11, or merged out of existence under [Article 11], the limited partnership is bound by an act of the person only if:

(1) the act would have bound the limited partnership under Section 402 before the dissociation; and

(2) at the time the other party enters into the transaction:

(A) less than two years has passed since the dissociation; and

(B) the other party does not have notice of the dissociation and reasonably believes that the person is a general partner.

(b) If a limited partnership is bound under subsection (a), the person dissociated as a general partner which caused the limited partnership to be bound is liable:

(1) to the limited partnership for any damage caused to the limited partnership arising from the obligation incurred under subsection (a); and

(2) if a general partner or another person dissociated as a general partner is liable for the obligation, to the general partner or other person for any damage caused to the general partner or other person arising from the liability.

Summary:　Provides for limited continuation of a dissociated partner's authority to bind the partnership, and for liability of a dissociated partner for damages resulting from his post-dissociation transactions.

Parallel U.L.P.A. 1985:   None.

Parallel R.U.P.A.:   § 702.

Parallel U.L.L.C.A.:   § 703.

Bromberg & Ribstein: §§ 17.15, 17.17.

Important Changes: Similar to the extent that R.U.P.A. linked to U.L.P.A. 1985, except for addition of liability to general partner or other person for damage arising from the liability incurred by the dissociating partner.

Analysis: The similar R.U.P.A. provision is discussed in § 8.702, above.

Subsection (a)(2)(B):   A person might have notice under Section 103(b) and (d)(1).

Subsection (b):   This provision covers liability to the partnership, while U.L.P.A. § 607 deals with liability to other persons. As discussed in the Comment, a dissociated partner may be liable under other law, such as under a guaranty. As discussed in § 8.702, above, the Act provides, in effect, for a special strict liability damage rule for post-dissociation transactions.

Waiver: This is not one of the non-waivable provisions under U.L.P.A. § 110. It is not clear why waiver of the general duty of care should be restricted under § 110(b)(6) but not the special duty under this section.

§ 9.607.   LIABILITY TO OTHER PERSONS OF PERSON DISSOCIATED AS GENERAL PARTNER

Section 607

(a) A person's dissociation as a general partner does not of itself discharge the person's liability as a general partner for an obligation of the limited partnership incurred before dissociation. Except as otherwise provided in subsections (b) and (c), the person is not liable for a limited partnership's obligation incurred after dissociation.

(b) A person whose dissociation as a general partner resulted in a dissolution and winding up of the limited partnership's activities is liable to the same extent as a general partner under Section 404 on an obligation incurred by the limited partnership under Section 804.

(c) A person that has dissociated as a general partner but whose dissociation did not result in a dissolution and winding up of the limited partnership's activities is liable on a transaction entered into by the limited partnership after the dissociation only if:

   (1) a general partner would be liable on the transaction; and

   (2) at the time the other party enters into the transaction:

      (A) less than two years has passed since the dissociation; and

      (B) the other party does not have notice of the dissociation and reasonably believes that the person is a general partner.

(d) By agreement with a creditor of a limited partnership and the limited partnership, a person dissociated as a general partner may be released from liability for an obligation of the limited partnership.

(e) A person dissociated as a general partner is released from liability for an obligation of the limited partnership if the limited partnership's creditor, with notice of the person's dissociation as a general partner but without the person's consent, agrees to a material alteration in the nature or time of payment of the obligation.

Summary: Provides for the dissociated partner's post-dissociation liability for pre-dissociation and post-dissociation debts.

Parallel U.L.P.A. 1985:   None.

Parallel R.U.P.A.:   § 703.

Parallel U.L.L.C.A.:   None.

Bromberg & Ribstein: §§ 17.14–17.16.

Important Changes: Similar to the R.U.P.A. rules linked to U.L.P.A. except to the extent described below.

Analysis:

Subsection (a):   This provision applies to a partner's liability under U.L.P.A. § 404 for partnership obligations. A partner that has no liability under U.L.P.A. § 404 because the firm is an LLLP obviously has no lingering liability under this section.

Subsection (b):   U.L.P.A. § 804, discussed in § 9.804, below, determines when a partnership is liable on a post-dissolution transaction. A partner whose dissociation caused the dissolution is liable even if a statement of dissociation or amended certificate reflecting the dissociation has been filed. It is not clear why the third party should be able to recover from the partner despite the notice that the partner has dissociated. U.L.P.A. § 804(b) curtails the dissociated partner's power to bind the partnership even to one who lacks the requisite notice of dissociation and reasonably believes that the partner has not dissociated if the standards for binding the partnership after dissolution are not met.

Subsection (c): This section applies where the partnership has not dissolved. Unlike under R.U.P.A. § 702, a person can recover under this section only if the person *both* lacks notice of the dissociation *and* reasonably believes that the person is a general partner. A person might have notice under Section 103(d)(1) as well as under Section 103(b).

Subsection (d)–(e): *See* R.U.P.A. § 703(c)–(d), discussed in § 8.703, above.

§ 9.701. PARTNER'S TRANSFERABLE INTEREST

Section 701

The only interest of a partner which is transferable is the partner's transferable interest. A transferable interest is personal property.

Summary: Identifies partner's transferable interest and provides that it is personal property.

Parallel U.L.P.A. 1985: §§ 701, 702.

Parallel R.U.P.A.: § 502.

Parallel U.L.L.C.A.: §§ 101(6); 501.

Bromberg & Ribstein: § 13.04(d)–(e).

Important Changes: None.

Analysis: This definition is consistent with basic partnership concept that a partner can freely transfer financial but not management rights. U.L.P.A. § 102(22) defines "transferable interest" as a partner's right to receive distributions, and therefore excludes other payments such as salaries that partners may receive other than in their capacity purely as partners. This is what a partner can transfer without co-partner consent under U.L.P.A. § 702, consistent with U.L.P.A. (1985) § 702. By contrast, R.U.P.A. § 502 provides that a partner's transferable interest also includes the partner's share of partnership profits and losses. Although U.L.P.A. (1985) § 503 provides for a default allocation of profits and losses, U.L.P.A. 1985 does not provide for transfer of this share. As discussed in § 9.503, U.L.P.A. has no provision equivalent to U.L.P.A. (1985) § 503. The partner's right to distributions is defined in U.L.P.A. § 504.

§ 9.702. TRANSFER OF PARTNER'S TRANSFERABLE INTEREST

Section 702

(a) A transfer, in whole or in part, of a partner's transferable interest:

(1) is permissible;

(2) does not by itself cause the partner's dissociation or a dissolution and winding up of the limited partnership's activities; and

(3) does not, as against the other partners or the limited partnership, entitle the transferee to participate in the management or conduct of the limited partnership's activities, to require access to information concerning the limited partnership's transactions except as otherwise provided in subsection (c), or to inspect or copy the required information or the limited partnership's other records.

(b) A transferee has a right to receive, in accordance with the transfer:

(1) distributions to which the transferor would otherwise be entitled; and

(2) upon the dissolution and winding up of the limited partnership's activities the net amount otherwise distributable to the transferor.

(c) In a dissolution and winding up, a transferee is entitled to an account of the limited partnership's transactions only from the date of dissolution.

(d) Upon transfer, the transferor retains the rights of a partner other than the interest in distributions transferred and retains all duties and obligations of a partner.

(e) A limited partnership need not give effect to a transferee's rights under this section until the limited partnership has notice of the transfer.

(f) A transfer of a partner's transferable interest in the limited partnership in violation of a restriction on transfer contained in the partnership agreement is ineffective as to a person having notice of the restriction at the time of transfer.

(g) A transferee that becomes a partner with respect to a transferable interest is liable for the transferor's obligations under Sections 502 and 509. However, the transferee is not obligated for liabilities unknown to the transferee at the time the transferee became a partner.

Summary: Provides for the effect of a transfer of a partner's transferable interest.

Parallel U.L.P.A. 1985: §§ 702, 704.

Parallel R.U.P.A.: § 503.

Parallel U.L.L.C.A.: §§ 502–503.

Bromberg & Ribstein: § 13.06(d)–(e).

Important Changes: Assignment does not cause dissociation; provides for right of account; requires notice of transfer.

Analysis: This section follows through on the basic partnership principle that partners can transfer financial but not management or other rights. It is based on R.U.P.A. § 503, discussed in § 8.503, above, except as indicated below. This Section, in turn, is basically consistent with U.L.P.A. (1985) § 702 and § 704, as discussed below. The provisions in § 704 relating to an assignee's becoming a limited partner now are effectively covered by U.L.P.A. § 301 and § 401 on becoming a limited and general partner, discussed in §§ 9.301 and 9.401, above. Because of the U.L.P.A. 1985 provisions on transfer, the R.U.P.A. provision probably was not linked with U.L.P.A.

Subsection (a)(1): This is consistent with the first sentence of U.L.P.A. (1985) § 702.

Subsection (a)(2): This differs from the last sentence of U.L.P.A. (1985) § 702 regarding dissociation. Detaching management and financial rights might cause incentive problems, as discussed in § 8.503. However, these are alleviated by the possibility of dissociation by expulsion pursuant to U.L.P.A. § 601(b)(4)(B) or § 603(4)(B).

Subsection (a)(3): This is consistent with the second sentence of U.L.P.A. (1985) § 702. A transferee has no information rights under U.L.P.A. § 304(k) and § 407(i), partners' fiduciary and good faith duties are owed only to the partnership and the partners under U.L.P.A. § 305 and § 408, and only a partner can bring a derivative suit under U.L.P.A. § 1003.

Subsection (b):   This is consistent with U.L.P.A. (1985) § 702, third sentence.

Subsection (c):   Although no comparable provision was included in U.L.P.A. 1985, it may have applied by linkage with R.U.P.A. § 503(c).

Subsection (d):   The retention of transferor rights is inconsistent with U.L.P.A. (1985) § 702 as discussed above concerning subsection (a)(2). However, retention of obligations is consistent with U.L.P.A. (1985) § 704(c).

Subsection (e)–(f):   These provisions, based on R.U.P.A. § 503(e)–(f), were not included in U.L.P.A. 1985, although they may have been implicit.

Subsection (g):   This is consistent with U.L.P.A. (1985) § 704(b).

§ 9.703.   RIGHTS OF CREDITOR OF PARTNER OR TRANSFEREE

Section 703

(a) On application to a court of competent jurisdiction by any judgment creditor of a partner or transferee, the court may charge the transferable interest of the judgment debtor with payment of the unsatisfied amount of the judgment with interest. To the extent so charged, the judgment creditor has only the rights of a transferee. The court may appoint a receiver of the share of the distributions due or to become due to the judgment debtor in respect of the partnership and make all other orders, directions, accounts, and inquiries the judgment debtor might have made or which the circumstances of the case may require to give effect to the charging order.

(b) A charging order constitutes a lien on the judgment debtor's transferable interest. The court may order a foreclosure upon the interest subject to the charging order at any time. The purchaser at the foreclosure sale has the rights of a transferee.

(c) At any time before foreclosure, an interest charged may be redeemed:

   (1) by the judgment debtor;

   (2) with property other than limited partnership property, by one or more of the other partners; or

   (3) with limited partnership property, by the limited partnership with the consent of all partners whose interests are not so charged.

(d) This [Act] does not deprive any partner or transferee of the benefit of any exemption laws applicable to the partner's or transferee's transferable interest.

(e) This section provides the exclusive remedy by which a judgment creditor of a partner or transferee may satisfy a judgment out of the judgment debtor's transferable interest.

Summary: Provides for the rights of partners' creditors to reach partners' transferable interests.

Parallel U.L.P.A. 1985: § 703.

Parallel R.U.P.A.: § 504.

Parallel U.L.L.C.A.: § 504.

Bromberg & Ribstein: § 13.07(d)–(e).

Important Changes: The first two sentences and subsection (d) are included in U.L.P.A. 1985, except for the reference to charging a transferee's interest. The rest, based on R.U.P.A., may or may not have applied by linkage.

Analysis: The Analysis of R.U.P.A. § 504 in § 8.504 generally applies here. However, subsection (a) expands slightly on R.U.P.A. § 504 by limiting court orders to those that "give effect to the charging order." The Comment says that this would permit an order determining whether a payment made to a partner is a distribution that is part of the partner's transferable interest and, if so, requiring the firm to make the payment to the creditor pursuant to the charging order. However, the Act does not empower the court to compel the firm to follow a particular policy concerning distributions.

State variation: **California** provides that "[n]o creditor of a partner shall have any right to obtain possession or otherwise exercise legal or equitable remedies with respect to the property of the limited partnership."[75]

§ 9.704. POWER OF ESTATE OF DECEASED PARTNER

Section 704

If a partner dies, the deceased partner's personal representative or other legal representative may exercise the rights of a transferee as provided in Section 702

---

[75] Cal. Corp. Code § 15907.03.

and, for the purposes of settling the estate, may exercise the rights of a current limited partner under Section 304.

Summary: Specifies rights of representative of deceased partner's estate.

Parallel U.L.P.A. 1985:   § 705.

Parallel R.U.P.A.:   None.

Parallel U.L.L.C.A.:   None.

Bromberg & Ribstein: § 13.09(f).

Important Changes: Applies to representative of incompetent's estate and to "all of the partner's rights for the purpose of settling his [or her] estate or administering his [or her] property."

Analysis: This section contrasts with the limits on transferees' rights generally under U.L.P.A. § 702. This section clarifies that the representative's rights are those of a limited partner even if the estate is that of a general partner.

§ 9.801.   NONJUDICIAL DISSOLUTION

Section 801

Except as otherwise provided in Section 802, a limited partnership is dissolved, and its activities must be wound up, only upon the occurrence of any of the following:

(1) the happening of an event specified in the partnership agreement;

(2) the consent of all general partners and of limited partners owning a majority of the rights to receive distributions as limited partners at the time the consent is to be effective;

(3) after the dissociation of a person as a general partner:

(A) if the limited partnership has at least one remaining general partner, the consent to dissolve the limited partnership given within 90 days after the dissociation by partners owning a majority of the rights to receive distributions as partners at the time the consent is to be effective; or

(B) if the limited partnership does not have a remaining general partner, the passage of 90 days after the dissociation, unless before the end of the period:

(i) consent to continue the activities of the limited partnership and admit at least one general partner is given by limited partners owning a majority of the rights to receive distributions as limited partners at the time the consent is to be effective; and

(ii) at least one person is admitted as a general partner in accordance with the consent;

(4) the passage of 90 days after the dissociation of the limited partnership's last limited partner, unless before the end of the period the limited partnership admits at least one limited partner; or

(5) the signing and filing of a declaration of dissolution by the [Secretary of State] under Section 809(c).

Summary: Provides for events other than judicial decree that cause the dissolution of the partnership.

Parallel U.L.P.A. 1985:   § 801.

Parallel R.U.P.A.:   § 801.

Parallel U.L.L.C.A.:   § 801(1)–(3).

Bromberg & Ribstein: §§ 17.01–17.05.

Important Changes: No writing requirements for consent or dissolution provisions; dissolution by consent requires consent of all general partners but only of the majority of limited partner distribution rights; no dissolution on dissociation of general partner where there is at least one general partner unless vote to dissolve by holders of a majority of distribution rights; dissolution on dissociation of last general partner unless holders of a majority of limited partner distribution rights vote to continue and admit a general partner; provision for dissolution if there are no limited partners unless the limited partnership appoints a limited partner; provision for administrative dissolution.

Analysis: Because of detailed coverage of dissolution in U.L.P.A. 1985, there was no linkage with R.U.P.A. (*but see* Bromberg & Ribstein, Section 17.02, n.6a) U.L.P.A. 2001 has removed default writing requirements but requires a record of dissolution events under U.L.P.A. § 111(9)(D). The effect of that provision is discussed in § 9.111. Pursuant to U.L.P.A. § 110, this section is subject to waiver in the partnership agreement, including by addition of writing requirements. The Comment gives examples of computation of voting rights attributable to holding different distribution rights in dual capacities as general and limited partners under U.L.P.A. § 113. Note that U.L.P.A. does not have a provision for dissolution waiver comparable to that in R.U.P.A. § 802.

§ 9.802.   JUDICIAL DISSOLUTION

Section 802

On application by a partner the [appropriate court] may order dissolution of a limited partnership if it is not reasonably practicable to carry on the activities of the limited partnership in conformity with the partnership agreement.

Summary: Provides for the ground of judicial dissolution.

Parallel U.L.P.A. 1985:   § 802.

Parallel R.U.P.A.:   § 801(5)–(6).

Parallel U.L.L.C.A.:   § 801(4)–(5).

Bromberg & Ribstein: § 17.06.

Important Changes: Prohibition of waiver under U.L.P.A. § 110(b)(9).

Analysis: Because of the coverage of judicial dissolution in U.L.P.A. 1985, there was no linkage with R.U.P.A., although many of the R.U.P.A. causes have been deemed relevant to applying the general basis of judicial dissolution in U.L.P.A. 1985. It is not clear precisely when judicial dissolution occurs—that is, initial order, a final resolution, or some other stage of the proceeding (*see* Bromberg & Ribstein, § 7.06(a)(3)). However, this provision does clarify that only a partner can sue for judicial dissolution, thereby eliminating uncertainty created by linkage with R.U.P.A. as to whether an action can be brought by a transferee, including a partner's judgment creditor who has obtained a charging order (*see* R.U.P.A. §§ 504, 801(5), and 8.802, above).

It is not clear why the firm should be prohibited from contracting around this provision, since the firm might reasonably seek to avoid the uncertainty inherent in judicial dissolution. The Comment to § 110(b)(9) says that the provision does not prevent arbitration clauses, the validity of which is mandated by federal law. However, the Federal Arbitration Act does not apply to all arbitration clauses. Moreover, this provision appears in terms to require court resolution of dissolution, which is inconsistent with mandatory arbitration.

State variation: **California** adds a provision permitting partners to avoid judicial dissolution by buying out the moving parties' interests for fair market value, to be fixed by court-supervised appraisal if the parties cannot agree on the price.[76]

---

[76] *Id.* § 15908.02.

§ 9.803. WINDING UP

Section 803

(a) A limited partnership continues after dissolution only for the purpose of winding up its activities.

(b) In winding up its activities, the limited partnership:

(1) may amend its certificate of limited partnership to state that the limited partnership is dissolved, preserve the limited partnership business or property as a going concern for a reasonable time, prosecute and defend actions and proceedings, whether civil, criminal, or administrative, transfer the limited partnership's property, settle disputes by mediation or arbitration, file a statement of termination as provided in Section 203, and perform other necessary acts; and

(2) shall discharge the limited partnership's liabilities, settle and close the limited partnership's activities, and marshal and distribute the assets of the partnership.

(c) If a dissolved limited partnership does not have a general partner, a person to wind up the dissolved limited partnership's activities may be appointed by the consent of limited partners owning a majority of the rights to receive distributions as limited partners at the time the consent is to be effective. A person appointed under this subsection:

(1) has the powers of a general partner under Section 804; and

(2) shall promptly amend the certificate of limited partnership to state:

(A) that the limited partnership does not have a general partner;

(B) the name of the person that has been appointed to wind up the limited partnership; and

(C) the street and mailing address of the person.

(d) On the application of any partner, the [appropriate court] may order judicial supervision of the winding up, including the appointment of a person to wind up the dissolved limited partnership's activities, if:

(1) a limited partnership does not have a general partner and within a reasonable time following the dissolution no person has been appointed pursuant to subsection (c); or

(2) the applicant establishes other good cause.

Summary: Provides for who may wind up a limited partnership after dissolution and what happens during winding up.

Parallel U.L.P.A. 1985: § 803.

Parallel R.U.P.A.: § 802(a) and § 803.

Parallel U.L.L.C.A.: § 803.

Bromberg & Ribstein: § 17.08.

Important Changes: Provides more specifically for activities of winding up partnership.

Analysis:

Subsection (a): This states a basic partnership rule, which applied under U.L.P.A. 1985 by linkage with R.U.P.A. § 802(a).

Subsection (b): This provision is generally consistent with R.U.P.A. § 803 except for the references to certificates and statements provided for in U.L.P.A. R.U.P.A. probably applied by linkage under U.L.P.A. 1985. The problem of the potentially open-ended scope of the power to "preserve the limited partnership business or property as a going concern for a reasonable time" is discussed in § 8.803. Note that, unlike U.L.P.A. 1985, this section does not exclude wrongfully dissolving partners from winding up. Such partners may be expelled under § 603(5), after which they have no further rights as general partners under § 605. Like U.L.P.A. 1985 and R.U.P.A. § 803, there is no specification of allocation of internal governance powers among general partners during winding up (*see* § 8.803).

Subsection (c): This section is generally consistent with U.L.P.A. (1985) § 803, which permitted winding up by the limited partners in this situation, and therefore by implication a person appointed by the limited partners. This section adds a voting rule, specifies the powers of the person appointed, and provides for a certificate amendment to reflect the appointment (*see* U.L.P.A. § 202(b)(3)). As stated in the Comment, a person appointed under this subsection is not subject to general partners' duties under U.L.P.A. § 408, although the partnership agreement can provide for such duties. It is not clear why such persons should not have the same default duties as general partners engaged in winding up under § 408.

Subsection (d): Although this provision does not specify assignees' or legal representatives' right to apply for judicial winding up, representatives of estates can exercise partners' powers under U.L.P.A. § 704. This section includes a specific ground for judicial winding up where the limited partnership does not have a general partner and no winding up person has been appointed under to subsection (c).

Waiver: U.L.P.A. § 110(b)(10) provides that the partnership agreement may not "vary the requirement to wind up the partnership's business as specified in Section 803." To the extent that winding up and payment of debts affects third-party rights, this appears to duplicate § 110(b)(13). To the extent that this section governs the method of winding up, particularly including the appointment of a winding up person under subsection (c) or winding up by the court under (d), the section may not, and probably should not, preclude contrary agreements.

§ 9.804. POWER OF GENERAL PARTNER AND PERSON DISSOCIATED AS GENERAL PARTNER TO BIND PARTNERSHIP AFTER DISSOLUTION

Section 804

(a) A limited partnership is bound by a general partner's act after dissolution which:

(1) is appropriate for winding up the limited partnership's activities; or

(2) would have bound the limited partnership under Section 402 before dissolution, if, at the time the other party enters into the transaction, the other party does not have notice of the dissolution.

(b) A person dissociated as a general partner binds a limited partnership through an act occurring after dissolution if:

(1) at the time the other party enters into the transaction:

(A) less than two years has passed since the dissociation; and

(B) the other party does not have notice of the dissociation and reasonably believes that the person is a general partner; and

(2) the act:

(A) is appropriate for winding up the limited partnership's activities; or

(B) would have bound the limited partnership under Section 402 before dissolution and at the time the other party enters into the transaction the other party does not have notice of the dissolution.

Summary: Provides for partners' and dissociated partners' authority to bind the partnership after dissolution as to winding up acts and as to those who lack notice of the dissolution and dissociation.

Parallel U.L.P.A. 1985: None.

Parallel R.U.P.A.: §§ 804–805.

Parallel U.L.L.C.A.: §§ 703–704.

Bromberg & Ribstein: §§ 17.15–17.16.

Important Changes: Similar to the effect of R.U.P.A., which may have been linked to U.L.P.A. 1985.

Analysis:

Subsection (a):   This subsection provides for the power of a partner to bind the partnership after dissolution. It is similar to the effect of R.U.P.A. § 804 and § 805, discussed in § 8.804–§ 8.805. Notice is provided for under U.L.P.A. § 103(b), and specifically under U.L.P.A. § 103(d)(2) concerning the effect of amending to certificate to reflect the partnership's dissolution.

Subsection (b):   This subsection states the power of a person dissociated as a partner to bind a partnership after dissolution. It provides in effect that the person can bind the partnership only if the act satisfies *both* the tests for binding the partnership by a dissociated partner *and* the test for binding a dissolved partnership. U.L.P.A. § 607(b) provides for the liability of a dissociated partner if the transaction binds the partnership. The requisite notice can be provided by U.L.P.A. § 103(b) or U.L.P.A. § 103(d)(1) (for § 804(b)(1)(B)) or U.L.P.A. § 103(d)(2) (for U.L.P.A. § 804(B)(2)(B)).

§ 9.805.   LIABILITY AFTER DISSOLUTION OF GENERAL PARTNER AND PERSON DISSOCIATED AS GENERAL PARTNER TO LIMITED PARTNERSHIP, OTHER GENERAL PARTNERS, AND PERSONS DISSOCIATED AS GENERAL PARTNER

Section 805

(a) If a general partner having knowledge of the dissolution causes a limited partnership to incur an obligation under Section 804(a) by an act that is not appropriate for winding up the partnership's activities, the general partner is liable:

(1) to the limited partnership for any damage caused to the limited partnership arising from the obligation; and

(2) if another general partner or a person dissociated as a general partner is liable for the obligation, to that other general partner or person for any damage caused to that other general partner or person arising from the liability.

(b) If a person dissociated as a general partner causes a limited partnership to incur an obligation under Section 804(b), the person is liable:

(1) to the limited partnership for any damage caused to the limited partnership arising from the obligation; and

(2) if a general partner or another person dissociated as a general partner is liable for the obligation, to the general partner or other person for any damage caused to the general partner or other person arising from the liability.

Summary: Provides for intra-partnership liability for post-dissolution debts incurred by general partners or persons dissociated as general partners.

Parallel U.L.P.A. 1985:   None.

Parallel R.U.P.A.:   § 806.

Parallel U.L.L.C.A.:   None.

Bromberg & Ribstein: § 17.17.

Important Changes: Similar to R.U.P.A. § 806, which may have been linked to U.L.P.A. 1985, except that it provides for liability of dissociated partners and for liability for damage to general partners or dissociated general partners who are liable for the post-dissolution obligation.

Analysis: A general partner is liable only if the partner, knowing of the dissolution, caused the partnership to enter into a transaction that was not appropriate for winding up. By contrast, a dissociated partner is liable for any acts of the partner that trigger partnership liability under U.L.P.A. § 804(b). This liability is comparable to a dissociated partner's liability under U.L.P.A. § 606(b). Since liability under that provision depends on whether the act is appropriate for winding up, the main difference between the two situations is that the dissociated partner need not know of the dissolution since the partner's post-dissociation act breaches a duty to the partnership or the other partners irrespective of such knowledge. As discussed in the Comment, it is not clear how the liability will be apportioned if more than one partner is liable.

§ 9.806.   KNOWN CLAIMS AGAINST DISSOLVED LIMITED PARTNERSHIP

Section 806

(a) A dissolved limited partnership may dispose of the known claims against it by following the procedure described in subsection (b).

(b) A dissolved limited partnership may notify its known claimants of the dissolution in a record. The notice must:

(1) specify the information required to be included in a claim;

(2) provide a mailing address to which the claim is to be sent;

(3) state the deadline for receipt of the claim, which may not be less than 120 days after the date the notice is received by the claimant;

(4) state that the claim will be barred if not received by the deadline; and

(5) unless the limited partnership has been throughout its existence a limited liability limited partnership, state that the barring of a claim against the limited partnership will also bar any corresponding claim against any general partner or person dissociated as a general partner which is based on Section 404.

(c) A claim against a dissolved limited partnership is barred if the requirements of subsection (b) are met and:

(1) the claim is not received by the specified deadline; or

(2) in the case of a claim that is timely received but rejected by the dissolved limited partnership, the claimant does not commence an action to enforce the claim against the limited partnership within 90 days after the receipt of the notice of the rejection.

(d) This section does not apply to a claim based on an event occurring after the effective date of dissolution or a liability that is contingent on that date.

Summary: Sets forth a procedure for notifying known claimants of the dissolved firm, setting a deadline for making claims and barring claims not made by the deadline.

Parallel U.L.P.A. 1985:   None.

Parallel R.U.P.A.:   None.

Parallel U.L.L.C.A.:   § 807.

Bromberg & Ribstein: § 17.14.

Important Changes: New provision.

Analysis: This is based on U.L.L.C.A. § 807 and is similar to the procedure in M.B.C.A. § 14.06.

§ 9.807.   OTHER CLAIMS AGAINST DISSOLVED LIMITED PARTNERSHIP

Section 807

(a) A dissolved limited partnership may publish notice of its dissolution and request persons having claims against the limited partnership to present them in accordance with the notice.

(b) The notice must:

(1) be published at least once in a newspaper of general circulation in the [county] in which the dissolved limited partnership's principal office is located or, if it has none in this State, in the [county] in which the limited partnership's designated office is or was last located;

(2) describe the information required to be contained in a claim and provide a mailing address to which the claim is to be sent;

(3) state that a claim against the limited partnership is barred unless an action to enforce the claim is commenced within five years after publication of the notice; and

(4) unless the limited partnership has been throughout its existence a limited liability limited partnership, state that the barring of a claim against the limited partnership will also bar any corresponding claim against any general partner or person dissociated as a general partner which is based on Section 404.

(c) If a dissolved limited partnership publishes a notice in accordance with subsection (b), the claim of each of the following claimants is barred unless the claimant commences an action to enforce the claim against the dissolved limited partnership within five years after the publication date of the notice:

(1) a claimant that did not receive notice in a record under Section 806;

(2) a claimant whose claim was timely sent to the dissolved limited partnership but not acted on; and

(3) a claimant whose claim is contingent or based on an event occurring after the effective date of dissolution.

(d) A claim not barred under this section may be enforced:

(1) against the dissolved limited partnership, to the extent of its undistributed assets;

(2) if the assets have been distributed in liquidation, against a partner or transferee to the extent of that person's proportionate share of the claim or the limited partnership's assets distributed to the partner or transferee in liquidation, whichever is less, but a person's total liability for all claims under this paragraph does not exceed the total amount of assets distributed to the person as part of the winding up of the dissolved limited partnership; or

(3) against any person liable on the claim under Section 404.

Summary: Sets forth a procedure for publishing notice of dissolution and requesting that claims be made, paying timely claims, and barring claims that are not made within five years.

Parallel U.L.P.A. 1985: None.

Parallel R.U.P.A.: None.

Parallel U.L.L.C.A.: § 808.

Bromberg & Ribstein: None.

Important Changes: New provision.

Analysis: This is based on U.L.L.C.A. § 808 and is similar to M.B.C.A. § 14.07.

§ 9.808. LIABILITY OF GENERAL PARTNER AND PERSON DISSOCIATED AS GENERAL PARTNER WHEN CLAIM AGAINST LIMITED PARTNERSHIP BARRED

Section 808

If a claim against a dissolved limited partnership is barred under Section 806 or 807, any corresponding claim under Section 404 is also barred.

Summary: Provides that, if a claim against a dissolved limited partnership is barred under the foregoing sections, a claim against a partner under U.L.P.A. § 404 is also barred.

Parallel U.L.P.A. 1985: None.

Parallel R.U.P.A.: None.

Parallel U.L.L.C.A.: § 808(d).

Bromberg & Ribstein: None.

Important Changes: New provision.

§ 9.809. ADMINISTRATIVE DISSOLUTION

Section 809

(a) The [Secretary of State] may dissolve a limited partnership administratively if the limited partnership does not, within 60 days after the due date:

(1) pay any fee, tax, or penalty due to the [Secretary of State] under this [Act] or other law; or

(2) deliver its annual report to the [Secretary of State].

(b) If the [Secretary of State] determines that a ground exists for administratively dissolving a limited partnership, the [Secretary of State] shall file a record of the determination and serve the limited partnership with a copy of the filed record.

(c) If within 60 days after service of the copy the limited partnership does not correct each ground for dissolution or demonstrate to the reasonable satisfaction of the [Secretary of State] that each ground determined by the [Secretary of State] does not exist, the [Secretary of State] shall administratively dissolve the limited partnership by preparing, signing and filing a declaration of dissolution that states the grounds for dissolution. The [Secretary of State] shall serve the limited partnership with a copy of the filed declaration.

(d) A limited partnership administratively dissolved continues its existence but may carry on only activities necessary to wind up its activities and liquidate its assets under Sections 803 and 812 and to notify claimants under Sections 806 and 807.

(e) The administrative dissolution of a limited partnership does not terminate the authority of its agent for service of process.

Summary: Provides for an action by the appropriate administrator to dissolve a limited partnership that has not paid fees or filed an annual report after an opportunity to correct the deficiency.

Parallel U.L.P.A. 1985: None.

Parallel R.U.P.A.: None.

Parallel U.L.L.C.A.: §§ 809–810.

Bromberg & Ribstein: None.

Important Changes: New provision.

Analysis: This is based on U.L.L.C.A. §§ 809–810 and is similar to M.B.C.A. §§ 14.20–14.21. The Comment notes that the declaration of dissolution by the administrator does not provide notice under U.L.P.A. § 103(d). It follows that, for example, the dissolution does not affect partners' power to bind the partnership for non–winding up acts. This is consistent with the possibility of reinstatement under the following sections, which relates back to the dissolution.

§ 9.810.   REINSTATEMENT FOLLOWING ADMINISTRATIVE DISSOLUTION

Section 810

(a) A limited partnership that has been administratively dissolved may apply to the [Secretary of State] for reinstatement within two years after the effective date of dissolution. The application must be delivered to the [Secretary of State] for filing and state:

(1) the name of the limited partnership and the effective date of its administrative dissolution;

(2) that the grounds for dissolution either did not exist or have been eliminated; and

(3) that the limited partnership's name satisfies the requirements of Section 108.

(b) If the [Secretary of State] determines that an application contains the information required by subsection (a) and that the information is correct, the [Secretary of State] shall prepare a declaration of reinstatement that states this determination, sign, and file the original of the declaration of reinstatement, and serve the limited partnership with a copy.

(c) When reinstatement becomes effective, it relates back to and takes effect as of the effective date of the administrative dissolution and the limited partnership may resume its activities as if the administrative dissolution had never occurred.

Summary: Provides for reinstatement within two years of dissolution if the grounds for dissolution either did not exist or have been eliminated.

Parallel U.L.P.A. 1985:   None.

Parallel R.U.P.A.:   None.

Parallel U.L.L.C.A.:   § 811.

Bromberg & Ribstein: None.

Important Changes: New provision.

Analysis: This is based on U.L.L.C.A. § 811 and is similar to M.B.C.A. § 14.22.

§ 9.811. APPEAL FROM DENIAL OF REINSTATEMENT

Section 811

(a) If the [Secretary of State] denies a limited partnership's application for reinstatement following administrative dissolution, the [Secretary of State] shall prepare, sign and file a notice that explains the reason or reasons for denial and serve the limited partnership with a copy of the notice.

(b) Within 30 days after service of the notice of denial, the limited partnership may appeal from the denial of reinstatement by petitioning the [appropriate court] to set aside the dissolution. The petition must be served on the [Secretary of State] and contain a copy of the [Secretary of State's] declaration of dissolution, the limited partnership's application for reinstatement, and the [Secretary of State's] notice of denial.

(c) The court may summarily order the [Secretary of State] to reinstate the dissolved limited partnership or may take other action the court considers appropriate.

Summary: Provides for judicial action on appeal from reinstatement filed within 30 days after service of the notice of denial.

Parallel U.L.P.A. 1985: None.

Parallel R.U.P.A.: None.

Parallel U.L.L.C.A.: § 812.

Bromberg & Ribstein: None.

Important Changes: New provision.

Analysis: This is based on U.L.L.C.A. § 812.

§ 9.812.   DISPOSITION OF ASSETS; WHEN CONTRIBUTIONS REQUIRED

Section 812

(a) In winding up a limited partnership's activities, the assets of the limited partnership, including the contributions required by this section, must be applied to satisfy the limited partnership's obligations to creditors, including, to the extent permitted by law, partners that are creditors.

(b) Any surplus remaining after the limited partnership complies with subsection (a) must be paid in cash as a distribution.

(c) If a limited partnership's assets are insufficient to satisfy all of its obligations under subsection (a), with respect to each unsatisfied obligation incurred when the limited partnership was not a limited liability limited partnership, the following rules apply:

(1) Each person that was a general partner when the obligation was incurred and that has not been released from the obligation under Section 607 shall contribute to the limited partnership for the purpose of enabling the limited partnership to satisfy the obligation. The contribution due from each of those persons is in proportion to the right to receive distributions in the capacity of general partner in effect for each of those persons when the obligation was incurred.

(2) If a person does not contribute the full amount required under paragraph (1) with respect to an unsatisfied obligation of the limited partnership, the other persons required to contribute by paragraph (1) on account of the obligation shall contribute the additional amount necessary to discharge the obligation. The additional contribution due from each of those other persons is in proportion to the right to receive distributions in the capacity of general partner in effect for each of those other persons when the obligation was incurred.

(3) If a person does not make the additional contribution required by paragraph (2), further additional contributions are determined and due in the same manner as provided in that paragraph.

(d) A person that makes an additional contribution under subsection (c)(2) or (3) may recover from any person whose failure to contribute under subsection (c)(1) or (2) necessitated the additional contribution. A person may not recover under this subsection more than the amount additionally contributed. A person's liability under this subsection may not exceed the amount the person failed to contribute.

(e) The estate of a deceased individual is liable for the person's obligations under this section.

(f) An assignee for the benefit of creditors of a limited partnership or a partner, or a person appointed by a court to represent creditors of a limited partnership or a partner, may enforce a person's obligation to contribute under subsection (c).

Summary: Provides for the distribution of partnership assets and for general partners' obligation to contribute toward payment of partnership debts.

Parallel U.L.P.A. 1985: § 804.

Parallel R.U.P.A.: § 807.

Parallel U.L.L.C.A.: § 806.

Bromberg & Ribstein: § 17.10.

Important Changes: U.L.P.A. 1985 provided priority for outside creditors and for payment of contribution obligations. It did not provide for contribution to payment of debts other then by possible linkage with R.U.P.A. § 807.

Analysis:

Subsection (a)–(b): Payments to partners as creditors would include distribution liabilities pursuant to U.L.P.A. § 507. Unlike under U.L.P.A. 1985, partners are on a parity with other creditors as to those obligations, consistent with U.L.P.A. § 508(e), but subject to other law, including the law on insider preferences. The "surplus" is distributed to the partners under subsection (b). "Surplus" is undefined but appears to refer to the amount exceeding obligations to creditors. It is not clear whether obligations to partner-creditors include amounts representing partner contributions. Unlike U.L.P.A. 1985, U.L.P.A. does not explicitly prioritize return of contributions, and unlike R.U.P.A. § 807 (to the extent that provision was linked to U.L.P.A.) does not refer to partner capital accounts. However, under U.L.P.A. § 503, distributions are shared according to contributions, which has an effect similar to U.L.P.A. 1985 and R.U.P.A. § 807 as long as the partners do not vary the Act with respect to allocation of interim distributions.

Subsection (c): This subsection provides for partner contributions to obligations incurred when the partnership was not an LLLP and when they were general partners. This is similar in effect to R.U.P.A. § 807, which provides that partners must contribute for obligations for which they are personally liable under § 306(c), which in turn refers to "an obligation incurred while the partnership is a limited liability partnership." The Act leaves determination of when the obligation was incurred to other law, thus creating ambiguity as to continuing obligations such as leases and lines of credit (*see* § 3.12). The partners share in these obligations, and in any obligation to pick up the "slack" for non-contributing partners under U.L.P.A. § 812(c)(2)-(3) and (d), in proportion to distribution shares rather than loss shares under R.U.P.A. § 807. It is not clear whether partners' contribution obligations include amounts owed to partners on account of capital contributions—i.e., "capital losses." The Comment states that contributions for capital losses are not part of "the limited partnership's obligations to creditors." But that is not obvious, since obligation is undefined. Thus, the black letter would seem to raise issues similar to those under R.U.P.A. § 807, discussed in § 8.807.

Waiver: This section is not one of the non-waivable provisions listed in U.L.P.A. § 110. However, under U.L.P.A. § 110(b)(13), the partnership agreement cannot contract around this section to the extent that would restrict third party rights, including the right to recover out of partner contributions.

§ 9.901.   GOVERNING LAW

Section 901

(a) The laws of the State or other jurisdiction under which a foreign limited partnership is organized govern relations among the partners of the foreign limited partnership and between the partners and the foreign limited partnership and the liability of partners as partners for an obligation of the foreign limited partnership.

(b) A foreign limited partnership may not be denied a certificate of authority by reason of any difference between the laws of the jurisdiction under which the foreign limited partnership is organized and the laws of this State.

(c) A certificate of authority does not authorize a foreign limited partnership to engage in any business or exercise any power that a limited partnership may not engage in or exercise in this State.

Summary: (a) The laws of the organization state govern relations among the partners and between the partners and the firm and the partners' liability for the firm's obligations; (b) a foreign limited partnership may not be denied a certificate of authority by reason of any difference between the laws of the formation jurisdiction and of this State; (c) a foreign limited partnership is not authorized to engage in any business or exercise any power that a domestic limited partnership may not engage in or exercise.

Parallel U.L.P.A. 1985: § 901.

Parallel R.U.P.A.: None.

Parallel U.L.L.C.A.: § 1001.

Bromberg & Ribstein: § 1.04.

Important Changes: Adds subsection (c).

Analysis: This section is based on ULLA § 1001. U.L.P.A. § 901(c) is a counterpart to U.L.P.A. § 106, which provides for the same effect of domestic law for domestic limited partnerships.

§ 9.902. APPLICATION FOR CERTIFICATE OF AUTHORITY

Section 902

(a) A foreign limited partnership may apply for a certificate of authority to transact business in this State by delivering an application to the [Secretary of State] for filing. The application must state:

(1) the name of the foreign limited partnership and, if the name does not comply with Section 108, an alternate name adopted pursuant to Section 905(a).

(2) the name of the State or other jurisdiction under whose law the foreign limited partnership is organized;

(3) the street and mailing address of the foreign limited partnership's principal office and, if the laws of the jurisdiction under which the foreign limited partnership is organized require the foreign limited partnership to maintain an office in that jurisdiction, the street and mailing address of the required office;

(4) the name and street and mailing address of the foreign limited partnership's initial agent for service of process in this State;

(5) the name and street and mailing address of each of the foreign limited partnership's general partners; and

(6) whether the foreign limited partnership is a foreign limited liability limited partnership.

(b) A foreign limited partnership shall deliver with the completed application a certificate of existence or a record of similar import signed by the [Secretary of State] or other official having custody of the foreign limited partnership's publicly filed records in the State or other jurisdiction under whose law the foreign limited partnership is organized.

§ 9.903.　ACTIVITIES NOT CONSTITUTING TRANSACTING BUSINESS

Section 903

(a) Activities of a foreign limited partnership which do not constitute transacting business in this State within the meaning of this [article] include:

(1) maintaining, defending, and settling an action or proceeding;

(2) holding meetings of its partners or carrying on any other activity concerning its internal affairs;

(3) maintaining accounts in financial institutions;

(4) maintaining offices or agencies for the transfer, exchange, and registration of the foreign limited partnership's own securities or maintaining trustees or depositories with respect to those securities;

(5) selling through independent contractors;

(6) soliciting or obtaining orders, whether by mail or electronic means or through employees or agents or otherwise, if the orders require acceptance outside this State before they become contracts;

(7) creating or acquiring indebtedness, mortgages, or security interests in real or personal property;

(8) securing or collecting debts or enforcing mortgages or other security interests in property securing the debts, and holding, protecting, and maintaining property so acquired;

(9) conducting an isolated transaction that is completed within 30 days and is not one in the course of similar transactions of a like manner; and

(10) transacting business in interstate commerce.

(b) For purposes of this [article], the ownership in this State of income-producing real property or tangible personal property, other than property excluded under subsection (a), constitutes transacting business in this State.

(c) This section does not apply in determining the contacts or activities that may subject a foreign limited partnership to service of process, taxation, or regulation under any other law of this State.

§ 9.904. FILING OF CERTIFICATE OF AUTHORITY

Section 904

Unless the [Secretary of State] determines that an application for a certificate of authority does not comply with the filing requirements of this [Act], the [Secretary of State], upon payment of all filing fees, shall file the application, prepare, sign and file a certificate of authority to transact business in this State, and send a copy of the filed certificate, together with a receipt for the fees, to the foreign limited partnership or its representative.

§ 9.905. NONCOMPLYING NAME OF FOREIGN LIMITED PARTNERSHIP

Section 905

(a) A foreign limited partnership whose name does not comply with Section 108 may not obtain a certificate of authority until it adopts, for the purpose of transacting business in this State, an alternate name that complies with Section 108. A foreign limited partnership that adopts an alternate name under this subsection and then obtains a certificate of authority with the name need not comply with [fictitious name statute]. After obtaining a certificate of authority with an alternate name, a foreign limited partnership shall transact business in this State under the name unless the foreign limited partnership is authorized under [fictitious name statute] to transact business in this State under another name.

(b) If a foreign limited partnership authorized to transact business in this State changes its name to one that does not comply with Section 108, it may not thereafter transact business in this State until it complies with subsection (a) and obtains an amended certificate of authority.

§ 9.906. REVOCATION OF CERTIFICATE OF AUTHORITY

Section 906

(a) A certificate of authority of a foreign limited partnership to transact business in this State may be revoked by the [Secretary of State] in the manner provided in subsections (b) and (c) if the foreign limited partnership does not:

(1) pay, within 60 days after the due date, any fee, tax or penalty due to the [Secretary of State] under this [Act] or other law;

(2) deliver, within 60 days after the due date, its annual report required under Section 210;

(3) appoint and maintain an agent for service of process as required by Section 114(b); or

(4) deliver for filing a statement of a change under Section 115 within 30 days after a change has occurred in the name or address of the agent.

(b) In order to revoke a certificate of authority, the [Secretary of State] must prepare, sign, and file a notice of revocation and send a copy to the foreign limited partnership's agent for service of process in this State, or if the foreign limited partnership does not appoint and maintain a proper agent in this State, to the foreign limited partnership's designated office. The notice must state:

(1) the revocation's effective date, which must be at least 60 days after the date the [Secretary of State] sends the copy; and

(2) the foreign limited partnership's failures to comply with subsection (a) which are the reason for the revocation.

(c) The authority of the foreign limited partnership to transact business in this State ceases on the effective date of the notice of revocation unless before that date the foreign limited partnership cures each failure to comply with subsection (a) stated in the notice. If the foreign limited partnership cures the failures, the [Secretary of State] shall so indicate on the filed notice.

§ 9.907.   CANCELLATION OF CERTIFICATE OF AUTHORITY; EFFECT OF FAILURE TO HAVE CERTIFICATE

Section 907

(a) In order to cancel its certificate of authority to transact business in this State, a foreign limited partnership must deliver to the [Secretary of State] for filing a notice of cancellation. The certificate is canceled when the notice becomes effective under Section 206.

(b) A foreign limited partnership transacting business in this State may not maintain an action or proceeding in this State unless it has a certificate of authority to transact business in this State.

(c) The failure of a foreign limited partnership to have a certificate of authority to transact business in this State does not impair the validity of a contract or act of the foreign limited partnership or prevent the foreign limited partnership from defending an action or proceeding in this State.

(d) A partner of a foreign limited partnership is not liable for the obligations of the foreign limited partnership solely by reason of the foreign limited partnership's having transacted business in this State without a certificate of authority.

(e) If a foreign limited partnership transacts business in this State without a certificate of authority or cancels its certificate of authority, it appoints the [Secretary of State] as its agent for service of process for rights of action arising out of the transaction of business in this State.

§ 9.908.   ACTION BY [ATTORNEY GENERAL]

Section 908

The [Attorney General] may maintain an action to restrain a foreign limited partnership from transacting business in this State in violation of this [article].

Summary: These sections provide for application for, and filing, revocation and cancellation of certificate of authority to transact business in the state by a foreign limited partnership; define conduct that does not constitute transacting business; provide for compliance with U.L.P.A. § 108 regarding the firm's name.

Parallel U.L.P.A. 1985:   §§ 902, 903, 904, 906, 907 and 908.

Parallel R.U.P.A.:   None.

Parallel U.L.L.C.A.:   §§ 1002–1006, 1008–1009.

Bromberg & Ribstein: § 12.12.

Important Changes: Provides for list of activities not constituting the transaction of business.

Analysis: These sections are similar to U.L.P.A. 1985 but are based more closely on the U.L.L.C.A. provisions noted above, and are similar to existing law in many states for LLCs and limited partnerships.[77]

---

[77] *See* Ribstein & Keatinge, ch. 13.

§ 9.1001.   DIRECT ACTION BY PARTNER

Section 1001

(a) Subject to subsection (b), a partner may maintain a direct action against the limited partnership or another partner for legal or equitable relief, with or without an accounting as to the partnership's activities, to enforce the rights and otherwise protect the interests of the partner, including rights and interests under the partnership agreement or this [Act] or arising independently of the partnership relationship.

(b) A partner commencing a direct action under this section is required to plead and prove an actual or threatened injury that is not solely the result of an injury suffered or threatened to be suffered by the limited partnership.

(c) The accrual of, and any time limitation on, a right of action for a remedy under this section is governed by other law. A right to an accounting upon a dissolution and winding up does not revive a claim barred by law.

Summary: Provides for partner's direct action against limited partnership or another partner with or without an accounting for actual or threatened injury that is not solely the result of an injury suffered or threatened to be suffered by the limited partnership; accounting action does not revive a claim barred by law.

Parallel U.L.P.A. 1985:   None.

Parallel R.U.P.A.:   § 405(b).

Parallel U.L.L.C.A.:   § 410.

Bromberg & Ribstein: §§ 5.04(d); 6.08; 15.04(e)–(i)

Important Changes: New, except to the extent R.U.P.A. § 405(b) is linked to U.L.P.A.

Analysis: This section provides for direct actions against the partnership or another partner. U.L.P.A. §§ 1002–1005 concern derivative actions.

Subsection (a):   This section is based on R.U.P.A. § 405(b), discussed in § 8.405. It clarifies partners' right to sue outside of an accounting, contrary to the case law under U.P.A. § 22. As discussed in § 8.405, eliminating the exclusivity of the accounting remedy for direct suits is not necessarily a good idea because this permits partners unilaterally to burden the firm with costly litigation.

Subsection (b): This section provides that the partner must show "an actual or threatened injury that is not solely the result of an injury suffered or threatened to be suffered by the limited partnership." This is the first statutory provision attempting to distinguish direct and derivative actions, an issue that was formerly left to common law development. The issue is obviously important given the special requirements for derivative suits in U.L.P.A. §§ 1002–1005. The test under this section is generally consistent with the general standard applied in partnership cases. However, the distinction is hazy. Thus, a rigid statutory definition may affect the results in some individual cases because it differs from the flexible common law approach developed in the case law discussed in Bromberg & Ribstein. One possible change is made by this provision's reference to "threatened" harm, which suggests that the same direct/derivative distinction applied to damage suits also is applied to claims for injunctive relief. Such suits arguably ought to be distinguished from other claims because the lack of a need to apportion damages makes derivative recovery less necessary.

Provisions or commentary elsewhere in U.L.P.A. refer to the distinction in this section. *See* the Comment to § 408 and the language of 604(c) making liability of a wrongfully dissociating partner to the other partners "subject to Section 1001." Although this language attempts to preserve the distinction between direct and derivative claims, it only highlights the difficulty of making this distinction.

Waiver: U.L.P.A. § 110(b)(11) provides that the partnership agreement may not "unreasonably restrict the right to maintain an action under [Article] 10." This would include the right to sue directly under U.L.P.A. § 1001. The wisdom of restricting the power to contract regarding partnership litigation is discussed in § 9.1002, below.

§ 9.1002. DERIVATIVE ACTION

Section 1002

A partner may maintain a derivative action to enforce a right of a limited partnership if:

(1) the partner first makes a demand on the general partners, requesting that they cause the limited partnership to bring an action to enforce the right, and the general partners do not bring the action within a reasonable time; or

(2) a demand would be futile.

Summary: A partner may maintain a derivative action to enforce a limited partnership right upon demand or if a demand would be futile.

Parallel U.L.P.A. 1985:   § 1001.

Parallel R.U.P.A.:   None.

Parallel U.L.L.C.A.:   §§ 1101–1104.

Bromberg & Ribstein: § 15.05.

Important Changes: Permits "partner," which would include a general partner, to bring a derivative suit.

Analysis: A new uniform law would have been a good opportunity to reconsider the appropriateness of derivative suit provisions long provided for in limited partnership law.[78] Instead, U.L.P.A. substantially replicates prior law. Although similar provisions are included in U.L.L.C.A., approximately a third of LLC statutes do not include such provisions.[79] This serves as a possible precedent for limited partnerships, particularly since the elimination of the limited partnership "control" rule (*see* U.L.P.A. § 303) increases the resemblance between LLCs and limited partnerships.

The costs of the derivative remedy may well outweigh the benefits even in the corporate context for which the remedy was designed.[80] The problem is that the derivative remedy permits an individual owner to decide to burden the firm with significant litigation expense. But the need for a derivative remedy is significantly greater in a publicly held firm where shareholders otherwise would have to gain authority to sue from many other shareholders, and where it may be particularly difficult to apportion the recovery among individual members. In firms that seek to be taxed as partnerships, on the other hand, tax rules inhibit widespread ownership.[81] A default derivative remedy is particularly unjustified in LLCs, where members are protected by information, veto and removal rights that exceed those of corporate shareholders.[82] A better alternative in this situation is that provided for in the Prototype Act[83] permitting suit by one or more members

---

[78] For an analysis of derivative suits in LLCs and a comparison between LLCs and limited partnerships, see Ribstein, Reforming Limited Liability Company Fiduciary Litigation, *available at* http://papers.ssrn.com/sol3/papers.cfm?abstract_id=1146662.

[79] *See* Ribstein & Keatinge, App. 10-1.

[80] *See generally* Fischel & Bradley, The Role of Liability Rules and the Derivative Suit in Corporate Law: A Theoretical and Empirical Analysis, 71 Cornell L. Rev. 261 (1986).

[81] *See* I.R.C. § 7704.

[82] *See* Ribstein & Keatinge, § 10.03; U.L.L.C.A. Comments, at 383–86.

[83] *See* Prototype LLC Act, § 1102.

of a member-managed LLC or by managers of a manager-managed LLC, if authorized by a majority of disinterested members or managers.

It is less clear whether to provide by default for derivative suits in limited partnerships. Although limited partners can now contract to participate in management (*see* U.L.P.A. § 303), in the default limited partnership they can vote only on important transactions (*see* § 9.302, above). Also, limited partners have somewhat less right to information under U.L.P.A. § 304 than do LLC members under U.L.L.C.A. § 408. More importantly, limited partners under U.L.P.A. lack a power to dissociate at any time and receive payment for their interest (*see* U.L.P.A. §§ 505 and 601), in contrast to the dissociation and dissolution rights of LLC members (*see* U.L.L.C.A. §§ 601 and 603). This makes limited partners significantly more vulnerable, and therefore arguably more in need of a right to sue, than LLC members. Moreover, even if LLC members should have a right to sue for injuries to the firm, the right arguably should be direct rather than derivative. Note that in close corporations the American Law Institute has recommended that courts treat derivative claims as direct actions in certain circumstances.[84] A derivative claim may do the members little good because the recovery goes to the firm under U.L.P.A. § 1005 and therefore is subject to misuse by the very managers who were the subject of the suit. Unlike in a public corporation, the partners cannot take advantage of the recovery by selling their shares in a public market.

Waiver: Under U.L.P.A. § 110(b)(11) the partnership agreement may not "unreasonably restrict the right to maintain an action under [Article] 10." It is not clear what an "unreasonable" restriction would be. The Comment says that this would prohibit a provision subjecting derivative claims to final determination by a special litigation committee. This raises many questions concerning variations on a special litigation committee's power, the types of actions that a special litigation committee may be able to block, and other procedural requirements. It is also not clear whether the agreement may substitute other remedies for derivative suits, particularly including arbitration. The Comment to U.L.P.A. § 110(b)(9) says that federal law precludes elimination of arbitration, but leaves unclear U.L.P.A.'s effect on intrastate arbitration contracts that federal law does not cover. Would substituting arbitration for a derivative remedy be "unreasonable"? Alternatively, could the parties "reasonably" provide for a remedy similar to that under the Prototype Act discussed above?

Apart from these issues, there is little justification for any restriction on the partners' power to contract regarding derivative suits. Particularly given the above reservations concerning the appropriateness of the derivative remedy for some firms, there is a strong argument the parties to the firm should be able to contract out of the derivative remedy. U.L.L.C.A. § 103 does not make the

---

[84] *See* Principles of Corporate Governance, § 7.01(d).

remedy non-waivable.[85] To be sure, the U.L.L.C.A. drafters suggested that limitations on contracting out of fiduciary duties may apply to contracting out of the remedy as well.[86] But whether or not such limitations are justifiable (*see* § 9.408), a remedy may be non-mandatory even if it relates to a mandatory duty.

State variation: **California** explicitly authorizes arbitration and choice-of-forum clauses, but specifies that the clause may not exclude jurisdiction in California courts.[87]

§ 9.1003.   PROPER PLAINTIFF

Section 1003

A derivative action may be maintained only by a person that is a partner at the time the action is commenced and:
(1) that was a partner when the conduct giving rise to the action occurred; or
(2) whose status as a partner devolved upon the person by operation of law or pursuant to the terms of the partnership agreement from a person that was a partner at the time of the conduct.

Summary: Derivative action may be maintained by a person that is a partner at the time the action is commenced and was a partner at the time of the conduct giving rise to the action or obtained such status from such a partner by operation of law or the partnership agreement.

Parallel U.L.P.A. 1985:   § 1002.

Parallel R.U.P.A.:   None.

Parallel U.L.L.C.A.:   § 1002.

Bromberg & Ribstein: § 15.05.

Important Changes: None.

Analysis: *See* Bromberg & Ribstein, § 15.05(g).

---

[85] *See* U.L.L.C.A. Comments, at 386.
[86] *See* Comment to U.L.L.C.A. § 1101.
[87] Cal. Corp. Code § 15901.17.

State variation: California provides for the court to allow a partner who does not meet the statutory standing requirements to bring suit based on evidence of a strong prima facie case in favor of the claim, no other similar action has been or is likely to be instituted, the plaintiff acquired the shares before disclosure of the wrongdoing, allowing the action is necessary to prevent defendant to gain from a wilful breach of fiduciary duty, and the relief request by plaintiff will not result in unjust enrichment of the partnership or any partner.[88]

§ 9.1004. PLEADING

Section 1004

In a derivative action, the complaint must state with particularity:
(1) the date and content of plaintiff's demand and the general partners' response to the demand; or
(2) why demand should be excused as futile.

Summary: Complaint must plead demand or why demand should be excused as futile.

Parallel U.L.P.A. 1985: § 1003.

Parallel R.U.P.A.: None.

Parallel U.L.L.C.A.: § 1103.

Bromberg & Ribstein: § 15.05.

Important Changes: None.

Analysis: *See* Bromberg & Ribstein, § 15.05(g).

State variation: California requires a derivative suit complaint to state with particularity the date and content of plaintiff's demand and the general partners' response to the demand or why demand is excused as futile.[89]

---

[88] *Id.* § 15910.03.
[89] *Id.* § 15910.04.

§ 9.1005.   PROCEEDS AND EXPENSES

Section 1005

(a) Except as otherwise provided in subsection (b):

(1) any proceeds or other benefits of a derivative action, whether by judgment, compromise, or settlement, belong to the limited partnership and not to the derivative plaintiff;

(2) if the derivative plaintiff receives any proceeds, the derivative plaintiff shall immediately remit them to the limited partnership.

(b) If a derivative action is successful in whole or in part, the court may award the plaintiff reasonable expenses, including reasonable attorney's fees, from the recovery of the limited partnership.

Summary: Proceeds belong to the limited partnership except for reasonable expenses, including attorney's fees, paid from the recovery.

Parallel U.L.P.A. 1985:   § 1004.

Parallel R.U.P.A.:   None.

Parallel U.L.L.C.A.:   § 1104.

Bromberg & Ribstein: § 15.05.

Important Changes: None.

Analysis: *See* Bromberg & Ribstein, § 15.05(g).

State variation: **California** permits the limited partnership or a general partner to move to require plaintiff to post a bond for reasonable expenses, including attorneys' fees, up to $50,000 if there is no reasonable possibility that the prosecution of the alleged cause of action will benefit the limited partnership or its partners, or the partner did not participate in the transaction complained of.[90]

---

[90] *Id.* § 15910.06.

§ 9.1101.   DEFINITIONS

Section 1101

In this [article]:

(1) "Constituent limited partnership" means a constituent organization that is a limited partnership.

(2) "Constituent organization" means an organization that is party to a merger.

(3) "Converted organization" means the organization into which a converting organization converts pursuant to Sections 1102 through 1105.

(4) "Converting limited partnership" means a converting organization that is a limited partnership.

(5) "Converting organization" means an organization that converts into another organization pursuant to Section 1102.

(6) "General partner" means a general partner of a limited partnership.

(7) "Governing statute" of an organization means the statute that governs the organization's internal affairs.

(8) "Organization" means a general partnership, including a limited liability partnership; limited partnership, including a limited liability limited partnership; limited liability company; business trust; corporation; or any other person having a governing statute. The term includes domestic and foreign organizations whether or not organized for profit.

(9) "Organizational documents" means:

(A) for a domestic or foreign general partnership, its partnership agreement;

(B) for a limited partnership or foreign limited partnership, its certificate of limited partnership and partnership agreement;

(C) for a domestic or foreign limited liability company, its articles of organization and operating agreement, or comparable records as provided in its governing statute;

(D) for a business trust, its agreement of trust and declaration of trust;

(E) for a domestic or foreign corporation for profit, its articles of incorporation, bylaws, and other agreements among its shareholders which are authorized by its governing statute, or comparable records as provided in its governing statute; and

(F) for any other organization, the basic records that create the organization and determine its internal governance and the relations among the persons that own it, have an interest in it, or are members of it.

(10) "Personal liability" means personal liability for a debt, liability, or other obligation of an organization which is imposed on a person that co-owns, has an interest in, or is a member of the organization:

(A) by the organization's governing statute solely by reason of the person co-owning, having an interest in, or being a member of the organization; or

(B) by the organization's organizational documents under a provision of the organization's governing statute authorizing those documents to make one or more specified persons liable for all or specified debts, liabilities, and other obligations of the organization solely by reason of the person or persons co-owning, having an interest in, or being a member of the organization.

(11) "Surviving organization" means an organization into which one or more other organizations are merged. A surviving organization may preexist the merger or be created by the merger.

Summary: Defines terms for purposes of this Article.

Parallel U.L.P.A. 1985:   None.

Parallel R.U.P.A.:   § 901.

Parallel U.L.L.C.A.:   § 901.

Bromberg & Ribstein: § 17.21.

Important Changes: New provision, except to the extent R.U.P.A. Article 9 is linked to U.L.P.A. 1985.

Analysis: Specific definitions are discussed below to the extent relevant.

§ 9.1102.   CONVERSION

Section 1102

(a) An organization other than a limited partnership may convert to a limited partnership, and a limited partnership may convert to another organization pursuant to this section and Sections 1103 through 1105 and a plan of conversion, if:

(1) the other organization's governing statute authorizes the conversion;

(2) the conversion is not prohibited by the law of the jurisdiction that enacted the governing statute; and

(3) the other organization complies with its governing statute in effecting the conversion.

(b) A plan of conversion must be in a record and must include:

(1) the name and form of the organization before conversion;

(2) the name and form of the organization after conversion; and

(3) the terms and conditions of the conversion, including the manner and basis for converting interests in the converting organization into any combination of money, interests in the converted organization, and other consideration; and

(4) the organizational documents of the converted organization.

Summary: Permits conversion between "organization" (defined very broadly in U.L.P.A. 1101(8)) and limited partnership.

Parallel U.L.P.A. 1985: None.

Parallel R.U.P.A.: §§ 902–903.

Parallel U.L.L.C.A.: §§ 902–903.

Bromberg & Ribstein: § 17.21.

Important Changes: New provision, except to the extent R.U.P.A. §§ 902–903 (permitting conversion between general and limited partnership) are linked to U.L.P.A. 1985.

Analysis: A conversion, in contrast with a merger, involves only a single business entity, although the effect may be virtually the same as a merger that involves a shell entity.

Subsection (a): A converting domestic limited partnership must comply with this Act, including provisions regarding fiduciary duties and information and voting rights, while an organization other than a domestic limited partnership must comply with the applicable statute. This applies, among other things, to determining any rules regarding squeeze-outs that might result from conversion of ownership interests under subsection (b)(3). Also, as the Comment notes, the applicable law includes any prohibition on the form of the converted entity, as where a non-profit limited partnership permitted by U.L.P.A. seeks to convert into a limited partnership formed under a statute that does not allow non-profit limited partnerships.

Subsection (b): The plan of conversion, which is dealt with in § 1103, must be in writing. It is not clear what the effect is of not having a plan, or of having a plan that is not in a "record." Even if the transaction is not effective as a "conversion" under this section, it may be effective by its terms under U.L.P.A. § 110 discussed immediately below.

Waiver: This section is not one of the nonwaivable provisions listed in § 110(b). It seems to follow that the agreement may, for example, prohibit all or certain forms of conversions or change the requirements regarding the plan in subsection (b), perhaps including the writing requirement. Alternatively, pursuant to the non-exclusivity provision in U.L.P.A. § 1113, the firm may be able to pursue procedures other than statutory conversion that have similar effects (*see* § 8.904). Section 110(b)(13) prohibits the agreement from restricting non-partner rights, which might affect contracts waiving subsection (b). Also, U.L.P.A. obviously cannot effectively authorize agreements that violate the statutes of other states. An alternative procedure might be authorized under the non-exclusivity provision of U.L.P.A. § 1113 even if it does affect third parties. But given the uncertainty of the effects of non-complying procedures, this provision serves as a safe harbor for conversions.

§ 9.1103.   ACTION ON PLAN OF CONVERSION BY CONVERTING LIMITED PARTNERSHIP

Section 1103

(a) Subject to Section 1110, a plan of conversion must be consented to by all the partners of a converting limited partnership.

(b) Subject to Section 1110 and any contractual rights, after a conversion is approved, and at any time before a filing is made under Section 1104, a converting limited partnership may amend the plan or abandon the planned conversion:

(1) as provided in the plan; and

(2) except as prohibited by the plan, by the same consent as was required to approve the plan.

Summary: Provides for unanimous approval of plan of conversion and for amendment of the plan.

Parallel U.L.P.A. 1985:   None.

Parallel R.U.P.A.:   § 902(b); § 903(b).

Parallel U.L.L.C.A.:   § 902.

Bromberg & Ribstein: §17.21.

Important Changes: New provision, except to the extent R.U.P.A. is linked to U.L.P.A. 1985.

Analysis: This section is subject to contrary agreement under U.L.P.A. 110(b). It follows that the parties may be able to waive the unanimity voting rule, subject to §1110 (*see* U.L.P.A. §110(b)(12) and §9.1110, below), or perhaps even the requirement of a plan. Moreover, a procedure that does not comply with this section may be enforceable under the non-exclusivity provision of U.L.P.A. §1113, making this provision in effect a safe harbor. Since agreements varying the requirements in this section need not be in writing pursuant to U.L.P.A. §102(13) and 110, dispensing with a written plan may itself be viewed as an enforceable agreement to do so, thereby casting in doubt the effectiveness of the writing requirement.

State variation: **California** provides for appraisal rights for limited partners dissenting from a reorganization, which includes a conversion.

§9.1104. FILINGS REQUIRED FOR CONVERSION; EFFECTIVE DATE

Section 1104

(a) After a plan of conversion is approved:

(1) a converting limited partnership shall deliver to the [Secretary of State] for filing articles of conversion, which must include:

(A) a statement that the limited partnership has been converted into another organization;

(B) the name and form of the organization and the jurisdiction of its governing statute;

(C) the date the conversion is effective under the governing statute of the converted organization;

(D) a statement that the conversion was approved as required by this [Act];

(E) a statement that the conversion was approved as required by the governing statute of the converted organization; and

(F) if the converted organization is a foreign organization not authorized to transact business in this State, the street and mailing address of an office which the [Secretary of State] may use for the purposes of Section 1105(c); and

(2) if the converting organization is not a converting limited partnership, the converting organization shall deliver to the [Secretary of State] for filing a certificate of limited partnership, which must include, in addition to the information required by Section 201:

(A) a statement that the limited partnership was converted from another organization;

(B) the name and form of the organization and the jurisdiction of its governing statute; and

(C) a statement that the conversion was approved in a manner that complied with the organization's governing statute.

(b) A conversion becomes effective:

(1) if the converted organization is a limited partnership, when the certificate of limited partnership takes effect; and

(2) if the converted organization is not a limited partnership, as provided by the governing statute of the converted organization.

Summary: Requires delivery for filing of a statement that firm has converted into or from a limited partnership.

Parallel U.L.P.A. 1985:   None.

Parallel R.U.P.A.:   § 902(c), 903(c)–(d).

Parallel U.L.L.C.A.:   § 902(d)–(f).

Bromberg & Ribstein: § 17.21.

Important Changes: New provision, unless R.U.P.A. linked to U.L.P.A. 1985 regarding partnership conversions.

Analysis: It is not clear what the effect is of failure to file the statement of conversion.[91] The conversion should be effective at least among the members. Note that this provision is not one of the non-waivable provisions under U.L.P.A. § 110(b), although it may be subject to U.L.P.A. § 110(b)(13) regarding restriction of third party rights. The effectiveness under U.L.P.A. § 1113 of an alternative procedure having similar effects but without a filing is not clear.

---

[91] *See* U.L.L.C.A. Comments, at 382.

§ 9.1105. EFFECT OF CONVERSION

Section 1105

(a) An organization that has been converted pursuant to this [article] is for all purposes the same entity that existed before the conversion.

(b) When a conversion takes effect:

(1) all property owned by the converting organization remains vested in the converted organization;

(2) all debts, liabilities, and other obligations of the converting organization continue as obligations of the converted organization;

(3) an action or proceeding pending by or against the converting organization may be continued as if the conversion had not occurred;

(4) except as prohibited by other law, all of the rights, privileges, immunities, powers, and purposes of the converting organization remain vested in the converted organization;

(5) except as otherwise provided in the plan of conversion, the terms and conditions of the plan of conversion take effect; and

(6) except as otherwise agreed, the conversion does not dissolve a converting limited partnership for the purposes of [Article] 8.

(c) A converted organization that is a foreign organization consents to the jurisdiction of the courts of this State to enforce any obligation owed by the converting limited partnership, if before the conversion the converting limited partnership was subject to suit in this State on the obligation. A converted organization that is a foreign organization and not authorized to transact business in this State appoints the [Secretary of State] as its agent for service of process for purposes of enforcing an obligation under this subsection. Service on the [Secretary of State] under this subsection is made in the same manner and with the same consequences as in Section 117(c) and (d).

Summary: Provides that the converted firm continues to be the same entity, that all property and liabilities of the old firm become that of the new one, and for suits against foreign converted organizations.

Parallel U.L.P.A. 1985: None.

Parallel R.U.P.A.: § 904.

Parallel U.L.L.C.A.: § 903.

Bromberg & Ribstein: § 17.21.

Important Changes: New provision, unless R.U.P.A. provisions similar to § 1105(a)–(b) linked to U.L.P.A. 1985 regarding conversion between general and limited partnership.

Analysis:

Subsection (a):   The Comment provides that "a conversion changes an entity's legal type, but does not create a new entity." As discussed in § 8.904, it is not clear what this means—for example, whether conversion triggers an obligation to pay real estate transfer fees on the theory that real property transfers to the converted firm. Although, pursuant to U.L.P.A. § 1111(b), the creditor does not lose the vicarious liability of existing owners, the creditor may not be able to sue post-conversion members who might otherwise have been personally liable as partners for continuing obligations such as post-admission lease payments.[92]

Subsection (b):   The Comment points out that a conversion, unlike a merger, does not transfer any of the entity's rights or obligations. It arguably follows that a conversion does not involve a fraudulent conveyance.[93]

Waiver: This section is not listed as non-waivable under U.L.P.A. § 110(b), except to the extent that a provision restricts third-party rights under § 110(b)(13). Thus, the parties may be able to contract for different effects of the conversion, or for a procedure other than a conversion that has different effects pursuant to the non-exclusivity provision in U.L.P.A. § 1113. Also, this section provides for the effects of the conversion alone as distinguished from agreements or other transactions associated with the conversion.

§ 9.1106.   MERGER

Section 1106

(a) A limited partnership may merge with one or more other constituent organizations pursuant to this section and Sections 1107 through 1109 and a plan of merger, if:

---

[92] *See* U.L.L.C.A. Comments, at 381. For cases involving the effect of conversions into LLCs, see Ribstein & Keatinge, § 11.13.

[93] *See* § 8.904; Kanefield v. SP Distrib. Co., LLC, 25 S.W.3d 492 (Mo. App. 2000) (involving conversion of LLC). *But see* Baker v. Dorfman, 2000 WL 1010285 (S.D.N.Y. 2000) (LLC formed by a sole proprietor liable as successor for sole proprietor's debts as a fraudulent attempt to escape sole proprietor's obligations).

(1) the governing statute of each the other organizations authorizes the merger;

(2) the merger is not prohibited by the law of a jurisdiction that enacted any of those governing statutes; and

(3) each of the other organizations complies with its governing statute in effecting the merger.

(b) A plan of merger must be in a record and must include:

(1) the name and form of each constituent organization;

(2) the name and form of the surviving organization and, if the surviving organization is to be created by the merger, a statement to that effect;

(3) the terms and conditions of the merger, including the manner and basis for converting the interests in each constituent organization into any combination of money, interests in the surviving organization, and other consideration;

(4) if the surviving organization is to be created by the merger, the surviving organization's organizational documents; and

(5) if the surviving organization is not to be created by the merger, any amendments to be made by the merger to the surviving organization's organizational documents.

Summary: A limited partnership may merge with one or more business organizations by a plan of merger if the transaction complies with the organizations' governing statutes.

Parallel U.L.P.A. 1985:   None.

Parallel R.U.P.A.:   § 905.

Parallel U.L.L.C.A.:   § 904.

Bromberg & Ribstein: § 17.21.

Important Changes: New provision, except to the extent that R.U.P.A. was linked to U.L.P.A. (1985) regarding partnership mergers.

Analysis: This provision is similar to U.L.P.A. § 1102, and the **Analysis** in § 9.1102 is also relevant here.[94]

---

[94] *See also* U.L.L.C.A. § 904; U.L.L.C.A. Comments.

§ 9.1107. ACTION ON PLAN OF MERGER BY CONSTITUENT LIMITED PARTNERSHIP

Section 1107

(a) Subject to Section 1110, a plan of merger must be consented to by all the partners of a constituent limited partnership.

(b) Subject to Section 1110 and any contractual rights, after a merger is approved, and at any time before a filing is made under Section 1108, a constituent limited partnership may amend the plan or abandon the planned merger:

(1) as provided in the plan; and

(2) except as prohibited by the plan, with the same consent as was required to approve the plan.

Summary: Provides for unanimous approval of plan of merger by members of constituent limited partnership and for amendment of the plan.

Parallel U.L.P.A. 1985:   None.

Parallel R.U.P.A.:   § 905.

Parallel U.L.L.C.A.:   None.

Important Changes: New provision, except to the extent R.U.P.A. is linked to U.L.P.A. 1985 regarding partnership mergers.

Analysis: This provision is similar to U.L.P.A. § 1103, and the **Analysis** in § 9.1103 also relates to this provision.[95]

State variations:

California provides for appraisal rights for limited partners dissenting from a reorganization, which includes a merger.[96]

Washington provides for appraisal rights for limited partners dissenting from a merger.[97]

---

[95] *See also* U.L.L.C.A. Comments, at 382.

[96] *Id.* §§ 15911.20–15911.33.

[97] 2009 Washington House Bill No. 1067, 61st Legislature, 2009 Regular Session, §§ 1201–1212.

§ 9.1108. FILINGS REQUIRED FOR MERGER; EFFECTIVE DATE

Section 1108

(a) After each constituent organization has approved a merger, articles of merger must be signed on behalf of:

(1) each preexisting constituent limited partnership, by each general partner listed in the certificate of limited partnership; and

(2) each other preexisting constituent organization, by an authorized representative.

(b) The articles of merger must include:

(1) the name and form of each constituent organization and the jurisdiction of its governing statute;

(2) the name and form of the surviving organization, the jurisdiction of its governing statute, and, if the surviving organization is created by the merger, a statement to that effect;

(3) the date the merger is effective under the governing statute of the surviving organization;

(4) if the surviving organization is to be created by the merger:

(A) if it will be a limited partnership, the limited partnership's certificate of limited partnership; or

(B) if it will be an organization other than a limited partnership, the organizational document that creates the organization;

(5) if the surviving organization preexists the merger, any amendments provided for in the plan of merger for the organizational document that created the organization;

(6) a statement as to each constituent organization that the merger was approved as required by the organization's governing statute;

(7) if the surviving organization is a foreign organization not authorized to transact business in this State, the street and mailing address of an office which the [Secretary of State] may use for the purposes of Section 1109(b); and

(8) any additional information required by the governing statute of any constituent organization.

(c) Each constituent limited partnership shall deliver the articles of merger for filing in the [office of the Secretary of State].

(d) A merger becomes effective under this [article]:

(1) if the surviving organization is a limited partnership, upon the later of:

(i) compliance with subsection (c); or

(ii) subject to Section 206(c), as specified in the articles of merger; or

(2) if the surviving organization is not a limited partnership, as provided by the governing statute of the surviving organization.

Summary: Requires articles of merger signed and filed on behalf of pre-existing constituent organizations; provides for effectiveness of the merger for surviving limited partnership upon filing or otherwise under U.L.P.A. § 206(c), or per the governing statute of surviving organization that is not a limited partnership.

Parallel U.L.P.A. 1985:   None.

Parallel R.U.P.A.:   § 905(e).

Parallel U.L.L.C.A.:   § 905.

Bromberg & Ribstein: § 17.21.

Important Changes: New provision, except to the extent that R.U.P.A. was linked to U.L.P.A. 1985 with respect to partnership mergers.

Analysis: This provision is similar to U.L.P.A. § 1104, and the **Analysis** in § 9.1103 is also relevant here.[98]

§ 9.1109.   EFFECT OF MERGER

Section 1109

(a) When a merger becomes effective:
   (1) the surviving organization continues or comes into existence;
   (2) each constituent organization that merges into the surviving organization ceases to exist as a separate entity;
   (3) all property owned by each constituent organization that ceases to exist vests in the surviving organization;
   (4) all debts, liabilities, and other obligations of each constituent organization that ceases to exist continue as obligations of the surviving organization;
   (5) an action or proceeding pending by or against any constituent organization that ceases to exist may be continued as if the merger had not occurred;
   (6) except as prohibited by other law, all of the rights, privileges, immunities, powers, and purposes of each constituent organization that ceases to exist vest in the surviving organization;
   (7) except as otherwise provided in the plan of merger, the terms and conditions of the plan of merger take effect; and

---

[98] *See also* U.L.L.C.A. Comments, at 382.

(8) except as otherwise agreed, if a constituent limited partnership ceases to exist, the merger does not dissolve the limited partnership for the purposes of [Article] 8;

(9) if the surviving organization is created by the merger:

(A) if it is a limited partnership, the certificate of limited partnership becomes effective; or

(B) if it is an organization other than a limited partnership, the organizational document that creates the organization becomes effective; and

(10) if the surviving organization preexists the merger, any amendments provided for in the articles of merger for the organizational document that created the organization become effective.

(b) A surviving organization that is a foreign organization consents to the jurisdiction of the courts of this State to enforce any obligation owed by a constituent organization, if before the merger the constituent organization was subject to suit in this State on the obligation. A surviving organization that is a foreign organization and not authorized to transact business in this State appoints the [Secretary of State] as its agent for service of process for the purposes of enforcing an obligation under this subsection. Service on the [Secretary of State] under this subsection is made in the same manner and with the same consequences as in Section 117(c) and (d).

Summary: Specifies what happens when a merger becomes effective, including formation of surviving organization, cessation as separate entity of each merging organization, vesting and continuation of property, debts, rights and actions of disappearing organizations; enforcement in local state court of obligations of surviving foreign organizations.

Parallel U.L.P.A. 1985: None.

Parallel R.U.P.A.: § 906.

Parallel U.L.L.C.A.: § 906.

Bromberg & Ribstein: § 17.21.

Important Changes: New provision, except to the extent that R.U.P.A. is linked with U.L.P.A. 1985 concerning partnership mergers.

Analysis: Unlike dissolution, there is an immediate cessation of the disappearing firm rather than dissolution and winding up (*see* U.L.P.A. § 1109(a)(8) because the business is continued in the form of the surviving entity. However, it is not clear what this means apart from the specific effects listed in the section, and specifically whether termination of "separate existence" in this section means something different from saying that a firm that converts "is for all purposes the same entity" as before a conversion, pursuant to U.L.P.A. § 1105, discussed above in § 9.1105.[99] Issues concerning the effect of alternative procedures are the same as those discussed above in § 9.1105. Note that, unlike a conversion, there may be a transfer of the entity's debts and obligations for fraudulent transfer purposes.[100]

§ 9.1110.   RESTRICTIONS ON APPROVAL OF CONVERSIONS AND MERGERS AND ON RELINQUISHING LLLP STATUS

Section 1110

(a) If a partner of a converting or constituent limited partnership will have personal liability with respect to a converted or surviving organization, approval and amendment of a plan of conversion or merger are ineffective without the consent of the partner, unless:

(1) the limited partnership's partnership agreement provides for the approval of the conversion or merger with the consent of fewer than all the partners; and

(2) the partner has consented to the provision of the partnership agreement.

(b) An amendment to a certificate of limited partnership which deletes a statement that the limited partnership is a limited liability limited partnership is ineffective without the consent of each general partner unless:

(1) the limited partnership's partnership agreement provides for the amendment with the consent of less than all the general partners; and

(2) each general partner that does not consent to the amendment has consented to the provision of the partnership agreement.

(c) A partner does not give the consent required by subsection (a) or (b) merely by consenting to a provision of the partnership agreement which permits the partnership agreement to be amended with the consent of fewer than all the partners.

Summary: Approval or amendment of conversion or merger, or certificate amendment deleting LLLP designation, is ineffective without the consent of a partner who will have personal liability as a result of the transaction unless the partner has consented to a partnership agreement providing for sub-unanimous consent to such approval or amendment.

---

[99] *See also* U.L.L.C.A. Comments, at 382.
[100] *Cf.* Comment to § 1105(b).

Parallel U.L.P.A. 1985: None.

Parallel R.U.P.A.: §§ 902–903.

Parallel U.L.L.C.A.: None.

Bromberg & Ribstein: § 17.21.

Important Changes: New provision, except to the extent that R.U.P.A. is linked to U.L.P.A. 1985 with respect to partnership mergers and conversions (*see* § 9.903, above).

Analysis: As elaborated in the Comment, this section attempts to distinguish between a general amendment provision and one that specifically permits non-unanimous amendment to confer personal liability. It seems unlikely that many agreements will include this specific type of authorization. Also, it may not be clear when the amendment provision is specific enough to qualify under this section.

This protection may not be waived pursuant to U.L.P.A. § 110(b)(12). U.L.P.A. § 1110 apparently applies specifically to conversion and merger, and not to one of the procedures implicitly authorized under the non-exclusivity provision of U.L.P.A. § 1113. However, a court probably will apply the principle underlying this section to a procedure that has a similar effect. The question of the effect as to third parties of an amendment that did not receive the requisite consent is discussed above in § 9.202.

§ 9.1111. LIABILITY OF GENERAL PARTNER AFTER CONVERSION OR MERGER

Section 1111

(a) A conversion or merger under this [article] does not discharge any liability under Sections 404 and 607 of a person that was a general partner in or dissociated as a general partner from a converting or constituent limited partnership, but:

(1) the provisions of this [Act] pertaining to the collection or discharge of the liability continue to apply to the liability;

(2) for the purposes of applying those provisions, the converted or surviving organization is deemed to be the converting or constituent limited partnership; and

(3) if a person is required to pay any amount under this subsection:

(A) the person has a right of contribution from each other person that was liable as a general partner under Section 404 when the obligation was incurred and has not been released from the obligation under Section 607; and

(B) the contribution due from each of those persons is in proportion to the right to receive distributions in the capacity of general partner in effect for each of those persons when the obligation was incurred.

(b) In addition to any other liability provided by law:

(1) a person that immediately before a conversion or merger became effective was a general partner in a converting or constituent limited partnership that was not a limited liability limited partnership is personally liable for each obligation of the converted or surviving organization arising from a transaction with a third party after the conversion or merger becomes effective, if, at the time the third party enters into the transaction, the third party:

(A) does not have notice of the conversion or merger; and

(B) reasonably believes that:

(i) the converted or surviving business is the converting or constituent limited partnership;

(ii) the converting or constituent limited partnership is not a limited liability limited partnership; and

(iii) the person is a general partner in the converting or constituent limited partnership; and

(2) a person that was dissociated as a general partner from a converting or constituent limited partnership before the conversion or merger became effective is personally liable for each obligation of the converted or surviving organization arising from a transaction with a third party after the conversion or merger becomes effective, if:

(A) immediately before the conversion or merger became effective the converting or surviving limited partnership was a not a limited liability limited partnership; and

(B) at the time the third party enters into the transaction less than two years have passed since the person dissociated as a general partner and the third party:

(i) does not have notice of the dissociation;

(ii) does not have notice of the conversion or merger; and

(iii) reasonably believes that the converted or surviving organization is the converting or constituent limited partnership, the converting or constituent limited partnership is not a limited liability limited partnership, and the person is a general partner in the converting or constituent limited partnership.

Summary: Provides that a conversion or merger does not discharge the liability under this Act of a partner or dissociated partner under § 404 and

§ 607(b); a person who before the conversion or merger was a general partner with personal liability, or was a general partner dissociated from a non-LLLP general partnership, is personally liable for obligations of the converted or surviving organization to third parties without notice of the conversion or merger (dissociated partners are liable for transactions within two years of the disso-ciation to third parties who lacked notice of the dissociation) who reasonably believe that the person is general partner in a non-LLLP converting or constituent limited partnership.

Parallel U.L.P.A. 1985: None.

Parallel R.U.P.A.: § 906(c).

Parallel U.L.L.C.A.: § 906(c).

Bromberg & Ribstein: § 17.21.

Important Changes: New provision, except to the extent that R.U.P.A. was linked to U.L.P.A. 1985 with respect to partnership mergers.

Analysis: This section has an effect of continuing a partner's liability similar to that under U.L.P.A. § 607 for dissociated general partners who have liability in non-LLLP partnerships. *See* the **Analysis** in § 9.607. Although this provision is not non-waivable under U.L.P.A. § 110(b), waiver restricting third party rights is prohibited under U.L.P.A. § 110(b)(13). As with other provisions in this Article, this provision explicitly applies only to the procedures specified in this Article, although it may apply to an analogous transaction permitted under the non-exclusivity provision of U.L.P.A. § 1113.

§ 9.1112. POWER OF GENERAL PARTNERS AND PERSONS DISSOCIATED AS GENERAL PARTNERS TO BIND ORGANIZATION AFTER CONVERSION OR MERGER

Section 1112

(a) An act of a person that immediately before a conversion or merger became effective was a general partner in a converting or constituent limited partnership binds the converted or surviving organization after the conversion or merger becomes effective, if:

(1) before the conversion or merger became effective, the act would have bound the converting or constituent limited partnership under Section 402; and

(2) at the time the third party enters into the transaction, the third party:

(A) does not have notice of the conversion or merger; and

(B) reasonably believes that the converted or surviving business is the converting or constituent limited partnership and that the person is a general partner in the converting or constituent limited partnership.

(b) An act of a person that before a conversion or merger became effective was dissociated as a general partner from a converting or constituent limited partnership binds the converted or surviving organization after the conversion or merger becomes effective, if:

(1) before the conversion or merger became effective, the act would have bound the converting or constituent limited partnership under Section 402 if the person had been a general partner; and

(2) at the time the third party enters into the transaction, less than two years have passed since the person dissociated as a general partner and the third party:

(A) does not have notice of the dissociation;

(B) does not have notice of the conversion or merger; and

(C) reasonably believes that the converted or surviving organization is the converting or constituent limited partnership and that the person is a general partner in the converting or constituent limited partnership.

(c) If a person having knowledge of the conversion or merger causes a converted or surviving organization to incur an obligation under subsection (a) or (b), the person is liable:

(1) to the converted or surviving organization for any damage caused to the organization arising from the obligation; and

(2) if another person is liable for the obligation, to that other person for any damage caused to that other person arising from the liability.

Summary: Provides for the continuing power to bind of general partners in or partners dissociated from converting or merging partnerships.

Parallel U.L.P.A. 1985:   None.

Parallel R.U.P.A.:   None.

Parallel U.L.L.C.A.:   None.

Bromberg & Ribstein: § 17.21.

Important Changes: New provision.

Analysis: This section has an effect of continuing a partner's or dissociated partner's power to bind similar to that under U.L.P.A. § 606 for dissociated general partners. *See* the **Analysis** in § 9.606.

§ 9.1113.   [ARTICLE] NOT EXCLUSIVE

Section 1113

This [article] does not preclude an entity from being converted or merged under other law.

Summary: Provides that this Article does not preclude an entity from being converted or merged under other law.

Parallel U.L.P.A. 1985:   None.

Parallel R.U.P.A.:   § 908.

Parallel U.L.L.C.A.:   § 907.

Bromberg & Ribstein: § 17.21.

Important Changes: New provision, except to the extent that R.U.P.A. is linked to U.L.P.A. 1985 regarding partnership mergers and conversions.

Analysis:[101]   As discussed in the Analysis of the other provisions in this Article, this provision apparently has the effect of providing a "safe harbor" for mergers and conversions while not precluding analogous procedures. However, as discussed in § 8.901 regarding the similar R.U.P.A. provision, the Comments to R.U.P.A. suggest that the R.U.P.A. conversion and merger procedures are virtually exclusive and mandatory, in the sense that non-complying procedures will be ineffective or will not have the effects prescribed for complying procedures, particularly regarding partners' liability. Thus, converting or merging partnerships likely will follow the U.L.P.A. procedures even if they might have proceeded by asset sale/dissolution or similar transactions under prior law.

---

[101] *See also* U.L.L.C.A. Comments, at 382–83.

§ 9.1201.   UNIFORMITY OF APPLICATION AND CONSTRUCTION

Section 1201

In applying and construing this Uniform Act, consideration must be given to the need to promote uniformity of the law with respect to its subject matter among States that enact it.

Summary: Provides that, in applying and construing this Act, consideration must be given to the need to promote uniformity.

Parallel U.L.P.A. 1985:   § 1101.

Parallel R.U.P.A.:   § 1201.

Parallel U.L.L.C.A.:   § 1201.

Bromberg & Ribstein: §§ 1.02(b), 11.02.

Important Changes: None.

Analysis: This is a standard provision in uniform acts, consistent with the mission of uniform law drafters. It is not clear how this provision should be applied to the extent that U.L.P.A. 2001 changes *existing* uniform law.[102]

§ 9.1202.   SEVERABILITY CLAUSE

Section 1202

If any provision of this [Act] or its application to any person or circumstance is held invalid, the invalidity does not affect other provisions or applications of this [Act] which can be given effect without the invalid provision or application, and to this end the provisions of this [Act] are severable.

Summary: Provides that invalidity of any provision or application of this Act does not affect other provisions or applications.

Parallel U.L.P.A. 1985:   § 1103.

---

[102] *See* Revisited, at 998.

Parallel R.U.P.A.:   § 1203.

Parallel U.L.L.C.A.:   § 1203.

Bromberg & Ribstein: None.

Important Changes: None.

§ 9.1203.   RELATION TO ELECTRONIC SIGNATURES IN GLOBAL AND NATIONAL COMMERCE ACT

Section 1203

This [Act] modifies, limits, or supersedes the federal Electronic Signatures in Global and National Commerce Act, 15 U.S.C. Section 7001 *et seq.,* but this [Act] does not modify, limit, or supersede Section 101(c) of that Act or authorize electronic delivery of any of the notices described in Section 103(b) of that Act.

Summary: This Act modifies, limits, or supersedes the Electronic Signatures in Global and National Commerce Act, 15 U.S.C. Section 7001 *et seq.,* except for § 101(c) of that Act, but does not authorize electronic delivery of any of the notices described in § 103(b) of that Act.

Parallel U.L.P.A. 1985:   None.

Parallel R.U.P.A.:   None.

Parallel U.L.L.C.A.:   None.

Bromberg & Ribstein: None.

Important Changes: New provision.

§ 9.1204.   EFFECTIVE DATE

Section 1204

This [Act] takes effect [effective date].

Summary: Provides for effective date.

Parallel U.L.P.A. 1985:   § 1104 (first clause).

Parallel R.U.P.A.:   § 1204.

Important Changes and Analysis: *See* § 9.1206.

§ 9.1205.   REPEALS

Section 1205

Effective [all-inclusive date], the following acts and parts of acts are repealed: [the State Limited Partnership Act as amended and in effect immediately before the effective date of this [Act]].

Summary: Provides for repeal on the effective date of the state's limited partnership act.

Parallel U.L.P.A. 1985:   § 1104, second clause.

Parallel R.U.P.A.:   § 1205.

Important Changes and Analysis: *See* § 9.1206.

§ 9.1206.   APPLICATION TO EXISTING RELATIONSHIPS

Section 1206

(a) Before [all-inclusive date], this [Act] governs only:

(1) a limited partnership formed on or after [the effective date of this [Act]]; and

(2) except as otherwise provided in subsections (c) and (d), a limited partnership formed before [the effective date of this [Act]] which elects, in the manner provided in its partnership agreement or by law for amending the partnership agreement, to be subject to this [Act].

(b) Except as otherwise provided in subsection (c), on and after [all-inclusive date] this [Act] governs all limited partnerships.

(c) With respect to a limited partnership formed before [the effective date of this [Act]], the following rules apply except as the partners otherwise elect in the manner provided in the partnership agreement or by law for amending the partnership agreement:

(1) Section 104(c) does not apply and the limited partnership has whatever duration it had under the law applicable immediately before [the effective date of this [Act]].

(2) the limited partnership is not required to amend its certificate of limited partnership to comply with Section 201(a)(4).

(3) Sections 601 and 602 do not apply and a limited partner has the same right and power to dissociate from the limited partnership, with the same consequences, as existed immediately before [the effective date of this [Act].

(4) Section 603(4) does not apply.

(5) Section 603(5) does not apply and a court has the same power to expel a general partner as the court had immediately before [the effective date of this [Act]].

(6) Section 801(3) does not apply and the connection between a person's dissociation as a general partner and the dissolution of the limited partnership is the same as existed immediately before [the effective date of this [Act]].

(d) With respect to a limited partnership that elects pursuant to subsection (a)(2) to be subject to this [Act], after the election takes effect the provisions of this [Act] relating to the liability of the limited partnership's general partners to third parties apply:

(1) before [all-inclusive date], to:

(A) a third party that had not done business with the limited partnership in the year before the election took effect; and

(B) a third party that had done business with the limited partnership in the year before the election took effect only if the third party knows or has received a notification of the election; and

(2) on and after [all-inclusive date], to all third parties, but those provisions remain inapplicable to any obligation incurred while those provisions were inapplicable under paragraph (1)(B).

Summary: Provides for application of U.L.P.A. to existing limited partnerships.

Parallel U.L.P.A. 1985: § 1104.

Parallel R.U.P.A.: § 1206.

Parallel U.L.L.C.A.: § 1205.

Bromberg & Ribstein: § 1.04(e).

Analysis: There are competing policy considerations regarding transition.[103] On the one hand, changing the law may be costly for members of firms and third parties who have relied on existing law. U.L.P.A. changes, among other things, members' rights to dissociate (*see* § 507 and § 601); the limited partner "control" rule (*see* § 303); the effect of the partnership agreement (*see* § 110(b), applied fiduciary duties (*see* § 408) and notice to third parties (*see* § 103(d)). On the other hand, these transition costs must be balanced against the benefits of legal evolution.

U.L.P.A. provides that, as to a limited partnership, which U.L.P.A. § 102(11) defines as one formed under this statute—that is, a *domestic* limited partnership—a limited partnership formed prior to the effective date in U.L.P.A. § 1204 is subject to prior law until the later "all-inclusive" date in U.L.P.A. § 1206 unless it elects to be subject to U.L.P.A.. Even after the "all-inclusive" date, a non-electing pre-existing partnership is not subject to the new law as to the matters specified in subsection (c). Conversely, pursuant to subsection (d), even an electing partnership may continue to be subject to existing law in some respects. These provisions are discussed in more detail below.

Although, as provided in § 1206(c)(2), *automatic* application of the certificate election requirement on the effective date could be a trap for existing firms, that is not necessarily the case for firms that elect coverage. On the other hand, these firms may not realize the need to amend the certificate or to change the firm's name to comply with § 108 (i.e., contain "limited liability limited partnership" or "LLLP" or "L.L.L.P." and not "L.P." or "LP"). Also, automatic application of the election requirement on the *all-inclusive date* might itself be a trap. Accordingly, paragraph 4 of the Note suggests that a filing under the prior LLLP provisions can constitute the necessary certificate amendment under U.L.P.A. § 201(a)(4) *if* the pre-existing firm would comply with the name requirements under U.L.P.A. § 108(c). However, paragraph 4(c) notes that, in the (probably rare) situation that the name requirements of the prior law differ significantly from those of new law, "it will be impossible both to enforce Section 108(c) and provide for automatic transition to LLLP status under this Act."

Subsection (a): Note that this provision does not prevent the Act's effectiveness as to a *foreign* limited partnership. Existing domestic partnerships

---

[103] *See* Revisited, at 997–98; Ribstein, Changing Statutory Forms, 1 J. Small & Emerging Bus. L. 11 (1997), *reprinted in* 39 Corp. Prac. Commentator 703 (1998). For the potential Constitutional implications of change, see Butler & Ribstein, The Contract Clause and the Corporation, 55 Brooklyn L. Rev. 767 (1989).

can, by following the contractual or statutory amendment procedure, elect to be governed by the new law. This means, in effect, that unanimity will be required under U.L.P.A. § 406(b) unless the agreement provides for sub-unanimous amendment.

Subsection (c): This section protects partners in existing firms from certain important changes in their contract rights on the all-inclusive date that would result from application of U.L.P.A., including perpetual duration (§ 104(c)); conditioning LLLP status on specification in the certificate (§ 201(a)(4)); barring dissociation as a limited partner in the absence of contrary agreement (§§ 601–602); providing for expulsion of a general partner by the unanimous consent of the other partners or in other specified circumstances (§ 603(4)–(5)); and restricting dissolution upon a general partner's dissociation (§ 801(3)). It is not clear why other rights are not also included, particularly including payment upon dissociation pursuant to U.L.P.A. (1985) § 604.

Subsection (d): This section prevents binding existing creditors to any limited liability of general partners created by the election.

The **Legislative Note** recommends transition provisions to protect partnerships that have formed as LLLPs under existing law that might otherwise be applied to subject partners to personal liability upon the effective date or upon electing coverage of the statute. But paragraph 3 of the Note suggests that the legislature compel preexisting LLLPs that elect coverage under the Act to comply with the certificate amendment provision in U.L.P.A. § 201(a)(4) and the name requirements in § 108(c).

§ 9.1207. SAVINGS CLAUSE

Section 1207

This [Act] does not affect an action commenced, proceeding brought, or right accrued before this [Act] takes effect.

Summary: Provides that U.L.P.A. does not affect an action commenced, proceeding brought, or right accrued before U.L.P.A. takes effect.

Parallel U.L.P.A. 1985: § 1106.

Parallel R.U.P.A.: § 1210.

Parallel U.L.L.C.A.: § 1206.

≡ *APPENDICES* ≡

≡ *Appendix A* ≡
UNIFORM PARTNERSHIP ACT (1997) [1]

[The 1997 version of R.U.P.A indicates by underlining and strikeout the 1996 changes and the 1997 amendment to Section 801, Events Causing Dissolution and Winding Up. Each section includes the official comment to the 1994 version, if any, followed by any additional comment to the 1996 version.]

[1] Drafted by the National Conference of Commissioners on Uniform State Laws and by it approved and recommended for enactment in all the states at its annual conference, July 12–July 19, 1996. Approved by the American Bar Association, San Antonio, Texas, February 4, 1997. This act has been printed through the permission of the National Conference of Commissioners on Uniform State Laws, and copies of the act may be ordered from them at 211 East Ontario Street, Suite 1300, Chicago, Illinois, 60611.

PREFATORY NOTE

The National Conference of Commissioners on Uniform State Laws first considered a uniform law of partnership in 1902. Although early drafts had proceeded along the mercantile or "entity" theory of partnerships, later drafts were based on the common-law "aggregate" theory. The resulting Uniform Partnership Act ("U.P.A."), which embodied certain aspects of each theory, was finally approved by the Conference in 1914. The U.P.A. governs general partnerships, and also governs limited partnerships except where the limited partnership statute is inconsistent. The U.P.A. has been adopted in every State other than Louisiana and has been the subject of remarkably few amendments in those States over the past 80 years.

In January of 1986, an American Bar Association subcommittee issued a detailed report that recommended extensive revisions to the U.P.A. *See* U.P.A. Revision Subcommittee of the Committee on Partnerships and Unincorporated Business Organizations, Section of Business Law, American Bar Association, Should the Uniform Partnership Act be Revised?, 43 Bus. Law. 121 (1987) ("ABA Report"). The ABA Report recommended that the entity theory "should be incorporated into any revision of the U.P.A. whenever possible." *Id.* at 124.

In 1987, the Conference appointed a Drafting Committee to Revise the Uniform Partnership Act and named a Reporter. The Committee held its initial meeting in January of 1988 and a first reading of the Committee's draft was begun at the Conference's 1989 Annual Meeting in Kauai, Hawaii. The first reading was completed at the 1990 Annual Meeting in Milwaukee. The second reading was begun at Naples, Florida, in 1991 and completed at San Francisco in 1992. The Revised Uniform Partnership Act (1992) was adopted unanimously by a vote of the States on August 6, 1992. The following year, in response to suggestions from various groups, including an American Bar Association subcommittee and several state bar associations, the Drafting Committee recommended numerous revisions to the Act. Those were adopted at the Charleston, South Carolina, Annual Meeting in 1993, and the Act was restyled as the Uniform Partnership Act (1993). Subsequently, a final round of changes was incorporated, and the Conference unanimously adopted the Uniform Partnership Act (1994) at its 1994 Annual Meeting in Chicago. The Revised Act was approved by the American Bar Association House of Delegates in August, 1994.

The Uniform Partnership Act (1994) ("Revised Act" or "R.U.P.A.") gives supremacy to the partnership agreement in almost all situations. The Revised Act is, therefore, largely a series of "default rules" that govern the relations among partners in situations they have not addressed in a partnership agreement. The primary focus of R.U.P.A. is the small, often informal, partnership. Larger partnerships generally have a partnership agreement addressing, and often modifying, many of the provisions of the partnership act.

The Revised Act enhances the entity treatment of partnerships to achieve simplicity for state law purposes, particularly in matters concerning title to partnership property. R.U.P.A. does not, however, relentlessly apply the entity approach. The aggregate approach is retained for some purposes, such as partners' joint and several liability.

The Drafting Committee spent significant effort on the rules governing partnership breakups. R.U.P.A.'s basic thrust is to provide stability for partnerships that have continuation agreements. Under the U.P.A., a partnership is dissolved every time a member leaves. The Revised Act provides that there are many departures or "dissociations" that do not result in a dissolution.

Under the Revised Act, the withdrawal of a partner is a "dissociation" that results in a dissolution of the partnership only in certain limited circumstances. Many dissociations result merely in a buyout of the withdrawing partner's interest rather than a winding up of the partnership's business. R.U.P.A. defines both the substance and procedure of the buyout right.

Article 6 of the Revised Act covers partner dissociations; Article 7 covers buyouts; and Article 8 covers dissolution and the winding up of the partnership business. *See generally* Donald J. Weidner & John W. Larson, The Revised Uniform Partnership Act: The Reporters' Overview, 49 Bus. Law. 1 (1993).

The Revised Act also includes a more extensive treatment of the fiduciary duties of partners. Although R.U.P.A. continues the traditional rule that a partner is a fiduciary, it also makes clear that a partner is not required to be a disinterested trustee. Provision is made for the legitimate pursuit of self-interest, with a counterbalancing irreducible core of fiduciary duties.

Another significant change introduced by R.U.P.A. is provision for the public filing of statements containing basic information about a partnership, such as the agency authority of its partners. Because of the informality of many partnerships, and the inadvertence of some, mandatory filings were eschewed in favor of a voluntary regime. It was the Drafting Committee's belief, however, that filings would become routine for sophisticated partnerships and would be required by lenders and others for major transactions.

Another innovation is found in Article 9. For the first time, the merger of two or more partnerships and the conversion of partnerships to limited partnerships (and the reverse) is expressly authorized, and a "safe harbor" procedure for effecting such transactions is provided.

One final change deserves mention. Partnership law no longer governs limited partnerships pursuant to the provisions of R.U.P.A. itself. First, limited partnerships are not "partnerships" within the R.U.P.A. definition. Second, U.P.A. Section 6(2), which provides that the U.P.A. governs limited partnerships in cases not provided for in the Uniform Limited Partnership Act (1976) (1985) ("RULPA") has been deleted. No substantive change in result is intended, however. Section 1105 of RULPA already provides that the U.P.A. governs in any case not provided for in RULPA, and thus the express linkage in R.U.P.A. is unnecessary. Structurally, it is more appropriately left to RULPA to determine the applicability of R.U.P.A. to limited partnerships. It is contemplated that the Conference will review the linkage question carefully, although no changes in RULPA may be necessary despite the many changes in R.U.P.A.

Finally, the Drafting Committee wishes to express its deep appreciation for the extraordinary time and effort that has been devoted to this project by its Reporter, Donald J. Weidner, Dean of the Florida State University College of Law; by its Assistant Reporter, Professor John W. Larson of the Florida State University College of Law; by its American Bar Association Advisors Allan G. Donn, of Norfolk, Virginia (ABA Section of Taxation and later the ABA Advisor, and a member of the original ABA subcommittee that recommended revising the U.P.A.), Harry J. Haynsworth, Dean of the Southern Illinois University School of Law (the original ABA Advisor until he became a Commissioner and member of the Drafting Committee in 1992 and who was also a member of the original ABA subcommittee), S. Stacy Eastland, of Houston, Texas (Probate and Trust Division of the ABA Section of Real Property, Probate and Trust Law), and Caryl B. Welborn, of San Francisco, California (Real Property Division of the ABA Section of Real Property, Probate and Trust Law); and by a number of other advisors and observers without whose assistance the successful completion of this project would not have been possible: Edward S. Merrill of Walnut Creek, California, Gregory P.L. Pierce of Chicago, Illinois, Paul L. Lion, III, of San Jose, California, Professor Robert W. Hillman of the University of California at Davis School of Law, John Goode of Richmond, Virginia, Ronald H. Wilcomes of New York, New York, Professor Gary S. Rosin of the South Texas College of Law, James F. Fotenos of San Francisco, California, and Joel S. Adelman of Detroit, Michigan (who also was a member of the original ABA subcommittee). The Drafting Committee also would like to express its appreciation to the members of the ABA Committee on Partnerships and Unincorporated Business Organizations, and its chairs, Thurston R. Moore of Richmond, Virginia, and John H. Small of Wilmington, Delaware, for all the time and effort they devoted to this project, and to that Committee's special Subcommittee on the Revised Uniform Partnership Act, the chairs of that subcommittee, Lauris G.L. Rall of New York, New York, and Gerald V. Niesar of San Francisco, California, and its members, in particular, Robert R. Keatinge of Denver, Colorado, Professor Larry E. Ribstein of the George Mason University School of Law, and Anthony van Westrum of Denver, Colorado. Each of these individuals added immeasurably to the Drafting Committee's discussion and consideration of both the major policy issues and the technical drafting issues raised by the Act.

App. A. Uniform Partnership Act (1997)

[ARTICLE] 1. GENERAL PROVISIONS

Section 101. Definitions

In this [Act]:
    (1) "Business" includes every trade, occupation, and profession.
    (2) "Debtor in bankruptcy" means a person who is the subject of:
    (i) an order for relief under Title 11 of the United States Code or a comparable order under a successor statute of general application; or
    (ii) a comparable order under federal, state, or foreign law governing insolvency.
    (3) "Distribution" means a transfer of money or other property from a partnership to a partner in the partner's capacity as a partner or to the partner's transferee.
    <u>(4) "Foreign limited liability partnership" means a partnership that:</u>
    <u>(i) is formed under laws other than the laws of this State;</u>

(ii) has the status of a limited liability partnership under those laws; and

(iii) does not file a statement of election not to be a foreign limited liability partnership.

(5) "Limited liability partnership" means a partnership that has filed a statement of qualification under Section 1001 and has not filed a similar statement in any other jurisdiction.

—— (4) (6) "Partnership" means an association of two or more persons to carry on as co-owners a business for profit formed under Section 202, predecessor law, or comparable law of another jurisdiction.

—— (5) (7) "Partnership agreement" means the agreement, whether written, oral, or implied, among the partners concerning the partnership, including amendments to the partnership agreement.

—— (6) (8) "Partnership at will" means a partnership in which the partners have not agreed to remain partners until the expiration of a definite term or the completion of a particular undertaking.

—— (7) (9) "Partnership interest" or "partner's interest in the partnership" means all of a partner's interests in the partnership, including the partner's transferable interest and all management and other rights.

—— (8) (10) "Person" means an individual, corporation, business trust, estate, trust, partnership, association, joint venture, government, governmental subdivision, agency, or instrumentality, or any other legal or commercial entity.

—— (9) (11) "Property" means all property, real, personal, or mixed, tangible or intangible, or any interest therein.

—— (10) (12) "State" means a State of the United States, the District of Columbia, the Commonwealth of Puerto Rico, or any territory or insular possession subject to the jurisdiction of the United States.

—— (11) (13) "Statement" means a statement of election not to be a foreign limited liability partnership under Section 101(4), a statement of partnership authority under Section 303, a statement of denial under Section 304, a statement of dissociation under Section 704, a statement of dissolution under Section 805, a statement of merger under Section 907, a statement of qualification under Section 1001, a statement of foreign qualification under Section 1102, or an amendment or cancellation of any of the foregoing.

—— (12) (14) "Transfer" includes an assignment, conveyance, lease, mortgage, deed, and encumbrance.

Comment to Original Section 101

The Revised Uniform Partnership Act (RUPA or the Act) continues the definition of "business" from Section 2 of the Uniform Partnership Act (UPA).

RUPA uses the more contemporary term "debtor in bankruptcy" instead of "bankrupt." The definition is adapted from the new Georgia Partnership Act, Ga.

Code Ann. § 14-8-2(1). The definition does not distinguish between a debtor whose estate is being liquidated under Chapter 7 of the Bankruptcy Code and a debtor who is being rehabilitated under Chapter 11, 12, or 13 and includes both. The filing of a voluntary petition under Section 301 of the Bankruptcy Code constitutes an order for relief, but the debtor is entitled to notice and an opportunity to be heard before the entry of an order for relief in an involuntary case under Section 303 of the Code. The term also includes a debtor who is the subject of a comparable order under state or foreign law.

The definition of "distribution" is new and adds precision to the accounting rules established in Sections 401 and 807 and related sections. Transfers to a partner in the partner's capacity as a creditor, lessor, or employee of the partnership, for example, are not "distributions."

"Partnership" is defined to mean an association of two or more persons to carry on as co-owners a business for profit formed under Section 202 (or predecessor law or comparable law of another jurisdiction), that is, a general partnership. Thus, as used in RUPA, the term "partnership" does not encompass limited partnerships, contrary to the use of the term in the UPA. Section 901(3) defines "limited partnership" for the purpose of Article 9, which deals with conversions and mergers of general and limited partnerships.

The definition of "partnership agreement" is adapted from Section 101(9) of the Revised Uniform Limited Partnership Act (RULPA). The RUPA definition is intended to include the agreement among the partners, including amendments, concerning either the affairs of the partnership or the conduct of its business. It does not include other agreements between some or all of the partners, such as a lease or loan agreement. The partnership agreement need not be written; it may be oral or inferred from the conduct of the parties.

Any partnership in which the partners have not agreed to remain partners until the expiration of a definite term or the completion of a particular undertaking is a "partnership at will." The distinction between an "at-will" partnership and a partnership for "a definite term or the completion of a particular undertaking" is important in determining the rights of dissociating and continuing partners following the dissociation of a partner. *See* Sections 601, 602, 701(b), 801(a), 802(b), and 803.

It is sometimes difficult to determine whether a partnership is at will or is for a definite term or the completion of a particular undertaking. Presumptively, every partnership is an at-will partnership. *See, e.g., Stone v. Stone*, 292 So. 2d 686 (La. 1974); *Frey v. Hauke*, 171 Neb. 852, 108 N.W.2d 228 (1961). To constitute a partnership for a term or a particular undertaking, the partners must agree (i) that the partnership will continue for a definite term or until a particular undertaking is completed *and* (ii) that they will remain partners until the expiration of the term or the completion of the undertaking. Both are necessary for a term partnership; if the partners have the unrestricted right, as distinguished from the power, to withdraw from a partnership formed for a term or particular undertaking, the partnership is one at will, rather than a term partnership.

To find that the partnership is formed for a definite term or a particular undertaking, there must be clear evidence of an agreement among the partners that the partnership (i) has a minimum or maximum duration or (ii) terminates at the conclusion of a particular venture whose time is indefinite but certain to occur. *See, e.g., Stainton v. Tarantino*, 637 F. Supp. 1051 (E.D. Pa. 1986) (partnership to dissolve no later than December 30, 2020); *Abel v. American Art Analog, Inc.*, 838 F.2d 691 (3d Cir. 1988) (partnership purpose to market an art book); *68th Street Apts., Inc. v. Lauricella*, 362 A.2d 78 (N.J. Super. Ct. 1976) (partnership purpose to construct an apartment building). A partnership to conduct a business which may last indefinitely, however, is an at-will partnership, even though there may be an obligation of the partnership, such as a mortgage, which must be repaid by a certain date, absent a specific agreement that no partner can rightfully withdraw until the obligation is repaid. *See, e.g., Page v. Page*, 55 Cal. 2d 192, 359 P.2d 41 (1961) (partnership purpose to operate a linen supply business); *Frey v. Hauke, supra* (partnership purpose to contract and operate a bowling alley); *Girard Bank v. Haley*, 460 Pa. 237, 332 A.2d 443 (1975) (partnership purpose to maintain and lease buildings).

"Partnership interest" or "partner's interest in the partnership" is defined to mean all of a partner's interests in the partnership, including the partner's transferable interest and all management and other rights. A partner's "transferable interest" is a more limited concept and means only his share of the profits and losses and right to receive distributions, that is, the partner's economic interests. *See* Section 502 and Comment. *Compare* RULPA § 101(10) ("partnership interest" includes partner's economic interests only).

The definition of "person" is the usual definition used by the National Conference of Commissioners on Uniform State Laws (NCCUSL or the Conference). The definition includes other legal or commercial entities such as limited liability companies.

"Property" is defined broadly to include all types of property, as well as any interest in property.

The definition of "State" is the Conference's usual definition.

The definition of "statement" is new and refers to one of the various statements authorized by RUPA to enhance or limit the agency authority of a partner, to deny the authority or status of a partner, or to give notice of certain events, such as the dissociation of a partner or the dissolution of the partnership. *See* Sections 303, 304, 704, 805, and 907. Generally, Section 105 governs the execution, filing, and recording of all statements.

"Transfer" is defined broadly to include all manner of conveyances, including leases and encumbrances.

Comment to Amendments

If the Amendments to Add Limited Liability Partnership Provisions to the Uniform Partnership Act (1994) are adopted in your State and the Revised Uniform Limited Partnership Act is also in effect in your State, you may want to consider amending your Revised Uniform Limited Partnership Act to provide appropriate linkage to the Uniform Partnership Act (1994), as now amended. The amendment to the Revised Uniform Limited Partnership Act is intended to make clear that limited partnerships may also become a limited liability partnership. A suggested form of the amendment is as follows:

Section 1107. Limited Liability Limited Partnership
(a) A limited partnership may become a limited liability partnership by:
(1) obtaining approval of the terms and conditions of the limited partnership becoming a limited liability limited partnership by the vote necessary to amend the limited partnership agreement except, in the case of a limited partnership agreement that expressly considers contribution obligations, the vote necessary to amend those provisions;
(2) filing a statement of qualification under Section 1001(c) of the Uniform Partnership Act (1994); and
(3) complying with the name requirements of Section 1002 of the Uniform Partnership Act (1994).
(b) A limited liability limited partnership continues to be the same entity that existed before the filing of a statement of qualification under Section 1001(c) of the Uniform Partnership Act (1994).
(c) Sections 306(c) and 307(f) of the Uniform Partnership Act (1994) apply to both general and limited partners of a limited liability limited partnership.

The definition of a "foreign limited liability partnership" includes a general partnership formed under the laws of another jurisdiction provided it also has the status of a limited liability partnership in the other jurisdiction and it has not filed a statement of election not to be a foreign limited liability partnership. Since the scope and nature of foreign limited liability partnership liability shields may vary in different jurisdictions, the definition avoids reference to similar or comparable laws. Rather, the definition incorporates the concept of a limited liability partnership in the foreign jurisdiction, however defined in that jurisdiction.

The definition of a "limited liability partnership" makes clear that a partnership may adopt the special liability shield characteristics of this Act simply by filing a statement of qualification under Section 1001. A partnership may file the statement regardless of where formed. When coupled with the governing law provisions of Section 106, this definition simplifies the choice of law issues applicable to partnerships with multistate activities and contacts. Once a statement of qualification is filed, a partnership's internal affairs and the liability of its partners are determined by the law of the State where the statement is filed. Section 106(b). The partnership may not vary this particular requirement. Section 103(b)(10).

Section 101(13) makes clear that a statement of qualification under Section 1001 and a statement of foreign qualification under Section 1102 are included in the definition of "statement". Both qualification statements are therefore subject to the execution, filing, and recordation rules of Section 105.

Section 102.　Knowledge and Notice

(a) A person knows a fact if the person has actual knowledge of it.

(b) A person has notice of a fact if the person:

(1) knows of it;

(2) has received a notification of it; or

(3) has reason to know it exists from all of the facts known to the person at the time in question.

(c) A person notifies or gives a notification to another by taking steps reasonably required to inform the other person in ordinary course, whether or not the other person learns of it.

(d) A person receives a notification when the notification:

(1) comes to the person's attention; or

(2) is duly delivered at the person's place of business or at any other place held out by the person as a place for receiving communications.

(e) Except as otherwise provided in subsection (f), a person other than an individual knows, has notice, or receives a notification of a fact for purposes of a particular transaction when the individual conducting the transaction knows, has notice, or receives a notification of the fact, or in any event when the fact would have been brought to the individual's attention if the person had exercised reasonable diligence. The person exercises reasonable diligence if it maintains reasonable routines for communicating significant information to the individual conducting the transaction and there is reasonable compliance with the routines. Reasonable diligence does not require an individual acting for the person to communicate information unless the communication is part of the individual's regular duties or the individual has reason to know of the transaction and that the transaction would be materially affected by the information.

(f) A partner's knowledge, notice, or receipt of a notification of a fact relating to the partnership is effective immediately as knowledge by, notice to, or receipt of a notification by the partnership, except in the case of a fraud on the partnership committed by or with the consent of that partner.

Comment to Original Section 102

The concepts and definitions of "knowledge," "notice," and "notification" draw heavily on Section 1-201(25) to (27) of the Uniform Commercial Code (UCC). The UCC text has been altered somewhat to improve clarity and style, but in general no substantive changes are intended from the UCC concepts. "A notification" replaces the UCC's redundant phrase, "a notice or notification," throughout the Act.

A person "knows" a fact only if that person has actual knowledge of it. Knowledge is cognitive awareness. That is solely an issue of fact. This is a change from the UPA Section 3(1) definition of "knowledge" which included the concept of "bad faith" knowledge arising from other known facts.

"Notice" is a lesser degree of awareness than "knows" and is based on a person's: (i) actual knowledge; (ii) receipt of a notification; or (iii) reason to know based on actual knowledge of other facts and the circumstances at the time. The latter is the traditional concept of inquiry notice.

Generally, under RUPA, statements filed pursuant to Section 105 do not constitute constructive knowledge or notice, except as expressly provided in the Act. *See* Section 301(1) (generally requiring knowledge of limitations on partner's apparent authority). Properly recorded statements of limitation on a partner's authority, on the other hand, generally constitute constructive knowledge with respect to the transfer of real property held in the partnership name. *See* Sections 303(d)(1), 303(e), 704(b), and 805(b). The other exceptions are Sections 704(c) (statement of dissociation effective 90 days after filing) and 805(c) (statement of dissolution effective 90 days after filing).

A person "receives" a notification when (i) the notification is delivered to the person's place of business (or other place for receiving communications) or (ii) the recipient otherwise actually learns of its existence.

The sender "notifies" or gives a notification by making an effort to inform the recipient, which is reasonably calculated to do so in ordinary course, even if the recipient does not actually learn of it.

The Official Comment to UCC Section 1-201(26), on which this subsection is based, explains that "notifies" is the word used when the essential fact is the proper dispatch of the notice, not its receipt. When the essential fact is the other party's receipt of the notice, that is stated.

A notification is not required to be in writing. That is a change from UPA Section 3(2)(b). As under the UCC, the time and circumstances under which a notification may cease to be effective are not determined by RUPA.

Subsection (e) determines when an agent's knowledge or notice is imputed to an organization, such as a corporation. In general, only the knowledge or notice of the agent conducting the particular transaction is imputed to the organization.

Organizations are expected to maintain reasonable internal routines to insure that important information reaches the individual agent handling a transaction. If, in the exercise of reasonable diligence on the part of the organization, the agent should have known or had notice of a fact, or received a notification of it, the organization is bound. The Official Comment to UCC Section 1-201(27) explains:

> This makes clear that reason to know, knowledge, or a notification, although "received" for instance by a clerk in Department A of an organization, is effective for a transaction conducted in Department B only from the time when it was or should have been communicated to the individual conducting that transaction.

Subsection (e) uses the phrase "person other than an individual" in lieu of the UCC term "organization."

Subsection (f) continues the rule in UPA Section 12 that a partner's knowledge or notice of a fact relating to the partnership is imputed to the partnership, except in the case of fraud on the partnership. Limited partners, however, are not "partners" within the meaning of RUPA. *See* Comment 4 to Section 202. It is anticipated that RULPA will address the issue of whether notice to a limited partner is imputed to a limited partnership.

Section 103.   Effect of Partnership Agreement; Nonwaivable Provisions

(a) Except as otherwise provided in subsection (b), relations among the partners and between the partners and the partnership are governed by the partnership agreement. To the extent the partnership agreement does not otherwise provide, this [Act] governs relations among the partners and between the partners and the partnership.

(b) The partnership agreement may not:

(1) vary the rights and duties under Section 105 except to eliminate the duty to provide copies of statements to all of the partners;

(2) unreasonably restrict the right of access to books and records under Section 403(b);

(3) eliminate the duty of loyalty under Section 404(b) or 603(b)(3), but:

(i) the partnership agreement may identify specific types or categories of activities that do not violate the duty of loyalty, if not manifestly unreasonable; or

(ii) all of the partners or a number or percentage specified in the partnership agreement may authorize or ratify, after full disclosure of all material facts, a specific act or transaction that otherwise would violate the duty of loyalty;

(4) unreasonably reduce the duty of care under Section 404(c) or 603(b)(3);

(5) eliminate the obligation of good faith and fair dealing under Section 404(d), but the partnership agreement may prescribe the standards by which the performance of the obligation is to be measured, if the standards are not manifestly unreasonable;

(6) vary the power to dissociate as a partner under Section 602(a), except to require the notice under Section 601(1) to be in writing;

(7) vary the right of a court to expel a partner in the events specified in Section 601(5);

(8) vary the requirement to wind up the partnership business in cases specified in Section 801(4), (5), or (6); or

(9) vary the law applicable to a limited liability partnership under Section 106(b); or

(10) restrict rights of third parties under this [Act].

Comment to Original Section 103

1. The general rule under Section 103(a) is that relations among the partners and between the partners and the partnership are governed by the partnership agreement. *See* Section 101(5). To the extent that the partners fail to agree upon a contrary rule, RUPA provides the default rule. Only the rights and duties listed in Section 103(b), and implicitly the corresponding liabilities and remedies under Section 405, are mandatory and cannot be waived or varied by agreement beyond what is authorized. Those are the only exceptions to the general principle that the provisions of RUPA with respect to the rights of the partners *inter se* are merely default rules, subject to modification by the partners. All modifications must also, of course, satisfy the general standards of contract validity. *See* Section 104.

2. Under subsection (b)(1), the partnership agreement may not vary the requirements for executing, filing, and recording statements under Section 105, except the duty to provide copies to all the partners. A statement that is not executed, filed, and recorded in accordance with the statutory requirements will not be accorded the effect prescribed in the Act, except as provided in Section 303(d).

The following paragraphs 3 through 11 were formerly part of 2 above.

3. Subsection (b)(2) provides that the partnership agreement may not unreasonably restrict a partner or former partner's access rights to books and records under Section 403(b). It is left to the courts to determine what restrictions are reasonable. *See* Comment 2 to Section 403. Other information rights in Section 403 can be varied or even eliminated by agreement.

4. Subsection (b)(3) through (5) are intended to ensure a fundamental core of fiduciary responsibility. Neither the fiduciary duties of loyalty or care, nor the obligation of good faith and fair dealing, may be eliminated entirely. However, the statutory requirements of each can be modified by agreement, subject to the limitation stated in subsection (b)(3) through (5).

The following underlined section up to #5 was formerly under #2 after the paragraph discussing Subsection (b)(3)(ii). Now the discussion of subsections (b)(3)(i) and (b)(3)(ii) come after the underlined section below.

There has always been a tension regarding the extent to which a partner's fiduciary duty of loyalty can be varied by agreement, as contrasted with the other partners' consent to a particular and known breach of duty. On the one hand, courts have been loathe to enforce agreements broadly "waiving" in advance a partner's fiduciary duty of loyalty, especially where there is unequal bargaining power, information, or sophistication. For this reason, a very broad provision in a partnership agreement in effect negating any duty of loyalty, such as a provision giving a managing partner complete discretion to manage the business with no liability except for acts and omissions that constitute wilful misconduct, will not likely be enforced. *See, e.g., Labovitz v. Dolan,* 189 Ill. App. 3d 403, 136 Ill. Dec. 780, 545 N.E.2d 304 (1989). On the other hand, it is clear that the remaining partners can "consent" to a particular conflicting interest transaction or other breach of duty, after the fact, provided there is full disclosure.

RUPA attempts to provide a standard that partners can rely upon in drafting exculpatory agreements. It is not necessary that the agreement be restricted to a particular transaction. That would require bargaining over every transaction or opportunity, which would be excessively burdensome. The agreement may be drafted in terms of types or categories of activities or transactions, but it should be reasonably specific.

A provision in a real estate partnership agreement authorizing a partner who is a real estate agent to retain commissions on partnership property bought and sold by that partner would be an example of a "type or category" of activity that is not manifestly unreasonable and thus should be enforceable under the Act. Likewise, a provision authorizing that partner to buy or sell real property for his own account without prior disclosure to the other partners or without first offering it to the partnership would be enforceable as a valid category of partnership activity.

Ultimately, the courts must decide the outer limits of validity of such agreements, and context may be significant. It is intended that the risk of judicial refusal to enforce manifestly unreasonable exculpatory clauses will discourage sharp practices while accommodating the legitimate needs of the parties in structuring their relationship.

5. Subsection (b)(3)(i) permits the partners, in their partnership agreement, to identify specific types or categories of partnership activities that do not violate the duty of loyalty. A modification of the statutory standard must not, however, be manifestly unreasonable. This is intended to discourage overreaching by a partner with superior bargaining power since the courts may refuse to enforce an overly broad exculpatory clause. *See, e.g., Vlases v. Montgomery Ward & Co.,* 377 F.2d 846, 850 (3d Cir. 1967) (limitation prohibits unconscionable agree-

ments); *PPG Industries, Inc. v. Shell Oil Co.*, 919 F.2d 17, 19 (5th Cir. 1990) (apply limitation deferentially to agreements of sophisticated parties).

Subsection (b)(3)(ii) is intended to clarify the right of partners, recognized under general law, to consent to a known past or anticipated violation of duty and to waive their legal remedies for redress of that violation. This is intended to cover situations where the conduct in question is not specifically authorized by the partnership agreement. It can also be used to validate conduct that might otherwise not satisfy the "manifestly unreasonable" standard. Clause (ii) provides that, after full disclosure of all material facts regarding a specific act or transaction that otherwise would violate the duty of loyalty, it may be authorized or ratified by the partners. That authorization or ratification must be unanimous unless a lesser number or percentage is specified for this purpose in the partnership agreement.

6. Under subsection (b)(4), the partners' duty of care may not be unreasonably reduced below the statutory standard set forth in Section 404(d), that is, to refrain from engaging in grossly negligent or reckless conduct, intentional misconduct, or a knowing violation of law.

For example, partnership agreements frequently contain provisions releasing a partner from liability for actions taken in good faith and in the honest belief that the actions are in the best interests of the partnership and indemnifying the partner against any liability incurred in connection with the business of the partnership if the partner acts in a good faith belief that he has authority to act. Many partnership agreements reach this same result by listing various activities and stating that the performance of these activities is deemed not to constitute gross negligence or wilful misconduct. These types of provisions are intended to come within the modifications authorized by subsection (b)(4). On the other hand, absolving partners of intentional misconduct is probably unreasonable. As with contractual standards of loyalty, determining the outer limit in reducing the standard of care is left to the courts.

The standard may, of course, be increased by agreement to one of ordinary care or an even higher standard of care.

7. Subsection (b)(5) authorizes the partners to determine the standards by which the performance of the obligation of good faith and fair dealing is to be measured. The language of subsection (b)(5) is based on UCC Section 1-102(3). The partners can negotiate and draft specific contract provisions tailored to their particular needs (*e.g.*, five days notice of a partners' meeting is adequate notice), but blanket waivers of the obligation are unenforceable. *See, e.g., PPG Indus., Inc. v. Shell Oil Co.*, 919 F.2d 17 (5th Cir. 1990); *First Security Bank v. Mountain View Equip. Co.*, 112 Idaho 158, 730 P.2d 1078 (Ct. App. 1986), *aff'd*, 112 Idaho 1078, 739 P.2d 377 (1987); *American Bank of Commerce v. Covolo*, 88 N.M. 405, 540 P.2d 1294 (1975).

8. Section 602(a) continues the traditional UPA Section 31(2) rule that every partner has the power to withdraw from the partnership at any time, which power

cannot be bargained away. Section 103(b)(6) provides that the partnership agreement may not vary the power to dissociate as a partner under Section 602(a), except to require that the notice of withdrawal under Section 601(1) be in writing. The UPA was silent with respect to requiring a written notice of withdrawal.

9. Under subsection (b)(7), the right of a partner to seek court expulsion of another partner under Section 601(5) can not be waived or varied (e.g., requiring a 90-day notice) by agreement. Section 601(5) refers to judicial expulsion on such grounds as misconduct, breach of duty, or impracticability.

10. Under subsection (b)(8), the partnership agreement may not vary the right of partners to have the partnership dissolved and its business wound up under Section 801(4), (5), or (6). Section 801(4) provides that the partnership must be wound up if its business is unlawful. Section 801(5) provides for judicial winding up in such circumstances as frustration of the firm's economic purpose, partner misconduct, or impracticability. Section 801(6) accords standing to transferees of an interest in the partnership to seek judicial dissolution of the partnership in specified circumstances.

11. Although stating the obvious, subsection (b)(9) provides expressly that the rights of a third party under the Act may not be restricted by an agreement among the partners to which the third party has not agreed. A non-partner who is a party to an agreement among the partners is, of course, bound. *Cf.* Section 703(c) (creditor joins release).

12. The Article 9 rules regarding conversions and mergers are not listed in Section 103(b) as mandatory. Indeed, Section 907 states expressly that partnerships may be converted and merged in any other manner provided by law. The effect of compliance with Article 9 is to provide a "safe harbor" assuring the legal validity of such conversions and mergers. Although not immune from variation in the partnership agreement, noncompliance with the requirements of Article 9 in effecting a conversion or merger is to deny that "safe harbor" validity to the transaction. In this regard, Sections 903(b) and 905(c)(2) require that the conversion or merger of a limited partnership be approved by all of the partners, notwithstanding a contrary provision in the limited partnership agreement. Thus, in effect, the agreement cannot vary the voting requirement without sacrificing the benefits of the "safe harbor."

Comment to Amendments

Section 103(b)(9) makes clear that a limited liability partnership may not designate the law of a State other than the State where it filed its statement of qualification to govern its internal affairs and the liability of its partners. *See* Sections 101(5), 106(b), and 202(a).

Section 104.   Supplemental Principles of Law

(a) Unless displaced by particular provisions of this [Act], the principles of law and equity supplement this [Act].

(b) If an obligation to pay interest arises under this [Act] and the rate is not specified, the rate is that specified in [applicable statute].

Comment to Original Section 104

The principles of law and equity supplement RUPA unless displaced by a particular provision of the Act. This broad statement combines the separate rules contained in UPA Sections 4(2), 4(3), and 5. These supplementary principles encompass not only the law of agency and estoppel and the law merchant mentioned in the UPA, but all of the other principles listed in UCC Section 1-103: the law relative to capacity to contract, fraud, misrepresentation, duress, coercion, mistake, bankruptcy, and other common law validating or invalidating causes, such as unconscionability. No substantive change from either the UPA or the UCC is intended.

It was thought unnecessary to repeat the UPA Section 4(1) admonition that statutes in derogation of the common law are not to be strictly construed. This principle is now so well established that it is not necessary to so state in the Act. No change in the law is intended. *See* the Comment to RULPA Section 1101.

Subsection (b) is new. It is based on the definition of "interest" in Section 14-8-2(5) of the Georgia act and establishes the applicable rate of interest in the absence of an agreement among the partners. Adopting States can select the State's legal rate of interest or other statutory interest rate, such as the rate for judgments.

Section 105.   Execution, Filing, and Recording of Statements

(a) A statement may be filed in the office of [the Secretary of State]. A certified copy of a statement that is filed in an office in another State may be filed in the office of [the Secretary of State]. Either filing has the effect provided in this [Act] with respect to partnership property located in or transactions that occur in this State.

(b) A certified copy of a statement that has been filed in the office of the [Secretary of State] and recorded in the office for recording transfers of real property has the effect provided for recorded statements in this [Act]. A recorded statement that is not a certified copy of a statement filed in the office of the [Secretary of State] does not have the effect provided for recorded statements in this [Act].

(c) A statement filed by a partnership must be executed by at least two partners. Other statements must be executed by a partner or other person authorized by this [Act]. An individual who executes a statement as, or on behalf of, a partner or other person named as a partner in a statement shall personally declare under penalty of perjury that the contents of the statement are accurate.

(d) A person authorized by this [Act] to file a statement may amend or cancel the statement by filing an amendment or cancellation that names the partnership, identifies the statement, and states the substance of the amendment or cancellation.

(e) A person who files a statement pursuant to this section shall promptly send a copy of the statement to every nonfiling partner and to any other person named as a partner in the statement. Failure to send a copy of a statement to a partner or other person does not limit the effectiveness of the statement as to a person not a partner.

(f) The [Secretary of State] may collect a fee for filing or providing a certified copy of a statement. The [officer responsible for recording transfers of real property] may collect a fee for recording a statement.

Comment to Original Section 105

1. Section 105 is new. It mandates the procedural rules for the execution, filing, and recording of the various "statements" (*see* Section 101(11)) authorized by RUPA.

No filings are mandatory under RUPA. In all cases, the filing of a statement is optional and voluntary. A system of mandatory filing and disclosure for partnerships, similar to that required for corporations and limited partnerships, was rejected for several reasons. First, RUPA is designed to accommodate the needs of small partnerships, which often have unwritten or sketchy agreements and limited resources. Furthermore, inadvertent partnerships are also governed by the Act, as the default form of business organization, in which case filing would be unlikely.

The RUPA filing provisions are, however, likely to encourage the voluntary use of partnership statements. There are a number of strong incentives for the partnership or the partners to file statements or for third parties, such as lenders or transferees of partnership property, to compel them to do so.

Only statements that are executed, filed, and, if appropriate (such as the authority to transfer real property), recorded in conformity with Section 105 have the legal consequences accorded statements by RUPA. The requirements of Section 105 cannot be varied in the partnership agreement, except the duty to provide copies of statements to all the partners. *See* Section 103(b)(1).

In most States today, the filing and recording of statements requires written documents. As technology advances, alternatives suitable for filing and recording may be developed. RUPA itself does not impose any requirement that statements be in writing. It is intended that the form or medium for filing and recording be left to the general law of adopting States.

2. Section 105(a) provides for a single, central filing of all statements, as is the case with corporations, limited partnerships, and limited liability companies. The expectation is that most States will assign to the Secretary of State the responsibility of maintaining the filing system for partnership statements. Since a partnership is an entity under RUPA, all statements should be indexed by partnership name, not by the names of the individual partners.

Partnerships transacting business in more than one State will want to file copies of statements in each State because subsection (a) limits the legal effect of filed statements to property located or transactions occurring within the state. The filing of a certified copy of a statement originally filed in another State is permitted, and indeed encouraged, in order to avoid inconsistencies between statements filed in different States.

3. Subsection (b), in effect, mandates the use of certified copies of filed statements for local recording in the real estate records by limiting the legal effect of recorded statements under the Act to those copies. The reason for recording only certified copies of filed statements is to eliminate the possibility of inconsistencies affecting the title to real property.

Subsection (c) requires that statements filed on behalf of a partnership, that is, the entity, be executed by at least two partners. Individual partners and other persons authorized by the Act to file a statement may execute it on their own behalf. To protect the partners and the partnership from unauthorized or improper filings, an individual who executes a statement as a partner must personally declare under penalty of perjury that the statement is accurate.

The amendment or cancellation of statements is authorized by subsection (d).

As a further safeguard against inaccurate or unauthorized filings, subsection (e) requires that a copy of every statement filed be sent to each partner, although the failure to do so does not limit the effectiveness of the statement. This requirement may, however, be eliminated in the partnership agreement. *See* Section 103(b)(1). Partners may also file a statement of denial under Section 304.

4. A filed statement may be amended or canceled by any person authorized by the Act to file an original statement. The amendment or cancellation must state the name of the partnership so that it can be properly indexed and found, identify the statement being amended or canceled, and the substance of the amendment or cancellation. An amendment generally has the same operative effect as an original statement. A cancellation of extraordinary authority terminates that authority. A cancellation of a limitation on authority revives a previous grant of authority. *See* Section 303(d). The subsequent filing of a statement similar in kind to a statement already of record is treated as an amendment, even if not so denominated. Any substantive conflict between filed statements operates as a cancellation of authority under Section 303.

Comment to Amendments

Section 101(13) makes clear that a statement of qualification filed by a partnership to become a limited liability partnership is defined as a statement. Therefore, the execution, filing, and recording rules of this section must be followed. However, the decision to file the statement must be approved by the vote of the partners necessary to amend the partnership agreement as to contribution requirements. *See* Section 1001(b).

Section 106.   *Governing Law* ~~Governing Internal Relations~~

(a) ~~The~~ Except as otherwise provided in subsection (b), the law of the jurisdiction in which a partnership has its chief executive office governs relations among the partners and between the partners and the partnership.

(b) The law of this State governs relations among the partners and between the partners and the partnership and the liability of partners for an obligation of a limited liability partnership.

Comment to Original Section 106

The internal relations rule is new. *Cf.* RULPA § 901 (internal affairs governed by law of State in which limited partnership organized).

RUPA looks to the jurisdiction in which a partnership's chief executive office is located to provide the law governing the internal relations among the partners and between the partners and the partnership. The concept of the partnership's "chief executive office" is drawn from UCC Section 9-103(3)(d). It was chosen in lieu of the State of organization because no filing is necessary to form a general partnership, and thus the situs of its organization is not always clear, unlike a limited partnership, which is organized in the State where its certificate is filed.

The term "chief executive office" is not defined in the Act, nor is it defined in the UCC. Paragraph 5 of the Official Comment to UCC Section 9-103(3)(d) explains:

> "Chief executive office" . . . means the place from which in fact the debtor manages the main part of his business operations. . . . Doubt may arise as to which is the "chief executive office" of a multi-state enterprise, but it would be rare that there could be more than two possibilities. . . . [The rule] will be simple to apply in most cases. . . .

In the absence of any other clear rule for determining a partnership's legal situs, it seems convenient to use that rule for choice of law purposes as well.

The choice-of-law rule provided by Section 106 is only a default rule, and the partners may by agreement select the law of another State to govern their internal affairs, subject to generally applicable conflict of laws requirements. For example, where the partners may not resolve a particular issue by an explicit provision of the partnership agreement, such as the rights and duties set forth in Section 103(b), the law chosen will not be applied if the partners or the partnership have no substantial relationship to the chosen State or other reasonable basis for their choice or if application of the law of the chosen State would be contrary to a fundamental policy of a State that has a materially greater interest than the chosen State. *See* Restatement (Second) of Conflict of Laws § 187(2) (1971). The partners must, however, select only one State to govern their internal relations. They cannot select one State for some aspects of their internal relations and another State for others.

Comment to the Amendment

The filing of a statement of qualification may change the law applicable to a partnership. *See* Section 101(5). Accordingly, if a statement is revoked or canceled, the law of the State of filing would continue to apply unless the partnership agreement thereafter altered the applicable law rule. Subsection (b) merely confirms that the law of the State where the statement is filed governs the partnership.

Section 107. Partnership Subject to Amendment or Repeal of [Act]

A partnership governed by this [Act] is subject to any amendment to or repeal of this [Act].

Comment to Original Section 107

The reservation of power provision is new. It is adapted from Section 1.02 of the Revised Model Business Corporation Act (RMBCA) and Section 1106 of RULPA.

As explained in the Official Comment to the RMBCA, the genesis of those provisions is *Trustees of Dartmouth College v. Woodward,* 17 U.S. (4 Wheat) 518 (1819), which held that the United States Constitution prohibits the application of newly enacted statutes to existing corporations, while suggesting the efficacy of a reservation of power provision. Its purpose is to avoid any possible argument that a legal entity created pursuant to statute or its members have a contractual or vested right in any specific statutory provision and to ensure that the State may in the future modify its enabling statute as it deems appropriate and require existing entities to comply with the statutes as modified.

[ARTICLE] 2.   NATURE OF PARTNERSHIP

Section 201.   Partnership as Entity
Section 202.   Formation of Partnership
Section 203.   Partnership Property
Section 204.   When Property Is Partnership Property

Section 201.   Partnership as Entity

(a) A partnership is an entity distinct from its partners.

(b) The law of this State governs relations among the partners and between the partners and the partnership and the liability of partners for an obligation of a limited liability partnership.

Comment to Original Section 201

RUPA embraces the entity theory of the partnership. In light of the UPA's ambivalence on the nature of partnerships, an explicit statement is deemed appropriate as an expression of the increased emphasis on the entity theory as the dominant model. *But see* Section 305 (partners' liability joint and several).

Giving clear expression to the entity nature of a partnership is intended to allay previous concerns stemming from the aggregate theory, such as the necessity of a deed to convey title from the "old" partnership to the "new" partnership every time there is a change of cast among the partners. Under RUPA, there is no "new" partnership just because of membership changes. That will avoid the result in cases such as *Fairway Development Co. v. Title Insurance Co.*, 621 F. Supp. 120 (N.D. Ohio 1985), which held that the "new" partnership resulting from a partner's death did not have standing to enforce a title insurance policy issued to the "old" partnership.

Comment to Amendments

The filing of a statement of qualification may change the law applicable to a partnership. *See* Section 101(5). Accordingly, if a statement is revoked or canceled, the law of the State of filing would continue to apply unless the partnership agreement thereafter altered the applicable law rule. Subsection (b) merely confirms that the law of the State where the statement is filed governs the partnership.

Section 202.   Formation of Partnership

(a) Except as otherwise provided in subsection (b), the association of two or more persons to carry on as co-owners a business for profit forms a partnership, whether or not the persons intend to form a partnership.

(b) An association formed under a statute other than this [Act], a predecessor statute, or a comparable statute of another jurisdiction is not a partnership under this [Act].

(c) In determining whether a partnership is formed, the following rules apply:

(1) Joint tenancy, tenancy in common, tenancy by the entireties, joint property, common property, or part ownership does not by itself establish a partnership, even if the co-owners share profits made by the use of the property.

(2) The sharing of gross returns does not by itself establish a partnership, even if the persons sharing them have a joint or common right or interest in property from which the returns are derived.

(3) A person who receives a share of the profits of a business is presumed to be a partner in the business, unless the profits were received in payment:

(i) of a debt by installments or otherwise;

(ii) for services as an independent contractor or of wages or other compensation to an employee;

(iii) of rent;

(iv) of an annuity or other retirement or health benefit to a beneficiary, representative, or designee of a deceased or retired partner;

(v) of interest or other charge on a loan, even if the amount of payment varies with the profits of the business, including a direct or indirect present or future ownership of the collateral, or rights to income, proceeds, or increase in value derived from the collateral; or

(vi) for the sale of the goodwill of a business or other property by installments or otherwise.

Comment to Original Section 202

1. Section 202 combines UPA Sections 6 and 7. The traditional UPA Section 6(1) "definition" of a partnership is recast as an operative rule of law. No substantive change in the law is intended. The UPA "definition" has always been understood as an operative rule, as well as a definition. The addition of the phrase, "whether or not the persons intend to form a partnership," merely codifies the universal judicial construction of UPA Section 6(1) that a partnership is created by the association of persons whose intent is to carry on as co-owners a business for profit, regardless of their subjective intention to be "partners." Indeed, they may inadvertently create a partnership despite their expressed

subjective intention not to do so. The new language alerts readers to this possibility.

As under the UPA, the attribute of co-ownership distinguishes a partnership from a mere agency relationship. A business is a series of acts directed toward an end. Ownership involves the power of ultimate control. To state that partners are co-owners of a business is to state that they each have the power of ultimate control. *See* Official Comment to UPA § 6(1). On the other hand, as subsection (c)(1) makes clear, passive co-ownership of property by itself, as distinguished from the carrying on of a business, does not establish a partnership.

2. Subsection (b) provides that business associations organized under other statutes are not partnerships. Those statutory associations include corporations, limited partnerships, and limited liability companies. That continues the UPA concept that general partnership is the residual form of for profit business association, existing only if another form does not.

A limited partnership is not a partnership under this definition. Nevertheless, certain provisions of RUPA will continue to govern limited partnerships because RULPA itself, in Section 1105, so requires "in any case not provided for" in RULPA. In light of that section, UPA Section 6(2), which provides that limited partnerships are governed by the UPA, is redundant and has not been carried over to RUPA. It is also more appropriate that the applicability of RUPA to limited partnerships be governed exclusively by RULPA.

It is not intended that RUPA change any common law rules concerning special types of associations, such as mining partnerships, which in some jurisdictions are not governed by the UPA.

Relationships that are called "joint ventures" are partnerships if they otherwise fit the definition of a partnership. An association is not classified as a partnership, however, simply because it is called a "joint venture."

An unincorporated nonprofit organization is not a partnership under RUPA, even if it qualifies as a business, because it is not a "for profit" organization.

3. Subsection (c) provides three rules of construction that apply in determining whether a partnership has been formed under subsection (a). They are largely derived from UPA Section 7, and to that extent no substantive change is intended. The sharing of profits is recast as a rebuttable presumption of a partnership, a more contemporary construction, rather than as prima facie evidence thereof. The protected categories, in which receipt of a share of the profits is not presumed to create a partnership, apply whether the profit share is a single flat percentage or a ratio that varies, for example, after reaching a dollar floor or different levels of profits.

Like its predecessor, RUPA makes no attempt to answer in every case whether a partnership is formed. Whether a relationship is more properly characterized as that of borrower and lender, employer and employee, or landlord and tenant is left to the trier of fact. As under the UPA, a person may function in both partner and nonpartner capacities.

Paragraph (3)(v) adds a new protected category to the list. It shields from the presumption a share of the profits received in payment of interest or other charges on a loan, "including a direct or indirect present or future ownership in the collateral, or rights to income, proceeds, or increase in value derived from the collateral." The quoted language is taken from Section 211 of the Uniform Land Security Interest Act. The purpose of the new language is to protect shared-appreciation mortgages, contingent or other variable or performance-related mortgages, and other equity participation arrangements by clarifying that contingent payments do not presumptively convert lending arrangements into partnerships.

4. Section 202(e) of the 1993 Act stated that partnerships formed under RUPA are general partnerships and that the partners are general partners. That section has been deleted as unnecessary. Limited partners are not "partners" within the meaning of RUPA, however.

Section 203.   Partnership Property

Property acquired by a partnership is property of the partnership and not of the partners individually.

Comment to Original Section 203

All property acquired by a partnership, by transfer or otherwise, becomes partnership property and belongs to the partnership as an entity, rather than to the individual partners. This expresses the substantive result of UPA Sections 8(1) and 25.

Neither UPA Section 8(1) nor RUPA Section 203 provides any guidance concerning when property is "acquired by" the partnership. That problem is dealt with in Section 204.

UPA Sections 25(2)(c) and (e) also provide that partnership property is not subject to exemptions, allowances, or rights of a partner's spouse, heirs, or next of kin. Those provisions have been omitted as unnecessary. No substantive change is intended. Those exemptions and rights inure to the property of the partners, and not to partnership property.

Section 204.   When Property Is Partnership Property

(a) Property is partnership property if acquired in the name of:

(1) the partnership; or

(2) one or more partners with an indication in the instrument transferring title to the property of the person's capacity as a partner or of the existence of a partnership but without an indication of the name of the partnership.

(b) Property is acquired in the name of the partnership by a transfer to:

(1) the partnership in its name; or

(2) one or more partners in their capacity as partners in the partnership, if the name of the partnership is indicated in the instrument transferring title to the property.

(c) Property is presumed to be partnership property if purchased with partnership assets, even if not acquired in the name of the partnership or of one or more partners with an indication in the instrument transferring title to the property of the person's capacity as a partner or of the existence of a partnership.

(d) Property acquired in the name of one or more of the partners, without an indication in the instrument transferring title to the property of the person's capacity as a partner or of the existence of a partnership and without use of partnership assets, is presumed to be separate property, even if used for partnership purposes.

Comment to Original Section 204

1. Section 204 sets forth the rules for determining when property is acquired by the partnership and, hence, becomes partnership property. It is based on UPA Section 8(3), as influenced by the recent Alabama and Georgia modifications. The rules govern the acquisition of personal property, as well as real property, that is held in the partnership name. *See* Section 101(9).

2. Subsection (a) governs the circumstances under which property becomes "partnership property," and subsection (b) clarifies the circumstances under which property is acquired "in the name of the partnership." The concept of record title is emphasized, although the term itself is not used. Titled personal property, as well as all transferable interests in real property acquired in the name of the partnership, are covered by this section.

Property becomes partnership property if acquired (1) in the name of the partnership or (2) in the name of one or more of the partners with an indication in the instrument transferring title of either (i) their capacity as partners or (ii) of the existence of a partnership, even if the name of the partnership is not indicated. Property acquired "in the name of the partnership" includes property acquired in the name of one or more partners in their capacity as partners, but only if the name of the partnership is indicated in the instrument transferring title.

Property transferred to a partner is partnership property, even though the name of the partnership is not indicated, if the instrument transferring title indicates either (i) the partner's capacity as a partner or (ii) the existence of a partnership. This is consonant with the entity theory of partnership and resolves the troublesome issue of a conveyance to fewer than all the partners but which nevertheless indicates their partner status.

3. Ultimately, it is the intention of the partners that controls whether property belongs to the partnership or to one or more of the partners in their individual

capacities, at least as among the partners themselves. RUPA sets forth two rebuttable presumptions that apply when the partners have failed to express their intent.

First, under subsection (c), property purchased with partnership funds is presumed to be partnership property, notwithstanding the name in which title is held. The presumption is intended to apply if partnership credit is used to obtain financing, as well as the use of partnership cash or property for payment. Unlike the rule in subsection (b), under which property is *deemed* to be partnership property if the partnership's name or the partner's capacity as a partner is disclosed in the instrument of conveyance, subsection (c) raises only a *presumption* that the property is partnership property if it is purchased with partnership assets.

That presumption is also subject to an important caveat. Under Section 302(b), partnership property held in the name of individual partners, without an indication of their capacity as partners or of the existence of a partnership, which is transferred by the partners in whose name title is held to a purchaser without knowledge that it is partnership property is free of any claims of the partnership.

Second, under subsection (d), property acquired in the name of one or more of the partners, without an indication of their capacity as partners and without use of partnership funds or credit, is presumed to be the partners' separate property, even if used for partnership purposes. In effect, it is presumed in that case that only the use of the property is contributed to the partnership.

4. Generally, under RUPA, partners and third parties dealing with partnerships will be able to rely on the record to determine whether property is owned by the partnership. The exception is property purchased with partnership funds without any reference to the partnership in the title documents. The inference concerning the partners' intent from the use of partnership funds outweighs any inference from the state of the title, subject to the overriding reliance interest in the case of a purchaser without notice of the partnership's interest. This allocation of risk should encourage the partnership to eliminate doubt about ownership by putting title in the partnership.

5. UPA Section 8(4) provides, "A transfer to a partnership in the partnership name, even without words of inheritance, passes the entire estate or interest of the grantor unless a contrary intent appears." It has been omitted from RUPA as unnecessary because modern conveyancing law deems all transfers to pass the entire estate or interest of the grantor unless a contrary intent appears.

[ARTICLE] 3.   RELATIONS OF PARTNERS TO PERSONS DEALING WITH PARTNERSHIP

Section 301.   Partner Agent of Partnership

Subject to the effect of a statement of partnership authority under Section 303:

(1) Each partner is an agent of the partnership for the purpose of its business. An act of a partner, including the execution of an instrument in the partnership name, for apparently carrying on in the ordinary course the partnership business or business of the kind carried on by the partnership binds the partnership, unless the partner had no authority to act for the partnership in the particular matter and the person with whom the partner was dealing knew or had received a notification that the partner lacked authority.

(2) An act of a partner which is not apparently for carrying on in the ordinary course the partnership business or business of the kind carried on by the partnership binds the partnership only if the act was authorized by the other partners.

Comment to Original Section 301

1. Section 301 sets forth a partner's power, as an agent of the firm, to bind the partnership entity to third parties. The rights of the partners among themselves, including the right to restrict a partner's authority, are governed by the partnership agreement and by Section 401.

The agency rules set forth in Section 301 are subject to an important qualification. They may be affected by the filing or recording of a statement of partnership authority. The legal effect of filing or recording a statement of partnership authority is set forth in Section 303.

2. Section 301(1) retains the basic principles reflected in UPA Section 9(1). It declares that each partner is an agent of the partnership and that, by virtue of partnership status, each partner has apparent authority to bind the partnership in ordinary course transactions. The effect of Section 301(1) is to characterize a partner as a general managerial agent having both actual and apparent authority co-extensive in scope with the firm's ordinary business, at least in the absence of a contrary partnership agreement.

Section 301(1) effects two changes from UPA Section 9(1). First, it clarifies that a partner's apparent authority includes acts for carrying on in the ordinary course "business of the kind carried on by the partnership," not just the business of the particular partnership in question. The UPA is ambiguous on this point, but there is some authority for an expanded construction in accordance with the so-called English rule. *See, e.g., Burns v. Gonzalez,* 439 S.W.2d 128, 131 (Tex. Civ. App. 1969) (dictum); *Commercial Hotel Co. v. Weeks,* 254 S.W. 521 (Tex. Civ. App. 1923). No substantive change is intended by use of the more customary phrase "carrying on in the ordinary course" in lieu of the UPA phrase "in the usual way." The UPA and the case law use both terms without apparent distinction.

The other change from the UPA concerns the allocation of risk of a partner's lack of authority. RUPA draws the line somewhat differently from the UPA.

Under UPA Section 9(1) and (4), only a person with knowledge of a restriction on a partner's authority is bound by it. Section 301(1) provides that a person who has received a notification of a partner's lack of authority is also bound. The meaning of "receives a notification" is explained in Section 102(d). Thus, the partnership may protect itself from unauthorized acts by giving a notification of a restriction on a partner's authority to a person dealing with that partner. A notification may be effective upon delivery, whether or not it actually comes to the other person's attention. To that extent, the risk of lack of authority is shifted to those dealing with partners.

On the other hand, as used in the UPA, the term "knowledge" embodies the concept of "bad faith" knowledge arising from other known facts. As used in RUPA, however, "knowledge" is limited to actual knowledge. *See* Section 102(a). Thus, RUPA does not expose persons dealing with a partner to the greater risk of being bound by a restriction based on their purported reason to know of the partner's lack of authority from all the facts they did know. *Compare* Section 102(b)(3) (notice).

With one exception, this result is not affected even if the partnership files a statement of partnership authority containing a limitation on a partner's authority. Section 303(f) makes clear that a person dealing with a partner is not deemed to know of such a limitation merely because it is contained in a filed statement of authority. Under Section 303(e), however, all persons are deemed to know of a limitation on the authority of a partner to transfer real property contained in a recorded statement. Thus, a recorded limitation on authority concerning real property constitutes constructive knowledge of the limitation to the whole world.

3. Section 301(2) is drawn directly from UPA Section 9(2), with conforming changes to mirror the new language of subsection (1). Subsection (2) makes it clear that the partnership is bound by a partner's actual authority, even if the partner has no apparent authority. Section 401(j) requires the unanimous consent of the partners for a grant of authority outside the ordinary course of business, unless the partnership agreement provides otherwise. Under general agency principles, the partners can subsequently ratify a partner's unauthorized act. *See* Section 104(a).

4. UPA Section 9(3) contains a list of five extraordinary acts that require unanimous consent of the partners before the partnership is bound. RUPA omits that section. That leaves it to the courts to decide the outer limits of the agency power of a partner. Most of the acts listed in UPA Section 9(3) probably remain outside the apparent authority of a partner under RUPA, such as disposing of the goodwill of the business, but elimination of a statutory rule will afford more flexibility in some situations specified in UPA Section 9(3). In particular, it seems archaic that the submission of a partnership claim to arbitration always requires unanimous consent. *See* UPA § 9(3)(e).

5. Section 301(1) fully reflects the principle embodied in UPA Section 9(4) that the partnership is not bound by an act of a partner in contravention of a restriction on his authority known to the other party.

Section 302. Transfer of Partnership Property

(a) Partnership property may be transferred as follows:

(1) Subject to the effect of a statement of partnership authority under Section 303, partnership property held in the name of the partnership may be transferred by an instrument of transfer executed by a partner in the partnership name.

(2) Partnership property held in the name of one or more partners with an indication in the instrument transferring the property to them of their capacity as partners or of the existence of a partnership, but without an indication of the name of the partnership, may be transferred by an instrument of transfer executed by the persons in whose name the property is held.

(3) Partnership property held in the name of one or more persons other than the partnership, without an indication in the instrument transferring the property to them of their capacity as partners or of the existence of a partnership, may be transferred by an instrument of transfer executed by the persons in whose name the property is held.

(b) A partnership may recover partnership property from a transferee only if it proves that execution of the instrument of initial transfer did not bind the partnership under Section 301 and:

(1) as to a subsequent transferee who gave value for property transferred under subsection (a)(1) and (2), proves that the subsequent transferee knew or had received a notification that the person who executed the instrument of initial transfer lacked authority to bind the partnership; or

(2) as to a transferee who gave value for property transferred under subsection (a)(3), proves that the transferee knew or had received a notification that the property was partnership property and that the person who executed the instrument of initial transfer lacked authority to bind the partnership.

(c) A partnership may not recover partnership property from a subsequent transferee if the partnership would not have been entitled to recover the property, under subsection (b), from any earlier transferee of the property.

(d) If a person holds all of the partners' interests in the partnership, all of the partnership property vests in that person. The person may execute a document in the name of the partnership to evidence vesting of the property in that person and may file or record the document.

Comment to Original Section 302

1. Section 302 replaces UPA Section 10 and provides rules for the transfer and recovery of partnership property. The language is adapted in part from Section 14-8-10 of the Georgia partnership statute.

2. Subsection (a)(1) deals with the transfer of partnership property held in the name of the partnership and subsection (a)(2) with property held in the name of one or more of the partners with an indication either of their capacity as partners or of the existence of a partnership. Subsection (a)(3) deals with partnership property held in the name of one or more of the partners without an indication of their capacity as partners or of the existence of a partnership. Like the general agency rules in Section 301, the power of a partner to transfer partnership property under subsection (a)(1) is subject to the effect under Section 303 of the filing or recording of a statement of partnership authority. These rules are intended to foster reliance on record title.

UPA Section 10 covers only real property. Section 302, however, also governs the transfer of partnership personal property acquired by instrument and held in the name of the partnership or one or more of the partners.

3. Subsection (b) deals with the right of the partnership to recover partnership property transferred by a partner without authority. Subsection (b)(1) deals with the recovery of property held in either the name of the partnership or the name of one or more of the partners with an indication of their capacity as partners or of the existence of a partnership, while subsection (b)(2) deals with the recovery of property held in the name of one or more persons without an indication of their capacity as partners or of the existence of a partnership.

In either case, a transfer of partnership property may be avoided only if the partnership proves that it was not bound under Section 301 by the execution of the instrument of initial transfer. Under Section 301, the partnership is bound by a transfer in the ordinary course of business, unless the transferee actually knew or had received a notification of the partner's lack of authority. *See* Section 102(a) and (d). The reference to Section 301, rather than Section 301(1), is intended to clarify that a partner's actual authority is not revoked by Section 302. *Compare* UPA § 10(1) (refers to partner's authority under Section 9(1)).

The burden of proof is on the partnership to prove the partner's lack of authority and, in the case of a subsequent transferee, the transferee's knowledge or notification thereof. Thus, even if the transfer to the initial transferee could be avoided, the partnership may not recover the property from a subsequent purchaser or other transferee for value unless it also proves that the subsequent transferee knew or had received a notification of the partner's lack of authority with respect to the initial transfer. Since knowledge is required, rather than notice, a remote purchaser has no duty to inquire as to the authority for the initial transfer, even if he knows it was partnership property.

The burden of proof is on the transferee to show that value was given. Value, as used in this context, is synonymous with valuable consideration and means any consideration sufficient to support a simple contract.

The burden of proof on all other issues is allocated to the partnership because it is generally in a better position than the transferee to produce the evidence. Moreover, the partnership may protect itself against unauthorized transfers by ensuring that partnership real property is held in the name of the partnership and that a statement of partnership authority is recorded specifying any limitations on the partners' authority to convey real property. Under Section 303(e), transferees of real property held in the partnership name are conclusively bound by those limitations. On the other hand, transferees can protect themselves by insisting that the partnership record a statement specifying who is authorized to transfer partnership property. Under Section 303(d), transferees for value, without actual knowledge to the contrary, may rely on that grant of authority.

4. Subsection (b)(2) replaces UPA Section 10(3) and provides that partners who hold partnership property in their own names, without an indication in the record of their capacity as partners or of the existence of a partnership, may transfer good title to a transferee for value without knowledge or a notification that it was partnership property. To recover the property under this subsection, the partnership has the burden of proving that the transferee knew or had received a notification of the partnership's interest in the property, as well as of the partner's lack of authority for the initial transfer.

5. Subsection (c) is new and provides that property may not be recovered by the partnership from a remote transferee if any intermediate transferee of the property would have prevailed against the partnership. *Cf.* Uniform Fraudulent Transfer Act, §§ 8(a) (subsequent transferee from bona fide purchaser protected), 8(b)(2) (same).

6. Subsection (d) is new. The UPA does not have a provision dealing with the situation in which all of the partners' interests in the partnership are held by one person, such as a surviving partner or a purchaser of all the other partners' interests. Subsection (d) allows for clear record title, even though the partnership no longer exists as a technical matter. When a partnership becomes a sole proprietorship by reason of the dissociation of all but one of the partners, title vests in the remaining "partner," although there is no "transfer" of the property. The

remaining "partner" may execute a deed or other transfer of record in the name of the non-existent partnership to evidence vesting of the property in that person's individual capacity.

7. UPA Section 10(2) provides that, where title to real property is in the partnership name, a conveyance by a partner in his own name transfers the partnership's equitable interest in the property. It has been omitted as was done in Georgia and Florida. In this situation, the conveyance is clearly outside the chain of title and so should not pass title or any interest in the property. UPA Section 10(2) dilutes, albeit slightly, the effect of record title and is, therefore, inconsistent with RUPA's broad policy of fostering reliance on the record.

UPA Section 10(4) and (5) have also been omitted. Those situations are now adequately covered by Section 302(a).

Section 303.   Statement of Partnership Authority

(a) A partnership may file a statement of partnership authority, which:
(1) must include:
(i) the name of the partnership;
(ii) the street address of its chief executive office and of one office in this State, if there is one;
(iii) the names and mailing addresses of all of the partners or of an agent appointed and maintained by the partnership for the purpose of subsection (b); and
(iv) the names of the partners authorized to execute an instrument transferring real property held in the name of the partnership; and
(2) may state the authority, or limitations on the authority, of some or all of the partners to enter into other transactions on behalf of the partnership and any other matter.

(b) If a statement of partnership authority names an agent, the agent shall maintain a list of the names and mailing addresses of all of the partners and make it available to any person on request for good cause shown.

(c) If a filed statement of partnership authority is executed pursuant to Section 105(c) and states the name of the partnership but does not contain all of the other information required by subsection (a), the statement nevertheless operates with respect to a person not a partner as provided in subsections (d) and (e).

(d) Except as otherwise provided in subsection (g), a filed statement of partnership authority supplements the authority of a partner to enter into transactions on behalf of the partnership as follows:
(1) Except for transfers of real property, a grant of authority contained in a filed statement of partnership authority is conclusive in favor of a person who gives value without knowledge to the contrary, so long as and to the extent that a limitation on that authority is not then contained in another filed state-

ment. A filed cancellation of a limitation on authority revives the previous grant of authority.

(2) A grant of authority to transfer real property held in the name of the partnership contained in a certified copy of a filed statement of partnership authority recorded in the office for recording transfers of that real property is conclusive in favor of a person who gives value without knowledge to the contrary, so long as and to the extent that a certified copy of a filed statement containing a limitation on that authority is not then of record in the office for recording transfers of that real property. The recording in the office for recording transfers of that real property of a certified copy of a filed cancellation of a limitation on authority revives the previous grant of authority.

(e) A person not a partner is deemed to know of a limitation on the authority of a partner to transfer real property held in the name of the partnership if a certified copy of the filed statement containing the limitation on authority is of record in the office for recording transfers of that real property.

(f) Except as otherwise provided in subsections (d) and (e) and Sections 704 and 805, a person not a partner is not deemed to know of a limitation on the authority of a partner merely because the limitation is contained in a filed statement.

(g) Unless earlier canceled, a filed statement of partnership authority is canceled by operation of law five years after the date on which the statement, or the most recent amendment, was filed with the [Secretary of State].

Comment to Original Section 303

1. Section 303 is new. It provides for an optional statement of partnership authority specifying the names of the partners authorized to execute instruments transferring real property held in the name of the partnership. It may also grant supplementary authority to partners, or limit their authority, to enter into other transactions on behalf of the partnership. The execution, filing, and recording of statements is governed by Section 105.

RUPA follows the lead of California and Georgia in authorizing the optional filing of statements of authority. Filing a statement of partnership authority may be deemed to satisfy the disclosure required by a State's fictitious name statute, if the State so chooses.

Section 105 provides for the central filing of statements, rather than local filing. However, to be effective in connection with the transfer of real property, a statement of partnership authority must also be recorded locally with the land records.

2. The most important goal of the statement of authority is to facilitate the transfer of real property held in the name of the partnership. A statement must specify the names of the partners authorized to execute an instrument transferring that property.

Under subsection (d)(2), a recorded grant of authority to transfer real property held in the name of the partnership is conclusive in favor of a transferee for value without actual knowledge to the contrary. A partner's authority to transfer partnership real property is affected by a recorded statement only if the property is held in the name of the partnership. A recorded statement has no effect on the partners' authority to transfer partnership real property that is held other than in the name of the partnership. In that case, by definition, the record will not indicate the name of the partnership, and thus the partnership's interest would not be disclosed by a title search. *See* Section 204. To be effective, the statement recorded with the land records must be a certified copy of the original statement filed with the secretary of state. *See* Section 105(b).

The presumption of authority created by subsection (d)(2) operates only so long as and to the extent that a limitation on the partner's authority is not contained in another recorded statement. This is intended to condition reliance on the record to situations where there is no conflict among recorded statements, amendments, or denials of authority. *See* Section 304. If the record is in conflict regarding a partner's authority, transferees must go outside the record to determine the partners' actual authority. This rule is modified slightly in the case of a cancellation of a limitation on a partner's authority, which revives the previous grant of authority.

Under subsection (e), third parties are deemed to know of a recorded limitation on the authority of a partner to transfer real property held in the partnership name. Since transferees are bound under Section 301 by knowledge of a limitation on a partner's authority, they are bound by such a recorded limitation. Of course, a transferee with actual knowledge of a limitation on a partner's authority is bound under Section 301, whether or not there is a recorded statement of limitation.

3. A statement of partnership authority may have effect beyond the transfer of real property held in the name of the partnership. Under subsection (a)(2), a statement of authority may contain any other matter the partnership chooses, including a grant of authority, or a limitation on the authority, of some or all of the partners to enter into other transactions on behalf of the partnership. Since Section 301 confers authority on all partners to act for the partnership in ordinary matters, the real import of such a provision is to grant extraordinary authority, or to limit the ordinary authority, of some or all of the partners.

The effect given to such a provision is different from that accorded a provision regarding the transfer of real property. Under subsection (d)(1), a filed grant of authority is binding on the partnership, in favor of a person who gives value without actual knowledge to the contrary, unless limited by another filed statement. That is the same rule as for statements involving real property under subsection 301(d)(2). There is, however, no counterpart to subsection (e) regarding a filed limitation of authority. To the contrary, subsection (f) makes clear that filing a limitation of authority does *not* operate as constructive knowledge of a partner's lack of authority with respect to non-real property transactions.

Under Section 301, only a third party who knows or has received a notification of a partner's lack of authority in an ordinary course transaction is bound. Thus, a limitation on a partner's authority to transfer personal property or to enter into other non-real property transactions on behalf of the partnership, contained in a filed statement of partnership authority, is effective only against a third party who knows or has received a notification of it. The fact of the statement being filed has no legal significance in those transactions, although the filed statement is a potential source of actual knowledge to third parties.

4. It should be emphasized that Section 303 concerns the authority of partners to bind the partnership to third persons. As among the partners, the authority of a partner to take any action is governed by the partnership agreement, or by the provisions of RUPA governing the relations among partners, and is not affected by the filing or recording of a statement of partnership authority.

5. The exercise of the option to file a statement of partnership authority imposes a further disclosure obligation on the partnership. Under subsection (a)(1), a filed statement must include the street address of its chief executive office and of an office in the State (if any), as well as the names and mailing addresses of all of the partners or, alternatively, of an agent appointed and maintained by the partnership for the purpose of maintaining such a list. If an agent is appointed, subsection (b) provides that the agent shall maintain a list of all of the partners and make it available to any person on request for good cause shown. Under subsection (c), the failure to make all of the required disclosures does not affect the statement's operative effect, however.

6. Under subsection (g), a statement of authority is canceled by operation of law five years after the date on which the statement, or the most recent amendment, was filed.

7. Section 308(c) makes clear that a person does not become a partner solely because he is named as a partner in a statement of partnership authority filed by another person. *See also* Section 304 ("person named as a partner" may file statement of denial).

8. Under certain circumstances a statement of authority can potentially affect the tax status of a partnership. Under the classification regulations in the Internal Revenue Code, centralization of management may exist if there is any limitation on the normal agency authority of partners. *See* Treas. Reg. § 301.7701-2(c). A statement of authority that simply names the partners who are authorized to execute deeds or other instruments transferring partnership real property, pursuant to Section 303(a)(1)(iv), does not create a tax classification problem because that designation has no effect on the agency power of the partners to bind the partnership by entering into the transaction. The mere execution of the instruments transferring partnership property is essentially a ministerial act and presupposes that the underlying transaction has already been approved and is

binding on the partnership. If the statement of authority goes further and grants some partners more power than other partners to bind the partnership or limits the normal agency authority of one or more partners, however, a potential centralization of management issue exists. The distinction is between saying "Partner John Smith is authorized to sign deeds and other instruments conveying interests in the partnership's real property" and "Partner John Smith has the exclusive power to enter into transactions on behalf of this partnership" or "Partner John Smith cannot enter into any transaction exceeding $5,000."

Even if the statement of partnership authority contains a special grant or limitation of authority, the potential adverse tax consequences are minimal for two reasons. First, whether the particular partnership will be held to have centralized management depends on all the facts and circumstances. The statement of authority is merely one factor in the analysis. Second, even if there is centralized management, the partnership will still be taxed under Subchapter K of the Internal Revenue Code unless it also possess at least two of the three other corporate characteristics deemed important by the Regulations: (1) continuity of life, (2) limited liability, and (3) free transferability of interests; that will rarely be the case.

Section 304.   Statement of Denial

A partner or other person named as a partner in a filed statement of partnership authority or in a list maintained by an agent pursuant to Section 303(b) may file a statement of denial stating the name of the partnership and the fact that is being denied, which may include denial of a person's authority or status as a partner. A statement of denial is a limitation on authority as provided in Section 303(d) and (e).

Comment to Original Section 304

Section 304 is new and complements Section 303. It provides partners (and persons named as partners) an opportunity to deny any fact asserted in a statement of partnership authority, including denial of a person's status as a partner or of another person's authority as a partner. A statement of denial must be executed, filed, and recorded pursuant to the requirements of Section 105.

Section 304 does not address the consequences of a denial of partnership. No adverse inference should be drawn from the failure of a person named as a partner to deny such status, however. *See* Section 308(c) (person not liable as a partner merely because named in statement as a partner).

A statement of denial operates as a limitation on a partner's authority to the extent provided in Section 303. Section 303(d) provides that a filed or recorded statement of partnership authority is conclusive, in favor of purchasers without knowledge to the contrary, so long as and to the extent that a limitation on that authority is not contained in another filed or recorded statement. A filed or recorded statement of denial operates as such a limitation on authority, thereby precluding reliance on an inconsistent grant of authority. Under Section 303(d), a filed or recorded cancellation of a statement of denial that operates as a limitation on authority revives the previous grant of authority.

Under Section 303(e), a recorded statement of denial of a partner's authority to transfer partnership real property held in the partnership name constitutes constructive knowledge of that limitation.

Section 305.   Partnership Liable for Partner's Actionable Conduct

(a) A partnership is liable for loss or injury caused to a person, or for a penalty incurred, as a result of a wrongful act or omission, or other actionable conduct, of a partner acting in the ordinary course of business of the partnership or with authority of the partnership.

(b) If, in the course of the partnership's business or while acting with authority of the partnership, a partner receives or causes the partnership to receive money or property of a person not a partner, and the money or property is misapplied by a partner, the partnership is liable for the loss.

Comment to Original Section 305

Section 305(a), which is derived from UPA Section 13, imposes liability on the partnership for the wrongful acts of a partner acting in the ordinary course of the partnership's business or otherwise within the partner's authority. The scope of the section has been expanded by deleting from UPA Section 13, "not being a partner in the partnership." This is intended to permit a partner to sue the partnership on a tort or other theory during the term of the partnership, rather than being limited to the remedies of dissolution and an accounting. *See also* Comment 2 to Section 405.

The section has also been broadened to cover no-fault torts by the addition of the phrase, "or other actionable conduct."

The partnership is liable for the actionable conduct or omission of a partner acting in the ordinary course of its business or "with the authority of the partnership." This is intended to include a partner's apparent, as well as actual, authority, thereby bringing within Section 305(a) the situation covered in UPA Section 14(a).

The phrase in UPA Section 13, "to the same extent as the partner so acting or omitting to act," has been deleted to prevent a partnership from asserting a partner's immunity from liability. This is consistent with the general agency rule that a principal is not entitled to its agent's immunities. *See* Restatement (Second) of Agency § 217(b) (1957). The deletion is not intended to limit a partnership's contractual rights.

Section 305(b) is drawn from UPA Section 14(b), but has been edited to improve clarity. It imposes strict liability on the partnership for the misapplication of money or property received by a partner in the course of the partnership's business or otherwise within the scope of the partner's actual authority.

Section 306.   Partner's Liability

(a) Except as otherwise provided in ~~subsection~~ subsections (b) <u>and (c)</u>, all partners are liable jointly and severally for all obligations of the partnership unless otherwise agreed by the claimant or provided by law.

(b) A person admitted as a partner into an existing partnership is not personally liable for any partnership obligation incurred before the person's admission as a partner.

<u>(c) An obligation of a partnership incurred while the partnership is a limited liability partnership, whether arising in contract, tort, or otherwise, is solely the obligation of the partnership. A partner is not personally liable, directly or indirectly, including by way of contribution or otherwise, for such a partnership obligation solely by reason of being or so acting as a partner. This subsection applies notwithstanding anything inconsistent in the partnership agreement that existed immediately before the vote required to become a limited liability partnership under Section 1001(b).</u>

Comment to Original Section 306

1. Section 306(a) changes the UPA rule by imposing joint and several liability on the partners for all partnership obligations. Under UPA Section 15, partners' liability for torts is joint and several, while their liability for contracts is joint but not several. About ten States that have adopted the UPA already provide for joint and several liability. The UPA reference to "debts and obligations" is redundant, and no change is intended by RUPA's reference solely to "obligations."

Joint and several liability under RUPA differs, however, from the classic model, which permits a judgment creditor to proceed immediately against any of the joint and several judgment debtors. Generally, Section 307(d) requires the judgment creditor to exhaust the partnership's assets before enforcing a judgment against the separate assets of a partner.

2. RUPA continues the UPA scheme of liability with respect to an incoming partner, but states the rule more clearly and simply. Under Section 306(a), an incoming partner becomes jointly and severally liable, as a partner, for all partnership obligations, except as otherwise provided in subsection (b). That subsection eliminates an incoming partner's personal liability for partnership obligations incurred before his admission as a partner. In effect, a new partner has no personal liability to existing creditors of the partnership, and only his investment in the firm is at risk for the satisfaction of existing partnership debts. That is presently the rule under UPA Sections 17 and 41(7), and no substantive change is intended. As under the UPA, a new partner's personal assets are at risk with respect to partnership liabilities incurred after his admission as a partner.

Comment to Amendments

Subject to the Section 307(d) partnership asset exhaustion rule, Section 306(a) imposes classic joint and several liability on all partners. Section 306(c) effaces this hallmark liability feature where the partnership is a limited liability partnership. Like shareholders of a corporation and members of a limited liability company, partners of a limited liability partnership are not personally liable for partnership obligations incurred while the partnership liability shield is in place solely because they are partners. As with shareholders of a corporation and members of a limited liability company, partners remain personally liable for personal misconduct. In cases of partner misconduct, Section 401(c) determines a partnership's obligation to indemnify the culpable partner where the liability was incurred in the ordinary course of the partnership's business. When indemnification occurs, the assets of the partnership as well as the culpable partner's assets are available to a creditor. However, Sections 306(c), 401(b), and 807(b) make clear that a partner who is not otherwise liable under Section 306(c) is not obligated to contribute assets in excess of agreed contributions to the partnership, to further share the loss with the culpable partner. (*See* Sections 401(b) and 807(b) cmts. regarding a slight variation on this theme in the context of priority of payment of partnership obligations. Accordingly, Section 306(c) makes clear that an innocent partner is not personally liable for specified partnership obligations, directly or indirectly, by way of contribution or otherwise.

Although the liability shield protections of Section 306(c) may be modified in part or in full in a partnership agreement (and certainly by way of private contractual guarantees), the modifications must constitute an intentional waiver of the liability protections. *See* Sections 103(b), 104(a), and 902(b). Since the mere act of filing a statement of qualification reflects the assumption that the partners intend to modify the otherwise applicable partner liability rules, the final sentence of subsection (c) makes clear that the filing negates inconsistent aspects of the partnership agreement that existed immediately before the vote to approve becoming a limited liability partnership. Of course, the sentence only applies to a partner's personal liability for future partnership obligations. For example, it has no effect as to previously created partner obligations to the partnership in the form of specific capital contribution requirements.

Partners of a limited liability partnership should be aware that inter se contribution agreements may erode part or all of the effects of the liability shield. For example, Section 807(f) provides that an assignee for the benefit of creditors of a partnership or a partner may enforce a partner's obligation to contribute to the partnership. The ultimate effect of such contribution obligations may make each partner jointly and severally liable for all partnership obligations — even those incurred while the partnership is a limited liability partnership.

The connection between partner status and personal liability for partnership obligations is severed only with respect to obligations that are incurred while the partnership is a limited liability partnership. Partnership obligations that are incurred before a partnership becomes a limited liability partnership or that are incurred after limited liability partnership status is revoked or canceled are treated as obligations of an ordinary partnership. *See* Sections 1001 (filing), 1003 (revocation), and 1006 (cancellation). Obligations incurred by a partnership during the period when its statement of qualification is administratively will nevertheless be considered as incurred by a limited liability partnership provided the partnership's status as such is reinstated within two years under Section 1003(e). *See* Section 1003(f).

For the limited purpose of determining when a partnership obligation relating to a contract claim is incurred, the reasonable expectations of creditors and the partners are paramount. Therefore, partnership obligations under or relating to a note, contract, or other agreement generally are incurred when the note, contract, or other agreement is made. Also, an amendment, modification, extension, or renewal of a note, contract, or other agreement should not affect or otherwise reset the time at which a partnership obligation under or relating to that note, contract, or other agreement is incurred, even as to a claim that relates to the subject matter of the amendment, modification, extension, or renewal. A note, contract, or other agreement may expressly modify these rules and fix the time a partnership obligation is incurred thereunder.

For the limited purpose of determining when a partnership obligation relating to a tort claim is incurred, a distinction is intended between injury and the conduct causing that injury. The purpose of the distinction is to prevent unjust results. Partnership obligations under or relating to a tort generally are incurred when the tortuous conduct occurs rather than at the time of the actual injury or harm. This interpretation prevents a culpable partnership from engaging in wrongful conduct and then filing a statement of qualification to sever vicarious responsibility of its partners for future injury or harm caused by conduct that occurred prior to the filing.

Section 307. Actions by and Against Partnership and Partners

(a) A partnership may sue and be sued in the name of the partnership.

(b) ~~An~~ Except as otherwise provided in subsection (f), action may be brought against the partnership and any or all of the partners in the same action or in separate actions.

(c) A judgment against a partnership is not by itself a judgment against a partner. A judgment against a partnership may not be satisfied from a partner's assets unless there is also a judgment against the partner.

(d) A judgment creditor of a partner may not levy execution against the assets of the partner to satisfy a judgment based on a claim against the partnership unless the partner is personally liable for the claim under Section 306 and:

(1) a judgment based on the same claim has been obtained against the partnership and a writ of execution on the judgment has been returned unsatisfied in whole or in part;

(2) the partnership is a debtor in bankruptcy;

(3) the partner has agreed that the creditor need not exhaust partnership assets;

(4) a court grants permission to the judgment creditor to levy execution against the assets of a partner based on a finding that partnership assets subject to execution are clearly insufficient to satisfy the judgment, that exhaustion of partnership assets is excessively burdensome, or that the grant of permission is an appropriate exercise of the court's equitable powers; or

(5) liability is imposed on the partner by law or contract independent of the existence of the partnership.

(e) This section applies to any partnership liability or obligation resulting from a representation by a partner or purported partner under Section 308.

(f) A partner is not a proper party to an action against a partnership if that partner is not personally liable for the claim under Section 306.

Comment to Original Section 307

1. Section 307 is new. Subsection (a) provides that a partnership may sue and be sued in the partnership name. That entity approach is designed to simplify suits by and against a partnership.

At common law, a partnership, not being a legal entity, could not sue or be sued in the firm name. The UPA itself is silent on this point, so in the absence of another enabling statute, it is generally necessary to join all the partners in an action against the partnership.

Most States have statutes or rules authorizing partnerships to sue or be sued in the partnership name. Many of those statutes, however, are found in the state provisions dealing with civil procedure rather than in the partnership act.

2. Subsection (b) provides that suit may be brought against the partnership and any or all of the partners in the same action or in separate actions. It is intended to clarify that the partners need not be named in an action against the partnership. In particular, in an action against a partnership, it is not necessary to name a partner individually in addition to the partnership. This will simplify and reduce the cost of litigation, especially in cases of small claims where there are known to be significant partnership assets and thus no necessity to collect the judgment out of the partners' assets.

3. Subsection (c) provides that a judgment against the partnership is not, standing alone, a judgment against the partners, and it cannot be satisfied from a partner's personal assets unless there is a judgment against the partner. Thus, a partner must be individually named and served, either in the action against the partnership or in a later suit, before his personal assets may be subject to levy for a claim against the partnership.

RUPA leaves it to the law of judgments, as did the UPA, to determine the collateral effects to be accorded a prior judgment for or against the partnership in a subsequent action against a partner individually. *See* Section 60 of the Second Restatement of Judgments (1982) and the Comments thereto.

4. Subsection (d) requires partnership creditors to exhaust the partnership's assets before levying on a judgment debtor partner's individual property. That rule respects the concept of the partnership as an entity and makes partners more in the nature of guarantors than principal debtors on every partnership debt. It is already the law in some States.

As a general rule, a final judgment against a partner cannot be enforced by a creditor against the partner's separate assets unless a writ of execution against the partnership has been returned unsatisfied. Under subsection (d), however, a creditor may proceed directly against the partner's assets if (i) the partnership is a debtor in bankruptcy (*see* Section 101(2)); (ii) the partner has consented; or (iii) the liability is imposed on the partner independently of the partnership. For example, a judgment creditor may proceed directly against the assets of a partner who is liable independently as the primary tortfeasor, but must exhaust the partnership's assets before proceeding against the separate assets of the other partners who are liable only as partners.

There is also a judicial override provision in subsection (d)(4). A court may authorize execution against the partner's assets on the grounds that (i) the partnership's assets are clearly insufficient; (ii) exhaustion of the partnership's assets would be excessively burdensome; or (iii) it is otherwise equitable to do so. For example, if the partners who are parties to the action have assets located in the forum State, but the partnership does not, a court might find that exhaustion of the partnership's assets would be excessively burdensome.

5. Although subsection (d) is silent with respect to pre-judgment remedies, the law of pre-judgment remedies already adequately embodies the principle that partnership assets should be exhausted before partners' assets are attached or

garnished. Attachment, for example, typically requires a showing that the partnership's assets are being secreted or fraudulently transferred or are otherwise inadequate to satisfy the plaintiff's claim. A showing of some exigent circumstance may also be required to satisfy due process. *See Connecticut v. Doehr*, 501 U.S. 1, 16 (1991).

6. Subsection (e) clarifies that actions against the partnership under Section 308, involving representations by partners or purported partners, are subject to Section 307.

Section 308.   Liability of Purported Partner

(a) If a person, by words or conduct, purports to be a partner, or consents to being represented by another as a partner, in a partnership or with one or more persons not partners, the purported partner is liable to a person to whom the representation is made, if that person, relying on the representation, enters into a transaction with the actual or purported partnership. If the representation, either by the purported partner or by a person with the purported partner's consent, is made in a public manner, the purported partner is liable to a person who relies upon the purported partnership even if the purported partner is not aware of being held out as a partner to the claimant. If partnership liability results, the purported partner is liable with respect to that liability as if the purported partner were a partner. If no partnership liability results, the purported partner is liable with respect to that liability jointly and severally with any other person consenting to the representation.

(b) If a person is thus represented to be a partner in an existing partnership, or with one or more persons not partners, the purported partner is an agent of persons consenting to the representation to bind them to the same extent and in the same manner as if the purported partner were a partner, with respect to persons who enter into transactions in reliance upon the representation. If all of the partners of the existing partnership consent to the representation, a partnership act or obligation results. If fewer than all of the partners of the existing partnership consent to the representation, the person acting and the partners consenting to the representation are jointly and severally liable.

(c) A person is not liable as a partner merely because the person is named by another in a statement of partnership authority.

(d) A person does not continue to be liable as a partner merely because of a failure to file a statement of dissociation or to amend a statement of partnership authority to indicate the partner's dissociation from the partnership.

(e) Except as otherwise provided in subsections (a) and (b), persons who are not partners as to each other are not liable as partners to other persons.

Comment to Original Section 308

Section 308 continues the basic principles of partnership by estoppel from UPA Section 16, now more accurately entitled "Liability of Purported Partner." Subsection (a) continues the distinction between representations made to specific persons and those made in a public manner. It is the exclusive basis for imposing liability as a partner on persons who are not partners in fact. As under the UPA, there is no duty of denial, and thus a person held out by another as a partner is not liable unless he actually consents to the representation. *See* the Official Comment to UPA Section 16. Also *see* Section 308(c) (no duty to file statement of denial) and Section 308(d) (no duty to file statement of dissociation or to amend statement of partnership authority).

Subsection (b) emphasizes that the persons being protected by Section 308 are those who enter into transactions in reliance upon a representation. If all of the partners of an existing partnership consent to the representation, a partnership obligation results. Apart from Section 308, the firm may be bound in other situations under general principles of apparent authority or ratification.

If a partnership liability results under Section 308, the creditor must exhaust the partnership's assets before seeking to satisfy the claim from the partners. *See* Section 307.

Subsections (c) and (d) are new and deal with potential negative inferences to be drawn from a failure to correct inaccurate or outdated filed statements. Subsection (c) makes clear that an otherwise innocent person is not liable as a partner for failing to deny his partnership status as asserted by a third person in a statement of partnership authority. Under subsection (d), a partner's liability as a partner does not continue after dissociation solely because of a failure to file a statement of dissociation.

Subsection (e) is derived from UPA Section 7(1). It means that only those persons who are partners as among themselves are liable as partners to third parties for the obligations of the partnership, except for liabilities incurred by purported partners under Section 308(a) and (b).

[ARTICLE] 4.   RELATIONS OF PARTNERS TO EACH OTHER AND TO PARTNERSHIP

Section 401.   Partner's Rights and Duties

(a) Each partner is deemed to have an account that is:

(1) credited with an amount equal to the money plus the value of any other property, net of the amount of any liabilities, the partner contributes to the partnership and the partner's share of the partnership profits; and

(2) charged with an amount equal to the money plus the value of any other property, net of the amount of any liabilities, distributed by the partnership to the partner and the partner's share of the partnership losses.

(b) Each partner is entitled to an equal share of the partnership profits and is chargeable with a share of the partnership losses in proportion to the partner's share of the profits.

(c) A partnership shall reimburse a partner for payments made and indemnify a partner for liabilities incurred by the partner in the ordinary course of the business of the partnership or for the preservation of its business or property.

(d) A partnership shall reimburse a partner for an advance to the partnership beyond the amount of capital the partner agreed to contribute.

(e) A payment or advance made by a partner which gives rise to a partnership obligation under subsection (c) or (d) constitutes a loan to the partnership which accrues interest from the date of the payment or advance.

(f) Each partner has equal rights in the management and conduct of the partnership business.

(g) A partner may use or possess partnership property only on behalf of the partnership.

(h) A partner is not entitled to remuneration for services performed for the partnership, except for reasonable compensation for services rendered in winding up the business of the partnership.

(i) A person may become a partner only with the consent of all of the partners.

(j) A difference arising as to a matter in the ordinary course of business of a partnership may be decided by a majority of the partners. An act outside the ordinary course of business of a partnership and an amendment to the partnership agreement may be undertaken only with the consent of all of the partners.

(k) This section does not affect the obligations of a partnership to other persons under Section 301.

Comment to Original Section 401

1. Section 401 is drawn substantially from UPA Section 18. It establishes many of the default rules that govern the relations among partners. All of these rules are, however, subject to contrary agreement of the partners as provided in Section 103.

2. Subsection (a) provides that each partner is deemed to have an account that is credited with the partner's contributions and share of the partnership profits and charged with distributions to the partner and the partner's share of partnership losses. In the absence of another system of partnership accounts, these rules establish a rudimentary system of accounts for the partnership. The rules regarding the settlement of the partners' accounts upon the dissolution and winding up of the partnership business are found in Section 807.

3. Subsection (b) establishes the default rules for the sharing of partnership profits and losses. The UPA Section 18(a) rules that profits are shared equally and that losses, whether capital or operating, are shared in proportion to each partner's share of the profits are continued. Thus, under the default rule, partners share profits per capita and not in proportion to capital contribution as do corporate shareholders or partners in limited partnerships. *Compare* RULPA Section 504. With respect to losses, the qualifying phrase, "whether capital or operating," has been deleted as inconsistent with contemporary partnership accounting practice and terminology; no substantive change is intended.

If partners agree to share profits other than equally, losses will be shared similarly to profits, absent agreement to do otherwise. That rule, carried over from the UPA, is predicated on the assumption that partners would likely agree to share losses on the same basis as profits, but may fail to say so. Of course, by agreement, they may share losses on a different basis from profits.

The default rules apply, as does UPA Section 18(a), where one or more of the partners contribute no capital, although there is case law to the contrary. *See, e.g., Kovacik v. Reed*, 49 Cal. 2d 166, 315 P.2d 314 (1957); *Becker v. Killarney*, 177 Ill. App. 3d 793, 523 N.E.2d 467 (1988). It may seem unfair that the contributor of services, who contributes little or no capital, should be obligated to contribute toward the capital loss of the large contributor who contributed no services. In entering a partnership with such a capital structure, the partners should foresee that application of the default rule may bring about unusual results and take advantage of their power to vary by agreement the allocation of capital losses.

Subsection (b) provides that each partner "is chargeable" with a share of the losses, rather than the UPA formulation that each partner shall "contribute" to losses. Losses are charged to each partner's account as provided in subsection (a)(2). It is intended to make clear that a partner is not obligated to contribute to partnership losses before his withdrawal or the liquidation of the partnership, unless the partners agree otherwise. In effect, a partner's negative account represents a debt to the partnership unless the partners agree to the contrary. Similarly, each partner's share of the profits is credited to his account under subsection (a)(1). Absent an agreement to the contrary, however, a partner does not have a right to receive a current distribution of the profits credited to his account, the interim distribution of profits being a matter arising in the ordinary course of business to be decided by majority vote of the partners.

4. Subsection (c) is derived from UPA Section 18(b) and provides that the partnership shall reimburse partners for payments made and indemnify them for liabilities incurred in the ordinary course of the partnership's business or for the preservation of its business or property. Reimbursement and indemnification is an obligation of the partnership. Indemnification may create a loss toward which the partners must contribute. Although the right to indemnification is usually enforced in the settlement of accounts among partners upon dissolution and winding up of the partnership business, the right accrues when the liability is incurred and thus may be enforced during the term of the partnership in an appropriate case. *See* Section 405 and Comment.

5. Subsection (d) is based on UPA Section 18(c). It makes explicit that the partnership must reimburse a partner for an advance of funds beyond the amount of the partner's agreed capital contribution, thereby treating the advance as a loan.

6. Subsection (e), which is also drawn from UPA Section 18(c), characterizes the partnership's obligation under subsections (c) or (d) as a loan to the partnership which accrues interest from the date of the payment or advance. *See* Section 104(b) (default rate of interest).

7. Under subsection (f), each partner has equal rights in the management and conduct of the business. It is based on UPA Section 18(e), which has been interpreted broadly to mean that, absent contrary agreement, each partner has a continuing right to participate in the management of the partnership and to be informed about the partnership business, even if his assent to partnership business decisions is not required.

8. Subsection (g) provides that partners may use or possess partnership property only for partnership purposes. That is the edited remains of UPA Section 25(2)(a), which deals in detail with the incidents of tenancy in partnership. That tenancy is abolished as a consequence of the entity theory of partnerships. *See* Section 501 and Comments.

9. Subsection (h) continues the UPA Section 18(f) rule that a partner is not entitled to remuneration for services performed, except in winding up the partnership. Subsection (h) deletes the UPA reference to a "surviving" partner. That means any partner winding up the business is entitled to compensation, not just a surviving partner winding up after the death of another partner. The exception is

not intended to apply in the hypothetical winding up that takes place if there is a buyout under Article 7.

10. Subsection (i) continues the substance of UPA Section 18(g) that no person can become a partner without the consent of all the partners.

11. Subsection (j) continues with one important clarification the UPA Section 18(h) scheme of allocating management authority among the partners. In the absence of an agreement to the contrary, matters arising in the ordinary course of the business may be decided by a majority of the partners. Amendments to the partnership agreement and matters outside the ordinary course of the partnership business require unanimous of the partners. Although the text of the UPA is silent regarding extraordinary matters, courts have generally required the consent of all partners for those matters. *See, e.g., Paciaroni v. Crane*, 408 A.2d 946 (Del. Ch. 1989); *Thomas v. Marvin E. Jewell & Co.*, 232 Neb. 261, 440 N.W.2d 437 (1989); *Duell v. Hancock*, 83 A.D.2d 762, 443 N.Y.S.2d 490 (1981).

It is not intended that subsection (j) embrace a claim for an objection to a partnership decision that is not discovered until after the fact. There is no cause of action based on that after-the-fact second-guessing.

12. Subsection (k) is new and was added to make it clear that Section 301 governs partners' agency power to bind the partnership to third persons, while Section 401 governs partners' rights among themselves.

Comment to Amendments

The absence of a liability shield amendment to Section 401(b) makes clear that a partnership remains liable for its obligations incurred while they are a limited liability partnership. However, a partner's obligation to contribute to a partnership's losses beyond previously agreed contributions is limited to the partner's share of partnership obligations for which that partner is personally liable under Section 306.

In the case of an operating limited liability partnership, the Section 306 liability shield may be partially eroded where the limited liability partnership incurs both shielded and unshielded liabilities. Where the limited liability partnership uses its assets to pay shielded liabilities before paying unshielded liabilities, each partner's obligation to contribute to the limited liability partnership for that partner's share of the unpaid and unshielded obligations remains intact. The same issue is less likely to occur in the context of the termination of a limited liability partnership since a partner's contribution obligation is based only on that partner's share of unshielded obligations and the partnership will ordinarily use the contributed assets to pay unshielded claims first as they were the basis of the contribution obligation. *See* Section 807(b) comment.

Section 401(c) makes clear that a partner's right to indemnification by the entity is not affected by a partnership becoming a limited liability partnership.

Accordingly, partners continue to share partnership losses to the extent of partnership assets.

Section 402.   Distributions in Kind

A partner has no right to receive, and may not be required to accept, a distribution in kind.

Comment to Original Section 402

Section 402 provides that a partner has no right to demand and receive a distribution in kind and may not be required to take a distribution in kind. That continues the "in kind" rule of UPA Section 38(*l*). The new language is suggested by RULPA Section 605.

This section is complemented by Section 807(a) which provides that, in winding up the partnership business on dissolution, any surplus after the payment of partnership obligations must be applied to pay in cash the net amount distributable to each partner.

Section 403.   Partner's Rights and Duties with Respect to Information

(a) A partnership shall keep its books and records, if any, at its chief executive office.

(b) A partnership shall provide partners and their agents and attorneys access to its books and records. It shall provide former partners and their agents and attorneys access to books and records pertaining to the period during which they were partners. The right of access provides the opportunity to inspect and copy books and records during ordinary business hours. A partnership may impose a reasonable charge, covering the costs of labor and material, for copies of documents furnished.

(c) Each partner and the partnership shall furnish to a partner, and to the legal representative of a deceased partner or partner under legal disability:

(1) without demand, any information concerning the partnership's business and affairs reasonably required for the proper exercise of the partner's rights and duties under the partnership agreement or this [Act]; and

(2) on demand, any other information concerning the partnership's business and affairs, except to the extent the demand or the information demanded is unreasonable or otherwise improper under the circumstances.

Comment to Original Section 403

1. Subsection (a) provides that the partnership's books and records, if any, shall be kept at its chief executive office. It continues the UPA Section 19 rule, modified to include partnership records other than its "books," i.e., financial records. The concept of "chief executive office" comes from UCC Section 9-103(3)(d). *See* the Comment to Section 106.

Since general partnerships are often informal or even inadvertent, no books and records are enumerated as mandatory, such as that found in RULPA Section 105. Any requirement in UPA Section 19 that the partnership keep books is oblique at best, since it states merely where the books shall be kept, not that they shall be kept. Under RUPA, there is no liability to either partners or third parties for the failure to keep partnership books. A partner who undertakes to keep books, however, must do so accurately and adequately.

In general, a partnership should, at a minimum, keep those books and records necessary to enable the partners to determine their share of the profits and losses, as well as their rights on withdrawal. An action for an accounting provides an adequate remedy in the event adequate records are not kept. The partnership must also maintain any books and records required by state or federal taxing or other governmental authorities.

2. Under subsection (b), partners are entitled to access to the partnership books and records. Former partners are expressly given a similar right, although limited to the books and records pertaining to the period during which they were partners. The line between partners and former partners is not a bright one for this purpose, however, and should be drawn in light of the legitimate interests of a dissociated partner in the partnership. For example, a withdrawing partner's liability is ongoing for pre-withdrawal liabilities and will normally be extended to new liabilities for at least 90 days. It is intended that a former partner be accorded access to partnership books and records as reasonably necessary to protect that partner's legitimate interests during the period his rights and liabilities are being wound down.

The right of access is limited to ordinary business hours, and the right to inspect and copy by agent or attorney is made explicit. The partnership may impose a reasonable charge for furnishing copies of documents. *Accord*, RULPA § 105(b).

A partner's right to inspect and copy the partnership's books and records is not conditioned on the partner's purpose or motive. *Compare* RMBCA Section 16.02(c)(*1*) (shareholder must have proper purpose to inspect certain corporate records). A partner's unlimited personal liability justifies an unqualified right of access to the partnership books and records. An abuse of the right to inspect and copy might constitute a violation of the obligation of good faith and fair dealing for which the other partners would have a remedy. *See* Sections 404(d) and 405.

Under Section 103(b)(2), a partner's right of access to partnership books and records may not be unreasonably restricted by the partnership agreement. Thus, to preserve a partner's core information rights despite unequal bargaining power, an agreement limiting a partner's right to inspect and copy partnership books and records is subject to judicial review. Nevertheless, reasonable restrictions on access to partnership books and records by agreement are authorized. For example, a provision in a partnership agreement denying partners access to the compensation of other partners should be upheld, absent any abuse such as fraud or duress.

3. Subsection (c) is a significant revision of UPA Section 20 and provides a more comprehensive, although not exclusive, statement of partners' rights and duties with respect to partnership information other than books and records. Both the partnership and the other partners are obligated to furnish partnership information.

Paragraph (1) is new and imposes an affirmative disclosure obligation on the partnership and partners. There is no express UPA provision imposing an affirmative obligation to disclose any information other than the partnership books. Under some circumstances, however, an affirmative disclosure duty has been inferred from other sections of the Act, as well as from the common law, such as the fiduciary duty of good faith. Under UPA Section 18(e), for example, all partners enjoy an equal right in the management and conduct of the partnership business, absent contrary agreement. That right has been construed to require that every partner be provided with ongoing information concerning the partnership business. *See* Comment 7 to Section 401. Paragraph (1) provides expressly that partners must be furnished, without demand, partnership information reasonably needed for them to exercise their rights and duties as partners. In addition, a disclosure duty may, under some circumstances, also spring from the Section 404(d) obligation of good faith and fair dealing. *See* Comment 4 to Section 404.

Paragraph (2) continues the UPA rule that partners are entitled, on demand, to any other information concerning the partnership's business and affairs. The demand may be refused if either the demand or the information demanded is unreasonable or otherwise improper. That qualification is new to the statutory formulation. The burden is on the partnership or partner from whom the information is requested to show that the demand is unreasonable or improper. The UPA admonition that the information furnished be "true and full" has been deleted as unnecessary, and no substantive change is intended.

The Section 403(c) information rights can be waived or varied by agreement of the partners, since there is no Section 103(b) limitation on the variation of those rights as there is with respect to the Section 403(b) access rights to books and records. *See* Section 103(b)(2).

Section 404. General Standards of Partner's Conduct

(a) The only fiduciary duties a partner owes to the partnership and the other partners are the duty of loyalty and the duty of care set forth in subsections (b) and (c).

(b) A partner's duty of loyalty to the partnership and the other partners is limited to the following:

(1) to account to the partnership and hold as trustee for it any property, profit, or benefit derived by the partner in the conduct and winding up of the partnership business or derived from a use by the partner of partnership property, including the appropriation of a partnership opportunity;

(2) to refrain from dealing with the partnership in the conduct or winding up of the partnership business as or on behalf of a party having an interest adverse to the partnership; and

(3) to refrain from competing with the partnership in the conduct of the partnership business before the dissolution of the partnership.

(c) A partner's duty of care to the partnership and the other partners in the conduct and winding up of the partnership business is limited to refraining from engaging in grossly negligent or reckless conduct, intentional misconduct, or a knowing violation of law.

(d) A partner shall discharge the duties to the partnership and the other partners under this [Act] or under the partnership agreement and exercise any rights consistently with the obligation of good faith and fair dealing.

(e) A partner does not violate a duty or obligation under this [Act] or under the partnership agreement merely because the partner's conduct furthers the partner's own interest.

(f) A partner may lend money to and transact other business with the partnership, and as to each loan or transaction the rights and obligations of the partner are the same as those of a person who is not a partner, subject to other applicable law.

(g) This section applies to a person winding up the partnership business as the personal or legal representative of the last surviving partner as if the person were a partner.

Comment to Original Section 404

1. Section 404 is new. The title, "General Standards of Partner's Conduct," is drawn from RMBCA Section 8.30. Section 404 is both comprehensive and exclusive. In that regard, it is structurally different from the UPA which touches only sparingly on a partner's duty of loyalty and leaves any further development of the fiduciary duties of partners to the common law of agency. *Compare* UPA Sections 4(3) and 21.

Section 404 begins by stating that the *only* fiduciary duties a partner owes to the partnership and the other partners are the duties of loyalty and care set forth in subsections (b) and (c) of the Act. Those duties may not be waived or eliminated in the partnership agreement, but the agreement may identify activities and determine standards for measuring performance of the duties, if not manifestly unreasonable. *See* Sections 103(b)(3)–(5).

Section 404 continues the term "fiduciary" from UPA Section 21, which is entitled "Partner Accountable as a Fiduciary." Arguably, the term "fiduciary" is inappropriate when used to describe the duties of a partner because a partner may legitimately pursue self-interest (*see* Section 404(e)) and not solely the interest of the partnership and the other partners, as must a true trustee. Nevertheless, partners have long been characterized as fiduciaries. *See, e.g., Meinhard v. Salmon*, 249 N.Y. 458, 463, 164 N.E. 545, 546 (1928) (Cardozo, J.). Indeed, the law of partnership reflects the broader law of principal and agent, under which every agent is a fiduciary. *See* Restatement (Second) of Agency § 13 (1957).

2. Section 404(b) provides three specific rules that comprise a partner's duty of loyalty. Those rules are exclusive and encompass the entire duty of loyalty.

Subsection (b)(1) is based on UPA Section 21(1) and continues the rule that partnership property usurped by a partner, including the misappropriation of a partnership opportunity, is held in trust for the partnership. The express reference to the appropriation of a partnership opportunity is new, but merely codifies case law on the point. *See, e.g., Meinhard v. Salmon, supra*; *Fouchek v. Janicek*, 190 Ore. 251, 225 P.2d 783 (1950). Under a constructive trust theory, the partnership can recover any money or property in the partner's hands that can be traced to the partnership. *See, e.g., Yoder v. Hooper*, 695 P.2d 1182 (Colo. App. 1984), *aff'd*, 737 P.2d 852 (Colo. 1987); *Fortugno v. Hudson Manure Co.*, 51 N.J. Super. 482, 144 A.2d 207 (1958); *Harestad v. Weitzel*, 242 Or. 199, 536 P.2d 522 (1975). As a result, the partnership's claim is greater than that of an ordinary creditor. *See* Official Comment to UPA Section 21.

UPA Section 21(1) imposes the duty on partners to account for profits and benefits in all transactions connected with "the formation, conduct, or liquidation of the partnership." Reference to the "formation" of the partnership has been eliminated by RUPA because of concern that the duty of loyalty could be inappropriately extended to the pre-formation period when the parties are really negotiating at arm's length. *Compare Herring v. Offutt*, 295 A.2d 876 (Ct. App. Md. 1972), *with Phoenix Mutual Life Ins. Co. v. Shady Grove Plaza Limited Partnership*, 734 F. Supp. 1181 (D. Md. 1990), *aff'd*, 937 F.2d 603 (4th Cir. 1991). Once a partnership is agreed to, each partner becomes a fiduciary in the "conduct" of the business. Pre-formation negotiations are, of course, subject to the general contract obligation to deal honestly and without fraud.

Upon a partner's dissociation, Section 603(b)(3) limits the application of the duty to account for personal profits to those derived from matters arising or events occurring before the dissociation, unless the partner participates in winding up the partnership's business. Thus, after withdrawal, a partner is free to appropriate to his own benefit any new business opportunity thereafter coming to his attention, even if the partnership continues.

Subsection (b)(2) provides that a partner must refrain from dealing with the partnership as or on behalf of a party having an interest adverse to the partnership. This rule is derived from Sections 389 and 391 of the Restatement (Second) of Agency. Comment c to Section 389 explains that the rule is not based upon the harm caused to the principal, but upon avoiding a conflict of opposing interests in the mind of an agent whose duty is to act for the benefit of his principal.

Upon a partner's dissociation, Section 603(b)(3) limits the application of the duty to refrain from representing interests adverse to the partnership to the same extent as the duty to account. Thus, after withdrawal, a partner may deal with the partnership as an adversary with respect to new matters or events.

Section 404(b)(3) provides that a partner must refrain from competing with the partnership in the conduct of its business. This rule is derived from Section 393 of the Restatement (Second) of Agency and is an application of the general duty of an agent to act solely on his principal's behalf.

The duty not to compete applies only to the "conduct" of the partnership business; it does not extend to winding up the business, as do the other loyalty rules. Thus, a partner is free to compete immediately upon an event of dissolution under Section 801, unless the partnership agreement otherwise provides. A partner who dissociates without a winding up of the business resulting is also free to compete, because Section 603(b)(2) provides that the duty not to compete terminates upon dissociation. A dissociated partner is not, however, free to use confidential partnership information after dissociation. *See* Restatement (Second) of Agency § 393 cmt. e (1957). Trade secret law also may apply. *See* the Uniform Trade Secrets Act.

Under Section 103(b)(3), the partnership agreement may not "eliminate" the duty of loyalty. Section 103(b)(3)(i) expressly empowers the partners, however, to identify specific types or categories of activities that do not violate the duty of loyalty, if not manifestly unreasonable. As under UPA Section 21, the other partners may also consent to a specific act or transaction that otherwise violates one of the rules. For the consent to be effective under Section 103(b)(3)(ii), there must be full disclosure of all material facts regarding the act or transaction and the partner's conflict of interest. *See* Comment 5 to Section 103.

3. Subsection (c) is new and establishes the duty of care that partners owe to the partnership and to the other partners. There is no statutory duty of care under the UPA, although a common law duty of care is recognized by some courts. *See, e.g., Rosenthal v. Rosenthal*, 543 A.2d 348, 352 (Me. 1988) (duty of care limited to acting in a manner that does not constitute gross negligence or wilful misconduct).

The standard of care imposed by RUPA is that of gross negligence, which is the standard generally recognized by the courts. *See, e.g., Rosenthal v. Rosenthal, supra.* Section 103(b)(4) provides that the duty of care may not be eliminated entirely by agreement, but the standard may be reasonably reduced. *See* Comment 6 to Section 103.

4. Subsection (d) is also new. It provides that partners have an obligation of good faith and fair dealing in the discharge of all their duties, including those arising under the Act, such as their fiduciary duties of loyalty and care, and those arising under the partnership agreement. The exercise of any rights by a partner is also subject to the obligation of good faith and fair dealing. The obligation runs to the partnership and to the other partners in all matters related to the conduct and winding up of the partnership business.

The obligation of good faith and fair dealing is a contract concept, imposed on the partners because of the consensual nature of a partnership. *See* Restatement (Second) of Contracts § 205 (1981). It is not characterized, in RUPA, as a fiduciary duty arising out of the partners' special relationship. Nor is it a separate and independent obligation. It is an ancillary obligation that applies whenever a partner discharges a duty or exercises a right under the partnership agreement or the Act.

The meaning of "good faith and fair dealing" is not firmly fixed under present law. "Good faith" clearly suggests a subjective element, while "fair dealing" implies an objective component. It was decided to leave the terms undefined in the Act and allow the courts to develop their meaning based on the experience of real cases. Some commentators, moreover, believe that good faith is more properly understood by what it excludes than by what it includes. *See* Robert S. Summers, *"Good Faith" in General Contract Law and the Sales Provisions of the Uniform Commercial Code*, 54 Va. L. Rev. 195, 262 (1968):

> Good faith, as judges generally use the term in matters contractual, is best understood as an "excluder"—a phrase with no general meaning or meanings of its own. Instead, it functions to rule out many different forms of bad faith. It is hard to get this point across to persons used to thinking that every word must have one or more general meanings of its own—must be either univocal or ambiguous.

The UCC definition of "good faith" is honesty in fact and, in the case of a merchant, the observance of reasonable commercial standards of fair dealing in the trade. *See* UCC §§ 1-201(19), 2-103(b). Those definitions were rejected as too narrow or not applicable.

In some situations the obligation of good faith includes a disclosure component. Depending on the circumstances, a partner may have an affirmative disclosure obligation that supplements the Section 403 duty to render information.

Under Section 103(b)(5), the obligation of good faith and fair dealing may not be eliminated by agreement, but the partners by agreement may determine the standards by which the performance of the obligation is to be measured, if the standards are not manifestly unreasonable. *See* Comment 7 to Section 103.

5. Subsection (e) is new and deals expressly with a very basic issue on which the UPA is silent. A partner as such is not a trustee and is not held to the same standards as a trustee. Subsection (e) makes clear that a partner's conduct is not deemed to be improper merely because it serves the partner's own individual interest.

That admonition has particular application to the duty of loyalty and the obligation of good faith and fair dealing. It underscores the partner's rights as an owner and principal in the enterprise, which must always be balanced against his duties and obligations as an agent and fiduciary. For example, a partner who, with consent, owns a shopping center may, under subsection (e), legitimately vote against a proposal by the partnership to open a competing shopping center.

6. Subsection (f) authorizes partners to lend money to and transact other business with the partnership and, in so doing, to enjoy the same rights and obligations as a nonpartner. That language is drawn from RULPA Section 107. The rights and obligations of a partner doing business with the partnership as an outsider are expressly made subject to the usual laws governing those transactions. They include, for example, rules limiting or qualifying the rights and remedies of inside creditors, such as fraudulent transfer law, equitable subordination, and the law of avoidable preferences, as well as general debtor-creditor law. The reference to "other applicable law" makes clear that subsection (f) is not intended to displace those laws, and thus they are preserved under Section 104(a).

It is unclear under the UPA whether a partner may, for the partner's own account, purchase the assets of the partnership at a foreclosure sale or upon the liquidation of the partnership. Those purchases are clearly within subsection (f)'s broad approval. It is also clear under that subsection that a partner may purchase partnership assets at a foreclosure sale, whether the partner is the mortgagee or the mortgagee is an unrelated third party. Similarly, a partner may purchase partnership property at a tax sale. The obligation of good faith requires disclosure of the partner's interest in the transaction, however.

7. Subsection (g) provides that the prescribed standards of conduct apply equally to a person engaged in winding up the partnership business as the personal or legal representative of the last surviving partner, as if the person were a partner. This is derived from UPA Section 21(2), but now embraces the duty of care and the obligation of good faith and fair dealing, as well as the duty of loyalty.

Section 405.   Actions by Partnership and Partners

(a) A partnership may maintain an action against a partner for a breach of the partnership agreement, or for the violation of a duty to the partnership, causing harm to the partnership.

(b) A partner may maintain an action against the partnership or another partner for legal or equitable relief, with or without an accounting as to partnership business, to:

    (1) enforce the partner's rights under the partnership agreement;

    (2) enforce the partner's rights under this [Act], including:

        (i) the partner's rights under Sections 401, 403, or 404;

        (ii) the partner's right on dissociation to have the partner's interest in the partnership purchased pursuant to Section 701 or enforce any other right under [Article] 6 or 7; or

        (iii) the partner's right to compel a dissolution and winding up of the partnership business under Section 801 or enforce any other right under [Article] 8; or

    (3) enforce the rights and otherwise protect the interests of the partner, including rights and interests arising independently of the partnership relationship.

(c) The accrual of, and any time limitation on, a right of action for a remedy under this section is governed by other law. A right to an accounting upon a dissolution and winding up does not revive a claim barred by law.

Comment to Original Section 405

1. Section 405(a) is new and reflects the entity theory of partnership. It provides that the partnership itself may maintain an action against a partner for any breach of the partnership agreement or for the violation of any duty owed to the partnership, such as a breach of fiduciary duty.

2. Section 405(b) is the successor to UPA Section 22, but with significant changes. At common law, an accounting was generally not available before dissolution. That was modified by UPA Section 22 which specifies certain circumstances in which an accounting action is available without requiring a partner to dissolve the partnership. Section 405(b) goes far beyond the UPA rule. It provides that, during the term of the partnership, partners may maintain a variety of legal or equitable actions, including an action for an accounting, as well as a final action for an accounting upon dissolution and winding up. It reflects a new policy choice that partners should have access to the courts during the term of the partnership to resolve claims against the partnership and the other partners, leaving broad judicial discretion to fashion appropriate remedies.

Under RUPA, an accounting is not a prerequisite to the availability of the other remedies a partner may have against the partnership or the other partners.

That change reflects the increased willingness courts have shown to grant relief without the requirement of an accounting, in derogation of the so-called "exclusivity rule." *See, e.g., Farney v. Hauser*, 109 Kan. 75, 79, 198 Pac. 178, 180 (1921) ("[For] all practical purposes a partnership may be considered as a business entity"); *Auld v. Estridge*, 86 Misc. 2d 895, 901, 382 N.Y.S.2d 897, 901 (1976) ("No purpose of justice is served by delaying the resolution here on empty procedural grounds").

Under subsection (b), a partner may bring a direct suit against the partnership or another partner for almost any cause of action arising out of the conduct of the partnership business. That eliminates the present procedural barriers to suits between partners filed independently of an accounting action. In addition to a formal account, the court may grant any other appropriate legal or equitable remedy. Since general partners are not passive investors like limited partners, RUPA does not authorize derivative actions, as does RULPA Section 1001.

Subsection (b)(3) makes it clear that a partner may recover against the partnership and the other partners for personal injuries or damage to the property of the partner caused by another partner. *See, e.g., Duffy v. Piazza Construction Co.*, 815 P.2d 267 (Wash. App. 1991); *Smith v. Hensley*, 354 S.W.2d 744 (Ky. App.). One partner's negligence is not imputed to bar another partner's action. *See, e.g., Reeves v. Harmon*, 475 P.2d 400 (Okla. 1970); *Eagle Star Ins. Co. v. Bean*, 134 F.2d 755 (9th Cir. 1943) (fire insurance company not subrogated to claim against partners who negligently caused fire that damaged partnership property).

3. Generally, partners may limit or contract away their Section 405 remedies. They may not, however, eliminate entirely the remedies for breach of those duties that are mandatory under Section 103(b). *See* Comment 1 to Section 103.

4. Section 405(c) replaces UPA Section 43 and provides that other (i.e., non-partnership) law governs the accrual of a cause of action for which subsection (b) provides a remedy. The statute of limitations on such claims is also governed by other law, and claims barred by a statute of limitations are not revived by reason of the partner's right to an accounting upon dissolution, as they were under the UPA. The effect of those rules is to compel partners to litigate their claims during the life of the partnership or risk losing them. Because an accounting is an equitable proceeding, it may also be barred by laches where there is an undue delay in bringing the action. Under general law, the limitations periods may be tolled by a partner's fraud.

5. UPA Section 39 grants ancillary remedies to a person who rescinds his participation in a partnership because it was fraudulently induced, including the right to a lien on surplus partnership property for the amount of that person's interest in the partnership. RUPA has no counterpart provision to UPA Section 39, and leaves it to the general law of rescission to determine the rights of a person fraudulently induced to invest in a partnership. *See* Section 104(a).

Section 406.   Continuation of Partnership Beyond Definite Term or Particular Undertaking

(a) If a partnership for a definite term or particular undertaking is continued, without an express agreement, after the expiration of the term or completion of the undertaking, the rights and duties of the partners remain the same as they were at the expiration or completion, so far as is consistent with a partnership at will.

(b) If the partners, or those of them who habitually acted in the business during the term or undertaking, continue the business without any settlement or liquidation of the partnership, they are presumed to have agreed that the partnership will continue.

Comment to Original Section 406

Section 406 continues UPA Section 23, with no substantive change. Subsection (a) provides that, if a term partnership is continued without an express agreement beyond the expiration of its term or the completion of the undertaking, the partners' rights and duties remain the same as they were, so far as is consistent with a partnership at will.

Subsection (b) provides that if the partnership is continued by the partners without any settlement or liquidation of the business, it is presumed that the partners have agreed not to wind up the business. The presumption is rebuttable. If the partnership is continued under this subsection, there is no dissolution under Section 801(2)(iii). As a partnership at will, however, the partnership may be dissolved under Section 801(1) at any time.

[ARTICLE] 5.   TRANSFEREES AND CREDITORS OF PARTNER

Section 501.   Partner Not Co-Owner of Partnership Property

A partner is not a co-owner of partnership property and has no interest in partnership property which can be transferred, either voluntarily or involuntarily.

Comment to Original Section 501

Section 501 provides that a partner is not a co-owner of partnership property and has no interest in partnership property that can be transferred, either voluntarily or involuntarily. Thus, the section abolishes the UPA Section 25(1) concept of tenants in partnership and reflects the adoption of the entity theory. Partnership property is owned by the entity and not by the individual partners. *See also* Section 203, which provides that property transferred to or otherwise acquired by the partnership is property of the partnership and not of the partners individually.

RUPA also deletes the references in UPA Sections 24 and 25 to a partner's "right in specific partnership property," although those rights are largely defined away by the detailed rules of UPA Section 25 itself. Thus, it is clear that a partner who misappropriates partnership property is guilty of embezzlement the same as a shareholder who misappropriates corporate property.

Adoption of the entity theory also has the effect of protecting partnership property from execution or other process by a partner's personal creditors. That continues the result under UPA Section 25(2)(c). Those creditors may seek a charging order under Section 504 to reach the partner's transferable interest in the partnership.

RUPA does not interfere with a partner's exemption claim in nonpartnership property. As under the UPA, disputes over whether specific property belongs to the partner or to the firm will likely arise in the context of an exemption claim by a partner.

A partner's spouse, heirs, or next of kin are not entitled to allowances or other rights in partnership property. That continues the result under UPA Section 25(2)(e).

Section 502. *Partner's Transferable Interest in Partnership*

The only transferable interest of a partner in the partnership is the partner's share of the profits and losses of the partnership and the partner's right to receive distributions. The interest is personal property.

Comment to Original Section 502

Section 502 continues the UPA Section 26 concept that a partner's only transferable interest in the partnership is the partner's share of profits and losses and right to receive distributions, that is, the partner's financial rights. The term "distribution" is defined in Section 101(3). *Compare* RULPA Section 101(10) ("partnership interest").

The partner's transferable interest is deemed to be personal property, regardless of the nature of the underlying partnership assets.

Under Section 503(b)(3), a transferee of a partner's transferable interest has standing to seek judicial dissolution of the partnership business.

A partner has other interests in the partnership that may not be transferred, such as the right to participate in the management of the business. Those rights are included in the broader concept of a "partner's interest in the partnership." *See* Section 101(7).

Section 503.   *Transfer of Partner's Transferable Interest*

(a) A transfer, in whole or in part, of a partner's transferable interest in the partnership:

(1) is permissible;

(2) does not by itself cause the partner's dissociation or a dissolution and winding up of the partnership business; and

(3) does not, as against the other partners or the partnership, entitle the transferee, during the continuance of the partnership, to participate in the management or conduct of the partnership business, to require access to information concerning partnership transactions, or to inspect or copy the partnership books or records.

(b) A transferee of a partner's transferable interest in the partnership has a right:

(1) to receive, in accordance with the transfer, distributions to which the transferor would otherwise be entitled;

(2) to receive upon the dissolution and winding up of the partnership business, in accordance with the transfer, the net amount otherwise distributable to the transferor; and

(3) to seek under Section 801(6) a judicial determination that it is equitable to wind up the partnership business.

(c) In a dissolution and winding up, a transferee is entitled to an account of partnership transactions only from the date of the latest account agreed to by all of the partners.

(d) Upon transfer, the transferor retains the rights and duties of a partner other than the interest in distributions transferred.

(e) A partnership need not give effect to a transferee's rights under this section until it has notice of the transfer.

(f) A transfer of a partner's transferable interest in the partnership in violation of a restriction on transfer contained in the partnership agreement is ineffective as to a person having notice of the restriction at the time of transfer.

Comment to Original Section 503

1. Section 503 is derived from UPA Section 27. Subsection (a)(1) states explicitly that a partner has the right to transfer his transferable interest in the partnership. The term "transfer" is used throughout RUPA in lieu of the term "assignment." *See* Section 101(10).

Subsection (a)(2) continues the UPA Section 27(1) rule that an assignment of a partner's interest in the partnership does not of itself cause a winding up of the partnership business. Under Section 601(4)(ii), however, a partner who has transferred substantially all of his partnership interest may be expelled by the other partners.

Subsection (a)(3), which is also derived from UPA Section 27(*l*), provides that a transferee is not, as against the other partners, entitled (i) to participate in the management or conduct of the partnership business; (ii) to inspect the partnership books or records; or (iii) to require any information concerning or an account of partnership transactions.

2. The rights of a transferee are set forth in subsection (b). Under subsection (b)(1), which is derived from UPA Section 27(*l*), a transferee is entitled to receive, in accordance with the terms of the assignment, any distributions to which the transferor would otherwise have been entitled under the partnership agreement before dissolution. After dissolution, the transferee is also entitled to receive, under subsection (b)(2), the net amount that would otherwise have been distributed to the transferor upon the winding up of the business.

Subsection (b)(3) confers standing on a transferee to seek a judicial dissolution and winding up of the partnership business as provided in Section 801(6), thus continuing the rule of UPA Section 32(2).

Section 504(b) accords the rights of a transferee to the purchaser at a sale foreclosing a charging order. The same rule should apply to creditors or other purchasers who acquire partnership interests by pursuing UCC remedies or statutory liens under federal or state law.

3. Subsection (c) is based on UPA Section 27(2). It grants to transferees the right to an account of partnership transactions, limited to the period since the date of the last account agreed to by all of the partners.

4. Subsection (d) is new. It makes clear that unless otherwise agreed the partner whose interest is transferred retains all of the rights and duties of a partner, other than the right to receive distributions. That means the transferor is entitled to participate in the management of the partnership and remains personally liable for all partnership obligations, unless and until he withdraws as a partner, is expelled under Section 601(4)(ii), or is otherwise dissociated under Section 601.

A divorced spouse of a partner who is awarded rights in the partner's partnership interest as part of a property settlement is entitled only to the rights of a
transferee. The spouse may instead be granted a money judgment in the amount
of the property award, enforceable by a charging order in the same manner as any
other money judgment against a partner. In neither case, however, would the
spouse become a partner by virtue of the property settlement or succeed to any of
the partner's management rights. *See, e.g., Warren v. Warren*, 12 Ark. App. 260,
675 S.W.2d 371 (1984).

5. Subsection (e) is new and provides that the partnership has no duty to
give effect to the transferee's rights until the partnership receives notice of the
transfer. This is consistent with UCC Section 9-318(3), which provides that an
"account debtor" is authorized to pay the assignor until the account debtor
receives notification that the amount due or to become due has been assigned and
that payment is to be made to the assignee. It further provides that the assignee,
on request, must furnish reasonable proof of the assignment.

6. Subsection (f) is new and provides that a transfer of a partner's transferable interest in the partnership in violation of a restriction on transfer contained
in a partnership agreement is ineffective as to a person with timely notice of the
restriction. Under Section 103(a), the partners may agree among themselves to
restrict the right to transfer their partnership interests. Subsection (f) makes
explicit that a transfer in violation of such a restriction is ineffective as to a transferee with notice of the restriction. *See* Section 102(b) for the meaning of
"notice." RUPA leaves to general law and the UCC the issue of whether a
transfer in violation of a valid restriction is effective as to a transferee without
notice of the restriction.

Whether a particular restriction will be enforceable, however, must be considered in light of other law. *See* 11 U.S.C. § 541(c)(1) (property owned by bankrupt passes to trustee regardless of restrictions on transfer); UCC § 9-318(4)
(agreement between account debtor and assignor prohibiting creation of security
interest in a general intangible or requiring account debtor's consent is ineffective); *Battista v. Carlo*, 57 Misc. 2d 495, 293 N.Y.S.2d 227 (1968) (restriction on
transfer of partnership interest subject to rules against unreasonable restraints on
alienation of property) (dictum); *Tupper v. Kroc*, 88 Nev. 146, 494 P.2d 1275
(1972) (partnership interest subject to charging order even if partnership agreement prohibits assignments). *Cf. Tu-Vu Drive-In Corp. v. Ashkins*, 61 Cal. 2d 283,
38 Cal. Rptr. 348, 391 P.2d 828 (1964) (restraints on transfer of corporate stock
must be reasonable). Even if a restriction on the transfer of a partner's transferable interest in a partnership were held to be unenforceable, the transfer might be
grounds for expelling the partner-transferor from the partnership under Section
601(5)(ii).

7. Other rules that apply in the case of transfers include Section 601(4)(ii)
(expulsion of partner who transfers substantially all of partnership interest);
Section 601(6) (dissociation of partner who makes an assignment for benefit of

creditors); and Section 801(6) (transferee has standing to seek judicial winding up).

Section 504.   *Partner's Transferable Interest Subject to Charging Order*

(a) On application by a judgment creditor of a partner or of a partner's transferee, a court having jurisdiction may charge the transferable interest of the judgment debtor to satisfy the judgment. The court may appoint a receiver of the share of the distributions due or to become due to the judgment debtor in respect of the partnership and make all other orders, directions, accounts, and inquiries the judgment debtor might have made or which the circumstances of the case may require.

(b) A charging order constitutes a lien on the judgment debtor's transferable interest in the partnership. The court may order a foreclosure of the interest subject to the charging order at any time. The purchaser at the foreclosure sale has the rights of a transferee.

(c) At any time before foreclosure, an interest charged may be redeemed:

(1) by the judgment debtor;

(2) with property other than partnership property, by one or more of the other partners; or

(3) with partnership property, by one or more of the other partners with the consent of all of the partners whose interests are not so charged.

(d) This [Act] does not deprive a partner of a right under exemption laws with respect to the partner's interest in the partnership.

(e) This section provides the exclusive remedy by which a judgment creditor of a partner or partner's transferee may satisfy a judgment out of the judgment debtor's transferable interest in the partnership.

Comment to Original Section 504

1. Section 504 continues the UPA Section 28 charging order as the proper remedy by which a judgment creditor of a partner may reach the debtor's transferable interest in a partnership to satisfy the judgment. Subsection (a) makes the charging order available to the judgment creditor of a transferee of a partnership interest. Under Section 503(b), the transferable interest of a partner or transferee is limited to the partner's right to receive distributions from the partnership and to seek judicial liquidation of the partnership. The court may appoint a receiver of the debtor's share of the distributions due or to become due and make all other orders that may be required.

2. Subsection (b) is new and codifies the case law under the UPA holding that a charging order constitutes a lien on the debtor's transferable interest. The lien may be foreclosed by the court at any time, and the purchaser at the foreclosure sale has the Section 503(b) rights of a transferee. For a general discussion of the charging order remedy, *see I Alan R. Bromberg & Larry E. Ribstein, Partnership* (1988), at 3:69.

3. Subsection (c) continues the UPA Section 28(2) right of the debtor or other partners to redeem the partnership interest before the foreclosure sale. Redemption by the partnership (i.e., with partnership property) requires the consent of all the remaining partners. Neither the UPA nor RUPA provide a statutory procedural framework for the redemption.

4. Subsection (d) provides that nothing in RUPA deprives a partner of his rights under the State's exemption laws. That is essentially the same as UPA Section 28(3).

5. Subsection (e) provides that the charging order is the judgment creditor's exclusive remedy. Although the UPA nowhere states that a charging order is the exclusive process for a partner's individual judgment creditor, the courts have generally so interpreted it. *See, e.g., Matter of Pischke*, 11 B.R. 913 (E.D. Va. 1981); *Baum v. Baum*, 51 Cal. 2d 610, 335 P.2d 481 (1959); *Atlantic Mobile Homes, Inc. v. LeFever*, 481 So. 2d 1002 (Fla. App. 1986).

Notwithstanding subsection (e), there may be an exception for the enforcement of family support orders. Some States have unique statutory procedures for the enforcement of support orders. In Florida, for example, a court may issue an "income deduction order" requiring any person or entity providing "income" to the obligor of a support order to remit to the obligee or a depository, as directed by the court, a specified portion of the income. Fla. Stat. § 61.1301 (1993). "Income" is broadly defined to include any form of payment to the obligor, including wages, salary, compensation as an independent contractor, dividends, interest, or other payment, regardless of source. Fla. Stat. § 61.046(4). That definition includes distributions payable to an obligor partner. A charging order under RUPA would still be necessary to reach the obligor's entire partnership interest, however.

[ARTICLE] 6.   PARTNER'S DISSOCIATION

Section 601. Events Causing Partner's Dissociation

A partner is dissociated from a partnership upon the occurrence of any of the following events:

(1) the partnership's having notice of the partner's express will to withdraw as a partner or on a later date specified by the partner;

(2) an event agreed to in the partnership agreement as causing the partner's dissociation;

(3) the partner's expulsion pursuant to the partnership agreement;

(4) the partner's expulsion by the unanimous vote of the other partners if:

(i) it is unlawful to carry on the partnership business with that partner;

(ii) there has been a transfer of all or substantially all of that partner's transferable interest in the partnership, other than a transfer for security purposes, or a court order charging the partner's interest, which has not been foreclosed;

(iii) within 90 days after the partnership notifies a corporate partner that it will be expelled because it has filed a certificate of dissolution or the equivalent, its charter has been revoked, or its right to conduct business has been suspended by the jurisdiction of its incorporation, there is no revocation of the certificate of dissolution or no reinstatement of its charter or its right to conduct business; or

(iv) a partnership that is a partner has been dissolved and its business is being wound up;

(5) on application by the partnership or another partner, the partner's expulsion by judicial determination because:

(i) the partner engaged in wrongful conduct that adversely and materially affected the partnership business;

(ii) the partner willfully or persistently committed a material breach of the partnership agreement or of a duty owed to the partnership or the other partners under Section 404; or

(iii) the partner engaged in conduct relating to the partnership business which makes it not reasonably practicable to carry on the business in partnership with the partner;

(6) the partner's:

(i) becoming a debtor in bankruptcy;

(ii) executing an assignment for the benefit of creditors;

(iii) seeking, consenting to, or acquiescing in the appointment of a trustee, receiver, or liquidator of that partner or of all or substantially all of that partner's property; or

(iv) failing, within 90 days after the appointment, to have vacated or stayed the appointment of a trustee, receiver, or liquidator of the partner or of all or substantially all of the partner's property obtained without the partner's consent or acquiescence, or failing within 90 days after the expiration of a stay to have the appointment vacated;

(7) in the case of a partner who is an individual:

　(i) the partner's death;

　(ii) the appointment of a guardian or general conservator for the partner; or

　(iii) a judicial determination that the partner has otherwise become incapable of performing the partner's duties under the partnership agreement;

(8) in the case of a partner that is a trust or is acting as a partner by virtue of being a trustee of a trust, distribution of the trust's entire transferable interest in the partnership, but not merely by reason of the substitution of a successor trustee;

(9) in the case of a partner that is an estate or is acting as a partner by virtue of being a personal representative of an estate, distribution of the estate's entire transferable interest in the partnership, but not merely by reason of the substitution of a successor personal representative; or

(10) termination of a partner who is not an individual, partnership, corporation, trust, or estate.

Comment to Original Section 601

1. RUPA dramatically changes the law governing partnership breakups and dissolution. An entirely new concept, "dissociation," is used in lieu of the UPA term "dissolution" to denote the change in the relationship caused by a partner's ceasing to be associated in the carrying on of the business. "Dissolution" is retained but with a different meaning. *See* Section 802. The entity theory of partnership provides a conceptual basis for continuing the firm itself despite a partner's withdrawal from the firm.

Under RUPA, unlike the UPA, the dissociation of a partner does not necessarily cause a dissolution and winding up of the business of the partnership. Section 801 identifies the situations in which the dissociation of a partner causes a winding up of the business. Section 701 provides that in all other situations there is a buyout of the partner's interest in the partnership, rather than a windup of the partnership business. In those other situations, the partnership entity continues, unaffected by the partner's dissociation.

A dissociated partner remains a partner for some purposes and still has some residual rights, duties, powers, and liabilities. Although Section 601 determines when a partner is dissociated from the partnership, the consequences of the partner's dissociation do not all occur at the same time. Thus, it is more useful to think of a dissociated partner as a partner for some purposes, but as a former partner for others. For example, *see* Section 403(b) (former partner's access to partnership books and records). The consequences of a partner's dissociation depend on whether the partnership continues or is wound up, as provided in Articles 6, 7, and 8.

Section 601 enumerates all of the events that cause a partner's dissociation. Section 601 is similar in approach to RULPA Section 402, which lists the events resulting in a general partner's withdrawal from a limited partnership.

2. Section 601(1) provides that a partner is dissociated when the partnership has notice of the partner's express will to withdraw as a partner, unless a later date is specified by the partner. If a future date is specified by the partner, other partners may dissociate before that date; specifying a future date does not bind the others to remain as partners until that date. *See also* Section 801(2)(i).

Section 602(a) provides that a partner has the power to withdraw at any time. The power to withdraw is immutable under Section 103(b)(6), with the exception that the partners may agree the notice must be in writing. This continues the present rule that a partner has the power to withdraw at will, even if not the right. *See* UPA Section 31(2). Since no writing is required to create a partner relationship, it was felt unnecessarily formalistic, and a trap for the unwary, to require a writing to end one. If a written notification is given, Section 102(d) clarifies when it is deemed received.

RUPA continues the UPA "express will" concept, thus preserving existing case law. Section 601(1) clarifies existing law by providing that the partnership must have notice of the partner's expression of will before the dissociation is effective. *See* Section 102(b) for the meaning of "notice."

3. Section 601(2) provides expressly that a partner is dissociated upon an event agreed to in the partnership agreement as causing dissociation. There is no such provision in the UPA, but that result has been assumed.

4. Section 601(3) provides that a partner may be expelled by the other partners pursuant to a power of expulsion contained in the partnership agreement. That continues the basic rule of UPA Section 31(1)(d). The expulsion can be with or without cause. As under existing law, the obligation of good faith under Section 404(d) does not require prior notice, specification of cause, or an opportunity to be heard. *See Holman v. Coie*, 11 Wn. App. 195, 522 P.2d 515, *cert. denied*, 420 U.S. 984 (1974).

5. Section 601(4) empowers the partners, by unanimous vote, to expel a partner for specified causes, even if not authorized in the partnership agreement. This changes the UPA Section 31(1)(d) rule that authorizes expulsion only if provided in the partnership agreement. A partner may be expelled from a term partnership, as well as from a partnership at will. Under Section 103(a), the partnership agreement may change or abolish the partners' power of expulsion.

Subsection (4)(i) is derived from UPA Section 31(3). A partner may be expelled if it is unlawful to carry on the business with that partner. Section 801(4), on the other hand, provides that the partnership itself is dissolved and must be wound up if substantially all of the business is unlawful.

Subsection (4)(ii) provides that a partner may be expelled for transferring substantially all of his transferable interest in the partnership, other than as security for a loan. (He may, however, be expelled upon foreclosure.) This rule is derived from UPA Section 31(1)(c). To avoid the presence of an unwelcome transferee, the remaining partners may dissolve the partnership under Section 801(2)(ii), after first expelling the transferor partner. A transfer of a partner's entire interest may, in some circumstances, evidence the transferor's intention to withdraw under Section 601(1).

Subsection (4)(iii) provides for the expulsion of a corporate partner if it has filed a certificate of dissolution, its charter has been revoked, or its right to conduct business has been suspended, unless cured within 90 days after notice. This provision is derived from RULPA Section 402(9). The cure proviso is important because charter revocation is very common in some States and partner status should not end merely because of a technical noncompliance with corporate law that can easily be cured. Withdrawal of a voluntarily filed notice of dissolution constitutes a cure.

Subsection (4)(iv) is the partnership analogue of paragraph (iii) and is suggested by RULPA Section 402(8). It provides that a partnership that is a partner may be expelled if it has been dissolved and its business is being wound up. It is intended that the right of expulsion not be triggered solely by the dissolution event, but only upon commencement of the liquidation process.

6. Section 601(5) empowers a court to expel a partner if it determines that the partner has engaged in specified misconduct. The enumerated grounds for judicial expulsion are based on the UPA Section 32(1) grounds for judicial dissolution. The application for expulsion may be brought by the partnership or any partner. The phrase "judicial determination" is intended to include an arbitration award, as well as any final court order or decree.

Subsection (5)(i) provides for the partner's expulsion if the court finds that the partner has engaged in wrongful conduct that adversely and materially affected the partnership business. That language is derived from UPA Section 32(1)(c).

Subsection (5)(ii) provides for expulsion if the court determines that the partner wilfully or persistently committed a material breach of the partnership agreement or of a duty owed to the partnership or to the other partners under Section 404. That would include a partner's breach of fiduciary duty. Paragraph (ii), together with paragraph (iii), carry forward the substance of UPA Section 32(1)(d).

Subsection (5)(iii) provides for judicial expulsion of a partner who engaged in conduct relating to the partnership business that makes it not reasonably practicable to carry on the business in partnership with that partner. Expulsion for such misconduct makes the partner's dissociation wrongful under Section 602(a)(ii) and may also support a judicial decree of dissolution under Section 801(5)(ii).

7. Section 601(6) provides that a partner is dissociated upon becoming a debtor in bankruptcy or upon taking or suffering other action evidencing the partner's insolvency or lack of financial responsibility.

Subsection (6)(i) is derived from UPA Section 31(5), which provides for dissolution upon a partner's bankruptcy. *Accord* RULPA § 402(4)(ii). There is some doubt as to whether UPA Section 31(1) is limited to so-called "straight bankruptcy" under Chapter 7 or includes other bankruptcy relief, such as Chapter 11. Under RUPA Section 101(2), however, "debtor in bankruptcy" includes a person who files a voluntary petition, or against whom relief is ordered in an involuntary case, under any chapter of the Bankruptcy Code.

Initially, upon the filing of the bankruptcy petition, the debtor partner's transferable interest in the partnership will pass to the bankruptcy trustee as property of the estate under Section 541(a)(1) of the Bankruptcy Code, notwithstanding any restrictions on transfer provided in the partnership agreement. In most Chapter 7 cases, that will result in the eventual buyout of the partner's interest.

The application of various provisions of the federal Bankruptcy Code to Section 601(6)(i) is unclear. In particular, there is uncertainty as to the validity of UPA Section 31(5), and thus its RUPA counterpart, under Sections 365(e) and 541(c)(1) of the Bankruptcy Code. Those sections generally invalidate so-called *ipso facto* laws that cause a termination or modification of the debtor's contract or property rights because of the bankruptcy filing. As a consequence, RUPA Section 601(6)(i), which provides for a partner's dissociation by operation of law upon becoming a debtor in bankruptcy, may be invalid under the Supremacy Clause. *See, e.g., In the Matter of Phillips*, 966 F.2d 926 (5th Cir. 1992); *In re Cardinal Industries, Inc.*, 105 B.R. 385 (Bankr. S.D. Ohio 1989), 116 B.R. 964 (Bankr. S.D. Ohio 1990); *In re Corky Foods Corp.*, 85 B.R. 903 (Bankr. S.D. Fla. 1988). *But see In re Catron*, 158 B.R. 629 (E.D. Va. 1993) (partnership agreement could not be assumed by debtor under Bankruptcy Code § 365(c)(1) because other partners excused by UPA from accepting performance by or rendering performance to party other than debtor and buyout option not invalid *ipso facto* clause under Code § 365(e)), *aff'd per curiam*, 25 F.3d 1038 (4th Cir. 1994). RUPA reflects the policy choice, as a matter of state partnership law, that a partner be dissociated upon becoming a debtor in bankruptcy.

Subsection (6)(ii) is new and provides for dissociation upon a general assignment for the benefit of a partner's creditors. The UPA says nothing about an assignment for the benefit of creditors or the appointment of a trustee, receiver, or liquidator. Subsection (6)(iii) and (iv) cover the latter and are based substantially on RULPA Section 402(4) and (5).

8. UPA Section 31(4) provides for the dissolution of a partnership upon the death of any partner, although by agreement the remaining partners may continue the partnership business. RUPA Section 601(7)(i), on the other hand, provides for dissociation upon the death of a partner who is an individual, rather than dissolution of the partnership. That changes existing law, except in those States previously adopting a similar non-uniform provision, such as California, Georgia, and Texas. Normally, under RUPA, the deceased partner's transferable interest in the partnership will pass to his estate and be bought out under Article 7.

Section 601(7)(ii) replaces UPA Section 32(1)(a) and provides for dissociation upon the appointment of a guardian or general conservator for partner who is an individual. The appointment itself operates as the event of dissociation, and no further order of the court is necessary.

Section 601(7)(iii) is based on UPA Section 32(1)(b) and provides for dissociation upon a judicial determination that an individual partner has in any other way become incapable of performing his duties under the partnership agreement. The intent is to include physical incapacity.

9. Section 601(8) is new and provides for the dissociation of a partner that is a trust, or is acting as a partner by virtue of being a trustee of a trust, upon the distribution by the trust of its entire transferable interest in the partnership, but not merely upon the substitution of a successor trustee. The provision is inspired by RULPA Section 402(7).

10. Section 601(9) is new and provides for the dissociation of a partner that is an estate, or is acting as a partner by virtue of being a personal representative of an estate, upon the distribution of the estate's entire transferable interest in the partnership, but not merely the substitution of a successor personal representative. It is based on RULPA Section 402(10). Under Section 601(7), a partner is dissociated upon death, however, and the estate normally becomes a transferee, not a partner.

11. Section 601(10) is new and provides that a partner that is not an individual, partnership, corporation, trust, or estate is dissociated upon its termination. It is the comparable "death" analogue for entity other types of entity partners, such as a limited liability company.

Section 602.   Partner's Power to Dissociate; Wrongful Dissociation

(a) A partner has the power to dissociate at any time, rightfully or wrongfully, by express will pursuant to Section 601(1).

(b) A partner's dissociation is wrongful only if:

(1) it is in breach of an express provision of the partnership agreement; or

(2) in the case of a partnership for a definite term or particular undertaking, before the expiration of the term or the completion of the undertaking:

(i) the partner withdraws by express will, unless the withdrawal follows within 90 days after another partner's dissociation by death or otherwise under Section 601(6) through (10) or wrongful dissociation under this subsection;

(ii) the partner is expelled by judicial determination under Section 601(5);

(iii) the partner is dissociated by becoming a debtor in bankruptcy; or

(iv) in the case of a partner who is not an individual, trust other than a business trust, or estate, the partner is expelled or otherwise dissociated because it willfully dissolved or terminated.

(c) A partner who wrongfully dissociates is liable to the partnership and to the other partners for damages caused by the dissociation. The liability is in addition to any other obligation of the partner to the partnership or to the other partners.

Comment to Original Section 602

1. Subsection (a) states explicitly what is implicit in UPA Section 31(2) and RUPA Section 601(1)—that a partner has the power to dissociate at any time by expressing a will to withdraw, even in contravention of the partnership agreement. The phrase "rightfully or wrongfully" reflects the distinction between a partner's *power* to withdraw in contravention of the partnership agreement and a partner's *right* to do so. In this context, although a partner cannot be enjoined from exercising the power to dissociate, the dissociation may be wrongful under subsection (b).

2. Subsection (b) provides that a partner's dissociation is wrongful only if it results from one of the enumerated events. The significance of a wrongful dissociation is that it may give rise to damages under subsection (c) and, if it results in the dissolution of the partnership, the wrongfully dissociating partner is not entitled to participate in winding up the business under Section 804.

Under subsection (b), a partner's dissociation is wrongful if (1) it breaches an express provision of the partnership agreement or (2), in a term partnership, before the expiration of the term or the completion of the undertaking (i) the partner voluntarily withdraws by express will, except a withdrawal following *another* partner's wrongful dissociation or dissociation by death or otherwise under Section 601(6) through (10); (ii) the partner is expelled for misconduct under Section 601(5); (iii) the partner becomes a debtor in bankruptcy (*see* Section 101(2)); or (iv) a partner that is an entity (other than a trust or estate) is expelled or otherwise dissociated because its dissolution or termination was willful. Since subsection (b) is merely a default rule, the partnership agreement may eliminate or expand the dissociations that are wrongful or modify the effects of wrongful dissociation.

The exception in subsection (b)(2)(i) is intended to protect a partner's reactive withdrawal from a term partnership after the premature departure of another partner, such as the partnership's rainmaker or main supplier of capital, under the same circumstances that may result in the dissolution of the partnership under Section 801(2)(i). Under that section, a term partnership is dissolved 90 days after the bankruptcy, incapacity, death (or similar dissociation of a partner that is an entity), or wrongful dissociation of any partner, unless a majority in interest (*see* Comment 5(i) to Section 801 for a discussion of the term "majority in interest") of the remaining partners agree to continue the partnership. Under Section 602(b)(2)(i), a partner's exercise of the right of withdrawal by express will under those circumstances is rendered "rightful," even if the partnership is continued by others, and does not expose the withdrawing partner to damages for wrongful dissociation under Section 602(c).

A partner wishing to withdraw prematurely from a term partnership for any other reason, such as another partner's misconduct, can avoid being treated as a wrongfully dissociating partner by applying to a court under Section 601(5)(iii) to have the offending partner expelled. Then, the partnership could be dissolved under Section 801(2)(i) or the remaining partners could, by unanimous vote, dissolve the partnership under Section 801(2)(ii).

3. Subsection (c) provides that a wrongfully dissociating partner is liable to the partnership and to the other partners for any damages caused by the wrongful nature of the dissociation. That liability is in addition to any other obligation of the partner to the partnership or to the other partners. For example, the partner would be liable for any damage caused by breach of the partnership agreement or other misconduct. The partnership might also incur substantial expenses resulting from a partner's premature withdrawal from a term partnership, such as replacing the partner's expertise or obtaining new financing. The wrongfully dissociating partner would be liable to the partnership for those and all other expenses and damages that are causally related to the wrongful dissociation.

Section 701(c) provides that any damages for wrongful dissociation may be offset against the amount of the buyout price due to the partner under Section 701(a), and Section 701(h) provides that a partner who wrongfully dissociates from a term partnership is not entitled to payment of the buyout price until the term expires.

Under UPA Section 38(2)(c)(II), in addition to an offset for damages, the goodwill value of the partnership is excluded in determining the value of a wrongfully dissociating partner's partnership interest. Under RUPA, however, unless the partnership's goodwill is damaged by the wrongful dissociation, the value of the wrongfully dissociating partner's interest will include any goodwill value of the partnership. If the firm's goodwill is damaged, the amount of the damages suffered by the partnership and the remaining partners will be offset against the buyout price. *See* Section 701 and Comments.

Section 603.   Effect of Partner's Dissociation

(a) If a partner's dissociation results in a dissolution and winding up of the partnership business, [Article] 8 applies; otherwise, [Article] 7 applies.

(b) Upon a partner's dissociation:

(1) the partner's right to participate in the management and conduct of the partnership business terminates, except as otherwise provided in Section 803;

(2) the partner's duty of loyalty under Section 404(b)(3) terminates; and

(3) the partner's duty of loyalty under Section 404(b)(1) and (2) and duty of care under Section 404(c) continue only with regard to matters arising and events occurring before the partner's dissociation, unless the partner participates in winding up the partnership's business pursuant to Section 803.

Comment to Original Section 603

1. Section 603(a) is a "switching" provision. It provides that, after a partner's dissociation, the partner's interest in the partnership must be purchased pursuant to the buyout rules in Article 7 *unless* there is a dissolution and winding up of the partnership business under Article 8. Thus, a partner's dissociation will always result in either a buyout of the dissociated partner's interest or a dissolution and winding up of the business.

By contrast, under the UPA, every partner dissociation results in the dissolution of the partnership, most of which trigger a right to have the business wound up unless the partnership agreement provides otherwise. *See* UPA § 38. The only exception in which the remaining partners have a statutory right to continue the business is when a partner wrongfully dissolves the partnership in breach of the partnership agreement. *See* UPA § 38(2)(b).

2. Section 603(b) is new and deals with some of the internal effects of a partner's dissociation. Subsection (b)(1) makes it clear that one of the consequences of a partner's dissociation is the immediate loss of the right to participate in the management of the business, unless it results in a dissolution and winding up of the business. In that case, Section 804(a) provides that all of the partners who have not wrongfully dissociated may participate in winding up the business.

Subsection (b)(2) and (3) clarify a partner's fiduciary duties upon dissociation. No change from current law is intended. With respect to the duty of loyalty, the Section 404(b)(3) duty not to compete terminates upon dissociation, and the dissociated partner is free immediately to engage in a competitive business, without any further consent. With respect to the partner's remaining loyalty duties under Section 404(b) and duty of care under Section 404(c), a withdrawing partner has a continuing duty after dissociation, but it is limited to matters that arose or events that occurred before the partner dissociated. For example, a partner who leaves a brokerage firm may immediately compete with the firm for new clients, but must exercise care in completing on-going client transactions and must account to the firm for any fees received from the old clients on account of those transactions. As the last clause makes clear, there is no contraction of a dissociated partner's duties under subsection (b)(3) if the partner thereafter participates in the dissolution and winding up the partnership's business.

[ARTICLE] 7.   PARTNER'S DISSOCIATION WHEN BUSINESS NOT WOUND UP

Section 701.   Purchase of Dissociated Partner's Interest

(a) If a partner is dissociated from a partnership without resulting in a dissolution and winding up of the partnership business under Section 801, the partnership shall cause the dissociated partner's interest in the partnership to be purchased for a buyout price determined pursuant to subsection (b).

(b) The buyout price of a dissociated partner's interest is the amount that would have been distributable to the dissociating partner under Section 807(b) if, on the date of dissociation, the assets of the partnership were sold at a price equal to the greater of the liquidation value or the value based on a sale of the entire business as a going concern without the dissociated partner and the partnership were wound up as of that date. Interest must be paid from the date of dissociation to the date of payment.

(c) Damages for wrongful dissociation under Section 602(b), and all other amounts owing, whether or not presently due, from the dissociated partner to the partnership, must be offset against the buyout price. Interest must be paid from the date the amount owed becomes due to the date of payment.

(d) A partnership shall indemnify a dissociated partner whose interest is being purchased against all partnership liabilities, whether incurred before or after the dissociation, except liabilities incurred by an act of the dissociated partner under Section 702.

(e) If no agreement for the purchase of a dissociated partner's interest is reached within 120 days after a written demand for payment, the partnership shall pay, or cause to be paid, in cash to the dissociated partner the amount the partnership estimates to be the buyout price and accrued interest, reduced by any offsets and accrued interest under subsection (c).

(f) If a deferred payment is authorized under subsection (h), the partnership may tender a written offer to pay the amount it estimates to be the buyout price and accrued interest, reduced by any offsets under subsection (c), stating the time of payment, the amount and type of security for payment, and the other terms and conditions of the obligation.

(g) The payment or tender required by subsection (e) or (f) must be accompanied by the following:

(1) a statement of partnership assets and liabilities as of the date of dissociation;

(2) the latest available partnership balance sheet and income statement, if any;

(3) an explanation of how the estimated amount of the payment was calculated; and

(4) written notice that the payment is in full satisfaction of the obligation to purchase unless, within 120 days after the written notice, the dissociated partner commences an action to determine the buyout price, any offsets under subsection (c), or other terms of the obligation to purchase.

(h) A partner who wrongfully dissociates before the expiration of a definite term or the completion of a particular undertaking is not entitled to payment of any portion of the buyout price until the expiration of the term or completion of the undertaking, unless the partner establishes to the satisfaction of the court that earlier payment will not cause undue hardship to the business of the partnership. A deferred payment must be adequately secured and bear interest.

(i) A dissociated partner may maintain an action against the partnership, pursuant to Section 405(b)(2)(ii), to determine the buyout price of that partner's interest, any offsets under subsection (c), or other terms of the obligation to purchase. The action must be commenced within 120 days after the partnership has tendered payment or an offer to pay or within one year after written demand for payment if no payment or offer to pay is tendered. The court shall determine the buyout price of the dissociated partner's interest, any offset due under subsection (c), and accrued interest, and enter judgment for any additional payment or refund. If deferred payment is authorized under subsection (h), the court shall also determine the security for payment and other terms of the obligation to purchase. The court may assess reasonable attorney's fees and the fees and expenses of appraisers or other experts for a party to the action, in amounts the court finds equitable, against a party that the court finds acted arbitrarily, vexatiously, or not in good faith. The finding may be based on the partnership's failure to tender payment or an offer to pay or to comply with subsection (g).

Comment to Original Section 701

1. Article 7 is new and provides for the buyout of a dissociated partner's interest in the partnership when the partner's dissociation does not result in a dissolution and winding up of its business under Article 8. *See* Section 603(a). If there is no dissolution, the remaining partners have a right to continue the business and the dissociated partner has a right to be paid the value of his partnership interest. These rights can, of course, be varied in the partnership agreement. *See*

Section 103. A dissociated partner has a continuing relationship with the partnership and third parties as provided in Sections 603(b), 702, and 703. *See also* Section 403(b) (former partner's access to partnership books and records).

2. Subsection (a) provides that, if a partner's dissociation does not result in a windup of the business, the partnership shall cause the interest of the dissociating partner to be purchased for a buyout price determined pursuant to subsection (b). The buyout is mandatory. The "cause to be purchased" language is intended to accommodate a purchase by the partnership, one or more of the remaining partners, or a third party.

For federal income tax purposes, a payment to a partner for his interest can be characterized either as a purchase of the partner's interest or as a liquidating distribution. The two have different tax consequences. RUPA permits either option by providing that the payment may come from either the partnership, some or all of the continuing partners, or a third party purchaser.

3. Subsection (b) provides how the "buyout price" is to be determined. The terms "fair market value" or "fair value" were not used because they are often considered terms of art having a special meaning depending on the context, such as in tax or corporate law. "Buyout price" is a new term. It is intended that the term be developed as an independent concept appropriate to the partnership buyout situation, while drawing on valuation principles developed elsewhere.

Under subsection (b), the buyout price is the amount that would have been distributable to the dissociating partner under Section 807(b) if, on the date of dissociation, the assets of the partnership were sold at a price equal to the greater of liquidation value or going concern value without the departing partner. Liquidation value is not intended to mean distress sale value. Under general principles of valuation, the hypothetical selling price in either case should be the price that a willing and informed buyer would pay a willing and informed seller, with neither being under any compulsion to deal. The notion of a minority discount in determining the buyout price is negated by valuing the business as a going concern. Other discounts, such as for a lack of marketability or the loss of a key partner, may be appropriate, however.

Since the buyout price is based on the value of the business at the time of dissociation, the partnership must pay interest on the amount due from the date of dissociation until payment to compensate the dissociating partner for the use of his interest in the firm. Section 104(b) provides that interest shall be at the legal rate unless otherwise provided in the partnership agreement. The UPA Section 42 option of electing a share of the profits in lieu of interest has been eliminated.

UPA Section 38(2)(c)(II) provides that the good will of the business not be considered in valuing a wrongfully dissociating partner's interest. The forfeiture of good will rule is implicitly rejected by RUPA. *See* Section 602(c) and Comment 3.

The Section 701 rules are merely default rules. The partners may, in the partnership agreement, fix the method or formula for determining the buyout price and all of the other terms and conditions of the buyout right. Indeed, the very right to a buyout itself may be modified, although a provision providing for a complete forfeiture would probably not be enforceable. *See* Section 104(a).

4. Subsection (c) provides that the partnership may offset against the buyout price all amounts owing by the dissociated partner to the partnership, whether or not presently due, including any damages for wrongful dissociation under Section 602(c). This has the effect of accelerating payment of amounts not yet due from the departing partner to the partnership, including a long-term loan by the partnership to the dissociated partner. Where appropriate, the amounts not yet due should be discounted to present value. A dissociating partner, on the other hand, is not entitled to an add-on for amounts owing to him by the partnership. Thus, a departing partner who has made a long-term loan to the partnership must wait for repayment, unless the terms of the loan agreement provide for acceleration upon dissociation.

It is not intended that the partnership's right of setoff be construed to limit the amount of the damages for the partner's wrongful dissociation and any other amounts owing to the partnership to the value of the dissociated partner's interest. Those amounts may result in a net sum due to the partnership from the dissociated partner.

5. Subsection (d) follows the UPA Section 38 rule and provides that the partnership must indemnify a dissociated partner against all partnership liabilities, whether incurred before or after the dissociation, except those incurred by the dissociated partner under Section 702.

6. Subsection (e) provides that, if no agreement for the purchase of the dissociated partner's interest is reached within 120 days after the dissociated partner's written demand for payment, the partnership must pay, or cause to be paid, in cash the amount it estimates to be the buyout price, adjusted for any offsets allowed and accrued interest. Thus, the dissociating partner will receive in cash within 120 days of dissociation the undisputed minimum value of the partner's partnership interest. If the dissociated partner claims that the buyout price should be higher, suit may thereafter be brought as provided in subsection (i) to have the amount of the buyout price determined by the court. This is similar to the procedure for determining the value of dissenting shareholders' shares under RMBCA Sections 13.20–13.28.

The "cause to be paid" language of subsection (a) is repeated here to permit either the partnership, one or more of the continuing partners, or a third-party purchaser to tender payment of the estimated amount due.

7. Subsection (f) provides that, when deferred payment is authorized in the case of a wrongfully dissociating partner, a written offer stating the amount the partnership estimates to be the purchase price should be tendered within the 120-day period, even though actual payment of the amount may be deferred, possibly for many years. *See* Comment 8. The dissociated partner is entitled to know at the time of dissociation what amount the remaining partners think is due,

including the estimated amount of any damages allegedly caused by the partner's wrongful dissociation that may be offset against the buyout price.

8. Subsection (g) provides that the payment of the estimated price (or tender of a written offer under subsection (f)) by the partnership must be accompanied by (1) a statement of the partnership's assets and liabilities as of the date of the partner's dissociation; (2) the latest available balance sheet and income statement, if the partnership maintains such financial statements; (3) an explanation of how the estimated amount of the payment was calculated; and (4) a written notice that the payment will be in full satisfaction of the partnership's buyout obligation unless the dissociated partner commences an action to determine the price within 120 days of the notice. Subsection (g) is based in part on the dissenters' rights provisions of RMBCA Section 13.25(b).

Those disclosures should serve to identify and narrow substantially the items of dispute between the dissociated partner and the partnership over the valuation of the partnership interest. They will also serve to pin down the parties as to their claims of partnership assets and values and as to the existence and amount of all known liabilities. *See* Comment 4. Lastly, it will force the remaining partners to consider thoughtfully the difficult and important questions as to the appropriate method of valuation under the circumstances, and in particular, whether they should use going concern or liquidation value. Simply getting that information on the record in a timely fashion should increase the likelihood of a negotiated resolution of the parties' differences during the 120-day period within which the dissociated partner must bring suit.

9. Subsection (h) replaces UPA Section 38(2)(c) and provides a somewhat different rule for payment to a partner whose dissociation before the expiration of a definite term or the completion of a particular undertaking is wrongful under Section 602(b). Under subsection (h), a wrongfully dissociating partner is not entitled to receive any portion of the buyout price before the expiration of the term or completion of the undertaking, unless the dissociated partner establishes to the satisfaction of the court that earlier payment will not cause undue hardship to the business of the partnership. In all other cases, there must be an immediate payment in cash.

10. Subsection (i) provides that a dissociated partner may maintain an action against the partnership to determine the buyout price, any offsets, or other terms of the purchase obligation. The action must be commenced within 120 days after the partnership tenders payment of the amount it estimates to be due or, if deferred payment is authorized, its written offer. This provision creates a 120-day "cooling off" period. It also allows the parties an opportunity to negotiate their differences after disclosure by the partnership of its financial statements and other required information.

If the partnership fails to tender payment of the estimated amount due (or a written offer, if deferred payment is authorized), the dissociated partner has one year after written demand for payment in which to commence suit.

If the parties fail to reach agreement, the court must determine the buyout price of the partner's interest, any offsets, including damages for wrongful dissociation, and the amount of interest accrued. If payment to a wrongfully dissociated partner is deferred, the court may also require security for payment and determine the other terms of the obligation.

Under subsection (i), attorney's fees and other costs may be assessed against any party found to have acted arbitrarily, vexatiously, or not in good faith in connection with the valuation dispute, including the partnership's failure to tender payment of the estimated price or to make the required disclosures. This provision is based in part on RMBCA Section 13.31(b).

Section 702.   Dissociated Partner's Power to Bind and Liability to Partnership

(a) For two years after a partner dissociates without resulting in a dissolution and winding up of the partnership business, the partnership, including a surviving partnership under [Article] 9, is bound by an act of the dissociated partner which would have bound the partnership under Section 301 before dissociation only if at the time of entering into the transaction the other party:

(1) reasonably believed that the dissociated partner was then a partner;

(2) did not have notice of the partner's dissociation; and

(3) is not deemed to have had knowledge under Section 303(e) or notice under Section 704(c).

(b) A dissociated partner is liable to the partnership for any damage caused to the partnership arising from an obligation incurred by the dissociated partner after dissociation for which the partnership is liable under subsection (a).

Comment to Original Section 702

1. Section 702 deals with a dissociated partner's lingering apparent authority to bind the partnership in ordinary course partnership transactions and the partner's liability to the partnership for any loss caused thereby. It also applies to partners who withdraw incident to a merger under Article 9. *See* Section 906(e).

A dissociated partner has no *actual* authority to act for the partnership. *See* Section 603(b)(1). Nevertheless, in order to protect innocent third parties, Section 702(a) provides that the partnership remains bound, for two years after a partner's dissociation, by that partner's acts that would, before his dissociation, have bound the partnership under Section 301 if, and only if, the other party to the transaction reasonably believed that he was still a partner, did not have notice of the partner's dissociation, and is not deemed to have had knowledge of the dissociation under Section 303(e) or notice thereof under Section 704(c).

Under Section 301, every partner has *apparent* authority to bind the partnership by any act for carrying on the partnership business in the ordinary course, unless the other party knows that the partner has no actual authority to act for the partnership or has received a notification of the partner's lack of authority. Section 702(a) continues that general rule for two years after a partner's dissociation, subject to three modifications.

After a partner's dissociation, the general rule is modified, first, by requiring the other party to show reasonable reliance on the partner's status as a partner. Section 301 has no explicit reliance requirement, although the partnership is bound only if the partner purports to act on its behalf. Thus, the other party will normally be aware of the partnership and presumably the partner's status as such.

The second modification is that, under Section 702(a), the partnership is not bound if the third party has *notice* of the partner's dissociation, while under the general rule of Section 301 the partnership is bound unless the third party *knows* of the partner's lack of authority. Under Section 102(b), a person has "notice" of a fact if he knows or has reason to know it exists from all the facts that are known to him or he has received a notification of it. Thus, the partnership may protect itself by sending a notification of the dissociation to a third party, and a third party may, in any event, have a duty to inquire further based on what is known. That provides the partnership with greater protection from the unauthorized acts of a dissociated partner than from those of partners generally.

The third modification of the general apparent authority rule under Section 702(a) involves the effect of a statement of dissociation. Section 704(c) provides that, for the purposes of Sections 702(a)(3) and 703(b)(3), third parties are deemed to have notice of a partner's dissociation 90 days after the filing of a statement of dissociation. Thus, the filing of a statement operates as constructive notice of the dissociated partner's lack of authority after 90 days, conclusively terminating the dissociated partner's Section 702 apparent authority.

With respect to a dissociated partner's authority to transfer partnership real property, Section 303(e) provides that third parties are deemed to have knowledge of a limitation on a partner's authority to transfer real property held in the partnership name upon the proper recording of a statement containing such a limitation. Section 704(b) provides that a statement of dissociation operates as a limitation on the dissociated partner's authority for the purposes of Section 303(e). Thus, a properly recorded statement of dissociation operates as constructive knowledge of a dissociated partner's lack of authority to transfer real property held in the partnership name, effective immediately upon recording.

Under RUPA, therefore, a partnership should notify all known creditors of a partner's dissociation and may, by filing a statement of dissociation, conclusively limit to 90 days a dissociated partner's lingering agency power. Moreover, under Section 703(b), a dissociated partner's lingering liability for post-dissociation partnership liabilities may be limited to 90 days by filing a statement of dissocia-

tion. These incentives should encourage both partnerships and dissociating partners to file statements routinely. Those transacting substantial business with
partnerships can protect themselves from the risk of dealing with dissociated
partners, or relying on their credit, by checking the partnership records at least
every 90 days.

2. Section 702(b) is a corollary to subsection (a) and provides that a dissociated partner is liable to the partnership for any loss resulting from an obligation
improperly incurred by the partner under subsection (a). In effect, the dissociated
partner must indemnify the partnership for any loss, meaning a loss net of any
gain from the transaction. The dissociated partner is also personally liable to the
third party for the unauthorized obligation.

Section 703.   Dissociated Partner's Liability to Other Persons

(a) A partner's dissociation does not of itself discharge the partner's liability
for a partnership obligation incurred before dissociation. A dissociated partner is
not liable for a partnership obligation incurred after dissociation, except as otherwise provided in subsection (b).

(b) A partner who dissociates without resulting in a dissolution and winding
up of the partnership business is liable as a partner to the other party in a
transaction entered into by the partnership, or a surviving partnership under
[Article] 9, within two years after the partner's dissociation, only if the partner is
liable for the obligation under Section 306 and at the time of entering into the
transaction the other party:

(1) reasonably believed that the dissociated partner was then a partner;

(2) did not have notice of the partner's dissociation; and

(3) is not deemed to have had knowledge under Section 303(e) or notice
under Section 704(c).

(c) By agreement with the partnership creditor and the partners continuing
the business, a dissociated partner may be released from liability for a partnership
obligation.

(d) A dissociated partner is released from liability for a partnership obligation
if a partnership creditor, with notice of the partner's dissociation but without the
partner's consent, agrees to a material alteration in the nature or time of payment
of a partnership obligation.

Comment to Original Section 703

Section 703(a) is based on UPA Section 36(1) and continues the basic rule
that the departure of a partner does not of itself discharge the partner's liability to

third parties for any partnership obligation incurred before dissociation. The word "obligation" is used instead of "liability" and is intended to include broadly both tort and contract liability incurred before dissociation. The second sentence states affirmatively that a dissociating partner is not liable for any partnership obligation incurred after dissociation except as expressly provided in subsection (b).

Section 703(b) is new and deals with the problem of protecting third parties who extend credit to the partnership after a partner's dissociation, believing that he is still a partner. It provides that the dissociated partner remains liable as a partner for transactions entered into by the partnership within two years after departure, if the other party does not have notice of the partner's dissociation and reasonably believes when entering the transaction that the dissociated partner is still a partner. The dissociated partner is not personally liable, however, if the other party is deemed to know of the dissociation under Section 303(e) or to have notice thereof under Section 704(c).

Section 703(b) operates similarly to Section 702(a) in that it requires reliance on the departed partner's continued partnership status, as well as lack of notice. Under Section 704(c), a statement of dissociation operates conclusively as constructive notice 90 days after filing for the purposes of Section 703(b)(3) and, under Section 704(b), as constructive knowledge when recorded for the purposes of Section 303(d) and (e).

Section 703(c) continues the rule of UPA Section 36(2) that a departing partner can bargain for a contractual release from personal liability for a partnership obligation, but it requires the consent of both the creditor and the remaining partners.

Section 703(d) continues the rule of UPA Section 36(3) that a dissociated partner is released from liability for a partnership obligation if the creditor, with notice of the partner's departure, agrees to a material alteration in the nature or time of payment, without that partner's consent. This rule covers all partner dissociations and is not limited, as is the UPA rule, to situations in which a third party "agrees to assume the existing obligations of a dissolved partnership."

In general under RUPA, as a result of the adoption of the entity theory, relationships between a partnership and its creditors are not affected by the dissociation of a partner or by the addition of a new partner, unless otherwise agreed. Therefore, there is no need under RUPA, as there is under the UPA, for an elaborate provision deeming the new partnership to assume the liabilities of the old partnership. See UPA Section 41.

The "dual priority" rule in UPA Section 36(4) is eliminated to reflect the abolition of the "jingle rule," providing that separate debts have first claim on separate property, in order to conform to the Bankruptcy Code. See Comment 2 to Section 807. A deceased partner's estate, and thus all of his individual property, remains liable for partnership obligations incurred while he was a partner, however.

Section 704.   Statement of Dissociation

(a) A dissociated partner or the partnership may file a statement of dissociation stating the name of the partnership and that the partner is dissociated from the partnership.

(b) A statement of dissociation is a limitation on the authority of a dissociated partner for the purposes of Section 303(d) and (e).

(c) For the purposes of Sections 702(a)(3) and 703(b)(3), a person not a partner is deemed to have notice of the dissociation 90 days after the statement of dissociation is filed.

Comment to Original Section 704

Section 704 is new and provides for a statement of dissociation and its effects. Subsection (a) authorizes either a dissociated partner or the partnership to file a statement of dissociation. Like other RUPA filings, the statement of dissociation is voluntary. Both the partnership and the departing partner have an incentive to file, however, and it is anticipated that those filings will become routine upon a partner's dissociation. The execution, filing, and recording of the statement is governed by Section 105.

Filing or recording a statement of dissociation has threefold significance:

(1) It is a statement of limitation on the dissociated partner's authority to the extent provided in Section 303(d) and (e). Under Section 303(d), a filed or recorded limitation on the authority of a partner destroys the conclusive effect of a prior grant of authority to the extent it contradicts the prior grant. Under Section 303(e), nonpartners are conclusively bound by a limitation on the authority of a partner to transfer real property held in the partnership name, if the statement is properly recorded in the real property records.

(2) Ninety days after the statement is filed, nonpartners are deemed to have notice of the dissociation and thus conclusively bound for purposes of cutting off the partner's apparent authority under Sections 301 and 702(a)(3).

(3) Ninety days after the statement is filed, third parties are conclusively bound for purposes of cutting off the dissociated partner's continuing liability under Section 703(b)(3) for transactions entered into by the partnership after dissociation.

Section 705.   Continued Use of Partnership Name

Continued use of a partnership name, or a dissociated partner's name as part thereof, by partners continuing the business does not of itself make the dissociated partner liable for an obligation of the partners or the partnership continuing the business.

Comment to Original Section 705

Section 705 is an edited version of UPA Section 41(10) and provides that a dissociated partner is not liable for the debts of the continuing business simply because of continued use of the partnership name or the dissociated partner's name as a part thereof. That prevents forcing the business to forego the good will associated with its name.

[ARTICLE] 8.   WINDING UP PARTNERSHIP BUSINESS

Section 801.   Events Causing Dissolution and Winding Up of Partnership Business

A partnership is dissolved, and its business must be wound up, only upon the occurrence of any of the following events:

(1) in a partnership at will, the partnership's having notice from a partner, other than a partner who is dissociated under Section 601(2) through (10), of that partner's express will to withdraw as a partner, or on a later date specified by the partner;

(2) in a partnership for a definite term or particular undertaking:

(i) ~~the expiration of~~ within 90 days after a partner's dissociation by death or otherwise under Section 601(6) through (10) or wrongful dissociation under Section 602(b), ~~unless before that time a majority in interest of the remaining partners, including partners who have rightfully dissociated pursuant to Section 602(b)(2)(i), agree to continue the partnership~~ the express will of at least half of the remaining partners to wind up the partnership business for which purpose a partner's rightful dissociation pursuant to Section 602(b)(2)(i), constitutes the expression of that partner's will to wind up the partnership business;

(ii) the express will of all of the partners to wind up the partnership business; or

(iii) the expiration of the term or the completion of the undertaking;

(3) an event agreed to in the partnership agreement resulting in the winding up of the partnership business;

(4) an event that makes it unlawful for all or substantially all of the business of the partnership to be continued, but a cure of illegality within 90 days after notice to the partnership of the event is effective retroactively to the date of the event for purposes of this section;

(5) on application by a partner, a judicial determination that:

(i) the economic purpose of the partnership is likely to be unreasonably frustrated;

(ii) another partner has engaged in conduct relating to the partnership business which makes it not reasonably practicable to carry on the business in partnership with that partner; or

(iii) it is not otherwise reasonably practicable to carry on the partnership business in conformity with the partnership agreement; or

(6) on application by a transferee of a partner's transferable interest, a judicial determination that it is equitable to wind up the partnership business:

(i) after the expiration of the term or completion of the undertaking, if the partnership was for a definite term or particular undertaking at the time of the transfer or entry of the charging order that gave rise to the transfer; or

(ii) at any time, if the partnership was a partnership at will at the time of the transfer or entry of the charging order that gave rise to the transfer.

Comment to Original Section 801

1. Under UPA Section 29, a partnership is dissolved every time a partner leaves. That reflects the aggregate nature of the partnership under the UPA. Even if the business of the partnership is continued by some of the partners, it is technically a new partnership. The dissolution of the old partnership and creation of a new partnership causes many unnecessary problems.

Under RULPA, limited partnerships dissolve far less readily than do general partnerships under the UPA. A limited partnership does not dissolve on the withdrawal of a limited partner, nor does it necessarily dissolve on the withdrawal of a general partner. *See* RULPA § 801(4).

RUPA's move to the entity theory is driven in part by the need to prevent a technical dissolution or its consequences. Under RUPA, not every partner dissociation causes a dissolution of the partnership. Only certain departures trigger a dissolution. The basic rule is that a partnership is dissolved, and its business must be wound up, only upon the occurrence of one of the events listed in Section 801. All other dissociations result in a buyout of the partner's interest under Article 7 and a continuation of the partnership entity and business by the remaining partners. *See* Section 603(a).

With only three exceptions, the provisions of Section 801 are merely default rules and may by agreement be varied or eliminated as grounds for dissolution. The first exception is dissolution under Section 801(4) resulting from carrying on an illegal business. The other two exceptions cover the power of a court to dissolve a partnership under Section 801(5) on application of a partner and under Section 801(6) on application of a transferee. *See* Comments 6-8 for further explanation of these provisions.

2. Under RUPA, "dissolution" is merely the commencement of the winding up process. The partnership continues for the limited purpose of winding up the business. In effect, that means the scope of the partnership business contracts to completing work in process and taking such other actions as may be necessary to wind up the business. Winding up the partnership business entails selling its assets, paying its debts, and distributing the net balance, if any, to the partners in cash according to their interests. The partnership entity continues, and the partners are associated in the winding up of the business until winding up is completed. When the winding up is completed, the partnership entity terminates.

3. Section 801 continues two basic rules from the UPA. First, it continues the rule that any member of an *at-will* partnership has the right to force a liquidation. Second, by negative implication, it continues the rule that the partners who wish to continue the business of a *term* partnership can not be forced to liquidate the business by a partner who withdraws prematurely in violation of the partnership agreement.

Those rules are gleaned from the separate UPA provisions governing dissolution and its consequences. Under UPA Section 31(1)(b), dissolution is caused by the express will of any partner when no definite term or particular undertaking is specified. UPA Section 38(1) provides that upon dissolution any partner has the right to have the business wound up. That is a default rule and applies only in the absence of an agreement affording the other partners a right to continue the business.

UPA Section 31(2) provides that a term partnership may be dissolved at any time, in contravention of the partnership agreement, by the express will of any partner. In that case, however, UPA Section 38(2)(b) provides that the nonbreaching partners may by unanimous consent continue the business. If the business is continued, they must buy out the breaching partner.

4. Section 801(1) provides that a partnership at will is dissolved and its business must be wound up upon the partnership's having notice of a partner's express will to withdraw as a partner, unless a later effective date is specified by the partner. A partner at will who has already been dissociated in some other manner, such as a partner who has been expelled, does not thereafter have a right to cause the partnership to be dissolved and its business wound up.

If, after dissolution, none of the partners wants the partnership wound up, Section 802(b) provides that, with the consent of all the partners, including the withdrawing partner, the remaining partners may continue the business. In that event, although there is a technical dissolution of the partnership and, at least in theory, a temporary contraction of the scope of the business, the partnership entity continues and the scope of its business is restored. *See* Section 802(b) and Comment 2.

5. Section 801(2) provides three ways in which a term partnership may be dissolved before the expiration of the term:

(i) Subsection (2)(i) provides for dissolution ~~upon the expiration of 90 days after any~~ after a partner's dissociation by death or otherwise under Section 601(6) to (10) or wrongful dissociation under Section 602(b), ~~unless~~ if within ~~that~~ 90 days ~~period a majority in interest of the remaining partners agree to continue the partnership.~~ after the dissociation at least half of the remaining partners express their will, to dissolve the partnership. Thus if a term partnership had six partners and one of the partners dies or wrongfully dissociates before the end of the term, the partnership will, as a result of the dissociation, be dissolved only if three of the remaining five partners affirmatively vote in favor of dissolution within 90 days after the dissociation.* This reactive dissolution of a term partnership protects the remaining partners where the dissociating partner is crucial to the successful continuation of the business. The corresponding UPA Section 38(2)(b) rule requires unanimous consent of the remaining partners to continue the business, thus giving each partner an absolute right to a reactive liquidation. Under ~~RUPA~~ UPA 1994, if the partnership is continued by the majority, any dissenting partner who wants to withdraw may do so rightfully under the exception to Section 602(b)(2)(i), in which case his interest in the partnership will be bought out under Article 7. By itself, however, a partner's vote not to continue the business is not necessarily an expression of the partner's will to withdraw, and a dissenting partner may still elect to remain a partner and continue in the business.

The Section 601 dissociations giving rise to a reactive dissolution are: (6) a partner's bankruptcy or similar financial impairment; (7) a partner's death or

*Prior to August 1997, Section 801(2)(i) provided that upon the dissociation of a partner in a term partnership by death or otherwise under Section 601(6) through (10) or wrongful dissociation under 602(b) the partnership would dissolve unless "a majority in interest of the remaining partners (including partners who have rightfully dissociated pursuant to Section 602(b)(2)(i)), agree to continue the partnership." This language was thought to be necessary for a term partnership to lack continuity of life under the Internal Revenue Act tax classification regulations. These regulations were repealed effective January 1, 1997. The current language, approved at the 1997 annual meeting of the National Conference of Commissioners on Uniform State Laws, allows greater continuity in a term partnership than the prior version of this subsection and UPA Section 38(2)(b).

incapacity; (8) the distribution by a trust-partner of its entire partnership interest; (9) the distribution by an estate-partner of its entire partnership interest; and (10) the termination of an entity-partner. Any dissociation during the term of the partnership that is wrongful under Section 602(b), including a partner's voluntary withdrawal, expulsion or bankruptcy, also gives rise to a reactive dissolution. Those statutory grounds may be varied by agreement or the reactive dissolution may be abolished entirely.

~~Under subsection (2)(i), a term partnership is dissolved 90 days after the first partner's dissociation unless within that time a majority in interest of the remaining partners have agreed to continue the partnership. Continuation under subsection (2)(i) requires the agreement of at least a majority in interest of the remaining partners. The interest and vote of a partner who dissociates rightfully under Section 602(b)(2)(i) is counted in determining whether a majority in interest agrees to continue.~~

~~Decision making by a majority in interest is not the normal RUPA~~ <u>UPA 1994</u> ~~default rule. Section 401(j) requires a majority in number, rather than a majority in interest, for ordinary business decisions and unanimity for extraordinary matters and amendments to the partnership agreement. Requiring only majority approval to continue the partnership, rather than unanimity, in effect treats the decision as an ordinary business matter, thereby enhancing firm stability. At the same time, requiring a majority in interest, rather than a majority in number, satisfies Internal Revenue Service concerns regarding a partnership's continuity of life.~~

~~*See* Treas. Reg. § 301.7701-2(b)(1).~~

~~"Majority in interest" is not defined in the Act, but is intended to satisfy Internal Revenue Service regulations regarding continuity of life. Under Rev. Proc. 94-46 (June 29, 1994), the "in interest" concept refers to the partners' economic interests in both the profits and capital of the partnership.~~

Under Section 601(6)(i), a partner is dissociated upon becoming a debtor in bankruptcy. The bankruptcy of a partner or of the partnership is not, however, an event of dissolution under Section 801. That is a change from UPA Section 31(5). A partner's bankruptcy does, however, cause dissolution of a term partnership under Section 801(2)(i), unless a majority in interest of the remaining partners thereafter agree to continue the partnership. Affording the other partners the option of buying out the bankrupt partner's interest avoids the necessity of winding up a term partnership every time a partner becomes a debtor in bankruptcy.

Similarly, under Section 801(2)(i), the death of any partner will result in the dissolution of a term partnership, ~~unless a majority in interest of the remaining partners agree to continue the business. In that case,~~ <u>only if at least half of the remaining partners express their will to wind up the partnership's business. If dissolution does occur,</u> the deceased partner's transferable interest in the partnership passes to his estate and must be bought out under Article 7. *See* Comment 8 to Section 601.

(ii) Section 801(2)(ii) provides that a term partnership may be dissolved and wound up at any time by the express will of all the partners. That is merely an expression of the general rule that the partnership agreement may override the statutory default rules and that the partnership agreement, like any contract, can be amended at any time by unanimous consent.

UPA Section 31(1)(c) provides that a term partnership may be wound up by the express will of all the partners whose transferable interests have not been assigned or charged for a partner's separate debts. That rule reflects the belief that the remaining partners may find transferees very intrusive. This provision has been deleted, however, because the liquidation is easily accomplished under Section 801(2)(ii) by first expelling the transferor partner under Section 601(4)(ii).

(iii) Section 801(2)(iii) is based on UPA Section 31(1)(a) and provides for winding up a term partnership upon the expiration of the term or the completion of the undertaking.

Subsection (2)(iii) must be read in conjunction with Section 406. Under Section 406(a), if the partners continue the business after the expiration of the term or the completion of the undertaking, the partnership will be treated as a partnership at will. Moreover, if the partners continue the business without any settlement or liquidation of the partnership, under Section 406(b) they are presumed to have agreed that the partnership will continue, despite the lack of a formal agreement. The partners may also agree to ratify all acts taken since the end of the partnership's term.

6. Section 801(3) provides for dissolution upon the occurrence of an event specified in the partnership agreement as resulting in the winding up of the partnership business. The partners may, however, agree to continue the business and to ratify all acts taken since dissolution.

7. Section 801(4) continues the basic rule in UPA Section 31(3) and provides for dissolution if it is unlawful to continue the business of the partnership, unless cured. The "all or substantially all" proviso is intended to avoid dissolution for insubstantial or innocent regulatory violations. If the illegality is cured within 90 days after notice to the partnership, it is effective retroactively for purposes of this section. The requirement that an uncured illegal business be wound up cannot be varied in the partnership agreement. *See* Section 103(b)(8).

8. Section 801(5) provides for judicial dissolution on application by a partner. It is based in part on UPA Section 32(1), and the language comes in part from RULPA Section 802. A court may order a partnership dissolved upon a judicial determination that: (i) the economic purpose of the partnership is likely to be unreasonably frustrated; (ii) another partner has engaged in conduct relating to the partnership business which makes it not reasonably practicable to carry on

the business in partnership with that partner; or (iii) it is not otherwise reasonably practicable to carry on the partnership business in conformity with the partnership agreement. The court's power to wind up the partnership under Section 801(5) cannot be varied in the partnership agreement. *See* Section 103(b)(8).

RUPA deletes UPA Section 32(1)(e) which provides for dissolution when the business can only be carried on at a loss. That provision might result in a dissolution contrary to the partners' expectations in a start-up or tax shelter situation, in which case "book" or "tax" losses do not signify business failure. Truly poor financial performance may justify dissolution under subsection (5)(i) as a frustration of the partnership's economic purpose.

RUPA also deletes UPA Section 32(1)(f) which authorizes a court to order dissolution of a partnership when "other circumstances render a dissolution equitable." That provision was regarded as too open-ended and, given RUPA's expanded remedies for partners, unnecessary. No significant change in result is intended, however, since the interpretation of UPA Section 32(1)(f) is comparable to the specific grounds expressed in subsection (5). *See, e.g., Karber v. Karber*, 145 Ariz. 293, 701 P.2d 1 (Ct. App. 1985) (partnership dissolved on basis of suspicion and ill will, citing UPA §§ 32(1)(d) and (f)); *Fuller v. Brough*, 159 Colo. 147, 411 P.2d 18 (1966) (not equitable to dissolve partnership for trifling causes or temporary grievances that do not render it impracticable to carry on partnership business); *Lau v. Wong*, 1 Haw. App. 217, 616 P.2d 1031 (1980) (partnership dissolved where business operated solely for benefit of managing partner).

9. Section 801(6) provides for judicial dissolution on application by a transferee of a partner's transferable interest in the partnership, including the purchaser of a partner's interest upon foreclosure of a charging order. It is based on UPA Section 32(2) and authorizes dissolution upon a judicial determination that it is equitable to wind up the partnership business (i) after the expiration of the partnership term or completion of the undertaking or (ii) at any time, if the partnership were a partnership at will at the time of the transfer or when the charging order was issued. The requirement that the court determine that it is equitable to wind up the business is new. The rights of a transferee under this section cannot be varied in the partnership agreement. *See* Section 103(b)(8).

Section 802.   Partnership Continues After Dissolution

(a) Subject to subsection (b), a partnership continues after dissolution only for the purpose of winding up its business. The partnership is terminated when the winding up of its business is completed.

(b) At any time after the dissolution of a partnership and before the winding up of its business is completed, all of the partners, including any dissociating partner other than a wrongfully dissociating partner, may waive the right to have the partnership's business wound up and the partnership terminated. In that event:

(1) the partnership resumes carrying on its business as if dissolution had never occurred, and any liability incurred by the partnership or a partner after the dissolution and before the waiver is determined as if dissolution had never occurred; and

(2) the rights of a third party accruing under Section 804(1) or arising out of conduct in reliance on the dissolution before the third party knew or received a notification of the waiver may not be adversely affected.

Comment to Original Section 802

1. Section 802(a) is derived from UPA Section 30 and provides that a partnership continues after dissolution only for the purpose of winding up its business, after which it is terminated. RUPA continues the concept of "termination" to mark the completion of the winding up process. Since no filing or other formality is required, the date will often be determined only by hindsight. No legal rights turn on the partnership's termination or the date thereof. Even after termination, if a previously unknown liability is asserted, all of the partners are still liable.

2. Section 802(b) makes explicit the right of the remaining partners to continue the business after an event of dissolution if all of the partners, including the dissociating partner or partners, waive the right to have the business wound up and the partnership terminated. Only those "dissociating" partners whose dissociation was the immediate cause of the dissolution must waive the right to have the business wound up. The consent of wrongfully dissociating partners is not required.

3. Upon waiver of the right to have the business wound up, Paragraph (1) of the subsection provides that the partnership entity may resume carrying on its business as if dissolution had never occurred, thereby restoring the scope of its business to normal. "Resumes" is intended to mean that acts appropriate to winding up, authorized when taken, are in effect ratified, and the partnership remains liable for those acts, as provided explicitly in paragraph (2).

If the business is continued following a waiver of the right to dissolution, any liability incurred by the partnership or a partner after the dissolution and before the waiver is to be determined as if dissolution had never occurred. That has the effect of validating transactions entered into after dissolution that might not have been appropriate for winding up the business, because, upon waiver, any liability incurred by either the partnership or a partner in those transactions will be determined under Sections 702 and 703, rather than Sections 804 and 806.

As to the liability for those transactions among the partners themselves, the partners by agreement may provide otherwise. Thus, a partner who, after dissolution, incurred an obligation appropriate for winding up, but *not* appropriate for continuing the business, may protect himself by conditioning his consent to the continuation of the business on the ratification of the transaction by the continuing partners.

Paragraph (2) of the subsection provides that the rights of third parties accruing under Section 804(1) before they knew (or were notified) of the waiver may not be adversely affected by the waiver. That is intended to mean the partnership is bound, notwithstanding a subsequent waiver of dissolution and resumption of its business, by a transaction entered into after dissolution that was appropriate for winding up the partnership business, even if *not* appropriate for continuing the business. Similarly, any rights of a third party arising out of conduct in reliance on the dissolution are protected, absent knowledge (or notification) of the waiver. Thus, for example, a partnership loan, callable upon dissolution, that has been called is not reinstated by a subsequent waiver. If the loan has not been called before the lender learns (or is notified) of the waiver, however, it may not thereafter be called because of the dissolution. On the other hand, a waiver does not reinstate a lease that is terminated by the dissolution itself.

Section 803.   Right to Wind Up Partnership Business

(a) After dissolution, a partner who has not wrongfully dissociated may participate in winding up the partnership's business, but on application of any partner, partner's legal representative, or transferee, the [designate the appropriate court], for good cause shown, may order judicial supervision of the winding up.

(b) The legal representative of the last surviving partner may wind up a partnership's business.

(c) A person winding up a partnership's business may preserve the partnership business or property as a going concern for a reasonable time, prosecute and defend actions and proceedings, whether civil, criminal, or administrative, settle and close the partnership's business, dispose of and transfer the partnership's property, discharge the partnership's liabilities, distribute the assets of the partnership pursuant to Section 807, settle disputes by mediation or arbitration, and perform other necessary acts.

Comment to Original Section 803

Section 803(a) is drawn from UPA Section 37. It provides that the partners who have not wrongfully dissociated may participate in winding up the partnership business. Wrongful dissociation is defined in Section 602. On application of any partner, a court may for good cause judicially supervise the winding up.

Section 803(b) continues the rule of UPA Section 25(2)(d) that the legal representative of the last surviving partner may wind up the business. It makes clear that the representative of the last surviving partner will not be forced to go to court for authority to wind up the business. On the other hand, the legal representative of a deceased partner, other than the last surviving partner, has only the rights of a transferee of the deceased partner's transferable interest. *See* Comment 8 to Section 601.

Section 803(c) is new and provides further guidance on the powers of a person who is winding up the business. It is based on Delaware Laws, Title, 6 Del. C. Section 17-803. The powers enumerated are not intended to be exclusive.

Subsection (c) expressly authorizes the preservation of the partnership's business or property as a going concern for a reasonable time. Some courts have reached that result without benefit of statutory authority. *See, e.g., Paciaroni v. Crane*, 408 A.2d 946 (Del. Ch. 1979). An agreement to continue the partnership business in order to preserve its going-concern value until sale is not a waiver of a partner's right to have the business liquidated.

The authorization of mediation and arbitration implements Conference policy to encourage alternative dispute resolution.

A partner's fiduciary duties of care and loyalty under Section 404 extend to winding up the business, except as modified by Section 603(b).

Section 804.   Partner's Power to Bind Partnership After Dissolution

Subject to Section 805, a partnership is bound by a partner's act after dissolution that:

(1) is appropriate for winding up the partnership business; or

(2) would have bound the partnership under Section 301 before dissolution, if the other party to the transaction did not have notice of the dissolution.

Comment to Original Section 804

Section 804 is the successor to UPA Sections 33(2) and 35, which wind down the authority of partners to bind the partnership to third persons.

Section 804(1) provides that partners have the authority to bind the partnership after dissolution in transactions that are appropriate for winding-up the partnership business. Section 804(2) provides that partners also have the power after dissolution to bind the partnership in transactions that are inconsistent with winding up. The partnership is bound in a transaction not appropriate for winding up, however, only if the partner's act would have bound the partnership under

Section 301 before dissolution and the other party to the transaction did not have notice of the dissolution. *See* Section 102(b) (notice). *Compare* Section 301(1) (partner has apparent authority unless other party knows or has received a notification of lack of authority).

Section 804(2) attempts to balance the interests of the partners to terminate their mutual agency authority against the interests of outside creditors who have no notice of the partnership's dissolution. Even if the partnership is not bound under Section 804, the faithless partner who purports to act for the partnership after dissolution may be liable individually to an innocent third party under the law of agency. *See* Section 330 of the Restatement (Second) of Agency (agent liable for misrepresentation of authority), applicable under RUPA as provided in Section 104(a).

RUPA eliminates the special and confusing UPA rules limiting the authority of partners after dissolution. The special protection afforded by UPA Section 35(1)(b)(I) to former creditors and the lesser special protection afforded by UPA Section 35(1)(b)(II) to other parties who knew of the partnership before dissolution are both abolished. RUPA eschews these cumbersome notice provisions in favor of the general apparent authority rules of Section 301, subject to the effect of a filed or recorded statement of dissolution under Section 805. This enhances the protection of innocent third parties and imposes liability on the partnership and the partners who choose their fellow partner-agents and are in the best position to protect others by providing notice of the dissolution.

Also deleted are the special rules for unknown partners in UPA Section 35(2) and for certain causes of dissolution in UPA Section 35(3). Those, too, are inconsistent with RUPA's policy of adhering more closely to the general agency rules of Section 301.

Section 804 should be contrasted with Section 702, which winds down the power of a partner being bought out. The power of a dissociating partner is limited to transactions entered into within two years after the partner's dissociation. Section 804 has no time limitation. However, the apparent authority of partners in both situations is now subject to the filing of a statement of dissociation or dissolution, as the case may be, which operates to cut off such authority after 90 days.

Section 805.   Statement of Dissolution

(a) After dissolution, a partner who has not wrongfully dissociated may file a statement of dissolution stating the name of the partnership and that the partnership has dissolved and is winding up its business.

(b) A statement of dissolution cancels a filed statement of partnership authority for the purposes of Section 303(d) and is a limitation on authority for the purposes of Section 303(e).

(c) For the purposes of Sections 301 and 804, a person not a partner is deemed to have notice of the dissolution and the limitation on the partners' authority as a result of the statement of dissolution 90 days after it is filed.

(d) After filing and, if appropriate, recording a statement of dissolution, a dissolved partnership may file and, if appropriate, record a statement of partnership authority which will operate with respect to a person not a partner as provided in Section 303(d) and (e) in any transaction, whether or not the transaction is appropriate for winding up the partnership business.

Comment to Original Section 805

1. Section 805 is new. Subsection (a) provides that, after an event of dissolution, any partner who has not wrongfully dissociated may file a statement of dissolution on behalf of the partnership. The filing and recording of a statement of dissolution is optional. The execution, filing, and recording of the statement is governed by Section 105. The legal consequences of filing a statement of dissolution are similar to those of a statement of dissociation under Section 704.

2. Subsection (b) provides that a statement of dissolution cancels a filed statement of partnership authority for the purposes of Section 303(d), thereby terminating any extraordinary grant of authority contained in that statement.

A statement of dissolution also operates as a limitation on authority for the purposes of Section 303(e). That section provides that third parties are deemed to know of a limitation on the authority of a partner to transfer real property held in the name of the partnership if a certified copy of the statement containing the limitation is recorded with the real estate records. In effect, a properly recorded statement of dissolution restricts the authority of all partners to real property transfers that are appropriate for winding up the business. Thus, third parties must inquire of the partnership whether a contemplated real property transfer is appropriate for winding up. After dissolution, the partnership may, however, file and record a new statement of authority that will bind the partnership under Section 303(d).

3. Subsection (c) operates in conjunction with Sections 301 and 804 to wind down partners' apparent authority after dissolution. It provides that, for purposes of those sections, 90 days after the filing of a statement of dissolution nonpartners are deemed to have notice of the dissolution and the corresponding limitation on the authority of all partners. Sections 301 and 804 provide that a partner's lack of authority is binding on persons with notice thereof. Thus, after 90 days the statement of dissolution operates as constructive notice conclusively limiting the apparent authority of partners to transactions that are appropriate for winding up the business.

4. Subsection (d) provides that, after filing and, if appropriate, recording a statement of dissolution, the partnership may file and record a new statement of

partnership authority that will operate as provided in Section 303(d). A grant of authority contained in that statement is conclusive and may be relied upon by a person who gives value without knowledge to the contrary, whether or not the transaction is appropriate for winding up the partnership business. That makes the partners' record authority conclusive after dissolution, and precludes going behind the record to inquire into whether or not the transaction was appropriate for winding up.

Section 806.   *Partner's Liability to Other Partners After Dissolution*

(a) Except as otherwise provided in subsection (b) <u>and Section 306</u>, after dissolution a partner is liable to the other partners for the partner's share of any partnership liability incurred under Section 804.

(b) A partner who, with knowledge of the dissolution, incurs a partnership liability under Section 804(2) by an act that is not appropriate for winding up the partnership business is liable to the partnership for any damage caused to the partnership arising from the liability.

Comment to Original Section 806

Section 806 is the successor to UPA Sections 33(1) and 34, which govern the rights of partners among themselves with respect to post-dissolution liability.

Subsection (a) provides that, except as provided in subsection (b), after dissolution each partner is liable to the other partners by way of contribution for his share of any partnership liability incurred under Section 804. That includes not only obligations that are appropriate for winding up the business, but also obligations that are inappropriate if within the partner's apparent authority.

Subsection (a) draws no distinction as to the cause of dissolution. Thus, as among the partners, their liability is treated alike in all events of dissolution. That is a change from UPA Section 33(1).

Subsection (b) creates an exception to the general rule in subsection (a). It provides that a partner, who with knowledge of the winding up nevertheless incurs a liability binding on the partnership by an act that is inappropriate for winding up the business, is liable to the partnership for any loss caused thereby.

Section 806 is merely a default rule and may be varied in the partnership agreement. *See* Section 103(a).

Comment to Amendments

Consistent with other provisions of this Act, Section 806(a) makes clear that a partner does not have a contribution obligation with regard to partnership obligations for which the partner is not liable under Section 306. *See* Section 401(b) cmt.

Section 807.   Settlement of Accounts and Contributions Among Partners

(a) In winding up a partnership's business, the assets of the partnership, including the contributions of the partners required by this section, must be applied to discharge its obligations to creditors, including, to the extent permitted by law, partners who are creditors. Any surplus must be applied to pay in cash the net amount distributable to partners in accordance with their right to distributions under subsection (b).

(b) Each partner is entitled to a settlement of all partnership accounts upon winding up the partnership business. In settling accounts among the partners, ~~the~~ profits and losses that result from the liquidation of the partnership assets must be credited and charged to the partners' accounts. The partnership shall make a distribution to a partner in an amount equal to any excess of the credits over the charges in the partner's account. A partner shall contribute to the partnership an amount equal to any excess of the charges over the credits in the partner's account but excluding from the calculation charges attributable to an obligation for which the partner is not personally liable under Section 306.

(c) If a partner fails to contribute the full amount required under subsection (b), all of the other partners shall contribute, in the proportions in which those partners share partnership losses, the additional amount necessary to satisfy the partnership obligations for which they are personally liable under Section 306. A partner or partner's legal representative may recover from the other partners any contributions the partner makes to the extent the amount contributed exceeds that partner's share of the partnership obligations for which the partner is personally liable under Section 306.

(d) After the settlement of accounts, each partner shall contribute, in the proportion in which the partner shares partnership losses, the amount necessary to satisfy partnership obligations that were not known at the time of the settlement and for which the partner is personally liable under Section 306.

(e) The estate of a deceased partner is liable for the partner's obligation to contribute to the partnership.

(f) An assignee for the benefit of creditors of a partnership or a partner, or a person appointed by a court to represent creditors of a partnership or a partner, may enforce a partner's obligation to contribute to the partnership.

Comment to Original Section 807

1. Section 807 provides the default rules for the settlement of accounts and contributions among the partners in winding up the business. It is derived in part from UPA Sections 38(1) and 40.

2. Subsection (a) continues the rule in UPA Section 38(1) that, in winding up the business, the partnership assets must first be applied to discharge partnership liabilities to creditors. For this purpose, any required contribution by the partners is treated as an asset of the partnership. After the payment of all partnership liabilities, any surplus must be applied to pay in cash the net amount due the partners under subsection (b) by way of a liquidating distribution.

RUPA continues the "in-cash" rule of UPA Section 38(1) and is consistent with Section 402, which provides that a partner has no right to receive, and may not be required to accept, a distribution in kind, unless otherwise agreed. The in-cash rule avoids the valuation problems that afflict unwanted in-kind distributions.

The partnership must apply its assets to discharge the obligations of partners who are creditors on a parity with other creditors. *See* Section 404(f) and Comment 6. In effect, that abolishes the priority rules in UPA Section 40(b) and (c) which subordinate the payment of inside debt to outside debt. Both RULPA and the RMBCA do likewise. *See* RULPA § 804; RMBCA §§ 6.40(f), 14.05(a). Ultimately, however, a partner whose "debt" has been repaid by the partnership is personally liable, as a partner, for any outside debt remaining unsatisfied, unlike a limited partner or corporate shareholder. Accordingly, the obligation to contribute sufficient funds to satisfy the claims of outside creditors may result in the equitable subordination of inside debt when partnership assets are insufficient to satisfy all obligations to non-partners.

RUPA in effect abolishes the "dual priority" or "jingle" rule of UPA Section 40(h) and (i). Those sections gave partnership creditors priority as to partnership property and separate creditors priority as to separate property. The jingle rule has already been preempted by the Bankruptcy Code, at least as to Chapter 7 partnership liquidation proceedings. Under Section 723(c) of the Bankruptcy Code, and under RUPA, partnership creditors share pro rata with the partners' individual creditors in the assets of the partners' estates.

3. Subsection (b) provides that each partner is entitled to a settlement of all partnership accounts upon winding up. It also establishes the default rules for closing out the partners' accounts. First, the profits and losses resulting from the liquidation of the partnership assets must be credited or charged to the partners' accounts, according to their respective shares of profits and losses. Then, the

partnership must make a final liquidating distribution to those partners with a positive account balance. That distribution should be in the amount of the excess of credits over the charges in the account. Any partner with a negative account balance must contribute to the partnership an amount equal to the excess of charges over the credits in the account. The partners may, however, agree that a negative account does not reflect a debt to the partnership and need not be repaid in settling the partners' accounts.

RUPA eliminates the distinction in UPA Section 40(b) between the liability owing to a partner in respect of capital and the liability owing in respect of profits. Section 807(b) speaks simply of the right of a partner to a liquidating distribution. That implements the logic of RUPA Sections 401(a) and 502 under which contributions to capital and shares in profits and losses combine to determine the right to distributions. The partners may, however, agree to share "operating" losses differently from "capital" losses, thereby continuing the UPA distinction.

4. Subsection (c) continues the UPA Section 40(d) rule that solvent partners share proportionately in the shortfall caused by insolvent partners who fail to contribute their proportionate share. The partnership may enforce a partner's obligation to contribute. *See* Section 405(a). A partner is entitled to recover from the other partners any contributions in excess of that partner's share of the partnership's liabilities. *See* Section 405(b)(iii).

5. Subsection (d) provides that, after settling the partners' accounts, each partner must contribute, in the proportion in which he shares losses, the amount necessary to satisfy partnership obligations that were not known at the time of the settlement. That continues the basic rule of UPA Section 40(d) and underscores that the obligation to contribute exists independently of the partnership's books of account. It specifically covers the situation of a partnership liability that was unknown when the partnership books were closed.

6. Under subsection (e), the estate of a deceased partner is liable for the partner's obligation to contribute to partnership losses. That continues the rule of UPA Section 40(g).

7. Subsection (f) provides that an assignee for the benefit of creditors of the partnership or of a partner (or other court appointed creditor representative) may enforce any partner's obligation to contribute to the partnership. That continues the rules of UPA Sections 36(4) and 40(e).

Comment to Amendments

Section 807(b) makes clear that a partner's contribution obligation in dissolution only considers the partner's share of unshielded obligations. *See* Section 401(b) cmt. (contribution to an operating partnership). Properly determined, the total contributions will be sufficient to satisfy the partnership's total unshielded claims. In addition, there may be excess remaining partnership assets with which to liquidate some portion of partnership-shielded obligations. Of course, if the partners' required contributions for unshielded partnership liabilities are used in part by the partnership to liquidate shielded claims, an unshielded and unpaid creditor retains an action against the partnership and the partners. Therefore, this section does not attempt to eliminate a partnership's obligation to an unshielded creditor.

[ARTICLE] 9.   CONVERSIONS AND MERGERS

Section 901.   Definitions

In this [article]:

(1) "General partner" means a partner in a partnership and a general partner in a limited partnership.

(2) "Limited partner" means a limited partner in a limited partnership.

(3) "Limited partnership" means a limited partnership created under the [State Limited Partnership Act], predecessor law, or comparable law of another jurisdiction.

(4) "Partner" includes both a general partner and a limited partner.

Comment to Original Section 901

1. Article 9 is new. The UPA is silent with respect to the conversion or merger of partnerships, and thus it is necessary under the UPA to structure those types of transactions as asset transfers. RUPA provides specific statutory authority for conversions and mergers. It provides for continuation of the partnership entity, thereby simplifying those transactions and adding certainty to the legal consequences.

A number of States currently authorize the merger of limited partnerships, and some authorize them to merge with other business entities such as corporations and limited liability companies. A few States currently authorize the merger of a general and a limited partnership or the conversion of a general to a limited partnership.

2. As Section 908 makes clear, the requirements of Article 9 are not mandatory, and a partnership may convert or merge in any other manner provided by law. Article 9 is merely a "safe harbor." If the requirements of the article are followed, the conversion or merger is legally valid. Since most States have no other established procedure for the conversion or merger of partnerships, it is likely that the Article 9 procedures will be used in virtually all cases.

3. Article 9 does not restrict the provisions authorizing conversions and mergers to domestic partnerships. Since no filing is required for the creation of a partnership under RUPA, it is often unclear where a partnership is domiciled. Moreover, a partnership doing business in the State satisfies the definition of a partnership created under this Act since it is an association of two or more co-owners carrying on a business for profit. Even a partnership clearly domiciled in another State could easily amend its partnership agreement to provide that its internal affairs are to be governed by the laws of a jurisdiction that has enacted Article 9 of RUPA. No harm is likely to result from extending to foreign partnerships the right to convert or merge under local law.

4. Because Article 9 deals with the conversion and merger of both general and limited partnerships, Section 901 sets forth four definitions distinguishing between the two types of partnerships solely for the purposes of Article 9. "Partner" includes both general and limited partners, and "general partner" includes general partners in both general and limited partnerships.

Section 902. Conversion of Partnership to Limited Partnership

(a) A partnership may be converted to a limited partnership pursuant to this section.

(b) The terms and conditions of a conversion of a partnership to a limited partnership must be approved by all of the partners or by a number or percentage specified for conversion in the partnership agreement.

(c) After the conversion is approved by the partners, the partnership shall file a certificate of limited partnership in the jurisdiction in which the limited partnership is to be formed. The certificate must include:

(1) a statement that the partnership was converted to a limited partnership from a partnership;

(2) its former name; and

(3) a statement of the number of votes cast by the partners for and against the conversion and, if the vote is less than unanimous, the number or percentage required to approve the conversion under the partnership agreement.

(d) The conversion takes effect when the certificate of limited partnership is filed or at any later date specified in the certificate.

(e) A general partner who becomes a limited partner as a result of the conversion remains liable as a general partner for an obligation incurred by the partnership before the conversion takes effect. If the other party to a transaction with the limited partnership reasonably believes when entering the transaction that the limited partner is a general partner, the limited partner is liable for an obligation incurred by the limited partnership within 90 days after the conversion takes effect. The limited partner's liability for all other obligations of the limited partnership incurred after the conversion takes effect is that of a limited partner as provided in the [State Limited Partnership Act].

Comment to Original Section 902

Section 902(a) authorizes the conversion of a "partnership" to a "limited partnership." Section 202(b) limits the usual RUPA definition of "partnership" to general partnerships. That definition is applicable to Article 9. If a limited partnership is contemplated, Article 9 uses the term "limited partnership." *See* Section 901(3).

Subsection (b) provides that the terms and conditions of the conversion must be approved by all the partners, unless the partnership agreement specifies otherwise for a conversion.

Subsection (c) provides that, after approval, the partnership must file a certificate of limited partnership which includes the requisite information concerning the conversion.

Subsection (d) provides that the conversion takes effect when the certificate is filed, unless a later effective date is specified.

Subsection (e) establishes the partners' liabilities following a conversion. A partner who becomes a limited partner as a result of the conversion remains fully liable as a general partner for any obligation arising before the effective date of the conversion, both to third parties and to other partners for contribution. Third parties who transact business with the converted partnership unaware of a partner's new status as a limited partner are protected for 90 days after the conversion. Since RULPA Section 201(a)(3) requires the certificate of limited partnership to name all of the general partners, and under RUPA Section 902(c) the certificate must also include a statement of the conversion, parties transacting business with the converted partnership can protect themselves by checking the record of the State where the limited partnership is formed (the State where the conversion takes place). A former general partner who becomes a limited partner as a result of the conversion can avoid the lingering 90-day exposure to liability as a general partner by notifying those transacting business with the partnership of his limited partner status.

Although Section 902 does not expressly provide that a partner's withdrawal upon a term partnership's conversion to a limited partnership is rightful, it was assumed that the unanimity requirement for the approval of a conversion would afford a withdrawing partner adequate opportunity to protect his interest as a condition of approval. This question is left to the partnership agreement if it provides for conversion without the approval of all the partners.

Section 903.   *Conversion of Limited Partnership to Partnership*

(a) A limited partnership may be converted to a partnership pursuant to this section.

(b) Notwithstanding a provision to the contrary in a limited partnership agreement, the terms and conditions of a conversion of a limited partnership to a partnership must be approved by all of the partners.

(c) After the conversion is approved by the partners, the limited partnership shall cancel its certificate of limited partnership.

(d) The conversion takes effect when the certificate of limited partnership is canceled.

(e) A limited partner who becomes a general partner as a result of the conversion remains liable only as a limited partner for an obligation incurred by the limited partnership before the conversion takes effect. ~~The~~ Except as otherwise provided in Section 306, the partner is liable as a general partner for an obligation of the partnership incurred after the conversion takes effect.

Comment to Original Section 903

Section 903(a) authorizes the conversion of a limited partnership to a general partnership.

Subsection (b) provides that the conversion must be approved by all of the partners, even if the partnership agreement provides to the contrary. That includes all of the general and limited partners. *See* Section 901(4). The purpose of the unanimity requirement is to protect a limited partner from exposure to personal liability as a general partner without clear and knowing consent at the time of conversion. Despite a general voting provision to the contrary in the partnership agreement, conversion to a general partnership may never have been contemplated by the limited partner when the partnership investment was made.

Subsection (c) provides that, after approval of the conversion, the converted partnership must cancel its certificate of limited partnership. *See* RULPA § 203.

Subsection (d) provides that the conversion takes effect when the certificate of limited partnership is canceled.

Subsection (e) provides that a limited partner who becomes a general partner is liable as a general partner for all obligations incurred after the effective date of the conversion, but still has only limited liability for obligations incurred before the conversion.

Section 904.   *Effect of Conversion; Entity Unchanged*

(a) A partnership or limited partnership that has been converted pursuant to this [article] is for all purposes the same entity that existed before the conversion.

(b) When a conversion takes effect:

(1) all property owned by the converting partnership or limited partnership remains vested in the converted entity;

(2) all obligations of the converting partnership or limited partnership continue as obligations of the converted entity; and

(3) an action or proceeding pending against the converting partnership or limited partnership may be continued as if the conversion had not occurred.

Comment to Original Section 904

Section 904 sets forth the effect of a conversion on the partnership. Subsection (a) provides that the converted partnership is for all purposes the same entity as before the conversion.

Subsection (b) provides that upon conversion: (1) all partnership property remains vested in the converted entity; (2) all obligations remain the obligations of the converted entity; and (3) all pending legal actions may be continued as if the conversion had not occurred. The term "entity" as used in Article 9 refers to either or both general and limited partnerships as the context requires.

Under subsection (b)(1), title to partnership property remains vested in the converted partnership. As a matter of general property law, title remains vested without further act or deed and without reversion or impairment.

Section 905.   *Merger of Partnerships*

(a) Pursuant to a plan of merger approved as provided in subsection (c), a partnership may be merged with one or more partnerships or limited partnerships.

(b) The plan of merger must set forth:

(1) the name of each partnership or limited partnership that is a party to the merger;

(2) the name of the surviving entity into which the other partnerships or limited partnerships will merge;

(3) whether the surviving entity is a partnership or a limited partnership and the status of each partner;

(4) the terms and conditions of the merger;

(5) the manner and basis of converting the interests of each party to the merger into interests or obligations of the surviving entity, or into money or other property in whole or part; and

(6) the street address of the surviving entity's chief executive office.

(c) The plan of merger must be approved:

(1) in the case of a partnership that is a party to the merger, by all of the partners, or a number or percentage specified for merger in the partnership agreement; and

(2) in the case of a limited partnership that is a party to the merger, by the vote required for approval of a merger by the law of the State or foreign jurisdiction in which the limited partnership is organized and, in the absence of such a specifically applicable law, by all of the partners, notwithstanding a provision to the contrary in the partnership agreement.

(d) After a plan of merger is approved and before the merger takes effect, the plan may be amended or abandoned as provided in the plan.

(e) The merger takes effect on the later of:

(1) the approval of the plan of merger by all parties to the merger, as provided in subsection (c);

(2) the filing of all documents required by law to be filed as a condition to the effectiveness of the merger; or

(3) any effective date specified in the plan of merger.

Comment to Original Section 905

Section 905 provides a "safe harbor" for the merger of a general partnership and one or more general or limited partnerships. The surviving entity may be either a general or a limited partnership.

The plan of merger must set forth the information required by subsection (b), including the status of each partner and the manner and basis of converting the interests of each party to the merger into interests or obligations of the surviving entity.

Subsection (c) provides that the plan of merger must be approved: (1) by all the partners of each general partnership that is a party to the merger, unless its partnership agreement specifically provides otherwise for mergers; and (2) by all the partners, including both general and limited partners, of each limited partnership that is a party to the merger, notwithstanding a contrary provision in its partnership agreement, unless specifically authorized by the law of the jurisdiction in which that limited partnership is organized. Like Section 902(b), the purpose of the unanimity requirement is to protect limited partners from exposure to liability as general partners without their clear and knowing consent.

Subsection (d) provides that the plan of merger may be amended or abandoned at any time before the merger takes effect, if the plan so provides.

Subsection (e) provides that the merger takes effect on the later of: (1) approval by all parties to the merger; (2) filing of all required documents; or (3) the effective date specified in the plan. The surviving entity must file all notices and documents relating to the merger required by other applicable statutes governing the entities that are parties to the merger, such as articles of merger or a certificate of limited partnership. It may also amend or cancel a statement of partnership authority previously filed by any party to the merger.

Section 906.   Effect of Merger

(a) When a merger takes effect:

(1) the separate existence of every partnership or limited partnership that is a party to the merger, other than the surviving entity, ceases;

(2) all property owned by each of the merged partnerships or limited partnerships vests in the surviving entity;

(3) all obligations of every partnership or limited partnership that is a party to the merger become the obligations of the surviving entity; and

(4) an action or proceeding pending against a partnership or limited partnership that is a party to the merger may be continued as if the merger had not occurred, or the surviving entity may be substituted as a party to the action or proceeding.

(b) The [Secretary of State] of this State is the agent for service of process in an action or proceeding against a surviving foreign partnership or limited partnership to enforce an obligation of a domestic partnership or limited partnership that is a party to a merger. The surviving entity shall promptly notify the [Secretary of State] of the mailing address of its chief executive office and of any change of address. Upon receipt of process, the [Secretary of State] shall mail a copy of the process to the surviving foreign partnership or limited partnership.

(c) A partner of the surviving partnership or limited partnership is liable for:

(1) all obligations of a party to the merger for which the partner was personally liable before the merger;

(2) all other obligations of the surviving entity incurred before the merger by a party to the merger, but those obligations may be satisfied only out of property of the entity; and

(3) all obligations of the surviving entity incurred after the merger takes effect, but those obligations may be satisfied only out of property of the entity if the partner is a limited partner.

(d) If the obligations incurred before the merger by a party to the merger are not satisfied out of the property of the surviving partnership or limited partnership, the general partners of that party immediately before the effective date of the merger shall contribute the amount necessary to satisfy that party's obligations to the surviving entity, in the manner provided in Section 807 or in the [Limited Partnership Act] of the jurisdiction in which the party was formed, as the case may be, as if the merged party were dissolved.

(e) A partner of a party to a merger who does not become a partner of the surviving partnership or limited partnership is dissociated from the entity, of which that partner was a partner, as of the date the merger takes effect. The surviving entity shall cause the partner's interest in the entity to be purchased under Section 701 or another statute specifically applicable to that partner's interest with respect to a merger. The surviving entity is bound under Section 702 by an act of a general partner dissociated under this subsection, and the partner is liable under Section 703 for transactions entered into by the surviving entity after the merger takes effect.

Comment to Original Section 906

Section 906 states the effect of a merger on the partnerships that are parties to the merger and on the individual partners.

Subsection (a) provides that when the merger takes effect: (1) the separate existence of every partnership that is a party to the merger (other than the surviving entity) ceases; (2) all property owned by the parties to the merger vests in the surviving entity; (3) all obligations of every party to the merger become the obligations of the surviving entity; and (4) all legal actions pending against a party to the merger may be continued as if the merger had not occurred or the surviving entity may be substituted as a party. Title to partnership property vests in the surviving entity without further act or deed and without reversion or impairment.

Subsection (b) makes the secretary of state the agent for service of process in any action against the surviving entity, if it is a foreign entity, to enforce an obligation of a domestic partnership that is a party to the merger. The purpose of this rule is to make it more convenient for local creditors to sue a foreign surviving entity when the credit was extended to a domestic partnership that has disappeared as a result of the merger.

Subsection (c) provides that a general partner of the surviving entity is liable for (1) all obligations for which the partner was personally liable before the merger; (2) all other obligations of the surviving entity incurred before the merger by a party to the merger, which obligations may be satisfied only out of the surviving entity's partnership property; and (3) all obligations incurred by the surviving entity after the merger, limited to the surviving entity's property in the case of limited partners.

This scheme of liability is similar to that of an incoming partner under Section 306(b). Only the surviving partnership itself is liable for all obligations, including obligations incurred by every constituent party before the merger. A general partner of the surviving entity is personally liable for obligations of the surviving entity incurred before the merger by the partnership of which he was a partner and those incurred by the surviving entity after the merger. Thus, a general partner of the surviving entity is liable only to the extent of his partnership interest for obligations incurred before the merger by a constituent party of which he was not a general partner.

Subsection (d) requires general partners to contribute the amount necessary to satisfy all obligations for which they were personally liable before the merger, if such obligations are not satisfied out of the partnership property of the surviving entity, in the same manner as provided in Section 807 or the limited partnership act of the applicable jurisdiction, as if the merged party were then dissolved. *See* RULPA §§ 502, 608.

Subsection (e) provides for the dissociation of a partner of a party to the merger who does not become a partner in the surviving entity. The surviving entity must buy out that partner's interest in the partnership under Section 701 or other specifically applicable statute. If the state limited partnership act has a dissenter's rights provision providing a different method of determining the amount due a dissociating limited partner, it would apply, rather than Section 701, since the two statutes should be read *in pari materia.*

Although subsection (e) does not expressly provide that a partner's withdrawal upon the merger of a term partnership is rightful, it was assumed that the unanimity requirement for the approval of a merger would afford a withdrawing partner adequate opportunity to protect his interest as a condition of approval. This question is left to the partnership agreement if it provides for merger without the approval of all the partners.

Under subsection (e), a dissociating general partner's lingering agency power is wound down, pursuant to Section 702, the same as in any other dissociation. Moreover, a dissociating general partner may be liable, under Section 703, for obligations incurred by the surviving entity for up to two years after the merger. A dissociating general partner can, however, limit to 90 days his exposure to liability by filing a statement of dissociation under Section 704.

Section 907. Statement of Merger

(a) After a merger, the surviving partnership or limited partnership may file a statement that one or more partnerships or limited partnerships have merged into the surviving entity.

(b) A statement of merger must contain:

(1) the name of each partnership or limited partnership that is a party to the merger;

(2) the name of the surviving entity into which the other partnerships or limited partnership were merged;

(3) the street address of the surviving entity's chief executive office and of an office in this State, if any; and

(4) whether the surviving entity is a partnership or a limited partnership.

(c) Except as otherwise provided in subsection (d), for the purposes of Section 302, property of the surviving partnership or limited partnership which before the merger was held in the name of another party to the merger is property held in the name of the surviving entity upon filing a statement of merger.

(d) For the purposes of Section 302, real property of the surviving partnership or limited partnership which before the merger was held in the name of another party to the merger is property held in the name of the surviving entity upon recording a certified copy of the statement of merger in the office for recording transfers of that real property.

(e) A filed and, if appropriate, recorded statement of merger, executed and declared to be accurate pursuant to Section 105(c), stating the name of a partnership or limited partnership that is a party to the merger in whose name property was held before the merger and the name of the surviving entity, but not containing all of the other information required by subsection (b), operates with respect to the partnerships or limited partnerships named to the extent provided in subsections (c) and (d).

Comment to Original Section 907

Section 907(a) provides that the surviving entity may file a statement of merger. The execution, filing, and recording of the statement are governed by Section 105.

Subsection (b) requires the statement to contain the name of each party to the merger, the name and address of the surviving entity, and whether it is a general or limited partnership.

Subsection (c) provides that, for the purpose of the Section 302 rules regarding the transfer of partnership property, all personal and intangible property which before the merger was held in the name of a party to the merger becomes, upon the filing of the statement of merger with the secretary of state, property held in the name of the surviving entity.

Subsection (d) provides a similar rule for real property, except that real property does not become property held in the name of the surviving entity until a certified copy of the statement of merger is recorded in the office for recording transfers of that real property under local law.

Subsection (e) is a savings provision in the event a statement of merger fails to contain all of the information required by subsection (b). The statement will have the operative effect provided in subsections (c) and (d) if it is executed and declared to be accurate pursuant to Section 105(e) and correctly states the name of the party to the merger in whose name the property was held before the merger, so that it would be found by someone searching the record. *Compare* Section 303(c) (statement of partnership authority).

Section 908.   Nonexclusive

This [article] is not exclusive. Partnerships or limited partnerships may be converted or merged in any other manner provided by law.

Comment to Original Section 908

Section 908 provides that Article 9 is not exclusive. It is merely a "safe harbor." Partnerships may be converted or merged in any other manner provided by statute or common law. Existing statutes in a few States already authorize the conversion or merger of general partnerships and limited partnerships. *See* Comment 1 to Section 901. Those procedures may be followed in lieu of Article 9.

[ARTICLE] 10.   LIMITED LIABILITY PARTNERSHIP

Section 1001. Statement of Qualification

(a) A partnership may become a limited liability partnership pursuant to this section.

(b) The terms and conditions on which a partnership becomes a limited liability partnership must be approved by the vote necessary to amend the partnership agreement except, in the case of a partnership agreement that expressly considers contribution obligations, the vote necessary to amend those provisions.

(c) After the approval required by subsection (b), a partnership may become a limited liability partnership by filing a statement of qualification. The statement must contain:

(1) the name of the partnership;

(2) the street address of the partnership's chief executive office and, if different, the street address of an office in this State, if any;

(3) if there is no office in this State, the name and street address of the partnership's agent for service of process who must be an individual resident of this State or any other person authorized to do business in this State;

(4) a statement that the partnership is applying for status as a limited liability partnership; and

(5) a deferred effective date, if any.

(d) The status of a partnership as a limited liability partnership is effective on the later of the filing of the statement or a date specified in the statement. The status remains effective, regardless of changes in the partnership, until it is canceled pursuant to Section 105(d) or revoked pursuant to Section 1003.

(e) The status of a partnership as a limited liability partnership and the liability of its partners is not affected by errors or later changes in the information required to be contained in the statement of qualification under subsection (c).

(f) The filing of a statement of qualification establishes that a partnership has satisfied all conditions precedent to the qualification of the partnership as a limited liability partnership.

(g) An amendment or cancellation of a statement of qualification is effective when it is filed or on a deferred effective date specified in the amendment or cancellation.

Comment to Amendments

The vote required under Section 1001(b) to approve the partnership filing of a statement of qualification to become a limited liability partnership is generally the vote necessary to amend the partnership agreement. Where the partnership agreement is silent as to amendment, the required vote must be unanimous. Where the partnership agreement has a general amendment provision, that vote will apply unless the agreement has a provision that considers the contribution obligations of the partners, then that vote will be required. The specific "contribution" vote is preferred because the filing of the statement directly affects those partner obligations. Therefore, the language "considers contribution" should be broadly interpreted to include any amendment vote that indirectly affects any partner's contribution obligation such as a partner's obligation to "indemnify" other partners.

Section 1001(c) sets forth the requirements of a statement of qualification. A partnership must state forth the address of its chief executive office and, if different, the street address of an office in this State. A partnership need state the name and street address of an agent for service of process only if it does not have any office in this State.

A statement of qualification is a "statement" under this Act. Section 101(13). Accordingly, it is executed, filed, and recorded with the office of the [Secretary of State] along with all other defined statements. *See* Section 105. Regardless of the approval authority necessary to file a statement of qualification, it must be executed by at least two partners under penalties of perjury that the contents of the statement are accurate. *See* Section 105(c). A person who files the statement must promptly send a copy of the statement to every nonfiling partner but failure to send the copy does not limit the effectiveness of the filed statement to a nonpartner. Section 105(e). The filing must be accompanied by the fee required by the [Secretary of State]. Section 105(f).

Section 1001(d) makes clear that, once effective, status as a limited liability partnership remains effective "regardless of changes in the partnership" until the partnership status is either canceled or revoked. Accordingly, a partnership that dissolves but whose business is continued under a business continuation agreement retains its status as a limited liability partnership without the need to refile. Also, limited liability partnership status remains even though a partnership may be dissolved, wound up, and terminated. Therefore, even after the termination of the partnership, the former partners of a terminated partnership would not be personally liable for partnership obligations incurred while the partnership was a limited liability partnership.

Section 1001(f) makes clear that once a completed statement of qualification is properly executed under Section 105 and filed under Section 1001(c), the partnership assumes the status of a limited liability partnership. This status is intended to be conclusive with regard to third parties dealing with the partnership. It is not intended to affect the rights of partners. For example, a properly executed and filed statement of qualification conclusively establishes the limited liability shield described in Section 306(c). If the partners executing and filing the statement exceed their authority, the internal abuse of authority has no effect on the liability shield with regard to third parties. Partners may challenge the abuse of authority for purposes of establishing the liability of the culpable partners but may not effect the liability shield as to third parties. Likewise, third parties may not challenge the existence of the liability shield because the decision to file the statement lacked the proper vote. As a result, the filing of the statement creates the liability shield even when the required Section 1001(b) vote is not obtained.

Section 1002. Name

The name of a limited liability partnership must end with "Registered Limited Liability Partnership," "Limited Liability Partnership," "R.L.L.P.," "L.L.P.," "RLLP," or "LLP."

Comment to Amendments

The name provisions are intended to alert persons dealing with a partnership of the presence of the liability shield. Because many jurisdictions have adopted the naming concept of a "registered" limited liability partnership, this aspect has been retained. A limited partnership filing a statement of qualification under an amendment to the State Uniform Limited Partnership Act law, will also be distinguishable from a general partnership filing a statement of qualification since these name requirements are required at the end of and in addition to the general or limited partnership's regular name. Since the name identification rules of this section do not alter the regular name of the partnership, they also do not disturb historic notions of apparent authority in general partners but not in limited partners.

Section 1003. Annual Report

(a) A limited liability partnership, and a foreign limited liability partnership authorized to transact business in this State, shall file an annual report in the office of the [Secretary of State] which contains:

(1) the name of the limited liability partnership and the State or other jurisdiction under whose laws the foreign limited liability partnership is formed;

(2) the current street address of the partnership's chief executive office and, if different, the current street address of an office in this State, if any; and

(3) if there is no current office in this State, the name and street address of the partnership's current agent for service of process who must be an individual resident of this State or any other person authorized to do business in this State.

(b) An annual report must be filed between [January 1 and April 1] of each year following the calendar year in which a partnership files a statement of qualification or a foreign partnership becomes authorized to transact business in this State.

(c) The [Secretary of State] may administratively revoke the statement of qualification of a partnership that fails to file an annual report when due or to pay the required filing fee. The [Secretary of State] shall provide the partnership at least 60 days' written notice of intent to revoke the statement. The notice must be mailed to the partnership at its chief executive office set forth in the last filed statement of qualification or annual report. The notice must specify the annual report that has not been filed, the fee that has not been paid, and the effective date of the revocation. The revocation is not effective if the annual report is filed and the fee is paid before the effective date of the revocation.

(d) A revocation under subsection (c) only affects a partnership's status as a limited liability partnership and is not an event of dissolution of the partnership.

(e) A partnership whose statement of qualification has been administratively revoked may apply to the [Secretary of State] for reinstatement within two years after the effective date of the revocation. The application must state:

(1) the name of the partnership and the effective date of the revocation; and

(2) that the ground for revocation either did not exist or has been corrected.

(f) A reinstatement under subsection (e) relates back to and takes effect as of the effective date of the revocation, and the partnership's status as a limited liability partnership continues as if the revocation had never occurred.

[ARTICLE] 11.　FOREIGN LIMITED LIABILITY PARTNERSHIP

Section 1101.　Law Governing Foreign Limited Liability Partnership
Section 1102.　Statement of Foreign Qualification
Section 1103.　Effect of Failure to Qualify
Section 1104.　Activities Not Constituting Transacting Business
Section 1005.　Action by [Attorney General]

Section 1101.　Law Governing Foreign Limited Liability Partnership

(a) The laws under which a foreign limited liability partnership is formed govern relations among the partners and between the partners and the partnership and the liability of partners for obligations of the partnership.

(b) A foreign limited liability partnership may not be denied a statement of foreign qualification by reason of any difference between the laws under which the partnership was formed and the laws of this State.

(c) A statement of foreign qualification does not authorize a foreign limited liability partnership to engage in any business or exercise any power that a partnership may not engage in or exercise in this State as a limited liability partnership.

Comment to Amendments

Section 1101(b) and (c) together make clear that although a foreign limited liability partnership may not be denied a statement of foreign qualification simply because of a difference between the laws of its foreign jurisdiction and the laws of this State, it may not conduct a business or exercise in this State that a domestic limited liability partnership may not conduct. In the latter case, the foreign limited liability partnership would be considered doing business in this

State without the benefit of the limited liability partnership liability shield set forth in Section 306(c). *See also* Section 101(13) (a foreign limited liability partnership may file a statement of election not to be considered a foreign limited liability partnership).

Section 1102. Statement of Foreign Qualification

(a) Before transacting business in this State, a foreign limited liability partnership must file a statement of foreign qualification. The statement must contain:

(1) the name of the foreign limited liability partnership which satisfies the requirements of the State or other jurisdiction under whose laws it is formed and ends with "Registered Limited Liability Partnership," "Limited Liability Partnership," "R.L.L.P.," "L.L.P.," "RLLP," or "LLP";

(2) the street address of the partnership's chief executive office and, if different, the street address of an office in this State, if any;

(3) if there is no office in this State, the name and street address of the partnership's agent for service of process who must be an individual resident of this State or any other person authorized to do business in this State; and

(4) a deferred effective date, if any.

(b) The status of a partnership as a foreign limited liability partnership is effective on the later of the filing of the statement of foreign qualification or a date specified in the statement. The status remains effective, regardless of changes in the partnership, until it is canceled pursuant to Section 105(d) or revoked pursuant to Section 1003.

(c) An amendment or cancellation of a statement of foreign qualification is effective when it is filed or on a deferred effective date specified in the amendment or cancellation.

Section 1103. Effect of Failure to Qualify

(a) A foreign limited liability partnership transacting business in this State may not maintain an action or proceeding in this State unless it has in effect a statement of foreign qualification.

(b) The failure of a foreign limited liability partnership to have in effect a statement of foreign qualification does not impair the validity of a contract or act of the foreign limited liability partnership or preclude it from defending an action or proceeding in this State.

(c) Limitations on personal liability of partners are not waived solely by transacting business in this State without a statement of foreign qualification.

(d) If a foreign limited liability partnership transacts business in this State without a statement of foreign qualification, the [Secretary of State] is its agent for service of process with respect to [claims for relief] arising out of the transaction of business in this State.

Section 1104. Activities Not Constituting Transacting Business

(a) Activities of a foreign limited liability partnership which do not constitute transacting business within the meaning of this [article] include:

(1) maintaining, defending, or settling an action or proceeding;

(2) holding meetings of its partners or carrying on any other activity concerning its internal affairs;

(3) maintaining bank accounts;

(4) maintaining offices or agencies for the transfer, exchange, and registration of the partnership's own securities or maintaining trustees or depositories with respect to those securities;

(5) selling through independent contractors;

(6) soliciting or obtaining orders, whether by mail or through employees or agents or otherwise, if the orders require acceptance outside this State before they become contracts;

(7) creating or acquiring indebtedness, mortgages, or security interests in real or personal property;

(8) securing or collecting debts or foreclosing mortgages or other security interests in property securing the debts, and holding, protecting, and maintaining property so acquired;

(9) conducting an isolated transaction that is completed within 30 days and is not one in the course of similar transactions of like nature; and

(10) transacting business in interstate commerce.

(b) For purposes of this [article], the ownership in this State of income-producing real property or tangible personal property, other than property excluded under subsection (a), constitutes transacting business in this State.

(c) This section does not apply in determining the contacts or activities that may subject a foreign limited liability partnership to service of process, taxation, or regulation under any other law of this State.

Section 1105. Action by [Attorney General]

The [Attorney General] may maintain an action to restrain a foreign limited liability partnership from transacting business in this State in violation of this [article].

[ARTICLE] ~~10~~ 12.   MISCELLANEOUS PROVISIONS

Section ~~1001~~ *1201*.   *Uniformity of Application and Construction*

This [Act] shall be applied and construed to effectuate its general purpose to make uniform the law with respect to the subject of this [Act] among States enacting it.

Section ~~1002~~ *1202*.   *Short Title*

This [Act] may be cited as the Uniform Partnership Act (1994).

Section ~~1003~~ *1203*.   *Severability Clause*

If any provision of this [Act] or its application to any person or circumstance is held invalid, the invalidity does not affect other provisions or applications of this [Act] which can be given effect without the invalid provision or application, and to this end the provisions of this [Act] are severable.

Section ~~1004~~ *1204*.   *Effective Date*

This [Act] takes effect _____.

Comment to Original Section ~~1004~~ 1204

The effective date of the Act established by an adopting State has operative effects under Section 1006, which defers mandatory application of the Act to existing partnerships.

Section ~~1005~~ *1205.* *Repeals*

Effective January 1, 199___, the following acts and parts of acts are repealed: [the State Partnership Act as amended and in effect immediately before the effective date of this [Act]].

Comment to Original Section ~~1005~~ 1205

This section repeals the adopting State's present general partnership act. The effective date of the repealer should not be any earlier than the date selected by that State in Section 1006(b) for the application of the Act to all partnerships.

Section ~~1006~~ *1206.* *Applicability*

(a) Before January 1, 199___, this [Act] governs only a partnership formed:

(1) after the effective date of this [Act], unless that partnership is continuing the business of a dissolved partnership under [Section 41 of the prior Uniform Partnership Act]; and

(2) before the effective date of this [Act], that elects, as provided by subsection (c), to be governed by this [Act].

(b) After January 1, 199___, this [Act] governs all partnerships.

(c) Before January 1, 199___, a partnership voluntarily may elect, in the manner provided in its partnership agreement or by law for amending the partnership agreement, to be governed by this [Act]. The provisions of this [Act] relating to the liability of the partnership's partners to third parties apply to limit those partners' liability to a third party who had done business with the partnership within one year preceding the partnership's election to be governed by this [Act], only if the third party knows or has received a notification of the partnership's election to be governed by this [Act].

Comment to Original ~~1006~~ 1206

This section provides for a transition period in the applicability of the Act to existing partnerships, similar to that provided in the revised Texas partnership act. *See* Tex. Rev. Civ. Stat. Ann. art. 6132b-10.03 (Vernon Supp. 1994). Subsection (a) makes application of the Act mandatory for all partnerships formed after the effective date of the Act and permissive, by election, for existing partnerships. That affords existing partnerships and partners an opportunity to consider the changes effected by RUPA and to amend their partnership agreements, if appropriate.

Under subsection (b), application of the Act becomes mandatory for all partnerships, including existing partnerships that did not previously elect to be governed by it, upon a future date to be established by the adopting State. Texas, for example, deferred for five years mandatory compliance by existing partnerships.

Subsection (c) provides that an existing partnership may voluntarily elect to be governed by RUPA in the manner provided for amending its partnership agreement. Under UPA Section 18(h), that requires the consent of all the partners, unless otherwise agreed. Third parties doing business with the partnership must know or be notified of the election before RUPA's rules limiting a partner's liability become effective as to them. Those rules would include, for example, the provisions of Section 704 limiting the liability of a partner 90 days after the filing of a statement of dissociation. Without knowledge of the partnership's election, third parties would not be aware that they must check the record to ascertain the extent of a dissociated partner's personal liability.

Section ~~1007~~ *1207*.   Savings Clause

This [Act] does not affect an action or proceeding commenced or right accrued before this [Act] takes effect.

Comment to Original Section ~~1007~~ 1207

This section continues the prior law after the effective date of the Act with respect to a pending action or proceeding or a right accrued at the time of the effective date. Since courts generally apply the law that exists at the time an action is commenced, in many circumstances the new law of this Act would displace the old law, but for this section.

Almost all States have general savings statutes, usually as part of their statutory construction acts. These are often very broad. *Compare* Uniform Statute and Rule Construction Act § 16(a) (narrow savings clause). As RUPA is remedial, the more limited savings provisions in Section 1007 are more appropriate than the broad savings provisions of the usual general savings clause. *See generally,* Comment to Uniform Statute and Rule Construction Act § 16.

Pending "action" refers to a judicial proceeding, while "proceeding" is broader and includes administrative proceedings. Although it is not always clear whether a right has "accrued," the term generally means that a cause of action has matured and is ripe for legal redress. *See, e.g., Estate of Hoover v. Iowa Dept. of Social Services*, 299 Iowa 702, 251 N.W.2d 529 (1977); *Nielsen v. State of Wisconsin*, 258 Wis. 1110, 141 N.W.2d 194 (1966). An inchoate right is not enough, and thus, for example, there is no accrued right under a contract until it is breached.

Section 1208.   Effective Date

This [Act] takes effect _____ .

Section 1209.   Applicability

(a) This [Act] does not govern a partnership that becomes a limited liability partnership before this [Act] takes effect, except (i) a partnership that is continuing the business of a dissolved limited liability partnership or (ii) a limited liability partnership that elects, before January 1, 199___, in the manner provided by the partnership agreement or by law for amending the agreement, to be governed by this [Act]. If an election is made, the provisions of this [Act] relating to the liability of a partner to a third party apply to limit the partner's liability to a third party who had done business with the partnership within 12 months next preceding the election only if the third party at the time of the election, knew or had received notification of the election.

(b) After January 1, 199___, this [Act] governs all limited liability partnerships.

(c) The existing provisions for execution and filing a statement of qualification of a limited liability partnership continue until either the limited liability partnership elects to have this [Act] apply or January 1, 199___.

Section 1210.   Savings Clause

This [Act] does not affect an action or proceeding commenced or right accrued before this [Act] takes effect.

Section 1211.   Repeals

Effective January 1, 199___, the following acts and parts of acts are repealed: [the Limited Liability Partnership amendments to the State Partnership Act as amended and in effect immediately before the effective date of this [Act].]

≡ *Appendix B* ≡
PROTOTYPE REGISTERED LIMITED LIABILITY PARTNERSHIP ACT[1]

ARTICLE 1.
GENERAL PROVISIONS

Section 101 is amended to read as follows:

§ 101. *Definitions*

In This [Act]:
  (1) "Business" includes every trade, occupation, and profession.
  (2) "Debtor in bankruptcy" means a person who is the subject of:
       (i) an order for relief under Title 11 of the United States Code or a comparable order under a successor statute of general application; or
       (ii) a comparable order under federal, state, or foreign law governing insolvency.

---

[1] This was a working document prepared in 1995 by the American Bar Association Section of Business Law, Committee on Partnerships and Unincorporated Business Organizations, Working Group on Registered Limited Liability Partnerships. Copyright 1995 American Bar Association. Reprinted with permission. All rights reserved.

The document is based on the Revised Uniform Partnership Act (1994). Additions to and deletions from that act are represented, respectively, by underscoring and strikeouts. The views expressed in the Proposed Prototype Registered Limited Liability Partnership Act have not been approved by the House of Delegates or the Board of Governors of the American Bar Association and, accordingly, should not be construed as representing the policy of the American Bar Association.

Based on Revised Uniform Partnership Act (1994). Additions to and deletions from that act are represented, respectively, by underscores and strike-overs.

(3) "Distribution" means a transfer of money or other property from a partnership to a partner in the partner's capacity as a partner or to the partner's transferee.

(4) "Foreign registered limited liability partnership" means a limited liability partnership or registered limited liability partnership, or the functional equivalent thereof, formed pursuant to an agreement governed by the laws of any State or jurisdiction other than this State and registered as a limited liability partnership under the laws of such State or jurisdiction.

(4)(5) "Partnership" means an association of two or more persons to carry on as co-owners a business for profit formed under Section 202, predecessor law, or comparable law of another jurisdiction, and includes, for all purposes of the laws of this State, a registered limited liability partnership.

(5)(6) "Partnership agreement" means the agreement, whether written, oral, or implied, among the partners concerning the partnership, including amendments to the partnership agreement.

(6)(7) "Partnership at will" means a partnership in which the partners have not agreed to remain partners until the expiration of a definite term or the completion of a particular undertaking.

(7)(8) "Partnership interest" or "partner's interest in the partnership" means all of a partner's interests in the partnership, including the partner's transferable interest and all management and other rights.

(8)(9) "Person" means an individual, corporation, business trust, estate, trust, partnership, association, joint venture, government, governmental subdivision, agency, or instrumentality, or any other legal or commercial entity.

(9)(10) "Property" means all property, real, personal, or mixed, tangible or intangible, or any interest therein.

(11) "Registered limited liability partnership" means a partnership formed pursuant to an agreement governed by the laws of this State, registered under Section 910.

(12) "Secretary of State" means the Secretary of State of the State of _____.

(10)(13) "State" means a State of the United States, the District of Columbia, the Commonwealth of Puerto Rico, or any territory or insular possession subject to the jurisdiction of the United States.

(11)(14) "Statement" means a statement of partnership authority under Section 303, a statement of denial under Section 304, a statement of dissociation under Section 704, a statement of dissolution under Section 805, a statement of merger under Section 907, a statement of registration as a limited liability partnership under Section 910, a statement of qualification as a foreign limited liability partnership under Section 916 or an amendment or cancellation of any of the foregoing.

——(12)(15) "Transfer" includes an assignment, conveyance, lease, mortgage, deed, and encumbrance.

Section 103 is amended to read as follows:

§ 103.   *Effect of Partnership Agreement; Nonwaivable Provisions*

(a) Except as otherwise provided in subsection (b), relations among the partners and between the partners and the partnership are governed by the partnership agreement. To the extent the partnership agreement does not otherwise provide, this [Act] governs relations among the partners and between the partners and the partnership.

(b)   The partnership agreement may not:

(1) vary the rights and duties under Section 105 except to eliminate the duty to provide copies of statements to all of the partners;

(2) unreasonably restrict the right of access to books and records under Section 403(b);

(3) eliminate the duty of loyalty under Section 404(b) or 603(b)(3), but:

(i) the partnership agreement may identify specific types or categories of activities that do not violate the duty of loyalty, if not manifestly unreasonable; or

(ii) all of the partners or a number or percentage specified in the partnership agreement may authorize or ratify, after full disclosure of all material facts, a specific act or transaction that otherwise would violate the duty of loyalty;

(4) unreasonably reduce the duty of care under Section 404(c) or 603(b)(3);

(5) eliminate the obligation of good faith and fair dealing under Section 404(d), but the partnership agreement may prescribe the standards by which the performance of the obligation is to be measured, if the standards are not manifestly unreasonable;

(6) vary the power to dissociate as a partner under Section 602(a), except to require the notice under Section 601(1) to be in writing;

(7) vary the right of a court to expel a partner in the events specified in Section 601(5);

(8) vary the requirement to wind up the partnership business in cases specified in Section 801(4), (5), or (6); or

(9) restrict rights of third parties under this [Act]; or

(10) vary the law applicable to registered limited liability partnerships as set forth in Section 106(b).

Section 106 is amended to read as follows:

§ 106.   Law Governing Internal Relations

(a) Except as provided in subsection (b), the law of the jurisdiction in which a partnership has its chief executive office governs relations among the partners and between the partners and the partnership.

(b) The law of this State shall govern relations among the partners and between the partners and the partnership, and the liability of partners for debts, obligations and liabilities chargeable to the partnership, in a partnership that has filed a statement of registration as a registered limited liability partnership in this State.

ARTICLE 3.   RELATIONS OF PARTNERS TO PERSONS DEALING WITH PARTNERSHIP

Section 306 is amended to read as follows:

§ 306.   Partner's Liability

(a) Except as otherwise provided in subsection (b) or subsection (c), all partners are liable jointly and severally for all obligations of the partnership unless otherwise agreed by the claimant or provided by law.

(b) A person admitted as a partner into an existing partnership is not personally liable for any partnership obligation incurred before the person's admission as a partner.

(c) A person is not, solely by reason of being a partner, liable, directly or indirectly, including by way of indemnification, contribution, assessment or otherwise, for debts, obligations or liabilities of, or chargeable to, the partnership, whether sounding in tort, contract or otherwise, which are incurred, created or assumed by the partnership while the partnership is a registered limited liability partnership.

(d) A person is not, solely by reason of being a partner, a proper party to a proceeding by or against a registered limited liability partnership, the object of which is to recover damages, collect the debts or liabilities or enforce the obligations of the partnership with respect to which the partner is not liable under subsection (c) of this section.

Comment:

The Working Group considered and rejected as unnecessary the proposal that additional language be added to affirmatively state that the exculpatory language proposed for Section 306(c) would not affect the liability of a partner for his own negligence, misconduct, wrongful acts, etc. If a legislature insists that such language be included to clarify the point, an additional sentence could be added to Section 306(c) which would state that "Nothing in this subsection (c) shall affect the liability of a partner in a registered limited liability partnership for his own negligence, malpractice, wrongful acts or misconduct."

§ 307.   Actions By and Against Partnership and Partners

(a) A partnership may sue and be sued in the name of the partnership.

(b) An action may be brought against the partnership and, except as provided in Section 306, against any or all of the partners in the same action or in separate actions.

(c) A judgment against a partnership is not by itself a judgment against a partner. A judgment against a partnership may not be satisfied from a partner's assets unless there is also a judgment against the partner.

(d) A judgment creditor of a partner may not levy execution against the assets of the partner to satisfy a judgment based on a claim against the partnership unless:

(1) the claim is for a debt, obligation or liability for which the partner is liable as provided in Section 306 and either:

—(1)(a) a judgment based on the same claim has been obtained against the partnership and a writ of execution on the judgment has been returned unsatisfied in whole or in part;

—(2)(b) the partnership is a debtor in bankruptcy;

—(3)(c) the partner has agreed that the creditor need not exhaust partnership assets; or

—(4)(d) a court grants permission to the judgment creditor to levy execution against the assets of a partner based on a finding that partnership assets subject to execution are clearly insufficient to satisfy the judgment, that exhaustion of partnership assets is excessively burdensome, or that the grant of permission is an appropriate exercise of the court's equitable powers; or

—(5)(2) liability is imposed on the partner by law or contract independent of the existence of the partnership.

(e) This section applies to any partnership liability or obligation resulting from a representation by a partner or purported partner under Section 308.

ARTICLE 4.   RELATIONS OF PARTNERS TO EACH OTHER AND TO PARTNERSHIP

Section 401 is amended to read as follows:

§ 401.   *Partner's Rights and Duties*

(a) Each partner is deemed to have an account that is:

(1) credited with an amount equal to the money plus the value of any other property, net of the amount of any liabilities, the partner contributes to the partnership and the partner's share of the partnership profits; and

(2) charged with an amount equal to the money plus the value of any other property, net of the amount of any liabilities, distributed by the partnership to the partner and the partner's share of the partnership losses.

(b) Each partner is entitled to an equal share of the partnership profits and is chargeable with a share of the partnership losses in proportion to the partner's share of the profits.

(c) A partnership shall reimburse a partner for payments made and indemnify a partner for liabilities incurred by the partner in the ordinary course of the business of the partnership or for the preservation of its business or property; however, no person shall be required as a consequence of the indemnification to make any payment to the extent that the payment would be inconsistent with subsections (b) and (c) of Section 306.

(d) A partnership shall reimburse a partner for an advance to the partnership beyond the amount of capital the partner agreed to contribute.

(e) A payment or advance made by a partner which gives rise to a partnership obligation under subsection (c) or (d) constitutes a loan to the partnership which accrues interest from the date of the payment or advance.

(f) Each partner has equal rights in the management and conduct of the partnership business.

(g) A partner may use or possess partnership property only on behalf of the partnership.

(h) A partner is not entitled to remuneration for services performed for the partnership, except for reasonable compensation for services rendered in winding up the business of the partnership.

(i) A person may become a partner only with the consent of all of the partners.

(j) A difference arising as to a matter in the ordinary course of business of a partnership may be decided by a majority of the partners. An act outside the ordinary course of business of a partnership and an amendment to the partnership agreement may be undertaken only with the consent of all of the partners.

(k) This section does not affect the obligations of a partnership to other persons under Section 301.

ARTICLE 7.   PARTNER'S DISSOCIATION WHEN BUSINESS NOT WOUND UP

Section 703 is amended to read as follows:

§ 703.   *Dissociated Partner's Liability to Other Persons*

(a) A partner's dissociation does not of itself discharge the partner's liability for a partnership obligation incurred before dissociation. A dissociated partner is not liable for a partnership obligation incurred after dissociation, except as otherwise provided in subsection (b).

(b) A partner who dissociates without resulting in a dissolution and winding up of the partnership business is liable as a partner to the other party in a transaction entered into by the partnership, or a surviving partnership under [Article] 9, within two years after the partner's dissociation, only if the obligation is one for which he is liable under Section 306 and at the time of entering into the transaction the other party:

(1) reasonably believed that the dissociated partner was then a partner;

(2) did not have notice of the partner's dissociation; and

(3) is not deemed to have had knowledge under Section 303(e) or notice under Section 704(c).

(c) By agreement with the partnership creditor and the partners continuing the business, a dissociated partner may be released from liability for a partnership obligation.

(d) A dissociated partner is released from liability for a partnership obligation if a partnership creditor, with notice of the partner's dissociation but without the partner's consent, agrees to a material alteration in the nature or time of payment of a partnership obligation.

ARTICLE 8.   WINDING UP PARTNERSHIP BUSINESS

§ 806.   *Partner's Liability to Other Partners After Dissolution*

(a) Except as otherwise provided in subsection (b) of this Section 806 or in subsection (c) of Section 306, after dissolution a partner is liable to the other partners for the partner's share of any partnership liability incurred under Section 804.

(b) A partner who, with knowledge of the dissolution, incurs a partnership liability under Section 804(2) by an act that is not appropriate for winding up the partnership business is liable to the partnership for any damage caused to the partnership arising from the liability.

§ 807. *Settlement of Accounts and Contributions Among Partners*

(a) In winding up a partnership's business, the assets of the partnership, including the contributions of the partners required by this section, must be applied to discharge its obligations to creditors, including, to the extent permitted by law, partners who are creditors. Any surplus must be applied to pay in cash the net amount distributable to partners in accordance with their right to distributions under subsection (b).

(b) Each partner is entitled to a settlement of all partnership accounts upon winding up the partnership business. In settling accounts among the partners, the profits and losses that result from the liquidation of the partnership assets must be credited and charged to the partners' accounts. The partnership shall make a distribution to a partner in an amount equal to any excess of the credits over the charges in the partner's account. A partner shall contribute to the partnership an amount equal to any excess of the charges over the credits in the partner's account that is attributable to an obligation for which the partner is liable under Section 306.

(c) If a partner fails or is not obligated to contribute, ~~all of the~~ each other ~~partners~~ partner shall contribute, in the ~~proportions~~ proportion in which ~~those partners share~~ such partner shares partnership losses, the additional amount necessary to satisfy ~~the~~ any partnership obligations for which the partner is liable under Section 306.

(d) A partner or partner's legal representative may recover from the other partners any contributions on account of obligations for which the other partners are liable under Section 306 that the partner or legal representative ~~the partner~~ makes to the extent the amount contributed exceeds the amount for which the partner or legal representative is personally liable under Section 306. ~~that partner's share of the partnership obligations.~~

(d̶e) After the settlement of accounts, each partner shall contribute, in the proportion in which the partner shares partnership losses, the amount necessary to satisfy partnership obligations for which the partner is liable under Section 306 and that were not known at the time of the settlement.

(e̶f) The estate of a deceased partner is liable for the partner's obligation to contribute to the partnership.

(fg) An assignee for the benefit of creditors of a partnership or a partner, or a person appointed by a court to represent creditors of a partnership or a partner, may enforce a partner's obligation to contribute to the partnership.

ARTICLE 9.   CONVERSIONS AND MERGERS

§ 903.   *Conversion of Limited Partnership to Partnership*

(a) A limited partnership may be converted to a partnership pursuant to this section.

(b) Notwithstanding a provision to the contrary in a limited partnership agreement, the terms and conditions of a conversion of a limited partnership to a partnership must be approved by all of the partners.

(c) After the conversion is approved by the partners, the limited partnership shall cancel its certificate of limited partnership.

(d) The conversion takes effect when the certificate of limited partnership is canceled.

(e) A limited partner who becomes a general partner as a result of the conversion remains liable only as a limited partner for an obligation incurred by the limited partnership before the conversion takes effect. Subject to the provisions of Section 306, the The partner is liable as a general partner for an obligation of the partnership incurred after the conversion takes effect.

§ 906.   *Effect of Merger*

(a) When a merger takes effect:

(1) the separate existence of every partnership or limited partnership that is a party to the merger, other than the surviving entity, ceases;

(2) all property owned by each of the merged partnerships or limited partnerships vests in the surviving entity;

(3) all obligations of every partnership or limited partnership that is a party to the merger become the obligations of the surviving entity; and

(4) an action or proceeding pending against a partnership or limited partnership that is a party to the merger may be continued as if the merger had not occurred, or the surviving entity may be substituted as a party to the action or proceeding.

(b) The [Secretary of State] of this State is the agent for service of process in an action or proceeding against a surviving foreign partnership or limited partnership to enforce an obligation of a domestic partnership or limited partnership that is a party to a merger. The surviving entity shall promptly notify the [Secretary of State] of the mailing address of its chief executive office and of any change of address. Upon receipt of process, the [Secretary of State] shall mail a copy of the process to the surviving foreign partnership or limited partnership.

(c) Subject to the provisions of Section 306, a A partner of the surviving partnership or limited partnership is liable for:

(1) all obligations of a party to the merger for which the partner was personally liable before the merger;

(2) all other obligations of the surviving entity incurred before the merger by a party to the merger, but those obligations may be satisfied only out of property of the entity; and

(3) all obligations of the surviving entity incurred after the merger takes effect, but those obligations may be satisfied only out of property of the entity if the partner is a limited partner.

(d) If the obligations incurred before the merger by a party to the merger are not satisfied out of the property of the surviving partnership or limited partnership, the general partners of that party immediately before the effective date of the merger shall contribute the amount necessary to satisfy that party's obligations to the surviving entity, in the manner provided in Section 807 or in the [Limited Partnership Act] of the jurisdiction in which the party was formed, as the case may be, as if the merged party were dissolved.

(e) A partner of a party to a merger who does not become a partner of the surviving partnership or limited partnership is dissociated from the entity, of which that partner was a partner, as of the date the merger takes effect. The surviving entity shall cause the partner's interest in the entity to be purchased under Section 701 or another statute specifically applicable to that partner's interest with respect to a merger. The surviving entity is bound under Section 702 by an act of a general partner dissociated under this subsection, and the partner is liable under Section 703 for transactions entered into by the surviving entity after the merger takes effect.

ARTICLE 9.1. REGISTERED LIMITED LIABILITY PARTNERSHIPS

§ 910.   *Registered Limited Liability Partnerships*

(a) To become a registered limited liability partnership, a partnership shall file with the [Secretary of State] a statement of registration as a registered limited liability partnership stating: the name of the partnership; the address of its principal office (which may, but need not be, located within the State); the post office address, including the street and number, if any, of its initial registered office; the name of the [city or] county in which the registered office is located; the name of its initial registered agent at that office and that the agent is either (i) an individual who is a resident of this State and is either a general partner of the registered limited liability partnership, an officer or director of a corporate general partner of the registered limited liability partnership, a general partner of a general partner of the registered limited liability partnership; a member or manager of the limited liability company that is a general partner of the registered limited liability partnership, or a member of the _____ State Bar or (ii) a professional corporation or professional limited liability company registered under Section _____; any other matters that the partnership determines to include; and that the partnership thereby applies for status as a registered limited liability partnership. A partnership becomes a registered limited liability partnership at the time of the filing of the initial statement of registration in the Office of the [Secretary of State] or at any later date or time specified in the statement of registration.

(b) The [Secretary of State] shall register as a registered limited liability partnership any partnership that submits a completed statement of registration with the required fee.

(c) Unless the partnership agreement provides otherwise, the registration of a partnership as a registered limited liability partnership shall require the consent of a majority of the partners in the partnership at the time the statement of registration is filed.

　　(d) A partnership that has registered shall continue to be a registered limited liability partnership until:

　　　　(1) the registration statement is revoked pursuant to section 912(d); or

　　　　(2) the partnership or limited partnership files with the [Secretary of State] a statement of cancellation of registration under Section 915.

　　(e) A partnership that has been registered as a registered limited liability partnership under this chapter is, for all purposes, the same entity that existed before it registered.

　　(f) The [Secretary of State] may provide forms for a statement of registration.

§ 911.　Name of Registered Limited Liability Partnership

The name of a registered limited liability partnership shall contain the words 'Registered Limited Liability Partnership' or 'Limited Liability Partnership', or the abbreviation 'R.L.L.P.' or 'L.L.P.' or the designation 'RLLP' or 'LLP' as the last words or letters of its name.

Comment:

The Working Group determined that the number of partners in a registered limited liability partnership should not be required to be disclosed in the statement of registration, nor should it be the basis for calculating the registration fee. Disclosure of the number of partners creates numerous problems, including reliance by third parties. If, notwithstanding this recommendation, a statute uses the number of partners as either a disclosure or revenue item, protective language such as that used in Section 1544(f) of the Delaware Act should also be included.

§ 912.　Registered Limited Liability Partnership Annual Reports

　　(a) On or before _____ of each year, each registered limited liability partnership and each foreign registered limited liability partnership authorized to transact business in this State shall file an annual report with the [Secretary of State] setting forth the name of the partnership, the partnership's current principal office address and, if a foreign registered limited liability partnership, the jurisdiction in which it is registered as a registered limited liability partnership.

　　(b) The [Secretary of State] shall initiate the report process by issuing a report form to the registered limited liability partnership or foreign registered limited liability partnership at its principal office as shown on his records on or before _____, but failure to receive such form shall not relieve a registered limited liability partnership or foreign registered limited liability partnership of the requirement of filing the report as required in this section. The partnership shall return the report to the [Secretary of State], hand-delivered or postmarked on or before _____. The information required shall be given as of the date of the execution of the report, and it shall be executed by a partner in the registered limited liability partnership or foreign registered limited liability partnership or, if the partnership is in the hands of a receiver or trustee, by the receiver or trustee on behalf of the registered limited liability partnership or foreign registered limited liability partnership. The report shall be accompanied by a fee in the amount determined by the [Secretary of State].

   (c) If the [Secretary of State] finds that a report conforms to the requirements of this Chapter, the [Secretary of State] shall file the same, or, upon finding that it does not so conform, shall promptly return it to the registered limited liability partnership for any necessary corrections. No penalty fee for late filing shall be assessed if such report was timely delivered, is corrected to conform to the requirements of this Chapter, and is returned to the [Secretary of State] no later than thirty days after the date the report was mailed back to the registered limited liability partnership or foreign registered limited liability partnership.

   (d) If any registered limited liability partnership or foreign registered limited liability partnership has failed to pay the fees or to file any report required pursuant to this section, the [Secretary of State] shall give notice by first-class mail to the partnership of such failure. Thirty days after the date of mailing of such notice, unless the report with the fee and penalty, if due, have been delivered and paid to the [Secretary of State], the statement of registration of such partnership shall be revoked and such partnership shall cease to be a registered limited liability partnership or foreign registered limited liability partnership but shall continue to be a partnership or limited partnership, as the case may be, under this [Title].

   (e) Any registered limited liability partnership which ceases to be a registered limited liability partnership under subsection (d) of this section shall not be considered to have dissolved as a result of ceasing to be a registered limited liability partnership.

   (f) A registered limited liability partnership or foreign registered limited liability partnership that has ceased to be a registered limited liability partnership or a foreign registered limited liability partnership, as the case may be, under subsection (d) of this section may restore its status as such by taking some or all of the following steps, as applicable:

      (1) Paying a reinstatement fee as determined by the [Secretary of State];

691

(2) Making and delivering a report and paying the fee due upon filing such report for the year in which it is to be reinstated;

(3) Paying a late filing penalty for the current year's report if filed after the required reporting date; and

(4) Paying an amount equal to the fee charged and collected for filing of reports for registered limited liability partnerships plus a late filing penalty for each year a required report was not filed.

(g) A registered limited liability partnership or foreign registered limited liability partnership that has ceased to be a registered limited liability partnership or foreign registered limited liability partnership under this section that restores its status as a registered limited liability partnership or foreign registered limited liability partnership within two years after the date on which its status as such has ceased shall be deemed not to have lost its status as a registered limited liability partnership or foreign registered limited liability partnership under this section.

§ 913.   Registered Office and Registered Agent

(a) Each registered limited liability partnership and each foreign registered limited liability partnership registered pursuant to this Article shall continuously maintain in this State:

(1) A registered office that may be the same as any of its places of business; and

(2) A registered agent who shall be either:

(i) An individual who is a resident of this State and is either a general partner of the registered limited liability partnership, an officer or director of a corporate general partner of the registered limited liability partnership, a general partner of a general partner of the registered limited liability partnership, a member or manager of a limited liability company that is a general partner of the registered limited liability partnership, or a member of the _____ State Bar, and whose business office is identical with the registered office; or

(ii) A professional corporation or professional limited liability company registered under Section _____, the business office of which is identical with the registered office.

(b) The sole duty of the registered agent is to forward to the registered limited liability partnership or foreign registered limited liability partnership at its last known address any process, notice or demand that is served on the registered agent.

(c) A registered limited liability partnership or a foreign registered limited liability partnership may change its registered agent or the address of its registered office, or both, upon filing with the [Secretary of State] a certificate of change on a form supplied by the [Secretary of State] that sets forth:

    (1) The name of the partnership;

    (2) The address of its current registered office;

    (3) If the current address of its registered office is to be changed, the post-office address, including the street and number, if any, of the new address of its registered office, and the name of the city or county in which it is to be located;

    (4) The name of its current registered agent;

    (5) If the current registered agent is to be changed, the name of the new registered agent;

    (6) That after the change or changes are made, the partnership will be in compliance with the requirements of Section 913.

    (d) A certificate of change shall promptly be executed by a registered limited liability partnership or foreign registered limited liability partnership whenever its registered agent dies, resigns or ceases to satisfy the requirements of Section 913.

    (e) If a registered agent changes his business address to another place within this State, he shall change his address for any registered limited liability partnership or foreign registered limited liability partnership of which he is a registered agent by filing a certificate of change as required above except that it need be signed, either manually or in facsimile, only by the registered agent and must recite that a copy of the certificate has been mailed to the partnership at its principal office.

    (f) A registered agent may resign his agency appointment by signing and filing with the [Secretary of State] a certificate of resignation accompanied by his certification that he has mailed a copy thereof by certified mail to the address of the principal office of the partnership set forth in the statement of registration for the registered limited liability partnership or foreign registered limited liability partnership. The agency appointment is terminated on the thirty-first day after the date on which the certificate was filed.

    (g) The [Secretary of State] may collect a fee for the filing of a certificate of change of registered agent or registered office address pursuant to subsection (c), (d) or (e), or certificate of resignation pursuant to subsection (f) of this section.

    (h) The registered agent of a registered limited liability partnership or foreign registered limited liability partnership is the partnership's agent for service of process, notice, or demand required or permitted by law to be served on the partnership.

    (i) Whenever a registered limited liability partnership or a foreign registered limited liability partnership fails to appoint or maintain a registered agent in this State or whenever its registered agent cannot with reasonable diligence be found at his address, then the [Secretary of State] shall be the agent of the partnership upon whom service may be made in accordance with Section _____.

(j) This section does not prescribe the only means, or necessarily the required means, of serving a registered limited liability partnership or a foreign registered limited liability partnership.

§ 914.   Amendment of Statement of Registration; Effect of Statement of Registration

(a) Notwithstanding the provisions of subsection (d) of this section or any other provision of this Chapter, the status of a partnership as a registered limited liability partnership or a foreign registered limited liability partnership, and the liability of the partners thereof, shall not be affected by (i) errors in the information stated in the statement of registration, provided that the statement was filed in good faith, or (ii) changes after the filing of a statement of registration in the information stated in such statement.

(b) A statement of registration or any amendment thereto may also serve as a statement of partnership authority under Section 303, a statement of denial under Section 304, a statement of dissociation under Section 704, or a statement of dissolution under Section 805 if (i) the title of the statement indicates each purpose for which it is filed and (ii) if the statement of registration otherwise meets the requirements of the particular other statement and, to the extent that it serves as such an other statement, it may be amended, cancelled or limited, in accordance with the provisions of Sections 303, 304, 704 and 805, but any amendment, cancellation or limitation shall not affect the validity of the statement of registration of the partnership as a registered limited liability partnership, which may only be amended as provided in Section 914 or cancelled in accordance with Section 915.

(c) The filing of a statement of registration shall be conclusive as to third parties, and it shall be incontestable by third parties that all conditions precedent to registration as a registered limited liability partnership or foreign registered limited liability partnership have been met.

(d) A statement of registration for a registered limited liability partnership or foreign limited liability partnership is amended by filing an amendment thereto with the [Secretary of State]. The amendment shall set forth: the name of the registered limited liability partnership or foreign registered limited liability partnership, the date of filing of the initial statement of registration; in the case of a foreign registered limited liability partnership, the jurisdiction in which it is registered as a limited liability partnership; and the amendment to the statement of registration. An amendment to the statement of registration shall be filed by a registered limited liability partnership or foreign registered limited liability partnership not later than ___ days after (i) a change in the name of the partnership, (ii) a change in the address of the principal office of the partnership or (iii) the partnership has knowledge that a material statement in the statement of registration was false or inaccurate when made or that any facts described therein have changed, making the statement of registration inaccurate in any material respect. An amendment to the statement of registration may be filed for any other proper purpose. Unless otherwise provided in this Chapter or in the amendment to the statement of registration, an amendment to a statement of registration shall be effective at the time of its filing with the [Secretary of State].

   (e) In an action or proceeding brought against a registered limited liability partnership or foreign registered limited liability partnership that has not complied with the provisions of subsection (d) of this section, the plaintiff or other party bringing the suit or proceeding may recover, if the court shall so determine, expenses incurred in locating and effecting service of process on such partnership as a result of the failure to comply with such provisions.

§ 915.   Cancellation of a Registered Limited Liability Partnership

   (a) A registered limited liability partnership registered under this Chapter may cancel its registration by filing with the [Secretary of State] a statement of cancellation of registration as a registered limited liability partnership, which shall set forth:
   (1) The name of the registered limited liability partnership;
   (2) The date of filing of the initial statement of registration;
   (3) The reason for filing the statement of cancellation of registration;
   (4) The effective date (which shall be a date certain) of cancellation of registration if it is not to be effective on the filing of the statement of cancellation, provided that any effective date other than the date of filing of the statement of cancellation must be a date subsequent to the filing; and
   (5) Any other information the partners determine to include therein.
   (b) The filing of a statement of cancellation of registration by or on behalf of a partnership pursuant to this Section 915 shall be effective only to cancel the partnership's registration as a limited liability partnership, and shall not, unless it specifically so provides, indicate the dissolution of the partnership.
   (c) Unless the partnership agreement provides otherwise, cancellation of the registration of a partnership as a registered limited liability partnership shall require the consent of a majority of the partners in the partnership at the time the statement of cancellation of registration is filed.

§ 916.   *Registration of Foreign Registered Limited Liability Partnerships*

(a) Before transacting business in this State as such, a foreign registered limited liability partnership shall register with the [Secretary of State]. An applicant for registration as a foreign registered limited liability partnership shall file with the [Secretary of State] a certificate of status from the filing office in the jurisdiction in which the foreign registered limited liability partnership is registered and a statement of registration as a foreign limited liability partnership setting forth the information described in subsection (b) below.

(b) A statement of registration as a foreign registered limited liability partnership shall set forth the following:

(1) The name of the foreign registered limited liability partnership and, if different, the name under which it proposes to transact business in this State. The name under which such foreign registered limited liability partnership proposes to transact business in this State shall comply with Section 911;

(2) The jurisdiction in which it is registered as a limited liability partnership and the laws of which govern the agreement pursuant to which it was formed;

(3) The address of its principal office;

(4) The address of a registered office and the name and address of a registered agent for service of process in this State required to be maintained in accordance with Section 913; and

(5) That the partnership thereby applies for status as a foreign registered limited liability partnership.

(c) The [Secretary of State] shall register as a foreign registered limited liability partnership any partnership that submits a completed statement of registration with the required fee.

(d) Registration as a foreign registered limited liability partnership is effective until:

(1) the registration statement is revoked pursuant to section 912(d); or

(2) the partnership files with the [Secretary of State] a statement of cancellation of registration under Section 917.

(e) The [Secretary of State] may provide forms for a statement of registration of a foreign registered limited liability partnership.

§ 917.   *Withdrawal of a Foreign Registered Limited Liability Partnership*

A foreign registered limited liability partnership authorized to transact business in this State may withdraw from this State by filing with the [Secretary of

State] a statement of cancellation of registration as a foreign registered limited liability partnership, which shall set forth:

(a) The name of the foreign registered limited liability partnership and the State or other jurisdiction under whose jurisdiction it was registered as a limited liability partnership and the laws of which govern the agreement pursuant to which it was formed;

(b) That the foreign registered limited liability partnership is not transacting business in this State and that it surrenders its registration to transact business in this state;

(c) That the foreign registered limited liability partnership revokes the authority of its registered agent in this State to accept service of process and appoints the [Secretary of State] as its agent for service of process in any action, suit, or proceeding based upon any cause of action arising during the time the foreign registered limited liability partnership was authorized to transact business in this state; and

(d) A mailing address to which the [Secretary of State] may mail a copy of any process served on him under subsection (c).

§ 918.   Effect of Failure of Foreign Registered Limited Liability Partnership to Register

The failure of a foreign registered limited liability partnership to file a statement of registration or to maintain such registration or to appoint and maintain a registered agent in this State shall not impair the validity of any contract or act of the foreign registered limited liability partnership and shall neither prevent the foreign registered limited liability partnership from defending any action or proceeding in any court of this State nor affect the application of the laws of the jurisdiction governing the agreement under which it was formed as provided in Section 919(e), but the foreign registered limited liability partnership may not maintain any action or proceeding in any court of this State until it has filed an application for registration. A foreign registered limited liability partnership, by transacting business in this State without registration, appoints the [Secretary of State] as its agent for service of process with respect to causes of action arising out of the transaction of business in this State.

§ 919.   Applicability of Chapter to Foreign and Interstate Commerce

(a) A registered limited liability partnership may conduct its business, carry on its operations, and have and exercise the powers granted by this Act in any state, territory, district, or possession of the United States or in any foreign country.

(b) It is the intent of the legislature that registered limited liability partnerships formed pursuant to agreements governed by the laws of this State be recognized outside the boundaries of this State and that the laws of this State governing registered limited liability partnerships transacting business outside of this State be granted the protection of full faith and credit under the Constitution of the United States.

(c) It is the policy of this State that in the case of a registered limited liability partnership the relations among the partners and between the partners and the partnership, and the liability of partners for debts, obligations and liabilities chargeable to the partnership, shall be subject to and governed by the laws of this State.

(d) Subject to any statutes for the regulation and control of specific types of business, foreign registered limited liability partnerships may do business in this State.

(e) It is the policy of this State that in the case of a foreign registered limited liability partnership (whether or not registered under Section 918) the relations among the partners and between the partners and the partnership, and the liability of partners for debts, obligations and liabilities chargeable to the partnership, shall be subject to and governed by the laws of the jurisdiction which govern the agreement under which it was formed.

§ 920.   *Limited Partnerships as Registered Limited Liability Partnerships*

A domestic limited partnership may become a registered limited liability limited partnership by complying with the applicable provisions of the _____ Revised Uniform Limited Partnership Act.

Comment

See page 79 for proposed amendment to RULPA.

[Amendment to RULPA:

§ _____ LIMITED PARTNERSHIP AS REGISTERED LIMITED LIABILITY PARTNERSHIP:

(a) A limited partnership is a registered limited liability partnership as well as a limited partnership if it:

(1) registers as a limited liability partnership as provided in Section 910 of the _____ Uniform Partnership Act (199), as permitted by its written partnership agreement or, if its written partnership agreement is silent, with the consent of partners required to amend its written partnership agreement; and

(2) has a name which complies with the requirements of Section 102 of this Act and the requirements of Section 911 of the _____ Uniform Partnership Act (199_).

(b) In applying Section 910 of the _____ Uniform Partnership Act (199) to a limited partnership, all references to partners mean general partners.

(c) If a limited partnership is a registered limited liability partnership, Section 306 of the _____ Uniform Partnership Act (199_) applies to its general partners and to any of its limited partners who, under other provisions of this Act, are liable for the debts or obligations of the partnership.]

≡*Appendix C*≡
SELECTED STATE STATUTES

CALIFORNIA CORPORATION CODE
TITLE 2.   PARTNERSHIPS
CHAPTER 5.   UNIFORM PARTNERSHIP ACT OF 1994
(CAL. CORP. CODE §§ 16100–16962)

ARTICLE 1.
GENERAL PROVISIONS

§ 16100.   *Citation of Chapter*

This chapter may be cited as the Uniform Partnership Act of 1994.

§ 16101.   *Definitions*

As used in this chapter, the following terms and phrases have the following meanings:

(1) "Business" includes every trade, occupation, and profession.

(2) "Debtor in bankruptcy" means a person who is the subject of either of the following:

(A) An order for relief under Title 11 of the United States Code or a comparable order under a successor statute of general application.

(B) A comparable order under federal, state, or foreign law governing insolvency.

(3) "Distribution" means a transfer of money or other property from a partnership to a partner in the partner's capacity as a partner or to the partner's transferee.

(4) "Electronic transmission by the partnership" means a communication (a) delivered by (1) facsimile telecommunication or electronic mail when directed to the facsimile number or electronic mail address, respectively, for that recipient on record with the partnership, (2) posting on an electronic message board or network that the partnership has designated for those communications, together with a separate notice to the recipient of the posting, which transmission shall be validly delivered upon the later of the posting or delivery of the separate notice thereof, or (3) other means of electronic communication, (b) to a recipient who has provided an unrevoked consent to the use of those means of transmission, and (c) that creates a record that is capable of retention, retrieval, and review, and that may thereafter be rendered into clearly legible tangible form. However, an electronic transmission by a partnership to an individual partner is not authorized unless, in addition to satisfying the requirements of this section, the transmission satisfies the requirements applicable to consumer consent to electronic records as set forth in the Electronic Signatures in Global and National Commerce Act (15 U.S.C. Sec. 7001(c)(1)).

(5) "Electronic transmission to the partnership" means a communication (a) delivered by (1) facsimile telecommunication or electronic mail when directed to the facsimile number or electronic mail address, respectively, which the partnership has provided from time to time to partners for sending communications to the partnership, (2) posting on an electronic message board or network that the partnership has designated for those communications, and which transmission shall be validly delivered upon the posting, or (3) other means of electronic communication, (b) as to which the partnership has placed in effect reasonable measures to verify that the sender is the partner (in person or by proxy) purporting to send the transmission, and (c) that creates a record that is capable of retention, retrieval, and review, and that may thereafter be rendered into clearly legible tangible form.

(6) (A) "Foreign limited liability partnership" means a partnership, other than a limited partnership, formed pursuant to an agreement governed by the laws of another jurisdiction and denominated or registered as a limited liability partnership or registered limited liability partnership under the laws of that jurisdiction (i) in which each partner is a licensed person or a person licensed or authorized to provide professional limited liability partnership services in a jurisdiction or jurisdictions other than this state, (ii) which is licensed under the laws of the state to engage in the practice of architecture, the practice of public accountancy, the practice of engineering, the practice of land surveying, or the practice of law, or (iii) which (I) is related to a registered limited liability partnership that practices public accountancy or, to the extent permitted by the State Bar, practices law or is related to a foreign limited liability partnership and (II) provides services related or complementary to the professional limited liability

partnership services provided by, or provides services or facilities to, that registered limited liability partnership or foreign limited liability partnership.

(B) For the purposes of clause (iii) of subparagraph (A), a partnership is
related to a registered limited liability partnership or foreign limited liability
partnership if (i) at least a majority of the partners in one partnership are also
partners in the other partnership, or (ii) at least a majority in interest in each
partnership hold interests in or are members of another person, except an individual, and each partnership renders services pursuant to an agreement
with that other person, or (iii) one partnership, directly or indirectly through
one or more intermediaries, controls, is controlled by, or is under common
control with, the other partnership.

(7) "Licensed person" means any person who is duly licensed, authorized, or
registered under the provisions of the Business and Professions Code to provide
professional limited liability partnership services or who is lawfully able to render professional limited liability partnership services in this state.

(8) (A) "Registered limited liability partnership" means a partnership, other
than a limited partnership, formed pursuant to an agreement governed by Article
10 (commencing with Section 16951), that is registered under Section 16953 and
(i) each of the partners of which is a licensed person or a person licensed or authorized to provide professional limited liability partnership services in a jurisdiction or jurisdictions other than this state, (ii) is licensed under the laws of the
state to engage in the practice of architecture, the practice of public accountancy,
the practice of engineering, the practice of land surveying, or the practice of law,
or (iii) (I) is related to a registered limited liability partnership that practices
public accountancy or, to the extent permitted by the State Bar, practices law or
is related to a foreign limited liability partnership and (II) provides services related or complementary to the professional limited liability partnership services
provided by, or provides services or facilities to, that registered limited liability
partnership or foreign limited liability partnership.

(B) For the purposes of clause (iii) of subparagraph (A), a partnership is
related to a registered limited liability partnership or foreign limited liability
partnership if (i) at least a majority of the partners in one partnership are also
partners in the other partnership, or (ii) at least a majority in interest in each
partnership hold interests in or are members of another person, other than an
individual, and each partnership renders services pursuant to an agreement
with that other person, or (iii) one partnership, directly or indirectly through
one or more intermediaries, controls, is controlled by, or is under common
control with, the other partnership.

(9) "Partnership" means an association of two or more persons to carry on as
coowners a business for profit formed under Section 16202, predecessor law, or
comparable law of another jurisdiction, and includes, for all purposes of the laws
of this state, a registered limited liability partnership, and excludes any partner-

ship formed under Chapter 2 (commencing with Section 15501), Chapter 3 (commencing with Section 15611), or Chapter 5.5 (commencing with Section 15900).

(10) "Partnership agreement" means the agreement, whether written, oral, or implied, among the partners concerning the partnership, including amendments to the partnership agreement.

(11) "Partnership at will" means a partnership in which the partners have not agreed to remain partners until the expiration of a definite term or the completion of a particular undertaking.

(12) "Partnership interest" or "partner's interest in the partnership" means all of a partner's interests in the partnership, including the partner's transferable interest and all management and other rights.

(13) "Person" means an individual, corporation, business trust, estate, trust, partnership, limited partnership, limited liability partnership, limited liability company, association, joint venture, government, governmental subdivision, agency, or instrumentality, or any other legal or commercial entity.

(14) "Professional limited liability partnership services" means the practice of architecture, the practice of public accountancy, the practice of engineering, the practice of land surveying, or the practice of law.

(15) "Property" means all property, real, personal, or mixed, tangible or intangible, or any interest therein.

(16) "State" means a state of the United States, the District of Columbia, the Commonwealth of Puerto Rico, or any territory or insular possession subject to the jurisdiction of the United States.

(17) "Statement" means a statement of partnership authority under Section 16303, a statement of denial under Section 16304, a statement of dissociation under Section 16704, a statement of dissolution under Section 16805, a statement of conversion or a certificate of conversion under Section 16906, a statement of merger under Section 16915, or an amendment or cancellation of any of the foregoing.

(18) "Transfer" includes an assignment, conveyance, lease, mortgage, deed, and encumbrance.

(19) The inclusion of the practice of architecture as a professional limited liability partnership service permitted by this section shall extend only until January 1, 2012.

(20) This section shall remain in effect only until January 1, 2016, and as of that date is repealed, unless a later enacted statute, that is enacted before January 1, 2016, deletes or extends that date.

§ 16101.   Definitions (This section shall become operative on January 1, 2016.)

As used in this chapter, the following terms and phrases have the following meanings:

(1) "Business" includes every trade, occupation, and profession.

(2) "Debtor in bankruptcy" means a person who is the subject of either of the following:

   (A) An order for relief under Title 11 of the United States Code or a comparable order under a successor statute of general application.

   (B) A comparable order under federal, state, or foreign law governing insolvency.

(3) "Distribution" means a transfer of money or other property from a partnership to a partner in the partner's capacity as a partner or to the partner's transferee.

(4) "Electronic transmission by the partnership" means a communication (a) delivered by (1) facsimile telecommunication or electronic mail when directed to the facsimile number or electronic mail address, respectively, for that recipient on record with the partnership, (2) posting on an electronic message board or network that the partnership has designated for those communications, together with a separate notice to the recipient of the posting, which transmission shall be validly delivered upon the later of the posting or delivery of the separate notice thereof, or (3) other means of electronic communication, (b) to a recipient who has provided an unrevoked consent to the use of those means of transmission, and (c) that creates a record that is capable of retention, retrieval, and review, and that may thereafter be rendered into clearly legible tangible form. However, an electronic transmission by a partnership to an individual partner is not authorized unless, in addition to satisfying the requirements of this section, the transmission satisfies the requirements applicable to consumer consent to electronic records as set forth in the Electronic Signatures in Global and National Commerce Act (15 U.S.C. Sec. 7001(c)(1)).

(5) "Electronic transmission to the partnership" means a communication (a) delivered by (1) facsimile telecommunication or electronic mail when directed to the facsimile number or electronic mail address, respectively, which the partnership has provided from time to time to partners for sending communications to the partnership, (2) posting on an electronic message board or network that the partnership has designated for those communications, and which transmission shall be validly delivered upon the posting, or (3) other means of electronic communication, (b) as to which the partnership has placed in effect reasonable measures to verify that the sender is the partner (in person or by proxy) purporting to send the transmission, and (c) that creates a record that is capable of reten-

tion, retrieval, and review, and that may thereafter be rendered into clearly legible tangible form.

(6) (A) "Foreign limited liability partnership" means a partnership, other than a limited partnership, formed pursuant to an agreement governed by the laws of another jurisdiction and denominated or registered as a limited liability partnership or registered limited liability partnership under the laws of that jurisdiction (i) in which each partner is a licensed person or a person licensed or authorized to provide professional limited liability partnership services in a jurisdiction or jurisdictions other than this state, (ii) which is licensed under the laws of the state to engage in the practice of architecture, the practice of public accountancy, or the practice of law, or (iii) which (I) is related to a registered limited liability partnership that practices public accountancy or, to the extent permitted by the State Bar, practices law or is related to a foreign limited liability partnership and (II) provides services related or complementary to the professional limited liability partnership services provided by, or provides services or facilities to, that registered limited liability partnership or foreign limited liability partnership.

(B) For the purposes of clause (iii) of subparagraph (A), a partnership is related to a registered limited liability partnership or foreign limited liability partnership if (i) at least a majority of the partners in one partnership are also partners in the other partnership, or (ii) at least a majority in interest in each partnership hold interests in or are members of another person, except an individual, and each partnership renders services pursuant to an agreement with that other person, or (iii) one partnership, directly or indirectly through one or more intermediaries, controls, is controlled by, or is under common control with, the other partnership.

(7) "Licensed person" means any person who is duly licensed, authorized, or registered under the provisions of the Business and Professions Code to provide professional limited liability partnership services or who is lawfully able to render professional limited liability partnership services in this state.

(8) (A) "Registered limited liability partnership" means a partnership, other than a limited partnership, formed pursuant to an agreement governed by Article 10 (commencing with Section 16951), that is registered under Section 16953 and (i) each of the partners of which is a licensed person or a person licensed or authorized to provide professional limited liability partnership services in a jurisdiction or jurisdictions other than this state, (ii) is licensed under the laws of the state to engage in the practice of architecture, practice of public accountancy, or the practice of law, or (iii) (I) is related to a registered limited liability partnership that practices public accountancy or, to the extent permitted by the State Bar, practices law or is related to a foreign limited liability partnership and (II) provides services related or complementary to the professional limited liability

partnership services provided by, or provides services or facilities to, that registered limited liability partnership or foreign limited liability partnership.

(B) For the purposes of clause (iii) of subparagraph (A), a partnership is related to a registered limited liability partnership or foreign limited liability partnership if (i) at least a majority of the partners in one partnership are also partners in the other partnership, or (ii) at least a majority in interest in each partnership hold interests in or are members of another person, other than an individual, and each partnership renders services pursuant to an agreement with that other person, or (iii) one partnership, directly or indirectly through one or more intermediaries, controls, is controlled by, or is under common control with, the other partnership.

(9) "Partnership" means an association of two or more persons to carry on as coowners a business for profit formed under Section 16202, predecessor law, or comparable law of another jurisdiction, and includes, for all purposes of the laws of this state, a registered limited liability partnership, and excludes any partnership formed under Chapter 2 (commencing with Section 15501), Chapter 3 (commencing with Section 15611), or Chapter 5.5 (commencing with Section 15900).

(10) "Partnership agreement" means the agreement, whether written, oral, or implied, among the partners concerning the partnership, including amendments to the partnership agreement.

(11) "Partnership at will" means a partnership in which the partners have not agreed to remain partners until the expiration of a definite term or the completion of a particular undertaking.

(12) "Partnership interest" or "partner's interest in the partnership" means all of a partner's interests in the partnership, including the partner's transferable interest and all management and other rights.

(13) "Person" means an individual, corporation, business trust, estate, trust, partnership, limited partnership, limited liability partnership, limited liability company, association, joint venture, government, governmental subdivision, agency, or instrumentality, or any other legal or commercial entity.

(14) "Professional limited liability partnership services" means the practice of architecture, the practice of public accountancy, or the practice of law.

(15) "Property" means all property, real, personal, or mixed, tangible or intangible, or any interest therein.

(16) "State" means a state of the United States, the District of Columbia, the Commonwealth of Puerto Rico, or any territory or insular possession subject to the jurisdiction of the United States.

(17) "Statement" means a statement of partnership authority under Section 16303, a statement of denial under Section 16304, a statement of dissociation under Section 16704, a statement of dissolution under Section 16805, a statement of conversion or a certificate of conversion under Section 16906, a state-

ment of merger under Section 16915, or an amendment or cancellation of any of the foregoing.

(18) "Transfer" includes an assignment, conveyance, lease, mortgage, deed, and encumbrance.

(19) The inclusion of the practice of architecture as a professional limited liability partnership service permitted by this section shall extend only until January 1, 2012.

(20) This section shall become operative on January 1, 2016.

§ 16102.   Knowledge of Fact; Notice; Notification

(a) A person knows a fact if the person has actual knowledge of it.

(b) A person has notice of a fact if any of the following apply:

(1) The person knows of it.

(2) The person has received a notification of it.

(3) The person has reason to know it exists from all of the facts known to the person at the time in question.

(4) Subdivision (f) of Section 16953 or subdivision (f) of Section 16959 as applicable.

(c) A person notifies or gives a notification to another by taking steps reasonably required to inform the other person in ordinary course, whether or not the other person knows of it.

(d) A person receives a notification when either of the following apply:

(1) The person knows of the notification.

(2) The notification is duly delivered at the person's place of business or at any other place held out by the person as a place for receiving communications.

(e) Except as otherwise provided in subdivision (f), a person other than an individual knows, has notice, or receives a notification of a fact for purposes of a particular transaction when the individual conducting the transaction knows, has notice, or receives a notification of the fact, or in any event when the fact would have been brought to the individual's attention if the person had exercised reasonable diligence. The person exercises reasonable diligence if it maintains reasonable routines for communicating significant information to the individual conducting the transaction and there is reasonable compliance with the routines. Reasonable diligence does not require an individual acting for the person to communicate information unless the communication is part of the individual's regular duties or the individual has reason to know of the transaction and that the transaction would be materially affected by the information.

(f) A partner's knowledge, notice, or receipt of a notification of a fact relating to the partnership is effective immediately as knowledge by, notice to, or receipt of a notification by the partnership, except in the case of a fraud on the partnership committed by or with the consent of that partner.

§ 16103.   Partnership Agreement

(a) Except as otherwise provided in subdivision (b), relations among the partners and between the partners and the partnership are governed by the partnership agreement. To the extent the partnership agreement does not otherwise provide, this chapter governs relations among the partners and between the partners and the partnership.

(b) The partnership agreement may not do any of the following:

(1) Vary the rights and duties under Section 16105 except to eliminate the duty to provide copies of statements to all of the partners.

(2) Unreasonably restrict the right of access to books and records under subdivision (b) of Section 16403, or the right to be furnished with information under subdivision (c) of Section 16403.

(3) Eliminate the duty of loyalty under subdivision (b) of Section 16404 or paragraph (3) of subdivision (b) of Section 16603, but, if not manifestly unreasonable, may do either of the following:

(A) The partnership agreement may identify specific types or categories of activities that do not violate the duty of loyalty.

(B) All of the partners or a number or percentage specified in the partnership agreement may authorize or ratify, after full disclosure of all material facts, a specific act or transaction that otherwise would violate the duty of loyalty.

(4) Unreasonably reduce the duty of care under subdivision (c) of Section 16404 or paragraph (3) of subdivision (b) of Section 16603.

(5) Eliminate the obligation of good faith and fair dealing under subdivision (d) of Section 16404, but the partnership agreement may prescribe the standards by which the performance of the obligation is to be measured, if the standards are not manifestly unreasonable.

(6) Vary the power to dissociate as a partner under subdivision (a) Section 16602, except to require the notice under paragraph (1) of Section 16601 to be in writing.

(7) Vary the right of a court to expel a partner in the events specified in paragraph (5) of Section 16601.

(8) Vary the requirement to wind up the partnership business in cases specified in paragraph (4), (5), or (6) of Section 16801.

(9) Restrict rights of third parties under this chapter.

(10) Vary the law applicable to a registered limited liability partnership under subdivision (b) of Section 16106.

§ 16104.   Principles of Law and Equity; Interest Rate

(a) Unless displaced by particular provisions of this chapter, the principles of law and equity supplement this chapter.

(b) If an obligation to pay interest arises under this chapter and the rate is not specified, the rate is that specified in Section 3289 of the Civil Code.

§ 16105.   Filing of Statement

(a) A statement may be filed in the office of the Secretary of State. A certified copy of a statement that is filed in an office in another state may be filed in the office of the Secretary of State. Either filing has the effect provided in this chapter with respect to partnership property located in or transactions that occur in this state.

(b) A certified copy of a statement that has been filed in the office of the Secretary of State and recorded in the office for recording transfers of real property has the effect provided for recorded statements in this chapter. A recorded statement that is not a certified copy of a statement filed in the office of the Secretary of State does not have the effect provided for recorded statements in this chapter.

(c) A statement filed by a partnership shall be executed by at least two partners. Other statements shall be executed by a partner or other person authorized by this chapter. An individual who executes a statement as, or on behalf of, a partner or other person named as a partner in a statement shall personally declare under penalty of perjury that the contents of the statement are accurate.

(d) A person authorized by this chapter to file a statement may amend or cancel the statement by filing an amendment or cancellation that names the partnership, identifies the statement, and states the substance of the amendment or cancellation.

(e) A person who files a statement pursuant to this section shall promptly send a copy of the statement to every nonfiling partner and to any other person named as a partner in the statement. Failure to send a copy of a statement to a partner or other person does not limit the effectiveness of the statement as to a person not a partner.

(f) The Secretary of State may collect a fee for filing or providing a certified copy of a statement. The officer responsible for recording transfers of real property may collect a fee for recording a statement.

§ 16106.   Jurisdiction

(a) Except as otherwise provided in subdivision (b) of this section, or Section 16958, the law of the jurisdiction in which a partnership has its chief executive office governs relations among the partners and between the partners and the partnership.

(b) With respect to a registered limited liability partnership, the law of this state shall govern relations among the partners and between the partners and the partnership, and the liability of partners for obligations of the partnership.

§ 16107.   Effect of Amendment or Repeal of Chapter

A partnership governed by this chapter is subject to any amendment to or repeal of this chapter.

§ 16108.   Application and Construction of Chapter; Exception for Limited Liability Partnerships

Except with respect to the provisions of this chapter specifically relating to registered limited liability partnerships and foreign limited liability partnerships, this chapter shall be applied and construed to effectuate its general purpose to make uniform the law with respect to the subject of this chapter among states enacting it.

§ 16109.   Probate Code

The rights and duties of surviving partners, the legal representatives of deceased partners, the creditors of such partners, and the creditors of the partnership created by or defined in this chapter shall be given full force and effect notwithstanding any inconsistent provisions of the Probate Code, but nothing in this chapter shall otherwise affect any provision of the Probate Code.

§ 16110.   Severability of Provision

If any provision of this chapter or its application to any person or circumstance is held invalid, the invalidity does not affect other provisions or applications of this chapter that can be given effect without the invalid provision or application, and to this end the provisions of this chapter are severable.

§ 16111.   Applicability of Chapter

(a) Except as provided in Section 16955.5, before January 1, 1999, this chapter governs only a partnership formed (1) on or after the effective date of this chapter, unless that partnership is continuing the business of a dissolved partnership under Section 15041, or (2) before the effective date of this chapter if that partnership elects, in the manner provided in its partnership agreement or by law for amending the partnership agreement, to be governed by this chapter.

(b) On and after January 1, 1999, this chapter governs all partnerships.

(c) Except with respect to the provisions of this chapter specifically relating to registered limited liability partnerships and foreign limited liability partnerships, the provisions of this chapter relating to the liability of the partnership's partners to third parties apply to limit those partners' liability to a third party who had done business with the partnership within one year preceding the partnership's election to be governed by this chapter, only if the third party knows or has received a notification of the partnership's election to be governed by this chapter.

§ 16112.   Accrued Right

This chapter does not affect an action or proceeding commenced or right accrued before this chapter takes effect.

§ 16113.   Filing Fees

(a) The fee for filing a statement of partnership is seventy dollars ($70).

(b) Unless another fee is specified by law or the law specifies that no fee is to be charged, the fee for filing any partnership statement pursuant to this chapter is thirty dollars ($30).

(c) There is no fee for filing a statement of dissolution for the purposes of canceling a statement of partnership.

§ 16114.   Fee for Acceptance of Process

Unless another fee is specified by law or the law specifies that no fee is to be charged, the fee for acceptance of copies of process against a surviving foreign partnership or limited partnership pursuant to subdivision (b) of Section 16906 is fifty dollars ($50) for each surviving foreign partnership or limited partnership general partnership upon whom service is sought.

ARTICLE 2.
NATURE OF PARTNERSHIP

§ 16201.   Entity Distinct From Partners

A partnership is an entity distinct from its partners.

§ 16202.   Formation; Applicable Rules

(a) Except as otherwise provided in subdivision (b), the association of two or more persons to carry on as coowners a business for profit forms a partnership, whether or not the persons intend to form a partnership.

(b) An association formed under a statute other than this chapter, a predecessor statute, or a comparable statute of another jurisdiction is not a partnership under this chapter.

(c) In determining whether a partnership is formed, the following rules apply:

(1) Joint tenancy, tenancy in common, tenancy by the entireties, joint property, common property, or part ownership does not by itself establish a partnership, even if the coowners share profits made by the use of the property.

(2) The sharing of gross returns does not by itself establish a partnership, even if the persons sharing them have a joint or common right or interest in property from which the returns are derived.

(3) A person who receives a share of the profits of a business is presumed to be a partner in the business, unless the profits were received for any of the following reasons:

(A) In payment of a debt by installments or otherwise.

(B) In payment for services as an independent contractor or of wages or other compensation to an employee.

(C) In payment of rent.

(D) In payment of an annuity or other retirement benefit to a beneficiary, representative, or designee of a deceased or retired partner.

(E) In payment of interest or other charge on a loan, even if the amount of payment varies with the profits of the business, including a direct or indirect present or future ownership of the collateral, or rights to income, proceeds, or increase in value derived from the collateral.

(F) In payment for the sale of the goodwill of a business or other property by installments or otherwise.

§ 16203.   Property Acquired by Partnership

Property acquired by a partnership is property of the partnership and not of the partners individually.

§ 16204.   What Constitutes Partnership Property; Acquisition

(a) Property is partnership property if acquired in the name of either of the following:

(1) The partnership.

(2) One or more partners with an indication in the instrument transferring title to the property of the person's capacity as a partner or of the existence of a partnership but without an indication of the name of the partnership.

(b) Property is acquired in the name of the partnership by a transfer to either of the following:

(1) The partnership in its name.

(2) One or more partners in their capacity as partners in the partnership, if the name of the partnership is indicated in the instrument transferring title to the property.

(c) Property is presumed to be partnership property if purchased with partnership assets, even if not acquired in the name of the partnership or of one or more partners with an indication in the instrument transferring title to the property of the person's capacity as a partner or of the existence of a partnership.

(d) Property acquired in the name of one or more of the partners, without an indication in the instrument transferring title to the property of the person's capacity as a partner or of the existence of a partnership and without use of partnership assets, is presumed to be separate property, even if used for partnership purposes.

ARTICLE 3.
RELATIONS OF PARTNERS TO PERSONS
DEALING WITH PARTNERSHIP

§ 16301.   Partner as Agent

Subject to the effect of a statement of partnership authority under Section 16303 both of the following apply:

(1) Each partner is an agent of the partnership for the purpose of its business. An act of a partner, including the execution of an instrument in the partnership name, for apparently carrying on in the ordinary course the partnership business or business of the kind carried on by the partnership binds the partnership, unless the partner had no authority to act for the partnership in the particular matter and the person with whom the partner was dealing knew or had received a notification that the partner lacked authority.

(2) An act of a partner that is not apparently for carrying on in the ordinary course the partnership business or business of the kind carried on by the partnership binds the partnership only if the act was authorized by the other partners.

§ 16302.   Property Transfer

(a) Partnership property may be transferred as follows:

(1) Subject to the effect of a statement of partnership authority under Section 16303, partnership property held in the name of the partnership may be transferred by an instrument of transfer executed by a partner in the partnership name.

(2) Partnership property held in the name of one or more partners with an indication in the instrument transferring the property to them of their capacity as partners or of the existence of a partnership, but without an indication of the name of the partnership, may be transferred by an instrument of transfer executed by the persons in whose name the property is held.

(3) Partnership property held in the name of one or more persons other than the partnership, without an indication in the instrument transferring the property to them of their capacity as partners or of the existence of a partnership, may be transferred by an instrument of transfer executed by the persons in whose name the property is held.

(b) A partnership may recover partnership property from a transferee only if it proves that execution of the instrument of initial transfer did not bind the partnership under Section 16301 and either of the following applies:

(1) As to a subsequent transferee who gave value for property transferred under paragraph (1) or (2) of subdivision (a), proves that the subsequent transferee knew or had received a notification that the person who executed the instrument of initial transfer lacked authority to bind the partnership.

(2) As to a transferee who gave value for property transferred under paragraph (3) of subdivision (a), proves that the transferee knew or had received a notification that the property was partnership property and that the person who executed the instrument of initial transfer lacked authority to bind the partnership.

(c) A partnership may not recover partnership property from a subsequent transferee if the partnership would not have been entitled to recover the property, under subdivision (b), from any earlier transferee of the property.

(d) If a person holds all of the partners' interests in the partnership, all of the partnership property vests in that person. The person may execute a document in the name of the partnership to evidence vesting of the property in that person and may file or record the document.

§ 16303.   Statement of Authority

(a) A partnership may file a statement of partnership authority, which is subject to all of the following:
   (1) The statement shall include all of the following:
      (A) The name of the partnership.
      (B) The street address of its chief executive office and of one office in this state, if there is one.
      (C) The mailing address of its chief executive office, if different from the street addresses specified pursuant to subparagraph (B).
      (D) The names and mailing addresses of all of the partners or of an agent appointed and maintained by the partnership for the purpose of subdivision (b).
      (E) The names of the partners authorized to execute an instrument transferring real property held in the name of the partnership.
   (2) The statement may specify the authority, or limitations on the authority, of some or all of the partners to enter into other transactions on behalf of the partnership and any other matter.

(b) If a statement of partnership authority names an agent, the agent shall maintain a list of the names and mailing addresses of all of the partners and make it available to any person on request for good cause shown.

(c) If a filed statement of partnership authority is executed pursuant to subdivision (c) of Section 16105 and states the name of the partnership but does not contain all of the other information required by subdivision (a), the statement nevertheless operates with respect to a person not a partner as provided in subdivisions (d) and (e).

(d) A filed statement of partnership authority supplements the authority of a partner to enter into transactions on behalf of the partnership as follows:
   (1) Except for transfers of real property, a grant of authority contained in a filed statement of partnership authority is conclusive in favor of a person who gives value without knowledge to the contrary, so long as and to the extent that a limitation on that authority is not then contained in another filed state-

ment. A filed cancellation of a limitation on authority revives the previous grant of authority.

(2) A grant of authority to transfer real property held in the name of the partnership contained in a certified copy of a filed statement of partnership authority recorded in the office for recording transfers of that real property is conclusive in favor of a person who gives value without knowledge to the contrary, so long as and to the extent that a certified copy of a filed statement containing a limitation on that authority is not then of record in the office for recording transfers of that real property. The recording in the office for recording transfers of that real property of a certified copy of a filed cancellation of a limitation on authority revives the previous grant of authority.

(e) A person not a partner is deemed to know of a limitation on the authority of a partner to transfer real property held in the name of the partnership if a certified copy of the filed statement containing the limitation on authority is of record in the office for recording transfers of that real property.

(f) Except as otherwise provided in subdivisions (d) and (e) and Sections 16704 and 16805, a person not a partner is not deemed to know of a limitation on the authority of a partner merely because the limitation is contained in a filed statement.

§ 16304. Statement of Denial

A partner or other person named as a partner in a filed statement of partnership authority or in a list maintained by an agent pursuant to subdivision (b) of Section 16303 may file a statement of denial stating the name of the partnership as filed with the Secretary of State, any identification number issued by the Secretary of State, and the fact that is being denied, that may include denial of a person's authority or status as a partner. A statement of denial is a limitation on authority as provided in subdivisions (d) and (e) of Section 16303.

§ 16305. Partnership Liability

(a) A partnership is liable for loss or injury caused to a person, or for a penalty incurred, as a result of a wrongful act or omission, or other actionable conduct, of a partner acting in the ordinary course of business of the partnership or with authority of the partnership.

(b) If, in the course of the partnership's business or while acting with authority of the partnership, a partner receives or causes the partnership to receive money or property of a person not a partner, and the money or property is misapplied by a partner, the partnership is liable for the loss.

§ 16306.   Personal Liability

(a) Except as otherwise provided in subdivisions (b) and (c), all partners are liable jointly and severally for all obligations of the partnership unless otherwise agreed by the claimant or provided by law.

(b) A person admitted as a partner into an existing partnership is not personally liable for any partnership obligation incurred before the person's admission as a partner.

(c) Notwithstanding any other section of this chapter, and subject to subdivisions (d), (e), (f), and (h), a partner in a registered limited liability partnership is not liable or accountable, directly or indirectly, including by way of indemnification, contribution, assessment, or otherwise, for debts, obligations, or liabilities of or chargeable to the partnership or another partner in the partnership, whether arising in tort, contract, or otherwise, that are incurred, created, or assumed by the partnership while the partnership is a registered limited liability partnership, by reason of being a partner or acting in the conduct of the business or activities of the partnership.

(d) Notwithstanding subdivision (c), all or certain specified partners of a registered limited liability partnership, if the specified partners agree, may be liable in their capacity as partners for all or specified debts, obligations, or liabilities of the registered limited liability partnership if the partners possessing a majority of the interests of the partners in the current profits of the partnership, or a different vote as may be required in the partnership agreement, specifically agreed to the specified debts, obligations, or liabilities in writing, prior to the debt, obligation, or liability being incurred. That specific agreement may be modified or revoked if the partners possessing a majority of the interests of the partners in the current profits of the partnership, or a different vote as may be required in the partnership agreement, agree to the modification or revocation in writing; provided, however, that a modification or revocation shall not affect the liability of a partner for any debts, obligations, or liabilities of a registered limited liability partnership incurred, created, or assumed by the registered limited liability partnership prior to the modification or revocation.

(e) Nothing in subdivision (c) shall be construed to affect the liability of a partner of a registered limited liability partnership to third parties for that partner's tortious conduct.

(f) The limitation of liability in subdivision (c) shall not apply to claims based upon acts, errors, or omissions arising out of the rendering of professional limited liability partnership services of a registered limited liability partnership providing legal services unless that partnership has a currently effective certificate of registration issued by the State Bar.

(g) A partner in a registered limited liability partnership is not a proper party to a proceeding by or against a registered limited liability partnership in which personal liability for partnership debts, obligations, or liabilities is asserted against the partner, unless that partner is personally liable under subdivision (d) or (e).

(h) Nothing in this section shall affect or impair the ability of a partner to act as a guarantor or surety for, provide collateral for or otherwise be liable for, the debts, obligations, or liabilities of a registered limited liability partnership.

§ 16307.   Power to Sue and be Sued

(a) A partnership may sue and be sued in the name of the partnership.

(b) Except as otherwise provided in subdivision (g) of Section 16306, an action may be brought against the partnership and any or all of the partners in the same action or in separate actions.

(c) A judgment against a partnership is not by itself a judgment against a partner. A judgment against a partnership may not be satisfied from a partner's assets unless there is also a judgment against the partner.

(d) A judgment creditor of a partner may not levy execution against the assets of the partner to satisfy a judgment based on a claim against the partnership unless any of the following apply:

(1) A judgment based on the same claim has been obtained against the partnership and a writ of execution on the judgment has been returned unsatisfied in whole or in part.

(2) The partnership is a debtor in bankruptcy.

(3) The partner has agreed that the creditor need not exhaust partnership assets.

(4) A court grants permission to the judgment creditor to levy execution against the assets of a partner based on a finding that partnership assets subject to execution are clearly insufficient to satisfy the judgment, that exhaustion of partnership assets is excessively burdensome, or that the grant of permission is an appropriate exercise of the court's equitable powers.

(5) Liability is imposed on the partner by law or contract independent of the existence of the partnership.

(e) This section applies to any partnership liability or obligation resulting from a representation by a partner or purported partner under Section 16308.

§ 16308.   Purported Partner

Except with respect to registered limited liability partnerships and foreign limited liability partnerships:

(a) If a person, by words or conduct, purports to be a partner, or consents to being represented by another as a partner, in a partnership or with one or more persons not partners, the purported partner is liable to a person to whom the representation is made, if that person, relying on the representation, enters into a transaction with the actual or purported partnership. If the representation, either by the purported partner or by a person with the purported partner's consent, is made in a public manner, the purported partner is liable to a person who relies upon the purported partnership even if the purported partner is not aware of being held out as a partner to the claimant. If partnership liability results, the purported partner is liable with respect to that liability as if the purported partner were a partner. If no partnership liability results, the purported partner is liable with respect to that liability jointly and severally with any other person consenting to the representation.

(b) If a person is thus represented to be a partner in an existing partnership, or with one or more persons not partners, the purported partner is an agent of persons consenting to the representation to bind them to the same extent and in the same manner as if the purported partner were a partner, with respect to persons who enter into transactions in reliance upon the representation. If all of the partners of the existing partnership consent to the representation, a partnership act or obligation results. If fewer than all of the partners of the existing partnership consent to the representation, the person acting and the partners consenting to the representation are jointly and severally liable.

(c) A person is not liable as a partner merely because the person is named by another in a statement of partnership authority.

(d) A person does not continue to be liable as a partner merely because of a failure to file a statement of dissociation or to amend a statement of partnership authority to indicate the partner's dissociation from the partnership.

(e) Except as otherwise provided in subdivisions (a) and (b), persons who are not partners as to each other are not liable as partners to other persons.

§ 16309.   *Designation of Agent for Service of Process; Resignation, etc.; Amended Statement*

(a) The statement of partnership authority may designate an agent for service of process. The agent may be an individual residing in this state or a corporation that has complied with Section 1505 and whose capacity to act as an agent has not terminated. If an individual is designated, the statement shall include that person's complete business or residence street address in this state. If a corporate agent is designated, no address for that agent shall be set forth.

(b) An agent designated for service of process may file with the Secretary of State a signed and acknowledged written statement of resignation as an agent. On filing of the statement of resignation, the authority of the agent to act in that capacity shall cease and the Secretary of State shall give written notice of the filing of the statement of resignation by mail to the partnership, addressed to its principal executive office.

(c) If an individual who has been designated agent for service of process dies or resigns or no longer resides in the state, or if the corporate agent for that purpose resigns, dissolves, withdraws from the state, forfeits its right to transact intrastate business, has its corporate rights, powers, and privileges suspended, or ceases to exist, the partnership or foreign partnership shall promptly file an amended statement of partnership authority, designating a new agent.

§ 16310.   Service of Process on Partnership

(a) If a partnership has designated an agent for service of process, process may be served on the partnership as provided in this section and in Chapter 4 (commencing with Section 413.10) of Title 5 of Part 2 of the Code of Civil Procedure.

(b) Personal service of a copy of any process against the partnership by delivery to an individual designated by it as agent, or if the designated agent is a corporation, to a person named in the latest certificate of the corporate agent filed pursuant to Section 1505 at the office of the corporate agent, shall constitute valid service on the partnership.

(c) No change in the address of the agent for service of process or appointment of a new agent for service of process shall be effective until an amendment to the statement of partnership authority is filed.

(d)(1) If an agent for service of process has resigned and has not been replaced, or if the designated agent cannot with reasonable diligence be found at the address designated for personal delivery of the process, and it is shown by affidavit to the satisfaction of the court that process against a partnership cannot be served with reasonable diligence upon the designated agent by hand in the manner provided in Section 415.10, subdivision (a) of Section 415.20, or subdivision (a) of Section 415.30 of the Code of Civil Procedure, the court may make an order that the service shall be made on a partnership by delivering by hand to the Secretary of State, or to any person employed in the Secretary of State's office in the capacity of assistant or deputy, one copy of the process for each defendant to be served, together with a copy of the order authorizing the service. Service in this manner shall be deemed complete on the 10th day after delivery of the process to the Secretary of State.

(2) Upon receipt of the copy of process and the fee for service, the Secretary of State shall give notice of the service of the process to the partnership, at its principal executive office, by forwarding to that office, by registered mail with request for return receipt, the copy of the process.

(3) The Secretary of State shall keep a record of all process served on the Secretary of State under this section and shall record therein the time of service and the action taken by the Secretary of State. A certificate under the Secretary of State's official seal, certifying to the receipt of process, the giving of notice to the partnership, and the forwarding of the process pursuant to this section, shall be competent and prima facie evidence of the service of process.

ARTICLE 4.
RELATIONS OF PARTNERS TO EACH OTHER
AND TO PARTNERSHIP

§ 16401.   Account Reimbursement

(a) Each partner is deemed to have an account that is subject to both of the following:

(1) Credited with an amount equal to the money plus the value of any other property, net of the amount of any liabilities, the partner contributes to the partnership and the partner's share of the partnership profits.

(2) Subject to Sections 16306 and 16957, charged with an amount equal to the money plus the value of any other property, net of the amount of any liabilities, distributed by the partnership to the partner and the partner's share of the partnership losses.

(b) Each partner is entitled to an equal share of the partnership profits and, subject to Sections 16306 and 16957, is chargeable with a share of the partnership losses in proportion to the partner's share of the profits.

(c) A partnership shall reimburse a partner for payments made and indemnify a partner for liabilities incurred by the partner in the ordinary course of the business of the partnership or for the preservation of its business or property.

(d) A partnership shall reimburse a partner for an advance to the partnership beyond the amount of capital the partner agreed to contribute.

(e) A payment or advance made by a partner that gives rise to a partnership obligation under subdivision (c) or (d) constitutes a loan to the partnership that accrues interest from the date of the payment or advance.

(f) Each partner has equal rights in the management and conduct of the partnership business.

(g) A partner may use or possess partnership property only on behalf of the partnership.

(h) A partner is not entitled to remuneration for services performed for the partnership, except for reasonable compensation for services rendered in winding up the business of the partnership.

(i) A person may become a partner only with the consent of all of the partners.

(j) A difference arising as to a matter in the ordinary course of business of a partnership may be decided by a majority of the partners. An act outside the ordinary course of business of a partnership and an amendment to the partnership agreement may be undertaken only with the consent of all of the partners.

(k) This section does not affect the obligations of a partnership to other persons under Section 16301.

§ 16402.   Distribution

A partner has no right to receive, and may not be required to accept, a distribution in kind.

§ 16403.   Place of Keeping Books and Records; Access Thereto; Information to be Furnished to Partner or Legal Representative of Deceased or Disabled Partner

(a) A partnership shall keep its books and records, if any, in writing or in any other form capable of being converted into clearly legible tangible form, at its chief executive office.

(b) A partnership shall provide partners and their agents and attorneys access to its books and records. It shall provide former partners and their agents and attorneys access to books and records pertaining to the period during which they were partners. The right of access provides the opportunity to inspect and copy books and records during ordinary business hours. A partnership may impose a reasonable charge, covering the costs of labor and material, for copies of documents furnished.

(c) Each partner and the partnership shall furnish to a partner, and to the legal representative of a deceased partner or partner under legal disability, both of the following, which may be transmitted by electronic transmission by the partnership (subdivision (4) of Section 16101):

(1) Without demand, any information concerning the partnership's business and affairs reasonably required for the proper exercise of the partner's rights and duties under the partnership agreement or this chapter; and

(2) On demand, any other information concerning the partnership's business and affairs, except to the extent the demand or the information demanded is unreasonable or otherwise improper under the circumstances.

§ 16404. Partner's Fiduciary Duties

(a) The fiduciary duties a partner owes to the partnership and the other partners are the duty of loyalty and the duty of care set forth in subdivisions (b) and (c).

(b) A partner's duty of loyalty to the partnership and the other partners includes all of the following:

(1) To account to the partnership and hold as trustee for it any property, profit, or benefit derived by the partner in the conduct and winding up of the partnership business or derived from a use by the partner of partnership property or information, including the appropriation of a partnership opportunity.

(2) To refrain from dealing with the partnership in the conduct or winding up of the partnership business as or on behalf of a party having an interest adverse to the partnership.

(3) To refrain from competing with the partnership in the conduct of the partnership business before the dissolution of the partnership.

(c) A partner's duty of care to the partnership and the other partners in the conduct and winding up of the partnership business is limited to refraining from engaging in grossly negligent or reckless conduct, intentional misconduct, or a knowing violation of law.

(d) A partner shall discharge the duties to the partnership and the other partners under this chapter or under the partnership agreement and exercise any rights consistently with the obligation of good faith and fair dealing.

(e) A partner does not violate a duty or obligation under this chapter or under the partnership agreement merely because the partner's conduct furthers the partner's own interest.

(f) A partner may lend money to and transact other business with the partnership, and as to each loan or transaction, the rights and obligations of the partner regarding performance or enforcement are the same as those of a person who is not a partner, subject to other applicable law.

(g) This section applies to a person winding up the partnership business as the personal or legal representative of the last surviving partner as if the person were a partner.

§ 16405.   Actions

(a) A partnership may maintain an action against a partner for a breach of the partnership agreement, or for the violation of a duty to the partnership, causing harm to the partnership.

(b) A partner may maintain an action against the partnership or another partner for legal or equitable relief, with or without an accounting as to partnership business, to do any of the following:

(1) Enforce the partner's rights under the partnership agreement.

(2) Enforce the partner's rights under this chapter, including all of the following:

(A) The partner's rights under Section 16401, 16403, or 16404.

(B) The partner's right on dissociation to have the partner's interest in the partnership purchased pursuant to Section 16701 or 16701.5, or to enforce any other right under Article 6 (commencing with Section 16601) or 7 (commencing with Section 16701).

(C) The partner's right to compel a dissolution and winding up of the partnership business under Section 16801 or enforce any other right under Article 8 (commencing with Section 16801).

(3) Enforce the rights and otherwise protect the interests of the partner, including rights and interests arising independently of the partnership relationship.

(c) The accrual of, and any time limitation on, a right of action for a remedy under this section is governed by other law. A right to an accounting upon a dissolution and winding up does not revive a claim barred by law.

§ 16406.   Continuation of Business

(a) If a partnership for a definite term or particular undertaking is continued, without an express agreement, after the expiration of the term or completion of the undertaking, the rights and duties of the partners remain the same as they were at the expiration or completion, so far as is consistent with a partnership at will.

(b) If the partners, or those of them who habitually acted in the business during the term or undertaking, continue the business without any settlement or liquidation of the partnership, they are presumed to have agreed that the partnership will continue.

ARTICLE 5.
TRANSFEREES AND CREDITORS OF PARTNER

§ 16501. Coownership

A partner is not a coowner of partnership property and has no interest in partnership property that can be transferred, either voluntarily or involuntarily.

§ 16502. Transferable Interest

The only transferable interest of a partner in the partnership is the partner's share of the profits and losses of the partnership and the partner's right to receive distributions. The interest is personal property.

§ 16503. Effect of Transfer of Partner's Transferable Interest

(a) A transfer, in whole or in part, of a partner's transferable interest in the partnership is permissible. However, a transfer does not do either of the following:

(1) By itself cause the partner's dissociation or a dissolution and winding up of the partnership business.

(2) As against the other partners or the partnership, entitle the transferee, during the continuance of the partnership, to participate in the management or conduct of the partnership business, to require access to information concerning partnership transactions, or to inspect or copy the partnership books or records.

(b) A transferee of a partner's transferable interest in the partnership has a right to all of the following:

(1) To receive, in accordance with the transfer, distributions to which the transferor would otherwise be entitled.

(2) To receive upon the dissolution and winding up of the partnership business, in accordance with the transfer, the net amount otherwise distributable to the transferor.

(3) To seek under paragraph (6) of Section 16801 a judicial determination that it is equitable to wind up the partnership business.

(c) In a dissolution and winding up, a transferee is entitled to an account of partnership transactions only from the date of the latest account agreed to by all of the partners.

(d) Upon transfer, the transferor retains the rights and duties of a partner other than the interest in distributions transferred.

(e) A partnership need not give effect to a transferee's rights under this section until it has notice of the transfer.

(f) A transfer of a partner's transferable interest in the partnership in violation of a restriction on transfer contained in the partnership agreement is ineffective as to a person having notice of the restriction at the time of transfer.

§ 16504.   *Judgment*

(a) On application by a judgment creditor of a partner or of a partner's transferee, a court having jurisdiction may charge the transferable interest of the judgment debtor to satisfy the judgment. The court may appoint a receiver of the share of the distributions due or to become due to the judgment debtor in respect of the partnership and make all other orders, directions, accounts, and inquiries the judgment debtor might have made or that the circumstances of the case may require.

(b) A charging order constitutes a lien on the judgment debtor's transferable interest in the partnership. The court may order a foreclosure of the interest subject to the charging order at any time. The purchaser at the foreclosure sale has the rights of a transferee.

(c) At any time before foreclosure, an interest charged may be redeemed in any of the following manners:

(1) By the judgment debtor.

(2) With property other than partnership property, by one or more of the other partners.

(3) With partnership property, by one or more of the other partners with the consent of all of the partners whose interests are not so charged.

(d) This chapter does not deprive a partner of a right under exemption laws with respect to the partner's interest in the partnership.

(e) This section provides the exclusive remedy by which a judgment creditor of a partner or partner's transferee may satisfy a judgment out of the judgment debtor's transferable interest in the partnership.

ARTICLE 6.
PARTNER'S DISSOCIATION

§ 16601.   Events Resulting in Dissociation

A partner is dissociated from a partnership upon the occurrence of any of the following events:

(1) The partnership's having notice of the partner's express will to withdraw as a partner or on a later date specified by the partner.

(2) An event agreed to in the partnership agreement as causing the partner's dissociation.

(3) The partner's expulsion pursuant to the partnership agreement.

(4) The partner's expulsion by the unanimous vote of the other partners if any of the following apply:

(A) It is unlawful to carry on the partnership business with that partner.

(B) There has been a transfer of all or substantially all of that partner's transferable interest in the partnership, other than a transfer for security purposes, or a court order charging the partner's interest, that has not been foreclosed.

(C) Within 90 days after the partnership notifies a corporate partner that it will be expelled because it has filed a certificate of dissolution or the equivalent, its charter has been revoked, or its right to conduct business has been suspended by the jurisdiction of its incorporation, there is no revocation of the certificate of dissolution or no reinstatement of its charter or its right to conduct business.

(D) A partnership, limited partnership, or limited liability company that is a partner has been dissolved and its business is being wound up.

(5) On application by the partnership or another partner, the partner's expulsion by judicial determination because of any of the following:

(A) The partner engaged in wrongful conduct that adversely and materially affected the partnership business.

(B) The partner willfully or persistently committed a material breach of the partnership agreement or of a duty owed to the partnership or the other partners under Section 16404.

(C) The partner engaged in conduct relating to the partnership business that makes it not reasonably practicable to carry on the business in partnership with the partner.

(6) The partner's act or failure to act in any of the following instances:

(A) By becoming a debtor in bankruptcy.

(B) By executing an assignment for the benefit of creditors.

(C) By seeking, consenting to, or acquiescing in the appointment of a trustee, receiver, or liquidator of that partner or of all or substantially all of that partner's property.

(D) By failing, within 90 days after the appointment, to have vacated or stayed the appointment of a trustee, receiver, or liquidator of the partner or of all or substantially all of the partner's property obtained without the partner's consent or acquiescence, or failing within 90 days after the expiration of a stay to have the appointment vacated.

(7) In the case of a partner who is an individual, by any of the following:

(A) The partner's death.

(B) The appointment of a guardian or general conservator for the partner.

(C) A judicial determination that the partner has otherwise become incapable of performing the partner's duties under the partnership agreement.

(8) In the case of a partner that is a trust or is acting as a partner by virtue of being a trustee of a trust, distribution of the trust's entire transferable interest in the partnership, but not merely by reason of the substitution of a successor trustee.

(9) In the case of a partner that is an estate or is acting as a partner by virtue of being a personal representative of an estate, distribution of the estate's entire transferable interest in the partnership, but not merely by reason of the substitution of a successor personal representative.

(10) Termination of a partner who is not an individual, partnership, corporation, trust, or estate.

§ 16602.   *Partner's Power to Dissociate; Wrongful Dissociation*

(a) A partner has the power to dissociate at any time, rightfully or wrongfully, by express will pursuant to paragraph (1) of Section 16601.

(b) A partner's dissociation is wrongful only if any of the following apply:

(1) It is in breach of an express provision of the partnership agreement.

(2) In the case of a partnership for a definite term or particular undertaking, before the expiration of the term or the completion of the undertaking if any of the following apply:

(A) The partner withdraws by express will, unless the withdrawal follows within 90 days after another partner's dissociation by death or otherwise under paragraphs (6) to (10), inclusive, of Section 16601 or wrongful dissociation under this subdivision.

(B) The partner is expelled by judicial determination under paragraph (5) of Section 16601.

(C) The partner is dissociated by becoming a debtor in bankruptcy.

(D) In the case of a partner who is not an individual, trust other than a business trust, or estate, the partner is expelled or otherwise dissociated because it willfully dissolved or terminated.

(c) A partner who wrongfully dissociates is liable to the partnership and to the other partners for damages caused by the dissociation. The liability is in addition to any other obligation of the partner to the partnership or to the other partners.

§ 16603.   Effect of Dissociation

Upon a partner's dissociation, all of the following apply:

(1) The partner's right to participate in the management and conduct of the partnership business terminates.

(2) The partner's duty of loyalty under paragraph (3) of subdivision (b) of Section 16404 terminates.

(3) The partner's duty of loyalty under paragraphs (1) and (2) of subdivision (b) of Section 16404 and duty of care under subdivision (c) of Section 16404 continue only with regard to matters arising and events occurring before the partner's dissociation.

ARTICLE 7.
PARTNER'S DISSOCIATION WHEN
BUSINESS NOT WOUND UP

§ 16701.   Effect of Dissociation

Except as provided in Section 16701.5, all of the following shall apply:

(a) If a partner is dissociated from a partnership, the partnership shall cause the dissociated partner's interest in the partnership to be purchased for a buyout price determined pursuant to subdivision (b).

(b) The buyout price of a dissociated partner's interest is the amount that would have been distributable to the dissociating partner under subdivision (b) of Section 16807 if, on the date of dissociation, the assets of the partnership were sold at a price equal to the greater of the liquidation value or the value based on a sale of the entire business as a going concern without the dissociated partner and the partnership was wound up as of that date. Interest shall be paid from the date of dissociation to the date of payment.

(c) Damages for wrongful dissociation under Section 16602, and all other amounts owing, whether or not presently due, from the dissociated partner to the partnership, shall be offset against the buyout price. Interest shall be paid from the date the amount owed becomes due to the date of payment.

(d) A partnership shall indemnify a dissociated partner whose interest is being purchased against all partnership liabilities, whether incurred before or after the dissociation, except liabilities incurred by an act of the dissociated partner under Section 16702.

(e) If no agreement for the purchase of a dissociated partner's interest is reached within 120 days after a written demand for payment, the partnership shall pay, or cause to be paid, in cash to the dissociated partner the amount the partnership estimates to be the buyout price and accrued interest, reduced by any offsets and accrued interest under subdivision (c).

(f) If a deferred payment is authorized under subdivision (h), the partnership may tender a written offer to pay the amount it estimates to be the buyout price and accrued interest, reduced by any offsets under subdivision (c), stating the time of payment, the amount and type of security for payment, and the other terms and conditions of the obligation.

(g) The payment or tender required by subdivision (e) or (f) shall be accompanied by all of the following:

(1) A statement of partnership assets and liabilities as of the date of dissociation.

(2) The latest available partnership balance sheet and income statement, if any.

(3) An explanation of how the estimated amount of the payment was calculated.

(4) Written notice that the payment is in full satisfaction of the obligation to purchase unless, within 120 days after the written notice, the dissociated partner commences an action to determine the buyout price, any offsets under subdivision (c), or other terms of the obligation to purchase.

(h) A partner who wrongfully dissociates before the expiration of a definite term or the completion of a particular undertaking is not entitled to payment of any portion of the buyout price until the expiration of the term or completion of the undertaking, unless the partner establishes to the satisfaction of the court that earlier payment will not cause undue hardship to the business of the partnership. A deferred payment shall be adequately secured and bear interest.

(i) A dissociated partner may maintain an action against the partnership, pursuant to subparagraph (B) of paragraph (2) of subdivision (b) of Section 16405, to determine the buyout price of that partner's interest, any offsets under subdivision (c), or other terms of the obligation to purchase. The action shall be commenced within 120 days after the partnership has tendered payment or an offer to pay or within one year after written demand for payment if no payment or offer to pay is tendered. The court shall determine the buyout price of the dissociated partner's interest, any offset due under subdivision (c), and accrued interest, and enter judgment for any additional payment or refund. If deferred payment is authorized under subdivision (h), the court shall also determine the security for payment and other terms of the obligation to purchase. The court may assess reasonable attorney's fees and the fees and expenses of appraisers or other experts for a party to the action, in amounts the court finds equitable, against a party that the court finds acted arbitrarily, vexatiously, or not in good faith. The finding may be based on the partnership's failure to tender payment or an offer to pay or to comply with subdivision (g).

§ 16701.5.   Dissolution

(a) Section 16701 shall not apply to any dissociation that occurs within 90 days prior to a dissolution under Section 16801.

(b) For dissociations occurring within 90 days prior to the dissolution, both of the following shall apply:

(1) All partners who dissociated within 90 days prior to the dissolution shall be treated as partners under Section 16807.

(2) Any damages for wrongful dissociation under Section 16602 and all other amounts owed by the dissociated partner to the partnership, whether or not presently due, shall be taken into account in determining the amount distributable to the dissociated partner under Section 16807.

§ 16702.   Transactions

(a) For two years after a partner dissociates, the partnership, including a surviving partnership under Article 9 (commencing with Section 16901), is bound by an act of the dissociated partner that would have bound the partnership under Section 16301 before dissociation only if at the time of entering into the transaction all of the following apply to the other party:

(1) The other party reasonably believed that the dissociated partner was then a partner.

(2) The other party did not have notice of the partner's dissociation.

(3) The other party is not deemed to have had knowledge under subdivision (e) of Section 16303 or notice under subdivision (c) of Section 16704.

(b) A dissociated partner is liable to the partnership for any damage caused to the partnership arising from an obligation incurred by the dissociated partner after dissociation for which the partnership is liable under subdivision (a).

§ 16703.   Liability

(a) A partner's dissociation does not of itself discharge the partner's liability for a partnership obligation incurred before dissociation. A dissociated partner is not liable for a partnership obligation incurred after dissociation, except as otherwise provided in subdivision (b).

(b) Except for registered limited liability partnerships and foreign limited liability partnerships, a partner who dissociates is liable as a partner to the other party in a transaction entered into by the partnership, or a surviving partnership under Article 9 (commencing with Section 16901), within two years after the partner's dissociation, only if at the time of entering into the transaction all of the following apply to the other party:

(1) The other party reasonably believed that the dissociated partner was then a partner.

(2) The other party did not have notice of the partner's dissociation.

(3) The other party is not deemed to have had knowledge under subdivision (e) of Section 16303 or notice under subdivision (c) of Section 16704.

(c) By agreement with the partnership creditor and the partners continuing the business, a dissociated partner may be released from liability for a partnership obligation.

(d) A dissociated partner is released from liability for a partnership obligation if a partnership creditor, with notice of the partner's dissociation but without the partner's consent, agrees to a material alteration in the nature or time of payment of a partnership obligation.

§ 16704.   Statement

(a) A dissociated partner or the partnership may file a statement of dissociation stating the name of the partnership as filed with the Secretary of State, any identification number issued by the Secretary of State, and that the partner is dissociated from the partnership.

(b) A statement of dissociation is a limitation on the authority of a dissociated partner for the purposes of subdivisions (d) and (e) of Section 16303.

(c) For the purposes of paragraph (3) of subdivision (a) of Section 16702 and paragraph (3) of subdivision (b) of Section 16703, a person not a partner is deemed to have notice of the dissociation 90 days after the statement of dissociation is filed.

§ 16705.   Obligations

Continued use of a partnership name, or a dissociated partner's name as part thereof, by partners continuing the business does not of itself make the dissociated partner liable for an obligation of the partners or the partnership continuing the business.

ARTICLE 8.
WINDING UP PARTNERSHIP BUSINESS

§ 16801.   Events Resulting in Dissolution and Winding Up

A partnership is dissolved, and its business shall be wound up, only upon the occurrence of any of the following events:

(1) In a partnership at will, by the express will to dissolve and wind up the partnership business of at least half of the partners, including partners, other than wrongfully dissociating partners, who have dissociated within the preceding 90 days, and for which purpose a dissociation under paragraph (1) of Section 16601 constitutes an expression of that partner's will to dissolve and wind up the partnership business.

(2) In a partnership for a definite term or particular undertaking, when any of the following occurs:

(A) After the expiration of 90 days after a partner's dissociation by death or otherwise under paragraphs (6) to (10), inclusive, of Section 16601, or a partner's wrongful dissociation under subdivision (b) of Section 16602 unless before that time a majority in interest of the partners, including partners who have rightfully dissociated pursuant to subparagraph (A) of paragraph (2) of subdivision (b) of Section 16602, agree to continue the partnership.

(B) The express will of all of the partners to wind up the partnership business.

(C) The expiration of the term or the completion of the undertaking.

(3) An event agreed to in the partnership agreement resulting in the winding up of the partnership business.

(4) An event that makes it unlawful for all or substantially all of the business of the partnership to be continued, but a cure of illegality within 90 days after notice to the partnership of the event is effective retroactively to the date of the event for purposes of this section.

(5) On application by a partner, a judicial determination that any of the following apply:

(A) The economic purpose of the partnership is likely to be unreasonably frustrated.

(B) Another partner has engaged in conduct relating to the partnership business that makes it not reasonably practicable to carry on the business in partnership with that partner.

(C) It is not otherwise reasonably practicable to carry on the partnership business in conformity with the partnership agreement.

(6) On application by a transferee of a partner's transferable interest, a judicial determination that it is equitable to wind up the partnership business after the expiration of the term or completion of the undertaking, if the partnership was for a definite term or particular undertaking at the time of the transfer or entry of the charging order that gave rise to the transfer.

§ 16802. *Termination; Waiver of Right to Wind Up and Terminate*

(a) Subject to subdivision (b), a partnership continues after dissolution only for the purpose of winding up its business. The partnership is terminated when the winding up of its business is completed.

(b) At any time after the dissolution of a partnership and before the winding up of its business is completed, all of the partners, including any dissociating partner other than a wrongfully dissociating partner, may waive the right to have the partnership's business wound up and the partnership terminated. In that event both of the following apply:

(1) The partnership resumes carrying on its business as if dissolution had never occurred, and any liability incurred by the partnership or a partner after the dissolution and before the waiver is determined as if dissolution had never occurred.

(2) The rights of a third party accruing under paragraph (1) of Section 16804 or arising out of conduct in reliance on the dissolution before the third party knew or received a notification of the waiver may not be adversely affected.

§ 16803. *Participation*

(a) After dissolution, a partner who has not dissociated may participate in winding up the partnership's business, but on application of any partner, partner's legal representative, or transferee, the court, for good cause shown, may order judicial supervision of the winding up.

(b) The legal representative of the last surviving partner may wind up a partnership's business.

(c) A person winding up a partnership's business may preserve the partnership business or property as a going concern for a reasonable time, prosecute and defend actions and proceedings, whether civil, criminal, or administrative, settle and close the partnership's business, dispose of and transfer the partnership's property, discharge the partnership's liabilities, distribute the assets of the partnership pursuant to Section 16807, settle disputes by mediation or arbitration, and perform other necessary acts.

§ 16804.   Binding Act

Subject to Section 16805, a partnership is bound by a partner's act after dissolution that is either of the following:

(1) Appropriate for winding up the partnership business.

(2) Would have bound the partnership under Section 16301 before dissolution, if the other party to the transaction did not have notice of the dissolution.

§ 16805.   Statement of Dissolution

(a) After dissolution, a partner who has not wrongfully dissociated may file a statement of dissolution stating the name of the partnership as filed with the Secretary of State, any identification number issued by the Secretary of State, and that the partnership has dissolved and is winding up its business.

(b) A statement of dissolution cancels a filed statement of partnership authority for the purposes of subdivision (d) of Section 16303 and is a limitation on authority for the purposes of subdivision (e) of Section 16303.

(c) For the purposes of Sections 16301 and 16804, a person not a partner is deemed to have notice of the dissolution and the limitation on the partners' authority as a result of the statement of dissolution 90 days after it is filed.

(d) After filing and, if appropriate, recording a statement of dissolution, a dissolved partnership may file and, if appropriate, record a statement of partnership authority that will operate with respect to a person not a partner as provided in subdivisions (d) and (e) of Section 16303 in any transaction, whether or not the transaction is appropriate for winding up the partnership business.

§ 16806.   Liability

(a) Except as otherwise provided in subdivision (b) and except for registered limited liability partnerships and foreign limited liability partnerships, after dissolution a partner is liable to the other partners for the partner's share of any partnership liability incurred under Section 16804.

(b) Except for registered limited liability partnerships and foreign limited liability partnerships, a partner who, with knowledge of the dissolution, incurs a partnership liability under paragraph (2) of Section 16804 by an act that is not appropriate for winding up the partnership business is liable to the partnership for any damage caused to the partnership arising from the liability.

§ 16807.   Assets

(a) In winding up a partnership's business, the assets of the partnership, including the contributions of the partners required by this section, shall be applied to discharge its obligations to creditors, including, to the extent permitted by law, partners who are creditors. Any surplus shall be applied to pay in cash the net amount distributable to partners in accordance with their right to distributions under subdivision (b).

(b) Each partner is entitled to a settlement of all partnership accounts upon winding up the partnership business. In settling accounts among the partners, the profits and losses that result from the liquidation of the partnership assets shall be credited and charged to the partners' accounts. The partnership shall make a distribution to a partner in an amount equal to any excess of the credits over the charges in the partner's account. Except for registered limited liability partnerships and foreign limited liability partnerships, a partner shall contribute to the partnership an amount equal to any excess of the charges over the credits in the partner's account.

(c) If a partner fails to contribute the full amount that the partner is obligated to contribute under subdivision (b), all of the other partners shall contribute, in the proportions in which those partners share partnership losses, the additional amount necessary to satisfy the partnership obligations for which they are liable under Section 16306. A partner or partner's legal representative may recover from the other partners any contributions the partner makes to the extent the amount contributed exceeds that partner's share of the partnership obligations for which the partner is personally liable under Section 16306.

(d) After the settlement of accounts, each partner shall contribute, in the proportion in which the partner shares partnership losses, the amount necessary to satisfy partnership obligations that were not known at the time of the settlement and for which the partner is personally liable under Section 16306.

(e) The estate of a deceased partner is liable for the partner's obligation to contribute to the partnership.

(f) An assignee for the benefit of creditors of a partnership or a partner, or a person appointed by a court to represent creditors of a partnership or a partner, may enforce a partner's obligation to contribute to the partnership.

ARTICLE 9.
CONVERSIONS AND MERGERS

§ 16901.   Definitions

In this article, the following terms have the following meanings:

(1) "Constituent other business entity" means any other business entity that is merged with or into one or more partnerships and includes a surviving other business entity.

(2) "Constituent partnership" means a partnership that is merged with or into one or more other partnerships or other business entities and includes a surviving partnership.

(3) "Disappearing other business entity" means a constituent other business entity that is not the surviving other business entity.

(4) "Disappearing partnership" means a constituent partnership that is not the surviving partnership.

(5) "Domestic" means organized under the laws of this state when used in relation to any partnership, other business entity, or person (other than an individual).

(6) "Foreign other business entity" means any other business entity formed under the laws of any state other than this state or under the laws of the United States or of a foreign country.

(7) "Foreign partnership" means a partnership formed under the laws of any state other than this state or under the laws of a foreign country.

(8) "General partner" means a partner in a partnership and a general partner in a limited partnership.

(9) "Limited liability company" means a limited liability company created under Title 2.5 (commencing with Section 17000), or comparable law of another jurisdiction.

(10) "Limited partner" means a limited partner in a limited partnership.

(11) "Limited partnership" means a limited partnership created under Chapter 3 (commencing with Section 15611) or Chapter 5.5 (commencing with Section 15900), predecessor law, or comparable law of another jurisdiction.

(12) "Other business entity" means a limited partnership, limited liability company, corporation, business trust, real estate investment trust, or an unincorporated association (other than a nonprofit association), but excluding a partnership.

(13) "Partner" includes both a general partner and a limited partner.

(14) "Surviving other business entity" means an other business entity into which one or more partnerships are merged.

(15) "Surviving partnership" means a partnership into which one or more other partnerships or other business entities are merged.

§ 16902. Conversion of Partnership

(a) A partnership, other than a registered limited liability partnership, may be converted into a domestic other business entity or a foreign other business entity pursuant to this article if, (1) pursuant to a conversion into a domestic or foreign limited partnership or limited liability company, each of the partners of the converting partnership would receive a percentage interest in the profits and capital of the converted other business entity equal to the partner's percentage interest in profits and capital of the converting partnership as of the effective time of the conversion, and (2) pursuant to a conversion into an other business entity or foreign other business entity not specified in clause (1) above, each of the partnership interests of the same class is treated equally with respect to any distribution of cash, property, rights, interests, or securities of the converted other business entity unless all partners of the same class consent.

(b) Notwithstanding this section, the conversion of a partnership to a domestic or foreign other business entity may be effected only if: (1) the law under which that domestic or foreign other business entity will exist expressly permits the formation of that other entity pursuant to a conversion; and (2) the partnership complies with any and all other requirements of that other law that applies to conversion of the other business entity.

§ 16903. Plan of Conversion

(a) A partnership that desires to convert to a domestic or foreign other business entity shall approve a plan of conversion. The plan of conversion shall state the following:

(1) The terms and conditions of the conversion.

(2) The place of the organization of the converted entity and of the converting partnership and the name of the converted entity after conversion, if different from that of the converting partnership.

(3) The manner of converting the partnership interests of each of the partners into shares of, securities of, or interests in the converted entity.

(4) The provisions of the governing documents for the converted entity, including the limited partnership agreement, limited liability company articles of organization and operating agreement, or articles or certificate of incorporation if the converted entity is a corporation, to which the holders of interest in the converted entity are to be bound.

(5) Any other details or provisions as are required by laws under which the converted entity is organized.

(6) Any other details or provisions that are desired.

(b) The plan of conversion shall be approved by that number or percentage of partners required by the partnership agreement to approve a conversion of the partnership as set forth in the partnership agreement. If the partnership agreement fails to specify the required partner approval for a conversion of the partnership, the plan of conversion shall be approved by that number or percentage of partners required by the partnership agreement to approve an amendment to the partnership agreement unless the conversion effects a change for which the partnership agreement requires a greater number or percentage of partners than that required to amend the partnership agreement, in which case the plan of conversion shall be approved by that greater number or percentage. If the partnership agreement fails to specify the vote required to amend the partnership agreement, the plan of conversion shall be approved by all partners.

(c) If the partnership is converting into a limited partnership, in addition to the approval of the partners as set forth in subdivision (b), the plan of conversion shall be approved by all partners who will become general partners of the converted limited partnership pursuant to the plan of conversion.

(d) All partners of the converting partnership except those that dissociate upon effectiveness of the conversion pursuant to subdivision (e) of Section 16909 shall be deemed parties to any partnership or operating agreement, articles or certificate of incorporation, or organic document for the converted entity adopted as part of the plan of conversion, regardless of whether that partner has executed the plan of conversion or the operating agreement, articles or certificate of incorporation, partnership agreement, or other organic document for the converted entity. Any adoption of a new partnership or operating agreement, articles or certificate of incorporation, or other organic document made pursuant to the foregoing sentence shall be effective at the effective time or date of the conversion.

(e) Notwithstanding its prior approval, a plan of conversion may be amended before the conversion takes effect if the amendment is approved by the partnership in the same manner, and by the same number or percentage of partners, as was required for approval of the original plan of conversion.

(f) The partners of a converting partnership may, at any time before the conversion is effective, in their discretion, abandon a conversion, without further approval by the partners, in the same manner, and by the same number or percentage of partners, as was required for approval of the original plan of conversion at any time before the conversion is effective, subject to the contractual rights of third parties.

(g) The converted entity shall keep the plan of conversion at:

(1) the principal place of business of the converted entity, if the converted entity is a foreign other business entity or a corporation; or

(2) the office at which records are to be kept under Section 15614 or 15901.14 if the converted entity is a domestic limited partnership, or at the office at which records are to be kept under Section 17701.13 if the converted

entity is a domestic limited liability company. Upon the request of a partner of a converting partnership, the authorized person on behalf of the converted entity shall promptly deliver to the partner or the holder of interests or other securities, at the expense of the converted entity, a copy of the plan of conversion. A waiver by a partner of the rights provided in this subdivision shall be unenforceable.

§ 16904.   *Effective Date of Conversion*

(a) A conversion into a domestic other business entity shall become effective upon the earliest date that all of the following shall have occurred:

(1) The approval of the plan of conversion by the partners of the converting partnership as provided in Section 16903.

(2) The filing of all documents required by law to create the converted other business entity, which documents shall also contain a statement of conversion, if required under Section 16906.

(3) The effective date, if set forth in the plan of conversion, shall have occurred.

(b) A copy of the certificate of limited partnership, articles of organization, or articles of incorporation, complying with Section 16906, if applicable, duly certified by the Secretary of State, is conclusive evidence of the conversion of the partnership.

§ 16905.   *Laws Applicable to Conversion of Partnership into*
Foreign Other Business Entity

(a) The conversion of a partnership into a foreign other business entity shall comply with Section 16902.

(b) If the partnership is converting into a foreign other business entity, then the conversion proceedings shall be in accordance with the laws of the state or place of organization of the foreign other business entity and the conversion shall become effective in accordance with that law.

(c) (1) Unless a statement of conversion has been filed to effect the conversion, the converted foreign other business entity shall promptly notify the Secretary of State of the mailing address of its agent for service of process, its chief executive office, and of any change of address. To enforce an obligation of a partnership that has converted to a foreign other business entity, the Secretary of State shall only be the agent for service of process in an action or proceeding against the converted foreign other business entity, if the agent designated for the service of process for that entity is a natural person and cannot be found with due diligence or if the agent is a corporation and no person, to whom delivery may be made, may be located with due diligence, or if no agent has been designated and if no one of the officers, partners, managers, members, or agents of that entity may be located after diligent search, and it is so shown by affidavit to the satisfaction of the court. The court then may make an order that service be made by personal delivery to the Secretary of State or to an assistant or deputy Secretary of State of two copies of the process together with two copies of the order, and the order shall set forth an address to which the process shall be sent by the Secretary of State. Service in this manner is deemed complete on the 10th day after delivery of the process to the Secretary of State.

(2) Upon receipt of the process and order and the fee set forth in Section 12197 of the Government Code, the Secretary of State shall provide notice to the entity of the service of the process by forwarding by certified mail, return receipt requested, a copy of the process and order to the address specified in the order.

(3) The Secretary of State shall keep a record of all process served upon the Secretary of State and shall record therein the time of service and the Secretary of State's action with respect thereto. The certificate of the Secretary of State, under the Secretary of State's official seal, certifying to the receipt of process, the providing of notice thereof to the entity, and the forwarding of the process, shall be competent and prima facie evidence of the matters stated therein.

§ 16906. Statement of Conversion

(a) If the converting partnership has filed a statement of partnership authority under Section 16303 that is effective at the time of the conversion, then upon conversion to a domestic limited partnership, limited liability company, or corporation, the certificate of limited partnership, articles of organization, or articles of incorporation filed by the converted entity, as applicable, shall contain a statement of conversion, in that form as may be prescribed by the Secretary of State. If the converting partnership has not filed a statement of partnership authority under Section 16303 that is effective at the time of the conversion, upon conversion to a domestic limited partnership, limited liability company, or corporation, the converted entity may, but is not required to file, on its certificate of limited partnership, articles of organization, or articles of incorporation, a statement of conversion. A statement of conversion shall set forth all of the following:

(1) The name and the Secretary of State's file number, if any, of the converting partnership.

(2) A statement that the principal terms of the plan of conversion were approved by a vote of the partners, which equaled or exceeded the vote required under Section 16903.

(b) A partnership converting to a foreign other business entity that has filed a statement of partnership authority under Section 16303 that is effective at the time of conversion may file a certificate of conversion with the Secretary of State. The certificate of conversion shall contain the following:

(1) The names of the converting partnership and the converted entity.

(2) The street address of the converted entity's chief executive office and of an office in this state, if any.

(3) The form of organization of the converted entity.

(c) The filing with the Secretary of State of a certificate of limited partnership, articles of organization, or articles of incorporation containing a statement of conversion as set forth in subdivision (a) or a certificate of conversion filed pursuant to subdivision (b) shall have the effect of the filing of a cancellation by the converting partnership of any statement of partnership authority filed by it.

§ 16907.   *Real Property*

(a) Whenever a partnership or other business entity having any real property in this state converts into a partnership or an other business entity pursuant to the laws of this state or of the state or place in which the other business entity was organized, and the laws of the state or place of organization (including this state) of the converting partnership or other business entity provide substantially that the conversion of a converting entity vests in the converted partnership or other business entity all the real property of the converting partnership or converting other business entity, the filing for record in the office of the county recorder of any county in this state in which any of the real property of the converting partnership or converting other business entity is located of either (1) a certificate of conversion or a certificate of limited partnership, articles of organization, or articles of incorporation, complying with Section 16906, in the form prescribed by the Secretary of State, certified by the Secretary of State, or (2) a copy of a certificate of conversion or a certificate of limited partnership, articles of organization, articles or certificate of incorporation, or other certificate evidencing the creation of a foreign other business entity by conversion, containing a statement of conversion, certified by the Secretary of State or an authorized public official of the state or place pursuant to the laws of which the conversion is effected, shall evidence record ownership in the converted partnership or converted other business entity of all interest of the converting partnership or converting other business entity in and to the real property located in that county.

(b) A filed and, if appropriate, recorded certificate of conversion, certificate of limited partnership, articles of organization, articles or certificate of incorporation, or other certificate evidencing the creation of an other business entity by conversion, containing a statement of conversion, executed and declared to be accurate pursuant to subdivision (c) of Section 16105, stating the name of the converting partnership or converting other business entity in whose name property was held before the conversion and the name of the converted entity, but not containing all of the other information required by Section 16906, operates with respect to the entities named to the extent provided in subdivision (a).

(c) Recording of a certificate of conversion, a certificate of limited partnership, articles of organization, articles or certificate of incorporation, or other certificate evidencing the creation of another business entity by conversion, containing a statement of conversion, in accordance with Section 16902 shall create, in favor of bona fide purchasers or encumbrancers for value, a conclusive presumption that the conversion was validly completed.

§ 16908.   Effect of Laws under Which Converting Entity Is Organized

(a) A domestic limited partnership, limited liability company, or corporation, or a foreign other business entity may be converted to a domestic partnership pursuant to this article, but only if the converting entity is authorized by the laws under which it is organized to effect the conversion.

(b) An entity that desires to convert into a domestic partnership shall approve a plan of conversion or the instrument that is required to be approved to effect the conversion pursuant to the laws under which the entity is organized.

(c) The conversion of a domestic limited partnership, limited liability company, or corporation, or foreign other business entity shall be approved by the number or percentage of the partners, members, shareholders, or holders of interest of the converting entity as is required by the law under which the entity is organized, or a greater or lesser percentage (subject to applicable laws) as set forth in the limited partnership agreement, articles of organization, operating agreement, or articles or certificate of organization, or other governing document for the converting entity.

(d) The conversion by a domestic limited partnership, limited liability company, or corporation, or a foreign other business entity into a partnership shall be effective under this article at the time that the conversion is effective under the laws under which the converting entity is organized.

(e) The filing with the Secretary of State of a certificate of conversion or a statement of partnership authority containing a statement of conversion pursuant to subdivision (a) shall have the effect of the filing of a certificate of cancellation by the converting foreign limited partnership or foreign limited liability company, and no converting foreign limited partnership or foreign limited liability company that has made the filing is required to file a certificate of cancellation under Section 15696, 15909.07, or 17708.08 as a result of that conversion. If a converting other business entity is a foreign corporation qualified to transact business in this state, the foreign corporation shall, by virtue of the filing, automatically surrender its right to transact intrastate business.

§ 16909.   Effect of Conversion

(a) An entity that converts into another entity pursuant to this article is for all purposes the same entity that existed before the conversion.

(b) When a conversion takes effect, all of the following apply:

(1) All the rights and property, whether real, personal, or mixed, of the converting entity remains vested in the converted entity.

(2) All debts, liabilities, and obligations of the converting entity continue as debts, liabilities, and obligations of the converted entity.

(3) All rights of creditors and liens upon the property of the converting entity shall be preserved unimpaired and remain enforceable against the converted entity to the same extent as against the converting entity as if the conversion had not occurred.

(4) Any action or proceeding pending by or against the converting entity may be continued against the converted entity as if the conversion had not occurred.

(c) A partner of a converting partnership is liable for:

(1) All obligations of the converting partnership for which the partner was personally liable before the conversion.

(2) All obligations of the converted entity incurred after the conversion takes effect, but those obligations may be satisfied only out of property of the entity if (A) the converted other business entity is a limited partnership and the partner becomes a limited partner, (B) the converted other business entity is a limited liability company and the partner becomes a member, unless the articles of organization or the operating agreement of the limited liability company provide otherwise, or (C) the converted other business entity is a corporation and the partner becomes a shareholder.

(d) A partner of a partnership that converted from an other business entity is liable for any and all obligations of the converting other business entity for which the partner was personally liable before the conversion, but only to the extent the partner was liable for the obligation of the converting entity prior to the conversion.

(e) A partner of a converting partnership, who does not vote in favor of the conversion and does not agree to become a partner, member, shareholder, or holder of interest of the converted other business entity shall have the right to dissociate from the partnership, as of the date the conversion takes effect. Within 10 days after the approval of the conversion by the partners as required under this article, the converting partnership shall send notice of the approval of the conversion to each partner that has not approved the conversion, accompanied by copies of Section 16701 and a brief description of the procedure to be followed under that section if the partner wishes to dissociate from the partnership. A partner that desires to dissociate from the converting partnership shall send written notice of that dissociation within 30 days after the date of the notice of the approval of the conversion. The converting partnership shall cause the partner's interest in the entity to be purchased under Section 16701. The converting partnership is bound under Section 16702 by an act of a general partner dissociated under this subdivision, and the partner is liable under Section 16703 for transactions entered into by the converted entity after the conversion takes effect. The dissociation of a partner in connection with a conversion pursuant to the terms of this subdivision shall not be deemed to be a wrongful dissociation under Section 16602.

§ 16910.   Entities Merged

(a) The following entities may be merged pursuant to this article:

(1) Two or more partnerships into one partnership.

(2) One or more partnerships and one or more other business entities into one of those other business entities.

(3) One or more partnerships, other than a limited liability partnership, and one or more other business entities into one partnership.

(b) Notwithstanding subdivision (a), the merger of any number of partnerships with any number of other business entities may be effected only if the other business entities that are organized in California are authorized by the laws under which they are organized to effect the merger, and (1) if a domestic partnership is the surviving partnership, the foreign other business entities are not prohibited by the laws under which they are organized from effecting that merger and (2) if a foreign partnership or foreign other business entity is the survivor of the merger, the laws of the jurisdiction under which the survivor is organized authorize that merger.

§ 16911.   Agreement of Merger

(a) Each partnership and other business entity which desires to merge shall approve an agreement of merger. The agreement of merger shall be approved by the number or percentage of partners specified for merger in the partnership agreement of the constituent partnership. If the partnership agreement fails to specify the required partner approval for merger of the constituent partnership, then the agreement of merger shall be approved by that number or percentage of partners specified by the partnership agreement to approve an amendment to the partnership agreement. However, if the merger effects a change for which the partnership agreement requires a greater number or percentage of partners than that required to amend the partnership agreement, then the merger shall be approved by that greater number or percentage. If the partnership agreement contains no provision specifying the vote required to amend the partnership agreement, then the agreement of merger must be approved by all the partners. The agreement of merger shall be approved on behalf of each constituent other business entity by those persons required to approve the merger by the laws under which it is organized. Other persons may be parties to the agreement of merger. The agreement of merger shall state all of the following:

(1) The terms and conditions of the merger.

(2) The name and place of organization of the surviving partnership or surviving other business entity, and of each disappearing partnership and disappearing other business entity, and the agreement of merger may change the name of the surviving partnership, which new name may be the same as, or similar to, the name of a disappearing partnership.

(3) The manner of converting the partnership interests of each of the constituent partnerships into interests or other securities of the surviving partnership or surviving other business entity, and if partnership interests of any of the constituent partnerships are not to be converted solely into interest or other securities of the surviving partnership or surviving other business entity, the cash, property, rights, interests, or securities which the holders of the partnership interest are to receive in exchange for the partnership interests, which cash, property, rights, interests, or securities may be in addition to or in lieu of interests or other securities of the surviving partnership or surviving other business entity, or that the partnership interests are canceled without consideration.

(4) Any other details or provisions as are required by the laws under which any constituent other business entity is organized.

(5) Any other details or provisions that are desired, including, without limitation, a provision for the treatment of fractional partnership interests.

(b) If the partnership is merging into a limited partnership, then in addition to the approval of the partners as set forth under subdivision (a), the agreement of merger must be approved by all partners who will become general partners of the surviving limited partnership upon the effectiveness of the merger.

(c) Notwithstanding its prior approval, an agreement of merger may be amended before the merger takes effect if the amendment is approved by the partners of each constituent partnership, in the same manner as required for approval of the original agreement of merger, and by each of the constituent other business entities.

(d) The partners of a constituent partnership may in their discretion, abandon a merger, subject to the contractual rights, if any, of third parties, including other constituent partnerships and constituent other business entities, if the abandonment is approved by the partners of the constituent partnership in the same manner as required for approval of the original agreement of merger.

(e) An agreement of merger approved in accordance with subdivision (a) may (1) effect any amendment to the partnership agreement of any domestic constituent partnership or (2) effect the adoption of a new partnership agreement for a domestic constituent partnership if it is the surviving partnership in the merger. Any amendment to a partnership agreement or adoption of a new partnership agreement made pursuant to the foregoing sentence shall be effective at the effective time or date of the merger.

(f) The surviving partnership or surviving other business entity shall keep the agreement of merger at the principal place of business of the surviving entity if the surviving entity is a partnership or a foreign other business entity, at the office referred to in Section 1500 if the surviving entity is a domestic corporation, at the office referred to in subdivision (a) of Section 15614 or 15901.14 if the surviving entity is a domestic limited partnership or at the office referred to in Section 17701.13 if the surviving entity is a domestic limited liability company and, upon the request of a partner of a constituent partnership or a holder of interests or other securities of a constituent other business entity, the authorized person on behalf of the partnership or the surviving other business entity shall promptly deliver to the partner or the holder of interests or other securities, at the expense of the surviving partnership or surviving other business entity, a copy of the agreement of merger. A waiver by a partner or holder of interests or other securities of the rights provided in this subdivision shall be unenforceable.

§ 16912.   Effective Date of Merger

(a) Unless a future effective date or time is provided in a certificate of merger if a certificate of merger is required to be filed under Section 16915 in which event the merger shall be effective at the future effective date or time:

(1) A merger in which no domestic other business entity is a party to the merger shall be effective upon the later of any of the following:

(A) The approval of the agreement of merger by all parties to the merger as provided in Section 16911.

(B) The filing of all documents required by law to be filed as a condition to the effectiveness of the merger; or

(C) Any effective date specified in the agreement of merger; and

(2) A merger in which a domestic other business entity is a party to the merger shall be effective upon the filing of the certificate of merger in the office of the Secretary of State.

(b) For all mergers in which a certificate of merger is required to be filed under Section 16915, a copy of the certificate of merger duly certified by the Secretary of State is conclusive evidence of the merger of (A) the constituent partnerships (either by themselves or together with constituent other business entities) into the surviving other business entity, or (B) the constituent partnerships or the constituent other business entities, or both, into the surviving partnership.

§ 16913.   *Laws Applicable to Mergers*

(a) The merger of any number of domestic partnerships with any number of foreign partnerships or foreign other business entities shall be required to comply with Section 16910.

(b) If the surviving entity is a domestic partnership or a domestic other business entity, the merger proceedings with respect to that partnership or other business entity and any domestic disappearing partnership shall conform to the provisions of this chapter governing the merger of domestic partnerships, but if the surviving entity is a foreign partnership or a foreign other business entity, then, subject to the requirements of subdivision (d), the merger proceedings may be in accordance with the laws of the state or place of organization of the surviving partnership or surviving other business entity.

(c) If the surviving entity is a domestic other business entity or is a domestic partnership in a merger in which a domestic other business entity is also a party, the certificate of merger shall be filed as provided in subdivision (b) of Section 16915, and thereupon, subject to subdivision (a) of Section 16912, the merger shall be effective as to each domestic constituent partnership and domestic constituent other business entity.

(d) If the surviving entity is a foreign partnership or foreign other business entity, the merger shall become effective in accordance with the law of the jurisdiction in which the surviving partnership or surviving other business entity is organized, but shall be effective as to any domestic disappearing partnership as of the time of effectiveness in the foreign jurisdiction in accordance with Section 16912.

§ 16914. Effect of Merger

(a) When a merger takes effect, all of the following apply:

(1) The separate existence of the disappearing partnerships and disappearing other business entities ceases and the surviving partnership or surviving other business entity shall succeed, without other transfer, act, or deed, to all the rights and property whether real, personal, or mixed, of each of the disappearing partnerships and disappearing other business entities and shall be subject to all the debts and liabilities of each in the same manner as if the surviving partnership or surviving other business entity had itself incurred them.

(2) All rights of creditors and all liens upon the property of each of the constituent partnerships and constituent other business entities shall be preserved unimpaired and may be enforced against the surviving partnership or the surviving other business entity to the same extent as if the debt, liability, or duty that gave rise to that lien had been incurred or contracted by it, provided that those liens upon the property of a disappearing partnership or disappearing other business entity shall be limited to the property affected thereby immediately prior to the time the merger is effective.

(3) Any action or proceeding pending by or against any disappearing partnership or disappearing other business entity may be prosecuted to judgment, which shall bind the surviving partnership or surviving other business entity, or the surviving partnership or surviving other business entity may be proceeded against or be substituted in the disappearing partnership's or the disappearing other business entity's place.

(b) (1) Unless a certificate of merger has been filed to effect the merger, the surviving foreign entity shall promptly notify the Secretary of State of the mailing address of its agent for service of process and its chief executive office, and of any change of address. To enforce an obligation of a partnership that has merged with a foreign partnership or foreign other business entity, the Secretary of State shall only be the agent for service of process in an action or proceeding against the surviving foreign partnership or foreign other business entity, if the agent designated for the service of process for that entity is a natural person and cannot be located with due diligence or if the agent is a corporation and no person to whom delivery may be made can be located with due diligence, or if no agent has been designated and if no one of the officers, partners, managers, members, or agents of the entity can be located after diligent search, and it is so shown by affidavit to the satisfaction of the court. The court then may make an order that service be made by personal delivery to the Secretary of State or to an assistant or deputy Secretary of State of two copies of the process together with two copies of the order, and the order shall set forth an address to which the process shall be sent by the Secretary of State. Service in this manner is deemed complete on the 10th day after delivery of the process to the Secretary of State.

(2) Upon receipt of the process and order and the fee set forth in subdivision (c) of Section 12197 of the Government Code, the Secretary of State shall give notice to the entity of the service of the process by forwarding by certified mail, return receipt requested, a copy of the process and order to the address specified in the order.

(3) The Secretary of State shall keep a record of all process served upon the Secretary of State and shall record therein the time of service and the Secretary of State's action with respect thereto. The certificate of the Secretary of State, under the Secretary of State's official seal, certifying to the receipt of process, the giving of notice thereof to the entity, and the forwarding of the process, shall be competent and prima facie evidence of the matters stated therein.

(c) A partner of the surviving partnership or surviving limited partnership, a member of the surviving limited liability company, a shareholder of the surviving corporation, or a holder of equity securities of the surviving other business entity, is liable for all of the following:

(1) All obligations of a party to the merger for which that person was personally liable before the merger.

(2) All other obligations of the surviving entity incurred before the merger by a party to the merger, but those obligations may be satisfied only out of property of the entity.

(3) All obligations of the surviving entity incurred after the merger takes effect, but those obligations may be satisfied only out of property of the entity if that person is a limited partner, a shareholder in a corporation, or, unless expressly provided otherwise in the articles of organization or other constituent documents, a member of a limited liability company or a holder of equity securities in a surviving other business entity.

(d) If the obligations incurred before the merger by a party to the merger are not satisfied out of the property of the surviving partnership or surviving other business entity, the general partners of that party immediately before the effective date of the merger, to the extent that party was a partnership or a limited partnership, shall contribute the amount necessary to satisfy that party's obligations to the surviving entity in the manner provided in Section 16807 or in the limited partnership act of the jurisdiction in which the party was formed, as the case may be, as if the merged party were dissolved.

(e) A partner of a domestic disappearing partnership who does not vote in favor of the merger and does not agree to become a partner, member, shareholder, or holder of interest or equity securities of the surviving partnership or surviving other business entity shall have the right to dissociate from the partnership as of the date the merger takes effect. Within 10 days after the approval of the merger by the partners as required under this article, each domestic disappearing partnership shall send notice of the approval of the merger to each partner that has not approved the merger, accompanied by a copy of Section 16701 and a brief description of the procedure to be followed under that section if the partner wishes to dissociate from the partnership. A partner that desires to dissociate from a disappearing partnership shall send written notice of that dissociation within 30 days after the date of the notice of the approval of the merger. The disappearing partnership shall cause the partner's interest in the entity to be purchased under Section 16701. The surviving entity is bound under Section 16702 by an act of a general partner dissociated under this subdivision, and the partner is liable under Section 16703 for transactions entered into by the surviving entity after the merger takes effect. The dissociation of a partner in connection with a merger pursuant to the terms of this subdivision shall not be deemed a wrongful dissociation under Section 16602.

§ 16915.   Statement of Merger

(a) In a merger involving a domestic partnership, in which another partnership or a foreign other business entity is a party, but in which no other domestic other business entity is a party, the surviving partnership or surviving foreign other business entity may file with the Secretary of State a statement that one or more partnerships have merged into the surviving partnership or surviving foreign other business entity, or that one or more partnerships or foreign other business entities have merged into the surviving domestic partnership. A statement of merger shall contain the following:

(1) The name of each partnership or foreign other business entity that is a party to the merger.

(2) The name of the surviving entity into which the other partnerships or foreign other business entities were merged.

(3) The street address of the surviving entity's chief executive office and of an office in this state, if any.

(4) Whether the surviving entity is a partnership or a foreign other business entity, specifying the type of the entity.

(b) In a merger involving a domestic partnership in which a domestic other business entity is also a party, after approval of the merger by the constituent partnerships and any constituent other business entities, the constituent partnerships and constituent other business entities shall file a certificate of merger in the office of, and on a form prescribed by, the Secretary of State, but if the surviving entity is a domestic corporation or a foreign corporation in a merger in which a domestic corporation is a constituent party, the surviving corporation shall file in the office of the Secretary of State a copy of the agreement of merger and attachments required under paragraph (1) of subdivision (g) of Section 1113. The certificate of merger shall be executed and acknowledged by each domestic constituent partnership by two partners (unless a lesser number is provided in the partnership agreement) and by each foreign constituent partnership by one or more partners, and by each constituent other business entity by those persons required to execute the certificate of merger by the laws under which the constituent other business entity is organized. The certificate of merger shall set forth all of the following:

(1) The names and the Secretary of State's file numbers, if any, of each of the constituent partnerships and constituent other business entities, separately identifying the disappearing partnerships and disappearing other business entities and the surviving partnership or surviving other business entity.

(2) If a vote of the partners was required under Section 16911, a statement that the principal terms of the agreement of merger were approved by a vote of the partners, which equaled or exceeded the vote required.

(3) If the surviving entity is a domestic partnership and not an other business entity, any change to the information set forth in any filed statement of partnership authority of the surviving partnership resulting from the merger, including any change in the name of the surviving partnership resulting from the merger. The filing of a certificate of merger setting forth any changes to any filed statement of partnership authority of the surviving partnership shall have the effect of the filing of a certificate of amendment of the statement of partnership authority by the surviving partnership, and the surviving partnership need not file a certificate of amendment under Section 16015 to reflect those changes.

(4) The future effective date or time (which shall be a date or time certain not more than 90 days subsequent to the date of filing) of the merger, if the merger is not to be effective upon the filing of the certificate of merger with the office of the Secretary of State.

(5) If the surviving entity is an other business entity or a foreign partnership, the full name, type of entity, legal jurisdiction in which the entity was organized and by whose laws its internal affairs are governed, and the address of the principal place of business of the entity.

(6) Any other information required to be stated in the certificate of merger by the laws under which each constituent other business entity is organized.

(c) A statement of merger or a certificate of merger, as is applicable under subdivision (a) or (b), shall have the effect of the filing of a cancellation for each disappearing partnership of any statement of partnership authority filed by it.

§ 16915.5.   Liability of Surviving Partnership or Business Entity Upon Merger; Filing of Merger Without Tax Board Certificate of Satisfaction

(a) Upon merger pursuant to this article, a surviving domestic or foreign partnership or other business entity shall be deemed to have assumed the liability of each disappearing domestic or foreign partnership or other business entity that is taxed under Part 10 (commencing with Section 17001) of, or under Part 11 (commencing with Section 23001) of, Division 2 of the Revenue and Taxation Code for the following:

(1) To prepare and file, or to cause to be prepared and filed, tax and information returns otherwise required of that disappearing entity as specified in Chapter 2 (commencing with Section 18501) of Part 10.2 of Division 2 of the Revenue and Taxation Code.

(2) To pay any tax liability determined to be due.

(b) If the surviving entity is a domestic limited liability company, domestic corporation, or registered limited liability partnership or a foreign limited liability company, foreign limited liability partnership, or foreign corporation that is registered or qualified to do business in California, the Secretary of State shall notify the Franchise Tax Board of the merger.

§ 16916.   Real Property

(a) Whenever a domestic or foreign partnership or other business entity having any real property in this state merges with another partnership or other business entity pursuant to the laws of this state or of the state or place in which any constituent partnership or constituent other business entity was organized, and the laws of the state or place of organization (including this state) of any disappearing partnership or disappearing other business entity provide substantially that the making and filing of a statement of merger, agreement of merger or certificate of merger vests in the surviving partnership or surviving other business entity all the real property of any disappearing partnership and disappearing other business entity, the filing for record in the office of the county record of any county in this state in which any of the real property of the disappearing partnership or disappearing other business entity is located of either (1) a certificate of merger or agreement of merger certified by the Secretary of State, or other certificate prescribed by the Secretary of State, or (2) a copy of the statement of merger, agreement of merger or certificate of merger, certified by the Secretary of State or an authorized public official of the state or place pursuant to the laws of which the merger is effected, shall evidence record ownership in the surviving partnership or surviving other business entity of all interest of that disappearing partnership or disappearing other business entity in and to the real property located in that county.

(b) A filed and, if appropriate, recorded statement of merger, executed and declared to be accurate pursuant to subdivision (c) of Section 16105, stating the name of a partnership or other business entity that is a party to the merger in whose name property was held before the merger and the name of the surviving entity, but not containing all of the other information required by Section 16915, operates with respect to the partnerships or other business entities named to the extent provided in subdivision (a).

(c) Recording of the certificate of merger in accordance with subdivision (a) shall create, in favor of bona fide purchasers or encumbrancers for value, a conclusive presumption that the merger was validly completed.

§ 16917.   Article Nonexclusive

This article is not exclusive. Partnerships, other than limited liability partnerships, may be converted or merged in any other manner provided by law.

ARTICLE 10.
LIMITED LIABILITY PARTNERSHIPS

§ 16951.   Recognized Types

For purposes of this chapter, the only types of limited liability partnerships that shall be recognized are a registered limited liability partnership and a foreign limited liability partnership, as defined in Section 16101. No registered limited liability partnership or foreign limited liability partnership may render professional limited liability partnership services in this state except through licensed persons.

§ 16952.   Name

The name of a registered limited liability partnership shall contain the words "Registered Limited Liability Partnership" or "Limited Liability Partnership" or one of the abbreviations "L.L.P.," "LLP," "R.L.L.P.," or "RLLP" as the last words or letters of its name.

§ 16953.   Registration; Notice of Obligation to Pay Tax

(a) To become a registered limited liability partnership, a partnership, other than a limited partnership, shall file with the Secretary of State a registration, executed by one or more partners authorized to execute a registration, stating all of the following:

(1) The name of the partnership.

(2) The street address of its principal office.

(3) The mailing address of its principal office, if different from the street address.

(4) The name and street address of the agent for service of process on the limited liability partnership in California in accordance with subdivision (a) of Section 16309.

(5) A brief statement of the business in which the partnership engages.

(6) Any other matters that the partnership determines to include.

(7) That the partnership is registering as a registered limited liability partnership.

(b) The registration shall be accompanied by a fee as set forth in subdivision (a) of Section 12189 of the Government Code.

(c) The Secretary of State shall register as a registered limited liability partnership any partnership that submits a completed registration with the required fee.

(d) The Secretary of State may cancel the filing of the registration if a check or other remittance accepted in payment of the filing fee is not paid upon presentation. Upon receiving written notification that the item presented for payment has not been honored for payment, the Secretary of State shall give a first written notice of the applicability of this section to the agent for service of process or to the person submitting the instrument. Thereafter, if the amount has not been paid by cashier's check or equivalent, the Secretary of State shall give a second written notice of cancellation and the cancellation shall thereupon be effective. The second notice shall be given 20 days or more after the first notice and 90 days or less after the date of the original filing.

(e) A partnership becomes a registered limited liability partnership at the time of the filing of the initial registration with the Secretary of State or at any later date or time specified in the registration and the payment of the fee required by subdivision (b). A partnership continues as a registered limited liability partnership until a notice that it is no longer a registered limited liability partnership has been filed pursuant to subdivision (b) of Section 16954 or, if applicable, until it has been dissolved and finally wound up. The status of a partnership as a registered limited liability partnership and the liability of a partner of the registered limited liability partnership shall not be adversely affected by errors or subsequent changes in the information stated in a registration under subdivision (a) or an amended registration or notice under Section 16954.

(f) The fact that a registration or amended registration pursuant to this section is on file with the Secretary of State is notice that the partnership is a registered limited liability partnership and of those other facts contained therein that are required to be set forth in the registration or amended registration.

(g) The Secretary of State shall provide a form for a registration under subdivision (a), which shall include the form for confirming compliance with the optional security requirement pursuant to subdivision (c) of Section 16956. The Secretary of State shall include with instructional materials provided in conjunction with the form for a registration under subdivision (a) a notice that filing the registration will obligate the limited liability partnership to pay an annual tax for that taxable year to the Franchise Tax Board pursuant to Section 17948 of the Revenue and Taxation Code. That notice shall be updated annually to specify the dollar amount of the tax.

(h) A limited liability partnership providing professional limited liability partnership services in this state shall comply with all statutory and administrative registration or filing requirements of the state board, commission, or other agency that prescribes the rules and regulations governing the particular profession in which the partnership proposes to engage, pursuant to the applicable provisions of the Business and Professions Code relating to that profession. The state board, commission, or other agency shall not disclose, unless compelled by a subpoena or other order of a court of competent jurisdiction, any information it receives in the course of evaluating the compliance of a limited liability partnership with applicable statutory and administrative registration or filing requirements, provided that nothing in this section shall be construed to prevent a state board, commission, or other agency from disclosing the manner in which the limited liability partnership has complied with the requirements of Section 16956, or the compliance or noncompliance by the limited liability partnership with any other requirements of the state board, commission, or other agency.

§ 16954.   *Amendment of Registration; Notice of Cessation*
of Existence; Filing Fees; Forms

(a) The registration of a registered limited liability partnership may be amended by an amended registration executed by one or more partners authorized to execute an amended registration and filed with the Secretary of State, as soon as reasonably practical after any information set forth in the registration or previously filed amended registration becomes inaccurate or to add information to the registration or amended registration.

(b) If a registered limited liability partnership ceases to be a registered limited liability partnership, it shall file with the Secretary of State a notice, executed by one or more partners authorized to execute the notice, that it is no longer a registered limited liability partnership. The notice shall state that a final annual tax return, as described by Section 17948.3 of the Revenue and Taxation Code, has been or will be filed with the Franchise Tax Board, as required under Part 10.2 (commencing with Section 18401) of Division 2 of the Revenue and Taxation Code.

(c) An amendment pursuant to subdivision (a) and a notice pursuant to subdivision (b) shall each be accompanied by a fee as set forth in subdivision (c) of Section 12189 of the Government Code.

(d) The Secretary of State shall provide forms for an amended registration under subdivision (a) and a notice under subdivision (b).

(e) A notice of cessation, signed pursuant to subdivision (b), shall be filed with the Secretary of State. The Secretary of State shall notify the Franchise Tax Board of the cessation.

§ 16955.   *Conversion to Registered Limited Liability Partnership*

(a) A domestic partnership, other than a limited partnership, may convert to a registered limited liability by the vote of the partners possessing a majority of the interests of its partners in the current profits of the partnership or by a different vote as may be required in its partnership agreement.

(b) When such a conversion takes effect, all of the following apply:

(1) All property, real and personal, tangible and intangible, of the converting partnership remains vested in the converted registered limited liability partnership.

(2) All debts, obligations, liabilities, and penalties of the converting partnership continue as debts, obligations, liabilities, and penalties of the converted registered limited liability partnership.

(3) Any action, suit, or proceeding, civil or criminal, then pending by or against the converting partnership may be continued as if the conversion had not occurred.

(4) To the extent provided in the agreement of conversion and in this chapter, the partners of a partnership shall continue as partners in the converted registered limited liability partnership.

(5) A partnership that has been converted to a registered limited liability partnership pursuant to this chapter is the same person that existed prior to the conversion.

§ 16955.5.   [Section repealed 1999.]

§ 16956.   Security for Claims Against Partnership

(a) At the time of registration pursuant to Section 16953, in the case of a registered limited liability partnership, and Section 16959, in the case of a foreign limited liability partnership, and at all times during which those partnerships shall transact intrastate business, every registered limited liability partnership and foreign limited liability partnership, as the case may be, shall be required to provide security for claims against it as follows:

(1) For claims based upon acts, errors, or omissions arising out of the practice of public accountancy, a registered limited liability partnership or foreign limited liability partnership providing accountancy services shall comply with one, or pursuant to subdivision (b) some combination, of the following:

(A) Maintaining a policy or policies of insurance against liability imposed on or against it by law for damages arising out of claims; however, the total aggregate limit of liability under the policy or policies of insurance for partnerships with five or fewer licensed persons shall not be less than one million dollars ($1,000,000), and for partnerships with more than five licensees rendering professional services on behalf of the partnership, an additional one hundred thousand dollars ($100,000) of insurance shall be obtained for each additional licensee; however, the maximum amount of insurance is not required to exceed five million dollars ($5,000,000) in any one designated period, less amounts paid in defending, settling, or discharging claims as set forth in this subparagraph. The policy or policies may be issued on a claims-made or occurrence basis, and shall cover: (i) in the case of a claims-made policy, claims initially asserted in the designated period, and (ii) in the case of an occurrence policy, occurrences during the designated period. For purposes of this subparagraph, "designated period" means a policy year or any other period designated in the policy that is not greater than 12 months. The impairment or exhaustion of the aggregate limit of liability by amounts paid under the policy in connection with the settlement, discharge, or defense of claims applicable to a designated period shall not require the partnership to acquire additional insurance coverage for that designated period. The policy or policies of insurance may be in a form reasonably available in the commercial insurance market and may be subject to those terms, conditions, exclusions, and endorsements that are typically contained in those policies. A policy or policies of insurance maintained pursuant to this subparagraph may be subject to a deductible or self-insured retention.

Upon the dissolution and winding up of the partnership, the partnership shall, with respect to any insurance policy or policies then maintained pursuant to this subparagraph, maintain or obtain an extended reporting period endorsement or equivalent provision in the maximum total aggregate limit of liability required to comply with this subparagraph for a minimum of three years if reasonably available from the insurer.

(B) Maintaining in trust or bank escrow, cash, bank certificates of deposit, United States Treasury obligations, bank letters of credit, or bonds of insurance or surety companies as security for payment of liabilities imposed by law for damages arising out of all claims; however, the maximum amount of security for partnerships with five or fewer licensed persons shall not be less than one million dollars ($1,000,000), and for partnerships with more than five licensees rendering professional services on behalf of the partnership, an additional one hundred thousand dollars ($100,000) of security shall be obtained for each additional licensee; however, the maximum amount of security is not required to exceed five million dollars ($5,000,000). The partnership remains in compliance with this section during a calendar year notwithstanding amounts paid during that calendar year from the accounts, funds, Treasury obligations, letters of credit, or bonds in defending, settling, or discharging claims of the type described in this paragraph, provided that the amount of those accounts, funds, Treasury obligations, letters of credit, or bonds was at least the amount specified in the preceding sentence as of the first business day of that calendar year. Notwithstanding the pendency of other claims against the partnership, a registered limited liability partnership or foreign limited liability partnership shall be deemed to be in compliance with this subparagraph as to a claim if within 30 days after the time that a claim is initially asserted through service of a summons, complaint, or comparable pleading in a judicial or administrative proceeding, the partnership has provided the required amount of security by designating and segregating funds in compliance with the requirements of this subparagraph.

(C) Unless the partnership has satisfied subparagraph (D), each partner of a registered limited liability partnership or foreign limited liability partnership providing accountancy services, by virtue of that person's status as a partner, thereby automatically guarantees payment of the difference between the maximum amount of security required for the partnership by this paragraph and the security otherwise provided in accordance with subparagraphs (A) and (B), provided that the aggregate amount paid by all partners under these guarantees shall not exceed the difference. Neither withdrawal by a partner nor the dissolution and winding up of the partnership shall affect the rights or obligations of a partner arising prior to withdrawal or dissolution and winding up, and the guarantee provided for in this subparagraph shall apply only to conduct that occurred prior to the withdrawal or dissolution and winding up. Nothing contained in this subparagraph shall affect or impair the rights or obligations of the partners among themselves, or the partnership, including, but not limited to, rights of contribution, subrogation, or indemnification.

(D) Confirming, pursuant to the procedure in subdivision (c), that, as of the most recently completed fiscal year of the partnership, it had a net worth equal to or exceeding ten million dollars ($10,000,000).

(2) For claims based upon acts, errors, or omissions arising out of the practice of law, a registered limited liability partnership or foreign limited liability partnership providing legal services shall comply with one, or pursuant to subdivision (b) some combination, of the following:

(A) Each registered limited liability partnership or foreign limited liability partnership providing legal services shall maintain a policy or policies of insurance against liability imposed on or against it by law for damages arising out of claims; however, the total aggregate limit of liability under the policy or policies of insurance for partnerships with five or fewer licensed persons shall not be less than one million dollars ($1,000,000), and for partnerships with more than five licensees rendering professional services on behalf of the partnership, an additional one hundred thousand dollars ($100,000) of insurance shall be obtained for each additional licensee; however, the maximum amount of insurance is not required to exceed seven million five hundred thousand dollars ($7,500,000) in any one designated period, less amounts paid in defending, settling, or discharging claims as set forth in this subparagraph. The policy or policies may be issued on a claims-made or occurrence basis, and shall cover (i) in the case of a claims-made policy, claims initially asserted in the designated period, and (ii) in the case of an occurrence policy, occurrences during the designated period. For purposes of this subparagraph, "designated period" means a policy year or any other period designated in the policy that is not greater than 12 months. The impairment or exhaustion of the aggregate limit of liability by amounts paid under the policy in connection with the settlement, discharge, or defense of claims applicable to a designated period shall not require the partnership to acquire additional insurance coverage for that designated period. The policy or policies of insurance may be in a form reasonably available in the commercial insurance market and may be subject to those terms, conditions, exclusions, and endorsements that are typically contained in those policies. A policy or policies of insurance maintained pursuant to this subparagraph may be subject to a deductible or self-insured retention.

Upon the dissolution and winding up of the partnership, the partnership shall, with respect to any insurance policy or policies then maintained pursuant to this subparagraph, maintain or obtain an extended reporting period endorsement or equivalent provision in the maximum total aggregate limit of liability required to comply with this subparagraph for a minimum of three years if reasonably available from the insurer.

(B) Each registered limited liability partnership or foreign limited liability partnership providing legal services shall maintain in trust or bank escrow, cash, bank certificates of deposit, United States Treasury obligations, bank letters of credit, or bonds of insurance or surety companies as security for payment of liabilities imposed by law for damages arising out of all claims; however, the maximum amount of security for partnerships with five or fewer licensed persons shall not be less than one million dollars ($1,000,000), and for partnerships with more than five licensees rendering professional services on behalf of the partnership, an additional one hundred thousand dollars ($100,000) of security shall be obtained for each additional licensee; however, the maximum amount of security is not required to exceed seven million five hundred thousand dollars ($7,500,000). The partnership remains in compliance with this section during a calendar year notwithstanding amounts paid during that calendar year from the accounts, funds, Treasury obligations, letters of credit, or bonds in defending, settling, or discharging claims of the type described in this paragraph, provided that the amount of those accounts, funds, Treasury obligations, letters of credit, or bonds was at least the amount specified in the preceding sentence as of the first business day of that calendar year. Notwithstanding the pendency of other claims against the partnership, a registered limited liability partnership or foreign limited liability partnership shall be deemed to be in compliance with this subparagraph as to a claim if within 30 days after the time that a claim is initially asserted through service of a summons, complaint, or comparable pleading in a judicial or administrative proceeding, the partnership has provided the required amount of security by designating and segregating funds in compliance with the requirement of this subparagraph.

(C) Unless the partnership has satisfied the requirements of subparagraph (D), each partner of a registered limited liability partnership or foreign limited liability partnership providing legal services, by virtue of that person's status as a partner, thereby automatically guarantees payment of the difference between the maximum amount of security required for the partnership by this paragraph and the security otherwise provided in accordance with the provisions of subparagraphs (A) and (B), provided that the aggregate amount paid by all partners under these guarantees shall not exceed the difference. Neither withdrawal by a partner nor the dissolution and winding up of the partnership shall affect the rights or obligations of a partner arising prior to withdrawal or dissolution and winding up, and the guarantee provided for in this subparagraph shall apply only to conduct that occurred prior to the withdrawal or dissolution and winding up. Nothing contained in this subparagraph shall affect or impair the rights or obligations of the partners among themselves, or the partnership, including, but not limited to, rights of contribution, subrogation, or indemnification.

(D) Confirming, pursuant to the procedure in subdivision (c), that, as of the most recently completed fiscal year of the partnership, it had a net worth equal to or exceeding fifteen million dollars ($15,000,000).

(3) For claims based upon acts, errors, or omissions arising out of the practice of architecture, a registered limited liability partnership or foreign limited liability partnership providing architectural services shall comply with one, or pursuant to subdivision (b) some combination, of the following:

(A) Maintaining a policy or policies of insurance against liability imposed on or against it by law for damages arising out of claims; however, the total aggregate limit of liability under the policy or policies of insurance for partnerships with five or fewer licensees rendering professional services on behalf of the partnership shall not be less than one million dollars ($1,000,000), and for partnerships with more than five licensees rendering professional services on behalf of the partnership, an additional one hundred thousand dollars ($100,000) of liability coverage shall be obtained for each additional licensee; however, the total aggregate limit of liability under the policy or policies of insurance is not required to exceed five million dollars ($5,000,000). The policy or policies may be issued on a claims-made or occurrence basis, and shall cover: (i) in the case of a claims-made policy, claims initially asserted in the designated period, and (ii) in the case of an occurrence policy, occurrences during the designated period. For purposes of this subparagraph, "designated period" means a policy year or any other period designated in the policy that is not greater than 12 months. The impairment or exhaustion of the aggregate limit of liability by amounts paid under the policy in connection with the settlement, discharge, or defense of claims applicable to a designated period shall not require the partnership to acquire additional insurance coverage for that designated period. The policy or policies of insurance may be in a form reasonably available in the commercial insurance market and may be subject to those terms, conditions, exclusions, and endorsements that are typically contained in those policies. A policy or policies of insurance maintained pursuant to this sub-paragraph may be subject to a deductible or self-insured retention.

Upon the dissolution and winding up of the partnership, the partner-ship shall, with respect to any insurance policy or policies then main-tained pursuant to this subparagraph, maintain or obtain an extended reporting period endorsement or equivalent provision in the maximum total aggregate limit of liability required to comply with this subpara-graph for a minimum of three years if reasonably available from the in-surer.

(B) Maintaining in trust or bank escrow, cash, bank certificates of de-posit, United States Treasury obligations, bank letters of credit, or bonds of insurance or surety companies as security for payment of liabilities im-posed by law for damages arising out of all claims; however, the maximum amount of security for partnerships with five or fewer licensees rendering professional services on behalf of the partnership shall not be less than one million dollars ($1,000,000), and for partnerships with more than five li-censees rendering professional services on behalf of the partnership, an additional one hundred thousand dollars ($100,000) of security shall be obtained for each additional licensee; however, the maximum amount of security is not required to exceed five million dollars ($5,000,000). The partnership remains in compliance with this section during a calendar year notwithstanding amounts paid during that calendar year from the accounts, funds, Treasury obligations, letters of credit, or bonds in defending, set-tling, or discharging claims of the type described in this paragraph, pro-vided that the amount of those accounts, funds, Treasury obligations, letters of credit, or bonds was at least the amount specified in the preced-ing sentence as of the first business day of that calendar year. Notwith-standing the pendency of other claims against the partnership, a registered limited liability partnership or foreign limited liability partnership shall be deemed to be in compliance with this subparagraph as to a claim if within 30 days after the time that a claim is initially asserted through service of a summons, complaint, or comparable pleading in a judicial or administra-tive proceeding, the partnership has provided the required amount of secu-rity by designating and segregating funds in compliance with the requirements of this subparagraph.

(C) Unless the partnership has satisfied subparagraph (D), each part-ner of a registered limited liability partnership or foreign limited liability partnership providing architectural services, by virtue of that person's status as a partner, thereby automatically guarantees payment of the dif-ference between the maximum amount of security required for the part-nership by this paragraph and the security otherwise provided in accordance with subparagraphs (A) and (B), provided that the aggregate amount paid by all partners under these guarantees shall not exceed the difference. Neither withdrawal by a partner nor the dissolution and winding up of the partnership shall affect the rights or obligations of a partner arising prior to withdrawal or dissolution and winding up, and the guarantee provided for in this subparagraph shall apply only to conduct that occurred prior to the withdrawal or dissolution and winding up. Nothing contained in this subparagraph shall affect or impair the rights or obligations of the partners among themselves, or the partnership, including, but not limited to, rights of contribution, subrogation, or indemnification.

(D) Confirming, pursuant to the procedure in subdivision (c), that, as of the most recently completed fiscal year of the partnership, it had a net worth equal to or exceeding ten million dollars ($10,000,000).

(4) For claims based upon acts, errors, or omissions arising out of the practice of engineering or the practice of land surveying, a registered limited liability partnership or foreign limited liability partnership providing engineering or land surveying services shall comply with one, or pursuant to subdivision (b) some combination, of the following:

(A) Maintaining a policy or policies of insurance against liability imposed on or against it by law for damages arising out of claims; however, the total aggregate limit of liability under the policy or policies of insurance for partnerships with five or fewer licensees rendering professional services on behalf of the partnership shall not be less than two million dollars ($2,000,000), and for partnerships with more than five licensees rendering professional services on behalf of the partnership, an additional one hundred thousand dollars ($100,000) of liability coverage shall be obtained for each additional licensee; however, the total aggregate limit of liability under the policy or policies of insurance is not required to exceed five million dollars ($5,000,000). The policy or policies may be issued on a claims-made or occurrence basis, and shall cover: (i) in the case of a claims-made policy, claims initially asserted in the designated period, and (ii) in the case of an occurrence policy, occurrences during the designated period. For purposes of this subparagraph, "designated period" means a policy year or any other period designated in the policy that is not greater than 12 months. The impairment or exhaustion of the aggregate limit of liability by amounts paid under the policy in connection with the settlement, discharge, or defense of claims applicable to a designated period shall not require the partnership to acquire additional insurance coverage for that designated period. The policy or policies of insurance may be in a form reasonably available in the commercial insurance market and may be subject to those terms, conditions, exclusions, and endorsements that are typically contained in those policies. A policy or policies of insurance maintained pursuant to this subparagraph may be subject to a deductible or self-insured retention.

Upon the dissolution and winding up of the partnership, the partnership shall, with respect to any insurance policy or policies then maintained pursuant to this subparagraph, maintain or obtain an extended reporting period endorsement or equivalent provision in the maximum total aggregate limit of liability required to comply with this subparagraph for a minimum of three years if reasonably available from the insurer.

(B) Maintaining in trust or bank escrow, cash, bank certificates of deposit, United States Treasury obligations, bank letters of credit, or bonds of insurance or surety companies as security for payment of liabilities imposed by law for damages arising out of all claims; however, the maximum amount of security for partnerships with five or fewer licensees rendering professional services on behalf of the partnership shall not be less than two million dollars ($2,000,000), and for partnerships with more than five licensees rendering professional services on behalf of the partnership, an additional one hundred thousand dollars ($100,000) of security shall be obtained for each additional licensee; however, the maximum amount of security is not required to exceed five million dollars ($5,000,000). The partnership remains in compliance with this section during a calendar year, notwithstanding amounts paid during that calendar year from the accounts, funds, Treasury obligations, letters of credit, or bonds in defending, settling, or discharging claims of the type described in this paragraph, provided that the amount of those accounts, funds, Treasury obligations, letters of credit, or bonds was at least the amount specified in the preceding sentence as of the first business day of that calendar year. Notwithstanding the pendency of other claims against the partnership, a registered limited liability partnership or foreign limited liability partnership shall be deemed to be in compliance with this subparagraph as to a claim if, within 30 days after the time that a claim is initially asserted through service of a summons, complaint, or comparable pleading in a judicial or administrative proceeding, the partnership has provided the required amount of security by designating and segregating funds in compliance with the requirements of this subparagraph.

(C) Unless the partnership has satisfied subparagraph (D), each partner of a registered limited liability partnership or foreign limited liability partnership providing engineering services or land surveying services, by virtue of that person's status as a partner, thereby automatically guarantees payment of the difference between the maximum amount of security required for the partnership by this paragraph and the security otherwise provided in accordance with subparagraphs (A) and (B), provided that the aggregate amount paid by all partners under these guarantees shall not exceed the difference. Neither withdrawal by a partner nor the dissolution and winding up of the partnership shall affect the rights or obligations of a partner arising prior to withdrawal or dissolution and winding up, and the guarantee provided for in this subparagraph shall apply only to conduct that occurred prior to the withdrawal or dissolution and winding up. Nothing contained in this subparagraph shall affect or impair the rights or obligations of the partners among themselves, or the partnership, including, but not limited to, rights of contribution, subrogation, or indemnification.

(D) Confirming, pursuant to the procedure in subdivision (c), that, as of the most recently completed fiscal year of the partnership, it had a net worth equal to or exceeding ten million dollars ($10,000,000).

(b) For purposes of satisfying the security requirements of this section, a registered limited liability partnership or foreign limited liability partnership may aggregate the security provided by it pursuant to subparagraphs (A), (B), (C), and (D) of paragraph (1) of subdivision (a), subparagraphs (A), (B), (C), and (D) of paragraph (2) of subdivision (a), subparagraphs (A), (B), (C), and (D) of paragraph (3) of subdivision (a), or subparagraphs (A), (B), (C), and (D) of paragraph (4) of subdivision (a), as the case may be. Any registered limited liability partnership or foreign limited liability partnership intending to comply with the alternative security provisions set forth in subparagraph (D) of paragraph (1) of subdivision (a), subparagraph (D) of paragraph (2) of subdivision (a), subparagraph (D) of paragraph (3) of subdivision (a), or subparagraph (D) of paragraph (4) of subdivision (a), shall furnish the following information to the Secretary of State's office, in the manner prescribed in, and accompanied by all information required by, the applicable section:

TRANSMITTAL FORM FOR EVIDENCING COMPLIANCE
WITH SECTION 16956(a)(1)(D),
SECTION 16956(a)(2)(D),
SECTION 16956(a)(3)(D), OR SECTION
16956(a)(4)(D) OF THE CALIFORNIA
CORPORATIONS CODE

The undersigned hereby confirms the following:

1. _____
   Name of registered or foreign limited liability partnership

2. _____
   Jurisdiction where partnership is organized

3. _____
   Address of principal office

4. The registered or foreign limited liability partnership chooses to satisfy the requirements of Section 16956 by confirming, pursuant to Section 16956(a)(1)(D), 16956(a)(2)(D), 16956(a)(3)(D), or 16956 (a)(4)(D) and pursuant to Section 16956(c), that, as of the most recently completed fiscal year, the partnership had a net worth equal to or exceeding ten million dollars ($10,000,000), in the case of a partnership providing accountancy services, fifteen million dollars ($15,000,000) in the case of a partnership providing legal services, or ten million dollars ($10,000,000), in the case of a partnership providing architectural services, engineering services, or land surveying services.

5. _____
   Title of authorized person executing this form

6. _____
   Signature of authorized person executing this form

(c) Pursuant to subparagraph (D) of paragraph (1) of subdivision (a), subparagraph (D) of paragraph (2) of subdivision (a), subparagraph (D) of paragraph (3) of subdivision (a), or subparagraph (D) of paragraph (4) of subdivision (a), a registered limited liability partnership or foreign limited liability partnership may satisfy the requirements of this section by confirming that, as of the last day of its most recently completed fiscal year, it had a net worth equal to or exceeding the amount required. In order to comply with this alternative method of meeting the requirements established in this section, a registered limited liability partnership or foreign limited liability partnership shall file an annual confirmation with the Secretary of State's office, signed by an authorized member of the registered limited liability partnership or foreign limited liability partnership, accompanied by a transmittal form as prescribed by subdivision (b). In order to be current in a given year, the partnership form for confirming compliance with the optional security requirement shall be on file within four months of the completion of the fiscal year and, upon being filed, shall constitute full compliance with the financial security requirements for purposes of this section as of the beginning of the fiscal year. A confirmation filed during any particular fiscal year shall continue to be effective for the first four months of the next succeeding fiscal year.

(d) Neither the existence of the requirements of subdivision (a) nor the extent of the registered limited liability partnership's or foreign limited liability partnership's compliance with the alternative requirements in this section shall be admissible in court or in any way be made known to a jury or other trier of fact in determining an issue of liability for, or to the extent of, the damages in question.

(e) Notwithstanding any other provision of this section, if a registered limited liability partnership or foreign limited liability partnership is otherwise in compliance with the terms of this section at the time that a bankruptcy or other insolvency proceeding is commenced with respect to the registered limited liability partnership or foreign limited liability partnership, it shall be deemed to be in compliance with this section during the pendency of the proceeding. A registered limited liability partnership that has been the subject of a proceeding and that conducts business after the proceeding ends shall thereafter comply with paragraph (1), (2), (3), or (4) of subdivision (a), in order to obtain the limitations on liability afforded by subdivision (c) of Section 16306.

(f) This section shall remain in effect only until January 1, 2016, and as of that date is repealed, unless a later enacted statute, that is enacted before January 1, 2016, deletes or extends that date.

§ 16956.   Security for Claims Against Partnership (This section shall become operative on January 1, 2016.)

(a) At the time of registration pursuant to Section 16953, in the case of a registered limited liability partnership, and Section 16959, in the case of a foreign limited liability partnership, and at all times during which those partnerships shall transact intrastate business, every registered limited liability partnership and foreign limited liability partnership, as the case may be, shall be required to provide security for claims against it as follows:

(1) For claims based upon acts, errors, or omissions arising out of the practice of public accountancy, a registered limited liability partnership or foreign limited liability partnership providing accountancy services shall comply with one, or pursuant to subdivision (b) some combination, of the following:

(A) Maintaining a policy or policies of insurance against liability imposed on or against it by law for damages arising out of claims; however, the total aggregate limit of liability under the policy or policies of insurance for partnerships with five or fewer licensed persons shall not be less than one million dollars ($1,000,000), and for partnerships with more than five licensees rendering professional services on behalf of the partnership, an additional one hundred thousand dollars ($100,000) of insurance shall be obtained for each additional licensee; however, the maximum amount of insurance is not required to exceed five million dollars ($5,000,000) in any one designated period, less amounts paid in defending, settling, or discharging claims as set forth in this subparagraph. The policy or policies may be issued on a claims-made or occurrence basis, and shall cover: (i) in the case of a claims-made policy, claims initially asserted in the designated period, and (ii) in the case of an occurrence policy, occurrences during the designated period. For purposes of this subparagraph, "designated period" means a policy year or any other period designated in the policy that is not greater than 12 months. The impairment or exhaustion of the aggregate limit of liability by amounts paid under the policy in connection with the settlement, discharge, or defense of claims applicable to a designated period shall not require the partnership to acquire additional insurance coverage for that designated period. The policy or policies of insurance may be in a form reasonably available in the commercial insurance market and may be subject to those terms, conditions, exclusions, and endorsements that are typically contained in those policies. A policy or policies of insurance maintained pursuant to this subparagraph may be subject to a deductible or self-insured retention.

Upon the dissolution and winding up of the partnership, the partnership shall, with respect to any insurance policy or policies then maintained pursuant to this subparagraph, maintain or obtain an extended reporting period endorsement or equivalent provision in the maximum total aggregate limit of liability required to comply with this subparagraph for a minimum of three years if reasonably available from the insurer.

(B) Maintaining in trust or bank escrow, cash, bank certificates of deposit, United States Treasury obligations, bank letters of credit, or bonds of insurance or surety companies as security for payment of liabilities imposed by law for damages arising out of all claims; however, the maximum amount of security for partnerships with five or fewer licensed persons shall not be less than one million dollars ($1,000,000), and for partnerships with more than five licensees rendering professional services on behalf of the partnership, an additional one hundred thousand dollars ($100,000) of security shall be obtained for each additional licensee; however, the maximum amount of security is not required to exceed five million dollars ($5,000,000). The partnership remains in compliance with this section during a calendar year notwithstanding amounts paid during that calendar year from the accounts, funds, Treasury obligations, letters of credit, or bonds in defending, settling, or discharging claims of the type described in this paragraph, provided that the amount of those accounts, funds, Treasury obligations, letters of credit, or bonds was at least the amount specified in the preceding sentence as of the first business day of that calendar year. Notwithstanding the pendency of other claims against the partnership, a registered limited liability partnership or foreign limited liability partnership shall be deemed to be in compliance with this subparagraph as to a claim if within 30 days after the time that a claim is initially asserted through service of a summons, complaint, or comparable pleading in a judicial or administrative proceeding, the partnership has provided the required amount of security by designating and segregating funds in compliance with the requirements of this subparagraph.

(C) Unless the partnership has satisfied subparagraph (D), each partner of a registered limited liability partnership or foreign limited liability partnership providing accountancy services, by virtue of that person's status as a partner, thereby automatically guarantees payment of the difference between the maximum amount of security required for the partnership by this paragraph and the security otherwise provided in accordance with subparagraphs (A) and (B), provided that the aggregate amount paid by all partners under these guarantees shall not exceed the difference. Neither withdrawal by a partner nor the dissolution and winding up of the partnership shall affect the rights or obligations of a partner arising prior to withdrawal or dissolution and winding up, and the guarantee provided for in this subparagraph shall apply only to conduct that occurred prior to the withdrawal or dissolution and winding up. Nothing contained in this subparagraph shall affect or impair the rights or obligations of the partners among themselves, or the partnership, including, but not limited to, rights of contribution, subrogation, or indemnification.

(D) Confirming, pursuant to the procedure in subdivision (c), that, as of the most recently completed fiscal year of the partnership, it had a net worth equal to or exceeding ten million dollars ($10,000,000).

(2) For claims based upon acts, errors, or omissions arising out of the practice of law, a registered limited liability partnership or foreign limited liability partnership providing legal services shall comply with one, or pursuant to subdivision (b) some combination, of the following:

(A) Each registered limited liability partnership or foreign limited liability partnership providing legal services shall maintain a policy or policies of insurance against liability imposed on or against it by law for damages arising out of claims; however, the total aggregate limit of liability under the policy or policies of insurance for partnerships with five or fewer licensed persons shall not be less than one million dollars ($1,000,000), and for partnerships with more than five licensees rendering professional services on behalf of the partnership, an additional one hundred thousand dollars ($100,000) of insurance shall be obtained for each additional licensee; however, the maximum amount of insurance is not required to exceed seven million five hundred thousand dollars ($7,500,000) in any one designated period, less amounts paid in defending, settling, or discharging claims as set forth in this subparagraph. The policy or policies may be issued on a claims-made or occurrence basis, and shall cover (i) in the case of a claims-made policy, claims initially asserted in the designated period, and (ii) in the case of an occurrence policy, occurrences during the designated period. For purposes of this subparagraph, "designated period" means a policy year or any other period designated in the policy that is not greater than 12 months. The impairment or exhaustion of the aggregate limit of liability by amounts paid under the policy in connection with the settlement, discharge, or defense of claims applicable to a designated period shall not require the partnership to acquire additional insurance coverage for that designated period. The policy or policies of insurance may be in a form reasonably available in the commercial insurance market and may be subject to those terms, conditions, exclusions, and endorsements that are typically contained in those policies. A policy or policies of insurance maintained pursuant to this subparagraph may be subject to a deductible or self-insured retention.

Upon the dissolution and winding up of the partnership, the partnership shall, with respect to any insurance policy or policies then maintained pursuant to this subparagraph, maintain or obtain an extended reporting period endorsement or equivalent provision in the maximum total aggregate limit of liability required to comply with this subparagraph for a minimum of three years if reasonably available from the insurer.

(B) Each registered limited liability partnership or foreign limited liability partnership providing legal services shall maintain in trust or bank escrow, cash, bank certificates of deposit, United States Treasury obligations, bank letters of credit, or bonds of insurance or surety companies as security for payment of liabilities imposed by law for damages arising out of all claims; however, the maximum amount of security for partnerships with five or fewer licensed persons shall not be less than one million dollars ($1,000,000), and for partnerships with more than five licensees rendering professional services on behalf of the partnership, an additional one hundred thousand dollars ($100,000) of security shall be obtained for each additional licensee; however, the maximum amount of security is not required to exceed seven million five hundred thousand dollars ($7,500,000). The partnership remains in compliance with this section during a calendar year notwithstanding amounts paid during that calendar year from the accounts, funds, Treasury obligations, letters of credit, or bonds in defending, settling, or discharging claims of the type described in this paragraph, provided that the amount of those accounts, funds, Treasury obligations, letters of credit, or bonds was at least the amount specified in the preceding sentence as of the first business day of that calendar year. Notwithstanding the pendency of other claims against the partnership, a registered limited liability partnership or foreign limited liability partnership shall be deemed to be in compliance with this subparagraph as to a claim if within 30 days after the time that a claim is initially asserted through service of a summons, complaint, or comparable pleading in a judicial or administrative proceeding, the partnership has provided the required amount of security by designating and segregating funds in compliance with the requirement of this subparagraph.

(C) Unless the partnership has satisfied the requirements of subparagraph (D), each partner of a registered limited liability partnership or foreign limited liability partnership providing legal services, by virtue of that person's status as a partner, thereby automatically guarantees payment of the difference between the maximum amount of security required for the partnership by this paragraph and the security otherwise provided in accordance with the provisions of subparagraphs (A) and (B), provided that the aggregate amount paid by all partners under these guarantees shall not exceed the difference. Neither withdrawal by a partner nor the dissolution and winding up of the partnership shall affect the rights or obligations of a partner arising prior to withdrawal or dissolution and winding up, and the guarantee provided for in this subparagraph shall apply only to conduct that occurred prior to the withdrawal or dissolution and winding up. Nothing contained in this subparagraph shall affect or impair the rights or obligations of the partners among themselves, or the partnership, including, but not limited to, rights of contribution, subrogation, or indemnification.

(D) Confirming, pursuant to the procedure in subdivision (c), that, as of the most recently completed fiscal year of the partnership, it had a net worth equal to or exceeding fifteen million dollars ($15,000,000).

(3) For claims based upon acts, errors, or omissions arising out of the practice of architecture, a registered limited liability partnership or foreign limited liability partnership providing architectural services shall comply with one, or pursuant to subdivision (b) some combination, of the following:

(A) Maintaining a policy or policies of insurance against liability imposed on or against it by law for damages arising out of claims in an amount for each claim of at least one hundred thousand dollars ($100,000) multiplied by the number of licensed persons rendering professional services on behalf of the partnership; however, the total aggregate limit of liability under the policy or policies of insurance for partnerships with five or fewer licensees rendering professional services on behalf of the partnership shall not be less than five hundred thousand dollars ($500,000), and for all other partnerships is not required to exceed five million dollars ($5,000,000) in any one designated period, less amounts paid in defending, settling, or discharging claims as set forth in this subparagraph. On and after January 1, 2008, the total aggregate limit of liability under the policy or policies of insurance for partnerships with five or fewer licensees rendering professional services on behalf of the partnership shall not be less than one million dollars ($1,000,000), and for partnerships with more than five licensees rendering professional services on behalf of the partnership, an additional one hundred thousand dollars ($100,000) of liability coverage shall be obtained for each additional licensee; however, the total aggregate limit of liability under the policy or policies of insurance is not required to exceed five million dollars ($5,000,000). The policy or policies may be issued on a claims-made or occurrence basis, and shall cover: (i) in the case of a claims-made policy, claims initially asserted in the designated period, and (ii) in the case of an occurrence policy, occurrences during the designated period. For purposes of this subparagraph, "designated period" means a policy year or any other period designated in the policy that is not greater than 12 months. The impairment or exhaustion of the aggregate limit of liability by amounts paid under the policy in connection with the settlement, discharge, or defense of claims applicable to a designated period shall not require the partnership to acquire additional insurance coverage for that designated period. The policy or policies of insurance may be in a form reasonably available in the commercial insurance market and may be subject to those terms, conditions, exclusions, and endorsements that are typically contained in those policies. A policy or policies of insurance maintained pursuant to this subparagraph may be subject to a deductible or self-insured retention.

Upon the dissolution and winding up of the partnership, the partnership shall, with respect to any insurance policy or policies then maintained pursuant to this subparagraph, maintain or obtain an extended reporting period endorsement or equivalent provision in the maximum total aggregate limit of liability required to comply with this subparagraph for a minimum of three years if reasonably available from the insurer.

(B) Maintaining in trust or bank escrow, cash, bank certificates of deposit, United States Treasury obligations, bank letters of credit, or bonds of insurance or surety companies as security for payment of liabilities imposed by law for damages arising out of all claims in an amount of at least one hundred thousand dollars ($100,000) multiplied by the number of licensed persons rendering professional services on behalf of the partnership; however, the maximum amount of security for partnerships with five or fewer licensees rendering professional services on behalf of the partnership shall not be less than five hundred thousand dollars ($500,000), and for all other partnerships is not required to exceed five million dollars ($5,000,000). On and after January 1, 2008, the maximum amount of security for partnerships with five or fewer licensees rendering professional services on behalf of the partnership shall not be less than one million dollars ($1,000,000), and for partnerships with more than five licensees rendering professional services on behalf of the partnership, an additional one hundred thousand dollars ($100,000) of security shall be obtained for each additional licensee; however, the maximum amount of security is not required to exceed five million dollars ($5,000,000). The partnership remains in compliance with this section during a calendar year notwithstanding amounts paid during that calendar year from the accounts, funds, Treasury obligations, letters of credit, or bonds in defending, settling, or discharging claims of the type described in this paragraph, provided that the amount of those accounts, funds, Treasury obligations, letters of credit, or bonds was at least the amount specified in the preceding sentence as of the first business day of that calendar year. Notwithstanding the pendency of other claims against the partnership, a registered limited liability partnership or foreign limited liability partnership shall be deemed to be in compliance with this subparagraph as to a claim if within 30 days after the time that a claim is initially asserted through service of a summons, complaint, or comparable pleading in a judicial or administrative proceeding, the partnership has provided the required amount of security by designating and segregating funds in compliance with the requirements of this subparagraph.

(C) Unless the partnership has satisfied subparagraph (D), each partner of a registered limited liability partnership or foreign limited liability partnership providing architectural services, by virtue of that person's status as a partner, thereby automatically guarantees payment of the difference between the maximum amount of security required for the partnership by this paragraph and the security otherwise provided in accordance with subparagraphs (A) and (B), provided that the aggregate amount paid by all partners under these guarantees shall not exceed the difference. Neither withdrawal by a partner nor the dissolution and winding up of the partnership shall affect the rights or obligations of a partner arising prior to withdrawal or dissolution and winding up, and the guarantee provided for in this subparagraph shall apply only to conduct that occurred prior to the withdrawal or dissolution and winding up. Nothing contained in this subparagraph shall affect or impair the rights or obligations of the partners among themselves, or the partnership, including, but not limited to, rights of contribution, subrogation, or indemnification.

(D) Confirming, pursuant to the procedure in subdivision (c), that, as of the most recently completed fiscal year of the partnership, it had a net worth equal to or exceeding ten million dollars ($10,000,000).

(b) For purposes of satisfying the security requirements of this section, a registered limited liability partnership or foreign limited liability partnership may aggregate the security provided by it pursuant to subparagraphs (A), (B), (C), and (D) of paragraph (1) of subdivision (a), subparagraphs (A), (B), (C), and (D) of paragraph (2) of subdivision (a), or subparagraphs (A), (B), (C), and (D) of paragraph (3) of subdivision (a), as the case may be. Any registered limited liability partnership or foreign limited liability partnership intending to comply with the alternative security provisions set forth in subparagraph (D) of paragraph (1) of subdivision (a), subparagraph (D) of paragraph (2) of subdivision (a), or subparagraph (D) of paragraph (3) of subdivision (a) shall furnish the following information to the Secretary of State's office, in the manner prescribed in, and accompanied by all information required by, the applicable section:

TRANSMITTAL FORM FOR EVIDENCING COMPLIANCE WITH SECTION 16956(a)(1)(D), SECTION 16956(a)(2)(D), OR SECTION 16956(a)(3)(D) OF THE CALIFORNIA CORPORATIONS CODE

The undersigned hereby confirms the following:

1. _____
   Name of registered or foreign limited liability partnership

2. _____
   Jurisdiction where partnership is organized

3. _____
   Address of principal office

4. The registered or foreign limited liability partnership chooses to satisfy the requirements of Section 16956 by confirming, pursuant to Section 16956(a)(1)(D), 16956(a)(2)(D), or 16956(a)(3)(D) and pursuant to Section 16956(c), that, as of the most recently completed fiscal year, the partnership had a net worth equal to or exceeding ten million dollars ($10,000,000), in the case of a partnership providing accountancy services, fifteen million dollars ($15,000,000) in the case of a partnership providing legal services, or ten million dollars ($10,000,000), in the case of a partnership providing architectural services.

5. _____
   Title of authorized person executing this form

6. _____
   Signature of authorized person executing this form

(c) Pursuant to subparagraph (D) of paragraph (1) of subdivision (a), subparagraph (D) of paragraph (2) of subdivision (a), or subparagraph (D) of paragraph (3) of subdivision (a), a registered limited liability partnership or foreign limited liability partnership may satisfy the requirements of this section by confirming that, as of the last day of its most recently completed fiscal year, it had a net worth equal to or exceeding the amount required. In order to comply with this alternative method of meeting the requirements established in this section, a registered limited liability partnership or foreign limited liability partnership shall file an annual confirmation with the Secretary of State's office, signed by an authorized member of the registered limited liability partnership or foreign limited liability partnership, accompanied by a transmittal form as prescribed by subdivision (b). In order to be current in a given year, the partnership form for confirming compliance with the optional security requirement shall be on file within four months of the completion of the fiscal year and, upon being filed, shall constitute full compliance with the financial security requirements for purposes of this section as of the beginning of the fiscal year. A confirmation filed during any particular fiscal year shall continue to be effective for the first four months of the next succeeding fiscal year.

(d) Neither the existence of the requirements of subdivision (a) nor the extent of the registered limited liability partnership's or foreign limited liability partnership's compliance with the alternative requirements in this section shall be admissible in court or in any way be made known to a jury or other trier of fact in determining an issue of liability for, or to the extent of, the damages in question.

(e) Notwithstanding any other provision of this section, if a registered limited liability partnership or foreign limited liability partnership is otherwise in compliance with the terms of this section at the time that a bankruptcy or other insolvency proceeding is commenced with respect to the registered limited liability partnership or foreign limited liability partnership, it shall be deemed to be in compliance with this section during the pendency of the proceeding. A registered limited liability partnership that has been the subject of a proceeding and that conducts business after the proceeding ends shall thereafter comply with paragraph (1), (2), or (3) of subdivision (a), in order to obtain the limitations on liability afforded by subdivision (c) of Section 16306.

(f) This section shall become operative on January 1, 2016.

§ 16957.   *Laws Applicable to Foreign Partnership; Name*

(a) No distribution shall be made by a registered limited liability partnership if, after giving effect to the distribution:

(1) The registered limited liability partnership would not be able to pay its debts as they become due in the usual course of business.

(2) The registered limited liability partnership's total assets would be less than the sum of its total liabilities plus the amount that would be needed, if the registered limited liability partnership were to be dissolved at the time of the distribution, to satisfy the preferential rights of other partners upon dissolution that are superior to the rights of the partners receiving the distribution.

(b) A cause of action with respect to an obligation to return a distribution is extinguished unless the action is brought within four years after the distribution is made.

(c) A distribution for purposes of this section means the transfer of money or property by a registered limited liability partnership to its partners without consideration.

§ 16958. Foreign Partnership

(a)(1) The laws of the jurisdiction under which a foreign limited liability partnership is organized shall govern its organization and internal affairs and the liability and authority of its partners, subject to compliance with Section 16956, and

(2) a foreign limited liability partnership may not be denied registration by reason of any difference between those laws and the laws of this state.

(b) The name of a foreign limited liability partnership transacting intrastate business in this state shall contain the words "Registered Limited Liability Partnership" or "Limited Liability Partnership" or one of the abbreviations "L.L.P.," "LLP," "R.L.L.P.," or "RLLP," or such other similar words or abbreviations as may be required or authorized by the laws of the jurisdiction of formation of the foreign limited liability partnership, as the last words or letters of its name.

§ 16959.   Foreign Partnership Registration; Notice of Obligation to Pay Tax

(a) (1) Before transacting intrastate business in this state, a foreign limited liability partnership shall comply with all statutory and administrative registration or filing requirements of the state board, commission, or agency that prescribes the rules and regulations governing a particular profession in which the partnership proposes to be engaged, pursuant to the applicable provisions of the Business and Professions Code relating to the profession or applicable rules adopted by the governing board. A foreign limited liability partnership that transacts intrastate business in this state shall within 30 days after the effective date of the act enacting this section or the date on which the foreign limited liability partnership first transacts intrastate business in this state, whichever is later, register with the Secretary of State by submitting to the Secretary of State an application for registration as a foreign limited liability partnership, signed by a person with authority to do so under the laws of the jurisdiction of formation of the foreign limited liability partnership, stating the name of the partnership, the street address of its principal office, the mailing address of the principal office if different from the street address, the name and address of its agent for service of process in this state in accordance with subdivision (a) of Section 16309, a brief statement of the business in which the partnership engages, and any other matters that the partnership determines to include.

(2) Annexed to the application for registration shall be a certificate from an authorized public official of the foreign limited liability partnership's jurisdiction of organization to the effect that the foreign limited liability partnership is in good standing in that jurisdiction, if the laws of that jurisdiction permit the issuance of those certificates, or, in the alternative, a statement by the foreign limited liability partnership that the laws of its jurisdiction of organization do not permit the issuance of those certificates.

(b) The registration shall be accompanied by a fee as set forth in subdivision (b) of Section 12189 of the Government Code.

(c) The Secretary of State shall register as a foreign limited liability partnership any partnership that submits a completed application for registration with the required fee.

(d) The Secretary of State may cancel the filing of the registration if a check or other remittance accepted in payment of the filing fee is not paid upon presentation. Upon receiving written notification that the item presented for payment has not been honored for payment, the Secretary of State shall give a first written notice of the applicability of this section to the agent for service of process or to the person submitting the instrument. Thereafter, if the amount has not been paid by cashier's check or equivalent, the Secretary of State shall give a second written notice of cancellation and the cancellation shall thereupon be effective. The second notice shall be given 20 days or more after the first notice and 90 days or less after the original filing.

(e) A partnership becomes registered as a foreign limited liability partnership at the time of the filing of the initial registration with the Secretary of State or at any later date or time specified in the registration and the payment of the fee required by subdivision (b). A partnership continues to be registered as a foreign limited liability partnership until a notice that it is no longer so registered as a foreign limited liability partnership has been filed pursuant to Section 16960 or, if applicable, once it has been dissolved and finally wound up. The status of a partnership registered as a foreign limited liability partnership and the liability of a partner of that foreign limited liability partnership shall not be adversely affected by errors or subsequent changes in the information stated in an application for registration under subdivision (a) or an amended registration or notice under Section 16960.

(f) The fact that a registration or amended registration pursuant to Section 16960 is on file with the Secretary of State is notice that the partnership is a foreign limited liability partnership and of those other facts contained therein that are required to be set forth in the registration or amended registration.

(g) The Secretary of State shall provide a form for a registration under subdivision (a), which shall include the form for confirming compliance with the optional security requirement pursuant to subdivision (c) of Section 16956. The Secretary of State shall include with instructional materials, provided in conjunction with the form for registration under subdivision (a), a notice that filing the registration will obligate the limited liability partnership to pay an annual tax for that taxable year to the Franchise Tax Board pursuant to Section 17948 of the Revenue and Taxation Code. That notice shall be updated annually to specify the dollar amount of this tax.

(h) A foreign limited liability partnership transacting intrastate business in this state shall not maintain any action, suit, or proceeding in any court of this state until it has registered in this state pursuant to this section.

(i) Any foreign limited liability partnership that transacts intrastate business in this state without registration is subject to a penalty of twenty dollars ($20) for each day that unauthorized intrastate business is transacted, up to a maximum of ten thousand dollars ($10,000).

(j) A partner of a foreign limited liability partnership is not liable for the debts or obligations of the foreign limited liability partnership solely by reason of its having transacted business in this state without registration.

(k) A foreign limited liability partnership, transacting business in this state without registration, appoints the Secretary of State as its agent for service of process with respect to causes of action arising out of the transaction of business in this state.

(l) "Transact intrastate business" as used in this section means to repeatedly and successively provide professional limited liability partnership services in this state, other than in interstate or foreign commerce.

(m) Without excluding other activities that may not be considered to be transacting intrastate business, a foreign limited liability partnership shall not be considered to be transacting intrastate business merely because its subsidiary or affiliate transacts intrastate business, or merely because of its status as any one or more of the following:

(1) A shareholder of a domestic corporation.

(2) A shareholder of a foreign corporation transacting intrastate business.

(3) A limited partner of a foreign limited partnership transacting intrastate business.

(4) A limited partner of a domestic limited partnership.

(5) A member or manager of a foreign limited liability company transacting intrastate business.

(6) A member or manager of a domestic limited liability company.

(n) Without excluding other activities that may not be considered to be transacting intrastate business, a foreign limited liability partnership shall not be considered to be transacting intrastate business within the meaning of this subdivision solely by reason of carrying on in this state any one or more of the following activities:

(1) Maintaining or defending any action or suit or any administrative or arbitration proceeding, or effecting the settlement thereof or the settlement of claims or disputes.

(2) Holding meetings of its partners or carrying on any other activities concerning its internal affairs.

(3) Maintaining bank accounts.

(4) Maintaining offices or agencies for the transfer, exchange, and registration of the foreign limited liability partnership's securities or maintaining trustees or depositories with respect to those securities.

(5) Effecting sales through independent contractors.

(6) Soliciting or procuring orders, whether by mail or through employees or agents or otherwise, where those orders require acceptance without this state before becoming binding contracts.

(7) Creating or acquiring evidences of debt or mortgages, liens, or security interest in real or personal property.

(8) Securing or collecting debts or enforcing mortgages and security interests in property securing the debts.

(9) Conducting an isolated transaction that is completed within 180 days and not in the course of a number of repeated transactions of a like nature.

(o) A person shall not be deemed to be transacting intrastate business in this state merely because of its status as a partner of a registered limited liability partnership or a foreign limited liability company whether or not registered to transact intrastate business in this state.

(p) The Attorney General may bring an action to restrain a foreign limited liability partnership from transacting intrastate business in this state in violation of this chapter.

(q) Nothing in this section is intended to, or shall, augment, diminish, or otherwise alter existing provisions of law, statutes, or court rules relating to services by a California architect, California public accountant, California engineer, California land surveyor, or California attorney in another jurisdiction, or services by an out-of-state architect, out-of-state public accountant, out-of-state engineer, out-of-state land surveyor, or out-of-state attorney in California.

(r) This section shall remain in effect only until January 1, 2016, and as of that date is repealed, unless a later enacted statute, that is enacted before January 1, 2016, deletes or extends that date.

§ 16959.   *Foreign Partnership Registration; Notice of Obligation to Pay Tax (This section shall become operative on January 1, 2016.)*

(a) (1) Before transacting intrastate business in this state, a foreign limited liability partnership shall comply with all statutory and administrative registration or filing requirements of the state board, commission, or agency that prescribes the rules and regulations governing a particular profession in which the partnership proposes to be engaged, pursuant to the applicable provisions of the Business and Professions Code relating to the profession or applicable rules adopted by the governing board. A foreign limited liability partnership that transacts intrastate business in this state shall within 30 days after the effective date of the act enacting this section or the date on which the foreign limited liability partnership first transacts intrastate business in this state, whichever is later, register with the Secretary of State by submitting to the Secretary of State an application for registration as a foreign limited liability partnership, signed by a person with authority to do so under the laws of the jurisdiction of formation of the foreign limited liability partnership, stating the name of the partnership, the address of its principal office, the name and address of its agent for service of process in this state, a brief statement of the business in which the partnership engages, and any other matters that the partnership determines to include.

(2) Annexed to the application for registration shall be a certificate from an authorized public official of the foreign limited liability partnership's jurisdiction of organization to the effect that the foreign limited liability partnership is in good standing in that jurisdiction, if the laws of that jurisdiction permit the issuance of those certificates, or, in the alternative, a statement by the foreign limited liability partnership that the laws of its jurisdiction of organization do not permit the issuance of those certificates.

(b) The registration shall be accompanied by a fee as set forth in subdivision (b) of Section 12189 of the Government Code.

(c) The Secretary of State shall register as a foreign limited liability partnership any partnership that submits a completed application for registration with the required fee.

(d) The Secretary of State may cancel the filing of the registration if a check or other remittance accepted in payment of the filing fee is not paid upon presentation. Upon receiving written notification that the item presented for payment has not been honored for payment, the Secretary of State shall give a first written notice of the applicability of this section to the agent for service of process or to the person submitting the instrument. Thereafter, if the amount has not been paid by cashier's check or equivalent, the Secretary of State shall give a second written notice of cancellation and the cancellation shall thereupon be effective. The second notice shall be given 20 days or more after the first notice and 90 days or less after the original filing.

(e) A partnership becomes registered as a foreign limited liability partnership at the time of the filing of the initial registration with the Secretary of State or at any later date or time specified in the registration and the payment of the fee required by subdivision (b). A partnership continues to be registered as a foreign limited liability partnership until a notice that it is no longer so registered as a limited liability partnership has been filed pursuant to Section 16960 or, if applicable, once it has been dissolved and finally wound up. The status of a partnership registered as a foreign limited liability partnership and the liability of a partner of that foreign limited liability partnership shall not be adversely affected by errors or subsequent changes in the information stated in an application for registration under subdivision (a) or an amended registration or notice under Section 16960.

(f) The fact that a registration or amended registration pursuant to Section 16960 is on file with the Secretary of State is notice that the partnership is a foreign limited liability partnership and of those other facts contained therein that are required to be set forth in the registration or amended registration.

(g) The Secretary of State shall provide a form for a registration under subdivision (a), which shall include the form for confirming compliance with the optional security requirement pursuant to subdivision (c) of Section 16956. The Secretary of State shall include with instructional materials, provided in conjunction with the form for registration under subdivision (a), a notice that filing the registration will obligate the limited liability partnership to pay an annual tax for that taxable year to the Franchise Tax Board pursuant to Section 17948 of the Revenue and Taxation Code. That notice shall be updated annually to specify the dollar amount of this tax.

(h) A foreign limited liability partnership transacting intrastate business in this state shall not maintain any action, suit, or proceeding in any court of this state until it has registered in this state pursuant to this section.

(i) Any foreign limited liability partnership that transacts intrastate business in this state without registration is subject to a penalty of twenty dollars ($20) for each day that unauthorized intrastate business is transacted, up to a maximum of ten thousand dollars ($10,000).

(j) A partner of a foreign limited liability partnership is not liable for the debts or obligations of the foreign limited liability partnership solely by reason of its having transacted business in this state without registration.

(k) A foreign limited liability partnership, transacting business in this state without registration, appoints the Secretary of State as its agent for service of process with respect to causes of action arising out of the transaction of business in this state.

(l) "Transact intrastate business" as used in this section means to repeatedly and successively provide professional limited liability partnership services in this state, other than in interstate or foreign commerce.

(m) Without excluding other activities that may not be considered to be transacting intrastate business, a foreign limited liability partnership shall not be considered to be transacting intrastate business merely because its subsidiary or affiliate transacts intrastate business, or merely because of its status as any one or more of the following:

(1) A shareholder of a domestic corporation.

(2) A shareholder of a foreign corporation transacting intrastate business.

(3) A limited partner of a foreign limited partnership transacting intrastate business.

(4) A limited partner of a domestic limited partnership.

(5) A member or manager of a foreign limited liability company transacting intrastate business.

(6) A member or manager of a domestic limited liability company.

(n) Without excluding other activities that may not be considered to be transacting intrastate business, a foreign limited liability partnership shall not be considered to be transacting intrastate business within the meaning of this subdivision solely by reason of carrying on in this state any one or more of the following activities:

(1) Maintaining or defending any action or suit or any administrative or arbitration proceeding, or effecting the settlement thereof or the settlement of claims or disputes.

(2) Holding meetings of its partners or carrying on any other activities concerning its internal affairs.

(3) Maintaining bank accounts.

(4) Maintaining offices or agencies for the transfer, exchange, and registration of the foreign limited liability partnership's securities or maintaining trustees or depositories with respect to those securities.

(5) Effecting sales through independent contractors.

(6) Soliciting or procuring orders, whether by mail or through employees or agents or otherwise, where those orders require acceptance without this state before becoming binding contracts.

(7) Creating or acquiring evidences of debt or mortgages, liens, or security interest in real or personal property.

(8) Securing or collecting debts or enforcing mortgages and security interests in property securing the debts.

(9) Conducting an isolated transaction that is completed within 180 days and not in the course of a number of repeated transactions of a like nature.

(o) A person shall not be deemed to be transacting intrastate business in this state merely because of its status as a partner of a registered limited liability partnership or a foreign limited liability company whether or not registered to transact intrastate business in this state.

(p) The Attorney General may bring an action to restrain a foreign limited liability partnership from transacting intrastate business in this state in violation of this chapter.

(q) Nothing in this section is intended to, or shall, augment, diminish, or otherwise alter existing provisions of law, statutes, or court rules relating to services by a California architect, California public accountant, or California attorney in another jurisdiction, or services by an out-of-state architect, out-of-state public accountant, or out-of-state attorney in California.

(r) This section shall become operative on January 1, 2016.

§ 16960. Amendment of Registration of Foreign Partnership; Notice of Cessation of Existence; Withdrawal of Registration; Forms; Filing Fees

(a) The registration of a foreign limited partnership may be amended by an amended registration executed by one or more partners authorized to execute an amended registration and filed with the Secretary of State, as soon as reasonably practical after any information set forth in the registration or previously filed amended registration becomes inaccurate, to add information to the registration or amended registration or to withdraw its registration as a foreign limited liability partnership.

(b) If a foreign limited partnership ceases to be a limited liability partnership, it shall file with the Secretary of State a notice, executed by one or more partners authorized to execute the notice, that it is no longer a foreign limited liability partnership. The notice shall state that a final annual tax return, as described by Section 17948.3 of the Revenue and Taxation Code, has been or will be filed with the Franchise Tax Board, as required under Part 10.2 (commencing with Section 18401) of the Revenue and Taxation Code.

(c) A foreign limited liability partnership that is, but is no longer required to be, registered under Section 16959 may withdraw its registration by filing a notice with the Secretary of State, executed by one or more partners authorized to execute the notice.

(d) The Secretary of State shall provide forms for an amended registration under subdivision (a) and notices under subdivisions (b) and (c).

(e) The filing of amended registration forms pursuant to subdivision (a) and a notice pursuant to subdivision (b) or (c) shall each be accompanied by a fee as set forth in subdivision (d) of Section 12189 of the Government Code.

(f) A notice of cessation, signed pursuant to subdivision (b), shall be filed with the Secretary of State. The Secretary of State shall notify the Franchise Tax Board of the cessation.

§ 16961.   *Filings*

The filing of a registration with the Secretary of State under Section 16953 or 16959 shall make it unnecessary for all purposes for the registered limited liability partnership or foreign limited liability partnership to make any of the filings referred to in Chapter 5 (commencing with Section 17900) of Part 3 of Division 7 of the Business and Professions Code.

§ 16962.   *Agent for Service*

(a) Each registered limited liability partnership whose principal office is not in this state and each foreign limited liability partnership registered under Section 16959 shall designate as its agent for service of process any natural person or a domestic or foreign corporation entitled to be designated as agent for the service of process pursuant to Section 1505.

(b) In addition to service that may be made as provided in Section 416.40 of the Code of Civil Procedure, delivery by hand of a copy of any process against a registered limited liability partnership or foreign limited liability partnership registered under Section 16959 (1) to any natural person designated by it as agent or (2), if a corporate agent has been designated, to any person named in the latest certificate of the corporate agent filed pursuant to Section 1505 at the office of that corporate agent shall constitute valid service on the registered limited liability partnership or foreign limited liability partnership.

(c) If an agent for the purpose of service of process has resigned and has not been replaced or if the agent designated cannot with reasonable diligence be found at the address designated for personally delivering the process, or if no agent has been designated, and it is shown by affidavit to the satisfaction of the court that process against a registered limited liability partnership or foreign limited liability partnership required to be registered under Section 16959 cannot be served with reasonable diligence upon the designated agent by hand in the manner provided in Section 415.10, subdivision (a) of Section 415.20, or subdivision (a) of Section 415.30 of the Code of Civil Procedure or upon the registered limited liability partnership or foreign limited liability partnership in the manner provided in Section 416.40 of the Code of Civil Procedure, the court may make an order that the service be made upon the registered limited liability partnership or foreign limited liability partnership by delivering by hand to the

Secretary of State, or to any person employed in the Secretary of State's office in the capacity of assistant or deputy, one copy of the process for each defendant to be served, together with a copy of the order authorizing that service. If the court makes that order, the Secretary of State who receives the process, or the person employed in the Secretary of State's office in the capacity of assistant or deputy who receives the process, is required to accept the process. A fee as set forth in subdivision (b) of Section 12197 of the Government Code shall be paid to the Secretary of State for the use of the state upon receipt of the process. Service in this manner shall be deemed complete on the 10th day after delivery of the process to the Secretary of State.

(d) Upon the receipt of the copy of process and the fee therefor, the Secretary of State shall give notice of the service of process to the registered limited liability partnership or foreign limited liability partnership registered under Section 16959 at its principal executive office, by forwarding to that office, by registered mail with request for return receipt, the copy of the process or, if the records of the Secretary of State do not disclose an address for that principal executive office, by forwarding the copy in the same manner to the last designated agent for service of process who has not resigned. If the agent for service of process has resigned and has not been replaced and the records of the Secretary of State do not disclose an address for its principal executive office, no action need be taken by the Secretary of State.

(e) The Secretary of State shall keep a record of all process served upon the Secretary of State under this section and shall record therein the time of service and the Secretary of State's action with reference thereto. The certificate of the Secretary of State, under the Secretary of State's official seal, certifying to the receipt of process, the giving of notice thereof to the registered limited liability partnership or foreign limited liability partnership, and the forwarding of the process pursuant to this section shall be competent and prima facie evidence of the matters stated therein.

(f) The court order pursuant to subdivision (c) that service of process be made upon the registered limited liability partnership or foreign limited liability partnership by delivery to the Secretary of State may be a court order of a court of another state, or of any federal court, if the suit, action, or proceeding has been filed in that court.

DELAWARE CODE
TITLE 6.   COMMERCE AND TRADE
SUBTITLE II.   OTHER LAWS RELATING TO COMMERCE AND TRADE

CHAPTER 15.   DELAWARE REVISED UNIFORM PARTNERSHIP ACT
(6 DEL. C. §§ 15-101–15-1210)

SUBCHAPTER I.
GENERAL PROVISIONS

§ 15-101.   Definitions

As used in this chapter unless the context otherwise requires:

(1) "Business" includes every trade, occupation and profession, the holding or ownership of property and any other activity for profit.

(2) "Certificate" means a certificate of conversion to partnership under § 15-901 of this title, a certificate of conversion to a non-Delaware entity under § 15-903 of this title, a certificate of merger or consolidation or a certificate of ownership and merger under § 15-902 of this title, a certificate of partnership domestication under § 15-904 of this title, a certificate of transfer and a certificate of transfer and domestic continuance under § 15-905 of this title, a certificate of correction and a corrected certificate under § 15-118 of this title, and a certificate of termination of a certificate with a future effective date or time and a certificate of amendment of a certificate with a future effective date or time under § 15-105(i) of this title.

(3) "Debtor in bankruptcy" means a person who is the subject of:

(i) an order for relief under Title 11 of the United States Code or a comparable order under a successor statute of general application; or

(ii) a comparable order under State of Delaware federal, state or foreign law governing insolvency.

(4) "Distribution" means a transfer of money or other property from a partnership to a partner in the partner's capacity as a partner or to a transferee of all or a part of a partner's economic interest.

(5) "Domestic partnership" means an association of two or more persons formed under § 15-202 of this title or predecessor law to carry on any lawful business, purpose or activity.

(6) "Economic interest" means a partner's share of the profits and losses of a partnership and the partner's right to receive distributions.

(7) "Foreign limited liability partnership" means a partnership that:

(i) is formed under laws other than the laws of the State of Delaware; and

(ii) has the status of a limited liability partnership under those laws.

(8) "Limited liability partnership" means a domestic partnership that has filed a statement of qualification under § 15-1001 of this title.

(9) "Liquidating Trustee" means a person, other than a partner, carrying out the winding up of a partnership.

(10) "Partner" means a person who is admitted to a partnership as a partner of the partnership.

(11) "Partnership" means an association of two or more persons formed under § 15-202 of this title, predecessor law or comparable law of another jurisdiction to carry on any business, purpose or activity.

(12) "Partnership agreement" means the agreement, whether written, oral or implied, among the partners concerning the partnership, including amendments to the partnership agreement. A partnership is not required to execute its partnership agreement. A partnership is bound by its partnership agreement whether or not the partnership executes the partnership agreement. A partnership agreement is not subject to any statute of frauds (including § 2714 of this title). A partnership agreement may provide rights to any person, including a person who is not a party to the partnership agreement, to the extent set forth therein. A partner of a partnership or a transferee of an economic interest is bound by the partnership agreement whether or not the partner or transferee executes the partnership agreement.

(13) "Partnership at will" means a partnership that is not a partnership for a definite term or particular undertaking.

(14) "Partnership for a definite term or particular undertaking" means a partnership in which the partners have agreed to remain partners until the expiration of a definite term or the completion of a particular undertaking.

(15) "Partnership interest" or "partner's interest in the partnership" means all of a partner's interests in the partnership, including the partner's economic interest and all management and other rights.

(16) "Person" means a natural person, partnership (whether general or limited), limited liability company, trust (including a common law trust, business trust, statutory trust, voting trust or any other form of trust), estate, association (including any group, organization, co-tenancy, plan, board, council or committee), corporation, government (including a country, state, county or any other governmental subdivision, agency or instrumentality), custodian, nominee or any other individual or entity (or series thereof) in its own or any representative capacity, in each case, whether domestic or foreign.

(17) "Property" means all property, real, personal or mixed, tangible or intangible, or any interest therein.

(18) "State" means the District of Columbia or the Commonwealth of Puerto Rico or any state, territory, possession or other jurisdiction of the United States other than the State of Delaware.

(19) "Statement" means a statement of partnership existence under § 15-303 of this title, a statement of denial under § 15-304 of this title, a statement of dissociation under § 15-704 of this title, a statement of dissolution under § 15-805 of this title, a statement of qualification under § 15-1001 of this title, a statement of foreign qualification under § 15-1102 of this title, and an amendment or cancellation of any of the foregoing under § 15-105 of this title and a statement of correction and a corrected statement under § 15-118 of this title.

(20) "Transfer" includes an assignment, conveyance, lease, mortgage, deed, and encumbrance.

§ 15-102.   Knowledge and Notice

(a) A person knows a fact if the person has actual knowledge of it.

(b) A person has notice of a fact:

(1) if the person knows of it;

(2) if the person has received a notification of it;

(3) if the person has reason to know it exists from all of the facts known to the person at the time in question; or

(4) by reason of a filing or recording of a statement or certificate to the extent provided by and subject to the limitations set forth in this chapter.

(c) A person notifies or gives a notification to another by taking steps reasonably required to inform the other person in the ordinary course, whether or not the other person obtains knowledge of it.

(d) A person receives a notification when the notification:

(1) comes to the person's attention; or

(2) is received at the person's place of business or at any other place held out by the person as a place for receiving communications.

(e) Except as otherwise provided in subsection (f), a person other than an individual knows, has notice, or receives a notification of a fact for purposes of a particular transaction when the individual conducting the transaction knows, has notice, or receives a notification of the fact, or in any event when the fact would have been brought to the individual's attention if the person had exercised reasonable diligence. The person exercises reasonable diligence if it maintains reasonable routines for communicating significant information to the individual conducting the transaction and there is reasonable compliance with the routines. Reasonable diligence does not require an individual acting for the person to communicate information unless the communication is part of the individual's regular duties or the individual has reason to know of the transaction and that the transaction would be materially affected by the information.

(f) A partner's knowledge, notice or receipt of a notification of a fact relating to the partnership is effective immediately as knowledge by, notice to or receipt of a notification by the partnership, except in the case of a fraud on the partnership committed by or with the consent of that partner.

§ 15-103.   *Effect of Partnership Agreement; Nonwaivable Provisions*

(a) Except as otherwise provided in subsection (b), relations among the partners and between the partners and the partnership are governed by the partnership agreement. To the extent the partnership agreement does not otherwise provide, this chapter governs relations among the partners and between the partners and the partnership.

(b) The partnership agreement may not:

(1) Vary the rights and duties under Section 15-105 except to eliminate the duty to provide copies of statements to all of the partners;

(2) Restrict a partner's rights to obtain information as provided in § 15-403 of this title, except as permitted by § 15-403(f) of this title;

(3) Eliminate the implied contractual covenant of good faith and fair dealing;

(4) Vary the power to dissociate as a partner under Section 15-602(a), except to require the notice under Section 15-601(1) to be in writing;

(5) Vary the right of a court to expel a partner in the events specified in Section 15-601(5);

(6) Vary the requirement to wind up the partnership business in cases specified in § 15-801(4), (5) or (6) of this title;

(7) Vary the law applicable to a limited liability partnership under § 15-106(b) of this title; or

(8) Vary the denial of partnership power to issue a certificate of partnership interest in bearer form under § 15-503(h) of this title.

(c) Notwithstanding anything to the contrary contained in this section, §§ 15-201, 15-203 and 15-501 of this title may be modified only to the extent provided in a statement of partnership existence or a statement of qualification and in a partnership agreement.

(d) It is the policy of this chapter to give maximum effect to the principle of freedom of contract and to the enforceability of partnership agreements.

(e) A partner or other person shall not be liable to a partnership or to another partner or to another person that is a party to or is otherwise bound by a partnership agreement for breach of fiduciary duty for the partner's or other person's good faith reliance on the provisions of the partnership agreement.

(f) A partnership agreement may provide for the limitation or elimination of any and all liabilities for breach of contract and breach of duties (including fiduciary duties) of a partner or other person to a partnership or to another partner or to another person that is a party to or is otherwise bound by a partnership agreement; provided, that a partnership agreement may not limit or eliminate liability for any act or omission that constitutes a bad faith violation of the implied contractual covenant of good faith and fair dealing.

§ 15-104.   Supplemental Principles of Law

(a) In any case not provided for in this chapter, the rules of law and equity, including the law merchant, shall govern.

(b) No obligation of a partner to a partnership or to a partner of a partnership, arising under a partnership agreement or a separate agreement or writing, and no note, instruction or other writing evidencing any such obligation of a partner, shall be subject to the defense of usury, and no partner shall interpose the defense of usury with respect to any such obligation in any action. If an obligation to pay interest arises under this chapter and the rate is not specified, the rate is that specified in § 2301 of this title.

(c) Sections 9-406 and 9-408 of this title do not apply to any interest in a domestic partnership, including all rights, powers and interests arising under a partnership agreement or this chapter. This provision prevails over §§ 9-406 and 9-408 of this title.

§ 15-105.   Execution, Filing and Recording of Statements and Certificates

(a) A statement or certificate may be filed with the Secretary of State by delivery to the Secretary of State of the signed copy of the statement or of the certificate. A certified copy of a statement that is filed in an office in another state may be filed with the Secretary of State. Either filing in the State of Delaware has the effect provided in this chapter with respect to partnership property located in or transactions that occur in the State of Delaware.

(b) Only a certified copy of a filed statement recorded in the office for recording transfers of real property has the effect provided for recorded statements in this chapter.

(c) A statement or certificate filed by a partnership must be executed by at least 1 partner or by 1 or more authorized persons. Other statements or certificates must be executed by a partner or 1 or more authorized persons or, in the case of a certificate of conversion to partnership or a certificate of partnership domestication, by any person authorized to execute such certificate on behalf of the other entity or non-United States entity, respectively, except that a certificate of merger or consolidation filed by a surviving or resulting other business entity shall be executed by any person authorized to execute such certificate on behalf of such other business entity. The execution of a statement or certificate by a person who is authorized by this chapter to execute such statement or certificate constitutes an oath or affirmation, under the penalties of perjury in the third degree, that, to the best of such person's knowledge and belief, the facts stated therein are true. A person who executes a statement or a certificate as an agent or fiduciary need not exhibit evidence of his authority as a prerequisite to filing. Any signature on any statement or certificate authorized to be filed with the Secretary of State under any provision of this chapter may be a facsimile, a conformed signature or an electronically transmitted signature. Upon delivery of any statement or certificate, the Secretary of State shall record the date and time of its delivery. Unless the Secretary of State finds that any statement or certificate does not conform to law, upon receipt of all filing fees required by law the Secretary of State shall:

(1) Certify that the statement or certificate has been filed with the Secretary of State by endorsing upon the original statement or certificate the word "Filed", and the date and time of the filing. This endorsement is conclusive of the date and time of its filing in the absence of actual fraud. Except as provided in paragraph (c)(5) or (c)(6) of this section, such date and time of filing of a statement or certificate shall be the date and time of delivery of the statement or certificate;

(2) File and index the endorsed statement or certificate;

(3) Prepare and return to the person who filed it or the person's representative a copy of the signed statement or certificate similarly endorsed, and shall certify such copy as a true copy of the signed statement or certificate; and

(4) Cause to be entered such information from the statement or certificate as the Secretary of State deems appropriate into the Delaware Corporation Information System or any system which is a successor thereto in the office of the Secretary of State, and such information and a copy of such statement or certificate shall be permanently maintained as a public record on a suitable medium. The Secretary of State is authorized to grant direct access to such system to registered agents subject to the execution of an operating agreement between the Secretary of State and such registered agent. Any registered agent granted such access shall demonstrate the existence of policies to ensure that information entered into the system accurately reflects the content of statements or certificates in the possession of the registered agent at the time of entry.

(5) Upon request made upon or prior to delivery, the Secretary of State may, to the extent deemed practicable, establish as the date and time of filing of a statement or certificate a date and time after its delivery. If the Secretary

of State refuses to file any statement or certificate due to an error, omission or other imperfection, the Secretary of State may hold such statement or certificate in suspension, and in such event, upon delivery of a replacement statement or certificate in proper form for filing and tender of the required fees within 5 business days after notice of such suspension is given to the filer, the Secretary of State shall establish as the date and time of filing of such statement or certificate the date and time that would have been the date and time of filing of the rejected statement or certificate had it been accepted for filing. The Secretary of State shall not issue a certificate of good standing with respect to any partnership with a statement or certificate held in suspension pursuant to this subsection. The Secretary of State may establish as the date and time of filing of a statement or certificate the date and time at which information from such statement or certificate is entered pursuant to paragraph (c)(4) of this section if such statement or certificate is delivered on the same date and within 4 hours after such information is entered.

(6) If:

a. Together with the actual delivery of a statement or certificate and tender of the required fees, there is delivered to the Secretary of State a separate affidavit (which in its heading shall be designated as an affidavit of extraordinary condition) attesting, on the basis of personal knowledge of the affiant or a reliable source of knowledge identified in the affidavit, that an earlier effort to deliver such statement or certificate and tender such fees was made in good faith, specifying the nature, date and time of such good faith effort and requesting that the Secretary of State establish such date and time as the date and time of filing of such statement or certificate; or

b. Upon the actual delivery of a statement or certificate and tender of the required fees, the Secretary of State in his or her discretion provides a written waiver of the requirement for such an affidavit stating that it appears to the Secretary of State that an earlier effort to deliver such statement or certificate and tender such fees was made in good faith and specifying the date and time of such effort; and

c. The Secretary of State determines that an extraordinary condition existed at such date and time, that such earlier effort was unsuccessful as a result of the existence of such extraordinary condition, and that such actual delivery and tender were made within a reasonable period (not to exceed 2 business days) after the cessation of such extraordinary condition, then the Secretary of State may establish such date and time as the date and time of filing of such statement or certificate. No fee shall be paid to the Secretary of State for receiving an affidavit of extraordinary condition. For purposes of this subsection, an extraordinary condition means: any emergency resulting from an attack on, invasion or occupation by foreign military forces of, or disaster, catastrophe, war or other armed conflict, revolution or insurrection or rioting or civil commotion in, the United States or a locality in which the Secretary of State conducts its business or in which the good faith effort to deliver the statement or certificate and tender the required fees is made, or the immediate threat of any of the foregoing; or any malfunction or outage of the electrical or telephone service to the Secretary of State's office, or weather or other condition in or about a locality in which the Secretary of State conducts its business, as a result of which the Secretary of State's office is not open for the purpose of the filing of statements and certificates under this chapter or such filing cannot be effected without extraordinary effort. The Secretary of State may require such proof as it deems necessary to make the determination required under this subparagraph c. of this subdivision, and any such determination shall be conclusive in the absence of actual fraud. If the Secretary of State establishes the date and time of filing of a statement or certificate pursuant to this subsection, the date and time of delivery of the affidavit of extraordinary condition or the date and time of the Secretary of State's written waiver of such affidavit shall be endorsed on such affidavit or waiver and such affidavit or waiver, so endorsed, shall be attached to the filed statement or certificate to which it relates. Such filed statement or certificate shall be effective as of the date and time established as the date and time of filing by the Secretary of State pursuant to this subsection, except as to those persons who are substantially and adversely affected by such establishment and, as to those persons, the statement or certificate shall be effective from the date and time endorsed on the affidavit of extraordinary condition or written waiver attached thereto.

(d)(1) A person authorized by this chapter to file a statement or certificate may amend or cancel the statement or certificate by filing an amendment or cancellation that names the partnership, identifies the statement or certificate, and states the substance of the amendment or cancellation. A person authorized by this chapter to file a statement or certificate who becomes aware that such statement or certificate was false when made, or that any matter described in the statement or certificate has changed, making the statement or certificate false in any material respect, shall promptly amend the statement or certificate. Upon the filing of a statement or a certificate amending or correcting a statement or a certificate (or judicial decree of amendment) with the Secretary of State, or upon the future effective date or time of a statement or a certificate amending or correcting a statement or a certificate (or judicial decree thereof), as provided for therein, the statement or the certificate being corrected or amended shall be corrected or amended as set forth therein. Upon the filing of a statement of cancellation of a statement of partnership existence (or judicial decree thereof), or a certificate of merger or consolidation or a certificate of ownership and merger which acts as a statement of cancellation of a statement of partnership existence, or a certificate of transfer, or a certificate of conversion to a non-Delaware entity, or upon the future effective date or time of a statement of cancellation of a statement of partnership existence (or a judicial decree thereof) or of a certificate of merger or consolidation or a certificate of ownership and merger which acts as a statement of cancellation of a statement of partnership existence, or a certificate of transfer, or a certificate of conversion to a non-Delaware entity, as provided for therein, or as specified in § 15-111(d), § 15-111(i)(4) or § 15-1209(a) of this title, the statement of partnership existence is canceled. Neither the filing of a statement of cancellation to accomplish the cancellation of a statement of qualification nor the revocation of a statement of qualification pursuant to § 15-1003 of this title cancels a statement of partnership existence for such partnership. A statement of partnership existence shall be canceled upon the dissolution and the completion of winding up of the partnership, or as provided in § 15-111(d), § 15-111(i)(4) or § 15-1209(a) of this title, or upon the filing of a certificate of merger or consolidation or a certificate of ownership and merger if the domestic partnership is not the surviving or resulting entity in a merger or consolidation, or upon the filing of a certificate of transfer, or upon the filing of a certificate of conversion to a non-Delaware entity. A statement of cancellation shall be filed with the Secretary of State to accomplish the cancellation of a statement of partnership existence upon the dissolution and the completion of winding up of a domestic partnership and shall set forth:

a. The name of the partnership;

b. The date of filing of its statement of partnership existence; and

c. Any other information the person filing the statement of cancellation determines.

(2) The Secretary of State shall not issue a certificate of good standing with respect to a domestic partnership if its statement of partnership existence is canceled.

(3) Upon the filing of a statement of cancellation of a statement of qualification (or judicial decree thereof), or a certificate of merger or consolidation or a certificate of ownership and merger which acts as a statement of cancellation of a statement of qualification, or a certificate of transfer, or a certificate of conversion to a non-Delaware entity, or upon the future effective date or time of a statement of cancellation of a statement of qualification (or a judicial decree thereof) or of a certificate of merger or consolidation or a certificate of ownership and merger which acts as a statement of cancella-

tion of a statement of qualification, or a certificate of transfer, or a certificate of conversion to a non-Delaware entity, as provided for therein, or as specified in § 15-111(d) or § 15-111(i)(4) of this title, the statement of qualification is canceled. Neither the filing of a statement of cancellation to accomplish the cancellation of a statement of partnership existence nor the cancellation of a statement of partnership existence pursuant to § 15-1209(a) of this title cancels a statement of qualification for such partnership. A statement of qualification shall be canceled upon the dissolution and the completion of winding up of the limited liability partnership, or as provided in § 15-111(d) or § 15-111(i)(4) of this title, or upon the filing of a certificate of merger or consolidation or a certificate of ownership and merger if the limited liability partnership is not the surviving or resulting entity in a merger or consolidation, or upon the filing of a certificate of transfer, or upon the filing of a certificate of conversion to a non-Delaware entity. A statement of cancellation shall be filed with the Secretary of State to accomplish the cancellation of a statement of qualification upon the dissolution and the completion of winding up of a limited liability partnership and shall set forth:

    a. The name of the limited liability partnership;

    b. The date of filing of its statement of qualification; and

    c. Any other information the person filing the statement of cancellation determines.

(4) If a statement of cancellation of a statement of qualification is filed, either a statement of cancellation of the partnership's statement of partnership existence (if any) or an amendment to the partnership's statement of partnership existence (if any) removing the "Limited Liability Partnership", "L.L.P." or "LLP" designation from the name of the partnership shall be filed simultaneously with the filing of such statement of cancellation of the statement of qualification.

(5) Upon the filing of a certificate of partnership domestication, or upon the future effective date or time of a certificate of partnership domestication, the entity filing the certificate of partnership domestication is domesticated as a partnership with the effect provided in § 15-904 of this title. Upon the filing of a certificate of conversion to partnership, or upon the future effective date or time of a certificate of conversion to partnership, the entity filing the certificate of conversion to partnership is converted to a partnership with the effect provided in § 15-901 of this title. Upon the filing of a certificate of transfer and domestic continuance, or upon the future effective date or time of a certificate of transfer and domestic continuance, as provided for therein, the partnership filing the certificate of transfer and domestic continuance shall continue to exist as a partnership of the State of Delaware with the effect provided in § 15-905 of this title.

(e) A person who files a statement or certificate pursuant to this section shall promptly send a copy of the statement or certificate to every nonfiling partner and to any other person named as a partner in the statement or certificate. Failure to send a copy of a statement or certificate to a partner or other person does not limit the effectiveness of the statement or certificate as to a person not a partner.

(f) The filing of a statement of partnership existence under § 15-303, a statement of qualification under § 15-1001 or a statement of foreign qualification under § 15-1102 with the Secretary of State shall make it unnecessary to file any other document under Chapter 31 of this Title.

(g) A statement or certificate filed with the Secretary of State shall be effective if there has been substantial compliance with the requirements of this chapter.

(h) Notwithstanding any other provision of this chapter, any statement or certificate filed under this chapter shall be effective at the time of its filing with the Secretary of State or at any later date or time (not later than a time on the one hundred and eightieth day after the date of its filing if such date of filing is on or after January 1, 2012) specified in the statement or certificate.

(i) If any certificate filed in accordance with this chapter provides for a future effective date or time and if, prior to such future effective date or time set forth in such certificate, the transaction is terminated or its terms are amended to change the future effective date or time or any other matter described in such certificate so as to make such certificate false or inaccurate in any respect, such certificate shall, prior to the future effective date or time set forth in such certificate, be terminated or amended by the filing of a certificate of termination or certificate of amendment of such certificate, executed in the same manner as the certificate being terminated or amended is required to be executed in accordance with this section, which shall identify the certificate which has been terminated or amended and shall state that the certificate has been terminated or the manner in which it has been amended. Upon the filing of a certificate of amendment of a certificate with a future effective date or time, the certificate identified in such certificate of amendment is amended. Upon the filing of a certificate of termination of a certificate with a future effective date or time, the certificate identified in such certificate of termination is terminated.

(j) A fee as set forth in § 15-1207 of this title shall be paid at the time of the filing of a statement or a certificate.

(k) A fee as set forth in § 15-1207 of this title shall be paid for a certified copy of any paper on file as provided for by this chapter, and a fee as set forth in § 15-1207 of this title shall be paid for each page copied.

(l) Notwithstanding any other provision of this chapter, it shall not be necessary for any partnership (including a limited liability partnership) or foreign partnership to amend its statement of partnership existence, its statement of qualification (as applicable), its statement of foreign qualification, or any other document that has been filed with the Secretary of State prior to August 1, 2011, to comply with § 15-111(k) of this title; notwithstanding the foregoing, any statement or other document filed

under this chapter on or after August 1, 2011, and changing the address of a registered agent or registered office shall comply with § 15-111(k) of this title.

§ 15-106.   Governing Law

(a) Except as otherwise provided in subsection (b), the law of the jurisdiction
governing a partnership agreement governs relations among the partners and
between the partners and the partnership.

(b) The law of the State of Delaware governs relations among the partners
and between the partners and the partnership and the liability of partners for an
obligation of a limited liability partnership.

(c) If (i) a partnership agreement provides for the application of the laws of the
State of Delaware, and (ii) the partnership files with the Secretary of State a statement
of partnership existence or a statement of qualification, then the partnership agreement shall be governed by and construed under the laws of the State of Delaware.

§ 15-107.   Reserved Power of State of Delaware to Alter or Repeal Chapter

All provisions of this chapter may be altered from time to time or repealed and all
rights of partners are subject to this reservation. Unless expressly stated to the contrary
in this chapter, all amendments of this chapter shall apply to partnerships and partners
whether or not existing at the time of the enactment of any such amendment.

§ 15-108.   Name of Partnership

(a) The name of a partnership: (i) may contain the name of a partner and (ii)
may contain the following words: "Company," "Association," "Club," "Foundation," "Fund," "Institute," "Society," "Union," "Syndicate," "Trust" (or abbreviations of like import).

(b) The name of a limited liability partnership shall contain as the last words
or letters of its name the words "Limited Liability Partnership," the abbreviation
"L.L.P." or the designation "LLP."

(c) The name of a partnership to be included in the statement of partnership existence, statement of qualification or statement of foreign qualification filed by
such partnership must be such as to distinguish it upon the records in the office of
the Secretary of State from the name on such records of any corporation, partnership (including a limited liability partnership), limited partnership (including a
limited liability limited partnership), statutory trust or limited liability company
organized under the laws of the State of Delaware and reserved, registered, formed
or organized with the Secretary of State or qualified to do business and registered
as a foreign corporation, foreign limited liability partnership, foreign limited partnership, foreign statutory trust or foreign limited liability company in the State of

Delaware; provided, however, that a domestic partnership may be registered under any name which is not such as to distinguish it upon the records of the Secretary of State from the name on such records of any domestic or foreign corporation, limited partnership (including a limited liability limited partnership), statutory trust or limited liability company or foreign limited liability partnership reserved, registered, formed or organized under the laws of the State of Delaware with the written consent of the other corporation, limited partnership (including a limited liability limited partnership), statutory trust, limited liability company, or foreign limited liability partnership which written consent shall be filed with the Secretary of State; provided further, that, if on July 31, 2011, a domestic partnership is registered (with the consent of another domestic partnership) under a name which is not such as to distinguish it upon the records in the office of the Secretary of State from the name on such records of such other domestic partnership, it shall not be necessary for any such domestic partnership to amend its statement of partnership existence or statement of qualification to comply with this subsection.

(d) The name of a partnership shall not contain the word "bank," or any variation thereof, except for the name of a bank reporting to and under the supervision of the State Bank Commissioner of this State or a subsidiary of a bank or savings association (as those terms are defined in the Federal Deposit Insurance Act, as amended, at 12 U.S.C. § 1813), or a partnership regulated under the Bank Holding Company Act of 1956, as amended, 12 U.S.C. § 1841 et seq., or the Home Owners' Loan Act, as amended, 12 U.S.C. § 1461 et seq.; provided, however, that this section shall not be construed to prevent the use of the word "bank," or any variation thereof, in a context clearly not purporting to refer to a banking business or otherwise likely to mislead the public about the nature of the business of the partnership or to lead to a pattern and practice of abuse that might cause harm to the interests of the public or the State as determined by the Division of Corporations in the Department of State.

§ 15-109. Reservation of Name

(a) The exclusive right to use of a specified name in a statement using the specified name may be reserved by: (1) any person intending to organize a partnership under this chapter and to adopt that name; (2) any partnership or any foreign limited liability partnership registered in the State of Delaware which, in either case, proposes to change its name; (3) any foreign limited liability partnership intending to register in the State of Delaware and adopt that name; and (4) any person intending to organize a foreign limited liability partnership and intending to have it register in the State of Delaware and adopt that name.

(b) The reservation of a specified name shall be made by filing with the Secretary of State an application, executed by the applicant, specifying the name to be reserved and the name and address of the applicant. If the Secretary of State finds that the name is available for use, the Secretary shall reserve the name for exclusive use of the applicant in a statement using the specified name for a period of 120 days. Once having so reserved a name, the same applicant may again reserve the same name for successive 120 day periods. The right to the exclusive use of a reserved name in a statement using the specified name may be transferred to any other person by filing with the Secretary of State a notice of the transfer, executed by the applicant for whom the name was reserved, specifying the name to be transferred and the name and address of the transferee. The reservation of a specified name may be canceled by filing with the Secretary of State a notice of cancellation, executed by the applicant or transferee, specifying the name reservation to be canceled and the name and address of the applicant or transferee. Unless the Secretary of State finds that any application, notice of transfer or notice of cancellation filed with the Secretary of State as required by this subsection does not conform to law, upon receipt of all filing fees required by law, the Secretary shall prepare and return to the person who filed such instrument a copy of the filed instrument with a notation thereon of the action taken by the Secretary of State.

(c) A fee as set forth in Section 15-1207 of this chapter shall be paid at the time of the initial reservation of any name, at the time of the renewal of any such reservation and at the time of the filing of a notice of the transfer or cancellation of any such reservation.

§ 15-110.   Indemnification

Subject to such standards and restrictions, if any, as are set forth in its partnership agreement, a partnership may, and shall have the power to, indemnify and hold harmless any partner or other person from and against any and all claims and demands whatsoever.

§ 15-111.   Registered Office; Registered Agent

(a) Each partnership that files a statement of partnership existence, a statement of qualification or a statement of foreign qualification shall have and maintain in the State of Delaware:

(1) A registered office, which may but need not be a place of its business in the State of Delaware; and

(2) A registered agent for service of process on the partnership, having a business office identical with such registered office, which agent may be any of

a. The partnership itself,

b. An individual resident in the State of Delaware,

c. A domestic limited liability company, a domestic corporation, a domestic partnership (other than the partnership itself) (whether general (including a limited liability partnership) or limited (including a limited liability limited partnership)), or a domestic statutory trust, or

d. A foreign corporation, a foreign partnership (whether general (including a limited liability partnership) or limited (including a limited liability limited partnership)), a foreign limited liability company, or a foreign statutory trust.

(b) A registered agent may change the address of the registered office of the partnership(s) for which it is a registered agent to another address in the State of Delaware by paying a fee as set forth in § 15-1207 of this title and filing with the Secretary of State a certificate, executed by such registered agent, setting forth the address at which such registered agent has maintained the registered office for each of the partnerships for which it is a registered agent, and further certifying to the new address to which each such registered office will be changed on a given day, and at which new address such registered agent will thereafter maintain the registered office for each of the partnerships for which it is a registered agent. Upon the filing of such certificate, the Secretary of State shall furnish to the registered agent a certified copy of the same under the Secretary's hand and seal of office, and thereafter, or until further change of address as authorized by law, the registered office in the State of Delaware of each of the partnerships for which the agent is a registered agent shall be located at the new address of the registered agent thereof as given in the certificate. In the event of a change of name of any person acting as a registered agent of a partnership, such registered agent shall file with the Secretary of State a certificate, executed by such registered agent, setting forth the new name of such registered agent, the name of such registered agent before it was changed and the address at which such registered agent has maintained the registered office for each of the partnerships for which it is a registered agent, and shall pay a fee as set forth in § 15-1207 of this title. Upon the filing of such certificate, the Secretary of State shall furnish to the registered agent a certified copy of the certificate under his or her hand and seal of office. A change of name of any person acting as a registered agent of a partnership as a result of a merger or consolidation of the registered agent, with or into another person which succeeds to its assets and liabilities by operation of law, shall be deemed a change of name for purposes of this section. Filing a certificate under this section shall be deemed to be an amendment of the statement of partnership existence, statement of qualification or statement of foreign qualification of each partnership affected thereby and each such partnership shall not be required to take any further action, with respect thereto, to amend its statement of partnership existence, statement of qualification or statement of foreign qualification under § 15-105(d) of this title. Any registered agent filing a certificate under this section shall promptly, upon such filing, deliver a copy of any such certificate to each partnership affected thereby.

(c) The registered agent of 1 or more partnerships may resign and appoint a successor registered agent by paying a fee as set forth in § 15-1207 of this title and filing a certificate with the Secretary of State, stating the name and address of the successor registered agent. There shall be attached to such certificate a statement of each affected partnership ratifying and approving such change of registered agent. Upon such filing, the successor registered agent shall become the registered agent of such partnerships as have ratified and approved such substitution and the successor registered agent's address, as stated in such certificate, shall become the address of each such partnership's registered office in the State of Delaware. The Secretary of State shall then issue a certificate that the successor registered agent has become the registered agent of the partnerships so ratifying and approving such change and setting out the names of such partnerships. Filing of such certificate of resignation shall be deemed to be an amendment of the statement of partnership existence, statement of qualification or statement of foreign qualification of each partnership affected thereby and each such partnership shall not be required to take any further action with respect thereto to amend its statement of partnership existence, statement of qualification or statement of foreign qualification under § 15-105(d) of this title.

(d) The registered agent of 1 or more partnerships may resign without appointing a successor registered agent by paying a fee as set forth in § 15-1207 of this title and filing a certificate of resignation with the Secretary of State, but such resignation shall not become effective until 30 days after the certificate is filed. The certificate shall contain a statement that written notice of resignation was given to each affected partnership at least 30 days prior to the filing of the certificate by mailing or delivering such notice to the partnership at its address last known to the registered agent and shall set forth the date of such notice. After receipt of the notice of the resignation of its registered agent, the partnership for which such registered agent was acting shall obtain and designate a new registered agent to take the place of the registered agent so resigning. If such partnership fails to obtain and designate a new registered agent as aforesaid prior to the expiration of the period of 30 days after the filing by the registered agent of the certificate of resignation, the statement of partnership existence and statement of qualification (in each case as applicable) or statement of foreign qualification of such partnership shall be canceled. After the resignation of the registered agent shall have become effective as provided in this section and if no new registered agent shall have been obtained and designated in the time and manner aforesaid, service of legal process against each partnership for which the resigned registered agent had been acting shall thereafter be upon the Secretary of State in accordance with § 15-113 of this title.

(e) Every registered agent shall:

(1) If an entity, maintain a business office in the State of Delaware which is generally open, or if an individual, be generally present at a designated loca-

tion in the State of Delaware, at sufficiently frequent times to accept service of process and otherwise perform the functions of a registered agent;

(2) If a foreign entity, be authorized to transact business in the State of Delaware;

(3) Accept service of process and other communications directed to the partnerships for which it serves as registered agent and forward same to the partnership to which the service or communication is directed; and

(4) Forward to the partnerships for which it serves as registered agent the statement for the annual tax described in § 15-1208 of this title or an electronic notification of same in a form satisfactory to the Secretary of State.

(f) Any registered agent who at any time serves as registered agent for more than 50 entities (a "commercial registered agent"), whether domestic or foreign, shall satisfy and comply with the following qualifications.

(1) A natural person serving as a commercial registered agent shall:

a. Maintain a principal residence or a principal place of business in the State of Delaware;

b. Maintain a Delaware business license;

c. Be generally present at a designated location within the State of Delaware during normal business hours to accept service of process and otherwise perform the functions of a registered agent as specified in subsection (e) of this section; and

d. Provide the Secretary of State upon request with such information identifying and enabling communication with such commercial registered agent as the Secretary of State shall require.

(2) A domestic or foreign corporation, a domestic or foreign partnership (whether general (including a limited liability partnership) or limited (including a limited liability limited partnership)), a domestic or foreign limited liability company, or a domestic or foreign statutory trust serving as a commercial registered agent shall:

a. Have a business office within the State of Delaware which is generally open during normal business hours to accept service of process and otherwise perform the functions of a registered agent as specified in subsection (e) of this section;

b. Maintain a Delaware business license;

c. Have generally present at such office during normal business hours an officer, director or managing agent who is a natural person; and

d. Provide the Secretary of State upon request with such information identifying and enabling communication with such commercial registered agent as the Secretary of State shall require.

(3) For purposes of this subsection and paragraph (i)(2)a. of this section, a "commercial registered agent" shall also include any registered agent which has an officer, director or managing agent in common with any other

registered agent or agents if such registered agents at any time during such common service as officer, director or managing agent collectively served as registered agents for more than 50 entities, whether domestic or foreign.

(g) Every partnership formed under the laws of the State of Delaware or qualified to do business in the State of Delaware that has and maintains a registered agent pursuant to this section shall provide to its registered agent update from time to time as necessary the name, business address and business telephone number of a natural person who is a partner, officer, employee or designated agent of the partnership, who is then authorized to receive communications from the registered agent. Such person shall be deemed the communications contact for the partnership. Every registered agent shall retain (in paper or electronic form) the above information concerning the current communications contact for each partnership for which he, she, or it serves as registered agent. If the partnership fails to provide the registered agent with a current communications contact, the registered agent may resign as the registered agent for such partnership pursuant to this section.

(h) The Secretary of State is authorized to issue such rules and regulations as may be necessary or appropriate to carry out the enforcement of subsections (e), (f) and (g) of this section, and to take actions reasonable and necessary to assure registered agents' compliance with subsections (e), (f) and (g) of this section. Such actions may include refusal to file documents submitted by a registered agent.

(i) Upon application of the Secretary of State, the Court of Chancery may enjoin any person or entity from serving as a registered agent or as an officer, director or managing agent of a registered agent.

(1) Upon the filing of a complaint by the Secretary of State pursuant to this section, the court may make such orders respecting such proceeding as it deems appropriate, and may enter such orders granting interim or final relief as it deems proper under the circumstances.

(2) Any 1 or more of the following grounds shall be a sufficient basis to grant an injunction pursuant to this section:

a. With respect to any registered agent who at any time within 1 year immediately prior to the filing of the Secretary of State's complaint is a commercial registered agent, failure after notice and warning to comply with the qualifications set forth in subsection (e) of this section and/or the requirements of subsection (f) or (g) of this section above;

b. The person serving as a registered agent, or any person who is an officer, director or managing agent of an entity registered agent, has been convicted of a felony or any crime which includes an element of dishonesty or fraud or involves moral turpitude; or

c. The registered agent has engaged in conduct in connection with acting as a registered agent that is intended to or likely to deceive or defraud the public.

(3) With respect to any order the court enters pursuant to this section with respect to an entity that has acted as a registered agent, the court may also direct such order to any person who has served as an officer, director or managing agent of such registered agent. Any person who, on or after January 1, 2007, serves as an officer, director or managing agent of an entity acting as a registered agent in the State of Delaware shall be deemed thereby to have consented to the appointment of such registered agent as agent upon whom service of process may be made in any action brought pursuant to this section, and service as an officer, director or managing agent of an entity acting as a registered agent in the State of Delaware shall be a signification of the consent of such person that any process when so served shall be of the same legal force and validity as if served upon such person within the State of Delaware, and such appointment of the registered agent shall be irrevocable.

(4) Upon the entry of an order by the court enjoining any person or entity from acting as a registered agent, the Secretary of State shall mail or deliver notice of such order to each affected partnership:

a. That has specified the address of a place of business in a record of the Secretary of State, to the address specified, or

b. To an address which the Secretary of State has obtained from the partnership's former registered agent, to the address obtained.

If such a partnership is a domestic partnership and fails to obtain and designate a new registered agent within 30 days after such notice is given, the statement of partnership existence and statement of qualification of such partnership (in each case as applicable) shall be canceled. If such a partnership is a foreign limited liability partnership and fails to obtain and designate a new registered agent within 30 days after such notice is given, such foreign limited liability partnership shall not be permitted to do business in the State of Delaware and its statement of foreign qualification shall be canceled. If any other affected partnership is a domestic partnership and fails to obtain and designate a new registered agent within 60 days after entry of an order by the court enjoining such partnership's registered agent from acting as a registered agent, the statement of partnership existence and statement of qualification of such partnership (in each case as applicable) shall be canceled. If any other affected partnership is a foreign limited liability partnership and fails to obtain and designate a new registered agent within 60 days after entry of an order by court enjoining such partnership's registered agent from acting as a registered agent, such foreign limited liability partnership shall not be permitted to do business in the State of Delaware and its statement of foreign qualification shall be canceled. If the court enjoins a person or entity from acting as a registered agent as provided in this section and no new registered agent shall have been obtained and designated in the time and manner aforesaid, service of legal process against the partnership for which the registered agent had been acting shall thereafter be upon the Secretary of State in accordance with § 15-113 of this title. The Court of Chancery may, upon application of the Secretary of State on notice to the former registered agent, enter such orders as it deems appropriate to give the Secretary of State access to information in the former registered agent's possession in order to facilitate communication with the partnerships the former registered agent served.

(j) The Secretary of State is authorized to make a list of registered agents available to the public, and to establish such qualifications and issue such rules and regulations with respect to such listing as the Secretary of State deems necessary or appropriate.

(k) As contained in any statement of partnership existence, statement of qualification, statement of foreign qualification, or other document filed with the Secretary of State under this chapter, the address of a registered agent or registered office shall include the street, number, city and postal code.

§ 15-112. *Service of Process on Partnership Filing a Statement*

(a) Service of legal process upon any partnership which has filed a statement of partnership existence, a statement of qualification or a statement of foreign qualification shall be made by delivering a copy personally to any partner of the partnership in the State of Delaware or any partner who signed a statement of partnership existence, a statement of qualification or a statement of foreign qualification or the registered agent of the partnership in the State of Delaware or by leaving it at the dwelling house or usual place of abode in the State of Delaware of any such partner or registered agent (if the registered agent be an individual), or at the registered office or any place of business of the partnership in the State of Delaware. Service by copy left at the dwelling house or usual place of abode of a partner, registered agent, or at the registered office or any place of business of the partnership in the State of Delaware, to be effective, must be delivered thereat at least 6 days before the return date of the process, and in the presence of an adult person, and the officer serving the process shall distinctly state the manner of service in the return thereto. Process returnable forthwith must be delivered personally to the partner or registered agent.

(b) In case the officer whose duty it is to serve legal process cannot by due diligence serve the process in any manner provided for by subsection (a) of this section, it shall be lawful to serve the process against the partnership upon the

Secretary of State, and such service shall be as effectual for all intents and purposes as if made in any of the ways provided for in subsection (a) of this section. Process may be served upon the Secretary of State under this subsection by means of electronic transmission but only as prescribed by the Secretary of State. The Secretary of State is authorized to issue such rules and regulations with respect to such service as the Secretary of State deems necessary or appropriate. In the event that service is effected through the Secretary of State in accordance with this subsection, the Secretary of State shall forthwith notify the partnership by letter, directed to the partnership at the address of any partner as it appears on the records relating to such partnership on file with the Secretary of State or, if no such address appears, at the last registered office. Such letter shall be sent by a mail or courier service that includes a record of mailing or deposit with the courier and a record of delivery evidenced by the signature of the recipient. Such letter shall enclose a copy of the process and any other papers served on the Secretary of State pursuant to this subsection. It shall be the duty of the plaintiff in the event of such service to serve process and any other papers in duplicate, to notify the Secretary of State that service is being effected pursuant to this subsection, and to pay the Secretary of State the sum of $50 for the use of the State of Delaware, which sum shall be taxed as part of the costs in the proceeding if the plaintiff shall prevail therein. The Secretary of State shall maintain an alphabetical record of any such service setting forth the name of the plaintiff and defendant, the title, docket number and nature of the proceeding in which process has been served upon him, the fact that service has been effected pursuant to this subsection, the return date thereof, and the day and hour when the service was made. The Secretary of State shall not be required to retain such information for a period longer than 5 years from receipt of the service of process.

§ 15-113.   *Service of Process on a Partnership Not Filing a Statement*

(a) Service of legal process upon any partnership which has not filed a statement of partnership existence, a statement of qualification or a statement of foreign qualification and which is formed under the laws of the State of Delaware or doing business in the State of Delaware shall be made by delivering a copy personally to any partner doing business in the State of Delaware or by leaving it at the dwelling house or usual place of abode in the State of Delaware of a partner or at a place of business of the partnership in the State of Delaware. Service by copy left at the dwelling house or usual place of abode of a partner or at a place of business of the partnership in the State of Delaware, to be effective, must be delivered thereat at least 6 days before the return date of the process, and in the presence of an adult person, and the officer serving the process shall distinctly state the manner of service in the return thereto. Process returnable forthwith must be delivered personally to the partner.

(b) In case the officer whose duty it is to serve legal process cannot by due diligence serve the process in any manner provided for by subsection (a) of this section, it shall be lawful to serve the process against the partnership upon the Secretary of State, and such service shall be as effectual for all intents and purposes as if made in any of the ways provided for in subsection (a) of this section. Process may be served upon the Secretary of State under this subsection by means of electronic transmission but only as prescribed by the Secretary of State. The Secretary of State is authorized to issue such rules and regulations with respect to such service as the Secretary of State deems necessary or appropriate. In the event that service is effected through the Secretary of State in accordance with this subsection, the Secretary of State shall forthwith notify the partnership by letter, directed to the partnership at the address of any partner or the partnership as it is furnished to the Secretary of State by the person desiring to make service. Such letter shall be sent by a mail or courier service that includes a record of mailing or deposit with the courier and a record of delivery evidenced by the signature of the recipient. Such letter shall enclose a copy of the process and any other papers served on the Secretary of State pursuant to this subsection. It shall be the duty of the plaintiff in the event of such service to serve process and any other papers in duplicate, to notify the Secretary of State that service is being effected pursuant to this subsection, and to pay the Secretary of State the sum of $50 for the use of the State of Delaware, which sum shall be taxed as part of the costs on the proceeding if the plaintiff shall prevail therein. The Secretary of State shall maintain an alphabetical record of any such service setting forth the name of the plaintiff and defendant, the title, docket number and nature of the proceeding in which process has been served upon the Secretary of State, the fact that service has been effected pursuant to this subsection, the return date thereof, and the day and hour when the service was made. The Secretary of State shall not be required to retain such information for a period longer than 5 years from the Secretary of State's receipt of the service of process.

§ 15-114. *Service of Process on a Partner and Liquidating Trustee*

(a) A partner or a liquidating trustee of a partnership which is formed under the laws of the State of Delaware or doing business in the State of Delaware may be served with process in the manner prescribed in this section in all civil actions or proceedings brought in the State of Delaware involving or relating to the business of the partnership or a violation by the partner or the liquidating trustee of a duty to the partnership or any partner of the partnership, whether or not the partner or the liquidating trustee is a partner or a liquidating trustee at the time suit is commenced. A person who is at the time of the effectiveness of this section or who becomes a partner or a liquidating trustee of a partnership thereby consents to the appointment of the registered agent of the partnership (or, if there is none, the Secretary of State) as such person's agent upon whom service of process may be made as provided in this section. Any process when so served shall be of the same legal force and validity as if served upon such partner or liquidating trustee within the State of Delaware and such appointment of the registered agent (or, if there is none, the Secretary of State) shall be irrevocable.

(b) Service of process shall be effected by serving the registered agent (or, if there is none, the Secretary of State) with 1 copy of such process in the manner provided by law for service of writs of summons. In the event service is made under this subsection upon the Secretary of State, the plaintiff shall pay to the Secretary of State the sum of $50 for the use of the State of Delaware, which sum shall be taxed as part of the costs of the proceeding if the plaintiff shall prevail therein. In addition, the Prothonotary or the Register in Chancery of the court in which the civil action or proceeding is pending shall, within 7 days of such service, deposit in the United States mails, by registered mail, postage prepaid, true and attested copies of the process, together with a statement that service is being made pursuant to this section, addressed to such partner or liquidating trustee at the partner's or liquidating trustee's address furnished to the Prothonotary or Register in Chancery by the person desiring to make service, which address shall be the partner's or the liquidating trustee's address as the same appears in any statement of the partnership or, if no such address appears, the partner's or the liquidating trustees's last known address.

(c) In any action in which any such partner or liquidating trustee has been served with process as hereinabove provided, the time in which a defendant shall be required to appear and file a responsive pleading shall be computed from the date of mailing by the Prothonotary or the Register in Chancery as provided in subsection (b) of the section; however, the court in which such action has been commenced may order such continuance or continuances as may be necessary to afford such partner or liquidating trustee reasonable opportunity to defend the action.

(d) In a written partnership agreement or other writing, a partner may consent to be subject to the nonexclusive jurisdiction of the courts of, or arbitration in, a specified jurisdiction, or the exclusive jurisdiction of the courts of the State of Delaware, or the exclusivity of arbitration in a specified jurisdiction or the State of Delaware, and to be served with legal process in the manner prescribed in such partnership agreement or other writing.

(e) Nothing herein contained limits or affects the right to serve process in any other manner now or hereafter provided by law. This section is an extension of and not a limitation upon the right otherwise existing of service of legal process upon nonresidents.

(f) The Court of Chancery and the Superior Court may make all necessary rules respecting the form of process, the manner of issuance and return thereof and such other rules which may be necessary to implement this section and are not inconsistent with this section.

§ 15-115.   *Doing Business*

A limited partnership, a partnership, a limited liability company, a business or other trust or association, or a corporation formed or organized under the laws of any foreign country or other foreign jurisdiction or the laws of any state shall not be deemed to be doing business in the State of Delaware solely by reason of its being a partner in a domestic partnership.

§ 15-116.   *Restated Statement of Partnership Existence*

(a) A statement of partnership existence may be restated by integrating into a single instrument all of the provisions of the statement of partnership existence which are then in effect and operative as a result of there having been theretofore filed 1 or more amendments pursuant to Section 15-105(d) or other instruments having the effect of amending a statement of partnership existence and the statement of partnership existence may be amended or further amended by the filing of a restated statement of partnership existence. The restated statement of partnership existence shall be specifically designated as such in its heading and shall set forth:

    (1) The present name of the partnership, and if it has been changed, the name under which the partnership was originally formed;

    (2) The date of filing of the original statement of partnership existence with the Secretary of State;

    (3) The information required to be included pursuant to Section 15-303(a); and

    (4) Any other information desired to be included therein.

(b) Upon the filing of the restated statement of partnership existence with the Secretary of State, or upon the future effective date or time of a restated statement of partnership existence as provided for therein, the initial statement of partnership existence, as theretofore amended, shall be superseded; thenceforth, the restated statement of partnership existence, including any further amendment made thereby, shall be the statement of partnership existence of the partnership, but the original date of formation of the partnership shall remain unchanged.

(c) Any amendment effected in connection with the restatement of the statement of partnership existence shall be subject to any other provision of this chapter, not inconsistent with this section, which would apply if a separate amendment were filed to effect such amendment.

§ 15-117.   *Execution, Amendment or Cancellation by Judicial Order*

(a) If a person required by this chapter to execute any statement or certificate fails or refuses to do so, any other person who is adversely affected by the failure or refusal may petition the Court of Chancery to direct the execution of the statement or certificate. If the Court finds that the execution of the statement or certificate is proper and that any person so designated has failed or refused to execute the statement or certificate, the Court shall order the Secretary of State to file an appropriate statement or certificate.

(b) If a person required to execute a partnership agreement or amendment thereof fails or refuses to do so, any other person who is adversely affected by the failure or refusal may petition the Court of Chancery to direct the execution of the partnership agreement or amendment thereof. If the Court finds that the partnership agreement or amendment thereof should be executed and that any person so designated has failed or refused to do so, the Court shall enter an order granting appropriate relief.

§ 15-118.   Statement or Certificate of Correction; Corrected Statement or Certificate

(a) Whenever any statement or certificate authorized to be filed with the Secretary of State under any provision of this chapter has been so filed and is an inaccurate record of the action therein referred to, or was defectively or erroneously executed, such statement or certificate may be corrected by filing with the Secretary of State a statement or certificate of correction of such statement or certificate. The statement or certificate of correction shall specify the inaccuracy or defect to be corrected, shall set forth the portion of the statement or certificate in corrected form and shall be executed and filed as required by this chapter. The statement or certificate of correction shall be effective as of the date the original statement or certificate was filed, except as to those persons who are substantially and adversely affected by the correction, and as to those persons the statement or certificate of correction shall be effective from the filing date.

(b) In lieu of filing a statement or certificate of correction, a statement or certificate may be corrected by filing with the Secretary of State a corrected statement or certificate which shall be executed and filed as if the corrected statement or certificate were the statement or certificate being corrected, and a fee equal to the fee payable to the Secretary of State if the statement or certificate being corrected were then being filed shall be paid to and collected by the Secretary of State for the use of the State of Delaware in connection with the filing of the corrected statement or certificate. The corrected statement or certificate shall be specifically designated as such in its heading, shall specify the inaccuracy or defect to be corrected, and shall set forth the entire statement or certificate in corrected form. A statement or certificate corrected in accordance with this section shall be effective as of the date the original statement or certificate was filed, except as to those persons who are substantially and adversely affected by the correction and as to those persons the statement or certificate as corrected shall be effective from the filing date.

§ 15-119.   Business Transactions of Partner with the Partnership

Except as provided in the partnership agreement, a partner may lend money to, borrow money from, act as a surety, guarantor or endorser for, guarantee or assume 1 or more specific obligations of, provide collateral for and transact other business with, the partnership and, subject to other applicable law, has the same rights and obligations with respect thereto as a person who is not a partner.

§ 15-120.   Contractual Appraisal Rights

A partnership agreement or an agreement of merger or consolidation or a plan of merger may provide that contractual appraisal rights with respect to a partnership interest or another interest in a partnership shall be available for any class or group of partners or partnership interests in connection with any amendment of a partnership agreement, any merger or consolidation in which the partnership is a constituent party to the merger or consolidation, any conversion of the partnership to another business form, any transfer to or domestication or continuance in any jurisdiction by the partnership, or the sale of all or substantially all of the partnership's assets. The Court of Chancery shall have jurisdiction to hear and determine any matter relating to any such appraisal rights.

§ 15-121.   Contested Matters Relating to Partners; Contested Votes

(a) Upon application of any partner of a partnership which is formed under the laws of the State of Delaware or doing business in the State of Delaware, the Court of Chancery may hear and determine the validity of any admission, election, appointment or dissociation of a partner of the partnership, and the right of any person to become or continue to be a partner of the partnership, and to that end make such order or decree in any such case as may be just and proper, with power to enforce the production of any books, papers and records relating to the issue. In any such application, the partnership shall be named as a party, and service of copies of the application upon the partnership shall be deemed to be service upon the partnership and upon the person or persons whose right to be a partner is contested and upon the person or persons, if any, claiming to be a partner or claiming the right to be a partner; and the person upon whom service is made shall forward immediately a copy of the application to the partnership and to the person or persons whose right to be a partner is contested and to the person or persons, if any, claiming to be a partner or the right to be a partner, in a postpaid, sealed, registered letter addressed to such partnership and such person or persons at their post-office addresses last known to the person upon whom service is made or furnished to the person upon whom service is made by the applicant partner. The Court may make such order respecting further or other notice of such application as it deems proper under the circumstances.

(b) Upon application of any partner of a partnership which is formed under the laws of the State of Delaware or doing business in the State of Delaware, the Court of Chancery may hear and determine the result of any vote of partners upon matters as to which the partners of the partnership, or any class or group of partners, have the right to vote pursuant to the partnership agreement or other agreement or this chapter (other than the admission, election, appointment or dissociation of partners). In any such application, the partnership shall be named as a party, and service of the application upon the person upon whom service is made shall be deemed to be service upon the partnership, and no other party need be joined in order for the Court to adjudicate the result of the vote. The Court may make such order respecting further or other notice of such application as it deems proper under the circumstances.

(c) Nothing herein contained limits or affects the right to serve process in any other manner now or hereafter provided by law. This section is an extension of and not a limitation upon the right otherwise existing of service of legal process upon nonresidents.

§ 15-122. Interpretation and Enforcement of Partnership Agreement

Any action to interpret, apply or enforce the provisions of a partnership agreement of a partnership which is formed under the laws of the State of Delaware or doing business in the State of Delaware, or the duties, obligations or liabilities of such partnership to the partners of the partnership, or the duties, obligations or liabilities among partners or of partners to such partnership, or the rights or powers of, or restrictions on, such partnership or partners, or any provision of this chapter, or any other instrument, document, agreement or certificate contemplated by any provision of this chapter, including actions authorized by § 15-405 of this title, may be brought in the Court of Chancery.

§ 15-123. Irrevocable Power of Attorney

For all purposes of the laws of the State of Delaware, a power of attorney with respect to matters relating to the organization, internal affairs or termination of a partnership or granted by a person as a partner or a transferee of an economic interest or by a person seeking to become a partner or a transferee of an economic interest shall be irrevocable if it states that it is irrevocable and it is coupled with an interest sufficient in law to support an irrevocable power. Such irrevocable power of attorney, unless otherwise provided therein, shall not be affected by subsequent death, disability, incapacity, dissolution, termination of existence or bankruptcy of, or any other event concerning, the principal. A power of attorney with respect to matters relating to the organization, internal affairs or termination of a partnership or granted by a person as a partner or a transferee of an economic interest or by a person seeking to become a partner or a transferee of an economic interest and, in either case, granted to the partnership, a partner thereof, or any of their respective officers, directors, managers, members, partners, trustees, employees or agents shall be deemed coupled with an interest sufficient in law to support an irrevocable power.

SUBCHAPTER II.
NATURE OF PARTNERSHIP

§ 15-201.   *Partnership as Entity*

(a) A partnership is a separate legal entity which is an entity distinct from its partners unless otherwise provided in a statement of partnership existence or a statement of qualification and in a partnership agreement.

(b) A limited liability partnership continues to be the same partnership that existed before the filing of a statement of qualification under § 15-1001 of this title.

§ 15-202.   *Formation of Partnership; Powers*

(a) Except as otherwise provided in subsection (b), the association of two or more persons (i) to carry on as co-owners a business for profit forms a partnership, whether or not the persons intend to form a partnership, and (ii) to carry on any purpose or activity not for profit, forms a partnership when the persons intend to form a partnership. A limited liability partnership is for all purposes a partnership.

(b) Subject to § 15-1206 of this title, an association formed under a statute other than (i) this chapter, (ii) a predecessor statute or (iii) a comparable statute of another jurisdiction, is not a partnership under this chapter.

(c) In determining whether a partnership is formed under Section 15-202(a)(i), the following rules apply:

(1) Joint tenancy, tenancy in common, tenancy by the entireties, joint property, common property or part ownership does not by itself establish a partnership, even if the co-owners share profits made by the use of the property.

(2) The sharing of gross returns does not by itself establish a partnership, even if the persons sharing them have a joint or common right or interest in property from which the returns are derived.

(3) A person who receives a share of the profits of a business is presumed to be a partner in the business, unless the profits were received in payment:

    (i) of a debt by installments or otherwise;

    (ii) for services as an independent contractor or of wages or other compensation to an employee;

    (iii) of rent;

    (iv) of an annuity or other retirement or health benefit to a beneficiary, representative or designee of a deceased or retired partner;

    (v) of interest or other charge on a loan, even if the amount of payment varies with the profits of the business, including a direct or indirect present or future ownership of the collateral, or rights to income, proceeds or increase in value derived from the collateral; or

    (vi) for the sale of the goodwill of a business or other property by installments or otherwise.

(d) A partnership shall possess and may exercise all the powers and privileges granted by this chapter or by any other law or by its partnership agreement, together with any powers incidental thereto, including such powers and privileges as are necessary or convenient to the conduct, promotion or attainment of the business, purposes or activities of the partnership.

(e) Notwithstanding any provision of this chapter to the contrary, without limiting the general powers enumerated in subsection (d) of this section, a partnership shall, subject to such standards and restrictions, if any, as are set forth in its partnership agreement, have the power and authority to make contracts of guaranty and suretyship and enter into interest rate, basis, currency, hedge or other swap agreements or cap, floor, put, call, option, exchange or collar agreements, derivative agreements, or other agreements similar to any of the foregoing.

(f) Unless otherwise provided in a partnership agreement, a partnership has the power and authority to grant, hold or exercise a power of attorney, including an irrevocable power of attorney.

§ 15-203. *Partnership Property*

Unless otherwise provided in a statement of partnership existence or a statement of qualification and in a partnership agreement, property acquired by a partnership is property of the partnership and not of the partners individually.

§ 15-204.   When Property Is Partnership Property

(a) Property is partnership property if acquired in the name of:
(1) the partnership; or
(2) one or more persons with an indication in the instrument transferring title to the property of the person's capacity as a partner or of the existence of a partnership but without an indication of the name of the partnership.
(b) Property is acquired in the name of the partnership by a transfer to:
(1) the partnership in its name; or
(2) one or more persons in their capacity as partners in the partnership, if the name of the partnership is indicated in the instrument transferring title to the property.
(c) Property is presumed to be partnership property if purchased with partnership assets, even if not acquired in the name of the partnership or of one or more persons with an indication in the instrument transferring title to the property of the person's capacity as a partner or of the existence of a partnership.
(d) Property acquired in the name of one or more persons, without an indication in the instrument transferring title to the property of the person's capacity as a partner or of the existence of a partnership and without use of partnership assets, is presumed to be separate property, even if used for partnership purposes.

§ 15-205.   Admission Without Contribution or Partnership Interest

Each person to be admitted as a partner to a partnership formed under either § 15-202(a)(i) or § 15-202(a)(ii) of this title may be admitted as a partner and may receive a partnership interest in the partnership without making a contribution or being obligated to make a contribution to the partnership. Each person to be admitted as a partner to a partnership formed under either § 15-202(a)(i) or § 15-202(a)(ii) of this title may be admitted as a partner without acquiring an economic interest in the partnership. Nothing contained in this section shall affect a partner's liability under § 15-306 of this title.

§ 15-206.   Form of Contribution

The contribution of a partner may be in cash, property or services rendered, or a promissory note or other obligation to contribute cash or property or to perform services.

§ 15-207.   Liability for Contribution

(a) A partner is obligated to the partnership to perform any promise to contribute cash or property or to perform services, even if the partner is unable to perform because of death, disability or any other reason. If a partner does not make the required contribution of property or services, the partner is obligated at the option of the partnership to contribute cash equal to that portion of the value of the contribution that has not been made. The foregoing option shall be in addition to, and not in lieu of, any other rights, including the right to specific performance, that the partnership may have against such partner under the partnership agreement or applicable law.

(b) A partnership agreement may provide that the partnership interest of any partner who fails to make any contribution that the partner is obligated to make shall be subject to specified penalties for, or specified consequences of, such failure. Such penalty or consequence may take the form of reducing or eliminating the defaulting partner's interest in the partnership, subordinating the partner's partnership interest to that of nondefaulting partners, a forced sale of the partner's partnership interest, forfeiture of the partner's partnership interest, the lending by other partners of the amount necessary to meet the partner's commitment, a fixing of the value of the partner's partnership interest by appraisal or by formula and redemption or sale of the partner's partnership interest at such value, or other penalty or consequence.

SUBCHAPTER III.
RELATIONS OF PARTNERS TO PERSONS
DEALING WITH PARTNERSHIP

§ 15-301.   *Partner Agent of Partnership*

Subject to the effect of a statement of partnership existence under Section 15-303:

(1) Each partner is an agent of the partnership for the purpose of its business, purposes or activities. An act of a partner, including the execution of an instrument in the partnership name, for apparently carrying on in the ordinary course the partnership's business, purposes or activities or business, purposes or activities of the kind carried on by the partnership binds the partnership, unless the partner had no authority to act for the partnership in the particular matter and the person with whom the partner was dealing had notice that the partner lacked authority.

(2) An act of a partner which is not apparently for carrying on in the ordinary course the partnership's business, purposes or activities or business, purposes or activities of the kind carried on by the partnership binds the partnership only if the act was authorized by the other partners.

§ 15-302.   *Transfer of Partnership Property*

(a) Partnership property may be transferred as follows:

(1) Subject to the effect of a statement of partnership existence under Section 15-303, partnership property held in the name of the partnership may be transferred by an instrument of transfer executed by a partner in the partnership name.

(2) Partnership property held in the name of one or more partners with an indication in the instrument transferring the property to them of their capacity as partners or of the existence of a partnership, but without an indication of the name of the partnership, may be transferred by an instrument of transfer executed by the persons in whose name the property is held.

(3) Partnership property held in the name of one or more persons other than the partnership, without an indication in the instrument transferring the property to them of their capacity as partners or of the existence of a partnership, may be transferred by an instrument of transfer executed by the persons in whose name the property is held.

(b) A partnership may recover partnership property from a transferee only if it proves that execution of the instrument of initial transfer did not bind the partnership under Section 15-301 and:

(1) as to a subsequent transferee who gave value for property transferred under Section 15-302(a)(1) and (2), proves that the subsequent transferee had notice that the person who executed the instrument of initial transfer lacked authority to bind the partnership; or

(2) as to a transferee who gave value for property transferred under subsection (a)(3), proves that the transferee had notice that the property was partnership property and that the person who executed the instrument of initial transfer lacked authority to bind the partnership.

(c) A partnership may not recover partnership property from a subsequent transferee if the partnership would not have been entitled to recover the property, under Section 15-302(b), from any earlier transferee of the property.

(d) If a person holds all of the partners' interests in the partnership, all of the partnership property vests in that person. The person may execute a document in the name of the partnership to evidence vesting of the property in that person and may file or record the document.

§ 15-303.   *Statement of Partnership Existence*

(a) A partnership may file a statement of partnership existence, which:
   (1) must include:
      (i) the name of the partnership; and

(ii) the address of the registered office and the name and address of the registered agent for service of process required to be maintained by Section 15-111 of this title; and

(2) may state (i) the names of the partners authorized to execute an instrument transferring real property held in the name of the partnership, (ii) the authority, or limitations on the authority, of some or all of the partners to enter into other transactions on behalf of the partnership and (iii) any other matter.

(b) A statement of partnership existence supplements the authority of a partner to enter into transactions on behalf of the partnership as follows:

(1) Except for transfers of real property, a grant of authority contained in a statement of partnership existence is conclusive in favor of a person who gives value without knowledge to the contrary, so long as and to the extent that a limitation on that authority is not then contained in another statement. A filed cancellation of a limitation on authority revives the previous grant of authority.

(2) A grant of authority to transfer real property held in the name of the partnership contained in a certified copy of a statement of partnership existence recorded in the office for recording transfers of that real property is conclusive in favor of a person who gives value without knowledge to the contrary, so long as and to the extent that a certified copy of a statement containing a limitation on that authority is not then of record in the office for recording transfers of that real property. The recording in the office for recording transfers of that real property of a certified copy of a cancellation of a limitation on authority revives the previous grant of authority.

(c) A person not a partner is deemed to know of a limitation on the authority of a partner to transfer real property held in the name of the partnership if a certified copy of the statement containing the limitation on authority is of record in the office for recording transfers of that real property.

(d) Except as otherwise provided in subsections (b) and (c) and Sections 15-704 and 15-805, a person not a partner is not deemed to know of a limitation on the authority of a partner merely because the limitation is contained in a statement.

§ 15-304.   Denial of Status as Partner

If a person named in a statement of partnership existence is or may be adversely affected by being so named, the person may petition the Court of Chancery to direct the correction of the statement. If the Court finds that correction of the statement is proper and that an authorized person has failed or refused to execute and file a certificate of correction or a corrected statement, the Court shall order the Secretary of State to file an appropriate correction.

§ 15-305.   *Partnership Liable for Partner's Actionable Conduct*

(a) A partnership is liable for loss or injury caused to a person, or for a penalty incurred, as a result of a wrongful act or omission, or other actionable conduct, of a partner acting in the ordinary course of business of the partnership or with authority of the partnership.

(b) If, in the course of the partnership's business or while acting with authority of the partnership, a partner receives or causes the partnership to receive money or property of a person not a partner, and the money or property is misapplied by a partner, the partnership is liable for the loss.

§ 15-306.   *Partner's Liability*

(a) Except as otherwise provided in subsections (b) and (c), all partners are liable jointly and severally for all obligations of the partnership unless otherwise agreed by the claimant or provided by law.

(b) A person admitted as a partner into an existing partnership is not personally liable for any obligation of the partnership incurred before the person's admission as a partner.

(c) An obligation of a partnership arising out of or related to circumstances or events occurring while the partnership is a limited liability partnership or incurred while the partnership is a limited liability partnership, whether arising in contract, tort or otherwise, is solely the obligation of the partnership. A partner is not personally liable, directly or indirectly, by way of indemnification, contribution, assessment or otherwise, for such an obligation solely by reason of being or so acting as a partner.

(d) The ability of an attorney-at-law, admitted to the practice of law in the State of Delaware, to practice law in Delaware in a limited liability partnership, shall be determined by the Rules of the Supreme Court of the State of Delaware.

(e) Notwithstanding the provisions of subsection (c) of this section, under a partnership agreement or under another agreement, a partner may agree to be personally liable, directly or indirectly, by way of indemnification, contribution, assessment or otherwise, for any or all of the obligations of the partnership incurred while the partnership is a limited liability partnership.

§ 15-307.   Actions By and Against Partnership and Partners

(a) A partnership may sue and be sued in the name of the partnership.

(b) An action may be brought against the partnership and, to the extent not inconsistent with Section 15-306, any or all of the partners in the same action or in separate actions.

(c) A judgment against a partnership is not by itself a judgment against a partner. A judgment against a partnership may not be satisfied from the assets of a partner liable as provided in Section 15-306 for a partnership obligation unless there is also a judgment against the partner for such obligation.

(d) A judgment creditor of a partner may not levy execution against the assets of the partner to satisfy a judgment based on a claim against the partnership unless:

(1) the claim is for an obligation of the partnership for which the partner is liable as provided in Section 15-306 and either:

(i) a judgment based on the same claim has been obtained against the partnership and a writ of execution on the judgment has been returned unsatisfied in whole or in part;

(ii) the partnership is a debtor in bankruptcy;

(iii) the partner has agreed that the creditor need not exhaust partnership assets; or

(iv) a court grants permission to the judgment creditor to levy execution against the assets of a partner based on a finding that partnership assets subject to execution are clearly insufficient to satisfy the judgment, that exhaustion of partnership assets is excessively burdensome, or that the grant of permission is an appropriate exercise of the court's equitable powers; or

(2) liability is imposed on the partner by law or contract independent of the existence of the partnership.

(e) This section applies to any obligation of the partnership resulting from a representation by a partner or purported partner under Section 15-308.

§ 15-308.   Liability of Purported Partner

(a) If a person, by words or conduct, purports to be a partner, or consents to being represented by another as a partner, in a partnership or with one or more persons not partners, the purported partner is liable to a person to whom the representation is made, if that person, relying on the representation, enters into a transaction with the actual or purported partnership. If the representation, either by the purported partner or by a person with the purported partner's consent, is made in a public manner, the purported partner is liable to a person who relies upon the purported partnership even if the purported partner is not aware of being held out as a partner to the claimant. If a partnership obligation results, the purported partner is liable with respect to that obligation as if the purported partner were a partner. If no partnership obligation results, the purported partner is liable with respect to that obligation jointly and severally with any other person consenting to the representation. In the case of a limited liability partnership, a person's liability under Section 15-308(a) is subject to Section 15-306 as if the person were a partner in the limited liability partnership.

(b) If a person is thus represented to be a partner in an existing partnership, or with one or more persons not partners, the purported partner is an agent of persons consenting to the representation to bind them to the same extent and in the same manner as if the purported partner were a partner, with respect to persons who enter into transactions in reliance upon the representation. If all of the partners of the existing partnership consent to the representation, a partnership act or obligation results. If fewer than all of the partners of the existing partnership consent to the representation, the person acting and the partners consenting to the representation are jointly and severally liable.

(c) A person is not liable as a partner merely because the person is named by another in a statement of partnership existence.

(d) A person does not continue to be liable as a partner merely because of a failure to file a statement of dissociation or to amend a statement of partnership existence to indicate the partner's dissociation from the partnership.

(e) Except as otherwise provided in subsections (a) and (b), persons who are not partners as to each other are not liable as partners to other persons.

§ 15-309.   Limitations on Distribution

(a) A limited liability partnership shall not make a distribution to a partner to the extent that at the time of the distribution, after giving effect to the distribution, all liabilities of the limited liability partnership, other than liabilities to partners on account of their economic interests and liabilities for which the recourse of creditors is limited to specified property of the limited liability partnership, exceed the fair value of the assets of the limited liability partnership, except that the fair value of property that is subject to a liability for which the recourse of creditors is limited shall be included in the assets of the limited liability partnership only to the extent that the fair value of that property exceeds that liability. For purposes of this subsection, the term "distribution" shall not include amounts constituting reasonable compensation for present or past services or reasonable payments made in the ordinary course of business pursuant to a bona fide retirement plan or other benefits program.

(b) A partner of a limited liability partnership who receives a distribution in violation of subsection (a) of this section, and who knew at the time of the distribution that the distribution violated subsection (a) of this section, shall be liable to the partnership for the amount of the distribution. A partner of a limited liability partnership who receives a distribution in violation of subsection (a) of this section, and who did not know at the time of the distribution that the distribution violated subsection (a) of this section, shall not be liable for the amount of the distribution. Subject to subsection (c) of this section, this subsection (b) shall not affect any obligation or liability of a partner of a limited liability partnership under an agreement or other applicable law for the amount of a distribution.

(c) Unless otherwise agreed, a partner of a limited liability partnership who receives a distribution from a partnership shall have no liability under this chapter or other applicable law for the amount of the distribution after the expiration of three years from the date of the distribution.

SUBCHAPTER IV.
RELATIONS OF PARTNERS TO EACH OTHER AND TO PARTNERSHIP

§ 15-401.   *Partner's Rights and Duties*

(a) Each partner is deemed to have an account that is:

(1) credited with an amount equal to the money plus the value of any other property, net of the amount of any liabilities, the partner contributes to the partnership and the partner's share of the partnership profits; and

(2) charged with an amount equal to the money plus the value of any other property, net of the amount of any liabilities, distributed by the partnership to the partner and the partner's share of the partnership losses.

(b) Each partner is entitled to an equal share of the partnership profits and is chargeable with a share of the partnership losses in proportion to the partner's share of the profits.

(c) In addition to indemnification under Section 15-110, a partnership shall reimburse a partner for payments made and indemnify a partner for liabilities incurred by the partner in the ordinary course of the business of the partnership or for the preservation of its business or property; however, no person shall be required as a consequence of any such indemnification to make any payment to the extent that the payment is inconsistent with Sections 15-306(b) or (c).

(d) A partnership shall reimburse a partner for an advance to the partnership beyond the amount of capital the partner agreed to contribute.

(e) A payment or advance made by a partner which gives rise to a partnership obligation under subsection (c) or (d) constitutes a loan to the partnership which accrues interest from the date of the payment or advance.

(f) Each partner has equal rights in the management and conduct of the partnership business and affairs.

(g) A partner may use or possess partnership property only on behalf of the partnership.

(h) A partner is not entitled to remuneration for services performed for the partnership, except for reasonable compensation for services rendered in winding up the partnership.

(i) A person may become a partner only with the consent of all of the partners.

(j) A difference arising as to a matter in the ordinary course of business of a partnership may be decided by a majority of the partners. An act outside the ordinary course of business of a partnership may be undertaken only with the consent of all of the partners.

(k) This section does not affect the obligations of a partnership to other persons under Section 15-301.

(l) A partner has the power and authority to delegate to one or more other persons the partner's rights and powers to manage and control the business and affairs of the partnership, including to delegate to agents, officers and employees of the partner or the partnership, and to delegate by a management agreement or other agreement with, or otherwise to, other persons. Such delegation by a partner shall not cause the partner to cease to be a partner of the partnership or cause the person to whom any such rights and powers have been delegated to be a partner of the partnership.

(m) Unless otherwise provided in a partnership agreement or another agreement, a partner shall have no preemptive right to subscribe to any additional issue of partnership interests or another interest in a partnership.

§ 15-402.   *Distributions in Kind*

A partner, regardless of the nature of the partner's contribution, has no right to demand and receive any distribution from a partnership in kind. A partner may not be compelled to accept a distribution of any asset in kind from a partnership to the extent that the percentage of the asset distributed to the partner exceeds a percentage of that asset which is equal to the percentage in which the partner shares in distributions from the partnership. A partner may be compelled to accept a distribution of any asset in kind from a partnership to the extent that the percentage of the asset distributed to the partner is equal to a percentage of that asset which is equal to the percentage in which the partner shares in distributions from the partnership.

§ 15-403.   *Partner's Rights and Duties with Respect to Information*

(a) Each partner and the partnership shall provide partners, former partners and the legal representative of a deceased partner or partner under a legal disability and their agents and attorneys, access to the books and records of the partnership and other information concerning the partnership's business and affairs (in the case of former partners, only with respect to the period during which they were partners) upon reasonable demand, for any purpose reasonably related to the partner's interest as a partner in the partnership. The right of access shall include access to:

(1) True and full information regarding the status of the business and financial condition of the partnership;

(2) Promptly after becoming available, a copy of the partnership's federal, state and local income tax returns for each year;

(3) A current list of the name and last known business, residence or mailing address of each partner;

(4) A copy of any statement and written partnership agreement and all amendments thereto, together with executed copies of any written powers of attorney pursuant to which the statement or the partnership agreement and any amendments thereto have been executed;

(5) True and full information regarding the amount of cash and a description and statement of the agreed value of any other property or services contributed by each partner and which each partner has agreed to contribute in the future, and the date on which each partner became a partner; and

(6) Other information regarding the affairs of the partnership as is just and reasonable.

The right of access includes the right to examine and make extracts from books and records and other information concerning the partnership's business and affairs. The partnership agreement may provide for, and in the absence of such provision in the partnership agreement, the partnership or the partner from whom access is sought may impose, reasonable standards (including standards governing what information and documents are to be furnished at what time and location and at whose expense) with respect to exercise of the right of access.

(b) A partnership agreement may provide that the partnership shall have the right to keep confidential from partners for such period of time as the partnership deems reasonable, any information which the partnership reasonably believes to be in the nature of trade secrets or other information the disclosure of which the partnership in good faith believes is not in the best interest of the partnership or could damage the partnership or its business or affairs or which the partnership is required by law or by agreement with a third party to keep confidential.

(c) A partnership and its partners may maintain the books and records and other information concerning the partnership in other than a written form if such form is capable of conversion into written form within a reasonable time.

(d) Any demand by a partner under this section shall be in writing and shall state the purpose of such demand.

(e) Any action to enforce any right arising under this section shall be brought in the Court of Chancery. If the partnership or a partner refuses to permit access as described in subsection (a) of this section or does not reply to a demand that has been made within 5 business days (or such shorter or longer period of time as is provided for in a partnership agreement but not longer than 30 business days) after the demand has been made, the demanding partner, former partner, or legal representative of a deceased partner or partner under a legal disability may apply to the Court of Chancery for an order to compel such disclosure. The Court of Chancery is hereby vested with exclusive jurisdiction to determine whether or not the person making the demand is entitled to the books and records or other information concerning the partnership's business and affairs sought. The Court of Chancery may summarily order the partnership or partner to permit the demanding partner, former partner or legal representative of a deceased partner or partner under a legal disability and their agents and attorneys to provide access to the information described in subsection (a) of this section and to make copies or extracts therefrom; or the Court of Chancery may summarily order the partnership or partner to furnish to the demanding partner, former partner or legal representative of a deceased partner or partner under a legal disability and their agents and attorneys the information described in subsection (a) of this section on the condition that the partner, former partner or legal representative of a deceased partner or partner under a legal disability first pay to the partnership or to the partner from whom access is sought the reasonable cost of obtaining and furnishing such information and on such other conditions as the Court of Chancery deems appropriate. When a demanding partner, former partner or legal representative of a deceased partner or partner under a legal disability seeks to obtain access to information described in subsection (a) of this section, the demanding partner, former partner or legal representative of a deceased partner or partner under a legal disability shall first establish (1) that the demanding partner, former partner or legal representative of a deceased partner or partner under a legal disability has complied with the provisions of this section respecting the form and manner of making demand for obtaining access to such information and (2) that the information the demanding partner, former partner or legal representative of a deceased partner or partner under a legal disability seeks is reasonably related to the partner's interest as a partner in the partnership. The Court of Chancery may, in its discretion, prescribe any limitations or conditions with reference to the access to information, or award such other or further relief as the Court of Chancery may deem just and proper. The Court of Chancery may order books, documents and records, pertinent extracts therefrom, or duly authenticated copies thereof, to be brought within the State of Delaware and kept in the State of Delaware upon such terms and conditions as the order may prescribe.

(f) The rights of a partner to obtain information as provided in this section may be restricted in an original partnership agreement or in any subsequent amendment approved or adopted by all of the partners or in compliance with any applicable requirements of the partnership agreement.

§ 15-404.   General Standards of Partner's Conduct

(a) The only fiduciary duties a partner owes to the partnership and the other partners are the duty of loyalty and the duty of care set forth in subsections (b) and (c).

(b) A partner's duty of loyalty to the partnership and the other partners is limited to the following:

(1) to account to the partnership and hold as trustee for it any property, profit or benefit derived by the partner in the conduct or winding up of the partnership business or affairs or derived from a use by the partner of partnership property, including the appropriation of a partnership opportunity;

(2) to refrain from dealing with the partnership in the conduct or winding up of the partnership business or affairs as or on behalf of a party having an interest adverse to the partnership; and

(3) to refrain from competing with the partnership in the conduct of the partnership business or affairs before the dissolution of the partnership.

(c) A partner's duty of care to the partnership and the other partners in the conduct and winding up of the partnership business or affairs is limited to refraining from engaging in grossly negligent or reckless conduct, intentional misconduct, or a knowing violation of law.

(d) A partner does not violate a duty or obligation under this chapter or under the partnership agreement solely because the partner's conduct furthers the partner's own interest.

(e) A partner may lend money to, borrow money from, act as a surety, guarantor or endorser for, guarantee or assume 1 or more specific obligations of, provide collateral for and transact other business with, the partnership and, subject to other applicable law, has the same rights and obligations with respect thereto as a person who is not a partner.

(f) This section applies to a person winding up the partnership business or affairs as the personal or legal representative of the last surviving partner as if the person were a partner.

§ 15-405.   *Actions by Partnership and Partners; Derivative Actions*

(a) A partnership may maintain an action against a partner for a breach of the partnership agreement, or for the violation of a duty to the partnership, causing harm to the partnership.

(b) A partner may maintain an action against the partnership or another partner for legal or equitable relief, with or without an accounting as to partnership business, to:

(1) enforce the partner's rights under the partnership agreement;

(2) enforce the partner's rights under this chapter, including:

(i) the partner's rights under Sections 15-401, 15-403 or 15-404;

(ii) the partner's right on dissociation to have the partner's interest in the partnership purchased pursuant to Section 15-701 or enforce any other right under Subchapter VI or VII; or

(iii) the partner's right to compel a dissolution and winding up of the partnership business under Section 15-801 or enforce any other right under Subchapter VIII; or

(3) enforce the rights and otherwise protect the interests of the partner, including rights and interests arising independently of the partnership relationship.

(c) The accrual of, and any time limitation on, a right of action for a remedy under this section is governed by other law. A right to an accounting upon a dissolution and winding up does not revive a claim barred by law.

(d) A partner may bring a derivative action in the Court of Chancery in the right of a partnership to recover a judgment in the partnership's favor.

(e) In a derivative action, the plaintiff must be a partner at the time of bringing the action and:

(1) At the time of the transaction of which the partner complains; or

(2) The partner's status as a partner had devolved upon the partner by operation of law or pursuant to the terms of the partnership agreement from a person who was a partner at the time of the transaction.

(f) In a derivative action, the complaint shall set forth with particularity the effort, if any, of the plaintiff to secure initiation of the action by the partnership or the reason for not making the effort.

(g) If a derivative action is successful, in whole or in part, as a result of a judgment, compromise or settlement of any such action, the court may award the plaintiff reasonable expenses, including reasonable attorney's fees, from any recovery in any such action or from a partnership.

§ 15-406.   Continuation of Partnership Beyond Definite Term or Particular Undertaking

(a) If a partnership for a definite term or particular undertaking is continued, without an express agreement, after the expiration of the term or completion of the undertaking, the rights and duties of the partners remain the same as they were at the expiration or completion, so far as is consistent with a partnership at will.

(b) If the partners, or those of them who habitually acted in the business or affairs during the term or undertaking, continue the business or affairs without any settlement or liquidation of the partnership, they are presumed to have agreed that the partnership will continue.

§ 15-407.   Classes and Voting

(a) A partnership agreement may provide for classes or groups of partners having such relative rights, powers and duties as the partnership agreement may provide, and may make provision for the future creation in the manner provided in the partnership agreement of additional classes or groups of partners having such relative rights, powers and duties as may from time to time be established, including rights, powers and duties senior to existing classes and groups of partners. A partnership agreement may provide for the taking of an action, including the amendment of the partnership agreement, without the vote or approval of any partner or class or group of partners, including an action to create under the provisions of the partnership agreement a class or group of partnership interests that was not previously outstanding. A partnership agreement may provide that any partner or class or group of partners shall have no voting rights.

(b) The partnership agreement may grant to all or certain identified partners or a specified class or group of the partners the right to vote separately or with all or any class or group of the partners on any matter. Voting by partners may be on a per capita, number, financial interest, class, group or any other basis.

(c) A partnership agreement may set forth provisions relating to notice of the time, place or purpose of any meeting at which any matter is to be voted on by any partners, waiver of any such notice, action by consent without a meeting, the establishment of a record date, quorum requirements, voting in person or by proxy, or any other matter with respect to the exercise of any such right to vote.

(d) Unless otherwise provided in a partnership agreement, meetings of partners may be held by means of conference telephone or other communications equipment by means of which all persons participating in the meeting can hear each other, and participation in a meeting pursuant to this subsection shall constitute presence in person at the meeting. On any matter that is to be voted on, consented to or approved by partners, the partners may take such action without a meeting, without prior notice and without a vote if consented to, in writing or by electronic transmission, by partners having not less than the minimum number of votes that would be necessary to authorize or take such action at a meeting at which all partners entitled to vote thereon were present and voted. On any matter that is to be voted on by partners, the partners may vote in person or by proxy, and such proxy may be granted in writing, by means of electronic transmission or as otherwise permitted by applicable law. Unless otherwise provided in a partnership agreement, a consent transmitted by electronic transmission by a partner or by a person or persons authorized to act for a partner shall be deemed to be written and signed for purposes of this subsection (d). For purposes of this subsection (d), the term "electronic transmission" means any form of communication not directly involving the physical transmission of paper that creates a record that may be retained, retrieved and reviewed by a recipient thereof and that may be directly reproduced in paper form by such a recipient through an automated process.

(e) If a partnership agreement provides for the manner in which it may be amended, including by requiring the approval of a person who is not a party to the partnership agreement or the satisfaction of conditions, it may be amended only in that manner or as otherwise permitted by law, including as permitted by § 15-902(g) of this title (provided that the approval of any person may be waived by such person and that any such conditions may be waived by all persons for whose benefit such conditions were intended). If a partnership agreement does not provide for the manner in which it may be amended, the partnership agreement may be amended with the approval of all the partners or as otherwise permitted by law, including as permitted by § 15-902(g) of this title. Unless otherwise provided in a partnership agreement, a supermajority amendment provision shall only apply to provisions of the partnership agreement that are expressly included in the partnership agreement. As used in this section, "supermajority amendment provision" means any amendment provision set forth in a partnership agreement requiring that an amendment to a provision of the partnership agreement be adopted by no less than the vote or consent required to take action under such latter provision.

§ 15-408. *Remedies for Breach of Partnership Agreement*

A partnership agreement may provide that (i) a partner who fails to perform in accordance with, or to comply with the terms and conditions of, the partnership agreement shall be subject to specified penalties or specified consequences, and (ii) at the time or upon the happening of events specified in the partnership agreement, a partner shall be subject to specified penalties or specified consequences. Such specified penalties or specified consequences may include and take the form of any penalty or consequence set forth in § 15-207(b) of this title.

§ 15-409.   *Reliance on Reports and Information by Partner or Liquidating Trustee*

(a) A liquidating trustee of a partnership (including a limited liability partnership) shall be fully protected in relying in good faith upon the records of the partnership and upon information, opinions, reports or statements presented by a partner of the partnership, an officer or employee of the partnership, another liquidating trustee, or committees of the partnership or partners, or by any other person as to matters the liquidating trustee reasonably believes are within such other person's professional or expert competence, including information, opinions, reports or statements as to the value and amount of assets, liabilities, profits or losses of the partnership, or the value and amount of assets or reserves or contracts, agreements or other undertakings that would be sufficient to pay claims and obligations of the partnership or to make reasonable provision to pay such claims and obligations, or any other facts pertinent to the existence and amount of assets from which distributions to partners or creditors might properly be paid.

(b) A partner of a limited liability partnership shall be fully protected in relying in good faith upon the records of the partnership and upon information, opinions, reports or statements presented by another partner of the partnership, an officer or employee of the partnership, a liquidating trustee, or committees of the partnership or partners, or by any other person as to matters the partner reasonably believes are within such other person's professional or expert competence, including information, opinions, reports or statements as to the value and amount of assets, liabilities, profits or losses of the partnership, or the value and amount of assets or reserves or contracts, agreements or other undertakings that would be sufficient to pay claims and obligations of the partnership or to make reasonable provision to pay such claims and obligations, or any other facts pertinent to the existence and amount of assets from which distributions to partners or creditors might properly be paid.

(c) A partner of a partnership that is not a limited liability partnership shall be fully protected from liability to the partnership, its partners or other persons party to or otherwise bound by the partnership agreement in relying in good faith upon the records of the partnership and upon information, opinions, reports or statements presented by another partner of the partnership, an officer or employee of the partnership, a liquidating trustee, or committees of the partnership or partners, or by any other person as to matters the partner reasonably believes are within such other person's professional or expert competence, including information, opinions, reports or statements as to the value and amount of assets, liabilities, profits or losses of the partnership, or the value and amount of assets or reserves or contracts, agreements or other undertakings that would be sufficient to pay claims and obligations of the partnership or to make reasonable provision to pay such claims and obligations, or any other facts pertinent to the existence and amount of assets from which distributions to partners or creditors might properly be paid.

SUBCHAPTER V.
TRANSFEREES AND CREDITORS OF PARTNER

§ 15-501. *Partner Not Co-Owner of Partnership Property*

Unless otherwise provided in a statement of partnership existence or a statement of qualification and in a partnership agreement, a partner is not a co-owner of partnership property and has no interest in specific partnership property.

§ 15-502. *Partner's Economic Interest in Partnership; Personal Property*

A partnership interest is personal property. Only a partner's economic interest may be transferred.

§ 15-503. *Transfer of Partner's Economic Interest*

(a) A transfer, in whole or in part, of a partner's economic interest in the partnership:
  (1) is permissible;
  (2) does not by itself cause the partner's dissociation or a dissolution and winding up of the partnership business or affairs; and
  (3) does not entitle the transferee to participate in the management or conduct of the partnership business or affairs, to require access to information concerning partnership transactions, or to inspect or copy the partnership books or records.
(b) A transferee of a partner's economic interest in the partnership has a right:
  (1) to receive, in accordance with the transfer, distributions to which the transferor would otherwise be entitled;
  (2) to receive upon the dissolution and winding up of the partnership business or affairs, in accordance with the transfer, the net amount otherwise distributable to the transferor; and
  (3) to seek under Section 15-801(6) a judicial determination that it is equitable to wind up the partnership business or affairs.
(c) In a dissolution and winding up, a transferee is entitled to an account of partnership transactions only from the date of the latest account agreed to by all of the partners.

(d) Upon transfer, the transferor retains the rights and duties of a partner other than the economic interest transferred.

(e) A partnership need not give effect to a transferee's rights under this section until it has notice of the transfer. Upon request of a partnership or a partner, a transferee must furnish reasonable proof of a transfer.

(f) A transfer of a partner's economic interest in the partnership in violation of a restriction on transfer contained in a partnership agreement is ineffective.

(g) Notwithstanding anything to the contrary under applicable law, a partnership agreement may provide that a partner's economic interest may not be transferred prior to the dissolution and winding up of the partnership.

(h) A partnership interest in a partnership may be evidenced by a certificate of partnership interest issued by the partnership. A partnership agreement may provide for the transfer of any partnership interest represented by such a certificate and make other provisions with respect to such certificates. A partnership shall not have the power to issue a certificate of partnership interest in bearer form.

(i) Except to the extent assumed by agreement, until a transferee of a partnership interest becomes a partner, the transferee shall have no liability as a partner solely as a result of the transfer.

(j) A partnership may acquire, by purchase, redemption or otherwise, any partnership interest or other interest of a partner in the partnership. Any such interest so acquired by the partnership shall be deemed canceled.

§ 15-504.   *Partner's Economic Interest Subject to Charging Order*

(a) On application by a judgment creditor of a partner or of a partner's transferee, a court having jurisdiction may charge the economic interest of the judgment debtor to satisfy the judgment. To the extent so charged, the judgment creditor has only the right to receive any distribution or distributions to which the judgment debtor would otherwise have been entitled in respect of such economic interest.

(b) A charging order constitutes a lien on the judgment debtor's economic interest in the partnership.

(c) This chapter does not deprive a partner or a partner's transferee of a right under exemption laws with respect to the judgment debtor's economic interest in the partnership.

(d) The entry of a charging order is the exclusive remedy by which a judgment creditor of a partner or of a partner's transferee may satisfy a judgment out of the judgment debtor's economic interest in the partnership and attachment, garnishment, foreclosure or other legal or equitable remedies are not available to the judgment creditor.

(e) No creditor of a partner or of a partner's transferee shall have any right to obtain possession of, or otherwise exercise legal or equitable remedies with respect to, the property of the partnership.

(f) The Court of Chancery shall have jurisdiction to hear and determine any matter relating to any such charging order.

SUBCHAPTER VI.
PARTNER'S DISSOCIATION

§ 15-601.   *Events Causing Partner's Dissociation*

A partner is dissociated from a partnership upon the occurrence of any of the following events:

(1) the partnership's having notice of the partner's express will to withdraw as a partner on a later date specified by the partner in the notice or, if no later date is specified, then upon receipt of notice;

(2) an event agreed to in the partnership agreement as causing the partner's dissociation;

(3) the partner's expulsion pursuant to the partnership agreement;

(4) the partner's expulsion by the unanimous vote of the other partners if:

(i) it is unlawful to carry on the partnership business or affairs with that partner; or

(ii) there has been a transfer of all or substantially all of that partner's economic interest, other than a transfer for security purposes, or a court order charging the partner's interest which, in either case, has not been foreclosed;

(5) on application by or for the partnership or another partner to the Court of Chancery, the partner's expulsion by determination by the Court of Chancery because:

(i) the partner engaged in wrongful conduct that adversely and materially affected the partnership business or affairs;

(ii) the partner willfully or persistently committed a material breach of either the partnership agreement or of a duty owed to the partnership or the other partners; or

(iii) the partner engaged in conduct relating to the partnership business or affairs which makes it not reasonably practicable to carry on the business or affairs in partnership with the partner;

(6) The partner's:

a. Making an assignment for the benefit of creditors;

b. Filing a voluntary petition in bankruptcy;

c. Being adjudged a bankrupt or insolvent, or having entered against that partner an order for relief in any bankruptcy or insolvency proceeding;

d. Filing a petition or answer seeking for that partner any reorganization, arrangement, composition, readjustment, liquidation, dissolution or similar relief under any statute, law or regulation;

e. Filing an answer or other pleading admitting or failing to contest the material allegations of a petition filed against that partner in any proceeding of this nature;

f. Seeking, consenting to or acquiescing in the appointment of a trustee, receiver or liquidator of that partner or of all or any substantial part of that partner's properties; or

g. Failing, within 120 days after its commencement, to have dismissed any proceeding against that partner seeking reorganization, arrangement, composition, readjustment, liquidation, dissolution or similar relief under any statute, law or regulation, or failing, within 90 days after the appointment without that partner's consent or acquiescence, to have vacated or stayed the appointment of a trustee, receiver or liquidator of that partner or of all or any substantial part of that partner's properties, or failing, within 90 days after the expiration of any such stay, to have the appointment vacated;

(7) in the case of a partner who is an individual:

(i) the partner's death;

(ii) the appointment of a guardian or general conservator for the partner; or

(iii) a judicial determination that the partner has otherwise become incapable of performing the partner's duties under the partnership agreement;

(8) in the case of a partner that is a trust or is acting as a partner by virtue of being a trustee of a trust, distribution of the trust's entire economic interest, but not merely by reason of the substitution of a successor trustee;

(9) in the case of a partner that is an estate or is acting as a partner by virtue of being a personal representative of an estate, distribution of the estate's entire economic interest, but not merely by reason of the substitution of a successor personal representative;

(10) the expiration of 90 days after the partnership notifies a corporate partner that it will be expelled because it has filed a certificate of dissolution or the equivalent, its existence has been terminated or its certificate of incorporation has been revoked, or its right to conduct business has been suspended by the jurisdiction of its incorporation, if there is no revocation of the certificate of dissolution or no reinstatement of its existence, its certificate of incorporation or its right to conduct business;

(11) a partnership, a limited liability company, a trust or a limited partnership that is a partner has been dissolved and its business is being wound up; or

(12) termination of a partner who is not an individual, partnership, corporation, trust, limited partnership, limited liability company or estate.

§ 15-602.   Partner's Power to Dissociate; Wrongful Dissociation

(a) A partner has the power to dissociate at any time, rightfully or wrong-fully, by express will pursuant to Section 15-601(1).

(b) A partner's dissociation is wrongful only if any of the following apply:

(1) it is in breach of an express provision of the partnership agreement; or

(2) in the case of a partnership for a definite term or particular undertak-ing, before the expiration of the term or the completion of the undertaking if any of the following apply:

(i) the partner withdraws by express will, unless the withdrawal fol-lows within 90 days after another partner's dissociation by death or oth-erwise under Section 15-601(6) through (12) or wrongful dissociation under this subsection;

(ii) the partner is expelled by judicial determination under Section 15-601(5);

(iii) the partner is dissociated under Section 15-601(6); or

(iv) in the case of a partner who is not an individual, trust (other than a statutory trust), or estate, the partner is expelled or otherwise dissoci-ated because it willfully dissolved or terminated.

(c) A partner who wrongfully dissociates is liable to the partnership and to the other partners for damages caused by the dissociation. Such liability is in addition to any other obligation of the partner to the partnership or to the other partners.

§ 15-603.   Effect of Partner's Dissociation

(a) If a partner's dissociation results in a dissolution and winding up of the partnership business, Subchapter VIII applies; otherwise, Subchapter VII applies.

(b) Upon a partner's dissociation:

(1) the partner's right to participate in the management and conduct of the partnership business terminates, except as otherwise provided in Section 15-803;

(2) the partner's duty of loyalty under Section 15-404(b)(3) terminates; and

(3) the partner's duty of loyalty under Section 15-404(b)(1) and (2) and duty of care under Section 15-404(c) continue only with regard to matters arising and events occurring before the partner's dissociation, unless the partner participates in winding up the partnership's business pursuant to Sec-tion 15-803.

SUBCHAPTER VII.
PARTNER'S DISSOCIATION WHEN BUSINESS
OR AFFAIRS NOT WOUND UP

§ 15-701.   *Purchase of Dissociated Partner's Partnership Interest*

(a) If a partner is dissociated from a partnership without resulting in a dissolution and winding up of the partnership business or affairs under Section 15-801, the partnership shall cause the dissociated partner's interest in the partnership to be purchased for a buyout price determined pursuant to subsection (b).

(b) The buyout price of a dissociated partner's partnership interest is an amount equal to the fair value of such partner's economic interest as of the date of dissociation based upon such partner's right to share in distributions from the partnership. Interest must be paid from the date of dissociation to the date of payment.

(c) Damages for wrongful dissociation under Section 15-602(b), and all other amounts owing, whether or not presently due, from the dissociated partner to the partnership, must be offset against the buyout price. Interest must be paid from the date the amount owed becomes due to the date of payment.

(d) A partnership shall indemnify a dissociated partner whose partnership interest is being purchased against all partnership obligations, whether incurred before or after the dissociation, except partnership obligations incurred by an act of the dissociated partner under Section 15-702.

(e) If no agreement for the purchase of a dissociated partner's partnership interest is reached within 120 days after a written demand for payment, the partnership shall pay, or cause to be paid, in cash to the dissociated partner the amount the partnership estimates to be the buyout price and accrued interest, reduced by any offsets and accrued interest under subsection (c).

(f) If a deferred payment is authorized under subsection (h), the partnership may tender a written offer to pay the amount it estimates to be the buyout price and accrued interest, reduced by any offsets under subsection (c), stating the time of payment, the amount and type of security for payment, and the other terms and conditions of the obligation.

(g) The payment or tender required by subsection (e) or (f) of this section must be accompanied by the following:

   (1) a written statement of partnership assets and liabilities as of the date of dissociation;

   (2) the latest available partnership balance sheet and income statement, if any;

   (3) a written explanation of how the estimated amount of the payment was calculated; and

(4) written notice which shall state that the payment is in full satisfaction of the obligation to purchase unless, within 120 days after the written notice, the dissociated partner commences an action in the Court of Chancery under (i) to determine the buyout price of that partner's partnership interest, any offsets under subsection (c) or other terms of the obligation to purchase.

(h) A partner who wrongfully dissociates before the expiration of a definite term or the completion of a particular undertaking is not entitled to payment of any portion of the buyout price until the expiration of the term or completion of the undertaking, unless the partner establishes to the satisfaction of the Court of Chancery that earlier payment will not cause undue hardship to the business of the partnership. A deferred payment must bear interest and, to the extent it would not cause undue hardship to the business of the partnership, be adequately secured.

(i) A dissociated partner may maintain an action against the partnership, pursuant to Section 15-405(b)(2)(ii), to determine the buyout price of that partner's partnership interest, any offsets under subsection (c), or other terms of the obligation to purchase. The action must be commenced within 120 days after the partnership has tendered payment or an offer to pay or within one year after written demand for payment if no payment or offer to pay is tendered. The Court of Chancery shall determine the buyout price of the dissociated partner's partnership interest, any offset due under subsection (c), and accrued interest, and enter judgment for any additional payment or refund. If deferred payment is authorized under subsection (h), the Court of Chancery shall also determine the security, if any, for payment and other terms of the obligation to purchase. The Court of Chancery may assess reasonable attorney's fees and the fees and expenses of appraisers or other experts for a party to the action, in amounts the Court of Chancery finds equitable, against a party that the Court of Chancery finds acted arbitrarily, vexatiously or not in good faith. The finding may be based on the partnership's failure to tender payment or an offer to pay or to comply with subsection (g).

§ 15-702.   *Dissociated Partner's Power to Bind and Liability to Partnership*

(a) For one year after a partner dissociates without resulting in a dissolution and winding up of the partnership business, the partnership, including a surviving partnership under Subchapter IX, is bound by an act of the dissociated partner which would have bound the partnership under Section 15-301 before dissociation only if at the time of entering into the transaction the other party:

(1) reasonably believed that the dissociated partner was then a partner and reasonably relied on such belief in entering into the transaction;

(2) did not have notice of the partner's dissociation; and

(3) is not deemed to have had knowledge under Section 15-303(c) or notice under Section 15-704(c).

(b) A dissociated partner is liable to the partnership for any damage caused to the partnership arising from an obligation incurred by the dissociated partner after dissociation for which the partnership is liable under subsection (a).

§ 15-703. *Dissociated Partner's Liability to Other Persons*

(a) A partner's dissociation does not of itself discharge the partner's liability for a partnership obligation incurred before dissociation. A dissociated partner is not liable for a partnership obligation incurred after dissociation, except as otherwise provided in subsection (b).

(b) A partner who dissociates without resulting in a dissolution and winding up of the partnership business is liable as a partner to the other party in a transaction entered into by the partnership, or a surviving partnership under Subchapter IX, within one year after the partner's dissociation, only if the partner is liable for the obligation under Section 15-306 and at the time of entering into the transaction the other party:

(1) reasonably believed that the dissociated partner was then a partner and reasonably relied on such belief in entering into the transaction;

(2) did not have notice of the partner's dissociation; and

(3) is not deemed to have had knowledge under Section 15-303(c) or notice under Section 15-704(c).

(c) By agreement with the partnership creditor and the partners continuing the business, a dissociated partner may be released from liability for a partnership obligation.

(d) A dissociated partner is released from liability for a partnership obligation if a partnership creditor, with notice of the partner's dissociation but without the partner's consent, agrees to a material alteration in the nature or time of payment of a partnership obligation.

§ 15-704. *Statement of Dissociation*

(a) A dissociated partner or, after the filing by the partnership of a statement of partnership existence, the partnership may file a statement of dissociation stating the name of the partnership and that the partner is dissociated from the partnership.

(b) A statement of dissociation is a limitation on the authority of a dissociated partner for the purposes of Section 15-303(b) and (c).

(c) For the purposes of Sections 15-702(a)(3) and 15-703(b)(3), a person not a partner is deemed to have notice of the dissociation 60 days after the statement of dissociation is filed.

§ 15-705.   *Continued Use of Partnership Name*

Continued use of a partnership name, or a dissociated partner's name as part thereof, by partners continuing the business does not of itself make the dissociated partner liable for an obligation of the partners or the partnership.

SUBCHAPTER VIII.
WINDING UP PARTNERSHIP BUSINESS
OR AFFAIRS

§ 15-801.   *Events Causing Dissolution and Winding Up of Partnership Business or Affairs*

A partnership is dissolved, and its business must be wound up, only upon the occurrence of any of the following events:

(1) In a partnership at will, the partnership's having notice from a partner, other than a partner who is dissociated under Section 15-601(2) through (12), of that partner's express will to withdraw as a partner, on a later date specified by the partner in the notice or, if no later date is specified, then upon receipt of notice;

(2) In a partnership for a definite term or particular undertaking:

(i) Within 90 days after a partner's dissociation by death or otherwise under Section 15-601(6) through (12) or wrongful dissociation under Section 15-602(b), at least half of the remaining partners express the will to wind up the partnership business, for which purpose a partner's rightful dissociation pursuant to Section 15-602(b)(2)(i) of this title constitutes the expression of that partner's will to wind up the partnership business;

(ii) The express will of all of the partners to wind up the partnership business or affairs; or

(iii) The expiration of the term or the completion of the undertaking;

(3) An event agreed to in the partnership agreement resulting in the winding up of the partnership business or affairs;

(4) An event that makes it unlawful for all or substantially all of the business or affairs of the partnership to be continued, but a cure of such illegality within 90 days after the partnership has notice of the event is effective retroactively to the date of the event for purposes of this section;

(5) On application by or for a partner to the Court of Chancery, the entry of a decree of dissolution of a partnership by the Court of Chancery upon a determination by the Court of Chancery that it is not reasonably practicable to carry on

the partnership business, purpose or activity in conformity with the partnership agreement; or

(6) On application by a transferee of a partner's economic interest to the Court of Chancery, a determination by the Court of Chancery that it is equitable to wind up the partnership business or affairs:

(i) After the expiration of the term or completion of the undertaking, if the partnership was for a definite term or particular undertaking at the time of the transfer or entry of the charging order that gave rise to the transfer; or

(ii) At any time, if the partnership was a partnership at will at the time of the transfer or entry of the charging order that gave rise to the transfer.

§ 15-802.   Partnership Continues After Dissolution

(a) Subject to subsection (b), a partnership continues after dissolution only for the purpose of winding up its business or affairs. The partnership is terminated when the winding up of its business or affairs is completed.

(b) At any time after the dissolution of a partnership and before the winding up of its business or affairs is completed, all of the partners, including any dissociating partner other than a wrongfully dissociating partner, may waive the right to have the partnership's business or affairs wound up and the partnership terminated. In that event:

(1) the partnership resumes carrying on its business or affairs as if dissolution had never occurred, and any liability incurred by the partnership or a partner after the dissolution and before the waiver is determined as if dissolution had never occurred; and

(2) the rights of a third party accruing under Section 15-804(1) or arising out of conduct in reliance on the dissolution before the third party knew or received a notification of the waiver may not be adversely affected.

§ 15-803.   Right to Wind Up Partnership Business or Affairs

(a) A partner at the time of dissolution, including a partner who has dissociated but not wrongfully, may participate in winding up the partnership's business or affairs, but on application of any partner or a partner's legal representative or transferee, the Court of Chancery for good cause shown, may order judicial supervision of the winding up.

(b) The legal representative of the last surviving partner may wind up a partnership's business or affairs.

(c) The persons winding up the partnership's business or affairs may, in the name of, and for and on behalf of, the partnership, prosecute and defend suits, whether civil, criminal or administrative, gradually settle and close the partnership's business or affairs, dispose of and convey the partnership's property, discharge or make reasonable provision for the partnership's liabilities, distribute to the partners pursuant to Section 15-807 any remaining assets of the partnership, and perform other acts which are necessary or convenient to the winding up of the partnership's business or affairs.

§ 15-804.   *Partner's Power to Bind Partnership After Dissolution*

Subject to Section 15-805, a partnership is bound by a partner's act after dissolution that:

(1) is appropriate for winding up the partnership business or affairs; or

(2) would have bound the partnership under Section 15-301 before dissolution, if the other party to the transaction did not have notice of the dissolution.

§ 15-805.   *Statement of Dissolution*

(a) After dissolution, a partnership may file a statement of dissolution stating the name of the partnership and that the partnership has dissolved and is winding up its business or affairs.

(b) A statement of dissolution cancels a filed statement of partnership existence for the purposes of Section 15-303(b) and is a limitation on authority for the purposes of Section 15-303(c).

(c) For the purposes of Sections 15-301 and 15-804, a person not a partner is deemed to have notice of the dissolution and the limitation on the partners' authority as a result of a statement of dissolution 60 days after it is filed.

(d) After filing a statement of dissolution, a dissolved partnership may file a statement of partnership existence which will operate with respect to a person not a partner as provided in Section 15-303(b) and (c) in any transaction, whether or not the transaction is appropriate for winding up the partnership business or affairs.

(e) If a partnership which has dissolved fails or refuses to file a statement of dissolution, any partner or dissociated partner who is or may be adversely affected by the failure or refusal may petition the Court of Chancery to direct the filing. If the Court finds that the statement of dissolution should be filed and that the partnership has failed or refused to do so, it shall enter an order granting appropriate relief.

§ 15-806.   *Partner's Liability to Other Partners After Dissolution*

(a) Except as otherwise provided in subsection (b) and Section 15-306, after dissolution a partner is liable to the other partners for the partner's share of any partnership obligation incurred under Section 15-804.

(b) A partner who, with knowledge of the dissolution, causes the partnership to incur an obligation under Section 15-804(2) by an act that is not appropriate for winding up the partnership business or affairs is liable to the partnership for any damage caused to the partnership arising from the obligation.

§ 15-807.   *Settlement of Accounts and Contributions Among Partners*

(a) In winding up a partnership's business or affairs, the assets of the partnership, including the contributions of the partners required by this section, must be applied to pay or make reasonable provision to pay the partnership's obligations to creditors, including, to the extent permitted by law, partners who are creditors. Any surplus must be applied to pay in cash the net amount distributable to partners in accordance with their right to distributions under subsection (b).

(b) Each partner is entitled to a settlement of all partnership accounts upon winding up the partnership business or affairs. In settling accounts among the partners, profits and losses that result from the liquidation of the partnership assets must be credited and charged to the partners' accounts. The partnership shall make a distribution to a partner in an amount equal to any excess of the credits over the charges in the partner's account. A partner shall contribute to the partnership an amount equal to any excess of the charges over the credits in the partner's account but excluding from the calculation charges attributable to an obligation for which the partner is not personally liable under Section 15-306.

(c) After the settlement of accounts, each partner shall contribute, in the proportion in which the partner shares partnership losses, the amount necessary to pay or make reasonable provision to pay partnership obligations that were not known at the time of the settlement and for which the partner is personally liable under Section 15-306.

(d) If a partner fails to contribute, all of the other partners shall contribute, in the proportions in which those partners share partnership losses, the additional amount necessary to pay or make reasonable provision to pay the partnership obligations for which they are personally liable under Section 15-306.

(e) A partner or partner's legal representative may recover from the other partners any contributions the partner makes to the extent the amount contributed exceeds that partner's share of the partnership obligations for which the partner is personally liable under Section 15-306.

(f) The estate of a deceased partner is liable for the partner's obligation to contribute to the partnership.

(g) An assignee for the benefit of creditors of a partnership or a partner, or a person appointed by a court to represent creditors of a partnership or a partner, may enforce a partner's obligation to contribute to the partnership.

(h) A limited liability partnership which has dissolved (i) shall pay or make reasonable provision to pay all claims and obligations, including all contingent, conditional or unmatured contractual claims, known to the limited liability partnership, (ii) shall make such provision as will be reasonably likely to be sufficient to provide compensation for any claim against the limited liability partnership which is the subject of a pending action, suit or proceeding to which the limited liability partnership is a party and (iii) shall make such provision as will be reasonably likely to be sufficient to provide compensation for claims that have not been made known to the limited liability partnership or that have not arisen but that, based on facts known to the limited liability partnership, are likely to arise or to become known to the limited liability partnership within 10 years after the date of dissolution. If there are sufficient assets, such claims and obligations shall be paid in full and any such provision for payment made shall be made in full. If there are insufficient assets, such claims and obligations shall be paid or provided for according to their priority and, among claims of equal priority, ratably to the extent of assets available therefor. Unless otherwise provided in the partnership agreement, any remaining assets shall be distributed as provided in this chapter. Any liquidating trustee winding up a limited liability partnership's affairs who has complied with this section shall not be personally liable to the claimants of the dissolved limited liability partnership by reason of such person's actions in winding up the limited liability partnership.

(i) A partner of a limited liability partnership who receives a distribution in violation of subsection (h) of this section, and who knew at the time of the distribution that the distribution violated subsection (h) of this section, shall be liable to the limited liability partnership for the amount of the distribution. For purposes of the immediately preceding sentence, the term "distribution" shall not include amounts constituting reasonable compensation for present or past services or reasonable payments made in the ordinary course of business pursuant to a bona fide retirement plan or other benefits program. A partner of a limited liability partnership who receives a distribution in violation of subsection (h) of this section, and who did not know at the time of the distribution that the distribution violated subsection (h) of this section, shall not be liable for the amount of the distribution. Subject to subsection (j) of this section, this subsection shall not affect any obligation or liability of a partner of a limited liability partnership under an agreement or other applicable law for the amount of a distribution.

(j) Unless otherwise agreed, a partner of a limited liability partnership who receives a distribution from a limited liability partnership shall have no liability under this chapter or other applicable law for the amount of the distribution after the expiration of 3 years from the date of the distribution.

(k) Section 15-309 of this chapter shall not apply to a distribution to which this section applies.

SUBCHAPTER IX.
CONVERSION; MERGER; DOMESTICATION;
AND TRANSFER

§ 15-901.   Conversion of Certain Entities to a Domestic Partnership

(a) As used in this section and in § 15-105 of this title, the term "other entity" means a corporation, a statutory trust, a business trust, an association, a real estate investment trust, a common-law trust or any other unincorporated business or entity, including a limited partnership (including a limited liability limited partnership), a foreign partnership or a limited liability company.

(b) Any other entity may convert to a domestic partnership (including a limited liability partnership) by complying with subsection (h) of this section and filing with the Secretary of State in accordance with § 15-105 of this chapter:

(1) A certificate of conversion to partnership that has been executed in accordance with § 15-105 of this chapter;

(2) A statement of partnership existence that complies with § 15-303 of this chapter and has been executed in accordance with § 15-105 of this chapter; and

(3) In the case of a conversion to a limited liability partnership, a statement of qualification in accordance with subsection (c) of § 15-1001 of this title.

Each of the certificate and statements required by this subsection (b) shall be filed simultaneously with the Secretary of State and, if such certificate and statements are not to become effective upon their filing as permitted by § 15-105(h) of this title, then such certificate and each such statement shall provide for the same effective date or time in accordance with § 15-105(h) of this title.

(c) The certificate of conversion to partnership shall state:

(1) The date on which and jurisdiction where the other entity was first created, formed or otherwise came into being and, if it has changed, its jurisdiction immediately prior to its conversion to a domestic partnership;

(2) The name and type of entity of the other entity immediately prior to the filing of the certificate of conversion to partnership;

(3) The name of the partnership as set forth in its statement of partnership existence filed in accordance with subsection (b) of this section;

(4) The future effective date or time (which shall be a date or time certain) of the conversion to a partnership if it is not to be effective upon the filing of the certificate of conversion to partnership and the statement of partnership existence; and

(5) In the case of a conversion to a limited liability partnership, that the partnership agreement of the partnership states that the partnership shall be a limited liability partnership.

(d) Upon the filing with the Secretary of State of the certificate of conversion to partnership, the statement of partnership existence and the statement of qualification (if applicable), or upon the future effective date or time of the certificate of conversion to partnership, the statement of partnership existence and the statement of qualification (if applicable), the other entity shall be converted into a domestic partnership (including a limited liability partnership, if applicable) and the partnership shall thereafter be subject to all of the provisions of this chapter, except that the existence of the partnership shall be deemed to have commenced on the date the other entity commenced its existence in the jurisdiction in which the other entity was first created, formed, incorporated or otherwise came into being.

(e) The conversion of any other entity into a domestic partnership (including a limited liability partnership) shall not be deemed to affect any obligations or liabilities of the other entity incurred prior to its conversion to a domestic partnership, or the personal liability of any person incurred prior to such conversion.

(f) When any conversion shall have become effective under this section, for all purposes of the laws of the State of Delaware, all of the rights, privileges and powers of the other entity that has converted, and all property, real, personal and mixed, and all debts due to such other entity, as well as all other things and causes of action belonging to such other entity, shall remain vested in the domestic partnership to which such other entity has converted and shall be the property of such domestic partnership, and the title to any real property vested by deed or otherwise in such other entity shall not revert or be in any way impaired by reason of this chapter; but all rights of creditors and all liens upon any property of such other entity shall be preserved unimpaired, and all debts, liabilities and duties of the other entity that has converted shall remain attached to the domestic partnership to which such other entity has converted, and may be enforced against it to the same extent as if said debts, liabilities and duties had originally been incurred or contracted by it in its capacity as a domestic partnership. The rights, privileges, powers and interests in property of the other entity, as well as the debts, liabilities and duties of the other entity, shall not be deemed, as a consequence of the conversion, to have been transferred to the domestic partnership to which such other entity has converted for any purpose of the laws of the State of Delaware.

(g) Unless otherwise agreed, for all purposes of the laws of the State of Delaware, the converting other entity shall not be required to wind up its affairs or pay its liabilities and distribute its assets, and the conversion shall not be deemed to constitute a dissolution of such other entity. When another entity has been converted to a domestic partnership pursuant to this section, for all purposes of the laws of the State of Delaware, the domestic partnership shall be deemed to be the same entity as the converting other entity and the conversion shall constitute a continuation of the existence of the converting other entity in the form of a domestic partnership.

(h) Prior to filing a certificate of conversion to partnership with the Secretary of State, the conversion shall be approved in the manner provided for by the document, instrument, agreement or other writing, as the case may be, governing the internal affairs of the other entity and the conduct of its business or by applicable law, as appropriate, and a partnership agreement shall be approved by the same authorization required to approve the conversion; provided, that in the event the continuing domestic partnership is not a limited liability partnership, such approval shall include the approval of any person who, at the effective date or time of the conversion, shall be a partner of the partnership.

(i) In connection with a conversion hereunder, rights or securities of, or interests in, the other entity which is to be converted to a domestic partnership may be exchanged for or converted into cash, property, rights or securities of or interests in such domestic partnership or, in addition to or in lieu thereof, may be exchanged for or converted into cash, property, rights or securities of or interests in another domestic partnership or other entity, may remain outstanding or may be cancelled.

(j) In connection with the conversion of any other entity to a domestic partnership (including a limited liability partnership), a person is admitted as a partner of the partnership as provided in the partnership agreement. For the purpose of subsection (b) of § 15-306 of this title, a person who, at the effective time or date of the conversion of any other entity to a domestic partnership (including a limited liability partnership), is a partner of the partnership, shall be deemed admitted as a partner of the partnership at the effective date or time of such conversion.

(k) The provisions of this section shall not be construed to limit the accomplishment of a change in the law governing, or the domicile of, another entity to the State of Delaware by any other means provided for in a document, instrument, agreement or other writing, including by the amendment of any such document, instrument, agreement or other writing, or by applicable law.

§ 15-902.   *Merger or Consolidation*

(a) As used in this section and in § 15-105 of this title, "other business entity" means a corporation, a statutory trust, a business trust, an association, a real estate investment trust, a common-law trust, or an unincorporated business or entity, including a limited liability company, a limited partnership (including a limited liability limited partnership) and a foreign partnership, but excluding a domestic partnership. As used in this section and in § 15-120 of this title, "plan of merger" means a writing approved by a domestic partnership, in the form of resolutions or otherwise, that states the terms and conditions of a merger under subsection (m) of this section.

(b) Pursuant to an agreement of merger or consolidation, 1 or more domestic partnerships may merge or consolidate with or into 1 or more domestic partnerships or 1 or more other business entities formed or organized under the laws of the State of Delaware or any other state or the United States or any foreign country or other foreign jurisdiction, or any combination thereof, with such domestic partnership or other business entity as the agreement shall provide being the surviving or resulting domestic partnership or other business entity. Unless otherwise provided in the partnership agreement, an agreement of merger or consolidation or a plan of merger shall be approved by each domestic partnership which is to merge or consolidate by all of its partners. In connection with a merger or consolidation hereunder, rights or securities of, or interests in, a domestic partnership or other business entity which is a constituent party to the merger or consolidation may be exchanged for or converted into cash, property, rights or securities of, or interests in, the surviving or resulting domestic partnership or other business entity or, in addition to or in lieu thereof, may be exchanged for or converted into cash, property, rights or securities of, or interests in a domestic partnership or other business entity which is not the surviving or resulting domestic partnership or other business entity in the merger or consolidation, may remain outstanding or may be cancelled. Notwithstanding prior approval, an agreement of merger or consolidation or a plan of merger may be terminated or amended pursuant to a provision for such termination or amendment contained in the agreement of merger or consolidation or plan of merger.

(c) Except in the case of a merger under subsection (m) of this section, if a domestic partnership is merging or consolidating under this section, (i) if the domestic partnership has not filed a statement of partnership existence, then the domestic partnership shall file a statement of partnership existence and (ii) the domestic partnership or other business entity surviving or resulting in or from the merger or consolidation shall file a certificate of merger or consolidation executed by at least 1 partner or by 1 or more authorized persons on behalf of the domestic partnership when it is the surviving or resulting entity with the Secretary of State. The certificate of merger or consolidation shall state:

(1) The name, jurisdiction of formation or organization and type of entity of each of the domestic partnerships and other business entities which is to merge or consolidate;

(2) That an agreement of merger or consolidation has been approved and executed by each of the domestic partnerships and other business entities which is to merge or consolidate;

(3) The name of the surviving or resulting domestic partnership or other business entity;

(4) In the case of a merger in which a domestic partnership is the surviving entity, such amendments, if any, to the statement of partnership existence of the surviving domestic partnership (and in the case of a surviving domestic partnership that is a limited liability partnership, to the statement of qualification of such surviving domestic partnership) to change its name, registered office or registered agent as are desired to be effected by the merger;

(5) The future effective date or time (which shall be a date or time certain) of the merger or consolidation if it is not to be effective upon the filing of the certificate of merger or consolidation;

(6) That the agreement of merger or consolidation is on file at a place of business of the surviving or resulting domestic partnership or other business entity, and shall state the address thereof;

(7) That a copy of the agreement of merger or consolidation will be furnished by the surviving or resulting domestic partnership or other business entity, on request and without cost, to any partner of any domestic partnership or any person holding an interest in any other business entity which is to merge or consolidate; and

(8) If the surviving or resulting entity is not formed, organized or created under the laws of the State of Delaware, a statement that such surviving or resulting entity agrees that it may be served with process in the State of Delaware in any action, suit or proceeding for the enforcement of any obligation of any domestic partnership which is to merge or consolidate, irrevocably appointing the Secretary of State as its agent to accept service of process in any such action, suit or proceeding and specifying the address to which a copy of such process shall be mailed to it by the Secretary of State. In the event of service hereunder upon the Secretary of State, the procedures set forth in § 15-113(b) of this title shall be applicable, except that the plaintiff in any such action, suit or proceeding shall furnish the Secretary of State with the address specified in the certificate of merger or consolidation provided for in this section and any other address which the plaintiff may elect to furnish, together with copies of each process as required by the Secretary of State, and the Secretary of State shall notify such surviving or resulting entity at all such addresses furnished by the plaintiff in accordance with the procedures set forth in § 15-113(b) of this title.

(d) Any failure to file a certificate of merger or consolidation in connection with a merger or consolidation which occurred prior to the effective date of this chapter shall not affect the validity or effectiveness of any such merger or consolidation.

(e) Unless a future effective date or time is provided in a certificate of merger or consolidation, or in the case of a merger under subsection (m) of this section in a certificate of ownership and merger, in which event a merger or consolidation shall be effective at any such future effective date or time, a merger or consolidation shall be effective upon the filing with the Secretary of State of a certificate of merger or consolidation or a certificate of ownership and merger.

(f) A certificate of merger or consolidation or a certificate of ownership and merger shall act as a statement of cancellation of the statement of partnership existence (and if applicable the statement of qualification) for a domestic partnership which is not the surviving or resulting entity in the merger or consolidation. A certificate of merger that sets forth any amendment in accordance with paragraph (c)(4) of this section shall be deemed to be an amendment to the statement of partnership existence (and if applicable to the statement of qualification) of the domestic partnership, and the domestic partnership shall not be required to take any further action to amend its statement of partnership existence (or if applicable its statement of qualification) under § 15-105 of this title with respect to such amendments set forth in the certificate of merger. Whenever this section requires the filing of a certificate of merger or consolidation, such requirement shall be deemed satisfied by the filing of an agreement of merger or consolidation containing the information required by this section to be set forth in the certificate of merger or consolidation.

(g) An agreement of merger or consolidation or a plan of merger approved in accordance with subsection (b) of this section may (1) effect any amendment to the partnership agreement or (2) effect the adoption of a new partnership agreement for a domestic partnership if it is the surviving or resulting partnership in the merger or consolidation. Any amendment to a partnership agreement or adoption of a new partnership agreement made pursuant to the foregoing sentence shall be effective at the effective time or date of the merger or consolidation and shall be effective notwithstanding any provision of the partnership agreement relating to amendment or adoption of a new partnership agreement, other than a provision that by its terms applies to an amendment to the partnership agreement or the adoption of a new partnership agreement, in either case, in connection with a merger or consolidation. The provisions of this subsection shall not be construed to limit the accomplishment of a merger or of any of the matters referred to herein by any other means provided for in a partnership agreement or other agreement or as otherwise permitted by law, including that the partnership agreement of any constituent domestic partnership to the merger or consolidation (including a domestic partnership formed for the purpose of consummating a merger or consolidation) shall be the partnership agreement of the surviving or resulting domestic partnership.

(h) When any merger or consolidation shall have become effective under this section, for all purposes of the laws of the State of Delaware, all of the rights, privileges and powers of each of the domestic partnerships and other business entities that have merged or consolidated, and all property, real, personal and mixed, and all debts due to any of said domestic partnerships and other business entities, as well as all other things and causes of action belonging to each of such domestic partnerships and other business entities, shall be vested in the surviving or resulting domestic partnership or other business entity, and shall thereafter be the property of the surviving or resulting domestic partnership or other business entity as they were of each of the domestic partnerships and other business entities that have merged or consolidated, and the title to any real property vested by deed or otherwise, under the laws of the State of Delaware, in any of such domestic partnerships and other business entities, shall not revert or be in any way impaired by reason of this chapter; but all rights of creditors and all liens upon any property of any of said domestic partnerships and other business entities shall be preserved unimpaired, and all debts, liabilities and duties of each of the said domestic partnerships and other business entities that have merged or consolidated shall thenceforth attach to the surviving or resulting domestic partnership or other business entity, and may be enforced against it to the same extent as if said debts, liabilities and duties had been incurred or contracted by it. Unless otherwise agreed, a merger or consolidation of a domestic partnership, including a domestic partnership which is not the surviving or resulting entity in the merger or consolidation, shall not require such domestic partnership to wind up its affairs under subchapter VIII of this chapter of this title or pay its liabilities and distribute its assets under subchapter VIII of this chapter of this title, and the merger or consolidation shall not constitute a dissolution of such partnership.

(i) Except as provided by agreement with a person to whom a partner of a domestic partnership is obligated, a merger or consolidation of a domestic partnership that has become effective shall not affect any obligation or liability existing at the time of such merger or consolidation of a partner of a domestic partnership which is merging or consolidating.

(j) If a domestic partnership is a constituent party to a merger or consolidation that shall have become effective, but the domestic partnership is not the surviving or resulting entity of the merger or consolidation, then a judgment creditor of a partner of such domestic partnership may not levy execution against the assets of the partner to satisfy a judgment based on a claim against the surviving entity of the merger or consolidation unless:

(1) The claim is for an obligation of the domestic partnership for which the partner is liable as provided in Section 15-306 and either:

(i) A judgment based on the same claim has been obtained against the surviving or resulting entity of the merger or consolidation and a writ of execution on the judgment has been returned unsatisfied in whole or in part;

(ii) The surviving or resulting entity of the merger or consolidation is a debtor in bankruptcy;

(iii) The partner has agreed that the creditor need not exhaust the assets of the domestic partnership that was not the surviving or resulting entity of the merger or consolidation;

(iv) The partner has agreed that the creditor need not exhaust the assets of the surviving or resulting entity of the merger or consolidation; or

(v) A court grants permission to the judgment creditor to levy execution against the assets of the partner based on a finding that the assets of the surviving or resulting entity of the merger or consolidation that are subject to execution are clearly insufficient to satisfy the judgment, that exhaustion of the assets of the surviving or resulting entity of the merger or consolidation is excessively burdensome, or that the grant of permission is an appropriate exercise of the court's equitable powers; or

(2) Liability is imposed on the partner by law or contract independent of the existence of the surviving or resulting entity of the merger or consolidation.

(k) A person is admitted as a partner of a surviving or resulting domestic partnership pursuant to a merger or consolidation approved in accordance with subsection (b) of this section as provided in the partnership agreement of the surviving or resulting domestic partnership or in the agreement of merger or consolidation or the plan of merger, and in the event of any inconsistency, the terms of the agreement of merger or consolidation or the plan of merger shall control. A person is admitted as a partner of a domestic partnership pursuant to a merger or consolidation in which such domestic partnership is not the surviving or resulting domestic partnership in the merger or consolidation as provided in the partnership agreement of such domestic partnership.

(l) A partnership agreement may provide that a domestic partnership shall not have the power to merge or consolidate as set forth in this section.

(m) In any case in which (i) at least 90% of the outstanding shares of each class of the stock of a corporation or corporations (other than a corporation which has in its certificate of incorporation the provision required by § 251(g)(7)(i) of Title 8), of which class there are outstanding shares that, absent § 267(a) of Title 8, would be entitled to vote on such merger, is owned by a domestic partnership, (ii) 1 or more of such corporations is a corporation of the State of Delaware, and (iii) any corporation that is not a corporation of the State of Delaware is a corporation of any other state or the District of Columbia or another jurisdiction, the laws of which do not forbid such merger, the domestic partnership having such stock ownership may either merge the corporation or corporations into itself and assume all of its or their obligations, or merge itself, or itself and 1 or more of such corporations, into 1 of the other corporations, pursuant to a plan of merger. If a domestic partnership is causing a merger under this subsection, the domestic partnership shall file a certificate of ownership and merger executed by at least 1 partner or by 1 or more authorized persons on behalf of the domestic partnership in the office of the Secretary of State. The certificate of ownership and merger shall certify that such merger was authorized in accordance with the domestic partnership's partnership agreement and this chapter, and if the domestic partnership shall not own all the outstanding stock of all the corporations that are parties to the merger, shall state the terms and conditions of the merger, including the securities, cash, property, or rights to be issued, paid, delivered or granted by the surviving domestic partnership or corporation upon surrender of each share of the corporation or corporations not owned by the domestic partnership, or the cancellation of some or all of such shares. The terms and conditions of the merger may not result in a holder of stock in a corporation becoming a partner in a surviving domestic partnership (other than a limited liability partnership). If a corporation surviving a merger under this subsection is not a corporation organized under the laws of the State of Delaware, then the terms and conditions of the merger shall obligate such corporation to agree that it may be served with process in the State of Delaware in any proceeding for enforcement of any obligation of the domestic partnership or any obligation of any constituent corporation of the State of Delaware, as well as for enforcement of any obligation of the surviving corporation, including any suit or other proceeding to enforce the right of any stockholders as determined in appraisal proceedings pursuant to § 262 of Title 8, and to irrevocably appoint the Secretary of State as its agent to accept service of process in any such suit or other proceedings, and to specify the address to which a copy of such process shall be mailed by the Secretary of State. Process may be served upon the Secretary of State under this subsection by means of electronic transmission but only as prescribed by the Secretary of State. The Secretary of State is authorized to issue such rules and regulations with respect to such service as the Secretary of State deems necessary or appropriate. In the event of such service upon the Secretary of State in accordance with this subsection, the Secretary of State shall forthwith notify such surviving corporation thereof by letter, directed to such surviving corporation at its address so specified, unless such surviving corporation shall have designated in writing to the Secretary of State a different address for such purpose, in which case it shall be mailed to the last address so designated. Such letter shall be sent by a mail or courier service that includes a record of mailing or deposit with the courier and a record of delivery evidenced by the signature of the recipient. Such letter shall enclose a copy of the process and any other papers served on the Secretary of State pursuant to this subsection. It shall be the duty of the plaintiff in the event of such service to serve process and any other papers in duplicate, to notify the Secretary of State that service is being effected pursuant to this subsection and to pay the Secretary of State the sum of $50 for the use of the State of Delaware, which sum shall be taxed as part of the costs in the proceeding, if the plaintiff shall prevail therein. The Secretary of State shall maintain an alphabetical record of any such service setting forth the name of the plaintiff and the defendant, the title, docket number and nature of the proceeding in which process has been served, the fact that service has been effected pursuant to this subsection, the return date thereof, and the day and hour service was made. The Secretary of State shall not be required to retain such information longer than 5 years from receipt of the service of process.

§ 15-903.   *Approval of Conversion of a Domestic Partnership*

(a) Upon compliance with this section, a domestic partnership may convert to a corporation, a statutory trust, a business trust, an association, a real estate investment trust, a common-law trust or any other unincorporated business or entity, including a limited partnership (including a limited liability limited partnership), a foreign partnership or a limited liability company. If a domestic partnership is converting under this section to another business form organized, formed or created under the laws of a jurisdiction other than the State of Delaware and has not filed a statement of partnership existence, then the domestic partnership shall file a statement of partnership existence prior to or at the time of the filing of the certificate of conversion to non-Delaware entity.

(b) If the partnership agreement specifies the manner of authorizing a conversion of the partnership, the conversion shall be authorized as specified in the partnership agreement. If the partnership agreement does not specify the manner of authorizing a conversion of the partnership and does not prohibit a conversion of the partnership, the conversion shall be authorized in the same manner as is specified in the partnership agreement for authorizing a merger or consolidation that involves the partnership as a constituent party to the merger or consolidation. If the partnership agreement does not specify the manner of authorizing a conversion of the partnership or a merger or consolidation that involves the partnership as a constituent party and does not prohibit a conversion of the partnership, the conversion shall be authorized by the approval by all the partners.

(c) Unless otherwise agreed, the conversion of a domestic partnership to another entity or business form pursuant to this section shall not require such partnership to wind up its affairs under subchapter VIII of this chapter or pay its liabilities and distribute its assets under subchapter VIII of this chapter, and the conversion shall not constitute a dissolution of such partnership. When a partnership has converted to another entity or business form pursuant to this section, for all purposes of the laws of the State of Delaware, the other entity or business form shall be deemed to be the same entity as the converting partnership and the conversion shall constitute a continuation of the existence of the partnership in the form of such other entity or business form.

(d) In connection with a conversion of a domestic partnership to another entity or business form pursuant to this section, rights or securities of or interests in the domestic partnership which is to be converted may be exchanged for or converted into cash, property, rights or securities of or interests in the entity or business form into which the domestic partnership is being converted or, in addition to or in lieu thereof, may be exchanged for or converted into cash, property, rights or securities of or interests in another entity or business form, may remain outstanding or may be cancelled.

(e) If a partnership shall convert in accordance with this section to another entity or business form organized, formed or created under the laws of a jurisdiction other than the State of Delaware, a certificate of conversion to non-Delaware entity executed in accordance with § 15-105 of this title shall be filed in the office of the Secretary of State in accordance with § 15-105 of this title. The certificate of conversion to non-Delaware entity shall state:

(1) The name of the partnership and, if it has been changed, the name under which its statement of partnership existence was originally filed;

(2) The date of the filing of its original statement of partnership existence with the Secretary of State;

(3) The jurisdiction in which the entity or business form, to which the partnership shall be converted, is organized, formed or created, and the name of such entity or business form;

(4) The future effective date or time (which shall be a date or time certain) of the conversion if it is not to be effective upon the filing of the certificate of conversion to non-Delaware entity;

(5) That the conversion has been approved in accordance with this section;

(6) The agreement of the partnership that it may be served with process in the State of Delaware in any action, suit or proceeding for enforcement of any obligation of the partnership arising while it was a partnership of the State of Delaware, and that it irrevocably appoints the Secretary of State as its agent to accept service of process in any such action, suit or proceeding;

(7) The address to which a copy of the process referred to in subdivision (e)(6) of this section shall be mailed to it by the Secretary of State. In the event of service hereunder upon the Secretary of State, the procedures set forth in § 15-112(b) of this title shall be applicable, except that the plaintiff in any such action, suit or proceeding shall furnish the Secretary of State with the address specified in this subdivision and any other address that the plaintiff may elect to furnish, together with copies of such process as required by the Secretary of State, and the Secretary of State shall notify the partnership that has converted out of the State of Delaware at all such addresses furnished by the plaintiff in accordance with the procedures set forth in § 15-112(b) of this title.

(f) Upon the filing in the office of the Secretary of State of the certificate of conversion to non-Delaware entity or upon the future effective date or time of the certificate of conversion to non-Delaware entity and payment to the Secretary of State of all fees prescribed in this chapter, the Secretary of State shall certify that the partnership has filed all documents and paid all fees required by this chapter, and thereupon the partnership shall cease to exist as a partnership of the State of Delaware. Such certificate of the Secretary of State shall be prima facie evidence of the conversion by such partnership out of the State of Delaware.

(g) The conversion of a partnership out of the State of Delaware in accordance with this section and the resulting cessation of its existence as a partnership of the State of Delaware pursuant to a certificate of conversion to non-Delaware entity shall not be deemed to affect any obligations or liabilities of the partnership incurred prior to such conversion or the personal liability of any person incurred prior to such conversion, nor shall it be deemed to affect the choice of law applicable to the partnership with respect to matters arising prior to such conversion.

(h) When a domestic partnership has been converted to another entity or business form pursuant to this section, the other entity or business form shall, for all purposes of the laws of the State of Delaware, be deemed to be the same entity as the domestic partnership. When any conversion shall have become effective under this section, for all purposes of the laws of the State of Delaware, all of the rights, privileges and powers of the domestic partnership that has converted, and all property, real, personal and mixed, and all debts due to such partnership, as well as all other things and causes of action belonging to such partnership, shall remain vested in the other entity or business form to which such partnership has converted and shall be the property of such other entity or business form, and the title to any real property vested by deed or otherwise in such partnership shall not revert or be in any way impaired by reason of this chapter; but all rights of creditors and all liens upon any property of such partnership shall be preserved unimpaired, and all debts, liabilities and duties of the domestic partnership that has converted shall remain attached to the other entity or business form to which such partnership has converted, and may be enforced against it to the same extent as if said debts, liabilities and duties had originally been incurred or contracted by it in its capacity as such other entity or business form. The rights, privileges, powers and interests in property of the domestic partnership that has converted, as well as the debts, liabilities and duties of such partnership, shall not be deemed, as a consequence of the conversion, to have been transferred to the other entity or business form to which such partnership has converted for any purpose of the laws of the State of Delaware.

(i) A partnership agreement may provide that a domestic partnership shall not have the power to convert as set forth in this section.

§ 15-904.   Domestication of Non-United States Entities

(a) As used in this section and in § 15-105 of this title, "non-United States entity" means a foreign limited partnership (other than 1 formed under the laws of a state) (including a foreign limited liability limited partnership (other than 1 formed under the laws of a state)), or a corporation, a statutory trust, a business trust, an association, a real estate investment trust, a common-law trust or any other unincorporated business or entity, including a general partnership (including a limited liability partnership) or a limited liability company, formed, incorporated, created or that otherwise came into being under the laws of any foreign country or other foreign jurisdiction (other than any state).

(b) Any non-United States entity may become domesticated as a partnership (including a limited liability partnership) in the State of Delaware by complying with subsection (g) of this section and filing with the Secretary of State in accordance with Section 15-105 of this chapter:

(1) A certificate of partnership domestication that has been executed in accordance with Section 15-105 of this chapter;

(2) A statement of partnership existence that complies with Section 15-303 of this chapter and has been executed in accordance with Section 15-105 of this; and

(3) In the case of a domestication as a limited liability partnership, a statement of qualification in accordance with § 15-1001(c) of this title. The certificate and the statements required by this subsection (b) shall be filed simultaneously with the Secretary of State and, if such certificate and such statements are not to become effective upon their filing as permitted by § 15-105(h) of this title, then such certificate and such statements shall provide for the same effective date or time in accordance with § 15-105(h) of this title.

(c) The certificate of partnership domestication shall state:

(1) The date on which and jurisdiction where the non-United States entity was first formed, incorporated, created or otherwise came into being;

(2) The name of the non-United States entity immediately prior to the filing of the certificate of partnership domestication;

(3) The name of the partnership as set forth in the statement of partnership existence filed in accordance with subsection (b) of this section;

(4) The future effective date or time (which shall be a date or time certain) of the domestication as a partnership if it is not to be effective upon the filing of the certificate of partnership domestication and the statement of partnership existence;

(5) The jurisdiction that constituted the seat, siege social, or principal place of business or central administration of the non-United States entity, or

any other equivalent thereto under applicable law, immediately prior to the filing of the certificate of partnership domestication; and

(6) That the domestication has been approved in the manner provided for by the document, instrument, agreement or other writing, as the case may be, governing the internal affairs of the non-United States entity and the conduct of its business or by applicable non-Delaware law, as appropriate.

(7) In the case of a domestication as a limited liability partnership, that the partnership agreement of the partnership states that the partnership shall be a limited liability partnership.

(d) Upon the filing with the Secretary of State of the certificate of partnership domestication, the statement of partnership existence and the statement of qualification (if applicable or upon the future effective date or time of the certificate of partnership domestication, the statement of partnership existence and the statement of qualification (if applicable, the non-United States entity shall be domesticated as a partnership including a limited liability partnership, if applicable in the State of Delaware and the partnership shall thereafter be subject to all of the provisions of this chapter, provided that the existence of the partnership shall be deemed to have commenced on the date the non-United States entity commenced its existence in the jurisdiction in which the non-United States entity was first formed, incorporated, created or otherwise came into being.

(e) The domestication of any non-United States entity as a partnership (including a limited liability partnership) in the State of Delaware shall not be deemed to affect any obligations or liabilities of the non-United States entity incurred prior to its domestication as a partnership in the State of Delaware, or the personal liability of any person therefor.

(f) The filing of a certificate of partnership domestication shall not affect the choice of law applicable to the non-United States entity, except that from the effective date or time of the domestication, the laws of the State of Delaware, including the provisions of this chapter, shall apply to the non-United States entity to the same extent as if the non-United States entity had been formed as a partnership on that date.

(g) Prior to the filing of a certificate of partnership domestication with the Secretary of State, the domestication shall be approved in the manner provided for by the document, instrument, agreement or other writing, as the case may be, governing the internal affairs of the non-United States entity and the conduct of its business or by applicable non-Delaware law, as appropriate, and a partnership agreement shall be approved by the same authorization required to approve the domestication; provided that, in the event the continuing domestic partnership is not a limited liability partnership, such approval shall include the approval of any person who, at the effective date or time of the domestication, shall be a partner of the partnership.

(h) When any domestication shall have become effective under this section, for all purposes of the laws of the State of Delaware, all of the rights, privileges and powers of the non-United States entity that has been domesticated, and all property, real, personal and mixed, and all debts due to such non-United States entity, as well as all other things and causes of action belonging to such non-United States entity, shall remain vested in the domestic partnership to which such non-United States entity has been domesticated (and also in the non-United States entity, if and for so long as the non-United States entity continues its existence in the foreign jurisdiction in which it was existing immediately prior to the domestication) and shall be the property of such domestic partnership (and also of the non-United States entity, if and for so long as the non-United States entity continues its existence in the foreign jurisdiction in which it was existing immediately prior to the domestication), and the title to any real property vested by deed or otherwise in such non-United States entity shall not revert or be in any way impaired by reason of this chapter; but all rights of creditors and all liens upon any property of such non-United States entity shall be preserved unimpaired, and all debts, liabilities and duties of the non-United States entity that has been domesticated shall remain attached to the domestic partnership to which such non-United States entity has been domesticated (and also to the non-United States entity, if and for so long as the non-United States entity continues its existence in the foreign jurisdiction in which it was existing immediately prior to the domestication), and may be enforced against it to the same extent as if said debts, liabilities and duties had originally been incurred or contracted by it in its capacity as a domestic partnership. The rights, privileges, powers and interests in property of the non-United States entity, as well as the debts, liabilities and duties of the non-United States entity, shall not be deemed, as a consequence of the domestication, to have been transferred to the domestic partnership to which such non-United States entity has domesticated for any purpose of the laws of the State of Delaware.

(i) When a non-United States entity has become domesticated as a domestic partnership pursuant to this section, for all purposes of the laws of the State of Delaware, the domestic partnership shall be deemed to be the same entity as the domesticating non-United States entity and the domestication shall constitute a continuation of the existence of the domesticating non-United States entity in the form of a domestic partnership. Unless otherwise agreed, for all purposes of the laws of the State of Delaware, the domesticating non-United States entity shall not be required to wind up its affairs or pay its liabilities and distribute its assets, and the domestication shall not be deemed to constitute a dissolution of such non-United States entity. If, following domestication, a non-United States entity that has become domesticated as a domestic partnership continues its existence in the foreign country or other foreign jurisdiction in which it was existing immediately prior to domestication, the domestic partnership and such non-United

States entity shall, for all purposes of the laws of the State of Delaware, constitute a single entity formed, incorporated, created or otherwise having come into
being, as applicable, and existing under the laws of the State of Delaware and the
laws of such foreign country or other foreign jurisdiction.

(j) In connection with a domestication hereunder, rights or securities of, or
interests in, the non-United States entity that is to be domesticated as a domestic
partnership may be exchanged for or converted into cash, property, rights or
securities of, or interests in, such domestic partnership or, in addition to or in
lieu thereof, may be exchanged for or converted into cash, property, rights or
securities of, or interests in, another domestic partnership or other entity, may
remain outstanding or may be cancelled.

(k) In connection with the domestication of a non-United States entity as a
domestic partnership (including a limited liability partnership), a person is admitted as a partner of the partnership as provided in the partnership agreement.
For the purpose of subsection (b) of § 15-306 of this title, a person who, at the
effective time or date of the domestication of any non-United States entity as a
domestic partnership (including a limited liability partnership), is a partner of the
partnership, shall be deemed admitted as a partner of the partnership at the effective date or time of such domestication.

§ 15-905.   *Transfer or Continuance of Domestic Partnerships*

(a) Upon compliance with the provisions of this section, any domestic partnership may transfer to or domesticate or continue in any jurisdiction, other than
any state, and, in connection therewith, may elect to continue its existence as a
partnership in the State of Delaware. If a domestic partnership is transferring or
domesticating or continuing under this section and has not filed a statement
of partnership existence, then the domestic partnership shall file a statement
of partnership existence prior to or at the time of the filing of the certificate of
transfer or certificate of transfer and domestic continuance.

(b) If the partnership agreement specifies the manner of authorizing a transfer or domestication or continuance described in subsection (a) of this section,
the transfer or domestication or continuance shall be authorized as specified in
the partnership agreement. If the partnership agreement does not specify the
manner of authorizing a transfer or domestication or continuance described in
subsection (a) of this section and does not prohibit such a transfer or domestication or continuance, the transfer or domestication or continuance shall be authorized in the same manner as is specified in the partnership agreement for
authorizing a merger or consolidation that involves the partnership as a constituent party to the merger or consolidation. If the partnership agreement does not
specify the manner of authorizing a transfer or domestication or continuance

described in subsection (a) of this section or a merger or consolidation that involves the partnership as a constituent party and does not prohibit such a transfer or domestication or continuance, the transfer or domestication or continuance shall be authorized by the approval by all the partners. If a transfer or domestication or continuance described in subsection (a) of this section shall be authorized as provided in this subsection (b), a certificate of transfer if the partnership's existence as a partnership of the State of Delaware is to cease, or a certificate of transfer and domestic continuance if the partnership's existence as a partnership in the State of Delaware is to continue, executed in accordance with § 15-105 of this title, shall be filed with the Secretary of State in accordance with § 15-105 of this title. The certificate of transfer or the certificate of transfer and domestic continuance shall state:

(1) The name of the partnership and, if it has been changed, the name under which its statement of partnership existence was originally filed;

(2) The date of the filing of its original statement of partnership existence with the Secretary of State;

(3) The jurisdiction to which the partnership shall be transferred or in which it shall be domesticated or continued and the name of the entity or business form formed, incorporated, created or that otherwise comes into being as a consequence of the transfer of the partnership to, or its domestication or continuance in, such foreign jurisdiction;

(4) The future effective date or time (which shall be a date or time certain) of the transfer to or domestication or continuance in the jurisdiction specified in paragraph (b)(3) of this section if it is not to be effective upon the filing of the certificate of transfer or the certificate of transfer and domestic continuance;

(5) That the transfer or domestication or continuance of the partnership has been approved in accordance with the provisions of this section;

(6) In the case of a certificate of transfer, (i) that the existence of the partnership as a partnership of the State of Delaware shall cease when the certificate of transfer becomes effective and (ii) the agreement of the partnership that it may be served with process in the State of Delaware in any action, suit or proceeding for enforcement of any obligation of the partnership arising while it was a partnership of the State of Delaware, and that it irrevocably appoints the Secretary of State as its agent to accept service of process in any such action, suit or proceeding;

(7) The address (which may not be that of the partnership's registered agent without the written consent of the partnership's registered agent, such consent to be filed with the certificate of transfer) to which a copy of the process referred to in paragraph (b)(6) of this section shall be mailed to it by the Secretary of State. In the event of service hereunder upon the Secretary of State, the procedures set forth in § 15-113(b) of this title shall be applica-

ble, except that the plaintiff in any such action, suit or proceeding shall furnish the Secretary of State with the address specified in this subsection and any other address that the plaintiff may elect to furnish, together with copies of such process as required by the Secretary of State, and the Secretary of State shall notify the partnership that has transferred or domesticated or continued out of the State of Delaware at all such addresses furnished by the plaintiff in accordance with the procedures set forth in § 15-113(b) of this title; and

(8) In the case of a certificate of transfer and domestic continuance, that the partnership will continue to exist as a partnership of the State of Delaware after the certificate of transfer and domestic continuance becomes effective.

(c) Upon the filing with the Secretary of State of the certificate of transfer or upon the future effective date or time of the certificate of transfer and payment to the Secretary of State of all fees prescribed in this chapter, the Secretary of State shall certify that the partnership has filed all documents and paid all fees required by this chapter, and thereupon the partnership shall cease to exist as a partnership of the State. Such certificate of the Secretary of State shall be prima facie evidence of the transfer or domestication or continuance by such partnership out of the State of Delaware.

(d) The transfer or domestication or continuance of a partnership out of the State of Delaware in accordance with this section and the resulting cessation of its existence as a partnership of the State of Delaware pursuant to a certificate of transfer shall not be deemed to affect any obligations or liabilities of the partnership incurred prior to such transfer or domestication or continuance or the personal liability of any person incurred prior to such transfer or domestication or continuance, nor shall it be deemed to affect the choice of law applicable to the partnership with respect to matters arising prior to such transfer or domestication or continuance. Unless otherwise agreed, the transfer or domestication or continuance of a partnership out of the State of Delaware in accordance with this section shall not require such partnership to wind up its affairs under subchapter VIII of this chapter or pay its liabilities and distribute its assets under subchapter VIII of this chapter and shall not be deemed to constitute a dissolution of such partnership.

(e) If a partnership files a certificate of transfer and domestic continuance, after the time the certificate of transfer and domestic continuance becomes effective, the partnership shall continue to exist as a partnership of the State of Delaware, and the laws of the State of Delaware, including the provisions of this chapter, shall apply to the partnership, to the same extent as prior to such time. So long as a partnership continues to exist as a partnership of the State of Delaware following the filing of a certificate of transfer and domestic continuance, the continuing domestic partnership and the entity or business form formed, incorporated, created or that otherwise came into being as a consequence of the transfer of the partnership to, or its domestication or continuance in, a foreign country or other foreign jurisdiction shall, for all purposes of the laws of the State of Delaware, constitute a single entity formed, incorporated, created or otherwise having come into being, as applicable, and existing under the laws of the State of Delaware and the laws of such foreign country or other foreign jurisdiction.

(f) In connection with a transfer or domestication or continuance of a domestic partnership to or in another jurisdiction pursuant to subsection (a) of this section, rights or securities of, or interests in, such partnership may be exchanged for or converted into cash, property, rights or securities of, or interests in, the entity or business form in which the partnership will exist in such other jurisdiction as a consequence of the transfer or domestication or continuance or, in addition to or in lieu thereof, may be exchanged for or converted into cash, property, rights or securities of, or interests in, another entity or business form, may remain outstanding or may be cancelled.

(g) When a domestic partnership has transferred or domesticated or continued out of the State of Delaware pursuant to this section, the transferred or domesticated or continued entity or business form shall, for all purposes of the laws of the State of Delaware, be deemed to be the same entity as the domestic partnership and shall constitute a continuation of the existence of such domestic partnership in the form of the transferred or domesticated or continued entity or business form. When any transfer or domestication or continuance of a domestic partnership out of the State of Delaware shall have become effective under this section, for all purposes of the laws of the State of Delaware, all of the rights, privileges and powers of the domestic partnership that has transferred or domesticated or continued, and all property, real, personal and mixed, and all debts due to such partnership, as well as all other things and causes of action belonging to such partnership, shall remain vested in the transferred or domesticated or continued entity or business form (and also in the domestic partnership that has transferred, domesticated or continued, if and for so long as such domestic partnership continues its existence as a domestic partnership) and shall be the property of such transferred or domesticated or continued entity or business form (and also of the domestic partnership that has transferred, domesticated or continued, if and for so long as such domestic partnership continues its existence as a domestic partnership), and the title to any real property vested by deed or otherwise in such partnership shall not revert or be in any way impaired by reason of this chapter; but all rights of creditors and all liens upon any property of such partnership shall be preserved unimpaired, and all debts, liabilities and duties of the domestic partnership that has transferred or domesticated or continued shall remain attached to the transferred or domesticated or continued entity or business form (and also to the domestic partnership that has transferred, domesticated or continued, if and for so long as such domestic partnership continues its existence as a domestic partnership), and may be enforced against it to the same extent as if said debts, liabilities and duties had originally been incurred or contracted by it in its capacity as the transferred or domesticated or continued entity or business form. The rights, privileges, powers and interests in property of the domestic partnership that has transferred or domesticated or continued, as well as the debts, liabilities and duties of such partnership, shall not be deemed, as a consequence of the transfer or domestication or continuance out of the State of Delaware, to have been transferred to the transferred or domesticated or continued entity or business form for any purpose of the laws of the State of Delaware.

(h) A partnership agreement may provide that a domestic partnership shall not have the power to transfer, domesticate or continue as set forth in this section.

SUBCHAPTER X.
LIMITED LIABILITY PARTNERSHIP

§ 15-1001.   *Statement of Qualification of a Domestic Partnership*

(a) A domestic partnership may be formed as, or may become, a limited liability partnership pursuant to this section.

(b) In order to form a limited liability partnership, the original partnership agreement of the partnership shall state that the partnership is formed as a limited liability partnership, and the partnership shall file a statement of qualification in accordance with subsection (c) of this section. In order for an existing partnership to become a limited liability partnership, the terms and conditions on which the partnership becomes a limited liability partnership must be approved by the vote necessary to amend the partnership agreement and, in the case of a partnership agreement that expressly considers obligations to contribute to the partnership, also the vote necessary to amend those provisions, and after such approval, the partnership shall file a statement of qualification in accordance with subsection (c) of this section.

(c) The statement of qualification must contain:

(1) The name of the partnership;

(2) The address of the registered office and the name and address of the registered agent for service of process required to be maintained by § 15-111 of this title;

(3) The number of partners of the partnership at the time of the effectiveness of the statement of qualification;

(4) A statement that the partnership elects to be a limited liability partnership; and

(5) The future effective date or time (which shall be a date or time certain) of the statement of qualification if it is not to be effective upon the filing of the statement of qualification.

(d) The status of a partnership as a limited liability partnership is effective on the later of the filing of the statement of qualification or a future effective date or time specified in the statement of qualification. The status as a limited liability partnership remains effective, regardless of changes in the partnership and regardless of cancellation of a statement of partnership existence for such partnership pursuant to the filing of a statement of cancellation to accomplish the cancellation of such statement of partnership existence or pursuant to § 15-1209(a) of this title, until the statement of qualification is canceled pursuant to § 15-105(d), § 15-111(d), or § 15-111(i)(4) of this chapter or revoked pursuant to § 15-1003 of this chapter.

(e) A partnership is a limited liability partnership if there has been substantial compliance with the requirements of this subchapter. The status of a partnership as a limited liability partnership and the liability of its partners is not affected by errors or later changes in the information required to be contained in the statement of qualification under subsection (c).

(f) The filing of a statement of qualification establishes that a partnership has satisfied all conditions precedent to the qualification of the partnership as a limited liability partnership.

(g) An amendment or cancellation of a statement of qualification is effective when it is filed or on a future effective date or time specified in the amendment or cancellation.

(h) If a person is included in the number of partners of a limited liability partnership set forth in a statement of qualification, a statement of foreign qualification or an annual report, the inclusion of such person shall not be admissible as evidence in any action, suit or proceeding, whether civil, criminal, administrative or investigative, for the purpose of determining whether such person is liable as a partner of such limited liability partnership. The status of a partnership as a limited liability partnership and the liability of a partner of such limited liability partnership shall not be adversely affected if the number of partners stated in a statement of qualification, a statement of foreign qualification or an annual report is erroneously stated provided that the statement of qualification, the statement of foreign qualification or the annual report was filed in good faith.

(i) Notwithstanding anything in this chapter to the contrary, a domestic partnership having, or that but for its election in accordance with § 15-1206(c) of this chapter, would have had, on December 31, 2001, the status of a registered limited liability partnership under predecessor law, shall have the status of a limited liability partnership under this chapter as of January 1, 2002, and to the extent such partnership has not filed a statement of qualification pursuant to this section, the latest application or renewal application filed by such partnership under such predecessor law shall constitute a statement of qualification filed under this section.

§ 15-1002.   Name

The name of a limited liability partnership shall comply with Section 15-108 of this chapter.

§ 15-1003.   Annual Report

(a) A limited liability partnership, and a foreign limited liability partnership authorized to transact business in the State of Delaware, shall file an annual report with the Secretary of State which contains:

(1) the name of the limited liability partnership and the state or other jurisdiction under whose laws the foreign limited liability partnership is formed and the number of partners of the partnership as of the date of the filing of the annual report or, in the case of a delinquent annual report, the number of partners as of June 1 of the year such annual report was due; and

(2) the address of the registered office and the name and address of the registered agent for service of process required to be maintained by § 15-111 of this chapter.

(b) An annual report must be filed by June 1 of each year following the calendar year in which a statement of qualification filed by a partnership becomes effective or a foreign partnership becomes authorized to transact business in the State of Delaware.

(c) On or before March 31 of each year, the Secretary of State shall mail to each partnership at its registered office set forth in the last filed statement of qualification or statement of foreign qualification or annual report a notice specifying that the annual report together with applicable fees shall be due on June 1 of the current year and stating that the statement of qualification or statement of foreign qualification of the partnership shall be revoked unless such report is filed and such filing fee is paid on or before June 1 of the following year. The Secretary of State shall not issue a certificate of good standing with respect to any limited liability partnership or foreign limited liability partnership which has not filed an annual report and paid the required filing fee pursuant to this section or with respect to any limited liability partnership or foreign limited liability partnership if its statement of qualification or statement of foreign qualification (as applicable) is canceled or revoked. The statement of qualification or statement of foreign qualification of any such partnership that fails to file such annual report or pay such required filing fee on or before June 1 of the following year shall be revoked.

(d) A revocation under subsection (c) only affects a partnership's status as a limited liability partnership and is not an event of dissolution of the partnership.

(e) A partnership whose statement of qualification or statement of foreign qualification has been revoked pursuant to subsection (c) may apply to the Secretary of State for reinstatement after the effective date of the revocation. The application must state:

> (1) the name of the partnership and the effective date of the revocation; and

> (2) that the ground for revocation either did not exist or has been corrected.

(f) A reinstatement under subsection (e) relates back to and takes effect as of the effective date of the revocation, and the partnership's status as a limited liability partnership continues as if the revocation had never occurred.

§ 15-1004.   Reinstatement of Statement of Qualification or Statement of Foreign Qualification

(a) A partnership whose statement of qualification or statement of foreign qualification has been canceled pursuant to §§ 15-111(d) or 15-111(i)(4) of this title may apply to the Secretary of State for reinstatement after the effective date of the cancellation. The application must state:

> (1) The name of the partnership and the effective date of the cancellation and, if such name is not available at the time of reinstatement, the name under which the statement of qualification or statement of foreign qualification is to be reinstated; and

> (2) That the partnership has obtained and designated a new registered agent as required by § 15-111(a) of this title and the name and address of such new registered agent and the address of the partnership's registered office in the State of Delaware.

(b) A cancellation of a partnership's statement of qualification or statement of foreign qualification pursuant to § 15-111(d) and § 15-111(i)(4) of this title only affects a partnership's status as a limited liability partnership or a foreign limited liability partnership and is not an event of dissolution of the partnership.

(c) A reinstatement under subsection (a) of this section relates back to and takes effect as of the effective date of the cancellation, and the partnership's status as a limited liability partnership or a foreign limited liability partnership continues as if the cancellation had never occurred.

SUBCHAPTER XI.
FOREIGN LIMITED LIABILITY PARTNERSHIP

§ 15-1101.   Law Governing Foreign Limited Liability Partnership

(a) The law under which a foreign limited liability partnership is formed governs relations among the partners and between the partners and the partnership and the liability of partners for obligations of the partnership.

(b) A foreign limited liability partnership may not be denied a statement of foreign qualification by reason of any difference between the law under which the partnership was formed and the law of the State of Delaware.

(c) A statement of foreign qualification does not authorize a foreign limited liability partnership to engage in any business or exercise any power that a partnership may not engage in or exercise in the State of Delaware as a limited liability partnership.

§ 15-1102.   Statement of Foreign Qualification

(a) Before doing business in the State of Delaware, a foreign limited liability partnership shall register with the Secretary of State by filing:

(1) A statement of foreign qualification which must contain:

a. The name of the foreign limited liability partnership which satisfies the requirements of the State or other jurisdiction under whose law it is formed and ends with the words "Registered Limited Liability Partnership" or "Limited Liability Partnership," the abbreviation "R.L.L.P." or "L.L.P." or the designation "RLLP" or "LLP";

b. The address of the registered office and the name and address of the registered agent for service of process required to be maintained by § 15-111 of this title;

c. The number of partners of the partnership; and

d. The future effective date or time (which shall be a date or time certain) of the statement of foreign qualification if it is not to be effective upon the filing of the statement of foreign qualification.

(2) A certificate, as of a date not earlier than 6 months prior to the filing date, issued by an authorized officer of the jurisdiction of its formation evidencing its existence. If such certificate is in a foreign language, a translation thereof, under oath of the translator, shall be attached thereto.

(b) The status of a partnership as a foreign limited liability partnership is effective on the later of the filing of the statement of foreign qualification or the future effective date or time specified in the statement of foreign qualification. The status remains effective, regardless of changes in the partnership, until it is canceled pursuant to § 15-105(d), § 15-111(d) or § 15-111(i)(4) of this title or revoked pursuant to § 15-1003 of this title.

(c) An amendment or cancellation of a statement of foreign qualification is effective when it is filed or on the future effective date or time specified in the amendment or cancellation.

§ 15-1103. *Effect of Failure to Qualify*

(a) A foreign limited liability partnership doing business in the State of Delaware may not maintain an action or proceeding in the State of Delaware until it has in effect a statement of foreign qualification and has paid to the State of Delaware all fees and penalties for the years or parts thereof during which it did business in the State of Delaware without such qualification.

(b) The failure of a foreign limited liability partnership to have in effect a statement of foreign qualification does not impair the validity of a contract or act of the foreign limited liability partnership or preclude it from defending an action or proceeding in the State of Delaware or does not impair the right of any other party to a contract to maintain any action, suit or proceeding on the contract.

(c) A limitation on personal liability of a partner is not waived solely by doing business in the State of Delaware without a statement of foreign qualification having been filed.

(d) If a foreign limited liability partnership does business in the State of Delaware without a statement of foreign qualification having been filed, the Secretary of State is its agent for service of process with respect to a right of action arising out of the doing of business in the State of Delaware and service of process may be made in accordance with the procedures set forth in Section 15-113 of this chapter.

§ 15-1104. *Activities Not Constituting Doing Business*

(a) Activities of a foreign limited liability partnership in the State of Delaware which do not constitute doing business for the purpose of this subchapter include:

(1) Maintaining, defending or settling an action or proceeding;

(2) Holding meetings of its partners or carrying on any other activity concerning its internal affairs;

(3) Maintaining bank accounts;

(4) Maintaining offices or agencies for the transfer, exchange or registration of the partnership's own securities or maintaining trustees or depositories with respect to those securities;

(5) Selling through independent contractors;

(6) Soliciting or obtaining orders, whether by mail or through employees or agents or otherwise, if the orders require acceptance outside the State of Delaware before they become contracts;

(7) Selling, by contract consummated outside the State of Delaware, and agreeing, by the contract, to deliver into the State of Delaware, machinery, plants or equipment, the construction, erection or installation of which within the State of Delaware requires the supervision of technical engineers or skilled employees performing services not generally available, and as part of the contract of sale agreeing to furnish such services, and such services only, to the vendee at the time of construction, erection or installation;

(8) Creating, as borrower or lender, or acquiring indebtedness with or without a mortgage or other security interest in property;

(9) Collecting debts or foreclosing mortgages or other security interests in property securing the debts, and holding, protecting and maintaining property so acquired;

(10) Conducting an isolated transaction that is not one in the course of similar transactions;

(11) Doing business in interstate commerce; and

(12) Doing business in the State of Delaware as an insurance company.

(b) A person shall not be deemed to be doing business in the State of Delaware solely by reason of being a partner in a partnership.

(c) This section does not apply in determining whether a foreign limited liability partnership is subject to service of process, taxation or regulation under any other law of the State of Delaware.

§ 15-1105. *Foreign Limited Liability Partnerships Doing Business Without Having Qualified; Injunctions*

(a) The Court of Chancery shall have jurisdiction to enjoin any foreign limited liability partnership, or any agent thereof, from doing any business in the State of Delaware if such foreign limited liability partnership has failed to register under this subchapter or if such foreign limited liability partnership's statement of foreign qualification contains false or misleading representations. The Attorney General shall, upon his own motion or upon the relation of proper parties, proceed for this purpose by complaint in any county in which such foreign limited liability partnership is doing or has done business.

(b) Any foreign limited liability partnership doing business in the State of Delaware without first having registered shall pay to the Secretary of State a fee of $200 for each year or part thereof during which the foreign limited liability partnership failed to register in the State of Delaware.

SUBCHAPTER XII.
MISCELLANEOUS PROVISIONS

§ 15-1201.   Uniformity of Application and Construction

This chapter shall be applied and construed to effectuate its general purpose to make uniform the law with respect to the subject of this chapter among states enacting it. The rule that statutes in derogation of the common law are to be strictly construed shall have no application to this chapter. Action validly taken pursuant to one provision of this chapter shall not be deemed invalid solely because it is identical or similar in substance to an action that could have been taken pursuant to some other provision of this chapter but fails to satisfy one or more requirements prescribed by such other provision.

§ 15-1202.   Short Title

This chapter may be cited as the Delaware Revised Uniform Partnership Act.

§ 15-1203.   Severability Clause

If any provision of this chapter or its application to any person or circumstance is held invalid, the invalidity does not affect other provisions or applications of this chapter which can be given effect without the invalid provision or application, and to this end the provisions of this chapter are severable.

§ 15-1204.   Effective Date

This chapter takes effect January 1, 2000.

§ 15-1205.   Repeals

Except with respect to limited partnerships (see 6 Del. C. § 17-1105), effective January 1, 2002, the Delaware Uniform Partnership Law, 6 Del. C. § 1501–§ 1553 is repealed.

§ 15-1206.   Applicability

(a) Before January 1, 2002, this chapter governs only a partnership formed:
    (1) after the effective date of this chapter, except a partnership that is continuing the business of a dissolved partnership under 6 Del. C. § 1541; and

(2) before the effective date of this chapter, that elects, as provided by subsection (c), to be governed by this chapter.

(b) On and after January 1, 2002, this chapter governs all partnerships.

(c) Before January 1, 2002, a partnership voluntarily may elect, in the manner provided in its partnership agreement or by law for amending the partnership agreement, to be governed by this chapter. The provisions of this chapter relating to the liability of the partnership's partners to third parties apply to limit those partners' liability to a third party who had done business with the partnership within one year before the partnership's election to be governed by this chapter only if the third party knows or has received a notification of the partnership's election to be governed by this chapter.

§ 15-1207.   Fees

(a) No document required to be filed under this chapter shall be effective until the applicable fee required by this section is paid. The following fees shall be paid to and collected by the Secretary of State for the use of the State of Delaware:

(1) Upon the receipt for filing of any statement or certificate, a fee in the amount of $200.

(2) Upon the receipt for filing of an application for reservation of name, an application for renewal of reservation or a notice of transfer or cancellation of reservation pursuant to Section 15-109 of this chapter, a fee in the amount of $75.

(3) Upon the receipt for filing of a statement of qualification, a statement of foreign qualification or an annual report for a limited liability partnership or a foreign limited liability partnership, a fee in the amount of $200 for each partner, but in no event shall the fee payable for any year with respect to a limited liability partnership or a foreign limited liability partnership under this section be more than $120,000.

(4) For certifying copies of any paper on file as provided for by this chapter, a fee in the amount of $50 for each copy certified.

(5) The Secretary of State may issue photocopies or electronic image copies of instruments on file, as well as instruments, documents and other papers not on file, and for all such photocopies or electronic image copies, whether certified or not, a fee of $10 shall be paid for the first page and $2 for each additional page. The Secretary of State may also issue microfiche copies of instruments on file as well as instruments, documents and other papers not on file, and for each such microfiche a fee of $2 shall be paid therefor. Notwithstanding the State of Delaware's Freedom of Information Act [Chapter 100 of Title 29] or other provision of this Code granting access

to public records, the Secretary of State shall issue only photocopies, microfiche or electronic image copies of records in exchange for the fees described above.

(6) Upon the receipt for filing of a certificate under § 15-111(b) of this title, a fee in the amount of $200, upon the receipt for filing of a certificate under § 15-111(c) of this title, a fee in the amount of $200, and upon the receipt for filing of a certificate under § 15-111(d) of this title, a fee in the amount of $2.00 for each partnership whose registered agent has resigned by such certificate.

(7) For preclearance of any document for filing, a fee in the amount of $250.

(8) For preparing and providing a written report of a record search, a fee in the amount of $50.

(9) For issuing any certificate of the Secretary of State, including but not limited to a certificate of good standing, other than a certification of a copy under paragraph (a)(2) of this section, a fee in the amount of $50, except that for issuing any certificate of the Secretary of State that recites all of a partnership's filings with the Secretary of State, a fee of $175 shall be paid for each such certificate.

(10) For receiving and filing and/or indexing any certificate, affidavit, agreement or any other paper provided for by this chapter, for which no different fee is specifically prescribed, a fee in the amount of $100. For filing any instrument submitted by a partnership that only changes the registered office or registered agent and is specifically captioned as a certificate or statement of amendment changing only the registered office or registered agent, a fee in the amount of $50.

(11) The Secretary of State may in the Secretary of State's discretion charge a fee of $60 for each check received for payment of any fee that is returned due to insufficient funds or the result of a stop payment order.

(b) In addition to those fees charged under subsection (a) of this section, there shall be collected by and paid to the Secretary of State the following:

(1) For all services described in subsection (a) of this section that are requested to be completed within 30 minutes on the same day as the day of the request, an additional sum of up to $7,500 and for all services described in subsection (a) of this section that are requested to be completed within 1 hour on the same day as the day of the request, an additional sum of up to $1,000 and for all services described in subsection (a) of this section that are requested to be completed within 2 hours on the same day as the day of the request, an additional sum of up to $500;

(2) For all services described in subsection (a) of this section that are requested to be completed within the same day as the day of the request, an additional sum of up to $300; and

(3) For all services described in subsection (a) of this section that are requested to be completed within a 24-hour period from the time of the request, an additional sum of up to $150.

The Secretary of State shall establish (and may from time to time amend) a schedule of specific fees payable pursuant to this subsection.

(c) The Secretary of State may in the Secretary of State's discretion permit the extension of credit for the fees required by this section upon such terms as the Secretary of State shall deem to be appropriate.

(d) The Secretary of State shall retain from the revenue collected from the fees required by this section a sum sufficient to provide at all times a fund of at least $500, but not more than $1,500, from which the Secretary of State may refund any payment made pursuant to this section to the extent that it exceeds the fees required by this section. The funds shall be deposited in a financial institution which is a legal depository of State of Delaware moneys to the credit of the Secretary of State and shall be disbursable on order of the Secretary of State.

(e) Except as provided in this section, the fees of the Secretary of State shall be as provided in Section 2315 of Title 29.

§ 15-1208.   *Annual Tax of Partnership*

(a) Every partnership that has filed a statement of partnership existence shall pay an annual tax, for the use of the State of Delaware, in the amount of $250.

(b) The annual tax shall be due and payable on the first day of June following the close of the calendar year or upon the cancellation of a statement of partnership existence. The Secretary of State shall receive the annual tax and pay over all taxes collected to the Department of Finance of the State of Delaware. If the annual tax remains unpaid after the due date established by subsection (d) of this section, the tax shall bear interest at the rate of 1 1/2% for each month or portion thereof until fully paid.

(c) The Secretary of State shall, at least 60 days prior to the first day of June of each year, cause to be mailed to each partnership required to comply with the provisions of this section in care of its registered agent in the State of Delaware an annual statement for the tax to be paid hereunder.

(d) In the event of neglect, refusal or failure on the part of any partnership to pay the annual tax to be paid hereunder on or before the first day of June in any year, such partnership shall pay the sum of $200 to be recovered by adding that amount to the annual tax, and such additional sum shall become a part of the tax and shall be collected in the same manner and subject to the same penalties.

(e) In case any partnership shall fail to pay the annual tax due within the time required by this section, and in case the agent in charge of the registered office of any partnership upon whom process against such partnership may be served shall die, resign, refuse to act as such, remove from the State of Delaware or cannot with due diligence be found, it shall be lawful while default continues to serve process against such partnership upon the Secretary of State. Such service upon the Secretary of State shall be made in the manner and shall have the effect stated in Section 15-113 of this chapter in the case of a partnership and shall be governed in all respects by said sections.

(f) The annual tax shall be a debt due from a partnership to the State of Delaware, for which an action at law may be maintained after the same shall have been in arrears for a period of one month. The tax shall also be a preferred debt in the case of insolvency.

(g) A partnership that neglects, refuses or fails to pay the annual tax when due shall cease to be in good standing as a partnership in the State of Delaware.

(h) A partnership that has ceased to be in good standing by reason of the failure to pay an annual tax shall be restored to and have the status of a partnership in good standing in the State of Delaware upon the payment of the annual tax and all penalties and interest thereon for each year for which such partnership neglected, refused or failed to pay an annual tax.

(i) The Attorney General, either on his own motion or upon request of the Secretary of State, whenever any annual tax due under this chapter from any partnership shall have remained in arrears for a period of 3 months after the tax shall have become payable, may apply to the Court of Chancery, by petition in the name of the State of Delaware, on 5 days' notice to such partnership, which notice may be served in such manner as the Court may direct, for an injunction to restrain such partnership from the transaction of any business within the State of Delaware or elsewhere, until the payment of the annual tax, and all penalties and interest due thereon and the cost of the application, which shall be fixed by the Court. The Court of Chancery may grant the injunction, if a proper case appears, and upon granting and service of the injunction, such partnership thereafter shall not transact any business until the injunction shall be dissolved.

(j) A partnership that has ceased to be in good standing by reason of its neglect, refusal or failure to pay an annual tax shall remain a partnership formed under this chapter. The Secretary of State shall not accept for filing any certificate (except a certificate of resignation of a registered agent when a successor registered agent is not being appointed) required or permitted by this chapter to be filed in respect of any partnership which has neglected, refused or failed to pay an annual tax, and shall not issue any certificate of good standing with respect to such partnership, unless and until such partnership shall have been restored to and have the status of a partnership in good standing in the State of Delaware.

(k) A partnership that has ceased to be in good standing in the State of Delaware by reason of its neglect, refusal or failure to pay an annual tax may not maintain any action, suit or proceeding in any court of the State of Delaware until such partnership has been restored to and has the status of a partnership in good standing in the State of Delaware. An action, suit or proceeding may not be maintained in any court of the State of Delaware by any successor or assignee of such partnership on any right, claim or demand arising out of the transaction of business by such partnership after it has ceased to be in good standing in the State of Delaware until such partnership, or any person that has acquired all or substantially all of its assets, has paid any annual tax then due and payable, together with penalties and interest thereon.

(l) The neglect, refusal or failure of a partnership to pay an annual tax shall not impair the validity of any contract, deed, mortgage, security interest, lien or act of such partnership or prevent such partnership from defending any action, suit, or proceeding in any court of the State of Delaware.

§ 15-1209. Cancellation of Statement of Partnership Existence for Failure to Pay Annual Tax

(a) The statement of partnership existence of a partnership shall be canceled if the partnership shall fail to pay the annual tax due under § 15-1208 of this title for a period of 3 years from the date it is due, such cancellation to be effective on the third anniversary of such due date.

(b) A list of those partnerships whose statement of partnership existence were canceled on June 1 of such calendar year pursuant to § 15-1209(a) of this title shall be filed in the office of the Secretary of State. On or before October 31 of each calendar year, the Secretary of State shall publish such list on the Internet or on a similar medium for a period of 1 week and shall advertise the website or other address where such list can be accessed in at least 1 newspaper of general circulation in the State of Delaware.

(c) A partnership whose statement of partnership existence has been canceled and has not been revived pursuant to § 15-1210 of this title shall be deemed, from the date such cancellation became effective, to be a partnership that has not filed a statement of partnership existence.

§ 15-1210. Revival of Statement of Partnership Existence

(a) A statement of partnership existence that has been canceled pursuant to § 15-111(d) or § 15-111(i)(4) or § 15-1209(a) of this title may be revived by filing in the office of the Secretary of State a certificate of revival accompanied by the payment of the fee required by § 15-1207 of this title and payment of the annual tax due under § 15-1208 of this title and all penalties and interest thereon due at the time of the cancellation of its statement of partnership existence. The certificate of revival shall set forth:

(1) The name of the partnership at the time its statement of partnership existence was canceled and, if such name is not available at the time of revival, the name under which the partnership is to be revived;

(2) The date of filing of the original statement of partnership existence of the partnership;

(3) The address of the partnership's registered office in the State of Delaware and the name and address of the partnership's registered agent in the State of Delaware;

(4) A statement that the certificate of revival is filed by one or more partners of the partnership authorized to execute and file the certificate of revival to revive the partnership; and

(5) Any other matters the partner or partners executing the certificate of revival determine to include therein.

(b) The certificate of revival shall be deemed to be an amendment to the statement of partnership existence of the partnership, and the partnership shall not be required to take any further action to amend its statement of partnership existence under Section 15-105 of this chapter with respect to the matters set forth in the certificate of revival.

(c) Upon the filing of a certificate of revival, the statement of partnership existence of the partnership shall be revived with the same force and effect as if its statement of partnership existence had not been canceled pursuant to § 15-111(d) or § 15-111(i)(4) or § 15-1209(a) of this title.

NEW YORK PARTNERSHIP LAW

Article 1. Short Title; Definitions; Construction

§ 2. General definitions

Article 2. Nature of a Partnership

§ 10. Partnership defined

Article 3. Relations of Partners to Persons Dealing with the Partnership

§ 26. Nature of partner's liability

Article 4. Relations of Partners to One Another

§ 40. Rules determining rights and duties of partners

Article 6.   *Dissolution and Winding Up*

Article 8-B.   *Registered Limited Liability Partnerships*

Article 1.   *Short Title; Definitions; Construction*

§ 2.   General definitions

As used in this chapter "court" includes every court and judge having jurisdiction in the case;

"Business" includes every trade, occupation, or profession;

"Person" includes individuals, partnerships, corporations, and other associations;

"Bankrupt" includes bankrupt under the federal bankruptcy act or insolvent under any state insolvent act;

"Conveyance" includes every assignment, lease, mortgage, or encumbrance;

"Real property" includes land and any interest or estate in land.

"Foreign professional service corporation" has the meaning given to it in subdivision (d) of section fifteen hundred twenty-five of the business corporation law.

"Foreign professional service limited liability company" has the meaning given to it in subdivision (a) of section thirteen hundred one of the limited liability company law.

"Foreign limited liability partnership" means (i) any partnership without limited partners operating under an agreement governed by the laws of any jurisdiction, other than this state, each of whose partners is a professional authorized by law to render a professional service within this state and who is or has been engaged in the practice of such profession in such partnership or a predecessor entity, or will engage in the practice of such profession in the foreign limited liability partnership within thirty days of the date of the effectiveness of the notice provided for in subdivision (a) of section 121-1502 of this chapter or each of whose partners is a professional, at least one of whom is authorized by law to render a professional service within this state and who is or has been engaged in the practice of such profession in such partnership or a predecessor entity, or will engage in the practice of such profession in the foreign limited liability partnership within thirty days of the date of the effectiveness of the notice provided for in subdivision (a) of section 121-1502 of this chapter, (ii) any partnership without limited partners operating under an agreement governed by the laws of any jurisdiction, other than this state, authorized by, or holding a license, certificate, registration or permit issued by the licensing authority pursuant to, the education law to render a professional service within this state, which renders or intends to render professional services within this state and which is denominated as a registered limited liability partnership or limited liability partnership under such laws, regardless of any difference between such laws and the laws of this state, or (iii) a foreign related limited liability partnership; except that all partners of a foreign limited liability partnership that provides health, professional engineering, land surveying, architectural and/or landscape architectural services in this state shall be licensed in this state.

"Licensing authority" means the regents of the university of the state of New York or the state education department, as the case may be, in the case of all professions licensed under title eight of the education law, and the appropriate appellate division of the supreme court in the case of the profession of law.

"New York registered foreign limited liability partnership" means a foreign limited liability partnership which has filed a notice pursuant to subdivision (a) of section 121-1502 of this chapter that has not been withdrawn or revoked and which complies with subdivision (1) of section 121-1502 of this chapter.

"Profession" includes any practice as an attorney and counsellor-at-law or as a licensed physician, and those professions designated in title eight of the education law.

"Professional" means an individual duly authorized to practice a profession, a professional service corporation, a professional service limited liability company, a foreign professional service limited liability company, a registered limited liability partnership, a foreign limited liability partnership, a foreign professional service corporation or a professional partnership.

"Professional partnership" means (1) a partnership without limited partners each of whose partners is a professional authorized by law to render a professional service within this state, (2) a partnership without limited partners each of whose partners is a professional, at least one of whom is authorized by law to render a professional service within this state or (3) a partnership without limited partners authorized by, or holding a license, certificate, registration or permit issued by the licensing authority pursuant to the education law to render a professional service within this state; except that all partners of a professional partnership that provides medical services in this state must be licensed pursuant to article 131 of the education law to practice medicine in this state and all partners of a professional partnership that provides dental services in this state must be licensed pursuant to article 133 of the education law to practice dentistry in this state; and further except that all partners of a professional partnership that provides professional engineering, land surveying, architectural and/or landscape architectural services in this state must be licensed pursuant to article 145, article 147 and/or article 148 of the education law to practice one or more of such professions in this state.

"Professional service" means any type of service to the public that may be lawfully rendered by a member of a profession within the purview of his or her profession.

"Professional service corporation" means (i) a corporation organized under article fifteen of the business corporation law and (ii) any other corporation organized under the business corporation law or any predecessor statute, which is authorized by, or holds a license, certificate, registration or permit issued by, the licensing authority pursuant to the education law to render professional services within this state.

"Professional service limited liability company" means a limited liability company organized under article twelve of the limited liability company law.

"Registered limited liability partnership" means a partnership without limited partners operating under an agreement governed by the laws of this state, registered under section 121-1500 of this chapter and complying with section 121-1501 of this chapter.

"Foreign related limited liability partnership" means a partnership without limited partners operating under an agreement governed by the laws of any jurisdiction, other than this state, which (i) is denominated as a limited liability partnership or registered limited liability partnership under such laws, (ii) is not a foreign limited liability partnership under clause (i) or (ii) of the paragraph defining foreign limited liability partnership in this section, (iii) is affiliated with a professional service limited liability company, foreign professional service limited liability company, professional service corporation, foreign professional service corporation, registered limited liability partnership that is a professional partnership under this section or a foreign limited liability partnership under clause (i) or (ii) of the paragraph defining foreign limited liability partnership in this section, and (iv) renders services related or complementary to the professional services rendered by, or provides services or facilities to, such professional service limited liability company, foreign professional service limited liability company, professional service corporation, foreign professional service corporation, registered limited liability partnership or foreign limited liability partnership. For purposes of this paragraph, such a partnership is affiliated with a professional service limited liability company, foreign professional service limited liability company, professional service corporation, foreign professional service corporation, registered limited liability partnership or foreign limited liability partnership if (1) at least a majority of partners in one partnership are partners in the other partnership, (2) at least a majority of the partners in each partnership also are partners, hold interests or are members in a limited liability company or other business entity, and each partnership renders services pursuant to an agreement with such limited liability company or other business entity, or (3) the partnerships or the partnership and such professional service limited liability company, such foreign professional service limited liability company, such professional service corporation, or such foreign professional service corporation are affiliates within the meaning of paragraph (a) of section nine hundred twelve of the business corporation law.

"Related limited liability partnership" means a partnership without limited partners operating under an agreement governed by the laws of this state, which (i) is not a professional partnership under this section, (ii) is affiliated with a professional service limited liability company, foreign professional service limited liability company, professional service corporation, foreign professional service corporation, registered limited liability partnership that is a professional partnership under this section or a foreign limited liability partnership under clause (i) or (ii) of the paragraph defining foreign limited liability partnership in this section, and (iii) renders services related or complementary to the professional services rendered by, or provides services or facilities to, such professional service limited liability company, foreign professional service limited liability company, professional service corporation, foreign professional service corporation, registered limited liability partnership or foreign limited liability partnership. For purposes of this paragraph, such a partnership is affiliated with a professional service limited liability company, foreign professional service limited liability company, professional service corporation, foreign professional service corporation, registered limited liability partnership or foreign limited liability partnership if (1) at least a majority of partners in one partnership are partners in the other partnership, (2) at least a majority of the partners in each partnership also are partners, hold interests or are members in a limited liability company or other business entity, and each partnership renders services pursuant to an agreement with such limited liability company or other business entity, or (3) the partnerships or the partnership and such professional service limited liability company, such foreign professional service limited liability company, such professional service corporation, or such foreign professional service corporation are affiliates within the meaning of paragraph (a) of section nine hundred twelve of the business corporation law.

Article 2.   Nature of a Partnership

§ 10.   Partnership defined

1. A partnership is an association of two or more persons to carry on as co-owners a business for profit and includes for all purposes of the laws of this state, a registered limited liability partnership.

2. But any association formed under any other statute of this state, or any statute adopted by authority, other than the authority of this state, is not a partnership under this chapter, unless such association would have been a partnership in this state prior to the adoption of this chapter; but this chapter shall apply to limited partnerships except in so far as the statutes relating to such partnerships are inconsistent herewith.

Article 3.   Relations of Partners to Persons Dealing with the Partnership

§ 26.   Nature of partner's liability

(a) Except as provided in subdivision (b) of this section, all partners are liable:

1. Jointly and severally for everything chargeable to the partnership under sections twenty-four and twenty-five.

2. Jointly for all other debts and obligations of the partnership; but any partner may enter into a separate obligation to perform a partnership contract.

(b) Except as provided by subdivisions (c) and (d) of this section, no partner of a partnership which is a registered limited liability partnership is liable or accountable, directly or indirectly (including by way of indemnification, contribution or otherwise), for any debts, obligations or liabilities of, or chargeable to, the registered limited liability partnership or each other, whether arising in tort, contract or otherwise, which are incurred, created or assumed by such partnership while such partnership is a registered limited liability partnership, solely by reason of being such a partner or acting (or omitting to act) in such capacity or rendering professional services or otherwise participating (as an employee, consultant, contractor or otherwise) in the conduct of the other business or activities of the registered limited liability partnership.

(c) Notwithstanding the provisions of subdivision (b) of this section, (i) each partner, employee or agent of a partnership which is a registered limited liability partnership shall be personally and fully liable and accountable for any negligent or wrongful act or misconduct committed by him or her or by any person under his or her direct supervision and control while rendering professional services on behalf of such registered limited liability partnership and (ii) each shareholder, director, officer, member, manager, partner, employee and agent of a professional service corporation, foreign professional service corporation, professional service limited liability company, foreign professional service limited liability company, registered limited liability partnership, foreign limited liability partnership or professional partnership that is a partner, employee or agent of a partnership which is a registered limited liability partnership shall be personally and fully liable and accountable for any negligent or wrongful act or misconduct committed by him or her or by any person under his or her direct supervision and control while rendering professional services in his or her capacity as a partner, employee or agent of such registered limited liability partnership. The relationship of a professional to a registered limited liability partnership with which such professional is associated, whether as a partner, employee or agent, shall not modify or diminish the jurisdiction over such professional of the licensing authority and in the case of an attorney and counsellor-at-law or a professional service corporation, professional service limited liability company, foreign professional service limited liability company, registered limited liability partnership, foreign limited liability partnership, foreign professional service corporation or professional partnership, engaged in the practice of law, the other courts of this state.

(d) Notwithstanding the provisions of subdivision (b) of this section, all or specified partners of a partnership which is a registered limited liability partnership may be liable in their capacity as partners for all or specified debts, obligations or liabilities of a registered limited liability partnership to the extent at least a majority of the partners shall have agreed unless otherwise provided in any agreement between the partners. Any such agreement may be modified or revoked to the extent at least a majority of the partners shall have agreed, unless otherwise provided in any agreement between the partners; provided, however, that (i) any such modification or revocation shall not affect the liability of a partner for any debts, obligations or liabilities of a registered limited liability partnership incurred, created or assumed by such registered limited liability partnership prior to such modification or revocation and (ii) a partner shall be liable for debts, obligations and liabilities of the registered limited liability partnership incurred, created or assumed after such modification or revocation only in accordance with this article and, if such agreement is further modified, such agreement as so further modified but only to the extent not inconsistent with subdivision (c) of this section. Nothing in this section shall in any way affect or impair the ability of a partner to act as a guarantor or surety for, provide collateral for or otherwise be liable for, the debts, obligations or liabilities of a registered limited liability partnership.

(e) Subdivision (b) of this section shall not affect the liability of a registered limited liability partnership out of partnership assets for partnership debts, obligations and liabilities.

(f) Neither the withdrawal or revocation of a registered limited liability partnership pursuant to subdivision (f) or (g), respectively, of section 121-1500 of this chapter nor the dissolution, winding up or termination of a registered limited liability partnership shall affect the applicability of the provisions of subdivision (b) of this section for any debt, obligation or liability incurred, created or assumed while the partnership was a registered limited liability partnership.

Article 4.   Relations of Partners to One Another

§ 40.   Rules determining rights and duties of partners

The rights and duties of the partners in relation to the partnership shall be determined, subject to any agreement between them, by the following rules:

1. Each partner shall be repaid his contributions, whether by way of capital or advances to the partnership property and share equally in the profits and surplus remaining after all liabilities, including those to partners, are satisfied; and except as provided in subdivision (b) of section twenty-six of this chapter, each partner must contribute toward the losses, whether of capital or otherwise, sustained by the partnership according to his share in the profits.

2. Except as provided in subdivision (b) of section twenty-six of this chapter, the partnership must indemnify every partner in respect of payments made and personal liabilities reasonably incurred by him in the ordinary and proper conduct of its business, or for the preservation of its business or property.

3. A partner, who in aid of the partnership makes any payment or advance beyond the amount of capital which he agreed to contribute, shall be paid interest from the date of the payment or advance.

4. A partner shall receive interest on the capital contributed by him only from the date when repayment should be made.

5. All partners have equal rights in the management and conduct of the partnership business.

6. No partner is entitled to remuneration for acting in the partnership business, except that a surviving partner is entitled to reasonable compensation for his services in winding up the partnership affairs.

7. No person can become a member of a partnership without the consent of all the partners.

8. Any difference arising as to ordinary matters connected with the partnership business may be decided by a majority of the partners; but no act in contravention of any agreement between the partners may be done rightfully without the consent of all the partners.

Article 6.   Dissolution and Winding Up

§ 65.   Right of partner to contribution from copartners after dissolution

Where the dissolution is caused by the act, death or bankruptcy of a partner, each partner is liable to his copartners for his share of any liability created by any partner acting for the partnership as if the partnership had not been dissolved unless

1. The dissolution being by act of any partner, the partner acting for the partnership had knowledge of the dissolution,

2. The dissolution being by the death or bankruptcy of a partner, the partner acting for the partnership had knowledge or notice of the death or bankruptcy, or

3. The liability is for a debt, obligation or liability for which the partner is not liable as provided in subdivision (b) of section twenty-six of this chapter.

§ 71.   Rules for distribution

In settling accounts between the partners after dissolution, the following rules shall be observed, subject to any agreement to the contrary:

(a) The assets of the partnership are:

I. The partnership property,

II. The contributions of the partners specified in paragraph (d) of this subdivision.

(b) The liabilities of the partnership shall rank in order of payment, as follows:

I. Those owing to creditors other than partners,

II. Those owing to partners other than for capital and profits,

III. Those owing to partners in respect of capital,

IV. Those owing to partners in respect of profits.

(c) The assets shall be applied in the order of their declaration in clause (a) of this paragraph to the satisfaction of the liabilities.

(d) Except as provided in subdivision (b) of section twenty-six of this section: (1) partners shall contribute, as provided by section forty, subdivision one, the amount necessary to satisfy the liabilities; and (2) if any, but not all, of the partners are insolvent, or, not being subject to process, refuse to contribute, the other partners shall contribute their share of the liabilities, and, in the relative proportions in which they share the profits, the additional amount necessary to pay the liabilities.

(e) An assignee for the benefit of creditors or any person appointed by the court shall have the right to enforce the contributions specified in paragraph (d) of this subdivision.

(f) Any partner or his legal representative shall have the right to enforce the contributions specified in paragraph (d) of this subdivision, to the extent of the amount which he has paid in excess of his share of the liability.

(g) The individual property of a deceased partner shall be liable for the contributions specified in paragraph (d) of this subdivision.

(h) When partnership property and the individual properties of the partners are in the possession of a court for distribution, partnership creditors shall have priority on partnership property and separate creditors on individual property, saving the rights of lien or secured creditors as heretofore.

(i) Where a partner has become bankrupt or his estate is insolvent the claims against his separate property shall rank in the following order:

    I. Those owing to separate creditors,

    II. Those owing to partnership creditors,

    III. Those owing to partners by way of contribution.

Article 8-B.   Registered Limited Liability Partnerships

§ 121-1500.   Registered limited liability partnership

(a)(I) Notwithstanding the education law or any other provision of law, (i) a partnership without limited partners each of whose partners is a professional authorized by law to render a professional service within this state and who is or has been engaged in the practice of such profession in such partnership or a predecessor entity, or will engage in the practice of such profession in the registered limited liability partnership within thirty days of the date of the effectiveness of the registration provided for in this subdivision or a partnership without limited partners each of whose partners is a professional, at least one of whom is authorized by law to render a professional service within this state and who is or has been engaged in the practice of such profession in such partnership or a predecessor entity, or will engage in the practice of such profession in the registered limited liability partnership within thirty days of the date of the effectiveness of the registration provided for in this subdivision, (ii) a partnership without limited partners authorized by, or holding a license, certificate, registration or permit issued by the licensing authority pursuant to the education law to render a professional service within this state, which renders or intends to render professional services within this state, or (iii) a related limited liability partnership may register as a registered limited liability partnership by filing with the department of state a registration which shall set forth:

    (1) the name of the registered limited liability partnership;

    (2) the address of the principal office of the partnership without limited partners;

(3) the profession or professions to be practiced by such partnership without limited partners and a statement that it is eligible to register as a registered limited liability partnership pursuant to subdivision (a) of this section;

(4) a designation of the secretary of state as agent of the partnership without limited partners upon whom process against it may be served and the post office address within or without this state to which the secretary of state shall mail a copy of any process against it or served upon it;

(5) if the partnership without limited partners is to have a registered agent, its name and address in this state and a statement that the registered agent is to be the agent of the partnership without limited partners upon whom process against it may be served;

(6) that the partnership without limited partners is filing a registration for status as a registered limited liability partnership;

(7) if the registration of the partnership without limited partners is to be effective on a date later than the time of filing, the date, not to exceed sixty days from the date of such filing, of such proposed effectiveness;

(8) if all or specified partners of the registered limited liability partnership are to be liable in their capacity as partners for all or specified debts, obligations or liabilities of the registered limited liability partnership as authorized pursuant to subdivision (d) of section twenty-six of this chapter, a statement that all or specified partners are so liable for such debts, obligations or liabilities in their capacity as partners of the registered limited liability partnership as authorized pursuant to subdivision (d) of section twenty-six of this chapter; and

(9) any other matters the partnership without limited partners determines to include in the registration.

(II)(A) Within one hundred twenty days after the effective date of the registration, a copy of the same or a notice containing the substance thereof shall be published once in each week for six successive weeks, in two newspapers of the county in which the principal office of the registered limited liability partnership is located in this state, one newspaper printed weekly and one newspaper to be printed daily, to be designated by the county clerk. When such county is located within a city with a population of one million or more, such designation shall be as though the copy or notice were a notice or advertisement of judicial proceedings. Proof of the publication required by this subparagraph, consisting of the certificate of publication of the registered limited liability partnership with the affidavits of publication annexed thereto, must be filed, with a fee of fifty dollars, with the department of state. Notwithstanding any other provision of law, if the office of the registered limited liability partnership is located in a county wherein a weekly or daily newspaper of the county, or both, has not been so designated by the county clerk, then the publication herein required shall be made in a weekly or daily newspaper of any county, or both, as the case may be, which is contiguous

to, such county, provided that any such newspaper meets all the other requirements of this subparagraph. A copy or notice published in a newspaper
other than the newspaper or newspapers designated by the county clerk shall
not be deemed to be one of the publications required by this paragraph. The
notice shall include: (1) the name of the registered limited liability partnership; (2) the date of filing of the registration with the department of state; (3)
the county within this state, in which the principal office of the registered
limited liability partnership is located; (3-a) the street address of the principal business location, if any; (4) a statement that the secretary of state has
been designated as agent of the registered limited liability partnership upon
whom process against it may be served and the post office address within or
without this state to which the secretary of state shall mail a copy of any
process against it served upon him or her; (5) if the registered limited liability partnership is to have a registered agent, his or her name and address
within this state and a statement that the registered agent is to be the agent of
the registered limited liability partnership upon whom process against it may
be served; (6) if the registered limited liability partnership is to have a specific date of dissolution in addition to the events of dissolution set forth in
section sixty-two of this chapter, the latest date upon which the registered
limited liability partnership is to dissolve; and (7) the character or purpose of
the business of such registered limited liability partnership. Where, at any
time after completion of the first of the six weekly publications required by
this subparagraph and prior to the completion of the sixth such weekly publication, there is a change in any of the information contained in the copy or
notice as published, the registered limited liability partnership may complete
the remaining publications of the original copy or notice, and the registered
limited liability partnership shall not be required to publish any further or
amended copy or notice. Where, at any time after completion of the six
weekly publications required by this subparagraph, there is a change to any
of the information contained in the copy or notice as published, no further or
amended publication or republication shall be required to be made. If within
one hundred twenty days after its formation, proof of such publication, consisting of the certificate of publication of the registered limited liability partnership with the affidavits of publication of the newspapers annexed thereto
has not been filed with the department of state, the authority of such registered limited liability partnership to carry on, conduct or transact any business in this state shall be suspended, effective as of the expiration of such
one hundred twenty day period. The failure of a registered limited liability
partnership to cause such copy or notice to be published and such certificate
of publication and affidavits of publication to be filed with the department of
state within such one hundred twenty day period or the suspension of such
registered limited liability partnership's authority to carry on, conduct or

transact business in this state pursuant to this subparagraph shall not limit or impair the validity of any contract or act of such registered limited liability partnership, or any right or remedy of any other party under or by virtue of any contract, act or omission of such registered limited liability partnership, or the right of any other party to maintain any action or special proceeding on any such contract, act or omission, or right of such registered limited liability partnership to defend any action or special proceeding in this state, or result in any partner or agent of such registered limited liability partnership becoming liable for the contractual obligations or other liabilities of the registered limited liability partnership. If, at any time following the suspension of a registered limited liability partnership's authority to carry on, conduct or transact business in this state pursuant to this subparagraph, such registered limited liability partnership shall cause proof of publication in substantial compliance with the provisions (other than the one hundred twenty day period) of this subparagraph, consisting of the certificate of publication of the registered limited liability partnership with the affidavits of publication of the newspapers annexed thereto, to be filed with the department of state, such suspension of such registered limited liability partnership's authority to carry on, conduct or transact business shall be annulled.

(B)(1) A registered limited liability partnership which was formed prior to the effective date of this subparagraph and which complied with the publication and filing requirements of this paragraph as in effect prior to such effective date shall not be required to make any publication or republication or any filing under subparagraph (A) of this paragraph, and shall not be subject to suspension pursuant to this paragraph.

(2) Within twelve months after the effective date of this subparagraph, a registered limited liability partnership which was formed prior to such effective date and which did not comply with the publication and filing requirements of this paragraph as in effect prior to such effective date shall publish a copy of its registration or a notice containing the substance thereof in the manner required (other than the one hundred twenty day period) by this paragraph as in effect prior to such effective date and file proof of such publication, consisting of the certificate of publication of the registered limited liability partnership with the affidavits of publication of the newspapers annexed thereto, with the department of state.

(3) If a registered limited liability partnership that is subject to the provisions of clause two of this subparagraph fails to file the required proof of publication with the department of state within twelve months after the effective date of this subparagraph, its authority to carry on, conduct or transact any business in this state shall be suspended, effective as of the expiration of such twelve month period.

(4) The failure of a registered limited liability partnership that is subject to the provisions of clause two of this subparagraph to fully comply with the provisions of said clause two or the suspension of such registered limited liability partnership's authority to carry on, conduct or transact any business in this state pursuant to clause three of this subparagraph shall not impair or limit the validity of any contract or act of such registered limited liability partnership, or any right or remedy of any other party under or by virtue of any contract, act or omission of such registered limited liability partnership, or the right of any other party to maintain any action or special proceeding on any such contract, act or omission, or right of such registered limited liability partnership to defend any action or special proceeding in this state, or result in any partner or agent of such registered limited liability partnership becoming liable for the contractual obligations or other liabilities of the registered limited liability partnership.

(5) If, at any time following the suspension of a registered limited liability partnership's authority to carry on, conduct or transact business in this state, pursuant to clause three of this subparagraph, such registered limited liability partnership shall cause proof of publication in substantial compliance with the provisions (other than the one hundred twenty day period) of subparagraph (A) of this paragraph, consisting of the certificate of publication of the registered limited liability partnership with the affidavits of publication of the newspapers annexed thereto, to be filed with the department of state, such suspension of such registered limited liability partnership's authority to carry on, conduct or transact business shall be annulled.

(6) For the purposes of this subparagraph, a registered limited liability partnership which was formed prior to the effective date of this subparagraph shall be deemed to have complied with the publication and filing requirements of this paragraph as in effect prior to such effective date if (A) the registered limited liability partnership was formed on or after January first, nineteen hundred ninety-nine and prior to such effective date and the registered limited liability partnership filed at least one affidavit of the printer or publisher of a newspaper with the department of state at any time prior to such effective date, or (B) the registered limited liability partnership was formed prior to January first, nineteen hundred ninety-nine, without regard to whether the registered limited liability partnership did or did not file any affidavit of the printer or publisher of a newspaper with the secretary of state.

(C) The information in a notice published pursuant to this paragraph shall be presumed to be in compliance with and satisfaction of the requirements of this paragraph.

(b) The registration shall be executed by one or more partners of the partnership without limited partners.

(c) The registration shall be accompanied by a fee of two hundred dollars.

(d) A partnership without limited partners is registered as a registered limited liability partnership at the time of the payment of the fee required by subdivision (c) of this section and the filing of a completed registration with the department of state or at the later date, if any, specified in such registration, not to exceed sixty days from the date of such filing. A partnership without limited partners that has been registered as a registered limited liability partnership is for all purposes the same entity that existed before the registration and continues to be a partnership without limited partners under the laws of this state. The status of a partnership without limited partners as a registered limited liability partnership shall not be affected by changes in the information stated in the registration after the filing of the registration. If a partnership without limited partners that is a registered limited liability partnership dissolves, a partnership without limited partners which is the successor to such registered limited liability partnership (i) shall not be required to file a new registration and shall be deemed to have filed the registration filed by the registered limited liability partnership pursuant to subdivision (a) of this section, as well as any withdrawal notice filed pursuant to subdivision (f) of this section, any statement or certificate of consent filed pursuant to subdivision (g) of this section or any certificate of amendment filed pursuant to subdivision (j) of this section and (ii) shall be bound by any revocation of registration pursuant to subdivision (g) of this section and any annulment thereof of the dissolved partnership without limited partners that was a registered limited liability partnership. For purposes of this section, a partnership without limited partners is a successor to a partnership without limited partners that was a registered limited liability partnership if a majority of the total interests in the current profits of such successor partnership without limited partners are held by partners of the predecessor partnership without limited partners that was a registered limited liability partnership who were partners of such predecessor partnership immediately prior to the dissolution of such predecessor partnership.

(e) If the signed registration delivered to the department of state for filing complies as to form with the requirements of law and the filing fee required by any statute of this state has been paid, the registration shall be filed and indexed by the department of state.

(f) A registration may be withdrawn by filing with the department of state a written withdrawal notice executed by one or more partners of the registered limited liability partnership, with a filing fee of sixty dollars. A withdrawal notice must include: (i) the name of the registered limited liability partnership (and if it has been changed since registration, the name under which it was registered); (ii) the date the registration was filed with the department of state pursuant to subdivision (a) of this section; (iii) the address of the registered limited liability partnership's principal office; (iv) if the withdrawal of the registered limited liability partnership is to be effective on a date later than the time of filing, the date, not to exceed sixty days from the date of such filing, of such proposed effectiveness; (v) a statement acknowledging that the withdrawal terminates the partnership's status as a registered limited liability partnership; and (vi) any other information determined by the registered limited liability partnership.

A withdrawal notice terminates the status of the partnership as a registered limited liability partnership as of the date of filing the notice or as of the later date, if any, specified in the notice, not to exceed sixty days from the date of such filing. The termination of registration shall not be affected by errors in the information stated in the withdrawal notice. If a registered limited liability partnership is dissolved, it shall within thirty days after the winding up of its affairs is completed file a withdrawal notice pursuant to this subdivision.

(g) Each registered limited liability partnership shall, within sixty days prior to the fifth anniversary of the effective date of its registration and every five years thereafter, furnish a statement to the department of state setting forth: (i) the name of the registered limited liability partnership, (ii) the address of the principal office of the registered limited liability partnership, (iii) the post office address within or without this state to which the secretary of state shall mail a copy of any process accepted against it served upon him or her, which address shall supersede any previous address on file with the department of state for this purpose, and (iv) a statement that it is eligible to register as a registered limited liability partnership pursuant to subdivision (a) of this section. The statement shall be executed by one or more partners of the registered limited liability partnership. The statement shall be accompanied by a fee of twenty dollars. If a registered limited liability partnership shall not timely file the statement required by this subdivision, the department of state may, upon sixty days' notice mailed to the address of such registered limited liability partnership as shown in the last registration or statement or certificate of amendment filed by such registered limited liability partnership, make a proclamation declaring the registration of such registered limited liability partnership to be revoked pursuant to this subdivision. The department of state shall file the original proclamation in its office and shall publish a copy thereof in the state register no later than three months following the date of such proclamation. Upon the publication of such proclamation in the manner aforesaid, the registration of each registered limited liability partnership named in such proclamation shall be deemed revoked without further legal proceedings. Any registered limited liability partnership whose registration was so revoked may file in the department of state a certificate of consent certifying that either a statement required by this subdivision has been filed or accompanies the certificate of consent and all fees imposed under this chapter on the registered limited liability partnership have been paid. The filing of such certificate of consent shall have the effect of annulling all of the proceedings theretofore taken for the revocation of the registration of such registered limited liability partnership under this subdivision and (1) the registered limited liability partnership shall thereupon have such powers, rights, duties and obligations as it had on the date of the publication of the proclamation, with the same force and effect as if such proclamation had not been made or published and (2) such publication shall not affect the applicability of the provisions of subdivision (b) of section twenty-six of this chapter to any debt, obligation or liability incurred, created or assumed from the date of publication of the proclamation through the date of the filing of the certificate of consent. The filing of a certificate of consent shall be accompanied by a fee of fifty dollars and if accompanied by a statement, the fee required by this subdivision. If, after the publication of such proclamation, it shall be determined by the department of state that the name of any registered limited liability partnership was erroneously included in such proclamation, the department of state shall make appropriate entry on its records, which entry shall have the effect of annulling all of the proceedings theretofore taken for the revocation of the registration of such registered limited liability partnership under this subdivision and (A) such registered limited liability partnership shall have such powers, rights, duties and obligations as it had on the date of the publication of the proclamation, with the same force and effect as if such proclamation had not been made or published and (B) such publication shall not affect the applicability of the provisions of subdivision (b) of section twenty-six of this chapter to any debt, obligation or liability incurred, created or assumed from the date of publication of the proclamation through the date of the making of the entry on the records of the department of state. Whenever a registered limited liability partnership shall have filed a certificate of consent pursuant to this subdivision or if the name of a registered limited liability partnership was erroneously included in a proclamation and such proclamation was annulled, the department of state shall publish a notice thereof in the state register.

(h) The filing of a withdrawal notice by a registered limited liability partnership pursuant to subdivision (f) of this section, a revocation of registration pursuant to subdivision (g) of this section and the filing of a certificate of amendment pursuant to subdivision (j) of this section shall not affect the applicability of the provisions of subdivision (b) of section twenty-six of this chapter to any debt, obligation or liability incurred, created or assumed while the partnership was a registered limited liability partnership. After a withdrawal or revocation of registration, the partnership without limited partners shall for all purposes remain the same entity that existed during registration and continues to be a partnership without limited partners under the laws of this state.

(i) The department of state shall remove from its active records the registration of a registered limited liability partnership whose registration has been withdrawn or revoked.

(j) A registration or statement filed with the department of state under this section may be amended or corrected by filing with the department of state a certificate of amendment executed by one or more partners of the registered limited liability partnership. No later than ninety days after (i) a change in the name of the registered limited liability partnership or (ii) a partner of the registered limited liability partnership becomes aware that any statement in a registration or statement was false in any material respect when made or that an event has occurred which makes the registration or statement inaccurate in any material respect, the registered limited liability partnership shall file a certificate of amendment. The filing of a certificate of amendment shall be accompanied by a fee of sixty dollars. The certificate of amendment shall set forth: (i) the name of the limited liability partnership and, if it has been changed, the name under which it was registered and (ii) the date of filing its initial registration or statement.

(j-1) A certificate of change which changes only the post office address to which the secretary of state shall mail a copy of any process against a registered limited liability partnership served upon him or the address of the registered agent, provided such address being changed is the address of a person, partnership or corporation whose address, as agent, is the address to be changed or who has been designated as registered agent for such registered limited liability partnership shall be signed and delivered to the department of state by such agent. The certificate of change shall set forth: (i) the name of the registered limited liability partnership and, if it has been changed, the name under which it was originally filed with the department of state; (ii) the date of filing of its initial registration or notice statement; (iii) each change effected thereby; (iv) that a notice of the proposed change was mailed to the limited liability partnership by the party signing the certificate not less than thirty days prior to the date of delivery to the department of state and that such limited liability partnership has not objected thereto; and (v) that the party signing the certificate is the agent of such limited liability partnership to whose address the secretary of state is required to mail copies of process or the registered agent, if such be the case. A certificate signed and delivered under this subdivision shall not be deemed to effect a change of location of the office of the limited liability partnership in whose behalf such certificate is filed. The certificate of change shall be accompanied by a fee of five dollars.

(k) The filing of a certificate of amendment pursuant to subdivision (j) of this section with the department of state shall not alter the effective date of the registration being amended or corrected.

(l) Except as otherwise provided in any agreement between the partners, the decision of a partnership without limited partners to file, withdraw or amend a registration pursuant to subdivision (a), (f) or (j), respectively, of this section is an ordinary matter connected with partnership business under subdivision eight of section forty of this chapter.

(m) A registered limited liability partnership, other than a registered limited liability partnership authorized to practice law, shall be under the supervision of the regents of the university of the state of New York and be subject to disciplinary proceedings and penalties in the same manner and to the same extent as is provided with respect to individuals and their licenses, certificates and registrations in title eight of the education law relating to the applicable profession. Notwithstanding the provisions of this subdivision, a registered limited liability partnership authorized to practice medicine shall be subject to the pre-hearing procedures and hearing procedures as are provided with respect to individual physicians and their licenses in title two-A of article two of the public health law. In addition to rendering the professional service or services the partners are authorized to practice in this state, a registered limited liability partnership may carry on, or conduct or transact any other business or activities as to which a partnership without limited partners may be formed. Notwithstanding any other provision of this section, a registered limited liability partnership (i) authorized to practice law may only engage in another profession or business or activities or (ii) which is engaged in a profession or other business or activities other than law may only engage in the practice of law, to the extent not prohibited by any other law of this state or any rule adopted by the appropriate appellate division of the supreme court or the court of appeals. Any registered limited liability partnership may invest its funds in real estate, mortgages, stocks, bonds or any other types of investments.

(n) No registered limited liability partnership may render a professional service except through individuals authorized by law to render such professional service as individuals, provided, that nothing in this chapter shall authorize a registered limited liability partnership to render a professional service in this state except through individuals authorized by law to render such professional service as individuals in this state.

(o) This section shall not repeal, modify or restrict any provision of the education law or the judiciary law or any rules or regulations adopted thereunder regulating the professions referred to in the education law or the judiciary law except to the extent in conflict herewith.

(p) A certified copy of the registration and of each certificate of amendment shall be filed by the registered limited liability partnership with the licensing authority within thirty days after the filing of such registration or amendment with the department of state.

(q) Each partner of a registered limited liability partnership formed to provide medical services in this state must be licensed pursuant to article 131 of the education law to practice medicine in this state and each partner of a registered limited liability partnership formed to provide dental services in this state must be licensed pursuant to article 133 of the education law to practice dentistry in this state.

Each partner of a registered limited liability partnership formed to provide veterinary services in this state must be licensed pursuant to article 135 of the education law to practice veterinary medicine in this state. Each partner of a registered limited liability partnership formed to provide professional engineering, land surveying, architectural and/or landscape architectural services in this state must be licensed pursuant to article 145, article 147 and/or article 148 of the education law to practice one or more of such professions in this state. Each partner of a registered limited liability partnership formed to provide licensed clinical social work services in this state must be licensed pursuant to article 154 of the education law to practice clinical social work in this state. Each partner of a registered limited liability partnership formed to provide creative arts therapy services in this state must be licensed pursuant to article 163 of the education law to practice creative arts therapy in this state. Each partner of a registered limited liability partnership formed to provide marriage and family therapy services in this state must be licensed pursuant to article 163 of the education law to practice marriage and family therapy in this state. Each partner of a registered limited liability partnership formed to provide mental health counseling services in this state must be licensed pursuant to article 163 of the education law to practice mental health counseling in this state. Each partner of a registered limited liability partnership formed to provide psychoanalysis services in this state must be licensed pursuant to article 163 of the education law to practice psychoanalysis in this state.

§ 121-1501.   Name of registered limited liability partnership

The name of each registered limited liability partnership shall contain without abbreviation the words "Registered Limited Liability Partnership" or "Limited Liability Partnership" or the abbreviations "R.L.L.P.", "RLLP", "L.L.P." or "LLP"; provided, however, the partnership may use any such words or abbreviation, without limitation, in addition to its registered name.

§ 121-1502.   New York registered foreign limited liability partnership

(a) In order for a foreign limited liability partnership to carry on or conduct or transact business or activities as a New York registered foreign limited liability partnership in this state, such foreign limited liability partnership shall file with the department of state a notice which shall set forth: (i) the name under which the foreign limited liability partnership intends to carry on or conduct or transact business or activities in this state; (ii) the date on which and the jurisdiction in which it registered as a limited liability partnership; (iii) the address of the principal office of the foreign limited liability partnership; (iv) the profession or professions to be practiced by such foreign limited liability partnership and a statement that it is a foreign limited liability partnership eligible to file a notice under this chapter; (v) a designation of the secretary of state as agent of the foreign limited liability partnership upon whom process against it may be served and the post office address within or without this state to which the secretary of state shall mail a copy of any process against it or served upon it; (vi) if the foreign limited liability partnership is to have a registered agent, its name and address in this state and a statement that the registered agent is to be the agent of the foreign limited liability partnership upon whom process against it may be served; (vii) a statement that its registration as a limited liability partnership is effective in the jurisdiction in which it registered as a limited liability partnership at the time of the filing of such notice; (viii) a statement that the foreign limited liability partnership is filing a notice in order to obtain status as a New York registered foreign limited liability partnership; (ix) if the registration of the foreign limited liability partnership is to be effective on a date later than the time of filing, the date, not to exceed sixty days from the date of filing, of such proposed effectiveness; and (x) any other matters the foreign limited liability partnership determines to include in the notice. Such notice shall be accompanied by either (1) a copy of the last registration or renewal registration (or similar filing), if any, filed by the foreign limited liability partnership with the jurisdiction where it registered as a limited liability partnership or (2) a certificate, issued by the jurisdiction where it registered as a limited liability partnership, substantially to the effect that such foreign limited liability partnership has filed a registration as a limited liability partnership which is effective on the date of the certificate (if such registration, renewal registration or certificate is in a foreign language, a translation thereof under oath of the translator shall be attached thereto). Such notice shall also be accompanied by a fee of two hundred fifty dollars.

(b) Without excluding other activities which may not constitute the carrying on or conducting or transacting of business or activities in this state, for purposes of determining whether a foreign limited liability partnership is required to file a notice pursuant to subdivision (a) of this section, a foreign limited liability partnership shall not be considered to be carrying on or conducting or transacting business or activities in this state by reason of carrying on in this state any one or more of the following activities:

> (i) maintaining or defending any action or proceeding, whether judicial, administrative, arbitrative or otherwise, or effecting settlement thereof or the settlement of claims or disputes;
>
> (ii) holding meetings of its partners; or
>
> (iii) maintaining bank accounts.

The specification in this subdivision does not establish a standard for activities which may subject a foreign limited liability partnership to service of process under this article or any other statute of this state. The filing of a notice pursuant to subdivision (a) of this section by a foreign limited liability partnership shall not by itself be deemed to be evidence that such foreign limited liability partnership is carrying on or conducting or transacting business or activities in this state.

(c) A notice shall be executed by one or more partners of the foreign limited liability partnership.

(d) If a signed notice delivered to the department of state for filing complies as to form with the requirements of law and the filing fee required by any statute of this state has been paid, the notice shall be filed and indexed by the department of state. If a foreign limited liability partnership that is a New York registered foreign limited liability partnership dissolves, a foreign limited liability partnership which is the successor to such New York registered foreign limited liability partnership (i) shall not be required to file a new notice and shall be deemed to have filed the notice filed by the New York registered foreign limited liability partnership pursuant to subdivision (a) of this section, as well as any withdrawal notice filed pursuant to subdivision (e) of this section, any statement or certificate of consent filed pursuant to subdivision (f) of this section and any notice of amendment filed pursuant to subdivision (i) of this section and (ii) shall be bound by any revocation of status pursuant to subdivision (f) of this section and any annulment thereof of the dissolved foreign limited liability partnership that was a New York registered foreign limited liability partnership. For purposes of this section, a foreign limited liability partnership is a successor to a foreign limited liability partnership that was a New York registered foreign limited liability partnership if a majority of the total interests in the current profits of such successor foreign limited liability partnership are held by partners of the predecessor foreign limited liability partnership that was a New York registered foreign limited liability partnership who were partners of such predecessor partnership immediately prior to the dissolution of such predecessor partnership.

(e) A notice may be withdrawn by filing with the department of state a written withdrawal notice executed by one or more partners of the New York registered foreign limited liability partnership, with a filing fee of sixty dollars. A withdrawal notice must include: (i) the name or names under which the New York registered foreign limited liability partnership carried on or conducted or transacted business or activities in this state (and if it has been changed since the filing of the notice, the name under which it filed such notice); (ii) the date a notice was filed with the department of state pursuant to subdivision (a) of this section; (iii) the address of the New York registered foreign limited liability partnership's principal office and the jurisdiction in which it is registered as a limited liability partnership; (iv) if the withdrawal of the New York registered foreign limited liability partnership is to be effective on a date later than the time of such filing, the date, not to exceed sixty days from the date of such filing, of such proposed effectiveness; (v) a statement acknowledging that the withdrawal terminates the foreign limited liability partnership's status as a New York registered foreign limited liability partnership; and (vi) any other information determined by the New York registered foreign limited liability partnership. A withdrawal notice terminates the status of the foreign limited liability partnership as a New York registered foreign limited liability partnership as of the date of filing of the notice or as of the later date, if any, specified in the notice, not to exceed sixty days from the date of such filing. The termination of status shall not be affected by errors in the information stated in the withdrawal notice. If a New York registered foreign limited liability partnership ceases to be denominated as a registered limited liability partnership or limited liability partnership under the laws of the jurisdiction governing the agreement under which such New York registered foreign limited liability partnership operates, it shall within thirty days after the occurrence of such event file a withdrawal notice pursuant to this subdivision.

(f)(I) Each New York registered foreign limited liability partnership shall, within sixty days prior to the fifth anniversary of the effective date of its notice and every five years thereafter, furnish a statement to the department of state setting forth: (i) the name under which the New York registered foreign limited liability partnership is carrying on or conducting or transacting business or activities in this state, (ii) the address of the principal office of the New York registered foreign limited liability partnership, (iii) the post office address within or without this state to which the secretary of state shall mail a copy of any process accepted against it served upon him or her, which address shall supersede any previous address on file with the department of state for this purpose, and (iv) a statement that it is a foreign limited liability partnership. The statement shall be executed by one or more partners of the New York registered foreign limited liability partnership. The statement shall be accompanied by a fee of fifty dollars. If a New York registered foreign limited liability partnership shall not timely file the statement required by this subdivision, the department of state may, upon sixty days' notice mailed to the address of such New York registered foreign limited liability partnership as shown in the last notice or statement or certificate of amendment filed by such New York registered foreign limited liability partnership, make a proclamation declaring the status of such New York registered foreign limited liability partnership to be revoked pursuant to this subdivision. The department of state shall file the original proclamation in its office and shall publish a copy thereof in the state register no later than three months following the date of such proclamation. Upon the publication of such proclamation in the manner aforesaid, the status of each New York registered foreign limited liability partnership named in such proclamation shall be deemed revoked without further legal proceedings. Any New York registered foreign limited liability partnership whose status was so revoked may file in the department of state a certificate of consent certifying that either a statement required by this subdivision has been filed or accompanies the certificate of consent and all fees imposed under this chapter on the New York registered foreign limited liability partnership have been paid. The filing of such certificate of consent shall have the effect of annulling all of the proceedings theretofore taken for the revocation of the status of such New York registered foreign limited liability partnership under this subdivision and (1) the New York registered foreign limited liability partnership shall thereupon have such powers, rights, duties and obligations as it had on the date of the publication of the proclamation, with the same force and effect as if such proclamation had not been made or published and (2) such publication shall not affect the applicability of the laws of the jurisdiction governing the agreement under which such New York registered foreign limited liability partnership is operating (including laws governing the liability of partners) to any debt, obligation or liability incurred, created or assumed from the date of publication of the proclamation through the date of the filing of the certificate of consent. The filing of a certificate of consent shall be accompanied by a fee of fifty dollars and if accompanied by a statement, the fee required by this subdivision. If, after the publication of such proclamation, it shall be determined by the department of state that the name of any New York registered foreign limited liability partnership was erroneously included in such proclamation, the department of state shall make appropriate entry on its records, which entry shall have the effect of annulling all of the proceedings theretofore taken for the revocation of the status of such New York registered foreign limited liability partnership under this subdivision and (1) such New York registered foreign limited liability partnership shall have such powers, rights, duties and obligations as it had on the date of the publication of the proclamation, with the same force and effect as if such proclamation had not been made or published and (2) such publication shall not affect the applicability of the laws of the jurisdiction governing the agreement under which such New York registered foreign limited liability partnership is operating (including laws governing the liability of partners) to any debt, obligation or liability incurred, created or assumed from the date of publication of the proclamation through the date of the making of the entry on the records of the department of state. Whenever a New York registered foreign limited liability partnership shall have filed a certificate of consent pursuant to this subdivision or if the name of a New York registered foreign limited liability partnership was erroneously included in a proclamation and such proclamation was annulled, the department of state shall publish a notice thereof in the state register.

(II)(A) Within one hundred twenty days after the effective date of the notice filed under subdivision (a) of this section, a copy of the same or a notice containing the substance thereof shall be published once in each week for six successive weeks, in two newspapers of the county within this state in which the principal office of the foreign limited liability partnership is located, one newspaper to be printed weekly and one newspaper to be printed daily, to be designated by the county clerk. When such county is located within a city with a population of one million or more, such designation shall be as though the copy or notice were a notice or advertisement of judicial proceedings. Proof of the publication required by this subparagraph, consisting of the certificate of publication of the foreign limited liability partnership with the affidavits of publication of such newspapers annexed thereto, must be filed with the department of state, with a filing fee of fifty dollars. Notwithstanding any other provision of law, if the office of the foreign limited liability partnership is located in a county wherein a weekly or daily newspaper of the county, or both, has not been so designated by the county clerk, then the publication herein required shall be made in a weekly or daily newspaper of any county, or both, as the case may be, which is contiguous to, such county, provided that any such newspaper meets all the other requirements of this subparagraph. A copy or notice published in a newspaper other than the newspaper or newspapers designated by the county clerk shall not be deemed to be one of the publications required by this subparagraph. The notice shall include: (1) the name of the foreign limited liability partnership; (2) the date of filing of such notice with the department of state; (3) the jurisdiction and date of its organization; (4) the county within this state, in which the principal office of the foreign limited liability partnership is located; (4-a) the street address of the principal business location, if any; (5) a statement that the secretary of state has been designated as agent of the foreign limited liability partnership upon whom process against it may be served and the post office address within or without this state to which the secretary of state shall mail a copy of any process against it served upon him or her; (6) if the foreign limited liability partnership is to have a registered agent, his or her name and address within this state and a statement that the registered agent is to be the agent of the foreign limited liability partnership upon whom process against it may be served; (7) the address of the office required to be maintained in the jurisdiction of its organization by the laws of that jurisdiction or, if not so required, of the principal office of the foreign limited liability partnership; (8) the name and address of the authorized officer in its jurisdiction in which it registered as a limited liability partnership where a copy of its registration is filed or, if no public filing of its registration is required by the law of its jurisdiction of organization, a statement that the foreign limited liability partnership shall provide, on request, a copy thereof with all amendments thereto (if such documents are in a foreign language, a translation thereof under oath of the translator shall be attached thereto), and the name and post office address of the person responsible for providing such copies; or (9) the character or purpose of the business of such foreign limited liability partnership. Where, at any time after completion of the first of the six weekly publications required by this subparagraph and prior to the completion of the sixth such weekly publication, there is a change in any of the information contained in the copy or notice as published, the foreign limited liability partnership may complete the remaining publications of the original copy or notice, and the foreign limited liability partnership shall not be required to publish any further or amended copy or notice. Where, at any time after completion of the six weekly publications required by this subparagraph, there is a change to any of the information contained in the copy or notice as published, no further or amended publication or republication shall be required to be made. If within one hundred twenty days after the effective date of the notice required to be filed under subdivision (a) of this section, proof of such publication, consisting of the certificate of publication of the foreign limited liability partnership with the affidavits of publication of the newspapers annexed thereto has not been filed with the department of state, the authority of such foreign limited liability partnership to carry on, conduct or transact any business in this state shall be suspended, effective as of the expiration of such one hundred twenty day period. The failure of a foreign limited liability partnership to cause such copy or notice to be published and such certificate of publication and affidavits of publication to be filed with the department of state within such one hundred twenty day period or the suspension of such foreign limited liability partnership's authority to carry on, conduct or transact business in this state pursuant to this subparagraph shall not limit or impair the validity of any contract or act of such foreign limited liability partnership, or any right or remedy of any other party under or by virtue of any contract, act or omission of such foreign limited liability partnership, or the right of any other party to maintain any action or special proceeding on any such contract, act or omission, or right of such foreign limited liability partnership to defend any action or special proceeding in this state, or result in any partner or agent of such foreign limited liability partnership becoming liable for the contractual obligations or other liabilities of the foreign limited liability partnership. If, at any time following the suspension of a foreign limited liability partnership's authority to carry on, conduct or transact business in this state pursuant to this subparagraph, such foreign limited liability partnership shall cause proof of publication in substantial compliance with the provisions (other than the one hundred twenty day period) of this subparagraph, consisting of the certificate of publication of the foreign limited liability partnership with the affidavits of publication of the newspapers annexed thereto, to be filed with the department of state, such suspension of such foreign limited liability partnership's authority to carry on, conduct or transact business shall be annulled.

(B)(1) A foreign limited liability partnership which was formed and filed the notice required to be filed under subdivision (a) of this section prior to the effective date of this subparagraph, and which filed a notice and complied with the publication and filing requirements of this paragraph as in effect prior to such effective date shall not be required to make any publication or republication or any filing under subparagraph (A) of this paragraph, and shall not be subject to suspension pursuant to this paragraph.

(2) Within twelve months after the effective date of this subparagraph, a foreign limited liability partnership which was formed and filed the notice required to be filed under subdivision (a) of this section prior to such effective date and which did not comply with the publication and filing requirements of this paragraph as in effect prior to such effective date shall publish a copy of its notice or a notice containing the substance thereof in the manner required (other than the one hundred twenty day period) by this paragraph as in effect prior to such effective date and file proof of such publication, consisting of the certificate of publication of the foreign limited liability partnership with the affidavits of publication of the newspapers annexed thereto, with the department of state.

(3) If a foreign limited liability partnership that is subject to the provisions of clause two of this subparagraph fails to file the required proof of publication with the department of state within twelve months after the effective date of this subparagraph, its authority to carry on, conduct or transact any business in this state shall be suspended, effective as of the expiration of such twelve month period.

(4) The failure of a foreign limited liability partnership that is subject to the provisions of clause two of this subparagraph to fully comply with the provisions of said clause two or the suspension of such foreign limited liability partnership's authority to carry on, conduct or transact any business in this state pursuant to clause three of this subparagraph shall not impair or limit the validity of any contract or act of such foreign limited liability partnership, or any right or remedy of any other party under or by virtue of any contract, act or omission of such foreign limited liability partnership, or the right of any other party to maintain any action or special proceeding on any such contract, act or omission, or right of such foreign limited liability partnership to defend any action or special proceeding in this state, or result in any partner or agent of such foreign limited liability partnership becoming liable for the contractual obligations or other liabilities of the foreign limited liability partnership.

(5) If, at any time following the suspension of a foreign limited liability partnership's authority to carry on, conduct or transact business in this state, pursuant to clause three of this subparagraph, such foreign limited liability partnership shall cause proof of publication in substantial compliance with the provisions (other than the one hundred twenty day period) of subparagraph (A) of this paragraph, consisting of the certificate of publication of the foreign limited liability partnership with the affidavits of publication of the newspapers annexed thereto, to be filed

with the department of state, such suspension of such foreign limited liability partnership's authority to carry on, conduct or transact business shall be annulled.

(6) For the purposes of this subparagraph, a foreign limited liability partnership which was formed and filed the notice required to be filed under subdivision (a) of this section prior to the effective date of this subparagraph shall be deemed to have complied with the publication and filing requirements of this paragraph as in effect prior to such effective date if (A) the foreign limited liability partnership was formed and filed the notice required to be filed under subdivision (a) of this section on or after January first, nineteen hundred ninety-nine and prior to such effective date and the foreign limited liability partnership filed at least one affidavit of the printer or publisher of a newspaper with the department of state at any time prior to such effective date, or (B) the foreign limited liability partnership was formed and filed the notice required to be filed under subdivision (a) of this section prior to January first, nineteen hundred ninety-nine, without regard to whether the foreign limited liability partnership did or did not file any affidavit of the printer or publisher of a newspaper with the secretary of state.

(C) The information in a notice published pursuant to this paragraph shall be presumed to be in compliance with and satisfaction of the requirements of this paragraph.

(g) The filing of a withdrawal notice by a New York registered foreign limited liability partnership pursuant to subdivision (e) of this section, a revocation of status pursuant to subdivision (f) of this section and the filing of a notice of amendment pursuant to subdivision (i) of this section shall not affect the applicability of the laws of the jurisdiction governing the agreement under which such foreign limited liability partnership is operating (including laws governing the liability of partners) to any debt, obligation or liability incurred, created or assumed while the foreign limited liability partnership was a New York registered foreign limited liability partnership. After a withdrawal or revocation of registration, the foreign limited liability partnership shall for all purposes continue to be a foreign partnership without limited partners under the laws of this state.

(h) The department of state shall remove from its active records the notice of any New York registered foreign limited liability partnership whose notice has been withdrawn or revoked.

(i) A notice or statement filed with the department of state under this section may be amended or corrected by filing with the department of state a notice of amendment executed in accordance with subdivision (c) of this section. No later than ninety days after (i) a change in the name of the New York registered foreign limited liability partnership or (ii) a partner of the New York registered foreign limited liability partnership becomes aware that any statement in a notice or statement was false in any material respect when made or that an event has occurred which makes the notice or statement inaccurate in any material respect, the New York registered foreign limited liability partnership shall file a notice of amendment. The filing of a notice of amendment shall be accompanied by a fee of sixty dollars. The certificate of amendment shall set forth: (i) the name of the limited liability partnership and, if it has been changed, the name under which it originally filed a notice under this section and (ii) the date of filing its initial registration or statement.

(i-1) A certificate of change which changes only the post office address to which the secretary of state shall mail a copy of any process against a New York registered foreign limited liability partnership served upon him or the address of the registered agent, provided such address being changed is the address of a person, partnership or corporation whose address, as agent, is the address to be changed or who has been designated as registered agent of such registered foreign limited liability partnership shall be signed and delivered to the department of state by such agent. The certificate of change shall set forth: (i) the name of the New York registered foreign limited liability partnership; (ii) the date of filing of its initial registration or notice statement; (iii) each change effected thereby; (iv) that a notice of the proposed change was mailed to the limited liability partnership by the party signing the certificate not less than thirty days prior to the date of delivery to the department of state and that such limited liability partnership has not objected thereto; and (v) that the party signing the certificate is the agent of such limited liability partnership to whose address the secretary of state is required to mail copies of process or the registered agent, if such be the case. A certificate signed and delivered under this subdivision shall not be deemed to effect a change of location of the office of the limited liability partnership in whose behalf such certificate is filed. The certificate of change shall be accompanied by a fee of five dollars.

(j) The filing of a notice of amendment pursuant to subdivision (i) of this section with the department of state shall not alter the effective date of the notice being amended or corrected.

(k) Each foreign limited liability partnership carrying on or conducting or transacting business or activities in this state shall use a name which contains without abbreviation the words "Registered Limited Liability Partnership" or "Limited Liability Partnership" or the abbreviations "R.L.L.P.", "RLLP", "P.L.L.", "PLL", "L.L.P." or "LLP"; provided, however, the partnership may use any such words or abbreviation, without limitation, in addition to its registered name.

(l) Subject to the constitution of this state, the laws of the jurisdiction that govern a foreign limited liability partnership shall determine its internal affairs and the liability of partners for debts, obligations and liabilities of, or chargeable to, the foreign limited liability partnership; provided that (i) each partner, employee or agent of a foreign limited liability partnership who performs professional services in this state on behalf of such foreign limited liability partnership shall be personally and fully liable and accountable for any negligent or wrongful act or misconduct committed by him or her or by any person under his or her direct supervision and control while rendering such professional services in this state and shall bear professional responsibility for compliance by such foreign limited liability partnership with all laws, rules and regulations governing the practice of a profession in this state and (ii) each shareholder, director, officer, member, manager, partner, employee or agent of a professional service corporation, foreign professional service corporation, professional service limited liability company, foreign professional service limited liability company, registered limited liability partnership, foreign limited liability partnership or professional partnership that is a partner, employee or agent of a foreign limited liability partnership who performs professional services in this state on behalf of such foreign limited liability partnership shall be personally and fully liable and accountable for any negligent or wrongful act or misconduct committed by him or her or by any person under his or her direct supervision and control while rendering professional services in this state in his or her capacity as a partner, employee or agent of such foreign limited liability partnership and shall bear professional responsibility for compliance by such foreign limited liability partnership with all laws, rules and regulations governing the practice of a profession in this state. The relationship of a professional to a foreign limited liability partnership with which such professional is associated, whether as a partner, employee or agent, shall not modify or diminish the jurisdiction over such professional of the licensing authority and, in the case of an attorney and counsellor-at-law or a professional service corporation, foreign professional service corporation, professional service limited liability company, foreign professional service limited liability company, registered limited liability partnership, foreign limited liability partnership or professional partnership engaged in the practice of law, the courts of this state. A limited partnership formed under the laws of any jurisdiction, other than this state, which is denominated as a registered limited liability partnership or limited liability partnership under such laws shall be recognized in this state as a foreign limited partnership but not as a foreign limited liability partnership or a New York registered foreign limited liability partnership. Except to the extent provided in article eight of the limited liability company law, a partnership without limited partners operating under an agreement governed by the laws of any jurisdiction, other than this state, which is denominated as a registered limited liability partnership or a limited liability partnership under such laws, but is not a foreign limited liability partnership, shall be recognized in this state as a foreign partnership without limited partners, but not as a foreign limited liability partnership or a New York registered foreign limited liability partnership.

(m) A foreign limited liability partnership carrying on or conducting or transacting business or activities in this state without having filed a notice pursuant to subdivision (a) of this section may not maintain any action, suit or special proceeding in any court of this state unless and until such foreign limited liability partnership shall have filed such notice and paid all fees that it would have been required to pay had it filed a notice pursuant to subdivision (a) of this section before carrying on or conducting or transacting business or activities as a New York registered foreign limited liability partnership in this state and shall have filed proof of publication pursuant to subdivision (f) of this section. The failure of a foreign limited liability partnership that is carrying on or conducting or transacting business or activities in this state to comply with the provisions of this section does not impair the validity of any contract or act of the foreign limited liability partnership or prevent the foreign limited liability partnership from defending any action or special proceeding in any court of this state.

(n) A foreign limited liability partnership, other than a foreign limited liability partnership authorized to practice law, shall be under the supervision of the regents of the university of the state of New York and be subject to disciplinary proceedings and penalties in the same manner and to the same extent as is provided with respect to individuals and their licenses, certificates and registrations in title eight of the education law relating to the applicable profession. Notwithstanding the provisions of this subdivision, a foreign limited liability partnership authorized to practice medicine shall be subject to the pre-hearing procedures and hearing procedures as are provided with respect to individual physicians and their licenses in title two-A of article two of the public health law. No foreign limited liability partnership shall engage in any profession or carry on, or conduct or transact any other business or activities in this state other than the rendering of the professional services or the carrying on, or conducting or transacting of any other business or activities for which it is formed and is authorized to do business in this state; provided that such foreign limited liability partnership may invest its funds in real estate, mortgages, stocks, bonds or any other type of investments; provided, further, that a foreign limited liability partnership (i) authorized to practice law may only engage in another profession or other business or activities in this state or (ii) which is engaged in a profession or other business or activities other than law may only engage in the practice of law in this state, to the extent not prohibited by any other law of this state or any rule adopted by the appropriate appellate division of the supreme court or the court of appeals.

(o) No foreign limited liability partnership may render a professional service in this state except through individuals authorized by law to render such professional service as individuals in this state.

(p) This section shall not repeal, modify or restrict any provision of the education law or the judiciary law or any rules or regulations adopted thereunder regulating the professions referred to in the education law or the judiciary law except to the extent in conflict herewith.

(q) Each partner of a foreign limited liability partnership which provides medical services in this state must be licensed pursuant to article 131 of the education law to practice medicine in the state and each partner of a foreign limited liability partnership which provides dental services in the state must be licensed pursuant to article 133 of the education law to practice dentistry in this state. Each partner of a foreign limited liability partnership which provides veterinary service in the state shall be licensed pursuant to article 135 of the education law to practice veterinary medicine in this state. Each partner of a foreign limited liability partnership which provides professional engineering, land surveying, architectural and/or landscape architectural services in this state must be licensed pursuant to article 145, article 147 and/or article 148 of the education law to practice one or more of such professions. Each partner of a foreign limited liability partnership which provides licensed clinical social work services in this state must be licensed pursuant to article 154 of the education law to practice licensed clinical social work in this state. Each partner of a foreign limited liability partnership which provides creative arts therapy services in this state must be licensed pursuant to article 163 of the education law to practice creative arts therapy in this state. Each partner of a foreign limited liability partnership which provides marriage and family therapy services in this state must be licensed pursuant to article 163 of the education law to practice marriage and family therapy in this state. Each partner of a foreign limited liability partnership which provides mental health counseling services in this state must be licensed pursuant to article 163 of the education law to practice mental health counseling in this state. Each partner of a foreign limited liability partnership which provides psychoanalysis services in this state must be licensed pursuant to article 163 of the education law to practice psychoanalysis in this state.

§ 121-1503.   Transaction of business outside the state

(a) It is the intent of the legislature that the registration of a partnership without limited partners as a registered limited liability partnership under this article shall be recognized beyond the limits of this state and that such registered limited liability partnership may conduct its business or activities, carry on its operations, and have and exercise the powers granted by this article in any state, territory, district or possession of the United States or in any foreign country and that, subject to any reasonable registration requirements any such registered limited liability partnership transacting business outside this state and the laws of this state governing such registered limited liability partnership shall be granted the protection of full faith and credit under section 1 of article IV of the Constitution of the United States.

(b) It is the policy of this state that the internal affairs of a partnership without limited partners registered as a registered limited liability partnership under this article and the liability of partners in a registered limited liability partnership for debts, obligations and liabilities of, or chargeable to, the registered limited liability partnership shall be subject to and governed by the laws of this state, including the provisions of this article.

§ 121-1504. Foreign related limited liability partnership

Any foreign related limited liability partnership that has filed a certificate of authority under and satisfied all the requirements of section eight hundred two of the limited liability company law shall be deemed to have filed a notice pursuant to section 121-1502 of this chapter until the fifth anniversary of filing its application for such certificate of authority, at which time the foreign related limited liability partnership shall file a notice pursuant to section 121-1502 of this chapter.

§ 121-1505. Service of process

(a) Service of process on the secretary of state as agent of a registered limited liability partnership under this article shall be made by personally delivering to and leaving with the secretary of state or a deputy, or with any person authorized by the secretary of state to receive such service, at the office of the department of state in the city of Albany, duplicate copies of such process together with the statutory fee, which fee shall be a taxable disbursement. Service of process on such registered limited liability partnership shall be complete when the secretary of state is so served. The secretary of state shall promptly send one of such copies by certified mail, return receipt requested, to such registered limited liability partnership, at the post office address on file in the department of state specified for such purpose.

(b) As used in this article, process shall mean judicial process and all orders, demands, notices or other papers required or permitted by law to be personally served on a registered limited liability partnership, for the purpose of acquiring jurisdiction of such registered limited liability partnership in any action or proceeding, civil or criminal, whether judicial, administrative, arbitrative or otherwise, in this state or in the federal courts sitting in or for this state.

(c) Nothing in this section shall affect the right to serve process in any other manner permitted by law.

§ 121-1506. Resignation for receipt of process

(a) A registered agent may resign as such agent. A certificate entitled "Certificate of resignation of registered agent of ...... (name of limited liability partnership) under section 121-1506 of the Partnership Law" shall be signed and delivered to the department of state. It shall set forth:

(1) That he resigns as registered agent for the designated limited liability partnership.

(2) The date the certificate of registration of the designated limited liability partnership was filed by the department of state.

(3) That he has sent a copy of the certificate of resignation by registered mail to the designating limited liability partnership at the post office address on file in the department of state specified for the mailing of process or if such address is the address of the registered agent, then to the office of the designating limited liability partnership in the jurisdiction of its formation.

(b) The party (or the party's legal representative) whose post address has been supplied by a limited liability partnership as its address for process may resign. A certificate entitled "Certificate of Resignation for Receipt of Process under Section 121-1506(b) of the Partnership Law" shall be signed by such party and delivered to the department of state. It shall set forth:

(1) The name of the limited liability partnership and the date that its certificate of registration was filed by the department of state.

(2) That the address of the party has been designated by the limited liability partnership as the post office address to which the secretary of state shall mail a copy of any process served on the secretary of state as agent for such limited liability partnership and that such party wishes to resign.

(3) That sixty days prior to the filing of the certificate of resignation with the department of state the party has sent a copy of the certificate of resignation for receipt of process by registered or certified mail to the address of the registered agent of the designated limited liability partnership, if other than the party filing the certificate of resignation, for receipt of process, or if the resigning limited liability partnership has no registered agent, then to the last address of the designated limited liability partnership, known to the party, specifying the address to which the copy was sent. If there is no registered agent and no known address of the designating limited liability partnership the party shall attach an affidavit to the certificate stating that a diligent but unsuccessful search was made by the party to locate the limited liability partnership, specifying what efforts were made.

(4) That the designated limited liability partnership is required to deliver to the department of state a certificate of amendment providing for the designation by the limited liability partnership of a new address and that upon

its failure to file such certificate, its authority to do business in this state shall be suspended.

(c) Upon the failure of the designating limited liability partnership to file a certificate of amendment providing for the designation by the limited liability partnership of the new address after the filing of a certificate of resignation for receipt of process with the secretary of state, its authority to do business in this state shall be suspended.

(d) The filing by the department of state of a certificate of amendment providing for a new address by a designating limited liability partnership shall annul the suspension and its authority to do business in this state shall be restored and continued as if no suspension had occurred.

(e) The resignation for receipt of process shall become effective upon the filing by the department of state of a certificate of resignation for receipt of process.

(f)(1) In any case in which a limited liability partnership suspended pursuant to this section would be subject to the personal or other jurisdiction of the courts of this state under article three of the civil practice law and rules, process against such limited liability partnership may be served upon the secretary of state as its agent pursuant to this section. Such process may be issued in any court in this state having jurisdiction of the subject matter.

(2) Service of such process upon the secretary of state shall be made by personally delivering to and leaving with him or his deputy, or with any person authorized by the secretary of state to receive such service, at the office of the department of state in the city of Albany, a copy of such process together with the statutory fee, which fee shall be a taxable disbursement. Such service shall be sufficient if notice thereof and a copy of the process are:

(i) delivered personally within or without this state to such limited liability partnership by a person and in the manner authorized to serve process by law of the jurisdiction in which service is made, or

(ii) sent by or on behalf of the plaintiff to such limited liability partnership by registered or certified mail with return receipt requested to the last address of such limited liability partnership known to the plaintiff.

(3)(i) Where service of a copy of process was effected by personal service, proof of service shall be by an affidavit of compliance with this section filed, together with the process, within thirty days after such service, with the clerk of the court in which the action or special proceeding is pending. Service of process shall be complete ten days after such papers are filed with the clerk of the court.

(ii) Where service of a copy of process was effected by mailing in accordance with this section, proof of service shall be by affidavit of compliance with this section filed, together with the process, within thirty days after receipt of the return receipt signed by the limited liability partnership, or other official proof of delivery or of the original envelope mailed. If a copy of the process is mailed in accordance with this section, there shall be filed with the affidavit of compliance either the return receipt signed by such limited liability partnership or other official proof of delivery, if acceptance was refused by it, the original envelope with a notation by the postal authorities that acceptance was refused. If acceptance was refused a copy of the notice and process together with notice of the mailing by registered or certified mail and refusal to accept shall be promptly sent to such limited liability partnership at the same address by ordinary mail and the affidavit of compliance shall so state. Service of process shall be complete ten days after such papers are filed with the clerk of the court. The refusal to accept delivery of the registered or certified mail or to sign the return receipt shall not affect the validity of the service and such limited liability partnership refusing to accept such registered or certified mail shall be charged with knowledge of the contents thereof.

(4) Service made as provided in this section without the state shall have the same force as personal service made within this state.

(5) Nothing in this section shall affect the right to serve process in any other manner permitted by law.

(g) The filing of a certificate of resignation of a registered agent pursuant to subdivision (a) of this section shall be accompanied by the fee of ten dollars, and the filing of a certificate of resignation for receipt of process pursuant to subdivision (b) of this section shall be accompanied by the fee of ten dollars.

§ 121-1507.   Definitions

For purposes of this article:

(a) "Partnership interest" means: (i) a partner's share of the profits and losses of a registered limited liability partnership; and (ii) the partner's right to receive distributions of a registered limited liability partnership.

(b) "Affidavit of publication" means the affidavit of the printer or publisher of a newspaper in which a publication required to be filed pursuant to sections 121-1500 and 121-1502 of this article has been made. The affidavit of publication shall be in a form substantially as follows:

"Affidavit of Publication Under Section (specify applicable section) of the Partnership Law State of New York, County of _____, ss.:

"The undersigned is the printer (or publisher) of _____ (name of newspaper), a _____ (daily or weekly) newspaper published in _____, New York. A notice regarding _____ (name of limited liability partnership) was published in said newspaper once in each week for six successive weeks, commencing on _____ and ending on _____. The text of the notice as published in said newspaper is as set forth below, or in the annexed exhibit. This newspaper has been designated by the Clerk of _____ County for this purpose.

_____(signature)

_____(printed name),
        (jurat)"

The text of the notice set forth in or annexed to each affidavit of publication shall: (i) include only the text of the published notice, (ii) be free of extraneous marks, and (iii) if submitted in paper form, be printed on paper of such size, weight and color, and in ink of such color, and in such fonts, and be in such other qualities and form not inconsistent with any other provision of law as, in the judgment of the secretary of state, will not impair the ability of the department of state to include a legible and permanent copy thereof in its official records. Nothing in this subdivision shall be construed as requiring the department of state to accept for filing a document submitted in electronic form.

(c) "Certificate of publication" means a certificate presented on behalf of the applicable limited liability partnership to the department of state together with the affidavits of publication pursuant to section 121-1500 or 121-1502 of this article. The certificate of publication shall be in a form substantially as follows:

"Certificate of Publication of _____ (name of limited partnership) Under Section (specify applicable section) of the Partnership Law. The undersigned is the _____ (title) of _____ (name of limited liability partnership). The published notices described in the annexed affidavits of publication contain all of the information required by the above-mentioned section of the partnership law. The newspapers described in such affidavits of publication satisfy the requirements set forth in the partnership law and the designation made by the county clerk. I certify the foregoing statements to be true under penalties of perjury.

Date
Signature
Printed Name"

≡*Appendix D*≡
UNIFORM LIMITED PARTNERSHIP ACT (2001)[1]

Drafted by the

NATIONAL CONFERENCE OF COMMISSIONERS
ON UNIFORM STATE LAWS

and by it

APPROVED AND RECOMMENDED FOR ENACTMENT
IN ALL THE STATES

at its

ANNUAL CONFERENCE
MEETING IN ITS ONE-HUNDRED-AND-TENTH YEAR
WHITE SULPHUR SPRINGS, WEST VIRGINIA
AUGUST 10–17, 2001

WITH PREFATORY NOTE AND COMMENTS

DRAFTING COMMITTEE TO REVISE
UNIFORM LIMITED PARTNERSHIP ACT

HOWARD J. SWIBEL, Suite 1200, 120 S. Riverside Plaza, Chicago, IL 60606, *Chair*

ANN CONAWAY ANKER, Widener University, School of Law, P.O. Box 7474, Wilmington, DE 19803

REX BLACKBURN, Suite 200, 1101 W. River Street, P.O. Box 959, Boise, ID 83701

HARRY J. HAYNSWORTH, IV, William Mitchell College of Law, 875 Summit Avenue, St. Paul, MN 55105

HARRIET LANSING, Court of Appeals, Judicial Building, 25 Constitution Avenue, St. Paul, MN 55155

REED L. MARTINEAU, P.O. Box 45000, 10 Exchange Place, Salt Lake City, UT 84145

JAMES C. McKAY, Office of Corporation Counsel, 6th Floor South, 441 4th Street, NW, Washington, DC 20001, *Committee on Style Liaison*

THOMAS A. SHIELS, P.O. Box 1401, Legislative Council, Legislative Hall, Dover, DE 19901

DAVID S. WALKER, Drake University Law School, Des Moines, IA 50311

DANIEL S. KLEINBERGER, William Mitchell College of Law, 875 Summit Avenue, St. Paul, MN 55105, *Reporter*

EX OFFICIO

JOHN L. McCLAUGHERTY, P.O. Box 553, Charleston, WV 25322, *President*

TERESA ANN BECK, House Legislative Services Office, P.O. Box 1018, Jackson, MS 39215, *Division Chair*

AMERICAN BAR ASSOCIATION ADVISORS

MARTIN I. LUBAROFF, American Bar Association (1997-2000)

ROBERT R. KEATINGE, American Bar Association

STEVEN G. FROST, American Bar Association Section of Taxation

THOMAS EARL GEU, American Bar Association Section of Real Property, Probate and Trust Law, Probate and Trust Division

SANFORD J. LIEBSCHUTZ, American Bar Association Section of Real Property, Probate and Trust Law, Real Property Division (1997–2000)

BARRY NEKRITZ, American Bar Association Section of Real Property, Probate and Trust Law, Real Property Division

LAURIS G. L. RALL, American Bar Association Section of Business Law

EXECUTIVE DIRECTOR

FRED H. MILLER, University of Oklahoma, College of Law, 300 Timberdell Road, Norman, OK 73019, *Executive Director*

WILLIAM J. PIERCE, 1505 Roxbury Road, Ann Arbor, MI 48104, *Executive Director Emeritus*

UNIFORM LIMITED PARTNERSHIP ACT

TABLE OF CONTENTS

ARTICLE 3.   LIMITED PARTNERS

ARTICLE 4.   GENERAL PARTNERS

ARTICLE 5.   CONTRIBUTIONS AND DISTRIBUTIONS

ARTICLE 6.   DISSOCIATION

ARTICLE 7.   TRANSFERABLE INTERESTS AND RIGHTS OF TRANSFEREES AND CREDITORS

ARTICLE 8.   DISSOLUTION

ARTICLE 9.   FOREIGN LIMITED PARTNERSHIPS

ARTICLE 10.   ACTIONS BY PARTNERS

ARTICLE 11.   CONVERSION AND MERGER

ARTICLE 12.   MISCELLANEOUS PROVISIONS

UNIFORM LIMITED PARTNERSHIP ACT (2001)

PREFATORY NOTE
The Act's Overall Approach

The new Limited Partnership Act is a "stand alone" act, "de-linked" from both the original general partnership act ("UPA") and the Revised Uniform Partnership Act ("RUPA"). To be able to stand alone, the Limited Partnership incorporates many provisions from RUPA and some from the Uniform Limited Liability Company Act ("ULLCA"). As a result, the new Act is far longer and more complex than its immediate predecessor, the Revised Uniform Limited Partnership Act ("RULPA").

The new Act has been drafted for a world in which limited liability partnerships and limited liability companies can meet many of the needs formerly met by limited partnerships. This Act therefore targets two types of enterprises that seem largely beyond the scope of LLPs and LLCs: (i) sophisticated, manager-entrenched commercial deals whose participants commit for the long term, and (ii) estate planning arrangements (family limited partnerships). This Act accordingly assumes that, more often than not, people utilizing it will want:

- strong centralized management, strongly entrenched, and
- passive investors with little control over or right to exit the entity

The Act's rules, and particularly its default rules, have been designed to reflect these assumptions.

The Decision to "De-Link" and Create a Stand Alone Act

Unlike this Act, RULPA is not a stand alone statute. RULPA was drafted to rest on and link to the UPA. RULPA Section 1105 states that "In any case not provided for in this [Act] the provisions of the Uniform Partnership Act govern." UPA Section 6(2) in turn provides that "this Act shall apply to limited partnerships except in so far as the statutes relating to such partnerships are inconsistent herewith." More particularly, RULPA Section 403 defines the rights, powers, restrictions and liabilities of a "general partner of a limited partnership" by equating them to the rights, powers, restrictions and liabilities of "a partner in a partnership without limited partners."

This arrangement has not been completely satisfactory, because the consequences of linkage are not always clear. *See, e.g., Frye v. Manacare Ltd.*, 431 So.2d 181, 183–84 (Fla. Dist. Ct. App. 1983) (applying UPA Section 42 in favor of a limited partner), *Porter v. Barnhouse*, 354 N.W.2d 227, 232–33 (Iowa 1984) (declining to apply UPA Section 42 in favor of a limited partner) and *Baltzell-Wolfe Agencies, Inc. v. Car Wash Investments No. 1, Ltd.*, 389 N.E.2d 517, 518-20 (Ohio App. 1978) (holding that neither the specific provisions of the general partnership statute nor those of the limited partnership statute determined the liability of a person who had withdrawn as general partner of a limited partnership). Moreover, in some instances the "not inconsistent" rules of the UPA can be inappropriate for the fundamentally different relations involved in a limited partnership.

In any event, the promulgation of RUPA unsettled matters. RUPA differs substantially from the UPA, and the drafters of RUPA expressly declined to decide whether RUPA provides a suitable base and link for the limited partnership statute. According to RUPA's Prefatory Note:

> Partnership law no longer governs limited partnerships pursuant to the provisions of RUPA itself. First, limited partnerships are not "partnerships" within the RUPA definition. Second, UPA Section 6(2), which provides that the UPA governs limited partnerships in cases not provided for in the Uniform Limited Partnership Act (1976) (1985) ("RULPA") has been deleted. No substantive change in result is intended, however. Section 1105 of RULPA already provides that the UPA governs in any case not provided for in RULPA, and thus the express linkage in RUPA is unnecessary. Structurally, it is more appropriately left to RULPA to determine the applicability of RUPA to limited partnerships. It is contemplated that the Conference will review the linkage question carefully, although no changes in RULPA may be necessary despite the many changes in RUPA.

The linkage question was the first major issue considered and decided by this Act's Drafting Committee. Since the Conference has recommended the repeal of the UPA, it made no sense to recommend retaining the UPA as the base and link for a revised or new limited partnership act. The Drafting Committee therefore had to choose between recommending linkage to the new general partnership act (i.e., RUPA) or recommending de-linking and a stand alone act.

The Committee saw several substantial advantages to de-linking. A stand alone statute would:

- be more convenient, providing a single, self-contained source of statutory authority for issues pertaining to limited partnerships;
- eliminate confusion as to which issues were solely subject to the limited partnership act and which required reference (i.e., linkage) to the general partnership act; and
- rationalize future case law, by ending the automatic link between the cases concerning partners in a general partnership and issues pertaining to general partners in a limited partnership.

Thus, a stand alone act seemed likely to promote efficiency, clarity, and coherence in the law of limited partnerships.

In contrast, recommending linkage would have required the Drafting Committee to (1) consider each provision of RUPA and determine whether the provision addressed a matter provided for in RULPA; (2) for each RUPA provision which addressed a matter not provided for in RULPA, determine whether the provision stated an appropriate rule for limited partnerships; and (3) for each matter addressed both by RUPA and RULPA, determine whether RUPA or RULPA stated the better rule for limited partnerships.

That approach was unsatisfactory for at least two reasons. No matter how exhaustive the Drafting Committee's analysis might be, the Committee could not guarantee that courts and practitioners would reach the same conclusions. Therefore, in at least some situations linkage would have produced ambiguity. In addition, the Drafting Committee could not guarantee that all currently appropriate links would remain appropriate as courts begin to apply and interpret RUPA. Even if the Committee recommended linkage, RUPA was destined to be interpreted primarily in the context of general partnerships. Those interpretations might not make sense for limited partnership law, because the modern limited partnership involves fundamentally different relations than those involved in "the small, often informal, partnership" that is "[t]he primary focus of RUPA." RUPA, Prefatory Note.

The Drafting Committee therefore decided to draft and recommend a stand alone act.

Availability of LLLP Status

Following the example of a growing number of States, this Act provides for limited liability limited partnerships. In a limited liability limited partnership ("LLLP"), no partner—whether general or limited—is liable on account of partner status for the limited partnership's obligations. Both general and limited partners benefit from a full, status-based liability shield that is equivalent to the shield enjoyed by corporate shareholders, LLC members, and partners in an LLP.

This Act is designed to serve preexisting limited partnerships as well as limited partnerships formed after the Act's enactment. Most of those preexisting limited partnership will not be LLLPs, and accordingly the Act does not prefer or presume LLLP status. Instead, the Act makes LLLP status available through a simple statement in the certificate of limited partnership. See Sections 102(9), 201(a)(4) and 404(c).

Liability Shield for Limited Partners

RULPA provides only a restricted liability shield for limited partners. The shield is at risk for any limited partner who "participates in the control of the business." RULPA Section 303(a). Although this "control rule" is subject to a lengthy list of safe harbors, RULPA Section 303(b), in a world with LLPs, LLCs and, most importantly, LLLPs, the rule is an anachronism. This Act therefore eliminates the control rule and provides a full, status-based shield against limited partner liability for entity obligations. The shield applies whether or not the limited partnership is an LLLP. See Section 303.

Transition Issues

Following RUPA's example, this Act provides (i) an effective date, after which all newly formed limited partnerships are subject to this Act; (ii) an optional period, during which limited partnerships formed under a predecessor statute may elect to become subject to this Act; and (iii) a mandatory date, on which all preexisting limited partnerships become subject to this Act by operation of law.

A few provisions of this Act differ so substantially from prior law that they should not apply automatically to a preexisting limited partnership. Section 1206(c) lists these provisions and states that each remains inapplicable to a preexisting limited partnership, unless the limited partnership elects for the provision to apply.

Comparison of RULPA and this Act

The following table compares some of the major characteristics of RULPA and this Act. In most instances, the rules involved are "default" rules—i.e., subject to change by the partnership agreement.

Characteristic	RULPA	This Act
relationship to general partnership act	linked, Sections 1105, 403; UPA Section 6(2)	de-linked (but many RULPA provisions incorporated)
permitted purposes	subject to any specified exceptions, "any business that a partnership without limited partners may carry on, " Section 106	any lawful purpose, Section 104(b)

Characteristic	RULPA	This Act
constructive notice via publicly filed documents	only that limited partnership exists and that designated general partners are general partners, Section 208	RULPA constructive notice provisions carried forward, Section 103(c), plus constructive notice, 90 days after appropriate filing, of: general partner dissociation and of limited partnership dissolution, termination, merger and conversion, Section 103(d)
duration	specified in certificate of limited partnership, Section 201(a)(4)	perpetual, Section 104(c); subject to change in partnership agreement
use of limited partner name in entity name	prohibited, except in unusual circumstances, Section 102(2)	permitted, Section 108(a)
annual report	none	required, Section 210
limited partner liability for entity debts	none unless limited partner "participates in the control of the business" and person "transact[s] business with the limited partnership reasonably believing . . . that the limited partner is a general partner," Section 303(a); safe harbor lists many activities that do not constitute participating in the control of the business, Section 303(b)	none, regardless of whether the limited partnership is an LLLP, "even if the limited partner participates in the management and control of the limited partnership," Section 303
limited partner duties	none specified	no fiduciary duties "solely by reason of being a limited partner," Section 305(a); each limited partner is obliged to "discharge duties . . . and exercise rights consistently with the obligation of good faith and fair dealing," Section 305(b)

Characteristic	RULPA	This Act
partner access to information—required records—information	all partners have right of access; no requirement of good cause; Act does not state whether partnership agreement may limit access; Sections 105(b) and 305(1)	list of required information expanded slightly; Act expressly states that partner does not have to show good cause; Sections 304(a), 407(a); however, the partnership agreement may set reasonable restrictions on access to and use of required information, Section 110(b)(4), and limited partnership may impose reasonable restrictions on the use of information, Sections 304(g) and 407(f)
partner access to information—other information	limited partners have the right to obtain other relevant information "upon reasonable demand," Section 305(2); general partner rights linked to general partnership act, Section 403	for limited partners, RULPA approach essentially carried forward, with procedures and standards for making a reasonable demand stated in greater detail, plus requirement that limited partnership supply known material information when limited partner consent sought, Section 304; general partner access rights made explicit, following ULLCA and RUPA, including obligation of limited partnership and general partners to volunteer certain information, Section 407; access rights provided for former partners, Sections 304 and 407

Characteristic	RULPA	This Act
general partner liability for entity debts	complete, automatic and formally inescapable, Section 403(b) (n.b.—in practice, most modern limited partnerships have used a general partner that has its own liability shield; *e.g.*, a corporation or limited liability company)	LLLP status available via a simple statement in the certificate of limited partnership, Sections 102(9), 201(a)(4); LLLP status provides a full liability shield to all general partners, Section 404(c); if the limited partnership is not an LLLP, general partners are liable just as under RULPA, Section 404(a)
general partner duties	linked to duties of partners in a general partnership, Section 403	RUPA general partner duties imported, Section 408; general partner's non-compete duty continues during winding up, Section 408(b)(3)
allocation of profits, losses and distributions	provides separately for sharing of profits and losses, Section 503, and for sharing of distributions, Section 504; allocates each according to contributions made and not returned	eliminates as unnecessary the allocation rule for profits and losses; allocates distributions according to contributions made, Section 503 (n.b.— in the default mode, the Act's formulation produces the same result as RULPA formulation)
partner liability for distributions	recapture liability if distribution involved "the return of . . . con- tribution"; one year recapture liability if distribution rightful, Section 608(a); six year recapture liability if wrongful, Section 608(b)	following ULLCA Sections 406 and 407, the Act adopts the RMBCA approach to improper distributions, Sections 508 and 509

Characteristic	RULPA	This Act
limited partner voluntary dissociation	theoretically, limited partner may withdraw on six months notice unless partnership agreement specifies a term for the limited partnership or withdrawal events for limited partner, Section 603; practically, virtually every partnership agreement specifies a term, thereby eliminating the right to withdraw (n.b.— due to estate planning concerns, several States have amended RULPA to prohibit limited partner withdrawal unless otherwise provided in the partnership agreement)	no "right to dissociate as a limited partner before the termination of the limited partnership," Section 601(a); power to dissociate expressly recognized, Section 601(b)(1), but can be eliminated by the partnership agreement
limited partner involuntary dissociation	not addressed	lengthy list of causes, Section 601(b), taken with some modification from RUPA
limited partner dissociation—payout	"fair value . . . based upon [the partner's] right to share in distributions," Section 604	no payout; person becomes transferee of its own transferable interest, Section 602(3)
general partner voluntary dissociation	right exists unless otherwise provided in partnership agreement, Section 602; power exists regardless of partnership agreement, Section 602	RULPA rule carried forward, although phrased differently, Section 604(a); dissociation before termination of the limited partnership is defined as wrongful, Section 604(b)(2)
general partner involuntary dissociation	Section 402 lists causes	following RUPA, Section 603 expands the list of causes, including expulsion by court order, Section 603(5)

Characteristic	RULPA	This Act
general partner dissociation—payout	"fair value . . . based upon [the partner's] right to share in distributions," Section 604, subject to offset for damages caused by wrongful withdrawal, Section 602	no payout; person becomes transferee of its own transferable interest, Section 605(5)
transfer of partner interest —nomenclature	"Assignment of Partnership Interest," Section 702	"Transfer of Partner's Transferable Interest," Section 702
transfer of partner interest —substance	economic rights fully transferable, but management rights and partner status are not transferable, Section 702	same rule, but Sections 701 and 702 follow RUPA's more detailed and less oblique formulation
rights of creditor of partner	limited to charging order, Section 703	essentially the same rule, but, following RUPA and ULLCA, the Act has a more elaborate provision that expressly extends to creditors of transferees, Section 703
dissolution by partner consent	requires unanimous written consent, Section 801(3)	requires consent of "all general partners and of limited partners owning a majority of the rights to receive distributions as limited partners at the time the consent is to be effective," Section 801(2)
dissolution following dissociation of a general partner	occurs automatically unless all partners agree to continue the business and, if there is no remaining general partner, to appoint a replacement general partner, Section 801(4)	if at least one general partner remains, no dissolution unless "within 90 days after the dissociation . . . partners owning a majority of the rights to receive distributions as partners" consent to dissolve the limited partnership; Section 801(3)(A); if no general partner remains, dissolution occurs upon the passage of 90 days

Characteristic	RULPA	This Act
		after the dissociation, unless before that deadline limited partners owning a majority of the rights to receive distributions owned by limited partners consent to continue the business and admit at least one new general partner and a new general partner is admitted, Section 801(3)(B)
filings related to entity termination	certificate of limited partnership to be cancelled when limited partnership dissolves and begins winding up, Section 203	limited partnership may amend certificate to indicate dissolution, Section 803(b)(1), and may file statement of termination indicating that winding up has been completed and the limited partnership is terminated, Section 203
procedures for barring claims against dissolved limited partnership	none	following ULLCA Sections 807 and 808, the Act adopts the RMBCA approach providing for giving notice and barring claims, Sections 806 and 807
conversions and mergers	no provision	Article 11 permits conversions to and from and mergers with any "organization," defined as "a general partnership, including a limited liability partnership; limited partnership, including a limited liability limited partnership; limited liability company; business trust; corporation; or any other entity having a governing statute . . . [including]

Characteristic	RULPA	This Act
		domestic and foreign entities regardless of whether organized for profit." Section 1101(8)
writing requirements	some provisions pertain only to written understandings; *see, e.g.,* Sections 401 (partnership agreement may "provide in writing for the admission of additional general partners"; such admission also permitted "with the written consent of all partners"), 502(a) (limited partner's promise to contribute "is not enforceable unless set out in a writing signed by the limited partner"), 801(2) and (3) (dissolution occurs "upon the happening of events specified in writing in the partnership agreement" and upon "written consent of all partners"), 801(4) (dissolution avoided following withdrawal of a general partner if "all partners agree in writing")	removes virtually all writing requirements; but does require that certain information be maintained in record form, Section 111

UNIFORM LIMITED PARTNERSHIP ACT (2001)

[ARTICLE] 1
GENERAL PROVISIONS

SECTION 101. SHORT TITLE. This [Act] may be cited as the Uniform Limited Partnership Act [year of enactment].

SECTION 102. DEFINITIONS. In this [Act]:

(1) "Certificate of limited partnership" means the certificate required by Section 201. The term includes the certificate as amended or restated.

(2) "Contribution", except in the phrase "right of contribution," means any benefit provided by a person to a limited partnership in order to become a partner or in the person's capacity as a partner.

(3) "Debtor in bankruptcy" means a person that is the subject of:

(A) an order for relief under Title 11 of the United States Code or a comparable order under a successor statute of general application; or

(B) a comparable order under federal, state, or foreign law governing insolvency.

(4) "Designated office" means:

(A) with respect to a limited partnership, the office that the limited partnership is required to designate and maintain under Section 114; and

(B) with respect to a foreign limited partnership, its principal office.

(5) "Distribution" means a transfer of money or other property from a limited partnership to a partner in the partner's capacity as a partner or to a transferee on account of a transferable interest owned by the transferee.

(6) "Foreign limited liability limited partnership" means a foreign limited partnership whose general partners have limited liability for the obligations of the foreign limited partnership under a provision similar to Section 404(c).

(7) "Foreign limited partnership" means a partnership formed under the laws of a jurisdiction other than this State and required by those laws to have one or more general partners and one or more limited partners. The term includes a foreign limited liability limited partnership.

(8) "General partner" means:

(A) with respect to a limited partnership, a person that:

(i) becomes a general partner under Section 401; or

(ii) was a general partner in a limited partnership when the limited partnership became subject to this [Act] under Section 1206(a) or (b); and

935

(B) with respect to a foreign limited partnership, a person that has rights, powers, and obligations similar to those of a general partner in a limited partnership.

(9) "Limited liability limited partnership", except in the phrase "foreign limited liability limited partnership", means a limited partnership whose certificate of limited partnership states that the limited partnership is a limited liability limited partnership.

(10) "Limited partner" means:

(A) with respect to a limited partnership, a person that:

(i) becomes a limited partner under Section 301; or

(ii) was a limited partner in a limited partnership when the limited partnership became subject to this [Act] under Section 1206(a) or (b); and

(B) with respect to a foreign limited partnership, a person that has rights, powers, and obligations similar to those of a limited partner in a limited partnership.

(11) "Limited partnership", except in the phrases "foreign limited partnership" and "foreign limited liability limited partnership", means an entity, having one or more general partners and one or more limited partners, which is formed under this [Act] by two or more persons or becomes subject to this [Act] under [Article] 11 or Section 1206(a) or (b). The term includes a limited liability limited partnership.

(12) "Partner" means a limited partner or general partner.

(13) "Partnership agreement" means the partners' agreement, whether oral, implied, in a record, or in any combination, concerning the limited partnership. The term includes the agreement as amended.

(14) "Person" means an individual, corporation, business trust, estate, trust, partnership, limited liability company, association, joint venture, government; governmental subdivision, agency, or instrumentality; public corporation, or any other legal or commercial entity.

(15) "Person dissociated as a general partner" means a person dissociated as a general partner of a limited partnership.

(16) "Principal office" means the office where the principal executive office of a limited partnership or foreign limited partnership is located, whether or not the office is located in this State.

(17) "Record" means information that is inscribed on a tangible medium or that is stored in an electronic or other medium and is retrievable in perceivable form.

(18) "Required information" means the information that a limited partnership is required to maintain under Section 111.

(19) "Sign" means:

(A) to execute or adopt a tangible symbol with the present intent to authenticate a record; or

(B) to attach or logically associate an electronic symbol, sound, or process to or with a record with the present intent to authenticate the record.

(20) "State" means a State of the United States, the District of Columbia, Puerto Rico, the United States Virgin Islands, or any territory or insular possession subject to the jurisdiction of the United States.

(21) "Transfer" includes an assignment, conveyance, deed, bill of sale, lease, mortgage, security interest, encumbrance, gift, and transfer by operation of law.

(22) "Transferable interest" means a partner's right to receive distributions.

(23) "Transferee" means a person to which all or part of a transferable interest has been transferred, whether or not the transferor is a partner.

Comment

This section contains definitions applicable throughout the Act. Section 1101 provides additional definitions applicable within Article 11.

Paragraph 8(A)(i) [General partner]—A partnership agreement may vary Section 401 and provide a process or mechanism for becoming a general partner which is different from or additional to the rules stated in that section. For the purposes of this definition, a person who becomes a general partner pursuant to a provision of the partnership agreement "becomes a general partner under Section 401."

Paragraph 10(A)(i) [Limited partner]—The Comment to Paragraph 8(A)(i) applies here as well. For the purposes of this definition, a person who becomes a limited partner pursuant to a provision of the partnership agreement "becomes a limited partner under Section 301."

Paragraph (11) [Limited partnership]—This definition pertains to what is commonly termed a "domestic" limited partnership. The definition encompasses: (i) limited partnerships originally formed under this Act, including limited partnerships formed under Section 1101(11) to be the surviving organization in a merger; (ii) any entity that becomes subject to this Act by converting into a limited partnership under Article 11; (iii) any preexisting domestic limited partnership that elects pursuant to Section 1206(a) to become subject to this Act; and (iv) all other preexisting domestic limited partnerships when they become subject to this Act under Section 1206(b).

Following the approach of predecessor law, RULPA Section 101(7), this definition contains two substantive requirements. First, it is of the essence of a limited partnership to have two classes of partners. Accordingly, under Section 101(11) a limited partnership must have at least one general and one limited partner. Section 801(3)(B) and (4) provide that a limited partnership dissolves if its sole general partner or sole limited partner dissociates and the limited partnership fails to admit a replacement within 90 days of the dissociation. The 90 day limitation is a default rule, but, in light of Section 101(11), a limited partnership may not indefinitely delay "having one or more general partners and one or more limited partners."

It is also of the essence of a limited partnership to have at least two partners. Section 101(11) codifies this requirement by referring to a limited partnership as "an entity . . . which is formed under this [Act] by two or more persons." Thus, while the same person may be both a general and limited partner, Section 113 (Dual Capacity), one person alone cannot be the "two persons" contemplated by this definition. However, nothing in this definition prevents two closely affiliated persons from satisfying the two person requirement.

Paragraph (13) [Partnership agreement]—Section 110 is essential to understanding the significance of the partnership agreement. See also Section 201(d) (resolving inconsistencies between the certificate of limited partnership and the partnership agreement).

Paragraph (21) [Transfer]—Following RUPA, this Act uses the words "transfer" and "transferee" rather than the words "assignment" and "assignee." See RUPA Section 503.

The reference to "transfer by operation of law" is significant in connection with Section 702 (Transfer of Partner's Transferable Interest). That section severely restricts a transferee's rights (absent the consent of the partners), and this definition makes those restrictions applicable, for example, to transfers ordered by a family court as part of a divorce proceeding and transfers resulting from the death of a partner.

Paragraph (23) [Transferee]—See comment to Paragraph 21 for an explanation of why this Act refers to "transferee" rather than "assignee."

SECTION 103. KNOWLEDGE AND NOTICE.
(a) A person knows a fact if the person has actual knowledge of it.
(b) A person has notice of a fact if the person:
  (1) knows of it;
  (2) has received a notification of it;
  (3) has reason to know it exists from all of the facts known to the person at the time in question; or
  (4) has notice of it under subsection (c) or (d).
(c) A certificate of limited partnership on file in the [office of the Secretary of State] is notice that the partnership is a limited partnership and the persons

designated in the certificate as general partners are general partners. Except as otherwise provided in subsection (d), the certificate is not notice of any other fact.

(d) A person has notice of:

(1) another person's dissociation as a general partner, 90 days after the effective date of an amendment to the certificate of limited partnership which states that the other person has dissociated or 90 days after the effective date of a statement of dissociation pertaining to the other person, whichever occurs first;

(2) a limited partnership's dissolution, 90 days after the effective date of an amendment to the certificate of limited partnership stating that the limited partnership is dissolved;

(3) a limited partnership's termination, 90 days after the effective date of a statement of termination;

(4) a limited partnership's conversion under [Article] 11, 90 days after the effective date of the articles of conversion; or

(5) a merger under [Article] 11, 90 days after the effective date of the articles of merger.

(e) A person notifies or gives a notification to another person by taking steps reasonably required to inform the other person in ordinary course, whether or not the other person learns of it.

(f) A person receives a notification when the notification:

(1) comes to the person's attention; or

(2) is delivered at the person's place of business or at any other place held out by the person as a place for receiving communications.

(g) Except as otherwise provided in subsection (h), a person other than an individual knows, has notice, or receives a notification of a fact for purposes of a particular transaction when the individual conducting the transaction for the person knows, has notice, or receives a notification of the fact, or in any event when the fact would have been brought to the individual's attention if the person had exercised reasonable diligence. A person other than an individual exercises reasonable diligence if it maintains reasonable routines for communicating significant information to the individual conducting the transaction for the person and there is reasonable compliance with the routines. Reasonable diligence does not require an individual acting for the person to communicate information unless the communication is part of the individual's regular duties or the individual has reason to know of the transaction and that the transaction would be materially affected by the information.

(h) A general partner's knowledge, notice, or receipt of a notification of a fact relating to the limited partnership is effective immediately as knowledge of, notice to, or receipt of a notification by the limited partnership, except in the case of a fraud on the limited partnership committed by or with the consent of the general partner. A limited partner's knowledge, notice, or receipt of a notification of a fact relating to the limited partnership is not effective as knowledge of, notice to, or receipt of a notification by the limited partnership.

Comment

Source—RUPA Section 102; RULPA Section 208.

Notice and the relationship among subsections (b), (c) and (d)—These subsections provide separate and independent avenues through which a person can have notice of a fact. A person has notice of a fact as soon as any of the avenues applies.

Example: A limited partnership dissolves and amends its certificate of limited partnership to indicate dissolution. The amendment is effective on March 1. On March 15, Person #1 has reason to know of the dissolution and therefore has "notice" of the dissolution under Section 103(b)(3) even though Section 103(d)(2) does not yet apply. Person #2 does not have actual knowledge of the dissolution until June 15. Nonetheless, under Section 103(d)(2) Person #2 has "notice" of the dissolution on May 30.

Subsection (c)—This subsection provides what is commonly called constructive notice and comes essentially verbatim from RULPA Section 208. As for the significance of constructive notice "that the partnership is a limited partnership," see *Water, Waste & Land, Inc. v. Lanham*, 955 P.2d 997, 1001-1003 (Colo. 1998) (interpreting a comparable provision of the Colorado LLC statute and holding the provision ineffective to change common law agency principles, including the rules relating to the liability of an agent that transacts business for an undisclosed principal).

As for constructive notice that "the persons designated in the certificate as general partners are general partners," Section 201(a)(3) requires the initial certificate of limited partnership to name each general partner, and Section 202(b) requires a limited partnership to promptly amend its certificate of limited partnership to reflect any change in the identity of its general partners. Nonetheless, it will be possible, albeit improper, for a person to be designated in the certificate of limited partnership as a general partner without having become a general partner as contemplated by Section 401. Likewise, it will be possible for a person to have become a general partner under Section 401 without being designated as a general partner in the certificate of limited partnership. According to the last clause of this subsection, the fact that a person is **not** listed as in the certificate as a general partner is **not** notice that the person is **not** a general partner. For further discussion of this point, see the Comment to Section 401.

If the partnership agreement and the public record are inconsistent, Section 201(d) applies (partnership agreement controls *inter se*; public record controls as to third parties who have relied). *See also* Section 202(b) (requiring the limited partnership to amend its certificate of limited partnership to keep accurate the listing of general partners), 202(c) (requiring a general partner to take corrective action when the general partner knows that the certificate of limited partnership contains false information), and 208 (imposing liability for false information in *inter alia* the certificate of limited partnership).

Subsection (d)—This subsection also provides what is commonly called constructive notice and works in conjunction with other sections of this Act to curtail the power to bind and personal liability of general partners and persons dissociated as general partners. *See* Sections 402, 606, 607, 804, 805, 1111, and 1112. Following RUPA (in substance, although not in form), the constructive notice begins 90 days after the effective date of the filed record. For the Act's rules on delayed effective dates, see Section 206(c).

The 90-day delay applies only to the constructive notice and not to the event described in the filed record.

> **Example:** On March 15 X dissociates as a general partner from XYZ Limited Partnership by giving notice to XYZ. See Section 603(1). On March 20, XYZ amends its certificate of limited partnership to remove X's name from the list of general partners. See Section 202(b)(2).
>
> X's **dissociation** is effective March 15. If on March 16 X purports to be a general partner of XYZ and under Section 606(a) binds XYZ to some obligation, X will be liable under Section 606(b) as a "person dissociated as a general partner."
>
> On June 13 (90 days after March 15), the world has constructive notice of X's dissociation as a general partner. Beginning on that date, X will lack the power to bind XYZ. See Section 606(a)(2)(B) (person dissociated as a general partner can bind the limited partnership only if, *inter alia*, "at the time the other party enters into the transaction . . . the other party does not have notice of the dissociation").

Constructive notice under this subsection applies to partners and transferees as well as other persons.

Subsection (e)—The phrase "person learns of it" in this subsection is equivalent to the phrase "knows of it" in subsection (b)(1).

Subsection (h)—Under this subsection and Section 302, information possessed by a person that is only a limited partner is not attributable to the limited partnership. However, information possessed by a person that is both a general partner and a limited partner is attributable to the limited partnership. See Section 113 (Dual Capacity).

SECTION 104. NATURE, PURPOSE, AND DURATION OF ENTITY.

(a) A limited partnership is an entity distinct from its partners. A limited partnership is the same entity regardless of whether its certificate states that the limited partnership is a limited liability limited partnership.

(b) A limited partnership may be organized under this [Act] for any lawful purpose.

(c) A limited partnership has a perpetual duration.

Comment

Subsection (a)—Acquiring or relinquishing an LLLP shield changes only the rules governing a general partner's liability for subsequently incurred obligations of the limited partnership. The underlying entity is unaffected.

Subsection (b)—In contrast with RULPA Section 106, this Act does not require a limited partnership to have a business purpose. However, many of the Act's default rules presuppose at least a profit-making purpose. See, e.g., Section 503 (providing for the sharing of distributions in proportion to the value of contributions), 701 (defining a transferable interest in terms of the right to receive distributions), 801 (allocating the right to consent to cause or avoid dissolution in proportion to partners' rights to receive distributions), and 812 (providing that, after a dissolved limited partnership has paid its creditors, "[a]ny surplus remaining . . . must be paid in cash as a distribution" to partners and transferees). If a limited partnership is organized for an essentially non-pecuniary purpose, the organizers should carefully review the Act's default rules and override them as necessary via the partnership agreement.

Subsection (c)—The partnership agreement has the power to vary this subsection, either by stating a definite term or by specifying an event or events which cause dissolution. Sections 110(a) and 801(1). Section 801 also recognizes several other occurrences that cause dissolution. Thus, the public record pertaining to a limited partnership will not necessarily reveal whether the limited partnership actually has a perpetual duration.

The public record might also fail to reveal whether the limited partnership has in fact dissolved. A dissolved limited partnership may amend its certificate of limited partnership to indicate dissolution but is not required to do so. Section 803(b)(1).

Predecessor law took a somewhat different approach. RULPA Section 201(4) required the certificate of limited partnership to state "the latest date upon which the limited partnership is to dissolve." Although RULPA Section 801(2) provided for a limited partnership to dissolve "upon the happening of events specified in writing in the partnership agreement," RULPA Section 203 required the limited partnership to file a certificate of cancellation to indicate that dissolution had occurred.

SECTION 105. POWERS. A limited partnership has the powers to do all things necessary or convenient to carry on its activities, including the power to sue, be sued, and defend in its own name and to maintain an action against a partner for harm caused to the limited partnership by a breach of the partnership agreement or violation of a duty to the partnership.

Comment

This Act omits as unnecessary any detailed list of specific powers. The power to sue and be sued is mentioned specifically so that Section 110(b)(1) can prohibit the partnership agreement from varying that power. The power to maintain an action against a partner is mentioned specifically to establish that the limited partnership itself has standing to enforce the partnership agreement.

SECTION 106. GOVERNING LAW. The law of this State governs relations among the partners of a limited partnership and between the partners and the limited partnership and the liability of partners as partners for an obligation of the limited partnership.

Comment

To partially define its scope, this section uses the phrase "relations among the partners of a limited partnership and between the partners and the limited partnership." Section 110(a) uses essentially identical language in defining the proper realm of the partnership agreement: "relations among the partners and between the partners and the partnership."

Despite the similarity of language, this section has no bearing on the power of a partnership agreement to vary other provisions of this Act. It is quite possible for a provision of this Act to involve "relations among the partners of a limited partnership and between the partners and the limited partnership" and thus come within this section, and yet not be subject to variation by the partnership agreement. Although Section 110(a) grants plenary authority to the partnership agreement to regulate "relations among the partners and between the partners and the partnership," that authority is subject to Section 110(b).

For example, Section 408 (General Standards of General Partner's Conduct) certainly involves "relations among the partners of a limited partnership and between the partners and the limited partnership." Therefore, according to this section, Section 408 applies to a limited partnership formed or otherwise subject to this Act. Just as certainly, Section 408 pertains to "relations among the partners and between the partners and the partnership" for the purposes of Section 110(a), and therefore the partnership agreement may properly address matters covered by Section 408. However, Section 110(b)(5), (6), and (7) limit the power of the partnership agreement to vary the rules stated in Section 408. See also, e.g., Section 502(c) (stating creditor's rights, which are protected under Section 110(b)(13) from being restricted by the partnership agreement) and Comment to Section 509.

This section also applies to "the liability of partners as partners for an obligation of a limited partnership." The phrase "as partners" contemplates the liability shield for limited partners under Section 303 and the rules for general partner liability stated in Section 404. Other grounds for liability can be supplied by other law, including the law of some other jurisdiction. For example, a partner's contractual guaranty of a limited partnership obligation might well be governed by the law of some other jurisdiction.

Transferees derive their rights and status under this Act from partners and accordingly this section applies to the relations of a transferee to the limited partnership.

The partnership agreement may not vary the rule stated in this section. See Section 110(b)(2).

SECTION 107. SUPPLEMENTAL PRINCIPLES OF LAW; RATE OF INTEREST.

(a) Unless displaced by particular provisions of this [Act], the principles of law and equity supplement this [Act].

(b) If an obligation to pay interest arises under this [Act] and the rate is not specified, the rate is that specified in [applicable statute].

Comment

Subsection (a)—This language comes from RUPA Section 104 and does not address an important question raised by the de-linking of this Act from the UPA and RUPA—namely, to what extent is the case law of general partnerships relevant to limited partnerships governed by this Act?

Predecessor law, RULPA Section 403, expressly equated the rights, powers, restrictions, and liabilities of a general partner in a limited partnership with the rights, powers, restrictions, and liabilities of a partner in a general partnership. This Act has no comparable provision. See Prefatory Note. Therefore, a court should not assume that a case concerning a general partnership is automatically relevant to a limited partnership governed by this Act. A general partnership case may be relevant by analogy, especially if (1) the issue in dispute involves a provision of this Act for which a comparable provision exists under the law of general partnerships; and (2) the fundamental differences between a general partnership and limited partnership are immaterial to the disputed issue.

SECTION 108. NAME.

(a) The name of a limited partnership may contain the name of any partner.

(b) The name of a limited partnership that is not a limited liability limited partnership must contain the phrase "limited partnership" or the abbreviation "L.P." or "LP" and may not contain the phrase "limited liability limited partnership" or the abbreviation "LLLP" or "L.L.L.P."

(c) The name of a limited liability limited partnership must contain the phrase "limited liability limited partnership" or the abbreviation "LLLP" or "L.L.L.P." and must not contain the abbreviation "L.P." or "LP."

(d) Unless authorized by subsection (e), the name of a limited partnership must be distinguishable in the records of the [Secretary of State] from:

(1) the name of each person other than an individual incorporated, organized, or authorized to transact business in this State; and

(2) each name reserved under Section 109 [or other state laws allowing the reservation or registration of business names, including fictitious name statutes].

(e) A limited partnership may apply to the [Secretary of State] for authorization to use a name that does not comply with subsection (d). The [Secretary of State] shall authorize use of the name applied for if, as to each conflicting name:

(1) the present user, registrant, or owner of the conflicting name consents in a signed record to the use and submits an undertaking in a form satisfactory to the [Secretary of State] to change the conflicting name to a name that complies with subsection (d) and is distinguishable in the records of the [Secretary of State] from the name applied for;

(2) the applicant delivers to the [Secretary of State] a certified copy of the final judgment of a court of competent jurisdiction establishing the applicant's right to use in this State the name applied for; or

(3) the applicant delivers to the [Secretary of State] proof satisfactory to the [Secretary of State] that the present user, registrant, or owner of the conflicting name:

(A) has merged into the applicant;

(B) has been converted into the applicant; or

(C) has transferred substantially all of its assets, including the conflicting name, to the applicant.

(f) Subject to Section 905, this section applies to any foreign limited partnership transacting business in this State, having a certificate of authority to transact business in this State, or applying for a certificate of authority.

Comment

Subsection (a)—Predecessor law, RULPA Section 102, prohibited the use of a limited partner's name in the name of a limited partnership except in unusual circumstances. That approach derived from the 1916 Uniform Limited Partnership Act and has become antiquated. In 1916, most business organizations were either unshielded (*e.g.*, general partnerships) or partially shielded (*e.g.*, limited partnerships), and it was reasonable for third parties to believe that an individual whose own name appeared in the name of a business would "stand behind" the business. Today most businesses have a full shield (*e.g.*, corporations, limited liability companies, most limited liability partnerships), and corporate, LLC and LLP statutes generally pose no barrier to the use of an owner's name in the name of the entity. This Act eliminates RULPA's restriction and puts limited partnerships on equal footing with these other "shielded" entities.

Subsection (d)(1)—If a sole proprietor registers or reserves a business name under a fictitious name statute, that name comes within this provision. For the purposes of this provision, a sole proprietor doing business under a registered or reserved name is a "person other than an individual."

Subsection (f)—Section 905 permits a foreign limited partnership to obtain a certificate of authority under an alternate name if the foreign limited partnership's actual name does not comply with this section.

SECTION 109. RESERVATION OF NAME.

(a) The exclusive right to the use of a name that complies with Section 108 may be reserved by:

(1) a person intending to organize a limited partnership under this [Act] and to adopt the name;

(2) a limited partnership or a foreign limited partnership authorized to transact business in this State intending to adopt the name;

(3) a foreign limited partnership intending to obtain a certificate of authority to transact business in this State and adopt the name;

(4) a person intending to organize a foreign limited partnership and intending to have it obtain a certificate of authority to transact business in this State and adopt the name;

(5) a foreign limited partnership formed under the name; or

(6) a foreign limited partnership formed under a name that does not comply with Section 108(b) or (c), but the name reserved under this paragraph may differ from the foreign limited partnership's name only to the extent necessary to comply with Section 108(b) and (c).

(b) A person may apply to reserve a name under subsection (a) by delivering to the [Secretary of State] for filing an application that states the name to be reserved and the paragraph of subsection (a) which applies. If the [Secretary of State] finds that the name is available for use by the applicant, the [Secretary of State] shall file a statement of name reservation and thereby reserve the name for the exclusive use of the applicant for a 120 days.

(c) An applicant that has reserved a name pursuant to subsection (b) may reserve the same name for additional 120-day periods. A person having a current reservation for a name may not apply for another 120-day period for the same name until 90 days have elapsed in the current reservation.

(d) A person that has reserved a name under this section may deliver to the [Secretary of State] for filing a notice of transfer that states the reserved name, the name and street and mailing address of some other person to which the reservation is to be transferred, and the paragraph of subsection (a) which applies to the other person. Subject to Section 206(c), the transfer is effective when the [Secretary of State] files the notice of transfer.

SECTION 110. EFFECT OF PARTNERSHIP AGREEMENT; NON-WAIVABLE PROVISIONS.

(a) Except as otherwise provided in subsection (b), the partnership agreement governs relations among the partners and between the partners and the partnership. To the extent the partnership agreement does not otherwise provide, this [Act] governs relations among the partners and between the partners and the partnership.

(b) A partnership agreement may not:

(1) vary a limited partnership's power under Section 105 to sue, be sued, and defend in its own name;

(2) vary the law applicable to a limited partnership under Section 106;

(3) vary the requirements of Section 204;

(4) vary the information required under Section 111 or unreasonably restrict the right to information under Sections 304 or 407, but the partnership agreement may impose reasonable restrictions on the availability and use of information obtained under those sections and may define appropriate remedies, including liquidated damages, for a breach of any reasonable restriction on use;

(5) eliminate the duty of loyalty under Section 408, but the partnership agreement may:

    (A) identify specific types or categories of activities that do not violate the duty of loyalty, if not manifestly unreasonable; and

    (B) specify the number or percentage of partners which may authorize or ratify, after full disclosure to all partners of all material facts, a specific act or transaction that otherwise would violate the duty of loyalty;

(6) unreasonably reduce the duty of care under Section 408(c);

(7) eliminate the obligation of good faith and fair dealing under Sections 305(b) and 408(d), but the partnership agreement may prescribe the standards by which the performance of the obligation is to be measured, if the standards are not manifestly unreasonable;

(8) vary the power of a person to dissociate as a general partner under Section 604(a) except to require that the notice under Section 603(1) be in a record;

(9) vary the power of a court to decree dissolution in the circumstances specified in Section 802;

(10) vary the requirement to wind up the partnership's business as specified in Section 803;

(11) unreasonably restrict the right to maintain an action under [Article] 10;

(12) restrict the right of a partner under Section 1110(a) to approve a conversion or merger or the right of a general partner under Section 1110(b) to consent to an amendment to the certificate of limited partnership which deletes a statement that the limited partnership is a limited liability limited partnership; or

(13) restrict rights under this [Act] of a person other than a partner or a transferee.

Comment

Source—RUPA Section 103.

Subject only to subsection (b), the partnership agreement has plenary power to structure and regulate the relations of the partners *inter se*. Although the certificate of limited partnership is a limited partnership's foundational document, among the partners the partnership agreement controls. See Section 201(d).

The partnership agreement has the power to control the manner of its own amendment. In particular, a provision of the agreement prohibiting oral modifications is enforceable, despite any common law antagonism to "no oral modification" provisions. Likewise, a partnership agreement can impose "made in a record" requirements on other aspects of the partners' relationship, such as requiring consents to be made in a record and signed, or rendering unenforceable oral promises to make contributions or oral understandings as to "events upon the happening of which the limited partnership is to be dissolved," Section 111(9)(D). See also Section 801(1).

Subsection (b)(3)—The referenced section states who must sign various documents.

Subsection (b)(4)—In determining whether a restriction is reasonable, a court might consider: (i) the danger or other problem the restriction seeks to avoid; (ii) the purpose for which the information is sought; and (iii) whether, in light of both the problem and the purpose, the restriction is reasonably tailored. Restricting access to or use of the names and addresses of limited partners is not per se unreasonable.

Under this Act, general and limited partners have sharply different roles. A restriction that is reasonable as to a limited partner is not necessarily reasonable as to a general partner.

Sections 304(g) and 407(f) authorize the limited partnership (as distinguished from the partnership agreement) to impose restrictions on the use of information. For a comparison of restrictions contained in the partnership agreement and restrictions imposed unilaterally by the limited partnership, see the Comment to Section 304(g).

Subsection (b)(5)(A)—It is not per se manifestly unreasonable for the partnership agreement to permit a general partner to compete with the limited partnership.

Subsection (b)(5)(B)—The Act does not require that the authorization or ratification be by **disinterested** partners, although the partnership agreement may so provide. The Act does require that the disclosure be made to all partners, even if the partnership agreement excludes some partners from the authorization or ratification process. An interested partner that participates in the authorization or ratification process is subject to the obligation of good faith and fair dealing. Sections 305(b) and 408(d).

Subsection (b)(8)—This restriction applies only to the power of a person to dissociate as a general partner. The partnership agreement may eliminate the power of a person to dissociate as a limited partner.

Subsection (b)(9)—This provision should not be read to limit a partnership agreement's power to provide for arbitration. For example, an agreement to arbitrate all disputes—including dissolution disputes—is enforceable. Any other interpretation would put this Act at odds with federal law. *See Southland Corp. v. Keating*, 465 U.S. 1 (1984) (holding that the Federal Arbitration Act preempts state statutes that seek to invalidate agreements to arbitrate) and *Allied-Bruce Terminix Cos., Inc. v. Dobson*, 513 U.S. 265 (1995) (same). This provision does prohibit any narrowing of the substantive grounds for judicial dissolution as stated in Section 802.

> **Example:** A provision of a partnership agreement states that no partner may obtain judicial dissolution without showing that a general partner is in material breach of the partnership agreement. The provision is ineffective to prevent a court from ordering dissolution under Section 802.

Subsection (b)(11)—Section 1001 codifies a partner's right to bring a direct action, and the rest of Article 10 provides for derivative actions. The partnership agreement may not restrict a partner's right to bring either type of action if the effect is to undercut or frustrate the duties and rights protected by Section 110(b).

The reasonableness of a restriction on derivative actions should be judged in light of the history and purpose of derivative actions. They originated as an equitable remedy, intended to protect passive owners against management abuses. A partnership agreement may not provide that all derivative claims will be subject to final determination by a special litigation committee appointed by the limited partnership, because that provision would eliminate, not merely restrict, a partner's right to bring a derivative *action*.

Subsection (b)(12)—Section 1110 imposes special consent requirements with regard to transactions that might make a partner personally liable for entity debts.

Subsection (b)(13)—The partnership agreement is a contract, and this provision reflects a basic notion of contract law—namely, that a contract can **directly** restrict rights only of parties to the contract and of persons who derive their rights from the contract. A provision of a partnership agreement can be determined to be unenforceable against third parties under paragraph (b)(13) without therefore and automatically being unenforceable *inter se* the partners and any transferees. How the former determination affects the latter question is a matter of other law.

SECTION 111. REQUIRED INFORMATION. A limited partnership shall maintain at its designated office the following information:

(1) a current list showing the full name and last known street and mailing address of each partner, separately identifying the general partners, in alphabetical order, and the limited partners, in alphabetical order;

(2) a copy of the initial certificate of limited partnership and all amendments to and restatements of the certificate, together with signed copies of any powers

of attorney under which any certificate, amendment, or restatement has been signed;

(3) a copy of any filed articles of conversion or merger;

(4) a copy of the limited partnership's federal, state, and local income tax returns and reports, if any, for the three most recent years;

(5) a copy of any partnership agreement made in a record and any amendment made in a record to any partnership agreement;

(6) a copy of any financial statement of the limited partnership for the three most recent years;

(7) a copy of the three most recent annual reports delivered by the limited partnership to the [Secretary of State] pursuant to Section 210;

(8) a copy of any record made by the limited partnership during the past three years of any consent given by or vote taken of any partner pursuant to this [Act] or the partnership agreement; and

(9) unless contained in a partnership agreement made in a record, a record stating:

(A) the amount of cash, and a description and statement of the agreed value of the other benefits, contributed and agreed to be contributed by each partner;

(B) the times at which, or events on the happening of which, any additional contributions agreed to be made by each partner are to be made;

(C) for any person that is both a general partner and a limited partner, a specification of what transferable interest the person owns in each capacity; and

(D) any events upon the happening of which the limited partnership is to be dissolved and its activities wound up.

Comment

Source—RULPA Section 105.

Sections 304 and 407 govern access to the information required by this section, as well as to other information pertaining to a limited partnership.

Paragraph (5)—This requirement applies to superseded as well as current agreements and amendments. An agreement or amendment is "made in a record" to the extent the agreement is "integrated" into a record and consented to in that memorialized form. It is possible for a partnership agreement to be made in part in a record and in part otherwise. See Comment to Section 110. An oral agreement that is subsequently inscribed in a record (but not consented to as such) was not "made in a record" and is not covered by paragraph (5). However, if the limited partnership happens to have such a record, Section 304(b) might and Section 407(a)(2) will provide a right of access.

Paragraph (8)—This paragraph does not require a limited partnership to make a record of consents given and votes taken. However, if the limited partnership has made such a record, this paragraph requires that the limited partnership maintain the record for three years. The requirement applies to any record made by the limited partnership, not just to records made contemporaneously with the giving of consent or voting. The three year period runs from when the record was made and not from when the consent was given or vote taken.

Paragraph (9)—Information is "contained in a partnership agreement made in a record" only to the extent that the information is "integrated" into a record and, in that memorialized form, has been consented to as part of the partnership agreement.

This paragraph is not a statute of frauds provision. For example, failure to comply with paragraph (9)(A) or (B) does not render unenforceable an oral promise to make a contribution. Likewise, failure to comply with paragraph (9)(D) does not invalidate an oral term of the partnership specifying "events upon the happening of which the limited partnership is to be dissolved and its activities wound up." See also Section 801(1).

Obversely, the mere fact that a limited partnership maintains a record in purported compliance with paragraph (9)(A) or (B) does not prove that a person has actually promised to make a contribution. Likewise, the mere fact that a limited partnership maintains a record in purported compliance with paragraph (9)(D) does not prove that the partnership agreement actually includes the specified events as causes of dissolution.

Consistent with the partnership agreement's plenary power to structure and regulate the relations of the partners *inter se*, a partnership agreement can impose "made in a record" requirements which render unenforceable oral promises to make contributions or oral understandings as to "events upon the happening of which the limited partnership is to be dissolved." See Comment to Section 110.

Paragraph (9)(A) and (B)—Often the partnership agreement will state in record form the value of contributions made and promised to be made. If not, these provisions require that the value be stated in a record maintained as part of the limited partnership's required information. The Act does not authorize the limited partnership or the general partners to set the value of a contribution without the concurrence of the person who has made or promised the contribution, although the partnership agreement itself can grant that authority.

Paragraph (9)(C)—The information required by this provision is essential for determining what happens to the transferable interests of a person that is both a general partner and a limited partner and that dissociates in one of those capacities but not the other. See Sections 602(3) and 605(5).

SECTION 112. BUSINESS TRANSACTIONS OF PARTNER WITH PARTNERSHIP. A partner may lend money to and transact other business with the limited partnership and has the same rights and obligations with respect to the loan or other transaction as a person that is not a partner.

Comment

Source—RULPA Section 107. See also RUPA Section 404(f) and ULLCA Section 409(f).

This section has no impact on a general partner's duty under Section 408(b)(2) (duty of loyalty includes refraining from acting as or for an adverse party) and means rather that this Act does not discriminate against a creditor of a limited partnership that happens also to be a partner. *See, e.g., BT-I v. Equitable Life Assurance Society of the United States*, 75 Cal. App. 4th 1406, 1415, 89 Cal. Rptr. 2d 811, 814 (Cal. App. 4 Dist. 1999). and *SEC v. DuPont, Homsey & Co.*, 204 F. Supp. 944, 946 (D. Mass. 1962), vacated and remanded on other grounds, 334 F2d 704 (1st Cir. 1964). This section does not, however, override other law, such as fraudulent transfer or conveyance acts.

SECTION 113. DUAL CAPACITY. A person may be both a general partner and a limited partner. A person that is both a general and limited partner has the rights, powers, duties, and obligations provided by this [Act] and the partnership agreement in each of those capacities. When the person acts as a general partner, the person is subject to the obligations, duties and restrictions under this [Act] and the partnership agreement for general partners. When the person acts as a limited partner, the person is subject to the obligations, duties and restrictions under this [Act] and the partnership agreement for limited partners.

Comment

Source—RULPA Section 404, redrafted for reasons of style.

SECTION 114. OFFICE AND AGENT FOR SERVICE OF PROCESS.
(a) A limited partnership shall designate and continuously maintain in this State:
   (1) an office, which need not be a place of its activity in this State; and
   (2) an agent for service of process.
(b) A foreign limited partnership shall designate and continuously maintain in this State an agent for service of process.
(c) An agent for service of process of a limited partnership or foreign limited partnership must be an individual who is a resident of this State or other person authorized to do business in this State.

Comment

Subsection (a)—The initial designation occurs in the original certificate of limited partnership. Section 201(a)(2). A limited partnership may change the designation in any of three ways: a statement of change, Section 115, an amendment to the certificate, Section 202, and the annual report, Section 210(e). If a limited partnership fails to maintain an agent for service of process, substituted service may be made on the Secretary of State. Section 117(b). Although a limited partnership's failure to maintain an agent for service of process is not immediate grounds for administrative dissolution, Section 809(a), the failure will prevent the limited partnership from delivering to the Secretary of State for filing an annual report that complies with Section 210(a)(2). Failure to deliver a proper annual report is grounds for administrative dissolution. Section 809(a)(2).

Subsection (b)—The initial designation occurs in the application for a certificate of authority. See Section 902(a)(4). A foreign limited partnership may change the designation in either of two ways: a statement of change, Section 115, and the annual report, Section 210(e). If a foreign limited partnership fails to maintain an agent for service of process, substituted service may be made on the Secretary of State. Section 117(b). A foreign limited partnership's failure to maintain an agent for service of process is grounds for administrative revocation of the certificate of authority. Section 906(a)(3).

A foreign limited partnership need not maintain an office in this State.

SECTION 115. CHANGE OF DESIGNATED OFFICE OR AGENT FOR SERVICE OF PROCESS.

(a) In order to change its designated office, agent for service of process, or the address of its agent for service of process, a limited partnership or a foreign limited partnership may deliver to the [Secretary of State] for filing a statement of change containing:

(1) the name of the limited partnership or foreign limited partnership;

(2) the street and mailing address of its current designated office;

(3) if the current designated office is to be changed, the street and mailing address of the new designated office;

(4) the name and street and mailing address of its current agent for service of process; and

(5) if the current agent for service of process or an address of the agent is to be changed, the new information.

(b) Subject to Section 206(c), a statement of change is effective when filed by the [Secretary of State].

Comment

Source—ULLCA Section 109.

Subsection (a)—The Act uses "may" rather than "shall" here because other avenues exist. A limited partnership may also change the information by an amendment to its certificate of limited partnership, Section 202, or through its annual report. Section 210(e). A foreign limited partnership may use its annual report. Section 210(e). However, neither a limited partnership nor a foreign limited partnership may wait for the annual report if the information described in the public record becomes inaccurate. See Sections 208 (imposing liability for false information in record) and 117(b) (providing for substitute service).

SECTION 116. RESIGNATION OF AGENT FOR SERVICE OF PROCESS.

(a) In order to resign as an agent for service of process of a limited partnership or foreign limited partnership, the agent must deliver to the [Secretary of State] for filing a statement of resignation containing the name of the limited partnership or foreign limited partnership.

(b) After receiving a statement of resignation, the [Secretary of State] shall file it and mail a copy to the designated office of the limited partnership or foreign limited partnership and another copy to the principal office if the address of the office appears in the records of the [Secretary of State] and is different from the address of the designated office.

(c) An agency for service of process is terminated on the 31st day after the [Secretary of State] files the statement of resignation.

Comment

Source—ULLCA Section 110.

This section provides the only way an agent can resign without cooperation from the limited partnership or foreign limited partnership and the only way the agent, rather than the limited partnership or foreign limited partnership, can effect a change in the public record. See Sections 115(a) (Statement of Change), 202 (Amendment or Restatement of Certificate), and 210(e) (Annual Report), all of which involve the limited partnership or foreign limited partnership designating a replacement agent for service of process.

Subsection (c)—In contrast to most records authorized or required to be delivered to the filing officer for filing under this Act, a statement of resignation may not provide for a delayed effective date. This subsection mandates the effective date, and an effective date included in a statement of resignation is disregarded. See also Section 206(c).

SECTION 117. SERVICE OF PROCESS.

(a) An agent for service of process appointed by a limited partnership or foreign limited partnership is an agent of the limited partnership or foreign limited partnership for service of any process, notice, or demand required or permitted by law to be served upon the limited partnership or foreign limited partnership.

(b) If a limited partnership or foreign limited partnership does not appoint or maintain an agent for service of process in this State or the agent for service of process cannot with reasonable diligence be found at the agent's address, the [Secretary of State] is an agent of the limited partnership or foreign limited partnership upon whom process, notice, or demand may be served.

(c) Service of any process, notice, or demand on the [Secretary of State] may be made by delivering to and leaving with the [Secretary of State] duplicate copies of the process, notice, or demand. If a process, notice, or demand is served on the [Secretary of State], the [Secretary of State] shall forward one of the copies by registered or certified mail, return receipt requested, to the limited partnership or foreign limited partnership at its designated office.

(d) Service is effected under subsection (c) at the earliest of:

(1) the date the limited partnership or foreign limited partnership receives the process, notice, or demand;

(2) the date shown on the return receipt, if signed on behalf of the limited partnership or foreign limited partnership; or

(3) five days after the process, notice, or demand is deposited in the mail, if mailed postpaid and correctly addressed.

(e) The [Secretary of State] shall keep a record of each process, notice, and demand served pursuant to this section and record the time of, and the action taken regarding, the service.

(f) This section does not affect the right to serve process, notice, or demand in any other manner provided by law.

Comment

Source—ULLCA Section 111.

Requiring a foreign limited partnership to name an agent for service of process is a change from RULPA. See RULPA Section 902(3).

SECTION 118. CONSENT AND PROXIES OF PARTNERS. Action requiring the consent of partners under this [Act] may be taken without a meeting,

and a partner may appoint a proxy to consent or otherwise act for the partner by signing an appointment record, either personally or by the partner's attorney in fact.

Comment

Source—ULLCA Section 404(d) and (e).

This Act imposes no meeting requirement and does not distinguish among oral, record, express and tacit consent. The partnership agreement may establish such requirements and make such distinctions.

[ARTICLE] 2
FORMATION; CERTIFICATE OF
LIMITED PARTNERSHIP AND OTHER FILINGS

SECTION 201. FORMATION OF LIMITED PARTNERSHIP; CERTIFICATE OF LIMITED PARTNERSHIP.

(a) In order for a limited partnership to be formed, a certificate of limited partnership must be delivered to the [Secretary of State] for filing. The certificate must state:

(1) the name of the limited partnership, which must comply with Section 108;

(2) the street and mailing address of the initial designated office and the name and street and mailing address of the initial agent for service of process;

(3) the name and the street and mailing address of each general partner;

(4) whether the limited partnership is a limited liability limited partnership; and

(5) any additional information required by [Article] 11.

(b) A certificate of limited partnership may also contain any other matters but may not vary or otherwise affect the provisions specified in Section 110(b) in a manner inconsistent with that section.

(c) If there has been substantial compliance with subsection (a), subject to Section 206(c) a limited partnership is formed when the [Secretary of State] files the certificate of limited partnership.

(d) Subject to subsection (b), if any provision of a partnership agreement is inconsistent with the filed certificate of limited partnership or with a filed statement of dissociation, termination, or change or filed articles of conversion or merger:

(1) the partnership agreement prevails as to partners and transferees; and

(2) the filed certificate of limited partnership, statement of dissociation, termination, or change or articles of conversion or merger prevail as to persons, other than partners and transferees, that reasonably rely on the filed record to their detriment.

Comment

Source—RULPA Section 201.

A limited partnership is a creature of statute, and this section governs how a limited partnership comes into existence. A limited partnership is formed only if (i) a certificate of limited partnership is prepared and delivered to the specified public official for filing, (ii) the public official files the certificate, and (iii) the certificate, delivery and filing are in "substantial compliance" with the requirements of subsection (a). Section 206(c) governs when a limited partnership comes into existence.

Despite its foundational importance, a certificate of limited partnership is far less powerful than a corporation's articles of incorporation. Among partners and transferees, for example, the partnership agreement is paramount. See Section 201(d).

Subsection (a)(1)—Section 108 contains name requirements. To be acceptable for filing, a certificate of limited partnership must state a name for the limited partnership which complies with Section 108.

Subsection (a)(3)—This provision should be read in conjunction with Section 103(c) and Section 401. See the Comment to those sections.

Subsection (a)(4) —This Act permits a limited partnership to be a limited liability limited partnership ("LLLP"), and this provision requires the certificate of limited partnership to state whether the limited partnership is an LLLP. The requirement is intended to force the organizers of a limited partnership to decide whether the limited partnership is to be an LLLP.

Subject to Sections 406(b)(2) and 1110, a limited partnership may amend its certificate of limited partnership to add or delete a statement that the limited partnership is a limited liability limited partnership. An amendment deleting such a statement must be accompanied by an amendment stating that the limited partnership is **not** a limited liability limited partnership. Section 201(a)(4) does not permit a certificate of limited partnership to be silent on this point, except for pre-existing partnerships that become subject to this Act under Section 1206. See Section 1206(c)(2).

Subsection (d)—Source: ULLCA Section 203(c).

A limited partnership is a creature of contract as well as a creature of statute. It will be possible, albeit improper, for the partnership agreement to be inconsistent with the certificate of limited partnership or other specified public filings relating to the limited partnership. For those circumstances, this subsection provides the rule for determining which source of information prevails.

For partners and transferees, the partnership agreement is paramount. For third parties seeking to invoke the public record, actual knowledge of that record is necessary and notice under Section 103(c) or (d) is irrelevant. A third party wishing to enforce the public record over the partnership agreement must show reasonable reliance on the public record, and reliance presupposes knowledge.

This subsection does not expressly cover a situation in which (i) one of the specified filed records contains information in addition to, but not inconsistent with, the partnership agreement, and (ii) a person, other than a partner or transferee, detrimentally relies on the additional information. However, the policy reflected in this subsection seems equally applicable to that situation.

Responsibility for maintaining a limited partnership's public record rests with the general partner or partners. Section 202(c). A general partner's failure to meet that responsibility can expose the general partner to liability to third parties under Section 208(a)(2) and might constitute a breach of the general partner's duties under Section 408. In addition, an aggrieved person may seek a remedy under Section 205 (Signing and Filing Pursuant to Judicial Order).

SECTION 202. AMENDMENT OR RESTATEMENT OF CERTIFICATE.

(a) In order to amend its certificate of limited partnership, a limited partnership must deliver to the [Secretary of State] for filing an amendment or, pursuant to [Article] 11, articles of merger stating:

(1) the name of the limited partnership;

(2) the date of filing of its initial certificate; and

(3) the changes the amendment makes to the certificate as most recently amended or restated.

(b) A limited partnership shall promptly deliver to the [Secretary of State] for filing an amendment to a certificate of limited partnership to reflect:

(1) the admission of a new general partner;

(2) the dissociation of a person as a general partner; or

(3) the appointment of a person to wind up the limited partnership's activities under Section 803(c) or (d).

(c) A general partner that knows that any information in a filed certificate of limited partnership was false when the certificate was filed or has become false due to changed circumstances shall promptly:

(1) cause the certificate to be amended; or

(2) if appropriate, deliver to the [Secretary of State] for filing a statement of change pursuant to Section 115 or a statement of correction pursuant to Section 207.

(d) A certificate of limited partnership may be amended at any time for any other proper purpose as determined by the limited partnership.

(e) A restated certificate of limited partnership may be delivered to the [Secretary of State] for filing in the same manner as an amendment.

(f) Subject to Section 206(c), an amendment or restated certificate is effective when filed by the [Secretary of State].

Comment

Source—RULPA Section 202.

Subsection (b)—This subsection lists changes in circumstances which require an amendment to the certificate. Neither a statement of change, Section 115, nor the annual report, Section 210(e), suffice to report the addition or deletion of a general partner or the appointment of a person to wind up a limited partnership that has no general partner.

This subsection states an obligation of the limited partnership. However, so long as the limited partnership has at least one general partner, the general partner or partners are responsible for managing the limited partnership's activities. Section 406(a). That management responsibility includes maintaining accuracy in the limited partnership's public record. Moreover, subsection (c) imposes direct responsibility on any general partner that knows that the filed certificate of limited partnership contains false information.

Acquiring or relinquishing LLLP status also requires an amendment to the certificate. See Sections 201(a)(4), 406(b)(2), and 1110(b)(2).

Subsection (c)—This provision imposes an obligation directly on the general partners rather than on the limited partnership. A general partner's failure to meet that responsibility can expose the general partner to liability to third parties under Section 208(a)(2) and might constitute a breach of the general partner's duties under Section 408. In addition, an aggrieved person may seek a remedy under Section 205 (Signing and Filing Pursuant to Judicial Order).

Subsection (d)—A limited partnership that desires to change its name will have to amend its certificate of limited partnership. The new name will have to comply with Section 108. See Section 201(a)(1).

SECTION 203. STATEMENT OF TERMINATION. A dissolved limited partnership that has completed winding up may deliver to the [Secretary of State] for filing a statement of termination that states:

(1) the name of the limited partnership;

(2) the date of filing of its initial certificate of limited partnership; and

(3) any other information as determined by the general partners filing the statement or by a person appointed pursuant to Section 803(c) or (d).

Comment

Under Section 103(d)(3), a filed statement of termination provides constructive notice, 90 days after the statement's effective date, that the limited partnership is terminated. That notice effectively terminates any apparent authority to bind the limited partnership.

However, this section is permissive. Therefore, it is not possible to use Section 205 (Signing and Filing Pursuant to Judicial Order) to cause a statement of termination to be filed.

This section differs from predecessor law, RULPA Section 203, which required the filing of a certificate of cancellation when a limited partnership dissolved.

SECTION 204. SIGNING OF RECORDS.

(a) Each record delivered to the [Secretary of State] for filing pursuant to this [Act] must be signed in the following manner:

(1) An initial certificate of limited partnership must be signed by all general partners listed in the certificate.

(2) An amendment adding or deleting a statement that the limited partnership is a limited liability limited partnership must be signed by all general partners listed in the certificate.

(3) An amendment designating as general partner a person admitted under Section 801(3)(B) following the dissociation of a limited partnership's last general partner must be signed by that person.

(4) An amendment required by Section 803(c) following the appointment of a person to wind up the dissolved limited partnership's activities must be signed by that person.

(5) Any other amendment must be signed by:

(A) at least one general partner listed in the certificate;

(B) each other person designated in the amendment as a new general partner; and

(C) each person that the amendment indicates has dissociated as a general partner, unless:

(i) the person is deceased or a guardian or general conservator has been appointed for the person and the amendment so states; or

(ii) the person has previously delivered to the [Secretary of State] for filing a statement of dissociation.

(6) A restated certificate of limited partnership must be signed by at least one general partner listed in the certificate, and, to the extent the restated certificate effects a change under any other paragraph of this subsection, the certificate must be signed in a manner that satisfies that paragraph.

(7) A statement of termination must be signed by all general partners listed in the certificate or, if the certificate of a dissolved limited partnership lists no general partners, by the person appointed pursuant to Section 803(c) or (d) to wind up the dissolved limited partnership's activities.

(8) Articles of conversion must be signed by each general partner listed in the certificate of limited partnership.

(9) Articles of merger must be signed as provided in Section 1108(a).

(10) Any other record delivered on behalf of a limited partnership to the [Secretary of State] for filing must be signed by at least one general partner listed in the certificate.

(11) A statement by a person pursuant to Section 605(a)(4) stating that the person has dissociated as a general partner must be signed by that person.

(12) A statement of withdrawal by a person pursuant to Section 306 must be signed by that person.

(13) A record delivered on behalf of a foreign limited partnership to the [Secretary of State] for filing must be signed by at least one general partner of the foreign limited partnership.

(14) Any other record delivered on behalf of any person to the [Secretary of State] for filing must be signed by that person.

(b) Any person may sign by an attorney in fact any record to be filed pursuant to this [Act].

Comment

Source—ULLCA Section 205.

This section pertains only to signing requirements and implies nothing about approval requirements. For example, Section 204(a)(2) requires that an amendment changing a limited partnership's LLLP status be signed by all **general** partners listed in the certificate, but under Section 406(b)(2) **all** partners must consent to that change unless otherwise provided in the partnership agreement.

A person who signs a record without ascertaining that the record has been properly authorized risks liability under Section 208.

Subsection (a)—The recurring reference to general partners "listed in the certificate" recognizes that a person might be admitted as a general partner under Section 401 without immediately being listed in the certificate of limited partnership. Such persons may have rights, powers and obligations despite their unlisted status, but they cannot act as general partners for the purpose of affecting the limited partnership's public record. See the Comment to Section 103(c) and the Comment to Section 401.

SECTION 205. SIGNING AND FILING PURSUANT TO JUDICIAL ORDER.

(a) If a person required by this [Act] to sign a record or deliver a record to the [Secretary of State] for filing does not do so, any other person that is aggrieved may petition the [appropriate court] to order:

(1) the person to sign the record;

(2) deliver the record to the [Secretary of State] for filing; or

(3) the [Secretary of State] to file the record unsigned.

(b) If the person aggrieved under subsection (a) is not the limited partnership or foreign limited partnership to which the record pertains, the aggrieved person shall make the limited partnership or foreign limited partnership a party to the action. A person aggrieved under subsection (a) may seek the remedies provided in subsection (a) in the same action in combination or in the alternative.

(c) A record filed unsigned pursuant to this section is effective without being signed.

Comment

Source—RULPA Section 205.

SECTION 206. DELIVERY TO AND FILING OF RECORDS BY [SECRETARY OF STATE]; EFFECTIVE TIME AND DATE.

(a) A record authorized or required to be delivered to the [Secretary of State] for filing under this [Act] must be captioned to describe the record's purpose, be in a medium permitted by the [Secretary of State], and be delivered to the [Secretary of State]. Unless the [Secretary of State] determines that a record does not comply with the filing requirements of this [Act], and if all filing fees have been paid, the [Secretary of State] shall file the record and:

(1) for a statement of dissociation, send:

(A) a copy of the filed statement and a receipt for the fees to the person which the statement indicates has dissociated as a general partner; and

(B) a copy of the filed statement and receipt to the limited partnership;

(2) for a statement of withdrawal, send:

(A) a copy of the filed statement and a receipt for the fees to the person on whose behalf the record was filed; and

(B) if the statement refers to an existing limited partnership, a copy of the filed statement and receipt to the limited partnership; and

(3) for all other records, send a copy of the filed record and a receipt for the fees to the person on whose behalf the record was filed.

(b) Upon request and payment of a fee, the [Secretary of State] shall send to the requester a certified copy of the requested record.

(c) Except as otherwise provided in Sections 116 and 207, a record delivered to the [Secretary of State] for filing under this [Act] may specify an effective time and a delayed effective date. Except as otherwise provided in this [Act], a record filed by the [Secretary of State] is effective:

(1) if the record does not specify an effective time and does not specify a delayed effective date, on the date and at the time the record is filed as evidenced by the [Secretary of State's] endorsement of the date and time on the record;

(2) if the record specifies an effective time but not a delayed effective date, on the date the record is filed at the time specified in the record;

(3) if the record specifies a delayed effective date but not an effective time, at 12:01 a.m. on the earlier of:

(A) the specified date; or

(B) the 90th day after the record is filed; or

(4) if the record specifies an effective time and a delayed effective date, at the specified time on the earlier of:

(A) the specified date; or

(B) the 90th day after the record is filed.

Comment

Source—ULLCA Section 206.

In order for a record prepared by a private person to become part of the public record under this Act, (i) someone must put a properly prepared version of the record into the possession of the public official specified in the Act as the appropriate filing officer, and (ii) that filing officer must determine that the record complies with the filing requirements of this Act and then officially make the record part of the public record. This Act refers to the first step as *delivery to the [Secretary of State] for filing* and refers to the second step as *filing*. Thus, under this Act "filing" is an official act.

   Subsection (a)—The caption need only indicate the title of the record; *e.g.*, Certificate of Limited Partnership, Statement of Change for Limited Partnership.
   Filing officers typically note on a filed record the fact, date and time of filing. The copies provided by the filing officer under this subsection should contain that notation.
   This Act does not provide a remedy if the filing officer wrongfully fails or refuses to file a record.

   Subsection (c)—This subsection allows most records to have a delayed effective date, up to 90 days after the date the record is filed by the filing officer. A record specifying a longer delay will **not** be rejected. Instead, under paragraph (c)(3) and (4), the delayed effective date is adjusted by operation of law to the "90th day after the record is filed." The Act does not require the filing officer to notify anyone of the adjustment.

SECTION 207. CORRECTING FILED RECORD.

   (a) A limited partnership or foreign limited partnership may deliver to the [Secretary of State] for filing a statement of correction to correct a record previously delivered by the limited partnership or foreign limited partnership to the [Secretary of State] and filed by the [Secretary of State], if at the time of filing the record contained false or erroneous information or was defectively signed.
   (b) A statement of correction may not state a delayed effective date and must:
      (1) describe the record to be corrected, including its filing date, or attach a copy of the record as filed;
      (2) specify the incorrect information and the reason it is incorrect or the manner in which the signing was defective; and
      (3) correct the incorrect information or defective signature.
   (c) When filed by the [Secretary of State], a statement of correction is effective retroactively as of the effective date of the record the statement corrects, but the statement is effective when filed:
      (1) for the purposes of Section 103(c) and (d); and
      (2) as to persons relying on the uncorrected record and adversely affected by the correction.

Comment

Source—ULLCA Section 207.

A statement of correction is appropriate only to correct inaccuracies that existed or signatures that were defective "at the time of filing." A statement of correction may not be used to correct a record that was accurate when filed but has become inaccurate due to subsequent events.

Subsection (c)—Generally, a statement of correction "relates back." However, there is no retroactive effect: (1) for the purposes of constructive notice under Section 103(c) and (d); and (2) against persons who have relied on the uncorrected record and would be adversely affected if the correction related back.

SECTION 208. LIABILITY FOR FALSE INFORMATION IN FILED RECORD.

(a) If a record delivered to the [Secretary of State] for filing under this [Act] and filed by the [Secretary of State] contains false information, a person that suffers loss by reliance on the information may recover damages for the loss from:

(1) a person that signed the record, or caused another to sign it on the person's behalf, and knew the information to be false at the time the record was signed; and

(2) a general partner that has notice that the information was false when the record was filed or has become false because of changed circumstances, if the general partner has notice for a reasonably sufficient time before the information is relied upon to enable the general partner to effect an amendment under Section 202, file a petition pursuant to Section 205, or deliver to the [Secretary of State] for filing a statement of change pursuant to Section 115 or a statement of correction pursuant to Section 207.

(b) Signing a record authorized or required to be filed under this [Act] constitutes an affirmation under the penalties of perjury that the facts stated in the record are true.

Comment

This section pertains to both limited partnerships and foreign limited partnerships.

LLLP status is irrelevant to this section. The LLLP shield protects only to the extent that (i) the obligation involved is an obligation of the limited partnership or foreign limited partnership, and (ii) a partner is claimed to be liable for that obligation by reason of being a partner. This section does not address the obligations of a limited partnership or foreign limited partnership and instead imposes direct liability on signers and general partners.

Subsection (a)—This subsection's liability rules apply only to records (i) created by private persons ("delivered to the [Secretary of State] for filing"), (ii) which actually become part of the public record ("filed by the [Secretary of State]"). This subsection does not preempt other law, which might provide remedies for misleading information contained, for example, in a record that is delivered to the filing officer for filing but withdrawn before the filing officer takes the official action of filing the record.

Records filed under this Act are signed subject to the penalties for perjury. See subsection (b). This subsection therefore does not require a party who relies on a record to demonstrate that the reliance was reasonable. Contrast Section 201(d)(2), which provides that, if the partnership agreement is inconsistent with the public record, the public record prevails in favor of a person that is neither a partner nor a transferee and that reasonably relied on the record.

SECTION 209. CERTIFICATE OF EXISTENCE OR AUTHORIZATION.

(a) The [Secretary of State], upon request and payment of the requisite fee, shall furnish a certificate of existence for a limited partnership if the records filed in the [office of the Secretary of State] show that the [Secretary of State] has filed a certificate of limited partnership and has not filed a statement of termination. A certificate of existence must state:

(1) the limited partnership's name;

(2) that it was duly formed under the laws of this State and the date of formation;

(3) whether all fees, taxes, and penalties due to the [Secretary of State] under this [Act] or other law have been paid;

(4) whether the limited partnership's most recent annual report required by Section 210 has been filed by the [Secretary of State];

(5) whether the [Secretary of State] has administratively dissolved the limited partnership;

(6) whether the limited partnership's certificate of limited partnership has been amended to state that the limited partnership is dissolved;

(7) that a statement of termination has not been filed by the [Secretary of State]; and

(8) other facts of record in the [office of the Secretary of State] which may be requested by the applicant.

(b) The [Secretary of State], upon request and payment of the requisite fee, shall furnish a certificate of authorization for a foreign limited partnership if the records filed in the [office of the Secretary of State] show that the [Secretary of State] has filed a certificate of authority, has not revoked the certificate of authority, and has not filed a notice of cancellation. A certificate of authorization must state:

(1) the foreign limited partnership's name and any alternate name adopted under Section 905(a) for use in this State;

(2) that it is authorized to transact business in this State;

(3) whether all fees, taxes, and penalties due to the [Secretary of State] under this [Act] or other law have been paid;

(4) whether the foreign limited partnership's most recent annual report required by Section 210 has been filed by the [Secretary of State];

(5) that the [Secretary of State] has not revoked its certificate of authority and has not filed a notice of cancellation; and

(6) other facts of record in the [office of the Secretary of State] which may be requested by the applicant.

(c) Subject to any qualification stated in the certificate, a certificate of existence or authorization issued by the [Secretary of State] may be relied upon as conclusive evidence that the limited partnership or foreign limited partnership is in existence or is authorized to transact business in this State.

Comment

Source—ULLCA Section 208.

A certificate of existence can reveal only information present in the public record, and under this Act significant information bearing on the status of a limited partnership may be outside the public record. For example, while this Act provides for a limited partnership to have a perpetual duration, Section 104(c), the partnership agreement may set a definite term or designate particular events whose occurrence will cause dissolution. Section 801(1). Dissolution is also possible by consent, Section 801(2), and, absent a contrary provision in the partnership agreement, will at least be at issue whenever a general partner dissociates. Section 801(3). Nothing in this Act requires a limited partnership to deliver to the filing officer for filing a record indicating that the limited partnership has dissolved.

A certificate of authorization furnished under this section is different than a certificate of authority filed under Section 904.

SECTION 210. ANNUAL REPORT FOR [SECRETARY OF STATE].

(a) A limited partnership or a foreign limited partnership authorized to transact business in this State shall deliver to the [Secretary of State] for filing an annual report that states:

(1) the name of the limited partnership or foreign limited partnership;

(2) the street and mailing address of its designated office and the name and street and mailing address of its agent for service of process in this State;

(3) in the case of a limited partnership, the street and mailing address of its principal office; and

(4) in the case of a foreign limited partnership, the State or other jurisdiction under whose law the foreign limited partnership is formed and any alternate name adopted under Section 905(a).

(b) Information in an annual report must be current as of the date the annual report is delivered to the [Secretary of State] for filing.

(c) The first annual report must be delivered to the [Secretary of State] between [January 1 and April 1] of the year following the calendar year in which a limited partnership was formed or a foreign limited partnership was authorized to transact business. An annual report must be delivered to the [Secretary of State] between [January 1 and April 1] of each subsequent calendar year.

(d) If an annual report does not contain the information required in subsection (a), the [Secretary of State] shall promptly notify the reporting limited partnership or foreign limited partnership and return the report to it for correction. If the report is corrected to contain the information required in subsection (a) and delivered to the [Secretary of State] within 30 days after the effective date of the notice, it is timely delivered.

(e) If a filed annual report contains an address of a designated office or the name or address of an agent for service of process which differs from the information shown in the records of the [Secretary of State] immediately before the filing, the differing information in the annual report is considered a statement of change under Section 115.

Comment

Source—ULLCA Section 211.

Subsection (d)—This subsection's rule affects only Section 809(a)(2) (late filing of annual report grounds for administrative dissolution) and any late fees that the filing officer might have the right to impose. For the purposes of subsection (e), the annual report functions as a statement of change only when "filed" by the filing officer. Likewise, a person cannot rely on subsection (d) to escape liability arising under Section 208.

[ARTICLE] 3
LIMITED PARTNERS

SECTION 301. BECOMING LIMITED PARTNER. A person becomes a limited partner:

(1) as provided in the partnership agreement;

(2) as the result of a conversion or merger under [Article] 11; or

(3) with the consent of all the partners.

Comment

Source—RULPA Section 301.

Although Section 801(4) contemplates the admission of a limited partner to avoid dissolution, that provision does not itself authorize the admission. Instead, this section controls. Contrast Section 801(3)(B), which itself authorizes the admission of a general partner in order to avoid dissolution.

SECTION 302. NO RIGHT OR POWER AS LIMITED PARTNER TO BIND LIMITED PARTNERSHIP. A limited partner does not have the right or the power as a limited partner to act for or bind the limited partnership.

Comment

In this respect a limited partner is analogous to a shareholder in a corporation; status as owner provides neither the right to manage nor a reasonable appearance of that right.

The phrase "as a limited partner" is intended to recognize that: (i) this section does not disable a general partner that also owns a limited partner interest, (ii) the partnership agreement may as a matter of contract allocate managerial rights to one or more limited partners; and (iii) a separate agreement can empower and entitle a person that is a limited partner to act for the limited partnership in another capacity; *e.g.*, as an agent. See Comment to Section 305.

The fact that a limited partner *qua* limited partner has no power to bind the limited partnership means that, subject to Section 113 (Dual Capacity), information possessed by a limited partner is not attributed to the limited partnership. See Section 103(h).

This Act specifies various circumstances in which limited partners have consent rights, including:

•   admission of a limited partner, Section 301(3)

- admission of a general partner, Section 401(4)
- amendment of the partnership agreement, Section 406(b)(1)
- the decision to amend the certificate of limited partnership so as to obtain or relinquish LLLP status, Section 406(b)(2)
- the disposition of all or substantially all of the limited partnership's property, outside the ordinary course, Section 406(b)(3)
- the compromise of a partner's obligation to make a contribution or return an improper distribution, Section 502(c)
- expulsion of a limited partner by consent of the other partners, Section 601(b)(4)
- expulsion of a general partner by consent of the other partners, Section 603(4)
- redemption of a transferable interest subject to charging order, using limited partnership property, Section 703(c)(3)
- causing dissolution by consent, Section 801(2)
- causing dissolution by consent following the dissociation of a general partner, when at least one general partner remains, Section 801(3)(A)
- avoiding dissolution and appointing a successor general partner, following the dissociation of the sole general partner, Section 801(3)(B)
- appointing a person to wind up the limited partnership when there is no general partner, Section 803(C)
- approving, amending or abandoning a plan of conversion, Section 1103(a) and (b)(2)
- approving, amending or abandoning a plan of merger, Section 1107(a) and (b)(2).

SECTION 303. NO LIABILITY AS LIMITED PARTNER FOR LIMITED PARTNERSHIP OBLIGATIONS. An obligation of a limited partnership, whether arising in contract, tort, or otherwise, is not the obligation of a limited partner. A limited partner is not personally liable, directly or indirectly, by way of contribution or otherwise, for an obligation of the limited partnership solely by reason of being a limited partner, even if the limited partner participates in the management and control of the limited partnership.

Comment

This section provides a full, status-based liability shield for each limited partner, "even if the limited partner participates in the management and control of the limited partnership." The section thus eliminates the so-called "control rule" with respect to personal liability for entity obligations and brings limited partners into parity with LLC members, LLP partners and corporate shareholders.

The "control rule" first appeared in an uniform act in 1916, although the concept is much older. Section 7 of the original Uniform Limited Partnership Act provided that "A limited partner shall not become liable as a general partner [i.e., for the obligations of the limited partnership] unless . . . he takes part in the control of the business." The 1976 Uniform Limited Partnership Act (ULPA-1976) "carrie[d] over the basic test from former Section 7," but recognized "the difficulty of determining when the 'control' line has been overstepped." Comment to ULPA-1976, Section 303. Accordingly, ULPA-1976 tried to buttress the limited partner's shield by (i) providing a safe harbor for a lengthy list of activities deemed not to constitute participating in control, ULPA-1976, Section 303(b), and (ii) limiting a limited partner's "control rule" liability "only to persons who transact business with the limited partnership with actual knowledge of [the limited partner's] participation in control." ULPA-1976, Section 303(a). However, these protections were complicated by a countervailing rule which made a limited partner generally liable for the limited partnership's obligations "if the limited partner's participation in the control of the business is . . . substantially the same as the exercise of the powers of a general partner." ULPA-1976, Section 303(a).

The 1985 amendments to ULPA-1976 (i.e., RULPA) further buttressed the limited partner's shield, removing the "substantially the same" rule, expanding the list of safe harbor activities and limiting "control rule" liability "only to persons who transact business with the limited partnership reasonably believing, based upon the limited partner's conduct, that the limited partner is a general partner."

In a world with LLPs, LLCs and, most importantly, LLLPs, the control rule has become an anachronism. This Act therefore takes the next logical step in the evolution of the limited partner's liability shield and renders the control rule extinct.

The shield established by this section protects only against liability for the limited partnership's obligations and only to the extent that the limited partner is claimed to be liable on account of being a limited partner. Thus, a person that is both a general and limited partner will be liable as a general partner for the limited partnership's obligations. Moreover, this section does not prevent a limited partner from being liable as a result of the limited partner's own conduct and is therefore inapplicable when a third party asserts that a limited partner's own wrongful conduct has injured the third party. This section is likewise inapplicable to claims by the limited partnership or another partner that a limited partner has breached a duty under this Act or the partnership agreement.

This section does not eliminate a limited partner's liability for promised contributions, Section 502 or improper distributions. Section 509. That liability pertains to a person's status as a limited partner but is not liability for an obligation of the limited partnership.

The shield provided by this section applies whether or not a limited partnership is a limited liability limited partnership.

SECTION 304. RIGHT OF LIMITED PARTNER AND FORMER LIMITED PARTNER TO INFORMATION.

(a) On 10 days' demand, made in a record received by the limited partnership, a limited partner may inspect and copy required information during regular business hours in the limited partnership's designated office. The limited partner need not have any particular purpose for seeking the information.

(b) During regular business hours and at a reasonable location specified by the limited partnership, a limited partner may obtain from the limited partnership and inspect and copy true and full information regarding the state of the activities and financial condition of the limited partnership and other information regarding the activities of the limited partnership as is just and reasonable if:

(1) the limited partner seeks the information for a purpose reasonably related to the partner's interest as a limited partner;

(2) the limited partner makes a demand in a record received by the limited partnership, describing with reasonable particularity the information sought and the purpose for seeking the information; and

(3) the information sought is directly connected to the limited partner's purpose.

(c) Within 10 days after receiving a demand pursuant to subsection (b), the limited partnership in a record shall inform the limited partner that made the demand:

(1) what information the limited partnership will provide in response to the demand;

(2) when and where the limited partnership will provide the information; and

(3) if the limited partnership declines to provide any demanded information, the limited partnership's reasons for declining.

(d) Subject to subsection (f), a person dissociated as a limited partner may inspect and copy required information during regular business hours in the limited partnership's designated office if:

(1) the information pertains to the period during which the person was a limited partner;

(2) the person seeks the information in good faith; and

(3) the person meets the requirements of subsection (b).

(e) The limited partnership shall respond to a demand made pursuant to subsection (d) in the same manner as provided in subsection (c).

(f) If a limited partner dies, Section 704 applies.

(g) The limited partnership may impose reasonable restrictions on the use of information obtained under this section. In a dispute concerning the reasonableness of a restriction under this subsection, the limited partnership has the burden of proving reasonableness.

(h) A limited partnership may charge a person that makes a demand under this section reasonable costs of copying, limited to the costs of labor and material.

(i) Whenever this [Act] or a partnership agreement provides for a limited partner to give or withhold consent to a matter, before the consent is given or withheld, the limited partnership shall, without demand, provide the limited partner with all information material to the limited partner's decision that the limited partnership knows.

(j) A limited partner or person dissociated as a limited partner may exercise the rights under this section through an attorney or other agent. Any restriction imposed under subsection (g) or by the partnership agreement applies both to the attorney or other agent and to the limited partner or person dissociated as a limited partner.

(k) The rights stated in this section do not extend to a person as transferee, but may be exercised by the legal representative of an individual under legal disability who is a limited partner or person dissociated as a limited partner.

Comment

This section balances two countervailing concerns relating to information: the need of limited partners and former limited partners for access versus the limited partnership's need to protect confidential business data and other intellectual property. The balance must be understood in the context of fiduciary duties. The general partners are obliged through their duties of care and loyalty to protect information whose confidentiality is important to the limited partnership or otherwise inappropriate for dissemination. See Section 408 (general standards of general partner conduct). A limited partner, in contrast, "does not have any fiduciary duty to the limited partnership or to any other partner solely by reason of being a limited partner." Section 305(a). (Both general partners and limited partners are subject to a duty of good faith and fair dealing. Section 305(b) and 408(d).)

Like predecessor law, this Act divides limited partner access rights into two categories—required information and other information. However, this Act builds on predecessor law by:

- expanding slightly the category of required information and stating explicitly that a limited partner may have access to that information without having to show cause

- specifying a procedure for limited partners to follow when demanding access to other information
- specifying how a limited partnership must respond to such a demand and setting a time limit for the response
- retaining predecessor law's "just and reasonable" standard for determining a limited partner's right to other information, while recognizing that, to be "just and reasonable," a limited partner's demand for other information must meet at minimum standards of relatedness and particularity
- expressly requiring the limited partnership to volunteer known, material information when seeking or obtaining consent from limited partners
- codifying (while limiting) the power of the partnership agreement to vary limited partner access rights
- permitting the limited partnership to establish other reasonable limits on access
- providing access rights for former limited partners.

The access rights stated in this section are personal to each limited partner and are enforceable through a direct action under Section 1001(a). These access rights are in addition to whatever discovery rights a party has in a civil suit.

Subsection (a)—The phrase "required information" is a defined term. See Sections 102(18) and 111. This subsection's broad right of access is subject not only to reasonable limitations in the partnership agreement, Section 110(b)(4), but also to the power of the limited partnership to impose reasonable limitations on use. Unless the partnership agreement provides otherwise, it will be the general partner or partners that have the authority to use that power. See Section 406(a).

Subsection (b)—The language describing the information to be provided comes essentially verbatim from RULPA Section 305(a)(2)(i) and (iii). The procedural requirements derive from RMBCA Section 16.02(c). This subsection does not impose a requirement of good faith, because Section 305(b) contains a generally applicable obligation of good faith and fair dealing for limited partners.

Subsection (d)—The notion that former owners should have information rights comes from RUPA Section 403(b) and ULLCA Section 408(a). The access is limited to the required information and is subject to certain conditions.

Example: A person dissociated as a limited partner seeks data which the limited partnership has compiled, which relates to the period when the person was a limited partner, but which is beyond the scope of the information required by Section 111. No matter how reasonable the person's purpose and how well drafted the person's demand, the limited partnership is not obliged to provide the data.

Example: A person dissociated as a limited partner seeks access to required information pertaining to the period during which the person was a limited partner. The person makes a bald demand, merely stating a desire to review the required information at the limited partnership's designated office. In particular, the demand does not describe "with reasonable particularity the information sought and the purpose for seeking the information." See subsection (b)(2). The limited partnership is not obliged to allow access. The person must first comply with subsection (d), which incorporates by reference the requirements of subsection (b).

Subsection (f) and Section 704 provide greater access rights for the estate of a deceased limited partner.

Subsection (d)(2)—A duty of good faith is needed here, because a person claiming access under this subsection is no longer a limited partner and is no longer subject to Section 305(b). See Section 602(a)(2) (dissociation as a limited partner terminates duty of good faith as to subsequent events).

Subsection (g)—This subsection permits the limited partnership—as distinguished from the partnership agreement—to impose use limitations. Contrast Section 110(b)(4). Under Section 406(a), it will be the general partner or partners that decide whether the limited partnership will impose use restrictions.

The limited partnership bears the burden of proving the reasonableness of any restriction imposed under this subsection. In determining whether a restriction is reasonable, a court might consider: (i) the danger or other problem the restriction seeks to avoid; (ii) the purpose for which the information is sought; and (iii) whether, in light of both the problem and the purpose, the restriction is reasonably tailored. Restricting use of the names and addresses of limited partners is not per se unreasonable.

The following table compares the limitations available through the partnership agreement with those available under this subsection.

	Partnership Agreement	**Section 304(g)**
how restrictions adopted	by the consent of partners when they adopt or amend the partnership agreement, unless the partnership agreement provides another method of amendment	by the general partners, acting under Section 406(a)
what restrictions may be imposed	"reasonable restrictions on the availability and use of information obtained," Section 110(b)(4)	"reasonable restrictions on the use of information obtained"
burden of proof	the person challenging the restriction must prove that the restriction will "unreasonably restrict the right of information," Section 110(b)(4)	"the limited partnership has the burden of proving reasonableness"

Subsection (h)—Source: RUPA Section 403(b) and ULLCA Section 408(a).

Subsection (i)—Source: ULLCA Section 408(b).

The duty stated in this subsection is at the core of the duties owed the limited partners by a limited partnership and its general partners. This subsection imposes an affirmative duty to volunteer information, but that obligation is limited to information which is both material and known by the limited partnership. The duty applies to known, material information, even if the limited partnership does not know that the information is material.

A limited partnership will "know" what its general partners know. Section 103(h). A limited partnership may also know information known by the "individual conducting the transaction for the [limited partnership]." Section 103(g).

A limited partner's right to information under this subsection is enforceable through the full panoply of "legal or equitable relief" provided by Section 1001(a), including in appropriate circumstances the withdrawal or invalidation of improperly obtained consent and the invalidation or recision of action taken pursuant to that consent.

Subsection (k)—Section 304 provides no information rights to a transferee as transferee. Transferee status brings only the very limited information rights stated in Section 702(c).

It is nonetheless possible for a person that happens to be a transferee to have rights under this section. For example, under Section 602(a)(3) a person dissociated as a limited partner becomes a "mere transferee" of its own transferable interest. While that status provides the person no rights under this section, the status of person dissociated as a limited partner triggers rights under subsection (d).

SECTION 305. LIMITED DUTIES OF LIMITED PARTNERS.

(a) A limited partner does not have any fiduciary duty to the limited partnership or to any other partner solely by reason of being a limited partner.

(b) A limited partner shall discharge the duties to the partnership and the other partners under this [Act] or under the partnership agreement and exercise any rights consistently with the obligation of good faith and fair dealing.

(c) A limited partner does not violate a duty or obligation under this [Act] or under the partnership agreement merely because the limited partner's conduct furthers the limited partner's own interest.

Comment

Subsection (a)—Fiduciary duty typically attaches to a person whose status or role creates significant power for that person over the interests of another person. Under this Act, limited partners have very limited power of any sort in the regular activities of the limited partnership and no power whatsoever justifying the imposition of fiduciary duties either to the limited partnership or fellow partners. It is possible for a partnership agreement to allocate significant managerial authority and power to a limited partner, but in that case the power exists not as a matter of status or role but rather as a matter of contract. The proper limit on such contract-based power is the obligation of good faith and fair dealing, not fiduciary duty, unless the partnership agreement itself expressly imposes a fiduciary duty or creates a role for a limited partner which, as a matter of other law, gives rise to a fiduciary duty. For example, if the partnership agreement makes a limited partner an agent for the limited partnership as to particular matters, the law of agency will impose fiduciary duties on the limited partner with respect to the limited partner's role as agent.

Subsection (b)—Source: RUPA Section 404(d). The same language appears in Section 408(d), pertaining to general partners.

The obligation of good faith and fair dealing is *not* a fiduciary duty, does not command altruism or self-abnegation, and does not prevent a partner from acting in the partner's own self-interest. Courts should not use the obligation to change *ex post facto* the parties' or this Act's allocation of risk and power. To the contrary, in light of the nature of a limited partnership, the obligation should be used only to protect agreed-upon arrangements from conduct that is manifestly beyond what a reasonable person could have contemplated when the arrangements were made.

The partnership agreement or this Act may grant discretion to a partner, and that partner may properly exercise that discretion even though another partner suffers as a consequence. Conduct does not violate the obligation of good faith and fair dealing merely because that conduct substantially prejudices a party. Indeed, parties allocate risk precisely because prejudice may occur. The exercise of discretion constitutes a breach of the obligation of good faith and fair dealing only when the party claiming breach shows that the conduct has no honestly-held purpose that legitimately comports with the parties' agreed-upon arrangements. Once such a purpose appears, courts should not second guess a party's choice of method in serving that purpose, unless the party invoking the obligation of good faith and fair dealing shows that the choice of method itself lacks any honestly-held purpose that legitimately comports with the parties' agreed-upon arrangements.

In sum, the purpose of the obligation of good faith and fair dealing is to protect the arrangement the partners have chosen for themselves, not to restructure that arrangement under the guise of safeguarding it.

SECTION 306. PERSON ERRONEOUSLY BELIEVING SELF TO BE LIMITED PARTNER.

(a) Except as otherwise provided in subsection (b), a person that makes an investment in a business enterprise and erroneously but in good faith believes that the person has become a limited partner in the enterprise is not liable for the enterprise's obligations by reason of making the investment, receiving distributions from the enterprise, or exercising any rights of or appropriate to a limited partner, if, on ascertaining the mistake, the person:

(1) causes an appropriate certificate of limited partnership, amendment, or statement of correction to be signed and delivered to the [Secretary of State] for filing; or

(2) withdraws from future participation as an owner in the enterprise by signing and delivering to the [Secretary of State] for filing a statement of withdrawal under this section.

(b) A person that makes an investment described in subsection (a) is liable to the same extent as a general partner to any third party that enters into a transaction with the enterprise, believing in good faith that the person is a general partner, before the [Secretary of State] files a statement of withdrawal, certificate of limited partnership, amendment, or statement of correction to show that the person is not a general partner.

(c) If a person makes a diligent effort in good faith to comply with subsection (a)(1) and is unable to cause the appropriate certificate of limited partnership, amendment, or statement of correction to be signed and delivered to the [Secretary of State] for filing, the person has the right to withdraw from the enterprise pursuant to subsection (a)(2) even if the withdrawal would otherwise breach an agreement with others that are or have agreed to become co-owners of the enterprise.

Comment

Source—RULPA Section 304, substantially redrafted for reasons of style.

Subsection (a)(2)—The requirement that a person "withdraw[] from future participation as an owner in the enterprise" means, in part, that the person refrain from taking any further profit from the enterprise. The requirement does not mean, however, that the person is required to return previously obtained profits or forfeit any investment.

[ARTICLE] 4
GENERAL PARTNERS

SECTION 401. BECOMING GENERAL PARTNER. A person becomes a general partner:

(1) as provided in the partnership agreement:

(2) under Section 801(3)(B) following the dissociation of a limited partnership's last general partner;

(3) as the result of a conversion or merger under [Article] 11; or

(4) with the consent of all the partners.

Comment

This section does not make a person's status as a general partner dependent on the person being so designated in the certificate of limited partnership. If a person does become a general partner under this section without being so designated:

- the limited partnership is obligated to promptly and appropriately amend the certificate of limited partnership, Section 202(b)(1);

- each general partner that knows of the anomaly is personally obligated to cause the certificate to be promptly and appropriately amended, Section 202(c)(1), and is subject to liability for failing to do so, Section 208(a)(2);
- the "non-designated" general partner has:
  - ~ all the rights and duties of a general partner to the limited partnership and the other partners, and
  - ~ the powers of a general partner to bind the limited partnership under Sections 402 and 403, but
  - ~ no power to sign records which are to be filed on behalf of the limited partnership under this Act

Example: By consent of the partners of XYZ Limited Partnership, G is admitted as a general partner. However, XYZ's certificate of limited partnership is not amended accordingly. Later, G—acting without actual authority —purports to bind XYZ to a transaction with Third Party. Third Party does not review the filed certificate of limited partnership before entering into the transaction. XYZ might be bound under Section 402.

Section 402 attributes to a limited partnership "[a]n act of a general partner . . . for apparently carrying on in the ordinary course the limited partnership's activities or activities of the kind carried on by the limited partnership." The limited partnership's liability under Section 402 does not depend on the "act of a general partner" being the act of a general partner designated in the certificate of limited partnership. Moreover, the notice provided by Section 103(c) does not undercut G's appearance of authority. Section 402 refers only to notice under Section 103(d) and, in any event, according to the second sentence of Section 103(c), the fact that a person is **not** listed as in the certificate as a general partner is **not** notice that the person is **not** a general partner. See Comment to Section 103(c).

Example: Same facts, except that Third Party does review the certificate of limited partnership before entering into the transaction. The result might still be the same.

The omission of a person's name from the certificate's list of general partners is **not** notice that the person is **not** a general partner. Therefore, Third Party's review of the certificate does not mean that Third Party knew, had received a notification or had notice that G lacked authority. At most, XYZ could argue that, because Third Party knew that G was not listed in the certificate, a transaction entered into by G could not appear to Third Party to be for apparently carrying on the limited partnership's activities in the ordinary course.

SECTION 402. GENERAL PARTNER AGENT OF LIMITED PARTNERSHIP.

(a) Each general partner is an agent of the limited partnership for the purposes of its activities. An act of a general partner, including the signing of a record in the partnership's name, for apparently carrying on in the ordinary course the limited partnership's activities or activities of the kind carried on by the limited partnership binds the limited partnership, unless the general partner did not have authority to act for the limited partnership in the particular matter and the person with which the general partner was dealing knew, had received a notification, or had notice under Section 103(d) that the general partner lacked authority.

(b) An act of a general partner which is not apparently for carrying on in the ordinary course the limited partnership's activities or activities of the kind carried on by the limited partnership binds the limited partnership only if the act was actually authorized by all the other partners.

Comment

Source—RUPA Section 301. For the meaning of "authority" in subsection (a) and "authorized" in subsection (b), see RUPA Section 301, Comment 3 (stating that "Subsection (2) [of RUPA Section 301] makes it clear that the partnership is bound by a partner's *actual* authority, even if the partner has no apparent authority"; emphasis added).

The fact that a person is not listed in the certificate of limited partnership as a general partner is **not** notice that the person is **not** a partner and is **not** notice that the person lacks authority to act for the limited partnership. See Comment to Section 103(c) and Comment to Section 401.

Section 103(f) defines receipt of notification. Section 103(d) lists various public filings, each of which provides notice 90 days after its effective date.

Example: For the past ten years, X has been a general partner of XYZ Limited Partnership and has regularly conducted the limited partnership's business with Third Party. However, 100 days ago the limited partnership expelled X as a general partner and the next day delivered for filing an amendment to XYZ's certificate of limited partnership which stated that X was no longer a general partner. On that same day, the filing officer filed the amendment.

Today X approaches Third Party, purports still be to a general partner of XYZ and purports to enter into a transaction with Third Party on XYZ's behalf. Third Party is unaware that X has been expelled and has no reason to doubt that X's bona fides. Nonetheless, XYZ is not liable on the transaction. Under Section 103(d), Third Party has notice that X is dissociated and perforce has notice that X is not a general partner authorized to bind XYZ.

SECTION 403. LIMITED PARTNERSHIP LIABLE FOR GENERAL PARTNER'S ACTIONABLE CONDUCT.

(a) A limited partnership is liable for loss or injury caused to a person, or for a penalty incurred, as a result of a wrongful act or omission, or other actionable conduct, of a general partner acting in the ordinary course of activities of the limited partnership or with authority of the limited partnership.

(b) If, in the course of the limited partnership's activities or while acting with authority of the limited partnership, a general partner receives or causes the limited partnership to receive money or property of a person not a partner, and the money or property is misapplied by a general partner, the limited partnership is liable for the loss.

Comment

Source—RUPA Section 305. For the meaning of "authority" in subsections (a) and (b), see RUPA Section 305, Comment. The third-to-last paragraph of that Comment states:

> The partnership is liable for the actionable conduct or omission of a partner acting in the ordinary course of its business or "with the authority of the partnership." This is intended to include a partner's apparent, as well as actual, authority, thereby bringing within Section 305(a) the situation covered in UPA Section 14(a).

The last paragraph of that Comment states:

> Section 305(b) is drawn from UPA Section 14(b), but has been edited to improve clarity. It imposes strict liability on the partnership for the misapplication of money or property received by a partner in the course of the partnership's business or otherwise within the scope of the partner's actual authority.

Section 403(a) of this Act is taken essentially verbatim from RUPA Section 305(a), and Section 403(b) of this Act is taken essentially verbatim from RUPA Section 305(b).

This section makes the limited partnership vicariously liable for a partner's misconduct. That vicariously liability in no way discharges or diminishes the partner's direct liability for the partner's own misconduct.

A general partner can cause a limited partnership to be liable under this section, even if the general partner is not designated as a general partner in the certificate of limited partnership. See Comment to Section 401.

SECTION 404. GENERAL PARTNER'S LIABILITY.

(a) Except as otherwise provided in subsections (b) and (c), all general partners are liable jointly and severally for all obligations of the limited partnership unless otherwise agreed by the claimant or provided by law.

(b) A person that becomes a general partner of an existing limited partnership is not personally liable for an obligation of a limited partnership incurred before the person became a general partner.

(c) An obligation of a limited partnership incurred while the limited partnership is a limited liability limited partnership, whether arising in contract, tort, or otherwise, is solely the obligation of the limited partnership. A general partner is not personally liable, directly or indirectly, by way of contribution or otherwise, for such an obligation solely by reason of being or acting as a general partner. This subsection applies despite anything inconsistent in the partnership agreement that existed immediately before the consent required to become a limited liability limited partnership under Section 406(b)(2).

Comment

Source—RUPA Section 306.

Following RUPA and the UPA, this Act leaves to other law the question of when a limited partnership obligation is incurred.

Subsection (c)—For an explanation of the decision to provide for limited liability limited partnerships, see the Prefatory Note.

SECTION 405. ACTIONS BY AND AGAINST PARTNERSHIP AND PARTNERS.

(a) To the extent not inconsistent with Section 404, a general partner may be joined in an action against the limited partnership or named in a separate action.

(b) A judgment against a limited partnership is not by itself a judgment against a general partner. A judgment against a limited partnership may not be satisfied from a general partner's assets unless there is also a judgment against the general partner.

(c) A judgment creditor of a general partner may not levy execution against the assets of the general partner to satisfy a judgment based on a claim against the limited partnership, unless the partner is personally liable for the claim under Section 404 and:

(1) a judgment based on the same claim has been obtained against the limited partnership and a writ of execution on the judgment has been returned unsatisfied in whole or in part;

(2) the limited partnership is a debtor in bankruptcy;

(3) the general partner has agreed that the creditor need not exhaust limited partnership assets;

(4) a court grants permission to the judgment creditor to levy execution against the assets of a general partner based on a finding that limited partnership assets subject to execution are clearly insufficient to satisfy the judgment, that exhaustion of limited partnership assets is excessively burdensome, or that the grant of permission is an appropriate exercise of the court's equitable powers; or

(5) liability is imposed on the general partner by law or contract independent of the existence of the limited partnership.

Comment

Source—RUPA Section 307.

If a limited partnership is a limited liability limited partnership throughout its existence, this section will bar a creditor of a limited partnership from impleading, suing or reaching the assets of a general partner unless the creditor can satisfy subsection (c)(5).

SECTION 406. MANAGEMENT RIGHTS OF GENERAL PARTNER.

(a) Each general partner has equal rights in the management and conduct of the limited partnership's activities. Except as expressly provided in this [Act], any matter relating to the activities of the limited partnership may be exclusively decided by the general partner or, if there is more than one general partner, by a majority of the general partners.

(b) The consent of each partner is necessary to:

(1) amend the partnership agreement;

(2) amend the certificate of limited partnership to add or, subject to Section 1110, delete a statement that the limited partnership is a limited liability limited partnership; and

(3) sell, lease, exchange, or otherwise dispose of all, or substantially all, of the limited partnership's property, with or without the good will, other than in the usual and regular course of the limited partnership's activities.

(c) A limited partnership shall reimburse a general partner for payments made and indemnify a general partner for liabilities incurred by the general partner in the ordinary course of the activities of the partnership or for the preservation of its activities or property.

(d) A limited partnership shall reimburse a general partner for an advance to the limited partnership beyond the amount of capital the general partner agreed to contribute.

(e) A payment or advance made by a general partner which gives rise to an obligation of the limited partnership under subsection (c) or (d) constitutes a loan to the limited partnership which accrues interest from the date of the payment or advance.

(f) A general partner is not entitled to remuneration for services performed for the partnership.

Comment

Source—RUPA Section 401 and ULLCA Section 404.

Subsection (a)—As explained in the Prefatory Note, this Act assumes that, more often than not, people utilizing the Act will want (i) strong centralized management, strongly entrenched, and (ii) passive investors with little control over the entity. Section 302 essentially excludes limited partners from the ordinary management of a limited partnership's activities. This subsection states affirmatively the general partners' commanding role. Only the partnership agreement and the express provisions of this Act can limit that role.

The authority granted by this subsection includes the authority to delegate. Delegation does not relieve the delegating general partner or partners of their duties under Section 408. However, the fact of delegation is a fact relevant to any breach of duty analysis.

Example: A sole general partner personally handles all "important paperwork" for a limited partnership. The general partner neglects to renew the fire insurance coverage on a building owned by the limited partnership, despite having received and read a warning notice from the insurance company. The building subsequently burns to the ground and is a total loss. The general partner might be liable for breach of the duty of care under Section 408(c) (gross negligence).

Example: A sole general partner delegates responsibility for insurance renewals to the limited partnership's office manager, and that manager neglects to renew the fire insurance coverage on the building. Even assuming that the office manager has been grossly negligent, the general partner is not necessarily liable under Section 408(c). The office manager's gross negligence is not automatically attributed to the general partner. Under Section 408(c), the question is whether the general partner was grossly negligent (or worse) in selecting the general manager, delegating insurance renewal matters to the general manager and supervising the general manager after the delegation.

For the consequences of delegating authority to a person that is a limited partner, see the Comment to Section 305.

The partnership agreement may also provide for delegation and, subject to Section 110(b)(5) – (7), may modify a general partner's Section 408 duties.

Subsection (b)—This subsection limits the managerial rights of the general partners, requiring the consent of each general and limited partner for the specified actions. The subsection is subject to change by the partnership agreement, except as provided in Section 110(b)(12) (pertaining to consent rights established by Section 1110).

Subsection (c)—This Act does not include any parallel provision for limited partners, because they are assumed to be passive. To the extent that by contract or other arrangement a limited partner has authority to act on behalf of the limited partnership, agency law principles will create an indemnity obligation. In other situations, principles of restitution might apply.

Subsection (f)—Unlike RUPA Section 401(h), this subsection provides no compensation for winding up efforts. In a limited partnership, winding up is one of the tasks for which the limited partners depend on the general partner. There is no reason for the Act to single out this particular task as giving rise to compensation.

SECTION 407. RIGHT OF GENERAL PARTNER AND FORMER GENERAL PARTNER TO INFORMATION.

(a) A general partner, without having any particular purpose for seeking the information, may inspect and copy during regular business hours:

(1) in the limited partnership's designated office, required information; and

(2) at a reasonable location specified by the limited partnership, any other records maintained by the limited partnership regarding the limited partnership's activities and financial condition.

(b) Each general partner and the limited partnership shall furnish to a general partner:

(1) without demand, any information concerning the limited partnership's activities and activities reasonably required for the proper exercise of the general partner's rights and duties under the partnership agreement or this [Act]; and

(2) on demand, any other information concerning the limited partnership's activities, except to the extent the demand or the information demanded is unreasonable or otherwise improper under the circumstances.

(c) Subject to subsection (e), on 10 days' demand made in a record received by the limited partnership, a person dissociated as a general partner may have access to the information and records described in subsection (a) at the location specified in subsection (a) if:

(1) the information or record pertains to the period during which the person was a general partner;

(2) the person seeks the information or record in good faith; and

(3) the person satisfies the requirements imposed on a limited partner by Section 304(b).

(d) The limited partnership shall respond to a demand made pursuant to subsection (c) in the same manner as provided in Section 304(c).

(e) If a general partner dies, Section 704 applies.

(f) The limited partnership may impose reasonable restrictions on the use of information under this section. In any dispute concerning the reasonableness of a restriction under this subsection, the limited partnership has the burden of proving reasonableness.

(g) A limited partnership may charge a person dissociated as a general partner that makes a demand under this section reasonable costs of copying, limited to the costs of labor and material.

(h) A general partner or person dissociated as a general partner may exercise the rights under this section through an attorney or other agent. Any restriction imposed under subsection (f) or by the partnership agreement applies both to the attorney or other agent and to the general partner or person dissociated as a general partner.

(i) The rights under this section do not extend to a person as transferee, but the rights under subsection (c) of a person dissociated as a general may be exercised by the legal representative of an individual who dissociated as a general partner under Section 603(7)(B) or (C).

Comment

This section's structure parallels the structure of Section 304 and the Comment to that section may be helpful in understanding this section.

Subsection (b)—Source: RUPA Section 403(c).

Subsection (b)(1)—If a particular item of material information is apparent in the limited partnership's records, whether a general partner is obliged to disseminate that information to fellow general partners depends on the circumstances.

Example: A limited partnership has two general partners: each of which is regularly engaged in conducting the limited partnership's activities; both of which are aware of and have regular access to all significant limited partnership records; and neither of which has special responsibility for or knowledge about any particular aspect of those activities or the partnership records pertaining to any particular aspect of those activities. Most likely, neither general partner is obliged to draw the other general partner's attention to information apparent in the limited partnership's records.

Example: Although a limited partnership has three general partners, one is the managing partner with day-to-day responsibility for running the limited partnership's activities. The other two meet periodically with the managing general partner, and together with that partner function in a manner analogous to a corporate board of directors. Most likely, the managing general partner has a duty to draw the attention of the other general partners to important information, even if that information would be apparent from a review of the limited partnership's records.

In all events under subsection (b)(1), the question is whether the disclosure by one general partner is "reasonably required for the proper exercise" of the other general partner's rights and duties.

Subsection (f)—This provision is identical to Section 304(g) and the Comment to Section 304(g) is applicable here. Under this Act, general and limited partners have sharply different roles. A restriction that is reasonable as to a limited partner is not necessarily reasonable as to a general partner.

Subsection (g)—No charge is allowed for current general partners, because in almost all cases they would be entitled to reimbursement under Section 406(c). Contrast Section 304(h), which authorizes charges to current limited partners.

Subsection (i)—The Comment to Section 304(k) is applicable here.

SECTION 408. GENERAL STANDARDS OF GENERAL PARTNER'S CONDUCT.

(a) The only fiduciary duties that a general partner has to the limited partnership and the other partners are the duties of loyalty and care under subsections (b) and (c).

(b) A general partner's duty of loyalty to the limited partnership and the other partners is limited to the following:

(1) to account to the limited partnership and hold as trustee for it any property, profit, or benefit derived by the general partner in the conduct and winding up of the limited partnership's activities or derived from a use by the general partner of limited partnership property, including the appropriation of a limited partnership opportunity;

(2) to refrain from dealing with the limited partnership in the conduct or winding up of the limited partnership's activities as or on behalf of a party having an interest adverse to the limited partnership; and

(3) to refrain from competing with the limited partnership in the conduct or winding up of the limited partnership's activities.

(c) A general partner's duty of care to the limited partnership and the other partners in the conduct and winding up of the limited partnership's activities is limited to refraining from engaging in grossly negligent or reckless conduct, intentional misconduct, or a knowing violation of law.

(d) A general partner shall discharge the duties to the partnership and the other partners under this [Act] or under the partnership agreement and exercise any rights consistently with the obligation of good faith and fair dealing.

(e) A general partner does not violate a duty or obligation under this [Act] or under the partnership agreement merely because the general partner's conduct furthers the general partner's own interest.

Comment

Source—RUPA Section 404.

This section does not prevent a general partner from delegating one or more duties, but delegation does not discharge the duty. For further discussion, see the Comment to Section 406(a).

If the partnership agreement removes a particular responsibility from a general partner, that general partner's fiduciary duty must be judged according to the rights and powers the general partner retains. For example, if the partnership agreement denies a general partner the right to act in a particular matter, the general partner's compliance with the partnership agreement cannot be a breach of fiduciary duty. However, the general partner may still have a duty to provide advice with regard to the matter. That duty could arise from the fiduciary duty of care under Section 408(c) and the duty to provide information under Sections 304(i) and 407(b).

For the partnership agreement's power directly to circumscribe a general partner's fiduciary duty, see Section 110(b)(5) and (6).

Subsection (a)—The reference to "the other partners" does not affect the distinction between direct and derivative claims. See Section 1001(b) (prerequisites for a partner bringing a direct claim).

Subsection (b)—A general partner's duty under this subsection continues through winding up, since the limited partners' dependence on the general partner does not end at dissolution. See Comment to Section 406(f) (explaining why this Act provides no remuneration for a general partner's winding up efforts).

Subsection (d)—This provision is identical to Section 305(b) and the Comment to Section 305(b) is applicable here.

[ARTICLE] 5
CONTRIBUTIONS AND DISTRIBUTIONS

SECTION 501. FORM OF CONTRIBUTION. A contribution of a partner may consist of tangible or intangible property or other benefit to the limited partnership, including money, services performed, promissory notes, other agreements to contribute cash or property, and contracts for services to be performed.

Comment

Source—ULLCA Section 401.

SECTION 502. LIABILITY FOR CONTRIBUTION.

(a) A partner's obligation to contribute money or other property or other benefit to, or to perform services for, a limited partnership is not excused by the partner's death, disability, or other inability to perform personally.

(b) If a partner does not make a promised non-monetary contribution, the partner is obligated at the option of the limited partnership to contribute money equal to that portion of the value, as stated in the required information, of the stated contribution which has not been made.

(c) The obligation of a partner to make a contribution or return money or other property paid or distributed in violation of this [Act] may be compromised only by consent of all partners. A creditor of a limited partnership which extends credit or otherwise acts in reliance on an obligation described in subsection (a), without notice of any compromise under this subsection, may enforce the original obligation.

Comment

In contrast with predecessor law, RULPA Section 502(a), this Act does not include a statute of frauds provision covering promised contributions. Section

111(9)(A) does require that the value of a promised contribution be memorialized, but that requirement does not affect enforceability. See Comment to Section 111(9).

Subsection (a)—Source: RULPA Section 502(b).

Under common law principles of impracticability, an individual's death or incapacity will sometimes discharge a duty to render performance. Restatement (Second) of Contracts, Sections 261 and 262. This subsection overrides those principles.

Subsection (b)—RULPA Section 502(b).

This subsection is a statutory liquidated damage provision, exercisable at the option of the limited partnership, with the damage amount set according to the value of the promised, non-monetary contribution as stated in the required information.

Example: In order to become a limited partner, a person promises to contribute to the limited partnership various assets which the partnership agreement values at $150,000. In return for the person's promise, and in light of the agreed value, the limited partnership admits the person as a limited partner with a right to receive 25% of the limited partnership's distributions.

The promised assets are subject to a security agreement, but the limited partner promises to contribute them "free and clear." Before the limited partner can contribute the assets, the secured party forecloses on the security interest and sells the assets at a public sale for $75,000. Even if the $75,000 reflects the actual fair market value of the assets, under this subsection the limited partnership has a claim against the limited partner for "the value, as stated in the required information, of the stated contribution which has not been made"—i.e, $150,000.

This section applies "at the option of the limited partnership" and does not affect other remedies which the limited partnership may have under other law.

Example: Same facts as the previous example, except that the public sale brings $225,000. The limited partnership is not obliged to invoke this subsection and may instead sue for breach of the promise to make the contribution, asserting the $225,000 figure as evidence of the actual loss suffered as a result of the breach.

Subsection (c)—Source: ULLCA Section 402(b); RULPA Section 502(c). The first sentence of this subsection applies not only to promised contributions but also to improper distributions. See Sections 508 and 509. The second sentence, pertaining to creditor's rights, applies only to promised contributions.

SECTION 503. SHARING OF DISTRIBUTIONS.

SECTION 503. SHARING OF DISTRIBUTIONS. A distribution by a limited partnership must be shared among the partners on the basis of the value, as stated in the required records when the limited partnership decides to make the distribution, of the contributions the limited partnership has received from each partner.

Comment

This Act has no provision allocating profits and losses among the partners. Instead, the Act directly apportions the right to receive distributions.

Nearly all limited partnerships will choose to allocate profits and losses in order to comply with applicable tax, accounting and other regulatory requirements. Those requirements, rather than this Act, are the proper source of guidance for that profit and loss allocation.

Unlike predecessor law, this section apportions distributions in relation to the value of contributions received from each partner without regard to whether the limited partnership has returned any of those contributions. Compare RULPA Sections 503 and 504. This Act's approach produces the same result as predecessor law, so long as the limited partnership does not vary this section's approach to apportioning distributions.

This section's rule for sharing distributions is subject to change under Section 110. A limited partnership that does vary the rule should be careful to consider not only the tax and accounting consequences but also the "ripple" effect on other provisions of this Act. See, e.g., Sections 801 and 803(c) (apportioning consent power in relation to the right to receive distributions).

SECTION 504. INTERIM DISTRIBUTIONS.

SECTION 504. INTERIM DISTRIBUTIONS. A partner does not have a right to any distribution before the dissolution and winding up of the limited partnership unless the limited partnership decides to make an interim distribution.

Comment

Under Section 406(a), the general partner or partners make this decision for the limited partnership.

SECTION 505. NO DISTRIBUTION ON ACCOUNT OF DISSOCIA-TION. A person does not have a right to receive a distribution on account of dissociation.

Comment

This section varies substantially from predecessor law. RULPA Sections 603 and 604 permitted a limited partner to withdraw on six months notice and receive the fair value of the limited partnership interest, unless the partnership agreement provided the limited partner with some exit right or stated a definite duration for the limited partnership.

Under this Act, a partner that dissociates becomes a transferee of its own transferable interest. See Sections 602(a)(3) (person dissociated as a limited partner) and 605(a)(5) (person dissociated as a general partner).

SECTION 506. DISTRIBUTION IN KIND. A partner does not have a right to demand or receive any distribution from a limited partnership in any form other than cash. Subject to Section 812(b), a limited partnership may distribute an asset in kind to the extent each partner receives a percentage of the asset equal to the partner's share of distributions.

Comment

Source—RULPA Section 605.

SECTION 507. RIGHT TO DISTRIBUTION. When a partner or transferee becomes entitled to receive a distribution, the partner or transferee has the status of, and is entitled to all remedies available to, a creditor of the limited partnership with respect to the distribution. However, the limited partnership's obligation to make a distribution is subject to offset for any amount owed to the limited partnership by the partner or dissociated partner on whose account the distribution is made.

Comment

Source—RULPA Section 606.
This section's first sentence refers to distributions generally. Contrast Section 508(e), which refers to indebtedness issued as a distribution.

The reference in the second sentence to "dissociated partner" encompasses circumstances in which the partner is gone and the dissociated partner's transferable interest is all that remains.

SECTION 508. LIMITATIONS ON DISTRIBUTION.

(a) A limited partnership may not make a distribution in violation of the partnership agreement.

(b) A limited partnership may not make a distribution if after the distribution:

(1) the limited partnership would not be able to pay its debts as they become due in the ordinary course of the limited partnership's activities; or

(2) the limited partnership's total assets would be less than the sum of its total liabilities plus the amount that would be needed, if the limited partnership were to be dissolved, wound up, and terminated at the time of the distribution, to satisfy the preferential rights upon dissolution, winding up, and termination of partners whose preferential rights are superior to those of persons receiving the distribution.

(c) A limited partnership may base a determination that a distribution is not prohibited under subsection (b) on financial statements prepared on the basis of accounting practices and principles that are reasonable in the circumstances or on a fair valuation or other method that is reasonable in the circumstances.

(d) Except as otherwise provided in subsection (g), the effect of a distribution under subsection (b) is measured:

(1) in the case of distribution by purchase, redemption, or other acquisition of a transferable interest in the limited partnership, as of the date money or other property is transferred or debt incurred by the limited partnership; and

(2) in all other cases, as of the date:

(A) the distribution is authorized, if the payment occurs within 120 days after that date; or

(B) the payment is made, if payment occurs more than 120 days after the distribution is authorized.

(e) A limited partnership's indebtedness to a partner incurred by reason of a distribution made in accordance with this section is at parity with the limited partnership's indebtedness to its general, unsecured creditors.

(f) A limited partnership's indebtedness, including indebtedness issued in connection with or as part of a distribution, is not considered a liability for purposes of subsection (b) if the terms of the indebtedness provide that payment of principal and interest are made only to the extent that a distribution could then be made to partners under this section.

(g) If indebtedness is issued as a distribution, each payment of principal or interest on the indebtedness is treated as a distribution, the effect of which is measured on the date the payment is made.

Comment

Source—ULLCA Section 406. See also RMBCA Section 6.40.

Subsection (c)—This subsection appears to impose a standard of ordinary care, in contrast with the general duty of care stated in Section 408(c). For a reconciliation of these two provisions, see Comment to Section 509(a).

SECTION 509. LIABILITY FOR IMPROPER DISTRIBUTIONS.
(a) A general partner that consents to a distribution made in violation of Section 508 is personally liable to the limited partnership for the amount of the distribution which exceeds the amount that could have been distributed without the violation if it is established that in consenting to the distribution the general partner failed to comply with Section 408.

(b) A partner or transferee that received a distribution knowing that the distribution to that partner or transferee was made in violation of Section 508 is personally liable to the limited partnership but only to the extent that the distribution received by the partner or transferee exceeded the amount that could have been properly paid under Section 508.

(c) A general partner against which an action is commenced under subsection (a) may:

(1) implead in the action any other person that is liable under subsection (a) and compel contribution from the person; and

(2) implead in the action any person that received a distribution in violation of subsection (b) and compel contribution from the person in the amount the person received in violation of subsection (b).

(d) An action under this section is barred if it is not commenced within two years after the distribution.

Comment

Source—ULLCA Section 407. See also RMBCA Section 8.33.

In substance and effect this section protects the interests of creditors of the limited partnership. Therefore, according to Section 110(b)(13), the partnership agreement may not change this section in a way that restricts the rights of those creditors. As for a limited partnership's power to compromise a claim under this section, see Section 502(c).

Subsection (a)—This subsection refers both to Section 508, which includes in its subsection (c) a standard of ordinary care ("reasonable in the circumstances"), and to Section 408, which includes in its subsection (c) a general duty of care that is limited to "refraining from engaging in grossly negligent or reckless conduct, intentional misconduct, or a knowing violation of law."

A limited partnership's failure to meet the standard of Section 508(c) cannot by itself cause a general partner to be liable under Section 509(a). *Both* of the following would have to occur before a failure to satisfy Section 508(c) could occasion personal liability for a general partner under Section 509(a):

- the limited partnership "base[s] a determination that a distribution is not prohibited . . . on financial statements prepared on the basis of accounting practices and principles that are [not] reasonable in the circumstances or on a [not] fair valuation or other method that is [not] reasonable in the circumstances" [Section 508(c)]

AND

- the general partner's decision to rely on the improper methodology in consenting to the distribution constitutes "grossly negligent or reckless conduct, intentional misconduct, or a knowing violation of law" [Section 408(c)] or breaches some other duty under Section 408.

To serve the protective purpose of Sections 508 and 509, in this subsection "consent" must be understood as encompassing any form of approval, assent or acquiescence, whether formal or informal, express or tacit.

Subsection (d)—The subsection's limitation applies to the commencement of an action under subsection (a) or (b) and not to subsection (c), under which a general partner may implead other persons.

[ARTICLE] 6
DISSOCIATION

SECTION 601. DISSOCIATION AS LIMITED PARTNER.

(a) A person does not have a right to dissociate as a limited partner before the termination of the limited partnership.

(b) A person is dissociated from a limited partnership as a limited partner upon the occurrence of any of the following events:

(1) the limited partnership's having notice of the person's express will to withdraw as a limited partner or on a later date specified by the person;

(2) an event agreed to in the partnership agreement as causing the person's dissociation as a limited partner;

(3) the person's expulsion as a limited partner pursuant to the partnership agreement;

(4) the person's expulsion as a limited partner by the unanimous consent of the other partners if:

(A) it is unlawful to carry on the limited partnership's activities with the person as a limited partner;

(B) there has been a transfer of all of the person's transferable interest in the limited partnership, other than a transfer for security purposes, or a court order charging the person's interest, which has not been foreclosed;

(C) the person is a corporation and, within 90 days after the limited partnership notifies the person that it will be expelled as a limited partner because it has filed a certificate of dissolution or the equivalent, its charter has been revoked, or its right to conduct business has been suspended by the jurisdiction of its incorporation, there is no revocation of the certificate of dissolution or no reinstatement of its charter or its right to conduct business; or

(D) the person is a limited liability company or partnership that has been dissolved and whose business is being wound up;

(5) on application by the limited partnership, the person's expulsion as a limited partner by judicial order because:

(A) the person engaged in wrongful conduct that adversely and materially affected the limited partnership's activities;

(B) the person willfully or persistently committed a material breach of the partnership agreement or of the obligation of good faith and fair dealing under Section 305(b); or

(C) the person engaged in conduct relating to the limited partnership's activities which makes it not reasonably practicable to carry on the activities with the person as limited partner;

(6) in the case of a person who is an individual, the person's death;

(7) in the case of a person that is a trust or is acting as a limited partner by virtue of being a trustee of a trust, distribution of the trust's entire transferable interest in the limited partnership, but not merely by reason of the substitution of a successor trustee;

(8) in the case of a person that is an estate or is acting as a limited partner by virtue of being a personal representative of an estate, distribution of the estate's entire transferable interest in the limited partnership, but not merely by reason of the substitution of a successor personal representative;

(9) termination of a limited partner that is not an individual, partnership, limited liability company, corporation, trust, or estate;

(10) the limited partnership's participation in a conversion or merger under [Article] 11, if the limited partnership:

    (A) is not the converted or surviving entity; or

    (B) is the converted or surviving entity but, as a result of the conversion or merger, the person ceases to be a limited partner.

Comment

Source—RUPA Section 601.

This section adopts RUPA's dissociation provision essentially verbatim, except for provisions inappropriate to limited partners. For example, this section does not provide for the dissociation of a person as a limited partner on account of bankruptcy, insolvency or incompetency.

This Act refers to *a person's dissociation as a limited partner* rather than to the *dissociation of a limited partner*, because the same person may be both a general and a limited partner. See Section 113 (Dual Capacity). It is possible for a dual capacity partner to dissociate in one capacity and not in the other.

Subsection (a)—This section varies substantially from predecessor law. See Comment to Section 505.

Subsection (b)(1)—This provision gives a person the power to dissociate as a limited partner even though the dissociation is wrongful under subsection (a). See, however, Section 110(b)(8) (prohibiting the partnership agreement from eliminating the power of a person to dissociate as a *general* partner but imposing no comparable restriction with regard to a person's dissociation as a *limited* partner).

Subsection (b)(5)—In contrast to RUPA, this provision may be varied or even eliminated by the partnership agreement.

SECTION 602. EFFECT OF DISSOCIATION AS LIMITED PARTNER.

(a) Upon a person's dissociation as a limited partner:

    (1) subject to Section 704, the person does not have further rights as a limited partner;

    (2) the person's obligation of good faith and fair dealing as a limited partner under Section 305(b) continues only as to matters arising and events occurring before the dissociation; and

(3) subject to Section 704 and [Article] 11, any transferable interest owned by the person in the person's capacity as a limited partner immediately before dissociation is owned by the person as a mere transferee.

(b) A person's dissociation as a limited partner does not of itself discharge the person from any obligation to the limited partnership or the other partners which the person incurred while a limited partner.

Comment

Source—RUPA Section 603(b).

Subsection (a)(1)—In general, when a person dissociates as a limited partner, the person's rights as a limited partner disappear and, subject to Section 113 (Dual Status), the person's status degrades to that of a mere transferee. However, Section 704 provides some special rights when dissociation is caused by an individual's death.

Subsection (a)(3)—For any person that is both a general partner and a limited partner, the required records must state which transferable interest is owned in which capacity. Section 111(9)(C).

Article 11 provides for conversions and mergers. A plan of conversion or merger may provide for the dissociation of a person as a limited partner and may override the rule stated in this paragraph.

SECTION 603. DISSOCIATION AS GENERAL PARTNER. A person is dissociated from a limited partnership as a general partner upon the occurrence of any of the following events:

(1) the limited partnership's having notice of the person's express will to withdraw as a general partner or on a later date specified by the person;

(2) an event agreed to in the partnership agreement as causing the person's dissociation as a general partner;

(3) the person's expulsion as a general partner pursuant to the partnership agreement;

(4) the person's expulsion as a general partner by the unanimous consent of the other partners if:

(A) it is unlawful to carry on the limited partnership's activities with the person as a general partner;

(B) there has been a transfer of all or substantially all of the person's transferable interest in the limited partnership, other than a transfer for security purposes, or a court order charging the person's interest, which has not been foreclosed;

(C) the person is a corporation and, within 90 days after the limited partnership notifies the person that it will be expelled as a general partner because it has filed a certificate of dissolution or the equivalent, its charter has been revoked, or its right to conduct business has been suspended by the jurisdiction of its incorporation, there is no revocation of the certificate of dissolution or no reinstatement of its charter or its right to conduct business; or

(D) the person is a limited liability company or partnership that has been dissolved and whose business is being wound up;

(5) on application by the limited partnership, the person's expulsion as a general partner by judicial determination because:

(A) the person engaged in wrongful conduct that adversely and materially affected the limited partnership activities;

(B) the person willfully or persistently committed a material breach of the partnership agreement or of a duty owed to the partnership or the other partners under Section 408; or

(C) the person engaged in conduct relating to the limited partnership's activities which makes it not reasonably practicable to carry on the activities of the limited partnership with the person as a general partner;

(6) the person's:

(A) becoming a debtor in bankruptcy;

(B) execution of an assignment for the benefit of creditors;

(C) seeking, consenting to, or acquiescing in the appointment of a trustee, receiver, or liquidator of the person or of all or substantially all of the person's property; or

(D) failure, within 90 days after the appointment, to have vacated or stayed the appointment of a trustee, receiver, or liquidator of the general partner or of all or substantially all of the person's property obtained without the person's consent or acquiescence, or failing within 90 days after the expiration of a stay to have the appointment vacated;

(7) in the case of a person who is an individual:

(A) the person's death;

(B) the appointment of a guardian or general conservator for the person; or

(C) a judicial determination that the person has otherwise become incapable of performing the person's duties as a general partner under the partnership agreement;

(8) in the case of a person that is a trust or is acting as a general partner by virtue of being a trustee of a trust, distribution of the trust's entire transferable interest in the limited partnership, but not merely by reason of the substitution of a successor trustee;

(9) in the case of a person that is an estate or is acting as a general partner by virtue of being a personal representative of an estate, distribution of the estate's entire transferable interest in the limited partnership, but not merely by reason of the substitution of a successor personal representative;

(10) termination of a general partner that is not an individual, partnership, limited liability company, corporation, trust, or estate; or

(11) the limited partnership's participation in a conversion or merger under [Article] 11, if the limited partnership:

(A) is not the converted or surviving entity; or

(B) is the converted or surviving entity but, as a result of the conversion or merger, the person ceases to be a general partner.

Comment

Source—RUPA Section 601.

This section adopts RUPA's dissociation provision essentially verbatim. This Act refers to *a person's dissociation as a general partner* rather than to the *dissociation of a general partner*, because the same person may be both a general and a limited partner. See Section 113 (Dual Capacity). It is possible for a dual capacity partner to dissociate in one capacity and not in the other.

Paragraph (1)—The partnership agreement may not eliminate this power to dissociate. See Section 110(b)(8).

Paragraph (5)—In contrast to RUPA, this provision may be varied or even eliminated by the partnership agreement.

SECTION 604. PERSON'S POWER TO DISSOCIATE AS GENERAL PARTNER; WRONGFUL DISSOCIATION.

(a) A person has the power to dissociate as a general partner at any time, rightfully or wrongfully, by express will pursuant to Section 603(1).

(b) A person's dissociation as a general partner is wrongful only if:

(1) it is in breach of an express provision of the partnership agreement; or

(2) it occurs before the termination of the limited partnership, and:

(A) the person withdraws as a general partner by express will;

(B) the person is expelled as a general partner by judicial determination under Section 603(5);

(C) the person is dissociated as a general partner by becoming a debtor in bankruptcy; or

(D) in the case of a person that is not an individual, trust other than a business trust, or estate, the person is expelled or otherwise dissociated as a general partner because it willfully dissolved or terminated.

(c) A person that wrongfully dissociates as a general partner is liable to the limited partnership and, subject to Section 1001, to the other partners for damages caused by the dissociation. The liability is in addition to any other obligation of the general partner to the limited partnership or to the other partners.

Comment

Source—RUPA Section 602.

Subsection (a)—The partnership agreement may not eliminate this power. See Section 110(b)(8).

Subsection (b)(1)—The reference to "an express provision of the partnership agreement" means that a person's dissociation as a general partner in breach of the obligation of good faith and fair dealing is not wrongful dissociation for the purposes of this section. The breach might be actionable on other grounds.

Subsection (b)(2)—The reference to "before the termination of the limited partnership" reflects the expectation that each general partner will shepherd the limited partnership through winding up. See Comment to Section 406(f). A person's obligation to remain as general partner through winding up continues even if another general partner dissociates and even if that dissociation leads to the limited partnership's premature dissolution under Section 801(3)(A).

Subsection (c)—The language "subject to Section 1001" is intended to preserve the distinction between direct and derivative claims.

SECTION 605. EFFECT OF DISSOCIATION AS GENERAL PARTNER.

(a) Upon a person's dissociation as a general partner:

(1) the person's right to participate as a general partner in the management and conduct of the partnership's activities terminates;

(2) the person's duty of loyalty as a general partner under Section 408(b)(3) terminates;

(3) the person's duty of loyalty as a general partner under Section 408(b)(1) and (2) and duty of care under Section 408(c) continue only with regard to matters arising and events occurring before the person's dissociation as a general partner;

(4) the person may sign and deliver to the [Secretary of State] for filing a statement of dissociation pertaining to the person and, at the request of the limited partnership, shall sign an amendment to the certificate of limited partnership which states that the person has dissociated; and

(5) subject to Section 704 and [Article] 11, any transferable interest owned by the person immediately before dissociation in the person's capacity as a general partner is owned by the person as a mere transferee.

(b) A person's dissociation as a general partner does not of itself discharge the person from any obligation to the limited partnership or the other partners which the person incurred while a general partner.

Comment

Source—RUPA Section 603(b).

Subsection (a)(1)—Once a person dissociates as a general partner, the person loses all management rights as a general partner regardless of what happens to the limited partnership. This rule contrasts with RUPA Section 603(b)(1), which permits a dissociated general partner to participate in winding up in some circumstances.

Subsection (a)(4)—Both records covered by this paragraph have the same effect under Section 103(d)—namely, to give constructive notice that the person has dissociated as a general partner. The notice benefits the person by curtailing any further personal liability under Sections 607, 805, and 1111. The notice benefits the limited partnership by curtailing any lingering power to bind under Sections 606, 804, and 1112.

The limited partnership is in any event obligated to amend its certificate of limited partnership to reflect the dissociation of a person as general partner. See Section 202(b)(2). In most circumstances, the amendment requires the signature of the person that has dissociated. Section 204(a)(5)(C). If that signature is required and the person refuses or fails to sign, the limited partnership may invoke Section 205 (Signing and Filing Pursuant to Judicial Order).

Subsection (a)(5)—In general, when a person dissociates as a general partner, the person's rights as a general partner disappear and, subject to Section 113 (Dual Status), the person's status degrades to that of a mere transferee. For any person that is both a general partner and a limited partner, the required records must state which transferable interest is owned in which capacity. Section 111(9)(C).

Section 704 provides some special rights when an individual dissociates by dying. Article 11 provides for conversions and mergers. A plan of conversion or merger may provide for the dissociation of a person as a general partner and may override the rule stated in this paragraph.

SECTION 606. POWER TO BIND AND LIABILITY TO LIMITED PARTNERSHIP BEFORE DISSOLUTION OF PARTNERSHIP OF PERSON DISSOCIATED AS GENERAL PARTNER.

(a) After a person is dissociated as a general partner and before the limited partnership is dissolved, converted under [Article] 11, or merged out of existence under [Article 11], the limited partnership is bound by an act of the person only if:

(1) the act would have bound the limited partnership under Section 402 before the dissociation; and

(2) at the time the other party enters into the transaction:

(A) less than two years has passed since the dissociation; and

(B) the other party does not have notice of the dissociation and reasonably believes that the person is a general partner.

(b) If a limited partnership is bound under subsection (a), the person dissociated as a general partner which caused the limited partnership to be bound is liable:

(1) to the limited partnership for any damage caused to the limited partnership arising from the obligation incurred under subsection (a); and

(2) if a general partner or another person dissociated as a general partner is liable for the obligation, to the general partner or other person for any damage caused to the general partner or other person arising from the liability.

Comment

Source—RUPA Section 702.

This Act contains three sections pertaining to the lingering power to bind of a person dissociated as a general partner:

- this section, which applies until the limited partnership dissolves, converts to another form of organization under Article 11, or is merged out of existence under Article 11;
- Section 804(b), which applies after a limited partnership dissolves; and
- Section 1112(b), which applies after a conversion or merger.

Subsection (a)(2)(B)—A person might have notice under Section 103(d)(1) as well as under Section 103(b).

Subsection (b)—The liability provided by this subsection is not exhaustive. For example, if a person dissociated as a general partner causes a limited partnership to be bound under subsection (a) and, due to a guaranty, some other person is liable on the resulting obligation, that other person may have a claim under other law against the person dissociated as a general partner.

SECTION 607. LIABILITY TO OTHER PERSONS OF PERSON DISSOCIATED AS GENERAL PARTNER.

(a) A person's dissociation as a general partner does not of itself discharge the person's liability as a general partner for an obligation of the limited partnership incurred before dissociation. Except as otherwise provided in subsections (b) and (c), the person is not liable for a limited partnership's obligation incurred after dissociation.

(b) A person whose dissociation as a general partner resulted in a dissolution and winding up of the limited partnership's activities is liable to the same extent as a general partner under Section 404 on an obligation incurred by the limited partnership under Section 804.

(c) A person that has dissociated as a general partner but whose dissociation did not result in a dissolution and winding up of the limited partnership's activities is liable on a transaction entered into by the limited partnership after the dissociation only if:

(1) a general partner would be liable on the transaction; and

(2) at the time the other party enters into the transaction:

(A) less than two years has passed since the dissociation; and

(B) the other party does not have notice of the dissociation and reasonably believes that the person is a general partner.

(d) By agreement with a creditor of a limited partnership and the limited partnership, a person dissociated as a general partner may be released from liability for an obligation of the limited partnership.

(e) A person dissociated as a general partner is released from liability for an obligation of the limited partnership if the limited partnership's creditor, with notice of the person's dissociation as a general partner but without the person's consent, agrees to a material alteration in the nature or time of payment of the obligation.

Comment

Source—RUPA Section 703.

A person's dissociation as a general partner does not categorically prevent the person from being liable as a general partner for subsequently incurred obligations of the limited partnership. If the dissociation results in dissolution, subsection (b) applies and the person will be liable as a general partner on any partnership obligation incurred under Section 804. In these circumstances, neither filing a statement of dissociation nor amending the certificate of limited partnership to state that the person has dissociated as a general partner will curtail the person's lingering exposure to liability.

If the dissociation does not result in dissolution, subsection (c) applies. In this context, filing a statement of dissociation or amending the certificate of limited partnership to state that the person has dissociated as a general partner will curtail the person's lingering liability. See subsection (c)(2)(B).

If the limited partnership subsequently dissolves as the result of some other occurrence (i.e., not a result of the person's dissociation as a general partner), subsection (c) continues to apply. In that situation, Section 804 will determine whether, for the purposes of subsection (c), the limited partnership has entered into a transaction after dissolution.

If the limited partnership is a limited liability limited partnership, these liability rules are moot.

Subsection (a)—The phrase "liability as a general partner for an obligation of the limited partnership" refers to liability under Section 404. Following RUPA and the UPA, this Act leaves to other law the question of when a limited partnership obligation is incurred.

Subsection (c)(2)(B)—A person might have notice under Section 103(d)(1) as well as under Section 103(b).

[ARTICLE] 7
TRANSFERABLE INTERESTS AND RIGHTS
OF TRANSFEREES AND CREDITORS

SECTION 701. PARTNER'S TRANSFERABLE INTEREST. The only interest of a partner which is transferable is the partner's transferable interest. A transferable interest is personal property.

Comment

Source—RUPA Section 502.

Like all other partnership statutes, this Act dichotomizes each partner's rights into economic rights and other rights. The former are freely transferable, as provided in Section 702. The latter are not transferable at all, unless the partnership agreement so provides.

Although a partner or transferee owns a transferable interest as a present right, that right only entitles the owner to distributions if and when made. See Sections 504 (subject to any contrary provision in the partnership agreement, no right to interim distribution unless the limited partnership decides to make an interim distribution) and the Comment to Section 812 (subject to any contrary provision in the partnership agreement, no partner obligated to contribute for the purpose of equalizing or otherwise allocating capital losses).

SECTION 702. TRANSFER OF PARTNER'S TRANSFERABLE INTEREST.

(a) A transfer, in whole or in part, of a partner's transferable interest:

(1) is permissible;

(2) does not by itself cause the partner's dissociation or a dissolution and winding up of the limited partnership's activities; and

(3) does not, as against the other partners or the limited partnership, entitle the transferee to participate in the management or conduct of the limited partnership's activities, to require access to information concerning the limited partnership's transactions except as otherwise provided in subsection (c), or to inspect or copy the required information or the limited partnership's other records.

(b) A transferee has a right to receive, in accordance with the transfer:

(1) distributions to which the transferor would otherwise be entitled; and

(2) upon the dissolution and winding up of the limited partnership's activities the net amount otherwise distributable to the transferor.

(c) In a dissolution and winding up, a transferee is entitled to an account of the limited partnership's transactions only from the date of dissolution.

(d) Upon transfer, the transferor retains the rights of a partner other than the interest in distributions transferred and retains all duties and obligations of a partner.

(e) A limited partnership need not give effect to a transferee's rights under this section until the limited partnership has notice of the transfer.

(f) A transfer of a partner's transferable interest in the limited partnership in violation of a restriction on transfer contained in the partnership agreement is ineffective as to a person having notice of the restriction at the time of transfer.

(g) A transferee that becomes a partner with respect to a transferable interest is liable for the transferor's obligations under Sections 502 and 509. However, the transferee is not obligated for liabilities unknown to the transferee at the time the transferee became a partner.

Comment

Source—RUPA Section 503, except for subsection (g), which derives from RULPA Section 704(b). Following RUPA, this Act uses the words "transfer" and "transferee" rather than the words "assignment" and "assignee." See RUPA Section 503.

Subsection (a)(2)—The phrase "by itself" is significant. A transfer of all of a person's transferable interest could lead to dissociation via expulsion, Sections 601(b)(4)(B) and 603(4)(B).

Subsection (a)(3)—Mere transferees have no right to intrude as the partners carry on their activities as partners. Moreover, a partner's obligation of good faith and fair dealing under Sections 305(b) and 408(d) is framed in reference to "the limited partnership and the other partners." See also Comment to Section 1102(b)(3) and Comment to Section 1106(b)(3).

SECTION 703. RIGHTS OF CREDITOR OF PARTNER OR TRANSFEREE.

(a) On application to a court of competent jurisdiction by any judgment creditor of a partner or transferee, the court may charge the transferable interest of the judgment debtor with payment of the unsatisfied amount of the judgment with interest. To the extent so charged, the judgment creditor has only the rights of a transferee. The court may appoint a receiver of the share of the distributions due or to become due to the judgment debtor in respect of the partnership and make all other orders, directions, accounts, and inquiries the judgment debtor might have made or which the circumstances of the case may require to give effect to the charging order.

(b) A charging order constitutes a lien on the judgment debtor's transferable interest. The court may order a foreclosure upon the interest subject to the charging order at any time. The purchaser at the foreclosure sale has the rights of a transferee.

(c) At any time before foreclosure, an interest charged may be redeemed:

(1) by the judgment debtor;

(2) with property other than limited partnership property, by one or more of the other partners; or

(3) with limited partnership property, by the limited partnership with the consent of all partners whose interests are not so charged.

(d) This [Act] does not deprive any partner or transferee of the benefit of any exemption laws applicable to the partner's or transferee's transferable interest.

(e) This section provides the exclusive remedy by which a judgment creditor of a partner or transferee may satisfy a judgment out of the judgment debtor's transferable interest.

Comment

Source—RUPA Section 504 and ULLCA Section 504.

This section balances the needs of a judgment creditor of a partner or transferee with the needs of the limited partnership and non-debtor partners and transferees. The section achieves that balance by allowing the judgment creditor to collect on the judgment through the transferable interest of the judgment debtor while prohibiting interference in the management and activities of the limited partnership.

Under this section, the judgment creditor of a partner or transferee is entitled to a charging order against the relevant transferable interest. While in effect, that order entitles the judgment creditor to whatever distributions would otherwise be due to the partner or transferee whose interest is subject to the order. The creditor has no say in the timing or amount of those distributions. The charging order does not entitle the creditor to accelerate any distributions or to otherwise interfere with the management and activities of the limited partnership.

Foreclosure of a charging order effects a permanent transfer of the charged transferable interest to the purchaser. The foreclosure does not, however, create any rights to participate in the management and conduct of the limited partnership's activities. The purchaser obtains nothing more than the status of a transferee.

Subsection (a)—The court's power to appoint a receiver and "make all other orders, directions, accounts, and inquiries the judgment debtor might have made or which the circumstances of the case may require" must be understood in the context of the balance described above. In particular, the court's power to make orders "which the circumstances may require" is limited to "giv[ing] effect to the charging order."

Example: A judgment creditor with a charging order believes that the limited partnership should invest less of its surplus in operations, leaving more funds for distributions. The creditor moves the court for an order directing the general partners to restrict re-investment. This section does not authorize the court to grant the motion.

Example: A judgment creditor with a judgment for $10,000 against a partner obtains a charging order against the partner's transferable interest. The limited partnership is duly served with the order. However, the limited partnership subsequently fails to comply with the order and makes a $3000 distribution to the partner. The court has the power to order the limited partnership to turn over $3000 to the judgment creditor to "give effect to the charging order."

The court also has the power to decide whether a particular payment is a distribution, because this decision determines whether the payment is part of a transferable interest subject to a charging order. (To the extent a payment is not a distribution, it is not part of the transferable interest and is not subject to subsection (e). The payment is therefore subject to whatever other creditor remedies may apply.)

Subsection (c)(3)—This provision requires the consent of all the limited as well as general partners.

SECTION 704. POWER OF ESTATE OF DECEASED PARTNER. If a partner dies, the deceased partner's personal representative or other legal representative may exercise the rights of a transferee as provided in Section 702 and, for the purposes of settling the estate, may exercise the rights of a current limited partner under Section 304.

Comment

Section 702 strictly limits the rights of transferees. In particular, a transferee has no right to participate in management in any way, no voting rights and, except following dissolution, no information rights. Even after dissolution, a transferee's information rights are limited. See Section 702(c).

This section provides special informational rights for a deceased partner's legal representative for the purposes of settling the estate. For those purposes, the legal representative may exercise the informational rights of a current limited partner under Section 304. Those rights are of course subject to the limitations and obligations stated in that section—*e.g.*, Section 304(g) (restrictions on use) and (h) (charges for copies)—as well as any generally applicable limitations stated in the partnership agreement.

[ARTICLE] 8
DISSOLUTION

SECTION 801. NONJUDICIAL DISSOLUTION. Except as otherwise provided in Section 802, a limited partnership is dissolved, and its activities must be wound up, only upon the occurrence of any of the following:

(1) the happening of an event specified in the partnership agreement;

(2) the consent of all general partners and of limited partners owning a majority of the rights to receive distributions as limited partners at the time the consent is to be effective;

(3) after the dissociation of a person as a general partner:

(A) if the limited partnership has at least one remaining general partner, the consent to dissolve the limited partnership given within 90 days after the dissociation by partners owning a majority of the rights to receive distributions as partners at the time the consent is to be effective; or

(B) if the limited partnership does not have a remaining general partner, the passage of 90 days after the dissociation, unless before the end of the period:

(i) consent to continue the activities of the limited partnership and admit at least one general partner is given by limited partners owning a majority of the rights to receive distributions as limited partners at the time the consent is to be effective; and

(ii) at least one person is admitted as a general partner in accordance with the consent;

(4) the passage of 90 days after the dissociation of the limited partnership's last limited partner, unless before the end of the period the limited partnership admits at least one limited partner; or

(5) the signing and filing of a declaration of dissolution by the [Secretary of State] under Section 809(c).

Comment

This Act does not require that any of the consents referred to in this section be given in the form of a signed record. The partnership agreement has the power to impose that requirement. See Comment to Section 110.

In several provisions, this section provides for consent in terms of rights to receive distributions. Distribution rights of non-partner transferees are not relevant. Mere transferees have no consent rights, and their distribution rights are not counted in determining whether majority consent has been obtained.

Paragraph (1)—There is no requirement that the relevant provision of the partnership agreement be made in a record, unless the partnership agreement creates that requirement. However, if the relevant provision is not "contained in a partnership agreement made in a record," Section 111(9)(D) includes among the limited partnership's required information "a record stating . . . any events upon the happening of which the limited partnership is to be dissolved and its activities wound up."

Paragraph (2)—Rights to receive distributions owned by a person that is both a general and a limited partner figure into the limited partner determination only to the extent those rights are owned in the person's capacity as a limited partner. See Section 111(9)(C).

Example: XYZ is a limited partnership with three general partners, each of whom is also a limited partner, and 5 other limited partners. Rights to receive distributions are allocated as follows:

Partner #1 as general partner—3%
Partner #2 as general partner—2%
Partner #3 as general partner—1%
Partner #1 as limited partner—7%
Partner #2 as limited partner—3%
Partner #3 as limited partner—4%
Partner #4 as limited partner—5%
Partner #5 as limited partner—5%
Partner #6 as limited partner—5%
Partner #7 as limited partner—5%
Partner #8 as limited partner—5%
Several non-partner transferees, in the aggregate—55%

Distribution rights owned by persons as limited partners amount to 39% of total distribution rights. A majority is therefore anything greater than 19.5%. If only Partners 1, 2, 3 and 4 consent to dissolve, the limited partnership is not dissolved. Together these partners own as limited partners 19% of the distribution rights owned by persons as limited partners—just short of the necessary majority. For purposes of this calculation, distribution rights owned by non-partner transferees are irrelevant. So, too, are distribution rights owned by persons as general partners. (However, dissolution under this provision requires "the consent of all general partners.")

Paragraph (3)(A)—Unlike paragraph (2), this paragraph makes no distinction between distribution rights owned by persons as general partners and distribution rights owned by persons as limited partners. Distribution rights owned by non-partner transferees are irrelevant.

SECTION 802. JUDICIAL DISSOLUTION. On application by a partner the [appropriate court] may order dissolution of a limited partnership if it is not reasonably practicable to carry on the activities of the limited partnership in conformity with the partnership agreement.

Comment

Source—RULPA Section 802.

Section 110(b)(9) limits the power of the partnership agreement with regard to this section.

SECTION 803. WINDING UP.

(a) A limited partnership continues after dissolution only for the purpose of winding up its activities.

(b) In winding up its activities, the limited partnership:

(1) may amend its certificate of limited partnership to state that the limited partnership is dissolved, preserve the limited partnership business or property as a going concern for a reasonable time, prosecute and defend actions and proceedings, whether civil, criminal, or administrative, transfer the limited partnership's property, settle disputes by mediation or arbitration, file a statement of termination as provided in Section 203, and perform other necessary acts; and

(2) shall discharge the limited partnership's liabilities, settle and close the limited partnership's activities, and marshal and distribute the assets of the partnership.

(c) If a dissolved limited partnership does not have a general partner, a person to wind up the dissolved limited partnership's activities may be appointed by the consent of limited partners owning a majority of the rights to receive distributions as limited partners at the time the consent is to be effective. A person appointed under this subsection:

(1) has the powers of a general partner under Section 804; and

(2) shall promptly amend the certificate of limited partnership to state:

(A) that the limited partnership does not have a general partner;

(B) the name of the person that has been appointed to wind up the limited partnership; and

(C) the street and mailing address of the person.

(d) On the application of any partner, the [appropriate court] may order judicial supervision of the winding up, including the appointment of a person to wind up the dissolved limited partnership's activities, if:

(1) a limited partnership does not have a general partner and within a reasonable time following the dissolution no person has been appointed pursuant to subsection (c); or

(2) the applicant establishes other good cause.

Comment

Source—RUPA Sections 802 and 803.

Subsection (b)(2)—A limited partnership may satisfy its duty to "discharge" a liability either by paying or by making an alternative arrangement satisfactory to the creditor.

Subsection (c)—The method for determining majority consent is analogous to the method applicable under Section 801(2). See the Comment to that paragraph.

A person appointed under this subsection is **not** a general partner and therefore is not subject to Section 408.

SECTION 804. POWER OF GENERAL PARTNER AND PERSON DISSOCIATED AS GENERAL PARTNER TO BIND PARTNERSHIP AFTER DISSOLUTION.

(a) A limited partnership is bound by a general partner's act after dissolution which:

(1) is appropriate for winding up the limited partnership's activities; or

(2) would have bound the limited partnership under Section 402 before dissolution, if, at the time the other party enters into the transaction, the other party does not have notice of the dissolution.

(b) A person dissociated as a general partner binds a limited partnership through an act occurring after dissolution if:

(1) at the time the other party enters into the transaction:

(A) less than two years has passed since the dissociation; and

(B) the other party does not have notice of the dissociation and reasonably believes that the person is a general partner; and

(2) the act:

(A) is appropriate for winding up the limited partnership's activities; or

(B) would have bound the limited partnership under Section 402 before dissolution and at the time the other party enters into the transaction the other party does not have notice of the dissolution.

Comment

Subsection (a)—Source: RUPA Section 804.

Subsection (a)(2)—A person might have notice under Section 103(d)(2) (amendment of certificate of limited partnership to indicate dissolution) as well as under Section 103(b).

Subsection (b)—This subsection deals with the post-dissolution power to bind of a person dissociated as a general partner. Paragraph (1) replicates the provisions of Section 606, pertaining to the pre-dissolution power to bind of a person dissociated as a general partner. Paragraph (2) replicates the provisions of subsection (a), which state the post-dissolution power to bind of a general partner. For a person dissociated as a general partner to bind a dissolved limited partnership, the person's act will have to satisfy both paragraph (1) and paragraph (2).

Subsection (b)(1)(B)—A person might have notice under Section 103(d)(1) as well as under Section 103(b).

Subsection (b)(2)(B)—A person might have notice under Section 103(d)(2) (amendment of certificate of limited partnership to indicate dissolution) as well as under Section 103(b).

SECTION 805. LIABILITY AFTER DISSOLUTION OF GENERAL PARTNER AND PERSON DISSOCIATED AS GENERAL PARTNER TO LIMITED PARTNERSHIP, OTHER GENERAL PARTNERS, AND PERSONS DISSOCIATED AS GENERAL PARTNER.

(a) If a general partner having knowledge of the dissolution causes a limited partnership to incur an obligation under Section 804(a) by an act that is not appropriate for winding up the partnership's activities, the general partner is liable:

    (1) to the limited partnership for any damage caused to the limited partnership arising from the obligation; and

    (2) if another general partner or a person dissociated as a general partner is liable for the obligation, to that other general partner or person for any damage caused to that other general partner or person arising from the liability.

(b) If a person dissociated as a general partner causes a limited partnership to incur an obligation under Section 804(b), the person is liable:

    (1) to the limited partnership for any damage caused to the limited partnership arising from the obligation; and

(2) if a general partner or another person dissociated as a general partner is liable for the obligation, to the general partner or other person for any damage caused to the general partner or other person arising from the liability.

Comment

Source—RUPA Section 806.

It is possible for more than one person to be liable under this section on account of the same limited partnership obligation. This Act does not provide any rule for apportioning liability in that circumstance.

Subsection (a)(2)—If the limited partnership is not a limited liability limited partnership, the liability created by this paragraph includes liability under Sections 404(a), 607(b), and 607(c). The paragraph also applies when a partner or person dissociated as a general partner suffers damage due to a contract of guaranty.

SECTION 806. KNOWN CLAIMS AGAINST DISSOLVED LIMITED PARTNERSHIP.

(a) A dissolved limited partnership may dispose of the known claims against it by following the procedure described in subsection (b).

(b) A dissolved limited partnership may notify its known claimants of the dissolution in a record. The notice must:

(1) specify the information required to be included in a claim;

(2) provide a mailing address to which the claim is to be sent;

(3) state the deadline for receipt of the claim, which may not be less than 120 days after the date the notice is received by the claimant;

(4) state that the claim will be barred if not received by the deadline; and

(5) unless the limited partnership has been throughout its existence a limited liability limited partnership, state that the barring of a claim against the limited partnership will also bar any corresponding claim against any general partner or person dissociated as a general partner which is based on Section 404.

(c) A claim against a dissolved limited partnership is barred if the requirements of subsection (b) are met and:

(1) the claim is not received by the specified deadline; or

(2) in the case of a claim that is timely received but rejected by the dissolved limited partnership, the claimant does not commence an action to enforce the claim against the limited partnership within 90 days after the receipt of the notice of the rejection.

(d) This section does not apply to a claim based on an event occurring after the effective date of dissolution or a liability that is contingent on that date.

Comment

Source—ULLCA Section 807. See also RMBCA Section 14.06.

Paragraph (b)(5)—If the limited partnership has always been a limited liability limited partnership, there can be no liability under Section 404 for any general partner or person dissociated as a general partner.

SECTION 807. OTHER CLAIMS AGAINST DISSOLVED LIMITED PARTNERSHIP.

(a) A dissolved limited partnership may publish notice of its dissolution and request persons having claims against the limited partnership to present them in accordance with the notice.

(b) The notice must:

(1) be published at least once in a newspaper of general circulation in the [county] in which the dissolved limited partnership's principal office is located or, if it has none in this State, in the [county] in which the limited partnership's designated office is or was last located;

(2) describe the information required to be contained in a claim and provide a mailing address to which the claim is to be sent;

(3) state that a claim against the limited partnership is barred unless an action to enforce the claim is commenced within five years after publication of the notice; and

(4) unless the limited partnership has been throughout its existence a limited liability limited partnership, state that the barring of a claim against the limited partnership will also bar any corresponding claim against any general partner or person dissociated as a general partner which is based on Section 404.

(c) If a dissolved limited partnership publishes a notice in accordance with subsection (b), the claim of each of the following claimants is barred unless the claimant commences an action to enforce the claim against the dissolved limited partnership within five years after the publication date of the notice:

(1) a claimant that did not receive notice in a record under Section 806;

(2) a claimant whose claim was timely sent to the dissolved limited partnership but not acted on; and

(3) a claimant whose claim is contingent or based on an event occurring after the effective date of dissolution.

(d) A claim not barred under this section may be enforced:

(1) against the dissolved limited partnership, to the extent of its undistributed assets;

(2) if the assets have been distributed in liquidation, against a partner or transferee to the extent of that person's proportionate share of the claim or the limited partnership's assets distributed to the partner or transferee in liquidation, whichever is less, but a person's total liability for all claims under this paragraph does not exceed the total amount of assets distributed to the person as part of the winding up of the dissolved limited partnership; or

(3) against any person liable on the claim under Section 404.

Comment

Source—ULLCA Section 808. See also RMBCA Section 14.07.

Paragraph (b)(4)—If the limited partnership has always been a limited liability limited partnership, there can be no liability under Section 404 for any general partner or person dissociated as a general partner.

SECTION 808. LIABILITY OF GENERAL PARTNER AND PERSON DISSOCIATED AS GENERAL PARTNER WHEN CLAIM AGAINST LIMITED PARTNERSHIP BARRED. If a claim against a dissolved limited partnership is barred under Section 806 or 807, any corresponding claim under Section 404 is also barred.

Comment

The liability under Section 404 of a general partner or person dissociated as a general partner is merely liability for the obligations of the limited partnership.

SECTION 809. ADMINISTRATIVE DISSOLUTION.

(a) The [Secretary of State] may dissolve a limited partnership administratively if the limited partnership does not, within 60 days after the due date:

(1) pay any fee, tax, or penalty due to the [Secretary of State] under this [Act] or other law; or

(2) deliver its annual report to the [Secretary of State].

(b) If the [Secretary of State] determines that a ground exists for administratively dissolving a limited partnership, the [Secretary of State] shall file a record of the determination and serve the limited partnership with a copy of the filed record.

(c) If within 60 days after service of the copy the limited partnership does not correct each ground for dissolution or demonstrate to the reasonable satisfaction of the [Secretary of State] that each ground determined by the [Secretary of State] does not exist, the [Secretary of State] shall administratively dissolve the limited partnership by preparing, signing and filing a declaration of dissolution that states the grounds for dissolution. The [Secretary of State] shall serve the limited partnership with a copy of the filed declaration.

(d) A limited partnership administratively dissolved continues its existence but may carry on only activities necessary to wind up its activities and liquidate its assets under Sections 803 and 812 and to notify claimants under Sections 806 and 807.

(e) The administrative dissolution of a limited partnership does not terminate the authority of its agent for service of process.

Comment

Source—ULLCA Sections 809 and 810. See also RMBCA Sections 14.20 and 14.21.

Subsection (a)(1)—This provision refers solely to money due the specified filing officer and does not apply to other money due to the State.

Subsection (c)—The filing of a declaration of dissolution does not provide notice under Section 103(d).

SECTION 810. REINSTATEMENT FOLLOWING ADMINISTRATIVE DISSOLUTION.

(a) A limited partnership that has been administratively dissolved may apply to the [Secretary of State] for reinstatement within two years after the effective date of dissolution. The application must be delivered to the [Secretary of State] for filing and state:

(1) the name of the limited partnership and the effective date of its administrative dissolution;

(2) that the grounds for dissolution either did not exist or have been eliminated; and

(3) that the limited partnership's name satisfies the requirements of Section 108.

(b) If the [Secretary of State] determines that an application contains the information required by subsection (a) and that the information is correct, the [Secretary of State] shall prepare a declaration of reinstatement that states this determination, sign, and file the original of the declaration of reinstatement, and serve the limited partnership with a copy.

(c) When reinstatement becomes effective, it relates back to and takes effect as of the effective date of the administrative dissolution and the limited partnership may resume its activities as if the administrative dissolution had never occurred.

Comment

Source—ULLCA Section 811. See also RMBCA Section 14.22.

SECTION 811. APPEAL FROM DENIAL OF REINSTATEMENT.

(a) If the [Secretary of State] denies a limited partnership's application for reinstatement following administrative dissolution, the [Secretary of State] shall prepare, sign and file a notice that explains the reason or reasons for denial and serve the limited partnership with a copy of the notice.

(b) Within 30 days after service of the notice of denial, the limited partnership may appeal from the denial of reinstatement by petitioning the [appropriate court] to set aside the dissolution. The petition must be served on the [Secretary of State] and contain a copy of the [Secretary of State's] declaration of dissolution, the limited partnership's application for reinstatement, and the [Secretary of State's] notice of denial.

(c) The court may summarily order the [Secretary of State] to reinstate the dissolved limited partnership or may take other action the court considers appropriate.

Comment

Source—ULLCA Section 812.

SECTION 812. DISPOSITION OF ASSETS; WHEN CONTRIBUTIONS REQUIRED.

(a) In winding up a limited partnership's activities, the assets of the limited partnership, including the contributions required by this section, must be applied to satisfy the limited partnership's obligations to creditors, including, to the extent permitted by law, partners that are creditors.

(b) Any surplus remaining after the limited partnership complies with subsection (a) must be paid in cash as a distribution.

(c) If a limited partnership's assets are insufficient to satisfy all of its obligations under subsection (a), with respect to each unsatisfied obligation incurred when the limited partnership was not a limited liability limited partnership, the following rules apply:

(1) Each person that was a general partner when the obligation was incurred and that has not been released from the obligation under Section 607 shall contribute to the limited partnership for the purpose of enabling the limited partnership to satisfy the obligation. The contribution due from each of those persons is in proportion to the right to receive distributions in the capacity of general partner in effect for each of those persons when the obligation was incurred.

(2) If a person does not contribute the full amount required under paragraph (1) with respect to an unsatisfied obligation of the limited partnership, the other persons required to contribute by paragraph (1) on account of the obligation shall contribute the additional amount necessary to discharge the obligation. The additional contribution due from each of those other persons is in proportion to the right to receive distributions in the capacity of general partner in effect for each of those other persons when the obligation was incurred.

(3) If a person does not make the additional contribution required by paragraph (2), further additional contributions are determined and due in the same manner as provided in that paragraph.

(d) A person that makes an additional contribution under subsection (c)(2) or (3) may recover from any person whose failure to contribute under subsection (c)(1) or (2) necessitated the additional contribution. A person may not recover under this subsection more than the amount additionally contributed. A person's liability under this subsection may not exceed the amount the person failed to contribute.

(e) The estate of a deceased individual is liable for the person's obligations under this section.

(f) An assignee for the benefit of creditors of a limited partnership or a partner, or a person appointed by a court to represent creditors of a limited partnership or a partner, may enforce a person's obligation to contribute under subsection (c).

Comment

In some circumstances, this Act requires a partner to make payments to the limited partnership. See, e.g., Sections 502(b), 509(a), 509(b), and 812(c). In other circumstances, this Act requires a partner to make payments to other partners. See, e.g., Sections 509(c) and 812(d). In no circumstances does this Act require a partner to make a payment for the purpose of equalizing or otherwise reallocating capital losses incurred by partners.

Example: XYZ Limited Partnership ("XYZ") has one general partner and four limited partners. According to XYZ's required information, the value of each partner's contributions to XYZ are:

General partner—$5,000
Limited partner #1—$10,000
Limited partner #2—$15,000
Limited partner #3—$20,000
Limited partner #4—$25,000

XYZ is unsuccessful and eventually dissolves without ever having made a distribution to its partners. XYZ lacks any assets with which to return to the partners the value of their respective contributions. No partner is obliged to make any payment either to the limited partnership or to fellow partners to adjust these capital losses. These losses are not part of "the limited partnership's obligations to creditors." Section 812(a).

Example: Same facts, except that Limited Partner #4 loaned $25,000 to XYZ when XYZ was not a limited liability limited partnership, and XYZ lacks the assets to repay the loan. The general partner must contribute to the limited partnership whatever funds are necessary to enable XYZ to satisfy the obligation owned to Limited Partner #4 on account of the loan. Section 812(a) and (c).

Subsection (c)—Following RUPA and the UPA, this Act leaves to other law the question of when a limited partnership obligation is incurred.

[ARTICLE] 9
FOREIGN LIMITED PARTNERSHIPS

SECTION 901. GOVERNING LAW.
(a) The laws of the State or other jurisdiction under which a foreign limited partnership is organized govern relations among the partners of the foreign limited partnership and between the partners and the foreign limited partnership and the liability of partners as partners for an obligation of the foreign limited partnership.

(b) A foreign limited partnership may not be denied a certificate of authority by reason of any difference between the laws of the jurisdiction under which the foreign limited partnership is organized and the laws of this State.

(c) A certificate of authority does not authorize a foreign limited partnership to engage in any business or exercise any power that a limited partnership may not engage in or exercise in this State.

Comment

Source—ULLCA Section 1001 for subsections (b) and (c).

Subsection (a)—This subsection parallels and is analogous in scope and effect to Section 106 (choice of law for domestic limited partnerships).

SECTION 902. APPLICATION FOR CERTIFICATE OF AUTHORITY.

(a) A foreign limited partnership may apply for a certificate of authority to transact business in this State by delivering an application to the [Secretary of State] for filing. The application must state:

(1) the name of the foreign limited partnership and, if the name does not comply with Section 108, an alternate name adopted pursuant to Section 905(a).

(2) the name of the State or other jurisdiction under whose law the foreign limited partnership is organized;

(3) the street and mailing address of the foreign limited partnership's principal office and, if the laws of the jurisdiction under which the foreign limited partnership is organized require the foreign limited partnership to maintain an office in that jurisdiction, the street and mailing address of the required office;

(4) the name and street and mailing address of the foreign limited partnership's initial agent for service of process in this State;

(5) the name and street and mailing address of each of the foreign limited partnership's general partners; and

(6) whether the foreign limited partnership is a foreign limited liability limited partnership.

(b) A foreign limited partnership shall deliver with the completed application a certificate of existence or a record of similar import signed by the [Secretary of State] or other official having custody of the foreign limited partnership's publicly filed records in the State or other jurisdiction under whose law the foreign limited partnership is organized.

Comment

Source—ULLCA Section 1002.

A certificate of authority applied for under this section is different than a certificate of authorization furnished under Section 209.

SECTION 903. ACTIVITIES NOT CONSTITUTING TRANSACTING BUSINESS.

(a) Activities of a foreign limited partnership which do not constitute transacting business in this State within the meaning of this [article] include:

(1) maintaining, defending, and settling an action or proceeding;

(2) holding meetings of its partners or carrying on any other activity concerning its internal affairs;

(3) maintaining accounts in financial institutions;

(4) maintaining offices or agencies for the transfer, exchange, and registration of the foreign limited partnership's own securities or maintaining trustees or depositories with respect to those securities;

(5) selling through independent contractors;

(6) soliciting or obtaining orders, whether by mail or electronic means or through employees or agents or otherwise, if the orders require acceptance outside this State before they become contracts;

(7) creating or acquiring indebtedness, mortgages, or security interests in real or personal property;

(8) securing or collecting debts or enforcing mortgages or other security interests in property securing the debts, and holding, protecting, and maintaining property so acquired;

(9) conducting an isolated transaction that is completed within 30 days and is not one in the course of similar transactions of a like manner; and

(10) transacting business in interstate commerce.

(b) For purposes of this [article], the ownership in this State of income-producing real property or tangible personal property, other than property excluded under subsection (a), constitutes transacting business in this State.

(c) This section does not apply in determining the contacts or activities that may subject a foreign limited partnership to service of process, taxation, or regulation under any other law of this State.

Comment

Source—ULLCA Section 1003.

SECTION 904. FILING OF CERTIFICATE OF AUTHORITY. Unless the [Secretary of State] determines that an application for a certificate of authority does not comply with the filing requirements of this [Act], the [Secretary of State], upon payment of all filing fees, shall file the application, prepare, sign and file a certificate of authority to transact business in this State, and send a copy of the filed certificate, together with a receipt for the fees, to the foreign limited partnership or its representative.

Comment

Source—ULLCA Section 1004 and RULPA Section 903.

A certificate of authority filed under this section is different than a certificate of authorization furnished under Section 209.

SECTION 905. NONCOMPLYING NAME OF FOREIGN LIMITED PARTNERSHIP.

(a) A foreign limited partnership whose name does not comply with Section 108 may not obtain a certificate of authority until it adopts, for the purpose of transacting business in this State, an alternate name that complies with Section 108. A foreign limited partnership that adopts an alternate name under this subsection and then obtains a certificate of authority with the name need not comply with [fictitious name statute]. After obtaining a certificate of authority with an alternate name, a foreign limited partnership shall transact business in this State under the name unless the foreign limited partnership is authorized under [fictitious name statute] to transact business in this State under another name.

(b) If a foreign limited partnership authorized to transact business in this State changes its name to one that does not comply with Section 108, it may not thereafter transact business in this State until it complies with subsection (a) and obtains an amended certificate of authority.

Comment

Source—ULLCA Section 1005.

SECTION 906. REVOCATION OF CERTIFICATE OF AUTHORITY.

(a) A certificate of authority of a foreign limited partnership to transact business in this State may be revoked by the [Secretary of State] in the manner provided in subsections (b) and (c) if the foreign limited partnership does not:

(1) pay, within 60 days after the due date, any fee, tax or penalty due to the [Secretary of State] under this [Act] or other law;

(2) deliver, within 60 days after the due date, its annual report required under Section 210;

(3) appoint and maintain an agent for service of process as required by Section 114(b); or

(4) deliver for filing a statement of a change under Section 115 within 30 days after a change has occurred in the name or address of the agent.

(b) In order to revoke a certificate of authority, the [Secretary of State] must prepare, sign, and file a notice of revocation and send a copy to the foreign limited partnership's agent for service of process in this State, or if the foreign limited partnership does not appoint and maintain a proper agent in this State, to the foreign limited partnership's designated office. The notice must state:

(1) the revocation's effective date, which must be at least 60 days after the date the [Secretary of State] sends the copy; and

(2) the foreign limited partnership's failures to comply with subsection (a) which are the reason for the revocation.

(c) The authority of the foreign limited partnership to transact business in this State ceases on the effective date of the notice of revocation unless before that date the foreign limited partnership cures each failure to comply with subsection (a) stated in the notice. If the foreign limited partnership cures the failures, the [Secretary of State] shall so indicate on the filed notice.

Comment

Source—ULLCA Section 1006.

SECTION 907. CANCELLATION OF CERTIFICATE OF AUTHORITY; EFFECT OF FAILURE TO HAVE CERTIFICATE.

(a) In order to cancel its certificate of authority to transact business in this State, a foreign limited partnership must deliver to the [Secretary of State] for filing a notice of cancellation. The certificate is canceled when the notice becomes effective under Section 206.

(b) A foreign limited partnership transacting business in this State may not maintain an action or proceeding in this State unless it has a certificate of authority to transact business in this State.

(c) The failure of a foreign limited partnership to have a certificate of authority to transact business in this State does not impair the validity of a contract or act of the foreign limited partnership or prevent the foreign limited partnership from defending an action or proceeding in this State.

(d) A partner of a foreign limited partnership is not liable for the obligations of the foreign limited partnership solely by reason of the foreign limited partnership's having transacted business in this State without a certificate of authority.

(e) If a foreign limited partnership transacts business in this State without a certificate of authority or cancels its certificate of authority, it appoints the [Secretary of State] as its agent for service of process for rights of action arising out of the transaction of business in this State.

Comment

Source—RULPA Section 907(d); ULLCA Section 1008.

SECTION 908. ACTION BY [ATTORNEY GENERAL]. The [Attorney General] may maintain an action to restrain a foreign limited partnership from transacting business in this State in violation of this [article].

Comment

Source—RULPA Section 908; ULLCA Section 1009.

[ARTICLE] 10
ACTIONS BY PARTNERS

SECTION 1001. DIRECT ACTION BY PARTNER.

(a) Subject to subsection (b), a partner may maintain a direct action against the limited partnership or another partner for legal or equitable relief, with or without an accounting as to the partnership's activities, to enforce the rights and otherwise protect the interests of the partner, including rights and interests under the partnership agreement or this [Act] or arising independently of the partnership relationship.

(b) A partner commencing a direct action under this section is required to plead and prove an actual or threatened injury that is not solely the result of an injury suffered or threatened to be suffered by the limited partnership.

(c) The accrual of, and any time limitation on, a right of action for a remedy under this section is governed by other law. A right to an accounting upon a dissolution and winding up does not revive a claim barred by law.

Comment

Subsection (a)—Source: RUPA Section 405(b).

Subsection (b)—In ordinary contractual situations it is axiomatic that each party to a contract has standing to sue for breach of that contract. Within a limited partnership, however, different circumstances may exist. A partner does not have a direct claim against another partner merely because the other partner has breached the partnership agreement. Likewise a partner's violation of this Act does not automatically create a direct claim for every other partner. To have standing in his, her, or its own right, a partner plaintiff must be able to show a harm that occurs independently of the harm caused or threatened to be caused to the limited partnership.

The reference to "threatened" harm is intended to encompass claims for injunctive relief and does not relax standards for proving injury.

SECTION 1002. DERIVATIVE ACTION. A partner may maintain a derivative action to enforce a right of a limited partnership if:

(1) the partner first makes a demand on the general partners, requesting that they cause the limited partnership to bring an action to enforce the right, and the general partners do not bring the action within a reasonable time; or

(2) a demand would be futile.

Comment

Source—RULPA Section 1001.

SECTION 1003. PROPER PLAINTIFF. A derivative action may be maintained only by a person that is a partner at the time the action is commenced and:

(1) that was a partner when the conduct giving rise to the action occurred; or

(2) whose status as a partner devolved upon the person by operation of law or pursuant to the terms of the partnership agreement from a person that was a partner at the time of the conduct.

Comment

Source—RULPA Section 1002.

SECTION 1004. PLEADING. In a derivative action, the complaint must state with particularity:

(1) the date and content of plaintiff's demand and the general partners' response to the demand; or

(2) why demand should be excused as futile.

Comment

Source—RULPA Section 1003.

SECTION 1005. PROCEEDS AND EXPENSES.

(a) Except as otherwise provided in subsection (b):

(1) any proceeds or other benefits of a derivative action, whether by judgment, compromise, or settlement, belong to the limited partnership and not to the derivative plaintiff;

(2) if the derivative plaintiff receives any proceeds, the derivative plaintiff shall immediately remit them to the limited partnership.

(b) If a derivative action is successful in whole or in part, the court may award the plaintiff reasonable expenses, including reasonable attorney's fees, from the recovery of the limited partnership.

Comment

Source—RULPA Section 1004.

[ARTICLE] 11
CONVERSION AND MERGER

SECTION 1101. DEFINITIONS. In this [article]:

(1) "Constituent limited partnership" means a constituent organization that is a limited partnership.

(2) "Constituent organization" means an organization that is party to a merger.

(3) "Converted organization" means the organization into which a converting organization converts pursuant to Sections 1102 through 1105.

(4) "Converting limited partnership" means a converting organization that is a limited partnership.

(5) "Converting organization" means an organization that converts into another organization pursuant to Section 1102.

(6) "General partner" means a general partner of a limited partnership.

(7) "Governing statute" of an organization means the statute that governs the organization's internal affairs.

(8) "Organization" means a general partnership, including a limited liability partnership; limited partnership, including a limited liability limited partnership; limited liability company; business trust; corporation; or any other person having a governing statute. The term includes domestic and foreign organizations whether or not organized for profit.

(9) "Organizational documents" means:

(A) for a domestic or foreign general partnership, its partnership agreement;

(B) for a limited partnership or foreign limited partnership, its certificate of limited partnership and partnership agreement;

(C) for a domestic or foreign limited liability company, its articles of organization and operating agreement, or comparable records as provided in its governing statute;

(D) for a business trust, its agreement of trust and declaration of trust;

(E) for a domestic or foreign corporation for profit, its articles of incorporation, bylaws, and other agreements among its shareholders which are authorized by its governing statute, or comparable records as provided in its governing statute; and

(F) for any other organization, the basic records that create the organization and determine its internal governance and the relations among the persons that own it, have an interest in it, or are members of it.

(10) "Personal liability" means personal liability for a debt, liability, or other obligation of an organization which is imposed on a person that co-owns, has an interest in, or is a member of the organization:

(A) by the organization's governing statute solely by reason of the person co-owning, having an interest in, or being a member of the organization; or

(B) by the organization's organizational documents under a provision of the organization's governing statute authorizing those documents to make one or more specified persons liable for all or specified debts, liabilities, and other obligations of the organization solely by reason of the person or persons co-owning, having an interest in, or being a member of the organization.

(11) "Surviving organization" means an organization into which one or more other organizations are merged. A surviving organization may preexist the merger or be created by the merger.

Comment

This section contains definitions specific to this Article.

SECTION 1102. CONVERSION.

(a) An organization other than a limited partnership may convert to a limited partnership, and a limited partnership may convert to another organization pursuant to this section and Sections 1103 through 1105 and a plan of conversion, if:

(1) the other organization's governing statute authorizes the conversion;

(2) the conversion is not prohibited by the law of the jurisdiction that enacted the governing statute; and

(3) the other organization complies with its governing statute in effecting the conversion.

(b) A plan of conversion must be in a record and must include:

(1) the name and form of the organization before conversion;

(2) the name and form of the organization after conversion; and

(3) the terms and conditions of the conversion, including the manner and basis for converting interests in the converting organization into any combination of money, interests in the converted organization, and other consideration; and

(4) the organizational documents of the converted organization.

Comment

In a statutory conversion an existing entity changes its form, the jurisdiction of its governing statute or both. For example, a limited partnership organized under the laws of one jurisdiction might convert to:

- a limited liability company (or other form of entity) organized under the laws of the same jurisdiction,
- a limited liability company (or other form of entity) organized under the laws of another jurisdiction, or
- a limited partnership organized under the laws of another jurisdiction (referred to in some statutes as "domestication").

In contrast to a merger, which involves at least two entities, a conversion involves only one. The converting and converted organization are the same entity. See Section 1105(a). For this Act to apply to a conversion, either the converting or converted organization must be a limited partnership subject to this Act. If the converting organization is a limited partnership subject to this Act, the partners of the converting organization are subject to the duties and obligations stated in this Act, including Sections 304 (informational rights of limited partners), 305(b) (limited partner's obligation of good faith and fair dealing), 407 (informational rights of general partners), and 408 (general partner duties).

Subsection (a)(2)—Given the very broad definition of "organization," Section 1101(8), this Act authorizes conversions involving non-profit organizations. This provision is intended as an additional safeguard for that context.

Subsection (b)(3)—A plan of conversion may provide that some persons with interests in the converting organization will receive interests in the converted organization while other persons with interests in the converting organization will receive some other form of consideration. Thus, a "squeeze out" conversion is possible. As noted above, if the converting organization is a limited partnership subject to this Act, the partners of the converting organization are subject to the duties and obligations stated in this Act. Those duties would apply to the process and terms under which a squeeze out conversion occurs.

If the converting organization is a limited partnership, the plan of conversion will determine the fate of any interests held by mere transferees. This Act does not state any duty or obligation owed by a converting limited partnership or its partners to mere transferees. That issue is a matter for other law.

SECTION 1103. ACTION ON PLAN OF CONVERSION BY CONVERTING LIMITED PARTNERSHIP.

(a) Subject to Section 1110, a plan of conversion must be consented to by all the partners of a converting limited partnership.

(b) Subject to Section 1110 and any contractual rights, after a conversion is approved, and at any time before a filing is made under Section 1104, a converting limited partnership may amend the plan or abandon the planned conversion:

(1) as provided in the plan; and

(2) except as prohibited by the plan, by the same consent as was required to approve the plan.

Comment

Section 1110 imposes special consent requirements for transactions which might cause a partner to have "personal liability," as defined in Section 1101(10) for entity debts. The partnership agreement may not restrict the rights provided by Section 1110. See Section 110(b)(12).

Subsection (a)—Like many of the rules stated in this Act, this subsection's requirement of unanimous consent is a default rule. Subject only to Section 1110, the partnership agreement may state a different quantum of consent or provide a completely different approval mechanism. Varying this subsection's rule means that a partner might be subject to a conversion (including a "squeeze out" conversion) without consent and with no appraisal remedy. If the converting organization is a limited partnership subject to this Act, the partners of the converting organization are subject to the duties and obligations stated in this Act. Those duties would apply to the process and terms under which the conversion occurs. However, if the partnership agreement allows for a conversion with less than unanimous consent, the mere fact a partner objects to a conversion does not mean that the partners favoring, arranging, consenting to or effecting the conversation have breached a duty under this Act.

SECTION 1104. FILINGS REQUIRED FOR CONVERSION; EFFECTIVE DATE.

(a) After a plan of conversion is approved:

(1) a converting limited partnership shall deliver to the [Secretary of State] for filing articles of conversion, which must include:

(A) a statement that the limited partnership has been converted into another organization;

(B) the name and form of the organization and the jurisdiction of its governing statute;

(C) the date the conversion is effective under the governing statute of the converted organization;

(D) a statement that the conversion was approved as required by this [Act];

(E) a statement that the conversion was approved as required by the governing statute of the converted organization; and

(F) if the converted organization is a foreign organization not authorized to transact business in this State, the street and mailing address of an office which the [Secretary of State] may use for the purposes of Section 1105(c); and

(2) if the converting organization is not a converting limited partnership, the converting organization shall deliver to the [Secretary of State] for filing a certificate of limited partnership, which must include, in addition to the information required by Section 201:

(A) a statement that the limited partnership was converted from another organization;

(B) the name and form of the organization and the jurisdiction of its governing statute; and

(C) a statement that the conversion was approved in a manner that complied with the organization's governing statute.

(b) A conversion becomes effective:

(1) if the converted organization is a limited partnership, when the certificate of limited partnership takes effect; and

(2) if the converted organization is not a limited partnership, as provided by the governing statute of the converted organization.

Comment

Subsection (b)—The effective date of a conversion is determined under the governing statute of the converted organization.

SECTION 1105. EFFECT OF CONVERSION.

(a) An organization that has been converted pursuant to this [article] is for all purposes the same entity that existed before the conversion.

(b) When a conversion takes effect:

(1) all property owned by the converting organization remains vested in the converted organization;

(2) all debts, liabilities, and other obligations of the converting organization continue as obligations of the converted organization;

(3) an action or proceeding pending by or against the converting organization may be continued as if the conversion had not occurred;

(4) except as prohibited by other law, all of the rights, privileges, immunities, powers, and purposes of the converting organization remain vested in the converted organization;

(5) except as otherwise provided in the plan of conversion, the terms and conditions of the plan of conversion take effect; and

(6) except as otherwise agreed, the conversion does not dissolve a converting limited partnership for the purposes of [Article] 8.

(c) A converted organization that is a foreign organization consents to the jurisdiction of the courts of this State to enforce any obligation owed by the converting limited partnership, if before the conversion the converting limited partnership was subject to suit in this State on the obligation. A converted organization that is a foreign organization and not authorized to transact business in this State appoints the [Secretary of State] as its agent for service of process for purposes of enforcing an obligation under this subsection. Service on the [Secretary of State] under this subsection is made in the same manner and with the same consequences as in Section 117(c) and (d).

Comment

Subsection (a)—A conversion changes an entity's legal type, but does not create a new entity.

Subsection (b)—Unlike a merger, a conversion involves a single entity, and the conversion therefore does not transfer any of the entity's rights or obligations.

SECTION 1106. MERGER.

(a) A limited partnership may merge with one or more other constituent organizations pursuant to this section and Sections 1107 through 1109 and a plan of merger, if:

(1) the governing statute of each the other organizations authorizes the merger;

(2) the merger is not prohibited by the law of a jurisdiction that enacted any of those governing statutes; and

(3) each of the other organizations complies with its governing statute in effecting the merger.

(b) A plan of merger must be in a record and must include:

(1) the name and form of each constituent organization;

(2) the name and form of the surviving organization and, if the surviving organization is to be created by the merger, a statement to that effect;

(3) the terms and conditions of the merger, including the manner and basis for converting the interests in each constituent organization into any combination of money, interests in the surviving organization, and other consideration;

(4) if the surviving organization is to be created by the merger, the surviving organization's organizational documents; and

(5) if the surviving organization is not to be created by the merger, any amendments to be made by the merger to the surviving organization's organizational documents.

Comment

For this Act to apply to a merger, at least one of the constituent organizations must be a limited partnership subject to this Act. The partners of any such limited partnership are subject to the duties and obligations stated in this Act, including Sections 304 (informational rights of limited partners), 305(b) (limited partner's obligation of good faith and fair dealing), 407 (informational rights of general partners), and 408 (general partner duties).

Subsection (a)(2)—Given the very broad definition of "organization," Section 1101(8), this Act authorizes mergers involving non-profit organizations. This provision is intended as an additional safeguard for that context.

Subsection (b)(3)—A plan of merger may provide that some persons with interests in a constituent organization will receive interests in the surviving organization, while other persons with interests in the same constituent organization will receive some other form of consideration. Thus, a "squeeze out" merger is possible. As noted above, the duties and obligations stated in this Act apply to the partners of a constituent organization that is a limited partnership subject to this Act. Those duties would apply to the process and terms under which a squeeze out merger occurs.

If a constituent organization is a limited partnership, the plan of merger will determine the fate of any interests held by mere transferees. This Act does not state any duty or obligation owed by a constituent limited partnership or its partners to mere transferees. That issue is a matter for other law.

SECTION 1107. ACTION ON PLAN OF MERGER BY CONSTITUENT LIMITED PARTNERSHIP.

(a) Subject to Section 1110, a plan of merger must be consented to by all the partners of a constituent limited partnership.

(b) Subject to Section 1110 and any contractual rights, after a merger is approved, and at any time before a filing is made under Section 1108, a constituent limited partnership may amend the plan or abandon the planned merger:

(1) as provided in the plan; and

(2) except as prohibited by the plan, with the same consent as was required to approve the plan.

Comment

Section 1110 imposes special consent requirements for transactions which might make a partner personally liable for entity debts. The partnership agreement may not restrict the rights provided by Section 1110. See Section 110(b)(12).

Subsection (a)—Like many of the rules stated in this Act, this subsection's requirement of unanimous consent is a default rule. Subject only to Section 1110, the partnership agreement may state a different quantum of consent or provide a completely different approval mechanism. Varying this subsection's rule means that a partner might be subject to a merger (including a "squeeze out" merger) without consent and with no appraisal remedy. The partners of a constituent limited partnership are subject to the duties and obligations stated in this Act, and those duties would apply to the process and terms under which the merger occurs. However, if the partnership agreement allows for a merger with less than unanimous consent, the mere fact a partner objects to a merger does not mean that the partners favoring, arranging, consenting to or effecting the merger have breached a duty under this Act.

SECTION 1108. FILINGS REQUIRED FOR MERGER; EFFECTIVE DATE.

(a) After each constituent organization has approved a merger, articles of merger must be signed on behalf of:

(1) each preexisting constituent limited partnership, by each general partner listed in the certificate of limited partnership; and

(2) each other preexisting constituent organization, by an authorized representative.

(b) The articles of merger must include:

(1) the name and form of each constituent organization and the jurisdiction of its governing statute;

(2) the name and form of the surviving organization, the jurisdiction of its governing statute, and, if the surviving organization is created by the merger, a statement to that effect;

(3) the date the merger is effective under the governing statute of the surviving organization;

(4) if the surviving organization is to be created by the merger:

(A) if it will be a limited partnership, the limited partnership's certificate of limited partnership; or

(B) if it will be an organization other than a limited partnership, the organizational document that creates the organization;

(5) if the surviving organization preexists the merger, any amendments provided for in the plan of merger for the organizational document that created the organization;

(6) a statement as to each constituent organization that the merger was approved as required by the organization's governing statute;

(7) if the surviving organization is a foreign organization not authorized to transact business in this State, the street and mailing address of an office which the [Secretary of State] may use for the purposes of Section 1109(b); and

(8) any additional information required by the governing statute of any constituent organization.

(c) Each constituent limited partnership shall deliver the articles of merger for filing in the [office of the Secretary of State].

(d) A merger becomes effective under this [article]:

(1) if the surviving organization is a limited partnership, upon the later of:

(i) compliance with subsection (c); or

(ii) subject to Section 206(c), as specified in the articles of merger; or

(2) if the surviving organization is not a limited partnership, as provided by the governing statute of the surviving organization.

Comment

Subsection (b)—The effective date of a merger is determined under the governing statute of the surviving organization.

SECTION 1109. EFFECT OF MERGER.

(a) When a merger becomes effective:

(1) the surviving organization continues or comes into existence;

(2) each constituent organization that merges into the surviving organization ceases to exist as a separate entity;

(3) all property owned by each constituent organization that ceases to exist vests in the surviving organization;

(4) all debts, liabilities, and other obligations of each constituent organization that ceases to exist continue as obligations of the surviving organization;

(5) an action or proceeding pending by or against any constituent organization that ceases to exist may be continued as if the merger had not occurred;

(6) except as prohibited by other law, all of the rights, privileges, immunities, powers, and purposes of each constituent organization that ceases to exist vest in the surviving organization;

(7) except as otherwise provided in the plan of merger, the terms and conditions of the plan of merger take effect; and

(8) except as otherwise agreed, if a constituent limited partnership ceases to exist, the merger does not dissolve the limited partnership for the purposes of [Article] 8;

(9) if the surviving organization is created by the merger:

(A) if it is a limited partnership, the certificate of limited partnership becomes effective; or

(B) if it is an organization other than a limited partnership, the organizational document that creates the organization becomes effective; and

(10) if the surviving organization preexists the merger, any amendments provided for in the articles of merger for the organizational document that created the organization become effective.

(b) A surviving organization that is a foreign organization consents to the jurisdiction of the courts of this State to enforce any obligation owed by a constituent organization, if before the merger the constituent organization was subject to suit in this State on the obligation. A surviving organization that is a foreign organization and not authorized to transact business in this State appoints the [Secretary of State] as its agent for service of process for the purposes of enforcing an obligation under this subsection. Service on the [Secretary of State] under this subsection is made in the same manner and with the same consequences as in Section 117(c) and (d).

SECTION 1110. RESTRICTIONS ON APPROVAL OF CONVERSIONS AND MERGERS AND ON RELINQUISHING LLLP STATUS.

(a) If a partner of a converting or constituent limited partnership will have personal liability with respect to a converted or surviving organization, approval and amendment of a plan of conversion or merger are ineffective without the consent of the partner, unless:

(1) the limited partnership's partnership agreement provides for the approval of the conversion or merger with the consent of fewer than all the partners; and

(2) the partner has consented to the provision of the partnership agreement.

(b) An amendment to a certificate of limited partnership which deletes a statement that the limited partnership is a limited liability limited partnership is ineffective without the consent of each general partner unless:

(1) the limited partnership's partnership agreement provides for the amendment with the consent of less than all the general partners; and

(2) each general partner that does not consent to the amendment has consented to the provision of the partnership agreement.

(c) A partner does not give the consent required by subsection (a) or (b) merely by consenting to a provision of the partnership agreement which permits the partnership agreement to be amended with the consent of fewer than all the partners.

Comment

This section imposes special consent requirements for transactions that might make a partner personally liable for entity debts. The partnership agreement may not restrict the rights provided by this section. See Section 110(b)(12).

Subsection (c)—This subsection prevents circumvention of the consent requirements of subsections (a) and (b).

Example: As initially a consented to, the partnership agreement of a limited partnership leaves in place the Act's rule requiring unanimous consent for a conversion or merger. The partnership agreement does provide, however, that the agreement may be amended with the affirmative vote of general partners owning 2/3 of the rights to receive distributions as general partners and of limited partners owning 2/3 of the rights to receive distributions as limited partners. The required vote is obtained for an amendment that permits approval of a conversion or merger by the same vote necessary to amend the partnership agreement. Partner X votes for the amendment. Partner Y votes against. Partner Z does not vote.

Subsequently the limited partnership proposes to convert to a limited partnership (not an LLLP) organized under the laws of another state, with Partners X, Y and Z each receiving interests as general partners. Under the amended partnership agreement, approval of the conversion does not require unanimous consent. However, since after the conversion, Partners X, Y and Z will each have "personal liability with respect to [the] converted . . . organization," Section 1110(a) applies.

As a result, the approval of the plan of conversion will require the consent of Partner Y and Partner Z. They did not consent to the amendment that provided for non-unanimous approval of a conversion or merger. Their initial consent to the partnership agreement, with its provision permitting non-unanimous consent for amendments, does _not_ satisfy the consent requirement of Subsection 1110(a)(2).

In contrast, Partner X's consent is not required. Partner X lost its Section 1110(a) veto right by consenting directly to the amendment to the partnership agreement which permitted non-unanimous consent to a conversion or merger.

SECTION 1111. LIABILITY OF GENERAL PARTNER AFTER CONVERSION OR MERGER.

(a) A conversion or merger under this [article] does not discharge any liability under Sections 404 and 607 of a person that was a general partner in or dissociated as a general partner from a converting or constituent limited partnership, but:

(1) the provisions of this [Act] pertaining to the collection or discharge of the liability continue to apply to the liability;

(2) for the purposes of applying those provisions, the converted or surviving organization is deemed to be the converting or constituent limited partnership; and

(3) if a person is required to pay any amount under this subsection:

(A) the person has a right of contribution from each other person that was liable as a general partner under Section 404 when the obligation was incurred and has not been released from the obligation under Section 607; and

(B) the contribution due from each of those persons is in proportion to the right to receive distributions in the capacity of general partner in effect for each of those persons when the obligation was incurred.

(b) In addition to any other liability provided by law:

(1) a person that immediately before a conversion or merger became effective was a general partner in a converting or constituent limited partnership that was not a limited liability limited partnership is personally liable for each obligation of the converted or surviving organization arising from a transaction with a third party after the conversion or merger becomes effective, if, at the time the third party enters into the transaction, the third party:

(A) does not have notice of the conversion or merger; and

(B) reasonably believes that:

(i) the converted or surviving business is the converting or constituent limited partnership;

(ii) the converting or constituent limited partnership is not a limited liability limited partnership; and

(iii) the person is a general partner in the converting or constituent limited partnership; and

(2) a person that was dissociated as a general partner from a converting or constituent limited partnership before the conversion or merger became effective is personally liable for each obligation of the converted or surviving organization arising from a transaction with a third party after the conversion or merger becomes effective, if:

(A) immediately before the conversion or merger became effective the converting or surviving limited partnership was a not a limited liability limited partnership; and

(B) at the time the third party enters into the transaction less than two years have passed since the person dissociated as a general partner and the third party:

(i) does not have notice of the dissociation;

(ii) does not have notice of the conversion or merger; and

(iii) reasonably believes that the converted or surviving organization is the converting or constituent limited partnership, the converting or constituent limited partnership is not a limited liability limited partnership, and the person is a general partner in the converting or constituent limited partnership.

Comment

This section extrapolates the approach of Section 607 into the context of a conversion or merger involving a limited partnership.

Subsection (a)—This subsection pertains to general partner liability for obligations which a limited partnership incurred before a conversion or merger. Following RUPA and the UPA, this Act leaves to other law the question of when a limited partnership obligation is incurred.

If the converting or constituent limited partnership was a limited liability limited partnership at all times before the conversion or merger, this subsection will not apply because no person will have any liability under Section 404 or 607.

Subsection (b)—This subsection pertains to entity obligations incurred after a conversion or merger and creates lingering exposure to personal liability for general partners and persons previously dissociated as general partners. In contrast to subsection (a)(3), this subsection does not provide for contribution among persons personally liable under this section for the same entity obligation. That issue is left for other law.

Subsection (b)(1)—If the converting or constituent limited partnership was a limited liability limited partnership immediately before the conversion or merger, there is no lingering exposure to personal liability under this subsection.

Subsection (b)(1)(A)—A person might have notice under Section 103(d)(4) or (5) as well as under Section 103(b).

Subsection (b)(2)(B)(i)—A person might have notice under Section 103(d)(1) as well as under Section 103(b).

Subsection (b)(2)(B)(ii)—A person might have notice under Section 103(d)(4) or (5) as well as under Section 103(b).

SECTION 1112. POWER OF GENERAL PARTNERS AND PERSONS DISSOCIATED AS GENERAL PARTNERS TO BIND ORGANIZATION AFTER CONVERSION OR MERGER.

(a) An act of a person that immediately before a conversion or merger became effective was a general partner in a converting or constituent limited partnership binds the converted or surviving organization after the conversion or merger becomes effective, if:

(1) before the conversion or merger became effective, the act would have bound the converting or constituent limited partnership under Section 402; and

(2) at the time the third party enters into the transaction, the third party:

(A) does not have notice of the conversion or merger; and

(B) reasonably believes that the converted or surviving business is the converting or constituent limited partnership and that the person is a general partner in the converting or constituent limited partnership.

(b) An act of a person that before a conversion or merger became effective was dissociated as a general partner from a converting or constituent limited partnership binds the converted or surviving organization after the conversion or merger becomes effective, if:

(1) before the conversion or merger became effective, the act would have bound the converting or constituent limited partnership under Section 402 if the person had been a general partner; and

(2) at the time the third party enters into the transaction, less than two years have passed since the person dissociated as a general partner and the third party:

(A) does not have notice of the dissociation;

(B) does not have notice of the conversion or merger; and

(C) reasonably believes that the converted or surviving organization is the converting or constituent limited partnership and that the person is a general partner in the converting or constituent limited partnership.

(c) If a person having knowledge of the conversion or merger causes a converted or surviving organization to incur an obligation under subsection (a) or (b), the person is liable:

(1) to the converted or surviving organization for any damage caused to the organization arising from the obligation; and

(2) if another person is liable for the obligation, to that other person for any damage caused to that other person arising from the liability.

Comment

This section extrapolates the approach of Section 606 into the context of a conversion or merger involving a limited partnership.

Subsection (a)(2)(A)—A person might have notice under Section 103(d)(4) or (5) as well as under Section 103(b).

Subsection (b)(2)(A)—A person might have notice under Section 103(d)(1) as well as under Section 103(b).

Subsection (b)(2)(B)—A person might have notice under Section 103(d)(4) or (5) as well as under Section 103(b).

SECTION 1113. [ARTICLE] NOT EXCLUSIVE. This [article] does not preclude an entity from being converted or merged under other law.

[ARTICLE] 12
MISCELLANEOUS PROVISIONS

SECTION 1201. UNIFORMITY OF APPLICATION AND CONSTRUCTION. In applying and construing this Uniform Act, consideration must be given to the need to promote uniformity of the law with respect to its subject matter among States that enact it.

SECTION 1202. SEVERABILITY CLAUSE. If any provision of this [Act] or its application to any person or circumstance is held invalid, the invalidity does not affect other provisions or applications of this [Act] which can be given effect without the invalid provision or application, and to this end the provisions of this [Act] are severable.

SECTION 1203. RELATION TO ELECTRONIC SIGNATURES IN GLOBAL AND NATIONAL COMMERCE ACT. This [Act] modifies, limits, or supersedes the federal Electronic Signatures in Global and National Commerce Act, 15 U.S.C. Section 7001 et seq., but this [Act] does not modify, limit, or supersede Section 101(c) of that Act or authorize electronic delivery of any of the notices described in Section 103(b) of that Act.

SECTION 1204. EFFECTIVE DATE. This [Act] takes effect [effective date].

Comment

Section 1206 specifies how this Act affects domestic limited partnerships, with special provisions pertaining to domestic limited partnerships formed before the Act's effective date. Section 1206 contains no comparable provisions for foreign limited partnerships. Therefore, once this Act is effective, it applies immediately to all foreign limited partnerships, whether formed before or after the Act's effective date.

SECTION 1205. REPEALS. Effective [all-inclusive date], the following acts and parts of acts are repealed: [the State Limited Partnership Act as amended and in effect immediately before the effective date of this [Act]].

SECTION 1206. APPLICATION TO EXISTING RELATIONSHIPS.
(a) Before [all-inclusive date], this [Act] governs only:
(1) a limited partnership formed on or after [the effective date of this [Act]]; and
(2) except as otherwise provided in subsections (c) and (d), a limited partnership formed before [the effective date of this [Act]] which elects, in the manner provided in its partnership agreement or by law for amending the partnership agreement, to be subject to this [Act].

(b) Except as otherwise provided in subsection (c), on and after [all-inclusive date] this [Act] governs all limited partnerships.

(c) With respect to a limited partnership formed before [the effective date of this [Act]], the following rules apply except as the partners otherwise elect in the manner provided in the partnership agreement or by law for amending the partnership agreement:

(1) Section 104(c) does not apply and the limited partnership has whatever duration it had under the law applicable immediately before [the effective date of this [Act]].

(2) the limited partnership is not required to amend its certificate of limited partnership to comply with Section 201(a)(4).

(3) Sections 601 and 602 do not apply and a limited partner has the same right and power to dissociate from the limited partnership, with the same consequences, as existed immediately before [the effective date of this [Act].

(4) Section 603(4) does not apply.

(5) Section 603(5) does not apply and a court has the same power to expel a general partner as the court had immediately before [the effective date of this [Act]].

(6) Section 801(3) does not apply and the connection between a person's dissociation as a general partner and the dissolution of the limited partnership is the same as existed immediately before [the effective date of this [Act]].

(d) With respect to a limited partnership that elects pursuant to subsection (a)(2) to be subject to this [Act], after the election takes effect the provisions of this [Act] relating to the liability of the limited partnership's general partners to third parties apply:

(1) before [all-inclusive date], to:

(A) a third party that had not done business with the limited partnership in the year before the election took effect; and

(B) a third party that had done business with the limited partnership in the year before the election took effect only if the third party knows or has received a notification of the election; and

(2) on and after [all-inclusive date], to all third parties, but those provisions remain inapplicable to any obligation incurred while those provisions were inapplicable under paragraph (1)(B).

Comment

Source—RUPA Section 1206.

This section pertains exclusively to domestic limited partnerships—i.e., to limited partnerships formed under this Act or a predecessor statute enacted by the same jurisdiction. For foreign limited partnerships, see the Comment to Section 1204.

This Act governs all limited partnerships formed on or after the Act's effective date. As for pre-existing limited partnerships, this section establishes an optional "elect in" period and a mandatory, all-inclusive date. The "elect in" period runs from the effective date, stated in Section 1204, until the all-inclusive date, stated in both subsection(a) and (b).

During the "elect in" period, a pre-existing limited partnership may elect to become subject to this Act. Subsection (d) states certain important consequences for a limited partnership that elects in. Beginning on the all-inclusive date, each pre-existing limited partnership that has not previously elected in becomes subject to this Act by operation of law.

Subsection (c)—This subsection specifies six provisions of this Act which never automatically apply to any pre-existing limited partnership. Except for subsection (c)(2), the list refers to provisions governing the relationship of the partners *inter se* and considered too different than predecessor law to be fairly applied to a preexisting limited partnership without the consent of its partners. Each of these *inter se* provisions is subject to change in the partnership agreement. However, many pre-existing limited partnerships may have taken for granted the analogous provisions of predecessor law and may therefore not have addressed the issues in their partnership agreements.

Subsection (c)(1)—Section 104(c) provides that a limited partnership has a perpetual duration.

Subsection (c)(2)—Section 201(a)(4) requires the certificate of limited partnership to state "whether the limited partnership is a limited liability limited partnership." The requirement is intended to force the organizers of a limited partnership to decide whether the limited partnership is to be an LLLP and therefore is inapposite to pre-existing limited partnerships. Moreover, applying the requirement to pre-existing limited partnerships would create a significant administrative burden both for limited partnerships and the filing officer and probably would result in many pre-existing limited partnerships being in violation of the requirement.

Subsection (c)(3)—Section 601 and 602 concern a person's dissociation as a limited partner.

Subsection (c)(4)—Section 603(4) provides for the expulsion of a general partner by the unanimous consent of the other partners in specified circumstances.

Subsection (c)(5)—Section 603(5) provides for the expulsion of a general partner by a court in specified circumstances.

Subsection (c)(6)—Section 801(3) concerns the continuance or dissolution of a limited partnership following a person's dissociation as a general partner.

Subsection (d)—Following RUPA Section 1206(c), this subsection limits the efficacy of the Act's liability protections for partners of an "electing in" limited partnership. The limitation:

- applies only to the benefit of "a third party that had done business with the limited partnership in the year before the election took effect," and
- ceases to apply when "the third party knows or has received a notification of the election" or on the "all-inclusive" date, whichever occurs first.

If the limitation causes a provision of this Act to be inapplicable with regard to a third party, the comparable provision of predecessor law applies.

Example: A pre-existing limited partnership elects to be governed by this Act before the "all-inclusive" date. Two months before the election, Third Party provided services to the limited partnership. Third Party neither knows nor has received a notification of the election. Until the "all inclusive" date, with regard to Third Party, Section 303's full liability shield does not apply to each limited partner. Instead, each limited partner has the liability shield applicable under predecessor law.

Subsection (d)(2)—To the extent subsection (d) causes a provision of this Act to be inapplicable when an obligation is incurred, the inapplicability continues as to that obligation even after the "all inclusive" date.

Legislative Note: In a State that has previously amended its existing limited partnership statute to provide for limited liability limited partnerships (LLLPs), this Act should include transition provisions specifically applicable to preexisting limited liability limited partnerships. The precise wording of those provisions must depend on the wording of the State's previously enacted LLLP provisions. However, the following principles apply generally:

1. In Sections 806(b)(5) and 807(b)(4) (notice by dissolved limited partnership to claimants), the phrase "the limited partnership has been throughout its existence a limited liability limited partnership" should be revised to en-

compass a limited partnership that was a limited liability limited partnership under the State's previously enacted LLLP provisions.

2. Section 1206(d) should provide that, if a preexisting limited liability limited partnership elects to be subject to this Act, this Act's provisions relating to the liability of general partners to third parties apply immediately to all third parties, regardless of whether a third party has previously done business with the limited liability limited partnership.

3. A preexisting limited liability limited partnership that elects to be subject to this Act should have to comply with Sections 201(a)(4) (requiring the certificate of limited partnership to state whether the limited partnership is a limited liability limited partnership) and 108(c) (establishing name requirements for a limited liability limited partnership).

4. As for Section 1206(b) (providing that, after a transition period, this Act applies to all preexisting limited partnerships):

a. if a State's previously enacted LLLP provisions have requirements essentially the same as Sections 201(a)(4) and 108(c), preexisting limited liability limited partnerships should automatically retain LLLP status under this Act.

b. if a State's previously enacted LLLP provisions have name requirements essentially the same as Section 108(c) and provide that a public filing other than the certificate of limited partnership establishes a limited partnership's status as a limited liability limited partnership:

i. that filing can be deemed to an amendment to the certificate of limited partnership to comply with Section 201(a)(4), and

ii. preexisting limited liability limited partnerships should automatically retain LLLP status under this Act.

c. if a State's previously enacted LLLP provisions do not have name requirements essentially the same as Section 108(c), it will be impossible both to enforce Section 108(c) and provide for automatic transition to LLLP status under this Act.

SECTION 1207. SAVINGS CLAUSE. This [Act] does not affect an action commenced, proceeding brought, or right accrued before this [Act] takes effect.

INDEX

References are to section numbers, Tables, and Appendices. For Chapter 8, the numbers after the decimal points refer to sections of the Revised Uniform Partnership Act discussed and analyzed in Chapter 8. For Chapter 9, the numbers after the decimal points refer to sections of the Uniform Limited Partnership Act (2001) discussed and analyzed in Chapter 9.

References are to section numbers, Tables, and Appendices. For Chapter 8, the numbers
after the decimal points refer to sections of the Revised Uniform Partnership Act
discussed and analyzed in Chapter 8. For Chapter 9, the numbers after the decimal points
refer to sections of the Uniform Limited Partnership Act (2001) discussed and analyzed in
Chapter 9.

1052

Index

References are to section numbers, Tables, and Appendices. For Chapter 8, the numbers
after the decimal points refer to sections of the Revised Uniform Partnership Act
discussed and analyzed in Chapter 8. For Chapter 9, the numbers after the decimal points
refer to sections of the Uniform Limited Partnership Act (2001) discussed and analyzed in
Chapter 9.

1053

References are to section numbers, Tables, and Appendices. For Chapter 8, the numbers
after the decimal points refer to sections of the Revised Uniform Partnership Act
discussed and analyzed in Chapter 8. For Chapter 9, the numbers after the decimal points
refer to sections of the Uniform Limited Partnership Act (2001) discussed and analyzed in
Chapter 9.

References are to section numbers, Tables, and Appendices. For Chapter 8, the numbers
after the decimal points refer to sections of the Revised Uniform Partnership Act
discussed and analyzed in Chapter 8. For Chapter 9, the numbers after the decimal points
refer to sections of the Uniform Limited Partnership Act (2001) discussed and analyzed in
Chapter 9.

References are to section numbers, Tables, and Appendices. For Chapter 8, the numbers
after the decimal points refer to sections of the Revised Uniform Partnership Act
discussed and analyzed in Chapter 8. For Chapter 9, the numbers after the decimal points
refer to sections of the Uniform Limited Partnership Act (2001) discussed and analyzed in
Chapter 9.

Index

References are to section numbers, Tables, and Appendices. For Chapter 8, the numbers
after the decimal points refer to sections of the Revised Uniform Partnership Act
discussed and analyzed in Chapter 8. For Chapter 9, the numbers after the decimal points
refer to sections of the Uniform Limited Partnership Act (2001) discussed and analyzed in
Chapter 9.

1057

References are to section numbers, Tables, and Appendices. For Chapter 8, the numbers after the decimal points refer to sections of the Revised Uniform Partnership Act discussed and analyzed in Chapter 8. For Chapter 9, the numbers after the decimal points refer to sections of the Uniform Limited Partnership Act (2001) discussed and analyzed in Chapter 9.

1058

References are to section numbers, Tables, and Appendices. For Chapter 8, the numbers after the decimal points refer to sections of the Revised Uniform Partnership Act discussed and analyzed in Chapter 8. For Chapter 9, the numbers after the decimal points refer to sections of the Uniform Limited Partnership Act (2001) discussed and analyzed in Chapter 9.

References are to section numbers, Tables, and Appendices. For Chapter 8, the numbers
after the decimal points refer to sections of the Revised Uniform Partnership Act
discussed and analyzed in Chapter 8. For Chapter 9, the numbers after the decimal points
refer to sections of the Uniform Limited Partnership Act (2001) discussed and analyzed in
Chapter 9.

1060

Index

References are to section numbers, Tables, and Appendices. For Chapter 8, the numbers
after the decimal points refer to sections of the Revised Uniform Partnership Act
discussed and analyzed in Chapter 8. For Chapter 9, the numbers after the decimal points
refer to sections of the Uniform Limited Partnership Act (2001) discussed and analyzed in
Chapter 9.

References are to section numbers, Tables, and Appendices. For Chapter 8, the numbers after the decimal points refer to sections of the Revised Uniform Partnership Act discussed and analyzed in Chapter 8. For Chapter 9, the numbers after the decimal points refer to sections of the Uniform Limited Partnership Act (2001) discussed and analyzed in Chapter 9.

1062

Index

References are to section numbers, Tables, and Appendices. For Chapter 8, the numbers
after the decimal points refer to sections of the Revised Uniform Partnership Act
discussed and analyzed in Chapter 8. For Chapter 9, the numbers after the decimal points
refer to sections of the Uniform Limited Partnership Act (2001) discussed and analyzed in
Chapter 9.

1063

References are to section numbers, Tables, and Appendices. For Chapter 8, the numbers after the decimal points refer to sections of the Revised Uniform Partnership Act discussed and analyzed in Chapter 8. For Chapter 9, the numbers after the decimal points refer to sections of the Uniform Limited Partnership Act (2001) discussed and analyzed in Chapter 9.

Index

References are to section numbers, Tables, and Appendices. For Chapter 8, the numbers after the decimal points refer to sections of the Revised Uniform Partnership Act discussed and analyzed in Chapter 8. For Chapter 9, the numbers after the decimal points refer to sections of the Uniform Limited Partnership Act (2001) discussed and analyzed in Chapter 9.

1065

References are to section numbers, Tables, and Appendices. For Chapter 8, the numbers after the decimal points refer to sections of the Revised Uniform Partnership Act discussed and analyzed in Chapter 8. For Chapter 9, the numbers after the decimal points refer to sections of the Uniform Limited Partnership Act (2001) discussed and analyzed in Chapter 9.

1066

Index

References are to section numbers, Tables, and Appendices. For Chapter 8, the numbers after the decimal points refer to sections of the Revised Uniform Partnership Act discussed and analyzed in Chapter 8. For Chapter 9, the numbers after the decimal points refer to sections of the Uniform Limited Partnership Act (2001) discussed and analyzed in Chapter 9.

References are to section numbers, Tables, and Appendices. For Chapter 8, the numbers after the decimal points refer to sections of the Revised Uniform Partnership Act discussed and analyzed in Chapter 8. For Chapter 9, the numbers after the decimal points refer to sections of the Uniform Limited Partnership Act (2001) discussed and analyzed in Chapter 9.

1068

Index

Loss sharing agreements, 2.09(c)

Louisiana
 changes, Table 2-3
 definition of LLP, Table 2-1
 foreign LLPs, Tables 6-1 to 6-2
 full statutory citations, Tables 2-10,
  3-3, 5-2, 6-3
 history, 1.01(b)
 limited liability, Tables 3-1 to 3-2
 LLLP provisions, Table 5-1
 names, Table 2-9
 periodic renewals or reports, Table 2-7
 registration
  contents, Table 2-2
  effectiveness, Table 2-6
  fees, Table 2-5
  partner approval, Table 2-8
 signatures, Table 2-4

M

Maine
 changes, Table 2-3
 definition of LLP, Table 2-1
 foreign LLPs, Tables 6-1 to 6-2
 full statutory citations, Tables 2-10,
  3-3, 5-2, 6-3
 limited liability, Tables 3-1 to 3-2
 LLLP provisions, Table 5-1
 names, Table 2-9
 periodic renewals or reports,
  Table 2-7
 registration
  contents, Table 2-2
  effectiveness, Table 2-6
  fees, Table 2-5
  partner approval, Table 2-8
 signatures, Table 2-4

Management and control, 4.02
 choice of form, 1.07(a)(9)
 decision in the event of disagreement,
  4.02(c)

"delectus personae" rule, 4.02(d)
 LLLPs, 5.02(b), 5.03
 new members, 4.02(d)
 participation in management, 4.02(a)
 partner liability for partnership debts,
  3.01(e)
 partnership agreements, 2.09(f)
 voting rights, 4.02(b)
 U.L.P.A. provisions
  partnership agreements, 9.110

Maryland
 changes, Table 2-3
 definition of LLP, Table 2-1
 foreign LLPs, Tables 6-1 to 6-2
 full statutory citations, Tables 2-10,
  5-2, 6-3
 history, 1.01(c)
 limited liability, Tables 3-1 to 3-2
 LLLP provisions, Table 5-1
 names, Table 2-9
 partner liability for partnership debts,
  3.11(b)
 periodic renewals or reports, Table 2-7
 registration
  contents, Table 2-2
  effectiveness, Table 2-6
  fees, Table 2-5
  partner approval, Table 2-8
 signatures, Table 2-4

Massachusetts
 changes, Table 2-3
 definition of LLP, Table 2-1
 foreign LLPs, Tables 6-1 to 6-2
 formation, 2.06(a), 2.06(c)
 full statutory citations, Tables 2-10,
  3-3, 5-2, 6-3
 history, 1.01(c)
 limited liability, Tables 3-1 to 3-2
 LLLP provisions, Table 5-1
 names, Table 2-9
 periodic renewals or reports, Table 2-7
 registration

References are to section numbers, Tables, and Appendices. For Chapter 8, the numbers after the decimal points refer to sections of the Revised Uniform Partnership Act discussed and analyzed in Chapter 8. For Chapter 9, the numbers after the decimal points refer to sections of the Uniform Limited Partnership Act (2001) discussed and analyzed in Chapter 9.

References are to section numbers, Tables, and Appendices. For Chapter 8, the numbers
after the decimal points refer to sections of the Revised Uniform Partnership Act
discussed and analyzed in Chapter 8. For Chapter 9, the numbers after the decimal points
refer to sections of the Uniform Limited Partnership Act (2001) discussed and analyzed in
Chapter 9.

1070

Index

References are to section numbers, Tables, and Appendices. For Chapter 8, the numbers after the decimal points refer to sections of the Revised Uniform Partnership Act discussed and analyzed in Chapter 8. For Chapter 9, the numbers after the decimal points refer to sections of the Uniform Limited Partnership Act (2001) discussed and analyzed in Chapter 9.

1071

References are to section numbers, Tables, and Appendices. For Chapter 8, the numbers after the decimal points refer to sections of the Revised Uniform Partnership Act discussed and analyzed in Chapter 8. For Chapter 9, the numbers after the decimal points refer to sections of the Uniform Limited Partnership Act (2001) discussed and analyzed in Chapter 9.

References are to section numbers, Tables, and Appendices. For Chapter 8, the numbers after the decimal points refer to sections of the Revised Uniform Partnership Act discussed and analyzed in Chapter 8. For Chapter 9, the numbers after the decimal points refer to sections of the Uniform Limited Partnership Act (2001) discussed and analyzed in Chapter 9.

O

References are to section numbers, Tables, and Appendices. For Chapter 8, the numbers after the decimal points refer to sections of the Revised Uniform Partnership Act discussed and analyzed in Chapter 8. For Chapter 9, the numbers after the decimal points refer to sections of the Uniform Limited Partnership Act (2001) discussed and analyzed in Chapter 9.

1074

Index

References are to section numbers, Tables, and Appendices. For Chapter 8, the numbers
after the decimal points refer to sections of the Revised Uniform Partnership Act
discussed and analyzed in Chapter 8. For Chapter 9, the numbers after the decimal points
refer to sections of the Uniform Limited Partnership Act (2001) discussed and analyzed in
Chapter 9.

1075

References are to section numbers, Tables, and Appendices. For Chapter 8, the numbers after the decimal points refer to sections of the Revised Uniform Partnership Act discussed and analyzed in Chapter 8. For Chapter 9, the numbers after the decimal points refer to sections of the Uniform Limited Partnership Act (2001) discussed and analyzed in Chapter 9.

References are to section numbers, Tables, and Appendices. For Chapter 8, the numbers
after the decimal points refer to sections of the Revised Uniform Partnership Act
discussed and analyzed in Chapter 8. For Chapter 9, the numbers after the decimal points
refer to sections of the Uniform Limited Partnership Act (2001) discussed and analyzed in
Chapter 9.

1077

References are to section numbers, Tables, and Appendices. For Chapter 8, the numbers
after the decimal points refer to sections of the Revised Uniform Partnership Act
discussed and analyzed in Chapter 8. For Chapter 9, the numbers after the decimal points
refer to sections of the Uniform Limited Partnership Act (2001) discussed and analyzed in
Chapter 9.

1078

References are to section numbers, Tables, and Appendices. For Chapter 8, the numbers after the decimal points refer to sections of the Revised Uniform Partnership Act discussed and analyzed in Chapter 8. For Chapter 9, the numbers after the decimal points refer to sections of the Uniform Limited Partnership Act (2001) discussed and analyzed in Chapter 9.

References are to section numbers, Tables, and Appendices. For Chapter 8, the numbers after the decimal points refer to sections of the Revised Uniform Partnership Act discussed and analyzed in Chapter 8. For Chapter 9, the numbers after the decimal points refer to sections of the Uniform Limited Partnership Act (2001) discussed and analyzed in Chapter 9.

1080

Index

References are to section numbers, Tables, and Appendices. For Chapter 8, the numbers after the decimal points refer to sections of the Revised Uniform Partnership Act discussed and analyzed in Chapter 8. For Chapter 9, the numbers after the decimal points refer to sections of the Uniform Limited Partnership Act (2001) discussed and analyzed in Chapter 9.

References are to section numbers, Tables, and Appendices. For Chapter 8, the numbers
after the decimal points refer to sections of the Revised Uniform Partnership Act
discussed and analyzed in Chapter 8. For Chapter 9, the numbers after the decimal points
refer to sections of the Uniform Limited Partnership Act (2001) discussed and analyzed in
Chapter 9.

1082

Index

References are to section numbers, Tables, and Appendices. For Chapter 8, the numbers
after the decimal points refer to sections of the Revised Uniform Partnership Act
discussed and analyzed in Chapter 8. For Chapter 9, the numbers after the decimal points
refer to sections of the Uniform Limited Partnership Act (2001) discussed and analyzed in
Chapter 9.

References are to section numbers, Tables, and Appendices. For Chapter 8, the numbers
after the decimal points refer to sections of the Revised Uniform Partnership Act
discussed and analyzed in Chapter 8. For Chapter 9, the numbers after the decimal points
refer to sections of the Uniform Limited Partnership Act (2001) discussed and analyzed in
Chapter 9.

1084

References are to section numbers, Tables, and Appendices. For Chapter 8, the numbers
after the decimal points refer to sections of the Revised Uniform Partnership Act
discussed and analyzed in Chapter 8. For Chapter 9, the numbers after the decimal points
refer to sections of the Uniform Limited Partnership Act (2001) discussed and analyzed in
Chapter 9.

1085

References are to section numbers, Tables, and Appendices. For Chapter 8, the numbers
after the decimal points refer to sections of the Revised Uniform Partnership Act
discussed and analyzed in Chapter 8. For Chapter 9, the numbers after the decimal points
refer to sections of the Uniform Limited Partnership Act (2001) discussed and analyzed in
Chapter 9.

Index

References are to section numbers, Tables, and Appendices. For Chapter 8, the numbers after the decimal points refer to sections of the Revised Uniform Partnership Act discussed and analyzed in Chapter 8. For Chapter 9, the numbers after the decimal points refer to sections of the Uniform Limited Partnership Act (2001) discussed and analyzed in Chapter 9.